Texas Criminal Procedure— Code and Rules

2018 Edition

[Supersedes 2016 Edition]

WITH TABLES
AND INDEX

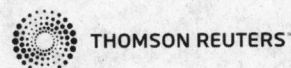

THOMSON REUTERS™

Mat #41883689

ISBN 978–0–314–68894–1

PREFACE

———

Designed for use in the office or courtroom, this pamphlet brings together in one convenient publication statutes and court rules relating to criminal procedure in Texas.

WHAT'S NEW

This product brings up to date statutes through the 2017 Regular and First Called Sessions of the Texas 85th Legislature and court rules with amendments received through September 1, 2017.

This pamphlet includes new enactments or important amendments to:

- The Code of Criminal Procedure
- Chapter 508 of the Government Code Relating to Parole and Mandatory Supervision
- Rules of Evidence
- Rules of Appellate Procedure

Article on Charging Instruments

Included in this pamphlet is a revised article on State Law of Charging Instruments, written by Helena F. Faulkner, discussing the content of accusatory pleadings through post-conviction review, and joinder and severance of offenses and defendants, updated through September 2017, including materials passed by the 2017 Regular and First Called Sessions of the Texas 85th Legislature.

CONTACT US

For additional information or research assistance call the Reference Attorneys at 1-800-REF-ATTY (1-800-733-2889). Contact our U.S. legal editorial department directly with your questions and suggestions by e-mail at editors.us-legal@tr.com.

Thank you for subscribing to this product. Should you have any questions regarding this product, please contact Customer Service at 1-800-328-4880 or by fax at 1-800-340-9378. If you would like to inquire about related publications, or to place an order, please contact us at 1-888-728-7677 or visit us at legalsolutions.thomsonreuters.com.

THE PUBLISHER

October, 2017

THOMSON REUTERS PROVIEW™

This title is one of many now available on your tablet as an eBook.

Take your research mobile. Powered by the Thomson Reuters ProView™ app, our eBooks deliver the same trusted content as your print resources, but in a compact, on-the-go format.

ProView eBooks are designed for the way you work. You can add your own notes and highlights to the text, and all of your annotations will transfer electronically to every new edition of your eBook.

You can also instantly verify primary authority with built-in links to WestlawNext® and KeyCite®, so you can be confident that you're accessing the most current and accurate information.

To find out more about ProView eBooks and available discounts, call 1-800-344-5009.

EFFECTIVE DATES

The following table shows the date of adjournment and the effective date of ninety day bills enacted at sessions of the legislature beginning with the year 1945:

Year	Leg.	Session	Adjournment Date	Effective Date
1945	49	Regular	June 5, 1945	September 4, 1945
1947	50	Regular	June 6, 1947	September 5, 1947
1949	51	Regular	June 6, 1949	September 5, 1949
1951	52	Regular	June 8, 1951	September 7, 1951
1953	53	Regular	May 27, 1953	August 26, 1953
1954	53	1st C.S.	May 13, 1954	August 12, 1954
1955	54	Regular	June 7, 1955	September 6, 1955
1957	55	Regular	May 23, 1957	August 22, 1957
1957	55	1st C.S.	November 12, 1957	February 11, 1958
1957	55	2nd C.S.	December 3, 1957	March 4, 1958
1959	56	Regular	May 12, 1959	August 11, 1959
1959	56	1st C.S.	June 16, 1959	September 15, 1959
1959	56	2nd C.S.	July 16, 1959	October 15, 1959
1959	56	3rd C.S.	August 6, 1959	November 5, 1959
1961	57	Regular	May 29, 1961	August 28, 1961
1961	57	1st C.S.	August 8, 1961	November 7, 1961
1961	57	2nd C.S.	August 14, 1961	November 13, 1961
1962	57	3rd C.S.	February 1, 1962	May 3, 1962
1963	58	Regular	May 24, 1963	August 23, 1963
1965	59	Regular	May 31, 1965	August 30, 1965
1966	59	1st C.S.	February 23, 1966	*
1967	60	Regular	May 29, 1967	August 28, 1967
1968	60	1st C.S.	July 3, 1968	*
1969	61	Regular	June 2, 1969	September 1, 1969
1969	61	1st C.S.	August 26, 1969	*
1969	61	2nd C.S.	September 9, 1969	December 9, 1969
1971	62	Regular	May 31, 1971	August 30, 1971
1971	62	1st C.S.	June 4, 1971	September 3, 1971
1972	62	2nd C.S.	March 30, 1972	June 29, 1972
1972	62	3rd C.S.	July 7, 1972	*
1972	62	4th C.S.	October 17, 1972	January 16, 1973
1973	63	Regular	May 28, 1973	August 27, 1973
1973	63	1st C.S.	December 20, 1973	*
1975	64	Regular	June 2, 1975	September 1, 1975
1977	65	Regular	May 30, 1977	August 29, 1977
1977	65	1st C.S.	July 21, 1977	*
1978	65	2nd C.S.	August 8, 1978	November 7, 1978
1979	66	Regular	May 28, 1979	August 27, 1979
1981	67	Regular	June 1, 1981	August 31, 1981

EFFECTIVE DATES

Year	Leg.	Session	Adjournment Date	Effective Date
1981	67	1st C.S.	August 11, 1981	November 10, 1981
1982	67	2nd C.S.	May 28, 1982	*
1982	67	3rd C.S.	September 9, 1982	*
1983	68	Regular	May 30, 1983	August 29, 1983
1983	68	1st C.S.	June 25, 1983	September 23, 1983
1984	68	2nd C.S.	July 3, 1984	October 2, 1984
1985	69	Regular	May 27, 1985	August 26, 1985
1985	69	1st C.S.	May 30, 1985	August 29, 1985
1986	69	2nd C.S.	September 4, 1986	December 4, 1986
1986	69	3rd C.S.	September 30, 1986	December 30, 1986
1987	70	Regular	June 1, 1987	August 31, 1987
1987	70	1st C.S.	June 3, 1987	September 2, 1987
1987	70	2nd C.S.	July 21, 1987	October 20, 1987
1989	71	Regular	May 29, 1989	August 28, 1989
1989	71	1st C.S.	July 19, 1989	October 18, 1989
1989	71	2nd C.S.	December 12, 1989	*
1990	71	3rd C.S.	March 28, 1990	*
1990	71	4th C.S.	May 1, 1990	*
1990	71	5th C.S.	May 30, 1990	*
1990	71	6th C.S.	June 7, 1990	September 6, 1990
1991	72	Regular	May 27, 1991	August 26, 1991
1991	72	1st C.S.	August 13, 1991	November 12, 1991
1991	72	2nd C.S.	August 25, 1991	November 24, 1991
1992	72	3rd C.S.	January 8, 1992	April 8, 1992
1992	72	4th C.S.	December 3, 1992	*
1993	73	Regular	May 31, 1993	August 30, 1993
1995	74	Regular	May 29, 1995	August 28, 1995
1997	75	Regular	June 2, 1997	September 1, 1997
1999	76	Regular	May 31, 1999	August 30, 1999
2001	77	Regular	May 28, 2001	September 1, 2001
2003	78	Regular	June 2, 2003	September 1, 2003
2003	78	1st C.S.	July 28, 2003	*
2003	78	2nd C.S.	August 26, 2003	*
2005	79	2nd C.S.	August 19, 2005	November 18, 2005
2006	79	3rd C.S.	May 16, 2006	August 15, 2006
2007	80	Regular	May 28, 2007	August 27, 2007
2009	81	Regular	June 1, 2009	August 31, 2009
2009	81	1st C.S.	July 2, 2009	*
2011	82	Regular	May 30, 2011	August 29, 2011
2011	82	1st C.S.	June 29, 2011	September 28, 2011**
2013	83	Regular	May 27, 2013	August 26, 2013
2013	83	1st C.S.	June 25, 2013	September 24, 2013**
2013	83	2nd C.S.	July 30, 2013	October 29, 2013**
2013	83	3rd C.S.	August 5, 2013	*
2015	84	Regular	June 1, 2015	August 31, 2015

EFFECTIVE DATES

Year	Leg.	Session	Adjournment Date	Effective Date
2017	85	Regular	May 29, 2017	August 28, 2017
2017	85	1st C.S.	August 15, 2017	November 14, 2017

* No legislation for which the ninety day effective date is applicable.

** Legislation effective on the 91st day after session.

DISPOSITION TABLE

Listing in Column 1 all articles in the Texas Code of Criminal Procedure of 1925, as amended and supplemented through the 1965 Regular Session of the Texas Legislature.

Showing in Column 2 where the subject matter of articles listed in Column 1 is incorporated in Vernon's Texas Code of Criminal Procedure or in Vernon's Texas Civil Statutes, as amended through the 1977 Regular Session of the Texas Legislature.

References in Column 2 are to 1965 C.C.P. Articles unless otherwise indicated.

1925 C.C.P. Article	1965 C.C.P. Article	1925 C.C.P. Article	1965 C.C.P. Article
1	1.03	47	2.23
2	1.04	48	3.01
3	1.05	49	3.02
4	1.06	50	3.03
4a, 4b	Repealed 1929	51	4.01
5	1.07	52	Civ.St. 1926–1
6	1.08	52–1 to 52–7	Civ.St. 1926–11
7	1.09	52–8 to 52–11	Civ.St. 1926–13
8	1.10	52–12	Civ.St. 1926–12
9	1.11	52–13	Civ.St. 1926–13
10	1.12	52–14	Civ.St. 1926–13
10a	1.13		See Civ.St. 199 (14th and 86th
11	1.14	52–15	Dists.)
12	1.15	52–16 to 52–22	Civ.St. 1926–21
13	1.16	52–23	Civ.St. 1926–26
14	1.17	52–24	Civ.St. 1926–27
15	1.18	52–24a	Civ.St. 1926–22
16	1.19	52–24b	Civ.St. 1926–16
17	1.20	52–24c	Civ.St. 1926–14
18	1.21	52–24d	Civ.St. 1926–15
19	1.22	52–25 to 52–48	Civ.St. 199 (174th Dist.)
20	1.23	52–49 to 52–61	Civ.St. 1926–51
21	1.24	52–61a	Civ.St. 199 (147th Dist.)
22	1.25		See Civ.St. 199 (28th and
23	1.26	52–62	107th Dists.)
24	1.27	52–63	Civ.St. 1926–41
25	2.01	52–64	Civ.St. 1926–42
26	2.02	52–65 to 52–80	Civ.St. 1926–41
27	2.03	52–81 to 52–87	Civ.St. 1926–42
28	2.04	52–87a 1 to 52–87a 10a	Civ.St. 1926–43
29	2.05	52–87b	Civ.St. 1926–44
30	2.06	52–88	Civ.St. 1960–1
31	2.07	52–89	Civ.St. 1960–2
32	2.08	52–90	Civ.St. 1960–3
33	2.09	52–91	Civ.St. 1960–4
34	2.10	52–92 to 52–104	See Civ.St. 1970–1 to 1970–14
35	2.11	52–105 to 52–117	Civ.St. 1970–301g
36	2.12	52–118 to 52–124	See Civ.St. 1970–76 et seq.
37	2.13	52–125 to 52–140	See Civ.St. 1970–95 et seq.
38	2.14	52–141 to 52–144	See Civ.St. 1970–111 et seq.
39	2.15	52–145 to 52–156	Repealed 1933
40	2.16	52–157	Civ.St. 2455–1
41	2.17	52–158	Civ.St. 199 (176th Dist.)
42	2.18	52–158a	Civ.St. 199 (177th Dist.)
43	2.19		Civ.St. 199 (178th and 179th
44	2.20	52–158b	Dists.)
45	2.21	52–158c	Civ.St. 199 (180th Dist.)
46	2.22	52–159	Civ.St. 1970–31.10

DISPOSITION TABLE

DISPOSITION TABLE

1925 C.C.P. Article	1965 C.C.P. Article	1925 C.C.P. Article	1965 C.C.P. Article
180	12.01	246	16.02
181	12.02	247	16.03
182	12.04	248	16.04
183	12.05	249	16.05
184	12.06	250	16.06
185	12.07	251	16.07
186	13.01	252	16.08
187	13.02	253	16.09
188	13.02	254	16.10
189	13.03	255	16.11
190	13.04	256	16.12
191	13.05	257	16.13
192	13.05	258	16.14
193	13.05	259	16.15
194	13.06	260	16.16
195	13.07	261	16.17
196	13.04	262	16.18
197	13.08	263	16.19
198	13.09	264	16.20
199	13.08 note	265	16.21
200	13.08 note	266	
201	13.10 note	267	17.01
202	13.11	268	
203	13.08 note	269	17.02
204	13.12	270	17.05
205	13.13	271	
206	13.14	271a	17.06
207	13.15	271b	17.07
208	13.01 note	272	
209	13.01 note	273	17.08
210	13.17	274	17.38
211	13.18	275	
212	14.01	275a	17.09
213	14.02	276	17.10
214	14.03	277	17.11
215	14.04	278	17.12
216	14.05	279	17.13
217	14.06	280	17.14
218	15.01	281	17.15
219	15.02	282	17.16
220	15.03	283	17.17
221	15.04	284	17.18
222	15.05	285	17.19
223	15.06	286	17.20
224	15.07	287	17.21
225	15.08	288	17.22
226	15.09	289	17.23
227	15.10	290	17.24
228	15.11	291	17.25
229	15.12	292	17.26
230	15.13	293	17.27
231	15.14	294	17.28
232	15.15	295	17.29
233	15.16	296	17.30
234		297	17.31
235	15.18	298	17.32
236	15.19	299	
237	15.20	300	17.34
238	15.21	301	17.35
239	15.22	302	17.36
240	15.23	303	17.37
241	15.24	304	18.01
242	15.25	305	18.02
243	15.26	306	18.03 note
244	15.27	307	18.04 note
245	16.01	308	18.05 note

DISPOSITION TABLE

DISPOSITION TABLE

1925 C.C.P. Article	1965 C.C.P. Article	1925 C.C.P. Article	1965 C.C.P. Article
425	22.02	492	26.02
426	22.03	493	26.03
427	22.04	494	26.04
428	22.05	494a	26.05
429	22.06	494b	26.06
430	22.07	495	26.07
431	22.08	496	26.08
432	22.09	497	26.09
433	22.10	498	26.10
434	22.11	499	26.11
435	22.12	500	26.12
436	22.13	501	26.13
437	22.14	502	26.14
438	22.15	503	26.15
439	22.16	504	27.01
440	22.17	505	27.02
441	23.01	506	27.03
442	23.02	507	27.04
445	23.05	508	27.05
446	23.06	509	27.06
447	23.07	510	27.07
448	23.08	511	27.08
449	23.09	512	27.09
450	23.10	513	27.10
451	23.11	514	27.11
452	23.12	515	27.12
453	23.13	516	27.11 note
454	23.14	517	27.13
455	23.15	518	27.14
456	23.16	519	27.15
457	23.17	520	27.16
458		521	27.17
459		522	28.01
460	23.18	523	28.01 note
461	24.01	524	28.02
462	24.02	525	28.12
463	24.03	526	28.03
464	24.04	527	28.04
465	24.05	528	28.05
466	24.06	529	28.06
467	24.07	530	28.07
468	24.08	531	28.08
469	24.09	532	28.09
470	24.10	533	28.10
471	24.11	534	28.11
472	24.12	535	28.12
473	24.14	536	28.13
474	24.15	537	28.14
475	24.16	538	29.01
476	24.17	539	29.02
477	24.18	540	29.03
478	24.19	541	29.04
479	24.20	542	29.05
480	24.21	543	29.06
481	24.22	544	29.07
482	24.23	545	29.08
483	24.24	546	
484	24.25	547	29.09
485	24.26	548	29.10
486	24.27	549	29.11
486a	24.28	550	29.12
487	25.01	551	29.13
488	25.02	552	30.01
489	25.03	553	30.02
490	25.04	554	30.03
491	26.01	555	30.04

DISPOSITION TABLE

1925 C.C.P. Article	1965 C.C.P. Article	1925 C.C.P. Article	1965 C.C.P. Article
556	30.05	621	35.21
557	30.06	622	35.22
558	30.07	623	35.23
559	30.08	624	35.20 note
560	31.01	625	See Civ.St. 2122
561	31.02	626	33.09
562	31.03	627	35.11 note
563	31.03 note	628	35.11 note
564	31.03 note	629	35.11 note
565	31.03 note	630	35.16 note
566	31.03 note	631	33.09 note
567	31.04	632	35.16 note
568	Repealed 1926	633	35.14 note
569	31.03 note	634	35.15
570	31.05	635	35.15
571	31.05 note	636	35.25
572	31.05 note	637	35.26
573	31.06	638	33.09 note
574	31.06 note	639	35.22 note
575	31.07	640	33.09 note
576	32.01	641	35.07 note
577	32.02	642	36.01
578	33.01	643	36.02
579	33.02	644	36.03
580	33.03	645	36.04
581	33.04	646	36.05
582	33.05	647	36.06
583	33.06	648	36.07
584	33.07	649	36.08
585	33.08	650	36.09
586	33.08	651	36.09 note
587	34.01	652	36.10
588	34.01 note	653	36.09 note
589	34.01 note	654	36.09 note
590	34.01 note	655	36.11
591	33.09	656	36.12
592	34.01 note	657	36.13
593	34.01 note	658	36.14
594	34.01 note	659	36.15
595	34.01 note	660	36.16
596	34.02	661	36.17
597	34.01	662	Repealed 1953
598	34.01 note	663	Repealed 1953
599	34.03 note	664	36.15 note
600	34.04 note	665	36.18
601	34.04	666	36.19
601a	34.01	667	36.20
602	35.01	668	35.23 note
603	35.02	670	36.21
604	35.03	671	36.22
605	35.04	672	36.23
606	35.05	673	36.24
607	35.06	674	36.25
608	35.07	675	36.26
609	35.08	676	36.27
610	35.09	677	36.27 note
611	35.10	678	36.28
612	35.12	679	36.27 note
613	35.13	680	36.29 note
614	35.14	681	36.30
615	35.15	682	36.31
616	35.16	683	36.32
617	35.18	684	36.33
618	35.18 note	685	36.27 note
619	35.19	686	37.01
620	35.20	687	36.29 note

DISPOSITION TABLE

1925 C.C.P. Article	1965 C.C.P. Article	1925 C.C.P. Article	1965 C.C.P. Article
688	37.02	751	40.01
689	37.03	752	40.02
690	37.04	753	40.03
691	37.05	754	40.04
692	37.06	755	40.05
693	37.07	756	40.05 note
694	37.08	757	40.06
695	37.09	758	40.07
696	37.10	759	40.08
697	37.11	759a	40.09 note
698	37.12		Repealed 1951 as "originally
699	37.07 note	760	enacted"
700	37.13 note	760a	40.09 note
701	37.13	760b	40.09 note
702	37.14	760c	40.10
703	38.01	760d	40.09 note
704	38.02	760e	40.09 note
705	38.03	761	41.01
706	38.04	762	41.02
707	38.05	763	41.03
708	38.06	764	41.04
709	38.07	765	41.05
710	38.08	766	42.01
711	38.06 note	767	42.02
712	38.09	768	42.03
713	38.10	769	42.04
714	38.11	770	42.05 note
715	38.12	771	42.05 note
716	38.06 note	772	42.06
717	38.13	773	42.07
718	38.14	774	42.08
719	38.06 note	775	42.09
720	38.15	775a	Repealed 1957
721	38.16	776	42.12 note
722	38.17	776a	42.12 note
723	38.18	777	42.12 note
724	38.19	778	42.12 note
725	38.20	779	42.12 note
726	38.21	780	42.12 note
727	38.22	781	42.12 note
727a	38.23	781a	42.10
728	38.24	781b	Repealed 1957
729	38.25	781b–1	Civ.St. 2292–1
730	38.26	781b–2	Civ.St. 2292–2
731	38.27	781c	42.11
732	38.28	781d	42.12
732a	38.29	782	42.14
733	38.30	783	42.15
733a	38.31	784	42.16
734	39.01	784a	42.13 note
735	39.02	785	43.01
736	39.03	786	43.02
737	39.09	787	43.03
738	39.09	788	43.04
739	39.04	789	43.05
740	39.05	790	43.06
741	39.02 note	791	43.07
742	39.06	792	43.08
743	39.07	793	43.09
744	39.08	793a	Unconstitutional 1939
745	39.01 note	794	43.10
746	39.01 note	794a	Unconstitutional 1939
747	39.01 note	794b	Unconstitutional 1939
748	39.10	794c	Unconstitutional 1939
749	39.12	794d	Unconstitutional 1939
750	39.01 note	795	43.11

DISPOSITION TABLE

DISPOSITION TABLE

1925 C.C.P. Article	1965 C.C.P. Article	1925 C.C.P. Article	1965 C.C.P. Article
936	47.04	1006	51.10
937	47.05	1007	51.11
938	47.06	1008	51.12
939	47.07	1008a	51.13
940	47.08	1009	1009
941	47.09	1010	1010
942	47.10	1010a	1010a
943	47.11	1011	1011
944	1001	1012	1012
945	1002	1013	1013
946	1003	1014	1014
947	1004	1015	1015
948	1005	1016	1016
949	1006	1017	1017
950	1007	1018	1018
951	1008	1019	1019
952	48.01	1019a	1019a
953	48.01 note	1020	1020
954	48.04	1021	1021
955	48.01 note	1022	1022
956	48.01 note	1023	1023
957	48.02	1024	1024
958	48.03	1025	1025
959 to 966	Repealed 1957	1026	1026
967	48.05	1027	1027
968	49.01	1028	1028
969	49.02	1029	1029
970	49.03	1030	1030
970a	49.04	1030a	1030a
970b	49.05	1031	1031
971	49.06	1032	1032
972	49.07	1033	1033
973	49.08	1034	1034
974	49.09	1035	1035
975	49.10	1036	35.27
976	49.11	1037	1037
977	49.12	1038	1038
978	49.13	1039	1039
979	49.14	1040	1040
980	49.15	1041	1041
981	49.16	1041a	1041a
982	49.17	1042	1042
983	49.18	1043	1043
984	49.19	1044	1044
985	49.20	1045	1045
986	49.21	1046	1046
987	49.22	1047	1047
988	49.23	1048	1048
989	49.24	1049	1049
989a	49.25	1050	1050
990	50.01	1051	1051
991	50.02	1052	1052
992	50.03	1053	1053
993	50.04	1054	1054
994	50.05	1055	1055
995	50.06	1056	See Civ.St. 2122
996	50.07	1057	Repealed 1945
997	51.01	1058	1058
998	51.02	1058a	1058a
999	51.03	1059	1059
1000	51.04	1060	1060
1001	51.05	1061	1061
1002	51.06	1062	1062
1003	51.07	1063	1063
1004	51.08	1064	1064
1005	51.09	1065	53.01

DISPOSITION TABLE

DISPOSITION TABLE

Showing where former provisions of the Rules of Civil Procedure, the Rules of Post Trial and Appellate Procedure in Criminal Cases, and the Code of Criminal Procedure are covered in the Texas Rules of Appellate Procedure.

RULES OF CIVIL PROCEDURE

Former Rule	Appellate Procedure Rule
18b	15
21c	54(c), 100, 130
352	3(a)
353	40(a)(4)
354	46(a) to (e)
355	40(a)(3)
356(a)	41(a)(1)
(b)	41(a)(2)
(c)	40(a)(2)
357	40(a)(5)
358	9(c)
360	45
363	40(a)(1)
363a	46(f)
364	47(a) to (i)
365	49(a), (b)
366	49(c)
367	49(c)
368	47(j)
369	10
369a	9a
371	50
372	52
373	52
375	50
376	51(a) to (c), 52
376b	11
376c	12(b), (c)
377	53(a) to (i), 55(a)
377a	58
378	50
379	51(d)
380	53(j)
381	50(f)
383	121
383a	120
385	42
385a	16
385b	43
386	54(a)
387	60(a)
387a	59(a)
388	56(a)
388a	13
389	56(a)
389a	56(b)
393	18(c)
394	17
395 to 398	18(d)

Former Rule	Appellate Procedure Rule
399	61
401	6
402	57
402a	7
403	8
404	71
405	72
407	70
408	19(b)
409	19(c), (e)
410	77
411	76, 77
413	50
414	4(a), (b), 74
419	74(f)
420	74(e)
422	74(p)
423	75
428	55(b)
429	55(c)
433	80
434	81
435	82
436	87(a)
437	83
438	84
439	85(a)
440	85(b)
441	85(c)
442	86(a)
446	86(e)
447	88
448	89
452	90
456	91
457	5(e)
458	100
461(a)	110
462(b)	110
466(c)	110
468	130
469	4(a), (b), 131(a) to (g), (i)
472	132(a), (b)
474	121
475	120
477	111
478	112
479	113
480	132(c)
480a	4(c), (d)
481	131(h), 136(f)

DISPOSITION TABLE

RULES OF POST TRIAL AND APPELLATE PROCEDURE IN CRIMINAL CASES

CODE OF CRIMINAL PROCEDURE

DERIVATION TABLE

Showing the source provisions for the Texas Rules of Appellate Procedure. As used in this table, R.Civ.P. means the Rules of Civil Procedure, Crim.App.R. means the Texas Rules of Post Trial and Appellate Procedure in Criminal Cases, C.C.P. means the Code of Criminal Procedure of 1965, and R.Evid. means the Texas Rules of Evidence.

Rule of Appellate Procedure	Source Provisions
1(a)	Crim.App.R. 3(a)
(b)	R.App.P. 3a
2	Crim.App.R. 3(b)
3(a)	R.Civ.P. 352
(b)	Crim.App.R. 8
4(a), (b)	R.Civ.P. 414, 469
(c), (d)	R.Civ.P. 480a, 492
5(a)	R.Civ.P. 4
	Crim.App.R. 7
(b) to (d)	R.Civ.P. 306a
(e)	R.Civ.P. 457
6	R.Civ.P. 401, 499
7	R.Civ.P. 402a
8	R.Civ.P. 403
9(a)	R.Civ.P. 369a
(c)	R.Civ.P. 358
10	R.Civ.P. 369
11	R.Civ.P. 376b
12(b), (c)	R.Civ.P. 376c
13	R.Civ.P. 388a, 485
14	R.Civ.P. 514
15	R.Civ.P. 18b
16	R.Civ.P. 385a
17	R.Civ.P. 394, 488
18(a)	Crim.App.R. 203(b) to (d)
(c)	R.Civ.P. 393
(d)	R.Civ.P. 395 to 398, 490 Crim.App.R. 203(b) to (d)
19(b)	R.Civ.P. 408
(c), (e)	R.Civ.P. 409
20	R.Civ.P. 496
40(a)(1)	R.Civ.P. 363
(a)(2)	R.Civ.P. 356(c)
(a)(3)	R.Civ.P. 355
(a)(4)	R.Civ.P. 353
(a)(5)	R.Civ.P. 357
(b)(1)	C.C.P. Art. 44.08
(b)(2)	C.C.P. Art. 44.11
41(a)(1)	R.Civ.P. 356(a)
(a)(2)	R.Civ.P. 356(b)
(b)	C.C.P. Art. 44.08
(c)	R.Civ.P. 306c
42	R.Civ.P. 385
43	R.Civ.P. 385b
44(a)	C.C.P. Art. 44.34
(b)	C.C.P. Art. 44.36
(c)	C.C.P. Art. 44.37
(d)	C.C.P. Art. 44.38
44(e)	C.C.P. Art. 44.39
(f)	C.C.P. Art. 44.40
45	R.Civ.P. 360
46(a) to (e)	R.Civ.P. 354
(f)	R.Civ.P. 363a
47(a) to (i)	R.Civ.P. 364
(j)	R.Civ.P. 368
48	R.Civ.P. 14c
49(a), (b)	R.Civ.P. 365
(c)	R.Civ.P. 366, 367
50	R.Civ.P. 371, 375, 378, 413
(e)	C.C.P. Art. 44.11
(f)	R.Civ.P. 381
51(a) to (c)	R.Civ.P. 376
(d)	R.Civ.P. 379
52	R.Civ.P. 372, 373, 376 R.Evid. 103
53(a) to (i)	R.Civ.P. 377
(j)	R.Civ.P. 380
54(a)	R.Civ.P. 386
(c)	R.Civ.P. 21c
55(a)	R.Civ.P. 377
(b)	R.Civ.P. 428
(c)	R.Civ.P. 429
56(a)	R.Civ.P. 388, 389
(b)	R.Civ.P. 389a
57	R.Civ.P. 402
(a)	Crim.App.R. 203(a)
58	R.Civ.P. 377a
59(a)	R.Civ.P. 387a
(b)	C.C.P. Art. 44.08
60(a)	R.Civ.P. 387
(b)	C.C.P. Art. 44.09
61	R.Civ.P. 399
70	R.Civ.P. 407
71	R.Civ.P. 404
72	R.Civ.P. 405
73	Crim.App.R. 6
74	R.Civ.P. 414
(e)	R.Civ.P. 420
(f)	R.Civ.P. 419
(l)	C.C.P. Art. 44.33(b)
(p)	R.Civ.P. 422
75	R.Civ.P. 423
76	R.Civ.P. 411
76	Crim.App.R. 204
77	R.Civ.P. 410, 411
78	C.C.P. Art. 44.23
79	Crim.App.R. 206

DERIVATION TABLE

Rule of Appellate Procedure	Source Provisions	Rule of Appellate Procedure	Source Provisions
80	R.Civ.P. 433	113	R.Civ.P. 479
	C.C.P. Art. 44.24(a), (b)	120	R.Civ.P. 383a, 475, 486
81	R.Civ.P. 434	121	R.Civ.P. 383, 474, 486
82	R.Civ.P. 435	122	R.Civ.P. 483
83	R.Civ.P. 437	130	R.Civ.P. 21c, 468
84	R.Civ.P. 438	131(a) to (g)	R.Civ.P. 469
85(a)	R.Civ.P. 439	(h)	R.Civ.P. 481
(b)	R.Civ.P. 440	(i)	R.Civ.P. 469
(c)	R.Civ.P. 441	132(a), (b)	R.Civ.P. 472
86(a)	R.Civ.P. 442	(c)	R.Civ.P. 480
(d)	C.C.P. Art. 44.27	133	R.Civ.P. 483
(e)	R.Civ.P. 446	134	R.Civ.P. 484
87(a)	R.Civ.P. 436	135	R.Civ.P. 486
(b)	C.C.P. Arts. 44.05, 44.06, 44.29, 44.31	136(a) to (e)	R.Civ.P. 496
		(f)	R.Civ.P. 481
88	R.Civ.P. 447	140	R.Civ.P. 499a
89	R.Civ.P. 448	170	R.Civ.P. 497
90	R.Civ.P. 452	171	R.Civ.P. 493
	Crim.App.R. 207(a)	172	R.Civ.P. 498
91	R.Civ.P. 456	180	R.Civ.P. 505
	C.C.P. Art. 44.24(e)	181	R.Civ.P. 500
100	R.Civ.P. 21c, 458	182	R.Civ.P. 501
	Crim.App.R. 208	183	R.Civ.P. 502
110	R.Civ.P. 461(a), 462(b), 466(c)	184	R.Civ.P. 503
111	R.Civ.P. 477	185	R.Civ.P. 504
112	R.Civ.P. 478	186	R.Civ.P. 507, 510
		190	R.Civ.P. 515

CODE OF CRIMINAL PROCEDURE
TABLE OF ARTICLES AFFECTED
BY THE 85th LEGISLATURE,
REGULAR AND FIRST CALLED SESSIONS

TABLE OF ARTICLES AFFECTED

TABLE OF ARTICLES AFFECTED

TABLE OF ARTICLES AFFECTED

CODE OF CRIMINAL PROCEDURE

TABLE OF ARTICLES AFFECTED

TABLE OF ARTICLES AFFECTED

TABLE OF ARTICLES AFFECTED

TABLE OF CONTENTS

_____

CODE OF CRIMINAL PROCEDURE
TITLE 1

Article Analysis, see beginning of each Chapter.

INTRODUCTORY

COURTS AND CRIMINAL JURISDICTION

PREVENTION AND SUPPRESSION OF OFFENSES

HABEAS CORPUS

LIMITATION AND VENUE

ARREST, COMMITMENT AND BAIL

XXXV

TABLE OF CONTENTS

TABLE OF CONTENTS

APPEAL AND WRIT OF ERROR

JUSTICE AND MUNICIPAL COURTS

MISCELLANEOUS PROCEEDINGS

TITLE 2

TABLE OF CONTENTS

GOVERNMENT CODE

RULES OF EVIDENCE

RULES OF APPELLATE PROCEDURE

APPENDIXES TO THE TEXAS RULES OF APPELLATE PROCEDURE

INDEX

(Page I–1)

STATE LAW OF CHARGING INSTRUMENTS

HELENA F. FAULKNER, Assistant Criminal District Attorney
Tarrant County, Texas*

October, 2017

Table of Contents

* Helena F. Faulkner has been an assistant criminal district attorney in the post-conviction section of the Tarrant County Criminal District Attorney's Office since January 1994. Prior to that, she spent a year in private practice and worked for three and a half years in Dallas, Texas, as a briefing attorney and then a research attorney at the Court of Appeals for the Fifth District of Texas. She is a graduate of Texas Tech University School of Law and Texas Christian University.

A special word of thanks to Marvin Collins and Candyce Howell, attorneys at law, for allowing me in 2008 to begin rewriting and updating their previous paper on this topic.

STATE LAW OF CHARGING INSTRUMENTS

I. SCOPE OF ARTICLE

This article discusses state law governing charging instruments, as well as joinder and severance of offenses and defendants. It does not address grand-jury proceedings.

II. CHARGING INSTRUMENTS

A. INDICTMENTS, INFORMATIONS, AND COMPLAINTS GENERALLY

1.   The preliminary pleading in a criminal action on the part of the State is the indictment or information. Tex. Code Crim. Proc. art. 27.01.

2.   An indictment is the written instrument presented to a court by a grand jury charging the named person with an offense. Tex. Const. art. V, § 12(b); Tex. Code Crim. Proc. art. 21.01.

3.   An information is a written instrument presented to a court by an attorney for the State charging a person with the commission of an offense. Tex. Const. art. V, § 12(b); Tex. Code Crim. Proc. art. 21.20. It is normally the pleading that initiates a misdemeanor prosecution in county court. *See* Tex. Code Crim. Proc. art. 2.05. An information is considered "presented" when it has been "filed by the proper officer in the proper court." *Id*. art. 12.07.

4.   A complaint is an affidavit of a credible person made before the magistrate or district or county attorney charging the commission of an offense. Tex. Code Crim. Proc. arts. 15.05, 21.22. The complaint must be filed with the information. Id. art. 21.22; *State v. Drummond*, 501 S.W.3d 78 (Tex. Crim. App. 2016). A valid complaint is a prerequisite to a valid information. Tex. Code Crim. Proc. art. 21.22; *State v. Zorilla*, 404 S.W.3d 734 (Tex. App.—San Antonio 2013, no pet.).

5.   The rules with respect to allegations in an indictment and the certainty required apply also to an information. Tex. Code Crim. Proc. 21.23.

6.   An indictment is required in all felony prosecutions unless it is expressly and voluntarily waived by the defendant while represented by counsel. Tex. Const. art. I, § 10; Tex. Code Crim. Proc. art. 1.141. An indictment cannot be waived for a capital felony. Tex. Code Crim. Proc. art. 1.141.

7.   The presentment of an indictment or information vests the trial court with jurisdiction. Tex. Const. art. V, § 12(b). Absent an indictment or a valid waiver, however, a district court does not have jurisdiction over the case. *Teal v. State*, 230 S.W.3d 172 (Tex. Crim. App. 2007). An instrument which is not an indictment or information under Tex. Const. art. V, § 12 will not vest the trial court with jurisdiction. *Smith v. State*, 494 S.W.3d 243 (Tex. App.—Texarkana 2015, no pet.). A defect of substance (*e.g.,* the absence of an element) does not deprive the court of jurisdiction. *Id*.; *Duron v. State*, 956 S.W.2d 547 (Tex. Crim. App. 1997); *Studer v. State*, 799 S.W.2d 263 (Tex. Crim. App. 1990).

8.   A felony court may still acquire jurisdiction over a case if the indictment, because of its defects, alleges only a misdemeanor. *Kirkpatrick v. State*, 279 S.W.3d 324 (Tex. Crim. App. 2009) (indictments charging two counts of misdemeanor tampering with government record were sufficient to show State's intent to charge felony offenses of tampering with government record and vested district court with subject-matter jurisdiction); *Nix v. State*, 401 S.W.3d 656 (Tex. App.—Houston [14th Dist.] 2013, pet. ref'd). The test for assessing a trial court's jurisdiction is not whether the indictment actually alleges a felony, but whether the indictment, despite its substantive defects, is "capable of being construed as intending to

charge a felony (or a misdemeanor for which the district court has jurisdiction)." *Kirkpatrick*, supra; *Nix*, supra.

9.   A defect in the underlying complaint is not jurisdictional. *Ramirez v. State*, 105 S.W.3d 628 (Tex. Crim. App. 2003); *Aguilar v. State*, 846 S.W.2d 318 (Tex. Crim. App. 1993). A trial court that "finds fault with an information or indictment does not 'dismiss' the complaint on which the indictment or information was based, but sets aside the information or indictment." *State v. Drummond*, 472 S.W.3d 857 (Tex. App.—Houston [1st Dist.] 2015) (quoting *State v. Boseman*, 830 S.W.2d 588 (Tex. Crim. App. 1992)), *rev'd on other grounds*, 501 S.W.3d 78 (Tex. Crim. App. 2016).

10.   While indictment by a grand jury is guaranteed by Tex. Const. art. I, § 10, it is not part of the due process guaranteed by the Fourteenth Amendment of the United States Constitution. *Branzburg v. Hayes*, 408 U.S. 665 (1972); *Hurtado v. California*, 110 U.S. 516 (1884).

B.   WAIVER ISSUES–Tex. Code Crim. Proc. art. 1.14(b)

1.   An accused who does not raise a defect, error, or irregularity of form or substance in an indictment or information before the date on which the trial on the merits commences waives and forfeits the right to object, and he may not raise the objection on appeal or in any other post-conviction proceeding. Tex. Code Crim. Proc. art. 1.14(b); *see Teal v. State*, 230 S.W.3d 172 (Tex. Crim. App. 2007); *Ortega v. State*, 472 S.W.3d 779 (Tex. App.—Houston [14th Dist.] 2015, no pet.). Because defects in indictments are subject to waiver, the existence of such defects does not render the indictment void. *Smith v. State*, 494 S.W.3d 243 (Tex. App.—Texarkana 2015, no pet.).

2.   For purposes of art. 1.14(b), trial commences on the date when the jury is seated and sworn. *Ledesma v. State*, 993 S.W.2d 361 (Tex. App.—Fort Worth 1999, pet. ref'd); *Satterwhite v. State*, 952 S.W.2d 613 (Tex. App.—Corpus Christi 1997), *aff'd*, 979 S.W.2d 626 (Tex. Crim. App. 1998); *Hinojosa v. State*, 875 S.W.2d 339 (Tex. App.—Corpus Christi 1994, no pet.); *see Freeman v. State*, 74 S.W.3d 913 (Tex. App.—Amarillo 2002, pet. ref'd) (objection made at pretrial hearing "immediately prior to the commencement of trial" held untimely).

3.   A defect that prevents the charging instrument from qualifying as an indictment under Tex. Const. art. V, § 12(b) does not vest the trial court with jurisdiction, and such defect need not be raised pursuant to art. 1.14(b). *See Cook v. State*, 902 S.W.2d 471 (Tex. Crim. App. 1995).

4.   A complaint that a charging instrument is so defective that it deprives the trial court of jurisdiction can be raised for the first time on appeal. *Smith v. State*, 494 S.W.3d 243 (Tex. App.—Texarkana 2015, no pet.).

5.   Generally, if state law requires a constitutional defect to be raised in a particular manner, the failure to timely object cannot be reviewed in federal court. *Wainwright v. Sykes*, 433 U.S. 72 (1977). This rule applies to indictments. *Johnson v. Estelle*, 704 F.2d 232 (5th Cir. 1983).

C.   STRUCTURAL REQUIREMENTS

1.   Commencement and Conclusion

a.   An indictment must commence, "In the name and by authority of The State of Texas." Tex. Code Crim. Proc. art. 21.02(1).

b.   The indictment must conclude, "Against the peace and dignity of the State." Tex. Code Crim. Proc. art. 21.02(8).

c.   An objection to the omission of a formal commencement or conclusion is waived if it is not raised pretrial pursuant to Tex. Code Crim. Proc. art. 1.14(b).

2.   Presentment

a.   The indictment must show that it "was presented in the district court of the county where the grand jury is in session." Tex. Code Crim. Proc. art. 21.02(2).

b.   An exception to the form of an indictment or information may be taken on the grounds that it "does not appear to have been presented in the proper court as required by law." Tex. Code Crim. Proc. art. 27.09(1).

c.   An indictment may be amended to allege the court in which it is presented as long as the amendment complies with Tex. Code Crim. Proc. art. 28.10. Tex. Code crim. Proc. art. 28.09–.11.

3.   Act of the Grand Jury

a.   The indictment must "appear to be the act of a grand jury of the proper county." Tex. Code Crim. Proc. art. 21.02(3).

b.   The indictment need not allege that the grand jurors were sworn or that the presentment was made on their oaths or affirmations. *Lamar v. State*, 149 S.W.2d 89 (Tex. Crim. App. 1941).

c.   An exception to the form of an indictment or information may be taken on the grounds that it "was not returned by a lawfully chosen or empaneled grand jury." Tex. Code Crim. Proc. art. 27.09(3).

4.   Name of the Accused

a.   An indictment "must contain the name of the accused, or state that his name is unknown and give a reasonably accurate description of him." Tex. Code Crim. Proc. art. 21.02(4); *see id.* art. 21.07.

b.   A charging instrument that completely fails to charge a person is not an indictment as defined by Tex. Const. art. V, § 12(b). *Cook v. State*, 902 S.W.2d 471 (Tex. Crim. App. 1995).

c.   In alleging the name of the defendant, it is sufficient to state one or more of the initials of the given name and the surname of the defendant. Tex. Code Crim. Proc. art. 21.07.

d.   When a person is known by two or more names, it is sufficient to state either name. Tex. Code Crim. Proc. art. 21.07.

e.   Use of the word "Defendant" in part of the indictment is appropriate if it obviously refers back to the accused individual named in the indictment. *King v. State*, 649 S.W.2d 42 (Tex. Crim. App. 1983).

f.   Unless the defendant or his counsel suggests when he is arraigned that he is not indicted by his true name, it will be taken that he is correctly named in the indictment, and he cannot later deny the same by way of a defense. Tex. Code Crim. Proc. art. 26.07.

g.   If the defendant or his counsel timely suggests that his name is misspelled or that he bears a different name from the one stated in the charging instrument, the trial court is authorized to correct the indictment to reflect his true name. Tex. Code Crim. Proc. art. 26.08. The cause then proceeds as if the true name had been first recited in the indictment. *Id.* Changing a defendant's name in the indictment is a ministerial act. *Wynn v. State*, 864 S.W.2d 539 (Tex. Crim. App. 1993); *Kelley v. State*, 823 S.W.2d 300 (Tex. Crim. App. 1992).

h.   If the defendant alleges that he is not indicted by his true name, and refuses to say what his real name is, the cause shall proceed as if the name stated in the indictment were true; and the defendant shall not be allowed to contradict the same by way of defense. Tex. Code Crim. Proc. art. 26.09.

i.   A defendant described as a person whose name is unknown may have the indictment corrected to reflect his true name. Tex. Code Crim. Proc. art. 26.10.

j.   Because Tex. Code Crim. Proc. arts. 26.07 and 26.08 provide a specific method and time for changing a defendant's name in the indictment, the more general provisions for amending indictments found in Tex. Code Crim. Proc. arts. 28.09 *et seq.* do not apply. *Kelley v. State*, 823 S.W.2d 300 (Tex. Crim. App. 1992).

k.   If the defendant is charged by a different name in a prior indictment used for enhancement, the enhancement portion of the present indictment is sufficient if the State proves that the defendant is the person named in the prior indictment. *Rios v. State*, 557 S.W.2d 87 (Tex. Crim. App. 1977); *Garza v. State*, 548 S.W.2d 55 (Tex. Crim. App. 1977).

5. Venue

a.   The indictment must show "that the place where the offense was committed is within the jurisdiction of the court in which the indictment is presented." Tex. Code Crim. Proc. art. 21.02(5).

b.   Presentment of an indictment omitting the venue allegation vests the trial court with jurisdiction of the cause, Tex. Const. art. V, § 12, and such a defect is waived by failure to raise a pretrial objection. Tex. Code Crim. Proc. art. 1.14(b).

c.   Use of words such as "then and there" or "in the County and State aforesaid" is sufficient to allege that the offense occurred in the county previously named in the indictment. *Ex parte Hunter*, 604 S.W.2d 188 (Tex. Crim. App. 1980).

d.   When the charged offense may be prosecuted in either of two or more counties, the indictment may allege that the offense was committed in the county where it is prosecuted or in any county or place where the offense was actually committed. Tex. Code Crim. Proc. art. 21.06.

6. Date of the Offense

a.   The indictment must allege a "date anterior to the presentment of the indictment, and not so remote that the prosecution of the offense is barred by limitation." Tex. Code Crim. Proc. art. 21.02(6); *see Tita v. State*, 267 S.W.3d 33 (Tex. Crim. App. 2008) (charging instrument must reflect on its face that prosecution is not barred by applicable statute of limitations); *State v. Schunior*, 467 S.W.3d 79 (Tex. App.—San Antonio 2015), *aff'd*, 506 S.W.3d 29 (Tex. Crim. App. 2016).

b.   An allegation that the offense was committed "anterior to the presentment of this indictment" satisfies Tex. Code Crim. Proc. art. 21.02(6).

c.   When the offense is alleged to have occurred "on or about" a specific date, the State may prove a date other than the one alleged if the date proven is anterior to presentment of the indictment and within the statutory limitation period. *Sanchez v. State*, 400 S.W.3d 595 (Tex. Crim. App. 2013); *Rodriguez v. State*, 446 S.W.3d 520 (Tex. App.—San Antonio 2014, no pet.).

d.   Before trial, a defendant may challenge the substance of the charging instrument if it shows on its face that the prosecution is barred by lapse of time or that the offense was committed after the finding of the indictment. Tex. Code Crim. Proc. art. 27.08(2).

e. Purported defects in a tolling paragraph may not be raised in a pretrial petition for writ of habeas corpus because they do not deprive the trial court of jurisdiction. *Ex parte Smith*, 178 S.W.3d 797 (Tex. Crim. App. 2005) (per curiam). Only when the indictment shows on its face that prosecution is absolutely barred by the statute of limitations, and the pleading is not reparable, may a defendant seek relief through a pretrial writ of habeas corpus. *Id.*; *State v. Schunior*, 467 S.W.3d 79 (Tex. App.—San Antonio 2015), *aff'd*, 506 S.W.3d 29 (Tex. Crim. App. 2016).

f. Including a "tolling paragraph," "explanatory averments," or even "innuendo allegations" in the indictment suffices to show that the charged offense is not, at least on its face, barred by limitations. *Tita v. State*, 267 S.W.3d 33 (Tex. Crim. App. 2008); *Ex parte Smith*, 178 S.W.3d 797 (Tex. Crim. App. 2005) (per curiam). A tolling paragraph need not be alleged with the same degree of particularity as an allegation of the charged offense. *Ex parte Smith*, supra. Pleading tolling facts avoids a defect in the charging instrument. *Tita*, supra.

g. The State must plead its reliance on a tolling provision if the indictment does not demonstrate on its face that the crime alleged occurred within the limitations period. *Tita v. State*, 267 S.W.3d 33 (Tex. Crim. App. 2008); *State v. Schunior*, 467 S.W.3d 79 (Tex. App.—San Antonio 2015), *aff'd*, 506 S.W.3d 29 (Tex. Crim. App. 2016).

h. A defendant may object to the substance of an indictment and obtain dismissal of the indictment if "it appears from the face thereof that a prosecution for the offense is barred by a lapse of time." Tex. Code Crim. Proc. 27.08(2); *Tita v. State*, 267 S.W.3d 33 (Tex. Crim. App. 2008). In order to avoid dismissal, the State must plead any tolling factors to prevent the indictment from giving the appearance that the prosecution is barred by a lapse of time. *Tita*, supra.

i. A harm analysis under Tex. R. App. P. 44.2(b) is necessary when an indictment is defective due to the lack of a tolling provision. *Mercier v. State*, 322 S.W.3d 258 (Tex. Crim. App. 2010). There may be some overlap between Tex. R. App. P. 44.2(b) and Tex. Code Crim. Proc. art. 21.19. *Mercier*, supra. Rule 44.2(b) deals with other error in general, including defects of substance, while art. 21.19 is specific to defects of form and applies before, during, or after the trial. *Id.*

7. Specificity of the Allegations

a. An accused is guaranteed the right to be informed of the nature and cause of the accusations against him in all criminal actions. *See* U.S. Const. amend. VI; Tex. Const. art. I, § 10.

b. The charged offense "must be set forth in plain and intelligible words." Tex. Code Crim. Proc. art. 21.02(7).

c. The accused is not required to look beyond the face of the indictment for notice of the nature and cause of the accusation. *Riney v. State*, 28 S.W.3d 561 (Tex. Crim. App. 2000).

d. Accusations must be set forth with enough clarity and specificity to identify the penal statute under which the State intends to prosecute, even if the instrument is otherwise defective. *Teal v. State*, 230 S.W.3d 172 (Tex. Crim. App. 2007); *Duron v. State*, 956 S.W.2d 547 (Tex. Crim. App. 1997).

e. A charging instrument is sufficient if, on its face, it charges the offense in plain and intelligible words that would enable a person of common understanding to know what offense he will be required to defend himself against and to enable him to plead the judgment that may be given on it in bar of any further prosecution. Tex. Code Crim. Proc. arts. 21.02(7), 21.03, 21.04, 21.11; *see Lawrence v. State*, 240 S.W.3d 912 (Tex. Crim. App. 2007); *State v.*

Moff, 154 S.W.3d 599 (Tex. Crim. App. 2004); *Nix v. State*, 401 S.W.3d 656 (Tex. App.—Houston [14th Dist.] 2013, no pet.).

f. In analyzing whether a charging instrument provides adequate notice, courts must engage in a two-step analysis. *State v. Barbernell*, 257 S.W.3d 248 (Tex. Crim. App. 2008). First, the court must identify the elements of the offense. *Id*. The elements of an offense include: the forbidden conduct; the required culpability, if any; any required result; and the negation of any exception to the offense. *Id*. Second, if the definition of an offense provides for alternative manners or means of committing an actor or omission, the charging instrument must allege the specific manner and means of commission that the State intends to rely on at trial. *Id*.

8. Signature of Grand Jury Foreman

a. The grand jury foreman must officially sign the indictment. Tex. Code Crim. Proc. art. 21.02(9). This requirement "is to insure that the indictment presented is in fact the one voted on and returned by the grand jury." *Stigers v. State*, 702 S.W.2d 301 (Tex. App.—Houston [1st Dist.] 1985, no pet.).

b. In certain circumstances, the grand jury foreman need not personally sign the indictment. *E.g., Paulus v. State*, 633 S.W.2d 827 (Tex. Crim. App. [Panel Op.] 1981) (foreman's signature affixed by rubber stamp); *Owens v. State*, 540 S.W.2d 324 (Tex. Crim. App. 1976) (foreman authorized another grand juror to sign latter's name for him); *Nwosoucha v. State*, 325 S.W.3d 816 (Tex. App.—Houston [14th Dist.] 2010, pet. ref'd) (assistant foreman's signature); *Stigers v. State*, 702 S.W.2d 301 (Tex. App.—Houston [1st Dist.] 1985, no pet.) (foreman's signature made with facsimile stamp).

c. The lack of the grand-jury foreman's signature will not invalidate an otherwise validly-presented indictment. *Riney v. State*, 28 S.W.3d 561 (Tex. Crim. App. 2000); *Tatmon v. State*, 815 S.W.2d 588 (Tex. Crim. App. 1991).

D. DRAFTING AND CHARGING ISSUES

1. Paragraphs and Counts

a. Two or more offenses may be joined and alleged in separate counts of a single charging instrument if the offenses arise out of the same criminal episode as defined in chapter 3 of the Texas Penal Code. Tex. Code Crim. Proc. art. 21.24(a); *Martinez v. State*, 225 S.W.3d 550 (Tex. Crim. App. 2007).

b. When the State wishes to charge multiple offenses in a single indictment, it is required to set out each separate offense in a separate count. *Martinez v. State*, 225 S.W.3d 550 (Tex. Crim. App. 2007).

c. Different methods of committing the same offense are alleged in separate paragraphs within a single count. Tex. Code Crim. Proc. art. 21.24(b); Martinez v. State, 225 S.W.3d 550 (Tex. Crim. App. 2007). A count may contain as many separate paragraphs charging the same offense as necessary, but no paragraph may contain more than one offense. Tex. Code Crim. Proc. art. 21.24(b); *see Bennett v. State*, 471 S.W.3d 5 (Tex. App.—El Paso 2015, pet. ref'd).

d. The State need not elect between counts, and a conviction on each count is permissible.[1] *Patterson v. State*, 96 S.W.3d 427 (Tex. App.—Austin 2002), *aff'd*, 152 S.W.3d 88 (Tex. Crim. App. 2004); *Willeford v. State*, 72 S.W.3d 820 (Tex. App.—Fort Worth 2002, pet. ref'd). However, once the State has closed its evidence, and upon the timely request by the

---

[1] This assumes, of course, that the convictions do not violate the prohibition against double jeopardy, as they would, for example, if the defendant were convicted of both a greater and a lesser offense. *See Landers v. State*, 957 S.W.2d 558 (Tex. Crim. App. 1997), *overruled on other grounds, Ex parte Cavazos*, 203 S.W.3d 333 (Tex. Crim. App. 2006).

defendant, a trial court must order the State to elect the occurrence upon which it intends to rely for a conviction for each alleged offense. *Phillips v. State,* 193 S.W.3d 904 (Tex. Crim. App. 2006).

e. Because each count alleges a single offense, an indictment cannot authorize more convictions than there are counts listed in the indictment. Martinez v. State, 225 S.W.3d 550 (Tex. Crim. App. 2007). Permitting more convictions than the indictment authorizes constitutes an implied amendment and, therefore, implicates the defendant's constitutional right to a grand-jury screening of the charges. Id.

f. Punishment is assessed on each count on which a finding of guilt has been returned. Tex. Code Crim. Proc. art. 37.07, § 2(c).

2. Duplicity[2]

a. "A count may contain as many separate paragraphs charging the same offense as necessary, but no paragraph may charge more than one offense." Tex. Code Crim. Proc. art. 21.24(b).

b. The State may conjunctively charge several ways or means of committing a single offense in one count of an indictment without rendering the charging instrument duplicitous. *Quinones v. State,* 592 S.W.2d 933 (Tex. Crim. App. 1980) (capital-murder indictment alleging in one count that defendant committed murder while in course of committing and attempting to commit kidnapping and robbery); *Sidney v. State,* 560 S.W.2d 679 (Tex. Crim. App. 1978) (aggravated robbery indictment may allege conjunctively in one count that robbery was effected by use and exhibition of deadly weapon and by infliction of serious bodily injury); *Carlock v. State,* 8 S.W.3d 717 (Tex. App.—Waco 1999, pet. ref'd) (alleging commission of burglary by entering habitation with intent to commit felony and committing or attempting to commit felony offense of robbery, or aggravated robbery, or injury to an elderly disabled person); *Gahl v. State,* 721 S.W.2d 888 (Tex. App.—Dallas 1986, pet. ref'd) (alleging different manner and means of committing bribery in single paragraph).

c. When the definition of one offense so includes another that proof of the one necessarily includes or makes out the other, both may be charged in the same count. *Nichols v. State,* 653 S.W.2d 768 (Tex. Crim. App. [Panel Op.] 1981) (allegation of engaging in organized criminal activity also included allegations of specific overt acts that happened to be allegations of other offenses); *Faulks v. State,* 528 S.W.2d 607 (Tex. Crim. App. 1975) (alleging burglary included allegation of theft in same count).

d. A single conspiracy may be charged in one count, even if the subject of the conspiracy involved multiple crimes. *Mutscher v. State,* 514 S.W.2d 905 (Tex. Crim. App. 1974) (charging members of legislature with conspiracy to accept bribe with understanding they would use their vote, influence, and powers of office to pass certain legislation brought before them in official capacities; even if instrument charged two or more separate offenses within count, there was only one act consisting of one agreement among conspirators, one offer constituting bribe, and one acceptance); *Nisbet v. State,* 170 Tex. Crim. 1, 336 S.W.2d 142 (1959) (conspiracy to commit number of crimes included in single count; gist of crime was conspiracy and could include single offense or several).

e. Failure to timely object on the grounds of duplicity waives the error. Tex. Code Crim. Proc. art. 1.14(b); *Lebo v. State,* 100 S.W.3d 417 (Tex. App.—San Antonio 2002, pet. ref'd).

---

[2] "Duplicity" is the technical fault of uniting two or more distinct and separate offenses in the same count of an indictment. *Brock v. State,* 495 S.W.3d 1 (Tex. App.—Waco 2016, pet. ref'd). The long-standing rule against duplicity was codified by Tex. Code Crim. Proc. art. 21.24(b).

3. Unconstitutional Statute

a. An indictment is void if it is based on an unconstitutional statute. *Crumpton v. State*, 977 S.W.2d 763 (Tex. App.—Fort Worth 1998, no pet.).

b. A complaint that a statute is unconstitutional as applied to the defendant must be raised in the trial court, but a complaint below is not required if the statute is facially invalid or void *ab initio*. *Garcia v. State*, 887 S.W.2d 846 (Tex. Crim. App. 1994); *Lawson v. State*, 283 S.W.3d 438 (Tex. App.—Fort Worth 2009, pet. ref'd).

c. A prior conviction alleged for enhancement may be collaterally attacked if it is void or tainted by a constitutional defect. Galloway v. State, 578 S.W.2d 142 (Tex. Crim. App. [Panel Op.] 1979). Other lesser infirmities in a prior conviction may not be collaterally attacked even if they would have resulted in a reversal had they been raised on appeal. Id. (sufficiency of juvenile court's transfer order does not subject prior conviction to collateral attack); *Egger v. State*, 62 S.W.3d 221 (Tex. App.—San Antonio 2001, no pet.) (prior conviction may not be collaterally attacked on basis defendant failed to execute proper jury-waiver form); *Dunbar v. State*, 761 S.W.2d 133 (Tex. App.—Fort Worth 1988, no pet.) (prior conviction may not be collaterally attacked on basis State failed to sign jury-waiver form).

4. Nature of Allegations

a. A charging instrument must charge a person with the commission of an offense against the laws of Texas. Tex. Const. art. V, § 12(b); *Ex parte Patterson,* 969 S.W.2d 16 (Tex. Crim. App. 1998).

b. A charging instrument is not rendered invalid merely because it contains additional information arguably indicating the accused's innocence. *Teal v. State*, 230 S.W.3d 172 (Tex. Crim. App. 2007); *Duron v. State*, 956 S.W.2d 547 (Tex. Crim. App. 1997).

c. If the charging instrument fails to satisfy constitutional requisites, it fails to vest the trial court with jurisdiction, and a judgment of conviction based on it is void. *Nix v. State*, 65 S.W.3d 664 (Tex. Crim. App. 2001). For a judgment to be void, the record must leave no question about the existence of the fundamental defect. *Id.* If the record is incomplete, and the missing portion could conceivably show that the defect does not in fact exist, then the judgment is not void, even though the available portions of the record tend to support the existence of the defect. *Id.*

d. An indictment must state everything that is necessary to be proved. Tex. Code Crim. Proc. art. 21.03. The accused is not required to look beyond the face of the indictment for notice of the nature and cause of the accusation. *Riney v. State*, 28 S.W.3d 561 (Tex. Crim. App. 2000).

e. A charging instrument must be specific enough to inform the defendant of the nature of the accusations against him so that he may prepare a defense. *Smith v. State*, 297 S.W.3d 260 (Tex. Crim. App. 2009); *Buxton v. State*, 2017 WL 2872490 (Tex. App.—Houston [1st Dist.] July 6, 2017, no pet. h.); *Turner v. State*, 435 S.W.3d 280 (Tex. App.—Waco 2014, pet. ref'd).

f. A charging instrument is sufficient if, on its face, it charges the offense in plain and intelligible words that would enable a person of common understanding to know what offense he will be required to defend himself against and to enable him to plead the judgment that may be given on it in bar of any further prosecution for the same offense. Tex. Code Crim. Proc. arts. 21.02(7), 21.03, 21.04, 21.11; *State v. Zuniga*, 512 S.W.3d 902, 906 (Tex. Crim. App. 2017); *Livingston v. State*, 739 S.W.2d 311 (Tex. Crim. App. 1987).

g. Definitions of terms, elements, and other evidentiary facts not required for notice need not be alleged in the charging instrument. *Crenshaw v. State*, 378 S.W.3d 460 (Tex. Crim.

App. 2012) (DWI indictment or information provides adequate notice when it sets out elements of offense as provided in Tex. Penal Code § 49.04; definitions of intoxicated are purely evidentiary and need not be alleged to provide sufficient notice); *State v. Barbernell*, 257 S.W.3d 248 (Tex. Crim. App. 2008) (DWI information need not specify manner of intoxication or whether defendant intoxicated due to loss of faculties or alcohol concentration); *Gray v. State*, 152 S.W.3d 125 (Tex. Crim. App. 2004) (DWI charging instrument need not specify substance that caused intoxication); *Daniels v. State*, 754 S.W.2d 214 (Tex. Crim. App. 1988) (alleging term "constructive transfer" sufficient); *Moreno v. State*, 721 S.W.2d 295 (Tex. Crim. App. 1986) (indictment need not allege facts proving trooper in lawful discharge of duties when killed); *Marrs v. State*, 647 S.W.2d 286 (Tex. Crim. App. 1983) (alleging terms "enter," "habitation," "effective consent," and "owner" sufficient); *Thompson v. State*, 12 S.W.3d 915 (Tex. App.—Beaumont 2000, pet. ref'd) (allegation defendant did "receive notice to depart" sufficient without identifying words used or person who gave notice).

h.   The charging instrument need not allege the evidence on which the State relies unless the additional information is required for notice or a plea in bar. *Compare Livingston v. State*, 739 S.W.2d 311 (Tex. Crim. App. 1987) (alleging murder weapon as "gun" sufficient without description of type of gun); *Moreno v. State*, 721 S.W.2d 295 (Tex. Crim. App. 1986) (capital-murder indictment need not allege specific acts of peace officer that constituted acting in discharge of duties); *George v. State*, 841 S.W.2d 544 (Tex. App.—Houston [1st Dist.] 1992) (indictment for terroristic threat need not allege actual words used), *aff'd*, 890 S.W.2d 73 (Tex. Crim. App. 1994) *with Doyle v. State*, 661 S.W.2d 726 (Tex. Crim. App. 1984) (retaliation indictment should allege how and to whom threat made); *Cruise v. State*, 587 S.W.2d 403 (Tex. Crim. App. [Panel Op.] 1979) (aggravated robbery indictment should allege manner and means of causing bodily injury); *State v. Goodman*, 221 S.W.3d 116 (Tex. App.—Fort Worth 2006, no pet.) (information for violation of Clear Air Act alleging defendant burned "illegal burning materials" should identify items burned illegally).

i.   A legally sufficient indictment may nonetheless be subject to a motion to quash when additional notice is necessary to allow the defendant to adequately prepare a defense or to prevent subsequent prosecution for the same act. *State v. Moff*, 154 S.W.3d 599 (Tex. Crim. App. 2004) (indictment alleging misapplication of fiduciary property held insufficient for failing to state specific transactions alleged to violate statute); *Swabado v. State*, 597 S.W.2d 361 (Tex. Crim. App. 1980) (indictment alleging tampering with government record held insufficient for failing to identify specific monthly staffing report on which State would rely); *Amaya v.* State, 551 S.W.2d 385 (Tex. Crim. App. 1977) (information held insufficient for failing to allege defendant's false statements). A motion to quash should be granted only when the language regarding the accused's conduct is so vague or indefinite that it fails to give the accused adequate notice of the acts that he allegedly committed. *Miller v. State*, 333 S.W.3d 352 (Tex. App.—Fort Worth 2010, pet. ref'd).

j.   When a criminal statute sets forth statutorily-defined alternative methods of committing an offense, the defendant is entitled, upon timely request, to an allegation of which statutory method the State intends to prove. *Geter v. State*, 779 S.W.2d 403 (Tex. Crim. App. 1989) (theft indictment, in face of motion to quash, must allege which statutory negative vitiated consent); *Gorman v. State*, 634 S.W.2d 681 (Tex. Crim. App. [Panel Op.] 1982) (indictment for unlawful appropriation provided insufficient notice for failure to allege type of appropriation); *Ferguson v. State*, 622 S.W.2d 846 (Tex. Crim. App. [Panel Op.] 1981) (op. on reh'g) (indictment alleging delivery of controlled substance must, upon timely motion to quash for lack of notice, specify which statutory definition of deliver the State will try to prove); *Deschenes v. State*, 253 S.W.3d 374 (Tex. App.—Amarillo 2008, pet. ref'd) (indictment for money laundering must specify offense State contends to be the relevant "criminal activity"; however, defendant failed to object at trial).

k. If a particular intent is a material element of the charged offense, the charging instrument must state the required intent. Tex. Code Crim. Proc. art. 21.05; *Victory v. State*, 547 S.W.2d 1 (Tex. Crim. App. 1976) (indictment for indecency with child must allege defendant acted with intent to arouse or gratify sexual desire of any person); *Smith v. State*, 517 S.W.2d 917 (Tex. Crim. App. [Panel Op.] 1978) (indictment for theft must allege intent to deprive).

l. The charging instrument need not negate the existence of a defense or an affirmative defense. Tex. Penal Code §§ 2.03(b), 2.04(b). However, the State must plead its reliance on a tolling provision if the indictment does not demonstrate on its face that the crime alleged occurred within the limitations period. *Tita v. State*, 267 S.W.3d 33 (Tex. Crim. App. 2008).

m. The State must negate the existence of an exception in the accusation charging commission of the offense. Tex. Penal Code § 2.02(b).

n. If an offense criminalizes an omission to act, the indictment must allege that the defendant had a duty to act or that a law as defined by Tex. Penal Code § 1.07 provides that the omission is an offense. *See Billingslea v. State*, 780 S.W.2d 271 (Tex. Crim. App. 1989).[3]

o. The sufficiency of an indictment is a question of law reviewed *de novo* on appeal. *Holton v. State*, 487 S.W.3d 600, 608 (Tex. App.—El Paso 2015, no pet.); *Turner v. State*, 435 S.W.3d 280 (Tex. App.—Waco 2014, pet. ref'd).

p. When a motion to quash is overruled, a defendant is not harmed unless he did not receive notice of the State's theory against which he must defend. *Brown v. State*, 468 S.W.3d 158 (Tex. App.—Houston [14th Dist.] 2015, pet. ref'd).

5. Conjunctive Pleadings

a. An indictment may allege alternative methods of committing the same offense in the conjunctive, and the jury may be charged in the disjunctive. *Martinez v. State*, 129 S.W.3d 101 (Tex. Crim. App. 2004); *Kitchens v. State*, 823 S.W.2d 256 (Tex. Crim. App. 1991); *Hernandez v. State*, 470 S.W.3d 862 (Tex. App.—Fort Worth 2015, pet. ref'd); *Wert v. State*, 383 S.W.3d 747 (Tex. App.—Houston [14th Dist.] 2012, no pet.).

b. When alternative methods are submitted in the disjunctive, the jury can return a general verdict if the evidence is sufficient to support a finding under any of the theories submitted. *E.g., Gamboa v. State*, 296 S.W.3d 574 (Tex. Crim. App. 2009) (alleging in first paragraph that defendant shot victim with firearm while committing or attempting to commit robbery and in second paragraph that defendant caused death of the predicate victim and murdered another individual during same criminal transaction); *Luna v. State*, 268 S.W.3d 594 (Tex. Crim. App. 2008) (alleging murder during burglary, robbery, and arson in capital-murder indictment); *Martinez v. State*, 129 S.W.3d 101 (Tex. Crim. App. 2004) (alleging alternative theories of murder committed in course of committing and attempting to commit robbery and murder committed in course of committing and attempting to commit aggravated sexual assault); *Garrett v. State*, 682 S.W.2d 301 (Tex. Crim. App. 1984) (alleging "choking and strangling" in capital-murder indictment).

---

[3] *Billingslea*'s requirement of a statutory duty to act has been overruled by the amendment of Tex. Penal Code § 6.01(c), which now provides that one who fails to act does not commit an offense unless a law as defined by Tex. Penal Code § 1.07 provides that the omission is an offense or otherwise provides that he has a duty to perform the act. *Oler v. State*, 998 S.W.2d 363 (Tex. App.—Dallas 1999, pet. ref'd, untimely filed); *see State v. Taylor*, 322 S.W.3d 702 (Tex. App.—Texarkana 2010, pet. ref'd). "Law" as currently defined by § 1.07 is not limited to statute. *Oler, supra; Taylor, supra.*

6. General versus Special Statutes

a. If a general provision conflicts with a special or local provision, the provisions are construed, if possible, to give effect to both. Tex. Gov't Code § 311.026(a). If the conflict between the general provision and the special or local provision is irreconcilable, the special or local provision prevails as an exception to the general provision, unless the general provision is the later enactment and the manifest intent is that the general provision prevail. Id. § (b).

b. The doctrine of in *pari materia* is a rule of statutory construction that seeks to carry out the Legislature's intent. *Jones v. State*, 396 S.W.3d 558 (Tex. Crim. App. 2013). The doctrine arises when one statute deals with a subject in comprehensive terms and another deals with a portion of the same subject in a more definite way. *Id.*; *Lomax v. State*, 233 S.W.3d 302 (Tex. Crim. App. 2007).

c. To determine whether statutes are in *pari materia*, courts consider whether the statutes: (1) involve different penalties; (2) are contained in the same legislative act; (3) require the same elements of proof; and (4) are intended to achieve the same purpose or objective. *Burke v. State*, 28 S.W.3d 545 (Tex. Crim. App. 2000); *Patterson v. State*, 496 S.W.3d 919, 926 (Tex. App.—Houston [1st Dist.] 2016, pet. ref'd).

d. Similarity of purpose or objective is the most important factor in determining whether two provisions are in *pari materia*. *Jones v. State*, 396 S.W.3d 558 (Tex. Crim. App. 2013); *Burke v. State*, 28 S.W.3d 545 (Tex. Crim. App. 2000). The two provisions must have been enacted with the same purpose in mind in order for the doctrine to apply, and the provisions must be closely enough related to justify interpreting one in light of the other. *Burke*, supra. Even statutes regulating the same conduct are not in *pari materia* if they have different objects and are intended to cover different situations. *Cheney v. State*, 755 S.W.2d 123 (Tex. Crim. App. 1988).

e. Cases where provisions were held to be in *pari materia*: *Azeez v. State*, 248 S.W.3d 182 (Tex. Crim. App. 2008) (defendant who failed to appear to answer to speeding citation should have been prosecuted under Tex. Transp. Code § 543.009(b) rather than Tex. Penal Code § 38.10(a)); *Cheney v. State*, 755 S.W.2d 123 (Tex. Crim. App. 1988) (State should have pursued conviction for false statement to obtain property or credit under Tex. Penal Code § 32.32 instead of general theft conviction under § 31.03); *Tawfik v. State*, 643 S.W.2d 127 (Tex. Crim. App. 1982) (prosecution should have proceeded under Tex. Penal Code § 32.22 for the offense of criminal simulation, a misdemeanor, rather than under felony theft); *Williams v. State*, 641 S.W.2d 236 (Tex. Crim. App. 1982) (prosecution should have proceeded for offense of hindering a secured creditor under Tex. Penal Code § 32.33 rather than broader theft offense); *Jones v. State*, 552 S.W.2d 836 (Tex. Crim. App. 1977) (district court lacked jurisdiction where defendant should have been prosecuted under narrower proscription against welfare fraud rather than under provisions of felony theft); *Ex parte Harrell*, 542 S.W.2d 169 (Tex. Crim. App. 1976) (prosecution should have proceeded for more specific misdemeanor offense of forgery under Tex. Penal Code § 32.21 rather than broader felony offense of unlawful use of a criminal instrument under § 16.01); *Jones v. State*, 225 S.W.3d 772 (Tex. App.—Houston [14th Dist.] 2007, no pet.) (defendant properly sentenced under Tex. Penal Code § 12.42(c), providing sentence enhancement for defendants twice convicted of specific sex crimes, rather than § 12.42(b), the general sentencing provision for second-degree felonies).

f. Cases where provisions were held not to be in *pari materia*: *Jones v. State*, 396 S.W.3d 558 (Tex. Crim. App. 2013) (statutes governing failure to identify and fraudulent use or possession of identifying information not in *pari materia*); *Lomax v. State*, 233 S.W.3d 302

(Tex. Crim. App. 2007) (statutes defining felony murder and intoxication manslaughter not in *pari materia*); *Burke v. State*, 28 S.W.3d 545 (Tex. Crim. App. 2000) (statute defining aggravated assault with serious bodily injury and intoxication assault not in *pari materia)*; *Mills v. State*, 722 S.W.2d 411 (Tex. Crim. App. 1986) (securing execution of a document by deception and theft not in *pari materia*); *Alejos v. State*, 555 S.W.2d 444 (Tex. Crim. App. 1977) (op. on reh'g) (statutes defining evading arrest and fleeing or attempting to allude police officer not in *pari materia*); *Patterson v. State*, 496 S.W.3d 919 (Tex. App.—Houston [1st Dist.] 2016, pet. ref'd) (murder and organized crime statutes not in *pari materia*); *State v. Allen*, 346 S.W.3d 713 (Tex. App. 2011, pet. ref'd) (third-degree forgery of government document [a driver's license] not in *pari materia* with provisions of Transportation Code relating to misdemeanor displaying driver's licenses person knows are fictitious or have been altered) *Haywood v. State*, 344 S.W.3d 454 (Tex. App.—Dallas 2011, pet. ref'd) (statutes setting forth offenses of tampering with physical evidence and tampering with a governmental record not in *pari materia*); *Fernandez v. State*, 269 S.W.3d 63 (Tex. App.—Texarkana 2008, no pet.) (felony "child abandonment" statute and misdemeanor "leaving a child in a vehicle" statute not in *pari materia* in determining whether defendant who left infant unattended in vehicle should be prosecuted under "leaving a child in a vehicle" statute); *Segura v. State*, 100 S.W.3d 652 (Tex. App.—Dallas 2003, no pet.) (harassment and stalking not in *pari materia*); *Cullen v. State*, 832 S.W.2d 788 (Tex. App.–Austin 1992, pet. ref'd) (criminal mischief and statute prohibiting desecration of venerated objects not in *pari materia*); *Raney v. State*, 769 S.W.2d 698 (Tex. App.—Corpus Christi 1989, no pet.) (theft and theft of service not in *pari materia*).

7. Terms with Alternate Meanings

a. When a statutory term goes to the act or omission of the defendant and the definition provides for more than one manner or means to commit the act or omission, upon timely request the State must allege the particular manner or means it seeks to establish. *E.g.*, *Curry v. State*, 30 S.W.3d 394 (Tex. Crim. App. 2000) (must allege type of abduction), *overruled in part on other grounds*, *Gollihar v. State*, 46 S.W.3d 243 (Tex. Crim. App. 2001); *Reynolds v. State*, 723 S.W.2d 685 (Tex. Crim. App. 2000) (must allege type of restraint); *Coats v. State*, 712 S.W.2d 520 (Tex. Crim. App. 1986) (must allege type of appropriation); *Kass v. State*, 642 S.W.2d 463 (Tex. Crim. App. [Panel Op.] 1981) (op. on reh'g) (must specify type of sexual conduct); *Ferguson v. State*, 622 S.W.2d 846 (Tex. Crim. App. [Panel Op.] 1980) (must specify method of delivering controlled substance); *Buxton v. State*, 2017 WL 2872490 (Tex. App.—Houston [1st Dist.] July 6, 2017, no pet. h.) (must identify specific "act of sexual abuse" for continuous sexual abuse).

b. An indictment or information may allege different ways of committing the offense in the conjunctive, and the jury may be charged in the disjunctive. *Martinez v. State*, 129 S.W.3d 101 (Tex. Crim. App. 2004); *Kitchens v. State*, 823 S.W.2d 256 (Tex. Crim. App. 1991); *Hernandez v. State*, 470 S.W.3d 862 (Tex. App.—Fort Worth 2015, pet. ref'd); *Wert v. State*, 383 S.W.3d 747 (Tex. App.—Houston [14th Dist.] 2012, no pet.).

c. An error in overruling a timely exception on the ground that the indictment fails to specify which of the statutory definitions of an act is relied upon will not result in a reversal unless it meets the test of harm set forth in *Adams v. State*, 707 S.W.2d 900 (Tex. Crim. App. 1986).

8. Tracking Statutory Language

a. Subject to rare exceptions, an indictment tracking the language of the statute satisfies constitutional and statutory requirements. *State v. Zuniga*, 512 S.W.3d 902 (Tex. Crim. App.

2017); *Smith v. State*, 309 S.W.3d 10 (Tex. Crim. App. 2010); *State v. Barbernell*, 257 S.W.3d 248 (Tex. Crim. App. 2008); *State v. Moff*, 154 S.W.3d 599 (Tex. Crim. App. 2004); *Curry v. State*, 30 S.W.3d 394 (Tex. Crim. App. 2000), *overruled in part on other grounds, Gollihar v. State*, 46 S.W.3d 243 (Tex. Crim. App. 2001). However, the trial court can require the State to amend an indictment which tracks the language of the statute when more notice is needed to allow the accused to adequately prepare a defense, *Moff*, supra, and the information sought for greater particularity relates to the defendant's acts, omissions, or conduct constituting the offense. *Curry,* supra.

b. If the statutory language is itself completely descriptive of the offense, the charging instrument is sufficient if it follows the statutory language. *State v. Mays*, 967 S.W.2d 404 (Tex. Crim. App. 1998) (indictment tracking statutory definition of a manner or means of committing barratry provided ample notice); *Moreno v. State*, 721 S.W.2d 295 (Tex. Crim. App. 1986) (indictment not defective for failing to allege specific acts of peace officer that constituted acting in discharge of duties).

c. If the statutory language is not completely descriptive, so that more particularity is required to afford the defendant notice as required, merely tracking the language of the statute is insufficient. *Olurebi v. State*, 870 S.W.2d 58 (Tex. Crim. App. 1994) (indictment tracking statutory language insufficient for failing to specify how credit card was fictitious); *Haecker v. State*, 571 S.W.2d 920 (Tex. Crim. App. [Panel Op.] 1978) (indictment alleging statutory language "torture an animal" held insufficient); *Sanchez v. State*, 182 S.W.3d 34 (Tex. App.—San Antonio 2005) (indictment for official oppression involving sexual harassments failed to inform defendant of complainant's "rights, privileges, powers, and immunities" he allegedly made conditional upon complainant's submission to sexual harassment), *aff'd*, 209 S.W.3d 117 (Tex. Crim. App. 2006).

d. A statute that uses an undefined term of indeterminate or variable meaning requires more specific pleading in order to notify the defendant of the nature of the charges against him. *State v. Zuniga*, 512 S.W.3d 902, 907 (Tex. Crim. App. 2017); *State v. Mays*, 967 S.W.2d 404 (Tex. Crim. App. 1998).

e. When a criminal statute defines the manner or means of committing an offense in several alternative ways, a defendant is entitled, upon timely request, to an allegation of which statutory method the State intends to prove. *Curry v. State*, 30 S.W.3d 394 (Tex. Crim. App. 2000) (type of abduction), *overruled in part on other grounds, Gollihar v. State*, 46 S.W.3d 243 (Tex. Crim. App. 2001); *Olurebi v. State*, 870 S.W.2d 58 (Tex. Crim. App. 1994) (how credit card fictitious); *Coleman v. State*, 643 S.W.2d 124 (Tex. Crim. App. 1982) (type of appropriation); *Ferguson v. State*, 622 S.W.2d 846 (Tex. Crim. App. [Panel Op.] 1980) (type of delivery); *State v. Cordell*, 34 S.W.3d 719 (Tex. App.—Fort Worth 2000, pet. ref'd) (type of intoxicant).

f. When a statute defines the manner or means of committing an offense, an indictment based upon that statute need not allege additional facts beyond that definition. *State v. Mays*, 967 S.W.2d 404 (Tex. Crim. App. 1998) (barratry indictment sufficient because tracked statutory definition of "solicit employment" as sole manner and means); *State v. Edmond*, 933 S.W.2d 120 (Tex. Crim. App. 1996) (indictment for official oppression sufficient because used statutory definition of sexual harassment and conjunctively alleged two statutory acts or omissions constituting offense); *State v. Shuck*, 222 S.W.3d 113 (Tex. App.—Houston [14th Dist.] 2006, no pet.) (indictment for indecency with child sufficient because tracked statutory definition of "sexual contact").

g. In rare instances, the courts may imply an element that is not literally expressed in the statute, and such element must be included in the charging instrument. *E.g., Green v. State*,

951 S.W.2d 3 (Tex. Crim. App. 1997) (requiring State to prove defendant who refused to identify himself knew person requesting information was peace officer).

h. It is permissible to plead as a legal conclusion an element other than the main act charged. For example, theft may be stated as a conclusion in an indictment charging the offense of burglary, and it is not necessary to plead the separate elements of theft. *Davila v. State*, 547 S.W.2d 606 (Tex. Crim. App. 1977). Likewise, in a capital-murder indictment, the State need not allege the constituent elements of an offense constituting the aggravating feature of a capital murder, even in the face of a motion to quash. *Dinkins v. State*, 894 S.W.2d 330 (Tex. Crim. App.1995).

i. Whenever recklessness or criminal negligence enters into or is a part or element of any offense, or it is charged that the accused acted recklessly or with criminal negligence in the commission of an offense, the charging instrument must allege, with reasonable certainty, the act or acts relied upon to constitute recklessness or criminal negligence. Tex. Code Crim. Proc. art. 21.15; *Smith v. State*, 309 S.W.3d 10 (Tex. Crim. App. 2010); *Reed v. State*, 117 S.W.3d 260 (Tex. Crim. App. 2003). However, an indictment is sufficient, even if it fails to allege the acts relied on to constitute recklessness, when it further alleges that the accused acted intentionally or knowingly. *Crawford v. State*, 646 S.W.2d 936 (Tex. Crim. App. 1983); *State v. Castorena*, 486 S.W.3d 630 (Tex. App.—San Antonio 2016, no pet.); *Bartlett v. State*, 249 S.W.3d 658 (Tex. App.—Austin 2008, pet. ref'd).

j. When a statute defining any offense uses special or particular terms, the indictment may use the general term which, in common language, embraces the special term. Tex. Code Crim. Proc. art. 21.12; *see Thomas v. State*, 621 S.W.2d 158 (Tex. Crim. App. [Panel Op.] 1981) (art. 21.12 requires only general term "owner" to be alleged).

k. Words used in a statute to define an offense need not be strictly pursued in the indictment, but substituted words must convey the same meaning or include the sense of the statutory word. Tex. Code Crim. Proc. art. 21.17.

9. Manner and Means

a. The phrase "manner or means" describes how the defendant committed the specific criminal act, which is the *actus reus*. *Munoz v. State*, 2017 WL 32892 (Tex. App.—San Antonio January 4, 2017, pet. ref'd); *Moreno v. State*, 413 S.W.3d 119 (Tex. App.—San Antonio 2013, no pet.).

b. The State may anticipate variances in proof by pleading alternative manner and means in the conjunctive, and proof of any one of the manner and means will support a guilty verdict. *Swearingen v. State*, 101 S.W.3d 89 (Tex. Crim. App. 2003); *Kitchens v. State*, 823 S.W.2d 256 (Tex. Crim. App. 1991); *Munoz v. State*, 2017 WL 32892 (Tex. App.—San Antonio January 4, 2017, pet. ref'd); *Desormeaux v. State*, 362 S.W.3d 233 (Tex. App.—Beaumont 2012, no pet.).

c. The defendant is entitled, upon timely exception, to a specific allegation of the manner and means of committing the offense in order to bar subsequent prosecution for the same offense and to give him precise notice of the offense with which he is charged. *Castillo v. State*, 689 S.W.2d 443 (Tex. Crim. App. 1985) (failure to allege manner and means used to start a fire in arson case); *Doyle v. State*, 661 S.W.2d 726 (Tex. Crim. App. 1984) (failure to allege manner and means used to communicate threat in retaliation case); *Miller v. State*, 647 S.W.2d 266 (Tex. Crim. App. 1983) (failure to more specifically allege "damage and destroy" in criminal mischief case); *Cruise v. State*, 587 S.W.2d 403 (Tex. Crim. App. 1979) (failure to allege manner and means of causing bodily injury in aggravated robbery).

d.   If the manner and means of doing an act makes otherwise innocent conduct a criminal offense, the State must allege facts showing the manner and means that make the act a criminal offense. *Posey v. State*, 545 S.W.2d 162 (Tex. Crim. App. 1977) (indictment alleging only that defendant presented pharmacist with prescription purporting to prescribe controlled substance for another alleged only non-criminal act; must show substance obtained by misrepresentation, fraud, deception, or subterfuge); *State v. Campbell*, 113 S.W.3d 9 (Tex. App.—Tyler 2000, pet. ref'd) (indictment for abuse of official capacity must allege more than failing to go to work because intent to obtain benefit or to harm or defraud raises the act to a crime).

e.   When a statute does not include manner and means, it is not considered material, the State is not required to prove it, and it need not be included in the indictment. *Brown v. State*, 468 S.W.3d 168 (Tex. App.—Houston [14th Dist.] 2015, pet. ref'd) (Tex. Penal Code § 38.122 provided no manner and means by which one could hold himself out as lawyer; therefore, indictment not required to allege manner and means).

f.   An indictment need not allege the manner of committing an aggravating element of the offense, the underlying offense, or the attempted offense. *Beathard v. State*, 767 S.W.2d 423 (Tex. Crim. App. 1989) (capital murder in course of burglary); *Young v. State*, 675 S.W.2d 770 (Tex. Crim. App. 1984) (attempted burglary of habitation with intent to commit theft); *Kitchens v. State*, 279 S.W.3d 733 (Tex. App.—Amarillo 2007, pet. ref'd) (capital murder in course of burglary).

g.   An accused indicted specifically as a party under Tex. Penal Code § 7.02(a)(2) is not entitled to an allegation of the manner and means whereby he supposedly solicited, encouraged, directed, aided or attempted to aid the primary actor in committing the offense. *Swope v. State*, 805 S.W.2d 442 (Tex. Crim. App. 1991).

h.   Statutory alternatives do not constitute manner and means of committing an offense if they do not relate to an act, omission, or conduct of the defendant. *Curry v. State*, 30 S.W.3d 394 (Tex. Crim. App. 2000), *overruled in part on other grounds*, *Gollihar v. State*, 46 S.W.3d 243 (Tex. Crim. App. 2001); *see Thomas v. State*, 621 S.W.2d 158 (Tex. Crim. App. [Panel Op.] 1981) (State need not allege which statutory definition of "owner" it seeks to prove in theft case because term "owner" does not "go to an act or omission of the defendant"; similarly, state need not define phrase "without effective consent" because it does not constitute an act or omission on defendant's part).

10.   Negating Statutory Exceptions

a.   An exception to an offense in the Penal Code is labeled by the phrase: "It is an exception to the application of. . . . " Tex. Penal Code § 2.02(a).

b.   The negation of an exception to an offense is an element of the offense. Tex. Penal Code § 1.07(a)(22)(D).

c.   The State must negate the existence of an exception in the charging instrument and prove beyond a reasonable doubt that the defendant or his conduct does not fall within the exception. Tex. Penal Code § 2.02(b). Failing to negate an exception is the same as failing to allege an essential element of the offense. *Baumgart v. State*, 2015 WL 3986153 (Tex. App.—Houston [14th Dist.] June 30, 2015), *aff'd*, 512 S.W.3d 335 (Tex. Crim. App. 2017).

d.   The State need not negate exceptions in the Texas Controlled Substances Act or the Texas Alcoholic Beverage Code. Tex. Alcoholic Bev. Code § 101.05; Tex. Health & Safety Code § 481.184.

e.   The charging instrument need not negate an exception to a penal statute that is placed in a separate section or article from the one defining the offense. *Baumgart v. State*, 510 S.W.3d 335 (Tex. Crim. App. 2017) (State not required to negate law-enforcement exception in indictments for violating Private Security Act); *Hicks v. State*, 18 S.W.3d 743 (Tex. App.—San Antonio 2000, no pet.) (complaint for driving without license need not negate exceptions to requirement that driver carry license); *Bragg v. State*, 740 S.W.2d 574 (Tex. App.—Houston [1st Dist.] 1987, pet. ref'd) (indictment charging violation of Private Investigators and Private Security Agencies Act need not negate exception that defendant was full-time peace officer).

f.   The State may implicitly negate an exception. *State v. Laird*, 208 S.W.3d 667 (Tex. App.—Fort Worth 2006, no pet.) (allegation that outdoor burning not authorized by exception contained in listed provisions of Administrative Code sufficient to negate exceptions); *Tarlton v. State*, 93 S.W.3d 168 (Tex. App.—Houston [14th Dist.] 2002, pet. ref'd) (allegation defendant acted "knowingly" negated statutory exception for one who "unknowingly disposes" of certain products into environment); *Priego v. State*, 658 S.W.2d 655 (Tex. App.—El Paso 1983, no pet.) (alleging term "parent" to describe defendant's relationship to child implicitly negated exception for individuals whose parental rights were relinquished or terminated by judicial order).

g.   The State can amend a charging instrument to add language negating a statutory exception by following Tex. Code Crim. Proc. art. 28.10.

11.   Mental States

a.   A person does not commit an offense unless he intentionally, knowingly, recklessly, or with criminal negligence engages in conduct as the definition of the offense requires, unless the definition of an offense does not require a culpable mental state. Tex. Penal Code § 6.02(a), (b). If the definition of an offense does not provide a culpable mental state, but one is nevertheless required, intent, knowledge, or recklessness will suffice to establish criminal responsibility. *Id.* at § (c).

b.   Application of Tex. Penal Code § 6.02 is not limited to Penal Code offenses. Tex. Penal Code § 1.03(b) (Penal Code Titles 1, 2, and 3 apply to offenses defined by other laws unless statute defining offense provides otherwise). *E.g.*, *Koah v. State*, 604 S.W.2d 156 (Tex. Crim. App. [Panel Op.] 1980) ("Blue Sky Law"); *Goss v. State*, 582 S.W.2d 782 (Tex.Crim.App.1979) (failure to stop and render aid, now found in Tex. Transp. Code § 550.021(a)); *Haddad v. State*, 9 S.W.3d 454 (Tex. App.—Houston [1st Dist.] 1999, no pet.) (city ordinance regulating sexually oriented businesses); *Diggles v. State*, 641 S.W.2d 667 (Tex. App.—Dallas 1982, pet. ref'd) (unlawful voter assistance, now found in Tex. Elec. Code § 64.036).

c.   Whenever recklessness or criminal negligence enters into or is a part or element of any offense, or it is charged that the accused acted recklessly or with criminal negligence in the commission of an offense, the charging instrument must allege, with reasonable certainty, the act or acts relied upon to constitute recklessness or criminal negligence. Tex. Code Crim. Proc. art. 21.15; *Smith v. State*, 309 S.W.3d 10 (Tex. Crim. App. 2010); *Reed v. State*, 117 S.W.3d 260 (Tex. Crim. App. 2003). However, it is not necessary to allege the act or acts relied on to constitute recklessness if the State alleges other culpable mental states such as intentionally or knowingly. *Crawford v. State*, 646 S.W.2d 936 (Tex. Crim. App. 1983); *State v. Castorena*, 486 S.W.3d 630 (Tex. App.—San Antonio 2016, no pet.); *Bartlett v. State*, 249 S.W.3d 658 (Tex. App.—2008, pet. ref'd).

d.   A culpable mental state is required, even if the definition of the offense does not provide a mental state, unless the definition plainly dispenses with any mental element. Tex. Penal

Code § 6.02(b); *see Aguirre v. State*, 22 S.W.3d 463 (Tex. Crim. App. 1999) (ordinance prohibiting conducting business in nude live entertainment club within 1,000 feet of school required allegation of culpable mental state even though ordinance did not so state); *State v. Walker*, 195 S.W.3d 293 (Tex. App.—Tyler 2006, no pet.) (statute defining offense of filing for record of unapproved plat and subdivision of real property required allegation of culpable mental state); *Thompson v. State*, 44 S.W.3d 171 (Tex. App.—Houston [14th Dist.] 2001, no pet.) (ordinance requiring entertainer employed by sexually oriented enterprise to conspicuously display permit upon her person not strict liability offense).

e.   Examples of strict liability offenses include DWI, intoxication manslaughter, intoxication assault, and water pollution. *American Plant Food Corp. v. State*, 587 S.W.2d 679 (Tex. Crim. App. 1979) (water pollution); *Owen v. State*, 525 S.W.2d 164 (Tex. Crim. App. 1975) (DWI); *Ex parte Ross*, 522 S.W.2d 214 (Tex. Crim. App. 1975) (DWI and involuntary manslaughter [now intoxication manslaughter]); *Stidman v. State*, 981 S.W.2d 227 (Tex. App.—Houston [1st Dist.] 1998, no pet.) (intoxication assault); *see Tovar v. State*, 978 S.W.2d 584 (Tex. Crim. App. 1998) (Tex. Gov't Code § 551.144 allowed member of governmental body to be held criminally responsible in holding closed meeting regardless of his mental state with respect to whether closed meeting permitted under Open Meetings Act).

f.   A court must look for a manifest intent to dispense with the requirement of a culpable mental state, and silence of a statute about whether a culpable mental state is an element of the offense leaves a presumption that one is. *Aguirre v. State*, 22 S.W.3d 463 (Tex. Crim. App. 1999).

g.   Absent an express intent to dispense with the requirement of a culpable mental state, courts ask whether such an intent is manifested by other features of the statute. *Aguirre v. State*, 22 S.W.3d 463 (Tex. Crim. App. 1999). Among the considerations are: (1) the subject of the statute; (2) the legislative history or title of the statute; (3) severity of the punishment provided; (4) the seriousness of harm to the public from the forbidden conduct; (5) the defendant's opportunity to ascertain the true facts; (6) the difficulty prosecuting officials would have in proving a mental state for this type of crime; and (7) the number of prosecutions to be expected. *Id.*

h.   The felony-murder rule found in Tex. Penal Code § 19.02(b)(3) dispenses with a culpable mental state. *Lomax v. State*, 233 S.W.3d 302 (Tex. Crim. App. 2007). However, it is not completely accurate to characterize § 19.02(b)(3) as defining a "strict liability" offense. *Id.* While it does not require a culpable mental state, it still requires a defendant to commit a felony involving a clearly dangerous act, which requires some element of "voluntariness." *Id.*

i.   Generally, there are two categories of mental elements: (1) general culpable mental states as defined by Tex. Penal Code § 6.03 (*i.e.*, intentional, knowing, reckless, or criminally negligent); and (2) particular intents as required by Tex. Code Crim. Proc. art. 21.05 (*e.g.*, taking property with intent to deprive the owner of property or committing an act with intent to commit a felony or theft). If the statute creating the offense requires both a general culpable mental state and a particular intent, both must be alleged. *Slavin v. State*, 548 S.W.2d 30 (Tex. Crim. App. 1977); *Victory v. State*, 547 S.W.2d 1 (Tex. Crim. App. 1977).

j.   For those statutes that do not contain a general culpable mental state, but do require a particular intent, allegation of the particular intent is required and is all that is necessary. *Chavez v. State*, 657 S.W.2d 146 (Tex. Crim. App. 1983); *Lugo-Lugo v. State*, 650 S.W.2d 72 (Tex. Crim. App. 1983). Allegation of the particular intent suffices for the more general culpable mental state as well. Martinez v. State, 565 S.W.2d 70 (Tex. Crim. App. [Panel Op.] 1978) (allegation defendant "with intent to commit theft, enter[ed] a building not then open to the public, owned by [Complainant] without the effective consent of the Complainant" not subject to motion to quash on ground it failed to allege culpable mental state).

k.   When a particular intent is a material fact in the description of the offense, it must be stated in the indictment. Tex. Code Crim. Proc. art. 21.05; *Victory v. State*, 547 S.W.2d 1 (Tex. Crim. App. 1976) (indictment for indecency with child must allege intent to arouse or gratify the sexual desire of any person).

l.   The charging instrument need not allege a culpable mental state of an underlying, attempted, or aggravating offense. *Dinkins v. State*, 894 S.W.2d 330 (Tex. Crim. App. 1995) (capital-murder indictment need not allege culpable mental state of second murder); *Ex parte Bartmess*, 739 S.W.2d 51 (Tex. Crim. App. 1987) (indictment alleging defendant attempted to cause death of individual necessarily incorporated allegation of intent to murder and satisfied *mens rea* requirement for attempted murder); *State v. Hernandez*, 395 S.W.3d 258 (Tex. App.—San Antonio 2012, no pet.) (indictment for first-degree-felony sexual-assault charge under Tex. Penal Code § 22.011(f) not required to plead elements of bigamy under § 25.01); *Jarnigan v. State*, 57 S.W.3d 76, 92 (Tex. App.—Houston [14th Dist.] 2001, pet. ref'd) (organized crime indictment need not allege manner and means of underlying theft).

m.   An indictment charging intoxication manslaughter must allege that death was caused by "accident or mistake" because the language is contained in the statute, even though it is not classifiable as either a general culpable mental state or a particular intent. *See* Tex. Penal Code § 49.08(a)(2). The terms "accident" and "mistake" refer to the state of mind of the accused and do not require further enumeration or description. *Crume v. State*, 658 S.W.2d 607 (Tex. Crim. App. 1983).

n.   If the required mental state is omitted from the charging instrument, it may be supplied by its necessary inclusion within a broader expressed word, term, or phrase. *Murphy v. State*, 665 S.W.2d 116 (Tex. Crim. App. 1983) (allegation of intent to collect insurance for damage and destruction of structure necessarily alleged defendant knew structure was insured against damage or destruction).

o.   Failure to allege a culpable mental state renders the charging instrument subject to a motion to quash. *Ex parte Weise*, 55 S.W.3d 617 (Tex. Crim. App. 2001). Failure to allege a culpable mental state when one is required does not render the charging instrument void. *Id*.

12. Description of Property

a.   Tex. Code Crim. Proc. art. 21.09 describes the degree of detail to which an indictment is required to describe property that is alleged by the State to have been stolen.

b.   If known, personal property alleged in the charging instrument must be identified by name, kind, number, and ownership. Tex. Code Crim. Proc. art. 21.09. When the information is unknown, that fact shall be stated, and a general classification, describing and identifying the property as near as may be, shall suffice. Id.

c.   Real estate alleged in the charging instrument should be identified by a description of its general locality in the county and the name of the owner, occupant, or claimant thereof. Tex. Code Crim. Proc. art. 21.09. The requirements of art. 21.09 apply only to real estate that is the object of the offense, not to real estate alleged only as the location of the offense. *Franks v. State*, 688 S.W.2d 502 (Tex. Crim. App. 1985) (in prosecution for burglary of habitation, indictment not required to allege location of habitation that is simply location of offense); *Chunn v. State*, 821 S.W.2d 718, 721 (Tex. App.—Houston [1st Dist.] 1991, pet. ref'd) (in prosecution for criminal trespass, information not required to allege specific location of real property; alleging offense date, county, and owner sufficient).

d. A generic description of personal property is adequate if it alleges: (1) quantity; (2) the general type of property (as long as it is more specific than merely stating "property" or "merchandise"); (3) "ownership"; and (4) if necessary, the jurisdictional value of the property. *Wood v. State*, 632 S.W.2d 734 (Tex. Crim. App. [Panel Op.] 1982).

e. Too general a description of property is insufficient to satisfy Tex. Code Crim. Proc. art. 21.09 and may be subject to a motion to quash. *E.g., Harris v. State*, 587 S.W.2d 429 (Tex. Crim. App. [Panel Op.] 1979) (alleging "property" was appropriated held insufficient); *State v. Leverett*, 400 S.W.3d 195 (Tex. App.—Beaumont 2013, no pet.) (alleging theft of "gold and jewelry" insufficiently specific; even if description sufficiently established type of articles stolen, indictment silent about number of articles of gold and jewelry stolen and did not state property allegedly stolen was unknown).

f. Descriptions that do not strictly comply with Tex. Code Crim. Proc. art. 21.09 have been held to be sufficient. *E.g., Inman v. State*, 650 S.W.2d 417 (Tex. Crim. App. 1983) ("automobile"); *Wood v. State*, 632 S.W.2d 734 (Tex. Crim. App. [Panel Op.] 1982) ("one truck tractor" and "one automobile"); *Rhodes v. State*, 560 S.W.2d 665 (Tex. Crim. App. 1978) ("wall paneling"); *State v. Czaplinski*, 956 S.W.2d 839 (Tex. App.—Austin 1997, no pet.) ("Two (2) pairs of shorts, one (1) shirt and one (1) dress of the value of $50 or more but less than $500"); *Caro v. State*, 771 S.W.2d 610 (Tex. App.—Dallas 1989, pet. ref'd) (describing automobile in terms of its owner).

g. If the charging instrument states that the name, kind, number, and ownership of personal property are unknown, a general classification describing and identifying the property as near as possible will withstand a motion to quash. Tex. Code Crim. Proc. art. 21.09; *Gentry v. State*, 608 S.W.2d 643 (Tex. Crim. App. [Panel Op.] 1980) (alleging theft of "merchandise" sufficient where charging instrument further stated exact name, kind, and number unknown); *Roberson v. State*, 741 S.W.2d 563 (Tex. App.—Texarkana 1987, no pet.) (same).

h. No property description is required in an indictment alleging robbery or aggravated robbery because robbery is a form of assault. *Ex parte Lucas*, 574 S.W.2d 162 (Tex. Crim. App. [Panel Op.] 1978); *Hammons v. State*, 856 S.W.2d 797 (Tex. App.—Fort Worth 1993, pet. ref'd); *see Ex parte Hawkins*, 6 S.W.3d 554 (Tex. Crim. App. 1999) (robbery is form of assault).

i. Where credit-card abuse is charged "with intent to obtain property," the State need not describe the property. *Ortega v. State*, 668 S.W.2d 701 (Tex. Crim. App. 1983), *overruled on other grounds*, *Gollihar v. State*, 46 S.W.3d 243 (Tex. Crim. App. 2001). However, if the indictment alleges that defendant received or obtained property in committing credit-card abuse, the indictment must contain an adequate description of the property. Id.

j. A burglary indictment alleging the attempt to commit theft and an actual completed theft under Tex. Penal Code § 30.02(a)(3) must, upon proper request, describe the property allegedly stolen or attempted to be stolen. *DeVaughn v. State*, 749 S.W.2d 62 (Tex. Crim. App. 1988). Burglary prosecutions under § 30.02(a)(1) do not require an allegation of what specific property the defendant allegedly intended to steal. *Id.*

k. A defect in the description of property must be raised by pretrial objection. Tex. Code Crim. Proc. art. 1.14(b).

13. Ownership of Property

a. An "owner" of property is anyone who has a possessory interest in the property through title or possession (whether lawful or not) or who has a greater right to possession of the property than the defendant. Tex. Penal Code § 1.07(a)(35)(A).

b. With regard to alleging ownership of property, Tex. Code Crim. Proc. art. 21.08 provides the following guidelines:

(1) Where one person owns the property, and another person has the possession of the same, the ownership thereof may be alleged to be in either.

(2) Where property is owned in common, or jointly, by two or more persons, the ownership may be alleged to be in all or either of them.

(3) When the property belongs to the estate of a deceased person, the ownership may be alleged to be in the executor, administrator or heirs of such deceased person, or in any one of such heirs.

(4) Where the ownership of the property is unknown to the grand jury, it shall be sufficient to allege that fact.

c. Ownership of property stolen must be established as of the date of the offense, not the date of the indictment. *Castillo v. State*, 469 S.W.2d 849 (Tex. Crim. App. 1971); *Skillern v. State*, 890 S.W.2d 849 (Tex. App.—Austin 1994, pet. ref'd).

d. Ownership may be alleged in either the actual owner or a special owner. *Freeman v. State*, 707 S.W.2d 597 (Tex. Crim. App. 1986); *Jackson v. State*, 270 S.W.3d 649 (Tex. App.—Fort Worth 2008, pet. ref'd). A special owner is an individual who is in custody or control of property belonging to another person. *Garza v. State*, 344 S.W.3d 409 (Tex. Crim. App. 2011). "Owner" has an expansive meaning: an owner of property is anyone having a possessory interest in the property through title or possession, whether lawful or not, or a greater right to possession of the property than the defendant. *Id.*

e. When an entity owns the property stolen, it is permissible for the State to allege special ownership in a natural person acting for the corporation (the actual owner). *Garza v. State*, 344 S.W.3d 409 (Tex. Crim. App. 2011) (employee alleged as owner of money obtained through warranty fraud); *Dingler v. State*, 705 S.W.2d 144 (Tex. Crim. App. 1984) (store manager alleged as special owner of stolen vehicle owned by corporation); *Binnion v. State*, 2017 WL 2812495 (Tex. App.—Houston [1st Dist.] June 29, 2017, pet. filed) (investigation manager for company alleged as special owner of funds stolen from company); *Jackson v. State*, 270 S.W.3d 649 (Tex. App.—Fort Worth 2008, pet. ref'd) (finance director alleged as special owner of stolen vehicle owned by dealership); *Garth v. State*, 3 S.W.3d 218 (Tex. App.—Dallas 1999, no pet.) (shift supervisor alleged as owner of gasoline appropriated by undercover officer). However, nothing prevents alleging the name of a corporation or a governmental entity as the owner of the property. *State v. Bartee*, 894 S.W.2d 34 (Tex. App.—San Antonio 1994, no pet.) (indictment for theft of white-tailed deer and deer antlers alleged owner as "State of Texas").

f. The State may allege that a deceased's heir is the owner of the deceased's property, even if the heir does not have actual ownership. *Gerhardt v. State*, 965 S.W.2d 55 (Tex. App.—Houston [1st Dist.] 1998, pet. ref'd) (State allowed to allege and prove deceased's daughter, who was complainant, did not give defendant permission to keep funds while acting as alleged executor of decedent's estate; State not required to prove daughter owned the funds to convict defendant for theft of the funds).

g. Alleging that real property was under the actual care, custody, and control of the person specified in the charging instrument is sufficient to identify such person as the owner. *Ruiz v. State*, 654 S.W.2d 488 (Tex. App.—Corpus Christi 1983, no pet.).

h. An indictment charging credit-card abuse under Tex. Penal Code § 32.31 should allege lack of consent of the true "cardholder," *i.e.*, the person named on the face of the credit card;

the "special owner" concept is inapplicable. *Harrell v. State*, 852 S.W.2d 521 (Tex. Crim. App. 1993); *Hayden v. State*, 818 S.W.2d 194 (Tex. App.—Corpus Christi 1991, no pet.).

i.   A burglary indictment alleging the attempt to commit theft and an actual completed theft under Tex. Penal Code § 30.02(a)(3) must, upon proper request, describe the name of the owner if known. *DeVaughn v. State*, 749 S.W.2d 62 (Tex. Crim. App. 1988).

j.   Even in the face of a motion to quash, the charging instrument need not specify the particular type of ownership upon which the prosecution will rely. *Rico v. State*, 707 S.W.2d 549 (Tex. Crim. App. 1983); *State v. Bartee*, 894 S.W.2d 34 (Tex. App.—San Antonio 1994, no pet.).

k.   An indictment or information may be amended in accordance with Tex. Code Crim. Proc. art. 28.10 to change the name of the alleged owner. *Flowers v. State*, 815 S.W.2d 724 (Tex. Crim. App. 1991).

14.   Location within County

a.   Notwithstanding Tex. Code Crim. Proc. art. 21.09, only the county need be alleged as the place where the offense occurred if: (1) the offense could be committed anywhere within the county; (2) the place the offense was committed is not an element of the offense; and (3) the court in which the offense is tried has countywide jurisdiction. *Ex parte Hunter*, 604 S.W.2d 188 (Tex. Crim. App. 1980); *see, e.g., Rivera v. State*, 808 S.W.2d 80 (Tex. Crim. App. 1991) (indictment for capital murder in course of burglary need not allege specific address of victim's burglarized habitation); *Santana v. State*, 658 S.W.2d 612 (Tex. Crim. App. 1983) (indictment need not allege specific location of burglary); *Ex parte Hyett*, 610 S.W.2d 787 (Tex. Crim. App. 1981) (charging instrument for possession of controlled substance need not allege where within county possession occurred); *Reed v. State*, 762 S.W.2d 640 (Tex. App.—Texarkana 1988, pet. ref'd) (charging instrument for trespass need not allege specific location of property).

b.   Tex. Code Crim. Proc. art. 21.09 applies to real estate alleged to be the object of the offense (such as arson), but not to real estate alleged only as the location of the offense (such as the location in a burglary case). *Franks v. State*, 688 S.W.2d 502 (Tex. Crim. App. 1985);[4] *see Chunn v. State*, 821 S.W.2d 718, 721 (Tex. App.—Houston [1st Dist.] 1991, pet. ref'd).

c.   Murder, burglary, theft, false imprisonment, and misdemeanor UCW are examples of offenses that can be committed anywhere within the county. *Pinkerton v. State*, 660 S.W.2d 58 (Tex. Crim. App. 1983) (capital murder in course of burglary with intent to commit rape); *Denison v. State*, 651 S.W.2d 754 (Tex. Crim. App. 1983) (burglary of a habitation); *Ward v. State*, 642 S.W.2d 782 (Tex. Crim. App. [Panel Op.] 1982) (false imprisonment); *Law v. State*, 574 S.W.2d 82 (Tex. Crim. App. [Panel Op.] 1978) (carrying handgun); *Nevarez v. State*, 503 S.W.2d 767 (Tex. Crim. App. 1974) (carrying pistol on premises licensed to sell alcohol).

d.   When an offense may be committed only in a certain type or class of places within a county, it is sufficient to allege its commission in that type or class of place without alleging the specific place within the type or class. *Nevarez v. State*, 503 S.W.2d 767 (Tex. Crim. App. 1974). For example, an indictment for unlawfully carrying a handgun on licensed premises must allege that the offense was committed on premises within the county for which a license or permit to sell or serve alcoholic beverages has issued. *Id.* Likewise, in prosecutions for DWI, it is necessary to allege that the offense occurred on a public highway or road, but no greater particularity is required. *Id.*

---

[4]   *Franks* cites *Lane v. State*, 621 S.W.2d 172 (Tex. Crim. App. [Panel Op.] 1981), as an arson case, but it was in fact a criminal mischief case for damage caused by fire. Furthermore, the *Franks* Court attempted to reconcile *Lane*, although *Lane*'s holding on the issue already had been expressly overruled by *Santana v. State*, 658 S.W.2d 612 (Tex. Crim. App. 1983).

e. An offense committed on the boundaries of two or more counties, or within 400 yards thereof, may be prosecuted and punished in any one of such counties and any offense committed on the premises of any airport operated jointly by two municipalities and situated in two counties may be prosecuted and punished in either county. Tex. Code Crim. Proc. art. 13.04.

f. The failure to identify property in accordance with Tex. Code Crim. Proc. art. 21.09 is a defect of form. *See* Tex. Code Crim. Proc. art. 27.09(2); *Bonner v. State*, 640 S.W.2d 601 (Tex. Crim. App. 1982).

15. Victim's Name

a. In the face of a motion to quash, the State must specify the name of the victim if the offense necessarily involves a victim. Even where the offense statute does not specifically mention a victim, an indictment must allege an injured party if the crime is one in which there is a victim. *Ex parte Munoz*, 657 S.W.2d 105 (Tex. Crim. App. 1983).

b. A charging instrument that fails to name the victim is valid and sufficient to vest the trial court with jurisdiction. *Ferguson v. State*, 335 S.W.3d 676 (Tex. App.—Houston [14th Dist.] 2011, no pet.); *Morelli v. State*, 9 S.W.3d 909 (Tex. App.—Austin 2000, pet. ref'd).

c. It is sufficient to state one or more initials of the given name and the surname of the victim. Tex. Code Crim. Proc. art. 21.07.

d. A victim known by two or more names may be identified by any one of such names. Tex. Code Crim. Proc. art. 21.07. The victim need not be commonly known by the other name; it is sufficient if the victim has been known by the other name. *Blankenship v. State*, 785 S.W.2d 158 (Tex. Crim. App. 1990).

e. If the victim's name is unknown to the grand jury, the indictment or information should allege that fact. Tex. Code Crim. Proc. art. 21.07. The requirement of a description applies only to descriptions of the defendant himself, not to others named in the indictment. *See id.*; *Saunders v. State*, 794 S.W.2d 91 (Tex. App.—San Antonio 1990), *aff'd*, 817 S.W.2d 688 (Tex. Crim. App. 1991).

f. The indictment should allege the victim of the underlying or aggravating felony when the criminal conduct is directed at a person other than the victim of the primary offense. *Rougeau v. State*, 738 S.W.2d 651 (Tex. Crim. App. 1987) (capital-murder indictment should allege victim of underlying aggravated robbery if it was someone other than murder victim), *overruled on other grounds*, *Harris v. State*, 784 S.W.2d 5 (Tex. Crim. App. 1989). However, the indictment is not subject to a motion to quash if it is open to no other interpretation than that the victim of the aggravating offense is the same person alleged as the victim of the primary offense. *Burks v. State*, 876 S.W.2d 877 (Tex. Crim. App. 1994); *Pinkerton v. State*, 660 S.W.2d 58 (Tex. Crim. App. 1983).

g. Theft of services involves a victim whose interest in obtaining compensation for services is jeopardized by the accused's conduct. *Ex parte Munoz*, 657 S.W.2d 105 (Tex. Crim. App. 1983) (op. on reh'g) (in theft of service case, indictment defective for not alleging owner or provider of services taken). In contrast, no victim need be alleged in an indictment for credit-card abuse because the offense does not require there to be a cardholder whose financial interest was placed at risk. *Moallen v. State*, 690 S.W.2d 244 (Tex. Crim. App. 1985).

h. Indecency with a child by exposure or indecent exposure are not victim-oriented offenses such as indecency by contact or aggravated rape because they focus on the mental state of the perpetrator and not the harm done to the victim. *Yanes v. State*, 149 S.W.3d 708 (Tex. App.—Austin 2004, pet. ref'd) (indecency with a child by exposure); *State v. York*, 31 S.W.3d 798

(Tex. App.—Dallas 2000, pet. ref'd) (indecent exposure). The gravamen of the offense of indecency with a child by exposure is the act of exposure; consequently, the child-victim's name is not a necessary element of proof. *Harris v. State*, 359 S.W.3d 625 (Tex. Crim. App. 2011).

i.   An indictment for burglary by entry with intent to commit an offense need not specify the victim of the offense that the defendant intended to commit. *Vaughn v. State*, 530 S.W.2d 558 (Tex. Crim. App. 1975).

j.   An indictment for retaliation should name the person to whom the threat was made, as well as the nature of the threat and the person against whom the threat was made. *Doyle v. State*, 661 S.W.2d 726 (Tex. Crim. App. 1983) (retaliation indictment stating only nature of threat and name of public servant threatened subject to motion to quash for failure to state how and to whom threat against judge made).

k.   In cases of sexual assault and aggravated sexual assault under Tex. Penal Code §§ 22.011 and 22.021, a victim may use a pseudonym in all public files and records concerning the offense. Tex. Code Crim. Proc. art. 57.02(b). If the prosecutor has notice of a pseudonym before indictment, the victim should presumably be named in the indictment by the designated pseudonym, and the pseudonym form shown confidentially to the defendant and his attorney. If the prosecutor receives notice of a pseudonym after indictment, the prosecutor should either return a superseding indictment and move to seal the original indictment or make a formal motion to amend pursuant to Tex. Code Crim. Proc. art. 28.10.

16.   Criminal Attempt

a.   A person commits the offense of criminal attempt if, with specific intent to commit an offense, he does an act amounting to more than mere preparation that tends but fails to effect the commission of the offense intended. Tex. Penal Code § 15.01(a).

b.   The charging instrument need not allege the constituent elements of the offense attempted. *Young v. State*, 675 S.W.2d 770 (Tex. Crim. App. 1984); *Farris v. State*, 506 S.W.3d 102 (Tex. App.—Corpus Christi 2016, pet. ref'd); *McCay v. State*, 476 S.W.3d 640 (Tex. App.—Dallas 2015, pet. ref'd).

c.   The charging instrument need not allege the statutory phrase "amounting to more than mere preparation that tends but fails to effect the commission of the offense intended" if it alleges facts which adequately show that the act is of that character. *Ex parte Todd*, 669 S.W.2d 738 (Tex. Crim. App. 1984) (indictment for attempted aggravated rape alleging "attempt to have sexual intercourse . . . and . . . attempt to compel the complainant to submit to the said act of sexual intercourse by threatening serious bodily injury" not deficient); *McCravy v. State*, 642 S.W.2d 450 (Tex. Crim. App. 1980) (indictment for attempted burglary alleging defendant attempted to enter building by turning off electrical power to building and climbing to roof to gain access with specific intent to commit burglary held sufficient).

d.   A charging instrument that alleges neither the statutory phrase "amounting to more than mere preparation that tends but fails to effect the commission of the offense intended" nor facts to show that element is insufficient to allege criminal attempt. *Molenda v. State*, 715 S.W.2d 651 (Tex. Crim. App. 1986) (alleging attempt to enter building "by prying a lock off of a fence surrounding said building with a screwdriver" held insufficient); *Ex parte Carter*, 618 S.W.2d 331 (Tex. Crim. App. 1981) (alleging "attempt to start a fire" held insufficient); *Hobbs v. State*, 548 S.W.2d 884 (Tex. Crim. App. 1977) (alleging "promise to pay" named individual to kill victim by shooting him held insufficient).

e.   Alleging that the defendant acted with intent to commit the underlying offense suffices to allege a culpable mental state for attempt. *Ex parte Prophet*, 601 S.W.2d 372 (Tex. Crim. App. 1980). Where the gravamen of an offense is an act coupled with a specific intent, pleading the requisite specific intent is sufficient to allege a culpable mental state. Id.

17. Conspiracy

a.   A person commits criminal conspiracy if, with intent that a felony be committed (1) he agrees with one or more persons that they or one or more of them engage in conduct that would constitute the offense, and (2) he or one or more of them performs an overt act in pursuance of the agreement. Tex. Penal Code § 15.02(a).

b.   An indictment charging conspiracy to commit an offense need not allege the offense intended with the particularity required to charge only the intended offense. *Farrington v. State*, 489 S.W.2d 607 (Tex. Crim. App. 1973); *Smith v. State*, 781 S.W.2d 418 (Tex. App.— Houston [1st Dist.] 1989, no pet.).

c.   An indictment alleging the essential elements of conspiracy, specifying each conspirator involved and the overt acts committed in furtherance of the conspiracy, is adequately specific. *Smith v. State*, 781 S.W.2d 418 (Tex. App.—Houston [1st Dist.] 1989, no pet.).

d.   A conspiracy to commit a number of crimes may be included in a single count of the indictment because the gist of the crime is the conspiracy. *Nisbet v. State*, 170 Tex. Crim. 1, 336 S.W.2d 142 (Tex. Crim. App. 1959); *see Woods v. State*, 801 S.W.2d 932 (Tex. App.— Austin 1990, pet. ref'd) (indictment alleging 22 overt acts).

18. Parties

a.   The indictment need not allege that the defendant acted as a party to the commission of a crime. Tex. Penal Code § 7.01(c); *In re State ex rel. Weeks*, 391 S.W.3d 117 (Tex. Crim. App. 2013); *Adames v. State*, 353 S.W.3d 854 (Tex. Crim. App. 2011); *Marable v. State*, 85 S.W.3d 287 (Tex. Crim. App. 2002). A charge on the law of parties may nevertheless be included in the trial court's jury charge if the issue is raised by the evidence. *Marable*, supra; *see* Tex. Penal Code § 7.01(c).

b.   A defendant specifically indicted as a party is not entitled to further allegation of the manner and means whereby he solicited, encouraged, directed, aided, or attempted to aid the primary actor in commission of the offense. *Swope v. State*, 805 S.W.2d 442 (Tex. Crim. App. 1991).

c.   An indictment allegation that the defendant "personally" committed the acts constituting the charged offense does not necessarily foreclose a charge on the law of parties based on the evidence at trial. *Igo v. State*, 723 S.W.2d 290 (Tex. App.—Fort Worth 1987, pet. ref'd) (submission of parties charge appropriate although burglary indictment alleged defendant "personally" entered habitation without consent).

d.   If the State chooses to specifically plead party liability, party liability becomes as much an element of an offense as the enumerated elements prescribed in a statute that defines a particular crime and is required to be proven as alleged. *Williams v. State*, 410 S.W.3d 411 (Tex. App.—Texarkana 2013, no pet.).

19. Judicial Notice

a.   At any stage of a proceeding, whether requested or not, a court may take judicial notice of adjudicative facts not subject to reasonable dispute in that it is either (1) generally known within the jurisdiction of the court or (2) capable of accurate and ready determination by resort to sources whose accuracy cannot reasonably be questioned. Tex. R. Evid. 201(b)(1), (2).

b. Presumptions of law and matters of which judicial notice is taken need not be stated in a charging instrument. Tex. Code Crim. Proc. art. 21.18. *E.g., Gonzales v. State*, 723 S.W.2d 746 (Tex. Crim. App. 1987) (judicial notice of incorporation of city of San Antonio); *Legg v. State*, 594 S.W.2d 429 (Tex. Crim. App. [Panel Op.] 1980) (judicial notice Taylor County Jail is "penal institution"); *Benton v. State*, 336 S.W.3d 355 (Tex. App.—Texarkana 2011, no pet.) (judicial notice of distances between two geographical locations); *Trujillo v. State*, 809 S.W.2d 593 (Tex. App.—San Antonio 1991, no pet.) (judicial notice high school accredited by Texas Education Agency).

20. Penalty Allegations

a. Prior convictions used as enhancements must be pled in some form, but they need not be pled in the indictment if they are not jurisdictional; however, it is permissible and perhaps preferable to include such allegations in the indictment. *Brooks v. State*, 957 S.W.2d 30 (Tex. Crim. App. 1997); *see Wilson v. State*, 267 S.W.3d 215 (Tex. App.—Waco 2008, pet. ref'd).

b. Because the purpose of an enhancement paragraph is to provide notice, it is not necessary to allege prior convictions for the purpose of enhancement with the same particularity used in charging the primary offense. *Freda v. State*, 704 S.W.2d 41 (Tex. Crim. App. 1986); *Derichsweiler v. State*, 359 S.W.3d 342 (Tex. App.—Fort Worth 2012, pet. ref'd). For example, the date on which the prior conviction became final and the sequence of prior convictions need not be alleged. *Derichsweiler*, supra. Rather, the notice must enable the accused "to find the record and make preparation for a trial of the question whether he is the convict named therein." *Id.* (quoting *Brown v. State*, 636 S.W.2d 867 (Tex. App.—Fort Worth 1982, no pet.)).

c. The State cannot use the same prior conviction more than once in the same prosecution. *Hernandez v. State*, 929 S.W.2d 11 (Tex. Crim. App. 1996) (per curiam) (alleging robbery conviction to increase charged drug offense from state-jail felony to third-degree felony barred using same robbery conviction to enhance defendant's punishment); *McWilliams v. State*, 782 S.W.2d 871 (Tex. Crim. App. 1990) (alleging prior burglary conviction to prove essential element of charged escape barred using same prior to enhance punishment).

d. A defendant is entitled to notice that the State will seek an affirmative deadly-weapon finding, but such notice need not be contained in the indictment under which the defendant is ultimately tried. *Brooks v. State*, 847 S.W.2d 247 (Tex. Crim. App. 1993) (per curiam). The defendant is simply entitled to written notice in "some form" that the use of a deadly weapon will be a fact issue at the time of prosecution. *Id.*; *Turner v. State*, 2016 WL 7030489 (Tex. App.—Texarkana December 2, 2016, no pet.).

e. Alleging that defendant caused death or serious bodily injury by using a named weapon or instrument provides sufficient notice that the State will seek a deadly-weapon finding. *Johnson v. State*, 815 S.W.2d 707 (Tex. Crim. App. 1991) ("causing death by striking with [his] feet and hands" held sufficient); *Mixon v. State*, 804 S.W.2d 107 (Tex. Crim. App. 1991) (death caused by unknown object held sufficient); *Gilbert v. State*, 769 S.W.2d 535 (Tex. Crim. App. 1989) ("serious bodily injury caused by placing complainant in hot liquid" held sufficient).

f. Notice is adequate even if it is contained in a dismissed or abandoned portion of the indictment. *Brooks v. State*, 847 S.W.2d 247 (Tex. Crim. App. 1993) (per curiam) (notice sufficient where defendant had actual notice of State's intent to seek affirmative deadly-weapon finding by virtue of separate aggravated sexual assault indictment arising from same criminal episode, which State agreed not to prosecute under plea agreement); *Grettenberg v. State*, 790 S.W.2d 613 (Tex. Crim. App. 1990) (notice sufficient where State voluntarily abandoned portion of indictment containing deadly weapon allegation; theories of prosecution were so interrelated that State's election to pursue only one count did not vitiate notice given in original form of indictment).

g.   An indictment alleging that the defendant committed or attempted to commit aggravated assault is adequate notice that there will be an issue of whether the defendant used or exhibited a deadly weapon since each manner of committing aggravated assault involves use of a deadly weapon. *Crumpton v. State*, 301 S.W.3d 663 (Tex. Crim. App. 2009). Further, the State may seek an affirmative deadly-weapon finding when an indictment alleges a burglary of a habitation in which, after entering, the defendant committed or attempted to commit a felony of aggravated assault. *Blount v. State*, 257 S.W.3d 712 (Tex. Crim. App. 2008).

h.   A capital-murder indictment need not allege the special issues contained in Tex. Code Crim. Proc. art. 37.071, even in the face of a motion to quash. *Joubert v. State*, 235 S.W.3d 729 (Tex. Crim. App. 2007); *Russeau v. State*, 171 S.W.3d 871 (Tex. Crim. App. 2005).

21. Complaints

a.   A complaint must: (1) state the name of the accused or, if the name is unknown, provide a reasonably definite description of the accused; (2) show that the accused has committed an offense against the laws of the state; (3) state the time and place of the commission of the offense; and (4) be signed by the affiant. Tex. Code Crim. Proc. art. 15.05.

b.   The complaint may be sworn before the district or county attorney who, for that purpose, shall have power to administer the oath, or it may be made before any officer authorized by law to administer oaths. Tex. Code Crim. Proc. art. 21.22.

c.   A person authorized to present informations and conduct prosecutions cannot be the affiant to the complaint supporting an information. *Wells v. State*, 516 S.W.2d 663 (Tex. Crim. App. 1974).

d.   A defect in the underlying complaint is not jurisdictional. *Aguilar v. State*, 846 S.W.2d 318 (Tex. Crim. App. 1993).

e.   Defects in complaints must be raised before trial. *Ramirez v. State*, 105 S.W.3d 628 (Tex. Crim. App. 2003); *Aguilar v. State*, 846 S.W.2d 318 (Tex. Crim. App. 1993).

22. Merger Doctrine

a.   The merger doctrine holds that, "[w]here there exists no general *mens rea* based upon proof of the commission of a separate felony which may be transferred from that crime to an independent homicide committed in the course thereof, the felony-murder rule cannot apply because there is a 'merger' of the two offenses." *Johnson v. State*, 4 S.W.3d 254 (Tex. Crim. App. 1999).

b.   There is no general merger doctrine in Texas. *Johnson v. State*, 4 S.W.3d 254 (Tex. Crim. App. 1999).

c.   The merger doctrine exists only to the extent consistent with Tex. Penal Code § 19.02(b)(3), meaning that a felony-murder conviction will not lie when the underlying felony is manslaughter or a lesser-included offense of manslaughter. *Johnson v. State*, 4 S.W.3d 254 (Tex. Crim. App. 1999). Otherwise, under § 19.02(a)(3), the State is allowed to transfer the mental state from the commission of a separate felony to an independent homicide committed in the course of a separate felony. *Homan v. State*, 19 S.W.3d 847 (Tex. Crim. App. 2000).

d.   Aggravated assault may serve as the predicate offense for felony murder. *Lawson v. State*, 64 S.W.3d 396 (Tex. Crim. App. 2001).

e.   The Seventh Court of Appeals in *Fraser v. State*, 2017 WL 2536861 (Tex. App.—Amarillo June 9, 2017, pet. filed), held that the merger doctrine did not allow the defendant's prosecution for felony murder under the State's theory that the defendant committed an act clearly dangerous to human life (administering diphenhydramine to an infant or causing the infant to ingest diphenhydramine) while in the course of committing the felony offense of reckless or criminally negligent injury to a child or reckless or criminally negligent child endangerment. The conviction potentially allowed a reckless or criminally negligent act to bootstrap what would otherwise be a manslaughter offense into a § 19.02(b)(3) felony murder. *Id.*

23.   Defects of Form and Substance

a.   Defects of form that may be raised by an exception are that the indictment: (1) does not appear to have been presented in the proper court; (2) lacks any requisite described by Tex. Code Crim. Proc. arts. 21.02 and 21.21; and (3) was not returned by a lawfully chosen or empanelled grand jury. Tex. Code Crim. Proc. art. 27.09.

b.   An indictment is not rendered insufficient by a defect of form that does not prejudice the defendant's substantial rights. Tex. Code Crim. Proc. art. 21.19.

c.   There is no exception to the substance of a charging instrument except that it: (1) does not appear therefrom that an offense against the law was committed by the defendant; (2) appears from the face thereof that a prosecution for the offense is barred by a lapse of time, or that the offense was committed after the finding of the indictment; (3) contains a matter which is a legal defense or bar to the prosecution; and (4) shows upon its face that the court trying the case lacks jurisdiction thereof. Tex. Code Crim. Proc. art. 27.08.

E.   AMENDMENT OF CHARGING INSTRUMENTS

1.   TEX. CODE CRIM. PROC. art. 28.10

a.   At any time before the date the trial on the merits commences, a matter of form or substance in a charging instrument may be amended after notice to the defendant. Tex. Code Crim. Proc. art. 28.10(a). Upon request, the defendant is entitled to not less than ten days (unless a shorter period is requested by the defendant) to respond to the amended charging instrument. *Id.* "Trial on the merits" as that phrase is used in art. 28.10(a) has been held to commence when the jury is impaneled and sworn. *Sanchez v. State*, 138 S.W.3d 324 (Tex. Crim. App. 2004); *Westfall v. State*, 970 S.W.2d 590 (Tex. App.—Waco 1998, pet. ref'd); *Hinojosa v. State*, 875 S.W.2d 339 (Tex. App.—Corpus Christi 1994, no pet.).

b.   A trial court errs by allowing the State to amend the indictment on the day of trial before jury selection, although a defendant waives this error by failing to object to the amendment. *Trevino v. State*, 470 S.W.3d 660 (Tex. App.—Houston [14th Dist.] 2015, pet. ref'd).

c.   After the trial on the merits commences, a matter of form or substance in a charging instrument may be amended if the defendant does not object. Tex. Code Crim. Proc. art. 28.10(b). A defendant has "an absolute veto power" over amendments to the indictment after trial begins; this includes amendments to an enhancement paragraph in the indictment. *Hamann v. State*, 428 S.W.3d 221 (Tex. App.—Houston [1st Dist.] 2014, pet. ref'd).

d.   A charging instrument may not be amended over the defendant's objection as to form or substance if the amended instrument charges the defendant with an additional or different offense or if the substantial rights of the defendant are prejudiced. Tex. Code Crim. Proc. art.

28.10(c). A "different offense" means a different statutory offense. *Flowers v. State*, 815 S.W.2d 724 (Tex. Crim. App. 1991) (per curiam) (change in element changes evidence required, but still same offense); *Gullatt v. State*, 368 S.W.3d 559 (Tex. App.—Waco 2011, pet. ref'd) (amendment lowering quantity of methamphetamine was possessed with intent to deliver did not charge "different offense"; both original and amended indictments contained identical offense, and fact that original allegations involved different punishment ranges and different subsections of same statute did not transform charge into "different offense"). *Compare Brown v. State*, 155 S.W.3d 625 (Tex. App.—Fort Worth 2004, pet. ref'd) (changing indictment charging burglary with intent to commit assault to charge burglary with attempted or completed assault did not charge different offense) *with Nichols v. State*, 52 S.W.3d 501 (Tex. App.—Dallas 2001, no pet.) (changing charge from possession of cocaine to possession of methamphetamine charged different offense). Amending a capital-murder indictment to allege that two murders were committed "during the same criminal transaction" does not violate Tex. Code Crim. Proc. art. 28.10(c). *Smith v. State*, 297 S.W.3d 260 (Tex. Crim. App. 2009).

e. The requirements of Tex. Code Crim. Proc. art. 28.10 are triggered only when the substance of the charging instrument is amended; they do not apply to nonsubstantive alterations to the charging instrument. *Auldridge v. State*, 228 S.W.3d 258 (Tex. App.—Fort Worth 2007, pet. ref'd).

f. A violation of Tex. Code Crim. Proc. art. 28.10 is subject to a harmless error analysis under Tex. R. App. P. 44.2(b). *See Hamann v. State*, 428 S.W.3d 221 (Tex. App.—Houston [1st Dist.] 2014, pet. ref'd).

2. Amendment versus Abandonment

a. An amendment is an alteration to the face of the charging instrument that affects its substance. *Ji Chen v. State*, 410 S.W.3d 394 (Tex. App.—Houston [1st Dist.] 2013, pet. ref'd); *Moore v. State*, 54 S.W.3d 529 (Tex. App.—Fort Worth 2001, pet. ref'd).

b. An abandonment is the deletion of unnecessary language that does not affect the substance of the charging instrument. *Ji Chen v. State*, 410 S.W.3d 394 (Tex. App.—Houston [1st Dist.] 2013, pet. ref'd); *Moore v. State*, 54 S.W.3d 529 (Tex. App.—Fort Worth 2001, pet. ref'd).

c. An alteration constitutes an abandonment, rather than an amendment, in three situations: (1) abandoning one or more ways or means of committing the offense; (2) reducing the charge to a lesser-included offense; and (3) eliminating surplusage.[5] *Eastep v. State*, 941 S.W.2d 130 (Tex. Crim. App. 1997), *overruled on other grounds*, *Riney v. State*, 28 S.W.3d 561 (Tex. Crim. App. 2000); *Ji Chen v. State*, 410 S.W.3d 394 (Tex. App.—Houston [1st Dist.] 2013, pet. ref'd); *Alston v. State*, 175 S.W.3d 853 (Tex. App.—Waco 2005, no pet.); *Mayfield v. State*, 117 S.W.3d 475 (Tex. App.—Texarkana 2003, pet. ref'd).

d. An abandonment (as opposed to an amendment) does not invoke the requirements of Tex. Code Crim. Proc. art. 28.10. *Ji Chen v. State*, 410 S.W.3d 394 (Tex. App.—Houston [1st Dist.] 2013, pet. ref'd); *Moore v. State*, 54 S.W.3d 529 (Tex. App.—Fort Worth 2001, pet. ref'd).

e. Although the Court of Criminal Appeals overruled surplusage law in favor of material-variance law when reviewing the sufficiency of the evidence, *Gollihar v. State*, 46 S.W.3d 243 (Tex. Crim. App. 2001), the surplusage doctrine likely still applies to issues of whether an

---

[5] Surplusage is unnecessary language that is not descriptive of what is legally essential to the validity of the indictment. *Curry v. State*, 30 S.W.3d 394 (Tex. Crim. App. 2000), *overruled in part on other grounds, Gollihar v. State*, 46 S.W.3d 243 (Tex. Crim. App. 2001). Extra language is descriptive of an element of the offense if it defines the offense more narrowly, places it in a specific setting, or describes the method by which it was committed. Id.

alteration constitutes an amendment under Tex. Code Crim. Proc. art. 28.10 or an abandonment to which art. 28.10 does not apply. *Auldridge v. State*, 228 S.W.3d 258 (Tex. App.—Fort
Worth 2007, pet. ref'd); *Mayfield v. State*, 117 S.W.3d 475 (Tex. App.—Texarkana 2003, pet.
ref'd); *Hall v. State*, 62 S.W.3d 918 (Tex. App.—Dallas 2001, pet. ref'd); *see Gollihar*, supra
(court's holding does not preclude defendant from raising purely "lack of notice" claim not
tied to legal sufficiency). Nevertheless, a logical extension of *Gollihar* to indictment cases
could allow any language in an indictment to be deleted as an abandonment if the deletion
would not result in a material variance. *Hall*, supra.

f.   Alteration or deletion of needlessly pled language, if such language is legally essential to
charge a crime, constitutes an amendment. *E.g.*, *Dukes v. State*, 239 S.W.3d 444 (Tex. App.—
Dallas 2007, pet. ref'd) (trial court erred in allowing State to amend information regarding
victim's address on day of trial for violation of protective order); *Garza v. State*, 50 S.W.3d
559 (Tex. App.—Houston [1st Dist.] 2001, no pet.) (deletion of "in a crowd of people" from
information charging misdemeanor offense of discharging a firearm in a metropolitan area
was an amendment because it described essential element of recklessness); *McCoy v. State*,
889 S.W.3d 354 (Tex. App.—Houston [14th Dist.] 1994, pet. ref'd) (amending language
describing manner of deception in theft case constituted amendment because descriptive of
element of effective consent).

g.   Changing the content of the charging instrument, as opposed to deleting an allegation,
has been held to constitute an amendment. *E.g.*, *Hillin v. State*, 808 S.W.2d 486 (Tex. Crim.
App. 1991) (altering weapon in aggravated assault indictment from "by throwing porcelain"
to "by throwing a commode"); *Garcia v. State*, 928 S.W.2d 666 (Tex. App.—Corpus Christi
1996, no pet.) (altering alleged date); *McCoy v. State*, 889 S.W.2d 354 (Tex. App.—Houston
[14th Dist.] 1994, pet. ref'd) (adding complainant); *Hilton v. State*, 879 S.W.2d 74 (Tex.
App.—Houston [14th Dist.] 1994, pet. ref'd) (altering indictment from "two facsimile
machines" to "one facsimile machine"); *Hinojosa v. State*, 875 S.W.2d 339 (Tex. App.—
Corpus Christi 1994, no pet.) (deleting "delivery" and replacing with "possession").

h.   Deleting surplusage, a manner or means of committing the offense, enhancement
allegations, or counts in the charging instrument constitute an abandonment, not an
amendment. *Garcia v. State*, 537 S.W.2d 930 (Tex. Crim. App. 1976) (State merely abandoned
theory that defendant escaped from custody after being convicted of a felony offense);
Stautzenberger v. State, 232 S.W.3d 323 (Tex. App.—Houston [14th Dist.] 2007, no pet.)
(enhancement allegations are mere surplusage which may be abandoned without invoking
requirements of art. 28.10); *Auldridge v. State*, 228 S.W.3d 258 (Tex. App.—Fort Worth 2007,
pet. filed) (omitting language "at a high rate of speed" did not change nature of manner or
means); *Johnson v. State*, 214 S.W.3d 157 (Tex. App.—Amarillo 2007, no pet.) (modifying
date in enhancement paragraph comparable to deleting surplusage); *Chavis v. State*, 177
S.W.3d 308 (Tex. App.—Houston [1st Dist.] 2005, pet. ref'd) (alteration removing convicting
court number in enhancement paragraph was abandonment because court number not
necessary to describe offense charged in enhancement paragraph); *Mayfield v. State*, 117
S.W.3d 475 (Tex. App.—Texarkana 2003, pet. ref'd) (abandoning allegations of prior theft
conviction and deleting language in enhancement paragraphs was abandonment of surplusage); *Chafin v. State*, 95 S.W.3d 549 (Tex. App.—Austin 2002, no pet.) (abandonment of
counts does not constitute amendment); *Hall v. State*, 62 S.W.3d 918 (Tex. App.—Dallas
2001, pet. ref'd) (deleting "without the consent of the complainant" where child under 14
years of age constituted abandonment because child's consent was not element of offense or
descriptive of any element); *Moore v. State*, 54 S.W.3d 529 (Tex. App.—Fort Worth 2001, pet.
ref'd) (deleting "or aggravated sexual assault of a child or injury to a child" from indictment
charging burglary of habitation constituted abandonment); *Williams v. State*, 946 S.W.2d 886

(Tex. App.—Waco 1997, no pet.) (deleting alternative allegation of intoxication constituted abandonment).

3. Procedure for Amending

a. Tex. Code Crim. Proc. art. 28.10(a) governs amendments "before the date the trial on the merits commences," while art. 28.10(b) deals with amendments "after the trial on the merits commences." The "trial on the merits" commences when the jury is impaneled and sworn. *Sanchez v. State*, 138 S.W.3d 324 (Tex. Crim. App. 2004); *Westfall v. State*, 970 S.W.2d 590 (Tex. App.—Waco 1998, pet. ref'd); *Hinojosa v. State*, 875 S.W.2d 339 (Tex. App.—Corpus Christi 1994, no pet.).

b. Tex. Code Crim. Proc. art. 28.10 does not provide for amendments to an indictment made on the date of trial prior to jury selection. Thus, the State may not amend a charging instrument on the day of trial, even if it is done before the trial commences. *Sodipo v. State*, 815 S.W.2d 551 (Tex. Crim. App. 1991) (op. on reh'g), *overruled on other grounds*, *Wright v. State*, 28 S.W.3d 526 (Tex. Crim. App. 2000); *State v. Murk*, 815 S.W.2d 556 (Tex. Crim. App. 1991); *Trevino v. State*, 470 S.W.3d 660, 662 (Tex. App.—Houston [14th Dist.] 2015, pet. ref'd).

c. Although Tex. Code Crim. Proc. art. 28.10(b) specifies no procedures for amending a charging instrument during trial and does not provide for ten days to respond, it clearly requires that the defendant have an opportunity to object.

d. All amendments must be made with leave of the trial court and under its direction. Tex. Code Crim. Proc. art. 28.11. However, the Texas Code of Criminal Procedure offers little guidance about the procedures for amending a charging instrument.

e. Because Tex. Code Crim. Proc. art. 28.11 requires "leave of the court," the State must request the trial court's permission before amending a charging instrument. *Ward v. State*, 829 S.W.2d 787 (Tex. Crim. App. 1992), *overruled on other grounds*, *Riney v. State*, 28 S.W.3d 561 (Tex. Crim. App. 2000). A motion for leave to amend is an appropriate vehicle to put the amending process in motion. Id.

f. While there is no specific requirement that the motion for leave to amend be in writing, it is better practice to file a written motion delineating the desired changes and to serve it on the defense. This allows the trial court to determine if the proposed amendment is proper under Tex. Code Crim. Proc. art. 28.10 and, if so, to grant the State permission to amend. *Ward v. State*, 829 S.W.2d 787 (Tex. Crim. App. 1992), *overruled on other grounds*, *Riney v. State*, 28 S.W.3d 561 (Tex. Crim. App. 2000). "In this sense, the amendment is done with leave of the court (*i.e.*, the trial judge's permission) and under its direction (*i.e.*, the trial judge's knowledge of the specific changes to be made, and the manner of making them, which it has deemed proper under the law)." Id.

g. Neither the State's motion to amend nor the trial court's granting thereof is an amendment; rather the two comprise the authorization for the eventual amendment of the charging instrument. *Riney v. State*, 28 S.W.3d 561 (Tex. Crim. App. 2000); *Tata v. State*, 446 S.W.3d 456 (Tex. App.—Houston [1st Dist.] 2014, pet. ref'd); *Valenti v. State*, 49 S.W.3d 594 (Tex. App.—Fort Worth 2001, no pet.). A written amendment must be submitted to the trial court and included in the record to be valid. *Tata*, supra.

h. Physical interlineation of the original charging instrument is an acceptable, but not the exclusive, means of effecting an amendment. *Riney v. State*, 28 S.W.3d 561 (Tex. Crim. App. 2000). It is acceptable for the State to proffer, for the trial court's approval, its amended version of a photocopy of the original indictment. If approved, the amended photocopy of the original indictment need only be incorporated into the record under the direction of the court, pursuant to Tex. Code Crim. Proc. art. 28.11, with the knowledge and affirmative assent of the defense. This version of the charging instrument then would become the "official" charging instrument in the case, and it would continue to state, presumably in "plain and intelligible" language, the nature and cause of the accusation. *Id.*

i. In *Perez v. State*, 429 S.W.3d 639 (Tex. Crim. App. 2014), the day before trial, the State filed an agreed motion asking the trial court to amend the indictment by replacing the existing eleven counts with the five counts as set forth in an attached exhibit. The trial court held a hearing where the State explained it was abandoning several counts and reorganizing those remaining so they would be in order of severity. The exhibit to the motion was treated as the amended indictment; there was no amendment to the indictment or to a copy of the indictment. The Court of Criminal Appeals rejected the defendant's claim that the amendment in this manner was ineffective.

j. Failure to object to an improper amendment waives the error. *State v. Murk*, 815 S.W.2d 556 (Tex. Crim. App. 1991); *Tyson v. State*, 172 S.W.3d 172 (Tex. App.—Fort Worth 2005, pet. ref'd).

F. WAIVER OF INDICTMENT

1. An accused has a constitutional right to be indicted by a grand jury if he is charged with a felony. Tex. Const. art. I, § 10.

2. A person represented by legal counsel may, orally in open court or in writing, voluntarily waive the right to be accused by indictment for a noncapital felony offense. Tex. Code Crim. Proc. art. 1.141. Upon waiver of an indictment, the accused is charged by information. Id.

3. A waiver of indictment must be intelligently, voluntarily, and knowingly given personally by the accused while represented by counsel. *Lackey v. State*, 574 S.W.2d 97 (Tex. Crim. App. [Panel Op.] 1978); *King v. State*, 473 S.W.2d 43 (Tex. Crim. App. 1971).

4. The record must reflect a proper waiver of indictment. *Ex parte Smith*, 650 S.W.2d 68 (Tex. Crim. App. 1982).

5. When an indictment is waived, the prosecution is not required to file a complaint with the information. *Ex parte Hyett*, 610 S.W.2d 787 (Tex. Crim. App. 1981).

6. Waiver of an indictment is governed by statute; it is not of constitutional dimension. *Ex parte Long*, 910 S.W.2d 485 (Tex. Crim. App. 1995).

7. Absent an indictment or valid waiver, the district court does not have jurisdiction over the case. *Teal v. State*, 230 S.W.3d 172 (Tex. Crim. App. 2007). If an accused has not effectively waived his right to an indictment in full accordance with the statute, the felony information is void, and an indictment is still mandatory. *King v. State*, 473 S.W.2d 43 (Tex. Crim. App. 1971).

G. ATTACKING CHARGING INSTRUMENTS

1. An objection to a defect, error, or irregularity of form or substance in a charging instrument must be made before the date on which the trial commences. Tex. Code Crim. Proc. art. 1.14(b).

2. All objections and exceptions to the charging instrument must be made in writing. Tex. Crim. Proc. art. 27.10; *Faulks v. State*, 528 S.W.2d 607 (Tex. Crim. App. 1975). An oral motion to quash preserves nothing for review. *Faulks*, supra; *Stoutner v. State*, 36 S.W.3d 716 (Tex. App.—Houston [1st Dist.] 2001, pet. ref'd).

3. Exceptions to the form or substance of the charging instrument are determined at a pretrial hearing if one is set. Tex. Code Crim. Proc. art. 28.01, § 1(4). When a criminal case is set for such pretrial hearing, any such preliminary matters not raised or filed seven days before the hearing will not thereafter be allowed to be raised or filed, except by permission of the court for good cause shown. Id. § 2.

4. A defendant must have at least ten days notice of a pretrial hearing in order to allow him to raise or file an objection to the indictment. Tex. Code Crim. Proc. art. 28.01, § 2. Notice may be given through either an announcement in open court in the presence of the defendant or his attorney, personal service on the defendant or his attorney of record, or by mail to the defendant or his attorney of record. Id. § 3.

5. A motion to set aside, dismiss, or quash an indictment should be made at the first opportunity and must be presented to the trial court prior to that party's announcement of ready. *Neal v. State*, 150 S.W.3d 169 (Tex. Crim. App. 2004).

6. An objection or exception to the charging instrument must be sufficiently specific to alert the trial court to the precise nature of the defect alleged. *Whalon v. State*, 725 S.W.2d 181 (Tex. Crim. App. 1986). The motion must make clear to the trial court what specific language the defendant contends is inadequate, and generalized form allegations are insufficient. *Id.* (allegations that charging instrument failed to "state facts sufficient to constitute an offense against the State of Texas," was "vague and uncertain," failed to contain essential facts constituting offense charged, and "state[d] conclusions rather than facts" was inadequate).

7. A pretrial writ of habeas corpus is available to raise a claim that the indictment is, on its face, barred by the statute of limitations (but not to challenge the sufficiency of a tolling allegation), barred by double jeopardy, or based on a void statute. *Ex parte Smith*, 178 S.W.3d 797 (Tex. Crim. App. 2005); *Ex parte Weise*, 55 S.W.3d 617 (Tex. Crim. App. 2001); *Ex parte Matthews*, 873 S.W.2d 40 (Tex. Crim. App. 1994). Otherwise, the indictment should be challenged by a pretrial motion to quash, the denial of which may be challenged on direct appeal after conviction. *Ex parte Mattox*, 683 S.W.2d 93 (Tex. App.—Austin 1984), *pet. ref'd*, 685 S.W.2d 53 (Tex. Crim. App. 1985).

8. The State is entitled to appeal a trial court order that dismisses all or part of a charging instrument. Tex. Code Crim. Proc. art. 44.01(a)(1).

   a. The State may appeal an order short of an acquittal if it has the effect of terminating the prosecution, *i.e.*, if it forces any alteration of the indictment or information before the trial on the merits and the State is not willing to comply with that order. *State v. Stanley*, 201 S.W.3d 754 (Tex. Crim. App. 2006).

   b. The State need not amend the charging instrument before attempting an appeal. *State v. Moreno*, 807 S.W.2d 327 (Tex. Crim. App. 1991).

   c. For purposes of applying the plain language of art. 44.01(a)(1), there is no meaningful distinction between elements of the offense and enhancement allegations contained within an indictment; both constitute "portion[s] of the indictment" under art. 44.01(a)(1). *State v. Richardson*, 383 S.W.3d 544 (Tex. Crim. App. 2012). Whenever the quashed provisions are alleged in the indictment and, thus, are a portion of the indictment, art. 44.01(a)(1) may be invoked to permit the State's appeal. *State v. Rosseau*, 396 S.W.3d 550 (Tex. Crim. App. 2013); *Richardson*, supra.

9. The sufficiency of a charging instrument is a question of law. *State v. Moff*, 154 S.W.3d 599 (Tex. Crim. App. 2004). An indictment must be facially tested under the law as a pleading. Id. In the pretrial setting, there is neither constitutional nor statutory authority for

a defendant to test–or for a trial court to determine–the sufficiency of evidence to support or defeat an element alleged in the indictment. *Id.*

III. JOINDER OF OFFENSES

A. SAME CRIMINAL EPISODE

1. When available

a. A defendant may be prosecuted in a single criminal action for all offenses arising out of the same "criminal episode." Tex. Penal Code § 3.02(a); *see* Tex. Health & Safety Code § 481.132(b) (offenses under the Texas Controlled Substances Act).

b. A "criminal episode" is the commission of two or more offenses, regardless of whether the harm is directed toward or inflicted upon more than one person or item of property, if (1) the offenses are committed pursuant to the same transaction or pursuant to two or more transactions that are connected or constitute a common scheme or plan; or (2) the offenses are the repeated commission of the same or similar offenses. Tex. Penal Code § 3.01(1), (2); *see* Tex. Health & Safety Code § 481.132(a) (offenses under the Texas Controlled Substances Act).

2. Procedure–Separate Charging Instruments

a. When a single criminal action is based on more than one charging instrument within the trial court's jurisdiction, the State must file written notice of the intent to join the offenses not less than thirty days before trial. Tex. Penal Code § 3.02(b).

b. Tex. Penal Code § 3.02(b) is simply a notice provision for the consolidation procedure, and noncompliance does not prevent application of the provision prohibiting consecutive sentencing for consolidated offenses. *LaPorte v. State*, 840 S.W.2d 412 (Tex. Crim. App. 1992). The procedural requirements of Tex. Penal Code § 3.02(b) may be waived either affirmatively or by inaction. Id.

c. If notice is not given, a defendant may either object to the lack of notice when he discovers that the State intends to prosecute for offenses based upon more than one indictment in a single trial, may request the severance provided by Tex. Penal Code § 3.04, or may waive the notice and proceed to trial on any charges presented by the State by not objecting to the lack of notice. *LaPorte v. State*, 840 S.W.2d 412 (Tex. Crim. App. 1992). If a defendant objects to the lack of notice, the State would then have the option of proceeding on one indictment or of seeking a resetting of the trial so as to provide adequate notice. Id.

d. A defendant has no right to consolidate offenses committed in the same criminal episode. *Nelson v. State*, 864 S.W.2d 496 (Tex. Crim. App. 1993).

3. Procedure–Single Charging Instrument

a. Two or more offenses may be joined in separate counts of a single charging instrument if they arise out of the same criminal episode as defined in chapter 3 of the Penal Code. Tex. Code Crim. Proc. art. 21.24(a).

b. A count may contain as many separate paragraphs charging the same offense as necessary, but no paragraph may charge more than one offense. Tex. Code Crim. Proc. art. 21.24(b).

c. The charging instrument need not allege that the offenses arose from the same criminal episode. *Lucas v. State*, 721 S.W.2d 467 (Tex. App.—Houston [1st Dist.] 1986, pet. ref'd); *Benavidez v. State*, 655 S.W.2d 233 (Tex. App.—Beaumont 1983, pet. ref'd).

4. Severance

a. When two or more offenses have been consolidated or joined for trial under Tex. Penal Code § 3.02, the defendant has an absolute right to a severance of the offenses. Tex. Penal Code § 3.04(a); *Graham v. State*, 19 S.W.3d 851 (Tex. Crim. App. 2000); .

b. To be timely, the defendant's request for separate trials or objection to their consolidation must occur before the jury is sworn and jeopardy attaches. *Trevino v. State*, 228 S.W.3d 729 (Tex. App.—Corpus Christi 2006, pet. ref'd); *Dominguez v. State*, 62 S.W.3d 203 (Tex. App.—El Paso 2000, pet. ref'd).

c. The defendant's complaint is sufficient if it apprises the trial judge that he does not desire to have the offenses joined in a common trial. *Trevino v. State*, 228 S.W.3d 729 (Tex. App.—Corpus Christi 2006, pet. ref'd). A defendant may so inform the court by objection, request, or motion to sever. *Id*. It is error to refuse such a motion, even if it is made orally on the day of trial. *Id*.

d. Unless the defendant or the State would be unfairly prejudiced by a joinder, the right to severance does not apply to the offenses listed in Tex. Penal Code § 3.03(b). *See* Tex. Penal Code § 3.04(c).

e. A charging instrument alleging multiple theories for a single offense is not subject to a motion to sever. *Sperling v. State*, 924 S.W.2d 722 (Tex. App.—Amarillo 1996, pet. ref'd).

5. Punishment and Sentence

a. The trial court's general authority under Tex. Code Crim. Proc. art. 42.08 to order consecutive sentences is statutorily limited by Tex. Penal Code § 3.03 when a defendant is found guilty of more than one offense arising out of the same criminal episode prosecuted in a single criminal action,[6] whether based on a single charging instrument or several charging instruments. *LaPorte v. State*, 840 S.W.2d 412 (Tex. Crim. App. 1992).

b. In most cases, when offenses are joined because they occurred in the same criminal episode, a sentence for each offense must be pronounced and the sentences must be concurrent. Tex. Penal Code § 3.03(a); *see LaPorte v. State*, 840 S.W.2d 412 (Tex. Crim. App. 1992). However, consecutive sentences are permitted for offenses enumerated in Tex. Penal Code § 3.03(b).

c. A defendant can waive the benefit of the concurrent sentence provisions stated in Tex. Penal Code § 3.03. *Ex parte McJunkins*, 954 S.W.2d 39 (Tex. Crim. App. 1997) (defendant validly waived right to concurrent sentences where he specifically accepted consecutive sentences as part of plea agreement).

d. If the defendant secures a severance, the court has discretion to order the sentences to run either concurrently or consecutively. Tex. Penal Code § 3.04(b).

e. If the facts show that the proceeding is a single criminal action arising out of a single criminal episode, the trial court may not order consecutive sentences, even if the State failed to comply with the notice requirement of Tex. Penal Code § 3.02(b). *LaPorte v. State*, 840 S.W.2d 412 (Tex. Crim. App. 1992).

f. The imposition of consecutive sentences for multiple offenses will be upheld on appeal if the record does not reflect that the convictions and sentences resulted from a single criminal action, even if the sentences were imposed on the same day. *Duran v. State*, 844 S.W.2d 745 (Tex. Crim. App. 1993) (per curiam).

---

[6] A defendant is prosecuted in a single criminal action whenever allegations and evidence of more than one offense arising out of the same criminal episode, as that term is defined in chapter 3 of the Penal Code, are presented in a single trial or plea proceeding. *LaPorte v. State*, 840 S.W.2d 412 (Tex. Crim. App. 1992).

g. The appropriate remedy for a void cumulation order is to reform the judgment to delete the cumulation order. *Robbins v. State*, 914 S.W.2d 582 (Tex. Crim. App. 1996) (per curiam). When only part of a cumulation order is illegal, the remedy is to delete the illegal portion. *Sullivan v. State*, 387 S.W.3d 649 (Tex. Crim. App. 2013).

6. Remedy for Misjoinder

a. A complaint of improper joinder must comply with Tex. Code Crim. Proc. 1.14(b) in order to be preserved for appeal. *Tear v. State*, 74 S.W.3d 555 (Tex. App.—Dallas 2002, pet. ref'd); *Sanchez v. State*, 928 S.W.2d 255 (Tex. App.—Houston [14th Dist.] 1996, no pet.).

b. Misjoinder is corrected if the State proceeds on only one offense, if the trial court submits only one offense in the jury charge, or if the jury charge allows the jury to convict the defendant of only one offense.

c. When a defendant is convicted of two or more misjoined offenses, the remedy is to retain the most serious offense and to vacate the remaining offenses. *Ex parte Cavazos*, 203 S.W.3d 333 (Tex. Crim. App. 2006). The "most serious offense" is the one for which the greatest sentence was assessed. Id.

d. Failure to object to misjoinder before the date on which the trial on the merits commences forfeits the complaint on appeal. *Waddell v. State*, 456 S.W.3d 366 (Tex. App.—Corpus Christi 2015, no pet.).

B. AGGREGATION OF OFFENSES

1. When Allowed

a. Theft

When amounts are obtained in violation of chapter 31 of the Penal Code (theft) pursuant to one scheme or continuing course of conduct, whether from the same or several sources, the conduct may be considered as one offense and the amounts aggregated in determining the grade of the offense. Tex. Penal Code § 31.09. In hybrid service-property offenses arising from one scheme or continuing course of conduct, amounts related to thefts of property may be aggregated with amounts related to theft of services pursuant to § 31.09. *Chance v. State*, 579 S.W.2d 471 (Tex. Crim. App. 1979).

b. Fraud

Amounts obtained in violation of chapter 32 of the Penal Code (fraud) pursuant to one scheme or continuing course of conduct may be considered one offense and the amounts aggregated to determine the grade of offense. Tex. Penal Code § 32.03.

c. Insurance Fraud

When separate claims in violation of chapter 35 of the Penal Code (insurance fraud) are communicated to an insurer or group of insurers pursuant to one scheme or continuing course of conduct, the conduct may be considered as one offense and the value of the claims aggregated in determining the classification of the offense. Tex. Penal Code § 35.03(a). When three or more separate claims in violation of chapter 35 are communicated to an insurer or group of insurers pursuant to one scheme or continuing course of conduct, the conduct may be considered as one offense, and the classification of the offense shall be one category higher than the most serious single offense proven from the separate claims, except that if the most serious offense is a felony of the first degree, the offense is a felony of the first degree. Id. § (b). Subsection (b) does not apply if claims are aggregated under subsection (a). *Id.*

d. Securities Act

When amounts are obtained in violation of the Texas Securities Act in the course of one scheme or continuing course of conduct—whether from the same or several sources—the conduct may be considered as one offense and the amounts aggregated in determining the grade of the offense. Tex. Rev. Civ. Stats. art. 581–29–2.

e. Lottery Fraud

When amounts are claimed, or attempted to be claimed in violation of chapter 466 of the Government Code pursuant to one scheme or continuing course of conduct, whether from the same or several sources, the amounts may be aggregated in determining the level of the offense. Tex. Gov't Code § 466.3012.

f. Food Stamp Fraud

When cash, exchange value, or food stamp benefit permits of various values are obtained in violation of this section pursuant to one scheme or continuing course of conduct, whether from the same or several sources, the conduct may be considered as one offense and the values aggregated in determining the grade of the offense. Tex. Hum. Res. Code § 33.011(d).

g. Criminal Mischief

When more than one item of tangible property belonging to one or more owners is damaged, destroyed, or tampered with pursuant to one continuing course of conduct or scheme, the amount of the pecuniary loss may be aggregated in determining the grade of the offense. Tex. Penal Code § 28.03(e).

h. Graffiti

When more than one item of tangible property belonging to one or more owners is marked pursuant to one scheme or continuing course of conduct, the amount of pecuniary loss may be aggregated in determining the grade of the offense. Tex. Penal Code § 28.08(c).

i. Breach of Computer Security

When benefits are obtained, a victim is defrauded or harmed, or property is altered, damaged, or deleted, whether or not in a single incident, the conduct may be considered as one offense and the value of the benefits obtained and of the losses incurred because of the fraud, harm, or alteration, damage, or deletion of property may be aggregated in determining the grade of the offense. Tex. Penal Code § 33.02(c). There is no requirement of one scheme or continuing course of conduct as in other aggregation statutes.

2. Procedure for Aggregation

a. An indictment charging an aggregated offense must allege that each individual offense was committed "pursuant to one scheme or continuing course of conduct." *Kellar v. State*, 108 S.W.3d 311 (Tex. Crim. App. 2003); *Whitehead v. State*, 745 S.W.2d 374 (Tex. Crim. App. 1988).

b. The charging instrument need not plead each separate instance included in the aggregation. *Kent v. State*, 483 S.W.3d 557 (Tex. Crim. App. 2016); *State v. Moff*, 154 S.W.3d 599 (Tex. Crim. App. 2004); *Kellar v. State*, 108 S.W.3d 311 (Tex. Crim. App. 2003). However, the defendant is still entitled to some type of constitutional due-process notice. *Moff*, supra; *Kellar*, supra.

c. Aggregation is discretionary; the State is not required to consider the prohibited conduct as one offense. *Montgomery v. State*, 91 S.W.3d 426 (Tex. App.—Eastland 2002, pet. ref'd).

3. Severance

Aggregated transactions are considered "one offense," and the defendant has no right to severance. *Wages v. State*, 573 S.W.2d 804 (Tex. Crim. App. [Panel Op.] 1978); *see Graves v. State*, 795 S.W.2d 185 (Tex. Crim. App. 1990).

4. Punishment and Sentence

a.   Once the offense grade has been enhanced by aggregation, punishment may be assessed within the enhanced range.

b.   Aggregation may be used along with enhancement provisions for repeat and habitual offenders to enhance the punishment available. *See Wages v. State*, 573 S.W.2d 804 (Tex. Crim. App. [Panel Op.] 1978).

5. Statute of Limitations

a.   When offenses are aggregated, the statute of limitations for the felony offense applies. *Graves v. State*, 795 S.W.2d 185 (Tex. Crim. App. 1990) (expiration of two-year statute of limitations for misdemeanor theft did not bar prosecution of felony resulting from aggregation of amounts involved in individual misdemeanors).

b.   The statute of limitations for an aggregated offense does not begin to run until the date of the commission of the final incident alleged. *King v. State*, 17 S.W.3d 7 (Tex. App.—Houston [14th Dist.] 2000, pet. ref'd).

C.   ELECTIONS BY THE STATE

1.   An election is required when the indictment alleges the commission of a single offense, but the State offers evidence at trial that the accused committed the offense alleged more than once. *Scoggan v. State*, 799 S.W.2d 679 (Tex. Crim. App. 1990); *Moore v. State*, 143 S.W.2d 305 (Tex. App.—Waco 2004, no pet.).

2.   No election is required when multiple offenses are properly joined in a single indictment and each offense is alleged as a separate count.[7] Moore v. State, 143 S.W.3d 305 (Tex. App.—Waco 2004, no pet.); *Owens v. State*, 96 S.W.3d 668 (Tex. App.—Austin 2003, no pet.).

3.   When the charging instrument alleges several ways of committing the same offense, the State need not elect between the various theories alleged; rather, the jury may consider all theories and return a general verdict of guilty. *Gonzales v. State*, 270 S.W.3d 282 (Tex. App.—Amarillo 2008, pet. ref'd); *Renteria v. State*, 199 S.W.3d 499 (Tex. App.—Houston [1st Dist.] 2006, pet. ref'd).

4.   Where the State establishes an interrelated series of acts or transactions in order to show one completed offense, no election is required. *Crocker v. State*, 573 S.W.2d 190 (Tex. Crim. App. [Panel Op.] 1978) (series of acts whereby defendant exposed his son to radiation was one criminal transaction); *McClelland v. State*, 390 S.W.2d 777 (Tex. Crim. App. 1965) (bribery involving many transactions during 18–month period).

5.   No election is required when the defendant's acts are part of one criminal transaction, one continuous offense, or one offense involving many transactions. *McCaleb v. State*, 537 S.W.2d 728 (Tex. Crim. App. 1976) (several advances of money by victim to defendant were part of scheme to obtain money by false representation, and no election required); *Steele v. State*, 523 S.W.2d 685 (Tex. Crim. App. 1975) (two acts of intercourse occasioned by defendant's continuing and intervening actions were part of same criminal transaction, and

---

[7]   This assumes, of course, that the convictions do not violate the prohibition against double jeopardy as they would, for example, if the defendant was convicted of both a greater and a lesser offense. *See Landers v. State*, 957 S.W.2d 558 (Tex. Crim. App. 1997), *overruled on other grounds*, *Ex parte Cavazos*, 203 S.W.3d 333 (Tex. Crim. App. 2006).

no election required); *Powell v. State*, 502 S.W.2d 705 (Tex. Crim. App. 1974) (possession of marijuana in camper on back of pickup truck in which accused was passenger after marijuana moved from airplane to camper and possession of marihuana in accused's pockets constituted single possession offense, and no election required).

6. Elections are not limited to jury trials; they may serve an important purpose in bench trials, too. *Phillips v. State*, 193 S.W.3d 904 (Tex. Crim. App. 2006) (even in bench trial, election important for notice and to ensure trial judge assays evidence with view to whether defendant committed discrete offense and not potentially convict for being criminal generally).

7. Before the State rests, the trial court has discretion in directing the State to make an election. *Phillips v. State*, 193 S.W.3d 904 (Tex. Crim. App. 2006); *Isenhower v. State*, 261 S.W.3d 168 (Tex. App.—Houston [14th Dist.] 2008, no pet.). However, once the State rests its case-in-chief, in the face of a timely request, the trial court must order the State to make its election, and failure to do so constitutes error. *Phillips*, supra; *Isenhower*, supra.

8. A complaint that offenses are improperly joined must be raised pretrial pursuant to Tex. Code Crim. Proc. art. 1.14(b). *Tear v. State*, 74 S.W.3d 555 (Tex. App.—Dallas 2002, pet. ref'd); *Sanchez v. State*, 928 S.W.2d 255 (Tex. App.—Houston [14th Dist.] 1996, no pet.); *Anderson v. State*, 905 S.W.2d 367 (Tex. App.—Fort Worth 1995, pet. ref'd).

IV. JOINDER OF DEFENDANTS

A. WHEN ALLOWED

1. Two or more defendants who are jointly or separately indicted or complained against for the same offense or any offense growing out of the same transaction may be, in the discretion of the trial court, tried jointly or separately as to one or more defendants. Tex. Code Crim. Proc. art. 36.09. When defendants are tried jointly, either defendant may testify for the other or on behalf of the State. Id.

2. Upon timely motion to sever, when it is made known to the trial court that there is a previous admissible conviction against one defendant or that a joint trial would be prejudicial to any defendant, the trial court shall order a severance as to the defendant whose joint trial would prejudice the other defendant or defendants. Tex. Code Crim. Proc. art. 36.09.

3. In drafting Tex. Code Crim. Proc. art. 36.09 "the Legislature intended for defendants accused of the same offense to be tried together most of the time." *Qualley v. State*, 206 S.W.3d 624 (Tex. Crim. App. 2006).

4. The test of "same transaction" appears to be fairly narrow. *Ex parte Mitchell*, 608 S.W.2d 915 (Tex. Crim. App. [Panel Op.] 1980).

a. In *Ex parte Mitchell*, 608 S.W.2d 915 (Tex. Crim. App. [Panel Op.] 1980), six defendants were charged in six separate informations with soliciting drinks from six different complainants. Each defendant was charged in a separate information that made no reference to other charging instruments and failed to allege any joint action. All the informations alleged the offenses occurred on the same date, at the same address, and with a common employer. The court held the charges did not constitute the "same offense" and did not grow out of the "same transaction." Therefore it was not within the trial court's discretion to order a joint trial over the defendant's objection. The court noted that, while joinder of the defendant with one of the employees may have been proper, his joinder with all of the employees (who were misjoined among themselves) did not result in a fair trial for the defendant.

b. In *Hernandez v. State*, 862 S.W.2d 193 (Tex. App.—Beaumont 1993, pet. ref'd), the defendant was convicted of aggravated assault on a correctional officer. The indictment alleged that the defendant struck the prison guard during an altercation involving four other prisoners and four other prison guards. All of the offenses occurred at the same location at or near the same time. The trial court granted a motion for a joint trial of five defendants. Following the rationale of *Ex parte Mitchell*, supra, the court held that it was an abuse of discretion to grant the motion to consolidate over the defendants' objections.

B. SEVERANCE

1. The two grounds for severance are: (1) the codefendant has a previous admissible conviction; and (2) a joint trial would prejudice any defendant. Tex. Code Crim. Proc. art. 36.09.

2. In order to obtain a severance in a joint trial, the motion for severance must be timely, and at least one of the two grounds for severance must be alleged with supporting evidence. *Qualley v. State*, 206 S.W.3d 624 (Tex. Crim. App. 2006). It is not error to overrule a motion for severance absent evidence to support the motion. *Robinson v. State*, 449 S.W.2d 239 (Tex. Crim. App. 1969). Absent evidence of prejudice to one defendant in a joint trial, or evidence that one of the defendants has a prior admissible conviction, a motion for severance is left to the trial court's discretion. *Castillo v. State*, 186 S.W.3d 21 (Tex. App.—Corpus Christi 2005, pet. ref'd).

3. A motion to sever must be made before trial if the factual basis for seeking a severance was known prior to trial. *Qualley v. State*, 206 S.W.3d 624 (Tex. Crim. App. 2006). Otherwise, the motion must be made "at the first opportunity or as soon as the grounds for [severance] become apparent or should have become apparent." Id. A new ground for severance is considered a new motion, and its timeliness should be viewed accordingly. Id.

4. Upon timely motion, a trial court must order severance if one defendant has a previous admissible conviction. Tex. Code Crim. Proc. art. 36.09.

a. The "previous admissible conviction" portion of Tex. Code Crim. Proc. art. 36.09 acts only to shield a defendant from the introduction of the codefendant's conviction. *Qualley v. State*, 206 S.W.3d 624 (Tex. Crim. App. 2006). Severance on this basis is mandatory only when the moving defendant himself has no prior conviction that would be admissible at either the guilt or punishment stage of trial. Id.

b. If both defendants have admissible prior convictions, there is no absolute right to severance. *Id.*

5. Upon timely motion and evidence, the trial court shall order a severance if a joint trial would be prejudicial to any defendant. Tex. Code Crim. Proc. art. 36.09; *Qualley v. State*, 206 S.W.3d 624 (Tex. Crim. App. 2006); *see Lacy v. State*, 901 S.W.2d 518 (Tex. App.—Tyler 1995, no pet.) (right to a severance not absolute, but denial of motion to sever is abuse of discretion when movant shows joint trial clearly prejudicial to his case).

a. "Prejudicial" is undefined and somewhat ambiguous, but it does not mean the types of circumstances or disagreements between parties that normally would be expected to arise during any trial containing multiple defendants. *Qualley v. State*, 206 S.W.3d 624 (Tex. Crim. App. 2006).

b. The mere allegation that prejudice will result is not evidence of, or a sufficient showing of, prejudice under Tex. Code Crim. Proc. art. 36.09, particularly when the severance is discretionary with the trial judge. *King v. State*, 17 S.W.3d 7 (Tex. App.—Houston [14th Dist.] 2000, pet. ref'd).

c. To establish prejudice, the defendant must show a serious risk that a specific trial right would be compromised by a joint trial, or that a joint trial would prevent the jury from making a reliable judgment about guilt or innocence, and that the problem could not be adequately addressed by lesser curative measures, such as a limiting instruction. *Qualley v. State*, 206 S.W.3d 624 (Tex. Crim. App. 2006) (adopting *Zafiro v. United States*, 506 U.S. 534 (1993)).

d. Prejudice must be analyzed with regard to each defendant because one defendant may be entitled to a severance while the other is not. *Qualley v. State*, 206 S.W.3d 624 (Tex. Crim. App. 2006). While a severance at trial in that situation would in essence grant both defendants a separate trial, only the defendant entitled to the severance can obtain relief on appeal. Id.

e. The existence of antagonistic defenses does not, alone, warrant a severance on the grounds of prejudice. *Qualley v. State*, 206 S.W.3d 624 (Tex. Crim. App. 2006). "Mutually exclusive defenses are not necessarily prejudicial." Id.

f. Proof that defendants have different levels of culpability is not enough to require separate trials. *Morales v. State*, 466 S.W.2d 293 (Tex. Crim. App. 1970); *Davila v. State*, 4 S.W.3d 844 (Tex. App.—Eastland 1999, no pet.).

g. If a defendant seeks a severance because a joint trial will prevent him from calling the codefendant as a witness, the movant must establish a bona fide need for the testimony, the substance of the desired testimony, its exculpatory nature and effect, and the designated codefendant will in fact testify at a separate trial. *Lacy v. State*, 901 S.W.2d 518 (Tex. App.—Tyler 1995, no pet.); *Rajski v. State*, 715 S.W.2d 832 (Tex. App.—Houston [14th Dist.] 1986, no pet.), *overruled on other grounds*, *Rutledge v. State*, 749 S.W.2d 50 (Tex. Crim. App. 1988).

h. A defendant may establish prejudice mandating severance by showing that a non-testifying codefendant's confession implicating the defendant as the perpetrator of the crime charged will be admissible at the joint trial. *Chavez v. State*, 6 S.W.3d 56 (Tex. App.—San Antonio 1999, pet. ref'd). However, the prejudice caused by admission of a codefendant's statement may be avoided if the trial court instructs the jury to use the confession only against the confessing codefendant and the confession is redacted to eliminate the defendant's name and any reference to his existence. Id.

6. The trial court has a continuing duty to order a severance after trial begins upon a showing of sufficient prejudice. *Aguilar v. State*, 26 S.W.3d 901 (Tex. Crim. App. 2000).

C. ORDER OF TRIAL

1. If a severance is granted, the defendants may agree as to which defendant will be tried first; but, if they fail to do so, the court will specify the order of trial. Tex. Code Crim. Proc. art. 36.10.

2. When there are more than two defendants, merely agreeing on which defendant is to be tried first, without agreeing to the order of trial for all defendants, does not comply with Tex. Code Crim. Proc. art. 36.10. *Lafoon v. State*, 543 S.W.2d 617 (Tex. Crim. App. 1976).

3. A violation of Tex. Code Crim. Proc. art. 36.10 regarding the agreed order of trial mandates reversal unless the appellate court determines the error is harmless. *Roberts v. State*, 784 S.W.2d 430 (Tex. Crim. App. 1990).

CODE OF CRIMINAL PROCEDURE

1

TITLE 1. CODE OF CRIMINAL PROCEDURE OF 1965

INTRODUCTORY

CHAPTER ONE. GENERAL PROVISIONS

Art. 1.01. Short title

This Act shall be known, and may be cited, as the "Code of Criminal Procedure".

Acts 1965, 59th Leg., vol. 2, p. 317, ch. 722, eff. Jan. 1, 1966.

Art. 1.02. Effective date

This Code shall take effect and be in force on and after January 1, 1966. The procedure herein prescribed shall govern all criminal proceedings instituted after the effective date of this Act and all proceedings pending upon the effective date hereof insofar as are applicable.

Acts 1965, 59th Leg., vol. 2, p. 317, ch. 722, eff. Jan. 1, 1966.

Art. 1.03. Objects of this Code

This Code is intended to embrace rules applicable to the prevention and prosecution of offenses against the laws of this State, and to make the rules of procedure in respect to the prevention and punishment of offenses intelligible to the officers who are to act under them, and to all persons whose rights are to be affected by them. It seeks:

1. To adopt measures for preventing the commission of crime;

2. To exclude the offender from all hope of escape;

3. To insure a trial with as little delay as is consistent with the ends of justice;

4. To bring to the investigation of each offense on the trial all the evidence tending to produce conviction or acquittal;

5. To insure a fair and impartial trial; and

6. The certain execution of the sentence of the law when declared.

Acts 1965, 59th Leg., vol. 2, p. 317, ch. 722, eff. Jan. 1, 1966.

Art. 1.04. Due course of law

No citizen of this State shall be deprived of life, liberty, property, privileges or immunities, or in any manner disfranchised, except by the due course of the law of the land.

Acts 1965, 59th Leg., vol. 2, p. 317, ch. 722, eff. Jan. 1, 1966.

Art. 1.05. Rights of accused

In all criminal prosecutions the accused shall have a speedy public trial by an impartial jury. He shall have the right to demand the nature and cause of the accusation against him, and to have a copy thereof. He shall not be compelled to give evidence against himself. He shall have the right of being heard by himself, or counsel, or both; shall be confronted with the witnesses against him, and shall have compulsory process for obtaining witnesses in his favor. No person shall be held to answer for a felony unless on indictment of a grand jury.

Acts 1965, 59th Leg., vol. 2, p. 317, ch. 722, eff. Jan. 1, 1966.

Art. 1.051. Right to representation by counsel

(a) A defendant in a criminal matter is entitled to be represented by counsel in an adversarial judicial proceeding. The right to be represented by counsel includes the right to consult in private with counsel sufficiently in advance of a proceeding to allow adequate preparation for the proceeding.

(b) For the purposes of this article and Articles 26.04 and 26.05 of this code, "indigent" means a person who is not financially able to employ counsel.

(c) An indigent defendant is entitled to have an attorney appointed to represent him in any adversary judicial proceeding that may result in punishment by confinement and in any other criminal proceeding if the court concludes that the interests of justice require representation. Subject to Subsection (c–1), if an indigent defendant is entitled to and requests appointed counsel and if adversarial judicial proceedings have been initiated against the defendant, a court or the courts' designee authorized under Article 26.04 to appoint counsel for indigent defendants in the county in which the defendant is arrested shall appoint counsel as soon as possible, but not later than:

(1) the end of the third working day after the date on which the court or the courts' designee receives the defendant's request for appointment of counsel, if the defendant is arrested in a county with a population of less than 250,000; or

(2) the end of the first working day after the date on which the court or the courts' designee receives the defendant's request for appointment of counsel, if the defendant is arrested in a county with a population of 250,000 or more.

(c–1) If an indigent defendant is arrested under a warrant issued in a county other than the county in which the arrest was made and the defendant is entitled to and requests appointed counsel, a court or the courts' designee authorized under Article 26.04 to appoint counsel for indigent defendants in the county that issued the warrant shall appoint counsel within the periods prescribed by Subsection (c), regardless of whether the defendant is present within the county issuing the warrant and even if adversarial judicial proceedings have not yet been initiated against the defendant in the county issuing the warrant. However, if the defendant has not been transferred or released into the custody of the county issuing the warrant before the 11th day after the date of the arrest and if counsel has not otherwise been appointed for the defendant in the arresting county under this article, a court or the courts' designee authorized under Article 26.04 to appoint counsel for indigent defendants in the arresting county immediately shall appoint counsel to represent the defendant in any matter under Chapter 11 or 17, regardless of whether adversarial judicial proceedings have been initiated against the defendant in the arresting county. If counsel is appointed for the defendant in the arresting county as required by this subsection, the arresting county may seek from the county that issued the warrant reimbursement for the actual costs paid by the arresting county for the appointed counsel.

(d) An eligible indigent defendant is entitled to have the trial court appoint an attorney to represent him in the following appellate and postconviction habeas corpus matters:

(1) an appeal to a court of appeals;

(2) an appeal to the Court of Criminal Appeals if the appeal is made directly from the trial court or if a petition for discretionary review has been granted;

(3) a habeas corpus proceeding if the court concludes that the interests of justice require representation; and

(4) any other appellate proceeding if the court concludes that the interests of justice require representation.

(e) An appointed counsel is entitled to 10 days to prepare for a proceeding but may waive the preparation time with the consent of the defendant in writing or on the record in open court. If a nonindigent defendant appears without counsel at a proceeding after having been given a reasonable opportunity to retain counsel, the court, on 10 days' notice to the defendant of a dispositive setting, may proceed with the matter without securing a written waiver or appointing counsel. If an indigent defendant who has refused appointed counsel in order to retain private counsel appears without counsel after having been given an opportunity to retain counsel, the court, after giving the defendant a reasonable opportunity to request appointment of counsel or, if the defendant elects not to request appointment of counsel, after obtaining a waiver of the right to counsel pursuant to Subsections (f) and (g), may proceed with the matter on 10 days' notice to the defendant of a dispositive setting.

(f) A defendant may voluntarily and intelligently waive in writing the right to counsel. A waiver obtained in violation of Subsection (f–1) or (f–2) is presumed invalid.

(f–1) In any adversary judicial proceeding that may result in punishment by confinement, the attorney representing the state may not:

(1) initiate or encourage an attempt to obtain from a defendant who is not represented by counsel a waiver of the right to counsel; or

(2) communicate with a defendant who has requested the appointment of counsel, unless the court or the court's designee authorized under Article 26.04 to appoint counsel for indigent defendants in the county has denied the request and, subsequent to the denial, the defendant:

(A) has been given a reasonable opportunity to retain and has failed to retain private counsel; or

(B) waives or has waived the opportunity to retain private counsel.

(f–2) In any adversary judicial proceeding that may result in punishment by confinement, the court may not direct or encourage the defendant to communicate with the attorney representing the state until the court advises the defendant of the right to counsel and the procedure for requesting appointed counsel and the defendant has been given a reasonable opportunity to request appointed counsel. If the defendant has requested appointed counsel, the court may not direct or encourage the defendant to communicate with the attorney representing the state unless the court or the court's designee authorized under Article 26.04 to appoint counsel for indigent defendants in the county has denied the request and, subsequent to the denial, the defendant:

(1) has been given a reasonable opportunity to retain and has failed to retain private counsel; or

(2) waives or has waived the opportunity to retain private counsel.

(g) If a defendant wishes to waive the right to counsel for purposes of entering a guilty plea or proceeding to trial, the court shall advise the defendant of the nature of the charges against the defendant and, if the defendant is proceeding to trial, the dangers and disadvantages of self-representation. If the court determines that the waiver is voluntarily and intelligently made, the court shall provide the defendant with a statement substantially in the following form, which, if signed by the defendant, shall be filed with and become part of the record of the proceedings:

"I have been advised this _____ day of _____, 2 ____, by the (name of court) Court of my right to representation by counsel in the case pending against me. I have been further advised that if I am unable to afford counsel, one will be appointed for me free of charge. Understanding my right to have counsel appointed for me free of charge if I am not financially able to employ counsel, I wish to waive that right and request the court to proceed with my case without an attorney being appointed for me. I hereby waive my right to counsel. (signature of defendant)"

(h) A defendant may withdraw a waiver of the right to counsel at any time but is not entitled to repeat a proceeding previously held or waived solely on the grounds of the subsequent appointment or retention of counsel. If the defendant withdraws a waiver, the trial court, in its discretion, may provide the appointed counsel 10 days to prepare.

(i) Subject to Subsection (c–1), with respect to a county with a population of less than 250,000, if an indigent defendant is entitled to and requests appointed counsel and if adversarial judicial proceedings have not been initiated against the defendant, a court or the courts' designee authorized under Article 26.04 to appoint counsel for indigent defendants in the county in which the defendant is arrested shall appoint counsel immediately following the expiration of three working days after the date on which the court or the courts' designee receives the defendant's request for appointment of counsel. If adversarial judicial proceedings are initiated against the defendant before the expiration of the three working days, the court or the courts' designee shall appoint counsel as provided by Subsection (c). Subject to Subsection (c–1), in a county with a population of 250,000 or more, the court or the courts' designee shall appoint counsel as required by this subsection immediately following the expiration of one working day after the date on which the court or the courts' designee receives the defendant's request for appointment of counsel. If adversarial judicial proceedings are initiated against the defendant before the expiration of the one working day, the court or the courts' designee shall appoint counsel as provided by Subsection (c).

(j) Notwithstanding any other provision of this section, if an indigent defendant is released from custody prior to the appointment of counsel under this section, appointment of counsel is not required until the defendant's first court appearance or when adversarial judicial proceedings are initiated, whichever comes first.

(k) A court or the courts' designee may without unnecessary delay appoint new counsel to represent an indigent defendant for whom counsel is appointed under Subsection (c), (c–1), or (i) if:

(1) the defendant is subsequently charged in the case with an offense different from the offense with which the defendant was initially charged; and

(2) good cause to appoint new counsel is stated on the record as required by Article 26.04(j)(2).

Added by Acts 1987, 70th Leg., ch. 979, § 1, eff. Sept. 1, 1987. Amended by Acts 2001, 77th Leg., ch. 906, § 2, eff. Jan. 1, 2002; Acts 2007, 80th Leg., ch. 463, § 1, eff. Sept. 1, 2007; Acts 2015, 84th Leg., ch. 858 (S.B. 1517), § 1, eff. Sept. 1, 2015.

Section 5 of Acts 2015, 84th Leg., ch. 858 (S.B. 1517) provides:

"The change in law made by this Act applies only to a person who is arrested on or after the effective date [Sept. 1, 2015] of this Act. A person arrested before the effective date of this Act is governed by the law in effect on the date the person was arrested, and the former law is continued in effect for that purpose."

Art. 1.052. Signed Pleadings of Defendant

(a) A pleading, motion, and other paper filed for or on behalf of a defendant represented by an attorney must be signed by at least one attorney of record in the attorney's name and state the attorney's address. A defendant who is not represented by an attorney must sign any pleading, motion, or other paper filed for or on the defendant's behalf and state the defendant's address.

(b) The signature of an attorney or a defendant constitutes a certificate by the attorney or defendant that the person has read the pleading, motion, or other paper and that to the best of the person's knowledge, information, and belief formed after reasonable inquiry that the instrument is not groundless and brought in bad faith or groundless and brought for harassment, unnecessary delay, or other improper purpose.

(c) If a pleading, motion, or other paper is not signed, the court shall strike it unless it is signed promptly after the omission is called to the attention of the attorney or defendant.

(d) An attorney or defendant who files a fictitious pleading in a cause for an improper purpose described by Subsection (b) or who makes a statement in a pleading that the attorney or defendant knows to be groundless and false to obtain a delay of the trial of the cause or for the purpose of harassment shall be held guilty of contempt.

(e) If a pleading, motion, or other paper is signed in violation of this article, the court, on motion or on its own initiative, after notice and hearing, shall impose an appropriate sanction, which may include an order to pay to the other party or parties to the prosecution or to the general fund of the county in which the pleading, motion, or other paper was filed the amount of reasonable expenses incurred because of the filing of the pleading, motion, or other paper, including reasonable attorney's fees.

(f) A court shall presume that a pleading, motion, or other paper is filed in good faith. Sanctions under this article may not be imposed except for good cause stated in the sanction order.

(g) A plea of "not guilty" or "no contest" or "nolo contendere" does not constitute a violation of this article. An allegation that an event took place or occurred on or about a particular date does not constitute a violation of this article.

(h) In this article, "groundless" means without basis in law or fact and not warranted by a good faith argument for the extension, modification, or reversal of existing law.

Added by Acts 1997, 75th Leg., ch. 189, § 11, eff. May 21, 1997.

Art. 1.06. Searches and seizures

The people shall be secure in their persons, houses, papers and possessions from all unreasonable seizures or searches. No warrant to search any place or to seize any person or thing shall issue without describing them as near as may be, nor without probable cause supported by oath or affirmation.

Acts 1965, 59th Leg., vol. 2, p. 317, ch. 722, eff. Jan. 1, 1966.

Art. 1.07. Right to bail

All prisoners shall be bailable unless for capital offenses when the proof is evident. This provision shall not be so construed as to prevent bail after indictment found upon examination of the evidence, in such manner as may be prescribed by law.

Acts 1965, 59th Leg., vol. 2, p. 317, ch. 722, eff. Jan. 1, 1966.

Art. 1.08. Habeas Corpus

The writ of habeas corpus is a writ of right and shall never be suspended.

Acts 1965, 59th Leg., vol. 2, p. 317, ch. 722, eff. Jan. 1, 1966.

Art. 1.09. Cruelty forbidden

Excessive bail shall not be required, nor excessive fines imposed, nor cruel or unusual punishment inflicted.

Acts 1965, 59th Leg., vol. 2, p. 317, ch. 722, eff. Jan. 1, 1966.

Art. 1.10. Jeopardy

No person for the same offense shall be twice put in jeopardy of life or liberty; nor shall a person be again put upon trial for the same offense, after a verdict of not guilty in a court of competent jurisdiction.

Acts 1965, 59th Leg., vol. 2, p. 317, ch. 722, eff. Jan. 1, 1966.

Art. 1.11. Acquittal a bar

An acquittal of the defendant exempts him from a second trial or a second prosecution for the same offense, however irregular the proceedings may have been; but if the defendant shall have been acquitted upon trial in a court having no jurisdiction of the offense, he may be prosecuted again in a court having jurisdiction.

Acts 1965, 59th Leg., vol. 2, p. 317, ch. 722, eff. Jan. 1, 1966.

Art. 1.12. Right to jury

The right of trial by jury shall remain inviolate.

Acts 1965, 59th Leg., vol. 2, p. 317, ch. 722, eff. Jan. 1, 1966.

Art. 1.13. [10a] Waiver of trial by jury

(a) The defendant in a criminal prosecution for any offense other than a capital felony case in which the state notifies the court and the defendant that it will seek the death penalty shall have the right, upon entering a plea, to waive the right of trial by jury, conditioned, however, that, except as provided by Article 27.19, the waiver must be made in person by the defendant in writing in open court with the consent and approval of the court, and the attorney representing the state. The consent and approval by the court shall be entered of record on the minutes of the court, and the consent and approval of the attorney representing the state shall be in writing, signed by that attorney, and filed in the papers of the cause before the defendant enters the defendant's plea.

(b) In a capital felony case in which the attorney representing the State notifies the court and the defendant that it will not seek the death penalty, the defendant may waive the right to trial by jury but only if the attorney representing the State, in writing and in open court, consents to the waiver.

(c) A defendant may agree to waive a jury trial regardless of whether the defendant is represented by an attorney at the time of making the waiver, but before a defendant charged with a felony who has no attorney can agree to waive the jury, the court must appoint an attorney to represent him.

Acts 1965, 59th Leg., vol. 2, p. 317, ch. 722, eff. Jan. 1, 1966. Amended by Acts 1991, 72nd Leg., ch. 652, § 1, eff. Sept. 1, 1991; Acts 1997, 75th Leg., ch. 285, § 1, eff. Sept. 1, 1997; Acts 2011, 82nd Leg., ch. 1031 (H.B. 2847), § 1, eff. Sept. 1, 2011.

Art. 1.14. Waiver of rights

(a) The defendant in a criminal prosecution for any offense may waive any rights secured him by law except that a defendant in a capital felony case may waive the right of trial by jury only in the manner permitted by Article 1.13(b) of this code.

(b) If the defendant does not object to a defect, error, or irregularity of form or substance in an indictment or information before the date on which the trial on the merits commences, he waives and forfeits the right to object to the defect, error, or irregularity and he may not raise the objection on appeal or in any other postconviction proceeding. Nothing in this article prohibits a trial court from requiring that an objection to an indictment or information be made at an earlier time in compliance with Article 28.01 of this code.

Acts 1965, 59th Leg., vol. 2, p. 317, ch. 722, eff. Jan. 1, 1966. Amended by Acts 1967, 60th Leg., p. 1733, ch. 659, § 1, eff. Aug. 28, 1967; Acts 1973, 63rd Leg., p. 1127, ch. 426, art. 3, § 5, eff. June 14, 1973; Acts 1985, 69th Leg., ch. 577, § 1, eff. Dec. 1, 1985; Acts 1991, 72nd Leg., ch. 652, § 2, eff. Sept. 1, 1991.

Art. 1.141. Waiver of indictment for noncapital felony

A person represented by legal counsel may in open court or by written instrument voluntarily waive the right to be accused by indictment of any offense other than a capital felony. On waiver as provided in this article, the accused shall be charged by information.

Added by Acts 1971, 62nd Leg., p. 1148, ch. 260, § 1, eff. May 19, 1971.

Art. 1.15.   Jury in felony

No person can be convicted of a felony except upon the verdict of a jury duly rendered and recorded, unless the defendant, upon entering a plea, has in open court in person waived his right of trial by jury in writing in accordance with Articles 1.13 and 1.14; provided, however, that it shall be necessary for the state to introduce evidence into the record showing the guilt of the defendant and said evidence shall be accepted by the court as the basis for its judgment and in no event shall a person charged be convicted upon his plea without sufficient evidence to support the same. The evidence may be stipulated if the defendant in such case consents in writing, in open court, to waive the appearance, confrontation, and cross-examination of witnesses, and further consents either to an oral stipulation of the evidence and testimony or to the introduction of testimony by affidavits, written statements of witnesses, and any other documentary evidence in support of the judgment of the court. Such waiver and consent must be approved by the court in writing, and be filed in the file of the papers of the cause.

Acts 1965, 59th Leg., vol. 2, p. 317, ch. 722, eff. Jan. 1, 1966. Amended by Acts 1967, 60th Leg., p. 1733, ch. 659, § 2, eff. Aug. 28, 1967; Acts 1971, 62nd Leg., p. 3028, ch. 996, § 1, eff. June 15, 1971; Acts 1973, 63rd Leg., p. 1127, ch. 426, art. 3, § 5, eff. June 14, 1973; Acts 1991, 72nd Leg., ch. 652, § 3, eff. Sept. 1, 1991.

Art. 1.16.   Liberty of speech and press

Every person shall be at liberty to speak, write or publish his opinion on any subject, being liable for the abuse of that privilege; and no law shall ever be passed curtailing the liberty of speech or of the press. In prosecutions for the publication of papers investigating the conduct of officers or men in public capacity, or when the matter published is proper for public information, the truth thereof may be given in evidence. In all indictments for libels, the jury shall have the right to determine the law and the facts, under the direction of the court, as in other cases.

Acts 1965, 59th Leg., vol. 2, p. 317, ch. 722, eff. Jan. 1, 1966.

Art. 1.17.   Religious belief

No person shall be disqualified to give evidence in any court of this State on account of his religious opinions, or for the want of any religious belief; but

all oaths or affirmations shall be administered in the mode most binding upon the conscience, and shall be taken subject to the pains and penalties of perjury.

Acts 1965, 59th Leg., vol. 2, p. 317, ch. 722, eff. Jan. 1, 1966.

Art. 1.18.   Outlawry and transportation

No citizen shall be outlawed, nor shall any person be transported out of the State for any offense committed within the same.

Acts 1965, 59th Leg., vol. 2, p. 317, ch. 722, eff. Jan. 1, 1966.

Art. 1.19.   Corruption of blood, etc.

No conviction shall work corruption of blood or forfeiture of estate.

Acts 1965, 59th Leg., vol. 2, p. 317, ch. 722, eff. Jan. 1, 1966.

Art. 1.20.   Conviction of treason

No person shall be convicted of treason except on the testimony of two witnesses to the same overt act, or on confession in open court.

Acts 1965, 59th Leg., vol. 2, p. 317, ch. 722, eff. Jan. 1, 1966.

Art. 1.21.   Privilege of legislators

Senators and Representatives shall, except in cases of treason, felony or breach of the peace, be privileged from arrest during the session of the Legislature, and in going to and returning from the same, allowing one day for every twenty miles such member may reside from the place at which the Legislature is convened.

Acts 1965, 59th Leg., vol. 2, p. 317, ch. 722, eff. Jan. 1, 1966.

Art. 1.22.   Repealed by Acts 1985, 69th Leg., ch. 211, § 9(a)(6), eff. Jan. 1, 1986

Art. 1.23.   Dignity of State

All justices of the Supreme Court, judges of the Court of Criminal Appeals, justices of the Courts of Appeals and judges of the District Courts, shall, by virtue of their offices, be conservators of the peace throughout the State. The style of all writs and process shall be "The State of Texas". All prosecutions shall be carried on "in the name and by authority of The State of Texas", and conclude, "against the peace and dignity of the State".

Acts 1965, 59th Leg., vol. 2, p. 317, ch. 722, eff. Jan. 1, 1966. Amended by Acts 1981, 67th Leg., p. 801, ch. 291, § 97, eff. Sept. 1, 1981.

Art. 1.24. Public trial

The proceedings and trials in all courts shall be public.

Acts 1965, 59th Leg., vol. 2, p. 317, ch. 722, eff. Jan. 1, 1966.

Art. 1.25. Confronted by witnesses

The defendant, upon a trial, shall be confronted with the witnesses, except in certain cases provided for in this Code where depositions have been taken.

Acts 1965, 59th Leg., vol. 2, p. 317, ch. 722, eff. Jan. 1, 1966.

Art. 1.26. Construction of this Code

The provisions of this Code shall be liberally construed, so as to attain the objects intended by the Legislature: The prevention, suppression and punishment of crime.

Acts 1965, 59th Leg., vol. 2, p. 317, ch. 722, eff. Jan. 1, 1966.

Art. 1.27. Common law governs

If this Code fails to provide a rule of procedure in any particular state of case which may arise, the rules of the common law shall be applied and govern.

Acts 1965, 59th Leg., vol. 2, p. 317, ch. 722, eff. Jan. 1, 1966.

CHAPTER TWO. GENERAL DUTIES OF OFFICERS

Art. 2.01. Duties of district attorneys

Each district attorney shall represent the State in all criminal cases in the district courts of his district and in appeals therefrom, except in cases where he has been, before his election, employed adversely. When any criminal proceeding is had before an examining court in his district or before a judge upon habeas corpus, and he is notified of the same, and is at the time within his district, he shall represent the State therein, unless prevented by other official duties. It shall be the primary duty of all prosecuting attorneys, including any special prosecutors, not to convict, but to see that justice is done. They shall not suppress facts or secrete witnesses capable of establishing the innocence of the accused.

Acts 1965, 59th Leg., vol. 2, p. 317, ch. 722, eff. Jan. 1, 1966. Amended by Acts 1981, 67th Leg., p. 801, ch. 291, § 98, eff. Sept. 1, 1981.

Art. 2.02. Duties of county attorneys

The county attorney shall attend the terms of court in his county below the grade of district court, and shall represent the State in all criminal cases under examination or prosecution in said county; and in the absence of the district attorney he shall represent the State alone and, when requested, shall aid the district attorney in the prosecution of any case in behalf of the State in the district court. He shall represent the State in cases he has prosecuted which are appealed.

Acts 1965, 59th Leg., vol. 2, p. 317, ch. 722, eff. Jan. 1, 1966. Amended by Acts 1981, 67th Leg., p. 801, ch. 291, § 99, eff. Sept. 1, 1981.

Art. 2.021. Duties of Attorney General

Text of Art. 2.021 effective until Jan. 1, 2019. See, also, text of Art. 2.021 effective Jan. 1, 2019.

The attorney general may offer to a county or district attorney the assistance of the attorney general's office in the prosecution of an offense described by Article 60.051(g) the victim of which is younger than 17 years of age at the time the offense is committed. On request of a county or district attorney, the attorney general shall assist in the prosecution of an offense described by Article 60.051(g) the victim of which is younger than 17 years of age at the time the offense is committed. For purposes of this article, assistance includes investigative, technical, and litigation assistance of the attorney general's office.

Added by Acts 2007, 80th Leg., ch. 593, § 1.02, eff. Sept. 1, 2007.

Art. 2.021. Duties of Attorney General

Text of Art. 2.021 effective Jan. 1, 2019. See, also, text of Art. 2.021 effective until Jan. 1, 2019.

The attorney general may offer to a county or district attorney the assistance of the attorney general's office in the prosecution of an offense described by

Article 66.102(h) the victim of which is younger than 17 years of age at the time the offense is committed. On request of a county or district attorney, the attorney general shall assist in the prosecution of an offense described by Article 66.102(h) the victim of which is younger than 17 years of age at the time the offense is committed. For purposes of this article, assistance includes investigative, technical, and litigation assistance of the attorney general's office.

Added by Acts 2007, 80th Leg., ch. 593, § 1.02, eff. Sept. 1, 2007. Amended by Acts 2017, 85th Leg., ch. 1058 (H.B. 2931), § 4.01, eff. Jan. 1, 2019.

Art. 2.022. Assistance of Texas Rangers

(a) The attorney representing the state may request the Texas Rangers division of the Department of Public Safety to provide assistance to a local law enforcement agency investigating an offense that:

(1) is alleged to have been committed by an elected officer of the political subdivision served by the local law enforcement agency; and

(2) on conviction or adjudication, would subject the elected officer to registration as a sex offender under Chapter 62.

(b) For purposes of this article, "assistance" includes investigative, technical, and administrative assistance.

Added by Acts 2009, 81st Leg., ch. 431, § 1, eff. June 19, 2009.

Art. 2.023. Tracking Use of Certain Testimony

Text of article 2.023 as added by Acts 2017, 85th Leg., ch. 686 (H.B. 34), § 1. See, also, art. 2.023 as added by Acts 2017, 85th Leg., ch. 772 (H.B. 104), § 1.

(a) In this article:

(1) "Attorney representing the state" means a district attorney, a criminal district attorney, or a county attorney with criminal jurisdiction.

(2) "Correctional facility" has the meaning assigned by Section 1.07, Penal Code.

(b) An attorney representing the state shall track:

(1) the use of testimony of a person to whom a defendant made a statement against the defendant's interest while the person was imprisoned or confined in the same correctional facility as the defendant, if known by the attorney representing the state, regard-

less of whether the testimony is presented at trial; and

(2) any benefits offered or provided to a person in exchange for testimony described by Subdivision (1).

Added by Acts 2017, 85th Leg., ch. 686 (H.B. 34), § 1, eff. Sept. 1, 2017.

Art. 2.023. Notification to Texas Department of Criminal Justice

Text of article 2.023 as added by Acts 2017, 85th Leg., ch. 772 (H.B. 104), § 1. See, also, art. 2.023 as added by Acts 2017, 85th Leg., ch. 686 (H.B. 34), § 1.

(a) This article applies only to a defendant who, in connection with a previous conviction for an offense listed in Article 42A.054(a) or for which the judgment contains an affirmative finding under Article 42A.054(c) or (d):

(1) received a sentence that included imprisonment at a facility operated by or under contract with the Texas Department of Criminal Justice; and

(2) was subsequently released from the imprisonment, including a release on parole, to mandatory supervision, or following discharge of the defendant's sentence.

(b) Not later than the 10th day after the date that a defendant described by Subsection (a) is indicted for an offense listed in Article 42A.054(a) or for which the judgment contains an affirmative finding under Article 42A.054(c) or (d), the attorney representing the state shall notify an officer designated by the Texas Department of Criminal Justice of the offense charged in the indictment.

Added by Acts 2017, 85th Leg., ch. 772 (H.B. 104), § 1, eff. Sept. 1, 2017.

Section 4 of Acts 2017, 85th Leg., ch. 772 (H.B. 104) provides:

"Article 2.023, Code of Criminal Procedure, as added by this Act, applies only to a criminal case in which the indictment is presented to the court on or after December 1, 2017. A criminal case in which the indictment is presented to the court before December 1, 2017, is governed by the law in effect on the date the indictment is presented, and the former law is continued in effect for that purpose."

Art. 2.025. Special Duty of District or County Attorney Relating to Child Support

If a district or county attorney receives money from a person who is required by a court order to pay child support through a local registry or the Title IV-D agency and the money is presented to the attorney as payment for the court-ordered child support, the attorney shall transfer the money to the local registry or Title IV-D agency designated as the place of payment in the child support order.

Added by Acts 1999, 76th Leg., ch. 40, § 1, eff. Sept. 1, 1999.

Art. 2.03. Neglect of duty

(a) It shall be the duty of the attorney representing the State to present by information to the court having jurisdiction, any officer for neglect or failure of any duty enjoined upon such officer, when such neglect or failure can be presented by information, whenever it shall come to the knowledge of said attorney that there has been a neglect or failure of duty upon the part of said officer; and he shall bring to the notice of the grand jury any act of violation of law or neglect or failure of duty upon the part of any officer, when such violation, neglect or failure is not presented by information, and whenever the same may come to his knowledge.

(b) It is the duty of the trial court, the attorney representing the accused, the attorney representing the state and all peace officers to so conduct themselves as to insure a fair trial for both the state and the defendant, not impair the presumption of innocence, and at the same time afford the public the benefits of a free press.

Acts 1965, 59th Leg., vol. 2, p. 317, ch. 722, eff. Jan. 1, 1966. Amended by Acts 1967, 60th Leg., p. 1733, ch. 659, § 3, eff. Aug. 28, 1967.

Art. 2.04. Shall draw complaints

Upon complaint being made before a district or county attorney that an offense has been committed in his district or county, he shall reduce the complaint to writing and cause the same to be signed and sworn to by the complainant, and it shall be duly attested by said attorney.

Acts 1965, 59th Leg., vol. 2, p. 317, ch. 722, eff. Jan. 1, 1966.

Art. 2.05. When complaint is made

If the offense be a misdemeanor, the attorney shall forthwith prepare an information based upon such complaint and file the same in the court having jurisdiction; provided, that in counties having no county attorney, misdemeanor cases may be tried upon complaint alone, without an information, provided, however, in counties having one or more criminal district courts an information must be filed in each misdemeanor case. If the offense be a felony, he shall forthwith file the complaint with a magistrate of the county.

Acts 1965, 59th Leg., vol. 2, p. 317, ch. 722, eff. Jan. 1, 1966.

Art. 2.06. May administer oaths

For the purpose mentioned in the two preceding Articles, district and county attorneys are authorized to administer oaths.

Acts 1965, 59th Leg., vol. 2, p. 317, ch. 722, eff. Jan. 1, 1966.

Art. 2.07. Attorney pro tem

(a) Whenever an attorney for the state is disqualified to act in any case or proceeding, is absent from the county or district, or is otherwise unable to perform the duties of his office, or in any instance where there is no attorney for the state, the judge of the court in which he represents the state may appoint any competent attorney to perform the duties of the office during the absence or disqualification of the attorney for the state.

(b) Except as otherwise provided by this subsection, if the appointed attorney is also an attorney for the state, the duties of the appointed office are additional duties of his present office, and he is not entitled to additional compensation. Nothing herein shall prevent a commissioners court of a county from contracting with another commissioners court to pay expenses and reimburse compensation paid by a county to an attorney for the state who is appointed to perform additional duties.

(b–1) An attorney for the state who is not disqualified to act may request the court to permit him to recuse himself in a case for good cause and upon approval by the court is disqualified.

(c) If the appointed attorney is not an attorney for the state, he is qualified to perform the duties of the office for the period of absence or disqualification of the attorney for the state on filing an oath with the clerk of the court. He shall receive compensation in the same amount and manner as an attorney appointed to represent an indigent person.

(d) In this article, "attorney for the state" means a county attorney, a district attorney, or a criminal district attorney.

(e) In Subsections (b) and (c) of this article, "attorney for the state" includes an assistant attorney general.

(f) In Subsection (a) of this article, "competent attorney" includes an assistant attorney general.

(g) An attorney appointed under Subsection (a) of this article to perform the duties of the office of an attorney for the state in a justice or municipal court may be paid a reasonable fee for performing those duties.

Acts 1965, 59th Leg., vol. 2, p. 317, ch. 722, eff. Jan. 1, 1966. Amended by Acts 1967, 60th Leg., p. 1733, ch. 659, § 4, eff. Aug. 28, 1967; Acts 1973, 63rd Leg., p. 356, ch. 154, § 1, eff. May 23, 1973; Acts 1987, 70th Leg., ch. 918, § 1, eff. Aug. 31, 1987; Acts 1995, 74th Leg., ch. 785, § 1, eff. Sept. 1, 1995; Acts 1999, 76th Leg., ch. 1545, § 1, eff. Sept. 1, 1999.

Art. 2.08. Disqualified

(a) District and county attorneys shall not be of counsel adversely to the State in any case, in any court, nor shall they, after they cease to be such officers, be of counsel adversely to the State in any case in which they have been of counsel for the State.

(b) A judge of a court in which a district or county attorney represents the State shall declare the district or county attorney disqualified for purposes of Article 2.07 on a showing that the attorney is the subject of a criminal investigation by a law enforcement agency if that investigation is based on credible evidence of criminal misconduct for an offense that is within the attorney's authority to prosecute. A disqualification under this subsection applies only to the attorney's access to the criminal investigation pending against the attorney and to any prosecution of a criminal charge resulting from that investigation.

Acts 1965, 59th Leg., vol. 2, p. 317, ch. 722, eff. Jan. 1, 1966. Amended by Acts 2011, 82nd Leg., ch. 977 (H.B. 1638), § 1, eff. Sept. 1, 2011.

Art. 2.09. Who Are Magistrates

Each of the following officers is a magistrate within the meaning of this Code: The justices of the Supreme Court, the judges of the Court of Criminal Appeals, the justices of the Courts of Appeals, the judges of the District Court, the magistrates appointed by the judges of the district courts of Bexar County, Dallas County, or Tarrant County that give preference to criminal cases, the criminal law hearing officers for Harris County appointed under Subchapter L, Chapter 54, Government Code,[1] the criminal law hearing officers for Cameron County appointed under Subchapter BB, Chapter 54, Government Code,[2] the magistrates or associate judges appointed by the judges of the district courts of Lubbock County, Nolan County, or Webb County, the magistrates appointed by the judges of the criminal district courts of Dallas County or Tarrant County, the associate judges appointed by the judges of the district courts and the county courts at law that give preference to criminal cases in Jefferson County, the associate judges appointed by the judges of the district courts and the statutory county courts of Brazos County, Nueces County, or Williamson County, the magistrates appointed by the judges of the district courts and statutory county courts that give preference to criminal cases in Travis County, the criminal magistrates appointed by the Brazoria County Commissioners Court, the criminal magistrates appointed by the Burnet County Commissioners Court, the county judges, the judges of the county courts at law, judges of the county criminal courts, the judges of statutory probate courts, the associate judges appointed by the judges of the statutory probate courts under Chapter 54A, Government Code, the associate judges appointed by the judge of a district court under Chapter 54A, Government Code, the magistrates appointed under Subchapter JJ, Chapter 54, Government Code, as added by H.B. No. 2132, Acts of the 82nd Legislature, Regular Session, 2011, [3]the justices of the peace, and the mayors and recorders and the judges of the municipal courts of incorporated cities or towns.

Acts 1965, 59th Leg., vol. 2, p. 317, ch. 722, eff. Jan. 1, 1966. Amended by Acts 1981, 67th Leg., p. 801, ch. 291, § 100, eff. Sept. 1, 1981; Acts 1983, 68th Leg., p. 883, ch. 204, § 1, eff. Aug. 29, 1983; Acts 1989, 71st Leg., ch. 25, § 2, eff. Aug. 28, 1989; Acts 1989, 71st Leg., ch. 79, § 1, eff. May 15, 1989; Acts 1989, 71st Leg., ch. 916, § 1, eff. Sept. 1, 1989; Acts 1989, 71st Leg., ch. 1068, § 2, eff. Aug. 28, 1989; Acts 1991, 72nd Leg., ch. 16, § 4.01, eff. Aug. 26, 1991; Acts 1993, 73rd Leg., ch. 224, § 2, eff. Aug. 30, 1993; Acts 1993, 73rd Leg., ch. 413, § 1, eff. Sept. 1, 1993; Acts 1993, 73rd Leg., ch. 468, § 1, eff. June 9, 1993; Acts 1993, 73rd Leg., ch. 577, § 2, eff. Aug. 30, 1993; Acts 1999, 76th Leg., ch. 586, § 2, eff. June 18, 1999; Acts 1999, 76th Leg., ch. 1503, § 2, eff. Sept. 1, 1999; Acts 2003, 78th Leg., ch. 979, § 1, eff. Sept. 1, 2003; Acts 2003, 78th Leg., ch. 1066, § 9, eff. Sept. 1, 2003; Acts 2005, 79th Leg., ch. 109, § 2, eff. May 20, 2005; Acts 2005, 79th Leg., ch. 767, § 2, eff. Sept. 1, 2005; Acts 2005, 79th Leg., ch. 1331, § 1, eff. Sept. 1, 2005; Acts 2007, 80th Leg., ch. 1141, § 1, eff. Sept. 1, 2007; Acts 2009, 81st Leg., ch. 646, § 2, eff. June 19, 2009; Acts 2009, 81st Leg., ch. 964, § 2, eff. June 19, 2009; Acts 2011, 82nd Leg., ch. 863 (H.B. 3844), § 2, eff. June 17, 2011; Acts 2011, 82nd Leg., ch. 995 (H.B. 2132), § 2, eff. June 17, 2011; Acts 2011, 82nd Leg., 1st C.S., ch. 3 (H.B. 79), § 6.06, eff. Jan. 1, 2012.

[1] V.T.C.A. Government Code, § 54.851 et seq.

[2] V.T.C.A., Government Code § 54.1351 et seq.

[3] V.T.C.A., Government Code § 54.1951 et seq.

Art. 2.10.   Duty of magistrates

It is the duty of every magistrate to preserve the peace within his jurisdiction by the use of all lawful means; to issue all process intended to aid in preventing and suppressing crime; to cause the arrest of offenders by the use of lawful means in order that they may be brought to punishment.

Acts 1965, 59th Leg., vol. 2, p. 317, ch. 722, eff. Jan. 1, 1966.

Art. 2.11.   Examining court

When the magistrate sits for the purpose of inquiring into a criminal accusation against any person, this is called an examining court.

Acts 1965, 59th Leg., vol. 2, p. 317, ch. 722, eff. Jan. 1, 1966.

Art. 2.12.   Who Are Peace Officers

The following are peace officers:

(1) sheriffs, their deputies, and those reserve deputies who hold a permanent peace officer license issued under Chapter 1701, Occupations Code;

(2) constables, deputy constables, and those reserve deputy constables who hold a permanent peace officer license issued under Chapter 1701, Occupations Code;

(3) marshals or police officers of an incorporated city, town, or village, and those reserve municipal police officers who hold a permanent peace officer license issued under Chapter 1701, Occupations Code;

(4) rangers, officers, and members of the reserve officer corps commissioned by the Public Safety Commission and the Director of the Department of Public Safety;

(5) investigators of the district attorneys', criminal district attorneys', and county attorneys' offices;

(6) law enforcement agents of the Texas Alcoholic Beverage Commission;

(7) each member of an arson investigating unit commissioned by a city, a county, or the state;

(8) officers commissioned under Section 37.081, Education Code, or Subchapter E, Chapter 51, Education Code; [1]

(9) officers commissioned by the General Services Commission;

(10) law enforcement officers commissioned by the Parks and Wildlife Commission;

(11) airport police officers commissioned by a city with a population of more than 1.18 million located primarily in a county with a population of 2 million or more that operates an airport that serves commercial air carriers;

(12) airport security personnel commissioned as peace officers by the governing body of any political subdivision of this state, other than a city described by Subdivision (11), that operates an airport that serves commercial air carriers;

(13) municipal park and recreational patrolmen and security officers;

(14) security officers and investigators commissioned as peace officers by the comptroller;

(15) officers commissioned by a water control and improvement district under Section 49.216, Water Code;

(16) officers commissioned by a board of trustees under Chapter 54, Transportation Code;

(17) investigators commissioned by the Texas Medical Board;

(18) officers commissioned by:

(A) the board of managers of the Dallas County Hospital District, the Tarrant County Hospital District, the Bexar County Hospital District, or the El Paso County Hospital District under Section 281.057, Health and Safety Code;

(B) the board of directors of the Ector County Hospital District under Section 1024.117, Special District Local Laws Code; and

(C) the board of directors of the Midland County Hospital District of Midland County, Texas, under Section 1061.121, Special District Local Laws Code;

(19) county park rangers commissioned under Subchapter E, Chapter 351, Local Government Code; [2]

(20) investigators employed by the Texas Racing Commission;

(21) officers commissioned under Chapter 554, Occupations Code;

(22) officers commissioned by the governing body of a metropolitan rapid transit authority under Section 451.108, Transportation Code, or by a regional transportation authority under Section 452.110, Transportation Code;

(23) investigators commissioned by the attorney general under Section 402.009, Government Code;

(24) security officers and investigators commissioned as peace officers under Chapter 466, Government Code;

(25) officers appointed by an appellate court under Subchapter F, Chapter 53, Government Code; [3]

(26) officers commissioned by the state fire marshal under Chapter 417, Government Code;

(27) an investigator commissioned by the commissioner of insurance under Section 701.104, Insurance Code;

(28) apprehension specialists and inspectors general commissioned by the Texas Juvenile Justice Department as officers under Sections 242.102 and 243.052, Human Resources Code;

(29) officers appointed by the inspector general of the Texas Department of Criminal Justice under Section 493.019, Government Code;

(30) investigators commissioned by the Texas Commission on Law Enforcement under Section 1701.160, Occupations Code;

(31) commission investigators commissioned by the Texas Private Security Board under Section 1702.061, Occupations Code;

(32) the fire marshal and any officers, inspectors, or investigators commissioned by an emergency services district under Chapter 775, Health and Safety Code;

(33) officers commissioned by the State Board of Dental Examiners under Section 254.013, Occupations Code, subject to the limitations imposed by that section;

(34) investigators commissioned by the Texas Juvenile Justice Department as officers under Section 221.011, Human Resources Code; and

(35) the fire marshal and any related officers, inspectors, or investigators commissioned by a county

under Subchapter B, Chapter 352, Local Government Code.

Acts 1965, 59th Leg., vol. 2, p. 317, ch. 722, eff. Jan. 1, 1966. Amended by Acts 1967, 60th Leg., p. 1734, ch. 659, § 5, eff. Aug. 28, 1967; Acts 1971, 62nd Leg., p. 1116, ch. 246, § 3, eff. May 17, 1971; Acts 1973, 63rd Leg., p. 9, ch. 7, § 2, eff. Aug. 27, 1973; Acts 1973, 63rd Leg., p. 1259, ch. 459, § 1, eff. Aug. 27, 1973; Acts 1975, 64th Leg., p. 480, ch. 204, § 1, eff. Sept. 1, 1975; Acts 1977, 65th Leg., p. 618, ch. 227, § 2, eff. May 24, 1977; Acts 1977, 65th Leg., p. 1082, ch. 396, §1, eff. Aug. 29, 1977; Acts 1983, 68th Leg., p. 545, ch. 114, § 1, eff. May 17, 1983; Acts 1983, 68th Leg., p. 4358, ch. 699, § 11, eff. June 19, 1983; Acts 1983, 68th Leg., p. 4901, ch. 867, § 2, eff. June 19, 1983; Acts 1983, 68th Leg., p. 5303, ch. 974, § 11, eff. Aug. 29, 1983; Acts 1985, 69th Leg., ch. 384, § 2, eff. Aug. 26, 1985; Acts 1985, 69th Leg., ch. 907, § 6, eff. Sept. 1, 1985; Acts 1986, 69th Leg., 2nd C.S., ch. 19, § 4, eff. Dec. 4, 1986; Acts 1987, 70th Leg., ch. 262, § 20, eff. Sept. 1, 1987; Acts 1987, 70th Leg., ch. 350, § 1, eff. Aug. 31, 1987; Acts 1989, 71st Leg., ch. 277, § 4, eff. June 14, 1989; Acts 1989, 71st Leg., ch. 794, § 1, eff. Aug. 28, 1989; Acts 1989, 71st Leg., ch. 1104, § 4, eff. June 16, 1989; Acts 1991, 72nd Leg., ch. 16, § 4.02, eff. Aug. 26, 1991; Acts 1991, 72nd Leg., ch. 228, § 1, eff. Sept. 1, 1991; Acts 1991, 72nd Leg., ch. 287, § 24, eff. Sept. 1, 1991; Acts 1991, 72nd Leg., ch. 386, § 70, eff. Aug. 26, 1991; Acts 1991, 72nd Leg., ch. 446, § 1, eff. June 11, 1991; Acts 1991, 72nd Leg., ch. 544, § 1, eff. Aug. 26, 1991; Acts 1991, 72nd Leg., ch. 545, § 2, eff. Aug. 26, 1991; Acts 1991, 72nd Leg., ch. 597, § 57, eff. Sept. 1, 1991; Acts 1991, 72nd Leg., ch. 853, § 2, eff. Sept. 1, 1991; Acts 1991, 72nd Leg., 1st C.S., ch. 6, § 6; Acts 1991, 72nd Leg., 1st C.S., ch. 14, § 3.01, eff. Nov. 12, 1991; Acts 1993, 73rd Leg., ch. 107, § 4.07, eff. Aug. 30, 1993; Acts 1993, 73rd Leg., ch. 116, § 1, eff. Aug. 30, 1993; Acts 1993, 73rd Leg., ch. 339, § 2, eff. Sept. 1, 1993; Acts 1993, 73rd Leg., ch. 695, § 2, eff. Sept. 1, 1993; Acts 1993, 73rd Leg., ch. 912, § 25, eff. Sept. 1, 1993; Acts 1995, 74th Leg., ch. 260, § 10, eff. May 30, 1995; Acts 1995, 74th Leg., ch. 621, § 2, eff. Sept. 1, 1995; Acts 1995, 74th Leg., ch. 729, § 1, eff. Aug. 28, 1995; Acts 1997, 75th Leg., ch. 1423, § 4.01, eff. Sept. 1, 1997; Acts 1999, 76th Leg., ch. 90, § 1, eff. Sept. 1, 1999; Acts 1999, 76th Leg., ch. 322, § 2, eff. May 29, 1999; Acts 1999, 76th Leg., ch. 882, § 2, eff. June 18, 1999; Acts 1999, 76th Leg., ch. 974, § 37, eff. Sept. 1, 1999; Acts 2001, 77th Leg., ch. 272, § 7, eff. Sept. 1, 2001; Acts 2001, 77th Leg., ch. 442, § 1, eff. Sept. 1, 2001; Acts 2001, 77th Leg., ch. 669, § 8, eff. Sept. 1, 2001; Acts 2001, 77th Leg., ch. 1420, § 3.001, eff. Sept. 1, 2001; Acts 2003, 78th Leg., ch. 235, § 16, eff. Sept. 1, 2003; Acts 2003, 78th Leg., ch. 474, § 1, eff. June 20, 2003; Acts 2003, 78th Leg., ch. 930, § 12, eff. Sept. 1, 2003; Acts 2005, 79th Leg., ch. 728, § 4.001, eff. Sept. 1, 2005; Acts 2007, 80th Leg., ch. 263, § 1, eff. June 8, 2007; Acts 2007, 80th Leg., ch. 838, § 1, eff. June 15, 2007; Acts 2007, 80th Leg., ch. 908, § 1, eff. Sept. 1, 2007; Acts 2007, 80th Leg., ch. 1172, § 1, eff. June 15, 2007; Acts 2009, 81st Leg., ch. 1164, § 1, eff. June 19, 2009; Acts 2011, 82nd Leg., ch. 85 (S.B. 653), § 3.001, eff. Sept. 1, 2011; Acts 2011, 82nd Leg., ch. 402 (S.B. 601), § 2, eff. June 17, 2011; Acts 2011, 82nd Leg., ch. 584 (H.B. 3815), § 2, eff. June 17, 2011; Acts 2011, 82nd Leg., ch. 1163 (H.B. 2702), § 5, eff. Sept. 1, 2011; Acts 2013, 83rd Leg., ch. 8 (S.B. 543), § 2, eff. May 2, 2013; Acts 2013, 83rd Leg., ch. 93 (S.B. 686), § 2.01, eff. May 18, 2013; Acts 2015, 84th Leg., ch. 333 (H.B. 11), § 1, eff. Sept. 1, 2015.

[1] V.T.C.A., Education Code § 51.201 et seq.
[2] V.T.C.A., Local Government Code § 351.081 et seq.
[3] V.T.C.A., Government Code § 53.091 et seq.

Section 21 of Acts 2015, 84th Leg., ch. 333 (H.B. 11) provides:

"To the extent of any conflict, this Act prevails over another Act of the 84th Legislature, Regular Session, 2015, relating to nonsubstantive additions to and corrections in enacted codes."

Art. 2.121.   Railroad peace officers

(a) The director of the Department of Public Safety may appoint up to 250 railroad peace officers who are employed by a railroad company to aid law enforcement agencies in the protection of railroad property and the protection of the persons and property of railroad passengers and employees.

(b) Except as provided by Subsection (c) of this article, a railroad peace officer may make arrests and exercise all authority given peace officers under this code when necessary to prevent or abate the commission of an offense involving injury to passengers and employees of the railroad or damage to railroad property or to protect railroad property or property in the custody or control of the railroad.

(c) A railroad peace officer may not issue a traffic citation for a violation of Chapter 521, Transportation Code, or Subtitle C, Title 7, Transportation Code.[1]

(d) A railroad peace officer is not entitled to state benefits normally provided by the state to a peace officer.

(e) A person may not serve as a railroad peace officer for a railroad company unless:

(1) the Texas Railroad Association submits the person's application for appointment and certification as a railroad peace officer to the director of the Department of Public Safety and to the executive director of the Texas Commission on Law Enforcement;

(2) the director of the department issues the person a certificate of authority to act as a railroad peace officer; and

(3) the executive director of the commission determines that the person meets minimum standards required of peace officers by the commission relating to competence, reliability, education, training, morality, and physical and mental health and issues the person a license as a railroad peace officer; and

(4) the person has met all standards for certification as a peace officer by the Texas Commission on Law Enforcement.

(f) For good cause, the director of the department may revoke a certificate of authority issued under this article and the executive director of the commission may revoke a license issued under this article. Termination of employment with a railroad company, or the revocation of a railroad peace officer license, shall constitute an automatic revocation of a certificate of authority to act as a railroad peace officer.

(g) A railroad company is liable for any act or omission by a person serving as a railroad peace officer for the company that is within the person's scope of employment. Neither the state nor any political subdivision or agency of the state shall be liable for any act or omission by a person appointed as a railroad peace officer. All expenses incurred by the granting or revocation of a certificate of authority to act as a railroad peace officer shall be paid by the employing railroad company.

(h) A railroad peace officer who is a member of a railroad craft may not perform the duties of a member of any other railroad craft during a strike or labor dispute.

(i) The director of the department and the executive director of the commission shall have the authority to promulgate rules necessary for the effective administration and performance of the duties and responsibilities delegated to them by this article.

Added by Acts 1985, 69th Leg., ch. 531, § 1, eff. June 12, 1985. Amended by Acts 1999, 76th Leg., ch. 62, § 3.01, eff. Sept. 1, 1999. Amended by Acts 2013, 83rd Leg., ch. 93 (S.B. 686), § 2.02, eff. May 18, 2013.

[1] V.T.C.A., Transportation Code § 541.001 et seq.

Art. 2.122. Special Investigators

(a) The following named criminal investigators of the United States shall not be deemed peace officers, but shall have the powers of arrest, search, and seizure under the laws of this state as to felony offenses only:

(1) Special Agents of the Federal Bureau of Investigation;

(2) Special Agents of the Secret Service;

(3) Special Agents of the United States Immigration and Customs Enforcement;

(4) Special Agents of the Bureau of Alcohol, Tobacco, Firearms and Explosives;

(5) Special Agents of the United States Drug Enforcement Administration;

(6) Inspectors of the United States Postal Inspection Service;

(7) Special Agents of the Criminal Investigation Division of the Internal Revenue Service;

(8) Civilian Special Agents of the United States Naval Criminal Investigative Service;

(9) Marshals and Deputy Marshals of the United States Marshals Service;

(10) Special Agents of the United States Department of State, Bureau of Diplomatic Security;

(11) Special Agents of the Treasury Inspector General for Tax Administration;

(12) Special Agents of the Office of Inspector General of the United States Social Security Administration;

(13) Special Agents of the Office of Inspector General of the United States Department of Veterans Affairs; and

(14) a police officer with the Office of Security and Law Enforcement of the United States Department of Veterans Affairs.

(b) A person designated as a special policeman by the Federal Protective Services division of the General Services Administration under 40 U.S.C. Section 318 or 318d is not a peace officer but has the powers of arrest and search and seizure as to any offense under the laws of this state.

(c) A Customs and Border Protection Officer or Border Patrol Agent of the United States Customs and Border Protection or an immigration enforcement agent or deportation officer of the Department of Homeland Security is not a peace officer under the laws of this state but, on the premises of a port facility designated by the commissioner of the United States Customs and Border Protection as a port of entry for arrival in the United States by land transportation from the United Mexican States into the State of Texas or at a permanent established border patrol traffic check point, has the authority to detain a person pending transfer without unnecessary delay to a peace officer if the agent or officer has probable cause to believe that the person has engaged in conduct that is a violation of Section 49.02, 49.04, 49.07, or 49.08, Penal Code, regardless of whether the violation may be disposed of in a criminal proceeding or a juvenile justice proceeding.

(d) A commissioned law enforcement officer of the National Park Service is not a peace officer under the laws of this state, except that the officer has the powers of arrest, search, and seizure as to any offense under the laws of this state committed within the boundaries of a national park or national recreation area. In this subsection, "national park or national recreation area" means a national park or national recreation area included in the National Park System as defined by 16 U.S.C. Section 1c(a).

(e) A Special Agent or Law Enforcement Officer of the United States Forest Service is not a peace officer under the laws of this state, except that the agent or officer has the powers of arrest, search, and seizure as to any offense under the laws of this state committed within the National Forest System. In this subsection, "National Forest System" has the meaning assigned by 16 U.S.C. Section 1609.

(f) Security personnel working at a commercial nuclear power plant, including contract security personnel, trained and qualified under a security plan approved by the United States Nuclear Regulatory Commission, are not peace officers under the laws of this state, except that such personnel have the powers of arrest, search, and seizure, including the powers under Section 9.51, Penal Code, while in the performance of their duties on the premises of a commercial nuclear power plant site or under agreements entered into with local law enforcement regarding areas surrounding the plant site.

(g) In addition to the powers of arrest, search, and seizure under Subsection (a), a Special Agent of the Secret Service protecting a person described by 18 U.S.C. Section 3056(a) or investigating a threat against a person described by 18 U.S.C. Section 3056(a) has the powers of arrest, search, and seizure as to:

(1) misdemeanor offenses under the laws of this state; and

(2) any criminal offense under federal law.

Added by Acts 1985, 69th Leg., ch. 543, § 1, eff. Sept. 1, 1985. Renumbered from Vernon's Ann.C.C.P. art. 2.121 and amended by Acts 1987, 70th Leg., ch. 503, § 1, eff. Aug. 31, 1987; Acts 1987, 70th Leg., ch. 854, § 1, eff. Aug. 31, 1987. Amended by Acts 1989, 71st Leg., ch. 841, § 1, eff. June 14, 1989; Acts 1993, 73rd Leg., ch. 927, § 1, eff. June 19, 1993; Acts 1997, 75th Leg., ch. 290, § 1, eff. May 26, 1997; Acts 1997, 75th Leg., ch. 717, § 1, eff. June 17, 1997; Acts 1999, 76th Leg., ch. 197, § 1, eff. May 24, 1999; Acts 1999, 76th Leg., ch. 863, § 1, eff. June 18, 1999; Acts 1999, 76th Leg., ch. 628, § 1, eff. June 18, 1999; 2001, 77th Leg., ch. 1420, § 21.001(7), eff. Sept. 1, 2001; Acts 2003, 78th Leg., ch. 1237, § 1, eff. June 20, 2003; Acts 2005, 79th Leg., ch. 1337, § 5, eff. June 18, 2005; Acts 2009, 81st Leg., ch. 732, § 1, eff. Sept. 1, 2009; Acts 2011, 82nd Leg., ch. 1223 (S.B. 530), § 1, eff. June 17, 2011; Acts 2011, 82nd Leg., ch. 1319 (S.B. 150), § 1, eff. June 17, 2011; Acts 2013, 83rd Leg., ch. 161 (S.B. 1093), § 3.001, eff. Sept. 1, 2013; Acts 2013, 83rd Leg., ch. 741 (S.B. 284), § 1, eff. June 14, 2013.

Art. 2.123. Adjunct police officers

(a) Within counties under 200,000 population, the chief of police of a municipality or the sheriff of the county, if the institution is outside the corporate limits of a municipality, that has jurisdiction over the geographical area of a private institution of higher education, provided the governing board of such institution consents, may appoint up to 50 peace officers who are commissioned under Section 51.212, Education Code, and who are employed by a private institution of higher education located in the municipality or county, to serve as adjunct police officers of the municipality or county. Officers appointed under this article shall aid law enforcement agencies in the protection of the municipality or county in a geographical area that is designated by agreement on an annual basis between the appointing chief of police or sheriff and the private institution.

(b) The geographical area that is subject to designation under Subsection (a) of this article may include only the private institution's campus area and an area that:

(1) is adjacent to the campus of the private institution;

(2) does not extend further than a distance of one mile from the perimeter of the campus of the private institution; and

(3) is inhabited primarily by students or employees of the private institution.

(c) A peace officer serving as an adjunct police officer may make arrests and exercise all authority given peace officers under this code only within the geographical area designated by agreement between the appointing chief of police or sheriff and the private institution.

(d) A peace officer serving as an adjunct police officer has all the rights, privileges, and immunities of a peace officer but is not entitled to state compensation and retirement benefits normally provided by the state to a peace officer.

(e) A person may not serve as an adjunct police officer for a municipality or county unless:

(1) the institution of higher education submits the person's application for appointment and certification as an adjunct police officer to the chief of police of the municipality or, if outside a municipality, the sheriff of the county that has jurisdiction over the geographical area of the institution;

(2) the chief of police of the municipality or sheriff of the county to whom the application was made issues the person a certificate of authority to act as an adjunct police officer; and

(3) the person undergoes any additional training required for that person to meet the training standards of the municipality or county for peace officers employed by the municipality or county.

(f) For good cause, the chief of police or sheriff may revoke a certificate of authority issued under this article.

(g) A private institution of higher education is liable for any act or omission by a person while serving as an adjunct police officer outside of the campus of the institution in the same manner as the municipality or county governing that geographical area is liable for any act or omission of a peace officer employed by the municipality or county. This subsection shall not be construed to act as a limitation on the liability of a municipality or county for the acts or omissions of a person serving as an adjunct police officer.

(h) The employing institution shall pay all expenses incurred by the municipality or county in granting or revoking a certificate of authority to act as an adjunct police officer under this article.

(i) This article does not affect any duty of the municipality or county to provide law enforcement services to a geographical area designated under Subsection (a) of this article.

Added by Acts 1987, 70th Leg., ch. 1128, § 1, eff. Aug. 31, 1987.

Art. 2.124. Peace Officers From Adjoining States

(a) A commissioned peace officer of a state of the United States of America adjoining this state, while the officer is in this state, has under this subsection the same powers, duties, and immunities as a peace officer of this state who is acting in the discharge of an official duty, but only:

(1) during a time in which:

(A) the peace officer from the adjoining state has physical custody of an inmate or criminal defendant and is transporting the inmate or defendant from a county in the adjoining state that is on the border between the two states to a hospital or other medical facility in a county in this state that is on the border between the two states; or

(B) the peace officer has physical custody of the inmate or defendant and is returning the inmate or

defendant from the hospital or facility to the county in the adjoining state; and

(2) to the extent necessary to:

(A) maintain physical custody of the inmate or defendant while transporting the inmate or defendant; or

(B) regain physical custody of the inmate or defendant if the inmate or defendant escapes while being transported.

(b) A commissioned peace officer of a state of the United States of America adjoining this state, while the officer is in this state, has under this subsection the same powers, duties, and immunities as a peace officer of this state who is acting in the discharge of an official duty, but only in a municipality some part of the municipal limits of which are within one mile of the boundary between this state and the adjoining state and only at a time the peace officer is regularly assigned to duty in a county, parish, or municipality that adjoins this state. A peace officer described by this subsection may also as part of the officer's powers in this state enforce the ordinances of a Texas municipality described by this subsection but only after the governing body of the municipality authorizes that enforcement by majority vote at an open meeting.

Added by Acts 1995, 74th Leg., ch. 156, § 1, eff. May 19, 1995. Amended by Acts 1999, 76th Leg., ch. 107, § 1, eff. Sept. 1, 1999.

Art. 2.125. Special Rangers of Texas and Southwestern Cattle Raisers Association

(a) The director of the Department of Public Safety may appoint up to 50 special rangers who are employed by the Texas and Southwestern Cattle Raisers Association to aid law enforcement agencies in the investigation of the theft of livestock or related property.

(b) Except as provided by Subsection (c) of this article, a special ranger may make arrests and exercise all authority given peace officers under this code when necessary to prevent or abate the commission of an offense involving livestock or related property.

(c) A special ranger may not issue a traffic citation for a violation of Chapter 521, Transportation Code, or Subtitle C, Title 7, Transportation Code.

(d) A special ranger is not entitled to state benefits normally provided by the state to a peace officer.

(e) A person may not serve as a special ranger unless:

(1) the Texas and Southwestern Cattle Raisers Association submits the person's application for appointment and certification as a special ranger to the director of the Department of Public Safety and to the executive director of the Texas Commission on Law Enforcement;

(2) the director of the department issues the person a certificate of authority to act as a special ranger;

(3) the executive director of the commission determines that the person meets minimum standards required of peace officers by the commission relating to competence, reliability, education, training, morality, and physical and mental health and issues the person a license as a special ranger; and

(4) the person has met all standards for certification as a peace officer by the Texas Commission on Law Enforcement.

(f) For good cause, the director of the department may revoke a certificate of authority issued under this article and the executive director of the commission may revoke a license issued under this article. Termination of employment with the association, or the revocation of a special ranger license, shall constitute an automatic revocation of a certificate of authority to act as a special ranger.

(g) The Texas and Southwestern Cattle Raisers Association is liable for any act or omission by a person serving as a special ranger for the association that is within the person's scope of employment. Neither the state nor any political subdivision or agency of the state shall be liable for any act or omission by a person appointed as a special ranger. All expenses incurred by the granting or revocation of a certificate of authority to act as a special ranger shall be paid by the association.

(h) The director of the department and the executive director of the commission shall have the authority to promulgate rules necessary for the effective administration and performance of the duties and responsibilities delegated to them by this article.

Added by Acts 2005, 79th Leg., ch. 209, § 1, eff. Sept. 1, 2005. Amended by Acts 2013, 83rd Leg., ch. 93 (S.B. 686), § 2.03, eff. May 18, 2013.

Art. 2.126. Peace Officers Commissioned by the Alabama–Coushatta Indian Tribe

(a) The tribal council of the Alabama–Coushatta Indian Tribe is authorized to employ and commission peace officers for the purpose of enforcing state law within the boundaries of the tribe's reservation.

(b) Within the boundaries of the tribe's reservation, a peace officer commissioned under this article:

(1) is vested with all the powers, privileges, and immunities of peace officers;

(2) may, in accordance with Chapter 14, arrest without a warrant any person who violates a law of the state; and

(3) may enforce all traffic laws on streets and highways.

(c) Outside the boundaries of the tribe's reservation, a peace officer commissioned under this article is vested with all the powers, privileges, and immunities of peace officers and may arrest any person who violates any law of the state if the peace officer:

(1) is summoned by another law enforcement agency to provide assistance; or

(2) is assisting another law enforcement agency.

(d) Any officer assigned to duty and commissioned under this article shall take and file the oath required of peace officers and shall execute and file a good and sufficient bond in the sum of $1,000, payable to the governor, with two or more good and sufficient sureties, conditioned that the officer will fairly, impartially, and faithfully perform the duties as may be required of the officer by law. The bond may be sued on from time to time in the name of the person injured until the whole amount is recovered.

(e) Any person commissioned under this article must:

(1) meet the minimum standards required of peace officers by the commission relating to competence, reliability, education, training, morality, and physical and mental health; and

(2) meet all standards for certification as a peace officer by the Texas Commission on Law Enforcement.

(f) A peace officer commissioned under this article is not entitled to state benefits normally provided by the state to a peace officer.

Added by Acts 2011, 82nd Leg., ch. 1344 (S.B. 1378), § 1, eff. Sept. 1, 2011. Amended by Acts 2013, 83rd Leg., ch. 93 (S.B. 686), § 2.04, eff. May 18, 2013.

Art. 2.127. School Marshals

(a) Except as provided by Subsection (b), a school marshal may:

(1) make arrests and exercise all authority given peace officers under this code, subject to written regulations adopted by:

(A) the board of trustees of a school district or the governing body of an open-enrollment charter school under Section 37.0811, Education Code;

(B) the governing body of a private school under Section 37.0813, Education Code; or

(C) the governing board of a public junior college under Section 51.220, Education Code; and

(2) only act as necessary to prevent or abate the commission of an offense that threatens serious bodily injury or death of students, faculty, or visitors on school premises.

(a–1) In this section, "private school" means a school that:

(1) offers a course of instruction for students in one or more grades from prekindergarten through grade 12;

(2) is not operated by a governmental entity; and

(3) is not a school whose students meet the definition provided by Section 29.916(a)(1), Education Code.

(b) A school marshal may not issue a traffic citation for a violation of Chapter 521, Transportation Code, or Subtitle C, Title 7, Transportation Code.

(c) A school marshal is not entitled to state benefits normally provided by the state to a peace officer.

(d) A person may not serve as a school marshal unless the person is:

(1) licensed under Section 1701.260, Occupations Code; and

(2) appointed by:

(A) the board of trustees of a school district or the governing body of an open-enrollment charter school under Section 37.0811, Education Code;

(B) the governing body of a private school under Section 37.0813, Education Code; or

(C) the governing board of a public junior college under Section 51.220, Education Code.

Added by Acts 2013, 83rd Leg., ch. 655 (H.B. 1009), § 2, eff. June 14, 2013. Amended by Acts 2015, 84th Leg., ch. 1144 (S.B. 386), § 1, eff. Sept. 1, 2015; Acts 2017, 85th Leg., ch. 988 (H.B. 867), § 1, eff. June 15, 2017.

Art. 2.13. Duties and powers

(a) It is the duty of every peace officer to preserve the peace within the officer's jurisdiction. To effect this purpose, the officer shall use all lawful means.

(b) The officer shall:

(1) in every case authorized by the provisions of this Code, interfere without warrant to prevent or suppress crime;

(2) execute all lawful process issued to the officer by any magistrate or court;

(3) give notice to some magistrate of all offenses committed within the officer's jurisdiction, where the officer has good reason to believe there has been a violation of the penal law; and

(4) arrest offenders without warrant in every case where the officer is authorized by law, in order that they may be taken before the proper magistrate or court and be tried.

(c) It is the duty of every officer to take possession of a child under Article 63.009(g).

Text of (d), as added by Acts 2017, 85th Leg., ch. 4 (S.B. 4), § 6.01

(d) Subject to Subsection (e), in the course of investigating an alleged criminal offense, a peace officer may inquire as to the nationality or immigration status of a victim of or witness to the offense only if the officer determines that the inquiry is necessary to:

(1) investigate the offense; or

(2) provide the victim or witness with information about federal visas designed to protect individuals providing assistance to law enforcement.

Text of (d), as added by Acts 2017, 85th Leg., ch. 34 (S.B. 1576), § 3

(d) On a request made by that office, a peace officer shall execute an emergency detention order issued by the Texas Civil Commitment Office under Section 841.0837, Health and Safety Code.

(e) Subsection (d) does not prevent a peace officer from:

(1) conducting a separate investigation of any other alleged criminal offense; or

(2) inquiring as to the nationality or immigration status of a victim of or witness to a criminal offense if the officer has probable cause to believe that the

victim or witness has engaged in specific conduct constituting a separate criminal offense.

Acts 1965, 59th Leg., vol. 2, p. 317, ch. 722, eff. Jan. 1, 1966. Amended by Acts 1999, 76th Leg., ch. 685, § 1, eff. Sept. 1, 1999; Acts 2003, 78th Leg., ch. 1276, § 5.0005, eff. Sept. 1, 2003; Acts 2017, 85th Leg., ch. 4 (S.B. 4), § 6.01, eff. Sept. 1, 2017; Acts 2017, 85th Leg., ch. 34 (S.B. 1576), § 3, eff. Sept. 1, 2017.

Section 7.01 of Acts 2017, 85th Leg., ch. 4 (S.B. 4) provides:

"It is the intent of the legislature that every provision, section, subsection, sentence, clause, phrase, or word in this Act, and every application of the provisions in this Act to each person or entity, are severable from each other. If any application of any provision in this Act to any person, group of persons, or circumstances is found by a court to be invalid for any reason, the remaining applications of that provision to all other persons and circumstances shall be severed and may not be affected."

Art. 2.1305. Carrying Weapon on Certain Premises

(a) An establishment serving the public may not prohibit or otherwise restrict a peace officer or special investigator from carrying on the establishment's premises a weapon that the peace officer or special investigator is otherwise authorized to carry, regardless of whether the peace officer or special investigator is engaged in the actual discharge of the officer's or investigator's duties while carrying the weapon.

(b) For purposes of this article:

(1) "Establishment serving the public" means:

(A) a hotel, motel, or other place of lodging;

(B) a restaurant or other place where food is offered for sale to the public;

(C) a retail business or other commercial establishment or an office building to which the general public is invited;

(D) a sports venue; and

(E) any other place of public accommodation, amusement, convenience, or resort to which the general public or any classification of persons from the general public is regularly, normally, or customarily invited.

(2) "Sports venue" means an arena, coliseum, stadium, or other type of area or facility that is primarily used or is planned for primary use for one or more professional or amateur sports or athletics events and for which a fee is charged or is planned to be charged for admission to the sports or athletics events, other than occasional civic, charitable, or promotional events.

Added by Acts 2017, 85th Leg., ch. 124 (H.B. 873), § 1, eff. Sept. 1, 2017.

Section 2 of Acts 2017, 85th Leg., ch. 124 (H.B. 873) provides:

"The change in law made by this Act applies only to conduct that occurs on or after the effective date [Sept. 1, 2017] of this Act. Conduct that occurs before the effective date of this Act is governed by the law in effect on the date the conduct occurred, and the former law is continued in effect for that purpose."

Art. 2.131. Racial Profiling Prohibited

A peace officer may not engage in racial profiling.

Added by Acts 2001, 77th Leg., ch. 947, § 1, eff. Sept. 1, 2001.

Art. 2.132. Law Enforcement Policy on Racial Profiling

(a) In this article:

(1) "Law enforcement agency" means an agency of the state, or of a county, municipality, or other political subdivision of the state, that employs peace officers who make motor vehicle stops in the routine performance of the officers' official duties.

(2) "Motor vehicle stop" means an occasion in which a peace officer stops a motor vehicle for an alleged violation of a law or ordinance.

(3) "Race or ethnicity" means the following categories:

(A) Alaska native or American Indian;

(B) Asian or Pacific Islander;

(C) black;

(D) white; and

(E) Hispanic or Latino.

(b) Each law enforcement agency in this state shall adopt a detailed written policy on racial profiling. The policy must:

(1) clearly define acts constituting racial profiling;

(2) strictly prohibit peace officers employed by the agency from engaging in racial profiling;

(3) implement a process by which an individual may file a complaint with the agency if the individual believes that a peace officer employed by the agency has engaged in racial profiling with respect to the individual;

(4) provide public education relating to the agency's compliment and complaint process, including providing the telephone number, mailing address, and e-mail address to make a compliment or complaint with respect to each ticket, citation, or warning issued by a peace officer;

(5) require appropriate corrective action to be taken against a peace officer employed by the agency who, after an investigation, is shown to have engaged

in racial profiling in violation of the agency's policy adopted under this article;

(6) require collection of information relating to motor vehicle stops in which a ticket, citation, or warning is issued and to arrests made as a result of those stops, including information relating to:

(A) the race or ethnicity of the individual detained;

(B) whether a search was conducted and, if so, whether the individual detained consented to the search;

(C) whether the peace officer knew the race or ethnicity of the individual detained before detaining that individual;

(D) whether the peace officer used physical force that resulted in bodily injury, as that term is defined by Section 1.07, Penal Code, during the stop;

(E) the location of the stop; and

(F) the reason for the stop; and

(7) require the chief administrator of the agency, regardless of whether the administrator is elected, employed, or appointed, to submit an annual report of the information collected under Subdivision (6) to:

(A) the Texas Commission on Law Enforcement; and

(B) the governing body of each county or municipality served by the agency, if the agency is an agency of a county, municipality, or other political subdivision of the state.

(c) The data collected as a result of the reporting requirements of this article shall not constitute prima facie evidence of racial profiling.

(d) On adoption of a policy under Subsection (b), a law enforcement agency shall examine the feasibility of installing video camera and transmitter-activated equipment in each agency law enforcement motor vehicle regularly used to make motor vehicle stops and transmitter-activated equipment in each agency law enforcement motorcycle regularly used to make motor vehicle stops. The agency also shall examine the feasibility of equipping each peace officer who regularly detains or stops motor vehicles with a body worn camera, as that term is defined by Section 1701.651, Occupations Code. If a law enforcement agency installs video or audio equipment or equips peace officers with body worn cameras as provided by this subsection, the policy adopted by the agency under Subsection (b) must include standards for reviewing video and audio documentation.

(e) A report required under Subsection (b)(7) may not include identifying information about a peace officer who makes a motor vehicle stop or about an individual who is stopped or arrested by a peace officer. This subsection does not affect the collection of information as required by a policy under Subsection (b)(6).

(f) On the commencement of an investigation by a law enforcement agency of a complaint described by Subsection (b)(3) in which a video or audio recording of the occurrence on which the complaint is based was made, the agency shall promptly provide a copy of the recording to the peace officer who is the subject of the complaint on written request by the officer.

(g) On a finding by the Texas Commission on Law Enforcement that the chief administrator of a law enforcement agency intentionally failed to submit a report required under Subsection (b)(7), the commission shall begin disciplinary procedures against the chief administrator.

(h) A law enforcement agency shall review the data collected under Subsection (b)(6) to identify any improvements the agency could make in its practices and policies regarding motor vehicle stops.

Added by Acts 2001, 77th Leg., ch. 947, § 1, eff. Sept. 1, 2001. Amended by Acts 2009, 81st Leg., ch. 1172, § 25, eff. Sept. 1, 2009; Acts 2013, 83rd Leg., ch. 93 (S.B. 686), § 2.05, eff. May 18, 2013; Acts 2017, 85th Leg., ch. 173 (H.B. 3051), § 1, eff. Sept. 1, 2017; Acts 2017, 85th Leg., ch. 950 (S.B. 1849), § 5.01, eff. Sept. 1, 2017.

Section 5.07 of Acts 2017, 85th Leg., ch. 950 (S.B. 1849) provides:

"Articles 2.132 and 2.134, Code of Criminal Procedure, as amended by this article, apply only to a report covering a calendar year beginning on or after January 1, 2018."

Art. 2.133. Reports Required for Motor Vehicle Stops

(a) In this article, "race or ethnicity" has the meaning assigned by Article 2.132(a).

(b) A peace officer who stops a motor vehicle for an alleged violation of a law or ordinance shall report to the law enforcement agency that employs the officer information relating to the stop, including:

(1) a physical description of any person operating the motor vehicle who is detained as a result of the stop, including:

(A) the person's gender; and

(B) the person's race or ethnicity, as stated by the person or, if the person does not state the person's race or ethnicity, as determined by the officer to the best of the officer's ability;

(2) the initial reason for the stop;

(3) whether the officer conducted a search as a result of the stop and, if so, whether the person detained consented to the search;

(4) whether any contraband or other evidence was discovered in the course of the search and a description of the contraband or evidence;

(5) the reason for the search, including whether:

(A) any contraband or other evidence was in plain view;

(B) any probable cause or reasonable suspicion existed to perform the search; or

(C) the search was performed as a result of the towing of the motor vehicle or the arrest of any person in the motor vehicle;

(6) whether the officer made an arrest as a result of the stop or the search, including a statement of whether the arrest was based on a violation of the Penal Code, a violation of a traffic law or ordinance, or an outstanding warrant and a statement of the offense charged;

(7) the street address or approximate location of the stop;

(8) whether the officer issued a verbal or written warning or a ticket or citation as a result of the stop; and

(9) whether the officer used physical force that resulted in bodily injury, as that term is defined by Section 1.07, Penal Code, during the stop.

(c) The chief administrator of a law enforcement agency, regardless of whether the administrator is elected, employed, or appointed, is responsible for auditing reports under Subsection (b) to ensure that the race or ethnicity of the person operating the motor vehicle is being reported.

Added by Acts 2001, 77th Leg., ch. 947, § 1, eff. Sept. 1, 2001. Amended by Acts 2009, 81st Leg., ch. 1172, § 26, eff. Sept. 1, 2009; Acts 2017, 85th Leg., ch. 950 (S.B. 1849), § 5.02, eff. Sept. 1, 2017.

Art. 2.134. Compilation and Analysis of Information Collected

(a) In this article:

(1) "Motor vehicle stop" has the meaning assigned by Article 2.132(a).

(2) "Race or ethnicity" has the meaning assigned by Article 2.132(a).

(b) A law enforcement agency shall compile and analyze the information contained in each report received by the agency under Article 2.133. Not later than March 1 of each year, each law enforcement agency shall submit a report containing the incident-based data compiled during the previous calendar year to the Texas Commission on Law Enforcement and, if the law enforcement agency is a local law enforcement agency, to the governing body of each county or municipality served by the agency.

(c) A report required under Subsection (b) must be submitted by the chief administrator of the law enforcement agency, regardless of whether the administrator is elected, employed, or appointed, and must include:

(1) a comparative analysis of the information compiled under Article 2.133 to:

(A) evaluate and compare the number of motor vehicle stops, within the applicable jurisdiction, of persons who are recognized as racial or ethnic minorities and persons who are not recognized as racial or ethnic minorities;

(B) examine the disposition of motor vehicle stops made by officers employed by the agency, categorized according to the race or ethnicity of the affected persons, as appropriate, including any searches resulting from stops within the applicable jurisdiction; and

(C) evaluate and compare the number of searches resulting from motor vehicle stops within the applicable jurisdiction and whether contraband or other evidence was discovered in the course of those searches; and

(2) information relating to each complaint filed with the agency alleging that a peace officer employed by the agency has engaged in racial profiling.

(d) A report required under Subsection (b) may not include identifying information about a peace officer who makes a motor vehicle stop or about an individual who is stopped or arrested by a peace officer. This subsection does not affect the reporting of information required under Article 2.133(b)(1).

(e) The Texas Commission on Law Enforcement, in accordance with Section 1701.162, Occupations Code, shall develop guidelines for compiling and reporting information as required by this article.

(f) The data collected as a result of the reporting requirements of this article shall not constitute prima facie evidence of racial profiling.

(g) On a finding by the Texas Commission on Law Enforcement that the chief administrator of a law enforcement agency intentionally failed to submit a report required under Subsection (b), the commission shall begin disciplinary procedures against the chief administrator.

Added by Acts 2001, 77th Leg., ch. 947, § 1, eff. Sept. 1, 2001. Amended by Acts 2009, 81st Leg., ch. 1172, § 27, eff. Sept. 1, 2009; Acts 2013, 83rd Leg., ch. 93 (S.B. 686), § 2.06, eff. May 18, 2013; Acts 2017, 85th Leg., ch. 950 (S.B. 1849), § 5.03, eff. Sept. 1, 2017.

Section 5.07 of Acts 2017, 85th Leg., ch. 950 (S.B. 1849) provides:

"Articles 2.132 and 2.134, Code of Criminal Procedure, as amended by this article, apply only to a report covering a calendar year beginning on or after January 1, 2018."

Art. 2.135. Repealed by Acts 2017, 85th Leg., ch. 950 (S.B. 1849), § 5.06, eff. Sept. 1, 2017

Art. 2.136. Liability

A peace officer is not liable for damages arising from an act relating to the collection or reporting of information as required by Article 2.133 or under a policy adopted under Article 2.132.

Added by Acts 2001, 77th Leg., ch. 947, § 1, eff. Sept. 1, 2001.

Art. 2.137. Provision of Funding or Equipment

(a) The Department of Public Safety shall adopt rules for providing funds or video and audio equipment to law enforcement agencies for the purpose of installing video and audio equipment in law enforcement motor vehicles and motorcycles or equipping peace officers with body worn cameras, including specifying criteria to prioritize funding or equipment provided to law enforcement agencies. The criteria may include consideration of tax effort, financial hardship, available revenue, and budget surpluses. The criteria must give priority to:

(1) law enforcement agencies that employ peace officers whose primary duty is traffic enforcement;

(2) smaller jurisdictions; and

(3) municipal and county law enforcement agencies.

(b) The Department of Public Safety shall collaborate with an institution of higher education to identify law enforcement agencies that need funds or video and audio equipment for the purpose of installing video and audio equipment in law enforcement motor vehicles and motorcycles or equipping peace officers with body worn cameras. The collaboration may include the use of a survey to assist in developing criteria to prioritize funding or equipment provided to law enforcement agencies.

(c) To receive funds or video and audio equipment from the state for the purpose of installing video and audio equipment in law enforcement motor vehicles and motorcycles or equipping peace officers with body worn cameras, the governing body of a county or municipality, in conjunction with the law enforcement agency serving the county or municipality, shall certify to the Department of Public Safety that the law enforcement agency needs funds or video and audio equipment for that purpose.

(d) On receipt of funds or video and audio equipment from the state for the purpose of installing video and audio equipment in law enforcement motor vehicles and motorcycles or equipping peace officers with body worn cameras, the governing body of a county or municipality, in conjunction with the law enforcement agency serving the county or municipality, shall certify to the Department of Public Safety that the law enforcement agency has taken the necessary actions to use and is using video and audio equipment and body worn cameras for those purposes.

Added by Acts 2001, 77th Leg., ch. 947, § 1, eff. Sept. 1, 2001. Amended by Acts 2017, 85th Leg., ch. 950 (S.B. 1849), § 5.04, eff. Sept. 1, 2017.

Art. 2.138. Rules

The Department of Public Safety may adopt rules to implement Articles 2.131–2.137.

Added by Acts 2001, 77th Leg., ch. 947, § 1, eff. Sept. 1, 2001.

Art. 2.1385. Civil Penalty

(a) If the chief administrator of a local law enforcement agency intentionally fails to submit the incident-based data as required by Article 2.134, the agency is liable to the state for a civil penalty in an amount not to exceed $5,000 for each violation. The attorney general may sue to collect a civil penalty under this subsection.

(b) From money appropriated to the agency for the administration of the agency, the executive director of a state law enforcement agency that intentionally fails to submit the incident-based data as required by Article 2.134 shall remit to the comptroller the amount of $1,000 for each violation.

(c) Money collected under this article shall be deposited in the state treasury to the credit of the general revenue fund.

Added by Acts 2009, 81st Leg., ch. 1172, § 29, eff. Sept. 1, 2009. Amended by Acts 2017, 85th Leg., ch. 950 (S.B. 1849), § 5.05, eff. Sept. 1, 2017.

Art. 2.1386. Eyewitness identification protocols

(a) In this article, "law enforcement agency" means an agency of the state or an agency of a political subdivision of the state authorized by law to employ peace officers.

(b) The Texas Commission on Law Enforcement shall establish a comprehensive education and training program on eyewitness identification, including material regarding variables that affect a witness's vision and memory, practices for minimizing contamination, and effective eyewitness identification protocols.

(c) Each law enforcement agency shall require each peace officer who is employed by the agency and who performs eyewitness identification procedures to complete the education and training described by Subsection (b).

Added by Acts 2017, 85th Leg., ch. 686 (H.B. 34), § 2, eff. Sept. 1, 2017.

Art. 2.139. Reports Required for Officer–Involved Injuries or Deaths

(a) In this article:

(1) "Deadly weapon" means:

(A) a firearm or any object manifestly designed, made, or adapted for the purpose of inflicting death or serious bodily injury; or

(B) any object that in the manner of its use or intended use is capable of causing death or serious bodily injury.

(2) "Officer-involved injury or death" means an incident during which a peace officer discharges a firearm causing injury or death to another.

(b) The office of the attorney general by rule shall create a written and electronic form for the reporting by law enforcement agencies of an officer-involved injury or death. The form must include spaces to report only the following information:

(1) the date on which the incident occurred;

(2) the location where the incident occurred;

(3) the age, gender, and race or ethnicity of each peace officer involved in the incident;

(4) if known, the age, gender, and race or ethnicity of each injured or deceased person involved in the incident;

(5) whether the person was injured or died as a result of the incident;

(6) whether each injured or deceased person used, exhibited, or was carrying a deadly weapon during the incident;

(7) whether each peace officer involved in the incident was on duty during the incident;

(8) whether each peace officer involved in the incident was responding to an emergency call or a request for assistance and, if so, whether the officer responded to that call or request with one or more other peace officers; and

(9) whether the incident occurred during or as a result of:

(A) the execution of a warrant; or

(B) a hostage, barricade, or other emergency situation.

(c) Not later than the 30th day after the date of an officer-involved injury or death, the law enforcement agency employing an officer involved in the incident must complete and submit a written or electronic report, using the form created under Subsection (b), to the office of the attorney general. The report must include all information described in Subsection (b).

(d) Not later than the fifth day after the date of receipt of a report submitted under Subsection (c), the office of the attorney general shall post a copy of the report on the office's Internet website.

(e) Not later than March 1 of each year, the office of the attorney general shall submit a report regarding all officer-involved injuries or deaths that occurred during the preceding year to the governor and the standing legislative committees with primary jurisdiction over criminal justice matters. The report must include:

(1) the total number of officer-involved injuries or deaths;

(2) a summary of the reports submitted to the office under this article; and

(3) a copy of each report submitted to the office under this article.

Added by Acts 2015, 84th Leg., ch. 516 (H.B. 1036), § 1, eff. Sept. 1, 2015. Amended by Acts 2017, 85th Leg., ch. 808 (H.B. 245), § 1, eff. Sept. 1, 2017.

Section 5 of Acts 2017, 85th Leg., ch. 808 (H.B. 245) provides:

"The changes in law made by this Act to Chapter 2, Code of Criminal Procedure, apply only to a report required to be submitted on or after the effective date [Sept. 1, 2017] of this Act. A report required to be submitted before the effective date of this Act is subject to the law in effect at the time the report was required to be submitted, and the former law is continued in effect for that purpose."

Art. 2.1395. Reports Required for Certain Injuries or Deaths of Peace Officers

(a) The office of the attorney general by rule shall create a written and electronic form for the reporting by law enforcement agencies of incidents in which, while a peace officer is performing an official duty, a person who is not a peace officer discharges a firearm and causes injury or death to the officer. The form must include spaces to report only the following information:

(1) the date on which the incident occurred;

(2) the location where the incident occurred;

(3) the age, gender, and race or ethnicity of each injured or deceased peace officer involved in the incident;

(4) if known, the age, gender, and race or ethnicity of each person who discharged a firearm and caused injury or death to a peace officer involved in the incident; and

(5) whether the officer or any other person was injured or died as a result of the incident.

(b) Not later than the 30th day after the date of the occurrence of an incident described by Subsection (a), the law enforcement agency employing the injured or deceased officer at the time of the incident must complete and submit a written or electronic report, using the form created under that subsection, to the office of the attorney general. The report must include all information described in Subsection (a).

(c) Not later than March 1 of each year, the office of the attorney general shall submit a report regarding all incidents described by Subsection (a) that occurred during the preceding year to the governor and the standing legislative committees with primary jurisdiction over criminal justice matters. The report must include:

(1) the total number of incidents that occurred;

(2) a summary of the reports submitted to the office under this article; and

(3) a copy of each report submitted to the office under this article.

Added by Acts 2015, 84th Leg., ch. 516 (H.B. 1036), § 1, eff. Sept. 1, 2015. Amended by Acts 2017, 85th Leg., ch. 808 (H.B. 245), § 2, eff. Sept. 1, 2017.

Section 5 of Acts 2017, 85th Leg., ch. 808 (H.B. 245) provides:

"The changes in law made by this Act to Chapter 2, Code of Criminal Procedure, apply only to a report required to be submitted on or after the effective date [Sept. 1, 2017] of this Act. A report required to be submitted before the effective date of this Act is subject to the law in effect at the time the report was required to be submitted, and the former law is continued in effect for that purpose."

Art. 2.13951. Notice of Violation of Reporting Requirements for Certain Injuries or Deaths; Civil Penalty

(a) The office of the attorney general shall conduct an investigation after receiving a written and signed report, on a form prescribed by the office, asserting that a law enforcement agency failed to submit a report required by Article 2.139 or 2.1395. If the office determines that the law enforcement agency failed to submit the report, the office shall provide notice of the failure to the agency. The notice must summarize the applicable reporting requirement and state that the agency may be subject to a civil penalty as provided by Subsection (b) or (c), as applicable.

(b) Except as provided by Subsection (c), a law enforcement agency that fails to submit the required report on or before the seventh day after the date of receiving notice under Subsection (a) is liable for a civil penalty in the amount of $1,000 for each day after the seventh day that the agency fails to submit the report.

(c) Beginning on the day after the date of receiving notice under Subsection (a), a law enforcement agency that, in the five-year period preceding the date the agency received the notice, has been liable for a civil penalty under Subsection (b) or this subsection is liable for a civil penalty for each day the agency fails to submit the required report. The amount of a civil penalty under this subsection is $10,000 for the first day and $1,000 for each additional day that the agency fails to submit the report.

(d) The attorney general may sue to collect a civil penalty under this article.

(e) A civil penalty collected under this article shall be deposited to the credit of the compensation to victims of crime fund established under Subchapter B, Chapter 56.

Added by Acts 2017, 85th Leg., ch. 808 (H.B. 245), § 3, eff. Sept. 1, 2017.

Section 5 of Acts 2017, 85th Leg., ch. 808 (H.B. 245) provides:

"The changes in law made by this Act to Chapter 2, Code of Criminal Procedure, apply only to a report required to be submitted on or after the effective date [Sept. 1, 2017] of this Act. A report required to be submitted before the effective date of this Act is subject to the law in effect at the time the report was required to be submitted, and the former law is continued in effect for that purpose."

Art. 2.1396.   Video Recordings of Arrests for Intoxication Offenses

A person stopped or arrested on suspicion of an offense under Section 49.04, 49.045, 49.07, or 49.08, Penal Code, is entitled to receive from a law enforcement agency employing the peace officer who made the stop or arrest a copy of any video made by or at the direction of the officer that contains footage of:

(1) the stop;

(2) the arrest;

(3) the conduct of the person stopped during any interaction with the officer, including during the administration of a field sobriety test; or

(4) a procedure in which a specimen of the person's breath or blood is taken.

Added by Acts 2015, 84th Leg., ch. 1124 (H.B. 3791), § 1, eff. Sept. 1, 2015. Redesignated from Vernon's Ann. Texas C.C.P. art. 2.139 by Acts 2017, 85th Leg., ch. 324 (S.B. 1488), § 24.001(3), eff. Sept. 1, 2017; Acts 2017, 85th Leg., ch. 808 (H.B. 245), § 4, eff. Sept. 1, 2017.

Section 2 of Acts 2015, 84th Leg., ch. 1124 (H.B. 3791) provides:

"The change in law made by this Act applies only to a recording of conduct that occurs on or after the effective date of this Act."

Section 5 of Acts 2017, 85th Leg., ch. 808 (H.B. 245) provides:

"The changes in law made by this Act to Chapter 2, Code of Criminal Procedure, apply only to a report required to be submitted on or after the effective date [Sept. 1, 2017] of this Act. A report required to be submitted before the effective date of this Act is subject to the law in effect at the time the report was required to be submitted, and the former law is continued in effect for that purpose."

Art. 2.14.   May summon aid

Whenever a peace officer meets with resistance in discharging any duty imposed upon him by law, he shall summon a sufficient number of citizens of his county to overcome the resistance; and all persons summoned are bound to obey.

Acts 1965, 59th Leg., vol. 2, p. 317, ch. 722, eff. Jan. 1, 1966.

Art. 2.15.   Person refusing to aid

The peace officer who has summoned any person to assist him in performing any duty shall report such person, if he refuse to obey, to the proper district or county attorney, in order that he may be prosecuted for the offense.

Acts 1965, 59th Leg., vol. 2, p. 317, ch. 722, eff. Jan. 1, 1966.

Art. 2.16.   Neglecting to execute process

If any sheriff or other officer shall wilfully refuse or fail from neglect to execute any summons, subpoena or attachment for a witness, or any other legal process which it is made his duty by law to execute, he shall be liable to a fine for contempt not less than ten nor more than two hundred dollars, at the discretion of the court. The payment of such fine shall be enforced in the same manner as fines for contempt in civil cases.

Acts 1965, 59th Leg., vol. 2, p. 317, ch. 722, eff. Jan. 1, 1966.

Art. 2.17.   Conservator of the peace

Each sheriff shall be a conservator of the peace in his county, and shall arrest all offenders against the laws of the State, in his view or hearing, and take them before the proper court for examination or trial. He shall quell and suppress all assaults and batteries, affrays, insurrections and unlawful assemblies. He shall apprehend and commit to jail all offenders, until an examination or trial can be had.

Acts 1965, 59th Leg., vol. 2, p. 317, ch. 722, eff. Jan. 1, 1966.

Art. 2.18.   Custody of prisoners

When a prisoner is committed to jail by warrant from a magistrate or court, he shall be placed in jail by the sheriff. It is a violation of duty on the part of any sheriff to permit a defendant so committed to remain out of jail, except that he may, when a defendant is committed for want of bail, or when he arrests in a bailable case, give the person arrested a reasonable time to procure bail; but he shall so guard the accused as to prevent escape.

Acts 1965, 59th Leg., vol. 2, p. 317, ch. 722, eff. Jan. 1, 1966.

Art. 2.19.   Report as to prisoners

On the first day of each month, the sheriff shall give notice, in writing, to the district or county attorney, where there be one, as to all prisoners in his custody, naming them, and of the authority under which he detains them.

Acts 1965, 59th Leg., vol. 2, p. 317, ch. 722, eff. Jan. 1, 1966.

Art. 2.195.   Report of Warrant or Capias Information

Not later than the 30th day after the date the court clerk issues the warrant or capias, the sheriff:

(1) shall report to the national crime information center each warrant or capias issued for a defendant charged with a felony who fails to appear in court when summoned; and

(2) may report to the national crime information center each warrant or capias issued for a defendant charged with a misdemeanor other than a Class C

misdemeanor who fails to appear in court when summoned.

Added by Acts 2009, 81st Leg., ch. 578, § 1, eff. June 19, 2009. Amended by Acts 2011, 82nd Leg., ch. 531 (H.B. 2472), § 1, eff. Sept. 1, 2011.

Art. 2.20. Deputy

Wherever a duty is imposed by this Code upon the sheriff, the same duty may lawfully be performed by his deputy. When there is no sheriff in a county, the duties of that office, as to all proceedings under the criminal law, devolve upon the officer who, under the law, is empowered to discharge the duties of sheriff, in case of vacancy in the office.

Acts 1965, 59th Leg., vol. 2, p. 317, ch. 722, eff. Jan. 1, 1966.

Art. 2.21. Duty of clerks

(a) In a criminal proceeding, a clerk of the district or county court shall:

(1) receive and file all papers;

(2) receive all exhibits at the conclusion of the proceeding;

(3) issue all process;

(4) accept and file electronic documents received from the defendant, if the clerk accepts electronic documents from an attorney representing the state;

(5) accept and file digital multimedia evidence received from the defendant, if the clerk accepts digital multimedia evidence from an attorney representing the state; and

(6) perform all other duties imposed on the clerk by law.

(a–1) A district clerk is exempt from the requirements of Subsections (a)(4) and (5) if the electronic filing system used by the clerk for accepting electronic documents or electronic digital media from an attorney representing the state does not have the capability of accepting electronic filings from a defendant and the system was established or procured before June 1, 2009. If the electronic filing system described by this subsection is substantially upgraded or is replaced with a new system, the exemption provided by this subsection is no longer applicable.

(b) At any time during or after a criminal proceeding, the court reporter shall release for safekeeping any firearm or contraband received as an exhibit in that proceeding to:

(1) the sheriff; or

(2) in a county with a population of 500,000 or more, the law enforcement agency that collected, seized, or took possession of the firearm or contraband or produced the firearm or contraband at the proceeding.

(c) The sheriff or the law enforcement agency, as applicable, shall receive and hold the exhibits consisting of firearms or contraband and release them only to the person or persons authorized by the court in which such exhibits have been received or dispose of them as provided by Chapter 18.

(d) In this article, "eligible exhibit" means an exhibit filed with the clerk that:

(1) is not a firearm or contraband;

(2) has not been ordered by the court to be returned to its owner; and

(3) is not an exhibit in another pending criminal action.

(e) An eligible exhibit may be disposed of as provided by this article:

(1) on or after the first anniversary of the date on which a conviction becomes final in the case, if the case is a misdemeanor or a felony for which the sentence imposed by the court is five years or less;

(2) on or after the second anniversary of the date on which a conviction becomes final in the case, if the case is a non-capital felony for which the sentence imposed by the court is greater than five years;

(3) on or after the first anniversary of the date of the acquittal of a defendant; or

(4) on or after the first anniversary of the date of the death of a defendant.

(f) Subject to Subsections (g), (h), (i), and (j), a clerk may dispose of an eligible exhibit or may deliver the eligible exhibit to the county purchasing agent for disposal as surplus or salvage property under Section 263.152, Local Government Code, if on the date provided by Subsection (e) the clerk has not received a request for the exhibit from either the attorney representing the state in the case or the attorney representing the defendant.

(f–1) Notwithstanding Section 263.156, Local Government Code, or any other law, the commissioners court shall remit 50 percent of any proceeds of the disposal of an eligible exhibit as surplus or salvage property as described by Subsection (f), less the reasonable expense of keeping the exhibit before disposal and the costs of that disposal, to each of the following:

(1) the county treasury, to be used only to defray the costs incurred by the district clerk of the county for the management, maintenance, or destruction of eligible exhibits in the county; and

(2) the state treasury to the credit of the compensation to victims of crime fund established under Subchapter B, Chapter 56.

(g) A clerk in a county with a population of less than two million must provide written notice by mail to the attorney representing the state in the case and the attorney representing the defendant before disposing of an eligible exhibit.

(h) The notice under Subsection (g) of this article must:

(1) describe the eligible exhibit;

(2) give the name and address of the court holding the exhibit; and

(3) state that the eligible exhibit will be disposed of unless a written request is received by the clerk before the 31st day after the date of notice.

(i) If a request is not received by a clerk covered by Subsection (g) before the 31st day after the date of notice, the clerk may dispose of the eligible exhibit in the manner permitted by this article, including the delivery of the eligible exhibit for disposal as surplus or salvage property as described by Subsection (f).

(j) If a request is timely received, the clerk shall deliver the eligible exhibit to the person making the request if the court determines the requestor is the owner of the eligible exhibit.

(k) In this article, "digital multimedia evidence" means evidence stored or transmitted in a binary form and includes data representing documents, audio, video metadata, and any other information attached to a digital file.

Acts 1965, 59th Leg., vol. 2, p. 317, ch. 722, eff. Jan. 1, 1966. Amended by Acts 1979, 66th Leg., p. 212, ch. 119, § 1, eff. Aug. 27, 1979; Acts 1993, 73rd Leg., ch. 967, § 1, eff. Sept. 1, 1993; Acts 1999, 76th Leg., ch. 580, § 1, eff. Sept. 1, 1999; Acts 2005, 79th Leg., ch. 1026, § 1, eff. Sept. 1, 2005; Acts 2009, 81st Leg., ch. 795, § 10, eff. June 19, 2009; Acts 2009, 81st Leg., ch. 829, § 1, eff. Sept. 1, 2009; Acts 2011, 82nd Leg., ch. 911 (S.B. 1228), § 1, eff. June 17, 2011; Acts 2011, 82nd Leg., ch. 1163 (H.B. 2702), § 6, eff. Sept. 1, 2011; Acts 2013, 83rd Leg., ch. 946 (H.B. 1728), § 2, eff. June 14, 2013.

Art. 2.211.   Hate Crime Reporting

In addition to performing duties required by Article 2.21, a clerk of a district or county court in which an affirmative finding under Article 42.014 is requested shall report that request to the Texas Judicial Council, along with a statement as to whether the request was granted by the court and, if so, whether the affirmative finding was entered in the judgment in the case. The clerk shall make the report required by this article not later than the 30th day after the date the judgment is entered in the case.

Added by Acts 2001, 77th Leg., ch. 85, § 4.01, eff. Sept. 1, 2001.

Art. 2.212.   Writ of Attachment Reporting

Not later than the 30th day after the date a writ of attachment is issued in a district court, statutory county court, or county court, the clerk of the court shall report to the Texas Judicial Council:

(1) the date the attachment was issued;

(2) whether the attachment was issued in connection with a grand jury investigation, criminal trial, or other criminal proceeding;

(3) the names of the person requesting and the judge issuing the attachment; and

(4) the statutory authority under which the attachment was issued.

Added by Acts 2017, 85th Leg., ch. 292 (S.B. 291), § 1, eff. Sept. 1, 2017.

Section 9 of Acts 2017, 85th Leg., ch. 292 (S.B. 291) provides:

"The change in law made by this Act applies only to a writ of attachment issued on or after the effective date [Sept. 1, 2017] of this Act. A writ of attachment issued before the effective date of this Act is governed by the law in effect on the date the writ was issued, and the former law is continued in effect for that purpose."

Art. 2.22.   Power of deputy clerks

Whenever a duty is imposed upon the clerk of the district or county court, the same may be lawfully performed by his deputy.

Acts 1965, 59th Leg., vol. 2, p. 317, ch. 722, eff. Jan. 1, 1966.

Art. 2.23.   Report to Attorney General

(a) The clerks of the district and county courts shall, when requested in writing by the Attorney General, report to the Attorney General not later than the 10th day after the date the request is received, and in the form prescribed by the Attorney General, information in court records that relates to a criminal matter, including information requested by the Attorney General for purposes of federal habeas review.

(b) A state agency or the office of an attorney representing the state shall, when requested in writing by the Attorney General, provide to the Attorney General any record that is needed for purposes of federal habeas review. The agency or office must provide the record not later than the 10th day after the date the request is received and in the form prescribed by the Attorney General.

(c) A district court, county court, state agency, or office of an attorney representing the state may not restrict or delay the reproduction or delivery of a record requested by the Attorney General under this article.

Acts 1965, 59th Leg., vol. 2, p. 317, ch. 722, eff. Jan. 1, 1966. Amended by Acts 2005, 79th Leg., ch. 933, § 1, eff. Sept. 1, 2005.

Art. 2.24. Authenticating officer

(a) The governor may appoint an authenticating officer, in accordance with Subsection (b) of this article, and delegate to that officer the power to sign for the governor or to use the governor's facsimile signature for signing any document that does not have legal effect under this code unless it is signed by the governor.

(b) To appoint an authenticating officer under this article, the governor shall file with the secretary of state a document that contains:

(1) the name of the person to be appointed as authenticating officer and a copy of the person's signature;

(2) the types of documents the authenticating officer is authorized to sign for the governor; and

(3) the types of documents on which the authenticating officer is authorized to use the governor's facsimile signature.

(c) The governor may revoke an appointment made under this article by filing with the secretary of state a document that expressly revokes the appointment of the authenticating agent.

(d) If an authenticating officer signs a document described in Subsection (a) of this article, the officer shall sign in the following manner: "_____, Authenticating Officer for Governor _____."

(e) If a provision of this code requires the governor's signature on a document before that document has legal effect, the authorized signature of the authenticating officer or an authorized facsimile signature of the governor gives the document the same legal effect as if it had been signed manually by the governor.

Added by Acts 1983, 68th Leg., p. 4289, ch. 684, § 1, eff. June 19, 1983.

Art. 2.25. Reporting Certain Aliens to Federal Government

A judge shall report to the United States Immigration and Naturalization Service a person who has been convicted in the judge's court of a crime or has been placed on deferred adjudication for a felony and is an illegal criminal alien as defined by Section 493.015(a), Government Code.

Added by Acts 1995, 74th Leg., ch. 85, § 2, eff. May 16, 1995.

Art. 2.251. Duties Related to Immigration Detainer Requests

(a) A law enforcement agency that has custody of a person subject to an immigration detainer request issued by United States Immigration and Customs Enforcement shall:

(1) comply with, honor, and fulfill any request made in the detainer request provided by the federal government; and

(2) inform the person that the person is being held pursuant to an immigration detainer request issued by United States Immigration and Customs Enforcement.

(b) A law enforcement agency is not required to perform a duty imposed by Subsection (a) with respect to a person who has provided proof that the person is a citizen of the United States or that the person has lawful immigration status in the United States, such as a Texas driver's license or similar government-issued identification.

Added by Acts 2017, 85th Leg., ch. 4 (S.B. 4), § 2.01, eff. Sept. 1, 2017.

Section 7.01 of Acts 2017, 85th Leg., ch. 4 (S.B. 4) provides:

"It is the intent of the legislature that every provision, section, subsection, sentence, clause, phrase, or word in this Act, and every application of the provisions in this Act to each person or entity, are severable from each other. If any application of any provision in this Act to any person, group of persons, or circumstances is found by a court to be invalid for any reason, the remaining applications of that provision to all other persons and circumstances shall be severed and may not be affected."

Art. 2.26. Digital Signature and Electronic Documents

(a) In this section, "digital signature" means an electronic identifier intended by the person using it to have the same force and effect as the use of a manual signature.

(b) An electronically transmitted document issued or received by a court or a clerk of the court in a criminal matter is considered signed if a digital signature is transmitted with the document.

(b–1) An electronically transmitted document is a written document for all purposes and exempt from any additional writing requirement under this code or any other law of this state.

(c) This section does not preclude any symbol from being valid as a signature under other applicable law, including Section 1.201(39), Business & Commerce Code.

(d) The use of a digital signature under this section is subject to criminal laws pertaining to fraud and computer crimes, including Chapters 32 and 33, Penal Code.

Added by Acts 1999, 76th Leg., ch. 701, § 1, eff. Aug. 30, 1999. Amended by Acts 2005, 79th Leg., ch. 312, §§ 1, 2, eff. June 17, 2005.

Art. 2.27. Investigation of Certain Reports Alleging Abuse

(a) On receipt of a report that is assigned the highest priority in accordance with rules adopted by the Department of Family and Protective Services under Section 261.301(d), Family Code, and that alleges an immediate risk of physical or sexual abuse of a child that could result in the death of or serious harm to the child by a person responsible for the care, custody, or welfare of the child, a peace officer from the appropriate local law enforcement agency shall investigate the report jointly with the department or with the agency responsible for conducting an investigation under Subchapter E, Chapter 261, Family Code.[1] As soon as possible after being notified by the department of the report, but not later than 24 hours after being notified, the peace officer shall accompany the department investigator in initially responding to the report.

(b) On receipt of a report of abuse or neglect or other complaint of a resident of a nursing home, convalescent home, or other related institution under Section 242.126(c)(1), Health and Safety Code, the appropriate local law enforcement agency shall investigate the report as required by Section 242.135, Health and Safety Code.

Added by Acts 2001, 77th Leg., ch. 492, § 1, eff. Sept. 1, 2001. Amended by Acts 2003, 78th Leg., ch. 867, § 2, eff. Sept. 1, 2003; Acts 2003, 78th Leg., ch. 1210, § 5, eff. Sept. 1, 2003. Amended by Acts 2011, 82nd Leg., ch. 91 (S.B. 1303), § 6.001, eff. Sept. 1, 2011.

[1] V.T.C.A., Family Code § 261.401 et seq.

Art. 2.271. Investigation of Certain Reports Alleging Abuse, Neglect, or Exploitation

Notwithstanding Article 2.27, on receipt of a report of abuse, neglect, exploitation, or other complaint of a resident of a nursing home, convalescent home, or other related institution or an assisted living facility, under Section 260A.007(c)(1), Health and Safety Code, the appropriate local law enforcement agency shall investigate the report as required by Section 260A.017, Health and Safety Code.

Added by Acts 2011, 82nd Leg., 1st C.S., ch. 7 (S.B. 7), § 1.05(d), eff. Sept. 28, 2011.

Art. 2.272. Law Enforcement Response to Child Safety Check Alert

(a) If a peace officer locates a child or other person listed on the Texas Crime Information Center's child safety check alert list established under Section 261.3022, Family Code, the officer shall:

(1) immediately contact the Department of Family and Protective Services on the department's dedicated law-enforcement telephone number for statewide intake;

(2) request information from the department regarding the circumstances of the case involving the child or other person; and

(3) request information from the child and the other person regarding the child's safety, well-being, and current residence.

(b) The peace officer may temporarily detain the child or other person to ensure the safety and well-being of the child.

(c) If the peace officer determines that the circumstances described by Section 262.104, Family Code, exist, the officer may take temporary possession of the child without a court order as provided by Section 262.104, Family Code. If the peace officer does not take temporary possession of the child, the officer shall obtain the child's current address and any other relevant information and report that information to the Department of Family and Protective Services.

(d) A peace officer who locates a child or other person listed on the Texas Crime Information Center's child safety check alert list and who reports the child's or other person's current address and other relevant information to the Department of Family and Protective Services shall report to the Texas Crime Information Center that the child or other person has been located and to whom the child was released, as applicable.

Added by Acts 2015, 84th Leg., ch. 1056 (H.B. 2053), § 6, eff. Sept. 1, 2015.

Art. 2.273. Release of Child by Law Enforcement Officer

(a) A law enforcement officer who takes possession of a child under Section 262.104, Family Code, may release the child to:

(1) a residential child-care facility licensed by the Department of Family and Protective Services under Chapter 42, Human Resources Code, if the facility is authorized by the department to take possession of the child;

(2) a juvenile probation department;

(3) the Department of Family and Protective Services; or

(4) any other person authorized by law to take possession of the child.

(b) Before a law enforcement officer may release a child to a person authorized by law to take possession of the child other than a governmental entity, the officer shall:

(1) verify with the National Crime Information Center that the child is not a missing child;

(2) search the relevant databases of the National Crime Information Center system, including those pertaining to protection orders, historical protection orders, warrants, sex offender registries, and persons on supervised release to:

(A) verify that the person to whom the child is being released:

(i) does not have a protective order issued against the person; and

(ii) is not registered as a sex offender unless the person is the child's parent or guardian and there are no restrictions regarding the person's contact with the child; and

(B) obtain any other information the Department of Family and Protective Services considers:

(i) relevant to protect the welfare of the child; or

(ii) reflective of the responsibility of the person to whom the child is being released;

(3) call the Department of Family and Protective Services Texas Abuse Hotline to determine whether the person to whom the child is being released is

listed in the registry as a person who abused or neglected a child;

(4) verify that the person to whom the child is being released is at least 18 years of age; and

(5) maintain a record regarding the child's placement, including:

(A) identifying information about the child, including the child's name or pseudonyms; and

(B) the name and address of the person to whom the child is being released.

Added by Acts 2017, 85th Leg., ch. 926 (S.B. 1571), § 1, eff. Sept. 1, 2017.

Art. 2.28. Duties Regarding Misused Identity

On receipt of information to the effect that a person's identifying information was falsely given by a person arrested as the arrested person's identifying information, the local law enforcement agency responsible for collecting identifying information on arrested persons in the county in which the arrest was made shall:

(1) notify the person that:

(A) the person's identifying information was misused by another person arrested in the county;

(B) the person may file a declaration with the Department of Public Safety under Section 411.0421, Government Code; and

(C) the person is entitled to expunction of information contained in criminal records and files under Chapter 55 of this code; and

(2) notify the Department of Public Safety regarding:

(A) the misuse of the identifying information;

(B) the actual identity of the person arrested, if known by the agency; and

(C) whether the agency was able to notify the person whose identifying information was misused.

Added by Acts 2003, 78th Leg., ch. 339, § 1, eff. Sept. 1, 2003.

Art. 2.29. Report Required in Connection With Fraudulent Use or Possession of Identifying Information

(a) A peace officer to whom an alleged violation of Section 32.51, Penal Code, is reported shall make a written report to the law enforcement agency that employs the peace officer that includes the following information:

(1) the name of the victim;

(2) the name of the suspect, if known;

(3) the type of identifying information obtained, possessed, transferred, or used in violation of Section 32.51, Penal Code; and

(4) the results of any investigation.

(b) On the victim's request, the law enforcement agency shall provide the report created under Subsection (a) to the victim. In providing the report, the law enforcement agency shall redact any otherwise confidential information that is included in the report, other than the information described by Subsection (a).

Added by Acts 2005, 79th Leg., ch. 294, § 1(a), eff. Sept. 1, 2005.

Art. 2.295. Report required in connection with unauthorized acquisition or transfer of certain financial information

(a) A peace officer to whom an alleged violation of Section 31.17, Penal Code, is reported shall make a written report to the law enforcement agency that employs the peace officer that includes the following information:

(1) the name of the victim;

(2) the name of the suspect, if known;

(3) the type of financial sight order or payment card information obtained or transferred in violation of Section 31.17, Penal Code; and

(4) the results of any investigation.

(b) On the victim's request, the law enforcement agency shall provide the report created under Subsection (a) to the victim. In providing the report, the law enforcement agency shall redact any otherwise confidential information that is included in the report, other than the information described by Subsection (a).

Added by Acts 2011, 82nd Leg., ch. 260 (H.B. 1215), § 2, eff. Sept. 1, 2011.

Art. 2.30. Report Concerning Certain Assaultive or Terroristic Offenses

(a) This article applies only to the following offenses:

(1) assault under Section 22.01, Penal Code;

(2) aggravated assault under Section 22.02, Penal Code;

(3) sexual assault under Section 22.011, Penal Code;

(4) aggravated sexual assault under Section 22.021, Penal Code; and

(5) terroristic threat under Section 22.07, Penal Code.

(b) A peace officer who investigates the alleged commission of an offense listed under Subsection (a) shall prepare a written report that includes the information required under Article 5.05(a).

(c) On request of a victim of an offense listed under Subsection (a), the local law enforcement agency responsible for investigating the commission of the offense shall provide the victim, at no cost to the victim, with any information that is:

(1) contained in the written report prepared under Subsection (b);

(2) described by Article 5.05(a)(1) or (2); and

(3) not exempt from disclosure under Chapter 552, Government Code, or other law.

Added by Acts 2007, 80th Leg., ch. 1057, § 1, eff. Sept. 1, 2007.

Art. 2.31. County Jailers

If a jailer licensed under Chapter 1701, Occupations Code, has successfully completed a training program provided by the sheriff,[1] the jailer may execute lawful process issued to the jailer by any magistrate or court on a person confined in the jail at which the jailer is employed to the same extent that a peace officer is authorized to execute process under Article 2.13(b)(2), including:

(1) a warrant under Chapter 15, 17, or 18;

(2) a capias under Chapter 17 or 23;

(3) a subpoena under Chapter 20 or 24; or

(4) an attachment under Chapter 20 or 24.

Added by Acts 2011, 82nd Leg., ch. 176 (S.B. 604), § 1, eff. Sept. 1, 2011; Acts 2011, 82nd Leg., ch. 1341 (S.B. 1233), § 2, eff. June 17, 2011.

[1] The text as added by Acts 2011, 82nd Leg., ch. 1341 (S.B. 1233), § 2, did not include "has successfully completed a training program provided by the sheriff,".

Art. 2.32. Electronic recording of custodial interrogations

(a) In this article:

(1) "Electronic recording" means an audiovisual electronic recording, or an audio recording if an audiovisual electronic recording is unavailable, that is authentic, accurate, and unaltered.

(2) "Law enforcement agency" means an agency of the state, or of a county, municipality, or other political subdivision of this state, that employs peace officers who, in the routine performance of the officers' duties, conduct custodial interrogations of persons suspected of committing criminal offenses.

(3) "Place of detention" means a police station or other building that is a place of operation for a law enforcement agency, including a municipal police department or county sheriff's department, and is owned or operated by the law enforcement agency for the purpose of detaining persons in connection with the suspected violation of a penal law. The term does not include a courthouse.

(b) Unless good cause exists that makes electronic recording infeasible, a law enforcement agency shall make a complete and contemporaneous electronic recording of any custodial interrogation that occurs in a place of detention and is of a person suspected of committing or charged with the commission of an offense under:

(1) Section 19.02, Penal Code (murder);

(2) Section 19.03, Penal Code (capital murder);

(3) Section 20.03, Penal Code (kidnapping);

(4) Section 20.04, Penal Code (aggravated kidnapping);

(5) Section 20A.02, Penal Code (trafficking of persons);

(6) Section 20A.03, Penal Code (continuous trafficking of persons);

(7) Section 21.02, Penal Code (continuous sexual abuse of young child or children);

(8) Section 21.11, Penal Code (indecency with a child);

(9) Section 21.12, Penal Code (improper relationship between educator and student);

(10) Section 22.011, Penal Code (sexual assault);

(11) Section 22.021, Penal Code (aggravated sexual assault); or

(12) Section 43.25, Penal Code (sexual performance by a child).

(c) For purposes of Subsection (b), an electronic recording of a custodial interrogation is complete only if the recording:

(1) begins at or before the time the person being interrogated enters the area of the place of detention in which the custodial interrogation will take place or

receives a warning described by Section 2(a), Article 38.22, whichever is earlier; and

(2) continues until the time the interrogation ceases.

(d) For purposes of Subsection (b), good cause that makes electronic recording infeasible includes the following:

(1) the person being interrogated refused to respond or cooperate in a custodial interrogation at which an electronic recording was being made, provided that:

(A) a contemporaneous recording of the refusal was made; or

(B) the peace officer or agent of the law enforcement agency conducting the interrogation attempted, in good faith, to record the person's refusal but the person was unwilling to have the refusal recorded, and the peace officer or agent contemporaneously, in writing, documented the refusal;

(2) the statement was not made as the result of a custodial interrogation, including a statement that was made spontaneously by the accused and not in response to a question by a peace officer;

(3) the peace officer or agent of the law enforcement agency conducting the interrogation attempted, in good faith, to record the interrogation but the recording equipment did not function, the officer or agent inadvertently operated the equipment incorrectly, or the equipment malfunctioned or stopped operating without the knowledge of the officer or agent;

(4) exigent public safety concerns prevented or rendered infeasible the making of an electronic recording of the statement; or

(5) the peace officer or agent of the law enforcement agency conducting the interrogation reasonably believed at the time the interrogation commenced that the person being interrogated was not taken into custody for or being interrogated concerning the commission of an offense listed in Subsection (b).

(e) A recording of a custodial interrogation that complies with this article is exempt from public disclosure as provided by Section 552.108, Government Code.

Added by Acts 2017, 85th Leg., ch. 686 (H.B. 34), § 1, eff. Sept. 1, 2017; Acts 2017, 85th Leg., ch. 1122 (S.B. 1253), § 1, eff. Sept. 1, 2017.

Section 11 of Acts 2017, 85th Leg., ch. 686 (H.B. 34) provides:

"Article 2.32 and Section 9, Article 38.22, Code of Criminal Procedure, as added by this Act, apply to the use of a statement resulting from a custodial interrogation that occurs on or after March 1, 2018, regardless of whether the criminal offense giving rise to that interrogation is committed before, on, or after that date."

CHAPTER THREE. DEFINITIONS

Art. 3.01. Words and phrases

All words, phrases and terms used in this Code are to be taken and understood in their usual acceptation in common language, except where specially defined.

Acts 1965, 59th Leg., vol. 2, p. 317, ch. 722, eff. Jan. 1, 1966. Amended by Acts 1975, 64th Leg., p. 909, ch. 341, § 1, eff. June 19, 1975.

Art. 3.02. Criminal action

A criminal action is prosecuted in the name of the State of Texas against the accused, and is conducted by some person acting under the authority of the State, in accordance with its laws.

Acts 1965, 59th Leg., vol. 2, p. 317, ch. 722, eff. Jan. 1, 1966.

Art. 3.03. Officers

The general term "officers" includes both magistrates and peace officers.

Acts 1965, 59th Leg., vol. 2, p. 317, ch. 722, eff. Jan. 1, 1966.

Art. 3.04. Official misconduct

In this code:

(1) "Official misconduct" means an offense that is an intentional or knowing violation of a law committed by a public servant while acting in an official capacity as a public servant.

(2) "Public servant" has the meaning assigned by Section 1.07, Penal Code.

Added by Acts 1993, 73rd Leg., ch. 900, § 1.03, eff. Sept. 1, 1994.

Art. 3.05. Racial profiling

In this code, "racial profiling" means a law enforcement-initiated action based on an individual's race, ethnicity, or national origin rather than on the individual's behavior or on information identifying the individual as having engaged in criminal activity.

Added by Acts 2001, 77th Leg., ch. 947, § 2, eff. Sept. 1, 2001.

COURTS AND CRIMINAL JURISDICTION

CHAPTER FOUR. COURTS AND CRIMINAL JURISDICTION

Art. 4.01. What courts have criminal jurisdiction

The following courts have jurisdiction in criminal actions:

1. The Court of Criminal Appeals;

2. Courts of appeals;

3. The district courts;

4. The criminal district courts;

5. The magistrates appointed by the judges of the district courts of Bexar County, Dallas County, Tarrant County, or Travis County that give preference to criminal cases and the magistrates appointed by the judges of the criminal district courts of Dallas County or Tarrant County;

6. The county courts;

7. All county courts at law with criminal jurisdiction;

8. County criminal courts;

9. Justice courts;

10. Municipal courts; and

11. The magistrates appointed by the judges of the district courts of Lubbock County.

Acts 1965, 59th Leg., vol. 2, p. 317, ch. 722, eff. Jan. 1, 1966. Amended by Acts 1981, 67th Leg., p. 801, ch. 291, § 101, eff. Sept. 1, 1981; Acts 1983, 68th Leg., p. 883, ch. 204, § 2, eff. Aug. 29, 1983; Acts 1989, 71st Leg., ch. 25, § 3, eff. Aug. 28, 1989; Acts 1989, 71st Leg., ch. 79, § 2, eff. May 15, 1989; Acts 1989, 71st Leg., ch. 1068, § 3, eff. Aug. 28, 1989; Acts 1991, 72nd Leg., ch. 16, § 4.03, eff. Aug. 26, 1991; Acts 1993, 73rd Leg., ch. 413, § 2, eff. Sept. 1, 1993.

Art. 4.02. Existing courts continued

No existing courts shall be abolished by this Code and shall continue with the jurisdiction, organization, terms and powers currently existing unless otherwise provided by law.

Acts 1965, 59th Leg., vol. 2, p. 317, ch. 722, eff. Jan. 1, 1966.

Art. 4.03. Courts of Appeals

The Courts of Appeals shall have appellate jurisdiction coextensive with the limits of their respective districts in all criminal cases except those in which the death penalty has been assessed. This Article shall not be so construed as to embrace any case which has been appealed from any inferior court to the county court, the county criminal court, or county court at law, in which the fine imposed or affirmed by the county court, the county criminal court or county court at law does not exceed one hundred dollars, unless the sole issue is the constitutionality of the statute or ordinance on which the conviction is based.

Acts 1965, 59th Leg., vol. 2, p. 317, ch. 722, eff. Jan. 1, 1966. Amended by Acts 1981, 67th Leg., p. 802, ch. 291, § 102, eff. Sept. 1, 1981; Acts 2011, 82nd Leg., ch. 1324 (S.B. 480), § 1, eff. June 17, 2011.

Art. 4.04. Court of Criminal Appeals

Sec. 1. The Court of Criminal Appeals and each judge thereof shall have, and is hereby given, the power and authority to grant and issue and cause the issuance of writs of habeas corpus, and, in criminal law matters, the writs of mandamus, procedendo, prohibition, and certiorari. The court and each judge thereof shall have, and is hereby given, the power and authority to grant and issue and cause the issuance of such other writs as may be necessary to protect its jurisdiction or enforce its judgments.

Sec. 2. The Court of Criminal Appeals shall have, and is hereby given, final appellate and review jurisdiction in criminal cases coextensive with the limits of the state, and its determinations shall be final. The appeal of all cases in which the death penalty has been assessed shall be to the Court of Criminal Appeals. In addition, the Court of Criminal Appeals may, on its own motion, with or without a petition for such discretionary review being filed by one of the parties, review any decision of a court of appeals in a criminal case. Discretionary review by the Court of Criminal Appeals is not a matter of right, but of sound judicial discretion.

Acts 1965, 59th Leg., vol. 2, p. 317, ch. 722, eff. Jan. 1, 1966. Amended by Acts 1971, 62nd Leg., p. 2536, §6, eff. Aug. 30, 1971; Acts 1981, 67th Leg., p. 802, ch. 291, § 103, eff. Sept. 1, 1981.

Art. 4.05. Jurisdiction of district courts

District courts and criminal district courts shall have original jurisdiction in criminal cases of the grade of felony, of all misdemeanors involving official misconduct, and of misdemeanor cases transferred to the district court under Article 4.17 of this code.

Acts 1965, 59th Leg., vol. 2, p. 317, ch. 722, eff. Jan. 1, 1966. Amended by Acts 1983, 68th Leg., p. 1585, ch. 303, § 5, eff. Jan. 1, 1984.

Art. 4.06. When felony includes misdemeanor

Upon the trial of a felony case, the court shall hear and determine the case as to any grade of offense included in the indictment, whether the proof shows a felony or a misdemeanor.

Acts 1965, 59th Leg., vol. 2, p. 317, ch. 722, eff. Jan. 1, 1966.

Art. 4.07. Jurisdiction of county courts

The county courts shall have original jurisdiction of all misdemeanors of which exclusive original jurisdiction is not given to the justice court, and when the fine to be imposed shall exceed five hundred dollars.

Acts 1965, 59th Leg., vol. 2, p. 317, ch. 722, eff. Jan. 1, 1966. Amended by Acts 1991, 72nd Leg., ch. 108, § 3, eff. Sept. 1, 1991.

Art. 4.08. Appellate jurisdiction of county courts

The county courts shall have appellate jurisdiction in criminal cases of which justice courts and other inferior courts have original jurisdiction.

Acts 1965, 59th Leg., vol. 2, p. 317, ch. 722, eff. Jan. 1, 1966.

Art. 4.09. Appeals from inferior court

If the jurisdiction of any county court has been transferred to the district court or to a county court at law, then an appeal from a justice or other inferior court will lie to the court to which such appellate jurisdiction has been transferred.

Acts 1965, 59th Leg., vol. 2, p. 317, ch. 722, eff. Jan. 1, 1966.

Art. 4.10. To forfeit bail bonds

County courts and county courts at law shall have jurisdiction in the forfeiture and final judgment of all bail bonds and personal bonds taken in criminal cases of which said courts have jurisdiction.

Acts 1965, 59th Leg., vol. 2, p. 317, ch. 722, eff. Jan. 1, 1966.

Art. 4.11. Jurisdiction of justice courts

(a) Justices of the peace shall have original jurisdiction in criminal cases:

(1) punishable by fine only or punishable by:

(A) a fine; and

(B) as authorized by statute, a sanction not consisting of confinement or imprisonment; or

(2) arising under Chapter 106, Alcoholic Beverage Code, that do not include confinement as an authorized sanction.

(b) The fact that a conviction in a justice court has as a consequence the imposition of a penalty or sanction by an agency or entity other than the court, such as a denial, suspension, or revocation of a privilege, does not affect the original jurisdiction of the justice court.

(c) A justice court has concurrent jurisdiction with a municipal court in criminal cases that arise in the municipality's extraterritorial jurisdiction and that arise under an ordinance of the municipality applicable to the extraterritorial jurisdiction under Section 216.902, Local Government Code.

Acts 1965, 59th Leg., vol. 2, p. 317, ch. 722, eff. Jan. 1, 1966. Amended by Acts 1991, 72nd Leg., ch. 108, § 4, eff. Sept. 1, 1991; Acts 1995, 74th Leg., ch. 449, § 1, eff. Sept. 1, 1995; 1997, 75th Leg., ch. 533, § 1, eff. Sept. 1, 1997; Acts 1997, 75th Leg., ch. 1013, § 38, eff. Sept. 1, 1997; Acts 2007, 80th Leg., ch. 612, § 13, eff. Sept. 1, 2007.

Art. 4.12. Misdemeanor cases; precinct in which defendant to be tried in justice court

(a) Except as otherwise provided by this article, a misdemeanor case to be tried in justice court shall be tried:

(1) in the precinct in which the offense was committed;

(2) in the precinct in which the defendant or any of the defendants reside;

(3) with the written consent of the state and each defendant or the defendant's attorney, in any other precinct within the county; or

(4) if the offense was committed in a county with a population of 3.3 million or more, in any precinct in the county that is adjacent to the precinct in which the offense was committed.

(b) In any misdemeanor case in which the offense was committed in a precinct where there is no qualified justice court, then trial shall be held:

(1) in the next adjacent precinct in the same county which has a duly qualified justice court; or

(2) in the precinct in which the defendant may reside.

(c) In any misdemeanor case in which each justice of the peace in the precinct where the offense was committed is disqualified for any reason, such case may be tried in the next adjoining precinct in the same county having a duly qualified justice of the peace.

(d) A defendant who is taken before a magistrate in accordance with Article 15.18 may waive trial by jury and enter a written plea of guilty or nolo contendere.

(e) The justices of the peace in each county shall, by majority vote, adopt local rules of administration regarding the transfer of a pending misdemeanor case from one precinct to a different precinct.

Acts 1965, 59th Leg., vol. 2, p. 317, ch. 722, eff. Jan. 1, 1966. Amended by Acts 1999, 76th Leg., ch. 1545, § 2, eff. Sept. 1, 1999; Acts 2001, 77th Leg., ch. 145, § 1, eff. Sept. 1, 2001; Acts 2011, 82nd Leg., ch. 1086 (S.B. 1200), § 1, eff. Sept. 1, 2011; Acts 2011, 82nd Leg., 1st C.S., ch. 3 (H.B. 79), § 5.05, eff. Jan. 1, 2012.

Art. 4.13. Justice may forfeit bond

A justice of the peace shall have the power to take forfeitures of all bonds given for the appearance of any party at his court, regardless of the amount.

Acts 1965, 59th Leg., vol. 2, p. 317, ch. 722, eff. Jan. 1, 1966.

Art. 4.14. Jurisdiction of municipal court

(a) A municipal court, including a municipal court of record, shall have exclusive original jurisdiction within the territorial limits of the municipality in all criminal cases that:

(1) arise under the ordinances of the municipality; and

(2) are punishable by a fine not to exceed:

(A) $2,000 in all cases arising under municipal ordinances that govern fire safety, zoning, or public health and sanitation, other than the dumping of refuse;

(B) $4,000 in cases arising under municipal ordinances that govern the dumping of refuse; or

(C) $500 in all other cases arising under a municipal ordinance.

(b) The municipal court shall have concurrent jurisdiction with the justice court of a precinct in which the municipality is located in all criminal cases arising under state law that:

(1) arise within the territorial limits of the municipality and are punishable by fine only, as defined in Subsection (c) of this article; or

(2) arise under Chapter 106, Alcoholic Beverage Code, and do not include confinement as an authorized sanction.

(c) In this article, an offense which is punishable by "fine only" is defined as an offense that is punishable by fine and such sanctions, if any, as authorized by statute not consisting of confinement in jail or imprisonment.

(d) The fact that a conviction in a municipal court has as a consequence the imposition of a penalty or sanction by an agency or entity other than the court, such as a denial, suspension, or revocation of a privilege, does not affect the original jurisdiction of the municipal court.

(e) The municipal court has jurisdiction in the forfeiture and final judgment of all bail bonds and personal bonds taken in criminal cases of which the court has jurisdiction.

(f) A municipality with a population of 1.19 million or more and another municipality contiguous to that municipality may enter into an agreement providing concurrent jurisdiction for the municipal courts of either jurisdiction for all criminal cases arising from offenses under state law that are:

(1) committed on the boundary of those municipalities or in one or both of the following areas:

(A) within 200 yards of that boundary; or

(B) within 2.25 miles of that boundary on a segment of highway in the state highway system that traverses a major water supply reservoir; and

(2) punishable by fine only.

(g) A municipality may enter into an agreement with a contiguous municipality or a municipality with boundaries that are within one-half mile of the municipality seeking to enter into the agreement to establish concurrent jurisdiction of the municipal courts in the municipalities and provide original jurisdiction to a municipal court in which a case is brought as if the municipal court were located in the municipality in which the case arose, for:

(1) all cases in which either municipality has jurisdiction under Subsection (a); and

(2) cases that arise under Section 821.022, Health and Safety Code.

Acts 1965, 59th Leg., vol. 2, p. 317, ch. 722, eff. Jan. 1, 1966. Amended by Acts 1983, 68th Leg., p. 3840, ch. 601, § 3, eff. Sept. 1, 1983; Acts 1985, 69th Leg., ch. 329, § 3, eff. Sept. 1, 1985; Acts 1987, 70th Leg., ch. 641, § 2, eff. Sept. 1, 1987; Acts 1987, 70th Leg., ch. 680, § 1, eff. Sept. 1, 1987; Acts 1995, 74th Leg., ch. 449, § 3, eff. Sept. 1, 1995; Acts 1997, 75th Leg., ch. 533, § 2, eff. Sept. 1, 1997; Acts 1997, 75th Leg., ch. 1013, § 39, eff. Sept. 1, 1997; Acts 2009, 81st Leg., ch. 230, § 1, eff. Sept. 1, 2009; Acts 2011, 82nd Leg., ch. 76 (H.B. 984), § 2, eff. May 19, 2011; Acts 2015, 84th Leg., ch. 680 (H.B. 274), § 3, eff. Sept. 1, 2015; Acts 2015, 84th Leg., ch. 935 (H.B. 2398), § 1, eff. Sept. 1, 2015; Acts 2015, 84th Leg., ch. 1154 (S.B. 631), § 1, eff. June 19, 2015; Acts 2017, 85th Leg., ch. 1004 (H.B. 1264), § 1, eff. Sept. 1, 2017.

Section 4 of Acts 2015, 84th Leg., ch. 680 (H.B. 274) provides:
"The change in law made by this Act applies only to an offense committed on or after the effective date of this Act [Sept. 1, 2015]." An offense committed before the effective date of this Act is governed by the law in effect when the offense was committed, and the former law is continued in effect for that purpose. For purposes of this section, an offense was committed before the effective date of this Act if any element of the offense was committed before that date."

Sections 42 and 43 of Acts 2015, 84th Leg., ch. 935 (H.B. 2398) provide:
"Sec. 42. The changes in law made by this Act apply only to an offense committed or conduct that occurs on or after the effective date [Sept. 1, 2015] of this Act. An offense committed or conduct that occurs before the effective date of this Act is governed by the law in effect on the date the offense was committed or the conduct occurred, and the former law is continued in effect for that purpose. For purposes of this section, an offense is committed or conduct occurs before the effective date of this Act if any element of the offense or conduct occurs before that date.

"Sec. 43. To the extent of any conflict, this Act prevails over another Act of the 84th Legislature, Regular Session, 2015, relating to nonsubstantive additions to and corrections in enacted codes."

Section 3 of Acts 2015, 84th Leg., ch. 1154 (S.B. 631) provides:
"The change in law made by this Act applies only to an offense committed on or after the effective date [June 19, 2015] of this Act. An offense committed before the effective date of this Act is governed by the law in effect when the offense was committed, and the former law is continued in effect for that purpose. For purposes of this section, an offense was committed before the effective date of this Act if any element of the offense occurred before that date."

Art. 4.15. May sit at any time

Justice courts and corporation courts may sit at any time to try criminal cases over which they have jurisdiction. Any case in which a fine may be assessed shall be tried in accordance with the rules of evidence and this Code.

Acts 1965, 59th Leg., vol. 2, p. 317, ch. 722, eff. Jan. 1, 1966.

Art. 4.16. Concurrent jurisdiction

When two or more courts have concurrent jurisdiction of any criminal offense, the court in which an indictment or a complaint shall first be filed shall retain jurisdiction except as provided in Article 4.12.

Acts 1965, 59th Leg., vol. 2, p. 317, ch. 722, eff. Jan. 1, 1966.

Art. 4.17. Transfer of certain misdemeanors

On a plea of not guilty to a misdemeanor offense punishable by confinement in jail, entered in a county court of a judge who is not a licensed attorney, on the motion of the state or the defendant, the judge may transfer the case to a district court having jurisdiction in the county or to a county court at law in the county presided over by a judge who is a licensed attorney. The judge may make the transfer on his own motion. The attorney representing the state in the case in county court shall continue the prosecution in the court to which the case is transferred. Provided, in no case may any such case be transferred to a district court except with the written consent of the judge of the district court to which the transfer is sought.

Added by Acts 1983, 68th Leg., p. 1586, ch. 303, § 6, eff. Jan. 1, 1984. Amended by Acts 1989, 71st Leg., ch. 295, § 1, eff. Sept. 1, 1989.

Art. 4.18. Claim of underage

(a) A claim that a district court or criminal district court does not have jurisdiction over a person because jurisdiction is exclusively in the juvenile court and that the juvenile court could not waive jurisdiction under Section 8.07(a), Penal Code, or did not waive jurisdiction under Section 8.07(b), Penal Code, must be made by written motion in bar of prosecution filed with the court in which criminal charges against the person are filed.

(b) The motion must be filed and presented to the presiding judge of the court:

(1) if the defendant enters a plea of guilty or no contest, before the plea;

(2) if the defendant's guilt or punishment is tried or determined by a jury, before selection of the jury begins; or

(3) if the defendant's guilt is tried by the court, before the first witness is sworn.

(c) Unless the motion is not contested, the presiding judge shall promptly conduct a hearing without a jury and rule on the motion. The party making the motion has the burden of establishing by a preponderance of the evidence those facts necessary for the motion to prevail.

(d) A person may not contest the jurisdiction of the court on the ground that the juvenile court has exclusive jurisdiction if:

(1) the person does not file a motion within the time requirements of this article; or

(2) the presiding judge finds under Subsection (c) that a motion made under this article does not prevail.

(e) An appellate court may review a trial court's determination under this article, if otherwise authorized by law, only after conviction in the trial court.

(f) A court that finds that it lacks jurisdiction over a case because exclusive jurisdiction is in the juvenile court shall transfer the case to the juvenile court as provided by Section 51.08, Family Code.

(g) This article does not apply to a claim of a defect or error in a discretionary transfer proceeding in juvenile court. A defendant may appeal a defect or error only as provided by Chapter 56, Family Code.

Added by Acts 1995, 74th Leg., ch. 262, § 80, eff. Jan. 1, 1996. Amended by Acts 1999, 76th Leg., ch. 1477, §§ 27, 28, eff. Sept. 1, 1999; Acts 2015, 84th Leg., ch. 74 (S.B. 888), § 1, eff. Sept. 1, 2015.

Section 5 of Acts 2015, 84th Leg., ch. 74 (S.B. 888) provides:

"The change in law made by this Act applies only to an order of a juvenile court waiving jurisdiction and transferring a child to criminal court that is issued on or after the effective date [Sept. 1, 2015] of this Act. An order of a juvenile court waiving jurisdiction and transferring a child to criminal court that is issued before the effective date of this Act is governed by the law in effect on the date the order was issued, and the former law is continued in effect for that purpose."

Art. 4.19. Transfer of person certified to stand trial as an adult

(a) Notwithstanding the order of a juvenile court to detain a person under the age of 17 who has been certified to stand trial as an adult in a certified juvenile detention facility under Section 54.02(h), Family Code, the judge of the criminal court having jurisdiction over the person may order the person to be transferred to an adult facility. A child who is transferred to an adult facility must be detained under conditions meeting the requirements of Section 51.12, Family Code.

(b) On the 17th birthday of a person described by Subsection (a) who is detained in a certified juvenile detention facility under Section 54.02(h), Family Code, the judge of the criminal court having jurisdiction over the person shall order the person to be transferred to an adult facility.

Added by Acts 2011, 82nd Leg., ch. 1078 (S.B. 1209), § 5, eff. Sept. 1, 2011. Amended by Acts 2013, 83rd Leg., ch. 1299 (H.B. 2862), § 1, eff. Sept. 1, 2013.

PREVENTION AND SUPPRESSION OF OFFENSES

CHAPTER FIVE. FAMILY VIOLENCE PREVENTION

Art. 5.01.   Legislative statement

(a) Family violence is a serious danger and threat to society and its members. Victims of family violence are entitled to the maximum protection from harm or abuse or the threat of harm or abuse as is permitted by law.

(b) In any law enforcement, prosecutorial, or judicial response to allegations of family violence, the responding law enforcement or judicial officers shall protect the victim, without regard to the relationship between the alleged offender and victim.

Added by Acts 1985, 69th Leg., ch. 583, § 1, eff. Sept. 1, 1985.

Art. 5.02.   Definitions

Definitions

Art. 5.02. In this chapter, "family violence," "family," "household," and "member of a household" have the meanings assigned by Chapter 71, Family Code.

Added by Acts 1985, 69th Leg., ch. 583, § 1, eff. Sept. 1, 1985. Amended by Acts 2003, 78th Leg., ch. 1276, § 7.002(c), eff. Sept. 1, 2003.

Art. 5.03.   Family or household relationship does not create an exception to official duties

A general duty prescribed for an officer by Chapter 2 of this code is not waived or excepted in any family violence case or investigation because of a family or household relationship between an alleged violator and the victim of family violence. A peace officer's or a magistrate's duty to prevent the commission of criminal offenses, including acts of family violence, is not waived or excepted because of a family or household relationship between the potential violator and victim.

Added by Acts 1985, 69th Leg., ch. 583, § 1, eff. Sept. 1, 1985.

Art. 5.04.   Duties of peace officers

(a) The primary duties of a peace officer who investigates a family violence allegation or who responds to a disturbance call that may involve family violence are to protect any potential victim of family violence, enforce the law of this state, enforce a protective order from another jurisdiction as provided by Chapter 88, Family Code, and make lawful arrests of violators.

(a–1) A peace officer who investigates a family violence allegation or who responds to a disturbance call that may involve family violence shall determine whether the address of the persons involved in the allegation or call matches the address of a current licensed foster home or verified agency foster home listed in the Texas Crime Information Center.

(b) A peace officer who investigates a family violence allegation or who responds to a disturbance call that may involve family violence shall advise any possible adult victim of all reasonable means to prevent further family violence, including giving written notice of a victim's legal rights and remedies and of the availability of shelter or other community services for family violence victims.

(c) A written notice required by Subsection (b) of this article is sufficient if it is in substantially the following form with the required information in English and in Spanish inserted in the notice:

"It is a crime for any person to cause you any physical injury or harm EVEN IF THAT PERSON IS A MEMBER OR FORMER MEMBER OF YOUR FAMILY OR HOUSEHOLD.

"NOTICE TO ADULT VICTIMS OF FAMILY VIOLENCE

"Please tell the investigating peace officer:

"IF you, your child, or any other household resident has been injured; or

"IF you feel you are going to be in danger when the officer leaves or later.

"You have the right to:

"ASK the local prosecutor to file a criminal complaint against the person committing family violence; and

"APPLY to a court for an order to protect you (you should consult a legal aid office, a prosecuting attorney, or a private attorney). If a family or household member assaults you and is arrested, you may request that a magistrate's order for emergency protection be issued. Please inform the investigating officer if you want an order for emergency protection. You need not be present when the order is issued. You cannot be charged a fee by a court in connection with filing, serving, or entering a protective order. For example, the court can enter an order that:

"(1) the abuser not commit further acts of violence;

"(2) the abuser not threaten, harass, or contact you at home;

"(3) directs the abuser to leave your household; and

"(4) establishes temporary custody of the children and directs the abuser not to interfere with the children or any property.

"A VIOLATION OF CERTAIN PROVISIONS OF COURT-ORDERED PROTECTION (such as (1) and (2) above) MAY BE A FELONY.

"CALL THE FOLLOWING VIOLENCE SHELTERS OR SOCIAL ORGANIZATIONS IF YOU NEED PROTECTION:

"_____ /

"_____ ."

Added by Acts 1985, 69th Leg., ch. 583, § 1, eff. Sept. 1, 1985. Amended by Acts 1991, 72nd Leg., ch. 366, § 4, eff. Sept. 1, 1991; Acts 1995, 74th Leg., ch. 1024, § 24, eff. Sept. 1, 1995; Acts 1997, 75th Leg., ch. 610, § 2, eff. Sept. 1, 1997; Acts 1997, 75th Leg., ch. 1193, § 23, eff. Sept. 1, 1997; Acts 2007, 80th Leg., ch. 524, § 2, eff. June 16, 2007.

Art. 5.045. Standby assistance; liability

(a) In the discretion of a peace officer, the officer may stay with a victim of family violence to protect the victim and allow the victim to take the personal property of the victim or of a child in the care of the victim to a place of safety in an orderly manner.

(b) A peace officer who provides assistance under Subsection (a) of this article is not:

(1) civilly liable for an act or omission of the officer that arises in connection with providing the assistance or determining whether to provide the assistance; or

(2) civilly or criminally liable for the wrongful appropriation of any personal property by the victim.

Added by Acts 1995, 74th Leg., ch. 565, § 1, eff. June 14, 1995.

Art. 5.05. Reports and records

(a) A peace officer who investigates a family violence incident or who responds to a disturbance call that may involve family violence shall make a written report, including but not limited to:

(1) the names of the suspect and complainant;

(2) the date, time, and location of the incident;

(3) any visible or reported injuries;

(4) a description of the incident and a statement of its disposition; and

(5) whether the suspect is a member of the state military forces or is serving in the armed forces of the United States in an active-duty status.

(a-1) In addition to the written report required under Subsection (a), a peace officer who investigates a family violence incident or who responds to a disturbance call that may involve family violence shall make a report to the Department of Family and Protective Services if the location of the incident or call, or the known address of a person involved in the incident or call, matches the address of a current licensed foster home or a verified agency foster home as listed in the Texas Crime Information Center. The report under this subsection may be made orally or electronically and must:

(1) include the information required by Subsection (a); and

(2) be filed with the Department of Family and Protective Services within 24 hours of the beginning of the investigation or receipt of the disturbance call.

(a-2) If a suspect is identified as being a member of the military, as described by Subsection (a)(5), the peace officer shall provide written notice of the incident or disturbance call to the staff judge advocate at Joint Force Headquarters or the provost marshal of the military installation to which the suspect is assigned with the intent that the commanding officer will be notified, as applicable.

(b) Each local law enforcement agency shall establish a departmental code for identifying and retrieving family violence reports as outlined in Subsection (a) of this section. A district or county attorney or an assistant district or county attorney exercising authority in the county where the law enforcement agency maintains records under this section is entitled to access to the records. The Department of Family and Protective Services is entitled to access the records relating to any person who is 14 years of age or older and who resides in a licensed foster home or a verified agency foster home.

(c) In order to ensure that officers responding to calls are aware of the existence and terms of protective orders, each municipal police department and sheriff shall establish procedures within the department or office to provide adequate information or access to information for law enforcement officers of the names of persons protected by a protective order and of persons to whom protective orders are directed.

(d) Each law enforcement officer shall accept a certified copy of an original or modified protective order as proof of the validity of the order and it is presumed the order remains valid unless:

(1) the order contains a termination date that has passed;

(2) it is more than one year after the date the order was issued; or

(3) the law enforcement officer has been notified by the clerk of the court vacating the order that the order has been vacated.

(e) A peace officer who makes a report under Subsection (a) of this article shall provide information concerning the incident or disturbance to the bureau of identification and records of the Department of Public Safety for its recordkeeping function under Section 411.042, Government Code. The bureau shall prescribe the form and nature of the information required to be reported to the bureau by this article.

(f) On request of a victim of an incident of family violence, the local law enforcement agency responsible for investigating the incident shall provide the victim, at no cost to the victim, with any information that is:

(1) contained in the written report prepared under Subsection (a);

(2) described by Subsection (a)(1) or (2); and

(3) not exempt from disclosure under Chapter 552, Government Code, or other law.

Added by Acts 1985, 69th Leg., ch. 583, § 1, eff. Sept. 1, 1985. Amended by Acts 1989, 71st Leg., ch. 614, § 27, eff. Sept. 1, 1989; Acts 1989, 71st Leg., ch. 739, § 8, eff. Sept. 1, 1989; Acts 1993, 73rd Leg., ch. 900, § 8.01, eff. Sept. 1, 1993; Acts 2007, 80th Leg., ch. 524, § 3, eff. June 16, 2007; Acts 2007, 80th Leg., ch. 1057, § 2, eff. Sept. 1, 2007; Acts 2011, 82nd Leg., ch. 327 (H.B. 2624), § 2, eff. Sept. 1, 2011.

Art. 5.06. Duties of prosecuting attorneys and courts

(a) Neither a prosecuting attorney nor a court may:

(1) dismiss or delay any criminal proceeding that involves a prosecution for an offense that constitutes family violence because a civil proceeding is pending or not pending; or

(2) require proof that a complaining witness, victim, or defendant is a party to a suit for the dissolution of a marriage or a suit affecting the parent-child relationship before presenting a criminal allegation to a grand jury, filing an information, or otherwise proceeding with the prosecution of a criminal case.

(b) A prosecuting attorney's decision to file an application for a protective order under Chapter 71, Family Code, should be made without regard to whether a criminal complaint has been filed by the applicant. A prosecuting attorney may require the applicant to provide information for an offense report, relating to the facts alleged in the application, with a local law enforcement agency.

(c) The prosecuting attorney having responsibility under Section 71.04(c), Family Code, for filing applications for protective orders under Chapter 71, Family Code, shall provide notice of that responsibility [1] to all law enforcement agencies within the jurisdiction of the prosecuting attorney for the prosecuting attorney.

Added by Acts 1985, 69th Leg., ch. 583, § 1, eff. Sept. 1, 1985. Amended by Acts 1989, 71st Leg., ch. 614, § 28, eff. Sept. 1, 1989; Acts 1989, 71st Leg., ch. 739, § 9, eff. Sept. 1, 1989; Acts 1995, 74th Leg., ch. 564, § 2, eff. Sept. 1, 1995; Acts 1995, 74th Leg., ch. 1024, § 25, eff. Sept. 1, 1995.

[1] Acts 1995, 74th Leg., ch. 1024, § 25 here read "those responsibilities" in lieu of "that responsibility".

Art. 5.07. Venue for protective order offenses

The venue for an offense under Section 25.07 or 25.072, Penal Code, is in the county in which the order was issued or, without regard to the identity or location of the court that issued the protective order, in the county in which the offense was committed.

Added by Acts 1989, 71st Leg., ch. 614, § 29, eff. Sept. 1, 1989; Acts 1989, 71st Leg., ch. 739, § 10, eff. Sept. 1, 1989. Amended by Acts 1995, 74th Leg., ch. 76, § 14.16, eff. Sept. 1, 1995; Acts 2013, 83rd Leg., ch. 96 (S.B. 743), § 3, eff. Sept. 1, 2013.

Art. 5.08. Mediation in family violence cases

Notwithstanding Article 26.13(g) or 42A.301(15), in a criminal prosecution arising from family violence, as that term is defined by Section 71.004, Family Code, a court shall not refer or order the victim or the defendant involved to mediation, dispute resolution, arbitration, or other similar procedures.

Added by Acts 1999, 76th Leg., ch. 389, § 1, eff. Aug. 30, 1999. Amended by Acts 2015, 84th Leg., ch. 770 (H.B. 2299), § 2.04, eff. Jan. 1, 2017.

CHAPTER SIX. PREVENTING OFFENSES BY THE ACT OF MAGISTRATES AND OTHER OFFICERS; EDUCATION CONCERNING CONSEQUENCES OF CERTAIN OFFENSES

Art. 6.01.   When magistrate hears threat

It is the duty of every magistrate, when he may have heard, in any manner, that a threat has been made by one person to do some injury to himself or the person or property of another, including the person or property of his spouse, immediately to give notice to some peace officer, in order that such peace officer may use lawful means to prevent the injury.

Acts 1965, 59th Leg., vol. 2, p. 317, ch. 722, eff. Jan. 1, 1966. Amended by Acts 1979, 66th Leg., p. 366, ch. 164, § 1, eff. Sept. 1, 1979.

Art. 6.02.   Threat to take life

If, within the hearing of a magistrate, one person shall threaten to take the life of another, including that of his spouse, or himself, the magistrate shall issue a warrant for the arrest of the person making the threat, or in case of emergency, he may himself immediately arrest such person.

Acts 1965, 59th Leg., vol. 2, p. 317, ch. 722, eff. Jan. 1, 1966. Amended by Acts 1979, 66th Leg., p. 366, ch. 164, § 1, eff. Sept. 1, 1979.

Art. 6.03.   On attempt to injure

Whenever, in the presence or within the observation of a magistrate, an attempt is made by one person to inflict an injury upon himself or to the person or property of another, including the person or property of his spouse, it is his duty to use all lawful means to prevent the injury. This may be done, either by verbal order to a peace officer to interfere and prevent the injury, or by the issuance of an order of arrest against the offender, or by arresting the offender; for which purpose he may call upon all persons present to assist in making the arrest.

Acts 1965, 59th Leg., vol. 2, p. 317, ch. 722, eff. Jan. 1, 1966. Amended by Acts 1979, 66th Leg., p. 366, ch. 164, § 1, eff. Sept. 1, 1979.

Art. 6.04.   May compel offender to give security

When the person making such threat is brought before a magistrate, he may compel him to give security to keep the peace, or commit him to custody.

Acts 1965, 59th Leg., vol. 2, p. 317, ch. 722, eff. Jan. 1, 1966.

Art. 6.05.   Duty of peace officer as to threats

It is the duty of every peace officer, when he may have been informed in any manner that a threat has been made by one person to do some injury to himself or to the person or property of another, including the person or property of his spouse, to prevent the threatened injury, if within his power; and, in order to do this, he may call in aid any number of citizens in his county. He may take such measures as the person about to be injured might for the prevention of the offense.

Acts 1965, 59th Leg., vol. 2, p. 317, ch. 722, eff. Jan. 1, 1966. Amended by Acts 1979, 66th Leg., p. 366, ch. 164, § 1, eff. Sept. 1, 1979.

Art. 6.06.   Peace officer to prevent injury

Whenever, in the presence of a peace officer, or within his view, one person is about to commit an offense against the person or property of another, including the person or property of his spouse, or injure himself, it is his duty to prevent it; and, for this purpose the peace officer may summon any number of the citizens of his county to his aid. The peace officer must use the amount of force necessary to prevent the commission of the offense, and no greater.

Acts 1965, 59th Leg., vol. 2, p. 317, ch. 722, eff. Jan. 1, 1966. Amended by Acts 1979, 66th Leg., p. 366, ch. 164, § 1, eff. Sept. 1, 1979.

Art. 6.07.   Conduct of peace officer

The conduct of peace officers, in preventing offenses about to be committed in their presence, or within their view, is to be regulated by the same rules as are prescribed to the action of the person about to be injured. They may use all force necessary to repel the aggression.

Acts 1965, 59th Leg., vol. 2, p. 317, ch. 722, eff. Jan. 1, 1966.

Art. 6.08.   Protective order prohibiting offense caused by bias or prejudice

(a) At any proceeding in which the defendant appears in constitutional county court, statutory county court, or district court that is related to an offense under Title 5, Penal Code,[1] or Section 28.02, 28.03, or 28.08, Penal Code, in which it is alleged that the defendant committed the offense because of bias or prejudice as described by Article 42.014, a person may request the court to render a protective order under Title 4, Family Code, for the protection of the person.

(b) The court shall render a protective order in the manner provided by Title 4, Family Code,[2] if, in lieu of the finding that family violence occurred and is likely to occur in the future as required by Section 85.001, Family Code, the court finds that probable cause exists to believe that an offense under Title 5, Penal

Code,[1] or Section 28.02, 28.03, or 28.08, Penal Code, occurred, that the defendant committed the offense because of bias or prejudice, and that the nature of the scheme or course of conduct engaged in by the defendant in the commission of the offense indicates that the defendant is likely to engage in the future in conduct prohibited by Title 5, Penal Code,[1] or Section 28.02, 28.03, or 28.08, Penal Code, and committed because of bias or prejudice.

(c) The procedure for the enforcement of a protective order under Title 4, Family Code,[2] applies to the fullest extent practicable to the enforcement of a protective order under this article, including provisions relating to findings, contents, duration, warning, delivery, law enforcement duties, and modification, except that:

(1) the printed statement on the warning must refer to the prosecution of subsequent offenses committed because of bias or prejudice;

(2) the court shall require a constable to serve a protective order issued under this article; and

(3) the clerk of the court shall forward a copy of a protective order issued under this article to the Department of Public Safety with a designation indicating that the order was issued to prevent offenses committed because of bias or prejudice.

(d) For an original or modified protective order rendered under this article, on receipt of the order from the clerk of the court, a law enforcement agency shall immediately, but not later than the 10th day after the date the order is received, enter the information required by Section 411.042(b)(6), Government Code, into the statewide law enforcement information system maintained by the Department of Public Safety.

Added by Acts 2001, 77th Leg., ch. 85, § 3.01, eff. Sept. 1, 2001.

[1] V.T.C.A., Penal Code § 19.01 et seq.
[2] V.T.C.A., Family Code § 71.001 et seq.

Art. 6.09. Stalking protective order

(a) At any proceeding related to an offense under Section 42.072, Penal Code, in which the defendant appears before the court, a person may request the court to render a protective order under Title 4, Family Code,[1] for the protection of the person. The request is made by filing "An Application for a Protective Order" in the same manner as an application for a protective order under Title 4, Family Code.

(b) The court shall render a protective order in the manner provided by Title 4, Family Code, if, in lieu of the finding that family violence occurred and is likely to occur in the future as required by Section 85.001, Family Code, the court finds that probable cause exists to believe that an offense under Section 42.072, Penal Code, occurred and that the nature of the scheme or course of conduct engaged in by the defendant in the commission of the offense indicates that the defendant is likely to engage in the future in conduct prohibited by Section 42.072(a)(1), (2), or (3), Penal Code.

(c) The procedure for the enforcement of a protective order under Title 4, Family Code, applies to the fullest extent practicable to the enforcement of a protective order under this article, including provisions relating to findings, contents, duration, warning, delivery, law enforcement duties, and modification.

Added by Acts 2011, 82nd Leg., ch. 981 (H.B. 1721), § 1, eff. Sept. 1, 2011.

[1] V.T.C.A., Family Code § 71.001 et seq.

Art. 6.10. Educational programs concerning certain offenses committed by minors; mandatory court attendance

(a) In this article, "parent" means a natural or adoptive parent, managing or possessory conservator, or legal guardian. The term does not include a parent whose parental rights have been terminated.

(b) This article applies to a defendant who has not had the disabilities of minority removed and has been charged with an offense under Section 43.261, Penal Code.

(c) The judge of a county court:

(1) must take the defendant's plea in open court; and

(2) shall issue a summons to compel the defendant's parent to be present during:

(A) the taking of the defendant's plea; and

(B) all other proceedings relating to the case.

(d) If a county court finds that a defendant has committed an offense under Section 43.261, Penal Code, the court may enter an order requiring the defendant to attend and successfully complete an educational program described by Section 37.218, Education Code, or another equivalent educational program.

(e) A court that enters an order under Subsection (d) shall require the defendant or the defendant's parent to pay the cost of attending an educational program under Subsection (d) if the court determines that the defendant or the defendant's parent is financially able to make payment.

Added by Acts 2011, 82nd Leg., ch. 1322 (S.B. 407), § 6, eff. Sept. 1, 2011. Redesignated from Vernon's Ann.C.C.P. art. 6.09 by Acts 2013, 83rd Leg., ch. 161 (S.B. 1093), § 22.001(5), eff. Sept. 1, 2013.

CHAPTER SEVEN. PROCEEDINGS BEFORE MAGISTRATES TO PREVENT OFFENSES

Art. 7.01. Shall issue warrant

Whenever a magistrate is informed upon oath that an offense is about to be committed against the person or property of the informant, or of another, or that any person has threatened to commit an offense, the magistrate shall immediately issue a warrant for the arrest of the accused; that he may be brought before such magistrate or before some other named in the warrant.

Acts 1965, 59th Leg., vol. 2, p. 317, ch. 722, eff. Jan. 1, 1966.

Art. 7.02. Appearance bond pending peace bond hearing

In proceedings under this Chapter, the accused shall have the right to make an appearance bond; such bond shall be conditioned as appearance bonds in other cases, and shall be further conditioned that the accused, pending the hearing, will not commit such offense and that he will keep the peace toward the person threatened or about to be injured, and toward all others, pending the hearing. Should the accused enter into such appearance bond, such fact shall not constitute any evidence of the accusation brought against him at the hearing on the merits before the magistrate.

Acts 1965, 59th Leg., vol. 2, p. 317, ch. 722, eff. Jan. 1, 1966.

Art. 7.03. Accused brought before magistrate

When the accused has been brought before the magistrate, he shall hear proof as to the accusation, and if he be satisfied that there is just reason to apprehend that the offense was intended to be committed, or that the threat was seriously made, he shall make an order that the accused enter into bond in such sum as he may in his discretion require, conditioned that he will not commit such offense, and that he will keep the peace toward the person threatened or about to be injured, and toward all others named in the bond for any period of time, not to exceed one year from the date of the bond. The magistrate shall admonish the accused that if the accused violates a condition of the bond, the court, in addition to ordering forfeiture of the bond, may punish the accused for contempt under Section 21.002(c), Government Code.

Acts 1965, 59th Leg., vol. 2, p. 317, ch. 722, eff. Jan. 1, 1966. Amended by Acts 1997, 75th Leg., ch. 773, § 1, eff. Sept. 1, 1997.

Art. 7.04. Form of peace bond

Such bond shall be sufficient if it be payable to the State of Texas, conditioned as required in said order of the magistrate, be for some certain sum, and be signed by the defendant and his surety or sureties and dated, and the provisions of Article 17.02 permitting the deposit of current United States money in lieu of sureties is applicable to this bond. No error of form shall vitiate such bond, and no error in the proceedings prior to the execution of the bond shall be a defense in a suit thereon.

Acts 1965, 59th Leg., vol. 2, p. 317, ch. 722, eff. Jan. 1, 1966.

Art. 7.05. Oath of surety; bond filed

The officer taking such bond shall require the sureties of the accused to make oath as to the value of their property as pointed out with regard to bail bonds. Such officer shall forthwith deposit such bond and oaths in the office of the clerk of the county where such bond is taken.

Acts 1965, 59th Leg., vol. 2, p. 317, ch. 722, eff. Jan. 1, 1966.

Art. 7.06. Amount of bail

The magistrate, in fixing the amount of such bonds, shall be governed by the pecuniary circumstances of the accused and the nature of the offense threatened or about to be committed.

Acts 1965, 59th Leg., vol. 2, p. 317, ch. 722, eff. Jan. 1, 1966.

Art. 7.07. Surety may exonerate himself

A surety upon any such bond may, at any time before a breach thereof, exonerate himself from the obligations of the same by delivering to any magistrate of the county where such bond was taken, the person of the defendant; and such magistrate shall in that case again require of the defendant bond, with other security in the same amount as the first bond; and the same proceeding shall be had as in the first instance, but the one year's time shall commence to run from the date of the first order.

Acts 1965, 59th Leg., vol. 2, p. 317, ch. 722, eff. Jan. 1, 1966.

Art. 7.08. Failure to give bond

If the defendant fail to give bond, he shall be committed to jail for one year from the date of the first order requiring such bond.

Acts 1965, 59th Leg., vol. 2, p. 317, ch. 722, eff. Jan. 1, 1966.

Art. 7.09. Discharge of defendant

A defendant committed for failing to give bond shall be discharged by the officer having him in custody, upon giving the required bond, or at the expiration of the time for which he has been committed.

Acts 1965, 59th Leg., vol. 2, p. 317, ch. 722, eff. Jan. 1, 1966.

Art. 7.10. May discharge defendant

If the magistrate believes from the evidence that there is no good reason to apprehend that the offense was intended or will be committed, or that no serious threat was made by the defendant, he shall discharge the accused, and may, in his discretion, tax the cost of the proceeding against the party making the complaint.

Acts 1965, 59th Leg., vol. 2, p. 317, ch. 722, eff. Jan. 1, 1966.

Arts. 7.11, 7.12. Repealed by Acts 1973, 63rd Leg., p. 995, ch. 399, § 3(b), eff. Jan. 1, 1974

Art. 7.13. When the defendant has committed a crime

If it appears from the evidence before the magistrate that the defendant has committed a criminal offense, the same proceedings shall be had as in other cases where parties are charged with crime.

Acts 1965, 59th Leg., vol. 2, p. 317, ch. 722, eff. Jan. 1, 1966.

Art. 7.14. Costs

If the accused is found subject to the charge and required to give bond, the costs of the proceedings shall be adjudged against him.

Acts 1965, 59th Leg., vol. 2, p. 317, ch. 722, eff. Jan. 1, 1966.

Art. 7.15. May order protection

When, from the nature of the case and the proof offered to the magistrate, it may appear necessary and proper, he shall have a right to order any peace officer to protect the person or property of any individual threatened; and such peace officer shall have the right to summon aid by requiring any number of citizens of his county to assist in giving the protection.

Acts 1965, 59th Leg., vol. 2, p. 317, ch. 722, eff. Jan. 1, 1966.

Art. 7.16. Suit on bond

A suit to forfeit any bond taken under the provisions of this Chapter shall be brought in the name of the State by the district or county attorney in the county where the bond was taken.

Acts 1965, 59th Leg., vol. 2, p. 317, ch. 722, eff. Jan. 1, 1966.

Art. 7.17. Limitation and procedure

Suits upon such bonds shall be commenced within two years from the breach of the same, and not thereafter, and shall be governed by the same rules as civil actions, except that the sureties may be sued without joining the principal. To entitle the State to recover, it shall only be necessary to prove that the accused violated any condition of said bond. The full amount of such bond may be recovered of the accused and the sureties.

Acts 1965, 59th Leg., vol. 2, p. 317, ch. 722, eff. Jan. 1, 1966.

Art. 7.18. Contempt

Violation of a condition of bond imposed under this chapter is punishable by:

(1) forfeiture of the bond;

(2) imposition of the fine and confinement for contempt under Section 21.002(c), Government Code; or

(3) both forfeiture of the bond and imposition of the fine and confinement.

Added by Acts 1997, 75th Leg., ch. 773, § 2, eff. Sept. 1, 1997.

CHAPTER 7A. PROTECTIVE ORDER FOR VICTIMS OF SEXUAL ASSAULT OR ABUSE, STALKING, OR TRAFFICKING

Article

Art. 7A.01.   Application for protective order

(a) The following persons may file an application for a protective order under this chapter without regard to the relationship between the applicant and the alleged offender:

(1) a person who is the victim of an offense under Section 21.02, 21.11, 22.011, 22.021, or 42.072, Penal Code;

(2) a person who is the victim of an offense under Section 20A.02, 20A.03, or 43.05, Penal Code;

(3) a parent or guardian acting on behalf of a person younger than 17 years of age who is the victim of an offense listed in Subdivision (1);

(4) a parent or guardian acting on behalf of a person younger than 18 years of age who is the victim of an offense listed in Subdivision (2); or

(5) a prosecuting attorney acting on behalf of a person described by Subdivision (1), (2), (3), or (4).

(b) An application for a protective order under this chapter may be filed in:

(1) a district court, juvenile court having the jurisdiction of a district court, statutory county court, or constitutional county court in:

(A) the county in which the applicant resides;

(B) the county in which the alleged offender resides; or

(C) any county in which an element of the alleged offense occurred; or

(2) any court with jurisdiction over a protective order under Title 4, Family Code,[1] involving the same parties named in the application.

Added by Acts 2003, 78th Leg., ch. 836, § 1, eff. Sept. 1, 2003. Amended by Acts 2007, 80th Leg., ch. 593, § 3.05, eff. Sept. 1, 2007; Acts 2007, 80th Leg., ch. 882, § 1, eff. Sept. 1, 2007; Acts 2011, 82nd Leg., ch. 1 (S.B. 24), § 2.02, eff. Sept. 1, 2011; Amended by Acts 2011, 82nd Leg., ch. 135 (S.B. 250), § 2, eff. Sept. 1, 2011; Acts 2013, 83rd Leg., ch. 520 (S.B. 357), § 2, eff. Sept. 1, 2013; Acts 2013, 83rd Leg., ch. 1252 (H.B. 8), § 2, eff. Sept. 1, 2013; Acts 2015, 84th Leg., ch. 1032 (H.B. 1447), § 1, eff. Sept. 1, 2015; Acts 2015, 84th Leg., ch. 1153 (S.B. 630), § 1, eff. Sept. 1, 2015.

[1] V.T.C.A., Family Code § 71.001 et seq.

Section 4 of Acts 2015, 84th Leg., ch. 1032 (H.B. 1447) provides:
"The change in law made by this Act applies to a victim of criminally injurious conduct for which a judgment of conviction is entered or a grant of deferred adjudication is made on or after the effective date [Sept. 1, 2015] of this Act, regardless of whether the criminally injurious conduct occurred before, on, or after the effective date of this Act."

Section 4 of Acts 2015, 84th Leg., ch. 1153 (S.B. 630) provides:
"The change in law made by this Act applies to a victim of criminally injurious conduct for which a judgment of conviction is entered or a grant of deferred adjudication is made on or after the effective date [Sept. 1, 2015] of this Act, regardless of whether the criminally injurious conduct occurred before, on, or after the effective date of this Act."

Art. 7A.02.   Temporary ex parte order

If the court finds from the information contained in an application for a protective order that there is a clear and present danger of sexual assault or abuse, stalking, trafficking, or other harm to the applicant, the court, without further notice to the alleged offender and without a hearing, may enter a temporary ex parte order for the protection of the applicant or any other member of the applicant's family or household.

Added by Acts 2003, 78th Leg., ch. 836, § 1, eff. Sept. 1, 2003. Amended by Acts 2011, 82nd Leg., ch. 135 (S.B. 250), § 3, eff. Sept. 1, 2011; Acts 2013, 83rd Leg., ch. 1252 (H.B. 8), § 3, eff. Sept. 1, 2013.

Art. 7A.03.   Required findings; issuance of protective order

(a) At the close of a hearing on an application for a protective order under this chapter, the court shall find whether there are reasonable grounds to believe that the applicant is the victim of sexual assault or abuse, stalking, or trafficking.

(b) If the court makes a finding described by Subsection (a), the court shall issue a protective order that includes a statement of the required findings.

Added by Acts 2003, 78th Leg., ch. 836, § 1, eff. Sept. 1, 2003. Amended by Acts 2007, 80th Leg., ch. 882, § 2, eff. Sept. 1, 2007; Acts 2011, 82nd Leg., ch. 135 (S.B. 250), § 4, eff. Sept. 1, 2011; Acts 2011, 82nd Leg., ch. 238 (H.B. 649), § 1, eff. Sept. 1, 2011; Acts 2013, 83rd Leg., ch. 520 (S.B. 357), § 3, eff. Sept. 1, 2013; Acts 2013, 83rd Leg., ch. 1252 (H.B. 8), § 4, eff. Sept. 1, 2013.

Art. 7A.035. Hearsay statement of child victim

In a hearing on an application for a protective order under this chapter, a statement that is made by a child younger than 14 years of age who is the victim of an offense under Section 21.02, 21.11, 22.011, or 22.021, Penal Code, and that describes the offense committed against the child is admissible as evidence in the same manner that a child's statement regarding alleged abuse against the child is admissible under Section 104.006, Family Code, in a suit affecting the parent-child relationship.

Added by Acts 2011, 82nd Leg., ch. 981 (H.B. 1721), § 2, eff. Sept. 1, 2011.

Art. 7A.04. Application of other law

To the extent applicable, except as otherwise provided by this chapter, Title 4, Family Code,[1] applies to a protective order issued under this chapter.

Added by Acts 2003, 78th Leg., ch. 836, § 1, eff. Sept. 1, 2003.

[1] V.T.C.A., Family Code § 71.001 et seq.

Art. 7A.05. Conditions specified by order

(a) In a protective order issued under this chapter, the court may:

(1) order the alleged offender to take action as specified by the court that the court determines is necessary or appropriate to prevent or reduce the likelihood of future harm to the applicant or a member of the applicant's family or household; or

(2) prohibit the alleged offender from:

(A) communicating:

(i) directly or indirectly with the applicant or any member of the applicant's family or household in a threatening or harassing manner; or

(ii) in any manner with the applicant or any member of the applicant's family or household except through the applicant's attorney or a person appointed by the court, if the court finds good cause for the prohibition;

(B) going to or near the residence, place of employment or business, or child-care facility or school of the applicant or any member of the applicant's family or household;

(C) engaging in conduct directed specifically toward the applicant or any member of the applicant's family or household, including following the person, that is reasonably likely to harass, annoy, alarm, abuse, torment, or embarrass the person; and

(D) possessing a firearm, unless the alleged offender is a peace officer, as defined by Section 1.07, Penal Code, actively engaged in employment as a sworn, full-time paid employee of a state agency or political subdivision.

(b) In an order under Subsection (a)(2)(B), the court shall specifically describe each prohibited location and the minimum distance from the location, if any, that the alleged offender must maintain. This subsection does not apply to an order with respect to which the court has received a request to maintain confidentiality of information revealing the locations.

(c) In a protective order, the court may suspend a license to carry a handgun issued under Section 411.177, Government Code, that is held by the alleged offender.

Added by Acts 2003, 78th Leg., ch. 836, § 1, eff. Sept. 1, 2003. Amended by Acts 2013, 83rd Leg., ch. 520 (S.B. 357), § 4, eff. Sept. 1, 2013; Acts 2013, 83rd Leg., ch. 760 (S.B. 893), § 2, eff. Sept. 1, 2013; Acts 2015, 84th Leg., ch. 437 (H.B. 910), § 5, eff. Jan. 1, 2016.

Section 51 of Acts 2015, 84th Leg., ch. 437 (H.B. 910) provides:

"The change in law made by this Act relating to the authority of a license holder to openly carry a holstered handgun applies to the carrying of a handgun on or after the effective date [Jan. 1, 2016] of this Act by any person who:

"(1) holds a license issued under Subchapter H, Chapter 411, Government Code, regardless of whether the person's license was issued before, on, or after the effective date of this Act; or

"(2) applies for the issuance of a license under that subchapter, regardless of whether the person applied for the license before, on, or after the effective date of this Act."

Art. 7A.06. Warning on protective order

(a) Each protective order issued under this chapter, including a temporary ex parte order, must contain the following prominently displayed statements in boldfaced type, capital letters, or underlined:

"A PERSON WHO VIOLATES THIS ORDER MAY BE PUNISHED FOR CONTEMPT OF COURT BY A FINE OF AS MUCH AS $500 OR BY CONFINEMENT IN JAIL FOR AS LONG AS SIX MONTHS, OR BOTH."

"NO PERSON, INCLUDING A PERSON WHO IS PROTECTED BY THIS ORDER, MAY GIVE PERMISSION TO ANYONE TO IGNORE OR VIOLATE ANY PROVISION OF THIS ORDER. DURING THE TIME IN WHICH THIS ORDER IS VALID, EVERY PROVISION OF THIS ORDER IS IN FULL FORCE AND EFFECT UNLESS A COURT CHANGES THE ORDER."

"IT IS UNLAWFUL FOR ANY PERSON, OTHER THAN A PEACE OFFICER, AS DEFINED BY

SECTION 1.07, PENAL CODE, ACTIVELY ENGAGED IN EMPLOYMENT AS A SWORN, FULL–TIME PAID EMPLOYEE OF A STATE AGENCY OR POLITICAL SUBDIVISION, WHO IS SUBJECT TO A PROTECTIVE ORDER TO POSSESS A FIREARM OR AMMUNITION."

(b) Each protective order issued under this chapter, except for a temporary ex parte order, must contain the following prominently displayed statement in bold-faced type, capital letters, or underlined:

"A VIOLATION OF THIS ORDER BY COMMISSION OF AN ACT PROHIBITED BY THE ORDER MAY BE PUNISHABLE BY A FINE OF AS MUCH AS $4,000 OR BY CONFINEMENT IN JAIL FOR AS LONG AS ONE YEAR, OR BOTH. AN ACT THAT RESULTS IN A SEPARATE OFFENSE MAY BE PROSECUTED AS A SEPARATE OFFENSE IN ADDITION TO A VIOLATION OF THIS ORDER."

Added by Acts 2003, 78th Leg., ch. 836, § 1, eff. Sept. 1, 2003.

Art. 7A.07. Duration of protective order

(a) A protective order issued under Article 7A.03 may be effective for the duration of the lives of the offender and victim or for any shorter period stated in the order. If a period is not stated in the order, the order is effective until the second anniversary of the date the order was issued.

(b) The following persons may file at any time an application with the court to rescind the protective order:

(1) a victim of an offense listed in Article 7A.01(a)(1) who is 17 years of age or older or a parent or guardian acting on behalf of a victim who is younger than 17 years of age; or

(2) a victim of an offense listed in Article 7A.01(a)(2) or a parent or guardian acting on behalf of a victim who is younger than 18 years of age.

(c) Repealed by Acts 2017, 85th Leg., ch. 97 (S.B. 257), § 2.

(d) To the extent of any conflict with Section 85.025, Family Code, this article prevails.

Added by Acts 2007, 80th Leg., ch. 882, § 3, eff. Sept. 1, 2007. Amended by Acts 2011, 82nd Leg., ch. 238 (H.B. 649), § 2, eff. Sept. 1, 2011; Acts 2013, 83rd Leg., ch. 1252 (H.B. 8), § 5, eff. Sept. 1, 2013; Acts 2017, 85th Leg., ch. 97 (S.B. 257), § 2, eff. Sept. 1, 2017.

Section 3 of Acts 2017, 85th Leg., ch. 97 (S.B. 257) provides:

"The changes in law made by this Act apply only to a protective order issued on or after the effective date [Sept. 1, 2017] of this Act. A protective order issued before the effective date of this Act is governed by the law in effect on the date the order is issued, and the former law is continued in effect for that purpose."

CHAPTER 7B. PROTECTIVE ORDER FOR VICTIM OF TRAFFICKING OF PERSONS [REPEALED]

Arts. 7B.01 to 7B.08. Repealed by Acts 2013, 83rd Leg., ch. 1252 (H.B. 8), § 22, eff. Sept. 1, 2013

CHAPTER EIGHT. SUPPRESSION OF RIOTS AND OTHER DISTURBANCES

Article
8.01. Officer may require aid.
8.02. Military aid in executing process.
8.03. Military aid in suppressing riots.
8.04. Dispersing riot.
8.05. Officer may call aid.
8.06. Means adopted to suppress.
8.07. Unlawful assembly.
8.08. Suppression at election.
8.09. Power of special constable.

Art. 8.01. Officer may require aid

When any officer authorized to execute process is resisted, or when he has sufficient reason to believe that he will meet with resistance in executing the same, he may command as many of the citizens of his county as he may think proper; and the sheriff may call any military company in the county to aid him in overcoming the resistance, and if necessary, in seizing and arresting the persons engaged in such resistance.

Acts 1965, 59th Leg., vol. 2, p. 317, ch. 722, eff. Jan. 1, 1966.

Art. 8.02. Military aid in executing process

If it be represented to the Governor in such manner as to satisfy him that the power of the county is not sufficient to enable the sheriff to execute process, he may, on application, order any military company of volunteers or militia company from another county to aid in overcoming such resistance.

Acts 1965, 59th Leg., vol. 2, p. 317, ch. 722, eff. Jan. 1, 1966.

Art. 8.03. Military aid in suppressing riots

Whenever, for the purpose of suppressing riots or unlawful assemblies, the aid of military or militia companies is called, they shall obey the orders of the civil officer who is engaged in suppressing the same.

Acts 1965, 59th Leg., vol. 2, p. 317, ch. 722, eff. Jan. 1, 1966.

Art. 8.04. Dispersing riot

Whenever a number of persons are assembled together in such a manner as to constitute a riot, according to the penal law of the State, it is the duty of every magistrate or peace officer to cause such persons to disperse. This may either be done by commanding them to disperse or by arresting the persons engaged, if necessary, either with or without warrant.

Acts 1965, 59th Leg., vol. 2, p. 317, ch. 722, eff. Jan. 1, 1966.

Art. 8.05. Officer may call aid

In order to enable the officer to disperse a riot, he may call to his aid the power of the county in the same manner as is provided where it is necessary for the execution of process.

Acts 1965, 59th Leg., vol. 2, p. 317, ch. 722, eff. Jan. 1, 1966.

Art. 8.06. Means adopted to suppress

The officer engaged in suppressing a riot, and those who aid him are authorized and justified in adopting such measures as are necessary to suppress the riot, but are not authorized to use any greater degree of force than is requisite to accomplish that object.

Acts 1965, 59th Leg., vol. 2, p. 317, ch. 722, eff. Jan. 1, 1966.

Art. 8.07. Unlawful assembly

The Articles of this Chapter relating to the suppression of riots apply equally to an unlawful assembly and other unlawful disturbances, as defined by the Penal Code.

Acts 1965, 59th Leg., vol. 2, p. 317, ch. 722, eff. Jan. 1, 1966.

Art. 8.08. Suppression at election

To suppress riots, unlawful assemblies and other disturbances at elections, any magistrate may appoint a sufficient number of special constables. Such appointments shall be made to each special constable, shall be in writing, dated and signed by the magistrate, and shall recite the purposes for which such appointment is made, and the length of time it is to continue. Before the same is delivered to such special constable, he shall take an oath before the magistrate to suppress, by lawful means, all riots, unlawful assemblies and breaches of the peace of which he may receive information, and to act impartially between all parties and persons interested in the result of the election.

Acts 1965, 59th Leg., vol. 2, p. 317, ch. 722, eff. Jan. 1, 1966.

Art. 8.09. Power of special constable

Special constables so appointed shall, during the time for which they are appointed, exercise the powers and perform the duties properly belonging to peace officers.

Acts 1965, 59th Leg., vol. 2, p. 317, ch. 722, eff. Jan. 1, 1966.

CHAPTER NINE. OFFENSES INJURIOUS TO PUBLIC HEALTH

Article
9.01. Trade injurious to health.
9.02. Refusal to give bond.
9.03. Requisites of bond.
9.04. Suit upon bond.
9.05. Proof.
9.06. Unwholesome food.

Art. 9.01. Trade injurious to health

After an indictment or information has been presented against any person for carrying on a trade, business or occupation injurious to the health of those in the neighborhood, the court shall have power, on the application of anyone interested, and after hearing proof both for and against the accused, to restrain the defendant, in such penalty as may be deemed proper, from carrying on such trade, business or occupation, or may make such order respecting the manner and place of carrying on the same as may be deemed advisable; and if upon trial, the defendant be convicted, the restraint shall be made perpetual, and the party shall be required to enter into bond, with security, not to continue such trade, business or occupation to the detriment of the health of such neighborhood, or of any other neighborhood within the county.

Acts 1965, 59th Leg., vol. 2, p. 317, ch. 722, eff. Jan. 1, 1966.

Art. 9.02. Refusal to give bond

If the party refuses to give bond when required under the provisions of the preceding Article, the court may either commit him to jail, or make an order requiring the sheriff to seize upon the implements of such trade, business or occupation, or the goods and property used in conducting such trade, business or occupation, and destroy the same.

Acts 1965, 59th Leg., vol. 2, p. 317, ch. 722, eff. Jan. 1, 1966.

Art. 9.03. Requisites of bond

Such bond shall be payable to the State of Texas, in a reasonable amount to be fixed by the court, conditioned that the defendant will not carry on such trade, business or occupation, naming the same, at such place, naming the place, or at any other place in the county, to the detriment of the health of the neighborhood. The bond shall be signed by the defendant and his sureties and dated, and shall be approved by the court taking the same, and filed in such court.

Acts 1965, 59th Leg., vol. 2, p. 317, ch. 722, eff. Jan. 1, 1966.

Art. 9.04. Suit upon bond

Any such bond, upon the breach thereof, may be sued upon by the district or county attorney, in the name of the State of Texas, within two years after such breach, and not afterwards; and such suits shall be governed by the same rules as civil actions.

Acts 1965, 59th Leg., vol. 2, p. 317, ch. 722, eff. Jan. 1, 1966.

Art. 9.05. Proof

It shall be sufficient proof of the breach of any such bond to show that the party continued after executing the same, to carry on the trade, business or occupation which he bound himself to discontinue; and the full amount of such bond may be recovered of the defendant and his sureties.

Acts 1965, 59th Leg., vol. 2, p. 317, ch. 722, eff. Jan. 1, 1966.

Art. 9.06. Unwholesome food

After conviction for selling unwholesome food or adulterated medicine, the court shall enter and issue an order to the sheriff or other proper officer to seize and destroy such as remains in the hands of the defendant.

Acts 1965, 59th Leg., vol. 2, p. 317, ch. 722, eff. Jan. 1, 1966.

CHAPTER TEN. OBSTRUCTIONS OF PUBLIC HIGHWAYS

Art. 10.01. Order to remove

After prosecution begun against any person for obstructing any highway, any one, in behalf of the public, may apply to the county judge of the county in which such highway is situated; and upon hearing proof, such judge, either in term time or in vacation, may issue his written order to the sheriff or other proper officer of the county, directing him to remove the obstruction. Before the issuance of such order, the applicant therefor shall give bond with security in an amount to be fixed by the judge, to indemnify the accused, in case of his acquittal, for the loss he

sustains. Such bond shall be approved by the county judge and filed with the papers in the cause.

Acts 1965, 59th Leg., vol. 2, p. 317, ch. 722, eff. Jan. 1, 1966.

Art. 10.02. Bond of applicant

If the defendant be acquitted after a trial upon the merits of the case, he may maintain a civil action against the applicant and his sureties upon such bond, and may recover the full amount of the bond, or such damages, less than the full amount thereof, as may be assessed by a court or jury; provided, he shows on the trial that the place was not in fact, at the time he placed the obstruction or impediment thereupon, a public highway established by proper authority, but was in fact his own property or in his lawful possession.

Acts 1965, 59th Leg., vol. 2, p. 317, ch. 722, eff. Jan. 1, 1966.

Art. 10.03. Removal

Upon the conviction of a defendant for obstructing a public highway, if such obstruction still exists, the court shall order the sheriff or other proper officer to forthwith remove the same at the cost of the defendant, to be taxed and collected as other costs in the case.

Acts 1965, 59th Leg., vol. 2, p. 317, ch. 722, eff. Jan. 1, 1966.

HABEAS CORPUS
CHAPTER ELEVEN. HABEAS CORPUS

Art. 11.01. What writ is

The writ of habeas corpus is the remedy to be used when any person is restrained in his liberty. It is an order issued by a court or judge of competent jurisdiction, directed to any one having a person in his custody, or under his restraint, commanding him to produce such person, at a time and place named in the writ, and show why he is held in custody or under restraint.

Acts 1965, 59th Leg., vol. 2, p. 317, ch. 722, eff. Jan. 1, 1966.

Art. 11.02. To whom directed

The writ runs in the name of "The State of Texas". It is addressed to a person having another under restraint, or in his custody, describing, as near as may be, the name of the office, if any, of the person to whom it is directed, and the name of the person said to be detained. It shall fix the time and place of return, and be signed by the judge, or by the clerk with his seal, where issued by a court.

Acts 1965, 59th Leg., vol. 2, p. 317, ch. 722, eff. Jan. 1, 1966.

Art. 11.03. Want of form

The writ of habeas corpus is not invalid, nor shall it be disobeyed for any want of form, if it substantially appear that it is issued by competent authority, and the writ sufficiently show the object of its issuance.

Acts 1965, 59th Leg., vol. 2, p. 317, ch. 722, eff. Jan. 1, 1966.

Art. 11.04. Construction

Every provision relating to the writ of habeas corpus shall be most favorably construed in order to give effect to the remedy, and protect the rights of the person seeking relief under it.

Acts 1965, 59th Leg., vol. 2, p. 317, ch. 722, eff. Jan. 1, 1966.

Art. 11.05. By whom writ may be granted

The Court of Criminal Appeals, the District Courts, the County Courts, or any Judge of said Courts, have power to issue the writ of habeas corpus; and it is their duty, upon proper motion, to grant the writ under the rules prescribed by law.

Acts 1965, 59th Leg., vol. 2, p. 317, ch. 722, eff. Jan. 1, 1966.

Art. 11.051. Filing Fee Prohibited

Notwithstanding any other law, a clerk of a court may not require a filing fee from an individual who files an application or petition for a writ of habeas corpus.

Added by Acts 1999, 76th Leg., ch. 392, § 1, eff. Aug. 30, 1999.

Art. 11.06. Returnable to any county

Before indictment found, the writ may be made returnable to any county in the State.

Acts 1965, 59th Leg., vol. 2, p. 317, ch. 722, eff. Jan. 1, 1966.

Art. 11.07. Procedure after conviction without death penalty

Sec. 1. This article establishes the procedures for an application for writ of habeas corpus in which the applicant seeks relief from a felony judgment imposing a penalty other than death.

Sec. 2.   After indictment found in any felony case, other than a case in which the death penalty is imposed, and before conviction, the writ must be made returnable in the county where the offense has been committed.

Sec. 3.   (a) After final conviction in any felony case, the writ must be made returnable to the Court of Criminal Appeals of Texas at Austin, Texas.

(b) An application for writ of habeas corpus filed after final conviction in a felony case, other than a case in which the death penalty is imposed, must be filed with the clerk of the court in which the conviction being challenged was obtained, and the clerk shall assign the application to that court. When the application is received by that court, a writ of habeas corpus, returnable to the Court of Criminal Appeals, shall issue by operation of law. The clerk of that court shall make appropriate notation thereof, assign to the case a file number (ancillary to that of the conviction being challenged), and forward a copy of the application by certified mail, return receipt requested, by secure electronic mail, or by personal service to the attorney representing the state in that court, who shall answer the application not later than the 15th day after the date the copy of the application is received. Matters alleged in the application not admitted by the state are deemed denied.

(c) Within 20 days of the expiration of the time in which the state is allowed to answer, it shall be the duty of the convicting court to decide whether there are controverted, previously unresolved facts material to the legality of the applicant's confinement. Confinement means confinement for any offense or any collateral consequence resulting from the conviction that is the basis of the instant habeas corpus. If the convicting court decides that there are no such issues, the clerk shall immediately transmit to the Court of Criminal Appeals a copy of the application, any answers filed, and a certificate reciting the date upon which that finding was made. Failure of the court to act within the allowed 20 days shall constitute such a finding.

(d) If the convicting court decides that there are controverted, previously unresolved facts which are material to the legality of the applicant's confinement, it shall enter an order within 20 days of the expiration of the time allowed for the state to reply, designating the issues of fact to be resolved. To resolve those issues the court may order affidavits, depositions,

interrogatories, additional forensic testing, and hearings, as well as using personal recollection. The state shall pay the cost of additional forensic testing ordered under this subsection, except that the applicant shall pay the cost of the testing if the applicant retains counsel for purposes of filing an application under this article. The convicting court may appoint an attorney or a magistrate to hold a hearing and make findings of fact. An attorney so appointed shall be compensated as provided in Article 26.05 of this code. It shall be the duty of the reporter who is designated to transcribe a hearing held pursuant to this article to prepare a transcript within 15 days of its conclusion. On completion of the transcript, the reporter shall immediately transmit the transcript to the clerk of the convicting court. After the convicting court makes findings of fact or approves the findings of the person designated to make them, the clerk of the convicting court shall immediately transmit to the Court of Criminal Appeals, under one cover, the application, any answers filed, any motions filed, transcripts of all depositions and hearings, any affidavits, and any other matters such as official records used by the court in resolving issues of fact.

(e) For the purposes of Subsection (d), "additional forensic testing" does not include forensic DNA testing as provided for in Chapter 64.

Sec. 4.   (a) If a subsequent application for writ of habeas corpus is filed after final disposition of an initial application challenging the same conviction, a court may not consider the merits of or grant relief based on the subsequent application unless the application contains sufficient specific facts establishing that:

(1) the current claims and issues have not been and could not have been presented previously in an original application or in a previously considered application filed under this article because the factual or legal basis for the claim was unavailable on the date the applicant filed the previous application; or

(2) by a preponderance of the evidence, but for a violation of the United States Constitution no rational juror could have found the applicant guilty beyond a reasonable doubt.

(b) For purposes of Subsection (a)(1), a legal basis of a claim is unavailable on or before a date described by Subsection (a)(1) if the legal basis was not recognized by and could not have been reasonably formulated from a final decision of the United States Supreme Court, a court of appeals of the United States, or a court of appellate jurisdiction of this state on or before that date.

(c) For purposes of Subsection (a)(1), a factual basis of a claim is unavailable on or before a date described by Subsection (a)(1) if the factual basis was not ascertainable through the exercise of reasonable diligence on or before that date.

Sec. 5. The Court of Criminal Appeals may deny relief upon the findings and conclusions of the hearing judge without docketing the cause, or may direct that the cause be docketed and heard as though originally presented to said court or as an appeal. Upon reviewing the record the court shall enter its judgment remanding the applicant to custody or ordering his release, as the law and facts may justify. The mandate of the court shall issue to the court issuing the writ, as in other criminal cases. After conviction the procedure outlined in this Act shall be exclusive and any other proceeding shall be void and of no force and effect in discharging the prisoner.

Sec. 6. Upon any hearing by a district judge by virtue of this Act, the attorney for applicant, and the state, shall be given at least seven full days' notice before such hearing is held.

Sec. 7. When the attorney for the state files an answer, motion, or other pleading relating to an application for a writ of habeas corpus or the court issues an order relating to an application for a writ of habeas corpus, the clerk of the court shall mail or deliver to the applicant a copy of the answer, motion, pleading, or order.

Acts 1965, 59th Leg., vol. 2, p. 317, ch. 722, eff. Jan. 1, 1966. Amended by Acts 1967, 60th Leg., p. 1734, ch. 659, § 7, eff. Aug. 28, 1967; Acts 1973, 63rd Leg., p. 1271, ch. 465, § 2, eff. June 14, 1973; Acts 1977, 65th Leg., p. 1974, ch. 789, § 1, eff. Aug. 29, 1977; Acts 1979, 66th Leg., p. 1017, ch. 451, § 1, eff. Sept. 1, 1979; Acts 1995, 74th Leg., ch. 319, § 5, eff. Sept. 1, 1995; Acts 1999, 76th Leg., ch. 580, § 2, eff. Sept. 1, 1999; Acts 2007, 80th Leg., ch. 1006, § 1, eff. Sept. 1, 2007; Acts 2013, 83rd Leg., ch. 78 (S.B. 354), § 1, eff. May 18, 2013; Acts 2013, 83rd Leg., ch. 648 (H.B. 833), § 1, eff. Sept. 1, 2013.

Art. 11.071. Procedure in death penalty case

Application to Death Penalty Case

Sec. 1. Notwithstanding any other provision of this chapter, this article establishes the procedures for an application for a writ of habeas corpus in which the applicant seeks relief from a judgment imposing a penalty of death.

Representation by Counsel

Sec. 2. (a) An applicant shall be represented by competent counsel unless the applicant has elected to proceed pro se and the convicting trial court finds, after a hearing on the record, that the applicant's election is intelligent and voluntary.

(b) If a defendant is sentenced to death the convicting court, immediately after judgment is entered under Article 42.01, shall determine if the defendant is indigent and, if so, whether the defendant desires appointment of counsel for the purpose of a writ of habeas corpus. If the defendant desires appointment of counsel for the purpose of a writ of habeas corpus, the court shall appoint the office of capital and forensic writs to represent the defendant as provided by Subsection (c).

(c) At the earliest practical time, but in no event later than 30 days, after the convicting court makes the findings required under Subsections (a) and (b), the convicting court shall appoint the office of capital and forensic writs or, if the office of capital and forensic writs does not accept or is prohibited from accepting an appointment under Section 78.054, Government Code, other competent counsel under Subsection (f), unless the applicant elects to proceed pro se or is represented by retained counsel. On appointing counsel under this section, the convicting court shall immediately notify the court of criminal appeals of the appointment, including in the notice a copy of the judgment and the name, address, and telephone number of the appointed counsel.

(d) Repealed by Acts 2009, 81st Leg., ch. 781, § 11.

(e) If the court of criminal appeals denies an applicant relief under this article, an attorney appointed under this section to represent the applicant shall, not later than the 15th day after the date the court of criminal appeals denies relief or, if the case is filed and set for submission, the 15th day after the date the court of criminal appeals issues a mandate on the initial application for a writ of habeas corpus under this article, move for the appointment of counsel in federal habeas review under 18 U.S.C. Section 3599. The attorney shall immediately file a copy of the motion with the court of criminal appeals, and if the attorney fails to do so, the court may take any action to ensure that the applicant's right to federal habeas review is protected, including initiating contempt proceedings against the attorney.

(f) If the office of capital and forensic writs does not accept or is prohibited from accepting an appointment under Section 78.054, Government Code, the convicting court shall appoint counsel from a list of competent counsel maintained by the presiding judges of the administrative judicial regions under Section 78.056, Government Code. The convicting court shall reasonably compensate as provided by Section 2A an attorney appointed under this section, other than an attorney employed by the office of capital and forensic writs, regardless of whether the attorney is appointed by the convicting court or was appointed by the court of criminal appeals under prior law. An attorney appointed under this section who is employed by the office of capital and forensic writs shall be compensated in accordance with Subchapter B, Chapter 78, Government Code. [1]

State Reimbursement; County Obligation

Sec. 2A.   (a) The state shall reimburse a county for compensation of counsel under Section 2, other than for compensation of counsel employed by the office of capital and forensic writs, and for payment of expenses under Section 3, regardless of whether counsel is employed by the office of capital and forensic writs. The total amount of reimbursement to which a county is entitled under this section for an application under this article may not exceed $25,000. Compensation and expenses in excess of the $25,000 reimbursement provided by the state are the obligation of the county.

(b) A convicting court seeking reimbursement for a county shall certify to the comptroller of public accounts the amount of compensation that the county is entitled to receive under this section. The comptroller of public accounts shall issue a warrant to the county in the amount certified by the convicting court, not to exceed $25,000.

(c) The limitation imposed by this section on the reimbursement by the state to a county for compensation of counsel and payment of reasonable expenses does not prohibit a county from compensating counsel and reimbursing expenses in an amount that is in excess of the amount the county receives from the state as reimbursement, and a county is specifically granted discretion by this subsection to make payments in excess of the state reimbursement.

(d) The comptroller shall reimburse a county for the compensation and payment of expenses of an attorney appointed by the court of criminal appeals under prior law. A convicting court seeking reimbursement for a county as permitted by this subsection shall certify the amount the county is entitled to receive under this subsection for an application filed

under this article, not to exceed a total amount of $25,000.

Investigation of Grounds for Application

Sec. 3.   (a) On appointment, counsel shall investigate expeditiously, before and after the appellate record is filed in the court of criminal appeals, the factual and legal grounds for the filing of an application for a writ of habeas corpus.

(b) Not later than the 30th day before the date the application for a writ of habeas corpus is filed with the convicting court, counsel may file with the convicting court an ex parte, verified, and confidential request for prepayment of expenses, including expert fees, to investigate and present potential habeas corpus claims. The request for expenses must state:

(1) the claims of the application to be investigated;

(2) specific facts that suggest that a claim of possible merit may exist; and

(3) an itemized list of anticipated expenses for each claim.

(c) The court shall grant a request for expenses in whole or in part if the request for expenses is timely and reasonable. If the court denies in whole or in part the request for expenses, the court shall briefly state the reasons for the denial in a written order provided to the applicant.

(d) Counsel may incur expenses for habeas corpus investigation, including expenses for experts, without prior approval by the convicting court or the court of criminal appeals. On presentation of a claim for reimbursement, which may be presented ex parte, the convicting court shall order reimbursement of counsel for expenses, if the expenses are reasonably necessary and reasonably incurred. If the convicting court denies in whole or in part the request for expenses, the court shall briefly state the reasons for the denial in a written order provided to the applicant. The applicant may request reconsideration of the denial for reimbursement by the convicting court.

(e) Materials submitted to the court under this section are a part of the court's record.

(f) This section applies to counsel's investigation of the factual and legal grounds for the filing of an application for a writ of habeas corpus, regardless of whether counsel is employed by the office of capital and forensic writs.

Filing of Application

Sec. 4. (a) An application for a writ of habeas corpus, returnable to the court of criminal appeals, must be filed in the convicting court not later than the 180th day after the date the convicting court appoints counsel under Section 2 or not later than the 45th day after the date the state's original brief is filed on direct appeal with the court of criminal appeals, whichever date is later.

(b) The convicting court, before the filing date that is applicable to the applicant under Subsection (a), may for good cause shown and after notice and an opportunity to be heard by the attorney representing the state grant one 90-day extension that begins on the filing date applicable to the defendant under Subsection (a). Either party may request that the court hold a hearing on the request. If the convicting court finds that the applicant cannot establish good cause justifying the requested extension, the court shall make a finding stating that fact and deny the request for the extension.

(c) An application filed after the filing date that is applicable to the applicant under Subsection (a) or (b) is untimely.

(d) If the convicting court receives an untimely application or determines that after the filing date that is applicable to the applicant under Subsection (a) or (b) no application has been filed, the convicting court immediately, but in any event within 10 days, shall send to the court of criminal appeals and to the attorney representing the state:

(1) a copy of the untimely application, with a statement of the convicting court that the application is untimely, or a statement of the convicting court that no application has been filed within the time periods required by Subsections (a) and (b); and

(2) any order the judge of the convicting court determines should be attached to an untimely application or statement under Subdivision (1).

(e) A failure to file an application before the filing date applicable to the applicant under Subsection (a) or (b) constitutes a waiver of all grounds for relief that were available to the applicant before the last date on which an application could be timely filed, except as provided by Section 4A.

Untimely Application; Application Not Filed

Sec. 4A. (a) On command of the court of criminal appeals, a counsel who files an untimely application or fails to file an application before the filing date applicable under Section 4(a) or (b) shall show cause as to why the application was untimely filed or not filed before the filing date.

(b) At the conclusion of the counsel's presentation to the court of criminal appeals, the court may:

(1) find that good cause has not been shown and dismiss the application;

(2) permit the counsel to continue representation of the applicant and establish a new filing date for the application, which may be not more than 180 days from the date the court permits the counsel to continue representation; or

(3) appoint new counsel to represent the applicant and establish a new filing date for the application, which may be not more than 270 days after the date the court appoints new counsel.

(c) The court of criminal appeals may hold in contempt counsel who files an untimely application or fails to file an application before the date required by Section 4(a) or (b). The court of criminal appeals may punish as a separate instance of contempt each day after the first day on which the counsel fails to timely file the application. In addition to or in lieu of holding counsel in contempt, the court of criminal appeals may enter an order denying counsel compensation under Section 2A.

(d) If the court of criminal appeals establishes a new filing date for the application, the court of criminal appeals shall notify the convicting court of that fact and the convicting court shall proceed under this article.

(e) Sections 2A and 3 apply to compensation and reimbursement of counsel appointed under Subsection (b)(3) in the same manner as if counsel had been appointed by the convicting court, unless the attorney is employed by the office of capital and forensic writs, in which case the compensation of that attorney is governed by Subchapter B, Chapter 78, Government Code.

(f) Notwithstanding any other provision of this article, the court of criminal appeals shall appoint counsel and establish a new filing date for application, which may be no later than the 270th day after the date on which counsel is appointed, for each applicant who before September 1, 1999, filed an untimely application or failed to file an application before the date required by Section 4(a) or (b). Section 2A applies to the compensation and payment of expenses of counsel appointed by the court of criminal appeals under this subsection, unless the attorney is employed by the office of capital and forensic writs, in which case the compensation of that attorney is governed by Subchapter B, Chapter 78, Government Code.

Subsequent Application

Sec. 5.   (a) If a subsequent application for a writ of habeas corpus is filed after filing an initial application, a court may not consider the merits of or grant relief based on the subsequent application unless the application contains sufficient specific facts establishing that:

(1) the current claims and issues have not been and could not have been presented previously in a timely initial application or in a previously considered application filed under this article or Article 11.07 because the factual or legal basis for the claim was unavailable on the date the applicant filed the previous application;

(2) by a preponderance of the evidence, but for a violation of the United States Constitution no rational juror could have found the applicant guilty beyond a reasonable doubt; or

(3) by clear and convincing evidence, but for a violation of the United States Constitution no rational juror would have answered in the state's favor one or more of the special issues that were submitted to the jury in the applicant's trial under Article 37.071, 37.0711, or 37.072.

(b) If the convicting court receives a subsequent application, the clerk of the court shall:

(1) attach a notation that the application is a subsequent application;

(2) assign to the case a file number that is ancillary to that of the conviction being challenged; and

(3) immediately send to the court of criminal appeals a copy of:

(A) the application;

(B) the notation;

(C) the order scheduling the applicant's execution, if scheduled; and

(D) any order the judge of the convicting court directs to be attached to the application.

(c) On receipt of the copies of the documents from the clerk, the court of criminal appeals shall determine whether the requirements of Subsection (a) have been satisfied. The convicting court may not take further action on the application before the court of criminal appeals issues an order finding that the requirements

have been satisfied. If the court of criminal appeals determines that the requirements have not been satisfied, the court shall issue an order dismissing the application as an abuse of the writ under this section.

(d) For purposes of Subsection (a)(1), a legal basis of a claim is unavailable on or before a date described by Subsection (a)(1) if the legal basis was not recognized by or could not have been reasonably formulated from a final decision of the United States Supreme Court, a court of appeals of the United States, or a court of appellate jurisdiction of this state on or before that date.

(e) For purposes of Subsection (a)(1), a factual basis of a claim is unavailable on or before a date described by Subsection (a)(1) if the factual basis was not ascertainable through the exercise of reasonable diligence on or before that date.

(f) If an amended or supplemental application is not filed within the time specified under Section 4(a) or (b), the court shall treat the application as a subsequent application under this section.

Issuance of Writ

Sec. 6.   (a) If a timely application for a writ of habeas corpus is filed in the convicting court, a writ of habeas corpus, returnable to the court of criminal appeals, shall issue by operation of law.

(b) If the convicting court receives notice that the requirements of Section 5 for consideration of a subsequent application have been met, a writ of habeas corpus, returnable to the court of criminal appeals, shall issue by operation of law.

(b–1) If the convicting court receives notice that the requirements of Section 5(a) for consideration of a subsequent application have been met and if the applicant has not elected to proceed pro se and is not represented by retained counsel, the convicting court shall appoint, in order of priority:

(1) the attorney who represented the applicant in the proceedings under Section 5, if the attorney seeks the appointment;

(2) the office of capital and forensic writs, if the office represented the applicant in the proceedings under Section 5 or otherwise accepts the appointment; or

(3) counsel from a list of competent counsel maintained by the presiding judges of the administrative judicial regions under Section 78.056, Government Code, if the office of capital and forensic writs:

(A) did not represent the applicant as described by Subdivision (2); or

(B) does not accept or is prohibited from accepting the appointment under Section 78.054, Government Code.

(b–2) Regardless of whether the subsequent application is ultimately dismissed, compensation and reimbursement of expenses for counsel appointed under Subsection (b–1) shall be provided as described by Section 2, 2A, or 3, including compensation for time previously spent and reimbursement of expenses previously incurred with respect to the subsequent application.

(c) The clerk of the convicting court shall:

(1) make an appropriate notation that a writ of habeas corpus was issued;

(2) assign to the case a file number that is ancillary to that of the conviction being challenged; and

(3) send a copy of the application by certified mail, return receipt requested, or by secure electronic mail to the attorney representing the state in that court.

(d) The clerk of the convicting court shall promptly deliver copies of documents submitted to the clerk under this article to the applicant and the attorney representing the state.

Answer to Application

Sec. 7. (a) The state shall file an answer to the application for a writ of habeas corpus not later than the 120th day after the date the state receives notice of issuance of the writ. The state shall serve the answer on counsel for the applicant or, if the applicant is proceeding pro se, on the applicant. The state may request from the convicting court an extension of time in which to answer the application by showing particularized justifying circumstances for the extension, but in no event may the court permit the state to file an answer later than the 180th day after the date the state receives notice of issuance of the writ.

(b) Matters alleged in the application not admitted by the state are deemed denied.

Findings of Fact Without Evidentiary Hearing

Sec. 8. (a) Not later than the 20th day after the last date the state answers the application, the convicting court shall determine whether controverted, previously unresolved factual issues material to the legality of the applicant's confinement exist and shall issue a written order of the determination.

(b) If the convicting court determines the issues do not exist, the parties shall file proposed findings of fact and conclusions of law for the court to consider on or before a date set by the court that is not later than the 30th day after the date the order is issued.

(c) After argument of counsel, if requested by the court, the convicting court shall make appropriate written findings of fact and conclusions of law not later than the 15th day after the date the parties filed proposed findings or not later than the 45th day after the date the court's determination is made under Subsection (a), whichever occurs first.

(d) The clerk of the court shall immediately send to:

(1) the court of criminal appeals a copy of the:

(A) application;

(B) answer;

(C) orders entered by the convicting court;

(D) proposed findings of fact and conclusions of law; and

(E) findings of fact and conclusions of law entered by the court; and

(2) counsel for the applicant or, if the applicant is proceeding pro se, to the applicant, a copy of:

(A) orders entered by the convicting court;

(B) proposed findings of fact and conclusions of law; and

(C) findings of fact and conclusions of law entered by the court.

Hearing

Sec. 9. (a) If the convicting court determines that controverted, previously unresolved factual issues material to the legality of the applicant's confinement exist, the court shall enter an order, not later than the 20th day after the last date the state answers the application, designating the issues of fact to be resolved and the manner in which the issues shall be resolved. To resolve the issues, the court may require affidavits, depositions, interrogatories, and evidentiary hearings and may use personal recollection.

(b) The convicting court shall hold the evidentiary hearing not later than the 30th day after the date on which the court enters the order designating issues under Subsection (a). The convicting court may grant a motion to postpone the hearing, but not for more than 30 days, and only if the court states, on the record, good cause for delay.

(c) The presiding judge of the convicting court shall conduct a hearing held under this section unless another judge presided over the original capital felony trial, in which event that judge, if qualified for assignment under Section 74.054 or 74.055, Government Code, may preside over the hearing.

(d) The court reporter shall prepare a transcript of the hearing not later than the 30th day after the date the hearing ends and file the transcript with the clerk of the convicting court.

(e) The parties shall file proposed findings of fact and conclusions of law for the convicting court to consider on or before a date set by the court that is not later than the 30th day after the date the transcript is filed. If the court requests argument of counsel, after argument the court shall make written findings of fact that are necessary to resolve the previously unresolved facts and make conclusions of law not later than the 15th day after the date the parties file proposed findings or not later than the 45th day after the date the court reporter files the transcript, whichever occurs first.

(f) The clerk of the convicting court shall immediately transmit to:

(1) the court of criminal appeals a copy of:

(A) the application;

(B) the answers and motions filed;

(C) the court reporter's transcript;

(D) the documentary exhibits introduced into evidence;

(E) the proposed findings of fact and conclusions of law;

(F) the findings of fact and conclusions of law entered by the court;

(G) the sealed materials such as a confidential request for investigative expenses; and

(H) any other matters used by the convicting court in resolving issues of fact; and

(2) counsel for the applicant or, if the applicant is proceeding pro se, to the applicant, a copy of:

(A) orders entered by the convicting court;

(B) proposed findings of fact and conclusions of law; and

(C) findings of fact and conclusions of law entered by the court.

(g) The clerk of the convicting court shall forward an exhibit that is not documentary to the court of criminal appeals on request of the court.

Rules of Evidence

Sec. 10. The Texas Rules of Criminal Evidence apply to a hearing held under this article.

Review by Court of Criminal Appeals

Sec. 11. The court of criminal appeals shall expeditiously review all applications for a writ of habeas corpus submitted under this article. The court may set the cause for oral argument and may request further briefing of the issues by the applicant or the state. After reviewing the record, the court shall enter its judgment remanding the applicant to custody or ordering the applicant's release, as the law and facts may justify.

Added by Acts 1995, 74th Leg., ch. 319, § 1, eff. Sept. 1, 1995. Amended by Acts 1997, 75th Leg., ch. 1336, §§ 1 to 5, eff. Sept. 1, 1997; Acts 1999, 76th Leg., ch. 803, §§ 1 to 10, eff. Sept. 1, 1999; Acts 2003, 78th Leg., ch. 315, §§ 1 to 3, eff. Sept. 1, 2003; Acts 2005, 79th Leg., ch. 787, § 13, eff. Sept. 1, 2005; Acts 2005, 79th Leg., ch. 965, § 5, eff. Sept. 1, 2005; Acts 2007, 80th Leg., ch. 593, § 3.06, eff. Sept. 1, 2007; Acts 2009, 81st Leg., ch. 781, §§ 2 to 5, eff. Sept. 1, 2009; Acts 2009, 81st Leg., ch. 781, § 11, eff. Jan. 1, 2010; Acts 2011, 82nd Leg., ch. 1139 (H.B. 1646), § 1, eff. Sept. 1, 2011; Acts 2013, 83rd Leg., ch. 78 (S.B. 354), § 2, eff. May 18, 2013; Acts 2015, 84th Leg., ch. 1215 (S.B. 1743), §§ 1 to 5, eff. Sept. 1, 2015.

[1] V.T.C.A., Government Code § 78.051 et seq.

Art. 11.072. Procedure in community supervision case

Sec. 1. This article establishes the procedures for an application for a writ of habeas corpus in a felony or misdemeanor case in which the applicant seeks relief from an order or a judgment of conviction ordering community supervision.

Sec. 2. (a) An application for a writ of habeas corpus under this article must be filed with the clerk of the court in which community supervision was imposed.

(b) At the time the application is filed, the applicant must be, or have been, on community supervision, and the application must challenge the legal validity of:

(1) the conviction for which or order in which community supervision was imposed; or

(2) the conditions of community supervision.

Sec. 3. (a) An application may not be filed under this article if the applicant could obtain the requested relief by means of an appeal under Article 44.02 and Rule 25.2, Texas Rules of Appellate Procedure.

(b) An applicant seeking to challenge a particular condition of community supervision but not the legality of the conviction for which or the order in which community supervision was imposed must first attempt to gain relief by filing a motion to amend the conditions of community supervision.

(c) An applicant may challenge a condition of community supervision under this article only on constitutional grounds.

Sec. 4. (a) When an application is filed under this article, a writ of habeas corpus issues by operation of law.

(b) At the time the application is filed, the clerk of the court shall assign the case a file number ancillary to that of the judgment of conviction or order being challenged.

Sec. 5. (a) Immediately on filing an application, the applicant shall serve a copy of the application on the attorney representing the state, by either certified mail, return receipt requested, or personal service.

(b) The state may file an answer within the period established by Subsection (c), but is not required to file an answer.

(c) The state may not file an answer after the 30th day after the date of service, except that for good cause the convicting court may grant the state one 30–day extension.

(d) Any answer, motion, or other document filed by the state must be served on the applicant by certified mail, return receipt requested, or by personal service.

(e) Matters alleged in the application not admitted by the state are considered to have been denied.

Sec. 6. (a) Not later than the 60th day after the day on which the state's answer is filed, the trial court shall enter a written order granting or denying the relief sought in the application.

(b) In making its determination, the court may order affidavits, depositions, interrogatories, or a hearing, and may rely on the court's personal recollection.

(c) If a hearing is ordered, the hearing may not be held before the eighth day after the day on which the applicant and the state are provided notice of the hearing.

(d) The court may appoint an attorney or magistrate to hold a hearing ordered under this section and make findings of fact. An attorney appointed under this subsection is entitled to compensation as provided by Article 26.05.

Sec. 7. (a) If the court determines from the face of an application or documents attached to the application that the applicant is manifestly entitled to no relief, the court shall enter a written order denying the application as frivolous. In any other case, the court shall enter a written order including findings of fact and conclusions of law. The court may require the prevailing party to submit a proposed order.

(b) At the time an order is entered under this section, the clerk of the court shall immediately, by certified mail, return receipt requested, or by secure electronic mail, send a copy of the order to the applicant and to the state.

Sec. 8. If the application is denied in whole or part, the applicant may appeal under Article 44.02 and Rule 31, Texas Rules of Appellate Procedure. If the application is granted in whole or part, the state may appeal under Article 44.01 and Rule 31, Texas Rules of Appellate Procedure.

Sec. 9. (a) If a subsequent application for a writ of habeas corpus is filed after final disposition of an initial application under this article, a court may not consider the merits of or grant relief based on the subsequent application unless the application contains sufficient specific facts establishing that the current claims and issues have not been and could not have been presented previously in an original application or in a previously considered application filed under this article because the factual or legal basis for the claim was unavailable on the date the applicant filed the previous application.

(b) For purposes of Subsection (a), a legal basis of a claim is unavailable on or before a date described by that subsection if the legal basis was not recognized by and could not have been reasonably formulated from a final decision of the United States Supreme Court, a court of appeals of the United States, or a court of appellate jurisdiction of this state on or before that date.

(c) For purposes of Subsection (a), a factual basis of a claim is unavailable on or before a date described by that subsection if the factual basis was not ascertainable through the exercise of reasonable diligence on or before that date.

Added by Acts 2003, 78th Leg., ch. 587, § 1, eff. June 20, 2003. Amended by Acts 2013, 83rd Leg., ch. 78 (S.B. 354), § 3, eff. May 18, 2013.

Art. 11.073.　Procedure related to certain scientific evidence

(a) This article applies to relevant scientific evidence that:

(1) was not available to be offered by a convicted person at the convicted person's trial; or

(2) contradicts scientific evidence relied on by the state at trial.

(b) A court may grant a convicted person relief on an application for a writ of habeas corpus if:

(1) the convicted person files an application, in the manner provided by Article 11.07, 11.071, or 11.072, containing specific facts indicating that:

(A) relevant scientific evidence is currently available and was not available at the time of the convicted person's trial because the evidence was not ascertainable through the exercise of reasonable diligence by the convicted person before the date of or during the convicted person's trial; and

(B) the scientific evidence would be admissible under the Texas Rules of Evidence at a trial held on the date of the application; and

(2) the court makes the findings described by Subdivisions (1)(A) and (B) and also finds that, had the scientific evidence been presented at trial, on the preponderance of the evidence the person would not have been convicted.

(c) For purposes of Section 4(a)(1), Article 11.07, Section 5(a)(1), Article 11.071, and Section 9(a), Article 11.072, a claim or issue could not have been presented previously in an original application or in a previously considered application if the claim or issue is based on relevant scientific evidence that was not ascertainable through the exercise of reasonable diligence by the convicted person on or before the date on which the original application or a previously considered application, as applicable, was filed.

(d) In making a finding as to whether relevant scientific evidence was not ascertainable through the exercise of reasonable diligence on or before a specific date, the court shall consider whether the field of scientific knowledge, a testifying expert's scientific knowledge, or a scientific method on which the relevant scientific evidence is based has changed since:

(1) the applicable trial date or dates, for a determination made with respect to an original application; or

(2) the date on which the original application or a previously considered application, as applicable, was filed, for a determination made with respect to a subsequent application.

Added by Acts 2013, 83rd Leg., ch. 410 (S.B. 344), § 1, eff. Sept. 1, 2013. Amended by Acts 2015, 84th Leg., ch. 1263 (H.B. 3724), § 1, eff. Sept. 1, 2015.

Art. 11.0731.　Procedures Related to Certain Previously Tested Evidence

(a) This article applies to relevant evidence consisting of biological material described by Article 64.01(a) that was:

(1) presented by the state at the convicted person's trial; and

(2) subjected to testing:

(A) at a laboratory that ceased conducting DNA testing after an audit by the Texas Forensic Science Commission revealed the laboratory engaged in faulty testing practices; and

(B) during the period identified in the audit as involving faulty testing practices.

(b) A court may grant a convicted person relief on an application for a writ of habeas corpus if the convicted person files an application, in the manner provided by Article 11.07, 11.071, or 11.072, containing specific facts indicating that:

(1) the person previously filed a motion under Chapter 64 for forensic DNA testing of evidence described by Subsection (a) that was denied because of a negative finding under Article 64.03(a)(1)(A) or (B); and

(2) had the evidence not been presented at the person's trial, on the preponderance of the evidence the person would not have been convicted.

(c) For purposes of Section 4(a)(1), Article 11.07, Section 5(a)(1), Article 11.071, and Section 9(a), Article 11.072, a claim or issue could not have been presented previously in an original application or in a previously considered application if the claim or issue is based on evidence that has been determined by the Texas Forensic Science Commission to have been subjected to faulty DNA testing practices.

Added by Acts 2017, 85th Leg., ch. 903 (H.B. 3872), § 1, eff. June 15, 2017.

Art. 11.074.　Court–Appointed Representation Required in Certain Cases

(a) This article applies only to a felony or misdemeanor case in which the applicant seeks relief on a writ of habeas corpus from a judgment of conviction that:

(1) imposes a penalty other than death; or

(2) orders community supervision.

(b) If at any time the state represents to the convicting court that an eligible indigent defendant under Article 1.051 who was sentenced or had a sentence suspended is not guilty, is guilty of only a lesser offense, or was convicted or sentenced under a law that has been found unconstitutional by the court of criminal appeals or the United States Supreme Court, the court shall appoint an attorney to represent the indigent defendant for purposes of filing an application for a writ of habeas corpus, if an application has not been filed, or to otherwise represent the indigent defendant in a proceeding based on the application for the writ.

(c) An attorney appointed under this article shall be compensated as provided by Article 26.05.

Added by Acts 2015, 84th Leg., ch. 608 (S.B. 662), § 1, eff. June 16, 2015.

Section 2 of Acts 2015, 84th Leg., ch. 608 (S.B. 662) provides:

"The changes in law made by this Act relating to the application of writ of habeas corpus apply regardless of whether the offense for which the applicant is in custody was committed before, on, or after the effective date [June 16, 2015] of this Act."

Art. 11.08. Applicant charged with felony

If a person is confined after indictment on a charge of felony, he may apply to the judge of the court in which he is indicted; or if there be no judge within the district, then to the judge of any district whose residence is nearest to the court house of the county in which the applicant is held in custody.

Acts 1965, 59th Leg., vol. 2, p. 317, ch. 722, eff. Jan. 1, 1966.

Art. 11.09. Applicant charged with misdemeanor

If a person is confined on a charge of misdemeanor, he may apply to the county judge of the county in which the misdemeanor is charged to have been committed, or if there be no county judge in said county, then to the county judge whose residence is nearest to the courthouse of the county in which the applicant is held in custody.

Acts 1965, 59th Leg., vol. 2, p. 317, ch. 722, eff. Jan. 1, 1966.

Art. 11.10. Proceedings under the writ

When motion has been made to a judge under the circumstances set forth in the two preceding Articles, he shall appoint a time when he will examine the cause of the applicant, and issue the writ returnable at that time, in the county where the offense is charged in the indictment or information to have been committed. He shall also specify some place in the county where he will hear the motion.

Acts 1965, 59th Leg., vol. 2, p. 317, ch. 722, eff. Jan. 1, 1966.

Art. 11.11. Early hearing

The time so appointed shall be the earliest day which the judge can devote to hearing the cause of the applicant.

Acts 1965, 59th Leg., vol. 2, p. 317, ch. 722, eff. Jan. 1, 1966.

Art. 11.12. Who may present petition

Either the party for whose relief the writ is intended, or any person for him, may present a petition to the proper authority for the purpose of obtaining relief.

Acts 1965, 59th Leg., vol. 2, p. 317, ch. 722, eff. Jan. 1, 1966.

Art. 11.13. Applicant

The word applicant, as used in this Chapter, refers to the person for whose relief the writ is asked, though the petition may be signed and presented by any other person.

Acts 1965, 59th Leg., vol. 2, p. 317, ch. 722, eff. Jan. 1, 1966.

Art. 11.14. Requisites of petition

The petition must state substantially:

1. That the person for whose benefit the application is made is illegally restrained in his liberty, and by whom, naming both parties, if their names are known, or if unknown, designating and describing them;

2. When the party is confined or restrained by virtue of any writ, order or process, or under color of either, a copy shall be annexed to the petition, or it shall be stated that a copy cannot be obtained;

3. When the confinement or restraint is not by virtue of any writ, order or process, the petition may state only that the party is illegally confined or restrained in his liberty;

4. There must be a prayer in the petition for the writ of habeas corpus; and

5. Oath must be made that the allegations of the petition are true, according to the belief of the petitioner.

Acts 1965, 59th Leg., vol. 2, p. 317, ch. 722, eff. Jan. 1, 1966.

Art. 11.15. Writ granted without delay

The writ of habeas corpus shall be granted without delay by the judge or court receiving the petition, unless it be manifest from the petition itself, or some documents annexed to it, that the party is entitled to no relief whatever.

Acts 1965, 59th Leg., vol. 2, p. 317, ch. 722, eff. Jan. 1, 1966.

Art. 11.16. Writ may issue without motion

A judge of the district or county court who has knowledge that any person is illegally confined or restrained in his liberty within his district or county may, if the case be one within his jurisdiction, issue the writ of habeas corpus, without any motion being made for the same.

Acts 1965, 59th Leg., vol. 2, p. 317, ch. 722, eff. Jan. 1, 1966.

Art. 11.17. Judge may issue warrant of arrest

Whenever it appears by satisfactory evidence to any judge authorized to issue such writ that any one is held in illegal confinement or custody, and there is good reason to believe that he will be carried out of the State, or suffer some irreparable injury before he can obtain relief in the usual course of law, or whenever the writ of habeas corpus has been issued and disregarded, the said judge may issue a warrant to any peace officer, or to any person specially named by said judge, directing him to take and bring such person before such judge, to be dealt with according to law.

Acts 1965, 59th Leg., vol. 2, p. 317, ch. 722, eff. Jan. 1, 1966.

Art. 11.18. May arrest detainer

Where it appears by the proof offered, under circumstances mentioned in the preceding Article, that the person charged with having illegal custody of the prisoner is, by such act, guilty of an offense against the law, the judge may, in the warrant, order that he be arrested and brought before him; and upon examination, he may be committed, discharged, or held to bail, as the law and the nature of the case may require.

Acts 1965, 59th, Leg., vol. 2, p. 317, ch. 722, eff. Jan. 1, 1966.

Art. 11.19. Proceedings under the warrant

The officer charged with the execution of the warrant shall bring the persons therein mentioned before the judge or court issuing the same, who shall inquire into the cause of the imprisonment or restraint, and make an order thereon, as in cases of habeas corpus, either remanding into custody, discharging or admitting to bail the party so imprisoned or restrained.

Acts 1965, 59th Leg., vol. 2, p. 317, ch. 722, eff. Jan. 1, 1966.

Art. 11.20. Officer executing warrant

The same power may be exercised by the officer executing the warrant in cases arising under the foregoing Articles as is exercised in the execution of warrants of arrest.

Acts 1965, 59th Leg., vol. 2, p. 317, ch. 722, eff. Jan. 1, 1966.

Art. 11.21. Constructive custody

The words "confined", "imprisoned", "in custody", "confinement", "imprisonment", refer not only to the actual, corporeal and forcible detention of a person, but likewise to any coercive measures by threats, menaces or the fear of injury, whereby one person exercises a control over the person of another, and detains him within certain limits.

Acts 1965, 59th Leg., vol. 2, p. 317, ch. 722, eff. Jan. 1, 1966.

Art. 11.22. Restraint

By "restraint" is meant the kind of control which one person exercises over another, not to confine him within certain limits, but to subject him to the general authority and power of the person claiming such right.

Acts 1965, 59th Leg., vol. 2, p. 317, ch. 722, eff. Jan. 1, 1966.

Art. 11.23. Scope of writ

The writ of habeas corpus is intended to be applicable to all such cases of confinement and restraint, where there is no lawful right in the person exercising the power, or where, though the power in fact exists, it is exercised in a manner or degree not sanctioned by law.

Acts 1965, 59th Leg., vol. 2, p. 317, ch. 722, eff. Jan. 1, 1966.

Art. 11.24. One committed in default of bail

Where a person has been committed to custody for failing to enter into bond, he is entitled to the writ of habeas corpus, if it be stated in the petition that there was no sufficient cause for requiring bail, or that the bail required is excessive. If the proof sustains the petition, it will entitle the party to be discharged, or have the bail reduced.

Acts 1965, 59th Leg., vol. 2, p. 317, ch. 722, eff. Jan. 1, 1966.

Art. 11.25. Person afflicted with disease

When a judge or court authorized to grant writs of habeas corpus shall be satisfied, upon investigation, that a person in legal custody is afflicted with a disease which will render a removal necessary for the preservation of life, an order may be made for the removal of the prisoner to some other place where his health will not be likely to suffer; or he may be admitted to bail when it appears that any species of confinement will endanger his life.

Acts 1965, 59th Leg., vol. 2, p. 317, ch. 722, eff. Jan. 1, 1966.

Art. 11.26. Who may serve writ

The service of the writ may be made by any person competent to testify.

Acts 1965, 59th Leg., vol. 2, p. 317, ch. 722, eff. Jan. 1, 1966.

Art. 11.27. How writ may be served and returned

The writ may be served by delivering a copy of the original to the person who is charged with having the party under restraint or in custody, and exhibiting the original, if demanded; if he refuse to receive it, he shall be informed verbally of the purport of the writ. If he refuses admittance to the person wishing to make the service, or conceals himself, a copy of the writ may be fixed upon some conspicuous part of the house where such person resides or conceals himself, or of the place where the prisoner is confined; and the person serving the writ of habeas corpus shall, in all cases, state fully, in his return, the manner and the time of the service of the writ.

Acts 1965, 59th Leg., vol. 2, p. 317, ch. 722, eff. Jan. 1, 1966.

Art. 11.28. Return under oath

The return of a writ of habeas corpus, under the provisions of the preceding Article, if made by any person other than an officer, shall be under oath.

Acts 1965, 59th Leg., vol. 2, p. 317, ch. 722, eff. Jan. 1, 1966.

Art. 11.29. Must make return

The person on whom the writ of habeas corpus is served shall immediately obey the same, and make the return required by law upon the copy of the original writ served on him, and this, whether the writ be directed to him or not.

Acts 1965, 59th Leg., vol. 2, p. 317, ch. 722, eff. Jan. 1, 1966.

Art. 11.30. How return is made

The return is made by stating in plain language upon the copy of the writ or some paper connected with it:

1. Whether it is true or not, according to the statement of the petition, that he has in his custody, or under his restraint, the person named or described in such petition;

2. By virtue of what authority, or for what cause, he took and detains such person;

3. If he had such person in his custody or under restraint at any time before the service of the writ, and has transferred him to the custody of another, he shall state particularly to whom, at what time, for what reason or by what authority he made such transfer;

4. He shall annex to his return the writ or warrant, if any, by virtue of which he holds the person in custody; and

5. The return must be signed and sworn to by the person making it.

Acts 1965, 59th Leg., vol. 2, p. 317, ch. 722, eff. Jan. 1, 1966.

Art. 11.31. Applicant brought before judge

The person on whom the writ is served shall bring before the judge the person in his custody, or under his restraint, unless it be made to appear that by reason of sickness he cannot be removed; in which case, another day may be appointed by the judge or court for hearing the cause, and for the production of the person confined; or the application may be heard and decided without the production of the person detained, by the consent of his counsel.

Acts 1965, 59th Leg., vol. 2, p. 317, ch. 722, eff. Jan. 1, 1966.

Art. 11.32. Custody pending examination

When the return of the writ has been made, and the applicant brought before the court, he is no longer detained on the original warrant or process, but under the authority of the habeas corpus. The safekeeping of the prisoner, pending the examination or hearing, is entirely under the direction and authority of the judge or court issuing the writ, or to which the return is made. He may be bailed from day to day, or be remanded to the same jail whence he came, or to any other place of safekeeping under the control of the judge or court, till the case is finally determined.

Acts 1965, 59th Leg., vol. 2, p. 317, ch. 722, eff. Jan. 1, 1966.

Art. 11.33. Court shall allow time

The court or judge granting the writ of habeas corpus shall allow reasonable time for the production of the person detained in custody.

Acts 1965, 59th Leg., vol. 2, p. 317, ch. 722, eff. Jan. 1, 1966.

Art. 11.34.   Disobeying writ

When service has been made upon a person charged with the illegal custody of another, if he refuses to obey the writ and make the return required by law, or, if he refuses to receive the writ, or conceals himself, the court or judge issuing the writ shall issue a warrant directed to any officer or other suitable person willing to execute the same, commanding him to arrest the person charged with the illegal custody or detention of another, and bring him before such court or judge. When such person has been arrested and brought before the court or judge, if he still refuses to return the writ, or does not produce the person in his custody, he shall be committed to jail and remain there until he is willing to obey the writ of habeas corpus, and until he pays all the costs of the proceeding.

Acts 1965, 59th Leg., vol. 2, p. 317, ch. 722, eff. Jan. 1, 1966.

Art. 11.35.   Further penalty for disobeying writ

Any person disobeying the writ of habeas corpus shall also be liable to a civil action at the suit of the party detained, and shall pay in such suit fifty dollars for each day of illegal detention and restraint, after service of the writ. It shall be deemed that a person has disobeyed the writ who detains a prisoner a longer time than three days after service thereof, unless where further time is allowed in the writ for making the return thereto.

Acts 1965, 59th Leg., vol. 2, p. 317, ch. 722, eff. Jan. 1, 1966.

Art. 11.36.   Applicant may be brought before court

In case of disobedience of the writ of habeas corpus, the person for whose relief it is intended may also be brought before the court or judge having competent authority, by an order for that purpose, issued to any peace officer or other proper person specially named.

Acts 1965, 59th Leg., vol. 2, p. 317, ch. 722, eff. Jan. 1, 1966.

Art. 11.37.   Death, etc., sufficient return of writ

It is a sufficient return of the writ of habeas corpus that the person, once detained, has died or escaped, or that by some superior force he has been taken from the custody of the person making the return; but where any such cause shall be assigned, the court or judge shall proceed to hear testimony; and the facts stated in the return shall be proved by satisfactory evidence.

Acts 1965, 59th Leg., vol. 2, p. 317, ch. 722, eff. Jan. 1, 1966.

Art. 11.38.   When a prisoner dies

When a prisoner confined in jail, or who is in legal custody, shall die, the officer having charge of him shall forthwith report the same to a justice of the peace of the county, who shall hold an inquest to ascertain the cause of his death. All the proceedings had in such cases shall be reduced to writing, certified and returned as in other cases of inquest; a certified copy of which shall be sufficient proof of the death of the prisoner at the hearing of a motion under habeas corpus.

Acts 1965, 59th Leg., vol. 2, p. 317, ch. 722, eff. Jan. 1, 1966.

Art. 11.39.   Who shall represent the State

If neither the county nor the district attorney be present, the judge may appoint some qualified practicing attorney to represent the State, who shall be paid the same fee allowed district attorneys for like services.

Acts 1965, 59th Leg., vol. 2, p. 317, ch. 722, eff. Jan. 1, 1966.

Art. 11.40.   Prisoner discharged

The judge or court before whom a person is brought by writ of habeas corpus shall examine the writ and the papers attached to it; and if no legal cause be shown for the imprisonment or restraint, or if it appear that the imprisonment or restraint, though at first legal, cannot for any cause be lawfully prolonged, the applicant shall be discharged.

Acts 1965, 59th Leg., vol. 2, p. 317, ch. 722, eff. Jan. 1, 1966.

Art. 11.41.   Where party is indicted for capital offense

If it appears by the return and papers attached that the party stands indicted for a capital offense, the judge or court having jurisdiction of the case shall, nevertheless, proceed to hear such testimony as may be offered on the part of the State and the applicant, and may either remand or admit him to bail, as the law and the facts may justify.

Acts 1965, 59th Leg., vol. 2, p. 317, ch. 722, eff. Jan. 1, 1966.

Art. 11.42.   If court has no jurisdiction

If it appear by the return and papers attached that the judge or court has no jurisdiction, such court or judge shall at once remand the applicant to the person from whose custody he has been taken.

Acts 1965, 59th Leg., vol. 2, p. 317, ch. 722, eff. Jan. 1, 1966.

Art. 11.43. Presumption of innocence

No presumption of guilt arises from the mere fact that a criminal accusation has been made before a competent authority.

Acts 1965, 59th Leg., vol. 2, p. 317, ch. 722, eff. Jan. 1, 1966.

Art. 11.44. Action of court upon examination

The judge or court, after having examined the return and all documents attached, and heard the testimony offered on both sides, shall, according to the facts and circumstances of the case, proceed either to remand the party into custody, admit him to bail or discharge him; provided, that no defendant shall be discharged after indictment without bail.

Acts 1965, 59th Leg., vol. 2, p. 317, ch. 722, eff. Jan. 1, 1966.

Art. 11.45. Void or informal

If it appears that the applicant is detained or held under a warrant of commitment which is informal, or void; yet, if from the document on which the warrant was based, or from the proof on the hearing of the habeas corpus, it appears that there is probable cause to believe that an offense has been committed by the prisoner, he shall not be discharged, but shall be committed or held to bail.

Acts 1965, 59th Leg., vol. 2, p. 317, ch. 722, eff. Jan. 1, 1966.

Art. 11.46. If proof shows offense

Where, upon an examination under habeas corpus, it appears to the court or judge that there is probable cause to believe that an offense has been committed by the prisoner, he shall not be discharged, but shall be committed or admitted to bail.

Acts 1965, 59th Leg., vol. 2, p. 317, ch. 722, eff. Jan. 1, 1966.

Art. 11.47. May summon magistrate

To ascertain the grounds on which an informal or void warrant has been issued, the judge or court may cause to be summoned the magistrate who issued the warrant, and may, by an order, require him to bring with him all the papers and proceedings touching the matter. The attendance of such magistrate and the production of such papers may be enforced by warrant of arrest.

Acts 1965, 59th Leg., vol. 2, p. 317, ch. 722, eff. Jan. 1, 1966.

Art. 11.48. Written issue not necessary

It shall not be necessary, on the trial of any cause arising under habeas corpus, to make up a written issue, though it may be done by the applicant for the writ. He may except to the sufficiency of, or controvert the return or any part thereof, or allege any new matter in avoidance. If written denial on his part be not made, it shall be considered, for the purpose of investigation, that the statements of said return are contested by a denial of the same; and the proof shall be heard accordingly, both for and against the applicant for relief.

Acts 1965, 59th Leg., vol. 2, p. 317, ch. 722, eff. Jan. 1, 1966.

Art. 11.49. Order of argument

The applicant shall have the right by himself or counsel to open and conclude the argument upon the trial under habeas corpus.

Acts 1965, 59th Leg., vol. 2, p. 317, ch. 722, eff. Jan. 1, 1966.

Art. 11.50. Costs

The judge trying the cause under habeas corpus may make such order as is deemed right concerning the cost of bringing the defendant before him, and all other costs of the proceeding, awarding the same either against the person to whom the writ was directed, the person seeking relief, or may award no costs at all.

Acts 1965, 59th Leg., vol. 2, p. 317, ch. 722, eff. Jan. 1, 1966.

Art. 11.51. Record of proceedings

If a writ of habeas corpus be made returnable before a court in session, all the proceedings had shall be entered of record by the clerk thereof, as in any other case in such court. When the motion is heard out of the county where the offense was committed, or in the Court of Criminal Appeals, the clerk shall transmit a certified copy of all the proceedings upon the motion to the clerk of the court which has jurisdiction of the offense.

Acts 1965, 59th Leg., vol. 2, p. 317, ch. 722, eff. Jan. 1, 1966.

Art. 11.52. Proceedings had in vacation

If the return is made and the proceedings had before a judge of a court in vacation, he shall cause all of the proceedings to be written, shall certify to the same, and cause them to be filed with the clerk of the court which has jurisdiction of the offense, who shall keep them safely.

Acts 1965, 59th Leg., vol. 2, p. 317, ch. 722, eff. Jan. 1, 1966.

Art. 11.53. Construing the two preceding Articles

The two preceding Articles refer only to cases where an applicant is held under accusation for some offense; in all other cases the proceedings had before the judge shall be filed and kept by the clerk of the court hearing the case.

Acts 1965, 59th Leg., vol. 2, p. 317, ch. 722, eff. Jan. 1, 1966.

Art. 11.54.   Court may grant necessary orders

The court or judge granting a writ of habeas corpus may grant all necessary orders to bring before him the testimony taken before the examining court, and may issue process to enforce the attendance of witnesses.

Acts 1965, 59th Leg., vol. 2, p. 317, ch. 722, eff. Jan. 1, 1966.

Art. 11.55.   Meaning of "return"

The word "return", as used in this Chapter, means the report made by the officer or person charged with serving the writ of habeas corpus, and also the answer made by the person served with such writ.

Acts 1965, 59th Leg., vol. 2, p. 317, ch. 722, eff. Jan. 1, 1966.

Art. 11.56.   Effect of discharge before indictment

Where a person, before indictment found against him, has been discharged or held to bail on habeas corpus by order of a court or judge of competent jurisdiction, he shall not be again imprisoned or detained in custody on an accusation for the same offense, until after he shall have been indicted, unless surrendered by his bail.

Acts 1965, 59th Leg., vol. 2, p. 317, ch. 722, eff. Jan. 1, 1966.

Art. 11.57.   Writ after indictment

Where a person once discharged or admitted to bail is afterward indicted for the same offense for which he has been once arrested, he may be committed on the indictment, but shall be again entitled to the writ of habeas corpus, and may be admitted to bail, if the facts of the case render it proper; but in cases where, after indictment is found, the cause of the defendant has been investigated on habeas corpus, and an order made, either remanding him to custody, or admitting him to bail, he shall neither be subject to be again placed in custody, unless when surrendered by his bail, nor shall he be again entitled to the writ of habeas corpus, except in the special cases mentioned in this Chapter.

Acts 1965, 59th Leg., vol. 2, p. 317, ch. 722, eff. Jan. 1, 1966.

Art. 11.58.   Person committed for a capital offense

If the accusation against the defendant for a capital offense has been heard on habeas corpus before indictment found, and he shall have been committed after such examination, he shall not be entitled to the writ, unless in the special cases mentioned in Articles 11.25 and 11.59.

Acts 1965, 59th Leg., vol. 2, p. 317, ch. 722, eff. Jan. 1, 1966.

Art. 11.59.   Obtaining writ a second time

A party may obtain the writ of habeas corpus a second time by stating in a motion therefor that since the hearing of his first motion important testimony has been obtained which it was not in his power to produce at the former hearing. He shall also set forth the testimony so newly discovered; and if it be that of a witness, the affidavit of the witness shall also accompany such motion.

Acts 1965, 59th Leg., vol. 2, p. 317, ch. 722, eff. Jan. 1, 1966.

Art. 11.60.   Refusing to execute writ

Any officer to whom a writ of habeas corpus, or other writ, warrant or process authorized by this Chapter shall be directed, delivered or tendered, who refuses to execute the same according to his directions, or who wantonly delays the service or execution of the same, shall be liable to fine as for contempt of court.

Acts 1965, 59th Leg., vol. 2, p. 317, ch. 722, eff. Jan. 1, 1966.

Art. 11.61.   Refusal to obey writ

Any one having another in his custody, or under his power, control or restraint who refuses to obey a writ of habeas corpus, or who evades the service of the same, or places the person illegally detained under the control of another, removes him, or in any other manner attempts to evade the operation of the writ, shall be dealt with as provided in Article 11.34 of this Code.

Acts 1965, 59th Leg., vol. 2, p. 317, ch. 722, eff. Jan. 1, 1966.

Art. 11.62.   Refusal to give copy of process

Any jailer, sheriff or other officer who has a prisoner in his custody and refuses, upon demand, to furnish a copy of the process under which he holds the person, is guilty of an offense, and shall be dealt with as provided in Article 11.34 of this Code for refusal to return the writ therein required.

Acts 1965, 59th Leg., vol. 2, p. 317, ch. 722, eff. Jan. 1, 1966.

Art. 11.63.   Held under federal authority

No person shall be discharged under the writ of habeas corpus who is in custody by virtue of a commitment for any offense exclusively cognizable by the courts of the United States, or by order or process issuing out of such courts in cases where they have jurisdiction, or who is held by virtue of any legal engagement or enlistment in the army, or who, being rightfully subject to the rules and articles of war, is confined by any one legally acting under the authority thereof, or who is held as a prisoner of war under the authority of the United States.

Acts 1965, 59th Leg., vol. 2, p. 317, ch. 722, eff. Jan. 1, 1966.

Art. 11.64. Application of chapter

This Chapter applies to all cases of habeas corpus for the enlargement of persons illegally held in custody or in any manner restrained in their personal liberty, for the admission of prisoners to bail, and for the discharge of prisoners before indictment upon a hearing of the testimony. Instead of a writ of habeas corpus in other cases heretofore used, a simple order shall be substituted.

Acts 1965, 59th Leg., vol. 2, p. 317, ch. 722, eff. Jan. 1, 1966.

Art. 11.65. Bond for certain applicants

(a) This article applies to an applicant for a writ of habeas corpus seeking relief from the judgment in a criminal case, other than an applicant seeking relief from a judgment imposing a penalty of death.

(b) On making proposed findings of fact and conclusions of law jointly stipulated to by the applicant and the state, or on approving proposed findings of fact and conclusions of law made by an attorney or magistrate appointed by the court to perform that duty and jointly stipulated to by the applicant and the state, the convicting court may order the release of the applicant on bond, subject to conditions imposed by the convicting court, until the applicant is denied relief, remanded to custody, or ordered released.

(c) For the purposes of this chapter, an applicant released on bond under this article remains restrained in his liberty.

(d) Article 44.04(b) does not apply to the release of an applicant on bond under this article.

Added by Acts 2003, 78th Leg., ch. 197, § 1, eff. June 2, 2003.

LIMITATION AND VENUE

CHAPTER TWELVE. LIMITATION

Art. 12.01. Felonies

Except as provided in Article 12.03, felony indictments may be presented within these limits, and not afterward:

(1) no limitation:

(A) murder and manslaughter;

(B) sexual assault under Section 22.011(a)(2), Penal Code, or aggravated sexual assault under Section 22.021(a)(1)(B), Penal Code;

(C) sexual assault, if:

(i) during the investigation of the offense biological matter is collected and subjected to forensic DNA testing and the testing results show that the matter does not match the victim or any other person whose identity is readily ascertained; or

(ii) probable cause exists to believe that the defendant has committed the same or a similar sexual offense against five or more victims;

(D) continuous sexual abuse of young child or children under Section 21.02, Penal Code;

(E) indecency with a child under Section 21.11, Penal Code;

(F) an offense involving leaving the scene of an accident under Section 550.021, Transportation Code, if the accident resulted in the death of a person;

(G) trafficking of persons under Section 20A.02(a)(7) or (8), Penal Code;

(H) continuous trafficking of persons under Section 20A.03, Penal Code; or

(I) compelling prostitution under Section 43.05(a)(2), Penal Code;

(2) ten years from the date of the commission of the offense:

(A) theft of any estate, real, personal or mixed, by an executor, administrator, guardian or trustee, with intent to defraud any creditor, heir, legatee, ward, distributee, beneficiary or settlor of a trust interested in such estate;

(B) theft by a public servant of government property over which he exercises control in his official capacity;

(C) forgery or the uttering, using or passing of forged instruments;

(D) injury to an elderly or disabled individual punishable as a felony of the first degree under Section 22.04, Penal Code;

(E) sexual assault, except as provided by Subdivision (1);

(F) arson;

(G) trafficking of persons under Section 20A.02(a)(1), (2), (3), or (4), Penal Code; or

(H) compelling prostitution under Section 43.05(a)(1), Penal Code;

(3) seven years from the date of the commission of the offense:

(A) misapplication of fiduciary property or property of a financial institution;

(B) securing execution of document by deception;

(C) a felony violation under Chapter 162, Tax Code;

(D) false statement to obtain property or credit under Section 32.32, Penal Code;

(E) money laundering;

(F) credit card or debit card abuse under Section 32.31, Penal Code;

(G) fraudulent use or possession of identifying information under Section 32.51, Penal Code;

(H) exploitation of a child, elderly individual, or disabled individual under Section 32.53, Penal Code;

(I) Medicaid fraud under Section 35A.02, Penal Code; or

(J) bigamy under Section 25.01, Penal Code, except as provided by Subdivision (6);

(4) five years from the date of the commission of the offense:

(A) theft or robbery;

(B) except as provided by Subdivision (5), kidnapping or burglary;

(C) injury to an elderly or disabled individual that is not punishable as a felony of the first degree under Section 22.04, Penal Code;

(D) abandoning or endangering a child; or

(E) insurance fraud;

(5) if the investigation of the offense shows that the victim is younger than 17 years of age at the time the offense is committed, 20 years from the 18th birthday of the victim of one of the following offenses:

(A) sexual performance by a child under Section 43.25, Penal Code;

(B) aggravated kidnapping under Section 20.04(a)(4), Penal Code, if the defendant committed the offense with the intent to violate or abuse the victim sexually; or

(C) burglary under Section 30.02, Penal Code, if the offense is punishable under Subsection (d) of that section and the defendant committed the offense with the intent to commit an offense described by Subdivision (1)(B) or (D) of this article or Paragraph (B) of this subdivision;

(6) ten years from the 18th birthday of the victim of the offense:

(A) trafficking of persons under Section 20A.02(a)(5) or (6), Penal Code;

(B) injury to a child under Section 22.04, Penal Code; or

(C) bigamy under Section 25.01, Penal Code, if the investigation of the offense shows that the person, other than the legal spouse of the defendant, whom the defendant marries or purports to marry or with whom the defendant lives under the appearance of being married is younger than 18 years of age at the time the offense is committed; or

(7) three years from the date of the commission of the offense: all other felonies.

Amended by Acts 1973, 63rd Leg., p. 975, ch. 399, § 2(B), eff. Jan. 1, 1974; Acts 1975, 64th Leg., p. 478, ch. 203, § 5, eff. Sept. 1, 1975; Acts 1983, 68th Leg., p. 413, ch. 85, § 1, eff. Sept. 1, 1983; Acts 1983, 68th Leg., p. 5317, ch. 977, § 7, eff. Sept. 1, 1983; Acts 1985, 69th Leg., ch. 330, § 1, eff. Aug. 26, 1985; Acts 1987, 70th Leg., ch. 716, § 1, eff. Sept. 1, 1987; Acts 1991, 72nd Leg., ch. 565, § 6, eff. Sept. 1, 1991; Acts 1995, 74th Leg., ch. 476, § 1, eff. Sept. 1, 1995; Acts 1997, 75th Leg., ch. 740, § 1, eff. Sept. 1, 1997; Acts 1999, 76th Leg., ch. 39, § 1, eff. Sept. 1, 1999; Acts 1999, 76th Leg., ch. 1285, § 33, eff. Sept. 1, 2000; Acts 2001, 77th Leg., ch. 12, § 1, eff. Sept. 1, 2001; Acts 2001, 77th Leg., ch. 1479, § 1, eff. Sept. 1, 2001; Acts 2001, 77th Leg., ch. 1482, § 1, eff. Sept. 1, 2001; Acts 2003, 78th Leg., ch. 371, § 6, eff. Sept. 1, 2003; Acts 2003, 78th Leg., ch. 1276, § 5.001, eff. Sept. 1, 2003; Acts 2005, 79th Leg., ch. 1162, § 6, eff. Sept. 1, 2005; Acts 2007, 80th Leg., ch. 285, § 6, eff. Sept. 1, 2007; Acts 2007, 80th Leg., ch. 593, § 1.03, eff. Sept. 1, 2007; Acts 2007, 80th Leg., ch. 640, § 1, eff. Sept. 1, 2007; Acts 2007, 80th Leg., ch. 841, § 1, eff. Sept. 1, 2007; Acts 2009, 81st Leg., ch. 87, § 6.001, eff. Sept. 1, 2009; Acts 2009, 81st Leg., ch. 1227, § 38, eff. Sept. 1, 2009; Acts 2011, 82nd Leg., ch. 1 (S.B. 24), § 2.03, eff. Sept. 1, 2011; Acts 2011, 82nd Leg., ch. 122 (H.B. 3000), § 2, eff. Sept. 1, 2011; Acts 2011, 82nd Leg., ch. 222 (H.B. 253), § 1, eff. Sept. 1, 2011; Acts 2011, 82nd Leg., ch. 620 (S.B. 688), § 1, eff. Sept. 1, 2011; Acts 2013, 83rd Leg., ch. 161 (S.B. 1093), § 3.003, eff. Sept. 1, 2013; Acts 2015, 84th Leg., ch. 332 (H.B. 10), § 1, eff. Sept. 1, 2015; Acts 2015, 84th Leg., ch. 918 (H.B. 189), § 2, eff. Sept. 1, 2015; Acts 2017, 85th Leg., ch. 392 (S.B. 998), § 1, eff. Sept. 1, 2017.

Section 15 of Acts 2015, 84th Leg., ch. 332 (H.B. 10) provides:

"The change in law made by this Act to Article 12.01, Code of Criminal Procedure, does not apply to an offense if the prosecution of that offense becomes barred by limitation before the effective date [Sept. 1, 2015] of this Act. The prosecution of that offense remains barred as if this Act had not taken effect."

Section 4 of Acts 2015, 84th Leg., ch. 918 (H.B. 189) provides:

"Article 12.01, Code of Criminal Procedure, as amended by this Act, does not apply to an offense if the prosecution of that offense becomes barred by limitation before the effective date [Sept. 1, 2015] of this Act. The prosecution of that offense remains barred as if this Act had not taken effect."

Section 2 of Acts 2017, 85th Leg., ch. 392 (S.B. 998) provides:

"Article 12.01, Code of Criminal Procedure, as amended by this Act, does not apply to an offense if the prosecution of that offense becomes barred by limitation before the effective date [Sept. 1, 2017] of this Act. The prosecution of that offense remains barred as if this Act had not taken effect."

Art. 12.02. Misdemeanors

(a) An indictment or information for any Class A or Class B misdemeanor may be presented within two years from the date of the commission of the offense, and not afterward.

(b) A complaint or information for any Class C misdemeanor may be presented within two years from the date of the commission of the offense, and not afterward.

Amended by Acts 1973, 63rd Leg., p. 975, ch. 399, § 2(B), eff. Jan. 1, 1974; Acts 2009, 81st Leg., ch. 472, § 1, eff. Sept. 1, 2009.

Art. 12.03. Aggravated offenses, attempt, conspiracy, solicitation, organized criminal activity

(a) The limitation period for criminal attempt is the same as that of the offense attempted.

(b) The limitation period for criminal conspiracy or organized criminal activity is the same as that of the most serious offense that is the object of the conspiracy or the organized criminal activity.

(c) The limitation period for criminal solicitation is the same as that of the felony solicited.

(d) Except as otherwise provided by this chapter, any offense that bears the title "aggravated" shall carry the same limitation period as the primary crime.

Amended by Acts 1973, 63rd Leg., p. 975, ch. 399, § 2(B), eff. Jan. 1, 1974; Acts 1987, 70th Leg., ch. 1133, § 1, eff. Sept. 1, 1987; Acts 1997, 75th Leg., ch. 740, § 2, eff. Sept. 1, 1997.

Art. 12.04. Computation

The day on which the offense was committed and the day on which the indictment or information is presented shall be excluded from the computation of time.

Amended by Acts 1973, 63rd Leg., p. 976, ch. 399, § 2(B), eff. Jan. 1, 1974.

Art. 12.05. Absence from State and time of pendency of indictment, etc., not computed

(a) The time during which the accused is absent from the state shall not be computed in the period of limitation.

(b) The time during the pendency of an indictment, information, or complaint shall not be computed in the period of limitation.

(c) The term "during the pendency," as used herein, means that period of time beginning with the day the indictment, information, or complaint is filed in a court of competent jurisdiction, and ending with the day such accusation is, by an order of a trial court having jurisdiction thereof, determined to be invalid for any reason.

Amended by Acts 1973, 63rd Leg., p. 976, ch. 399, § 2(B), eff. Jan. 1, 1974.

Art. 12.06. An indictment is "presented," when

An indictment is considered as "presented" when it has been duly acted upon by the grand jury and received by the court.

Amended by Acts 1973, 63rd Leg., p. 976, ch. 399, § 2(B), eff. Jan. 1, 1974.

Art. 12.07. An information is "presented," when

An information is considered as "presented," when it has been filed by the proper officer in the proper court.

Amended by Acts 1973, 63rd Leg., p. 976, ch. 399, § 2(B), eff. Jan. 1, 1974.

CHAPTER THIRTEEN. VENUE

Article

CODE OF CRIMINAL PROCEDURE

A former Chapter 13, consisting of articles 13.01 to 13.26, was amended by Acts 1973, 63rd Leg., p. 976, ch. 399, § 2(C), effective January 1, 1974, to consist of Vernon's Ann. Texas C.C.P. arts. 13.01 to 13.19. Section 1 of said Act also enacted the Texas Penal Code.

Art. 13.01. Offenses committed outside this State

Offenses committed wholly or in part outside this State, under circumstances that give this State jurisdiction to prosecute the offender, may be prosecuted in any county in which the offender is found or in any county in which an element of the offense occurs.

Amended by Acts 1973, 63rd Leg., p. 976, ch. 399, § 2(C), eff. Jan. 1, 1974.

Art. 13.02. Forgery

Forgery may be prosecuted in any county where the writing was forged, or where the same was used or passed, or attempted to be used or passed, or deposited or placed with another person, firm, association, or corporation either for collection or credit for the account of any person, firm, association or corpo-

ration. In addition, a forging and uttering, using or passing of forged instruments in writing which concern or affect the title to land in this State may be prosecuted in the county in which such land, or any part thereof, is situated.

Amended by Acts 1973, 63rd Leg., p. 976, ch. 399, § 2(C), eff. Jan. 1, 1974.

Art. 13.03. Perjury

Perjury and aggravated perjury may be prosecuted in the county where committed, or in the county where the false statement is used or attempted to be used.

Amended by Acts 1973, 63rd Leg., p. 976, ch. 399, § 2(C), eff. Jan. 1, 1974.

Art. 13.04. On the boundaries of counties

An offense committed on the boundaries of two or more counties, or within four hundred yards thereof, may be prosecuted and punished in any one of such counties and any offense committed on the premises of any airport operated jointly by two municipalities and situated in two counties may be prosecuted and punished in either county.

Amended by Acts 1973, 63rd Leg., p. 977, ch. 399, § 2(C), eff. Jan. 1, 1974; Acts 1973, 63rd Leg., p. 1251, ch. 454, art. 2, § 1, eff. Jan. 1, 1974; Acts 1981, 67th Leg., p. 2239, ch. 534, § 1, eff. Aug. 31, 1981.

Art. 13.045. on the Boundaries of Certain Municipalities

An offense punishable by fine only that is committed on or near the boundary of contiguous municipalities that have entered into an agreement authorized by Article 4.14(f) and Section 29.003(h), Government Code, may be prosecuted in either of those municipalities as provided in the agreement.

Added by Acts 2009, 81st Leg., ch. 230, § 2, eff. Sept. 1, 2009. Amended by Acts 2017, 85th Leg., ch. 1004 (H.B. 1264), § 2, eff. Sept. 1, 2017.

Art. 13.05. Criminal homicide committed outside this State

The offense of criminal homicide committed wholly or in part outside this State, under circumstances that give this State jurisdiction to prosecute the offender, may be prosecuted in the county where the injury was inflicted, or in the county where the offender was located when he inflicted the injury, or in the county where the victim died or the body was found.

Amended by Acts 1973, 63rd Leg., p. 977, ch. 399, § 2(C), eff. Jan. 1, 1974.

Art. 13.06. Committed on a boundary stream

If an offense be committed upon any river or stream, the boundary of this State, it may be prosecuted in the county the boundary of which is upon such stream or river, and the county seat of which is nearest the place where the offense was committed.

Amended by Acts 1973, 63rd Leg., p. 977, ch. 399, § 2(C), eff. Jan. 1, 1974.

Art. 13.07. Injured in one county and dying in another

If a person receives an injury in one county and dies in another by reason of such injury, the offender may be prosecuted in the county where the injury was received or where the death occurred, or in the county where the dead body is found.

Amended by Acts 1973, 63rd Leg., p. 977, ch. 399, § 2(C), eff. Jan. 1, 1974.

Art. 13.075. Child injured in one county and residing in another

An offense under Title 5, Penal Code,[1] involving a victim younger than 18 years of age, or an offense under Section 25.03, Penal Code, that results in bodily injury to a child younger than 18 years of age, may be prosecuted in the county:

(1) in which an element of the offense was committed;

(2) in which the defendant is apprehended;

(3) in which the victim resides; or

(4) in which the defendant resides.

Added by Acts 2011, 82nd Leg., ch. 1100 (S.B. 1551), § 1, eff. Sept. 1, 2011.

[1] V.T.C.A., Penal Code § 19.01 et seq.

Art. 13.08. Theft; Organized Retail Theft; Cargo Theft

(a) Where property is stolen in one county and removed to another county, the offender may be prosecuted either in the county in which the property was stolen or in any other county through or into which the property was removed.

(b) An offense under Section 31.16 or 31.18, Penal Code, may be prosecuted in any county in which an underlying theft could have been prosecuted as a separate offense.

Amended by Acts 1973, 63rd Leg., p. 977, ch. 399, § 2(C), eff. Jan. 1, 1974; Acts 2007, 80th Leg., ch. 1274, § 2, eff. Sept. 1, 2007; Acts 2011, 82nd Leg., ch. 433 (S.B. 1103), § 1, eff. Sept. 1, 2011; Acts 2015, 84th Leg., ch. 1219 (S.B. 1828), §§ 1, 2, eff. Sept. 1, 2015.

Art. 13.09. Hindering secured creditors

If secured property is taken from one county and unlawfully disposed of in another county or state, the offender may be prosecuted either in the county in which such property was disposed of, or in the county from which it was removed, or in the county in which the security agreement is filed.

Amended by Acts 1973, 63rd Leg., p. 976, ch. 399, § 2(C), eff. Jan. 1, 1974.

Art. 13.10. Persons acting under authority of this State

An offense committed outside this State by any officer acting under the authority of this State, under circumstances that give this state jurisdiction to prosecute the offender, may be prosecuted in the county of his residence or, if a nonresident of this State, in Travis County.

Amended by Acts 1973, 63rd Leg., p. 977, ch. 399, § 2(C), eff. Jan. 1, 1974.

Art. 13.11. On vessels

An offense committed on board a vessel which is at the time upon any navigable water within the boundaries of this State, may be prosecuted in any county through which the vessel is navigated in the course of her voyage, or in the county where the voyage commences or terminates.

Amended by Acts 1973, 63rd Leg., p. 977, ch. 399, § 2(C), eff. Jan. 1, 1974.

Art. 13.12. Trafficking of persons, false imprisonment, kidnapping, and smuggling of persons

Venue for trafficking of persons, false imprisonment, kidnapping, and smuggling of persons is in:

(1) the county in which the offense was committed; or

(2) any county through, into, or out of which the person trafficked, falsely imprisoned, kidnapped, or transported may have been taken.

Amended by Acts 1973, 63rd Leg., p. 977, ch. 399, § 2(C), eff. Jan. 1, 1974; Acts 2011, 82nd Leg., ch. 1 (S.B. 24), § 2.04, eff. Sept. 1, 2011; Acts 2011, 82nd Leg., ch. 223 (H.B. 260), § 4, eff. Sept. 1, 2011; Acts 2013, 83rd Leg., ch. 161 (S.B. 1093), § 3.004, eff. Sept. 1, 2013.

Art. 13.13. Conspiracy

Criminal conspiracy may be prosecuted in the county where the conspiracy was entered into, in the county where the conspiracy was agreed to be executed, or in any county in which one or more of the conspirators does any act to effect an object of the conspiracy. If the object of the conspiracy is an offense classified as a felony under the Tax Code, regardless of whether the offense was committed, the conspiracy may be prosecuted in any county in which venue is proper under the Tax Code for the offense. If a conspiracy was entered into outside this State under circumstances that give this State jurisdiction to prosecute the offender, the offender may be prosecuted in the county where the conspiracy was agreed to be executed, in the county where any one of the conspirators was found, or in Travis County.

Amended by Acts 1973, 63rd Leg., p. 978, ch. 399, § 2(C), eff. Jan. 1, 1974; Acts 2011, 82nd Leg., ch. 68 (S.B. 934), § 1, eff. Sept. 1, 2011.

Art. 13.14.   Bigamy

Bigamy may be prosecuted:

(1) in the county where the bigamous marriage occurred;

(2) in any county in this State in which the parties to such bigamous marriage may live or cohabit together as man and wife; or

(3) in any county in this State in which a party to the bigamous marriage not charged with the offense resides.

Amended by Acts 1973, 63rd Leg., p. 978, ch. 399, § 2(C), eff. Jan. 1, 1974; Acts 1989, 71st Leg., ch. 1112, § 1, eff. Aug. 28, 1989.

Art. 13.15.   Sexual assault

Sexual assault may be prosecuted in the county in which it is committed, in the county in which the victim is abducted, or in any county through or into which the victim is transported in the course of the abduction and sexual assault. When it shall come to the knowledge of any district judge whose court has jurisdiction under this Article that sexual assault has probably been committed, he shall immediately, if his court be in session, and if not in session, then, at the first term thereafter in any county of the district, call the attention of the grand jury thereto; and if the court be in session, but the grand jury has been discharged, he shall immediately recall the grand jury to investigate the accusation. The district courts are authorized and directed to change the venue in such cases whenever it shall be necessary to secure a speedy trial.

Amended by Acts 1973, 63rd Leg., p. 978, ch. 399, § 2(C), eff. Jan. 1, 1974; Acts 1977, 65th Leg., p. 692, ch. 262, § 1, eff. May 25, 1977; Acts 1981, 67th Leg., p. 2636, ch. 707, § 4(17), eff. Aug. 31, 1981; Acts 1983, 68th Leg., p. 5317, ch. 977, § 7, eff. Sept. 1, 1983.

Art. 13.16.   Criminal nonsupport

Criminal nonsupport may be prosecuted in the county where the offended spouse or child is residing at the time the information or indictment is presented.

Amended by Acts 1973, 63rd Leg., p. 978, ch. 399, § 2(C), eff. Jan. 1, 1974.

Art. 13.17.   Proof of venue

In all cases mentioned in this Chapter, the indictment or information, or any pleading in the case, may allege that the offense was committed in the county where the prosecution is carried on. To sustain the allegation of venue, it shall only be necessary to prove by the preponderance of the evidence that by reason of the facts in the case, the county where such prosecution is carried on has venue.

Amended by Acts 1973, 63rd Leg., p. 978, ch. 399, § 2(C), eff. Jan. 1, 1974.

Art. 13.18.   Other offenses

If venue is not specifically stated, the proper county for the prosecution of offenses is that in which the offense was committed.

Amended by Acts 1973, 63rd Leg., p. 978, ch. 399, § 2(C), eff. Jan. 1, 1974.

Art. 13.19.   Where venue cannot be determined

If an offense has been committed within the state and it cannot readily be determined within which county or counties the commission took place, trial may be held in the county in which the defendant resides, in the county in which he is apprehended, or in the county to which he is extradited.

Amended by Acts 1973, 63rd Leg., p. 979, ch. 399, § 2(C), eff. Jan., 1, 1974.

Art. 13.20.   Venue by consent

The trial of all felony cases, without a jury, may, with the consent of the defendant in writing, his attorney, and the attorney for the state, be held in any county within the judicial district or districts for the county where venue is otherwise authorized by law.

Added by Acts 1975, 64th Leg., p. 242, ch. 91, § 1, eff. Sept. 1; 1975.

Art. 13.21.   Organized criminal activity

The offense of engaging in organized criminal activity may be prosecuted in any county in which any act is committed to effect an objective of the combination or, if the prosecution is based on a criminal offense classified as a felony under the Tax Code, in any county in which venue is proper under the Tax Code for the offense.

Added by Acts 1977, 65th Leg., p. 924, ch. 346, § 2, eff. June 10, 1977. Amended by Acts 2011, 82nd Leg., ch. 68 (S.B. 934), § 2, eff. Sept. 1, 2011.

Art. 13.22. Possession and delivery of marihuana

An offense of possession or delivery of marihuana may be prosecuted in the county where the offense was committed or with the consent of the defendant in a county that is adjacent to and in the same judicial district as the county where the offense was committed.

Added by Acts 1979, 66th Leg., p. 18, ch. 10, § 1, eff. March 7, 1979.

Art. 13.23. Unauthorized use of a vehicle

An offense of unauthorized use of a vehicle may be prosecuted in any county where the unauthorized use of the vehicle occurred or in the county in which the vehicle was originally reported stolen.

Added by Acts 1985, 69th Leg., ch. 719, § 1, eff. Aug. 26, 1985.

Art. 13.24. Illegal recruitment of athletes

An offense of illegal recruitment of an athlete may be prosecuted in any county in which the offense was committed or in the county in which is located the institution of higher education in which the athlete agreed to enroll or was influenced to enroll.

Added by Acts 1989, 71st Leg., ch. 125, § 2, eff. Sept. 1, 1989.

Art. 13.25. Computer crimes

(a) In this section "access," "computer," "computer network," "computer program," "computer system," and "owner" have the meanings assigned to those terms by Section 33.01, Penal Code.

(b) An offense under Chapter 33, Penal Code, may be prosecuted in:

(1) the county of the principal place of business of the owner or lessee of a computer, computer network, or computer system involved in the offense;

(2) any county in which a defendant had control or possession of:

(A) any proceeds of the offense; or

(B) any books, records, documents, property, negotiable instruments, computer programs, or other material used in furtherance of the offense;

(3) any county from which, to which, or through which access to a computer, computer network, computer program, or computer system was made in violation of Chapter 33, whether by wires, electromagnetic waves, microwaves, or any other means of communication; or

(4) any county in which an individual who is a victim of the offense resides.

Added by Acts 1989, 71st Leg., ch. 306, § 4, eff. Sept. 1, 1989. Renumbered from Vernon's Ann.C.C.P. art. 13.24 by Acts 1991, 72nd Leg., ch. 16, § 19.01(1), eff. Aug. 26, 1991. Amended by Acts 1993, 73rd Leg., ch. 900, § 3.01, eff. Sept. 1, 1994; Acts 1997, 75th Leg., ch. 306, § 4, eff. Sept. 1, 1997; Acts 2013, 83rd Leg., ch. 547 (S.B. 222), § 1, eff. Sept. 1, 2013.

Art. 13.26. Telecommunications crimes

An offense under Chapter 33A, Penal Code, may be prosecuted in the county in which the telecommunications service originated or terminated or in the county to which the bill for the telecommunications service was or would have been delivered.

Added by Acts 1997, 75th Leg., ch. 306, § 5, eff. Sept. 1, 1997.

Art. 13.27. Simulating legal process

An offense under Section 32.46, 32.48, 32.49, or 37.13, Penal Code, may be prosecuted either in the county from which any material document was sent or in the county in which it was delivered.

Added by Acts 1997, 75th Leg., ch. 189, § 12, eff. May 21, 1997. Renumbered from Vernon's Ann. Texas C.C.P. art. 13.26 by Acts 1999, 76th Leg., ch. 62, § 19.01(6), eff. Sept. 1, 1999.

Art. 13.271. Prosecution of mortgage fraud

(a) In this article, "real estate transaction" means a sale, lease, trade, exchange, gift, grant, or other conveyance of a real property interest.

(b) Any offense under Chapter 32, Penal Code, that involves a real estate transaction may be prosecuted in:

(1) the county where the property is located; or

(2) any county in which part of the transaction occurred, including the generation of documentation supporting the transaction.

(c) An offense under Section 32.46, 32.48, or 32.49, Penal Code, that involves a real estate transaction may also be prosecuted in any county authorized by Article 13.27.

Added by Acts 2011, 82nd Leg., ch. 389 (S.B. 485), § 1, eff. Sept. 1, 2011.

Art. 13.28.   Escape; unauthorized absence

An offense of escape under Section 38.06, Penal Code, or unauthorized absence under Section 38.113, Penal Code, may be prosecuted in:

(1) the county in which the offense of escape or unauthorized absence was committed; or

(2) the county in which the defendant committed the offense for which the defendant was placed in custody, detained, or required to submit to treatment.

Added by Acts 2003, 78th Leg., ch. 392, § 1, eff. Sept. 1, 2003.

Art. 13.29.   Fraudulent use or possession of identifying information

An offense under Section 32.51, Penal Code, may be prosecuted in any county in which the offense was committed or in the county of residence for the person whose identifying information was fraudulently obtained, possessed, transferred, or used.

Added by Acts 2003, 78th Leg., ch. 415, § 1, eff. Sept. 1, 2003. Renumbered from Vernon's Ann.C.C.P. art. 13.28 by Acts 2005, 79th Leg., ch. 728, § 23.001(7), eff. Sept. 1, 2005.

Art. 13.295.   Unauthorized acquisition or transfer of certain financial information

An offense under Section 31.17, Penal Code, may be prosecuted in any county in which the offense was committed or in the county of residence of the person whose financial sight order or payment card information was unlawfully obtained or transferred.

Added by Acts 2011, 82nd Leg., ch. 260 (H.B. 1215), § 3, eff. Sept. 1, 2011.

Art. 13.30.   Fraudulent, substandard, or fictitious degree

An offense under Section 32.52, Penal Code, may be prosecuted in the county in which an element of the offense occurs or in Travis County.

Added by Acts 2005, 79th Leg., ch. 1039, § 9, eff. Sept. 1, 2005.

Art. 13.31.   Failure to comply with sex offender registration statute

An offense under Chapter 62 may be prosecuted in:

(1) any county in which an element of the offense occurs;

(2) the county in which the person subject to Chapter 62 last registered, verified registration, or otherwise complied with a requirement of Chapter 62;

(3) the county in which the person required to register under Chapter 62 has indicated that the person intends to reside, regardless of whether the person establishes or attempts to establish residency in that county;

(4) any county in which the person required to register under Chapter 62 is placed under custodial arrest for an offense subsequent to the person's most recent reportable conviction or adjudication under Chapter 62; or

(5) the county in which the person required to register under Chapter 62 resides or is found by a peace officer, regardless of how long the person has been in the county or intends to stay in the county.

Added by Acts 2005, 79th Leg., ch. 1008, § 1.02, eff. Sept. 1, 2005. Renumbered from Vernon's Ann.C.C.P. art. 13.30 by Acts 2007, 80th Leg., ch. 921, § 17.001(8), eff. Sept. 1, 2007. Amended by Acts 2009, 81st Leg., ch. 661, § 1, eff. Sept. 1, 2009.

Art. 13.315.   Failure to Comply With Sexually Violent Predator Civil Commitment Requirement

An offense under Section 841.085, Health and Safety Code, may be prosecuted in the county in which any element of the offense occurs or in the court that retains jurisdiction over the civil commitment proceeding under Section 841.082, Health and Safety Code.

Added by Acts 2007, 80th Leg., ch. 1219, § 10, eff. Sept. 1, 2007. Amended by Acts 2015, 84th Leg., ch. 845 (S.B. 746), § 32, eff. June 17, 2015.

Section 43 of Acts 2015, 84th Leg., ch. 845 (S.B. 746) provides:

"To the extent of any conflict, this Act prevails over another Act of the 84th Legislature, Regular Session, 2015, relating to nonsubstantive additions to and corrections in enacted codes."

Art. 13.32.   Misapplication of certain property

(a) An offender who misapplies property held as a fiduciary or property of a financial institution in one county and removes the property to another county may be prosecuted in the county where the offender misapplied the property, in any other county through or into which the offender removed the property, or, as applicable, in the county in which the fiduciary was appointed to serve.

(b) An offense related to misapplication of construction trust funds under Chapter 162, Property Code, must be prosecuted in the county where the construction project is located.

Added by Acts 2005, 79th Leg., ch. 1275, § 1, eff. Sept. 1, 2005. Renumbered from Vernon's Ann.C.C.P. art. 13.30 by Acts 2007, 80th Leg., ch. 921, § 17.001(9).

Art. 13.34. Certain Offenses Committed Against a Child Committed to the Texas Juvenile Justice Department

An offense described by Article 104.003(a) committed by an employee or officer of the Texas Juvenile Justice Department or a person providing services under a contract with the department against a child committed to the department may be prosecuted in:

(1) any county in which an element of the offense occurred; or

(2) Travis County.

Added by Acts 2009, 81st Leg., ch. 947, § 1, eff. Sept. 1, 2009; Acts 2009, 81st Leg., ch. 1187, § 4.001, eff. June 1, 2009. Amended by Acts 2015, 84th Leg., ch. 734 (H.B. 1549), § 2, eff. Sept. 1, 2015.

Section 150 of Acts 2015, 84th Leg., ch. 734 (H.B. 1549) provides:

"If any provision of this Act conflicts with a provision of another Act of the 84th Legislature, Regular Session, 2015, the provision of the other Act controls to the extent of the conflict, regardless of the date of enactment."

Art. 13.35. Money laundering

Money laundering may be prosecuted in the county in which the offense was committed as provided by Article 13.18 or, if the prosecution is based on a criminal offense classified as a felony under the Tax Code, in any county in which venue is proper under the Tax Code for the offense.

Added by Acts 2011, 82nd Leg., ch. 68 (S.B. 934), § 3, eff. Sept. 1, 2011.

Art. 13.36. Stalking

The offense of stalking may be prosecuted in any county in which an element of the offense occurred.

Added by Acts 2011, 82nd Leg., ch. 591 (S.B. 82), § 2, eff. Sept. 1, 2011.

Art. 13.37. Obstruction or Retaliation

An offense under Section 36.06(a)(1), Penal Code, may be prosecuted in any county in which:

(1) the harm occurs; or

(2) the threat to do harm originated or was received.

Added by Acts 2017, 85th Leg., ch. 328 (H.B. 268), § 1, eff. Sept. 1, 2017.

Section 2 of Acts 2017, 85th Leg., ch. 328 (H.B. 268) provides:

"The change in law made by this Act applies only to venue for the trial of an offense committed on or after the effective date [Sept. 1, 2017] of this Act. Venue for the trial of an offense committed before the effective date of this Act is covered by the law in effect when the offense was committed, and the former law is continued in effect for that purpose. For purposes of this section, an offense was committed before the effective date of this Act if any element of the offense occurred before that date."

ARREST, COMMITMENT AND BAIL

CHAPTER FOURTEEN. ARREST WITHOUT WARRANT

Art. 14.01. Offense within view

(a) A peace officer or any other person, may, without a warrant, arrest an offender when the offense is committed in his presence or within his view, if the offense is one classed as a felony or as an offense against the public peace.

(b) A peace officer may arrest an offender without a warrant for any offense committed in his presence or within his view.

Acts 1965, 59th Leg., vol. 2, p. 317, ch. 722, eff. Jan. 1, 1966. Amended by Acts 1967, 60th Leg., p. 1735, ch. 659, § 8, eff. Aug. 28, 1967.

Art. 14.02. Within view of magistrate

A peace officer may arrest, without warrant, when a felony or breach of the peace has been committed in the presence or within the view of a magistrate, and such magistrate verbally orders the arrest of the offender.

Acts 1965, 59th Leg., vol. 2, p. 317, ch. 722, eff. Jan. 1, 1966.

Art. 14.03. Authority of peace officers

(a) Any peace officer may arrest, without warrant:

(1) persons found in suspicious places and under circumstances which reasonably show that such persons have been guilty of some felony, violation of Title 9, Chapter 42, Penal Code, breach of the peace, or offense under Section 49.02, Penal Code, or threaten, or are about to commit some offense against the laws;

(2) persons who the peace officer has probable cause to believe have committed an assault resulting in bodily injury to another person and the peace officer has probable cause to believe that there is danger of further bodily injury to that person;

(3) persons who the peace officer has probable cause to believe have committed an offense defined by Section 25.07, Penal Code, if the offense is not committed in the presence of the peace officer;

(4) persons who the peace officer has probable cause to believe have committed an offense involving family violence;

(5) persons who the peace officer has probable cause to believe have prevented or interfered with an individual's ability to place a telephone call in an emergency, as defined by Section 42.062(d), Penal Code, if the offense is not committed in the presence of the peace officer; or

(6) a person who makes a statement to the peace officer that would be admissible against the person under Article 38.21 and establishes probable cause to believe that the person has committed a felony.

(b) A peace officer shall arrest, without a warrant, a person the peace officer has probable cause to believe has committed an offense under Section 25.07, Penal Code, if the offense is committed in the presence of the peace officer.

(c) If reasonably necessary to verify an allegation of a violation of a protective order or of the commission of an offense involving family violence, a peace officer shall remain at the scene of the investigation to verify the allegation and to prevent the further commission of the violation or of family violence.

(d) A peace officer who is outside his jurisdiction may arrest, without warrant, a person who commits an offense within the officer's presence or view, if the offense is a felony, a violation of Chapter 42 or 49, Penal Code, or a breach of the peace. A peace officer making an arrest under this subsection shall, as soon as practicable after making the arrest, notify a law enforcement agency having jurisdiction where the arrest was made. The law enforcement agency shall then take custody of the person committing the offense and take the person before a magistrate in compliance with Article 14.06 of this code.

(e) The justification for conduct provided under Section 9.21, Penal Code, applies to a peace officer when the peace officer is performing a duty required by this article.

(f) In this article, "family violence" has the meaning assigned by Section 71.004, Family Code.

(g)(1) A peace officer listed in Subdivision (1), (2), or (5), Article 2.12, who is licensed under Chapter 1701, Occupations Code, and is outside of the officer's

jurisdiction may arrest without a warrant a person who commits any offense within the officer's presence or view, other than a violation of Subtitle C, Title 7, Transportation Code.[1]

(2) A peace officer listed in Subdivision (3), Article 2.12, who is licensed under Chapter 1701, Occupations Code, and is outside of the officer's jurisdiction may arrest without a warrant a person who commits any offense within the officer's presence or view, except that an officer described in this subdivision who is outside of that officer's jurisdiction may arrest a person for a violation of Subtitle C, Title 7, Transportation Code, only if the offense is committed in the county or counties in which the municipality employing the peace officer is located.

(3) A peace officer making an arrest under this subsection shall as soon as practicable after making the arrest notify a law enforcement agency having jurisdiction where the arrest was made. The law enforcement agency shall then take custody of:

(A) the person committing the offense and take the person before a magistrate in compliance with Article 14.06; and

(B) any property seized during or after the arrest as if the property had been seized by a peace officer of that law enforcement agency.

Acts 1965, 59th Leg., vol. 2, p. 317, ch. 722, eff. Jan. 1, 1966. Amended by Acts 1967, 60th Leg., p. 1735, ch. 659, § 9, eff. Aug. 28, 1967; Acts 1981, 67th Leg., p. 1865, ch. 442, § 1, eff. Aug. 31, 1981; Acts 1985, 69th Leg., ch. 583, § 2, eff. Sept. 1, 1985; Acts 1987, 70th Leg., ch. 68, § 1, eff. Sept. 1, 1987; Acts 1989, 71st Leg., ch. 740, § 1, eff. Aug. 28, 1989; Acts 1991, 72nd Leg., ch. 542, § 9, eff. Sept. 1, 1991; Acts 1993, 73rd Leg., ch. 900, § 3.02, eff. Sept. 1, 1994; Acts 1995, 74th Leg., ch. 76, § 14.17, eff. Sept. 1, 1995; Acts 1995, 74th Leg., ch. 829, § 1, eff. Aug. 28, 1995; Acts 1999, 76th Leg., ch. 62, § 3.02, eff. Sept. 1, 1999; Acts 1999, 76th Leg., ch. 210, § 2, eff. May 24, 1999; Acts 2003, 78th Leg., ch. 460, § 2, eff. Sept. 1, 2003; Acts 2003, 78th Leg., ch. 836, § 2, eff. Sept. 1, 2003; Acts 2003, 78th Leg., ch. 897, § 1, eff. Sept. 1, 2003; Acts 2003, 78th Leg., ch. 989, § 1, eff. Sept. 1, 2003; Acts 2003, 78th Leg., ch. 1164, § 2, eff. Sept. 1, 2003; Acts 2003, 78th Leg., ch. 1276, § 7.002(d), eff. Sept. 1, 2003; Acts 2005, 79th Leg., ch. 728, § 4.002, eff. Sept. 1, 2005; Acts 2005, 79th Leg., ch. 788, §§ 4, 5, eff. Sept. 1, 2005; Acts 2005, 79th Leg., ch. 847, § 1, eff. Sept. 1, 2005; Acts 2005, 79th Leg., ch. 1015 § 1, eff. Sept. 1, 2005; Acts 2015, 84th Leg., ch. 1133 (S.B. 147), § 5, eff. Sept. 1, 2015.

[1] V.T.C.A., Transportation Code § 541.001 et seq.

Section 8 of Acts 2015, 84th Leg., ch. 1133 (S.B. 147) provides:

"The change in law made by this Act applies only to an offense committed on or after the effective date [Sept. 1, 2015] of this Act. An offense committed before the effective date of this Act is governed by the law in effect on the date the offense was committed, and the former law is continued in effect for that purpose. For purposes of this section, an offense was committed before the effective date of this Act if any element of the offense occurred before that date."

Art. 14.031.   Public intoxication

(a) In lieu of arresting an individual who is not a child, as defined by Section 51.02, Family Code, and who commits an offense under Section 49. 02, Penal Code, a peace officer may release the individual if:

(1) the officer believes detention in a penal facility is unnecessary for the protection of the individual or others; and

(2) the individual:

(A) is released to the care of an adult who agrees to assume responsibility for the individual; or

(B) verbally consents to voluntary treatment for chemical dependency in a program in a treatment facility licensed and approved by the Texas Commission on Alcohol and Drug Abuse, and the program admits the individual for treatment.

(b) A magistrate may release from custody an individual who is not a child, as defined by Section 51.02, Family Code, and who is arrested under Section 49.02, Penal Code, if the magistrate determines the individual meets the conditions required for release in lieu of arrest under Subsection (a) of this article.

(c) The release of an individual under Subsection (a) or (b) of this article to an alcohol or drug treatment program may not be considered by a peace officer or magistrate in determining whether the individual should be released to such a program for a subsequent incident or arrest under Section 49.02, Penal Code.

(d) A peace officer and the agency or political subdivision that employs the peace officer may not be held liable for damage to persons or property that results from the actions of an individual released under Subsection (a) or (b) of this article.

Added by Acts 1993, 73rd Leg., ch. 900, § 1.04, eff. Sept. 1, 1994. Amended by Acts 2009, 81st Leg., ch. 311, § 1, eff. Sept. 1, 2009.

Art. 14.04.   When felony has been committed

Where it is shown by satisfactory proof to a peace officer, upon the representation of a credible person, that a felony has been committed, and that the offender is about to escape, so that there is no time to procure a warrant, such peace officer may, without warrant, pursue and arrest the accused.

Acts 1965, 59th Leg., vol. 2, p. 317, ch. 722, eff. Jan. 1, 1966.

Art. 14.05.   Rights of officer

In each case enumerated where arrests may be lawfully made without warrant, the officer or person making the arrest is justified in adopting all the measures which he might adopt in cases of arrest under warrant, except that an officer making an arrest without a warrant may not enter a residence to make the arrest unless:

(1) a person who resides in the residence consents to the entry; or

(2) exigent circumstances require that the officer making the arrest enter the residence without the consent of a resident or without a warrant.

Acts 1965, 59th Leg., vol. 2, p. 317, ch. 722, eff. Jan. 1, 1966. Amended by Acts 1987, 70th Leg., ch. 532, § 1, eff. Aug. 31, 1987.

Art. 14.051.   Arrest by peace officer from other jurisdiction

(a) A peace officer commissioned and authorized by another state to make arrests for felonies who is in fresh pursuit of a person for the purpose of arresting that person for a felony may continue the pursuit into this state and arrest the person.

(b) In this article, "fresh pursuit" means a pursuit without unreasonable delay by a peace officer of a person the officer reasonably suspects has committed a felony.

Added by Acts 1989, 71st Leg., ch. 997, § 2, eff. Aug. 28, 1989.

Art. 14.055.   Duty of Officer to Notify Probate Court

(a) In this article, "ward" has the meaning assigned by Section 22.033, Estates Code.

(b) As soon as practicable, but not later than the first working day after the date a peace officer detains or arrests a person who is a ward, the peace officer or the person having custody of the ward shall notify the court having jurisdiction over the ward's guardianship of the ward's detention or arrest.

Added by Acts 2017, 85th Leg., ch. 313 (S.B. 1096), § 1, eff. Sept. 1, 2017.

Section 14(b) of Acts 2017, 85th Leg., ch. 313 (S.B. 1096) provides:

"(b) A law enforcement officer or other person with custody of a ward is not required to comply with Articles 14.055 and 15.171, Code of Criminal Procedure, Section 52.011, Family Code, or Section 573.0021, Health and Safety Code, as added by this Act, as applicable, until July 1, 2018."

Art. 14.06. Must take offender before magistrate

(a) Except as otherwise provided by this article, in each case enumerated in this Code, the person making the arrest or the person having custody of the person arrested shall take the person arrested or have him taken without unnecessary delay, but not later than 48 hours after the person is arrested, before the magistrate who may have ordered the arrest, before some magistrate of the county where the arrest was made without an order, or, to provide more expeditiously to the person arrested the warnings described by Article 15.17 of this Code, before a magistrate in any other county of this state. The magistrate shall immediately perform the duties described in Article 15.17 of this Code.

(b) A peace officer who is charging a person, including a child, with committing an offense that is a Class C misdemeanor, other than an offense under Section 49.02, Penal Code, may, instead of taking the person before a magistrate, issue a citation to the person that contains:

(1) written notice of the time and place the person must appear before a magistrate;

(2) the name and address of the person charged;

(3) the offense charged;

(4) information regarding the alternatives to the full payment of any fine or costs assessed against the person, if the person is convicted of the offense and is unable to pay that amount; and

(5) the following admonishment, in boldfaced or underlined type or in capital letters:

"If you are convicted of a misdemeanor offense involving violence where you are or were a spouse, intimate partner, parent, or guardian of the victim or are or were involved in another, similar relationship with the victim, it may be unlawful for you to possess or purchase a firearm, including a handgun or long gun, or ammunition, pursuant to federal law under 18 U.S.C. Section 922(g)(9) or Section 46.04(b), Texas Penal Code. If you have any questions whether these laws make it illegal for you to possess or purchase a firearm, you should consult an attorney."

(c) If the person resides in the county where the offense occurred, a peace officer who is charging a person with committing an offense that is a Class A or B misdemeanor may, instead of taking the person before a magistrate, issue a citation to the person that contains written notice of the time and place the person must appear before a magistrate of this state as described by Subsection (a), the name and address of the person charged, and the offense charged.

(d) Subsection (c) applies only to a person charged with committing an offense under:

(1) Section 481.121, Health and Safety Code, if the offense is punishable under Subsection (b)(1) or (2) of that section;

(1–a) Section 481.1161, Health and Safety Code, if the offense is punishable under Subsection (b)(1) or (2) of that section;

(2) Section 28.03, Penal Code, if the offense is punishable under Subsection (b)(2) of that section;

(3) Section 28.08, Penal Code, if the offense is punishable under Subsection (b)(2) or (3) of that section;

(4) Section 31.03, Penal Code, if the offense is punishable under Subsection (e)(2)(A) of that section;

(5) Section 31.04, Penal Code, if the offense is punishable under Subsection (e)(2) of that section;

(6) Section 38.114, Penal Code, if the offense is punishable as a Class B misdemeanor; or

(7) Section 521.457, Transportation Code.

Acts 1965, 59th Leg., vol. 2, p. 317, ch. 722, eff. Jan. 1, 1966. Amended by Acts 1967, 60th Leg., p. 1735, ch. 659, § 10, eff. Aug. 28, 1967. Amended by Acts 1987, 70th Leg., ch. 455, § 1, eff. Aug. 31, 1987; Acts 1991, 72nd Leg., ch. 84, § 1, eff. Sept. 1, 1991; Acts 1993, 73rd Leg., ch. 900, § 1.05, eff. Sept. 1, 1994; Acts 1995, 74th Leg., ch. 262, § 81, eff. Jan. 1, 1996; Acts 2001, 77th Leg., ch. 906, § 3, eff. Jan. 1, 2002; Acts 2005, 79th Leg., ch. 1094, § 1, eff. Sept. 1, 2005; Acts 2007, 80th Leg., ch. 320, § 1, eff. Sept. 1, 2007; Acts 2009, 81st Leg., ch. 1379, § 1, eff. Sept. 1, 2009; Acts 2011, 82nd Leg., ch. 170 (S.B. 331), § 7, eff. Sept. 1, 2011; Acts 2015, 84th Leg., ch. 1251 (H.B. 1396), § 9, eff. Sept. 1, 2015; Acts 2017, 85th Leg., ch. 977 (H.B. 351), § 1, eff. Sept. 1, 2017; Acts 2017, 85th Leg., ch. 1127 (S.B. 1913), § 1, eff. Sept. 1, 2017.

Section 32 of Acts 2017, 85th Leg., ch. 977 (H.B. 351) provides:

"The changes in law made by this Act to Articles 14.06 and 27.14, Code of Criminal Procedure, and Section 502.010 and Chapter 706, Transportation Code, apply only to an offense committed on or after the effective date [Sept. 1, 2017] of this Act. An offense committed before the effective date of this Act is governed by the law in effect on the date the offense was committed, and the former law is continued in effect for that purpose. For purposes of this section, an offense was committed before the effective date of this Act if any element of the offense occurred before that date."

Section 28 of Acts 2017, 85th Leg., ch. 1127 (S.B. 1913) provides:

"The changes in law made by this Act to Articles 14.06 and 27.14, Code of Criminal Procedure, and Section 502.010 and Chapter 706, Transportation Code, apply only to an offense committed on or after the effective date [Sept. 1, 2017] of this Act. An offense committed before the effective date of this Act is governed by the law in effect on the date the offense was committed, and the former law is continued in effect for that purpose. For purposes of this section, an offense was committed before the effective date of this Act if any element of the offense occurred before that date."

CHAPTER FIFTEEN. ARREST UNDER WARRANT

Art. 15.01.   Warrant of arrest

A "warrant of arrest" is a written order from a magistrate, directed to a peace officer or some other person specially named, commanding him to take the body of the person accused of an offense, to be dealt with according to law.

Acts 1965, 59th Leg., vol. 2, p. 317, ch. 722, eff. Jan. 1, 1966.

Art. 15.02.   Requisites of warrant

It issues in the name of "The State of Texas", and shall be sufficient, without regard to form, if it have these substantial requisites:

1.   It must specify the name of the person whose arrest is ordered, if it be known, if unknown, then some reasonably definite description must be given of him.

2.   It must state that the person is accused of some offense against the laws of the State, naming the offense.

3.   It must be signed by the magistrate, and his office be named in the body of the warrant, or in connection with his signature.

Acts 1965, 59th Leg., vol. 2, p. 317, ch. 722, eff. Jan. 1, 1966.

Art. 15.03.   Magistrate may issue warrant or summons

(a) A magistrate may issue a warrant of arrest or a summons:

1.   In any case in which he is by law authorized to order verbally the arrest of an offender;

2.   When any person shall make oath before the magistrate that another has committed some offense against the laws of the State; and

3.   In any case named in this Code where he is specially authorized to issue warrants of arrest.

(b) A summons may be issued in any case where a warrant may be issued, and shall be in the same form as the warrant except that it shall summon the defendant to appear before a magistrate at a stated time and place. The summons shall be served upon a defendant by delivering a copy to him personally, or by leaving it at his dwelling house or usual place of abode with some person of suitable age and discretion then residing therein or by mailing it to the defendant's last known address. If a defendant fails to appear in response to the summons a warrant shall be issued.

(c) For purposes of Subdivision 2, Subsection (a), a person may appear before the magistrate in person or the person's image may be presented to the magistrate through an electronic broadcast system.

(d) A recording of the communication between the person and the magistrate must be made if the person's image is presented through an electronic broadcast system under Subsection (c). If the defendant is charged with the offense, the recording must be preserved until:

(1) the defendant is acquitted of the offense; or

(2) all appeals relating to the offense have been exhausted.

(e) The counsel for the defendant may obtain a copy of the recording on payment of an amount reasonably necessary to cover the costs of reproducing the recording.

(f) In this article, "electronic broadcast system" means a two-way electronic communication of image and sound between a person and magistrate and includes secure Internet videoconferencing.

Acts 1965, 59th Leg., vol. 2, p. 317, ch. 722, eff. Jan. 1, 1966. Amended by Acts 2011, 82nd Leg., ch. 248 (H.B. 976), § 1, eff. June 17, 2011.

Art. 15.04. Complaint

The affidavit made before the magistrate or district or county attorney is called a "complaint" if it charges the commission of an offense.

Acts 1965, 59th Leg., vol. 2, p. 317, ch. 722, eff. Jan. 1, 1966.

Art. 15.05. Requisites of complaint

The complaint shall be sufficient, without regard to form, if it have these substantial requisites:

1. It must state the name of the accused, if known, and if not known, must give some reasonably definite description of him.

2. It must show that the accused has committed some offense against the laws of the State, either directly or that the affiant has good reason to believe, and does believe, that the accused has committed such offense.

3. It must state the time and place of the commission of the offense, as definitely as can be done by the affiant.

4. It must be signed by the affiant by writing his name or affixing his mark.

Acts 1965, 59th Leg., vol. 2, p. 317, ch. 722, eff. Jan. 1, 1966.

Art. 15.051. Requiring polygraph examination of complainant prohibited

(a) A peace officer or an attorney representing the state may not require a polygraph examination of a person who charges or seeks to charge in a complaint the commission of an offense under Section 21.02, 21.11, 22.011, 22.021, or 25.02, Penal Code.

(b) If a peace officer or an attorney representing the state requests a polygraph examination of a person who charges or seeks to charge in a complaint the commission of an offense listed in Subsection (a), the officer or attorney must inform the complainant that the examination is not required and that a complaint may not be dismissed solely:

(1) because a complainant did not take a polygraph examination; or

(2) on the basis of the results of a polygraph examination taken by the complainant.

(c) A peace officer or an attorney representing the state may not take a polygraph examination of a person who charges or seeks to charge the commission of an offense listed in Subsection (a) unless the officer or attorney provides the information in Subsection (b) to the person and the person signs a statement indicating the person understands the information.

(d) A complaint may not be dismissed solely:

(1) because a complainant did not take a polygraph examination; or

(2) on the basis of the results of a polygraph examination taken by the complainant.

Added by Acts 1995, 74th Leg., ch. 24, § 1, eff. Sept. 1, 1995. Amended by Acts 1997, 75th Leg., ch. 608, § 1, eff. Sept. 1, 1997; Acts 2007, 80th Leg., ch. 593, § 3.07, eff. Sept. 1, 2007.

Art. 15.06. Warrant extends to every part of the state

A warrant of arrest, issued by any county or district clerk, or by any magistrate (except mayors of an incorporated city or town), shall extend to any part of the State; and any peace officer to whom said warrant is directed, or into whose hands the same has been transferred, shall be authorized to execute the same in any county in this State.

Acts 1965, 59th Leg., vol. 2, p. 317, ch. 722, eff. Jan. 1, 1966. Amended by Acts 1985, 69th Leg., ch. 666, § 1, eff. June 14, 1985.

Art. 15.07. Warrant issued by other magistrate

When a warrant of arrest is issued by any mayor of an incorporated city or town, it cannot be executed in another county than the one in which it issues, except:

1. It be endorsed by a judge of a court of record, in which case it may be executed anywhere in the State; or

2. If it be endorsed by any magistrate in the county in which the accused is found, it may be executed in such county. The endorsement may be: "Let this warrant be executed in the county of ....". Or, if the endorsement is made by a judge of a court of record, then the endorsement may be: "Let this warrant be executed in any county of the State of Texas". Any other words of the same meaning will be sufficient. The endorsement shall be dated, and signed officially by the magistrate making it.

Acts 1965, 59th Leg., vol. 2, p. 317, ch. 722, eff. Jan. 1, 1966. Amended by Acts 1985, 69th Leg., ch. 666, § 2, eff. June 14, 1985.

Art. 15.08. Warrant May Be Forwarded

A warrant of arrest may be forwarded by any method that ensures the transmission of a duplicate of the original warrant, including secure facsimile transmission or other secure electronic means. If issued by any magistrate named in Article 15.06, the peace officer receiving the same shall execute it without delay. If it be issued by any other magistrate than is named in Article 15.06, the peace officer receiving the same shall proceed with it to the nearest magistrate of the peace officer's county, who shall endorse thereon, in substance, these words:

"Let this warrant be executed in the county of..........", which endorsement shall be dated and signed officially by the magistrate making the same.

Acts 1965, 59th Leg., vol. 2, p. 317, ch. 722, eff. Jan. 1, 1966. Amended by Acts 2009, 81st Leg., ch. 345, § 1, eff. Sept. 1, 2009; Acts 2015, 84th Leg., ch. 771 (H.B. 2300), § 1, eff. Sept. 1, 2015.

Art. 15.09. Complaint may be forwarded

A complaint in accordance with Article 15.05, may be forwarded as provided by Article 15.08 to any magistrate in the State; and the magistrate who receives the same shall forthwith issue a warrant for the arrest of the accused; and the accused, when arrested, shall be dealt with as provided in this Chapter in similar cases.

Acts 1965, 59th Leg., vol. 2, p. 317, ch. 722, eff. Jan. 1, 1966. Amended by Acts 2009, 81st Leg., ch. 345, § 1, eff. Sept. 1, 2009.

Arts. 15.10 to 15.13. Repealed by Acts 2015, 84th Leg., ch. 771 (H.B. 2300), § 3, eff. Sept. 1, 2015

Art. 15.14. Arrest After Dismissal Because of Delay

If a prosecution of a defendant is dismissed under Article 32.01, the defendant may be rearrested for the same criminal conduct alleged in the dismissed prosecution only upon presentation of indictment or information for the offense and the issuance of a capias subsequent to the indictment or information.

Added by Acts 1997, 75th Leg., ch. 289, § 3, eff. May 26, 1997.

Art. 15.15. Repealed by Acts 1991, 72nd Leg., ch. 446, § 2, eff. June 11, 1991

Art. 15.16. How warrant is executed

(a) The officer or person executing a warrant of arrest shall without unnecessary delay take the person or have him taken before the magistrate who issued the warrant or before the magistrate named in the warrant, if the magistrate is in the same county where the person is arrested. If the issuing or named magistrate is in another county, the person arrested shall without unnecessary delay be taken before some magistrate in the county in which he was arrested.

(b) Notwithstanding Subsection (a), to provide more expeditiously to the person arrested the warnings described by Article 15.17, the officer or person executing the arrest warrant may as permitted by that article take the person arrested before a magistrate in a county other than the county of arrest.

Acts 1965, 59th Leg., vol. 2, p. 317, ch. 722, eff. Jan. 1, 1966. Amended by Acts 1967, 60th Leg., p. 1736, ch. 659, § 11, eff. Aug. 28, 1967; Acts 2005, 79th Leg., ch. 1094, § 2, eff. Sept. 1, 2005.

Art. 15.17. Duties of arresting officer and magistrate

(a) In each case enumerated in this Code, the person making the arrest or the person having custody of the person arrested shall without unnecessary delay, but not later than 48 hours after the person is arrested, take the person arrested or have him taken before some magistrate of the county where the accused was arrested or, to provide more expeditiously to the person arrested the warnings described by this article, before a magistrate in any other county of this state. The arrested person may be taken before the magistrate in person or the image of the arrested person may be presented to the magistrate by means of a videoconference. The magistrate shall inform in clear language the person arrested, either in person or through a videoconference, of the accusation against him and of any affidavit filed therewith, of his right to retain counsel, of his right to remain silent, of his right to have an attorney present during any interview with peace officers or attorneys representing the state, of his right to terminate the interview at any time, and of his right to have an examining trial. The magistrate shall also inform the person arrested of the person's right to request the appointment of counsel if the person cannot afford counsel. The magistrate shall inform the person arrested of the procedures for requesting appointment of counsel. If the person does not speak and understand the English language or is deaf, the magistrate shall inform the person in a manner consistent with Articles 38.30 and 38.31, as appropriate. The magistrate shall ensure that reasonable assistance in completing the necessary forms for requesting appointment of counsel is provided to the person at the same time. If the person arrested is indigent and requests appointment of counsel and if the magistrate is authorized under Article 26.04 to appoint counsel for indigent defendants in the county, the magistrate shall appoint counsel in accordance with Article 1.051. If the magistrate is not authorized to appoint counsel, the magistrate shall without unnecessary delay, but not later than 24 hours after the person arrested requests appointment of counsel, transmit, or cause to be transmitted to the court or to the courts' designee authorized under Article 26.04 to appoint counsel in the county, the forms requesting the appointment of counsel. The magistrate shall also inform the person arrested that he is not required to make a statement and that any statement made by him may be used against him. The magistrate shall allow the person arrested reasonable time and opportunity to consult counsel and shall, after determining whether the person is currently on bail for a separate criminal offense, admit the person arrested to bail if allowed by law. A record of the communication between the arrested person and the magistrate shall be made. The record shall be preserved until the earlier of the following dates: (1) the date on which the pretrial hearing ends; or (2) the 91st day after the date on which the record is made if the person is charged with a misdemeanor or the 120th day after the date on which the record is made if the person is charged with a felony. For purposes of this subsection, "videoconference" means a two-way electronic communication of image and sound between the arrested person and the magistrate and includes secure Internet videoconferencing.

(a–1) If a magistrate is provided written or electronic notice of credible information that may establish reasonable cause to believe that a person brought before the magistrate has a mental illness or is a person with an intellectual disability, the magistrate shall conduct the proceedings described by Article 16.22 or 17.032, as appropriate.

(b) After an accused charged with a misdemeanor punishable by fine only is taken before a magistrate under Subsection (a) and the magistrate has identified the accused with certainty, the magistrate may release the accused without bond and order the accused to appear at a later date for arraignment in the applicable justice court or municipal court. The order must state in writing the time, date, and place of the arraignment, and the magistrate must sign the order. The accused shall receive a copy of the order on release. If an accused fails to appear as required by the order, the judge of the court in which the accused is required to appear shall issue a warrant for the arrest of the accused. If the accused is arrested and brought before the judge, the judge may admit the accused to bail, and in admitting the accused to bail,

the judge should set as the amount of bail an amount double that generally set for the offense for which the accused was arrested. This subsection does not apply to an accused who has previously been convicted of a felony or a misdemeanor other than a misdemeanor punishable by fine only.

(c) When a deaf accused is taken before a magistrate under this article or Article 14.06 of this Code, an interpreter appointed by the magistrate qualified and sworn as provided in Article 38.31 of this Code shall interpret the warning required by those articles in a language that the accused can understand, including but not limited to sign language.

(d) If a magistrate determines that a person brought before the magistrate after an arrest authorized by Article 14.051 of this code was arrested unlawfully, the magistrate shall release the person from custody. If the magistrate determines that the arrest was lawful, the person arrested is considered a fugitive from justice for the purposes of Article 51.13 of this code, and the disposition of the person is controlled by that article.

(e) In each case in which a person arrested is taken before a magistrate as required by Subsection (a) or Article 15.18(a), a record shall be made of:

(1) the magistrate informing the person of the person's right to request appointment of counsel;

(2) the magistrate asking the person whether the person wants to request appointment of counsel; and

(3) whether the person requested appointment of counsel.

(f) A record required under Subsection (a) or (e) may consist of written forms, electronic recordings, or other documentation as authorized by procedures adopted in the county under Article 26.04(a). The counsel for the defendant may obtain a copy of the record on payment of a reasonable amount to cover the costs of reproduction or, if the defendant is indigent, the court shall provide a copy to the defendant without charging a cost for the copy.

(g) If a person charged with an offense punishable as a misdemeanor appears before a magistrate in compliance with a citation issued under Article 14.06(b) or (c), the magistrate shall perform the duties imposed by this article in the same manner as if the person had been arrested and brought before the magistrate by a peace officer. After the magistrate performs the duties imposed by this article, the magistrate except for good cause shown may release the person on personal bond. If a person who was issued a citation under Article 14.06(c) fails to appear as required by that citation, the magistrate before which the person is required to appear shall issue a warrant for the arrest of the accused.

Acts 1965, 59th Leg., vol. 2, p. 317, ch. 722, eff. Jan. 1, 1966. Amended by Acts 1967, 60th Leg., p. 1736, ch. 659, § 12, eff. Aug. 28, 1967; Acts 1979, 66th Leg., p. 398, ch. 186, § 3, eff. May 15, 1979; Acts 1987, 70th Leg., ch. 455, § 2, eff. Aug. 31, 1987; Acts 1989, 71st Leg., ch. 467, § 1, eff. Aug. 28, 1989; Acts 1989, 71st Leg., ch. 977, § 1, eff. Aug. 28, 1989; Acts 1989, 71st Leg., ch. 997, § 3, eff. Aug. 28, 1989; Acts 1991, 72nd Leg., ch. 16, § 19.01(2), eff. Aug. 26, 1991; Acts 2001, 77th Leg., ch. 906, § 4, eff. Jan. 1, 2002; Acts 2001, 77th Leg., ch. 1281, § 1, eff. Sept. 1, 2001; Acts 2005, 79th Leg., ch. 1094, § 3, eff. Sept. 1, 2005; Acts 2007, 80th Leg., ch. 320, § 2, eff. Sept. 1, 2007; Acts 2009, 81st Leg., ch. 735, § 1, eff. Sept. 1, 2009; Acts 2015, 84th Leg., ch. 858 (S.B. 1517), § 2, eff. Sept. 1, 2015; Acts 2017, 85th Leg., ch. 748 (S.B. 1326), § 1, eff. Sept. 1, 2017; Acts 2017, 85th Leg., ch. 1064 (H.B. 3165), § 1, eff. Sept. 1, 2017.

Section 5 of Acts 2015, 84th Leg., ch. 858 (S.B. 1517) provides:

"The change in law made by this Act applies only to a person who is arrested on or after the effective date [Sept. 1, 2015] of this Act. A person arrested before the effective date of this Act is governed by the law in effect on the date the person was arrested, and the former law is continued in effect for that purpose."

Section 37 of Acts 2017, 85th Leg., ch. 748 (S.B. 1326) provides:

"The changes in law made by this Act apply only to a defendant charged with an offense committed on or after the effective date [Sept. 1, 2017] of this Act. A defendant charged with an offense committed before the effective date of this Act is governed by the law in effect on the date the offense was committed, and the former law is continued in effect for that purpose. For purposes of this section, an offense was committed before the effective date of this Act if any element of the offense occurred before that date."

Section 11 of Acts 2017, 85th Leg., ch. 1064 (H.B. 3165) provides:

"Article 15.17, Code of Criminal Procedure, as amended by this Act, applies to an arrested person brought before a magistrate on or after the effective date [Sept. 1, 2017] of this Act, regardless of whether the offense for which the person was arrested was committed before, on, or after that date."

Art. 15.171. Duty of Officer to Notify Probate Court

(a) In this article, "ward" has the meaning assigned by Section 22.033, Estates Code.

(b) As soon as practicable, but not later than the first working day after the date a peace officer arrests a person who is a ward, the peace officer or the person having custody of the ward shall notify the court having jurisdiction over the ward's guardianship of the ward's arrest.

Added by Acts 2017, 85th Leg., ch. 313 (S.B. 1096), § 2, eff. Sept. 1, 2017.

Section 14(b) of Acts 2017, 85th Leg., ch. 313 (S.B. 1096) provides:

"(b) A law enforcement officer or other person with custody of a ward is not required to comply with Articles 14.055 and 15.171, Code of Criminal Procedure, Section 52.011, Family Code, or Section 573.0021, Health and Safety Code, as added by this Act, as applicable, until July 1, 2018."

Art. 15.18. Arrest for out-of-county offense

(a) A person arrested under a warrant issued in a county other than the one in which the person is arrested shall be taken before a magistrate of the county where the arrest takes place or, to provide more expeditiously to the arrested person the warnings described by Article 15.17, before a magistrate in any other county of this state, including the county where the warrant was issued. The magistrate shall:

(1) take bail, if allowed by law, and, if without jurisdiction, immediately transmit the bond taken to the court having jurisdiction of the offense; or

(2) in the case of a person arrested under warrant for an offense punishable by fine only, accept a written plea of guilty or nolo contendere, set a fine, determine costs, accept payment of the fine and costs, give credit for time served, determine indigency, or, on satisfaction of the judgment, discharge the defendant, as the case may indicate.

(a–1) If the arrested person is taken before a magistrate of a county other than the county that issued the warrant, the magistrate shall inform the person arrested of the procedures for requesting appointment of counsel and ensure that reasonable assistance in completing the necessary forms for requesting appointment of counsel is provided to the person at the same time. If the person requests the appointment of counsel, the magistrate shall, without unnecessary delay but not later than 24 hours after the person requested the appointment of counsel, transmit, or cause to be transmitted, the necessary request forms to a court or the courts' designee authorized under Article 26.04 to appoint counsel in the county issuing the warrant.

(b) Before the 11th business day after the date a magistrate accepts a written plea of guilty or nolo contendere in a case under Subsection (a)(2), the magistrate shall, if without jurisdiction, transmit to the court having jurisdiction of the offense:

(1) the written plea;

(2) any orders entered in the case; and

(3) any fine or costs collected in the case.

(c) The arrested person may be taken before a magistrate by means of an electronic broadcast system as provided by and subject to the requirements of Article 15.17.

(d) This article does not apply to an arrest made pursuant to a capias pro fine issued under Chapter 43 or Article 45.045.

Acts 1965, 59th Leg., vol. 2, p. 317, ch. 722, eff. Jan. 1, 1966. Amended by Acts 2001, 77th Leg., ch. 145, § 2, eff. Sept. 1, 2001; Acts 2005, 79th Leg., ch. 1094, § 4, eff. Sept. 1, 2005; Acts 2007, 80th Leg., ch. 1263, § 1, eff. Sept. 1, 2007; Acts 2015, 84th Leg., ch. 858 (S.B. 1517), § 3, eff. Sept. 1, 2015.

Section 5 of Acts 2015, 84th Leg., ch. 858 (S.B. 1517) provides:

"The change in law made by this Act applies only to a person who is arrested on or after the effective date [Sept. 1, 2015] of this Act. A person arrested before the effective date of this Act is governed by the law in effect on the date the person was arrested, and the former law is continued in effect for that purpose."

Art. 15.19. Notice of arrest

(a) If the arrested person fails or refuses to give bail, as provided in Article 15.18, the arrested person shall be committed to the jail of the county where the person was arrested. The magistrate committing the arrested person shall immediately provide notice to the sheriff of the county in which the offense is alleged to have been committed regarding:

(1) the arrest and commitment, which notice may be given by mail or other written means or by secure facsimile transmission or other secure electronic means; and

(2) whether the person was also arrested under a warrant issued under Section 508.251, Government Code.

(b) If a person is arrested and taken before a magistrate in a county other than the county in which the arrest is made and if the person is remanded to custody, the person may be confined in a jail in the county in which the magistrate serves for a period of not more than 72 hours after the arrest before being transferred to the county jail of the county in which the arrest occurred.

Acts 1965, 59th Leg., vol. 2, p. 317, ch. 722, eff. Jan. 1, 1966. Amended by Acts 1987, 70th Leg., 2nd C.S., ch. 40, § 1, eff. Oct. 20, 1987; Acts 2005, 79th Leg., ch. 1094, § 5, eff. Sept. 1, 2005; Acts 2007, 80th Leg., ch. 1308, § 1, eff. June 15, 2007; Acts 2009, 81st Leg., ch. 345, § 2, eff. Sept. 1, 2009; Acts 2015, 84th Leg., ch. 771 (H.B. 2300), § 2, eff. Sept. 1, 2015.

Art. 15.20. Duty of sheriff receiving notice

(a) Subject to Subsection (b), the sheriff receiving the notice of arrest and commitment under Article 15.19 shall forthwith go or send for the arrested person and have the arrested person brought before the proper court or magistrate.

(b) A sheriff who receives notice under Article 15.19(a)(2) of a warrant issued under Section 508.251, Government Code, shall have the arrested person brought before the proper magistrate or court before the 11th day after the date the person is committed to the jail of the county in which the person was arrested.

Acts 1965, 59th Leg., vol. 2, p. 317, ch. 722, eff. Jan. 1, 1966. Amended by Acts 2007, 80th Leg., ch. 1308, § 2, eff. June 15, 2007.

Art. 15.21. Release on Personal Bond If Not Timely Demanded

If the proper office of the county where the offense is alleged to have been committed does not demand an arrested person described by Article 15.19 and take charge of the arrested person before the 11th day after the date the person is committed to the jail of the county in which the person is arrested, a magistrate in the county where the person was arrested shall:

(1) release the arrested person on personal bond without sureties or other security; and

(2) forward the personal bond to:

(A) the sheriff of the county where the offense is alleged to have been committed; or

(B) the court that issued the warrant of arrest.

Acts 1965, 59th Leg., vol. 2, p. 317, ch. 722, eff. Jan. 1, 1966. Amended by Acts 2007, 80th Leg., ch. 1308, § 3, eff. June 15, 2007; Acts 2017, 85th Leg., ch. 1064 (H.B. 3165), § 2, eff. Sept. 1, 2017.

Section 12 of Acts 2017, 85th Leg., ch. 1064 (H.B. 3165) provides:

"Article 15.21, Code of Criminal Procedure, applies only to a person who is arrested on or after the effective date [Sept. 1, 2017] of this Act. A person arrested before the effective date of this Act is governed by the law in effect on the date the person was arrested, and the former law is continued in effect for that purpose."

Art. 15.22. When a person is arrested

A person is arrested when he has been actually placed under restraint or taken into custody by an officer or person executing a warrant of arrest, or by an officer or person arresting without a warrant.

Acts 1965, 59th Leg., vol. 2, p. 317, ch. 722, eff. Jan. 1, 1966.

Art. 15.23. Time of arrest

An arrest may be made on any day or at any time of the day or night.

Acts 1965, 59th Leg., vol. 2, p. 317, ch. 722, eff. Jan. 1, 1966.

Art. 15.24. What force may be used

In making an arrest, all reasonable means are permitted to be used to effect it. No greater force, however, shall be resorted to than is necessary to secure the arrest and detention of the accused.

Acts 1965, 59th Leg., vol. 2, p. 317, ch. 722, eff. Jan. 1, 1966.

Art. 15.25. May break door

In case of felony, the officer may break down the door of any house for the purpose of making an arrest, if he be refused admittance after giving notice of his authority and purpose.

Acts 1965, 59th Leg., vol. 2, p. 317, ch. 722, eff. Jan. 1, 1966.

Art. 15.26. Authority to arrest must be made known

In executing a warrant of arrest, it shall always be made known to the accused under what authority the arrest is made. The warrant shall be executed by the arrest of the defendant. The officer need not have the warrant in his possession at the time of the arrest, provided the warrant was issued under the provisions of this Code, but upon request he shall show the warrant to the defendant as soon as possible. If the officer does not have the warrant in his possession at the time of arrest he shall then inform the defendant of the offense charged and of the fact that a warrant has been issued. The arrest warrant, and any affidavit presented to the magistrate in support of the issuance of the warrant, is public information, and beginning immediately when the warrant is executed the magistrate's clerk shall make a copy of the warrant and the affidavit available for public inspection in the clerk's office during normal business hours. A person may request the clerk to provide copies of the warrant and affidavit on payment of the cost of providing the copies.

Acts 1965, 59th Leg., vol. 2, p. 317, ch. 722, eff. Jan. 1, 1966. Amended by Acts 1967, 60th Leg., p. 1736, ch. 659, § 13, eff. Aug. 28, 1967; Acts 2003, 78th Leg., ch. 390, § 1, eff. Sept. 1, 2003.

Art. 15.27. Notification to schools required

(a) A law enforcement agency that arrests any person or refers a child to the office or official designated by the juvenile board who the agency believes is enrolled as a student in a public primary or secondary school, for an offense listed in Subsection (h), shall attempt to ascertain whether the person is so enrolled. If the law enforcement agency ascertains that the individual is enrolled as a student in a public primary or secondary school, the head of the agency or a person designated by the head of the agency shall orally notify the superintendent or a person designated by the superintendent in the school district in

which the student is enrolled of that arrest or referral within 24 hours after the arrest or referral is made, or before the next school day, whichever is earlier. If the law enforcement agency cannot ascertain whether the individual is enrolled as a student, the head of the agency or a person designated by the head of the agency shall orally notify the superintendent or a person designated by the superintendent in the school district in which the student is believed to be enrolled of that arrest or detention within 24 hours after the arrest or detention, or before the next school day, whichever is earlier. If the individual is a student, the superintendent or the superintendent's designee shall immediately notify all instructional and support personnel who have responsibility for supervision of the student. All personnel shall keep the information received in this subsection confidential. The State Board for Educator Certification may revoke or suspend the certification of personnel who intentionally violate this subsection. Within seven days after the date the oral notice is given, the head of the law enforcement agency or the person designated by the head of the agency shall mail written notification, marked "PERSONAL and CONFIDENTIAL" on the mailing envelope, to the superintendent or the person designated by the superintendent. The written notification must include the facts contained in the oral notification, the name of the person who was orally notified, and the date and time of the oral notification. Both the oral and written notice shall contain sufficient details of the arrest or referral and the acts allegedly committed by the student to enable the superintendent or the superintendent's designee to determine whether there is a reasonable belief that the student has engaged in conduct defined as a felony offense by the Penal Code. The information contained in the notice shall be considered by the superintendent or the superintendent's designee in making such a determination.

(a–1) The superintendent or a person designated by the superintendent in the school district shall send to a school district employee having direct supervisory responsibility over the student the information contained in the confidential notice under Subsection (a).

(b) On conviction, deferred prosecution, or deferred adjudication or an adjudication of delinquent conduct of an individual enrolled as a student in a public primary or secondary school, for an offense or for any conduct listed in Subsection (h) of this article, the office of the prosecuting attorney acting in the case shall orally notify the superintendent or a person designated by the superintendent in the school district in which the student is enrolled of the conviction or adjudication and whether the student is required to register as a sex offender under Chapter 62. Oral notification must be given within 24 hours of the time of the order or before the next school day, whichever is earlier. The superintendent shall, within 24 hours of receiving notification from the office of the prosecuting attorney, or before the next school day, whichever is earlier, notify all instructional and support personnel who have regular contact with the student. Within seven days after the date the oral notice is given, the office of the prosecuting attorney shall mail written notice, which must contain a statement of the offense of which the individual is convicted or on which the adjudication, deferred adjudication, or deferred prosecution is grounded and a statement of whether the student is required to register as a sex offender under Chapter 62.

(c) A parole, probation, or community supervision office, including a community supervision and corrections department, a juvenile probation department, the paroles division of the Texas Department of Criminal Justice, and the Texas Juvenile Justice Department, having jurisdiction over a student described by Subsection (a), (b), or (e) who transfers from a school or is subsequently removed from a school and later returned to a school or school district other than the one the student was enrolled in when the arrest, referral to a juvenile court, conviction, or adjudication occurred shall within 24 hours of learning of the student's transfer or reenrollment, or before the next school day, whichever is earlier, notify the superintendent or a person designated by the superintendent of the school district to which the student transfers or is returned or, in the case of a private school, the principal or a school employee designated by the principal of the school to which the student transfers or is returned of the arrest or referral in a manner similar to that provided for by Subsection (a) or (e)(1), or of the conviction or delinquent adjudication in a manner similar to that provided for by Subsection (b) or (e)(2). The superintendent of the school district to which the student transfers or is returned or, in the case of a private school, the principal of the school to which the student transfers or is returned shall, within 24 hours of receiving notification under this subsection or before the next school day, whichever is earlier, notify all instructional and support personnel who have regular contact with the student.

(d) Repealed by Acts 2007, 80th Leg., ch. 1240, § 5; Acts 2007, 80th Leg., ch. 1291, § 8.

(e)(1) A law enforcement agency that arrests, or refers to a juvenile court under Chapter 52, Family Code, an individual who the law enforcement agency knows or believes is enrolled as a student in a private primary or secondary school shall make the oral and written notifications described by Subsection (a) to the principal or a school employee designated by the principal of the school in which the student is enrolled.

(2) On conviction, deferred prosecution, or deferred adjudication or an adjudication of delinquent conduct of an individual enrolled as a student in a private primary or secondary school, the office of prosecuting attorney shall make the oral and written notifications described by Subsection (b) of this article to the principal or a school employee designated by the principal of the school in which the student is enrolled.

(3) The principal of a private school in which the student is enrolled or a school employee designated by the principal shall send to a school employee having direct supervisory responsibility over the student the information contained in the confidential notice, for the same purposes as described by Subsection (a–1) of this article.

(f) A person who receives information under this article may not disclose the information except as specifically authorized by this article. A person who intentionally violates this article commits an offense. An offense under this subsection is a Class C misdemeanor.

(g) The office of the prosecuting attorney or the office or official designated by the juvenile board shall, within two working days, notify the school district that removed a student to a disciplinary alternative education program under Section 37.006, Education Code, if:

(1) prosecution of the student's case was refused for lack of prosecutorial merit or insufficient evidence and no formal proceedings, deferred adjudication, or deferred prosecution will be initiated; or

(2) the court or jury found the student not guilty or made a finding the child did not engage in delinquent conduct or conduct indicating a need for supervision and the case was dismissed with prejudice.

(h) This article applies to any felony offense and the following misdemeanors:

(1) an offense under Section 20.02, 21.08, 22.01, 22.05, 22.07, or 71.02, Penal Code;

(2) the unlawful use, sale, or possession of a controlled substance, drug paraphernalia, or marihuana,

as defined by Chapter 481, Health and Safety Code; or

(3) the unlawful possession of any of the weapons or devices listed in Sections 46.01(1)–(14) or (16), Penal Code, or a weapon listed as a prohibited weapon under Section 46.05, Penal Code.

(i) A person may substitute electronic notification for oral notification where oral notification is required by this article. If electronic notification is substituted for oral notification, any written notification required by this article is not required.

(j) The notification provisions of this section concerning a person who is required to register as a sex offender under Chapter 62 do not lessen the requirement of a person to provide any additional notification prescribed by that chapter.

(k) Oral or written notice required under this article must include all pertinent details of the offense or conduct, including details of any:

(1) assaultive behavior or other violence;

(2) weapons used in the commission of the offense or conduct; or

(3) weapons possessed during the commission of the offense or conduct.

(l) If a school district board of trustees learns of a failure by the superintendent of the district or a district principal to provide a notice required under Subsection (a), (a–1), or (b), the board of trustees shall report the failure to the State Board for Educator Certification. If the governing body of a private primary or secondary school learns of a failure by the principal of the school to provide a notice required under Subsection (e), and the principal holds a certificate issued under Subchapter B, Chapter 21, Education Code,[1] the governing body shall report the failure to the State Board for Educator Certification.

(m) If the superintendent of a school district in which the student is enrolled learns of a failure of the head of a law enforcement agency or a person designated by the head of the agency to provide a notification under Subsection (a), the superintendent or principal shall report the failure to notify to the Texas Commission on Law Enforcement.

(n) If a juvenile court judge or official designated by the juvenile board learns of a failure by the office of the prosecuting attorney to provide a notification required under Subsection (b) or (g), the official shall report the failure to notify to the elected prosecuting attorney responsible for the operation of the office.

(o) If the supervisor of a parole, probation, or community supervision department officer learns of a failure by the officer to provide a notification under Subsection (c), the supervisor shall report the failure to notify to the director of the entity that employs the officer.

Added by Acts 1993, 73rd Leg., ch. 461, § 1, eff. Sept. 1, 1993. Amended by Acts 1995, 74th Leg., ch. 76, § 14.18, eff. Aug. 28, 1995; Acts 1995, 74th Leg., ch. 626, § 1, eff. Sept. 1, 1995; Acts 1997, 75th Leg., ch. 165, § 12.02, eff. Sept. 1, 1997; Acts 1997, 75th Leg., ch. 1015, §§ 12 to 14, eff. June 19, 1997; Acts 1997, 75th Leg., ch. 1233, § 1, eff. June 20, 1997; Acts 2001, 77th Leg., ch. 1297, §§ 48, 49, eff. Sept. 1, 2001; Acts 2003, 78th Leg., ch. 1055, §§ 25 to 27, eff. June 20, 2003; Acts 2005, 79th Leg., ch. 949, § 31, eff. Sept. 1, 2005; Acts 2007, 80th Leg., ch. 492, § 1, eff. June 16, 2007; Acts 2007, 80th Leg., ch. 1240, §§ 4, 5, eff. June 15, 2007; Acts 2007, 80th Leg., ch. 1291, §§ 1, 8, eff. Sept. 1, 2007; Acts 2009, 81st Leg., ch. 87, § 6.002, eff. Sept. 1, 2009. Amended by Acts 2011, 82nd Leg., ch. 992 (H.B. 1907), §§ 1, 2, eff. Sept. 1, 2011; Acts 2013, 83rd Leg., ch. 93 (S.B. 686), § 2.07, eff. May 18, 2013; Acts 2015, 84th Leg., ch. 734 (H.B. 1549), § 3, eff. Sept. 1, 2015.

[1] V.T.C.A., Education Code § 21.031 et seq.

Section 150 of Acts 2015, 84th Leg., ch. 734 (H.B. 1549) provides:

"If any provision of this Act conflicts with a provision of another Act of the 84th Legislature, Regular Session, 2015, the provision of the other Act controls to the extent of the conflict, regardless of the date of enactment."

CHAPTER SIXTEEN. THE COMMITMENT OR DISCHARGE OF THE ACCUSED

Article

16.23.   Diversion of persons suffering mental health crisis or substance abuse issue.

Art. 16.01.   Examining trial

When the accused has been brought before a magistrate for an examining trial that officer shall proceed to examine into the truth of the accusation made, allowing the accused, however, sufficient time to procure counsel. In a proper case, the magistrate may appoint counsel to represent an accused in such examining trial only, to be compensated as otherwise provided in this Code. The accused in any felony case shall have the right to an examining trial before indictment in the county having jurisdiction of the offense, whether he be in custody or on bail, at which time the magistrate at the hearing shall determine the amount or sufficiency of bail, if a bailable case. If the accused has been transferred for criminal prosecution after a hearing under Section 54.02, Family Code, the accused may be granted an examining trial at the discretion of the court.

Acts 1965, 59th Leg., vol. 2, p. 317, ch. 722, eff. Jan. 1, 1966. Amended by Acts 1987, 70th Leg., ch. 140, § 4, eff. Sept. 1, 1987.

Art. 16.02.   Examination postponed

The magistrate may at the request of either party postpone the examination to procure testimony; but the accused shall in the meanwhile be detained in custody unless he give bail to be present from day to day before the magistrate until the examination is concluded, which he may do in all cases except murder and treason.

Acts 1965, 59th Leg., vol. 2, p. 317, ch. 722, eff. Jan. 1, 1966.

Art. 16.03.   Warning to accused

Before the examination of the witnesses, the magistrate shall inform the accused that it is his right to make a statement relative to the accusation brought against him, but at the same time shall also inform him that he cannot be compelled to make any statement whatever, and that if he does make such statement, it may be used in evidence against him.

Acts 1965, 59th Leg., vol. 2, p. 317, ch. 722, eff. Jan. 1, 1966.

Art. 16.04.   Voluntary statement

If the accused desires to make a voluntary statement, he may do so before the examination of any witness, but not afterward. His statement shall be reduced to writing by or under the direction of the magistrate, or by the accused or his counsel, and shall be signed by the accused by affixing his name or mark, but shall not be sworn to by him. The magistrate shall attest by his own certificate and signature to the execution and signing of the statement.

Acts 1965, 59th Leg., vol. 2, p. 317, ch. 722, eff. Jan. 1, 1966.

Art. 16.05.   Repealed by Texas Rules of Criminal Evidence effective September 1, 1986 [Acts 1985, 69th Leg., ch. 685, § 9(b)]

Art. 16.06.   Counsel may examine witness

The counsel for the State, and the accused or his counsel may question the witnesses on direct or cross examination. If no counsel appears for the State the magistrate may examine the witnesses.

Acts 1965, 59th Leg., vol. 2, p. 317, ch. 722, eff. Jan. 1, 1966.

Art. 16.07.   Same rules of evidence as on final trial

The same rules of evidence shall apply to and govern a trial before an examining court that apply to and govern a final trial.

Acts 1965, 59th Leg., vol. 2, p. 317, ch. 722, eff. Jan. 1, 1966.

Art. 16.08.   Presence of the accused

The examination of each witness shall be in the presence of the accused.

Acts 1965, 59th Leg., vol. 2, p. 317, ch. 722, eff. Jan. 1, 1966.

Art. 16.09.   Testimony reduced to writing

The testimony of each witness shall be reduced to writing by or under the direction of the magistrate, and shall then be read over to the witness, or he may read it over himself. Such corrections shall be made in the same as the witness may direct; and he shall then sign the same by affixing thereto his name or mark. All the testimony thus taken shall be certified to by the magistrate. In lieu of the above provision, a statement of facts authenticated by State and defense counsel and approved by the presiding magistrate may be used to preserve the testimony of witnesses.

Acts 1965, 59th Leg., vol. 2, p. 317, ch. 722, eff. Jan. 1, 1966.

Art. 16.10.   Attachment for witness

The magistrate has the power in all cases, where a witness resides or is in the county where the prosecution is pending, to issue an attachment for the purpose of enforcing the attendance of such witness; this he may do without having previously issued a subpoena for that purpose.

Acts 1965, 59th Leg., vol. 2, p. 317, ch. 722, eff. Jan. 1, 1966.

Art. 16.11. Attachment to another county

The magistrate may issue an attachment for a witness to any county in the State, when affidavit is made by the party applying therefor that the testimony of the witness is material to the prosecution, or the defense, as the case may be; and the affidavit shall further state the facts which it is expected will be proved by the witness; and if the facts set forth are not considered material by the magistrate, or if they be admitted to be true by the adverse party, the attachment shall not issue.

Acts 1965, 59th Leg., vol. 2, p. 317, ch. 722, eff. Jan. 1, 1966.

Art. 16.12. Witness need not be tendered his witness fees or expenses

A witness attached need not be tendered his witness fees or expenses.

Acts 1965, 59th Leg., vol. 2, p. 317, ch. 722, eff. Jan. 1, 1966.

Art. 16.13. Attachment executed forthwith

The officer receiving the attachment shall execute it forthwith by bringing before the magistrate the witness named therein, unless such witness shall give bail for his appearance before the magistrate at the time and place required by the writ.

Acts 1965, 59th Leg., vol. 2, p. 317, ch. 722, eff. Jan. 1, 1966.

Art. 16.14. Postponing examination

After examining the witness in attendance, if it appear to the magistrate that there is other important testimony which may be had by a postponement, he shall, at the request of the prosecutor or of the defendant, postpone the hearing for a reasonable time to enable such testimony to be procured; but in such case the accused shall remain in the custody of the proper officer until the day fixed for such further examination. No postponement shall take place, unless a sworn statement be made by the defendant, or the prosecutor, setting forth the name and residence of the witness, and the facts which it is expected will be proved. If it be testimony other than that of a witness, the statement made shall set forth the nature of the evidence. If the magistrate is satisfied that the testimony is not material, or if the same be admitted to be true by the adverse party, the postponement shall be refused.

Acts 1965, 59th Leg., vol. 2, p. 317, ch. 722, eff. Jan. 1, 1966.

Art. 16.15. Who may discharge capital offense

The examination of one accused of a capital offense shall be conducted by a justice of the peace, county judge, county court at law, or county criminal court. The judge may admit to bail, except in capital cases where the proof is evident.

Acts 1965, 59th Leg., vol. 2, p. 317, ch. 722, eff. Jan. 1, 1966.

Art. 16.16. If insufficient bail has been taken

Where it is made to appear by affidavit to a judge of the Court of Criminal Appeals, a justice of a court of appeals, or to a judge of the district or county court, that the bail taken in any case is insufficient in amount, or that the sureties are not good for the amount, or that the bond is for any reason defective or insufficient, such judge shall issue a warrant of arrest, and require of the defendant sufficient bond and security, according to the nature of the case.

Acts 1965, 59th Leg., vol. 2, p. 317, ch. 722, eff. Jan. 1, 1966. Amended by Acts 1981, 67th Leg., p. 802, ch. 291, § 104, eff. Sept. 1, 1981.

Art. 16.17. Decision of judge

After the examining trial has been had, the judge shall make an order committing the defendant to the jail of the proper county, discharging him or admitting him to bail, as the law and facts of the case may require. Failure of the judge to make or enter an order within 48 hours after the examining trial has been completed operates as a finding of no probable cause and the accused shall be discharged.

Acts 1965, 59th Leg., vol. 2, p. 317, ch. 722, eff. Jan. 1, 1966.

Art. 16.18. When no safe jail

If there is no safe jail in the county in which the prosecution is carried on, the magistrate may commit defendant to the nearest safe jail in any other county.

Acts 1965, 59th Leg., vol. 2, p. 317, ch. 722, eff. Jan. 1, 1966.

Art. 16.19. Warrant in such case

The commitment in the case mentioned in the preceding Article shall be directed to the sheriff of the county to which the defendant is sent, but the sheriff of the county from which the defendant is taken shall be required to deliver the prisoner into the hands of the sheriff to whom he is sent.

Acts 1965, 59th Leg., vol. 2, p. 317, ch. 722, eff. Jan. 1, 1966.

Art. 16.20. "Commitment"

A "commitment" is an order signed by the proper magistrate directing a sheriff to receive and place in jail the person so committed. It will be sufficient if it have the following requisites:

1. That it run in the name of "The State of Texas";

2. That it be addressed to the sheriff of the county to the jail of which the defendant is committed;

3. That it state in plain language the offense for which the defendant is committed, and give his name, if it be known, or if unknown, contain an accurate description of the defendant;

4. That it state to what court and at what time the defendant is to be held to answer;

5. When the prisoner is sent out of the county where the prosecution arose, the warrant of commitment shall state that there is no safe jail in the proper county; and

6. If bail has been granted, the amount of bail shall be stated in the warrant of commitment.

Acts 1965, 59th Leg., vol. 2, p. 317, ch. 722, eff. Jan. 1, 1966.

Art. 16.21.   Duty of sheriff as to prisoners

Every sheriff shall keep safely a person committed to his custody. He shall use no cruel or unusual means to secure this end, but shall adopt all necessary measures to prevent the escape of a prisoner. He may summon a guard of sufficient number, in case it becomes necessary to prevent an escape from jail, or the rescue of a prisoner.

Acts 1965, 59th Leg., vol. 2, p. 317, ch. 722, eff. Jan. 1, 1966.

Art. 16.22.   Early identification of defendant suspected of having mental illness or intellectual disability

Text of article as amended by Acts 2017, 85th Leg., ch. 748 (S.B. 1326), § 2. See, also, art. 16.22 as amended by Acts 2017, 85th Leg., ch. 950 (S.B. 1849), § 2.01.

(a)(1) Not later than 12 hours after the sheriff or municipal jailer having custody of a defendant for an offense punishable as a Class B misdemeanor or any higher category of offense receives credible information that may establish reasonable cause to believe that the defendant has a mental illness or is a person with an intellectual disability, the sheriff or municipal jailer shall provide written or electronic notice to the magistrate. The notice must include any information related to the sheriff's or municipal jailer's determination, such as information regarding the defendant's behavior immediately before, during, and after the defendant's arrest and, if applicable, the results of any previous assessment of the defendant. On a determination that there is reasonable cause to believe that the defendant has a mental illness or is a person with an intellectual disability, the magistrate, except as

provided by Subdivision (2), shall order the local mental health authority, local intellectual and developmental disability authority, or another qualified mental health or intellectual disability expert to:

(A) collect information regarding whether the defendant has a mental illness as defined by Section 571.003, Health and Safety Code, or is a person with an intellectual disability as defined by Section 591.003, Health and Safety Code, including, if applicable, information obtained from any previous assessment of the defendant and information regarding any previously recommended treatment; and

(B) provide to the magistrate a written assessment of the information collected under Paragraph (A) on the form approved by the Texas Correctional Office on Offenders with Medical or Mental Impairments under Section 614.0032(b), Health and Safety Code.

(2) The magistrate is not required to order the collection of information under Subdivision (1) if the defendant in the year preceding the defendant's applicable date of arrest has been determined to have a mental illness or to be a person with an intellectual disability by the local mental health authority, local intellectual and developmental disability authority, or another mental health or intellectual disability expert described by Subdivision (1). A court that elects to use the results of that previous determination may proceed under Subsection (c).

(3) If the defendant fails or refuses to submit to the collection of information regarding the defendant as required under Subdivision (1), the magistrate may order the defendant to submit to an examination in a jail or in another place determined to be appropriate by the local mental health authority or local intellectual and developmental disability authority for a reasonable period not to exceed 72 hours. If applicable, the county in which the committing court is located shall reimburse the local mental health authority or local intellectual and developmental disability authority for the mileage and per diem expenses of the personnel required to transport the defendant, calculated in accordance with the state travel regulations in effect at the time.

(b) Except as otherwise permitted by the magistrate for good cause shown, a written assessment of the information collected under Subsection (a)(1)(A) shall be provided to the magistrate:

(1) for a defendant held in custody, not later than 96 hours after the time an order was issued under Subsection (a); or

(2) for a defendant released from custody, not later than the 30th day after the date an order was issued under Subsection (a).

(b–1) The magistrate shall provide copies of the written assessment to the defense counsel, the attorney representing the state, and the trial court. The written assessment must include a description of the procedures used in the collection of information under Subsection (a)(1)(A) and the applicable expert's observations and findings pertaining to:

(1) whether the defendant is a person who has a mental illness or is a person with an intellectual disability;

(2) whether there is clinical evidence to support a belief that the defendant may be incompetent to stand trial and should undergo a complete competency examination under Subchapter B, Chapter 46B;[1] and

(3) any appropriate or recommended treatment or service.

(c) After the trial court receives the applicable expert's written assessment relating to the defendant under Subsection (b–1) or elects to use the results of a previous determination as described by Subsection (a)(2), the trial court may, as applicable:

(1) resume criminal proceedings against the defendant, including any appropriate proceedings related to the defendant's release on personal bond under Article 17.032 if the defendant is being held in custody;

(2) resume or initiate competency proceedings, if required, as provided by Chapter 46B or other proceedings affecting the defendant's receipt of appropriate court-ordered mental health or intellectual disability services, including proceedings related to the defendant's receipt of outpatient mental health services under Section 574.034, Health and Safety Code;

(3) consider the written assessment during the punishment phase after a conviction of the offense for which the defendant was arrested, as part of a presentence investigation report, or in connection with the impositions of conditions following placement on community supervision, including deferred adjudication community supervision; or

(4) refer the defendant to an appropriate specialty court established or operated under Subtitle K, Title 2, Government Code.

(d) This article does not prevent the applicable court from, before, during, or after the collection of information regarding the defendant as described by this article:

(1) releasing a defendant who has a mental illness or is a person with an intellectual disability from custody on personal or surety bond, including imposing as a condition of release that the defendant submit to an examination or other assessment; or

(2) ordering an examination regarding the defendant's competency to stand trial.

(e) The magistrate shall submit to the Office of Court Administration of the Texas Judicial System on a monthly basis the number of written assessments provided to the court under Subsection (a)(1)(B).

Added by Acts 1993, 73rd Leg., ch. 900, § 3.05, eff. Sept. 1, 1994. Amended by Acts 1997, 75th Leg., ch. 312, § 1, eff. Sept. 1, 1997; Acts 2001, 77th Leg., ch. 828, § 1, eff. Sept. 1, 2001; Acts 2003, 78th Leg., ch. 35, § 2, eff. Jan. 1, 2004; Acts 2007, 80th Leg., ch. 1307, § 1, eff. Sept. 1, 2007; Acts 2009, 81st Leg., ch. 1228, § 1, eff. Sept. 1, 2009; Acts 2017, 85th Leg., ch. 748 (S.B. 1326), § 2, eff. Sept. 1, 2017.

[1] Vernon's Ann. Texas C.C.P. art. 46B.021 et seq.

Section 37 of Acts 2017, 85th Leg., ch. 748 (S.B. 1326) provides:

"The changes in law made by this Act apply only to a defendant charged with an offense committed on or after the effective date [Sept. 1, 2017] of this Act. A defendant charged with an offense committed before the effective date of this Act is governed by the law in effect on the date the offense was committed, and the former law is continued in effect for that purpose. For purposes of this section, an offense was committed before the effective date of this Act if any element of the offense occurred before that date."

Art. 16.22. Early identification of defendant suspected of having mental illness or intellectual disability

Text of article as amended by Acts 2017, 85th Leg., ch. 950 (S.B. 1849), § 2.01. See, also, art. 16.22 as amended by Acts 2017, 85th Leg., ch. 748 (S.B. 1326), § 2.

(a)(1) Not later than 12 hours after receiving credible information that may establish reasonable cause to believe that a defendant committed to the sheriff's custody has a mental illness or is a person with an intellectual disability, including observation of the defendant's behavior immediately before, during, and after the defendant's arrest and the results of any previous assessment of the defendant, the sheriff shall provide written or electronic notice of the information to the magistrate. On a determination that there is reasonable cause to believe that the defendant has a mental illness or is a person with an intellectual disability, the magistrate, except as provided by Subdivision (2), shall order the local mental health or intellectual and developmental disability authority or another qualified mental health or intellectual disability expert to:

(A) collect information regarding whether the defendant has a mental illness as defined by Section 571.003, Health and Safety Code, or is a person with an intellectual disability as defined by Section 591.003, Health and Safety Code, including information obtained from any previous assessment of the defendant; and

(B) provide to the magistrate a written assessment of the information collected under Paragraph (A).

(2) The magistrate is not required to order the collection of information under Subdivision (1) if the defendant in the year preceding the defendant's applicable date of arrest has been determined to have a mental illness or to be a person with an intellectual disability by the local mental health or intellectual and developmental disability authority or another mental health or intellectual disability expert described by Subdivision (1). A court that elects to use the results of that previous determination may proceed under Subsection (c).

(3) If the defendant fails or refuses to submit to the collection of information regarding the defendant as required under Subdivision (1), the magistrate may order the defendant to submit to an examination in a mental health facility determined to be appropriate by the local mental health or intellectual and developmental disability authority for a reasonable period not to exceed 21 days. The magistrate may order a defendant to a facility operated by the Department of State Health Services or the Health and Human Services Commission for examination only on request of the local mental health or intellectual and developmental disability authority and with the consent of the head of the facility. If a defendant who has been ordered to a facility operated by the Department of State Health Services or the Health and Human Services Commission for examination remains in the facility for a period exceeding 21 days, the head of that facility shall cause the defendant to be immediately transported to the committing court and placed in the custody of the sheriff of the county in which the committing court is located. That county shall reimburse the facility for the mileage and per diem expenses of the personnel required to transport the defendant calculated in accordance with the state travel regulations in effect at the time.

(b) A written assessment of the information collected under Subsection (a)(1)(A) shall be provided to the magistrate not later than the 30th day after the date

of any order issued under Subsection (a) in a felony case and not later than the 10th day after the date of any order issued under that subsection in a misdemeanor case, and the magistrate shall provide copies of the written assessment to the defense counsel, the prosecuting attorney, and the trial court. The written assessment must include a description of the procedures used in the collection of information under Subsection (a)(1)(A) and the applicable expert's observations and findings pertaining to:

(1) whether the defendant is a person who has a mental illness or is a person with an intellectual disability;

(2) whether there is clinical evidence to support a belief that the defendant may be incompetent to stand trial and should undergo a complete competency examination under Subchapter B, Chapter 46B;[1] and

(3) recommended treatment.

(c) After the trial court receives the applicable expert's written assessment relating to the defendant under Subsection (b) or elects to use the results of a previous determination as described by Subsection (a)(2), the trial court may, as applicable:

(1) resume criminal proceedings against the defendant, including any appropriate proceedings related to the defendant's release on personal bond under Article 17.032;

(2) resume or initiate competency proceedings, if required, as provided by Chapter 46B or other proceedings affecting the defendant's receipt of appropriate court-ordered mental health or intellectual disability services, including proceedings related to the defendant's receipt of outpatient mental health services under Section 574.034, Health and Safety Code; or

(3) consider the written assessment during the punishment phase after a conviction of the offense for which the defendant was arrested, as part of a presentence investigation report, or in connection with the impositions of conditions following placement on community supervision, including deferred adjudication community supervision.

(d) This article does not prevent the applicable court from, before, during, or after the collection of information regarding the defendant as described by this article:

(1) releasing a defendant who has a mental illness or is a person with an intellectual disability from custody on personal or surety bond; or

(2) ordering an examination regarding the defendant's competency to stand trial.

Added by Acts 1993, 73rd Leg., ch. 900, § 3.05, eff. Sept. 1, 1994. Amended by Acts 1997, 75th Leg., ch. 312, § 1, eff. Sept. 1, 1997; Acts 2001, 77th Leg., ch. 828, § 1, eff. Sept. 1, 2001; Acts 2003, 78th Leg., ch. 35, § 2, eff. Jan. 1, 2004; Acts 2007, 80th Leg., ch. 1307, § 1, eff. Sept. 1, 2007; Acts 2009, 81st Leg., ch. 1228, § 1, eff. Sept. 1, 2009; Acts 2017, 85th Leg., ch. 950 (S.B. 1849), § 2.01, eff. Sept. 1, 2017.

[1] Vernon's Ann. Texas C.C.P. art. 46B.021 et seq.

Art. 16.23. Diversion of persons suffering mental health crisis or substance abuse issue

(a) Each law enforcement agency shall make a good faith effort to divert a person suffering a mental health crisis or suffering from the effects of substance abuse to a proper treatment center in the agency's jurisdiction if:

(1) there is an available and appropriate treatment center in the agency's jurisdiction to which the agency may divert the person;

(2) it is reasonable to divert the person;

(3) the offense that the person is accused of is a misdemeanor, other than a misdemeanor involving violence; and

(4) the mental health crisis or substance abuse issue is suspected to be the reason the person committed the alleged offense.

(b) Subsection (a) does not apply to a person who is accused of an offense under Section 49.04, 49.045, 49.05, 49.06, 49.065, 49.07, or 49.08, Penal Code.

Added by Acts 2017, 85th Leg., ch. 950 (S.B. 1849), § 2.02, eff. Sept. 1, 2017.

Section 1 of Acts 2017, 85th Leg., ch. 950 (S.B. 1849) provides:

"This Act shall be known as the Sandra Bland Act, in memory of Sandra Bland."

CHAPTER SEVENTEEN. BAIL

Art. 17.01.   Definition of "bail"

"Bail" is the security given by the accused that he will appear and answer before the proper court the accusation brought against him, and includes a bail bond or a personal bond.

Acts 1965, 59th Leg., vol. 2, p. 317, ch. 722, eff. Jan. 1, 1966.

Art. 17.02.   Definition of "bail bond"

A "bail bond" is a written undertaking entered into by the defendant and the defendant's sureties for the appearance of the principal therein before a court or magistrate to answer a criminal accusation; provided, however, that the defendant on execution of the bail bond may deposit with the custodian of funds of the court in which the prosecution is pending current money of the United States in the amount of the bond in lieu of having sureties signing the same. Any cash funds deposited under this article shall be receipted for by the officer receiving the funds and, on order of the court, be refunded in the amount shown on the face of the receipt less the administrative fee authorized by Section 117.055, Local Government Code, after the defendant complies with the conditions of the defendant's bond, to:

(1) any person in the name of whom a receipt was issued, including the defendant if a receipt was issued to the defendant; or

(2) the defendant, if no other person is able to produce a receipt for the funds.

Acts 1965, 59th Leg., vol. 2, p. 317, ch. 722, eff. Jan. 1, 1966. Amended by Acts 2011, 82nd Leg., ch. 978 (H.B. 1658), § 1, eff. Sept. 1, 2011; Acts 2015, 84th Leg., ch. 654 (H.B. 2182), § 1, eff. Sept. 1, 2015.

Section 7 of Acts 2015, 84th Leg., ch. 654 (H.B. 2182) provides:

"The changes in law made by this Act apply only to a fee that becomes payable on or after the effective date [Sept. 1, 2015] of this Act. A fee that becomes payable before that date is governed by the law in effect when the fee became payable, and the former law is continued in effect for that purpose."

Art. 17.025.   Officers taking bail bond

A jailer licensed under Chapter 1701, Occupations Code, is considered to be an officer for the purposes of taking a bail bond and discharging any other related powers and duties under this chapter.

Added by Acts 2011, 82nd Leg., ch. 736 (H.B. 1070), § 1, eff. June 17, 2011.

Art. 17.026.   Electronic Filing of Bail Bond

In any manner permitted by the county in which the bond is written, a bail bond may be filed electronically with the court, judge, magistrate, or other officer taking the bond.

Added by Acts 2015, 84th Leg., ch. 779 (H.B. 2499), § 1, eff. Sept. 1, 2015.

Art. 17.03.   Personal bond

(a) Except as provided by Subsection (b) or (b–1), a magistrate may, in the magistrate's discretion, release the defendant on personal bond without sureties or other security.

(b) Only the court before whom the case is pending may release on personal bond a defendant who:

(1) is charged with an offense under the following sections of the Penal Code:

(A) Section 19.03 (Capital Murder);

(B) Section 20.04 (Aggravated Kidnapping);

(C) Section 22.021 (Aggravated Sexual Assault);

(D) Section 22.03 (Deadly Assault on Law Enforcement or Corrections Officer, Member or Employee of Board of Pardons and Paroles,[1] or Court Participant);

(E) Section 22.04 (Injury to a Child, Elderly Individual, or Disabled Individual);

(F) Section 29.03 (Aggravated Robbery);

(G) Section 30.02 (Burglary);

(H) Section 71.02 (Engaging in Organized Criminal Activity);

(I) Section 21.02 (Continuous Sexual Abuse of Young Child or Children); or

(J) Section 20A.03 (Continuous Trafficking of Persons);

(2) is charged with a felony under Chapter 481, Health and Safety Code, or Section 485.033, Health and Safety Code, punishable by imprisonment for a minimum term or by a maximum fine that is more than a minimum term or maximum fine for a first degree felony; or

(3) does not submit to testing for the presence of a controlled substance in the defendant's body as requested by the court or magistrate under Subsection (c) of this article or submits to testing and the test shows evidence of the presence of a controlled substance in the defendant's body.

(b–1) A magistrate may not release on personal bond a defendant who, at the time of the commission

94

of the charged offense, is civilly committed as a sexually violent predator under Chapter 841, Health and Safety Code.

(c) When setting a personal bond under this chapter, on reasonable belief by the investigating or arresting law enforcement agent or magistrate of the presence of a controlled substance in the defendant's body or on the finding of drug or alcohol abuse related to the offense for which the defendant is charged, the court or a magistrate shall require as a condition of personal bond that the defendant submit to testing for alcohol or a controlled substance in the defendant's body and participate in an alcohol or drug abuse treatment or education program if such a condition will serve to reasonably assure the appearance of the defendant for trial.

(d) The state may not use the results of any test conducted under this chapter in any criminal proceeding arising out of the offense for which the defendant is charged.

(e) Costs of testing may be assessed as court costs or ordered paid directly by the defendant as a condition of bond.

(f) In this article, "controlled substance" has the meaning assigned by Section 481.002, Health and Safety Code.

(g) The court may order that a personal bond fee assessed under Section 17.42 be:

(1) paid before the defendant is released;

(2) paid as a condition of bond;

(3) paid as court costs;

(4) reduced as otherwise provided for by statute; or

(5) waived.

Acts 1965, 59th Leg., vol. 2, p. 317, ch. 722, eff. Jan. 1, 1966. Amended by Acts 1989, 71st Leg., ch. 374, § 1, eff. Sept. 1, 1989; Acts 1991, 72nd Leg., ch. 14, § 284(45), (57), eff. Sept. 1, 1991; Acts 1995, 74th Leg., ch. 76, § 14.19, eff. Sept. 1, 1995; Acts 2007, 80th Leg., ch. 593, § 3.08, eff. Sept. 1, 2007; Acts 2011, 82nd Leg., ch. 122 (H.B. 3000), § 3, eff. Sept. 1, 2011; Acts 2017, 85th Leg., ch. 34 (S.B. 1576), § 4, eff. Sept. 1, 2017.

[1] References to the Board of Pardons and Paroles shall mean either the Board of Pardons and Paroles or the pardons and paroles division of the Texas Department of Criminal Justice as provided by Acts 1989, 71st Leg., ch. 785, § 1.20(f)(2), as amended by Acts 1990, 71st Leg., 6th C.S., ch. 25, § 5.

Section 41 of Acts 2017, 85th Leg., ch. 34 (S.B. 1576) provides:

"Article 17.03, Code of Criminal Procedure, as amended by this Act, applies only to a personal bond that is executed on or after the effective date [Sept. 1, 2017] of this Act. A personal bond executed before the effective date of this Act is governed by the law in effect when the personal bond was executed, and the former law is continued in effect for that purpose."

Art. 17.031.   Release on personal bond

(a) Any magistrate in this state may release a defendant eligible for release on personal bond under Article 17.03 of this code on his personal bond where the complaint and warrant for arrest does not originate in the county wherein the accused is arrested if the magistrate would have had jurisdiction over the matter had the complaint arisen within the county wherein the magistrate presides. The personal bond may not be revoked by the judge of the court issuing the warrant for arrest except for good cause shown.

(b) If there is a personal bond office in the county from which the warrant for arrest was issued, the court releasing a defendant on his personal bond will forward a copy of the personal bond to the personal bond office in that county.

Added by Acts 1971, 62nd Leg., p. 2445, ch. 787, § 1, eff. June 8, 1971. Amended by Acts 1989, 71st Leg., ch. 374, § 2, eff. Sept. 1, 1989.

Art. 17.032.   Release on personal bond of certain defendants with mental illness or intellectual disability

(a) In this article, "violent offense" means an offense under the following sections of the Penal Code:

(1) Section 19.02 (murder);

(2) Section 19.03 (capital murder);

(3) Section 20.03 (kidnapping);

(4) Section 20.04 (aggravated kidnapping);

(5) Section 21.11 (indecency with a child);

(6) Section 22.01(a)(1) (assault), if the offense involved family violence as defined by Section 71.004, Family Code;

(7) Section 22.011 (sexual assault);

(8) Section 22.02 (aggravated assault);

(9) Section 22.021 (aggravated sexual assault);

(10) Section 22.04 (injury to a child, elderly individual, or disabled individual);

(11) Section 29.03 (aggravated robbery);

(12) Section 21.02 (continuous sexual abuse of young child or children); or

(13) Section 20A.03 (continuous trafficking of persons).

Text of (b), as amended by Acts 2017, 85th Leg., ch. 748 (S.B. 1326), § 3

(b) Notwithstanding Article 17.03(b), or a bond schedule adopted or a standing order entered by a judge, a magistrate shall release a defendant on personal bond unless good cause is shown otherwise if:

(1) the defendant is not charged with and has not been previously convicted of a violent offense;

(2) the defendant is examined by the local mental health authority, local intellectual and developmental disability authority, or another qualified mental health or intellectual disability expert under Article 16.22;

(3) the applicable expert, in a written assessment submitted to the magistrate under Article 16.22:

(A) concludes that the defendant has a mental illness or is a person with an intellectual disability and is nonetheless competent to stand trial; and

(B) recommends mental health treatment or intellectual disability services for the defendant, as applicable;

(4) the magistrate determines, in consultation with the local mental health authority or local intellectual and developmental disability authority, that appropriate community-based mental health or intellectual disability services for the defendant are available in accordance with Section 534.053 or 534.103, Health and Safety Code, or through another mental health or intellectual disability services provider; and

(5) the magistrate finds, after considering all the circumstances, a pretrial risk assessment, if applicable, and any other credible information provided by the attorney representing the state or the defendant, that release on personal bond would reasonably ensure the defendant's appearance in court as required and the safety of the community and the victim of the alleged offense.

Text of (b), as amended by Acts 2017, 85th Leg., ch. 950 (S.B. 1849), § 3.02

(b) A magistrate shall release a defendant on personal bond unless good cause is shown otherwise if the:

(1) defendant is not charged with and has not been previously convicted of a violent offense;

(2) defendant is examined by the local mental health or intellectual and developmental disability authority or another mental health expert under Article 16.22;

(3) applicable expert, in a written assessment submitted to the magistrate under Article 16.22:

(A) concludes that the defendant has a mental illness or is a person with an intellectual disability and is nonetheless competent to stand trial; and

(B) recommends mental health treatment or intellectual disability treatment for the defendant, as applicable; and

(4) magistrate determines, in consultation with the local mental health or intellectual and developmental disability authority, that appropriate community-based mental health or intellectual disability services for the defendant are available through the Department of State Health Services under Section 534.053, Health and Safety Code, or through another mental health or intellectual disability services provider.

Text of (c), as amended by Acts 2017, 85th Leg., ch. 748 (S.B. 1326), § 3

(c) The magistrate, unless good cause is shown for not requiring treatment, shall require as a condition of release on personal bond under this article that the defendant submit to outpatient or inpatient mental health treatment or intellectual disability services as recommended by the local mental health authority, local intellectual and developmental disability authority, or another qualified mental health or intellectual disability expert if the defendant's:

(1) mental illness or intellectual disability is chronic in nature; or

(2) ability to function independently will continue to deteriorate if the defendant is not treated.

(d) In addition to a condition of release imposed under Subsection (c), the magistrate may require the defendant to comply with other conditions that are reasonably necessary to ensure the defendant's appearance in court as required and the safety of the community and the victim of the alleged offense.

(e) In this article, a person is considered to have been convicted of an offense if:

(1) a sentence is imposed;

(2) the person is placed on community supervision or receives deferred adjudication; or

(3) the court defers final disposition of the case.

Text of (c), as amended by Acts 2017, 85th Leg., ch. 950 (S.B. 1849), § 3.02

(c) The magistrate, unless good cause is shown for not requiring treatment, shall require as a condition of release on personal bond under this article that the defendant submit to outpatient or inpatient mental health or intellectual disability treatment as recommended by the local mental health or intellectual and developmental disability authority if the defendant's:

(1) mental illness or intellectual disability is chronic in nature; or

(2) ability to function independently will continue to deteriorate if the defendant is not treated.

Added by Acts 1993, 73rd Leg., ch. 900, § 3.06, eff. Sept. 1, 1994. Amended by Acts 1995, 74th Leg., ch. 76, § 14.20, eff. Sept. 1, 1995; Acts 1997, 75th Leg., ch. 312, § 2, eff. Sept. 1, 1997; Acts 2001, 77th Leg., ch. 828, § 2, eff. Sept. 1, 2001; Acts 2007, 80th Leg., ch. 593, § 3.09, eff. Sept. 1, 2007; Acts 2009, 81st Leg., ch. 1228, § 2, eff. Sept. 1, 2009. Amended by Acts 2011, 82nd Leg., ch. 122 (H.B. 3000), § 4, eff. Sept. 1, 2011; Acts 2017, 85th Leg., ch. 748 (S.B. 1326), § 3, eff. Sept. 1, 2017; Acts 2017, 85th Leg., ch. 950 (S.B. 1849), §§ 3.01, 3.02, eff. Sept. 1, 2017.

Section 37 of Acts 2017, 85th Leg., ch. 748 (S.B. 1326) provides:

"The changes in law made by this Act apply only to a defendant charged with an offense committed on or after the effective date [Sept. 1, 2017] of this Act. A defendant charged with an offense committed before the effective date of this Act is governed by the law in effect on the date the offense was committed, and the former law is continued in effect for that purpose. For purposes of this section, an offense was committed before the effective date of this Act if any element of the offense occurred before that date."

Section 3.08 of Acts 2017, 85th Leg., ch. 950 (S.B. 1849) provides:

"The changes in law made by this article to Article 17.032, Code of Criminal Procedure, apply only to a personal bond that is executed on or after the effective date [Sept. 1, 2017] of this Act. A personal bond executed before the effective date of this Act is governed by the law in effect when the personal bond was executed, and the former law is continued in effect for that purpose."

Art. 17.033. Release on bond of certain persons arrested without a warrant

(a) Except as provided by Subsection (c), a person who is arrested without a warrant and who is detained in jail must be released on bond, in an amount not to exceed $5,000, not later than the 24th hour after the person's arrest if the person was arrested for a misdemeanor and a magistrate has not determined whether probable cause exists to believe that the person committed the offense. If the person is unable to obtain a surety for the bond or unable to deposit money in the amount of the bond, the person must be released on personal bond.

(a–1) Expired.

(b) Except as provided by Subsection (c), a person who is arrested without a warrant and who is detained in jail must be released on bond, in an amount not to exceed $10,000, not later than the 48th hour after the person's arrest if the person was arrested for a felony and a magistrate has not determined whether proba-

ble cause exists to believe that the person committed the offense. If the person is unable to obtain a surety for the bond or unable to deposit money in the amount of the bond, the person must be released on personal bond.

(c) On the filing of an application by the attorney representing the state, a magistrate may postpone the release of a person under Subsection (a) or (b) for not more than 72 hours after the person's arrest. An application filed under this subsection must state the reason a magistrate has not determined whether probable cause exists to believe that the person committed the offense for which the person was arrested.

(d) The time limits imposed by Subsections (a) and (b) do not apply to a person arrested without a warrant who is taken to a hospital, clinic, or other medical facility before being taken before a magistrate under Article 15.17. For a person described by this subsection, the time limits imposed by Subsections (a) and (b) begin to run at the time, as documented in the records of the hospital, clinic, or other medical facility, that a physician or other medical professional releases the person from the hospital, clinic, or other medical facility.

(e) Expired.

Added by Acts 2001, 77th Leg., ch. 906, § 5(a), eff. Jan. 1, 2002. Amended by Acts 2003, 78th Leg., ch. 298, § 1, eff. June 18, 2003. Amended by Acts 2011, 82nd Leg., ch. 1350 (H.B. 1173), § 1, eff. Sept. 1, 2011; Acts 2017, 85th Leg., ch. 324 (S.B. 1488), § 5.001, eff. Sept. 1, 2017.

Art. 17.0331. Expired

Art. 17.04. Requisites of a personal bond

A personal bond is sufficient if it includes the requisites of a bail bond as set out in Article 17.08, except that no sureties are required. In addition, a personal bond shall contain:

(1) the defendant's name, address, and place of employment;

(2) identification information, including the defendant's:

(A) date and place of birth;

(B) height, weight, and color of hair and eyes;

(C) driver's license number and state of issuance, if any; and

(D) nearest relative's name and address, if any; and

(3) the following oath sworn and signed by the defendant:

"I swear that I will appear before (the court or magistrate) at (address, city, county) Texas, on the (date), at the hour of (time, a.m. or p.m.) or upon notice by the court, or pay to the court the principal sum of (amount) plus all necessary and reasonable expenses incurred in any arrest for failure to appear."

Acts 1965, 59th Leg., vol. 2, p. 317, ch. 722, eff. Jan. 1, 1966. Amended by Acts 1987, 70th Leg., ch. 623, § 1, eff. Sept. 1, 1987.

Art. 17.045.   Bail bond certificates

A bail bond certificate with respect to which a fidelity and surety company has become surety as provided in the Automobile Club Services Act, or for any truck and bus association incorporated in this state, when posted by the person whose signature appears thereon, shall be accepted as bail bond in an amount not to exceed $200 to guarantee the appearance of such person in any court in this state when the person is arrested for violation of any motor vehicle law of this state or ordinance of any municipality in this state, except for the offense of driving while intoxicated or for any felony, and the alleged violation was committed prior to the date of expiration shown on such bail bond certificate.

Added by Acts 1969, 61st Leg., p. 2033, ch. 697, § 2, eff. Sept. 1, 1969.

Art. 17.05.   When a bail bond is given

A bail bond is entered into either before a magistrate, upon an examination of a criminal accusation, or before a judge upon an application under habeas corpus; or it is taken from the defendant by a peace officer or jailer if authorized by Article 17.20, 17.21, or 17.22.

Acts 1965, 59th Leg., vol. 2, p. 317, ch. 722, eff. Jan. 1, 1966. Amended by Acts 1971, 62nd Leg., p. 3045, ch. 1006, § 1, eff. Aug. 30, 1971; Acts 2011, 82nd Leg., ch. 736 (H.B. 1070), § 2, eff. June 17, 2011.

Art. 17.06.   Corporation as surety

Wherever in this Chapter, any person is required or authorized to give or execute any bail bond, such bail bond may be given or executed by such principal and any corporation authorized by law to act as surety, subject to all the provisions of this Chapter regulating and governing the giving of bail bonds by personal surety insofar as the same is applicable.

Acts 1965, 59th Leg., vol. 2, p. 317, ch. 722, eff. Jan. 1, 1966.

Art. 17.07.   Corporation to file with county clerk power of attorney designating agent

(a) Any corporation authorized by the law of this State to act as a surety, shall before executing any bail bond as authorized in the preceding Article, first file in the office of the county clerk of the county where such bail bond is given, a power of attorney designating and authorizing the named agent, agents or attorney of such corporation to execute such bail bonds and thereafter the execution of such bail bonds by such agent, agents or attorney, shall be a valid and binding obligation of such corporation.

(b) A corporation may limit the authority of an agent designated under Subsection (a) by specifying the limitation in the power of attorney that is filed with the county clerk.

Acts 1965, 59th Leg., vol. 2, p. 317, ch. 722, eff. Jan. 1, 1966. Amended by Acts 2011, 82nd Leg., ch. 769 (H.B. 1823), § 1, eff. Sept. 1, 2011.

Art. 17.08.   Requisites of a bail bond

A bail bond must contain the following requisites:

1.   That it be made payable to "The State of Texas";

2.   That the defendant and his sureties, if any, bind themselves that the defendant will appear before the proper court or magistrate to answer the accusation against him;

3.   If the defendant is charged with a felony, that it state that he is charged with a felony. If the defendant is charged with a misdemeanor, that it state that he is charged with a misdemeanor;

4.   That the bond be signed by name or mark by the principal and sureties, if any, each of whom shall write thereon his mailing address;

5.   That the bond state the time and place, when and where the accused binds himself to appear, and the court or magistrate before whom he is to appear. The bond shall also bind the defendant to appear before any court or magistrate before whom the cause may thereafter be pending at any time when, and place where, his presence may be required under this Code or by any court or magistrate, but in no event shall the sureties be bound after such time as the defendant receives an order of deferred adjudication or is acquitted, sentenced, placed on community supervision, or dismissed from the charge;

6.   The bond shall also be conditioned that the principal and sureties, if any, will pay all necessary and reasonable expenses incurred by any and all

sheriffs or other peace officers in rearresting the principal in the event he fails to appear before the court or magistrate named in the bond at the time stated therein. The amount of such expense shall be in addition to the principal amount specified in the bond. The failure of any bail bond to contain the conditions specified in this paragraph shall in no manner affect the legality of any such bond, but it is intended that the sheriff or other peace officer shall look to the defendant and his sureties, if any, for expenses incurred by him, and not to the State for any fees earned by him in connection with the rearresting of an accused who has violated the conditions of his bond.

Acts 1965, 59th Leg., vol. 2, p. 317, ch. 722, eff. Jan. 1, 1966. Amended by Acts 1999, 76th Leg., ch. 1506, § 1, eff. Sept. 1, 1999.

Art. 17.085. Notice of appearance date

The clerk of a court that does not provide online Internet access to that court's criminal case records shall post in a designated public place in the courthouse notice of a prospective criminal court docket setting as soon as the court notifies the clerk of the setting.

Added by Acts 2007, 80th Leg., ch. 1038, § 1, eff. Sept. 1, 2007. Amended by Acts 2011, 82nd Leg., ch. 278 (H.B. 1573), § 1, eff. Sept. 1, 2011.

Art. 17.09. Duration; original and subsequent proceedings; new bail

Sec. 1. Where a defendant, in the course of a criminal action, gives bail before any court or person authorized by law to take same, for his personal appearance before a court or magistrate, to answer a charge against him, the said bond shall be valid and binding upon the defendant and his sureties, if any, thereon, for the defendant's personal appearance before the court or magistrate designated therein, as well as before any other court to which same may be transferred, and for any and all subsequent proceedings had relative to the charge, and each such bond shall be so conditioned except as hereinafter provided.

Sec. 2. When a defendant has once given bail for his appearance in answer to a criminal charge, he shall not be required to give another bond in the course of the same criminal action except as herein provided.

Sec. 3. Provided that whenever, during the course of the action, the judge or magistrate in whose court such action is pending finds that the bond is defective, excessive or insufficient in amount, or that the sure-

ties, if any, are not acceptable, or for any other good and sufficient cause, such judge or magistrate may, either in term-time or in vacation, order the accused to be rearrested, and require the accused to give another bond in such amount as the judge or magistrate may deem proper. When such bond is so given and approved, the defendant shall be released from custody.

Sec. 4. Notwithstanding any other provision of this article, the judge or magistrate in whose court a criminal action is pending may not order the accused to be rearrested or require the accused to give another bond in a higher amount because the accused:

(1) withdraws a waiver of the right to counsel; or

(2) requests the assistance of counsel, appointed or retained.

Acts 1965, 59th Leg., vol. 2, p. 317, ch. 722, eff. Jan. 1, 1966. Amended by Acts 2007, 80th Leg., ch. 463, § 2, eff. Sept. 1, 2007.

Art. 17.091. Notice of Certain Bail Reductions Required

Before a judge or magistrate reduces the amount of bail set for a defendant charged with an offense listed in Article 42A.054, an offense described by Article 62.001(5), or an offense under Section 20A.03, Penal Code, the judge or magistrate shall provide:

(1) to the attorney representing the state, reasonable notice of the proposed bail reduction; and

(2) on request of the attorney representing the state or the defendant or the defendant's counsel, an opportunity for a hearing concerning the proposed bail reduction.

Added by Acts 2005, 79th Leg., ch. 671, § 1, eff. Sept. 1, 2005. Amended by Acts 2007, 80th Leg., ch. 593, § 3.10, eff. Sept. 1, 2007; Acts 2011, 82nd Leg., ch. 122 (H.B. 3000), § 5, eff. Sept. 1, 2011; Acts 2015, 84th Leg., ch. 770 (H.B. 2299), § 2.05, eff. Jan. 1, 2017.

Art. 17.10. Disqualified sureties

(a) A minor may not be surety on a bail bond, but the accused party may sign as principal.

(b) A person, for compensation, may not be a surety on a bail bond written in a county in which a county bail bond board regulated under Chapter 1704, Occupations Code, does not exist unless the person, within two years before the bail bond is given, completed in person at least eight hours of continuing legal education in criminal law courses or bail bond law courses that are:

(1) approved by the State Bar of Texas; and

(2) offered by an accredited institution of higher education in this state.

(c) A person, for compensation, may not act as a surety on a bail bond if the person has been finally convicted of:

(1) a misdemeanor involving moral turpitude; or

(2) a felony.

Acts 1965, 59th Leg., vol. 2, p. 317, ch. 722, eff. Jan. 1, 1966. Amended by Acts 2005, 79th Leg., ch. 743, § 1, eff. Sept. 1, 2005. Amended by Acts 2011, 82nd Leg., ch. 769 (H.B. 1823), § 2, eff. Sept. 1, 2011.

Art. 17.11.   How bail bond is taken

Sec. 1. Every court, judge, magistrate or other officer taking a bail bond shall require evidence of the sufficiency of the security offered; but in every case, one surety shall be sufficient, if it be made to appear that such surety is worth at least double the amount of the sum for which he is bound, exclusive of all property exempted by law from execution, and of debts or other encumbrances; and that he is a resident of this state, and has property therein liable to execution worth the sum for which he is bound.

Sec. 2. Provided, however, any person who has signed as a surety on a bail bond and is in default thereon shall thereafter be disqualified to sign as a surety so long as the person is in default on the bond. It shall be the duty of the clerk of the court where the surety is in default on a bail bond to notify in writing the sheriff, chief of police, or other peace officer of the default. If a bail bond is taken for an offense other than a Class C misdemeanor, the clerk of the court where the surety is in default on the bond shall send notice of the default by certified mail to the last known address of the surety.

Sec. 3. A surety is considered to be in default from the time execution may be issued on a final judgment in a bond forfeiture proceeding under the Texas Rules of Civil Procedure, unless the final judgment is superseded by the posting of a supersedeas bond.

Acts 1965, 59th Leg., vol. 2, p. 317, ch. 722, eff. Jan. 1, 1966. Amended by Acts 1967, 60th Leg., p. 1736, ch. 659, § 14, eff. Aug. 28, 1967; Acts 1999, 76th Leg., ch. 1506, § 2, eff. Sept. 1, 1999; Acts 2013, 83rd Leg., ch. 930 (H.B. 1562), § 1, eff. Sept. 1, 2013.

"The change in law made by this Act to Article 17.11, Code of Criminal Procedure, applies only to a bail bond that is executed on or after the effective date [Sept. 1, 2013] of this Act. A bail bond executed before the effective date of this Act is governed by the law in effect when the bail bond was executed, and the former law is continued in effect for that purpose."

Art. 17.12.   Exempt property

The property secured by the Constitution and laws from forced sale shall not, in any case, be held liable for the satisfaction of bail, either as to principal or sureties, if any.

Acts 1965, 59th Leg., vol. 2, p. 317, ch. 722, eff. Jan. 1, 1966.

Art. 17.13.   Sufficiency of sureties ascertained

To test the sufficiency of the security offered to any bail bond, unless the court or officer taking the same is fully satisfied as to its sufficiency, the following oath shall be made in writing and subscribed by the sureties: "I, do swear that I am worth, in my own right, at least the sum of (here insert the amount in which the surety is bound), after deducting from my property all that which is exempt by the Constitution and Laws of the State from forced sale, and after the payment of all my debts of every description, whether individual or security debts, and after satisfying all encumbrances upon my property which are known to me; that I reside in . . . . County, and have property in this State liable to execution worth said amount or more.

(Dated . . . ., and attested by the judge of the court, clerk, magistrate or sheriff.)"

Such affidavit shall be filed with the papers of the proceedings.

Acts 1965, 59th Leg., vol. 2, p. 317, ch. 722, eff. Jan. 1, 1966.

Art. 17.14.   Affidavit not conclusive

Such affidavit shall not be conclusive as to the sufficiency of the security; and if the court or officer taking the bail bond is not fully satisfied as to the sufficiency of the security offered, further evidence shall be required before approving the same.

Acts 1965, 59th Leg., vol. 2, p. 317, ch. 722, eff. Jan. 1, 1966.

Art. 17.141.   Eligible bail bond sureties in certain counties

In a county in which a county bail bond board regulated under Chapter 1704, Occupations Code, does not exist, the sheriff may post a list of eligible bail bond sureties whose security has been determined to be sufficient. Each surety listed under this article must file annually a sworn financial statement with the sheriff.

Added by Acts 2005, 79th Leg., ch. 743, § 2, eff. Sept. 1, 2005.

Art. 17.15. Rules for fixing amount of bail

The amount of bail to be required in any case is to be regulated by the court, judge, magistrate or officer taking the bail; they are to be governed in the exercise of this discretion by the Constitution and by the following rules:

1. The bail shall be sufficiently high to give reasonable assurance that the undertaking will be complied with.

2. The power to require bail is not to be so used as to make it an instrument of oppression.

3. The nature of the offense and the circumstances under which it was committed are to be considered.

4. The ability to make bail is to be regarded, and proof may be taken upon this point.

5. The future safety of a victim of the alleged offense and the community shall be considered.

Acts 1965, 59th Leg., vol. 2, p. 317, ch. 722, eff. Jan. 1, 1966. Amended by Acts 1985, 69th Leg., ch. 588, § 2, eff. Sept. 1, 1985; Acts 1993, 73rd Leg., ch. 396, § 1, eff. Sept. 1, 1993.

Art. 17.151. Release because of delay

Sec. 1. A defendant who is detained in jail pending trial of an accusation against him must be released either on personal bond or by reducing the amount of bail required, if the state is not ready for trial of the criminal action for which he is being detained within:

(1) 90 days from the commencement of his detention if he is accused of a felony;

(2) 30 days from the commencement of his detention if he is accused of a misdemeanor punishable by a sentence of imprisonment in jail for more than 180 days;

(3) 15 days from the commencement of his detention if he is accused of a misdemeanor punishable by a sentence of imprisonment for 180 days or less; or

(4) five days from the commencement of his detention if he is accused of a misdemeanor punishable by a fine only.

Sec. 2. The provisions of this article do not apply to a defendant who is:

(1) serving a sentence of imprisonment for another offense while the defendant is serving that sentence;

(2) being detained pending trial of another accusation against the defendant as to which the applicable period has not yet elapsed;

(3) incompetent to stand trial, during the period of the defendant's incompetence; or

(4) being detained for a violation of the conditions of a previous release related to the safety of a victim of the alleged offense or to the safety of the community under this article.

Sec. 3. Repealed by Acts 2005, 79th Leg., ch. 110, § 2.

Added by Acts 1977, 65th Leg., p. 1972, ch. 787, § 2, eff. July 1, 1978. Amended by Acts 2005, 79th Leg., ch. 110, §§ 1, 2, eff. Sept. 1, 2005.

Art. 17.152. Denial of bail for violation of certain court orders or conditions of bond in a family violence case

(a) In this article, "family violence" has the meaning assigned by Section 71.004, Family Code.

(b) Except as otherwise provided by Subsection (d), a person who commits an offense under Section 25.07, Penal Code, related to a violation of a condition of bond set in a family violence case and whose bail in the case under Section 25.07, Penal Code, or in the family violence case is revoked or forfeited for a violation of a condition of bond may be taken into custody and, pending trial or other court proceedings, denied release on bail if following a hearing a judge or magistrate determines by a preponderance of the evidence that the person violated a condition of bond related to:

(1) the safety of the victim of the offense under Section 25.07, Penal Code, or the family violence case, as applicable; or

(2) the safety of the community.

(c) Except as otherwise provided by Subsection (d), a person who commits an offense under Section 25.07, Penal Code, other than an offense related to a violation of a condition of bond set in a family violence case, may be taken into custody and, pending trial or other court proceedings, denied release on bail if following a hearing a judge or magistrate determines by a preponderance of the evidence that the person committed the offense.

(d) A person who commits an offense under Section 25.07(a)(3), Penal Code, may be held without bail under Subsection (b) or (c), as applicable, only if following a hearing the judge or magistrate determines by a preponderance of the evidence that the person went to or near the place described in the order or condition of bond with the intent to commit or threaten to commit:

(1) family violence; or

(2) an act in furtherance of an offense under Section 42.072, Penal Code.

(e) In determining whether to deny release on bail under this article, the judge or magistrate may consider:

(1) the order or condition of bond;

(2) the nature and circumstances of the alleged offense;

(3) the relationship between the accused and the victim, including the history of that relationship;

(4) any criminal history of the accused; and

(5) any other facts or circumstances relevant to a determination of whether the accused poses an imminent threat of future family violence.

(f) A person arrested for committing an offense under Section 25.07, Penal Code, shall without unnecessary delay and after reasonable notice is given to the attorney representing the state, but not later than 48 hours after the person is arrested, be taken before a magistrate in accordance with Article 15.17. At that time, the magistrate shall conduct the hearing and make the determination required by this article.

Added by Acts 2007, 80th Leg., ch. 1113, § 3, eff. Jan. 1, 2008.

Art. 17.153.   Denial of bail for violation of condition of bond where child alleged victim

(a) This article applies to a defendant charged with a felony offense under any of the following provisions of the Penal Code, if committed against a child younger than 14 years of age:

(1) Chapter 21 (Sexual Offenses);

(2) Section 25.02 (Prohibited Sexual Conduct);

(3) Section 43.25 (Sexual Performance by a Child);

(4) Section 20A.02 (Trafficking of Persons), if the defendant is alleged to have:

(A) trafficked the child with the intent or knowledge that the child would engage in sexual conduct, as defined by Section 43.25, Penal Code; or

(B) benefited from participating in a venture that involved a trafficked child engaging in sexual conduct, as defined by Section 43.25, Penal Code; or

(5) Section 43.05(a)(2) (Compelling Prostitution).

(b) A defendant described by Subsection (a) who violates a condition of bond set under Article 17.41

and whose bail in the case is revoked for the violation may be taken into custody and denied release on bail pending trial if, following a hearing, a judge or magistrate determines by a preponderance of the evidence that the defendant violated a condition of bond related to the safety of the victim of the offense or the safety of the community. If the magistrate finds that the violation occurred, the magistrate may revoke the defendant's bond and order that the defendant be immediately returned to custody. Once the defendant is placed in custody, the revocation of the defendant's bond discharges the sureties on the bond, if any, from any future liability on the bond. A discharge under this subsection from any future liability on the bond does not discharge any surety from liability for previous forfeitures on the bond.

Added by Acts 2009, 81st Leg., ch. 982, § 2, eff. Sept. 1, 2009. Amended by Acts 2011, 82nd Leg., ch. 515 (H.B. 2014), § 2.01, eff. Sept. 1, 2011.

Art. 17.16.   Discharge of liability; surrender or incarceration of principal before forfeiture; verification of incarceration

(a) A surety may before forfeiture relieve the surety of the surety's undertaking by:

(1) surrendering the accused into the custody of the sheriff of the county where the prosecution is pending; or

(2) delivering to the sheriff of the county in which the prosecution is pending and to the office of the prosecuting attorney an affidavit stating that the accused is incarcerated in:

(A) federal custody, subject to Subsection (a–1);

(B) the custody of any state; or

(C) any county of this state.

(a–1) For purposes of Subsection (a)(2), the surety may not be relieved of the surety's undertaking if the accused is in federal custody to determine whether the accused is lawfully present in the United States.

(b) On receipt of an affidavit described by Subsection (a)(2), the sheriff of the county in which the prosecution is pending shall verify whether the accused is incarcerated as stated in the affidavit. If the sheriff verifies the statement in the affidavit, the sheriff shall notify the magistrate before which the prosecution is pending of the verification.

(c) On a verification described by this article, the sheriff shall place a detainer against the accused with the appropriate officials in the jurisdiction in which the accused is incarcerated. On receipt of notice of a verification described by this article, the magistrate before which the prosecution is pending shall direct the clerk of the court to issue a capias for the arrest of the accused, except as provided by Subsection (d).

(d) A capias for the arrest of the accused is not required if:

(1) a warrant has been issued for the accused's arrest and remains outstanding; or

(2) the issuance of a capias would otherwise be unnecessary for the purpose of taking the accused into custody.

(e) For the purposes of Subsection (a)(2) of this article, the bond is discharged and the surety is absolved of liability on the bond on the verification of the incarceration of the accused.

(f) An affidavit described by Subsection (a)(2) and the documentation of any verification obtained under Subsection (b) must be:

(1) filed in the court record of the underlying criminal case in the court in which the prosecution is pending or, if the court record does not exist, in a general file maintained by the clerk of the court; and

(2) delivered to the office of the prosecuting attorney.

(g) A surety is liable for all reasonable and necessary expenses incurred in returning the accused into the custody of the sheriff of the county in which the prosecution is pending.

Acts 1965, 59th Leg., vol. 2, p. 317, ch. 722, eff. Jan. 1, 1966. Amended by Acts 1987, 70th Leg., ch. 1047, § 1, eff. June 20, 1987; Acts 2011, 82nd Leg., ch. 87 (S.B. 877), § 1, eff. May 19, 2011; Acts 2017, 85th Leg., ch. 4 (S.B. 4), § 4.01, eff. Sept. 1, 2017.

Section 7.01 of Acts 2017, 85th Leg., ch. 4 (S.B. 4) provides:

"It is the intent of the legislature that every provision, section, subsection, sentence, clause, phrase, or word in this Act, and every application of the provisions in this Act to each person or entity, are severable from each other. If any application of any provision in this Act to any person, group of persons, or circumstances is found by a court to be invalid for any reason, the remaining applications of that provision to all other persons and circumstances shall be severed and may not be affected."

Art. 17.17. When surrender is made during term

If a surrender of the accused be made during a term of the court to which he has bound himself to appear, the sheriff shall take him before the court; and if he is willing to give other bail, the court shall forthwith require him to do so. If he fails or refuses to give bail, the court shall make an order that he be committed to jail until the bail is given, and this shall be a sufficient commitment without any written order to the sheriff.

Acts 1965, 59th Leg., vol. 2, p. 317, ch. 722, eff. Jan. 1, 1966.

Art. 17.18. Surrender in vacation

When the surrender is made at any other time than during the session of the court, the sheriff may take the necessary bail bond, but if the defendant fails or refuses to give other bail, the sheriff shall take him before the nearest magistrate; and such magistrate shall issue a warrant of commitment, reciting the fact that the accused has been once admitted to bail, has been surrendered, and now fails or refuses to give other bail.

Acts 1965, 59th Leg., vol. 2, p. 317, ch. 722, eff. Jan. 1, 1966.

Art. 17.19. Surety may obtain a warrant

(a) Any surety, desiring to surrender his principal and after notifying the principal's attorney, if the principal is represented by an attorney, in a manner provided by Rule 21a, Texas Rules of Civil Procedure, of the surety's intention to surrender the principal, may file an affidavit of such intention before the court or magistrate before which the prosecution is pending. The affidavit must state:

(1) the court and cause number of the case;

(2) the name of the defendant;

(3) the offense with which the defendant is charged;

(4) the date of the bond;

(5) the cause for the surrender; and

(6) that notice of the surety's intention to surrender the principal has been given as required by this subsection.

(b) In a prosecution pending before a court, if the court finds that there is cause for the surety to surrender the surety's principal, the court shall issue a capias for the principal. In a prosecution pending before a magistrate, if the magistrate finds that there is cause for the surety to surrender the surety's principal, the magistrate shall issue a warrant of arrest for the principal. It is an affirmative defense to any liability on the bond that:

(1) the court or magistrate refused to issue a capias or warrant of arrest for the principal; and

(2) after the refusal to issue the capias or warrant of arrest, the principal failed to appear.

(c) If the court or magistrate before whom the prosecution is pending is not available, the surety may deliver the affidavit to any other magistrate in the county and that magistrate, on a finding of cause for the surety to surrender the surety's principal, shall issue a warrant of arrest for the principal.

(d) An arrest warrant or capias issued under this article shall be issued to the sheriff of the county in which the case is pending, and a copy of the warrant or capias shall be issued to the surety or his agent.

(e) An arrest warrant or capias issued under this article may be executed by a peace officer, a security officer, or a private investigator licensed in this state.

Acts 1965, 59th Leg., vol. 2, p. 317, ch. 722, eff. Jan. 1, 1966. Amended by Acts 1987, 70th Leg., ch. 1047, § 2, eff. June 20, 1987; Acts 1989, 71st Leg., ch. 374, § 3, eff. Sept. 1,1989; Acts 1999, 76th Leg., ch. 1506, § 3, eff. Sept. 1, 1999; Acts 2003, 78th Leg., ch. 942, § 4, eff. June 20, 2003; Acts 2007, 80th Leg., ch. 1263, § 2, eff. Sept. 1, 2007.

Art. 17.20.   Bail in misdemeanor

In cases of misdemeanor, the sheriff or other peace officer, or a jailer licensed under Chapter 1701, Occupations Code, may, whether during the term of the court or in vacation, where the officer has a defendant in custody, take of the defendant a bail bond.

Acts 1965, 59th Leg., vol. 2, p. 317, ch. 722, eff. Jan. 1, 1966. Amended by Acts 1971, 62nd Leg., p. 3046, ch. 1006, § 1, eff. Aug. 30, 1971; Acts 2011, 82nd Leg., ch. 736 (H.B. 1070), § 3, eff. June 17, 2011.

Art. 17.21.   Bail in felony

In cases of felony, when the accused is in custody of the sheriff or other officer, and the court before which the prosecution is pending is in session in the county where the accused is in custody, the court shall fix the amount of bail, if it is a bailable case and determine if the accused is eligible for a personal bond; and the sheriff or other peace officer, unless it be the police of a city, or a jailer licensed under Chapter 1701, Occupations Code, is authorized to take a bail bond of the accused in the amount as fixed by the court, to be approved by such officer taking the same, and will thereupon discharge the accused from custody. The defendant and the defendant's sureties are not required to appear in court.

Acts 1965, 59th Leg., vol. 2, p. 317, ch. 722, eff. Jan. 1, 1966. Amended by Acts 2011, 82nd Leg., ch. 736 (H.B. 1070), § 4, eff. June 17, 2011.

Art. 17.22.   May take bail in felony

In a felony case, if the court before which the same is pending is not in session in the county where the defendant is in custody, the sheriff or other peace officer, or a jailer licensed under Chapter 1701, Occu-

pations Code, who has the defendant in custody may take the defendant's bail bond in such amount as may have been fixed by the court or magistrate, or if no amount has been fixed, then in such amount as such officer may consider reasonable.

Acts 1965, 59th Leg., vol. 2, p. 317, ch. 722, eff. Jan. 1, 1966. Amended by Acts 2011, 82nd Leg., ch. 736 (H.B. 1070), § 5, eff. June 17, 2011.

Art. 17.23.   Sureties severally bound

In all bail bonds taken under any provision of this Code, the sureties shall be severally bound. Where a surrender of the principal is made by one or more of them, all the sureties shall be considered discharged.

Acts 1965, 59th Leg., vol. 2, p. 317, ch. 722, eff. Jan. 1, 1966.

Art. 17.24.   General rules applicable

All general rules in the Chapter are applicable to bail defendant before an examining court.

Acts 1965, 59th Leg., vol. 2, p. 317, ch. 722, eff. Jan. 1, 1966.

Art. 17.25.   Proceedings when bail is granted

After a full examination of the testimony, the magistrate shall, if the case be one where bail may properly be granted and ought to be required, proceed to make an order that the accused execute a bail bond with sufficient security, conditioned for his appearance before the proper court.

Acts 1965, 59th Leg., vol. 2, p. 317, ch. 722, eff. Jan. 1, 1966.

Art. 17.26.   Time given to procure bail

Reasonable time shall be given the accused to procure security.

Acts 1965, 59th Leg., vol. 2, p. 317, ch. 722, eff. Jan. 1, 1966.

Art. 17.27.   When bail is not given

If, after the allowance of a reasonable time, the security be not given, the magistrate shall make an order committing the accused to jail to be kept safely until legally discharged; and he shall issue a commitment accordingly.

Acts 1965, 59th Leg., vol. 2, p. 317, ch. 722, eff. Jan. 1, 1966.

Art. 17.28.   When ready to give bail

If the party be ready to give bail, the magistrate shall cause to be prepared a bond, which shall be signed by the accused and his surety or sureties, if any.

Acts 1965, 59th Leg., vol. 2, p. 317, ch. 722, eff. Jan. 1, 1966.

Art. 17.29. Accused liberated

(a) When the accused has given the required bond, either to the magistrate or the officer having him in custody, he shall at once be set at liberty.

(b) Before releasing on bail a person arrested for an offense under Section 42.072, Penal Code, or a person arrested or held without warrant in the prevention of family violence, the law enforcement agency holding the person shall make a reasonable attempt to give personal notice of the imminent release to the victim of the alleged offense or to another person designated by the victim to receive the notice. An attempt by an agency to give notice to the victim or the person designated by the victim at the victim's or person's last known telephone number or address, as shown on the records of the agency, constitutes a reasonable attempt to give notice under this subsection. If possible, the arresting officer shall collect the address and telephone number of the victim at the time the arrest is made and shall communicate that information to the agency holding the person.

(c) A law enforcement agency or an employee of a law enforcement agency is not liable for damages arising from complying or failing to comply with Subsection (b) of this article.

(d) In this article, "family violence" has the meaning assigned by Section 71.004, Family Code.

Acts 1965, 59th Leg., vol. 2, p. 317, ch. 722, eff. Jan. 1, 1966. Amended by Acts 1995, 74th Leg., ch. 656, § 1, eff. June 14, 1995; Acts 1995, 74th Leg., ch. 661, § 1, eff. Aug. 28, 1995; Acts 1997, 75th Leg., ch. 1, § 3, eff. Jan. 28, 1997; Acts 2003, 78th Leg., ch. 1276, § 7.002(e), eff. Sept. 1, 2003.

Art. 17.291. Further detention of certain persons

(a) In this article:

(1) "family violence" has the meaning assigned to that phrase by Section 71.004, Family Code; and

(2) "magistrate" has the meaning assigned to it by Article 2.09 of this code.

(b) Article 17.29 does not apply when a person has been arrested or held without a warrant in the prevention of family violence if there is probable cause to believe the violence will continue if the person is immediately released. The head of the agency arresting or holding such a person may hold the person for a period of not more than four hours after bond has been posted. This detention period may be extended for an additional period not to exceed 48 hours, but only if authorized in a writing directed to the person having custody of the detained person by a magistrate who concludes that:

(1) the violence would continue if the person is released; and

(2) if the additional period exceeds 24 hours, probable cause exists to believe that the person committed the instant offense and that, during the 10-year period preceding the date of the instant offense, the person has been arrested:

(A) on more than one occasion for an offense involving family violence; or

(B) for any other offense, if a deadly weapon, as defined by Section 1.07, Penal Code, was used or exhibited during commission of the offense or during immediate flight after commission of the offense.

Added by Acts 1991, 72nd Leg., ch. 552, § 2, eff. June 16, 1991. Amended by Acts 1999, 76th Leg., ch. 1341, § 1, eff. Sept. 1, 1999; Acts 2003, 78th Leg., ch. 1276, § 7.002(f), eff. Sept. 1, 2003.

Art. 17.292. Magistrate's order for emergency protection

(a) At a defendant's appearance before a magistrate after arrest for an offense involving family violence or an offense under Section 20A.02, 20A.03, 22.011, 22.021, or 42.072, Penal Code, the magistrate may issue an order for emergency protection on the magistrate's own motion or on the request of:

(1) the victim of the offense;

(2) the guardian of the victim;

(3) a peace officer; or

(4) the attorney representing the state.

(b) At a defendant's appearance before a magistrate after arrest for an offense involving family violence, the magistrate shall issue an order for emergency protection if the arrest is for an offense that also involves:

(1) serious bodily injury to the victim; or

(2) the use or exhibition of a deadly weapon during the commission of an assault.

(c) The magistrate in the order for emergency protection may prohibit the arrested party from:

(1) committing:

(A) family violence or an assault on the person protected under the order; or

(B) an act in furtherance of an offense under Section 20A.02 or 42.072, Penal Code;

(2) communicating:

(A) directly with a member of the family or household or with the person protected under the order in a threatening or harassing manner;

(B) a threat through any person to a member of the family or household or to the person protected under the order; or

(C) if the magistrate finds good cause, in any manner with a person protected under the order or a member of the family or household of a person protected under the order, except through the party's attorney or a person appointed by the court;

(3) going to or near:

(A) the residence, place of employment, or business of a member of the family or household or of the person protected under the order; or

(B) the residence, child care facility, or school where a child protected under the order resides or attends; or

(4) possessing a firearm, unless the person is a peace officer, as defined by Section 1.07, Penal Code, actively engaged in employment as a sworn, full-time paid employee of a state agency or political subdivision.

(c–1) In addition to the conditions described by Subsection (c), the magistrate in the order for emergency protection may impose a condition described by Article 17.49(b) in the manner provided by that article, including ordering a defendant's participation in a global positioning monitoring system or allowing participation in the system by an alleged victim or other person protected under the order.

(d) The victim of the offense need not be present when the order for emergency protection is issued.

(e) In the order for emergency protection the magistrate shall specifically describe the prohibited locations and the minimum distances, if any, that the party must maintain, unless the magistrate determines for the safety of the person or persons protected by the order that specific descriptions of the locations should be omitted.

(f) To the extent that a condition imposed by an order for emergency protection issued under this article conflicts with an existing court order granting possession of or access to a child, the condition imposed under this article prevails for the duration of the order for emergency protection.

(f–1) To the extent that a condition imposed by an order issued under this article conflicts with a condition imposed by an order subsequently issued under Chapter 85, Subtitle B, Title 4, Family Code, or under Title 1 [1] or Title 5, Family Code, [2] the condition imposed by the order issued under the Family Code prevails.

(f–2) To the extent that a condition imposed by an order issued under this article conflicts with a condition imposed by an order subsequently issued under Chapter 83, Subtitle B, Title 4, Family Code, the condition imposed by the order issued under this article prevails unless the court issuing the order under Chapter 83, Family Code:

(1) is informed of the existence of the order issued under this article; and

(2) makes a finding in the order issued under Chapter 83, Family Code, that the court is superseding the order issued under this article.

(g) An order for emergency protection issued under this article must contain the following statements printed in bold-face type or in capital letters:

"A VIOLATION OF THIS ORDER BY COMMISSION OF AN ACT PROHIBITED BY THE ORDER MAY BE PUNISHABLE BY A FINE OF AS MUCH AS $4,000 OR BY CONFINEMENT IN JAIL FOR AS LONG AS ONE YEAR OR BY BOTH. AN ACT THAT RESULTS IN FAMILY VIOLENCE OR A STALKING OR TRAFFICKING OFFENSE MAY BE PROSECUTED AS A SEPARATE MISDEMEANOR OR FELONY OFFENSE, AS APPLICABLE. IF THE ACT IS PROSECUTED AS A SEPARATE FELONY OFFENSE, IT IS PUNISHABLE BY CONFINEMENT IN PRISON FOR AT LEAST TWO YEARS. THE POSSESSION OF A FIREARM BY A PERSON, OTHER THAN A PEACE OFFICER, AS DEFINED BY SECTION 1.07, PENAL CODE, ACTIVELY ENGAGED IN EMPLOYMENT AS A SWORN, FULL–TIME PAID EMPLOYEE OF A STATE AGENCY OR POLITICAL SUBDIVISION, WHO IS SUBJECT TO THIS ORDER MAY BE PROSECUTED AS A SEPARATE OFFENSE PUNISHABLE BY CONFINEMENT OR IMPRISONMENT.

"NO PERSON, INCLUDING A PERSON WHO IS PROTECTED BY THIS ORDER, MAY GIVE PERMISSION TO ANYONE TO IGNORE OR VIOLATE ANY PROVISION OF THIS ORDER. DURING THE TIME IN WHICH THIS ORDER IS VALID, EVERY PROVISION OF THIS ORDER IS IN FULL FORCE AND EFFECT UNLESS A COURT CHANGES THE ORDER."

(h) As soon as possible but not later than the next business day after the date the magistrate issues an order for emergency protection under this article, the magistrate shall send a copy of the order to the chief of police in the municipality where the member of the family or household or individual protected by the order resides, if the person resides in a municipality, or to the sheriff of the county where the person resides, if the person does not reside in a municipality. If the victim of the offense is not present when the order is issued, the magistrate issuing the order shall order an appropriate peace officer to make a good faith effort to notify, within 24 hours, the victim that the order has been issued by calling the victim's residence and place of employment. The clerk of the court shall send a copy of the order to the victim at the victim's last known address as soon as possible but not later than the next business day after the date the order is issued.

(h–1) A magistrate or clerk of the court may delay sending a copy of the order under Subsection (h) only if the magistrate or clerk lacks information necessary to ensure service and enforcement.

(i) If an order for emergency protection issued under this article prohibits a person from going to or near a child care facility or school, the magistrate shall send a copy of the order to the child care facility or school.

(i–1) The copy of the order and any related information may be sent under Subsection (h) or (i) electronically or in another manner that can be accessed by the recipient.

(j) An order for emergency protection issued under this article is effective on issuance, and the defendant shall be served a copy of the order by the magistrate or the magistrate's designee in person or electronically. The magistrate shall make a separate record of the service in written or electronic format. An order for emergency protection issued under Subsection (a) or (b)(1) of this article remains in effect up to the 61st day but not less than 31 days after the date of issuance. An order for emergency protection issued under Subsection (b)(2) of this article remains in effect up to the 91st day but not less than 61 days after the date of issuance. After notice to each affected party and a hearing, the issuing court may modify all or part of an order issued under this article if the court finds that:

(1) the order as originally issued is unworkable;

(2) the modification will not place the victim of the offense at greater risk than did the original order; and

(3) the modification will not in any way endanger a person protected under the order.

(k) To ensure that an officer responding to a call is aware of the existence and terms of an order for emergency protection issued under this article, not later than the third business day after the date of receipt of the copy of the order by the applicable law enforcement agency with jurisdiction over the municipality or county in which the victim resides, the law enforcement agency shall enter the information required under Section 411.042(b)(6), Government Code, into the statewide law enforcement information system maintained by the Department of Public Safety.

(k–1) A law enforcement agency may delay entering the information required under Subsection (k) only if the agency lacks information necessary to ensure service and enforcement.

(l) In the order for emergency protection, the magistrate shall suspend a license to carry a handgun issued under Subchapter H, Chapter 411, Government Code,[3] that is held by the defendant.

(m) In this article:

(1) "Family," "family violence," and "household" have the meanings assigned by Chapter 71, Family Code.

(2) "Firearm" has the meaning assigned by Chapter 46, Penal Code.

(3) "Business day" means a day other than a Saturday, Sunday, or state or national holiday.

(n) On motion, notice, and hearing, or on agreement of the parties, an order for emergency protection issued under this article may be transferred to the court assuming jurisdiction over the criminal act giving rise to the issuance of the emergency order for protection. On transfer, the criminal court may modify all or part of an order issued under this subsection in the same manner and under the same standards as the issuing court under Subsection (j).

Added by Acts 1995, 74th Leg., ch. 658, § 1, eff. June 14, 1995. Amended by Acts 1997, 75th Leg., ch. 1, § 4, eff. Jan. 28, 1997; Acts 1997, 75th Leg., ch. 610, § 1, eff. Sept. 1, 1997; Acts 1999, 76th Leg., ch. 514, § 1, eff. Sept. 1, 1999; Acts 1999, 76th Leg., ch. 1412, § 1, eff. Sept. 1, 1999; Acts 2001, 77th Leg., ch. 23, § 4, eff. Sept. 1, 2001; Acts 2003, 78th Leg., ch. 424, § 1, eff. Sept. 1, 2003; Acts 2005, 79th Leg., ch. 361, § 1, eff. June 17, 2005; Acts 2007, 80th Leg., ch. 66, § 1, eff. May 11, 2007; Acts 2009, 81st Leg., ch. 1146, § 11.20, eff. Sept. 1, 2009; Acts 2009, 81st Leg., ch. 1276, § 1, eff. Sept. 1, 2009; Acts 2013, 83rd Leg., ch. 255 (H.B. 570), § 1, eff. June 14, 2013; Acts 2015, 84th Leg., ch. 108 (S.B. 112), § 1, eff. May 23, 2015; Acts 2015, 84th Leg., ch. 243 (S.B. 737), §§ 1, 2, eff. Sept. 1, 2015 Acts 2015, 84th Leg., ch. 437 (H.B. 910), § 6, eff. Jan. 1, 2016.

[1] V.T.C.A., Family Code § 1.001 et seq.

[2] V.T.C.A., Family Code § 101.001 et seq.

[3] V.T.C.A., Government Code § 411.171 et seq.

Section 6 of Acts 2015, 84th Leg., ch. 243 (S.B. 737) provides:

"The changes in law made by this Act apply to a protective order or magistrate's order of emergency protection issued on or after the effective date [Sept. 1, 2015] of this Act, regardless of whether the conduct on which the order is based occurred before, on, or after that date."

Section 51 of Acts 2015, 84th Leg., ch. 437 (H.B. 910) provides:

"The change in law made by this Act relating to the authority of a license holder to openly carry a holstered handgun applies to the carrying of a handgun on or after the effective date [Jan. 1, 2016] of this Act by any person who:

"(1) holds a license issued under Subchapter H, Chapter 411, Government Code, regardless of whether the person's license was issued before, on, or after the effective date of this Act; or

"(2) applies for the issuance of a license under that subchapter, regardless of whether the person applied for the license before, on, or after the effective date of this Act."

Art. 17.293. Delivery of order for emergency protection to other persons

The magistrate or the clerk of the magistrate's court issuing an order for emergency protection under Article 17.292 that suspends a license to carry a handgun shall immediately send a copy of the order to the appropriate division of the Department of Public Safety at its Austin headquarters. On receipt of the order suspending the license, the department shall:

(1) record the suspension of the license in the records of the department;

(2) report the suspension to local law enforcement agencies, as appropriate; and

(3) demand surrender of the suspended license from the license holder.

Added by Acts 1999, 76th Leg., ch. 1412, § 2, eff. Sept. 1, 1999. Amended by Acts 2015, 84th Leg., ch. 437 (H.B. 910), § 7, eff. Jan. 1, 2016.

Section 51 of Acts 2015, 84th Leg., ch. 437 (H.B. 910) provides:

"The change in law made by this Act relating to the authority of a license holder to openly carry a holstered handgun applies to the carrying of a handgun on or after the effective date [Jan. 1, 2016] of this Act by any person who:

"(1) holds a license issued under Subchapter H, Chapter 411, Government Code, regardless of whether the person's license was issued before, on, or after the effective date of this Act; or

"(2) applies for the issuance of a license under that subchapter, regardless of whether the person applied for the license before, on, or after the effective date of this Act."

Art. 17.30. Shall certify proceedings

The magistrate, before whom an examination has taken place upon a criminal accusation, shall certify to all the proceedings had before him, as well as where he discharges, holds to bail or commits, and transmit them, sealed up, to the court before which the defen-dant may be tried, writing his name across the seals of the envelope. The voluntary statement of the defendant, the testimony, bail bonds, and every other proceeding in the case, shall be thus delivered to the clerk of the proper court, without delay.

Acts 1965, 59th Leg., vol. 2, p. 317, ch. 722, eff. Jan. 1, 1966.

Art. 17.31. Duty of clerks who receive such proceedings

If the proceedings be delivered to a district clerk, he shall keep them safely and deliver the same to the next grand jury. If the proceedings are delivered to a county clerk, he shall without delay deliver them to the district or county attorney of his county.

Acts 1965, 59th Leg., vol. 2, p. 317, ch. 722, eff. Jan. 1, 1966.

Art. 17.32. In case of no arrest

Upon failure from any cause to arrest the accused the magistrate shall file with the proper clerk the complaint, warrant of arrest, and a list of the witnesses.

Acts 1965, 59th Leg., vol. 2, p. 317, ch. 722, eff. Jan. 1, 1966.

Art. 17.33. Request setting of bail

The accused may at any time after being confined request a magistrate to review the written statements of the witnesses for the State as well as all other evidence available at that time in determining the amount of bail. This setting of the amount of bail does not waive the defendant's right to an examining trial as provided in Article 16.01.

Acts 1965, 59th Leg., vol. 2, p. 317, ch. 722, eff. Jan. 1, 1966.

Art. 17.34. Witnesses to give bond

Witnesses for the State or defendant may be required by the magistrate, upon the examination of any criminal accusation before him, to give bail for their appearance to testify before the proper court. A personal bond may be taken of a witness by the court before whom the case is pending.

Acts 1965, 59th Leg., vol. 2, p. 317, ch. 722, eff. Jan. 1, 1966.

Art. 17.35. Security of witness

The amount of security to be required of a witness is to be regulated by his pecuniary condition, character and the nature of the offense with respect to which he is a witness.

Acts 1965, 59th Leg., vol. 2, p. 317, ch. 722, eff. Jan. 1, 1966.

Art. 17.36.   Effect of witness bond

The bond given by a witness for his appearance has the same effect as a bond of the accused and may be forfeited and recovered upon in the same manner.

Acts 1965, 59th Leg., vol. 2, p. 317, ch. 722, eff. Jan. 1, 1966.

Art. 17.37.   Witness may be committed

A witness required to give bail who fails or refuses to do so shall be committed to jail as in other cases of a failure to give bail when required, but shall be released from custody upon giving such bail.

Acts 1965, 59th Leg., vol. 2, p. 317, ch. 722, eff. Jan. 1, 1966.

Art. 17.38.   Rules applicable to all cases of bail

The rules in this Chapter respecting bail are applicable to all such undertakings when entered into in the course of a criminal action, whether before or after an indictment, in every case where authority is given to any court, judge, magistrate, or other officer, to require bail of a person accused of an offense, or of a witness in a criminal action.

Acts 1965, 59th Leg., vol. 2, p. 317, ch. 722, eff. Jan. 1, 1966.

Art. 17.39.   Records of bail

A magistrate or other officer who sets the amount of bail or who takes bail shall record in a well-bound book the name of the person whose appearance the bail secures, the amount of bail, the date bail is set, the magistrate or officer who sets bail, the offense or other cause for which the appearance is secured, the magistrate or other officer who takes bail, the date the person is released, and the name of the bondsman, if any.

Added by Acts 1977, 65th Leg., p. 1525, ch. 618, § 1, eff. Aug. 29, 1977.

Art. 17.40.   Conditions related to victim or community safety

(a) To secure a defendant's attendance at trial, a magistrate may impose any reasonable condition of bond related to the safety of a victim of the alleged offense or to the safety of the community.

(b) At a hearing limited to determining whether the defendant violated a condition of bond imposed under Subsection (a), the magistrate may revoke the defendant's bond only if the magistrate finds by a preponderance of the evidence that the violation occurred. If the magistrate finds that the violation occurred, the magistrate shall revoke the defendant's bond and order that the defendant be immediately returned to custody. Once the defendant is placed in custody, the revocation of the defendant's bond discharges the sureties on the bond, if any, from any future liability on the bond. A discharge under this subsection from any future liability on the bond does not discharge any surety from liability for previous forfeitures on the bond.

Added by Acts 1999, 76th Leg., ch. 768, § 1, eff. Sept. 1, 1999. Amended by Acts 2007, 80th Leg., ch. 1113, § 4, eff. Jan. 1, 2008.

Art. 17.41.   Condition where child alleged victim

(a) This article applies to a defendant charged with an offense under any of the following provisions of the Penal Code, if committed against a child younger than 14 years of age:

(1) Chapter 21 (Sexual Offenses) or 22 (Assaultive Offenses);

(2) Section 25.02 (Prohibited Sexual Conduct); or

(3) Section 43.25 (Sexual Performance by a Child).

(b) Subject to Subsections (c) and (d), a magistrate shall require as a condition of bond for a defendant charged with an offense described by Subsection (a) that the defendant not:

(1) directly communicate with the alleged victim of the offense; or

(2) go near a residence, school, or other location, as specifically described in the bond, frequented by the alleged victim.

(c) A magistrate who imposes a condition of bond under this article may grant the defendant supervised access to the alleged victim.

(d) To the extent that a condition imposed under this article conflicts with an existing court order granting possession of or access to a child, the condition imposed under this article prevails for a period specified by the magistrate, not to exceed 90 days.

Added by Acts 1985, 69th Leg., ch. 595, § 1, eff. Sept. 1, 1985. Amended by Acts 1995, 74th Leg., ch. 76, § 14.21, eff. Sept. 1, 1995; Acts 2009, 81st Leg., ch. 982, § 1, eff. Sept. 1, 2009.

Art. 17.42.   Personal bond office

Sec. 1.   Any county, or any judicial district with jurisdiction in more than one county, with the approval of the commissioners court of each county in the district, may establish a personal bond office to gather and review information about an accused that may have a bearing on whether he will comply with the conditions of a personal bond and report its findings to the court before which the case is pending.

Sec. 2. (a) The commissioners court of a county that establishes the office or the district and county judges of a judicial district that establishes the office may employ a director of the office.

(b) The director may employ the staff authorized by the commissioners court of the county or the commissioners court of each county in the judicial district.

Sec. 3. If a judicial district establishes an office, each county in the district shall pay its pro rata share of the costs of administering the office according to its population.

Sec. 4. (a) Except as otherwise provided by this subsection, if a court releases an accused on personal bond on the recommendation of a personal bond office, the court shall assess a personal bond fee of $20 or three percent of the amount of the bail fixed for the accused, whichever is greater. The court may waive the fee or assess a lesser fee if good cause is shown. A court that requires a defendant to give a personal bond under Article 45.016 may not assess a personal bond fee under this subsection.

(b) Fees collected under this article may be used solely to defray expenses of the personal bond office, including defraying the expenses of extradition.

(c) Fees collected under this article shall be deposited in the county treasury, or if the office serves more than one county, the fees shall be apportioned to each county in the district according to each county's pro rata share of the costs of the office.

Sec. 5. (a) A personal bond pretrial release office established under this article shall:

(1) prepare a record containing information about any accused person identified by case number only who, after review by the office, is released by a court on personal bond before sentencing in a pending case;

(2) update the record on a monthly basis; and

(3) file a copy of the record with the district or county clerk, as applicable based on court jurisdiction over the categories of offenses addressed in the records, in any county served by the office.

(b) In preparing a record under Subsection (a), the office shall include in the record a statement of:

(1) the offense with which the person is charged;

(2) the dates of any court appearances scheduled in the matter that were previously unattended by the person;

(3) whether a warrant has been issued for the person's arrest for failure to appear in accordance with the terms of the person's release;

(4) whether the person has failed to comply with conditions of release on personal bond; and

(5) the presiding judge or magistrate who authorized the personal bond.

(c) This section does not apply to a personal bond pretrial release office that on January 1, 1995, was operated by a community corrections and supervision department.

Sec. 6. (a) Not later than April 1 of each year, a personal bond office established under this article shall submit to the commissioners court or district and county judges that established the office an annual report containing information about the operations of the office during the preceding year.

(b) In preparing an annual report under Subsection (a), the office shall include in the report a statement of:

(1) the office's operating budget;

(2) the number of positions maintained for office staff;

(3) the number of accused persons who, after review by the office, were released by a court on personal bond before sentencing in a pending case; and

(4) the number of persons described by Subdivision (3):

(A) who failed to attend a scheduled court appearance;

(B) for whom a warrant was issued for the arrest of those persons for failure to appear in accordance with the terms of their release; or

(C) who, while released on personal bond, were arrested for any other offense in the same county in which the persons were released on bond.

(c) This section does not apply to a personal bond pretrial release office that on January 1, 1995, was operated by a community corrections and supervision department.

Added by Acts 1989, 71st Leg., ch. 2, § 5.01(a), eff. Aug. 28, 1989; Acts 1989, 71st Leg., ch. 1080, § 1, eff. Sept. 1, 1989. Amended by Acts 1995, 74th Leg., ch. 318, § 44, eff. Sept. 1, 1995; Acts 2011, 82nd Leg., ch. 420 (S.B. 882), § 1, eff. June 17, 2011; Acts 2015, 84th Leg., ch. 1174 (S.B. 965), § 1, eff. Sept. 1, 2015; Acts 2017, 85th Leg., ch. 977 (H.B. 351), § 2, eff. Sept. 1, 2017; Acts 2017, 85th Leg., ch. 1064 (H.B. 3165), §§ 3, 4, eff. Sept. 1, 2017; Acts 2017, 85th Leg., ch. 1127 (S.B. 1913), § 2, eff. Sept. 1, 2017.

Art. 17.43. Home curfew and electronic monitoring as condition

(a) A magistrate may require as a condition of release on personal bond that the defendant submit to home curfew and electronic monitoring under the supervision of an agency designated by the magistrate.

(b) Cost of monitoring may be assessed as court costs or ordered paid directly by the defendant as a condition of bond.

Added by Acts 1989, 71st Leg., ch. 374, § 4, eff. Sept. 1, 1989.

Art. 17.44. Home confinement, electronic monitoring, and drug testing as condition

(a) A magistrate may require as a condition of release on bond that the defendant submit to:

(1) home confinement and electronic monitoring under the supervision of an agency designated by the magistrate; or

(2) testing on a weekly basis for the presence of a controlled substance in the defendant's body.

(b) In this article, "controlled substance" has the meaning assigned by Section 481.002, Health and Safety Code.

(c) The magistrate may revoke the bond and order the defendant arrested if the defendant:

(1) violates a condition of home confinement and electronic monitoring;

(2) refuses to submit to a test for controlled substances or submits to a test for controlled substances and the test indicates the presence of a controlled substance in the defendant's body; or

(3) fails to pay the costs of monitoring or testing for controlled substances, if payment is ordered under Subsection (e) as a condition of bond and the magistrate determines that the defendant is not indigent and is financially able to make the payments as ordered.

(d) The community justice assistance division of the Texas Department of Criminal Justice may provide grants to counties to implement electronic monitoring programs authorized by this article.

(e) The cost of electronic monitoring or testing for controlled substances under this article may be assessed as court costs or ordered paid directly by the defendant as a condition of bond.

Added by Acts 1989, 71st Leg., ch. 785, § 4.03, eff. Sept. 1, 1989. Renumbered from Vernon's Ann.C.C.P. art. 17.42 by Acts 1991, 72nd Leg., ch. 16, § 19.01(3), eff. Aug. 26, 1991. Amended by Acts 1991, 72nd Leg., ch. 14, § 284(46), eff. Sept. 1, 1991; Acts 2009, 81st Leg., ch. 163, § 1, eff. Sept. 1, 2009.

Art. 17.441. Conditions requiring motor vehicle ignition interlock

(a) Except as provided by Subsection (b), a magistrate shall require on release that a defendant charged with a subsequent offense under Sections 49.04–49.06, Penal Code, or an offense under Section 49.07 or 49.08 of that code:

(1) have installed on the motor vehicle owned by the defendant or on the vehicle most regularly driven by the defendant, a device that uses a deep-lung breath analysis mechanism to make impractical the operation of a motor vehicle if ethyl alcohol is detected in the breath of the operator; and

(2) not operate any motor vehicle unless the vehicle is equipped with that device.

(b) The magistrate may not require the installation of the device if the magistrate finds that to require the device would not be in the best interest of justice.

(c) If the defendant is required to have the device installed, the magistrate shall require that the defendant have the device installed on the appropriate motor vehicle, at the defendant's expense, before the 30th day after the date the defendant is released on bond.

(d) The magistrate may designate an appropriate agency to verify the installation of the device and to monitor the device. If the magistrate designates an agency under this subsection, in each month during which the agency verifies the installation of the device or provides a monitoring service the defendant shall pay a fee to the designated agency in the amount set by the magistrate. The defendant shall pay the initial fee at the time the agency verifies the installation of the device. In each subsequent month during which the defendant is required to pay a fee the defendant shall pay the fee on the first occasion in that month that the agency provides a monitoring service. The magistrate shall set the fee in an amount not to exceed $10 as determined by the county auditor, or by the commissioners court of the county if the county does not have a county auditor, to be sufficient to cover the cost incurred by the designated agency in conducting the verification or providing the monitoring service, as applicable in that county.

Added by Acts 1995, 74th Leg., ch. 318, § 45, eff. Sept. 1, 1995. Amended by Acts 1999, 76th Leg., ch. 537, § 1, eff. Sept. 1, 1999.

Art. 17.45.   Conditions requiring AIDS and HIV instruction

A magistrate may require as a condition of bond that a defendant charged with an offense under Section 43.02, Penal Code, receive counseling or education, or both, relating to acquired immune deficiency syndrome or human immunodeficiency virus.

Added by Acts 1989, 71st Leg., ch. 1195, § 8, eff. Sept. 1, 1989. Renumbered from Vernon's Ann.C.C.P. art. 17.42 by Acts 1991, 72nd Leg., ch. 16, § 19.01(4), eff. Aug. 26, 1991.

Art. 17.46.   Conditions for a defendant charged with stalking

(a) A magistrate may require as a condition of release on bond that a defendant charged with an offense under Section 42.072, Penal Code, may not:

(1) communicate directly or indirectly with the victim; or

(2) go to or near the residence, place of employment, or business of the victim or to or near a school, day-care facility, or similar facility where a dependent child of the victim is in attendance.

(b) If the magistrate requires the prohibition contained in Subsection (a)(2) of this article as a condition of release on bond, the magistrate shall specifically describe the prohibited locations and the minimum distances, if any, that the defendant must maintain from the locations.

Added by Acts 1993, 73rd Leg., ch. 10, § 2, eff. March 19, 1993. Amended by Acts 1995, 74th Leg., ch. 657, § 3, eff. June 14, 1995; Acts 1997, 75th Leg., ch. 1, § 5, eff. Jan. 28, 1997.

Art. 17.47.   Conditions requiring submission of specimen

(a) A magistrate may require as a condition of release on bail or bond of a defendant that the defendant provide to a local law enforcement agency one or more specimens for the purpose of creating a DNA record under Subchapter G, Chapter 411, Government Code.[1]

(b) A magistrate shall require as a condition of release on bail or bond of a defendant described by Section 411.1471(a), Government Code, that the defendant provide to a local law enforcement agency one or more specimens for the purpose of creating a DNA record under Subchapter G, Chapter 411, Government Code.

Added by Acts 2001, 77th Leg., ch. 1490, § 5, eff. Sept. 1, 2001. Amended by Acts 2005, 79th Leg., ch. 1224, § 17, eff. Sept. 1, 2005.

[1] V.T.C.A., Government Code § 411.141 et seq.

Art. 17.48.   Posttrial actions

A convicting court on entering a finding favorable to a convicted person under Article 64.04, after a hearing at which the attorney representing the state and the counsel for the defendant are entitled to appear, may release the convicted person on bail under this chapter pending the conclusion of court proceedings or proceedings under Section 11, Article IV, Texas Constitution, and Article 48. 01.

Added by Acts 2001, 77th Leg., ch. 2, § 3, eff. April 5, 2001. Renumbered from Vernon's Ann.C.C.P. art. 17.47 by Acts 2003, 78th Leg., ch. 1275, § 2(6), eff. Sept. 1, 2003.

Art. 17.49.   Conditions for defendant charged with offense involving family violence

(a) In this article:

(1) "Family violence" has the meaning assigned by Section 71.004, Family Code.

(2) "Global positioning monitoring system" means a system that electronically determines and reports the location of an individual through the use of a transmitter or similar device carried or worn by the individual that transmits latitude and longitude data to a monitoring entity through global positioning satellite technology. The term does not include a system that contains or operates global positioning system technology, radio frequency identification technology, or any other similar technology that is implanted in or otherwise invades or violates the individual's body.

(b) A magistrate may require as a condition of release on bond that a defendant charged with an offense involving family violence:

(1) refrain from going to or near a residence, school, place of employment, or other location, as specifically described in the bond, frequented by an alleged victim of the offense;

(2) carry or wear a global positioning monitoring system device and, except as provided by Subsection (h), pay the costs associated with operating that system in relation to the defendant; or

(3) except as provided by Subsection (h), if the alleged victim of the offense consents after receiving

the information described by Subsection (d), pay the costs associated with providing the victim with an electronic receptor device that:

(A) is capable of receiving the global positioning monitoring system information from the device carried or worn by the defendant; and

(B) notifies the victim if the defendant is at or near a location that the defendant has been ordered to refrain from going to or near under Subdivision (1).

(c) Before imposing a condition described by Subsection (b)(1), a magistrate must afford an alleged victim an opportunity to provide the magistrate with a list of areas from which the victim would like the defendant excluded and shall consider the victim's request, if any, in determining the locations the defendant will be ordered to refrain from going to or near. If the magistrate imposes a condition described by Subsection (b)(1), the magistrate shall specifically describe the locations that the defendant has been ordered to refrain from going to or near and the minimum distances, if any, that the defendant must maintain from those locations.

(d) Before imposing a condition described by Subsection (b)(3), a magistrate must provide to an alleged victim information regarding:

(1) the victim's right to participate in a global positioning monitoring system or to refuse to participate in that system and the procedure for requesting that the magistrate terminate the victim's participation;

(2) the manner in which the global positioning monitoring system technology functions and the risks and limitations of that technology, and the extent to which the system will track and record the victim's location and movements;

(3) any locations that the defendant is ordered to refrain from going to or near and the minimum distances, if any, that the defendant must maintain from those locations;

(4) any sanctions that the court may impose on the defendant for violating a condition of bond imposed under this article;

(5) the procedure that the victim is to follow, and support services available to assist the victim, if the defendant violates a condition of bond or if the global positioning monitoring system equipment fails;

(6) community services available to assist the victim in obtaining shelter, counseling, education, child care, legal representation, and other assistance available to address the consequences of family violence; and

(7) the fact that the victim's communications with the court concerning the global positioning monitoring system and any restrictions to be imposed on the defendant's movements are not confidential.

(e) In addition to the information described by Subsection (d), a magistrate shall provide to an alleged victim who participates in a global positioning monitoring system under this article the name and telephone number of an appropriate person employed by a local law enforcement agency whom the victim may call to request immediate assistance if the defendant violates a condition of bond imposed under this article.

(f) In determining whether to order a defendant's participation in a global positioning monitoring system under this article, the magistrate shall consider the likelihood that the defendant's participation will deter the defendant from seeking to kill, physically injure, stalk, or otherwise threaten the alleged victim before trial.

(g) An alleged victim may request that the magistrate terminate the victim's participation in a global positioning monitoring system at any time. The magistrate may not impose sanctions on the victim for requesting termination of the victim's participation in or refusing to participate in a global positioning monitoring system under this article.

(h) If the magistrate determines that a defendant is indigent, the magistrate may, based on a sliding scale established by local rule, require the defendant to pay costs under Subsection (b)(2) or (3) in an amount that is less than the full amount of the costs associated with operating the global positioning monitoring system in relation to the defendant or providing the victim with an electronic receptor device.

(i) If an indigent defendant pays to an entity that operates a global positioning monitoring system the partial amount ordered by a magistrate under Subsection (h), the entity shall accept the partial amount as payment in full. The county in which the magistrate who enters an order under Subsection (h) is located is not responsible for payment of any costs associated with operating the global positioning monitoring system in relation to an indigent defendant.

(j) A magistrate that imposes a condition described by Subsection (b)(1) or (2) shall order the entity that operates the global positioning monitoring system to notify the court and the appropriate local law enforcement agency if a defendant violates a condition of bond imposed under this article.

(k) A magistrate that imposes a condition described by Subsection (b) may only allow or require the defendant to execute or be released under a type of bond that is authorized by this chapter.

(*l*) This article does not limit the authority of a magistrate to impose any other reasonable conditions of bond or enter any orders of protection under other applicable statutes.

Added by Acts 2009, 81st Leg., ch. 1276, § 2, eff. Sept. 1, 2009.

CHAPTER SEVENTEEN–A. CORPORATIONS AND ASSOCIATIONS

Art. 17A.01. Application and definitions

(a) This chapter sets out some of the procedural rules applicable to the criminal responsibility of corporations and associations. Where not in conflict with this chapter, the other chapters of this code apply to corporations and associations.

(b) In this code, unless the context requires a different definition:

(1) "Agent" means a director, officer, employee, or other person authorized to act in behalf of a corporation or association.

(2) "Association" means a government or governmental subdivision or agency, trust, partnership, or two or more persons having a joint or common economic interest.

(3) "High managerial agent" means:

(A) an officer of a corporation or association;

(B) a partner in a partnership; or

(C) an agent of a corporation or association who has duties of such responsibility that his conduct may reasonably be assumed to represent the policy of the corporation or association.

(4) "Person," "he," and "him" include corporation and association.

Added by Acts 1973, 63rd Leg., p. 979, ch. 399, § 2(D), eff. Jan. 1, 1974.

Art. 17A.02. Allegation of name

(a) In alleging the name of a defendant corporation, it is sufficient to state in the complaint, indictment, or information the corporate name, or to state any name or designation by which the corporation is known or may be identified. It is not necessary to allege that the defendant was lawfully incorporated.

(b) In alleging the name of a defendant association it is sufficient to state in the complaint, indictment, or information the association's name, or to state any name or designation by which the association is known or may be identified, or to state the name or names of one or more members of the association, referring to the unnamed members as "others." It is not necessary to allege the legal form of the association.

Added by Acts 1973, 63rd Leg., p. 979, ch. 399, § 2(D), eff. Jan. 1, 1974.

Art. 17A.03. Summoning corporation or association

(a) When a complaint is filed or an indictment or information presented against a corporation or association, the court or clerk shall issue a summons to the corporation or association. The summons shall be in the same form as a capias except that:

(1) it shall summon the corporation or association to appear before the court named at the place stated in the summons; and

(2) it shall be accompanied by a certified copy of the complaint, indictment, or information; and

(3) it shall provide that the corporation or association appear before the court named at or before 10 a.m. of the Monday next after the expiration of 20 days after it is served with summons, except when service is made upon the secretary of state or the Commissioner of Insurance, in which instance the summons shall provide that the corporation or association appear before the court named at or before 10 a.m. of the Monday next after the expiration of 30 days after the secretary of state or the Commissioner of Insurance is served with summons.

(b) No individual may be arrested upon a complaint, indictment, information, judgment, or sentence against a corporation or association.

Added by Acts 1973, 63rd Leg., p. 980, ch. 399, § 2(D), eff. Jan. 1, 1974. Amended by Acts 1987, 70th Leg., ch. 46, § 10, eff. Sept. 1, 1987.

Art. 17A.04. Service on corporation

(a) Except as provided in Paragraph (d) of this article, a peace officer shall serve a summons on a corporation by personally delivering a copy of it to the corporation's registered agent. However, if a registered agent has not been designated, or cannot with reasonable diligence be found at the registered office, then the peace officer shall serve the summons by personally delivering a copy of it to the president or a vice-president of the corporation.

(b) If the peace officer certifies on the return that he diligently but unsuccessfully attempted to effect service under Paragraph (a) of this article, or if the corporation is a foreign corporation that has no certificate of authority, then he shall serve the summons on the secretary of state by personally delivering a copy of it to him, or to the deputy secretary of state, or to any clerk in charge of the corporation department of his office. On receipt of the summons copy, the secretary of state shall immediately forward it by certified or registered mail, return receipt requested, addressed to the defendant corporation at its registered or principal office in the state or country under whose law it was incorporated.

(c) The secretary of state shall keep a permanent record of the date and time of receipt and his disposition of each summons served under Paragraph (b) of this article together with the return receipt.

(d) The method of service on a corporation regulated under the Insurance Code is governed by that code.

Added by Acts 1973, 63rd Leg., p. 980, ch. 399, § 2(D), eff. Jan. 1, 1974. Amended by Acts 2005, 79th Leg., ch. 41, § 15, eff. Sept. 1, 2005.

Art. 17A.05. Service on association

(a) Except as provided in Paragraph (b) of this article, a peace officer shall serve a summons on an association by personally delivering a copy of it:

(1) to a high managerial agent at any place where business of the association is regularly conducted; or

(2) if the peace officer certifies on the return that he diligently but unsuccessfully attempted to serve a high managerial agent, to any employee of suitable age and discretion at any place where business of the association is regularly conducted; or

(3) if the peace officer certifies on the return that he diligently but unsuccessfully attempted to serve a high managerial agent, or employee of suitable age and discretion, to any member of the association.

(b) The method of service on an association regulated under the Insurance Code is governed by that code.

Added by Acts 1973, 63rd Leg., p. 981, ch. 399, § 2(D), eff. Jan. 1, 1974.

Art. 17A.06. Appearance

(a) In all criminal actions instituted against a corporation or association, in which original jurisdiction is in a district or county-level court:

(1) appearance is for the purpose of arraignment;

(2) the corporation or association has 10 full days after the day the arraignment takes place and before the day the trial begins to file written pleadings.

(b) In all criminal actions instituted against a corporation or association, in which original jurisdiction is in a justice court or corporation court:

(1) appearance is for the purpose of entering a plea; and

(2) 10 full days must elapse after the day of appearance before the corporation or association may be tried.

Added by Acts 1973, 63rd Leg., p. 981, ch. 399, § 2(D), eff. Jan. 1, 1974.

Art. 17A.07. Presence of corporation or association

(a) A defendant corporation or association appears through counsel.

(b) If a corporation or association does not appear in response to summons, or appears but fails or refuses to plead:

(1) it is deemed to be present in person for all purposes; and

(2) the court shall enter a plea of not guilty in its behalf; and

(3) the court may proceed with trial, judgment, and sentencing.

(c) If, having appeared and entered a plea in response to summons, a corporation or association is absent without good cause at any time during later proceedings:

(1) it is deemed to be present in person for all purposes; and

(2) the court may proceed with trial, judgment, or sentencing.

Added by Acts 1973, 63rd Leg., p. 981, ch. 399, § 2(D), eff. Jan. 1, 1974.

Art. 17A.08. Probation

The benefits of the adult probation laws shall not be available to corporations and associations.

Added by Acts 1973, 63rd Leg., p. 981, ch. 399, § 2(D), eff. Jan. 1, 1974.

Art. 17A.09. Notifying attorney general of corporation's conviction

If a corporation is convicted of an offense, or if a high managerial agent is convicted of an offense committed in the conduct of the affairs of the corporation, the court shall notify the attorney general in writing of the conviction when it becomes final and unappealable. The notice shall include:

(1) the corporation's name, and the name of the corporation's registered agent and the address of the registered office, or the high managerial agent's name and address, or both; and

(2) certified copies of the judgment and sentence and of the complaint, information, or indictment on which the judgment and sentence were based.

Added by Acts 1973, 63rd Leg., p. 981, ch. 399, § 2(D), eff. Jan. 1, 1974.

SEARCH WARRANTS

CHAPTER EIGHTEEN. SEARCH WARRANTS

Art. 18.01. Search warrant

(a) A "search warrant" is a written order, issued by a magistrate and directed to a peace officer, commanding him to search for any property or thing and to seize the same and bring it before such magistrate or commanding him to search for and photograph a child and to deliver to the magistrate any of the film exposed pursuant to the order.

(b) No search warrant shall issue for any purpose in this state unless sufficient facts are first presented to satisfy the issuing magistrate that probable cause does in fact exist for its issuance. A sworn affidavit setting forth substantial facts establishing probable cause shall be filed in every instance in which a search warrant is requested. Except as provided by Article 18.011, the affidavit becomes public information when the search warrant for which the affidavit was presented is executed, and the magistrate's clerk shall make a copy of the affidavit available for public inspection in the clerk's office during normal business hours.

(b–1)(1) For purposes of this article, a magistrate may consider information communicated by telephone or other reliable electronic means in determining whether to issue a search warrant. The magistrate may examine an applicant for a search warrant and any person on whose testimony the application is based. The applicant or other person must be placed under oath before the examination.

(2) If an applicant for a search warrant attests to the contents of an affidavit submitted by reliable electronic means, the magistrate must acknowledge the attestation in writing on the affidavit. If the magistrate considers additional testimony or exhibits, the magistrate must:

(A) ensure that the testimony is recorded verbatim by an electronic recording device, by a court reporter, or in writing;

(B) ensure that any recording or reporter's notes are transcribed and that the transcription is certified as accurate and is preserved;

(C) sign, certify the accuracy of, and preserve any other written record; and

(D) ensure that the exhibits are preserved.

(3) An applicant for a search warrant who submits information as authorized by this subsection must prepare a proposed duplicate original of the warrant and must read or otherwise transmit its contents verbatim to the magistrate. A magistrate must enter into an original search warrant the contents of a proposed duplicate original that are read to the magistrate. If the applicant transmits the contents by reliable electronic means, the transmission received by the magistrate may serve as the original search warrant.

(4) The magistrate may modify a search warrant that is submitted as described by Subdivision (3). If the magistrate modifies the warrant, the magistrate must:

(A) transmit the modified version to the applicant by reliable electronic means; or

(B) file the modified original and direct the applicant to modify the proposed duplicate original accordingly.

(5) A magistrate who issues a search warrant for which information is provided by telephone or reliable electronic means must:

(A) sign the original documents;

(B) enter the date and time of issuance on the warrant; and

(C) transmit the warrant by reliable electronic means to the applicant or direct the applicant to sign the judge's name and enter the date and time on the duplicate original.

(6) Evidence obtained pursuant to a search warrant for which information was provided in accordance with this subsection is not subject to suppression on the ground that issuing the warrant in compliance with this subsection was unreasonable under the circumstances, absent a finding of bad faith.

(c) A search warrant may not be issued under Article 18.02(10) unless the sworn affidavit required by Subsection (b) sets forth sufficient facts to establish probable cause: (1) that a specific offense has been committed, (2) that the specifically described property or items that are to be searched for or seized constitute evidence of that offense or evidence that a particular person committed that offense, and (3) that the property or items constituting evidence to be

searched for or seized are located at or on the particular person, place, or thing to be searched. Except as provided by Subsections (d), (i), and (j), only a judge of a municipal court of record or a county court who is an attorney licensed by the State of Texas, a statutory county court judge, a district court judge, a judge of the Court of Criminal Appeals, including the presiding judge, a justice of the Supreme Court of Texas, including the chief justice, or a magistrate with jurisdiction over criminal cases serving a district court may issue warrants under Article 18.02(10).

(d) Only the specifically described property or items set forth in a search warrant issued under Subdivision (10) of Article 18.02 of this code or property, items or contraband enumerated in Subdivisions (1) through (9) or in Subdivision (12) of Article 18.02 of this code may be seized. A subsequent search warrant may be issued pursuant to Subdivision (10) of Article 18.02 of this code to search the same person, place, or thing subjected to a prior search under Subdivision (10) of Article 18.02 of this code only if the subsequent search warrant is issued by a judge of a district court, a court of appeals, the court of criminal appeals, or the supreme court.

(e) A search warrant may not be issued under Subdivision (10) of Article 18.02 of this code to search for and seize property or items that are not described in Subdivisions (1) through (9) of that article and that are located in an office of a newspaper, news magazine, television station, or radio station, and in no event may property or items not described in Subdivisions (1) through (9) of that article be legally seized in any search pursuant to a search warrant of an office of a newspaper, news magazine, television station, or radio station.

(f) A search warrant may not be issued pursuant to Article 18.021 of this code unless the sworn affidavit required by Subsection (b) of this article sets forth sufficient facts to establish probable cause:

(1) that a specific offense has been committed;

(2) that a specifically described person has been a victim of the offense;

(3) that evidence of the offense or evidence that a particular person committed the offense can be detected by photographic means; and

(4) that the person to be searched for and photographed is located at the particular place to be searched.

(g) A search warrant may not be issued under Subdivision (12), Article 18.02, of this code unless the sworn affidavit required by Subsection (b) of this article sets forth sufficient facts to establish probable cause that a specific felony offense has been committed and that the specifically described property or items that are to be searched for or seized constitute contraband as defined in Article 59.01 of this code and are located at or on the particular person, place, or thing to be searched.

(h) Except as provided by Subsection (i) of this article, a warrant under Subdivision (12), Article 18.02 of this code may only be issued by:

(1) a judge of a municipal court of record who is an attorney licensed by the state;

(2) a judge of a county court who is an attorney licensed by the state; or

(3) a judge of a statutory county court, district court, the court of criminal appeals, or the supreme court.

(i) In a county that does not have a municipal court of record with a courtroom located in that county and a judge who is an attorney licensed by the state, a county court judge who is an attorney licensed by the state, or a statutory county court judge, any magistrate may issue a search warrant under Article 18.02(a)(10) or (12). This subsection is not applicable to a subsequent search warrant under Article 18.02(a)(10).

(j) Any magistrate who is an attorney licensed by this state may issue a search warrant under Article 18.02(10) to collect a blood specimen from a person who:

(1) is arrested for an offense under Section 49.04, 49.045, 49.05, 49.06, 49.065, 49.07, or 49.08, Penal Code; and

(2) refuses to submit to a breath or blood alcohol test.

Amended by Acts 1973, 63rd Leg., p. 982, ch. 399, § 2(E), eff. Jan. 1, 1974; Acts 1977, 65th Leg., p. 640, ch. 237, § 1, eff. May 25, 1977; Acts 1979, 66th Leg., p. 1124, ch. 536, § 1, eff. June 11, 1979; Acts 1979, 66th Leg., p. 1076, ch. 505, § 1, eff. Sept. 1, 1979; Acts 1981, 67th Leg., p. 759, ch. 289, §§ 3, 4, eff. Sept. 1, 1981; Acts 1981, 67th Leg., p. 2789, ch. 755, § 1, eff. Sept. 1, 1981; Acts 1987, 70th Leg., ch. 686, § 1, eff. Sept. 1, 1987; Acts 1989, 71st Leg., 1st C.S., ch. 12, § 2, eff. Oct. 18, 1989; Acts 1991, 72nd Leg., ch. 73, § 1, eff. May 9, 1991; Acts 1995, 74th Leg., ch. 670, § 1, eff. Sept. 1, 1995; Acts 1997, 75th Leg., ch. 604, § 1, eff. Sept. 1, 1997; Acts 1999, 76th Leg., ch. 167, § 1, eff. Aug. 30, 1999; Acts 1999, 76th Leg., ch. 1469, § 1, eff. June 19, 1999; Acts 2001, 77th Leg., ch. 1395, § 1, eff. June 16, 2001; Acts 2007, 80th Leg., ch. 355, § 1, eff. Sept. 1, 2007; Acts 2007, 80th Leg., ch. 748, § 1, eff. Sept. 1, 2007; Acts 2009, 81st Leg., ch. 1348, § 5, eff. Sept. 1, 2009; Acts 2011, 82nd Leg., ch. 66 (S.B. 483), § 3, eff. Sept. 1, 2011; Acts 2015, 84th Leg., ch. 683 (H.B. 326), § 1, eff. Sept. 1, 2015; Acts 2017, 85th Leg., ch. 174 (H.B. 3237), § 1, eff. May 26, 2017; Acts 2017, 85th Leg., ch. 1035 (H.B. 1727), § 1, eff. Sept. 1, 2017.

Section 2 of Acts 2015, 84th Leg., ch. 683 (H.B. 326) provides:

"The change in law made by this Act applies only to a search warrant that is issued on or after the effective date of this Act. A search warrant that was issued before the effective date of this Act is governed by the law in effect on the date the warrant was issued, and the former law is continued in effect for that purpose."

Section 2 of Acts 2017, 85th Leg., ch. 1035 (H.B. 1727) provides:

"The change in law made by this Act applies only to a search warrant issued on or after the effective date [Sept. 1, 2017] of this Act. A search warrant issued before the effective date of this Act is governed by the law in effect on the date the warrant was issued, and the former law is continued in effect for that purpose."

Art. 18.011. Sealing of affidavit

(a) An attorney representing the state in the prosecution of felonies may request a district judge or the judge of an appellate court to seal an affidavit presented under Article 18.01(b). The judge may order the affidavit sealed if the attorney establishes a compelling state interest in that:

(1) public disclosure of the affidavit would jeopardize the safety of a victim, witness, or confidential informant or cause the destruction of evidence; or

(2) the affidavit contains information obtained from a court-ordered wiretap that has not expired at the time the attorney representing the state requests the sealing of the affidavit.

(b) An order sealing an affidavit under this section expires on the 31st day after the date on which the search warrant for which the affidavit was presented is executed. After an original order sealing an affidavit is issued under this article, an attorney representing the state in the prosecution of felonies may request, and a judge may grant, before the 31st day after the date on which the search warrant for which the affidavit was presented is executed, on a new finding of compelling state interest, one 30–day extension of the original order.

(c) On the expiration of an order issued under Subsection (b) and any extension, the affidavit must be unsealed.

(d) An order issued under this section may not:

(1) prohibit the disclosure of information relating to the contents of a search warrant, the return of a search warrant, or the inventory of property taken pursuant to a search warrant; or

(2) affect the right of a defendant to discover the contents of an affidavit.

Added by Acts 2007, 80th Leg., ch. 355, § 2, eff. Sept. 1, 2007.

Art. 18.02. Grounds for issuance

(a) A search warrant may be issued to search for and seize:

(1) property acquired by theft or in any other manner which makes its acquisition a penal offense;

(2) property specially designed, made, or adapted for or commonly used in the commission of an offense;

(3) arms and munitions kept or prepared for the purposes of insurrection or riot;

(4) weapons prohibited by the Penal Code;

(5) gambling devices or equipment, altered gambling equipment, or gambling paraphernalia;

(6) obscene materials kept or prepared for commercial distribution or exhibition, subject to the additional rules set forth by law;

(7) a drug, controlled substance, immediate precursor, chemical precursor, or other controlled substance property, including an apparatus or paraphernalia kept, prepared, or manufactured in violation of the laws of this state;

(8) any property the possession of which is prohibited by law;

(9) implements or instruments used in the commission of a crime;

(10) property or items, except the personal writings by the accused, constituting evidence of an offense or constituting evidence tending to show that a particular person committed an offense;

(11) persons;

(12) contraband subject to forfeiture under Chapter 59 of this code;

(13) electronic customer data held in electronic storage, including the contents of and records and other information related to a wire communication or electronic communication held in electronic storage; or

(14) a cellular telephone or other wireless communications device, subject to Article 18.0215.

Text of (b) effective until January 1, 2019

(b) For purposes of Subsection (a)(13), "electronic communication," "electronic storage," and "wire communication" have the meanings assigned by Article 18.20, and "electronic customer data" has the meaning assigned by Article 18.21.

Text of (b) effective January 1, 2019

(b) For purposes of Subsection (a)(13):

(1) "Electronic communication" and "wire communication" have the meanings assigned by Article 18A.001.

(2) "Electronic customer data" and "electronic storage" have the meanings assigned by Article 18B.001.

Amended by Acts 1973, 63rd Leg., p. 982, ch. 399, § 2(E), eff. Jan. 1, 1974; Acts 1977, 65th Leg., p. 640, ch. 237, § 2, eff. May 25, 1977; Amended by Acts 1981, 67th Leg., p. 2790, ch. 755, § 5, eff. Sept. 1, 1981; Acts 1989, 71st Leg., 1st C.S., ch. 12, § 3, eff. Oct. 18, 1989; Acts 2003, 78th Leg., ch. 1099, § 16, eff. Sept. 1, 2003; Acts 2013, 83rd Leg., ch. 1289 (H.B. 2268), § 1, eff. June 14, 2013; Acts 2015, 84th Leg., ch. 1251 (H.B. 1396), § 1, eff. Sept. 1, 2015; Acts 2017, 85th Leg., ch. 1058 (H.B. 2931), § 3.03, eff. Jan. 1, 2019.

Art. 18.021. Issuance of search warrant to photograph injured child

(a) A search warrant may be issued to search for and photograph a child who is alleged to be the victim of the offenses of injury to a child as prohibited by Section 22.04, Penal Code; sexual assault of a child as prohibited by Section 22.011(a), Penal Code; aggravated sexual assault of a child as prohibited by Section 22.021, Penal Code; or continuous sexual abuse of young child or children as prohibited by Section 21.02, Penal Code.

(b) The officer executing the warrant may be accompanied by a photographer who is employed by a law enforcement agency and who acts under the direction of the officer executing the warrant. The photographer is entitled to access to the child in the same manner as the officer executing the warrant.

(c) In addition to the requirements of Subdivisions (1), (4), and (5) of Article 18.04 of this code, a warrant issued under this article shall identify, as near as may be, the child to be located and photographed, shall name or describe, as near as may be, the place or thing to be searched, and shall command any peace officer of the proper county to search for and cause the child to be photographed.

(d) After having located and photographed the child, the peace officer executing the warrant shall take possession of the exposed film and deliver it forthwith to the magistrate. The child may not be removed from the premises on which he or she is located except under Subchapters A and B, Chapter 262, Family Code.[1]

(e) A search warrant under this section shall be executed by a peace officer of the same sex as the alleged victim or, if the officer is not of the same sex as the alleged victim, the peace officer must be assisted by a person of the same sex as the alleged victim. The person assisting an officer under this subsection must be acting under the direction of the officer and must be with the alleged victim during the taking of the photographs.

Added by Acts 1981, 67th Leg., p. 758, ch. 289, § 2, eff. Sept. 1, 1981. Amended by Acts 1983, 68th Leg., p. 5319, ch. 977, § 8, eff. Sept. 1, 1983; Acts 1997, 75th Leg., ch. 165, § 7.01, eff. Sept. 1, 1997; Acts 2007, 80th Leg., ch. 593, § 3.11, eff. Sept. 1, 2007; Acts 2015, 84th Leg., ch. 690 (H.B. 644), § 2, eff. Sept. 1, 2015.

[1] V.T.C.A., Family Code §§ 262.001, 262.101 et seq.

Section 4(a) of Acts 2015, 84th Leg., ch. 690 (H.B. 644) provides:

"(a) The changes in law made by this Act in amending Articles 18.04 and 18.021(c), Code of Criminal Procedure, apply to a search warrant issued on or after the effective date [Sept. 1, 2015] of this Act. A search warrant issued before the effective date of this Act is governed by the law in effect on the date the warrant was issued, and the former law is continued in effect for that purpose."

Art. 18.0215.   Access to Cellular Telephone or Other Wireless Communications Device

(a) A peace officer may not search a person's cellular telephone or other wireless communications device, pursuant to a lawful arrest of the person without obtaining a warrant under this article.

(b) A warrant under this article may be issued only by a judge in the same judicial district as the site of:

(1) the law enforcement agency that employs the peace officer, if the cellular telephone or other wireless communications device is in the officer's possession; or

(2) the likely location of the telephone or device.

(c) A judge may issue a warrant under this article only on the application of a peace officer. An application must be written and signed and sworn to or affirmed before the judge. The application must:

(1) state the name, department, agency, and address of the applicant;

(2) identify the cellular telephone or other wireless communications device to be searched;

(3) state the name of the owner or possessor of the telephone or device to be searched;

(4) state the judicial district in which:

(A) the law enforcement agency that employs the peace officer is located, if the telephone or device is in the officer's possession; or

(B) the telephone or device is likely to be located; and

(5) state the facts and circumstances that provide the applicant with probable cause to believe that:

(A) criminal activity has been, is, or will be committed; and

(B) searching the telephone or device is likely to produce evidence in the investigation of the criminal activity described in Paragraph (A).

Text of (d) effective until January 1, 2019

(d) Notwithstanding any other law, a peace officer may search a cellular telephone or other wireless communications device without a warrant if:

(1) the owner or possessor of the telephone or device consents to the search;

(2) the telephone or device is reported stolen by the owner or possessor; or

(3) the officer reasonably believes that:

(A) the telephone or device is in the possession of a fugitive from justice for whom an arrest warrant has been issued for committing a felony offense; or

(B) there exists an immediate life-threatening situation, as defined by Section 1, Article 18.20.

Text of (d) effective January 1, 2019

(d) Notwithstanding any other law, a peace officer may search a cellular telephone or other wireless communications device without a warrant if:

(1) the owner or possessor of the telephone or device consents to the search;

(2) the telephone or device is reported stolen by the owner or possessor; or

(3) the officer reasonably believes that:

(A) the telephone or device is in the possession of a fugitive from justice for whom an arrest warrant has been issued for committing a felony offense; or

(B) there exists an immediate life-threatening situation, as defined by Article 18A.201.

(e) A peace officer must apply for a warrant to search a cellular telephone or other wireless communications device as soon as practicable after a search is conducted under Subsection (d)(3)(A) or (B). If the judge finds that the applicable situation under Subsection (d)(3)(A) or (B) did not occur and declines to issue the warrant, any evidence obtained is not admissible in a criminal action.

Added by Acts 2015, 84th Leg., ch. 1251 (H.B. 1396), § 2, eff. Sept. 1, 2015. Amended by Acts 2017, 85th Leg., ch. 1058 (H.B. 2931), § 3.04, eff. Jan. 1, 2019.

Art. 18.03. Search warrant may order arrest

If the facts presented to the magistrate under Article 18.02 of this chapter also establish the existence of probable cause that a person has committed some offense under the laws of this state, the search warrant may, in addition, order the arrest of such person.

Amended by Acts 1973, 63rd Leg., p. 983, ch. 399, § 2(E), eff. Jan. 1, 1974.

Art. 18.04. Contents of Warrant

Text of Art. 18.04 effective until Jan. 1, 2019. See, also, text of Art. 18.04 effective Jan. 1, 2019.

A search warrant issued under this chapter shall be sufficient if it contains the following requisites:

(1) that it run in the name of "The State of Texas";

(2) that it identify, as near as may be, that which is to be seized and name or describe, as near as may be, the person, place, or thing to be searched;

(3) that it command any peace officer of the proper county to search forthwith the person, place, or thing named;

(4) that it be dated and signed by the magistrate; and

(5) that the magistrate's name appear in clearly legible handwriting or in typewritten form with the magistrate's signature.

Amended by Acts 1973, 63rd Leg., p. 983, ch. 399, § 2(E), eff. Jan. 1, 1974; Acts 2015, 84th Leg., ch. 690 (H.B. 644), § 1, eff. Sept. 1, 2015.

Art. 18.04. Contents of Warrant

Text of Art. 18.04 effective Jan. 1, 2019. See, also, text of Art. 18.04 effective until Jan. 1, 2019.

A search warrant issued under this chapter, Chapter 18A, or Chapter 18B shall be sufficient if it contains the following requisites:

(1) that it run in the name of "The State of Texas";

(2) that it identify, as near as may be, that which is to be seized and name or describe, as near as may be, the person, place, or thing to be searched;

(3) that it command any peace officer of the proper county to search forthwith the person, place, or thing named;

(4) that it be dated and signed by the magistrate; and

(5) that the magistrate's name appear in clearly legible handwriting or in typewritten form with the magistrate's signature.

Amended by Acts 1973, 63rd Leg., p. 983, ch. 399, § 2(E), eff. Jan. 1, 1974; Acts 2015, 84th Leg., ch. 690 (H.B. 644), § 1, eff. Sept. 1, 2015; Acts 2017, 85th Leg., ch. 1058 (H.B. 2931), § 3.05, eff. Jan. 1, 2019.

Section 4(a) of Acts 2015, 84th Leg., ch. 690 (H.B. 644) provides:

"(a) The changes in law made by this Act in amending Articles 18.04 and 18.021(c), Code of Criminal Procedure, apply to a search warrant issued on or after the effective date [Sept. 1, 2015] of this Act. A search warrant issued before the effective date of this Act is governed by the law in effect on the date the warrant was issued, and the former law is continued in effect for that purpose."

Art. 18.05. Warrants for fire, health, and code inspections

(a) Except as provided by Subsection (e) of this article, a search warrant may be issued to a fire marshal, health officer, or code enforcement official of the state or of any county, city, or other political subdivision for the purpose of allowing the inspection of any specified premises to determine the presence of a fire or health hazard or unsafe building condition or a violation of any fire, health, or building regulation, statute, or ordinance.

(b) A search warrant may not be issued under this article except upon the presentation of evidence of probable cause to believe that a fire or health hazard or violation or unsafe building condition is present in the premises sought to be inspected.

(c) In determining probable cause, the magistrate is not limited to evidence of specific knowledge, but may consider any of the following:

(1) the age and general condition of the premises;

(2) previous violations or hazards found present in the premises;

(3) the type of premises;

(4) the purposes for which the premises are used; and

(5) the presence of hazards or violations in and the general condition of premises near the premises sought to be inspected.

(d) Each city or county may designate one or more code enforcement officials for the purpose of being issued a search warrant as authorized by Subsection

(a) of this article. A political subdivision other than a city or county may designate not more than one code enforcement official for the purpose of being issued a search warrant as authorized by Subsection (a) of this article only if the political subdivision routinely inspects premises to determine whether there is a fire or health hazard or unsafe building condition or a violation of fire, health, or building regulation, statute, or ordinance.

(e) A search warrant may not be issued under this article to a code enforcement official of a county with a population of 3.3 million or more for the purpose of allowing the inspection of specified premises to determine the presence of an unsafe building condition or a violation of a building regulation, statute, or ordinance.

Amended by Acts 1973, 63rd Leg., p. 983, ch. 399, § 2(E), eff. Jan. 1, 1974; Acts 1989, 71st Leg., ch. 382, § 1, eff. Aug. 28, 1989; Acts 2007, 80th Leg., ch. 769, § 1, eff. Sept. 1, 2007; Acts 2011, 82nd Leg., ch. 1163 (H.B. 2702), § 7, eff. Sept. 1, 2011.

Art. 18.06. Execution of warrants

Text of (a) effective until January 1, 2019

(a) A peace officer to whom a search warrant is delivered shall execute the warrant without delay and forthwith return the warrant to the proper magistrate. A search warrant issued under Section 5A, Article 18.21, must be executed in the manner provided by that section not later than the 11th day after the date of issuance. In all other cases, a search warrant must be executed within three days from the time of its issuance. A warrant issued under this chapter shall be executed within a shorter period if so directed in the warrant by the magistrate.

Text of (a) effective January 1, 2019

(a) A peace officer to whom a search warrant is delivered shall execute the warrant without delay and forthwith return the warrant to the proper magistrate. A search warrant issued under Article 18B.354 must be executed in the manner provided by Article 18B.355 not later than the 11th day after the date of issuance. In all other cases, a search warrant must be executed within three days from the time of its issuance. A warrant issued under this chapter, Chapter 18A, or Chapter 18B shall be executed within a shorter period if so directed in the warrant by the magistrate.

(b) On searching the place ordered to be searched, the officer executing the warrant shall present a copy of the warrant to the owner of the place, if he is present. If the owner of the place is not present but a person who is present is in possession of the place, the officer shall present a copy of the warrant to the person. Before the officer takes property from the place, he shall prepare a written inventory of the property to be taken. He shall legibly endorse his name on the inventory and present a copy of the inventory to the owner or other person in possession of the property. If neither the owner nor a person in possession of the property is present when the officer executes the warrant, the officer shall leave a copy of the warrant and the inventory at the place.

Amended by Acts 1973, 63rd Leg., p. 983, ch. 399, § 2(E), eff. Jan. 1, 1974; Acts 1981, 67th Leg., p. 2789, ch. 755, § 2, eff. Sept. 1, 1981; Acts 2013, 83rd Leg., ch. 1289 (H.B. 2268), § 2, eff. June 14, 2013; Acts 2017, 85th Leg., ch. 1058 (H.B. 2931), § 3.06, eff. Jan. 1, 2019.

Art. 18.065. Execution of Warrant Issued by District Judge for DNA Specimen

(a) A warrant issued by the judge of a district court under Article 18.02(10) to collect a DNA specimen from a person for the purpose of connecting that person to an offense may be executed in any county in this state.

(b) This article does not apply to a warrant issued by a justice of the peace, judge, or other magistrate other than a judge of a district court.

Added by Acts 2015, 84th Leg., ch. 1063 (H.B. 2185), § 1, eff. Sept. 1, 2015.

Section 2 of Acts 2015, 84th Leg., ch. 1063 (H.B. 2185) provides:

"The change in law made by this Act applies only to a search warrant issued on or after the effective date of this Act. A search warrant issued before the effective date of this Act is governed by the law in effect on the date the warrant was issued, and the former law is continued in effect for that purpose."

Art. 18.07. Days allowed for warrant to run

Text of (a) effective until January 1, 2019

(a) The period allowed for the execution of a search warrant, exclusive of the day of its issuance and of the day of its execution, is:

(1) 15 whole days if the warrant is issued solely to search for and seize specimens from a specific person for DNA analysis and comparison, including blood and saliva samples;

(2) 10 whole days if the warrant is issued under Section 5A, Article 18. 21; or

(3) three whole days if the warrant is issued for a purpose other than that described by Subdivision (1) or (2).

Text of (a) effective January 1, 2019

(a) The period allowed for the execution of a search warrant, exclusive of the day of its issuance and of the day of its execution, is:

(1) 15 whole days if the warrant is issued solely to search for and seize specimens from a specific person for DNA analysis and comparison, including blood and saliva samples;

(2) 10 whole days if the warrant is issued under Article 18B.354; or

(3) three whole days if the warrant is issued for a purpose other than that described by Subdivision (1) or (2).

Text of (b) effective until January 1, 2019

(b) The magistrate issuing a search warrant under this chapter shall endorse on the search warrant the date and hour of its issuance.

Text of (b) effective January 1, 2019

(b) The magistrate issuing a search warrant under this chapter, Chapter 18A, or Chapter 18B shall endorse on the search warrant the date and hour of its issuance.

(c) If a warrant is issued to search for and seize data or information contained in or on a computer, disk drive, flash drive, cellular telephone, or other electronic, communication, or data storage device, the warrant is considered to have been executed within the time allowed under Subsection (a) if the device was seized before the expiration of the time allowed. Notwithstanding any other law, any data or information contained in or on a device seized may be recovered and analyzed after the expiration of the time allowed under Subsection (a).

Amended by Acts 1973, 63rd Leg., p. 984, ch. 399, § 2(E), eff. Jan. 1, 1974; Acts 2009, 81st Leg., ch. 761, § 1, eff. Sept. 1, 2009; Acts 2011, 82nd Leg., ch. 772 (H.B. 1891), § 1, eff. Sept. 1, 2011; Acts 2013, 83rd Leg., ch. 1289 (H.B. 2268), § 3, eff. June 14, 2013; Acts 2017, 85th Leg., ch. 1058 (H.B. 2931), § 3.07, eff. Jan. 1, 2019.

Art. 18.08. Power of officer executing warrant

In the execution of a search warrant, the officer may call to his aid any number of citizens in this county, who shall be bound to aid in the execution of the same.

Amended by Acts 1973, 63rd Leg., p. 984, ch. 399, § 2(E), eff. Jan. 1, 1974.

Art. 18.09. Shall seize accused and property

When the property which the officer is directed to search for and seize is found he shall take possession of the same and carry it before the magistrate. He shall also arrest any person whom he is directed to arrest by the warrant and immediately take such person before the magistrate. For purposes of this chapter, "seizure," in the context of property, means the restraint of property, whether by physical force or by a display of an officer's authority, and includes the collection of property or the act of taking possession of property.

Amended by Acts 1973, 63rd Leg., p. 984, ch. 399, § 2(E), eff. Jan. 1, 1974; Acts 2005, 79th Leg., ch. 1026, § 2, eff. Sept. 1, 2005.

Art. 18.095. Seizure of circuit board of gambling device, equipment, or paraphernalia

For purposes of this chapter, an officer directed under a search warrant to search for and seize a gambling device or equipment, altered gambling equipment, or gambling paraphernalia in the discretion of the officer may:

(1) seize only the programmable main circuit board of the device, equipment, or paraphernalia if that circuit board is designed as a subassembly or essential part of the device, equipment, or paraphernalia to provide the information necessary for the device, equipment, or paraphernalia to operate as a gambling device or equipment, altered gambling equipment, or gambling paraphernalia;

(2) carry the circuit board before the magistrate; and

(3) retain custody of the circuit board as the property seized pursuant to the warrant as required under this chapter.

Added by Acts 2009, 81st Leg., ch. 898, § 1, eff. Sept. 1, 2009.

Art. 18.10. How Return Made

Not later than three whole days after executing a search warrant, the officer shall return the search warrant. Upon returning the search warrant, the officer shall state on the back of the same, or on some paper attached to it, the manner in which the warrant has been executed. The officer shall also deliver to the magistrate a copy of the inventory of the property taken into his possession under the warrant. The failure of an officer to make a timely return of an executed search warrant or to submit an inventory of the property taken into the officer's possession under the warrant does not bar the admission of evidence under Article 38.23. The officer who seized the property shall retain custody of it until the magistrate issues an order directing the manner of safekeeping the property. The property may not be removed from the county in which it was seized without an order approving the removal, issued by a magistrate in the county in which the warrant was issued; provided, however, nothing herein shall prevent the officer, or his department, from forwarding any item or items seized to a laboratory for scientific analysis.

Amended by Acts 1973, 63rd Leg., p. 984, ch. 399, § 2(E), eff. Jan. 1, 1974; Acts 1981, 67th Leg., p. 2789, ch. 755, § 3, eff. Sept. 1, 1981; Acts 2017, 85th Leg., ch. 174 (H.B. 3237), § 2, eff. May 26, 2017.

Art. 18.11.　Custody of property found

Property seized pursuant to a search warrant shall be kept as provided by the order of a magistrate issued in accordance with Article 18.10 of this code.

Amended by Acts 1973, 63rd Leg., p. 984, ch. 399, § 2(E), eff. Jan. 1, 1974; Acts 1981, 67th Leg., p. 2789, ch. 755, § 4, eff. Sept. 1, 1981.

Art. 18.12.　Magistrate shall investigate

The magistrate, upon the return of a search warrant, shall proceed to try the questions arising upon the same, and shall take testimony as in other examinations before him.

Amended by Acts 1973, 63rd Leg., p. 984, ch. 399, § 2(E), eff. Jan. 1, 1974.

Art. 18.13.　Shall discharge defendant

If the magistrate be not satisfied, upon investigation, that there was good ground for the issuance of the warrant, he shall discharge the defendant and order restitution of the property taken from him, except for criminal instruments. In such case, the criminal instruments shall be kept by the sheriff subject to the order of the proper court.

Amended by Acts 1973, 63rd Leg., p. 984, ch. 399, § 2(E), eff. Jan. 1, 1974.

Art. 18.14.　Examining trial

The magistrate shall proceed to deal with the accused as in other cases before an examining court if he is satisfied there was good ground for issuing the warrant.

Amended by Acts 1973, 63rd Leg., p. 984, ch. 399, § 2(E), eff. Jan. 1, 1974.

Art. 18.15.　Certify record to proper court

The magistrate shall keep a record of all the proceedings had before him in cases of search warrants, and shall certify the same and deliver them to the clerk of the court having jurisdiction of the case, before the next term of said court, and accompany the same with all the original papers relating thereto, including the certified schedule of the property seized.

Amended by Acts 1973, 63rd Leg., p. 985, ch. 399, § 2(E), eff. Jan. 1, 1974.

Art. 18.16.　Preventing consequences of theft

Any person has a right to prevent the consequences of theft by seizing any personal property that has been stolen and bringing it, with the person suspected of committing the theft, if that person can be taken, before a magistrate for examination, or delivering the property and the person suspected of committing the theft to a peace officer for that purpose. To justify a seizure under this article, there must be reasonable ground to believe the property is stolen, and the seizure must be openly made and the proceedings had without delay.

Amended by Acts 1973, 63rd Leg., p. 985, ch. 399, § 2(E), eff. Jan. 1, 1974; Acts 2001, 77th Leg., ch. 109, § 2, eff. Sept. 1, 2001.

Art. 18.17.　Disposition of abandoned or unclaimed property

(a) All unclaimed or abandoned personal property of every kind, other than contraband subject to forfeiture under Chapter 59 of this code and whiskey, wine and beer, seized by any peace officer in the State of Texas which is not held as evidence to be used in any pending case and has not been ordered destroyed or returned to the person entitled to possession of the same by a magistrate, which shall remain unclaimed for a period of 30 days shall be delivered for disposition to a person designated by the municipality or the purchasing agent of the county in which the property was seized. If a peace officer of a municipality seizes the property, the peace officer shall deliver the property to a person designated by the municipality. If any other peace officer seizes the property, the peace officer shall deliver the property to the purchasing agent of the county. If the county has no purchasing agent, then such property shall be disposed of by the sheriff of the county.

(b) The county purchasing agent, the person designated by the municipality, or the sheriff of the county, as the case may be, shall mail a notice to the last known address of the owner of such property by certified mail. Such notice shall describe the property being held, give the name and address of the officer holding such property, and shall state that if the owner does not claim such property within 90 days from the date of the notice such property will be disposed of and the proceeds, after deducting the reasonable expense of keeping such property and the costs of the disposition, placed in the treasury of the municipality or county giving the notice.

(c) If the property has a fair market value of $500 or more and the owner or the address of the owner is unknown, the person designated by the municipality, the county purchasing agent, or the sheriff, as the case may be, shall cause to be published once in a paper of general circulation in the municipality or county a notice containing a general description of the property held, the name of the owner if known, the name and address of the officer holding such property, and a statement that if the owner does not claim such property within 90 days from the date of the publication such property will be disposed of and the proceeds, after deducting the reasonable expense of keeping such property and the costs of the disposition, placed in the treasury of the municipality or county disposing of the property. If the property has a fair market value of less than $500 and the owner or the address of the owner is unknown, the person designated by the municipality, the county purchasing agent, or the sheriff may sell or donate the property. The person designated by the municipality, the purchasing agent, or the sheriff shall deposit the sale proceeds, after deducting the reasonable expense of keeping the property and costs of the sale, in the treasury of the municipality or county selling or donating the property.

(d) The sale under this article of any property that has a fair market value of $500 or more shall be preceded by a notice published once at least 14 days prior to the date of such sale in a newspaper of general circulation in the municipality or county where the sale is to take place, stating the general description of the property, the names of the owner if known, and the date and place that such sale will occur. This article does not require disposition by sale.

(d-1) Notwithstanding Subsection (a), (b), (c), or (d), if property described by Subsection (a), other than money, is seized by a peace officer at the time the owner of the property is arrested for an offense punishable as a Class C misdemeanor, the law enforcement agency may provide notice to the owner at the time the owner is taken into or released from custody. On receiving the notice, the owner must sign the notice and attach a thumbprint to the notice. The notice must include:

(1) a description of the property being held;

(2) the address where the property is being held; and

(3) a statement that if the owner does not claim the property before the 31st day after the date the owner is released from custody, the property will be disposed of and the proceeds of the property, after deducting the reasonable expense of keeping and disposing of the property, will be placed in the treasury of the municipality or county providing the notice.

(d-2) If the property for which notice is provided under Subsection (d-1) is not claimed by the owner before the 31st day after the date the owner is released from custody, the law enforcement agency holding the property shall deliver the property for disposition to a person designated by the municipality or to the purchasing agent or sheriff of the county in which the property was seized, as applicable. The person designated by the municipality, the purchasing agent, or the sheriff may sell or donate the property without mailing or publishing an additional notice as required by Subsection (b), (c), or (d). The sale proceeds, after deducting the reasonable expense of keeping and disposing of the property, must be deposited in the treasury of the municipality or county disposing of the property.

(e) The real owner of any property disposed of shall have the right to file a claim to the proceeds with the commissioners court of the county or with the governing body of the municipality in which the disposition took place. A claim by the real owner must be filed not later than the 30th day after the date of disposition. If the claim is allowed by the commissioners court or the governing body of the municipality, the municipal or county treasurer shall pay the owner such funds as were paid into the treasury of the municipality or county as proceeds of the disposition. If the claim is denied by the commissioners court or the governing body or if said court or body fails to act upon such claim within 90 days, the claimant may sue the municipal or county treasurer in a court of competent jurisdiction in the county, and upon sufficient proof of ownership, recover judgment against such municipality or county for the recovery of the proceeds of the disposition.

(f) For the purposes of this article:

(1) "Person designated by a municipality" means an officer or employee of a municipality who is designated by the municipality to be primarily responsible for the disposition of property under this article.

(2) "Property held as evidence" means property related to a charge that has been filed or to a matter that is being investigated for the filing of a charge.

(g) If the provisions of this section have been met and the property is scheduled for disposition, the municipal or county law enforcement agency that originally seized the property may request and have the property converted to agency use. The agency at any time may transfer the property to another municipal or county law enforcement agency for the use of that agency. The agency last using the property shall return the property to the person designated by the municipality, county purchasing agent, or sheriff, as the case may be, for disposition when the agency has completed the intended use of the property.

(h) If the abandoned or unclaimed personal property is money, the person designated by the municipality, the county purchasing agent, or the sheriff of the county, as appropriate, may, after giving notice under Subsection (b) or (c) of this article, deposit the money in the treasury of the municipality or county giving notice without conducting the sale as required by Subsection (d) of this article.

(i) While offering the property for sale under this article, if a person designated by a municipality, county purchasing agent, or sheriff considers any bid as insufficient, the person, agent, or sheriff may decline the bid and reoffer the property for sale.

(j) Chapters 72, 74, 75, and 76, Property Code, do not apply to unclaimed or abandoned property to which this article applies.

Amended by Acts 1967, 60th Leg., p. 1737, ch. 659, § 15, eff. Aug. 27, 1967; Acts 1973, 63rd Leg., p. 985, ch. 399, § 2(E), eff. Jan. 1, 1974; Acts 1987, 70th Leg., ch. 1002, § 1, eff. Sept. 1, 1987; Acts 1989, 71st Leg., 1st C.S., ch. 12, § 4, eff. Oct. 18, 1989; Acts 1991, 72nd Leg., ch. 254, § 1, eff. June 5, 1991; Acts 1993, 73rd Leg., ch. 157, § 1, eff. Sept. 1, 1993; Acts 1993, 73rd Leg., ch. 321, §§ 1 to 4, eff. May 28, 1993; Acts 1995, 74th Leg., ch. 76, §§ 3.01 to 3.05, eff. Sept. 1, 1995; Acts 2001, 77th Leg., ch. 402, § 18, eff. Sept. 1, 2001; Acts 2013, 83rd Leg., ch. 81 (S.B. 367), § 1, eff. May 18, 2013.

Art. 18.18. Disposition of gambling paraphernalia, prohibited weapon, criminal instrument, and other contraband

(a) Following the final conviction of a person for possession of a gambling device or equipment, altered gambling equipment, or gambling paraphernalia, for an offense involving a criminal instrument, for an offense involving an obscene device or material, for an offense involving child pornography, or for an offense involving a scanning device or re-encoder, the court entering the judgment of conviction shall order that the machine, device, gambling equipment or gambling paraphernalia, instrument, obscene device or material, child pornography, or scanning device or re-encoder be destroyed or forfeited to the state. Not later than the 30th day after the final conviction of a person for an offense involving a prohibited weapon, the court entering the judgment of conviction on its own motion, on the motion of the prosecuting attorney in the case, or on the motion of the law enforcement agency initiating the complaint on notice to the prosecuting attorney in the case if the prosecutor fails to move for the order shall order that the prohibited weapon be destroyed or forfeited to the law enforcement agency that initiated the complaint. If the court fails to enter the order within the time required by this subsection, any magistrate in the county in which the offense occurred may enter the order. Following the final conviction of a person for an offense involving dog fighting, the court entering the judgment of conviction shall order that any dog-fighting equipment be destroyed or forfeited to the state. Destruction of dogs, if necessary, must be carried out by a veterinarian licensed in this state or, if one is not available, by trained personnel of a humane society or an animal shelter. If forfeited, the court shall order the contraband delivered to the state, any political subdivision of the state, or to any state institution or agency. If gambling proceeds were seized, the court shall order them forfeited to the state and shall transmit them to the grand jury of the county in which they were seized for use in investigating alleged violations of the Penal Code, or to the state, any political subdivision of the state, or to any state institution or agency.

(b) If there is no prosecution or conviction following seizure, the magistrate to whom the return was made shall notify in writing the person found in possession of the alleged gambling device or equipment, altered gambling equipment or gambling paraphernalia, gambling proceeds, prohibited weapon, obscene device or material, child pornography, scanning device or re-encoder, criminal instrument, or dog-fighting equipment to show cause why the property seized should not be destroyed or the proceeds forfeited. The magistrate, on the motion of the law enforcement agency seizing a prohibited weapon, shall order the weapon destroyed or forfeited to the law enforcement agency seizing the weapon, unless a person shows

agency holding the weapon or by a county forensic laboratory designated by the magistrate. If the magistrate does not order the return, destruction, sale, or forfeiture of the weapon within the applicable period prescribed by this subsection, the law enforcement agency holding the weapon may request an order of destruction, sale, or forfeiture of the weapon from the magistrate. Only a firearms dealer licensed under 18 U.S.C. Section 923 may purchase a weapon at public sale under this subsection. Proceeds from the sale of a seized weapon under this subsection shall be transferred, after the deduction of court costs to which a district court clerk is entitled under Article 59.05(f), followed by the deduction of auction costs, to the law enforcement agency holding the weapon.

(d) A person either convicted or receiving deferred adjudication under Chapter 46, Penal Code, is entitled to the weapon seized upon request to the court in which the person was convicted or placed on deferred adjudication. However, the court entering the judgment shall order the weapon destroyed, sold at public sale by the law enforcement agency holding the weapon or by an auctioneer licensed under Chapter 1802, Occupations Code, or forfeited to the state for use by the law enforcement agency holding the weapon or by a county forensic laboratory designated by the court if:

(1) the person does not request the weapon before the 61st day after the date of the judgment of conviction or the order placing the person on deferred adjudication;

(2) the person has been previously convicted under Chapter 46, Penal Code;

(3) the weapon is one defined as a prohibited weapon under Chapter 46, Penal Code;

(4) the offense for which the person is convicted or receives deferred adjudication was committed in or on the premises of a playground, school, video arcade facility, or youth center, as those terms are defined by Section 481.134, Health and Safety Code; or

(5) the court determines based on the prior criminal history of the defendant or based on the circumstances surrounding the commission of the offense that possession of the seized weapon would pose a threat to the community or one or more individuals.

(d-1) Only a firearms dealer licensed under 18 U.S.C. Section 923 may purchase a weapon at public sale under Subsection (d). Proceeds from the sale of a seized weapon under Subsection (d) shall be transferred, after the deduction of court costs to which a

district court clerk is entitled under Article 59.05(f), followed by the deduction of auction costs, to the law enforcement agency holding the weapon.

(e) If the person found in possession of a weapon is convicted of an offense involving the use of the weapon, before the 61st day after the date of conviction the court entering judgment of conviction shall order destruction of the weapon, sale at public sale by the law enforcement agency holding the weapon or by an auctioneer licensed under Chapter 1802, Occupations Code, or forfeiture to the state for use by the law enforcement agency holding the weapon or by a county forensic laboratory designated by the court. If the court entering judgment of conviction does not order the destruction, sale, or forfeiture of the weapon within the period prescribed by this subsection, the law enforcement agency holding the weapon may request an order of destruction, sale, or forfeiture of the weapon from a magistrate. Only a firearms dealer licensed under 18 U.S.C. Section 923 may purchase a weapon at public sale under this subsection. Proceeds from the sale of a seized weapon under this subsection shall be transferred, after the deduction of court costs to which a district court clerk is entitled under Article 59.05(f), followed by the deduction of auction costs, to the law enforcement agency holding the weapon.

Amended by Acts 1973, 63rd Leg., p. 987, ch. 399, § 2(E), eff. Jan. 1, 1974; Acts 1987, 70th Leg., ch. 980, § 2, eff. Sept. 1, 1987; Acts 1993, 73rd Leg., ch. 157, § 3, eff. Sept. 1, 1993; Acts 1995, 74th Leg., ch. 318, § 46(a), eff. Sept. 1, 1995; Acts 2001, 77th Leg., ch. 1083, § 1, eff. Sept. 1, 2001; Acts 2005, 79th Leg., ch. 509, § 1, eff. Sept. 1, 2005; Acts 2013, 83rd Leg., ch. 178 (H.B. 1421), § 1, eff. Sept. 1, 2013.

Art. 18.191. Disposition of firearm seized from certain persons with mental illness

(a) A law enforcement officer who seizes a firearm from a person taken into custody under Section 573.001, Health and Safety Code, and not in connection with an offense involving the use of a weapon or an offense under Chapter 46, Penal Code, shall immediately provide the person a written copy of the receipt for the firearm and a written notice of the procedure for the return of a firearm under this article.

(b) The law enforcement agency holding a firearm subject to disposition under this article shall, as soon as possible, but not later than the 15th day after the date the person is taken into custody under Section 573.001, Health and Safety Code, provide written notice of the procedure for the return of a firearm under this article to the last known address of the person's closest immediate family member as identified by the person or reasonably identifiable by the law enforcement agency, sent by certified mail, return receipt requested. The written notice must state the date by which a request for the return of the firearm must be submitted to the law enforcement agency as provided by Subsection (h).

(c) Not later than the 30th day after the date a firearm subject to disposition under this article is seized, the law enforcement agency holding the firearm shall contact the court in the county having jurisdiction to order commitment under Chapter 574, Health and Safety Code, and request the disposition of the case. Not later than the 30th day after the date of this request, the clerk of the court shall advise the requesting agency whether the person taken into custody was released under Section 573.023, Health and Safety Code, or was ordered to receive inpatient mental health services under Section 574.034 or 574.035, Health and Safety Code.

(d) Not later than the 30th day after the date the clerk of the court informs a law enforcement agency holding a firearm subject to disposition under this article that the person taken into custody was released under Section 573.023, Health and Safety Code, the law enforcement agency shall:

(1) conduct a check of state and national criminal history record information to verify whether the person may lawfully possess a firearm under 18 U.S.C. Section 922(g); and

(2) provide written notice to the person by certified mail that the firearm may be returned to the person on verification under Subdivision (1) that the person may lawfully possess the firearm.

(e) Not later than the 30th day after the date the clerk of the court informs a law enforcement agency holding a firearm subject to disposition under this article that the person taken into custody was ordered to receive inpatient mental health services under Section 574.034 or 574.035, Health and Safety Code, the law enforcement agency shall provide written notice to the person by certified mail that the person:

(1) is prohibited from owning, possessing, or purchasing a firearm under 18 U.S.C. Section 922(g)(4);

(2) may petition the court that entered the commitment order for relief from the firearms disability under Section 574.088, Health and Safety Code; and

(3) may dispose of the firearm in the manner provided by Subsection (f).

(f) A person who receives notice under Subsection (e) may dispose of the person's firearm by:

(1) releasing the firearm to the person's designee, if:

(A) the law enforcement agency holding the firearm conducts a check of state and national criminal history record information and verifies that the designee may lawfully possess a firearm under 18 U.S.C. Section 922(g);

(B) the person provides to the law enforcement agency a copy of a notarized statement releasing the firearm to the designee; and

(C) the designee provides to the law enforcement agency an affidavit confirming that the designee:

(i) will not allow access to the firearm by the person who was taken into custody under Section 573.001, Health and Safety Code, at any time during which the person may not lawfully possess a firearm under 18 U.S.C. Section 922(g); and

(ii) acknowledges the responsibility of the designee and no other person to verify whether the person has reestablished the person's eligibility to lawfully possess a firearm under 18 U.S.C. Section 922(g); or

(2) releasing the firearm to the law enforcement agency holding the firearm, for disposition under Subsection (h).

(g) If a firearm subject to disposition under this article is wholly or partly owned by a person other than the person taken into custody under Section 573.001, Health and Safety Code, the law enforcement agency holding the firearm shall release the firearm to the person claiming a right to or interest in the firearm after:

(1) the person provides an affidavit confirming that the person:

(A) wholly or partly owns the firearm;

(B) will not allow access to the firearm by the person who was taken into custody under Section 573.001, Health and Safety Code, at any time during which that person may not lawfully possess a firearm under 18 U.S.C. Section 922(g); and

(C) acknowledges the responsibility of the person and no other person to verify whether the person who was taken into custody under Section 573.001, Health and Safety Code, has reestablished the person's eligibility to lawfully possess a firearm under 18 U.S.C. Section 922(g); and

(2) the law enforcement agency holding the firearm conducts a check of state and national criminal history record information and verifies that the person claiming a right to or interest in the firearm may lawfully possess a firearm under 18 U.S.C. Section 922(g).

(h) If a person to whom written notice is provided under Subsection (b) or another lawful owner of a firearm subject to disposition under this article does not submit a written request to the law enforcement agency for the return of the firearm before the 121st day after the date the law enforcement agency holding the firearm provides written notice under Subsection (b), the law enforcement agency may have the firearm sold by a person who is a licensed firearms dealer under 18 U.S.C. Section 923. The proceeds from the sale of a firearm under this subsection shall be given to the owner of the seized firearm, less the cost of administering this subsection. An unclaimed firearm that was seized from a person taken into custody under Section 573.001, Health and Safety Code, may not be destroyed or forfeited to the state.

Added by Acts 2013, 83rd Leg., ch. 776 (S.B. 1189), § 2, eff. Sept. 1, 2013.

Art. 18.20. Detection, interception, and use of wire, oral, or electronic communications

Definitions

Sec. 1. In this article:

(1) "Wire communication" means an aural transfer made in whole or in part through the use of facilities for the transmission of communications by the aid of wire, cable, or other like connection between the point of origin and the point of reception, including the use of such a connection in a switching station, furnished or operated by a person authorized to engage in providing or operating the facilities for the transmission of communications as a communications common carrier.

(2) "Oral communication" means an oral communication uttered by a person exhibiting an expectation that the communication is not subject to interception under circumstances justifying that expectation. The term does not include an electronic communication.

(3) "Intercept" means the aural or other acquisition of the contents of a wire, oral, or electronic communication through the use of an electronic, mechanical, or other device.

(4) "Electronic, mechanical, or other device" means a device that may be used for the nonconsensual interception of wire, oral, or electronic communications. The term does not include a telephone or telegraph instrument, the equipment or a facility used for the transmission of electronic communications, or a component of the equipment or a facility used for the transmission of electronic communications if the instrument, equipment, facility, or component is:

(A) furnished to the subscriber or user by a provider of wire or electronic communications service in the ordinary course of the provider's business and being used by the subscriber or user in the ordinary course of its business;

(B) furnished by a subscriber or user for connection to the facilities of a wire or electronic communications service for use in the ordinary course of the subscriber's or user's business;

(C) being used by a communications common carrier in the ordinary course of its business; or

(D) being used by an investigative or law enforcement officer in the ordinary course of the officer's duties.

(5) "Investigative or law enforcement officer" means an officer of this state or of a political subdivision of this state who is empowered by law to conduct investigations of or to make arrests for offenses enumerated in Section 4 of this article or an attorney authorized by law to prosecute or participate in the prosecution of the enumerated offenses.

(6) "Contents," when used with respect to a wire, oral, or electronic communication, includes any information concerning the substance, purport, or meaning of that communication.

(7) "Judge of competent jurisdiction" means a judge from the panel of nine active district judges with criminal jurisdiction appointed by the presiding judge of the court of criminal appeals as provided by Section 3 of this article.

(8) "Prosecutor" means a district attorney, criminal district attorney, or county attorney performing the duties of a district attorney, with jurisdiction in the county within an administrative judicial district described by Section 3(b).

(9) "Director" means the director of the Department of Public Safety or, if the director is absent or unable to serve, the assistant director of the Department of Public Safety.

(10) "Communication common carrier" means a person engaged as a common carrier for hire in the transmission of wire or electronic communications.

(11) "Aggrieved person" means a person who was a party to an intercepted wire, oral, or electronic communication or a person against whom the interception was directed.

(12) "Covert entry" means any entry into or onto premises which if made without a court order allowing such an entry under this Act, would be a violation of the Penal Code.

(13) "Residence" means a structure or the portion of a structure used as a person's home or fixed place of habitation to which the person indicates an intent to return after any temporary absence.

(14) "Pen register," "ESN reader," "trap and trace device," and "mobile tracking device" have the meanings assigned by Article 18.21.

(15) "Electronic communication" means a transfer of signs, signals, writing, images, sounds, data, or intelligence of any nature transmitted in whole or in part by a wire, radio, electromagnetic, photoelectronic, or photo-optical system. The term does not include:

(A) a wire or oral communication;

(B) a communication made through a tone-only paging device; or

(C) a communication from a tracking device.

(16) "User" means a person who uses an electronic communications service and is authorized by the provider of the service to use the service.

(17) "Electronic communications system" means a wire, radio, electromagnetic, photo-optical or photoelectronic facility for the transmission of wire or electronic communications, and any computer facility or related electronic equipment for the electronic storage of those communications.

(18) "Electronic communications service" means a service that provides to users of the service the ability to send or receive wire or electronic communications.

(19) "Readily accessible to the general public" means, with respect to a radio communication, a communication that is not:

(A) scrambled or encrypted;

(B) transmitted using modulation techniques whose essential parameters have been withheld from the public with the intention of preserving the privacy of the communication;

(C) carried on a subcarrier or other signal subsidiary to a radio transmission;

(D) transmitted over a communication system provided by a common carrier, unless the communication is a tone-only paging system communication;

(E) transmitted on frequencies allocated under Part 25, Subpart D, E, or F of Part 74, or Part 94 of the rules of the Federal Communications Commission, unless, in the case of a communication transmitted on a frequency allocated under Part 74 that is not exclusively allocated to broadcast auxiliary services, the communication is a two-way voice communication by radio; or

(F) an electronic communication.

(20) "Electronic storage" means any storage of electronic customer data in a computer, computer network, or computer system, regardless of whether the data is subject to recall, further manipulation, deletion, or transmission, and includes any storage of a wire or electronic communication by an electronic communications service or a remote computing service.

(21) "Aural transfer" means a transfer containing the human voice at any point between and including the point of origin and the point of reception.

(22) "Immediate life-threatening situation" means a hostage, barricade, or other emergency situation in which a person unlawfully and directly:

(A) threatens another with death; or

(B) exposes another to a substantial risk of serious bodily injury.

(23) "Member of a law enforcement unit specially trained to respond to and deal with life-threatening situations" means a peace officer who, as evidenced by the submission of appropriate documentation to the Texas Commission on Law Enforcement:

(A) receives a minimum of 40 hours a year of training in hostage and barricade suspect situations; or

(B) has received a minimum of 24 hours of training on kidnapping investigations and is:

(i) the sheriff of a county with a population of 3.3 million or more or the sheriff's designee; or

(ii) the police chief of a police department in a municipality with a population of 500,000 or more or the police chief's designee.

(24) "Access," "computer," "computer network," "computer system," and "effective consent" have the meanings assigned by Section 33.01, Penal Code.

(25) "Computer trespasser" means a person who:

(A) is accessing a protected computer without effective consent of the owner; and

(B) has no reasonable expectation of privacy in any communication transmitted to, through, or from the protected computer. The term does not include a person who accesses the computer under an existing contractual relationship with the owner or operator of the protected computer.

(26) "Protected computer" means a computer, computer network, or computer system that is:

(A) owned by a financial institution or governmental entity; or

(B) used by or for a financial institution or governmental entity and conduct constituting an offense affects that use.

Prohibition of Use as Evidence of Intercepted Communications

Sec. 2. (a) The contents of an intercepted communication and evidence derived from an intercepted communication may be received in evidence in any trial, hearing, or other proceeding in or before any court, grand jury, department, officer, agency, regulatory body, legislative committee, or other authority of the United States or of this state or a political subdivision of this state unless:

(1) the communication was intercepted in violation of this article, Section 16.02, Penal Code, or federal law; or

(2) the disclosure of the contents of the intercepted communication or evidence derived from the communication would be in violation of this article, Section 16.02, Penal Code, or federal law.

(b) The contents of an intercepted communication and evidence derived from an intercepted communication may be received in a civil trial, hearing, or other proceeding only if the civil trial, hearing, or other proceeding arises out of a violation of a penal law.

(c) This section does not prohibit the use or admissibility of the contents of a communication or evidence derived from the communication if the communication was intercepted in a jurisdiction outside this state in compliance with the law of that jurisdiction.

Judges Authorized to Consider Interception Applications

Sec. 3. (a) The presiding judge of the court of criminal appeals, by order filed with the clerk of that court, shall appoint one district judge from each of the administrative judicial districts of this state to serve at his pleasure as the judge of competent jurisdiction within that administrative judicial district. The presiding judge shall fill vacancies, as they occur, in the same manner.

(b) Except as provided by Subsection (c), a judge appointed under Subsection (a) may act on an application for authorization to intercept wire, oral, or electronic communications if the judge is appointed as the judge of competent jurisdiction within the administrative judicial district in which the following is located:

(1) the site of:

(A) the proposed interception; or

(B) the interception device to be installed or monitored;

(2) the communication device to be intercepted;

(3) the billing, residential, or business address of the subscriber to the electronic communications service to be intercepted;

(4) the headquarters of the law enforcement agency that makes a request for or executes an order authorizing an interception; or

(5) the headquarters of the service provider.

(c) If the judge of competent jurisdiction for an administrative judicial district is absent or unable to serve or if exigent circumstances exist, the application may be made to the judge of competent jurisdiction in an adjacent administrative judicial district. Exigent circumstances does not include a denial of a previous application on the same facts and circumstances. To be valid, the application must fully explain the circumstances justifying application under this subsection.

Offenses for Which Interceptions May Be Authorized

Sec. 4. A judge of competent jurisdiction may issue an order authorizing interception of wire, oral, or electronic communications only if the prosecutor applying for the order shows probable cause to believe that the interception will provide evidence of the commission of:

(1) a felony under Section 19.02, 19.03, or 43.26, Penal Code;

(2) a felony under:

(A) Chapter 481, Health and Safety Code, other than felony possession of marihuana;

(B) Section 485.032, Health and Safety Code; or

(C) Chapter 483, Health and Safety Code;

(3) an offense under Section 20.03 or 20.04, Penal Code;

(4) an offense under Chapter 20A, Penal Code;

(5) an offense under Chapter 34, Penal Code, if the criminal activity giving rise to the proceeds involves the commission of an offense under Title 5, Penal Code, [1] or an offense under federal law or the laws of another state containing elements that are substantially similar to the elements of an offense under Title 5;

(6) an offense under Section 38.11, Penal Code;

(7) an offense under Section 43.04 or 43.05, Penal Code; or

(8) an attempt, conspiracy, or solicitation to commit an offense listed in this section.

Control of Intercepting Devices

Sec. 5. (a) Except as otherwise provided by this section and Sections 8A and 8B, only the Department of Public Safety is authorized by this article to own, possess, install, operate, or monitor an electronic, mechanical, or other device. The Department of Public Safety may be assisted by an investigative or law enforcement officer or other person in the operation and monitoring of an interception of wire, oral, or electronic communications, provided that the officer or other person:

(1) is designated by the director for that purpose; and

(2) acts in the presence and under the direction of a commissioned officer of the Department of Public Safety.

(b) The director shall designate in writing the commissioned officers of the Department of Public Safety who are responsible for the possession, installation, operation, and monitoring of electronic, mechanical, or other devices for the department.

(c) The Texas Department of Criminal Justice may own electronic, mechanical, or other devices for a use or purpose authorized by Section 500.008, Government Code, and the inspector general of the Texas Department of Criminal Justice, a commissioned officer of that office, or another person acting in the presence and under the direction of a commissioned officer of that office may possess, install, operate, or monitor those devices as provided by Section 500.008.

(d) The Texas Juvenile Justice Department may own electronic, mechanical, or other devices for a use or purpose authorized by Section 242.103, Human Resources Code, and the inspector general of the Texas Juvenile Justice Department, a commissioned officer of that office, or another person acting in the presence and under the direction of a commissioned officer of that office may possess, install, operate, or monitor those devices as provided by Section 242.103.

Request for Application for Interception

Sec. 6. (a) The director may, based on written affidavits, request in writing that a prosecutor apply for an order authorizing interception of wire, oral, or electronic communications.

(b) The head of a local law enforcement agency or, if the head of the local law enforcement agency is absent or unable to serve, the acting head of the local law enforcement agency may, based on written affidavits, request in writing that a prosecutor apply for an order authorizing interception of wire, oral, or electronic communications. Prior to the requesting of an application under this subsection, the head of a local law enforcement agency must submit the request and supporting affidavits to the director, who shall make a finding in writing whether the request and supporting affidavits establish that other investigative procedures have been tried and failed or they reasonably appear unlikely to succeed or to be too dangerous if tried, is feasible, is justifiable, and whether the Department of Public Safety has the necessary resources available. The prosecutor may file the application only after a written positive finding on all the above requirements by the director.

Authorization for Disclosure and Use of Intercepted Communications

Sec. 7. (a) An investigative or law enforcement officer who, by any means authorized by this article, obtains knowledge of the contents of a wire, oral, or electronic communication or evidence derived from the communication may disclose the contents or evidence to another investigative or law enforcement officer, including a federal law enforcement officer or agent or a law enforcement officer or agent of another state, to the extent that the disclosure is appropriate to the proper performance of the official duties of the officer making or receiving the disclosure.

(b) An investigative or law enforcement officer who, by any means authorized by this article, obtains knowledge of the contents of a wire, oral, or electronic communication or evidence derived from the communication may use the contents or evidence to the extent the use is appropriate to the proper performance of his official duties.

(c) A person who receives, by any means authorized by this article, information concerning a wire, oral, or electronic communication or evidence derived from a communication intercepted in accordance with the provisions of this article may disclose the contents of that communication or the derivative evidence while giving testimony under oath in any proceeding held under the authority of the United States, of this state, or of a political subdivision of this state.

(d) An otherwise privileged wire, oral, or electronic communication intercepted in accordance with, or in violation of, the provisions of this article does not lose its privileged character and any evidence derived from such privileged communication against the party to the privileged communication shall be considered privileged also.

(e) When an investigative or law enforcement officer, while engaged in intercepting wire, oral, or electronic communications in a manner authorized by this article, intercepts wire, oral, or electronic communications relating to offenses other than those specified in the order of authorization, the contents of and evidence derived from the communication may be disclosed or used as provided by Subsections (a) and (b) of this section. Such contents and any evidence derived therefrom may be used under Subsection (c) of this section when authorized by a judge of competent jurisdiction where the judge finds, on subsequent application, that the contents were otherwise intercepted in accordance with the provisions of this article. The application shall be made as soon as practicable.

Application for Interception Authorization

Sec. 8. (a) To be valid, an application for an order authorizing the interception of a wire, oral, or electronic communication must be made in writing under oath to a judge of competent jurisdiction and must state the applicant's authority to make the application. An applicant must include the following information in the application:

(1) the identity of the prosecutor making the application and of the officer requesting the application;

(2) a full and complete statement of the facts and circumstances relied on by the applicant to justify his belief that an order should be issued, including:

(A) details about the particular offense that has been, is being, or is about to be committed;

(B) a particular description of the nature and location of the facilities from which or the place where the communication is to be intercepted;

(C) a particular description of the type of communication sought to be intercepted; and

(D) the identity of the person, if known, committing the offense and whose communications are to be intercepted;

(3) a full and complete statement as to whether or not other investigative procedures have been tried and failed or why they reasonably appear to be unlikely to succeed or to be too dangerous if tried;

(4) a statement of the period of time for which the interception is required to be maintained and, if the nature of the investigation is such that the authorization for interception should not automatically terminate when the described type of communication is first obtained, a particular description of facts establishing probable cause to believe that additional communications of the same type will occur after the described type of communication is obtained;

(5) a statement whether a covert entry will be necessary to properly and safely install the wiretapping or electronic surveillance or eavesdropping equipment and, if a covert entry is requested, a statement as to why such an entry is necessary and proper under the facts of the particular investigation, including a full and complete statement as to whether other investigative techniques have been tried and have failed or why they reasonably appear to be unlikely to succeed or to be too dangerous if tried or are not feasible under the circumstances or exigencies of time;

(6) a full and complete statement of the facts concerning all applications known to the prosecutor making the application that have been previously made to a judge for authorization to intercept wire, oral, or electronic communications involving any of the persons, facilities, or places specified in the application and of the action taken by the judge on each application; and

(7) if the application is for the extension of an order, a statement setting forth the results already obtained from the interception or a reasonable explanation of the failure to obtain results.

(b) The judge may, in an ex parte hearing in chambers, require additional testimony or documentary evidence in support of the application, and such testimony or documentary evidence shall be preserved as part of the application.

Emergency Installation and Use of Intercepting Device

Sec. 8A. (a) The prosecutor in a county in which an electronic, mechanical, or other device is to be installed or used to intercept wire, oral, or electronic communications shall designate in writing each peace officer in the county, other than a commissioned officer of the Department of Public Safety, who:

(1) is a member of a law enforcement unit specially trained to respond to and deal with life-threatening situations; and

(2) is authorized to possess such a device and responsible for the installation, operation, and monitoring of the device in an immediate life-threatening situation.

(b) A peace officer designated under Subsection (a) or under Section 5(b) may possess, install, operate, or monitor an electronic, mechanical, or other device to intercept wire, oral, or electronic communications if the officer:

(1) reasonably believes an immediate life-threatening situation exists that:

(A) is within the territorial jurisdiction of the officer or another officer the officer is assisting; and

(B) requires interception of communications before an order authorizing the interception can, with due diligence, be obtained under this section;

(2) reasonably believes there are sufficient grounds under this section on which to obtain an order authorizing the interception; and

(3) obtains oral or written consent to the interception before beginning the interception from:

(A) a judge of competent jurisdiction;

(B) a district judge for the county in which the device will be installed or used; or

(C) a judge or justice of a court of appeals or of a higher court.

(c) An official described in Subsection (b)(3) may give oral or written consent to the interception of communications under this section to provide evidence of the commission of a felony, or of a threat, attempt, or conspiracy to commit a felony, in an immediate life-threatening situation. Oral or written consent given under this section expires 48 hours after the grant of consent or at the conclusion of the emergency justifying the interception, whichever occurs first.

(d) If an officer installs or uses a device under Subsection (b), the officer shall:

(1) promptly report the installation or use to the prosecutor in the county in which the device is installed or used; and

(2) within 48 hours after the installation is complete or the interception begins, whichever occurs first, obtain a written order from a judge of competent jurisdiction authorizing the interception.

(e) A judge of competent jurisdiction under Section 3 or under Subsection (b) may issue a written order authorizing interception of communications under this section during the 48–hour period prescribed by Subsection (d)(2). A written order under this section expires on the 30th day after execution of the order or at the conclusion of the emergency that initially justified the interception, whichever occurs first. If an order is denied or is not issued within the 48–hour period, the officer shall terminate use of and remove the device promptly on the earlier of:

(1) the denial;

(2) the end of the emergency that initially justified the interception; or

(3) the expiration of 48 hours.

(f) The state may not use as evidence in a criminal proceeding any information gained through the use of a device installed under this section if authorization for the device is not sought or is sought but not obtained.

(g) A peace officer may certify to a communications common carrier that the officer is acting lawfully under this section.

Detection of Cellular Telephone or Other Wireless Communications Device in Correctional or Detention Facility

Sec. 8B. (a) In this section, "correctional facility" means:

(1) any place described by Section 1.07(a)(14), Penal Code; or

(2) a "secure correctional facility" or "secure detention facility" as defined by Section 51.02, Family Code.

(b) Notwithstanding any other provision of this article or Article 18.21, the office of the inspector general of the Texas Department of Criminal Justice may:

(1) without a warrant, use electronic, mechanical, or other devices to detect the presence or use of a cellular telephone or other wireless communications device in a correctional facility;

(2) without a warrant, intercept, monitor, detect, or, as authorized by applicable federal laws and regulations, prevent the transmission of any communication transmitted through the use of a cellular telephone or

other wireless communications device in a correctional facility; and

(3) use, to the extent authorized by law, any information obtained under Subdivision (2), including the contents of an intercepted communication, in any criminal or civil proceeding before a court or other governmental agency or entity.

(c) Not later than the 30th day after the date on which the office of the inspector general uses an electronic, mechanical, or other device under Subsection (b), the inspector general shall report the use of the device to:

(1) a prosecutor with jurisdiction in the county in which the device was used; or

(2) the special prosecution unit established under Subchapter E, Chapter 41, Government Code,[2] if that unit has jurisdiction in the county in which the device was used.

(d) When using an electronic, mechanical, or other device under Subsection (b), the office of the inspector general shall minimize the impact of the device on any communication that is not reasonably related to the detection of the presence or use of a cellular telephone or other wireless communications device in a correctional facility.

(e) A person confined in a correctional facility does not have an expectation of privacy with respect to the possession or use of a cellular telephone or other wireless communications device located on the premises of the facility. The person who is confined, and any person with whom that person communicates through the use of a cellular telephone or other wireless communications device, does not have an expectation of privacy with respect to the contents of any communication transmitted by the cellular telephone or wireless communications device.

Action on Application for Interception Order

Sec. 9. (a) On receipt of an application, the judge may enter an ex parte order, as requested or as modified, authorizing interception of wire, oral, or electronic communications if the judge determines from the evidence submitted by the applicant that:

(1) there is probable cause to believe that a person is committing, has committed, or is about to commit a particular offense enumerated in Section 4 of this article;

(2) there is probable cause to believe that particular communications concerning that offense will be obtained through the interception;

(3) normal investigative procedures have been tried and have failed or reasonably appear to be unlikely to succeed or to be too dangerous if tried;

(4) there is probable cause to believe that the facilities from which or the place where the wire, oral, or electronic communications are to be intercepted are being used or are about to be used in connection with the commission of an offense or are leased to, listed in the name of, or commonly used by the person; and

(5) a covert entry is or is not necessary to properly and safely install the wiretapping or electronic surveillance or eavesdropping equipment.

(b) An order authorizing the interception of a wire, oral, or electronic communication must specify:

(1) the identity of the person, if known, whose communications are to be intercepted;

(2) the nature and location of the communications facilities as to which or the place where authority to intercept is granted;

(3) a particular description of the type of communication sought to be intercepted and a statement of the particular offense to which it relates;

(4) the identity of the officer making the request and the identity of the prosecutor;

(5) the time during which the interception is authorized, including a statement of whether or not the interception will automatically terminate when the described communication is first obtained; and

(6) whether or not a covert entry or surreptitious entry is necessary to properly and safely install wiretapping, electronic surveillance, or eavesdropping equipment.

(c) On request of the applicant for an order authorizing the interception of a wire, oral, or electronic communication, the judge may issue a separate order directing that a provider of wire or electronic communications service, a communication common carrier, landlord, custodian, or other person furnish the applicant all information, facilities, and technical assistance necessary to accomplish the interception unobtrusively and with a minimum of interference with the services that the provider, carrier, landlord, custodian, or other person is providing the person whose communications are to be intercepted. Any provider of wire or electronic communications service, communication common carrier, landlord, custodian, or other person furnishing facilities or technical assistance is entitled to compensation by the applicant for reasonable expenses incurred in providing the facilities or assistance at the prevailing rates. The interception order may include an order to:

(1) install or use a pen register, ESN reader, trap and trace device, or mobile tracking device, or similar equipment that combines the function of a pen register and trap and trace device;

(2) disclose a stored communication, information subject to an administrative subpoena, or information subject to access under Article 18.21, Code of Criminal Procedure.

(d) An order entered pursuant to this section may not authorize the interception of a wire, oral, or electronic communication for longer than is necessary to achieve the objective of the authorization and in no event may it authorize interception for more than 30 days. The issuing judge may grant extensions of an order, but only on application for an extension made in accordance with Section 8 and the court making the findings required by Subsection (a). The period of extension may not be longer than the authorizing judge deems necessary to achieve the purposes for which it is granted and in no event may the extension be for more than 30 days. To be valid, each order and extension of an order must provide that the authorization to intercept be executed as soon as practicable, be conducted in a way that minimizes the interception of communications not otherwise subject to interception under this article, and terminate on obtaining the authorized objective or within 30 days, whichever occurs sooner. If the intercepted communication is in code or a foreign language and an expert in that code or language is not reasonably available during the period of interception, minimization may be accomplished as soon as practicable after the interception.

(e) An order entered pursuant to this section may not authorize a covert entry into a residence solely for the purpose of intercepting a wire or electronic communication.

(f) An order entered pursuant to this section may not authorize a covert entry into or onto a premises for the purpose of intercepting an oral communication unless:

(1) the judge, in addition to making the determinations required under Subsection (a) of this section, determines that:

(A)(i) the premises into or onto which the covert entry is authorized or the person whose communications are to be obtained has been the subject of a pen register previously authorized in connection with the same investigation;

(ii) the premises into or onto which the covert entry is authorized or the person whose communications are to be obtained has been the subject of an interception of wire or electronic communications previously authorized in connection with the same investigation; and

(iii) that such procedures have failed; or

(B) that the procedures enumerated in Paragraph (A) reasonably appear to be unlikely to succeed or to be too dangerous if tried or are not feasible under the circumstances or exigencies of time; and

(2) the order, in addition to the matters required to be specified under Subsection (b) of this section, specifies that the covert entry is for the purpose of intercepting oral communications of two or more persons and that there is probable cause to believe they are committing, have committed, or are about to commit a particular offense enumerated in Section 4 of this article.

(g) Whenever an order authorizing interception is entered pursuant to this article, the order may require reports to the judge who issued the order showing what progress has been made toward achievement of the authorized objective and the need for continued interception. Reports shall be made at any interval the judge requires.

(h) A judge who issues an order authorizing the interception of a wire, oral, or electronic communication may not hear a criminal prosecution in which evidence derived from the interception may be used or in which the order may be an issue.

Interception Order for Communication by Specified Person

Sec. 9A. (a) The requirements of Sections 8(a)(2)(B) and 9(b)(2) relating to the specification of the facilities from which or the place where a communication is to be intercepted do not apply if:

(1) in the case of an application for an order authorizing the interception of an oral communication:

(A) the application contains a full and complete statement as to why the specification is not practical and identifies the person committing or believed to be committing the offense and whose communications are to be intercepted; and

(B) a judge of competent jurisdiction finds that the specification is not practical; and

(2) in the case of an application for an order authorizing the interception of a wire or electronic communication:

(A) the application identifies the person committing or believed to be committing the offense and whose communications are to be intercepted;

(B) a judge of competent jurisdiction finds that the applicant has made an adequate showing of probable cause to believe that the actions of the person identified in the application could have the effect of thwarting interception from a specified facility; and

(C) the authority to intercept a wire or electronic communication under the order is limited to a period in which it is reasonable to presume that the person identified in the application will be reasonably proximate to the interception device.

(b) A person implementing an order authorizing the interception of an oral communication that, in accordance with this section, does not specify the facility from which or the place where a communication is to be intercepted may begin interception only after the person ascertains the place where the communication is to be intercepted.

(c) A provider of wire or electronic communications that receives an order authorizing the interception of a wire or electronic communication that, in accordance with this section, does not specify the facility from which or the place where a communication is to be intercepted may move the court to modify or quash the order on the ground that the provider's assistance with respect to the interception cannot be performed in a timely or reasonable fashion. On notice to the state, the court shall decide the motion expeditiously.

Procedure for Preserving Intercepted Communications

Sec. 10. (a) The contents of a wire, oral, or electronic communication intercepted by means authorized by this article shall be recorded on tape, wire, or other comparable device. The recording of the contents of a wire, oral, or electronic communication under this subsection shall be done in a way that protects the recording from editing or other alterations.

(b) Immediately on the expiration of the period of the order and all extensions, if any, the recordings shall be made available to the judge issuing the order and sealed under his directions. Custody of the recordings shall be wherever the judge orders. The recordings may not be destroyed until at least 10 years after the date of expiration of the order and the last extension, if any. A recording may be destroyed only by order of the judge of competent jurisdiction for the administrative judicial district in which the interception was authorized.

(c) Duplicate recordings may be made for use or disclosure pursuant to Subsections (a) and (b), Section 7, of this article for investigations.

(d) The presence of the seal required by Subsection (b) of this section or a satisfactory explanation of its absence is a prerequisite for the use or disclosure of the contents of a wire, oral, or electronic communication or evidence derived from the communication under Subsection (c), Section 7, of this article.

Sealing of Orders and Applications

Sec. 11. The judge shall seal each application made and order granted under this article. Custody of the applications and orders shall be wherever the judge directs. An application or order may be disclosed only on a showing of good cause before a judge of competent jurisdiction and may not be destroyed until at least 10 years after the date it is sealed. An application or order may be destroyed only by order of the judge of competent jurisdiction for the administrative judicial district in which it was made or granted.

Contempt

Sec. 12. A violation of Section 10 or 11 of this article may be punished as contempt of court.

Notice and Disclosure of Interception to a Party

Sec. 13. (a) Within a reasonable time but not later than 90 days after the date an application for an order is denied or after the date an order or the last extension, if any, expires, the judge who granted or denied the application shall cause to be served on the persons named in the order or the application and any other parties to intercepted communications, if any, an inventory, which must include notice:

(1) of the entry of the order or the application;

(2) of the date of the entry and the period of authorized interception or the date of denial of the application; and

(3) that during the authorized period wire, oral, or electronic communications were or were not intercepted.

(b) The judge, on motion, may in his discretion make available to a person or his counsel for inspection any portion of an intercepted communication, application, or order that the judge determines, in the interest of justice, to disclose to that person.

(c) On an ex parte showing of good cause to the judge, the serving of the inventory required by this section may be postponed, but in no event may any evidence derived from an order under this article be disclosed in any trial, until after such inventory has been served.

Preconditions to Use as Evidence

Sec. 14. (a) The contents of an intercepted wire, oral, or electronic communication or evidence derived from the communication may not be received in evidence or otherwise disclosed in a trial, hearing, or other proceeding in a federal or state court unless each party, not later than the 10th day before the date of the trial, hearing, or other proceeding, has been furnished with a copy of the court order and application under which the interception was authorized or approved. This 10-day period may be waived by the judge if he finds that it is not possible to furnish the party with the information 10 days before the trial, hearing, or proceeding and that the party will not be prejudiced by the delay in receiving the information.

(b) An aggrieved person charged with an offense in a trial, hearing, or proceeding in or before a court, department, officer, agency, regulatory body, or other authority of the United States or of this state or a political subdivision of this state may move to suppress the contents of an intercepted wire, oral, or electronic communication or evidence derived from the communication on the ground that:

(1) the communication was unlawfully intercepted;

(2) the order authorizing the interception is insufficient on its face; or

(3) the interception was not made in conformity with the order.

(c) A person identified by a party to an intercepted wire, oral, or electronic communication during the course of that communication may move to suppress the contents of the communication on the grounds provided in Subsection (b) of this section or on the ground that the harm to the person resulting from his identification in court exceeds the value to the prosecution of the disclosure of the contents.

(d) The motion to suppress must be made before the trial, hearing, or proceeding unless there was no opportunity to make the motion or the person was not aware of the grounds of the motion. The hearing on the motion shall be held in camera upon the written request of the aggrieved person. If the motion is granted, the contents of the intercepted wire, oral, or electronic communication and evidence derived from the communication shall be treated as having been obtained in violation of this article. The judge, on the filing of the motion by the aggrieved person, shall make available to the aggrieved person or his counsel for inspection any portion of the intercepted communication or evidence derived from the communication that the judge determines, in the interest of justice, to make available.

(e) Any judge of this state, upon hearing a pretrial motion regarding conversations intercepted by wire pursuant to this article, or who otherwise becomes informed that there exists on such intercepted wire, oral, or electronic communication identification of a specific individual who is not a party or suspect to the subject of interception:

(1) shall give notice and an opportunity to be heard on the matter of suppression of references to that person if identification is sufficient so as to give notice; or

(2) shall suppress references to that person if identification is sufficient to potentially cause embarrassment or harm which outweighs the probative value, if any, of the mention of such person, but insufficient to require the notice provided for in Subdivision (1), above.

Reports concerning intercepted wire, oral, or electronic communications

Sec. 15. (a) Within 30 days after the date an order or the last extension, if any, expires or after the denial of an order, the issuing or denying judge shall report to the Administrative Office of the United States Courts:

(1) the fact that an order or extension was applied for;

(2) the kind of order or extension applied for;

(3) the fact that the order or extension was granted as applied for, was modified, or was denied;

(4) the period of interceptions authorized by the order and the number and duration of any extensions of the order;

(5) the offense specified in the order or application or extension;

(6) the identity of the officer making the request and the prosecutor; and

(7) the nature of the facilities from which or the place where communications were to be intercepted.

(b) In January of each year each prosecutor shall report to the Administrative Office of the United States Courts the following information for the preceding calendar year:

(1) the information required by Subsection (a) of this section with respect to each application for an order or extension made;

(2) a general description of the interceptions made under each order or extension, including the approximate nature and frequency of incriminating communications intercepted, the approximate nature and frequency of other communications intercepted, the approximate number of persons whose communications were intercepted, and the approximate nature, amount, and cost of the manpower and other resources used in the interceptions;

(3) the number of arrests resulting from interceptions made under each order or extension and the offenses for which arrests were made;

(4) the number of trials resulting from interceptions;

(5) the number of motions to suppress made with respect to interceptions and the number granted or denied;

(6) the number of convictions resulting from interceptions, the offenses for which the convictions were obtained, and a general assessment of the importance of the interceptions; and

(7) the information required by Subdivisions (2) through (6) of this subsection with respect to orders or extensions obtained.

(c) Any judge or prosecutor required to file a report with the Administrative Office of the United States Courts shall forward a copy of such report to the director of the Department of Public Safety. On or before March 1 of each year, the director shall submit to the governor; lieutenant governor; speaker of the house of representatives; chairman, senate jurisprudence committee; and chairman, house of representatives criminal jurisprudence committee a report of all intercepts as defined herein conducted pursuant to this article and terminated during the preceding calendar year. Such report shall include:

(1) the reports of judges and prosecuting attorneys forwarded to the director as required in this section;

(2) the number of Department of Public Safety personnel authorized to possess, install, or operate electronic, mechanical, or other devices;

(3) the number of Department of Public Safety and other law enforcement personnel who participated or engaged in the seizure of intercepts pursuant to this article during the preceding calendar year; and

(4) the total cost to the Department of Public Safety of all activities and procedures relating to the seizure of intercepts during the preceding calendar year, including costs of equipment, manpower, and expenses incurred as compensation for use of facilities or technical assistance provided to the department.

Recovery of Civil Damages Authorized

Sec. 16. (a) A person whose wire, oral, or electronic communication is intercepted, disclosed, or used in violation of this article, or in violation of Chapter 16, Penal Code, has a civil cause of action against any person who intercepts, discloses, or uses or solicits another person to intercept, disclose, or use the communication and is entitled to recover from the person:

(1) actual damages but not less than liquidated damages computed at a rate of $100 a day for each day of violation or $1,000, whichever is higher;

(2) punitive damages; and

(3) a reasonable attorney's fee and other litigation costs reasonably incurred.

(b) A good faith reliance on a court order or legislative authorization constitutes a complete defense to an action brought under this section.

(c) A person is subject to suit by the federal or state government in a court of competent jurisdiction for appropriate injunctive relief if the person engages in conduct that:

(1) constitutes an offense under Section 16.05, Penal Code, but is not for a tortious or illegal purpose or for the purpose of direct or indirect commercial advantage or private commercial gain; and

(2) involves a radio communication that is:

(A) transmitted on frequencies allocated under Subpart D of Part 74 of the rules of the Federal Communications Commission; and

(B) not scrambled or encrypted.

(d) A defendant is liable for a civil penalty of $500 if it is shown at the trial of the civil suit brought under Subsection (c) that the defendant:

(1) has been convicted of an offense under Section 16.05, Penal Code; or

(2) is found liable in a civil action brought under Subsection (a).

(e) Each violation of an injunction ordered under Subsection (c) is punishable by a fine of $500.

(f) The attorney general, or the county or district attorney of the county in which the conduct, as described by Subsection (c), is occurring, may file suit under Subsection (c) on behalf of the state.

(g) A computer trespasser or a user, aggrieved person, subscriber, or customer of a communications common carrier or electronic communications service does not have a cause of action against the carrier or service, its officers, employees, or agents, or other specified persons for providing information, facilities, or assistance as required by a good faith reliance on:

(1) legislative authority; or

(2) a court order, warrant, subpoena, or certification under this article.

Nonapplicability

Sec. 17. This article does not apply to conduct described as an affirmative defense under Section 16.02(c), Penal Code, except as otherwise specifically provided by that section.

Sec. 18. Repealed by Acts 2005, 79th Leg., ch. 889, § 2.

Added by Acts 1981, 67th Leg., p. 729, ch. 275, § 1, eff. Aug. 31, 1981. Amended by Acts 1983, 68th Leg., p. 4880, ch. 864, § 4, eff. June 19, 1983; Acts 1985, 69th Leg., ch. 587, §§ 2 to 4, eff. Aug. 26, 1985; Acts 1989, 71st Leg., ch. 1166, §§ 1 to 15, eff. Sept. 1, 1989; Acts 1991, 72nd Leg., ch. 14, § 284(38), (57), eff. Sept. 1, 1991; 1993, 73rd Leg., ch. 790, § 15, eff. Sept. 1, 1993; Acts 1993, 73rd Leg., ch. 900, § 1.06, eff. Sept. 1, 1994; Acts 1997, 75th Leg., ch. 1051, §§ 1 to 4, eff. Sept. 1, 1997; Acts 2001, 77th Leg., ch. 1270, §§ 1 to 6, eff. Sept. 1, 2001; Acts 2003, 78th Leg., ch. 678, §§ 2 to 7, eff. Sept. 1, 2003; Acts 2005, 79th Leg., ch. 390, § 1, eff. Sept. 1, 2005; Acts 2005, 79th Leg., ch. 889, § 2, eff. June 17, 2005; Acts 2007, 80th Leg., ch. 186, § 1, eff. May 23, 2007; Acts 2007, 80th Leg., ch. 258, § 6.01, eff. Sept. 1, 2007; Acts 2009, 81st Leg., ch. 1130, § 40, eff. Sept. 1, 2009; Acts 2009, 81st Leg., ch. 1169, §§ 2 to 6, eff. Sept. 1, 2009; Acts 2009, 81st Leg., ch. 1237, § 1, eff. Sept. 1, 2009; Acts 2009, 81st Leg., ch. 1356, § 1, eff. Sept. 1, 2009; Acts 2011, 82nd Leg., ch. 85 (S.B. 653), § 3.002, eff. Sept. 1, 2011; Acts 2013, 83rd Leg., ch. 93 (S.B. 686), § 2.08, eff. May 18, 2013; Acts 2013, 83rd Leg., ch. 1289 (H.B. 2268), § 4, eff. June 14, 2013; Acts 2015, 84th Leg., ch. 216 (H.B. 511), § 2, eff. Sept. 1, 2015; Acts 2015, 84th Leg., ch. 333 (H.B. 11), § 2, eff. Sept. 1, 2015.

[1] V.T.C.A., Penal Code § 19.01 et seq.

[2] V.T.C.A., Government Code § 411.301 et seq.

Repeal

This article is repealed by Acts 2017, 85th Leg., ch. 1058 (H.B. 2931), § 5.01(1), effective Jan. 1, 2019.

Section 3 of Acts 2015, 84th Leg., ch. 216 (H.B. 511) provides:

"The change in law made by this Act applies only to an offense committed on or after the effective date [Sept. 1, 2015] of this Act. An offense committed before the effective date of this Act is governed by the law in effect on the date the offense was committed, and the former law is continued in effect for that purpose. For purposes of

this section, an offense was committed before the effective date of this Act if any element of the offense occurred before that date."

Sections 18 and 21 of Acts 2015, 84th Leg., ch. 333 (H.B. 11) provide:

"Sec. 18. The change in law made by this Act to Section 4, Article 18.20, Code of Criminal Procedure, applies only to an application for an interception order filed on or after the effective date [Sept. 1, 2015] of this Act. An application for an interception order filed before the effective date of this Act is governed by the law in effect on the date the application was filed, and the former law is continued in effect for that purpose."

"Sec. 21. To the extent of any conflict, this Act prevails over another Act of the 84th Legislature, Regular Session, 2015, relating to nonsubstantive additions to and corrections in enacted codes."

Art. 18.21. Pen registers and trap and trace devices; access to stored communications; mobile tracking devices

Definitions

Sec. 1. In this article:

(1) "Aural transfer," "communication common carrier," "computer trespasser," "electronic communication," "electronic communications service," "electronic communications system," "electronic storage," "immediate life-threatening situation," "member of a law enforcement unit specially trained to respond to and deal with life-threatening situations," " readily accessible to the general public," " user," and "wire communication" have the meanings assigned by Article 18.20.

(2) "Authorized peace officer" means:

(A) a sheriff or a sheriff's deputy;

(B) a constable or deputy constable;

(C) a marshal or police officer of an incorporated city;

(D) a ranger or officer commissioned by the Public Safety Commission or the director of the Department of Public Safety;

(E) an investigator of a prosecutor's office;

(F) a law enforcement agent of the Alcoholic Beverage Commission;

(G) a law enforcement officer commissioned by the Parks and Wildlife Commission;

(H) an enforcement officer appointed by the inspector general of the Texas Department of Criminal Justice under Section 493.019, Government Code;

(I) an investigator commissioned by the attorney general under Section 402.009, Government Code; or

(J) a member of an arson investigating unit commissioned by a municipality, a county, or the state.

(3) "Department" means the Department of Public Safety.

(3–a) "Designated law enforcement office or agency" means:

(A) the sheriff's department of a county with a population of 3.3 million or more;

(B) a police department in a municipality with a population of 500,000 or more; or

(C) the office of inspector general of the Texas Department of Criminal Justice.

(3–b) "Domestic entity" has the meaning assigned by Section 1.002, Business Organizations Code.

(3–c) "Electronic customer data" means data or records that:

(A) are in the possession, care, custody, or control of a provider of an electronic communications service or a remote computing service; and

(B) contain:

(i) information revealing the identity of customers of the applicable service;

(ii) information about a customer's use of the applicable service;

(iii) information that identifies the recipient or destination of a wire communication or electronic communication sent to or by the customer;

(iv) the content of a wire communication or electronic communication sent to or by the customer; and

(v) any data stored by or on behalf of the customer with the applicable service provider.

(4) "ESN reader" means a device that records the electronic serial number from the data track of a wireless telephone, cellular telephone, or similar communication device that transmits its operational status to a base site, if the device does not intercept the contents of a communication.

(5) "Mobile tracking device" means an electronic or mechanical device that permits tracking the movement of a person, vehicle, container, item, or object.

(6) "Pen register" means a device or process that records or decodes dialing, routing, addressing, or signaling information transmitted by an instrument or facility from which a wire or electronic communication is transmitted, if the information does not include the contents of the communication. The term does not include a device used by a provider or customer of a wire or electronic communication service in the ordinary course of the provider's or customer's business for purposes of:

(A) billing or recording as an incident to billing for communications services; or

(B) cost accounting, security control, or other ordinary business purposes.

(7) "Prosecutor" means a district attorney, criminal district attorney, or county attorney performing the duties of a district attorney.

(8) "Remote computing service" means the provision to the public of computer storage or processing services by means of an electronic communications system.

(9) "Supervisory official" means:

(A) an investigative agent or an assistant investigative agent who is in charge of an investigation;

(B) an equivalent person at an investigating agency's headquarters or regional office; and

(C) the principal prosecuting attorney of the state or of a political subdivision of the state or the first assistant or chief assistant prosecuting attorney in the office of either.

(10) "Trap and trace device" means a device or process that records an incoming electronic or other impulse that identifies the originating number or other dialing, routing, addressing, or signaling information reasonably likely to identify the source of a wire or electronic communication, if the information does not include the contents of the communication. The term does not include a device or telecommunications network used in providing:

(A) a caller identification service authorized by the Public Utility Commission of Texas under Subchapter E, Chapter 55, Utilities Code;[1]

(B) the services referenced in Section 55.102(b), Utilities Code; or

(C) a caller identification service provided by a commercial mobile radio service provider licensed by the Federal Communications Commission.

Application and Order

Sec. 2. (a) A prosecutor with jurisdiction in a county within a judicial district described by this subsection may file an application for the installation and use of a pen register, ESN reader, trap and trace device, or similar equipment that combines the function of a pen register and a trap and trace device with a district judge in the judicial district. The judicial district must be a district in which is located:

(1) the site of the proposed installation or use of the device or equipment;

(2) the site of the communication device on which the device or equipment is proposed to be installed or used;

(3) the billing, residential, or business address of the subscriber to the electronic communications service on which the device or equipment is proposed to be installed or used;

(4) the headquarters of:

(A) the office of the prosecutor filing an application under this section; or

(B) a law enforcement agency that requests the prosecutor to file an application under this section or that proposes to execute an order authorizing installation and use of the device or equipment; or

(5) the headquarters of a service provider ordered to install the device or equipment.

(b) A prosecutor may file an application under this section or under federal law on the prosecutor's own motion or on the request of an authorized peace officer, regardless of whether the officer is commissioned by the department. A prosecutor who files an application on the prosecutor's own motion or who files an application for the installation and use of a pen register, ESN reader, or similar equipment on the request of an authorized peace officer not commissioned by the department, other than an authorized peace officer employed by a designated law enforcement office or agency, must make the application personally and may not do so through an assistant or some other person acting on the prosecutor's behalf. A prosecutor may make an application through an assistant or other person acting on the prosecutor's behalf if the prosecutor files an application for the installation and use of:

(1) a pen register, ESN reader, or similar equipment on the request of:

(A) an authorized peace officer who is commissioned by the department; or

(B) an authorized peace officer of a designated law enforcement office or agency; or

(2) a trap and trace device or similar equipment on the request of an authorized peace officer, regardless of whether the officer is commissioned by the department.

(c) The application must:

(1) be made in writing under oath;

(2) include the name of the subscriber and the telephone number and location of the communication device on which the pen register, ESN reader, trap and trace device, or similar equipment will be used, to the extent that information is known or is reasonably ascertainable; and

(3) state that the installation and use of the device or equipment will likely produce information that is material to an ongoing criminal investigation.

(d) On presentation of the application, the judge may order the installation and use of the pen register, ESN reader, or similar equipment by an authorized peace officer commissioned by the department or an authorized peace officer of a designated law enforcement office or agency, and, on request of the applicant, the judge shall direct in the order that a communication common carrier or a provider of electronic communications service furnish all information, facilities, and technical assistance necessary to facilitate the installation and use of the device or equipment by the department or designated law enforcement office or agency unobtrusively and with a minimum of interference to the services provided by the carrier or service. The carrier or service is entitled to compensation at the prevailing rates for the facilities and assistance provided to the department or a designated law enforcement office or agency.

(e) On presentation of the application, the judge may order the installation and use of the trap and trace device or similar equipment by the communication common carrier or other person on the appropriate line. The judge may direct the communication common carrier or other person, including any landlord or other custodian of equipment, to furnish all information, facilities, and technical assistance necessary to install or use the device or equipment unobtrusively and with a minimum of interference to the services provided by the communication common carrier, landlord, custodian, or other person. Unless otherwise ordered by the court, the results of the trap and trace device or similar equipment shall be furnished to the applicant, designated by the court, at reasonable intervals during regular business hours, for the duration of the order. The carrier is entitled to compensation at the prevailing rates for the facilities and assistance provided to the designated law enforcement office or agency.

(f) Except as otherwise provided by this subsection, an order for the installation and use of a device or equipment under this section is valid for not more than 60 days after the earlier of the date the device or equipment is installed or the 10th day after the date the order is entered, unless the prosecutor applies for and obtains from the court an extension of the order before the order expires. The period of extension may not exceed 60 days for each extension granted, except that with the consent of the subscriber or customer of the service on which the device or equipment is used, the court may extend an order for a period not to exceed one year.

(g) The district court shall seal an application and order granted under this article.

(h) A peace officer is not required to file an application or obtain an order under this section before the officer makes an otherwise lawful search, with or without a warrant, to determine the contents of a caller identification message, pager message, or voice message that is contained within the memory of an end-user's identification, paging, or answering device.

(i) A peace officer of a designated law enforcement office or agency is authorized to possess, install, operate, or monitor a pen register, ESN reader, or similar equipment if the officer's name is on the list submitted to the director of the department under Subsection (k).

(j) Each designated law enforcement office or agency shall:

(1) adopt a written policy governing the application of this article to the office or agency; and

(2) submit the policy to the director of the department, or the director's designee, for approval.

(k) If the director of the department or the director's designee approves the policy submitted under Subsection (j), the inspector general of the Texas Department of Criminal Justice or the inspector general's designee, or the sheriff or chief of a designated law enforcement agency or the sheriff's or chief's designee, as applicable, shall submit to the director a written list of all officers in the designated law enforcement office or agency who are authorized to possess, install, monitor, or operate pen registers, ESN readers, or similar equipment.

(l) The department may conduct an audit of a designated law enforcement office or agency to ensure compliance with this article. If the department determines from the audit that the designated law enforcement office or agency is not in compliance with the policy adopted by the office or agency under Subsection (j), the department shall notify the office or agency in writing that it is not in compliance. If the department determines that the office or agency still is not in compliance with the policy 90 days after the date the office or agency receives written notice under this subsection, the office or agency loses the authority granted by this article until:

(1) the office or agency adopts a new written policy governing the application of this article to the office or agency; and

(2) the department approves the written policy.

(m) The inspector general of the Texas Department of Criminal Justice or the sheriff or chief of a designated law enforcement agency, as applicable, shall submit to the director of the department a written report of expenditures made by the designated law enforcement office or agency for the purchase and maintenance of a pen register, ESN reader, or similar equipment, authorized under this article. The director of the department shall report those expenditures publicly on an annual basis via the department's website, or other comparable means.

Emergency Installation and Use of Pen Register or Trap and Trace Device

Sec. 3. (a) A peace officer authorized to possess, install, operate, or monitor a device under Section 8A, Article 18.20, may install and use a pen register or trap and trace device if the officer:

(1) reasonably believes an immediate life-threatening situation exists that:

(A) is within the territorial jurisdiction of the officer or another officer the officer is assisting; and

(B) requires the installation of a pen register or trap and trace device before an order authorizing the installation and use can, with due diligence, be obtained under this article; and

(2) reasonably believes there are sufficient grounds under this article on which to obtain an order authorizing the installation and use of a pen register or trap and trace device.

(b) If an officer installs or uses a pen register or trap and trace device under Subsection (a), the officer shall:

(1) promptly report the installation or use to the prosecutor in the county in which the device is installed or used; and

(2) within 48 hours after the installation is complete or the use of the device begins, whichever occurs first, obtain an order under Section 2 authorizing the installation and use.

(c) A judge may issue an order authorizing the installation and use of a device under this section during the 48-hour period prescribed by Subsection (b)(2). If an order is denied or is not issued within the 48-hour period, the officer shall terminate use of and remove the pen register or the trap and trace device promptly on the earlier of the denial or the expiration of 48 hours.

(d) The state may not use as evidence in a criminal proceeding any information gained through the use of a pen register or trap and trace device installed under this section if an authorized peace officer does not apply for or applies for but does not obtain authorization for the pen register or trap and trace device.

Requirements for government access to stored communications

Sec. 4. (a) An authorized peace officer may require a provider of an electronic communications service or a provider of a remote computing service to disclose electronic customer data that is in electronic storage by obtaining a warrant under Section 5A.

(b) An authorized peace officer may require a provider of an electronic communications service or a provider of a remote computing service to disclose only electronic customer data that is information revealing the identity of customers of the applicable service or information about a customer's use of the applicable service, without giving the subscriber or customer notice:

(1) by obtaining an administrative subpoena authorized by statute;

(2) by obtaining a grand jury subpoena;

(3) by obtaining a warrant under Section 5A;

(4) by obtaining the consent of the subscriber or customer to the disclosure of the data;

(5) by obtaining a court order under Section 5; or

(6) as otherwise permitted by applicable federal law.

(c) A provider of telephonic communications service shall disclose to an authorized peace officer, without any form of legal process, subscriber listing information, including name, address, and telephone number or similar access code that:

(1) the service provides to others in the course of providing publicly available directory or similar assistance; or

(2) is solely for use in the dispatch of emergency vehicles and personnel responding to a distress call directed to an emergency dispatch system or when the information is reasonably necessary to aid in the dispatching of emergency vehicles and personnel for the immediate prevention of death, personal injury, or destruction of property.

(d) A provider of telephonic communications service shall provide an authorized peace officer with the name of the subscriber of record whose published telephone number is provided to the service by an authorized peace officer.

Court order to obtain access to stored communications

Sec. 5. (a) A court shall issue an order authorizing disclosure of contents, records, or other information of a wire or electronic communication held in electronic storage if the court determines that there is reasonable belief that the information sought is relevant to a legitimate law enforcement inquiry.

(b) A court may grant a motion by the service provider to quash or modify the order issued under Subsection (a) of this section if the court determines that the information or records requested are unusually voluminous in nature or that compliance with the order would cause an undue burden on the provider.

Warrant Issued in This State for Stored Customer Data or Communications

Sec. 5A. (a) This section applies to a warrant required under Section 4 to obtain electronic customer data, including the contents of a wire communication or electronic communication.

(b) On the filing of an application by an authorized peace officer, a district judge may issue a search warrant under this section for electronic customer data held in electronic storage, including the contents of and records and other information related to a wire communication or electronic communication held in electronic storage, by a provider of an electronic communications service or a provider of a remote computing service described by Subsection (h), regardless of whether the customer data is held at a location in this state or at a location in another state. An application made under this subsection must demonstrate probable cause for the issuance of the warrant and must be supported by the oath or affirmation of the authorized peace officer.

(c) A search warrant may not be issued under this section unless the sworn affidavit required by Article 18.01(b) sets forth sufficient and substantial facts to establish probable cause that:

(1) a specific offense has been committed; and

(2) the electronic customer data sought:

(A) constitutes evidence of that offense or evidence that a particular person committed that offense; and

(B) is held in electronic storage by the service provider on which the warrant is served under Subsection (i).

(d) Only the electronic customer data described in the sworn affidavit required by Article 18.01(b) may be seized under the warrant.

(e) A warrant issued under this section shall run in the name of "The State of Texas."

(f) Article 18.011 applies to an affidavit presented under Article 18.01(b) for the issuance of a warrant under this section, and the affidavit may be sealed in the manner provided by that article.

(g) The peace officer shall execute the warrant not later than the 11th day after the date of issuance, except that the officer shall execute the warrant within a shorter period if so directed in the warrant by the district judge. For purposes of this subsection, a warrant is executed when the warrant is served in the manner described by Subsection (i).

(h) A warrant under this section may be served only on a service provider that is a domestic entity or a company or entity otherwise doing business in this state under a contract or a terms of service agreement with a resident of this state, if any part of that contract or agreement is to be performed in this state. The service provider shall produce all electronic customer data, contents of communications, and other information sought, regardless of where the information is held and within the period allowed for compliance with the warrant, as provided by Subsection (j). A court may find any designated officer, designated director, or designated owner of a company or entity in contempt of court if the person by act or omission is responsible for the failure of the company or entity to comply with the warrant within the period allowed for compliance. The failure of a company or entity to timely deliver the information sought in the warrant does not affect the admissibility of that evidence in a criminal proceeding.

(i) A search warrant issued under this section is served when the authorized peace officer delivers the warrant by hand, by facsimile transmission, or, in a manner allowing proof of delivery, by means of the United States mail or a private delivery service to:

(1) a person specified by Section 5.255, Business Organizations Code;

(2) the secretary of state in the case of a company or entity to which Section 5.251, Business Organizations Code, applies; or

(3) any other person or entity designated to receive the service of process.

(j) The district judge shall indicate in the warrant that the deadline for compliance by the provider of an electronic communications service or the provider of a remote computing service is the 15th business day after the date the warrant is served if the warrant is to be served on a domestic entity or a company or entity otherwise doing business in this state, except that the deadline for compliance with a warrant served in accordance with Section 5.251, Business Organizations Code, may be extended to a date that is not later than the 30th day after the date the warrant is served. The judge may indicate in a warrant that the deadline for compliance is earlier than the 15th business day after the date the warrant is served if the officer makes a showing and the judge finds that failure to comply with the warrant by the earlier deadline would cause serious jeopardy to an investigation, cause undue delay of a trial, or create a material risk of:

(1) danger to the life or physical safety of any person;

(2) flight from prosecution;

(3) the tampering with or destruction of evidence; or

(4) intimidation of potential witnesses.

(k) If the authorized peace officer serving the warrant under this section also delivers an affidavit form to the provider of an electronic communications service or the provider of a remote computing service responding to the warrant, and the peace officer also notifies the provider in writing that an executed affidavit is required, then the provider shall verify the authenticity of the customer data, contents of communications, and other information produced in compliance with the warrant by including with the information the affidavit form completed and sworn to by a person who is a custodian of the information or a person otherwise qualified to attest to its authenticity that states that the information was stored in the course of regularly conducted business of the provider and specifies whether it is the regular practice of the provider to store that information.

(*l*) On a service provider's compliance with a warrant under this section, an authorized peace officer shall file a return of the warrant and a copy of the inventory of the seized property as required under Article 18.10.

(m) The district judge shall hear and decide any motion to quash the warrant not later than the fifth business day after the date the service provider files the motion. The judge may allow the service provider to appear at the hearing by teleconference.

(n) A provider of an electronic communications service or a provider of a remote computing service responding to a warrant issued under this section may request an extension of the period for compliance with the warrant if extenuating circumstances exist to justify the extension. The district judge shall grant a request for an extension based on those circumstances if:

(1) the authorized peace officer who applied for the warrant or another appropriate authorized peace officer agrees to the extension; or

(2) the district judge finds that the need for the extension outweighs the likelihood that the extension will cause an adverse circumstance described by Subsection (j).

Warrant Issued in Another State for Stored Customer Data or Communications

Sec. 5B. Any domestic entity that provides electronic communications services or remote computing services to the public shall comply with a warrant issued in another state and seeking information described by Section 5A(b), if the warrant is served on the entity in a manner equivalent to the service of process requirements provided in Section 5A(h).

Backup preservation

Sec. 6. (a) A subpoena or court order for disclosure of certain electronic customer data held in electronic storage by a provider of an electronic communications service or a provider of a remote computing service under Section 4(b) may require that provider to create a copy of the customer data sought by the subpoena or court order for the purpose of preserving that data. The provider may not inform the subscriber or customer whose data is being sought that the subpoena or court order has been issued. The provider shall create the copy within a reasonable time as determined by the court issuing the subpoena or court order.

(b) The provider of an electronic communications service or the provider of a remote computing service shall immediately notify the authorized peace officer who presented the subpoena or court order requesting the copy when the copy has been created.

(c) The authorized peace officer shall notify the subscriber or customer whose electronic customer data is the subject of the subpoena or court order of the creation of the copy not later than three days after the date of the receipt of the notification from the applicable provider that the copy was created.

(d) The provider of an electronic communications service or the provider of a remote computing service shall release the copy to the requesting authorized peace officer not earlier than the 14th day after the date of the peace officer's notice to the subscriber or customer if the provider has not:

(1) initiated proceedings to challenge the request of the peace officer for the copy; or

(2) received notice from the subscriber or customer that the subscriber or customer has initiated proceedings to challenge the request.

(e) The provider of an electronic communications service or the provider of a remote computing service may not destroy or permit the destruction of the copy until the electronic customer data has been delivered to the applicable law enforcement agency or until the resolution of any court proceedings, including appeals of any proceedings, relating to the subpoena or court order requesting the creation of the copy, whichever occurs last.

(f) An authorized peace officer who reasonably believes that notification to the subscriber or customer of the subpoena or court order would result in the destruction of or tampering with electronic customer data sought may request the creation of a copy of the data. The peace officer's belief is not subject to challenge by the subscriber or customer or by a provider of an electronic communications service or a provider of a remote computing service.

(g)(1) A subscriber or customer who receives notification as described in Subsection (c) may file a written motion to quash the subpoena or vacate the court order in the court that issued the subpoena or court order not later than the 14th day after the date of the receipt of the notice. The motion must contain an affidavit or sworn statement stating:

(A) that the applicant is a subscriber or customer of the provider of an electronic communications service or the provider of a remote computing service from which the electronic customer data held in electronic storage for the subscriber or customer has been sought; and

(B) the applicant's reasons for believing that the customer data sought is not relevant to a legitimate law enforcement inquiry or that there has not been substantial compliance with the provisions of this article in some other respect.

(2) The subscriber or customer shall give written notice to the provider of an electronic communications service or the provider of a remote computing service of the challenge to the subpoena or court order. The authorized peace officer requesting the subpoena or court order must be served a copy of the papers filed by personal delivery or by registered or certified mail.

(h)(1) The court shall order the authorized peace officer to file a sworn response to the motion filed by the subscriber or customer if the court determines that the subscriber or customer has complied with the requirements of Subsection (g). On request of the peace officer, the court may permit the response to be filed in camera. The court may conduct any additional proceedings the court considers appropriate if the court is unable to make a determination on the motion on the basis of the parties' initial allegations and response.

(2) The court shall rule on the motion as soon after the filing of the officer's response as practicable. The court shall deny the motion if the court finds that the applicant is not the subscriber or customer whose electronic customer data held in electronic storage is the subject of the subpoena or court order or that there is reason to believe that the peace officer's inquiry is legitimate and that the customer data sought is relevant to that inquiry. The court shall quash the subpoena or vacate the order if the court finds that the applicant is the subscriber or customer whose data is the subject of the subpoena or court order and that there is not a reason to believe that the data is relevant to a legitimate law enforcement inquiry or that there has not been substantial compliance with the provisions of this article.

(3) A court order denying a motion or application under this section is not a final order and no interlocutory appeal may be taken from the denial.

Delay of notification

Sec. 7. Repealed by Acts 2013, 83rd Leg., ch. 1289 (H.B. 2268), § 13.

Preclusion of notification

Sec. 8. (a) An authorized peace officer seeking electronic customer data under Section 4 may apply to the court for an order commanding the service provider to whom a warrant, subpoena, or court order is directed not to disclose to any person the existence of the warrant, subpoena, or court order. The order is effective for the period the court considers appropriate. The court shall enter the order if the court determines that there is reason to believe that notification of the existence of the warrant, subpoena, or court order will have an adverse result.

(b) In this section, an "adverse result" means:

(1) endangering the life or physical safety of an individual;

(2) flight from prosecution;

(3) destruction of or tampering with evidence;

(4) intimidation of a potential witness; or

(5) otherwise seriously jeopardizing an investigation or unduly delaying a trial.

Reimbursement of costs

Sec. 9. (a) Except as provided by Subsection (c) of this section, an authorized peace officer who obtains electronic customer data under Section 4 or other information under this article shall reimburse the person assembling or providing the data or information for all costs that are reasonably necessary and that have been directly incurred in searching for, assembling, reproducing, or otherwise providing the data or information. These costs include costs arising from necessary disruption of normal operations of a provider of an electronic communications service or a provider of a remote computing service in which the electronic customer data may be held in electronic storage or in which the other information may be stored.

(b) The authorized peace officer and the person providing the electronic customer data or other information may agree on the amount of reimbursement. If there is no agreement, the court that issued the order for production of the data or information shall determine the amount. If no court order was issued for production of the data or information, the court before which the criminal prosecution relating to the data or information would be brought shall determine the amount.

(c) Subsection (a) of this section does not apply to records or other information maintained by a communications common carrier that relate to telephone toll records or telephone listings obtained under Section 4(e) of this article unless the court determines that the amount of information required was unusually voluminous or that an undue burden was imposed on the provider.

No cause of action

Sec. 10.   A subscriber or customer of a provider of an electronic communications service or a provider of a remote computing service does not have a cause of action against a provider or its officers, employees, or agents or against other specified persons for providing information, facilities, or assistance as required by a court order, warrant, subpoena, or certification under this article.

Disclosure of stored communications

Sec. 11.   (a) Except as provided by Subsection (c) of this section, a provider of an electronic communications service may not knowingly divulge the contents of a communication that is in electronic storage.

(b) Except as provided by Subsection (c) of this section, a provider of remote computing service may not knowingly divulge the contents of any communication that is:

(1) in electronic storage;

(2) stored on behalf of a subscriber or customer of the service and is received by means of electronic transmission from or created by means of computer processing of communications received by means of electronic transmission from the subscriber or customer; and

(3) solely for the purpose of providing storage or computer processing services to the subscriber or customer if the provider of the service is not authorized to obtain access to the contents of those communications for purposes of providing any service other than storage or computer processing.

(c) A provider of an electronic communications or remote computing service may divulge the contents of an electronically stored communication:

(1) to an intended recipient of the communication or that person's agent;

(2) to the addressee or that person's agent;

(3) with the consent of the originator, to the addressee or the intended recipient of the communication, or the subscriber of a remote computing service;

(4) to a person whose facilities are used to transmit the communication to its destination or the person's employee or authorized representative;

(5) as may be necessary to provide the service or to protect the property or rights of the provider of the service;

(6) to a law enforcement agency if the contents were obtained inadvertently by the service provider and the contents appear to pertain to the commission of a crime; or

(7) as authorized under federal or other state law.

Cause of action

Sec. 12.   (a) Except as provided by Section 10 of this article, a provider of an electronic communications service or a provider of a remote computing service, or a subscriber or customer of that provider, that is aggrieved by a violation of this article has a civil cause of action if the conduct constituting the violation was committed knowingly or intentionally and is entitled to:

(1) injunctive relief;

(2) a reasonable attorney's fee and other litigation costs reasonably incurred; and

(3) the sum of the actual damages suffered and any profits made by the violator as a result of the violation or $1,000, whichever is more.

(b) The reliance in good faith on a court order, warrant, subpoena, or legislative authorization is a complete defense to any civil action brought under this article.

(c) A civil action under this section may be presented within two years after the date the claimant first discovered or had reasonable opportunity to discover the violation, and not afterward.

Exclusivity of remedies

Sec. 13.   The remedies and sanctions described in this article are the exclusive judicial remedies and sanctions for a violation of this article other than a violation that infringes on a right of a party guaranteed by a state or federal constitution.

Mobile tracking devices

Sec. 14.   (a) A district judge may issue an order for the installation and use of a mobile tracking device in the same judicial district as the site of:

(1) the investigation; or

(2) the person, vehicle, container, item, or object the movement of which will be tracked by the mobile tracking device.

(b) The order may authorize the use of a mobile tracking device outside the judicial district but within the state, if the device is installed within the district.

(c) A district judge may issue the order only on the application of an authorized peace officer. An application must be written and signed and sworn to or affirmed before the judge. The affidavit must:

(1) state the name, department, agency, and address of the applicant;

(2) identify the vehicle, container, or item to which, in which, or on which the mobile tracking device is to be attached, placed, or otherwise installed;

(3) state the name of the owner or possessor of the vehicle, container, or item described in Subdivision (2);

(4) state the judicial jurisdictional area in which the vehicle, container, or item described in Subdivision (2) is expected to be found; and

(5) state the facts and circumstances that provide the applicant with a reasonable suspicion that:

(A) criminal activity has been, is, or will be committed; and

(B) the installation and use of a mobile tracking device is likely to produce information that is material to an ongoing criminal investigation of the criminal activity described in Paragraph (A).

(d) Within 72 hours after the time the mobile tracking device was activated in place on or within the vehicle, container, or item, the applicant shall notify in writing the judge who issued an order under this section.

(e) An order under this section expires not later than the 90th day after the date that the device has been activated in place on or within the vehicle, container, or item. For good cause shown, the judge may grant an extension for an additional 90–day period.

(f) The applicant shall remove or cause to be removed a mobile tracking device as soon as is practicable after the authorization period expires. If removal is not practicable, monitoring of the device shall cease on expiration of the authorization order.

(g) This section does not apply to a global positioning or similar device installed in or on an item of property by the owner or with the consent of the owner of the property. A device described by this subsection may be monitored by a private entity in an emergency.

Subpoena authority

Sec. 15. (a) The director of the department or the director's designee, the inspector general of the Texas Department of Criminal Justice or the inspector general's designee, or the sheriff or chief of a designated law enforcement agency or the sheriff's or chief's designee may issue an administrative subpoena to a communications common carrier or an electronic communications service to compel the production of the carrier's or service's business records that:

(1) disclose information about:

(A) the carrier's or service's customers; or

(B) users of the services offered by the carrier or service; and

(2) are material to a criminal investigation.

(b) Not later than the 30th day after the date on which the administrative subpoena is issued under Subsection (a), the inspector general of the Texas Department of Criminal Justice or the sheriff or chief of a designated law enforcement agency, as applicable, shall report the issuance of the subpoena to the department.

(c) If, based on reports received under Subsection (b), the department determines that a designated law enforcement office or agency is not in compliance with the policy adopted by the office or agency under Section 2(j), the department shall notify the office or agency in writing that it is not in compliance. If the department determines that the office or agency still is not in compliance with the policy 90 days after the date the office or agency receives written notice under this subsection, the office or agency loses the authority granted by this article until:

(1) the office or agency adopts a new written policy governing the application of this article to the office or agency; and

(2) the department approves the written policy.

Limitation

Sec. 16. A governmental agency authorized to install and use a pen register under this article or other law must use reasonably available technology to only record and decode electronic or other impulses used to identify the numbers dialed, routed, addressed, or otherwise processed or transmitted by a wire or electronic communication so as to not include the contents of the communication.

Added by Acts 1985, 69th Leg., ch. 587, § 5, eff. Aug. 26, 1985. Amended by Acts 1989, 71st Leg., ch. 958, § 1, eff. Sept. 1, 1989; Acts 1993, 73rd Leg., ch. 659, § 2, eff. Sept. 1, 1993; Acts 1995, 74th Leg., ch. 170, § 1, eff. Aug. 28, 1995; Acts 1995, 74th Leg., ch. 318, § 47, eff. Sept. 1, 1995; Acts 1997, 75th Leg., ch. 165, § 31.01(40), eff. Sept. 1, 1997; Acts 1997, 75th Leg., ch. 1051, §§ 5 to 8, eff. Sept. 1, 1997; Acts 1999, 76th Leg., ch. 62, § 18.20, eff. Sept. 1, 1999; Acts 2001, 77th Leg., ch. 1270, §§ 7 to 10, eff. Sept. 1, 2001; Acts 2003, 78th Leg., ch. 678, §§ 8 to 11, eff. Sept. 1, 2003; Acts 2007, 80th Leg., ch. 186, §§ 2 to 4, eff. May 23, 2007; Acts 2009, 81st Leg., ch. 1237, §§ 2 to 5, eff. Sept. 1, 2009; Acts 2011, 82nd Leg., ch. 316 (H.B. 2354), §§ 1 to 5, eff. Sept. 1, 2011; Acts 2011, 82nd Leg., ch. 620 (S.B. 688), § 2, eff. Sept. 1, 2011; Acts 2013, 83rd Leg., ch. 1289 (H.B. 2268), §§ 5 to 13, eff. June 14, 2013; Acts 2015, 84th Leg., ch. 1120 (H.B. 3668), § 1, eff. June 19, 2015.

[1] V.T.C.A., Utilities Code § 55.101 et seq.

Repeal

This article is repealed by Acts 2017, 85th Leg., ch. 1058 (H.B. 2931), § 5.01(2), effective Jan. 1, 2019.

Art. 18.22. Testing certain defendants or confined persons for communicable diseases

Text of (a), as amended by Acts 2015, 84th Leg., ch. 736 (H.B. 1595), § 2

(a) A person who is arrested for a misdemeanor or felony and who during the commission of that offense or the arrest, during a judicial proceeding or initial period of confinement following the arrest, or during the person's confinement after a conviction or adjudication resulting from the arrest causes the person's bodily fluids to come into contact with a peace officer, a magistrate, or an employee of a correctional facility where the person is confined shall, at the direction of the court having jurisdiction over the arrested person, undergo a medical procedure or test designed to show or help show whether the person has a communicable disease. The court may direct the person to undergo the procedure or test on its own motion or on the request of the peace officer, magistrate, or correctional facility employee. If the person refuses to submit voluntarily to the procedure or test, the court shall require the person to submit to the procedure or test. Notwithstanding any other law, the person performing the procedure or test shall make the test results available to the local health authority, and the local health authority shall notify the peace officer, magistrate, or correctional facility employee, as appropriate, of the test result. The state may not use the fact that a medical procedure or test was performed on a person under this article, or use the results of the procedure or test, in any criminal proceeding arising out of the alleged offense.

Text of (a), as amended by Acts 2015, 84th Leg., ch. 1278 (S.B. 1574), § 1

(a) A person who is arrested for a misdemeanor or felony and who during the commission of that offense or an arrest following the commission of that offense causes an emergency response employee or volunteer, as defined by Section 81.003, Health and Safety Code, to come into contact with the person's bodily fluids shall, at the direction of the court having jurisdiction over the arrested person, undergo a medical procedure or test designed to show or help show whether the person has a communicable disease. The court may direct the person to undergo the procedure or test on its own motion or on the request of the emergency response employee or volunteer. If the person refuses to submit voluntarily to the procedure or test, the court shall require the person to submit to the procedure or test. Notwithstanding any other law, the person performing the procedure or test shall make the test results available to the local health authority and the designated infection control officer of the entity that employs or uses the services of the affected emergency response employee or volunteer, and the local health authority or the designated infection control officer of the affected employee or volunteer shall notify the emergency response employee or volunteer of the test result. The state may not use the fact that a medical procedure or test was performed on a person under this article, or use the results of the procedure or test, in any criminal proceeding arising out of the alleged offense.

(b) Testing under this article shall be conducted in accordance with written infectious disease control protocols adopted by the Department of State Health Services that clearly establish procedural guidelines that provide criteria for testing and that respect the rights of the arrested person and the peace officer, magistrate, or correctional facility employee.

(c) Nothing in this article authorizes a court to release a test result to a person other than a person specifically authorized by this article, and Section 81.103(d), Health and Safety Code, does not authorize that disclosure.

(d) In this article, "correctional facility" means:

(1) any place described by Section 1.07(a)(14), Penal Code; or

(2) a "secure correctional facility" or "secure detention facility" as those terms are defined by Section 51.02, Family Code.

Added by Acts 2001, 77th Leg., ch. 1480, § 2, eff. Sept. 1, 2001. Amended by Acts 2003, 78th Leg., ch. 1250, § 1, eff. Sept. 1, 2003; Acts 2015, 84th Leg., ch. 736 (H.B. 1595), §§ 1, 2, eff. June 17, 2015; Acts 2015, 84th Leg., ch. 1278 (S.B. 1574), § 1, eff. Sept. 1, 2015.

Section 3 of Acts 2015, 84th Leg., ch. 736 (H.B. 1595) provides:

"The change in law made by this Act applies to a motion by the court or request of a magistrate or correctional facility employee made on or after the effective date [June 17, 2015] of this Act, regardless of whether the offense for which the person was arrested or the applicable contact with bodily fluids occurred before, on, or after that date."

Art. 18.23. Expenses for motor vehicle towed and stored for certain purposes

(a) A law enforcement agency that directs the towing and storage of a motor vehicle for an evidentiary or examination purpose shall pay the cost of the towing and storage.

(b) Subsection (a) applies whether the motor vehicle is taken to or stored on property that is:

(1) owned or operated by the law enforcement agency; or

(2) owned or operated by another person who provides storage services to the law enforcement agency, including:

(A) a governmental entity; and

(B) a vehicle storage facility, as defined by Section 2303.002, Occupations Code.

(c) Subsection (a) does not require a law enforcement agency to pay the cost of:

(1) towing or storing a motor vehicle for a purpose that is not an evidentiary or examination purpose, including towing or storing a vehicle that has been abandoned, illegally parked, in an accident, or recovered after being stolen; or

(2) storing a motor vehicle after the date the law enforcement agency authorizes the owner or operator of the property to which the vehicle was taken or on which the vehicle is stored to release the vehicle to the vehicle's owner.

(d) This subsection applies only to a motor vehicle taken to or stored on property described by Subsection (b)(2). After a law enforcement agency authorizes the release of a motor vehicle held for an evidentiary or examination purpose, the owner or operator of the storage property may not refuse to release the vehicle to the vehicle's owner because the law enforcement agency has not paid the cost of the towing and storage.

(e) Subchapter J, Chapter 2308, Occupations Code,[1] does not apply to a motor vehicle directed by a law enforcement agency to be towed and stored for an evidentiary or examination purpose.

Added by Acts 2005, 79th Leg., ch. 1197, § 1, eff. Sept. 1, 2005. Amended by Acts 2007, 80th Leg., ch. 1046, § 3.01, eff. Sept. 1, 2007.

[1] V.T.C.A., Occupations Code § 2308.451 et seq.

Art. 18.24. Body Cavity Search During Traffic Stop

(a) In this article, "body cavity search" means an inspection that is conducted of a person's anal or vaginal cavity in any manner, but the term does not include a pat-down.

(b) Notwithstanding any other law, a peace officer may not conduct a body cavity search of a person during a traffic stop unless the officer first obtains a search warrant pursuant to this chapter authorizing the body cavity search.

Added by Acts 2015, 84th Leg., ch. 997 (H.B. 324), § 1, eff. Sept. 1, 2015.

Art. 18.24 to 18.30. Deleted by Acts 1973, 63rd Leg., p. 982, ch. 399, § 2(E), eff. Jan. 1974

CHAPTER 18A. DETECTION, INTERCEPTION, AND USE OF WIRE, ORAL, AND ELECTRONIC COMMUNICATIONS

SUBCHAPTER A. GENERAL PROVISIONS

SUBCHAPTER B. APPLICATION FOR INTERCEPTION ORDER

SUBCHAPTER C. ISSUANCE OF INTERCEPTION ORDER AND RELATED ORDERS

SUBCHAPTER D. INTERCEPTION ORDER FOR COMMUNICATION BY SPECIFIED PERSON

SUBCHAPTER E. EMERGENCY INSTALLATION AND USE OF INTERCEPTION DEVICE

SUBCHAPTER A. GENERAL PROVISIONS

Art. 18A.001. Definitions

Text of article effective Jan. 1, 2019

In this chapter:

(1) "Access," "computer," "computer network," "computer system," and "effective consent" have the meanings assigned by Section 33.01, Penal Code.

(2) "Aggrieved person" means a person who was a party to an intercepted wire, oral, or electronic communication or a person against whom the interception was directed.

(3) "Aural transfer" means a transfer containing the human voice at any point between and including the point of origin and the point of reception.

(4) "Communication common carrier" means a person engaged as a common carrier for hire in the transmission of wire or electronic communications.

(5) "Computer trespasser" means a person who accesses a protected computer without effective consent of the owner and has no reasonable expectation of privacy in a communication transmitted to, through, or from the protected computer. The term does not include a person who accesses the protected computer under an existing contractual relationship with the owner or operator of the computer.

(6) "Contents," with respect to a wire, oral, or electronic communication, includes any information concerning the substance, purport, or meaning of that communication.

(7) "Covert entry" means an entry that is made into or onto premises and that, if not authorized by a court order under this chapter, would violate the Penal Code.

(8) "Department" means the Department of Public Safety of the State of Texas.

(9) "Director" means:

(A) the public safety director of the department; or

(B) if the public safety director is absent or unable to serve, the assistant director of the department.

(10) "Electronic communication" means a transfer of any signs, signals, writing, images, sounds, data, or intelligence transmitted wholly or partly by a wire, radio, electromagnetic, photoelectronic, or photo-optical system. The term does not include:

(A) a wire or oral communication;

(B) a communication made through a tone-only paging device; or

(C) a communication from a tracking device.

(11) "Electronic communications service" means a service that provides to users of the service the ability to send or receive wire or electronic communications.

(12) "ESN reader," "pen register," and "trap and trace device" have the meanings assigned by Article 18B.001.

(13) "Intercept" means the aural or other acquisition of the contents of a wire, oral, or electronic communication through the use of an interception device.

(14) "Interception device" means an electronic, mechanical, or other device that may be used for the nonconsensual interception of wire, oral, or electronic communications. The term does not include a telephone or telegraph instrument, the equipment or a facility used for the transmission of electronic communications, or a component of the equipment or a facility used for the transmission of electronic communications if the instrument, equipment, facility, or component is:

(A) provided to a subscriber or user by a provider of a wire or electronic communications service in the ordinary course of the service provider's business and used by the subscriber or user in the ordinary course of the subscriber's or user's business;

(B) provided by a subscriber or user for connection to the facilities of a wire or electronic communications service for use in the ordinary course of the subscriber's or user's business;

(C) used by a communication common carrier in the ordinary course of the carrier's business; or

(D) used by an investigative or law enforcement officer in the ordinary course of the officer's duties.

(15) "Interception order" means an order authorizing the interception of a wire, oral, or electronic communication.

(16) "Investigative or law enforcement officer" means:

(A) an officer of this state or a political subdivision of this state who is authorized by law to investigate or make arrests for offenses described by Article 18A.101; or

(B) an attorney authorized by law to prosecute or participate in the prosecution of those offenses.

(17) "Judge of competent jurisdiction" means a judge described by Article 18A.051.

(18) "Mobile tracking device" has the meaning assigned by Article 18B.201.

(19) "Oral communication" means a communication uttered by a person exhibiting an expectation that the communication is not subject to interception under circumstances justifying that expectation. The term does not include an electronic communication.

(20) "Prosecutor" means a district attorney, criminal district attorney, or county attorney performing the duties of a district attorney, with jurisdiction in the county within an administrative judicial region described by Article 18A.053.

(21) "Protected computer" means a computer, computer network, or computer system that is:

(A) owned by a financial institution or governmental entity; or

(B) used by or for a financial institution or governmental entity, if conduct constituting an offense affects that use.

(22) "Residence" means a structure or the portion of a structure used as a person's home or fixed place of habitation to which the person indicates an intent to return after a temporary absence.

(23) "User" means a person who uses an electronic communications service and is authorized by the service provider to use the service.

(24) "Wire communication" means an aural transfer made wholly or partly through the use of facilities for the transmission of communications by the aid of wire, cable, or other similar connection between the point of origin and the point of reception, including the use of the connection in a switching station, if those facilities are provided or operated by a person authorized to provide or operate the facilities for the transmission of communications as a communication common carrier.

Added by Acts 2017, 85th Leg., ch. 1058 (H.B. 2931), § 1.01, eff. Jan. 1, 2019.

Art. 18A.002. Nonapplicability

Text of article effective Jan. 1, 2019

This chapter does not apply to conduct described as an affirmative defense under Section 16.02(c), Penal Code, except as otherwise specifically provided by that section.

Added by Acts 2017, 85th Leg., ch. 1058 (H.B. 2931), § 1.01, eff. Jan. 1, 2019.

SUBCHAPTER B. APPLICATION FOR INTERCEPTION ORDER

Art. 18A.051. Judge of Competent Jurisdiction

Text of article effective Jan. 1, 2019

(a) For purposes of this chapter, a judge of competent jurisdiction is a judge from the panel of nine active district judges with criminal jurisdiction who is appointed by the presiding judge of the court of criminal appeals under this article.

(b) The presiding judge of the court of criminal appeals, by order filed with the clerk of that court, shall appoint one district judge from each of the administrative judicial regions of this state to serve at the presiding judge's pleasure as the judge of competent jurisdiction in that administrative judicial region.

(c) The presiding judge shall fill vacancies as those vacancies occur in the same manner.

Added by Acts 2017, 85th Leg., ch. 1058 (H.B. 2931), § 1.01, eff. Jan. 1, 2019.

Art. 18A.052. Request for Filing of Interception Application

Text of article effective Jan. 1, 2019

(a) The director may, based on written affidavits, request in writing that a prosecutor apply for an interception order.

(b) The head of a local law enforcement agency or, if the head of the agency is absent or unable to serve, the acting head of the local law enforcement agency may, based on written affidavits, request in writing that a prosecutor apply for an interception order.

(c) Before making a request under Subsection (b), the head of a local law enforcement agency must submit the request and supporting affidavits to the director. The director shall make a written finding as to whether the request and supporting affidavits establish that other investigative procedures have been attempted and have failed or those procedures reason-ably appear unlikely to succeed or to be too dangerous if attempted, is feasible, is justifiable, and whether the department has the necessary resources available.

(d) A prosecutor may file the application requested under Subsection (b) only after a written positive finding by the director on all of the requirements provided by Subsection (c).

Added by Acts 2017, 85th Leg., ch. 1058 (H.B. 2931), § 1.01, eff. Jan. 1, 2019.

Art. 18A.053. Jurisdiction

Text of article effective Jan. 1, 2019

Except as provided by Article 18A.054, a judge of competent jurisdiction may act on an application for an interception order if any of the following is located in the administrative judicial region with respect to which the judge is appointed:

(1) the site of:

(A) the proposed interception; or

(B) the interception device to be installed or monitored;

(2) the communication device to be intercepted;

(3) the billing, residential, or business address of the subscriber to the electronic communications service to be intercepted;

(4) the headquarters of the law enforcement agency that makes the request for or will execute the interception order; or

(5) the headquarters of the service provider.

Added by Acts 2017, 85th Leg., ch. 1058 (H.B. 2931), § 1.01, eff. Jan. 1, 2019.

Art. 18A.054. Alternate Jurisdiction

Text of article effective Jan. 1, 2019

(a) An application for an interception order may be made to the judge of competent jurisdiction in an administrative judicial region adjacent to a region described by Article 18A.053 if:

(1) the judge of competent jurisdiction for the administrative judicial region described by Article 18A.053 is absent or unable to serve; or

(2) exigent circumstances exist.

(b) Exigent circumstances under Subsection (a)(2) do not include a denial of a previous application on the same facts and circumstances.

Added by Acts 2017, 85th Leg., ch. 1058 (H.B. 2931), § 1.01, eff. Jan. 1, 2019.

Art. 18A.055. Application for Interception Order

Text of article effective Jan. 1, 2019

(a) A prosecutor applying for an interception order must make the application in writing under oath to a judge of competent jurisdiction.

(b) An application must:

(1) identify the prosecutor making the application and state the prosecutor's authority to make the application;

(2) identify the officer requesting the application;

(3) include a complete statement of the facts and circumstances relied on by the prosecutor to justify the prosecutor's belief that an order should be issued, including:

(A) details about the particular offense that has been, is being, or is about to be committed;

(B) except as otherwise provided by this chapter, a particular description of the nature and location of the facilities from which or the place where the communication is to be intercepted;

(C) a particular description of the type of communication sought to be intercepted; and

(D) the identity of the person, if known, committing the offense and whose communications are to be intercepted;

(4) include a complete statement as to whether other investigative procedures have been attempted and have failed or why those procedures reasonably appear to be unlikely to succeed or to be too dangerous if attempted;

(5) include a statement of the period for which the interception is required to be maintained and, if the nature of the investigation indicates that the interception order should not automatically terminate when the described type of communication is first obtained, a particular description of facts establishing probable cause to believe that additional communications of the same type will occur after the described type of communication is obtained;

(6) include a statement whether a covert entry will be necessary to properly and safely install wiretapping, electronic surveillance, or eavesdropping equipment and, if a covert entry is requested, a statement as to why a covert entry is necessary and proper under the facts of the particular investigation, including a complete statement as to whether other investigative techniques have been attempted and have failed or why those techniques reasonably appear to be unlikely to succeed or to be too dangerous if attempted or are not feasible under the circumstances or exigencies of time;

(7) include a complete statement of the facts concerning all applications known to the prosecutor that have been previously made to a judge for an interception order involving any persons, facilities, or places specified in the application and of the action taken by the judge on each application;

(8) if the application is for the extension of an order, include a statement providing the results already obtained from the interception or a reasonable explanation of the failure to obtain results; and

(9) if the application is made under Article 18A.054, fully explain the circumstances justifying application under that article.

(c) In an ex parte hearing in chambers, the judge may require additional testimony or documentary evidence to support the application. The testimony or documentary evidence must be preserved as part of the application.

Added by Acts 2017, 85th Leg., ch. 1058 (H.B. 2931), § 1.01, eff. Jan. 1, 2019.

SUBCHAPTER C. ISSUANCE OF INTERCEPTION ORDER AND RELATED ORDERS

Art. 18A.101. Offenses for Which Interception Order May Be Issued

Text of article effective Jan. 1, 2019

A judge of competent jurisdiction may issue an interception order only if the prosecutor applying for the order shows probable cause to believe that the interception will provide evidence of the commission of:

(1) a felony under any of the following provisions of the Health and Safety Code:

(A) Chapter 481, other than felony possession of marihuana;

(B) Chapter 483; or

(C) Section 485.032;

(2) an offense under any of the following provisions of the Penal Code:

(A) Section 19.02;

(B) Section 19.03;

(C) Section 20.03;

(D) Section 20.04;

(E) Chapter 20A;

(F) Chapter 34, if the criminal activity giving rise to the proceeds involves the commission of an offense under Title 5, Penal Code, or an offense under federal law or the laws of another state containing elements that are substantially similar to the elements of an offense under Title 5;

(G) Section 38.11;

(H) Section 43.04;

(I) Section 43.05; or

(J) Section 43.26; or

(3) an attempt, conspiracy, or solicitation to commit an offense listed in Subdivision (1) or (2).

Added by Acts 2017, 85th Leg., ch. 1058 (H.B. 2931), § 1.01, eff. Jan. 1, 2019.

Art. 18A.102. Judicial Determinations Required for Issuance of Interception Order

Text of article effective Jan. 1, 2019

On receipt of an application under Subchapter B, the judge may issue an ex parte interception order, as requested or as modified, if the judge determines from the evidence submitted by the prosecutor that:

(1) there is probable cause to believe that a person is committing, has committed, or is about to commit a particular offense described by Article 18A.101;

(2) there is probable cause to believe that particular communications concerning that offense will be obtained through the interception;

(3) normal investigative procedures have been attempted and have failed or reasonably appear to be unlikely to succeed or to be too dangerous if attempted;

(4) there is probable cause to believe that the facilities from which or the place where the wire, oral, or electronic communications are to be intercepted is being used or is about to be used in connection with the commission of an offense or is leased to, listed in the name of, or commonly used by the person; and

(5) a covert entry is or is not necessary to properly and safely install the wiretapping, electronic surveillance, or eavesdropping equipment.

Added by Acts 2017, 85th Leg., ch. 1058 (H.B. 2931), § 1.01, eff. Jan. 1, 2019.

Art. 18A.103. Contents of Interception Order

Text of article effective Jan. 1, 2019

(a) An interception order must specify:

(1) the identity of the person, if known, whose communications are to be intercepted;

(2) except as otherwise provided by this chapter, the nature and location of the communications facilities as to which or the place where authority to intercept is granted;

(3) a particular description of the type of communication sought to be intercepted and a statement of the particular offense to which the communication relates;

(4) the identity of the officer making the request and the identity of the prosecutor;

(5) the period during which the interception is authorized, including a statement of whether the interception will automatically terminate when the described communication is first obtained; and

(6) whether a covert entry or surreptitious entry is necessary to properly and safely install wiretapping, electronic surveillance, or eavesdropping equipment.

(b) Each interception order and extension of that order must provide that the authorization to intercept be executed as soon as practicable, be conducted in a way that minimizes the interception of communications not otherwise subject to interception under this chapter, and terminate on obtaining the authorized objective or within 30 days, whichever occurs sooner.

(c) For purposes of Subsection (b), if the intercepted communication is in code or a foreign language and an expert in that code or language is not reasonably available during the period of interception, minimization may be accomplished as soon as practicable after the interception.

Added by Acts 2017, 85th Leg., ch. 1058 (H.B. 2931), § 1.01, eff. Jan. 1, 2019.

Art. 18A.104. Limitation on Covert Entry

Text of article effective Jan. 1, 2019

(a) An interception order may not authorize a covert entry for the purpose of intercepting an oral communication unless:

(1) the judge, in addition to making the determinations required under Article 18A.102, determines:

(A) that:

(i) the premises into or onto which the covert entry is authorized or the person whose communications are to be obtained has been the subject of a pen register previously authorized in connection with the same investigation;

(ii) the premises into or onto which the covert entry is authorized or the person whose communications are to be obtained has been the subject of an interception of wire or electronic communications previously authorized in connection with the same investigation; and

(iii) the procedures under Subparagraphs (i) and (ii) have failed; or

(B) that the procedures under Paragraph (A) reasonably appear to be unlikely to succeed or to be too dangerous if attempted or are not feasible under the circumstances or exigencies of time; and

(2) the interception order, in addition to the matters required to be specified under Article 18A.103(a), specifies that:

(A) the covert entry is for the purpose of intercepting oral communications of two or more persons; and

(B) there is probable cause to believe that the persons described by Paragraph (A) are committing, have committed, or are about to commit a particular offense described by Article 18A.101.

(b) An interception order may not authorize a covert entry into a residence solely for the purpose of intercepting a wire or electronic communication.

Added by Acts 2017, 85th Leg., ch. 1058 (H.B. 2931), § 1.01, eff. Jan. 1, 2019.

Art. 18A.105. Authority to Issue Certain Ancillary Orders

Text of article effective Jan. 1, 2019

An interception order may include an order to:

(1) install or use a pen register, ESN reader, trap and trace device, or mobile tracking device or similar equipment that combines the function of a pen register and trap and trace device; or

(2) disclose a stored communication, information subject to an administrative subpoena, or information subject to access under Chapter 18B.

Added by Acts 2017, 85th Leg., ch. 1058 (H.B. 2931), § 1.01, eff. Jan. 1, 2019.

Art. 18A.106. Order to Third Party to Assist With Execution of Interception Order

Text of article effective Jan. 1, 2019

(a) On request of the prosecutor applying for an interception order, the judge may issue a separate order directing a provider of a wire or electronic communications service, communication common carrier, landlord, custodian, or other person to provide to the prosecutor all information, facilities, and technical assistance necessary to accomplish the interception unobtrusively and with a minimum of interference with the services that the service provider, carrier, landlord, custodian, or other person is providing the person whose communications are to be intercepted.

(b) A provider of a wire or electronic communications service, communication common carrier, landlord, custodian, or other person that provides facilities or technical assistance under an order described by Subsection (a) is entitled to compensation, at the prevailing rates, by the prosecutor for reasonable expenses incurred in providing the facilities or assistance.

Added by Acts 2017, 85th Leg., ch. 1058 (H.B. 2931), § 1.01, eff. Jan. 1, 2019.

Art. 18A.107. Duration of Interception Order

Text of article effective Jan. 1, 2019

An interception order may not authorize the interception of a communication for a period that:

(1) is longer than is necessary to achieve the objective of the authorization; or

(2) exceeds 30 days.

Added by Acts 2017, 85th Leg., ch. 1058 (H.B. 2931), § 1.01, eff. Jan. 1, 2019.

Art. 18A.108. Extension of Interception Order

Text of article effective Jan. 1, 2019

(a) A judge who issues an interception order may grant extensions of the order.

(b) An extension of an interception order may be granted only if:

(1) an application for an extension is made in accordance with Article 18A.055; and

(2) the judge makes the findings required by Article 18A.102.

(c) The period of extension may not:

(1) be longer than the judge considers necessary to achieve the purposes for which the extension is granted; or

(2) exceed 30 days.

Added by Acts 2017, 85th Leg., ch. 1058 (H.B. 2931), § 1.01, eff. Jan. 1, 2019.

Art. 18A.109. Report on Need for Continued Interception

Text of article effective Jan. 1, 2019

(a) An interception order may require reports to the judge who issued the order that show any progress toward achieving the authorized objective and the need for continued interception.

(b) Reports under this article must be made at any interval the judge requires.

Added by Acts 2017, 85th Leg., ch. 1058 (H.B. 2931), § 1.01, eff. Jan. 1, 2019.

Art. 18A.110. Subsequent Criminal Prosecution Related to Interception Order

Text of article effective Jan. 1, 2019

A judge who issues an interception order may not hear a criminal prosecution in which:

(1) evidence derived from the interception may be used; or

(2) the order may be an issue.

Added by Acts 2017, 85th Leg., ch. 1058 (H.B. 2931), § 1.01, eff. Jan. 1, 2019.

SUBCHAPTER D. INTERCEPTION ORDER FOR COMMUNICATION BY SPECIFIED PERSON

Art. 18A.151. Requirements Regarding Interception Order for Communication by Specified Person

Text of article effective Jan. 1, 2019

The requirements of Articles 18A.055(b)(3)(B) and 18A.103(a)(2) relating to the specification of the facilities from which or the place where a communication is to be intercepted do not apply if:

(1) in the case of an application for an interception order that authorizes the interception of an oral communication:

(A) the application contains a complete statement as to why the specification is not practical and identifies the person committing or believed to be committing the offense and whose communications are to be intercepted; and

(B) a judge of competent jurisdiction finds that the specification is not practical; or

(2) in the case of an application for an interception order that authorizes the interception of a wire or electronic communication:

(A) the application identifies the person committing or believed to be committing the offense and whose communications are to be intercepted;

(B) a judge of competent jurisdiction finds that the prosecutor has made an adequate showing of probable cause to believe that the actions of the person identified in the application could have the effect of preventing interception from a specified facility; and

(C) the authority to intercept a wire or electronic communication under the interception order is limited to a period in which it is reasonable to presume that the person identified in the application will be reasonably proximate to the interception device.

Added by Acts 2017, 85th Leg., ch. 1058 (H.B. 2931), § 1.01, eff. Jan. 1, 2019.

Art. 18A.152. Implementation of Interception Order

Text of article effective Jan. 1, 2019

A person implementing an interception order that authorizes the interception of an oral communication and that, as permitted by this subchapter, does not specify the facility from which or the place where a communication is to be intercepted may begin interception only after the person ascertains the place where the communication is to be intercepted.

Added by Acts 2017, 85th Leg., ch. 1058 (H.B. 2931), § 1.01, eff. Jan. 1, 2019.

Art. 18A.153. Motion to Modify or Quash Interception Order

Text of article effective Jan. 1, 2019

(a) provider of a wire or electronic communications service that receives an interception order that authorizes the interception of a wire or electronic communication and that, as permitted by this subchapter, does not specify the facility from which or the place where a communication is to be intercepted may move the court to modify or quash the order on the ground that the service provider's assistance with respect to the interception cannot be performed in a timely or reasonable manner.

(b) On notice to the state, the court shall decide the motion expeditiously.

Added by Acts 2017, 85th Leg., ch. 1058 (H.B. 2931), § 1.01, eff. Jan. 1, 2019.

SUBCHAPTER E. EMERGENCY INSTALLATION AND USE OF INTERCEPTION DEVICE

Art. 18A.201. Definitions

Text of article effective Jan. 1, 2019

In this subchapter:

(1) "Immediate life-threatening situation" means a hostage, barricade, or other emergency situation in which a person unlawfully and directly:

(A) threatens another with death; or

(B) exposes another to a substantial risk of serious bodily injury.

(2) "Member of a law enforcement unit specially trained to respond to and deal with life-threatening situations" means a peace officer who, as evidenced by the submission of appropriate documentation to the Texas Commission on Law Enforcement:

(A) receives each year a minimum of 40 hours of training in hostage and barricade suspect situations; or

(B) has received a minimum of 24 hours of training on kidnapping investigations and is:

(i) the sheriff of a county with a population of 3.3 million or more or the sheriff's designee; or

(ii) the police chief of a police department in a municipality with a population of 500,000 or more or the chief's designee.

Added by Acts 2017, 85th Leg., ch. 1058 (H.B. 2931), § 1.01, eff. Jan. 1, 2019.

Art. 18A.202. Possession and Use of Interception Device in Emergency Situation

Text of article effective Jan. 1, 2019

(a) The prosecutor in a county in which an interception device is to be installed or used shall designate in writing each peace officer in the county, other than a commissioned officer of the department, who is:

(1) a member of a law enforcement unit specially trained to respond to and deal with life-threatening situations; and

(2) authorized to possess an interception device and responsible for the installation, operation, and monitoring of the device in an immediate life-threatening situation.

(b) A peace officer designated under Subsection (a) or Article 18A.301(c) may possess, install, operate, or monitor an interception device if the officer:

(1) reasonably believes an immediate life-threatening situation exists that:

(A) is within the territorial jurisdiction of the officer or another officer the officer is assisting; and

(B) requires interception of communications before an interception order can, with due diligence, be obtained under this subchapter;

(2) reasonably believes there are sufficient grounds under this subchapter on which to obtain an interception order; and

(3) before beginning the interception, obtains oral or written consent to the interception from:

(A) a judge of competent jurisdiction;

(B) a district judge for the county in which the device will be installed or used; or

(C) a judge or justice of a court of appeals or of a higher court.

(c) If a peace officer installs or uses an interception device under Subsection (b), the officer shall:

(1) promptly report the installation or use to the prosecutor in the county in which the device is installed or used; and

(2) within 48 hours after the installation is complete or the interception begins, whichever occurs first, obtain a written interception order from a judge of competent jurisdiction.

(d) A peace officer may certify to a communication common carrier that the officer is acting lawfully under this subchapter.

Added by Acts 2017, 85th Leg., ch. 1058 (H.B. 2931), § 1.01, eff. Jan. 1, 2019.

Art. 18A.203. Consent for Emergency Interception

Text of article effective Jan. 1, 2019

(a) An official described by Article 18A.202(b)(3) may give oral or written consent to the interception of communications under this subchapter to provide evidence of the commission of a felony, or of a threat, attempt, or conspiracy to commit a felony, in an immediate life-threatening situation.

(b) Oral or written consent given under this subchapter expires on the earlier of:

(1) 48 hours after the grant of consent; or

(2) the conclusion of the emergency justifying the interception.

Added by Acts 2017, 85th Leg., ch. 1058 (H.B. 2931), § 1.01, eff. Jan. 1, 2019.

Art. 18A.204. Written Order Authorizing Interception

Text of article effective Jan. 1, 2019

(a) A judge of competent jurisdiction under Article 18A.051 or under Article 18A.202(b) may issue a written interception order under this subchapter during the 48–hour period prescribed by Article 18A.202(c)(2).

(b) A written interception order under this subchapter expires on the earlier of:

(1) the 30th day after the date of execution of the order; or

(2) the conclusion of the emergency that initially justified the interception.

(c) If an interception order is denied or is not issued within the 48–hour period, the officer shall terminate use of and remove the interception device promptly on the earlier of:

(1) the denial;

(2) the end of the emergency that initially justified the interception; or

(3) the expiration of 48 hours.

Added by Acts 2017, 85th Leg., ch. 1058 (H.B. 2931), § 1.01, eff. Jan. 1, 2019.

Art. 18A.205. Certain Evidence Not Admissible

Text of article effective Jan. 1, 2019

The state may not use as evidence in a criminal proceeding information gained through the use of an interception device installed under this subchapter if authorization for the device is not sought or is sought but not obtained.

Added by Acts 2017, 85th Leg., ch. 1058 (H.B. 2931), § 1.01, eff. Jan. 1, 2019.

SUBCHAPTER F. DETECTION OF CELLULAR TELEPHONE OR OTHER WIRELESS COMMUNICATIONS DEVICE IN CORRECTIONAL OR DETENTION FACILITY

Art. 18A.251. Definition

Text of article effective Jan. 1, 2019

In this subchapter, "correctional facility" means:

(1) a place described by Section 1.07(a)(14), Penal Code; or

(2) a "secure correctional facility" or "secure detention facility" as defined by Section 51.02, Family Code.

Added by Acts 2017, 85th Leg., ch. 1058 (H.B. 2931), § 1.01, eff. Jan. 1, 2019.

Art. 18A.252. Use of Interception Device by Inspector General

Text of article effective Jan. 1, 2019

(a) Notwithstanding any other provision of this chapter or Chapter 18B, the office of inspector general of the Texas Department of Criminal Justice may:

(1) without a warrant, use an interception device to detect the presence or use of a cellular telephone or other wireless communications device in a correctional facility;

(2) without a warrant, intercept, monitor, detect, or, as authorized by applicable federal laws and regulations, prevent the transmission of a communication through a cellular telephone or other wireless communications device in a correctional facility; and

(3) use, to the extent authorized by law, any information obtained under Subdivision (2), including the contents of an intercepted communication, in a criminal or civil proceeding before a court or other governmental agency or entity.

(b) When using an interception device under Subsection (a), the office of inspector general shall minimize the impact of the device on a communication that is not reasonably related to the detection of the presence or use of a cellular telephone or other wireless communications device in a correctional facility.

Added by Acts 2017, 85th Leg., ch. 1058 (H.B. 2931), § 1.01, eff. Jan. 1, 2019.

Art. 18A.253. Reporting Use of Interception Device

Text of article effective Jan. 1, 2019

Not later than the 30th day after the date on which the office of inspector general uses an interception device under Article 18A.252(a), the inspector general shall report the use of the device to:

(1) a prosecutor with jurisdiction in the county in which the device was used; or

(2) the special prosecution unit established under Subchapter E, Chapter 41, Government Code, if that

unit has jurisdiction in the county in which the device was used.

Added by Acts 2017, 85th Leg., ch. 1058 (H.B. 2931), § 1.01, eff. Jan. 1, 2019.

Art. 18A.254. No Expectation of Privacy

Text of article effective Jan. 1, 2019

(a) A person confined in a correctional facility does not have an expectation of privacy with respect to the possession or use of a cellular telephone or other wireless communications device located on the premises of the facility.

(b) A person confined in a correctional facility, and any person with whom the confined person communicates through the use of a cellular telephone or other wireless communications device, does not have an expectation of privacy with respect to the contents of a communication transmitted by the telephone or device.

Added by Acts 2017, 85th Leg., ch. 1058 (H.B. 2931), § 1.01, eff. Jan. 1, 2019.

SUBCHAPTER G. AGENCIES AND PERSONNEL AUTHORIZED TO POSSESS AND USE INTERCEPTION DEVICES

Art. 18A.301. Department of Public Safety Authorized to Possess and Use Interception Device

Text of article effective Jan. 1, 2019

(a) Except as otherwise provided by this subchapter and Subchapters E and F, only the department is authorized by this chapter to own, possess, install, operate, or monitor an interception device.

(b) An investigative or law enforcement officer or other person may assist the department in the operation and monitoring of an interception of wire, oral, or electronic communications if the officer or other person:

(1) is designated by the director for that purpose; and

(2) acts in the presence and under the direction of a commissioned officer of the department.

(c) The director shall designate in writing the commissioned officers of the department who are responsible for the possession, installation, operation, and monitoring of interception devices for the department.

Added by Acts 2017, 85th Leg., ch. 1058 (H.B. 2931), § 1.01, eff. Jan. 1, 2019.

Art. 18A.302. Texas Department of Criminal Justice Authorized to Possess and Use Interception Device

Text of article effective Jan. 1, 2019

(a) The Texas Department of Criminal Justice may own an interception device for a use or purpose authorized by Section 500.008, Government Code.

(b) The inspector general of the Texas Department of Criminal Justice, a commissioned officer of that office, or a person acting in the presence and under the direction of the commissioned officer may possess, install, operate, or monitor the interception device as provided by Section 500.008, Government Code.

Added by Acts 2017, 85th Leg., ch. 1058 (H.B. 2931), § 1.01, eff. Jan. 1, 2019.

Art. 18A.303. Texas Juvenile Justice Department Authorized to Possess and Use Interception Device

Text of article effective Jan. 1, 2019

(a) The Texas Juvenile Justice Department may own an interception device for a use or purpose authorized by Section 242.103, Human Resources Code.

(b) The inspector general of the Texas Juvenile Justice Department, a commissioned officer of that office, or a person acting in the presence and under the direction of the commissioned officer may possess, install, operate, or monitor the interception device as provided by Section 242.103, Human Resources Code.

Added by Acts 2017, 85th Leg., ch. 1058 (H.B. 2931), § 1.01, eff. Jan. 1, 2019.

SUBCHAPTER H. DISCLOSURE AND USE OF INTERCEPTED COMMUNICATIONS

Art. 18A.351. Disclosure or Use of Intercepted Communications

Text of article effective Jan. 1, 2019

An investigative or law enforcement officer who, by means authorized by this chapter, obtains knowledge of the contents of a wire, oral, or electronic communication or evidence derived from the communication may:

(1) use the contents or evidence to the extent the use is appropriate to the proper performance of the officer's official duties; or

(2) disclose the contents or evidence to another investigative or law enforcement officer, including a law enforcement officer or agent of the United States or of another state, to the extent that the disclosure is appropriate to the proper performance of the official duties of the officer making or receiving the disclosure.

Added by Acts 2017, 85th Leg., ch. 1058 (H.B. 2931), § 1.01, eff. Jan. 1, 2019.

Art. 18A.352. Disclosure Under Oath

Text of article effective Jan. 1, 2019

A person who receives, by means authorized by this chapter, information concerning a wire, oral, or electronic communication or evidence derived from a communication intercepted in accordance with this chapter may disclose the contents of that communication or evidence while giving testimony under oath in any proceeding held under the authority of the United States, this state, or a political subdivision of this state.

Added by Acts 2017, 85th Leg., ch. 1058 (H.B. 2931), § 1.01, eff. Jan. 1, 2019.

Art. 18A.353. Privileged Communications

Text of article effective Jan. 1, 2019

(a) An otherwise privileged wire, oral, or electronic communication intercepted in accordance with, or in violation of, this chapter does not lose its privileged character.

(b) Evidence derived from a privileged communication described by Subsection (a) against a party to that communication is privileged.

Added by Acts 2017, 85th Leg., ch. 1058 (H.B. 2931), § 1.01, eff. Jan. 1, 2019.

Art. 18A.354. Disclosure or Use of Incidentally Intercepted Communications

Text of article effective Jan. 1, 2019

(a) This article applies only to the contents of and evidence derived from wire, oral, or electronic communications that:

(1) are intercepted by an investigative or law enforcement officer while engaged in intercepting wire, oral, or electronic communications in a manner authorized by this chapter; and

(2) relate to offenses other than those specified by the interception order.

(b) The contents of and evidence derived from a communication described by Subsection (a) may be disclosed or used as provided by Article 18A.351.

(c) The contents of and evidence derived from a communication described by Subsection (a) may be used under Article 18A.352 when authorized by a judge of competent jurisdiction if the judge finds, on subsequent application, that the contents were otherwise intercepted in accordance with this chapter.

(d) An application under Subsection (c) must be made as soon as practicable.

Added by Acts 2017, 85th Leg., ch. 1058 (H.B. 2931), § 1.01, eff. Jan. 1, 2019.

Art. 18A.355. Notice and Disclosure of Interception Application, Interception Order, and Intercepted Communications

Text of article effective Jan. 1, 2019

(a) Within a reasonable period but not later than the 90th day after the date an application for an interception order is denied or after the date an interception order or the last extension, if any, expires, the judge who granted or denied the application shall cause to be served on each person named in the order or application and any other party to an intercepted communication, if any, an inventory that must include notice of:

(1) the application or the issuance of the order;

(2) the date of denial of the application, or the date of the issuance of the order and the authorized interception period; and

(3) whether during any authorized interception period wire, oral, or electronic communications were intercepted.

(b) The judge may, on motion, make available for inspection to a person or the person's counsel any portion of an intercepted communication, application, or order that the judge determines to disclose to that person in the interest of justice.

(c) On an ex parte showing of good cause to the judge, the serving of the inventory required under Subsection (a) may be postponed.

(d) Evidence derived from an order under this chapter may not be disclosed in a trial until after the inventory has been served.

Added by Acts 2017, 85th Leg., ch. 1058 (H.B. 2931), § 1.01, eff. Jan. 1, 2019.

Art. 18A.356. Notice of Interception Required

Text of article effective Jan. 1, 2019

(a) The contents of an intercepted wire, oral, or electronic communication or evidence derived from the communication may not be received in evidence or otherwise disclosed in a trial, hearing, or other proceeding in a federal or state court unless each party, not later than the 10th day before the date of the trial, hearing, or other proceeding, has been provided with a copy of the interception order and application under which the interception was authorized.

(b) The judge may waive the 10–day period described by Subsection (a) on a finding that:

(1) it is not possible to provide the party with the information 10 days before the trial, hearing, or proceeding; and

(2) the party will not be prejudiced by the delay in receiving the information.

Added by Acts 2017, 85th Leg., ch. 1058 (H.B. 2931), § 1.01, eff. Jan. 1, 2019.

Art. 18A.357. Communications Received in Evidence

Text of article effective Jan. 1, 2019

(a) The contents of an intercepted communication and evidence derived from the communication may be received in evidence in any trial, hearing, or other proceeding in or before any court, grand jury, department, officer, agency, regulatory body, legislative committee, or other authority of the United States, this state, or a political subdivision of this state unless:

(1) the communication was intercepted in violation of this chapter, Section 16.02, Penal Code, or federal law; or

(2) the disclosure of the contents of the communication or evidence derived from the communication would violate a law described by Subdivision (1).

(b) The contents of an intercepted communication and evidence derived from the communication may be received in a civil trial, hearing, or other proceeding only if the civil trial, hearing, or other proceeding arises out of a violation of a penal law.

(c) This article does not prohibit the use or admissibility of the contents of an intercepted communication or evidence derived from the communication if the communication was intercepted in a jurisdiction outside this state in compliance with the law of that jurisdiction.

Added by Acts 2017, 85th Leg., ch. 1058 (H.B. 2931), § 1.01, eff. Jan. 1, 2019.

Art. 18A.358. Suppression of Contents of Intercepted Communications

Text of article effective Jan. 1, 2019

(a) An aggrieved person charged with an offense in a trial, hearing, or proceeding in or before a court, department, officer, agency, regulatory body, or other authority of the United States, this state, or a political subdivision of this state may move to suppress the contents of an intercepted wire, oral, or electronic communication or evidence derived from the communication on the ground that:

(1) the communication was unlawfully intercepted;

(2) the interception order is insufficient on its face; or

(3) the interception was not made in conformity with the interception order.

(b) A person identified by a party to an intercepted wire, oral, or electronic communication during the course of that communication may move to suppress the contents of the communication on:

(1) a ground provided under Subsection (a); or

(2) the ground that the harm to the person resulting from the person's identification in court exceeds the value to the prosecution of the disclosure of the contents.

(c) The motion to suppress must be made before the trial, hearing, or proceeding unless:

(1) there was not an opportunity to make the motion; or

(2) the aggrieved person was not aware of the grounds of the motion.

(d) The hearing on the motion to suppress shall be held in camera on the written request of the aggrieved person.

(e) If the motion to suppress is granted, the contents of the intercepted wire, oral, or electronic communication and evidence derived from the communication shall be treated as having been obtained in violation of this chapter.

(f) The judge, on the filing of the motion to suppress by the aggrieved person, shall make available to the aggrieved person or the person's counsel for inspection any portion of the intercepted communication or evidence derived from the communication that the judge determines to make available in the interest of justice.

(g) A judge of this state, on hearing a pretrial motion regarding conversations intercepted by wire in accordance with this chapter, or who otherwise becomes informed that there exists on such an intercepted wire, oral, or electronic communication identification of a specific individual who is not a suspect or a party to the subject of interception shall:

(1) give notice and an opportunity to be heard on the matter of suppression of references to that individual if identification is sufficient to give notice; or

(2) suppress references to that individual if identification is:

(A) sufficient to potentially cause embarrassment or harm that outweighs the probative value, if any, of the mention of that individual; and

(B) insufficient to require the notice under Subdivision (1).

Added by Acts 2017, 85th Leg., ch. 1058 (H.B. 2931), § 1.01, eff. Jan. 1, 2019.

SUBCHAPTER I.   USE AND DISPOSITION OF APPLICATIONS AND ORDERS

Art. 18A.401.   Sealing of Application or Order

Text of article effective Jan. 1, 2019

The judge shall seal each application made and order issued under this chapter.

Added by Acts 2017, 85th Leg., ch. 1058 (H.B. 2931), § 1.01, eff. Jan. 1, 2019.

Art. 18A.402.   Custody of Applications and Orders

Text of article effective Jan. 1, 2019

Custody of applications and orders issued under this chapter shall be wherever the judge directs.

Added by Acts 2017, 85th Leg., ch. 1058 (H.B. 2931), § 1.01, eff. Jan. 1, 2019.

Art. 18A.403.   Disclosure of Application or Order

Text of article effective Jan. 1, 2019

An application made or order issued under this chapter may be disclosed only on a showing of good cause before a judge of competent jurisdiction.

Added by Acts 2017, 85th Leg., ch. 1058 (H.B. 2931), § 1.01, eff. Jan. 1, 2019.

Art. 18A.404.   Destruction of Application or Order

Text of article effective Jan. 1, 2019

An application made or order issued under this chapter may be destroyed only on or after the 10th anniversary of the date the application or order was sealed and only if the judge of competent jurisdiction for the administrative judicial region in which the application was made or the order was issued orders the destruction.

Added by Acts 2017, 85th Leg., ch. 1058 (H.B. 2931), § 1.01, eff. Jan. 1, 2019.

SUBCHAPTER J.   CREATION, USE, AND DISPOSITION OF RECORDINGS

Art. 18A.451.   Creation of Recordings

Text of article effective Jan. 1, 2019

The contents of a wire, oral, or electronic communication intercepted by means authorized by this chapter shall be recorded on tape, wire, or other comparable device in a way that protects the recording from editing or other alterations.

Added by Acts 2017, 85th Leg., ch. 1058 (H.B. 2931), § 1.01, eff. Jan. 1, 2019.

Art. 18A.452.   Duplication of Recordings

Text of article effective Jan. 1, 2019

Recordings under Article 18A.451 may be duplicated for use or disclosure under Article 18A.351 for investigations.

Added by Acts 2017, 85th Leg., ch. 1058 (H.B. 2931), § 1.01, eff. Jan. 1, 2019.

Art. 18A.453.   Sealing and Custody of Recordings

Text of article effective Jan. 1, 2019

(a) Immediately on the expiration of the period of an interception order and all extensions, if any, the recordings under Article 18A.451 shall be:

(1) made available to the judge issuing the order; and

(2) sealed under the judge's directions.

(b) Custody of the recordings shall be wherever the judge orders.

Added by Acts 2017, 85th Leg., ch. 1058 (H.B. 2931), § 1.01, eff. Jan. 1, 2019.

Art. 18A.454. Destruction of Recordings

Text of article effective Jan. 1, 2019

A recording under Article 18A.451 may be destroyed only on or after the 10th anniversary of the date of expiration of the interception order and the last extension, if any, and only if the judge of competent jurisdiction for the administrative judicial region in which the interception was authorized orders the destruction.

Added by Acts 2017, 85th Leg., ch. 1058 (H.B. 2931), § 1.01, eff. Jan. 1, 2019.

Art. 18A.455. Prerequisite for Use or Disclosure of Recording in Certain Proceedings

Text of article effective Jan. 1, 2019

The presence of the seal required by Article 18A.453(a) or a satisfactory explanation of the seal's absence is a prerequisite for the use or disclosure of the contents of a wire, oral, or electronic communication or evidence derived from the communication under Article 18A.352.

Added by Acts 2017, 85th Leg., ch. 1058 (H.B. 2931), § 1.01, eff. Jan. 1, 2019.

SUBCHAPTER K. VIOLATION; SANCTIONS

Art. 18A.501. Contempt

Text of article effective Jan. 1, 2019

A violation of Subchapter I or J may be punished as contempt of court.

Added by Acts 2017, 85th Leg., ch. 1058 (H.B. 2931), § 1.01, eff. Jan. 1, 2019.

Art. 18A.502. Recovery of Civil Damages by Aggrieved Person

Text of article effective Jan. 1, 2019

A person whose wire, oral, or electronic communication is intercepted, disclosed, or used in violation of this chapter or Chapter 16, Penal Code:

(1) has a civil cause of action against any person who intercepts, discloses, or uses or solicits another person to intercept, disclose, or use the communication; and

(2) is entitled to recover from the person:

(A) actual damages but not less than liquidated damages computed at a rate of $100 for each day the violation occurs or $1,000, whichever is higher;

(B) punitive damages; and

(C) reasonable attorney's fees and other litigation costs reasonably incurred.

Added by Acts 2017, 85th Leg., ch. 1058 (H.B. 2931), § 1.01, eff. Jan. 1, 2019.

Art. 18A.503. Action Brought by Federal or State Government; Injunction; Penalties

Text of article effective Jan. 1, 2019

(a) A person is subject to suit by the federal or state government in a court of competent jurisdiction for appropriate injunctive relief if the person engages in conduct that:

(1) constitutes an offense under Section 16.05, Penal Code, but is not for a tortious or illegal purpose or for the purpose of direct or indirect commercial advantage or private commercial gain; and

(2) involves a radio communication that is:

(A) transmitted on frequencies allocated under Subpart D of Part 74 of the rules of the Federal Communications Commission; and

(B) not scrambled or encrypted.

(b) The attorney general or the county or district attorney of the county in which the conduct described by Subsection (a) is occurring may file suit under that subsection on behalf of the state.

(c) A defendant is liable for a civil penalty of $500 if it is shown at the trial of the civil suit brought under Subsection (a) that the defendant has been:

(1) convicted of an offense under Section 16.05, Penal Code; or

(2) found liable in a civil action brought under Article 18A.502.

(d) Each violation of an injunction ordered under Subsection (a) is punishable by a fine of $500.

Added by Acts 2017, 85th Leg., ch. 1058 (H.B. 2931), § 1.01, eff. Jan. 1, 2019.

Art. 18A.504. Good Faith Defense Available

Text of article effective Jan. 1, 2019

A good faith reliance on a court order or legislative authorization constitutes a complete defense to an action brought under Article 18A.502 or 18A.503.

Added by Acts 2017, 85th Leg., ch. 1058 (H.B. 2931), § 1.01, eff. Jan. 1, 2019.

Art. 18A.505.　No Cause of Action

Text of article effective Jan. 1, 2019

A computer trespasser or a user, aggrieved person, subscriber, or customer of a communication common carrier or provider of an electronic communications service does not have a cause of action against the carrier or service provider, the officers, employees, or agents of the carrier or service provider, or other specified persons for providing information, facilities, or assistance as required by a good faith reliance on:

(1) legislative authority; or

(2) a court order, warrant, subpoena, or certification under this chapter.

Added by Acts 2017, 85th Leg., ch. 1058 (H.B. 2931), § 1.01, eff. Jan. 1, 2019.

SUBCHAPTER L.　REPORTS

Art. 18A.551.　Report of Intercepted Communications by Judge

Text of article effective Jan. 1, 2019

(a) Within 30 days after the date an interception order or the last extension, if any, expires or after the denial of an interception order, the issuing or denying judge shall report to the Administrative Office of the United States Courts:

(1) the fact that an order or extension was applied for;

(2) the kind of order or extension applied for;

(3) the fact that the order or extension was granted as applied for, was modified, or was denied;

(4) the period of interceptions authorized by the order and the number and duration of any extensions of the order;

(5) the offense specified in the order or application or extension;

(6) the identity of the requesting officer and the prosecutor; and

(7) the nature of the facilities from which or the place where communications were to be intercepted.

(b) A judge required to file a report under this article shall forward a copy of the report to the director.

Added by Acts 2017, 85th Leg., ch. 1058 (H.B. 2931), § 1.01, eff. Jan. 1, 2019.

Art. 18A.552.　Report of Intercepted Communications by Prosecutor

Text of article effective Jan. 1, 2019

(a) In January of each year each prosecutor shall report to the Administrative Office of the United States Courts the following information for the preceding calendar year:

(1) the information required by Article 18A.551(a) with respect to each application for an interception order or extension made;

(2) a general description of the interceptions made under each order or extension, including:

(A) the approximate nature and frequency of incriminating communications intercepted;

(B) the approximate nature and frequency of other communications intercepted;

(C) the approximate number of persons whose communications were intercepted; and

(D) the approximate nature, amount, and cost of the personnel and other resources used in the interceptions;

(3) the number of arrests resulting from interceptions made under each order or extension and the offenses for which the arrests were made;

(4) the number of trials resulting from interceptions;

(5) the number of motions to suppress made with respect to interceptions and the number granted or denied;

(6) the number of convictions resulting from interceptions, the offenses for which the convictions were obtained, and a general assessment of the importance of the interceptions; and

(7) the information required by Subdivisions (2) through (6) with respect to orders or extensions obtained.

(b) A prosecutor required to file a report under this article shall forward a copy of the report to the director.

Added by Acts 2017, 85th Leg., ch. 1058 (H.B. 2931), § 1.01, eff. Jan. 1, 2019.

Art. 18A.553.　Report of Intercepted Communications by Department of Public Safety

Text of article effective Jan. 1, 2019

(a) On or before March 1 of each year, the director shall submit a report of all intercepts conducted under this chapter and terminated during the preceding calendar year to:

(1) the governor;

(2) the lieutenant governor;

(3) the speaker of the house of representatives;

(4) the chair of the senate jurisprudence committee; and

(5) the chair of the house of representatives criminal jurisprudence committee.

(b) The report must include:

(1) the reports of judges and prosecuting attorneys forwarded to the director as required by Articles 18A.551(b) and 18A.552(b);

(2) the number of department personnel authorized to possess, install, or operate an interception device;

(3) the number of department and other law enforcement personnel who participated or engaged in the seizure of intercepts under this chapter during the preceding calendar year; and

(4) the total cost to the department of all activities and procedures relating to the seizure of intercepts during the preceding calendar year, including costs of equipment, personnel, and expenses incurred as compensation for use of facilities or technical assistance provided to the department.

Added by Acts 2017, 85th Leg., ch. 1058 (H.B. 2931), § 1.01, eff. Jan. 1, 2019.

CHAPTER 18B. INSTALLATION AND USE OF TRACKING EQUIPMENT; ACCESS TO COMMUNICATIONS

SUBCHAPTER A. GENERAL PROVISIONS

Art. 18B.001. Definitions

Text of article effective Jan. 1, 2019

In this chapter:

(1) "Authorized peace officer" means:

(A) a sheriff or deputy sheriff;

(B) a constable or deputy constable;

(C) a marshal or police officer of a municipality;

(D) a ranger or officer commissioned by the Public Safety Commission or the director of the department;

(E) an investigator of a prosecutor's office;

(F) a law enforcement agent of the Texas Alcoholic Beverage Commission;

(G) a law enforcement officer commissioned by the Parks and Wildlife Commission;

(H) an enforcement officer appointed by the inspector general of the Texas Department of Criminal Justice under Section 493.019, Government Code;

(I) an investigator commissioned by the attorney general under Section 402.009, Government Code; or

(J) a member of an arson investigating unit commissioned by a municipality, a county, or the state.

(2) "Communication common carrier," "electronic communication," "electronic communications service," "user," and "wire communication" have the meanings assigned by Article 18A.001.

(3) "Department" means the Department of Public Safety of the State of Texas.

(4) "Designated law enforcement office or agency" means:

(A) the sheriff's department of a county with a population of 3.3 million or more;

(B) a police department in a municipality with a population of 500,000 or more; or

(C) the office of inspector general of the Texas Department of Criminal Justice.

(5) "Domestic entity" has the meaning assigned by Section 1.002, Business Organizations Code.

(6) "Electronic communications system" means:

(A) a wire, radio, electromagnetic, photo-optical, or photoelectronic facility for the transmission of wire or electronic communications; and

(B) any computer facility or related electronic equipment for the electronic storage of wire or electronic communications.

(7) "Electronic customer data" means data or records that:

(A) are in the possession, care, custody, or control of a provider of an electronic communications service or provider of a remote computing service; and

(B) contain:

(i) information revealing the identity of customers of the applicable service;

(ii) information about a customer's use of the applicable service;

(iii) information that identifies the recipient or destination of a wire or electronic communication sent to or by a customer;

(iv) the content of a wire or electronic communication sent to or by a customer; and

(v) any data stored with the applicable service provider by or on behalf of a customer.

(8) "Electronic storage" means storage of electronic customer data in a computer, computer network, or computer system, regardless of whether the data is subject to recall, further manipulation, deletion, or transmission. The term includes storage of a wire or electronic communication by an electronic communications service or a remote computing service.

(9) "ESN reader" means a device that, without intercepting the contents of a communication, records the electronic serial number from the data track of a wireless telephone, cellular telephone, or similar com-

munication device that transmits its operational status to a base site.

(10) "Pen register" means a device or process that records or decodes dialing, routing, addressing, or signaling information transmitted by an instrument or facility from which a wire or electronic communication is transmitted, if the information does not include the contents of the communication. The term does not include a device used by a provider or customer of a wire or electronic communications service in the ordinary course of the service provider's or customer's business for purposes of:

(A) billing or recording incident to billing for communications services; or

(B) cost accounting, security control, or other ordinary business purposes.

(11) "Prosecutor" means a district attorney, criminal district attorney, or county attorney performing the duties of a district attorney.

(12) "Remote computing service" means the provision of computer storage or processing services to the public by means of an electronic communications system.

(13) "Trap and trace device" means a device or process that records an incoming electronic or other impulse that identifies the originating number or other dialing, routing, addressing, or signaling information reasonably likely to identify the source of a wire or electronic communication, if the information does not include the contents of the communication. The term does not include a device or telecommunications network used in providing:

(A) a caller identification service authorized by the Public Utility Commission of Texas under Subchapter E, Chapter 55, Utilities Code;

(B) the services referenced by Section 55.102(b), Utilities Code; or

(C) a caller identification service provided by a commercial mobile radio service provider licensed by the Federal Communications Commission.

Added by Acts 2017, 85th Leg., ch. 1058 (H.B. 2931), § 1.02, eff. Jan. 1, 2019.

SUBCHAPTER B. APPLICATION FOR ORDER AUTHORIZING INSTALLATION AND USE OF EQUIPMENT

Art. 18B.051. Requirements Regarding Request for and Filing of Application

Text of article effective Jan. 1, 2019

(a) A prosecutor with jurisdiction in a county within a judicial district described by Article 18B.052 may file with a district judge in the judicial district an application for the installation and use of a pen register, ESN reader, trap and trace device, or similar equipment that combines the function of a pen register and a trap and trace device.

(b) A prosecutor may file an application under this subchapter or under federal law on:

(1) the prosecutor's own motion; or

(2) the request of an authorized peace officer, regardless of whether the peace officer is commissioned by the department.

(c) A prosecutor must make an application personally and may not make the application through an assistant or other person acting on the prosecutor's behalf if the prosecutor:

(1) files an application on the prosecutor's own motion; or

(2) files an application for the installation and use of a pen register, ESN reader, or similar equipment on the request of an authorized peace officer not commissioned by the department, other than an authorized peace officer employed by a designated law enforcement office or agency.

(d) A prosecutor may make an application through an assistant or other person acting on the prosecutor's behalf if the prosecutor files an application for the installation and use of:

(1) a pen register, ESN reader, or similar equipment on the request of:

(A) an authorized peace officer who is commissioned by the department; or

(B) an authorized peace officer of a designated law enforcement office or agency; or

(2) a trap and trace device or similar equipment on the request of an authorized peace officer, regardless of whether the peace officer is commissioned by the department.

Added by Acts 2017, 85th Leg., ch. 1058 (H.B. 2931), § 1.02, eff. Jan. 1, 2019.

Art. 18B.052. Jurisdiction

Text of article effective Jan. 1, 2019

An application under this subchapter must be filed in a judicial district in which is located:

(1) the site of the proposed installation or use of the device or equipment;

(2) the site of the communication device on which the device or equipment is proposed to be installed or used;

(3) the billing, residential, or business address of the subscriber to the electronic communications service on which the device or equipment is proposed to be installed or used;

(4) the headquarters of:

(A) the office of the prosecutor filing an application under this subchapter; or

(B) a law enforcement agency that requests the prosecutor to file an application under this subchapter or that proposes to execute an order authorizing installation and use of the device or equipment; or

(5) the headquarters of a service provider ordered to install the device or equipment.

Added by Acts 2017, 85th Leg., ch. 1058 (H.B. 2931), § 1.02, eff. Jan. 1, 2019.

Art. 18B.053.   Application Requirements

Text of article effective Jan. 1, 2019

An application under this subchapter must:

(1) be made in writing under oath;

(2) include the name of the subscriber and the telephone number and location of the communication device on which the pen register, ESN reader, trap and trace device, or similar equipment will be used, to the extent that information is known or is reasonably ascertainable; and

(3) state that the installation and use of the device or equipment will likely produce information that is material to an ongoing criminal investigation.

Added by Acts 2017, 85th Leg., ch. 1058 (H.B. 2931), § 1.02, eff. Jan. 1, 2019.

SUBCHAPTER C.   ORDER AUTHORIZING
INSTALLATION AND USE OF
EQUIPMENT

Art. 18B.101.   Order Authorizing Installation and Use of Pen Register, ESN Reader, or Similar Equipment

Text of article effective Jan. 1, 2019

(a) On presentation of an application under Subchapter B, a judge may order the installation and use of a pen register, ESN reader, or similar equipment by an authorized peace officer commissioned by the department or an authorized peace officer of a designated law enforcement office or agency.

(b) On request of the applicant, the judge shall direct in the order that a communication common carrier or a provider of an electronic communications service provide all information, facilities, and technical assistance necessary to facilitate the installation and use of the device or equipment by the department or designated law enforcement office or agency unobtrusively and with a minimum of interference to the services provided by the carrier or service provider.

Added by Acts 2017, 85th Leg., ch. 1058 (H.B. 2931), § 1.02, eff. Jan. 1, 2019.

Art. 18B.102.   Order Authorizing Installation and Use of Trap and Trace Device or Similar Equipment

Text of article effective Jan. 1, 2019

(a) On presentation of an application under Subchapter B, a judge may order the installation and use of a trap and trace device or similar equipment on the appropriate line by a communication common carrier or other person.

(b) The judge may direct the communication common carrier or other person, including any landlord or other custodian of equipment, to provide all information, facilities, and technical assistance necessary to install or use the device or equipment unobtrusively and with a minimum of interference to the services provided by the communication common carrier, landlord, custodian, or other person.

(c) Unless otherwise ordered by the court, the results of the device or equipment shall be provided to the applicant, as designated by the court, at reasonable intervals during regular business hours, for the duration of the order.

Added by Acts 2017, 85th Leg., ch. 1058 (H.B. 2931), § 1.02, eff. Jan. 1, 2019.

Art. 18B.103.   Compensation for Carrier or Service Provider

Text of article effective Jan. 1, 2019

(a) A communication common carrier or a provider of an electronic communications service that provides facilities and assistance to the department or a designated law enforcement office or agency under Article 18B.101(b) is entitled to compensation at the prevailing rates for the facilities and assistance.

(b) A communication common carrier that provides facilities and assistance to a designated law enforcement office or agency under Article 18B.102(b) is entitled to compensation at the prevailing rates for the facilities and assistance. (Code Crim. Proc., Art. 18.21, Secs. 2(d) (part), (e) (part).)

Added by Acts 2017, 85th Leg., ch. 1058 (H.B. 2931), § 1.02, eff. Jan. 1, 2019.

Art. 18B.104. Duration of Order

Text of article effective Jan. 1, 2019

(a) An order for the installation and use of a device or equipment under this subchapter is valid for a period not to exceed 60 days after the earlier of the date the device or equipment is installed or the 10th day after the date the order is entered, unless the prosecutor applies for and obtains an extension of the order from the court before the order expires.

(b) Each extension granted under Subsection (a) may not exceed a period of 60 days, except that the court may extend an order for a period not to exceed one year with the consent of the subscriber or customer of the service on which the device or equipment is used.

Added by Acts 2017, 85th Leg., ch. 1058 (H.B. 2931), § 1.02, eff. Jan. 1, 2019.

Art. 18B.105. Sealing Records of Application and Order

Text of article effective Jan. 1, 2019

A district court shall seal an application and order granted under this chapter.

Added by Acts 2017, 85th Leg., ch. 1058 (H.B. 2931), § 1.02, eff. Jan. 1, 2019.

SUBCHAPTER D. EMERGENCY INSTALLATION AND USE OF CERTAIN EQUIPMENT

Art. 18B.151. Emergency Installation and Use of Pen Register or Trap and Trace Device

Text of article effective Jan. 1, 2019

(a) In this article, "immediate life-threatening situation" has the meaning assigned by Article 18A.201.

(b) A peace officer authorized to possess, install, operate, or monitor a device under Subchapter E, Chapter 18A, may install and use a pen register or trap and trace device if the peace officer reasonably believes:

(1) an immediate life-threatening situation exists that:

(A) is within the territorial jurisdiction of the peace officer or another officer the peace officer is assisting; and

(B) requires the installation of a pen register or trap and trace device before an order authorizing the installation and use can, with due diligence, be obtained under this chapter; and

(2) there are sufficient grounds under this chapter on which to obtain an order authorizing the installation and use of a pen register or trap and trace device. (Code Crim. Proc., Art. 18.21, Secs. 1(1) (part), 3(a).)

Added by Acts 2017, 85th Leg., ch. 1058 (H.B. 2931), § 1.02, eff. Jan. 1, 2019.

Art. 18B.152. Order Authorizing Emergency Installation and Use

Text of article effective Jan. 1, 2019

(a) A peace officer who installs or uses a pen register or trap and trace device under Article 18B.151 shall:

(1) promptly report the installation or use of the device to the prosecutor in the county in which the device is installed or used; and

(2) within 48 hours after the installation of the device is complete or the use of the device begins, whichever occurs first, obtain an order under Subchapter C authorizing the installation and use of the device.

(b) A judge may issue an order authorizing the installation and use of a device under this subchapter during the 48–hour period prescribed by Subsection (a)(2). If an order is denied or is not issued within the 48–hour period, the peace officer shall terminate use of and remove the pen register or trap and trace device promptly on the earlier of the denial or the expiration of 48 hours.

Added by Acts 2017, 85th Leg., ch. 1058 (H.B. 2931), § 1.02, eff. Jan. 1, 2019.

Art. 18B.153. Admissibility of Evidence Obtained

Text of article effective Jan. 1, 2019

The state may not use as evidence in a criminal proceeding any information gained through the use of a pen register or trap and trace device installed under this subchapter if an authorized peace officer:

(1) does not apply for authorization for the pen register or trap and trace device; or

(2) applies for but does not obtain that authorization.

Added by Acts 2017, 85th Leg., ch. 1058 (H.B. 2931), § 1.02, eff. Jan. 1, 2019.

SUBCHAPTER E. MOBILE TRACKING DEVICES

Art. 18B.201. Definition

Text of article effective Jan. 1, 2019

In this subchapter, "mobile tracking device" means an electronic or mechanical device that permits tracking the movement of a person, vehicle, container, item, or object.

Added by Acts 2017, 85th Leg., ch. 1058 (H.B. 2931), § 1.02, eff. Jan. 1, 2019.

Art. 18B.202. Order Authorizing Installation and Use of Mobile Tracking Device

Text of article effective Jan. 1, 2019

(a) A district judge may issue an order for the installation and use of a mobile tracking device only on the application of an authorized peace officer.

(b) An application must be written, signed, and sworn to before the judge.

(c) The affidavit must:

(1) state the name, department, agency, and address of the applicant;

(2) identify the vehicle, container, or item to which, in which, or on which the mobile tracking device is to be attached, placed, or otherwise installed;

(3) state the name of the owner or possessor of the vehicle, container, or item identified under Subdivision (2);

(4) state the judicial jurisdictional area in which the vehicle, container, or item identified under Subdivision (2) is expected to be found; and

(5) state the facts and circumstances that provide the applicant with a reasonable suspicion that:

(A) criminal activity has been, is, or will be committed; and

(B) the installation and use of a mobile tracking device is likely to produce information that is material to an ongoing criminal investigation of that criminal activity.

Added by Acts 2017, 85th Leg., ch. 1058 (H.B. 2931), § 1.02, eff. Jan. 1, 2019.

Art. 18B.203. Jurisdiction

Text of article effective Jan. 1, 2019

(a) A district judge may issue an order for the installation and use of a mobile tracking device in the same judicial district as the site of:

(1) the investigation; or

(2) the person, vehicle, container, item, or object the movement of which will be tracked by the device.

(b) The order may authorize the use of a mobile tracking device outside the judicial district but within the state, if the device is installed within the district.

Added by Acts 2017, 85th Leg., ch. 1058 (H.B. 2931), § 1.02, eff. Jan. 1, 2019.

Art. 18B.204. Notification of Judge Following Activation of Mobile Tracking Device

Text of article effective Jan. 1, 2019

Within 72 hours after the time a mobile tracking device is activated in place on or within a vehicle, container, or item, the applicant for whom an order was issued under this subchapter shall notify in writing the judge who issued the order.

Added by Acts 2017, 85th Leg., ch. 1058 (H.B. 2931), § 1.02, eff. Jan. 1, 2019.

Art. 18B.205. Duration of Order

Text of article effective Jan. 1, 2019

(a) An order under this subchapter expires not later than the 90th day after the date that the mobile tracking device was activated in place on or within the vehicle, container, or item.

(b) For good cause shown, the judge may grant an extension for an additional 90–day period. (Code Crim. Proc., Art. 18.21, Sec. 14(e).)

Added by Acts 2017, 85th Leg., ch. 1058 (H.B. 2931), § 1.02, eff. Jan. 1, 2019.

Art. 18B.206. Removal of Device

Text of article effective Jan. 1, 2019

(a) The applicant shall remove or cause to be removed the mobile tracking device as soon as is practicable after the authorization period expires.

(b) If removal is not practicable, the device may not be monitored after the expiration of the order.

Added by Acts 2017, 85th Leg., ch. 1058 (H.B. 2931), § 1.02, eff. Jan. 1, 2019.

Art. 18B.207. Nonapplicability

Text of article effective Jan. 1, 2019

(a) This subchapter does not apply to a global positioning or similar device installed in or on an item of property by the owner or with the consent of the owner of the property.

(b) In an emergency, a private entity may monitor a device described by Subsection (a).

Added by Acts 2017, 85th Leg., ch. 1058 (H.B. 2931), § 1.02, eff. Jan. 1, 2019.

SUBCHAPTER F. LAW ENFORCEMENT POWERS AND DUTIES

Art. 18B.251. Policy Required

Text of article effective Jan. 1, 2019

Each designated law enforcement office or agency shall:

(1) adopt a written policy governing the application of this chapter to the office or agency; and

(2) submit the policy to the director of the department, or the director's designee, for approval.

Added by Acts 2017, 85th Leg., ch. 1058 (H.B. 2931), § 1.02, eff. Jan. 1, 2019.

Art. 18B.252. Peace Officers Authorized to Possess, Install, Operate, or Monitor Equipment

Text of article effective Jan. 1, 2019

(a) A peace officer of a designated law enforcement office or agency is authorized to possess, install, operate, or monitor a pen register, ESN reader, or similar equipment if the peace officer's name is on the list submitted to the director of the department under Subsection (b).

(b) If the director of the department or the director's designee approves the policy submitted under Article 18B.251, the inspector general of the Texas Department of Criminal Justice or the inspector general's designee, or the sheriff or chief of a designated law enforcement agency or the sheriff's or chief's designee, as applicable, shall submit to the director a written list of all peace officers in the designated law enforcement office or agency who are authorized to possess, install, operate, or monitor pen registers, ESN readers, or similar equipment.

Added by Acts 2017, 85th Leg., ch. 1058 (H.B. 2931), § 1.02, eff. Jan. 1, 2019.

Art. 18B.253. Limitation: Pen Registers

Text of article effective Jan. 1, 2019

To prevent inclusion of the contents of a wire or electronic communication, a governmental agency authorized to install and use a pen register under this chapter or other law must use reasonably available technology to only record and decode electronic or other impulses used to identify the numbers dialed, routed, addressed, or otherwise processed or transmitted by the communication.

Added by Acts 2017, 85th Leg., ch. 1058 (H.B. 2931), § 1.02, eff. Jan. 1, 2019.

Art. 18B.254. Application or Order Not Required for Certain Searches

Text of article effective Jan. 1, 2019

A peace officer is not required to file an application under Subchapter B or obtain an order under Subchapter C before the peace officer makes an otherwise lawful search, with or without a warrant, to determine the contents of a caller identification message, pager message, or voice message that is contained within the memory of an end-user's identification, paging, or answering device.

Added by Acts 2017, 85th Leg., ch. 1058 (H.B. 2931), § 1.02, eff. Jan. 1, 2019.

SUBCHAPTER G. OVERSIGHT

Art. 18B.301. Compliance Audit

Text of article effective Jan. 1, 2019

(a) The department may conduct an audit of a designated law enforcement office or agency to ensure compliance with this chapter.

(b) If the department determines from the audit that the designated law enforcement office or agency is not in compliance with the policy adopted by the office or agency under Article 18B.251, the department shall notify the office or agency in writing that the office or agency, as applicable, is not in compliance.

(c) If the department determines that the office or agency still is not in compliance with the policy on the 90th day after the date the office or agency receives written notice under Subsection (b), the office or agency loses the authority granted by this chapter until:

(1) the office or agency adopts a new written policy governing the application of this chapter to the office or agency; and

(2) the department approves that policy.

Added by Acts 2017, 85th Leg., ch. 1058 (H.B. 2931), § 1.02, eff. Jan. 1, 2019.

Art. 18B.302.   Report of Expenditures

Text of article effective Jan. 1, 2019

(a) The inspector general of the Texas Department of Criminal Justice or the sheriff or chief of a designated law enforcement agency, as applicable, shall submit to the director of the department a written report of expenditures made by the designated law enforcement office or agency to purchase and maintain a pen register, ESN reader, or similar equipment authorized under this chapter.

(b) The director of the department shall report the expenditures publicly on an annual basis on the department's Internet website or by other comparable means.

Added by Acts 2017, 85th Leg., ch. 1058 (H.B. 2931), § 1.02, eff. Jan. 1, 2019.

SUBCHAPTER H.   ACCESS TO STORED COMMUNICATIONS AND OTHER STORED CUSTOMER DATA

Art. 18B.351.   Government Access to Electronic Customer Data

Text of article effective Jan. 1, 2019

(a) An authorized peace officer may require a provider of an electronic communications service or a provider of a remote computing service to disclose electronic customer data that is in electronic storage by obtaining a warrant under Article 18B.354.

(b) An authorized peace officer may require a provider of an electronic communications service or a provider of a remote computing service to disclose only electronic customer data that is information revealing the identity of customers of the applicable service or information about a customer's use of the applicable service, without giving the subscriber or customer notice:

(1) by obtaining an administrative subpoena authorized by statute;

(2) by obtaining a grand jury subpoena;

(3) by obtaining a court order under Article 18B.352;

(4) by obtaining a warrant under Article 18B.354;

(5) by obtaining the consent of the subscriber or customer to the disclosure of the data; or

(6) as otherwise permitted by applicable federal law.

Added by Acts 2017, 85th Leg., ch. 1058 (H.B. 2931), § 1.02, eff. Jan. 1, 2019.

Art. 18B.352.   Court Order for Government Access to Stored Customer Data

Text of article effective Jan. 1, 2019

(a) A court shall issue an order authorizing disclosure of contents, records, or other information of a wire or electronic communication held in electronic storage if the court determines that there is a reasonable belief that the information sought is relevant to a legitimate law enforcement inquiry.

(b) A court may grant a motion by the service provider to quash or modify the order issued under Subsection (a) if the court determines that:

(1) the information or records requested are unusually voluminous; or

(2) compliance with the order would cause an undue burden on the provider.

Added by Acts 2017, 85th Leg., ch. 1058 (H.B. 2931), § 1.02, eff. Jan. 1, 2019.

Art. 18B.353.   Warrant Issued in This State: Applicability

Text of article effective Jan. 1, 2019

Articles 18B.354–18B.357 apply to a warrant required under Article 18B.351 to obtain electronic customer data, including the contents of a wire or electronic communication.

Added by Acts 2017, 85th Leg., ch. 1058 (H.B. 2931), § 1.02, eff. Jan. 1, 2019.

Art. 18B.354.   Warrant Issued in This State: Application and Issuance of Warrant

Text of article effective Jan. 1, 2019

(a) On the filing of an application by an authorized peace officer, a district judge may issue a search warrant under this article for electronic customer data held in electronic storage, including the contents of and records and other information related to a wire or electronic communication held in electronic storage, by a provider of an electronic communications service or a provider of a remote computing service described by Article 18B.355(b), regardless of whether the customer data is held at a location in this state or another state. An application made under this subsection must demonstrate probable cause for the issuance of the warrant and must be supported by the oath of the authorized peace officer.

(b) A search warrant may not be issued under this article unless the sworn affidavit required by Article 18.01(b) provides sufficient and substantial facts to establish probable cause that:

(1) a specific offense has been committed; and

(2) the electronic customer data sought:

(A) constitutes evidence of that offense or evidence that a particular person committed that offense; and

(B) is held in electronic storage by the service provider on which the warrant is served under Article 18B.355(c).

(c) Only the electronic customer data described in the sworn affidavit required by Article 18.01(b) may be seized under the warrant.

(d) A warrant issued under this article shall run in the name of "The State of Texas."

(e) Article 18.011 applies to an affidavit presented under Article 18.01(b) for the issuance of a warrant under this article, and the affidavit may be sealed in the manner provided by that article.

Added by Acts 2017, 85th Leg., ch. 1058 (H.B. 2931), § 1.02, eff. Jan. 1, 2019.

Art. 18B.355. Warrant Issued in This State: Execution of Warrant

Text of article effective Jan. 1, 2019

(a) Not later than the 11th day after the date of issuance, an authorized peace officer shall execute a warrant issued under Article 18B.354, except that the peace officer shall execute the warrant within a shorter period if the district judge directs a shorter period in the warrant. For purposes of this subsection, a warrant is executed when the warrant is served in the manner described by Subsection (c).

(b) A warrant issued under Article 18B.354 may be served only on a provider of an electronic communications service or a provider of a remote computing service that is a domestic entity or a company or entity otherwise doing business in this state under a

contract or a terms of service agreement with a resident of this state, if any part of that contract or agreement is to be performed in this state.

(c) A search warrant issued under Article 18B.354 is served when an authorized peace officer delivers the warrant by hand, by facsimile transmission, or, in a manner allowing proof of delivery, by means of the United States mail or a private delivery service to:

(1) a person specified by Section 5.255, Business Organizations Code;

(2) the secretary of state in the case of a company or entity to which Section 5.251, Business Organizations Code, applies; or

(3) any other person or entity designated to receive the service of process.

(d) The district judge shall hear and decide any motion to quash the warrant not later than the fifth business day after the date the service provider files the motion. The judge may allow the service provider to appear at the hearing by teleconference.

Added by Acts 2017, 85th Leg., ch. 1058 (H.B. 2931), § 1.02, eff. Jan. 1, 2019.

Art. 18B.356. Warrant Issued in This State: Compliance With Warrant

Text of article effective Jan. 1, 2019

(a) A district judge shall indicate in a warrant issued under Article 18A.354 that the deadline for compliance by the provider of an electronic communications service or the provider of a remote computing service is the 15th business day after the date the warrant is served if the warrant is to be served on a domestic entity or a company or entity otherwise doing business in this state, except that the deadline for compliance with a warrant served in accordance with Section 5.251, Business Organizations Code, may be extended to a date that is not later than the 30th day after the date the warrant is served.

(b) The judge may indicate in the warrant that the deadline for compliance is earlier than the 15th business day after the date the warrant is served if the authorized peace officer who applies for the warrant makes a showing and the judge finds that failure to comply with the warrant by the earlier deadline would cause serious jeopardy to an investigation, cause undue delay of a trial, or create a material risk of:

(1) danger to the life or physical safety of any person;

(2) flight from prosecution;

(3) the tampering with or destruction of evidence; or

(4) intimidation of potential witnesses.

(c) The service provider shall produce all electronic customer data, contents of communications, and other information sought, regardless of where the information is held and within the period allowed for compliance with the warrant, as provided by Subsection (a) or (b).

(d) A court may find any designated officer, designated director, or designated owner of a company or entity in contempt of court if the person by act or omission is responsible for the failure of the company or entity to comply with the warrant within the period allowed for compliance.

(e) The failure of a company or entity to timely deliver the information sought in the warrant does not affect the admissibility of that evidence in a criminal proceeding.

(f) On a service provider's compliance with a warrant issued under Article 18B.354, an authorized peace officer shall file a return of the warrant and a copy of the inventory of the seized property as required under Article 18.10.

(g) A provider of an electronic communications service or a provider of a remote computing service responding to a warrant issued under Article 18B.354 may request an extension of the period for compliance with the warrant if extenuating circumstances exist to justify the extension. The district judge shall grant a request for an extension based on those circumstances if:

(1) the authorized peace officer who applied for the warrant or another appropriate authorized peace officer agrees to the extension; or

(2) the district judge finds that the need for the extension outweighs the likelihood that the extension will cause an adverse circumstance described by Subsection (b).

Added by Acts 2017, 85th Leg., ch. 1058 (H.B. 2931), § 1.02, eff. Jan. 1, 2019.

Art. 18B.357. Warrant Issued in This State: Authentication of Records by Service Provider

Text of article effective Jan. 1, 2019

If an authorized peace officer serving a warrant under Article 18B.355 also delivers an affidavit form to the provider of an electronic communications ser-

vice or the provider of a remote computing service responding to the warrant, and the peace officer also notifies the service provider in writing that an executed affidavit is required, the service provider shall verify the authenticity of the customer data, contents of communications, and other information produced in compliance with the warrant by including with the information an affidavit form that:

(1) is completed and sworn to by a person who is a custodian of the information or a person otherwise qualified to attest to the authenticity of the information; and

(2) states that the information was stored in the course of regularly conducted business of the service provider and specifies whether the regular practice of the service provider is to store that information.

Added by Acts 2017, 85th Leg., ch. 1058 (H.B. 2931), § 1.02, eff. Jan. 1, 2019.

Art. 18B.358. Warrant Issued in Another State

Text of article effective Jan. 1, 2019

Any domestic entity that provides electronic communications services or remote computing services to the public shall comply with a warrant issued in another state and seeking information described by Article 18B.354(a), if the warrant is served on the entity in a manner equivalent to the service of process requirements provided by Article 18B.355(b).

Added by Acts 2017, 85th Leg., ch. 1058 (H.B. 2931), § 1.02, eff. Jan. 1, 2019.

Art. 18B.359. Government Access to Certain Stored Customer Data Without Legal Process

Text of article effective Jan. 1, 2019

(a) A provider of a telephonic communications service shall disclose to an authorized peace officer, without legal process, subscriber listing information, including name, address, and telephone number or similar access code:

(1) that the service provider provides to others in the course of providing publicly available directory or similar assistance; or

(2) that is solely for use in the dispatch of emergency vehicles and personnel responding to a distress call directed to an emergency dispatch system or when the information is reasonably necessary to aid in the dispatching of emergency vehicles and personnel for

the immediate prevention of death, personal injury, or destruction of property.

(b) A provider of a telephonic communications service shall provide to an authorized peace officer the name of the subscriber of record whose published telephone number is provided to the service provider by an authorized peace officer.

Added by Acts 2017, 85th Leg., ch. 1058 (H.B. 2931), § 1.02, eff. Jan. 1, 2019.

SUBCHAPTER I. BACKUP PRESERVATION OF ELECTRONIC CUSTOMER DATA

Art. 18B.401. Backup Preservation of Electronic Customer Data

Text of article effective Jan. 1, 2019

(a) A subpoena or court order under Article 18B.351(b) for disclosure of certain electronic customer data held in electronic storage by a provider of an electronic communications service or a provider of a remote computing service may, for the purpose of preserving the customer data sought by the subpoena or court order, require that service provider to create a copy of that data.

(b) The service provider shall create the copy within a reasonable period as determined by the court issuing the subpoena or court order.

(c) On creating a copy under this article, the service provider shall immediately notify the authorized peace officer who presented the subpoena or court order requesting the copy.

(d) The service provider may not inform the subscriber or customer whose data is being sought that the subpoena or court order has been issued.

Added by Acts 2017, 85th Leg., ch. 1058 (H.B. 2931), § 1.02, eff. Jan. 1, 2019.

Art. 18B.402. Notice to Subscriber or Customer

Text of article effective Jan. 1, 2019

Not later than the third day after the date of the receipt of the notice under Article 18B.401(c) from the applicable service provider, the authorized peace officer who presented the subpoena or court order requesting the copy shall provide notice of the creation of the copy to the subscriber or customer whose electronic customer data is the subject of the subpoena or court order.

Added by Acts 2017, 85th Leg., ch. 1058 (H.B. 2931), § 1.02, eff. Jan. 1, 2019.

Art. 18B.403. Release of Copy of Electronic Customer Data

Text of article effective Jan. 1, 2019

The provider of an electronic communications service or the provider of a remote computing service shall release a copy created under this subchapter to the requesting authorized peace officer not earlier than the 14th day after the date of the peace officer's notice to the subscriber or customer if the service provider has not:

(1) initiated proceedings to challenge the request of the peace officer for the copy; or

(2) received notice from the subscriber or customer that the subscriber or customer has initiated proceedings to challenge the request.

Added by Acts 2017, 85th Leg., ch. 1058 (H.B. 2931), § 1.02, eff. Jan. 1, 2019.

Art. 18B.404. Destruction of Copy of Electronic Customer Data

Text of article effective Jan. 1, 2019

The provider of an electronic communications service or the provider of a remote computing service may not destroy or permit the destruction of a copy created under this subchapter until the later of:

(1) the delivery of electronic customer data to the applicable law enforcement agency; or

(2) the resolution of any court proceedings, including appeals of any proceedings, relating to the subpoena or court order requesting the creation of the copy.

Added by Acts 2017, 85th Leg., ch. 1058 (H.B. 2931), § 1.02, eff. Jan. 1, 2019.

Art. 18B.405. Request for Copy of Electronic Customer Data by Authorized Peace Officer

Text of article effective Jan. 1, 2019

(a) An authorized peace officer who reasonably believes that notice to a subscriber or customer regarding a subpoena or court order would result in the destruction of or tampering with the electronic customer data sought may request the creation of a copy of the data.

(b) The peace officer's belief is not subject to challenge by the subscriber or customer or by a provider of an electronic communications service or a provider of a remote computing service.

Added by Acts 2017, 85th Leg., ch. 1058 (H.B. 2931), § 1.02, eff. Jan. 1, 2019.

Art. 18B.406. Proceedings to Quash Subpoena or Vacate Court Order

Text of article effective Jan. 1, 2019

(a) Not later than the 14th day after the date a subscriber or customer receives notice under Article 18B.402, the subscriber or customer may file a written motion to quash the subpoena or vacate the court order in the court that issued the subpoena or court order. The motion must contain an affidavit or other sworn statement stating:

(1) that the applicant is a subscriber or customer of the provider of an electronic communications service or the provider of a remote computing service from which the electronic customer data held in electronic storage for the subscriber or customer has been sought; and

(2) the applicant's reasons for believing that the customer data sought is not relevant to a legitimate law enforcement inquiry or that there has not been substantial compliance with the provisions of this chapter in some other respect.

(b) The subscriber or customer shall give written notice to the applicable service provider of the challenge to the subpoena or court order. The authorized peace officer requesting the subpoena or court order must be served a copy of the filed papers by personal delivery or by registered or certified mail.

(c) The court shall order the authorized peace officer to file a sworn response to the motion filed by the subscriber or customer if the court determines that the subscriber or customer has complied with the requirements of Subsections (a) and (b). On request of the peace officer, the court may permit the response to be filed in camera. The court may conduct any additional proceedings the court considers appropriate if the court is unable to make a determination on the motion on the basis of the parties' initial allegations and response.

(d) The court shall rule on the motion as soon as practicable after the filing of the peace officer's response. The court shall deny the motion if the court finds that the applicant is not the subscriber or customer whose data is the subject of the subpoena or court order or that there is reason to believe that the peace officer's inquiry is legitimate and that the data

sought is relevant to that inquiry. The court shall quash the subpoena or vacate the court order if the court finds that the applicant is the subscriber or customer whose data is the subject of the subpoena or court order and that there is not a reason to believe that the data is relevant to a legitimate law enforcement inquiry or that there has not been substantial compliance with the provisions of this chapter.

(e) A court order denying a motion or application under this article is not a final order, and an interlocutory appeal may not be taken from the denial.

Added by Acts 2017, 85th Leg., ch. 1058 (H.B. 2931), § 1.02, eff. Jan. 1, 2019.

SUBCHAPTER J. PRODUCTION OF CERTAIN BUSINESS RECORDS

Art. 18B.451. Subpoena Authority

Text of article effective Jan. 1, 2019

The director of the department or the director's designee, the inspector general of the Texas Department of Criminal Justice or the inspector general's designee, or the sheriff or chief of a designated law enforcement agency or the sheriff's or chief's designee may issue an administrative subpoena to a communication common carrier or a provider of an electronic communications service to compel the production of any carrier's or service provider's business records that:

(1) disclose information about:

(A) the carrier's or service provider's customers; or

(B) users of the services offered by the carrier or service provider; and

(2) are material to a criminal investigation.

Added by Acts 2017, 85th Leg., ch. 1058 (H.B. 2931), § 1.02, eff. Jan. 1, 2019.

Art. 18B.452. Report of Issuance of Subpoena

Text of article effective Jan. 1, 2019

Not later than the 30th day after the date on which an administrative subpoena is issued under Article 18B.451, the inspector general of the Texas Department of Criminal Justice or the sheriff or chief of a designated law enforcement agency, as applicable, shall report to the department the issuance of the subpoena.

Added by Acts 2017, 85th Leg., ch. 1058 (H.B. 2931), § 1.02, eff. Jan. 1, 2019.

Art. 18B.453. Compliance With Policy for Installation and Use of Equipment

Text of article effective Jan. 1, 2019

(a) If, based on a report received under Article 18B.452, the department determines that a designated law enforcement office or agency is not in compliance with the policy adopted by the office or agency under Article 18B.251, the department shall notify the office or agency in writing that the office or agency, as applicable, is not in compliance.

(b) If the department determines that the office or agency still is not in compliance with the policy on the 90th day after the date the office or agency receives written notice under this article, the office or agency loses the authority granted by this chapter until:

(1) the office or agency adopts a new written policy governing the application of this chapter to the office or agency; and

(2) the department approves that policy.

Added by Acts 2017, 85th Leg., ch. 1058 (H.B. 2931), § 1.02, eff. Jan. 1, 2019.

SUBCHAPTER K. SERVICE PROVIDER POWERS AND DUTIES

Art. 18B.501. Preclusion of Notification

Text of article effective Jan. 1, 2019

(a) An authorized peace officer seeking electronic customer data under Article 18B.351 may apply to the court for an order commanding the service provider to whom a warrant, subpoena, or court order is directed not to disclose to any person the existence of the warrant, subpoena, or court order. The order is effective for the period the court considers appropriate.

(b) The court shall enter the order if the court determines that there is reason to believe that notification of the existence of the warrant, subpoena, or court order will have an adverse result.

(c) In this article, an "adverse result" means:

(1) endangering the life or physical safety of an individual;

(2) flight from prosecution;

(3) destruction of or tampering with evidence;

(4) intimidation of a potential witness; or

(5) otherwise seriously jeopardizing an investigation or unduly delaying a trial.

Added by Acts 2017, 85th Leg., ch. 1058 (H.B. 2931), § 1.02, eff. Jan. 1, 2019.

Art. 18B.502. Disclosure by Service Provider Prohibited

Text of article effective Jan. 1, 2019

(a) Except as provided by Subsection (c), a provider of an electronic communications service may not knowingly divulge the contents of a communication that is in electronic storage.

(b) Except as provided by Subsection (c), a provider of a remote computing service may not knowingly divulge the contents of a communication that:

(1) is in electronic storage on behalf of a subscriber or customer of the service provider;

(2) is received by means of electronic transmission from the subscriber or customer or created by means of computer processing of communications received by means of electronic transmission from the subscriber or customer; and

(3) is solely for the purpose of providing storage or computer processing services to the subscriber or customer, if the service provider is not authorized to obtain access to the contents of that communication for purposes of providing any service other than storage or computer processing.

(c) A provider of an electronic communications service or a provider of a remote computing service may disclose the contents of an electronically stored communication:

(1) to an intended recipient of the communication or the intended recipient's agent;

(2) to the addressee or the addressee's agent;

(3) with the consent of the originator, to the addressee or the intended recipient of the communication, or the subscriber of a remote computing service;

(4) to a person whose facilities are used to transmit the communication to its destination or the person's employee or authorized representative;

(5) as may be necessary to provide the service or to protect the property or rights of the service provider;

(6) to a law enforcement agency if the contents were obtained inadvertently by the service provider and the contents appear to pertain to the commission of an offense; or

(7) as authorized under federal or other state law.

Added by Acts 2017, 85th Leg., ch. 1058 (H.B. 2931), § 1.02, eff. Jan. 1, 2019.

Art. 18B.503. Reimbursement of Costs

Text of article effective Jan. 1, 2019

(a) Except as provided by Subsection (c), an authorized peace officer who obtains electronic customer data under Article 18B.351 or 18B.359 or other information under this chapter shall reimburse the person assembling or providing the data or information for all costs that are reasonably necessary and that have been directly incurred in searching for, assembling, reproducing, or otherwise providing the data or information, including costs arising from necessary disruption of normal operations of a provider of an electronic communications service or a provider of a remote computing service in which the electronic customer data may be held in electronic storage or in which the other information may be stored.

(b) The authorized peace officer and the person providing the electronic customer data or other information may agree on the amount of reimbursement. If there is not an agreement, the court that issued the order for production of the data or information shall determine the amount. If a court order was not issued for production of the data or information, the court before which any criminal prosecution relating to the data or information would be brought shall determine the amount.

(c) Subsection (a) does not apply to records or other information that is maintained by a communication common carrier and that relates to telephone toll records or telephone listings obtained under Article 18B.359(a), unless the court determines that:

(1) the amount of information required was unusually voluminous; or

(2) an undue burden was imposed on the service provider.

Added by Acts 2017, 85th Leg., ch. 1058 (H.B. 2931), § 1.02, eff. Jan. 1, 2019.

SUBCHAPTER L. REMEDIES

Art. 18B.551. Cause of Action

Text of article effective Jan. 1, 2019

(a) Except as provided by Article 18B.552, a provider of an electronic communications service or a provider of a remote computing service, or a subscriber or customer of that service provider, that is aggrieved by a violation of this chapter has a civil cause of action if the conduct constituting the violation was committed knowingly or intentionally and is entitled to:

(1) injunctive relief;

(2) reasonable attorney's fees and other litigation costs reasonably incurred; and

(3) the amount of the actual damages suffered and any profits made by the violator as a result of the violation or $1,000, whichever is more.

(b) The reliance in good faith on a court order, warrant, subpoena, or legislative authorization is a complete defense to any civil action brought under this chapter.

(c) A civil action under this article may be presented not later than the second anniversary of the date the claimant first discovered or had reasonable opportunity to discover the violation.

Added by Acts 2017, 85th Leg., ch. 1058 (H.B. 2931), § 1.02, eff. Jan. 1, 2019.

Art. 18B.552. No Cause of Action

Text of article effective Jan. 1, 2019

A subscriber or customer of a provider of an electronic communications service or a provider of a remote computing service does not have a cause of action against a service provider or the service provider's officers, employees, or agents or against other specified persons for providing information, facilities, or assistance as required by a court order, warrant, subpoena, or certification under this chapter.

Added by Acts 2017, 85th Leg., ch. 1058 (H.B. 2931), § 1.02, eff. Jan. 1, 2019.

Art. 18B.553. Exclusivity of Remedies

Text of article effective Jan. 1, 2019

The remedies and sanctions under this chapter are the exclusive judicial remedies and sanctions for a violation of this chapter, other than a violation that infringes on a right of a party that is guaranteed by a state or federal constitution.

Added by Acts 2017, 85th Leg., ch. 1058 (H.B. 2931), § 1.02, eff. Jan. 1, 2019.

AFTER COMMITMENT OR BAIL AND BEFORE THE TRIAL

CHAPTER NINETEEN. ORGANIZATION OF THE GRAND JURY

Article

Art. 19.01. Selection and Summons of Prospective Grand Jurors

The district judge shall direct that the number of prospective grand jurors the judge considers necessary to ensure an adequate number of jurors under Article 19.26 be selected and summoned, with return on summons, in the same manner as for the selection and summons of panels for the trial of civil cases in the district courts. The judge shall try the qualifications for and excuses from service as a grand juror and impanel the completed grand jury as provided by this chapter.

Acts 1965, 59th Leg., vol. 2, p. 317, ch. 722, eff. Jan. 1, 1966. Amended by Acts 1971, 62nd Leg., p. 905, ch. 131, § 1, eff. May 10, 1971; Acts 1979, 66th Leg., p. 393, ch. 184, § 1, eff. Sept. 1, 1979. Acts 1983, 68th Leg., p. 2983, ch. 514, § 1, eff. June 19, 1983; Acts 1991, 72nd Leg., ch. 67, § 1, eff. Sept. 1, 1991; Acts 2001, 77th Leg., ch. 344, § 1, eff. Sept. 1, 2001; Acts 2015, 84th Leg., ch. 929 (H.B. 2150), § 1, eff. Sept. 1, 2015; Acts 2017, 85th Leg., ch. 745 (S.B. 1298), § 1, eff. Sept. 1, 2017.

Section 22(a) of Acts 2015, 84th Leg., ch. 929 (H.B. 2150) provides:

"(a) Except as provided by Subsection (b) of this section, the changes in law made by this Act apply to a grand jury impaneled on or after the effective date [Sept. 1, 2015] of this Act. A grand jury impaneled before the effective date of this Act is governed by the law in effect on the date the grand jury was impaneled, and the former law is continued in effect for that purpose."

Section 3 of Acts 2017, 85th Leg., ch. 745 (S.B. 1298) provides:

"The changes in law made by this Act apply to a grand jury impaneled on or after the effective date [Sept. 1, 2017] of this Act. A grand jury impaneled before the effective date of this Act is governed by the law in effect on the date the grand jury was impaneled, and the former law is continued in effect for that purpose."

Arts. 19.02 to 19.06. Repealed by Acts 2015, 84th Leg., ch. 929 (H.B. 2150), § 21(1), eff. Sept. 1, 2015

Art. 19.07. Extension Beyond Term of Period for Which Grand Jurors Shall Sit

If prior to the expiration of the term for which the grand jury was impaneled, it is made to appear by a declaration of the foreman or of a majority of the grand jurors in open court, that the investigation by the grand jury of the matters before it cannot be concluded before the expiration of the term, the judge of the district court in which said grand jury was impaneled may, by the entry of an order on the minutes of said court, extend, from time to time, for the purpose of concluding the investigation of matters then before it, the period during which said grand jury shall sit, for not to exceed a total of ninety days after the expiration of the term for which it was impaneled, and all indictments pertaining thereto returned by the grand jury within said extended period shall be as valid as if returned before the expiration of the term.

Acts 1965, 59th Leg., vol. 2, p. 317, ch. 722, eff. Jan. 1, 1966. Amended by Acts 2015, 84th Leg., ch. 929 (H.B. 2150), § 2, eff. Sept. 1, 2015.

Section 22(a) of Acts 2015, 84th Leg., ch. 929 (H.B. 2150) provides:

"(a) Except as provided by Subsection (b) of this section, the changes in law made by this Act apply to a grand jury impaneled on or after the effective date [Sept. 1, 2015] of this Act. A grand jury impaneled before the effective date of this Act is governed by the law in effect on the date the grand jury was impaneled, and the former law is continued in effect for that purpose."

Art. 19.08. Qualifications

A person may be selected or serve as a grand juror only if the person:

(1) is at least 18 years of age;

(2) is a citizen of the United States;

(3) is a resident of this state, and of the county in which the person is to serve;

(4) is qualified under the Constitution and laws to vote in the county in which the grand jury is sitting, regardless of whether the person is registered to vote;

(5) is of sound mind and good moral character;

(6) is able to read and write;

(7) has not been convicted of misdemeanor theft or a felony;

(8) is not under indictment or other legal accusation for misdemeanor theft or a felony;

(9) is not related within the third degree of consanguinity or second degree of affinity, as determined under Chapter 573, Government Code, to any person selected to serve or serving on the same grand jury;

(10) has not served as grand juror in the year before the date on which the term of court for which the person has been selected as grand juror begins; and

(11) is not a complainant in any matter to be heard by the grand jury during the term of court for which the person has been selected as a grand juror.

Acts 1965, 59th Leg., vol. 2, p. 317, ch. 722, eff. Jan. 1, 1966. Amended by Acts 1969, 61st Leg., p. 1364, ch. 412, § 5, eff. Sept. 1, 1969; Acts 1981, 67th Leg., p. 3143, ch. 827, § 5, eff. Aug. 31, 1981; Acts 1989, 71st Leg., ch. 1065, § 1, eff. Sept. 1, 1989; Acts 1991, 72nd Leg., ch. 561, § 8, eff. Aug. 26, 1991; Acts 1995, 74th Leg., ch. 76, § 5.95(27), eff. Sept. 1, 1995; Acts 1999, 76th Leg., ch. 1177, § 1, eff. Sept. 1, 1999; Acts 2005, 79th Leg., ch. 801, § 2, eff. Sept. 1, 2005; Acts 2015, 84th Leg., ch. 929 (H.B. 2150), § 3, eff. Sept. 1, 2015; Acts 2017, 85th Leg., ch. 745 (S.B. 1298), § 2, eff. Sept. 1, 2017.

Section 22(a) of Acts 2015, 84th Leg., ch. 929 (H.B. 2150) provides:

"(a) Except as provided by Subsection (b) of this section, the changes in law made by this Act apply to a grand jury impaneled on or after the effective date [Sept. 1, 2015] of this Act. A grand jury impaneled before the effective date of this Act is governed by the law in effect on the date the grand jury was impaneled, and the former law is continued in effect for that purpose."

Section 3 of Acts 2017, 85th Leg., ch. 745 (S.B. 1298) provides:

"The changes in law made by this Act apply to a grand jury impaneled on or after the effective date [Sept. 1, 2017] of this Act. A grand jury impaneled before the effective date of this Act is governed by the law in effect on the date the grand jury was impaneled, and the former law is continued in effect for that purpose."

Arts. 19.09 to 19.15.   Repealed by Acts 2015, 84th Leg., ch. 929 (H.B. 2150), § 21(1), eff. Sept. 1, 2015

Art. 19.16.   Absent juror fined

A juror legally summoned, failing to attend without a reasonable excuse, may, by order of the court entered on the record, be fined not less than $100 nor more than $500.

Acts 1965, 59th Leg., vol. 2, p. 317, ch. 722, eff. Jan. 1, 1966. Amended by Acts 2009, 81st Leg., ch. 640, § 2, eff. Sept. 1, 2009.

Art. 19.17.   Repealed by Acts 2015, 84th Leg., ch. 929 (H.B. 2150), § 21(1), eff. Sept. 1, 2015

Art. 19.18.   If Less than Sixteen Attend

When less than sixteen of those summoned to serve as grand jurors are found to be in attendance and qualified to so serve, the court shall order the sheriff to summon such additional number of persons as may be deemed necessary to constitute a grand jury of twelve persons and four alternates.

Acts 1965, 59th Leg., vol. 2, p. 317, ch. 722, eff. Jan. 1, 1966. Amended by Acts 1999, 76th Leg., ch. 1065, § 1, eff. Sept. 1, 1999; Acts 2015, 84th Leg., ch. 929 (H.B. 2150), § 4, eff. Sept. 1, 2015.

Section 22(a) of Acts 2015, 84th Leg., ch. 929 (H.B. 2150) provides:

"(a) Except as provided by Subsection (b) of this section, the changes in law made by this Act apply to a grand jury impaneled on or after the effective date [Sept. 1, 2015] of this Act. A grand jury impaneled before the effective date of this Act is governed by the law in effect on the date the grand jury was impaneled, and the former law is continued in effect for that purpose."

Art. 19.19.   Jurors to Attend Forthwith

The jurors provided for in Article 19.18 shall be summoned in person to attend before the court forthwith.

Acts 1965, 59th Leg., vol. 2, p. 317, ch. 722, eff. Jan. 1, 1966. Amended by Acts 2015, 84th Leg., ch. 929 (H.B. 2150), § 5, eff. Sept. 1, 2015.

Section 22(a) of Acts 2015, 84th Leg., ch. 929 (H.B. 2150) provides:

"(a) Except as provided by Subsection (b) of this section, the changes in law made by this Act apply to a grand jury impaneled on or after the effective date [Sept. 1, 2015] of this Act. A grand jury impaneled before the effective date of this Act is governed by the law in effect on the date the grand jury was impaneled, and the former law is continued in effect for that purpose."

Art. 19.20.   To Summon Qualified Persons

On directing the sheriff to summon grand jurors, the court shall instruct the sheriff that the sheriff must not summon any person to serve as a grand juror who does not possess the qualifications prescribed by law.

Acts 1965, 59th Leg., vol. 2, p. 317, ch. 722, eff. Jan. 1, 1966. Amended by Acts 2015, 84th Leg., ch. 929 (H.B. 2150), § 6, eff. Sept. 1, 2015.

Section 22(a) of Acts 2015, 84th Leg., ch. 929 (H.B. 2150) provides:

"(a) Except as provided by Subsection (b) of this section, the changes in law made by this Act apply to a grand jury impaneled on or after the effective date [Sept. 1, 2015] of this Act. A grand jury impaneled before the effective date of this Act is governed by the law in effect on the date the grand jury was impaneled, and the former law is continued in effect for that purpose."

Art. 19.21.   To test qualifications

When as many as fourteen persons summoned to serve as grand jurors are in attendance upon the court, it shall proceed to test their qualifications as such.

Acts 1965, 59th Leg., vol. 2, p. 317, ch. 722, eff. Jan. 1, 1966. Amended by Acts 1999, 76th Leg., ch. 1065, § 2, eff. Sept. 1, 1999.

Art. 19.22. Interrogated

Each person who is presented to serve as a grand juror shall, before being impaneled, be interrogated on oath by the court or under his direction, touching his qualifications.

Acts 1965, 59th Leg., vol. 2, p. 317, ch. 722, eff. Jan. 1, 1966.

Art. 19.23. Mode of Test

In trying the qualifications of any person to serve as a grand juror, that person shall be asked:

1. Are you a citizen of this state and county, and qualified to vote in this county, under the Constitution and laws of this state?

2. Are you able to read and write?

3. Have you ever been convicted of misdemeanor theft or any felony?

4. Are you under indictment or other legal accusation for misdemeanor theft or for any felony?

Acts 1965, 59th Leg., vol. 2, p. 317, ch. 722, eff. Jan. 1, 1966. Amended by Acts 1969, 61st Leg., p. 1364, ch. 412, § 6, eff. Sept. 1, 1969; Acts 2015, 84th Leg., ch. 929 (H.B. 2150), § 7, eff. Sept. 1, 2015.

Section 22(a) of Acts 2015, 84th Leg., ch. 929 (H.B. 2150) provides:

"(a) Except as provided by Subsection (b) of this section, the changes in law made by this Act apply to a grand jury impaneled on or after the effective date [Sept. 1, 2015] of this Act. A grand jury impaneled before the effective date of this Act is governed by the law in effect on the date the grand jury was impaneled, and the former law is continued in effect for that purpose."

Art. 19.24. Qualified juror accepted

When, by the answer of the person, it appears to the court that he is a qualified juror, he shall be accepted as such, unless it be shown that he is not of sound mind or of good moral character, or unless it be shown that he is in fact not qualified to serve as a grand juror.

Acts 1965, 59th Leg., vol. 2, p. 317, ch. 722, eff. Jan. 1, 1966.

Art. 19.25. Excuses from service

Any person summoned who does not possess the requisite qualifications shall be excused by the court from serving. The following qualified persons may be excused from grand jury service:

(1) a person older than 70 years;

(2) a person responsible for the care of a child younger than 18 years;

(3) a student of a public or private secondary school;

(4) a person enrolled and in actual attendance at an institution of higher education; and

(5) any other person that the court determines has a reasonable excuse from service.

Acts 1965, 59th Leg., vol. 2, p. 317, ch. 722, eff. Jan. 1, 1966. Amended by Acts 1979, 66th Leg., p. 393, ch. 184, § 2, eff. Sept. 1, 1979; Acts 1999, 76th Leg., ch. 1177, § 2, eff. Sept. 1, 1999.

Art. 19.26. Jury Impaneled

(a) When at least sixteen qualified jurors are found to be present, the court shall select twelve fair and impartial persons to serve as grand jurors and four additional persons to serve as alternate grand jurors. The grand jurors and the alternate grand jurors shall be randomly selected from a fair cross section of the population of the area served by the court.

(b) The court shall proceed to impanel the grand jury, unless a challenge is made, which may be to the array or to any particular person presented to serve as a grand juror or an alternate. In addition, the court shall impanel four alternates to serve on disqualification or unavailability of a juror during the term of the grand jury. On learning that a grand juror has become disqualified or unavailable during the term of the grand jury, the attorney representing the state shall prepare an order for the court identifying the disqualified or unavailable juror, stating the basis for the disqualification or unavailability, dismissing the disqualified or unavailable juror from the grand jury, and naming one of the alternates as a member of the grand jury. The procedure established by this subsection may be used on disqualification or unavailability of a second or subsequent grand juror during the term of the grand jury. For purposes of this subsection, a juror is unavailable if the juror is unable to participate fully in the duties of the grand jury because of the death of the juror, a physical or mental illness of the juror, or any other reason the court determines constitutes good cause for dismissing the juror.

Acts 1965, 59th Leg., vol. 2, p. 317, ch. 722, eff. Jan. 1, 1966. Amended by Acts 1999, 76th Leg., ch. 1065, § 3, eff. Sept. 1, 1999; Acts 2003, 78th Leg., ch. 889, § 1, eff. Sept. 1, 2003; Acts 2015, 84th Leg., ch. 929 (H.B. 2150), § 8, eff. Sept. 1, 2015.

Section 22(a) of Acts 2015, 84th Leg., ch. 929 (H.B. 2150) provides:

"(a) Except as provided by Subsection (b) of this section, the changes in law made by this Act apply to a grand jury impaneled on or after the effective date [Sept. 1, 2015] of this Act. A grand jury impaneled before the effective date of this Act is governed by the law in effect on the date the grand jury was impaneled, and the former law is continued in effect for that purpose."

Art. 19.27. Any person may challenge

Before the grand jury has been impaneled, any person may challenge the array of jurors or any person presented as a grand juror. In no other way shall objections to the qualifications and legality of the grand jury be heard. Any person confined in jail in the county shall upon his request be brought into court to make such challenge.

Acts 1965, 59th Leg., vol. 2, p. 317, ch. 722, eff. Jan. 1, 1966.

Art. 19.28. "Array"

By the "array" of grand jurors is meant the whole body of persons summoned to serve as such before they have been impaneled.

Acts 1965, 59th Leg., vol. 2, p. 317, ch. 722, eff. Jan. 1, 1966.

Art. 19.29. "Impaneled" and "panel"

A grand juror is said to be "impaneled" after his qualifications have been tried and he has been sworn. By "panel" is meant the whole body of grand jurors.

Acts 1965, 59th Leg., vol. 2, p. 317, ch. 722, eff. Jan. 1, 1966.

Art. 19.30. Challenge to "array"

A challenge to the "array" shall be made in writing for these causes only:

1. That those summoned as grand jurors are not in fact those selected by the method provided by Article 19.01; and

2. That the officer who summoned the grand jurors acted corruptly in summoning any one or more of them.

Acts 1965, 59th Leg., vol. 2, p. 317, ch. 722, eff. Jan. 1, 1966. Amended by Acts 1979, 66th Leg., p. 394, ch. 184, § 3, eff. Sept. 1, 1979; Acts 2015, 84th Leg., ch. 929 (H.B. 2150), § 9, eff. Sept. 1, 2015.

Section 22(a) of Acts 2015, 84th Leg., ch. 929 (H.B. 2150) provides:

"(a) Except as provided by Subsection (b) of this section, the changes in law made by this Act apply to a grand jury impaneled on or after the effective date [Sept. 1, 2015] of this Act. A grand jury impaneled before the effective date of this Act is governed by the law in effect on the date the grand jury was impaneled, and the former law is continued in effect for that purpose."

Art. 19.31. Challenge to Juror

(a) A challenge to a particular grand juror may be made orally for any of the following causes:

1. That the juror is insane;

2. That the juror has such defect in the organs of feeling or hearing, or such bodily or mental defect or disease as to render the juror unfit for jury service, or that the juror is legally blind and the court in its discretion is not satisfied that the juror is fit for jury service in that particular case;

3. That the juror is a witness in or a target of an investigation of a grand jury;

4. That the juror served on a petit jury in a former trial of the same alleged conduct or offense that the grand jury is investigating;

5. That the juror has a bias or prejudice in favor of or against the person accused or suspected of committing an offense that the grand jury is investigating;

6. That from hearsay, or otherwise, there is established in the mind of the juror such a conclusion as to the guilt or innocence of the person accused or suspected of committing an offense that the grand jury is investigating as would influence the juror's vote on the presentment of an indictment;

7. That the juror is related within the third degree by consanguinity or affinity, as determined under Chapter 573, Government Code, to a person accused or suspected of committing an offense that the grand jury is investigating or to a person who is a victim of an offense that the grand jury is investigating;

8. That the juror has a bias or prejudice against any phase of the law upon which the state is entitled to rely for an indictment;

9. That the juror is not a qualified juror; and

10. That the juror is the prosecutor upon an accusation against the person making the challenge.

(b) A challenge under Subsection (a)(3) may be made ex parte and shall be reviewed and ruled on in an in camera proceeding. The court shall seal any record of the challenge.

(c) In this article, "legally blind" has the meaning assigned by Article 35.16(a).

Acts 1965, 59th Leg., vol. 2, p. 317, ch. 722, eff. Jan. 1, 1966. Amended by Acts 2015, 84th Leg., ch. 929 (H.B. 2150), § 10, eff. Sept. 1, 2015.

Section 22(a) of Acts 2015, 84th Leg., ch. 929 (H.B. 2150) provides:

"(a) Except as provided by Subsection (b) of this section, the changes in law made by this Act apply to a grand jury impaneled on or after the effective date [Sept. 1, 2015] of this Act. A grand jury impaneled before the effective date of this Act is governed by the law in effect on the date the grand jury was impaneled, and the former law is continued in effect for that purpose."

Art. 19.315.   Recusal of Juror

(a) If, during the course of a juror's service on the grand jury, the juror determines that the juror could be subject to a valid challenge for cause under Article 19.31, the juror shall recuse himself or herself from grand jury service until the cause no longer exists. A person who knowingly fails to recuse himself or herself under this subsection may be held in contempt of court. A person authorized to be present in the grand jury room shall report a known violation of this subsection to the court.

(b) The court shall instruct the grand jury as to the duty imposed by Subsection (a).

Added by Acts 2015, 84th Leg., ch. 929 (H.B. 2150), § 11, eff. Sept. 1, 2015.

Section 22(a) of Acts 2015, 84th Leg., ch. 929 (H.B. 2150) provides:

"(a) Except as provided by Subsection (b) of this section, the changes in law made by this Act apply to a grand jury impaneled on or after the effective date [Sept. 1, 2015] of this Act. A grand jury impaneled before the effective date of this Act is governed by the law in effect on the date the grand jury was impaneled, and the former law is continued in effect for that purpose."

Art. 19.32.   Summarily decided

When a challenge to the array or to any individual has been made, the court shall hear proof and decide in a summary manner whether the challenge be well-founded or not.

Acts 1965, 59th Leg., vol. 2, p. 317, ch. 722, eff. Jan. 1, 1966.

Art. 19.33.   Other jurors summoned

The court shall order another grand jury to be summoned if the challenge to the array be sustained, or order the panel to be completed if by challenge to any particular grand juror their number be reduced below twelve.

Acts 1965, 59th Leg., vol. 2, p. 317, ch. 722, eff. Jan. 1, 1966.

Art. 19.34.   Oath of grand jurors

When the grand jury is completed, the court shall appoint one of the number foreman; and the following oath shall be administered by the court, or under its direction, to the jurors: "You solemnly swear that you will diligently inquire into, and true presentment make, of all such matters and things as shall be given you in charge; the State's counsel, your fellows and your own, you shall keep secret, unless required to disclose the same in the course of a judicial proceeding in which the truth or falsity of evidence given in the grand jury room, in a criminal case, shall be under investigation. You shall present no person from envy, hatred or malice; neither shall you leave any person unpresented for love, fear, favor, affection or hope of reward; but you shall present things truly as they come to your knowledge, according to the best of your understanding, so help you God".

Acts 1965, 59th Leg., vol. 2, p. 317, ch. 722, eff. Jan. 1, 1966.

Art. 19.35.   To instruct jury

The court shall instruct the grand jury as to their duty.

Acts 1965, 59th Leg., vol. 2, p. 317, ch. 722, eff. Jan. 1, 1966.

Art. 19.36.   Bailiffs appointed

The court and the district attorney may each appoint one or more bailiffs to attend upon the grand jury, and at the time of appointment, the following oath shall be administered to each of them by the court, or under its direction: "You solemnly swear that you will faithfully and impartially perform all the duties of bailiff of the grand jury, and that you will keep secret the proceedings of the grand jury, so help you God". Such bailiffs shall be compensated in a sum to be set by the commissioners court of said county.

Acts 1965, 59th Leg., vol. 2, p. 317, ch. 722, eff. Jan. 1, 1966.

Art. 19.37.   Bailiff's duties

A bailiff is to obey the instructions of the foreman, to summon all witnesses, and generally, to perform all such duties as the foreman may require of him. One bailiff shall be always with the grand jury, if two or more are appointed.

Acts 1965, 59th Leg., vol. 2, p. 317, ch. 722, eff. Jan. 1, 1966.

Art. 19.38.   Bailiff violating duty

No bailiff shall take part in the discussions or deliberations of the grand jury nor be present when they are discussing or voting upon a question. The grand jury shall report to the court any violation of duty by a bailiff and the court may punish him for such violation as for contempt.

Acts 1965, 59th Leg., vol. 2, p. 317, ch. 722, eff. Jan. 1, 1966.

Art. 19.39.   Another foreman appointed

If the foreman of the grand jury is from any cause absent or unable or disqualified to act, the court shall appoint in his place some other member of the body.

Acts 1965, 59th Leg., vol. 2, p. 317, ch. 722, eff. Jan. 1, 1966.

Art. 19.40. Quorum

Nine members shall be a quorum for the purpose of discharging any duty or exercising any right properly belonging to the grand jury.

Acts 1965, 59th Leg., vol. 2, p. 317, ch. 722, eff. Jan. 1, 1966.

Art. 19.41. Reassembled

A grand jury discharged by the court for the term may be reassembled by the court at any time during the term.

Acts 1965, 59th Leg., vol. 2, p. 317, ch. 722, eff. Jan. 1, 1966. Amended by Acts 1999, 76th Leg., ch. 1065, § 4, eff. Sept. 1, 1999.

Art. 19.42. Personal information about grand jurors

(a) Except as provided by Subsection (b), information collected by the court, court personnel, or prosecuting attorney during the grand jury selection process about a person who serves as a grand juror, including the person's home address, home telephone number, social security number, driver's license number, and other personal information, is confidential and may not be disclosed by the court, court personnel, or prosecuting attorney.

(b) On a showing of good cause, the court shall permit disclosure of the information sought to a party to the proceeding.

Added by Acts 1999, 76th Leg., ch. 1177, § 3, eff. Sept. 1, 1999.

CHAPTER TWENTY. DUTIES AND POWERS OF THE GRAND JURY

Art. 20.01. Grand jury room

After the grand jury is organized they shall proceed to the discharge of their duties in a suitable place which the sheriff shall prepare for their sessions.

Acts 1965, 59th Leg., vol. 2, p. 317, ch. 722, eff. Jan. 1, 1966.

Art. 20.011. Who may be present in grand jury room

(a) Only the following persons may be present in a grand jury room while the grand jury is conducting proceedings:

(1) grand jurors;

(2) bailiffs;

(3) the attorney representing the state;

(4) witnesses while being examined or when necessary to assist the attorney representing the state in examining other witnesses or presenting evidence to the grand jury;

(5) interpreters, if necessary;

(6) a stenographer or person operating an electronic recording device, as provided by Article 20.012; and

(7) a person operating a video teleconferencing system for use under Article 20.151.

(b) Only a grand juror may be in a grand jury room while the grand jury is deliberating.

Added by Acts 1995, 74th Leg., ch. 1011, § 1, eff. Sept. 1, 1995. Amended by Acts 2011, 82nd Leg., ch. 1031 (H.B. 2847), § 2, eff. Sept. 1, 2011; Acts 2011, 82nd Leg., ch. 1341 (S.B. 1233), § 3, eff. June 17, 2011.

Art. 20.012. Recording of certain testimony

(a) Questions propounded by the grand jury or the attorney representing the state to a person accused or suspected and the testimony of that person to the grand jury shall be recorded either by a stenographer or by use of an electronic device capable of recording sound.

(b) The validity of a grand jury proceeding is not affected by an unintentional failure to record all or part of questions propounded or testimony made under Subsection (a).

(c) The attorney representing the state shall maintain possession of all records other than stenographer's notes made under this article and any typewritten transcription of those records, except as provided by Article 20.02.

Added by Acts 1995, 74th Leg., ch. 1011, § 1, eff. Sept. 1, 1995.

Art. 20.02. Proceedings secret

(a) The proceedings of the grand jury shall be secret.

(b) A grand juror, bailiff, interpreter, stenographer or person operating an electronic recording device, person preparing a typewritten transcription of a stenographic or electronic recording, or person operating a video teleconferencing system for use under Article 20.151 who discloses anything transpiring before the grand jury, regardless of whether the thing transpiring is recorded, in the course of the official duties of the grand jury, is liable to a fine as for contempt of the court, not exceeding $500, imprisonment not exceeding 30 days, or both the fine and imprisonment.

(c) A disclosure of a record made under Article 20.012, a disclosure of a typewritten transcription of that record, or a disclosure otherwise prohibited by Subsection (b) or Article 20.16 may be made by the attorney representing the state in performing the attorney's duties to a grand juror serving on the grand jury before whom the record was made, another grand jury, a law enforcement agency, or a prosecuting attorney, as permitted by the attorney representing the state and determined by the attorney as necessary to assist the attorney in the performance of the attorney's duties. The attorney representing the state shall warn any person the attorney authorizes to receive information under this subsection of the person's duty to maintain the secrecy of the information. Any person who receives information under this subsection and discloses the information for purposes other than those permitted by this subsection is subject to punishment for contempt in the same manner as persons who violate Subsection (b).

(d) The defendant may petition a court to order the disclosure of information otherwise made secret by this article or the disclosure of a recording or typewritten transcription under Article 20.012 as a matter preliminary to or in connection with a judicial proceeding. The court may order disclosure of the information, recording, or transcription on a showing by the defendant of a particularized need.

(e) A petition for disclosure under Subsection (d) must be filed in the district court in which the case is pending. The defendant must also file a copy of the petition with the attorney representing the state, the parties to the judicial proceeding, and any other persons required by the court to receive a copy of the petition. All persons receiving a petition under this subsection are entitled to appear before the court. The court shall provide interested parties with an opportunity to appear and present arguments for the continuation of or end to the requirement of secrecy.

(f) A person who receives information under Subsection (d) or (e) and discloses that information is subject to punishment for contempt in the same manner as a person who violates Subsection (b).

(g) The attorney representing the state may not disclose anything transpiring before the grand jury except as permitted by Subsections (c), (d), and (e).

(h) A subpoena or summons relating to a grand jury proceeding or investigation must be kept secret to the extent and for as long as necessary to prevent the unauthorized disclosure of a matter before the grand jury. This subsection may not be construed to limit a disclosure permitted by Subsection (c), (d), or (e).

Acts 1965, 59th Leg., vol. 2, p. 317, ch. 722, eff. Jan. 1, 1966. Amended by Acts 1995, 74th Leg., ch. 1011, § 2, eff. Sept. 1, 1995; Acts 2007, 80th Leg., ch. 628, § 1, eff. Sept. 1, 2007. Amended by Acts 2011, 82nd Leg., ch. 1031 (H.B. 2847), § 3, eff. Sept. 1, 2011; Acts 2011, 82nd Leg., ch. 1341 (S.B. 1233), § 4, eff. June 17, 2011.

Art. 20.03. Attorney representing State entitled to appear

"The attorney representing the State" means the Attorney General, district attorney, criminal district attorney, or county attorney. The attorney representing the State, is entitled to go before the grand jury and inform them of offenses liable to indictment at any time except when they are discussing the propriety of finding an indictment or voting upon the same.

Acts 1965, 59th Leg., vol. 2, p. 317, ch. 722, eff. Jan. 1, 1966.

Art. 20.04. Attorney may examine witnesses

The attorney representing the State may examine the witnesses before the grand jury and shall advise as to the proper mode of interrogating them. No person other than the attorney representing the State or a grand juror may question a witness before the grand jury. No person may address the grand jury about a matter before the grand jury other than the attorney representing the State, a witness, or the accused or suspected person or the attorney for the accused or suspected person if approved by the State's attorney.

Acts 1965, 59th Leg., vol. 2, p. 317, ch. 722, eff. Jan. 1, 1966. Amended by Acts 1989, 71st Leg., ch. 1065, § 2, eff. Sept. 1, 1989.

Art. 20.05. May send for attorney

The grand jury may send for the attorney representing the state and ask his advice upon any matter of law or upon any question arising respecting the proper discharge of their duties.

Acts 1965, 59th Leg., vol. 2, p. 317, ch. 722, eff. Jan. 1, 1966. Amended by Acts 1989, 71st Leg., ch. 1065, § 3, eff. Sept. 1, 1989.

Art. 20.06. Advice from court

The grand jury may also seek and receive advice from the court touching any matter before them, and for this purpose, shall go into court in a body; but they shall so guard the manner of propounding their questions as not to divulge the particular accusation that is pending before them; or they may propound their questions in writing, upon which the court may give them the desired information in writing.

Acts 1965, 59th Leg., vol. 2, p. 317, ch. 722, eff. Jan. 1, 1966.

Art. 20.07. Foreman shall preside

The foreman shall preside over the sessions of the grand jury, and conduct its business and proceedings in an orderly manner. He may appoint one or more members of the body to act as clerks for the grand jury.

Acts 1965, 59th Leg., vol. 2, p. 317, ch. 722, eff. Jan. 1, 1966.

Art. 20.08. Adjournments

The grand jury shall meet and adjourn at times agreed upon by a majority of the body; but they shall not adjourn, at any one time, for more than three days, unless by consent of the court. With the consent of the court, they may adjourn for a longer time, and shall as near as may be, conform their adjournments to those of the court.

Acts 1965, 59th Leg., vol. 2, p. 317, ch. 722, eff. Jan. 1, 1966.

Art. 20.09. Duties of grand jury

The grand jury shall inquire into all offenses liable to indictment of which any member may have knowledge, or of which they shall be informed by the attorney representing the State, or any other credible person.

Acts 1965, 59th Leg., vol. 2, p. 317, ch. 722, eff. Jan. 1, 1966.

Art. 20.10. Attorney or foreman may issue process

The attorney representing the state, or the foreman, in term time or vacation, may issue a summons or attachment for any witness in the county where they are sitting; which summons or attachment may require the witness to appear before them at a time fixed, or forthwith, without stating the matter under investigation.

Acts 1965, 59th Leg., vol. 2, p. 317, ch. 722, eff. Jan. 1, 1966.

Art. 20.11. Out-of-county witnesses

Sec. 1. The foreman or the attorney representing the State may, upon written application to the district court stating the name and residence of the witness and that his testimony is believed to be material, cause a subpoena or an attachment to be issued to any county in the State for such witness, returnable to the grand jury then in session, or to the next grand jury for the county from whence the same issued, as such foreman or attorney may desire. The subpoena may require the witness to appear and produce records and documents. An attachment shall command the sheriff or any constable of the county where the witness resides to serve the witness, and have him before the grand jury at the time and place specified in the writ.

Sec. 2. A subpoena or attachment issued pursuant to this article shall be served and returned in the manner prescribed in Chapter 24 of this code.

A witness subpoenaed pursuant to this article shall be compensated as provided in this code.

Acts 1965, 59th Leg., vol. 2, p. 317, ch. 722, eff. Jan. 1, 1966. Amended by Acts 1973, 63rd Leg., p. 787, ch. 350, § 1, eff. June 12, 1973.

Art. 20.12. Attachment in vacation

The attorney representing the state may cause an attachment for a witness to be issued, as provided in the preceding Article, either in term time or in vacation.

Acts 1965, 59th Leg., vol. 2, p. 317, ch. 722, eff. Jan. 1, 1966.

Art. 20.13. Execution of process

The bailiff or other officer who receives process to be served from a grand jury shall forthwith execute the same and return it to the foreman, if the grand jury be in session; and if the grand jury be not in session, the process shall be returned to the district clerk. If the process is returned not executed, the return shall state why it was not executed.

Acts 1965, 59th Leg., vol. 2, p. 317, ch. 722, eff. Jan. 1, 1966.

Art. 20.14. Evasion of process

If it be made to appear satisfactorily to the court that a witness for whom an attachment has been issued to go before the grand jury is in any manner wilfully evading the service of such summons or attachment, the court may fine such witness, as for contempt, not exceeding five hundred dollars.

Acts 1965, 59th Leg., vol. 2, p. 317, ch. 722, eff. Jan. 1, 1966.

Art. 20.15. When witness refuses to testify

When a witness, brought in any manner before a grand jury, refuses to testify, such fact shall be made known to the attorney representing the State or to the court; and the court may compel the witness to answer the question, if it appear to be a proper one, by imposing a fine not exceeding five hundred dollars, and by committing the party to jail until he is willing to testify.

Acts 1965, 59th Leg., vol. 2, p. 317, ch. 722, eff. Jan. 1, 1966.

Art. 20.151. Certain testimony by video teleconferencing

(a) With the consent of the foreman of the grand jury and the attorney representing the state, a peace officer summoned to testify before the grand jury may testify through the use of a closed circuit video teleconferencing system that provides an encrypted, simultaneous, compressed full motion video and interactive communication of image and sound between the peace officer, the attorney representing the state, and the grand jury.

(b) In addition to being administered the oath described by Article 20.16(a), before being interrogated, a peace officer testifying through the use of a closed circuit video teleconferencing system under this article shall affirm that:

(1) no person other than a person in the grand jury room is capable of hearing the peace officer's testimony; and

(2) the peace officer's testimony is not being recorded or otherwise preserved by any person at the location from which the peace officer is testifying.

(c) Testimony received from a peace officer under this article shall be recorded in the same manner as other testimony taken before the grand jury and shall be preserved.

Added by Acts 2011, 82nd Leg., ch. 1031 (H.B. 2847), § 4, eff. Sept. 1, 2011; Acts 2011, 82nd Leg., ch. 1341 (S.B. 1233), § 5, eff. June 17, 2011. Amended by Acts 2013, 83rd Leg., ch. 161 (S.B. 1093), § 3.005, eff. Sept. 1, 2013.

Art. 20.16. Oaths to witnesses

(a) The following oath shall be administered by the foreman, or under the foreman's direction, to each witness before being interrogated: "You solemnly swear that you will not reveal, by your words or conduct, and will keep secret any matter about which you may be interrogated or that you have observed during the proceedings of the grand jury, and that you will answer truthfully the questions asked of you by the grand jury, or under its direction, so help you God."

(b) A witness who reveals any matter about which the witness is interrogated or that the witness has observed during the proceedings of the grand jury, other than when required to give evidence thereof in due course, shall be liable to a fine as for contempt of court, not exceeding $500, and to imprisonment not exceeding six months.

Acts 1965, 59th Leg., vol. 2, p. 317, ch. 722, eff. Jan. 1, 1966. Amended by Acts 1973, 63rd Leg., p. 968, ch. 399, § 2(A), eff. Jan. 1, 1974; Acts 2007, 80th Leg., ch. 28, § 1, eff. Sept. 1, 2007.

Art. 20.17. How suspect or accused questioned

(a) The grand jury, in propounding questions to the person accused or suspected, shall first state the offense with which he is suspected or accused, the county where the offense is said to have been committed and as nearly as may be, the time of commission of the offense, and shall direct the examination to the offense under investigation.

(b) Prior to any questioning of an accused or suspected person who is subpoenaed to appear before the grand jury, the accused or suspected person shall be furnished a written copy of the warnings contained in Subsection (c) of this section and shall be given a reasonable opportunity to retain counsel or apply to the court for an appointed attorney and to consult with counsel prior to appearing before the grand jury.

(c) If an accused or suspected person is subpoenaed to appear before a grand jury prior to any questions before the grand jury, the person accused or suspected shall be orally warned as follows:

(1) "Your testimony before this grand jury is under oath";

(2) "Any material question that is answered falsely before this grand jury subjects you to being prosecuted for aggravated perjury";

(3) "You have the right to refuse to make answers to any question, the answer to which would incriminate you in any manner";

(4) "You have the right to have a lawyer present outside this chamber to advise you before making answers to questions you feel might incriminate you";

(5) "Any testimony you give may be used against you at any subsequent proceeding";

(6) "If you are unable to employ a lawyer, you have the right to have a lawyer appointed to advise you before making an answer to a question, the answer to which you feel might incriminate you."

Acts 1965, 59th Leg., vol. 2, p. 317, ch. 722, eff. Jan. 1, 1966. Amended by Acts 1989, 71st Leg., ch. 1065, § 4, eff. Sept. 1, 1989.

Art. 20.18. How witness questioned

When a felony has been committed in any county within the jurisdiction of the grand jury, and the name of the offender is known or unknown or where it is uncertain when or how the felony was committed, the grand jury shall first state to the witness called the subject matter under investigation, then may ask pertinent questions relative to the transaction in general terms and in such a manner as to determine whether he has knowledge of the violation of any particular law by any person, and if so, by what person.

Acts 1965, 59th Leg., vol. 2, p. 317, ch. 722, eff. Jan. 1, 1966.

Art. 20.19. Grand jury shall vote

After all the testimony which is accessible to the grand jury shall have been given in respect to any criminal accusation, the vote shall be taken as to the presentment of an indictment, and if nine members concur in finding the bill, the foreman shall make a memorandum of the same with such data as will enable the attorney who represents the State to write the indictment.

Acts 1965, 59th Leg., vol. 2, p. 317, ch. 722, eff. Jan. 1, 1966.

Art. 20.20. Indictment prepared

The attorney representing the State shall prepare all indictments which have been found, with as little delay as possible, and deliver them to the foreman, who shall sign the same officially, and said attorney shall endorse thereon the names of the witnesses upon whose testimony the same was found.

Acts 1965, 59th Leg., vol. 2, p. 317, ch. 722, eff. Jan. 1, 1966.

Art. 20.21. Indictment presented

When the indictment is ready to be presented, the grand jury shall through their foreman, deliver the indictment to the judge or clerk of the court. At least nine members of the grand jury must be present on such occasion.

Acts 1965, 59th Leg., vol. 2, p. 317, ch. 722, eff. Jan. 1, 1966. Amended by Acts 1979, 66th Leg., p. 1033, ch. 463, § 1, eff. June 7, 1979.

Art. 20.22. Presentment entered of record

(a) The fact of a presentment of indictment by a grand jury shall be entered in the record of the court, if the defendant is in custody or under bond, noting briefly the style of the criminal action, the file number of the indictment, and the defendant's name.

(b) If the defendant is not in custody or under bond at the time of the presentment of indictment, the indictment may not be made public and the entry in the record of the court relating to the indictment must be delayed until the capias is served and the defendant is placed in custody or under bond.

Acts 1965, 59th Leg., vol. 2, p. 317, ch. 722, eff. Jan. 1, 1966. Amended by Acts 1979, 66th Leg., p. 1033, ch. 463, § 2, eff. June 7, 1979; Acts 1999, 76th Leg., ch. 580, § 3, eff. Sept. 1, 1999; Acts 2007, 80th Leg., ch. 628, § 2, eff. Sept. 1, 2007. Amended by Acts 2011, 82nd Leg., ch. 278 (H.B. 1573), § 2, eff. Sept. 1, 2011.

CHAPTER TWENTY–ONE. INDICTMENT AND INFORMATION

Art. 21.01.   "Indictment"

An "indictment" is the written statement of a grand jury accusing a person therein named of some act or omission which, by law, is declared to be an offense.

Acts 1965, 59th Leg., p. 317, ch. 722, § 1, eff. Jan. 1, 1966.

Art. 21.011.   Filing of Charging Instrument or Related Document in Electronic Form

(a) An indictment, information, complaint, or other charging instrument or a related document in a criminal case may be filed in electronic form with a judge or clerk of the court authorized to receive the document.

(b) A judge or clerk of the court is authorized to receive for filing purposes an information, indictment, complaint, or other charging instrument or a related document in electronic form in accordance with Subchapter I, Chapter 51, Government Code, [1] if:

(1) the document complies with the requirements that would apply if the document were filed in hard-copy form;

(2) the clerk of the court has the means to electronically store the document for the statutory period of record retention;

(3) the judge or clerk of the court is able to reproduce the document in hard-copy form on demand; and

(4) the clerk of the court is able to display or otherwise make the document available in electronic form to the public at no charge.

(c) The person filing the document and the person receiving the document must complete the electronic filing as provided by Section 51.804, Government Code.

(d) Notwithstanding Section 51.806, Government Code, an indictment, information, complaint, or other charging instrument or a related document transmitted in electronic form is exempt from a requirement under this code that the pleading be endorsed by a natural person. The requirement of an oath under this code is satisfied if:

(1) all or part of the document was sworn to; and

(2) the electronic form states which parts of the document were sworn to and the name of the officer administering the oath.

(e) An electronically filed document described by this section may be amended or modified in compliance with Chapter 28 or other applicable law. The amended or modified document must reflect that the original document has been superseded.

(f) This section does not affect the application of Section 51.318, Government Code, Section 118.052(3), Local Government Code, or any other law permitting the collection of fees for the provision of services related to court documents.

Added by Acts 2005, 79th Leg., ch. 312, § 3, eff. June 17, 2005.

[1] V.T.C.A.Government Code § 51.801 et seq.

Art. 21.02.   Requisites of an indictment

An indictment shall be deemed sufficient if it has the following requisites:

1. It shall commence, "In the name and by authority of The State of Texas".

2. It must appear that the same was presented in the district court of the county where the grand jury is in session.

3. It must appear to be the act of a grand jury of the proper county.

4. It must contain the name of the accused, or state that his name is unknown and give a reasonably accurate description of him.

5. It must show that the place where the offense was committed is within the jurisdiction of the court in which the indictment is presented.

6. The time mentioned must be some date anterior to the presentment of the indictment, and not so remote that the prosecution of the offense is barred by limitation.

7. The offense must be set forth in plain and intelligible words.

8. The indictment must conclude, "Against the peace and dignity of the State".

9. It shall be signed officially by the foreman of the grand jury.

Acts 1965, 59th Leg., p. 317, ch. 722, § 1, eff. Jan. 1, 1966.

Art. 21.03. What should be stated

Everything should be stated in an indictment which is necessary to be proved.

Acts 1965, 59th Leg., p. 317, ch. 722, § 1, eff. Jan. 1, 1966.

Art. 21.04. The certainty required

The certainty required in an indictment is such as will enable the accused to plead the judgment that may be given upon it in bar of any prosecution for the same offense.

Acts 1965, 59th Leg., p. 317, ch. 722, § 1, eff. Jan. 1, 1966.

Art. 21.05. Particular intent; intent to defraud

Where a particular intent is a material fact in the description of the offense, it must be stated in the indictment; but in any case where an intent to defraud is required to constitute an offense, it shall be sufficient to allege an intent to defraud, without naming therein the particular person intended to be defrauded.

Acts 1965, 59th Leg., p. 317, ch. 722, § 1, eff. Jan. 1, 1966.

Art. 21.06. Allegation of venue

When the offense may be prosecuted in either of two or more counties, the indictment may allege the offense to have been committed in the county where the same is prosecuted, or in any county or place where the offense was actually committed.

Acts 1965, 59th Leg., p. 317, ch. 722, § 1, eff. Jan. 1, 1966.

Art. 21.07. Allegation of name

In alleging the name of the defendant, or of any other person necessary to be stated in the indictment, it shall be sufficient to state one or more of the initials of the given name and the surname. When a person is known by two or more names, it shall be sufficient to state either name. When the name of the person is unknown to the grand jury, that fact shall be stated, and if it be the accused, a reasonably accurate description of him shall be given in the indictment.

Acts 1965, 59th Leg., p. 317, ch. 722, § 1, eff. Jan. 1, 1966. Amended by Acts 1995, 74th Leg., ch. 830, § 1, eff. Sept. 1, 1995.

Art. 21.08. Allegation of ownership

Where one person owns the property, and another person has the possession of the same, the ownership thereof may be alleged to be in either. Where property is owned in common, or jointly, by two or more persons, the ownership may be alleged to be in all or either of them. When the property belongs to the estate of a deceased person, the ownership may be alleged to be in the executor, administrator or heirs of such deceased person, or in any one of such heirs. Where the ownership of the property is unknown to the grand jury, it shall be sufficient to allege that fact.

Acts 1965, 59th Leg., p. 317, ch. 722, § 1, eff. Jan. 1, 1966. Amended by Acts 1967, 60th Leg., p. 1738, ch. 659, § 16, eff. Aug. 28, 1967.

Art. 21.09. Description of property

If known, personal property alleged in an indictment shall be identified by name, kind, number, and ownership. When such is unknown, that fact shall be stated, and a general classification, describing and identifying the property as near as may be, shall suffice. If the property be real estate, its general locality in the county, and the name of the owner, occupant or claimant thereof, shall be a sufficient description of the same.

Acts 1965, 59th Leg., p. 317, ch. 722, § 1, eff. Jan. 1, 1966. Amended by Acts 1975, 64th Leg., p. 909, ch. 341, § 2, eff. June 19, 1975.

Art. 21.10. "Felonious" and "feloniously"

It is not necessary to use the words "felonious" or "feloniously" in any indictment.

Acts 1965, 59th Leg., p. 317, ch. 722, § 1, eff. Jan. 1, 1966.

Art. 21.11. Certainty; what sufficient

An indictment shall be deemed sufficient which charges the commission of the offense in ordinary and concise language in such a manner as to enable a person of common understanding to know what is meant, and with that degree of certainty that will give the defendant notice of the particular offense with which he is charged, and enable the court, on conviction, to pronounce the proper judgment; and in no case are the words "force and arms" or "contrary to the form of the statute" necessary.

Acts 1965, 59th Leg., p. 317, ch. 722, § 1, eff. Jan. 1, 1966.

Art. 21.12. Special and general terms

When a statute defining any offense uses special or particular terms, indictment on it may use the general term which, in common language, embraces the special term. To charge an unlawful sale, it is necessary to name the purchaser.

Acts 1965, 59th Leg., p. 317, ch. 722, § 1, eff. Jan. 1, 1966.

Art. 21.13.   Act with intent to commit an offense

An indictment for an act done with intent to commit some other offense may charge in general terms the commission of such act with intent to commit such other offense.

Acts 1965, 59th Leg., p. 317, ch. 722, § 1, eff. Jan. 1, 1966.

Art. 21.14.   Perjury and aggravated perjury

(a) An indictment for perjury or aggravated perjury need not charge the precise language of the false statement, but may state the substance of the same, and no such indictment shall be held insufficient on account of any variance which does not affect the subject matter or general import of such false statement; and it is not necessary in such indictment to set forth the pleadings, records or proceeding with which the false statement is connected, nor the commission or authority of the court or person before whom the false statement was made; but it is sufficient to state the name of the court or public servant by whom the oath was administered with the allegation of the falsity of the matter on which the perjury or aggravated perjury is assigned.

(b) If an individual is charged with aggravated perjury before a grand jury, the indictment may not be entered by the grand jury before which the false statement was alleged to have been made.

Acts 1965, 59th Leg., p. 317, ch. 722, § 1, eff. Jan. 1, 1966. Amended by Acts 1973, 63rd Leg., p. 968, ch. 399, § 2(A), eff. Jan. 1, 1974; Acts 1989, 71st Leg., ch. 1065, § 5, eff. Sept. 1, 1989.

Art. 21.15.   Must allege acts of recklessness or criminal negligence

Whenever recklessness or criminal negligence enters into or is a part or element of any offense, or it is charged that the accused acted recklessly or with criminal negligence in the commission of an offense, the complaint, information, or indictment in order to be sufficient in any such case must allege, with reasonable certainty, the act or acts relied upon to constitute recklessness or criminal negligence, and in no event shall it be sufficient to allege merely that the accused, in committing the offense, acted recklessly or with criminal negligence.

Acts 1965, 59th Leg., p. 317, ch. 722, § 1, eff. Jan. 1, 1966. Amended by Acts 1973, 63rd Leg., p. 968, ch. 399, § 2(A), eff. Jan. 1, 1974.

Art. 21.16.   Certain forms of indictments

The following form of indictments is sufficient:

"In the name and by authority of the State of Texas: The grand jury of .... County, State of Texas, duly organized at the .... term, A.D. ...., of the district court of said county, in said court at said term, do present that .... (defendant) on the .... day of .... A.D. ...., in said county and State, did .... (description of offense) against the peace and dignity of the State.

............, Foreman of the grand jury."

Acts 1965, 59th Leg., p. 317, ch. 722, § 1, eff. Jan. 1, 1966.

Art. 21.17.   Following statutory words

Words used in a statute to define an offense need not be strictly pursued in the indictment; it is sufficient to use other words conveying the same meaning, or which include the sense of the statutory words.

Acts 1965, 59th Leg., p. 317, ch. 722, § 1, eff. Jan. 1, 1966.

Art. 21.18.   Matters of judicial notice

Presumptions of law and matters of which judicial notice is taken (among which are included the authority and duties of all officers elected or appointed under the General Laws of this State) need not be stated in an indictment.

Acts 1965, 59th Leg., p. 317, ch. 722, § 1, eff. Jan. 1, 1966.

Art. 21.19.   Defects of form

An indictment shall not be held insufficient, nor shall the trial, judgment or other proceedings thereon be affected, by reason of any defect of form which does not prejudice the substantial rights of the defendant.

Acts 1965, 59th Leg., p. 317, ch. 722, § 1, eff. Jan. 1, 1966.

Art. 21.20.   "Information"

An "information" is a written statement filed and presented in behalf of the State by the district or county attorney, charging the defendant with an offense which may by law be so prosecuted.

Acts 1965, 59th Leg., p. 317, ch. 722, § 1, eff. Jan. 1, 1966.

Art. 21.21.   Requisites of an information

An information is sufficient if it has the following requisites:

1. It shall commence, "In the name and by authority of the State of Texas";

2. That it appear to have been presented in a court having jurisdiction of the offense set forth;

3. That it appear to have been presented by the proper officer;

4. That it contain the name of the accused, or state that his name is unknown and give a reasonably accurate description of him;

5. It must appear that the place where the offense is charged to have been committed is within the jurisdiction of the court where the information is filed;

6. That the time mentioned be some date anterior to the filing of the information, and that the offense does not appear to be barred by limitation;

7. That the offense be set forth in plain and intelligible words;

8. That it conclude, "Against the peace and dignity of the State"; and

9. It must be signed by the district or county attorney, officially.

Acts 1965, 59th Leg., p. 317, ch. 722, § 1, eff. Jan. 1, 1966.

Art. 21.22.　Information based upon complaint

No information shall be presented until affidavit has been made by some credible person charging the defendant with an offense. The affidavit shall be filed with the information. It may be sworn to before the district or county attorney who, for that purpose, shall have power to administer the oath, or it may be made before any officer authorized by law to administer oaths.

Acts 1965, 59th Leg., p. 317, ch. 722, § 1, eff. Jan. 1, 1966.

Art. 21.23.　Rules as to indictment apply to information

The rules with respect to allegations in an indictment and the certainty required apply also to an information.

Acts 1965, 59th Leg., p. 317, ch. 722, § 1, eff. Jan. 1, 1966.

Art. 21.24.　Joinder of certain offenses

(a) Two or more offenses may be joined in a single indictment, information, or complaint, with each offense stated in a separate count, if the offenses arise out of the same criminal episode, as defined in Chapter 3 of the Penal Code.

(b) A count may contain as many separate paragraphs charging the same offense as necessary, but no paragraph may charge more than one offense.

(c) A count is sufficient if any one of its paragraphs is sufficient. An indictment, information, or complaint is sufficient if any one of its counts is sufficient.

Acts 1965, 59th Leg., p. 317, ch. 722, § 1, eff. Jan. 1, 1966. Amended by Acts 1973, 63rd Leg., p. 968, ch. 399, § 2(A), eff. Jan. 1, 1974.

Art. 21.25.　When indictment has been lost, etc.

When an indictment or information has been lost, mislaid, mutilated or obliterated, the district or county attorney may suggest the fact to the court; and the same shall be entered upon the minutes of the court. In such case, another indictment or information may be substituted, upon the written statement of such attorney that it is substantially the same as that which has been lost, mislaid, mutilated, or obliterated. Or another indictment may be presented, as in the first instance; and in such case, the period for the commencement of the prosecution shall be dated from the time of making such entry.

Acts 1965, 59th Leg., p. 317, ch. 722, § 1, eff. Jan. 1, 1966.

Art. 21.26.　Order transferring cases

Upon the filing of an indictment in the district court which charges an offense over which such court has no jurisdiction, the judge of such court shall make an order transferring the same to such inferior court as may have jurisdiction, stating in such order the cause transferred and to what court transferred.

Acts 1965, 59th Leg., p. 317, ch. 722, § 1, eff. Jan. 1, 1966.

Art. 21.27.　Causes transferred to justice court

Causes over which justices of the peace have jurisdiction may be transferred to a justice of the peace at the county seat, or in the discretion of the judge, to a justice of the precinct in which the same can be most conveniently tried, as may appear by memorandum endorsed by the grand jury on the indictment or otherwise. If it appears to the judge that the offense has been committed in any incorporated town or city, the cause shall be transferred to a justice in said town or city, if there be one therein; and any justice to whom such cause may be transferred shall have jurisdiction to try the same.

Acts 1965, 59th Leg., p. 317, ch. 722, § 1, eff. Jan. 1, 1966.

Art. 21.28.　Duty on transfer

The clerk of the court, without delay, shall deliver the indictments in all cases transferred, together with all the papers relating to each case, to the proper court or justice, as directed in the order of transfer;

and shall accompany each case with a certified copy of all the proceedings taken therein in the district court, and with a bill of the costs that have accrued therein in the district court. The said costs shall be taxed in the court in which said cause is tried, in the event of a conviction.

Acts 1965, 59th Leg., p. 317, ch. 722, § 1, eff. Jan. 1, 1966.

Art. 21.29. Proceedings of inferior court

Any case so transferred shall be entered on the docket of the court to which it is transferred. All process thereon shall be issued and the defendant tried as if the case had originated in the court to which it was transferred.

Acts 1965, 59th Leg., p. 317, ch. 722, § 1, eff. Jan. 1, 1966.

Art. 21.30. Cause improvidently transferred

When a cause has been improvidently transferred to a court which has no jurisdiction of the same, the court to which it has been transferred shall order it to be re-transferred to the proper court; and the same proceedings shall be had as in the case of the original transfer. In such case, the defendant and the witnesses shall be held bound to appear before the court to which the case has been re-transferred, the same as they were bound to appear before the court so transferring the same.

Acts 1965, 59th Leg., p. 317, ch. 722, § 1, eff. Jan. 1, 1966.

Art. 21.31. Testing for AIDS and Certain Other Diseases

(a) A person who is indicted for or who waives indictment for an offense under Section 21.02, 21.11(a)(1), 22.011, or 22.021, Penal Code, shall, at the direction of the court on the court's own motion or on the request of the victim of the alleged offense, undergo a standard diagnostic test approved by the United States Food and Drug Administration for human immunodeficiency virus (HIV) infection and other sexually transmitted diseases. If the person refuses to submit voluntarily to the test, the court shall require the person to submit to the test. On request of the victim of the alleged offense, the court shall order the defendant to undergo the test not later than 48 hours after an indictment for the offense is presented against the defendant or the defendant waives indictment. Except as provided by Subsection (b–1), the court may require a defendant previously required under this article to undergo a diagnostic test on indictment for an offense to undergo a subsequent test only after conviction of the offense. A person per-

forming a test under this subsection shall make the test results available to the local health authority, and the local health authority shall be required to make the notification of the test results to the victim of the alleged offense and to the defendant.

(a–1) If the victim requests the testing of the defendant and a law enforcement agency is unable to locate the defendant during the 48–hour period allowed for that testing under Subsection (a), the running of the 48–hour period is tolled until the law enforcement agency locates the defendant and the defendant is present in the jurisdiction.

(b) The court shall order a person who is charged with an offense under Section 22.11, Penal Code, to undergo in the manner provided by Subsection (a) a diagnostic test designed to show or help show whether the person has HIV, hepatitis A, hepatitis B, tuberculosis, or any other disease designated as a reportable disease under Section 81.048, Health and Safety Code. The person charged with the offense shall pay the costs of testing under this subsection.

(b–1) If the results of a diagnostic test conducted under Subsection (a) or (b) are positive for HIV, the court shall order the defendant to undergo any necessary additional testing within a reasonable time after the test results are released.

(c) The state may not use the fact that a test was performed on a person under Subsection (a) or use the results of a test conducted under Subsection (a) in any criminal proceeding arising out of the alleged offense.

(d) Testing under this article shall be conducted in accordance with written infectious disease control protocols adopted by the Texas Board of Health that clearly establish procedural guidelines that provide criteria for testing and that respect the rights of the person accused and any victim of the alleged offense.

(e) This article does not permit a court to release a test result to anyone other than those authorized by law, and the provisions of Section 81.103(d), Health and Safety Code, may not be construed to allow that disclosure.

Acts 1987, 70th Leg., 2nd C.S., ch. 55, § 3, eff. Oct. 20, 1987. Amended by Acts 1991, 72nd Leg., ch. 14, § 284(7), eff. Sept. 1, 1991; Acts 1993, 73rd Leg., ch. 811, § 1, eff. Sept. 1, 1993; Acts 2005, 79th Leg., ch. 543, § 3, eff. Sept. 1, 2005; Acts 2007, 80th Leg., ch. 593, § 3.12, eff. Sept. 1, 2007; Acts 2009, 81st Leg., ch. 418, § 1, eff. Sept. 1, 2009.

CHAPTER TWENTY–TWO. FORFEITURE OF BAIL

Art. 22.01. Bail forfeited, when

When a defendant is bound by bail to appear and fails to appear in any court in which such case may be pending and at any time when his personal appearance is required under this Code, or by any court or magistrate, a forfeiture of his bail and a judicial declaration of such forfeiture shall be taken in the manner provided in Article 22.02 of this Code and entered by such court.

Acts 1965, 59th Leg., p. 317, ch. 722, § 1, eff. Jan. 1, 1966. Amended by Acts 1981, 67th Leg., p. 886, ch. 312, § 2, eff. Aug. 31, 1981.

Art. 22.01a. Repealed by Acts 1973, 63rd Leg., p. 995, ch. 399, § 3(b), eff. Jan. 1, 1974

Art. 22.02. Manner of taking a forfeiture

Bail bonds and personal bonds are forfeited in the following manner: The name of the defendant shall be called distinctly at the courthouse door, and if the defendant does not appear within a reasonable time after such call is made, judgment shall be entered that the State of Texas recover of the defendant the amount of money in which he is bound, and of his sureties, if any, the amount of money in which they are respectively bound, which judgment shall state that the same will be made final, unless good cause be shown why the defendant did not appear.

Acts 1965, 59th Leg., p. 317, ch. 722, § 1, eff. Jan. 1, 1966.

Art. 22.021. Repealed by Acts 2007, 80th Leg., ch. 1113, § 6, eff. Jan. 1, 2008

Art. 22.03. Citation to Sureties

(a) Upon entry of judgment, a citation shall issue forthwith notifying the sureties of the defendant, if any, that the bond has been forfeited, and requiring them to appear and show cause why the judgment of forfeiture should not be made final.

(b) A citation to a surety who is an individual shall be served to the individual at the address shown on the face of the bond or the last known address of the individual.

(c) A citation to a surety that is a corporation or other entity shall be served to the attorney designated for service of process by the corporation or entity under Chapter 804, Insurance Code.

(d) By filing the waiver or designation in writing with the clerk of the court, a surety may waive service of citation or may designate a person other than the surety or the surety's attorney to receive service of citation under this article. The waiver or designation is effective until a written revocation is filed with the clerk.

Acts 1965, 59th Leg., p. 317, ch. 722, § 1, eff. Jan. 1, 1966. Amended by Acts 2005, 79th Leg., ch. 743, § 3, eff. Sept. 1, 2005; Acts 2007, 80th Leg., ch. 657, § 1, eff. Sept. 1, 2007.

Art. 22.035. Citation to Defendant Posting Cash Bond

A citation to a defendant who posted a cash bond shall be served to the defendant at the address shown on the face of the bond or the last known address of the defendant.

Added by Acts 2007, 80th Leg., ch. 657, § 2, eff. Sept. 1, 2007.

Art. 22.04. Requisites of Citation

A citation shall be sufficient if it be in the form provided for citations in civil cases in such court; provided, however, that a copy of the judgment of forfeiture entered by the court, a copy of the forfeited bond, and a copy of any power of attorney attached to the forfeited bond shall be attached to the citation and the citation shall notify the parties cited to appear and show cause why the judgment of forfeiture should not be made final.

Acts 1965, 59th Leg., p. 317, ch. 722, § 1, eff. Jan. 1, 1966. Amended by Acts 2005, 79th Leg., ch. 743, § 4, eff. Sept. 1, 2005.

Art. 22.05. Citation as in Civil Actions

If service of citation is not waived under Article 22.03, a surety is entitled to notice by service of citation, the length of time and in the manner required in civil actions; and the officer executing the citation shall return the same as in civil actions. It shall not be necessary to give notice to the defendant unless he has furnished his address on the bond, in which event notice to the defendant shall be deposited in the United States mail directed to the defendant at the address shown on the bond or the last known address of the defendant.

Acts 1965, 59th Leg., p. 317, ch. 722, § 1, eff. Jan. 1, 1966. Amended by Acts 2005, 79th Leg., ch. 743, § 5, eff. Sept. 1, 2005; Acts 2007, 80th Leg., ch. 657, § 3, eff. Sept. 1, 2007.

Art. 22.06.   Citation by publication

Where the surety is a nonresident of the State, or where he is a transient person, or where his residence is unknown, the district or county attorney may, upon application in writing to the county clerk, stating the facts, obtain a citation to be served by publication; and the same shall be served by a publication and returned as in civil actions.

Acts 1965, 59th Leg., p. 317, ch. 722, § 1, eff. Jan. 1, 1966.

Art. 22.07.   Cost of publication

When service of citation is made by publication, the county in which the forfeiture has been taken shall pay the costs thereof, to be taxed as costs in the case.

Acts 1965, 59th Leg., p. 317, ch. 722, § 1, eff. Jan. 1, 1966.

Art. 22.08.   Service out of the state

Service of a certified copy of the citation upon any absent or non-resident surety may be made outside of the limits of this State by any person competent to make oath of the fact; and the affidavit of such person, stating the facts of such service, shall be a sufficient return.

Acts 1965, 59th Leg., p. 317, ch. 722, § 1, eff. Jan. 1, 1966.

Art. 22.09.   When surety is dead

If the surety is dead at the time the forfeiture is taken, the forfeiture shall nevertheless be valid. The final judgment shall not be rendered where a surety has died, either before or after the forfeiture has been taken, unless his executor, administrator or heirs, as the case may be, have been cited to appear and show cause why the judgment should not be made final, in the same manner as provided in the case of the surety.

Acts 1965, 59th Leg., p. 317, ch. 722, § 1, eff. Jan. 1, 1966.

Art. 22.10.   Scire facias docket

When a forfeiture has been declared upon a bond, the court or clerk shall docket the case upon the scire facias or upon the civil docket, in the name of the State of Texas, as plaintiff, and the principal and his sureties, if any, as defendants; and, except as otherwise provided by this chapter, the proceedings had therein shall be governed by the same rules governing other civil suits.

Acts 1965, 59th Leg., p. 317, ch. 722, § 1, eff. Jan. 1, 1966. Amended by Acts 1981, 67th Leg., p. 886, ch. 312, § 3, eff. Aug. 31, 1981; Acts 1999, 76th Leg., ch. 1506, § 4, eff. Sept. 1, 1999.

Art. 22.11.   Sureties may answer

After the forfeiture of the bond, if the sureties, if any, have been duly notified, the sureties, if any, may answer in writing and show cause why the defendant did not appear, which answer may be filed within the time limited for answering in other civil actions.

Acts 1965, 59th Leg., p. 317, ch. 722, § 1, eff. Jan. 1, 1966.

Art. 22.12.   Proceedings not set aside for defect of form

The bond, the judgment declaring the forfeiture, the citation and the return thereupon, shall not be set aside because of any defect of form; but such defect of form may, at any time, be amended under the direction of the court.

Acts 1965, 59th Leg., p. 317, ch. 722, § 1, eff. Jan. 1, 1966.

Art. 22.12a.   Renumbered as Vernon's Ann.C.C.P. art. 22.125 by Acts 1987, 69th Leg., ch. 167, § 5.02(1), eff. Sept. 1, 1987

Art. 22.125.   Powers of the Court

After a judicial declaration of forfeiture is entered, the court may proceed with the trial required by Article 22.14 of this code. The court may exonerate the defendant and his sureties, if any, from liability on the forfeiture, remit the amount of the forfeiture, or set aside the forfeiture only as expressly provided by this chapter. The court may approve any proposed settlement of the liability on the forfeiture that is agreed to by the state and by the defendant or the defendant's sureties, if any.

Acts 1981, 67th Leg., p. 886, ch. 312, § 4, eff. Aug. 31, 1981. Renumbered from art. 22.12a by Acts 1987, 70th Leg., ch. 167, § 5.02(1), eff. Sept. 1, 1987. Amended by Acts 1999, 76th Leg., ch. 1506, § 5, eff. Sept. 1, 1999.

Art. 22.13. Causes Which Will Exonerate

(a) The following causes, and no other, will exonerate the defendant and his sureties, if any, from liability upon the forfeiture taken:

1. That the bond is, for any cause, not a valid and binding undertaking in law. If it be valid and binding as to the principal, and one or more of his sureties, if any, they shall not be exonerated from liability because of its being invalid and not binding as to another surety or sureties, if any. If it be invalid and not binding as to the principal, each of the sureties, if any, shall be exonerated from liability. If it be valid and binding as to the principal, but not so as to the sureties, if any, the principal shall not be exonerated, but the sureties, if any, shall be.

2. The death of the principal before the forfeiture was taken.

3. The sickness of the principal or some uncontrollable circumstance which prevented his appearance at court, and it must, in every such case, be shown that his failure to appear arose from no fault on his part. The causes mentioned in this subdivision shall not be deemed sufficient to exonerate the principal and his sureties, if any, unless such principal appear before final judgment on the bond to answer the accusation against him, or show sufficient cause for not so appearing.

4. Failure to present an indictment or information at the first term of the court which may be held after the principal has been admitted to bail, in case where the party was bound over before indictment or information, and the prosecution has not been continued by order of the court.

5. The incarceration of the principal in any jurisdiction in the United States:

(A) in the case of a misdemeanor, at the time of or not later than the 180th day after the date of the principal's failure to appear in court; or

(B) in the case of a felony, at the time of or not later than the 270th day after the date of the principal's failure to appear in court.

(b) A surety exonerated under Subdivision 5, Subsection (a), remains obligated to pay costs of court, any reasonable and necessary costs incurred by a county to secure the return of the principal, and interest accrued on the bond amount from the date of the judgment nisi to the date of the principal's incarceration.

Acts 1965, 59th Leg., p. 317, ch. 722, § 1, eff. Jan. 1, 1966. Amended by Acts 2003, 78th Leg., ch. 942, § 1, eff. June 20, 2003.

Art. 22.14. Judgment final

When, upon a trial of the issues presented, no sufficient cause is shown for the failure of the principal to appear, the judgment shall be made final against him and his sureties, if any, for the amount in which they are respectively bound; and the same shall be collected by execution as in civil actions. Separate executions shall issue against each party for the amount adjudged against him. The costs shall be equally divided between the sureties, if there be more than one.

Acts 1965, 59th Leg., p. 317, ch. 722, § 1, eff. Jan. 1, 1966.

Art. 22.15. Judgment final by default

When the sureties have been duly cited and fail to answer, and the principal also fails to answer within the time limited for answering in other civil actions, the court shall enter judgment final by default.

Acts 1965, 59th Leg., p. 317, ch. 722, § 1, eff. Jan. 1, 1966.

Art. 22.16. Remittitur After Forfeiture

(a) After forfeiture of a bond and before entry of a final judgment, the court shall, on written motion, remit to the surety the amount of the bond, after deducting the costs of court and any reasonable and necessary costs to the county for the return of the principal, and the interest accrued on the bond amount as provided by Subsection (c) if the principal is released on new bail in the case or the case for which bond was given is dismissed.

(b) For other good cause shown and before the entry of a final judgment against the bond, the court in its discretion may remit to the surety all or part of the amount of the bond after deducting the costs of court and any reasonable and necessary costs to the county for the return of the principal, and the interest accrued on the bond amount as provided by Subsection (c).

(c) For the purposes of this article, interest accrues on the bond amount from the date of forfeiture in the same manner and at the same rate as provided for the accrual of prejudgment interest in civil cases.

Acts 1965, 59th Leg., p. 317, ch. 722, § 1, eff. Jan. 1, 1966. Amended by Acts 1981, 67th Leg., p. 886, ch. 312, § 5, eff. Aug. 31, 1981; Acts 1987, 70th Leg., ch. 1047, § 3, eff. June 20, 1987; Acts 2003, 78th Leg., ch. 942, § 2, eff. June 20, 2003.

Art. 22.17. Special bill of review

(a) Not later than two years after the date a final judgment is entered in a bond forfeiture proceeding, the surety on the bond may file with the court a special bill of review. A special bill of review may include a request, on equitable grounds, that the final judgment be reformed and that all or part of the bond amount be remitted to the surety, after deducting the costs of court, any reasonable costs to the county for the return of the principal, and the interest accrued on the bond amount from the date of forfeiture. The court in its discretion may grant or deny the bill in whole or in part.

(b) For the purposes of this article, interest accrues on the bond amount from the date of:

(1) forfeiture to the date of final judgment in the same manner and at the same rate as provided for the accrual of prejudgment interest in civil cases; and

(2) final judgment to the date of the order for remittitur at the same rate as provided for the accrual of postjudgment interest in civil cases.

Acts 1987, 70th Leg., ch. 1047, § 4, eff. June 20, 1987.

Art. 22.18. Limitation

An action by the state to forfeit a bail bond under this chapter must be brought not later than the fourth anniversary of the date the principal fails to appear in court.

Added by Acts 1999, 76th Leg., ch. 1506, § 6, eff. Sept. 1, 1999.

CHAPTER TWENTY–THREE. THE CAPIAS

Art. 23.01. Definition of a "capias"

In this chapter, a "capias" is a writ that is:

(1) issued by a judge of the court having jurisdiction of a case after commitment or bail and before trial, or by a clerk at the direction of the judge; and

(2) directed "To any peace officer of the State of Texas", commanding the officer to arrest a person accused of an offense and bring the arrested person before that court immediately or on a day or at a term stated in the writ.

Acts 1965, 59th Leg., p. 317, ch. 722, § 1, eff. Jan. 1, 1966. Amended by Acts 2007, 80th Leg., ch. 1263, § 3, eff. Sept. 1, 2007.

Art. 23.02. Its requisites

A capias shall be held sufficient if it have the following requisites:

1. That it run in the name of "The State of Texas";

2. That it name the person whose arrest is ordered, or if unknown, describe him;

3. That it specify the offense of which the defendant is accused, and it appear thereby that he is accused of some offense against the penal laws of the State;

4. That it name the court to which and the time when it is returnable; and

5. That it be dated and attested officially by the authority issuing the same.

Acts 1965, 59th Leg., p. 317, ch. 722, § 1, eff. Jan. 1, 1966.

Art. 23.03. Capias or summons in felony

(a) A capias shall be issued by the district clerk upon each indictment for felony presented, after bail has been set or denied by the judge of the court. Upon the request of the attorney representing the State, a summons shall be issued by the district clerk. The capias or summons shall be delivered by the clerk or mailed to the sheriff of the county where the defendant resides or is to be found. A capias or summons need not issue for a defendant in custody or under bond.

(b) Upon the request of the attorney representing the State a summons instead of a capias shall issue. If a defendant fails to appear in response to the summons a capias shall issue.

(c) Summons. The summons shall be in the same form as the capias except that it shall summon the defendant to appear before the proper court at a stated time and place. The summons shall be served upon a defendant by delivering a copy to him personally, or by leaving it at his dwelling house or usual place of abode with some person of suitable age and discretion then residing therein or by mailing it to the defendant's last known address.

(d) A summons issued to any person must clearly and prominently state in English and in Spanish the following:

"It is an offense for a person to intentionally influence or coerce a witness to testify falsely or to elude legal process. It is also a felony offense to harm or threaten to harm a witness or prospective witness in retaliation for or on account of the service of the person as a witness or to prevent or delay the person's service as a witness to a crime."

Acts 1965, 59th Leg., p. 317, ch. 722, § 1, eff. Jan. 1, 1966. Amended by Acts 1979, 66th Leg., p. 1034, ch. 463, § 3, eff. June 7, 1979; Acts 1995, 74th Leg., ch. 67, § 1, eff. Sept. 1, 1995.

Art. 23.031. Issuance of Capias in Electronic Form

A district clerk, county clerk, or court may issue in electronic form a capias for the failure of a person to appear before a court or comply with a court order.

Added by Acts 2005, 79th Leg., ch. 312, § 4, eff. June 17, 2005. Amended by Acts 2007, 80th Leg., ch. 1263, § 4, eff. Sept. 1, 2007.

Art. 23.04. In Misdemeanor Case

In misdemeanor cases, the capias or summons shall issue from a court having jurisdiction of the case on the filing of an information or complaint. The summons shall be issued only upon request of the attorney representing the State and on the determination of probable cause by the judge, and shall follow the same form and procedure as in a felony case.

Acts 1965, 59th Leg., p. 317, ch. 722, § 1, eff. Jan. 1, 1966. Amended by Acts 2007, 80th Leg., ch. 1263, § 5, eff. Sept. 1, 2007.

Art. 23.05. Capias After Surrender Or Forfeiture

(a) If a forfeiture of bail is declared by a court or a surety surrenders a defendant under Article 17.19, a capias shall be immediately issued for the arrest of the defendant, and when arrested, in its discretion, the court may require the defendant, in order to be released from custody, to deposit with the custodian of funds of the court in which the prosecution is pending current money of the United States in the amount of the new bond as set by the court, in lieu of a surety bond, unless a forfeiture is taken and set aside under

the third subdivision of Article 22.13, in which case the defendant and the defendant's sureties shall remain bound under the same bail.

(b) A capias issued under this article may be executed by a peace officer or by a private investigator licensed under Chapter 1702, Occupations Code.

(c) A capias under this article must be issued not later than the 10th business day after the date of the court's issuance of the order of forfeiture or order permitting surrender of the bond.

(d) The sheriff of each county shall enter a capias issued under this article into a local warrant system not later than the 10th business day after the date of issuance of the capias by the clerk of court.

Acts 1965, 59th Leg., p. 317, ch. 722, § 1, eff. Jan. 1, 1966. Amended by Acts 1971, 62nd Leg., p. 2383, ch. 740, § 1, eff. Aug. 30, 1971; Acts 1999, 76th Leg., ch. 1506, § 7, eff. Sept. 1, 1999; Acts 2001, 77th Leg., ch. 1420, § 14.733, eff. Sept. 1, 2001; Acts 2003, 78th Leg., ch. 942, § 5, eff. June 20, 2003; Acts 2007, 80th Leg., ch. 1263, § 6, eff. Sept. 1, 2007.

Art. 23.06. New bail in felony case

When a defendant who has been arrested for a felony under a capias has previously given bail to answer said charge, his sureties, if any, shall be released by such arrest, and he shall be required to give new bail.

Acts 1965, 59th Leg., p. 317, ch. 722, § 1, eff. Jan. 1, 1966.

Art. 23.07. Capias does not lose its force

A capias shall not lose its force if not executed and returned at the time fixed in the writ, but may be executed at any time afterward, and return made. All proceedings under such capias shall be as valid as if the same had been executed and returned within the time specified in the writ.

Acts 1965, 59th Leg., p. 317, ch. 722, § 1, eff. Jan. 1, 1966.

Art. 23.08. Reasons for retaining capias

When the capias is not returned at the time fixed in the writ, the officer holding it shall notify the court from whence it was issued, in writing, of his reasons for retaining it.

Acts 1965, 59th Leg., p. 317, ch. 722, § 1, eff. Jan. 1, 1966.

Art. 23.09. Capias to several counties

Capiases for a defendant may be issued to as many counties as the district or county attorney may direct.

Acts 1965, 59th Leg., p. 317, ch. 722, § 1, eff. Jan. 1, 1966.

Art. 23.10. Bail in felony

In cases of arrest for felony in the county where the prosecution is pending, during a term of court, the officer making the arrest may take bail as provided in Article 17.21.

Acts 1965, 59th Leg., p. 317, ch. 722, § 1, eff. Jan. 1, 1966.

Art. 23.11. Sheriff may take bail in felony

In cases of arrest for felony less than capital, made during vacation or made in another county than the one in which the prosecution is pending, the sheriff may take bail; in such cases the amount of the bail bond shall be the same as is endorsed upon the capias; and if no amount be endorsed on the capias, the sheriff shall require a reasonable amount of bail. If it be made to appear by affidavit, made by any district attorney, county attorney, or the sheriff approving the bail bond, to a judge of the Court of Criminal Appeals, a justice of a court of appeals, or to a judge of the district or county court, that the bail taken in any case after indictment is insufficient in amount, or that the sureties are not good for the amount, or that the bond is for any reason defective or insufficient, such judge shall issue a warrant of arrest and require of the defendant sufficient bond, according to the nature of the case.

Acts 1965, 59th Leg., p. 317, ch. 722, § 1, eff. Jan. 1, 1966. Amended by Acts 1981, 67th Leg., p. 803, ch. 291, § 105, eff. Sept. 1, 1981.

Art. 23.12. Court shall fix bail in felony

In felony cases which are bailable, the court shall, before adjourning, fix and enter upon the minutes the amount of the bail to be required in each case. The clerk shall endorse upon the capias the amount of bail required. In case of neglect to so comply with this Article, the arrest of the defendant, and the bail taken by the sheriff, shall be as legal as if there had been no such omission.

Acts 1965, 59th Leg., p. 317, ch. 722, § 1, eff. Jan. 1, 1966.

Art. 23.13. Who may arrest under capias

A capias may be executed by any peace officer. In felony cases, the defendant must be delivered immediately to the sheriff of the county where the arrest is made together, with the writ under which he was taken.

Acts 1965, 59th Leg., p. 317, ch. 722, § 1, eff. Jan. 1, 1966.

Art. 23.14. Bail in misdemeanor

Any officer making an arrest under a capias in a misdemeanor may in term time or vacation take a bail bond of the defendant.

Acts 1965, 59th Leg., p. 317, ch. 722, § 1, eff. Jan. 1, 1966.

Art. 23.15. Arrest in capital cases

Where an arrest is made under a capias in a capital case, the sheriff shall confine the defendant in jail, and the capias shall, for that purpose, be a sufficient commitment. This Article is applicable when the arrest is made in the county where the prosecution is pending.

Acts 1965, 59th Leg., p. 317, ch. 722, § 1, eff. Jan. 1, 1966.

Art. 23.16. Arrest in capital case in another county

In each capital case where a defendant is arrested under a capias in a county other than that in which the case is pending, the sheriff who arrests or to whom the defendant is delivered, shall convey him immediately to the county from which the capias issued and deliver him to the sheriff of such county.

Acts 1965, 59th Leg., p. 317, ch. 722, § 1, eff. Jan. 1, 1966.

Art. 23.17. Return of bail and capias

When an arrest has been made and a bail taken, such bond, together with the capias, shall be returned forthwith to the proper court.

Acts 1965, 59th Leg., p. 317, ch. 722, § 1, eff. Jan. 1, 1966.

Art. 23.18. Return of capias

The return of the capias shall be made to the court from which it is issued. If it has been executed, the return shall state what disposition has been made of the defendant. If it has not been executed, the cause of the failure to execute it shall be fully stated. If the defendant has not been found, the return shall further show what efforts have been made by the officer to find him, and what information he has as to the defendant's whereabouts.

Acts 1965, 59th Leg., p. 317, ch. 722, § 1, eff. Jan. 1, 1966.

CHAPTER TWENTY–FOUR. SUBPOENA AND ATTACHMENT

Art. 24.01. Issuance of subpoenas

(a) A subpoena may summon one or more persons to appear:

(1) before a court to testify in a criminal action at a specified term of the court or on a specified day; or

(2) on a specified day:

(A) before an examining court;

(B) at a coroner's inquest;

(C) before a grand jury;

(D) at a habeas corpus hearing; or

(E) in any other proceeding in which the person's testimony may be required in accordance with this code.

(b) The person named in the subpoena to summon the person whose appearance is sought must be:

(1) a peace officer; or

(2) a least 18 years old and, at the time the subpoena is issued, not a participant in the proceeding for which the appearance is sought.

(c) A person who is not a peace officer may not be compelled to accept the duty to execute a subpoena, but if he agrees in writing to accept that duty and neglects or refuses to serve or return the subpoena, he may be punished in accordance with Article 2.16 of this code.

(d) A court or clerk issuing a subpoena shall sign the subpoena and indicate on it the date it was issued, but the subpoena need not be under seal.

Acts 1965, 59th Leg., p. 317, ch. 722, § 1, eff. Jan. 1, 1966. Amended by Acts 1981, 67th Leg., p. 503, ch. 209, § 1, eff. Sept. 1, 1981.

Art. 24.011. Subpoenas; child witnesses

(a) If a witness is younger than 18 years, the court may issue a subpoena directing a person having custody, care, or control of the child to produce the child in court.

(b) If a person, without legal cause, fails to produce the child in court as directed by a subpoena issued under this article, the court may impose on the person penalties for contempt provided by this chapter. The court may also issue a writ of attachment for the person and the child, in the same manner as other writs of attachment are issued under this chapter.

(b–1) If the defendant or the attorney representing the state requests the issuance of an attachment under this article, other than an attachment for a witness described by Subsection (c), the request must include the applicable affidavit described by Article 24.12.

(c) If the witness is in a placement in the custody of the Texas Juvenile Justice Department, a juvenile secure detention facility, or a juvenile secure correctional facility, the court may issue a bench warrant or direct that an attachment issue to require a peace officer or probation officer to secure custody of the person at the placement and produce the person in court. When the person is no longer needed as a witness or the period prescribed by Subsection (d–1) has expired without extension, the court shall order the peace officer or probation officer to return the person to the placement from which the person was released.

(d) The court may order that the person who is the witness be detained in a certified juvenile detention facility if the person is younger than 17 years of age. If the person is at least 17 years of age, the court may order that the person be detained without bond in an appropriate county facility for the detention of adults accused of criminal offenses.

(d–1) A witness younger than 17 years of age held in custody under this article may be placed in a certified juvenile detention facility for a period not to exceed 30 days. The length of placement may be extended in increments of 30 days by the court that issued the original bench warrant. If the placement is not extended, the period under this article expires and the witness may be returned as provided by Subsection (c).

(e) In this article, "secure detention facility" and "secure correctional facility" have the meanings assigned by Section 51.02, Family Code.

Acts 1987, 70th Leg., ch. 520, § 1, eff. June 17, 1987. Amended by Acts 2005, 79th Leg., ch. 949, § 32, eff. Sept. 1, 2005; Acts 2013, 83rd Leg., ch. 1299 (H.B. 2862), § 2, eff. Sept. 1, 2013; Acts 2017, 85th Leg., ch. 292 (S.B. 291), § 2, eff. Sept. 1, 2017.

Section 9 of Acts 2017, 85th Leg., ch. 292 (S.B. 291) provides:

"The change in law made by this Act applies only to a writ of attachment issued on or after the effective date [Sept. 1, 2017] of this Act. A writ of attachment issued before the effective date of this Act is governed by the law in effect on the date the writ was issued, and the former law is continued in effect for that purpose."

Art. 24.02.   Subpoena duces tecum

If a witness have in his possession any instrument of writing or other thing desired as evidence, the subpoena may specify such evidence and direct that the witness bring the same with him and produce it in court.

Acts 1965, 59th Leg., p. 317, ch. 722, § 1, eff. Jan. 1, 1966.

Art. 24.03.   Subpoena and application therefor

(a) Before the clerk or his deputy shall be required or permitted to issue a subpoena in any felony case pending in any district or criminal district court of this State of which he is clerk or deputy, the defendant or his attorney or the State's attorney shall make an application in writing or by electronic means to such clerk for each witness desired. Such application shall state the name of each witness desired, the location and vocation, if known, and that the testimony of said witness is material to the State or to the defense. The application must be filed with the clerk and placed with the papers in the cause or, if the application is filed electronically, placed with any other electronic information linked to the number of the cause. The application must also be made available to both the State and the defendant. Except as provided by Subsection (b), as far as is practical such clerk shall include in one subpoena the names of all witnesses for the State and for defendant, and such process shall show that the witnesses are summoned for the State or for the defendant. When a witness has been served with a subpoena, attached or placed under bail at the instance of either party in a particular case, such execution of process shall inure to the benefit of the opposite party in such case in the event such opposite party desires to use such witness on the trial of the case, provided that when a witness has once been served with a subpoena, no further subpoena shall be issued for said witness.

(b) If the defendant is a member of a combination as defined by Section 71.01, Penal Code, the clerk shall issue for each witness a subpoena that does not include a list of the names of all other witnesses for the State or the defendant.

Acts 1965, 59th Leg., p. 317, ch. 722, § 1, eff. Jan. 1, 1966. Amended by Acts 1993, 73rd Leg., ch. 900, § 10.01, eff. Sept. 1, 1993; Acts 1999, 76th Leg., ch. 580, § 4, eff. Sept. 1, 1999; Acts 1999, 76th Leg., ch. 614, § 2, eff. June 18, 1999.

Art. 24.04.   Service and return of subpoena

(a) A subpoena is served by:

(1) reading the subpoena in the hearing of the witness;

(2) delivering a copy of the subpoena to the witness;

(3) electronically transmitting a copy of the subpoena, acknowledgment of receipt requested, to the last known electronic address of the witness; or

(4) mailing a copy of the subpoena by certified mail, return receipt requested, to the last known address of the witness unless:

(A) the applicant for the subpoena requests in writing that the subpoena not be served by certified mail; or

(B) the proceeding for which the witness is being subpoenaed is set to begin within seven business days after the date the subpoena would be mailed.

(b) The officer having the subpoena shall make due return thereof, showing the time and manner of service, if served under Subsection (a)(1) or (2) of this article, the acknowledgment of receipt, if served under Subsection (a)(3) of this article, or the return receipt, if served under Subsection (a)(4) of this article. If the subpoena is not served, the officer shall show in his return the cause of his failure to serve it. If receipt of an electronically transmitted subpoena is not acknowledged within a reasonable time or a mailed subpoena is returned undelivered, the officer shall use due diligence to locate and serve the witness. If the witness could not be found, the officer shall state the diligence he has used to find him, and what information he has as to the whereabouts of the witness.

(c) A subpoena served under Subsection (a)(3) of this article must be accompanied by notice that an acknowledgment of receipt of the subpoena must be made in a manner enabling verification of the person acknowledging receipt.

Acts 1965, 59th Leg., p. 317, ch. 722, § 1, eff. Jan. 1, 1966. Amended by Acts 1979, 66th Leg., p. 770, ch. 336, § 1, eff. Aug. 27, 1979; Acts 1995, 74th Leg., ch. 374, § 1, eff. June 8, 1995; Acts 1999, 76th Leg., ch. 580, § 5, eff. Sept. 1, 1999.

Art. 24.05.   Refusing to obey

If a witness refuses to obey a subpoena, he may be fined at the discretion of the court, as follows: In a felony case, not exceeding five hundred dollars; in a misdemeanor case, not exceeding one hundred dollars.

Acts 1965, 59th Leg., p. 317, ch. 722, § 1, eff. Jan. 1, 1966.

Art. 24.06.   What is disobedience of a subpoena

It shall be held that a witness refuses to obey a subpoena:

1. If he is not in attendance on the court on the day set apart for taking up the criminal docket or on any day subsequent thereto and before the final disposition or continuance of the particular case in which he is a witness;

2. If he is not in attendance at any other time named in a writ; and

3. If he refuses without legal cause to produce evidence in his possession which he has been summoned to bring with him and produce.

Acts 1965, 59th Leg., p. 317, ch. 722, § 1, eff. Jan. 1, 1966.

Art. 24.07.   Fine against witness conditional

When a fine is entered against a witness for failure to appear and testify, the judgment shall be conditional; and a citation shall issue to him to show cause, at the term of the court at which said fine is entered, or at the first term thereafter, at the discretion of the judge of said court, why the same should not be final; provided, citation shall be served upon said witness in the manner and for the length of time prescribed for citations in civil cases.

Acts 1965, 59th Leg., p. 317, ch. 722, § 1, eff. Jan. 1, 1966.

Art. 24.08.   Witness may show cause

A witness cited to show cause, as provided in the preceding Article, may do so under oath, in writing or verbally, at any time before judgment final is entered against him; but if he fails to show cause within the time limited for answering in civil actions, a judgment final by default shall be entered against him.

Acts 1965, 59th Leg., p. 317, ch. 722, § 1, eff. Jan. 1, 1966.

Art. 24.09.   Court may remit fine

It shall be within the discretion of the court to judge of the sufficiency of an excuse rendered by a witness, and upon the hearing the court shall render judgment against the witness for the whole or any part of the fine, or shall remit the fine altogether, as to the court may appear proper and right. Said fine shall be collected as fines in misdemeanor cases.

Acts 1965, 59th Leg., p. 317, ch. 722, § 1, eff. Jan. 1, 1966.

Art. 24.10.   When witness appears and testifies

When a fine has been entered against a witness, but no trial of the cause takes place, and such witness afterward appears and testifies upon the trial thereof, it shall be discretionary with the judge, though no good excuse be rendered, to reduce the fine or remit it altogether; but the witness, in such case, shall, nevertheless, be adjudged to pay all the costs accruing in the proceeding against him by reason of his failure to attend.

Acts 1965, 59th Leg., p. 317, ch. 722, § 1, eff. Jan. 1, 1966.

Art. 24.11.   Requisites of an "Attachment"

An "attachment" is a writ issued by a clerk of a court under seal, or by any magistrate, or by the foreman of a grand jury, in any criminal action or proceeding authorized by law, commanding some peace officer to take the body of a witness and bring him before such court, magistrate or grand jury on a day named, or forthwith, to testify in behalf of the State or of the defendant, as the case may be. It shall be dated and signed officially by the officer issuing it.

Acts 1965, 59th Leg., p. 317, ch. 722, § 1, eff. Jan. 1, 1966.

Art. 24.111.   Hearing Required Before Issuance of Certain Writs of Attachment

(a) This article applies only to an attachment that is requested to be issued under:

(1) Article 24.011, if an affidavit is required under Article 24.011(b–1); or

(2) Article 24.12, 24.14, or 24.22.

(b) Notwithstanding any other law, a writ of attachment to which this article applies may only be issued by the judge of the court in which the witness is to testify if the judge determines, after a hearing, that the issuance of the attachment is in the best interest of justice.

(c) In making a determination under Subsection (b), the judge shall consider the affidavit of the attorney representing the state or the defendant, as applicable, that was submitted with the request for the issuance of the attachment.

(d) The court shall appoint an attorney to represent the witness at the hearing under Subsection (b), including a hearing conducted outside the presence of the witness.

Added by Acts 2017, 85th Leg., ch. 292 (S.B. 291), § 3, eff. Sept. 1, 2017.

Section 9 of Acts 2017, 85th Leg., ch. 292 (S.B. 291) provides:

"The change in law made by this Act applies only to a writ of attachment issued on or after the effective date [Sept. 1, 2017] of this Act. A writ of attachment issued before the effective date of this Act is governed by the law in effect on the date the writ was issued, and the former law is continued in effect for that purpose."

Art. 24.12. When Attachment May Issue

When a witness who resides in the county of the prosecution has been duly served with a subpoena to appear and testify in any criminal action or proceeding fails to so appear, the attorney representing the state or the defendant may request that the court issue an attachment for the witness. The request must be filed with the clerk of the court and must include an affidavit of the attorney representing the state or the defendant, as applicable, stating that the affiant has good reason to believe, and does believe, that the witness is a material witness.

Acts 1965, 59th Leg., p. 317, ch. 722, § 1, eff. Jan. 1, 1966. Amended by Acts 2017, 85th Leg., ch. 292 (S.B. 291), § 4, eff. Sept. 1, 2017.

Section 9 of Acts 2017, 85th Leg., ch. 292 (S.B. 291) provides:

"The change in law made by this Act applies only to a writ of attachment issued on or after the effective date [Sept. 1, 2017] of this Act. A writ of attachment issued before the effective date of this Act is governed by the law in effect on the date the writ was issued, and the former law is continued in effect for that purpose."

Art. 24.13. Attachment for convict witnesses

All persons who have been or may be convicted in this state, and who are confined in an institution operated by the Texas Department of Criminal Justice or any jail in this state, shall be permitted to testify in person in any court for the state and the defendant when the presiding judge finds, after hearing, that the ends of justice require their attendance, and directs that an attachment issue to accomplish the purpose, notwithstanding any other provision of this code. Nothing in this article shall be construed as

limiting the power of the courts of this state to issue bench warrants.

Acts 1965, 59th Leg., p. 317, ch. 722, § 1, eff. Jan. 1, 1966. Amended by Acts 2009, 81st Leg., ch. 87, § 25.013, eff. Sept. 1, 2009.

Art. 24.131. Notification to Department of Criminal Justice

If after the Texas Department of Criminal Justice transfers a defendant or inmate to a county under Article 24.13 and before that person is returned to the department the person is released on bail or the charges on which the person was convicted and for which the person was transferred to the department are dismissed, the county shall immediately notify an officer designated by the department of the release on bail or the dismissal.

Added by Acts 2001, 77th Leg., ch. 857, § 1, eff. June 14, 2001.

Art. 24.14. Attachment for Resident Witness

(a) Regardless of whether the witness has disobeyed a subpoena, if a witness who resides in the county of the prosecution may be about to move out of the county, the defendant or the attorney representing the state may request that the court issue an attachment for the witness. The request must be filed with the clerk of the court and must include the applicable affidavit described by Article 24.12, except that the affidavit must additionally state that the affiant has good reason to believe, and does believe, that the witness is about to move out of the county.

(b) If an attachment is issued under this article in a misdemeanor case, when the witness makes oath that the witness cannot give surety, the officer executing the attachment shall take the witness's personal bond.

Acts 1965, 59th Leg., p. 317, ch. 722, § 1, eff. Jan. 1, 1966. Amended by Acts 2017, 85th Leg., ch. 292 (S.B. 291), § 5, eff. Sept. 1, 2017.

Section 9 of Acts 2017, 85th Leg., ch. 292 (S.B. 291) provides:

"The change in law made by this Act applies only to a writ of attachment issued on or after the effective date [Sept. 1, 2017] of this Act. A writ of attachment issued before the effective date of this Act is governed by the law in effect on the date the writ was issued, and the former law is continued in effect for that purpose."

Art. 24.15. [525a] To secure attendance before grand jury

At any time before the first day of any term of the district court, the clerk, upon application of the State's attorney, shall issue a subpoena for any witness who resides in the county. If at the time such application is made, such attorney files a sworn application that he has good reason to believe and does believe that such witness is about to move out of the county, then said clerk shall issue an attachment for such witness to be and appear before said district court on the first day thereof to testify as a witness before the grand jury. Any witness so summoned, or attached, who shall fail or refuse to obey a subpoena or attachment, shall be punished by the court by a fine not exceeding five hundred dollars, to be collected as fines and costs in other criminal cases.

Acts 1965, 59th Leg., p. 317, ch. 722, § 1, eff. Jan. 1, 1966.

Art. 24.16. Application for out-county witness

Where, in misdemeanor cases in which confinement in jail is a permissible punishment, or in felony cases, a witness resides out of the county in which the prosecution is pending, the State or the defendant shall be entitled, either in term-time or in vacation, to a subpoena to compel the attendance of such witness on application to the proper clerk or magistrate. Such application shall be in the manner and form as provided in Article 24.03. Witnesses in such misdemeanor cases shall be compensated in the same manner as in felony cases. This Article shall not apply to more than one character witness in a misdemeanor case.

Acts 1965, 59th Leg., p. 317, ch. 722, § 1, eff. Jan. 1, 1966.

Art. 24.17. Duty of officer receiving said subpoena

The officer receiving said subpoena shall execute the same by delivering a copy thereof to each witness therein named. He shall make due return of said subpoena, showing therein the time and manner of executing the same, and if not executed, such return shall show why not executed, the diligence used to find said witness, and such information as the officer has as to the whereabouts of said witness.

Acts 1965, 59th Leg., p. 317, ch. 722, § 1, eff. Jan. 1, 1966.

Art. 24.18. Subpoena returnable forthwith

When a subpoena is returnable forthwith, the officer shall immediately serve the witness with a copy of the same; and it shall be the duty of said witness to immediately make his appearance before the court, magistrate or other authority issuing the same. If said witness makes affidavit of his inability from lack of funds to appear in obedience to said subpoena, the officer executing the same shall provide said witness, if said subpoena be issued as provided in Article 24.16, with the necessary funds or means to appear in obedience to said subpoena, taking his receipt therefor, and showing in his return on said subpoena, under oath, the amount furnished to said witness, together with the amount of his fees for executing said subpoena.

Acts 1965, 59th Leg., p. 317, ch. 722, § 1, eff. Jan. 1, 1966.

Art. 24.19. Certificate to officer

The clerk, magistrate, or foreman of the grand jury issuing said process, immediately upon the return of said subpoena, if issued as provided in Article 24.16, shall issue to such officer a certificate for the amount furnished such witness, together with the amount of his fees for executing the same, showing the amount of each item; which certificate shall be approved by the district judge and recorded by the district clerk in a book kept for that purpose; and said certificate transmitted to the officer executing such subpoena, which amount shall be paid by the State, as costs are paid in other criminal matters.

Acts 1965, 59th Leg., p. 317, ch. 722, § 1, eff. Jan. 1, 1966.

Art. 24.20. Subpoena returnable at future date

If the subpoena be returnable at some future date, the officer shall have authority to take bail of such witness for his appearance under said subpoena, which bond shall be returned with such subpoena, and shall be made payable to the State of Texas, in the amount in which the witness and his surety, if any, shall be bound and conditioned for the appearance of the witness at the time and before the court, magistrate or grand jury named in said subpoena, and shall be signed by the witness and his sureties. If the witness refuses to give bond, he shall be kept in custody until such time as he starts in obedience to said subpoena, when he shall be, upon affidavit being made, provided with funds necessary to appear in obedience to said subpoena.

Acts 1965, 59th Leg., p. 317, ch. 722, § 1, eff. Jan. 1, 1966.

Art. 24.21. Stating bail in subpoena

The court or magistrate issuing said subpoena may direct therein the amount of the bail to be required. The officer may fix the amount if not specified, and in either case, shall require sufficient security, to be approved by himself.

Acts 1965, 59th Leg., p. 317, ch. 722, § 1, eff. Jan. 1, 1966.

Art. 24.22. Witness Fined and Attached

(a) If a witness summoned from outside the county refuses to obey a subpoena, the witness shall be fined by the court or magistrate not exceeding five hundred dollars, which fine and judgment shall be final, unless set aside after due notice to show cause why it should not be final, which notice may immediately issue, requiring the defaulting witness to appear at once or at the next term of the court, in the discretion of the magistrate issuing the subpoena, to answer for the default.

(b) At the time a fine is imposed under Subsection (a), on request of the defendant or the attorney representing the state, the court may cause to be issued an attachment for the witness, directed to the proper county, commanding the officer to whom the attachment is directed to take the witness into custody and have the witness before the court at the time specified in the attachment; in which case the witness shall receive no fees, unless it appears to the court that the disobedience is excusable, when the witness may receive the same pay as if the witness had not been attached.

(c) A request for the issuance of an attachment under Subsection (b) must include the applicable affidavit described by Article 24.12.

(d) The fine when made final and all related costs shall be collected in the same manner as in other criminal cases. The fine and judgment may be set aside in vacation or at the time or any subsequent term of the court for good cause shown, after the witness testifies or has been discharged.

(e) The following words shall be written or printed on the face of a subpoena for an out-of-county witness: "A disobedience of this subpoena is punishable by fine not exceeding five hundred dollars, to be collected as fines and costs in other criminal cases."

Acts 1965, 59th Leg., p. 317, ch. 722, § 1, eff. Jan. 1, 1966. Amended by Acts 2017, 85th Leg., ch. 292 (S.B. 291), § 6, eff. Sept. 1, 2017.

Section 9 of Acts 2017, 85th Leg., ch. 292 (S.B. 291) provides:

"The change in law made by this Act applies only to a writ of attachment issued on or after the effective date [Sept. 1, 2017] of this Act. A writ of attachment issued before the effective date of this Act is governed by the law in effect on the date the writ was issued, and the former law is continued in effect for that purpose."

Art. 24.221. Affidavit Regarding Confinement

As soon as practicable after the sheriff takes custody of a witness pursuant to an attachment issued as provided by Article 24.111, the sheriff shall submit an affidavit to the issuing court stating that the sheriff has taken custody of the witness.

Added by Acts 2017, 85th Leg., ch. 292 (S.B. 291), § 7, eff. Sept. 1, 2017.

Section 9 of Acts 2017, 85th Leg., ch. 292 (S.B. 291) provides:

"The change in law made by this Act applies only to a writ of attachment issued on or after the effective date [Sept. 1, 2017] of this Act. A writ of attachment issued before the effective date of this Act is governed by the law in effect on the date the writ was issued, and the former law is continued in effect for that purpose."

Art. 24.222. Hearing During Confinement of Witness

(a) A witness who has been confined for at least 24 hours pursuant to an attachment issued as provided by Article 24.111 may request a hearing in the issuing court regarding whether the continued confinement of the witness is necessary. The court shall grant the request and hold the hearing as soon as practicable.

(b) Any subsequent request for a hearing may be granted only if the court determines that holding the hearing is in the best interest of justice.

(c) The attorney appointed for the witness under Article 24.111 shall represent the witness at a hearing under this article.

Added by Acts 2017, 85th Leg., ch. 292 (S.B. 291), § 7, eff. Sept. 1, 2017.

Section 9 of Acts 2017, 85th Leg., ch. 292 (S.B. 291) provides:

"The change in law made by this Act applies only to a writ of attachment issued on or after the effective date [Sept. 1, 2017] of this Act. A writ of attachment issued before the effective date of this Act is governed by the law in effect on the date the writ was issued, and the former law is continued in effect for that purpose."

Art. 24.23. Witness released

A witness who is in custody for failing to give bail shall be at once released upon giving bail required.

Acts 1965, 59th Leg., p. 317, ch. 722, § 1, eff. Jan. 1, 1966.

Art. 24.24. Bail for witness

Witnesses on behalf of the State or defendant may, at the request of either party, be required to enter into bail in an amount to be fixed by the court to appear and testify in a criminal action; but if it shall appear to the court that any witness is unable to give security upon such bail, he shall be released without security.

Acts 1965, 59th Leg., p. 317, ch. 722, § 1, eff. Jan. 1, 1966.

Art. 24.25. Personal bond of witness

When it appears to the satisfaction of the court that personal bond of the witness will insure his attendance, no security need be required of him; but no bond without security shall be taken by any officer.

Acts 1965, 59th Leg., p. 317, ch. 722, § 1, eff. Jan. 1, 1966.

Art. 24.26.   Enforcing forfeiture

The bond of a witness may be enforced against him and his sureties, if any, in the manner pointed out in this Code for enforcing the bond of a defendant in a criminal case.

Acts 1965, 59th Leg., p. 317, ch. 722, § 1, eff. Jan. 1, 1966.

Art. 24.27.   No surrender after forfeiture

The sureties of a witness have no right to discharge themselves by the surrender of the witness after the forfeiture of their bond.

Acts 1965, 59th Leg., p. 317, ch. 722, § 1, eff. Jan. 1, 1966.

Art. 24.28.   Uniform Act to secure attendance of witnesses from without State

Short Title

Sec. 1.   This Act may be cited as the "Uniform Act to Secure the Attendance of Witnesses from Without the State in Criminal Proceedings".

Definitions

Sec. 2.   "Witness" as used in this Act shall include a person whose testimony is desired in any proceeding or investigation by a grand jury or in a criminal action, prosecution or proceeding.

The word "State" shall include any territory of the United States and the District of Columbia.

The word "summons" shall include a subpoena, order or other notice requiring the appearance of a witness.

Summoning witness in this State to testify in another State

Sec. 3.   (a) If a judge of a court of record in any State which by its laws has made provision for commanding persons within that State to attend and testify in this State certifies under the seal of such court that there is a criminal prosecution pending in such court, or that a grand jury investigation has commenced or is about to commence, that a person being within this State is a material witness in such prosecution, or grand jury investigation, and that his presence will be required for a specified number of days, upon presentation of such certificate to any judge of a court of record in the county in which such person is, such judge shall fix a time and place for a hearing, and shall make an order directing the witness to appear at a time and place certain for the hearing.

(b) If at a hearing the judge determines that the witness is material and necessary, that it will not cause undue hardship to the witness to be compelled to attend and testify in the prosecution or a grand jury investigation in the other State, and that the laws of the State in which the prosecution is pending, or grand jury investigation has commenced or is about to commence, (and of any other State through which the witness may be required to pass by ordinary course of travel), will give to him protection from arrest and the service of civil and criminal process, he shall issue a summons, with a copy of the certificate attached, directing the witness to attend and testify in the court where the prosecution is pending, or where a grand jury investigation has commenced or is about to commence at a time and place specified in the summons. In any such hearing the certificate shall be prima facie evidence of all the facts stated therein.

(c) If said certificate recommends that the witness be taken into immediate custody and delivered to an officer of the requesting State to assure his attendance in the requesting State, such judge may, in lieu of notification of the hearing, direct that such witness be forthwith brought before him for said hearing; and the judge at the hearing being satisfied of the desirability of such custody and delivery, for which determination the certificate shall be prima facie proof of such desirability may, in lieu of issuing subpoena or summons, order that said witness be forthwith taken into custody and delivered to an officer of the requesting State.

(d) If the witness, who is summoned as above provided, after being paid or tendered by some properly authorized person the compensation for nonresident witnesses authorized and provided for by Article 35.27 of this Code, fails without good cause to attend and testify as directed in the summons, he shall be punished in the manner provided for the punishment of any witness who disobeys a summons issued from a court of record in this State.

Witness from another State summoned to testify in this State

Sec. 4.   (a) If a person in any State, which by its laws has made provision for commanding persons within its borders to attend and testify in criminal prosecutions, or grand jury investigations commenced or about to commence, in this State, is a material witness in a prosecution pending in a court of record in this State, or in a grand jury investigation which has commenced or is about to commence, a judge of such court may issue a certificate under the seal of the court stating these facts and specifying the number of days the witness will be required. Said certificate may include a recommendation that the witness be taken into immediate custody and delivered to an officer of this State to assure his attendance in this State. This certificate shall be presented to a judge of a court of record in the county in which the witness is found.

(b) If the witness is summoned to attend and testify in this State he shall be tendered the compensation for nonresident witnesses authorized by Article 35.27 of this Code, together with such additional compensation, if any, required by the other State for compliance. A witness who has appeared in accordance with the provisions of the summons shall not be required to remain within this State a longer period of time than the period mentioned in the certificate, unless otherwise ordered by the court. If such witness, after coming into this State, fails without good cause to attend and testify as directed in the summons, he shall be punished in the manner provided for the punishment of any witness who disobeys a summons issued from a court of record in this State.

Exemption from arrest and service of process

Sec. 5. If a person comes into this State in obedience to a summons directing him to attend and testify in this State he shall not while in this State pursuant to such summons be subject to arrest or the service of process, civil or criminal, in connection with matters which arose before his entrance into this State under the summons.

If a person passes through this State while going to another State in obedience to a summons to attend and testify in that State or while returning therefrom, he shall not while so passing through this State be subject to arrest or the service of process, civil or criminal, in connection with matters which arose before his entrance into this State under the summons.

Acts 1965, 59th Leg., p. 317, ch. 722, § 1, eff. Jan. 1, 1966. Amended by Acts 1973, 63rd Leg., p. 1285, ch. 477, § 1, eff. Aug. 27, 1973.

Art. 24.29. Uniform Act to secure rendition of prisoners in criminal proceedings

Short title

Sec. 1. This article may be cited as the "Uniform Act to Secure Rendition of Prisoners in Criminal Proceedings."

Definitions

Sec. 2. In this Act:

(1) "Penal institution" means a jail, prison, penitentiary, house of correction, or other place of penal detention.

(2) "State" means a state of the United States, the District of Columbia, the Commonwealth of Puerto Rico, and any territory of the United States.

(3) "Witness" means a person who is confined in a penal institution in a state and whose testimony is desired in another state in a criminal proceeding or investigation by a grand jury or in any criminal action before a court.

Summoning witness in this state to testify in another state

Sec. 3. (a) A judge of a state court of record in another state, which by its laws has made provision for commanding persons confined in penal institutions within that state to attend and testify in this state, may certify that:

(1) there is a criminal proceeding or investigation by a grand jury or a criminal action pending in the court;

(2) a person who is confined in a penal institution in this state may be a material witness in the proceeding, investigation, or action; and

(3) his presence will be required during a specified time.

(b) On presentation of the certificate to any judge having jurisdiction over the person confined and on notice to the attorney general, the judge in this state shall fix a time and place for a hearing and shall make an order directed to the person having custody of the prisoner requiring that the prisoner be produced before him at the hearing.

Court order

Sec. 4. (a) A judge may issue a transfer order if at the hearing the judge determines that:

(1) the witness may be material and necessary;

(2) his attending and testifying are not adverse to the interest of this state or to the health or legal rights of the witness;

(3) the laws of the state in which he is requested to testify will give him protection from arrest and the service of civil and criminal process because of any act committed prior to his arrival in the state under the order; and

(4) as a practical matter the possibility is negligible that the witness may be subject to arrest or to the

service of civil or criminal process in any state through which he will be required to pass.

(b) If a judge issues an order under Subsection (a) of this section, the judge shall attach to the order a copy of a certificate presented under Section 3 of this Act. The order shall:

(1) direct the witness to attend and testify;

(2) except as provided by Subsection (c) of this section, direct the person having custody of the witness to produce him in the court where the criminal action is pending or where the grand jury investigation is pending at a time and place specified in the order; and

(3) prescribe such conditions as the judge shall determine.

(c) The judge, in lieu of directing the person having custody of the witness to produce him in the requesting jurisdiction's court, may direct and require in his order that:

(1) an officer of the requesting jurisdiction come to the Texas penal institution in which the witness is confined to accept custody of the witness for physical transfer to the requesting jurisdiction;

(2) the requesting jurisdiction provide proper safeguards on his custody while in transit;

(3) the requesting jurisdiction be liable for and pay all expenses incurred in producing and returning the witness, including but not limited to food, lodging, clothing, and medical care; and

(4) the requesting jurisdiction promptly deliver the witness back to the same or another Texas penal institution as specified by the Texas Department of Criminal Justice at the conclusion of his testimony.

Terms and conditions

Sec. 5. An order to a witness and to a person having custody of the witness shall provide for the return of the witness at the conclusion of his testimony, proper safeguards on his custody, and proper financial reimbursement or prepayment by the requesting jurisdiction for all expenses incurred in the production and return of the witness. The order may prescribe any other condition the judge thinks proper or necessary. The judge shall not require prepayment of expenses if the judge directs and requires the requesting jurisdiction to accept custody of the witness at the Texas penal institution in which the witness is confined and to deliver the witness back to the same or another Texas penal institution at the conclu-

sion of his testimony. An order does not become effective until the judge of the state requesting the witness enters an order directing compliance with the conditions prescribed.

Exceptions

Sec. 6. This Act does not apply to a person in this state who is confined as mentally ill or who is under sentence of death.

Prisoner from another state summoned to testify in this state

Sec. 7. (a) If a person confined in a penal institution in any other state may be a material witness in a criminal action pending in a court of record or in a grand jury investigation in this state, a judge of the court may certify that:

(1) there is a criminal proceeding or investigation by a grand jury or a criminal action pending in the court;

(2) a person who is confined in a penal institution in the other state may be a material witness in the proceeding, investigation, or action; and

(3) his presence will be required during a specified time.

(b) The judge of the court in this state shall:

(1) present the certificate to a judge of a court of record in the other state having jurisdiction over the prisoner confined; and

(2) give notice that the prisoner's presence will be required to the attorney general of the state in which the prisoner is confined.

Compliance

Sec. 8. A judge of the court in this state may enter an order directing compliance with the terms and conditions of an order specified in a certificate under Section 3 of this Act and entered by the judge of the state in which the witness is confined.

Exemption from arrest and service of process

Sec. 9. If a witness from another state comes into or passes through this state under an order directing him to attend and testify in this or another state, while in this state pursuant to the order he is not subject to arrest or the service of civil or criminal process because of any act committed prior to his arrival in this state under the order.

Uniformity of interpretation

Sec. 10.   This Act shall be so construed as to effect its general purpose to make uniform the laws of those states which enact it.

Acts 1983, 68th Leg., p. 1068, ch. 240, § 1, eff. Aug. 29, 1983. Amended by Acts 2009, 81st Leg., ch. 87, § 25.014, eff. Sept. 1, 2009.

CHAPTER TWENTY–FOUR–A. RESPONDING TO SUBPOENAS AND CERTAIN OTHER COURT ORDERS; PRESERVING CERTAIN INFORMATION

SUBCHAPTER A. RESPONDING TO SUBPOENAS AND CERTAIN OTHER COURT ORDERS

SUBCHAPTER A. RESPONDING TO SUBPOENAS AND CERTAIN OTHER COURT ORDERS

Art. 24A.001. Applicability of Subchapter

This subchapter applies only to a subpoena, search warrant, or other court order that:

(1) relates to the investigation or prosecution of a criminal offense under:

(A) Section 21.02, 21.11, 22.011, or 22.021, Penal Code;

(B) Chapter 20A, Penal Code;

(C) Section 33.021, Penal Code; or

(D) Chapter 43, Penal Code; and

(2) is served on or issued with respect to an online service provider that provides service in this state.

Added by Acts 2007, 80th Leg., ch. 1291, § 2, eff. Sept. 1, 2007. Amended by Acts 2017, 85th Leg., ch. 69 (S.B. 1203), § 1, eff. Sept. 1, 2017; Acts 2017, 85th Leg., ch. 685 (H.B. 29), § 8, eff. Sept. 1, 2017.

Section 6 of Acts 2017, 85th Leg., ch. 69 (S.B. 1203) provides:

"The change in law made by this Act to Chapter 24A, Code of Criminal Procedure, applies only to a subpoena, search warrant, or other court order issued on or after the effective date [Sept. 1, 2017] of this Act. A subpoena, search warrant, or other court order issued before the effective date of this Act is governed by the law in effect on the date the warrant was issued, and the former law is continued in effect for that purpose."

Sections 45 and 46 of Acts 2017, 85th Leg., ch. 685 (H.B. 29) provide:

"[Sec. 45](a) Except as provided by Subsection (b) of this section, the changes in law made by this Act apply only to an offense committed on or after the effective date [Sept. 1, 2017] of this Act. An offense committed before the effective date of this Act is governed by the law in effect on the date the offense was committed, and the former law is continued in effect for that purpose. For purposes of this subsection, an offense was committed before the effective date of this Act if any element of the offense occurred before that date.

"(b) The changes in law made by this Act in amending Chapter 62, Code of Criminal Procedure, apply only to a person who is required to register under Chapter 62, Code of Criminal Procedure, on the basis of a conviction or adjudication for or based on an offense committed on or after the effective date of this Act. A person who is required to register under Chapter 62, Code of Criminal Procedure, solely on the basis of a conviction or adjudication for or based on an offense committed before the effective date of this Act is governed by the law in effect on the date the offense was committed, and the former law is continued in effect for that purpose. For purposes of this subsection, an offense was committed before the effective date of this Act if any element of the offense occurred before that date."

"[Sec. 46.] The change in law made by this Act to Chapter 24A, Code of Criminal Procedure, applies only to a subpoena, search warrant, or other court order issued on or after the effective date [Sept. 1, 2017] of this Act. A subpoena, search warrant, or other court order issued before the effective date of this Act is governed by the law in effect on the date the warrant was issued, and the former law is continued in effect for that purpose."

Art. 24A.0015. Definition

In this chapter, "online service provider" means an Internet service provider, search engine, web hosting company, web browsing company, manufacturer of devices providing online application platforms, or company providing online social media platforms.

Added by Acts 2017, 85th Leg., ch. 69 (S.B. 1203), § 2, eff. Sept. 1, 2017; Acts 2017, 85th Leg., ch. 685 (H.B. 29), § 9, eff. Sept. 1, 2017.

Section 6 of Acts 2017, 85th Leg., ch. 69 (S.B. 1203) provides:

"The change in law made by this Act to Chapter 24A, Code of Criminal Procedure, applies only to a subpoena, search warrant, or other court order issued on or after the effective date [Sept. 1, 2017] of this Act. A subpoena, search warrant, or other court order issued before the effective date of this Act is governed by the law in effect on the date the warrant was issued, and the former law is continued in effect for that purpose."

Sections 45 and 46 of Acts 2017, 85th Leg., ch. 685 (H.B. 29) provide:

"[Sec. 45](a) Except as provided by Subsection (b) of this section, the changes in law made by this Act apply only to an offense committed on or after the effective date [Sept. 1, 2017] of this Act. An offense committed before the effective date of this Act is governed by the law in effect on the date the offense was committed, and the former law is continued in effect for that purpose. For purposes of this subsection, an offense was committed before the effective date of this Act if any element of the offense occurred before that date.

"(b) The changes in law made by this Act in amending Chapter 62, Code of Criminal Procedure, apply only to a person who is required to register under Chapter 62, Code of Criminal Procedure, on the basis of a conviction or adjudication for or based on an offense committed on or after the effective date of this Act. A person who is required to register under Chapter 62, Code of Criminal Procedure, solely on the basis of a conviction or adjudication for or based on an offense committed before the effective date of this Act is governed by the law in effect on the date the offense was committed, and the former law is continued in effect for that purpose. For purposes of this subsection, an offense was committed before the effective date of this Act if any element of the offense occurred before that date."

"[Sec. 46.] The change in law made by this Act to Chapter 24A, Code of Criminal Procedure, applies only to a subpoena, search warrant, or other court order issued on or after the effective date [Sept. 1, 2017] of this Act. A subpoena, search warrant, or other court order issued before the effective date of this Act is governed by the law in effect on the date the warrant was issued, and the former law is continued in effect for that purpose."

Art. 24A.002. Response Required; Deadline for Response

(a) Except as provided by Subsection (b), not later than the 10th day after the date on which an online service provider is served with or otherwise receives a subpoena, search warrant, or other court order described by Article 24A.001, the online service provider shall:

(1) fully comply with the subpoena, warrant, or order; or

(2) petition a court to excuse the online service provider from complying with the subpoena, warrant, or order.

(b) As soon as is practicable, and in no event later than the second business day after the date the online service provider is served with or otherwise receives a subpoena, search warrant, or other court order described by Article 24A.001, the online service provider shall fully comply with the subpoena, search warrant, or order if the subpoena, search warrant, or order indicates that full compliance is necessary to address a situation that threatens a person with death or other serious bodily injury.

(c) For the purposes of Subsection (a)(1), full compliance with the subpoena, warrant, or order includes:

(1) producing or providing, to the extent permitted under federal law, all documents or information requested under the subpoena, warrant, or order; or

(2) providing, to the extent permitted under federal law, electronic access to all documents or information requested under the subpoena, warrant, or order.

Added by Acts 2007, 80th Leg., ch. 1291, § 2, eff. Sept. 1, 2007. Amended by Acts 2017, 85th Leg., ch. 69 (S.B. 1203), § 3, eff. Sept. 1, 2017; Acts 2017, 85th Leg., ch. 685 (H.B. 29), § 10, eff. Sept. 1, 2017.

Section 6 of Acts 2017, 85th Leg., ch. 69 (S.B. 1203) provides:

"The change in law made by this Act to Chapter 24A, Code of Criminal Procedure, applies only to a subpoena, search warrant, or other court order issued on or after the effective date [Sept. 1, 2017] of this Act. A subpoena, search warrant, or other court order issued before the effective date of this Act is governed by the law in effect on the date the warrant was issued, and the former law is continued in effect for that purpose."

Sections 45 and 46 of Acts 2017, 85th Leg., ch. 685 (H.B. 29) provide:

"[Sec. 45](a) Except as provided by Subsection (b) of this section, the changes in law made by this Act apply only to an offense committed on or after the effective date [Sept. 1, 2017] of this Act. An offense committed before the effective date of this Act is governed by the law in effect on the date the offense was committed, and the former law is continued in effect for that purpose. For purposes of this subsection, an offense was committed before the effective date of this Act if any element of the offense occurred before that date.

"(b) The changes in law made by this Act in amending Chapter 62, Code of Criminal Procedure, apply only to a person who is required to register under Chapter 62, Code of Criminal Procedure, on the basis of a conviction or adjudication for or based on an offense committed on or after the effective date of this Act. A person who is required to register under Chapter 62, Code of Criminal Procedure, solely on the basis of a conviction or adjudication for or based on an offense committed before the effective date of this Act is governed by the law in effect on the date the offense was committed, and the former law is continued in effect for that purpose. For purposes of this subsection, an offense was committed before the effective date of this Act if any element of the offense occurred before that date."

"[Sec. 46] The change in law made by this Act to Chapter 24A, Code of Criminal Procedure, applies only to a subpoena, search warrant, or other court order issued on or after the effective date [Sept. 1, 2017] of this Act. A subpoena, search warrant, or other court order issued before the effective date of this Act is governed by the law in effect on the date the warrant was issued, and the former law is continued in effect for that purpose."

Art. 24A.003. Disobeying Subpoena, Warrant, or Order

An online service provider that disobeys a subpoena, search warrant, or other court order described by Article 24A.001 and that was not excused from complying with the subpoena, warrant, or order under Article 24A.002(a)(2) may be punished in any manner provided by law.

Added by Acts 2007, 80th Leg., ch. 1291, § 2, eff. Sept. 1, 2007. Amended by Acts 2017, 85th Leg., ch. 69 (S.B. 1203), § 4, eff. Sept. 1, 2017; Acts 2017, 85th Leg., ch. 685 (H.B. 29), § 11, eff. Sept. 1, 2017.

Section 6 of Acts 2017, 85th Leg., ch. 69 (S.B. 1203) provides:

"The change in law made by this Act to Chapter 24A, Code of Criminal Procedure, applies only to a subpoena, search warrant, or other court order issued on or after the effective date [Sept. 1, 2017] of this Act. A subpoena, search warrant, or other court order issued before the effective date of this Act is governed by the law in effect on the date the warrant was issued, and the former law is continued in effect for that purpose."

Sections 45 and 46 of Acts 2017, 85th Leg., ch. 685 (H.B. 29) provide:

"[Sec. 45](a) Except as provided by Subsection (b) of this section, the changes in law made by this Act apply only to an offense committed on or after the effective date [Sept. 1, 2017] of this Act. An offense committed before the effective date of this Act is governed by the law in effect on the date the offense was committed, and the former law is continued in effect for that purpose. For purposes of this subsection, an offense was committed before the effective date of this Act if any element of the offense occurred before that date.

"(b) The changes in law made by this Act in amending Chapter 62, Code of Criminal Procedure, apply only to a person who is required to register under Chapter 62, Code of Criminal Procedure, on the basis of a conviction or adjudication for or based on an offense committed on or after the effective date of this Act. A person who is required to register under Chapter 62, Code of Criminal Procedure, solely on the basis of a conviction or adjudication for or based on an offense committed before the effective date of this Act is governed by the law in effect on the date the offense was committed, and the former law is continued in effect for that purpose. For purposes of this subsection, an offense was committed before the effective date of this Act if any element of the offense occurred before that date."

"[Sec. 46] The change in law made by this Act to Chapter 24A, Code of Criminal Procedure, applies only to a subpoena, search warrant, or other court order issued on or after the effective date [Sept. 1, 2017] of this Act. A subpoena, search warrant, or other court order issued before the effective date of this Act is governed by the law in effect on the date the warrant was issued, and the former law is continued in effect for that purpose."

SUBCHAPTER B. PRESERVING CERTAIN INFORMATION

Art. 24A.051. Preserving Information

(a) On written request of a law enforcement agency in this state or a federal law enforcement agency and pending the issuance of a subpoena or other court order described by Article 24A.001, an online service provider that provides service in this state shall take all steps necessary to preserve all records or other potential evidence in a criminal trial that is in the possession of the online service provider.

(b) Subject to Subsection (c), an online service provider shall preserve information under Subsection (a) for a period of 90 days after the date the online service provider receives the written request described by Subsection (a).

(c) An online service provider shall preserve information under Subsection (a) for the 90–day period immediately following the 90–day period described by Subsection (b) if the requesting law enforcement agency in writing requests an extension of the preservation period.

Added by Acts 2007, 80th Leg., ch. 1291, § 2, eff. Sept. 1, 2007. Amended by Acts 2017, 85th Leg., ch. 69 (S.B. 1203), § 5, eff. Sept. 1, 2017; Acts 2017, 85th Leg., ch. 685 (H.B. 29), § 12, eff. Sept. 1, 2017.

Section 6 of Acts 2017, 85th Leg., ch. 69 (S.B. 1203) provides:

"The change in law made by this Act to Chapter 24A, Code of Criminal Procedure, applies only to a subpoena, search warrant, or other court order issued on or after the effective date [Sept. 1, 2017] of this Act. A subpoena, search warrant, or other court order issued before the effective date of this Act is governed by the law in effect on the date the warrant was issued, and the former law is continued in effect for that purpose."

Sections 45 and 46 of Acts 2017, 85th Leg., ch. 685 (H.B. 29) provide:

"[Sec. 45](a) Except as provided by Subsection (b) of this section, the changes in law made by this Act apply only to an offense committed on or after the effective date [Sept. 1, 2017] of this Act. An offense committed before the effective date of this Act is governed by the law in effect on the date the offense was committed, and the former law is continued in effect for that purpose. For purposes of

this subsection, an offense was committed before the effective date of this Act if any element of the offense occurred before that date.

"(b) The changes in law made by this Act in amending Chapter 62, Code of Criminal Procedure, apply only to a person who is required to register under Chapter 62, Code of Criminal Procedure, on the basis of a conviction or adjudication for or based on an offense committed on or after the effective date of this Act. A person who is required to register under Chapter 62, Code of Criminal Procedure, solely on the basis of a conviction or adjudication for or based on an offense committed before the effective date of this Act is governed by the law in effect on the date the offense was committed, and the former law is continued in effect for that purpose. For purposes of this subsection, an offense was committed before the effective date of this Act if any element of the offense occurred before that date."

"[Sec. 46] The change in law made by this Act to Chapter 24A, Code of Criminal Procedure, applies only to a subpoena, search warrant, or other court order issued on or after the effective date [Sept. 1, 2017] of this Act. A subpoena, search warrant, or other court order issued before the effective date of this Act is governed by the law in effect on the date the warrant was issued, and the former law is continued in effect for that purpose."

CHAPTER TWENTY–FIVE. SERVICE OF A COPY OF THE INDICTMENT

Art. 25.01. In felony

In every case of felony, when the accused is in custody, or as soon as he may be arrested, the clerk of the court where an indictment has been presented shall immediately make a certified copy of the same, and deliver such copy to the sheriff, together with a writ directed to such sheriff, commanding him forthwith to deliver such certified copy to the accused.

Acts 1965, 59th Leg., p. 317, ch. 722, § 1, eff. Jan. 1, 1966.

Art. 25.02. Service and return

Upon receipt of such writ and copy, the sheriff shall immediately deliver such certified copy of the indictment to the accused and return the writ to the clerk issuing the same, with his return thereon, showing when and how the same was executed.

Acts 1965, 59th Leg., p. 317, ch. 722, § 1, eff. Jan. 1, 1966.

Art. 25.03. If on bail in felony

When the accused, in case of felony, is on bail at the time the indictment is presented, the clerk shall deliver a copy of the indictment to the accused or the accused's counsel at the earliest possible time.

Acts 1965, 59th Leg., p. 317, ch. 722, § 1, eff. Jan. 1, 1966. Amended by Acts 2017, 85th Leg., ch. 950 (S.B. 1849), § 3.03, eff. Sept. 1, 2017.

Art. 25.04.   In Misdemeanor

In misdemeanors, the clerk shall deliver a copy of the indictment or information to the accused or the accused's counsel at the earliest possible time before trial.

Acts 1965, 59th Leg., p. 317, ch. 722, § 1, eff. Jan. 1, 1966. Amended by Acts 2017, 85th Leg., ch. 950 (S.B. 1849), § 3.04, eff. Sept. 1, 2017.

CHAPTER TWENTY–SIX.   ARRAIGNMENT

Art. 26.01.   Arraignment

In all felony cases, after indictment, and all misdemeanor cases punishable by imprisonment, there shall be an arraignment.

Acts 1965, 59th Leg., p. 317, ch. 722, § 1, eff. Jan. 1, 1966.

Art. 26.011.   Waiver of Arraignment

An attorney representing a defendant may present a waiver of arraignment, and the clerk of the court may not require the presence of the defendant as a condition of accepting the waiver.

Added by Acts 2001, 77th Leg., ch. 818, § 1, eff. June 14, 2001.

Art. 26.02.   Purpose of arraignment

An arraignment takes place for the purpose of fixing his identity and hearing his plea.

Acts 1965, 59th Leg., p. 317, ch. 722, § 1, eff. Jan. 1, 1966.

Art. 26.03.   Time of arraignment

No arraignment shall take place until the expiration of at least two entire days after the day on which a copy of the indictment was served on the defendant, unless the right to such copy or to such delay be waived, or unless the defendant is on bail.

Acts 1965, 59th Leg., p. 317, ch. 722, § 1, eff. Jan. 1, 1966.

Art. 26.04.   Procedures for Appointing Counsel

(a) The judges of the county courts, statutory county courts, and district courts trying criminal cases in each county, by local rule, shall adopt and publish written countywide procedures for timely and fairly appointing counsel for an indigent defendant in the county arrested for, charged with, or taking an appeal from a conviction of a misdemeanor punishable by confinement or a felony.   The procedures must be consistent with this article and Articles 1.051, 15.17, 15.18, 26.05, and 26.052.   A court shall appoint an attorney from a public appointment list using a system of rotation, unless the court appoints an attorney under Subsection (f), (f–1), (h), or (i).   The court shall appoint attorneys from among the next five names on the appointment list in the order in which the attorneys' names appear on the list, unless the court makes a finding of good cause on the record for appointing an attorney out of order.   An attorney who is not appointed in the order in which the attorney's name appears on the list shall remain next in order on the list.

(b) Procedures adopted under Subsection (a) shall:

(1) authorize only the judges of the county courts, statutory county courts, and district courts trying criminal cases in the county, or the judges' designee, to appoint counsel for indigent defendants in the county;

(2) apply to each appointment of counsel made by a judge or the judges' designee in the county;

(3) ensure that each indigent defendant in the county who is charged with a misdemeanor punishable by

confinement or with a felony and who appears in court without counsel has an opportunity to confer with appointed counsel before the commencement of judicial proceedings;

(4) require appointments for defendants in capital cases in which the death penalty is sought to comply with any applicable requirements under Articles 11.071 and 26.052;

(5) ensure that each attorney appointed from a public appointment list to represent an indigent defendant perform the attorney's duty owed to the defendant in accordance with the adopted procedures, the requirements of this code, and applicable rules of ethics; and

(6) ensure that appointments are allocated among qualified attorneys in a manner that is fair, neutral, and nondiscriminatory.

(c) Whenever a court or the courts' designee authorized under Subsection (b) to appoint counsel for indigent defendants in the county determines for purposes of a criminal proceeding that a defendant charged with or appealing a conviction of a felony or a misdemeanor punishable by confinement is indigent or that the interests of justice require representation of a defendant in the proceeding, the court or the courts' designee shall appoint one or more practicing attorneys to represent the defendant in accordance with this subsection and the procedures adopted under Subsection (a). If the court or the courts' designee determines that the defendant does not speak and understand the English language or that the defendant is deaf, the court or the courts' designee shall make an effort to appoint an attorney who is capable of communicating in a language understood by the defendant.

(d) A public appointment list from which an attorney is appointed as required by Subsection (a) shall contain the names of qualified attorneys, each of whom:

(1) applies to be included on the list;

(2) meets the objective qualifications specified by the judges under Subsection (e);

(3) meets any applicable qualifications specified by the Texas Indigent Defense Commission; and

(4) is approved by a majority of the judges who established the appointment list under Subsection (e).

(e) In a county in which a court is required under Subsection (a) to appoint an attorney from a public appointment list:

(1) the judges of the county courts and statutory county courts trying misdemeanor cases in the county, by formal action:

(A) shall:

(i) establish a public appointment list of attorneys qualified to provide representation in the county in misdemeanor cases punishable by confinement; and

(ii) specify the objective qualifications necessary for an attorney to be included on the list; and

(B) may establish, if determined by the judges to be appropriate, more than one appointment list graduated according to the degree of seriousness of the offense, the attorneys' qualifications, and whether representation will be provided in trial court proceedings, appellate proceedings, or both; and

(2) the judges of the district courts trying felony cases in the county, by formal action:

(A) shall:

(i) establish a public appointment list of attorneys qualified to provide representation in felony cases in the county; and

(ii) specify the objective qualifications necessary for an attorney to be included on the list; and

(B) may establish, if determined by the judges to be appropriate, more than one appointment list graduated according to the degree of seriousness of the offense, the attorneys' qualifications, and whether representation will be provided in trial court proceedings, appellate proceedings, or both.

(f) In a county in which a public defender's office is created or designated under Article 26.044, the court or the courts' designee shall give priority in appointing that office to represent the defendant. However, the court is not required to appoint the public defender's office if:

(1) the court has reason to appoint other counsel; or

(2) a managed assigned counsel program also exists in the county and an attorney will be appointed under that program.

(f–1) In a county in which a managed assigned counsel program is operated in accordance with Article 26.047, the managed assigned counsel program may appoint counsel to represent the defendant in accordance with the guidelines established for the program.

(g) A countywide alternative program for appointing counsel for indigent defendants in criminal cases is established by a formal action in which two-thirds of the judges of the courts designated under this subsection vote to establish the alternative program. An alternative program for appointing counsel in misdemeanor and felony cases may be established in the manner provided by this subsection by the judges of the county courts, statutory county courts, and district courts trying criminal cases in the county. An alternative program for appointing counsel in misdemeanor cases may be established in the manner provided by this subsection by the judges of the county courts and statutory county courts trying criminal cases in the county. An alternative program for appointing counsel in felony cases may be established in the manner provided by this subsection by the judges of the district courts trying criminal cases in the county. In a county in which an alternative program is established:

(1) the alternative program may:

(A) use a single method for appointing counsel or a combination of methods; and

(B) use a multicounty appointment list using a system of rotation; and

(2) the procedures adopted under Subsection (a) must ensure that:

(A) attorneys appointed using the alternative program to represent defendants in misdemeanor cases punishable by confinement:

(i) meet specified objective qualifications for that representation, which may be graduated according to the degree of seriousness of the offense and whether representation will be provided in trial court proceedings, appellate proceedings, or both; and

(ii) are approved by a majority of the judges of the county courts and statutory county courts trying misdemeanor cases in the county;

(B) attorneys appointed using the alternative program to represent defendants in felony cases:

(i) meet specified objective qualifications for that representation, which may be graduated according to the degree of seriousness of the offense and whether representation will be provided in trial court proceedings, appellate proceedings, or both; and

(ii) are approved by a majority of the judges of the district courts trying felony cases in the county;

(C) appointments for defendants in capital cases in which the death penalty is sought comply with the requirements of Article 26.052; and

(D) appointments are reasonably and impartially allocated among qualified attorneys.

(h) Subject to Subsection (f), in a county in which an alternative program for appointing counsel is established as provided by Subsection (g) and is approved by the presiding judge of the administrative judicial region, a court or the courts' designee may appoint an attorney to represent an indigent defendant by using the alternative program. In establishing an alternative program under Subsection (g), the judges of the courts establishing the program may not, without the approval of the commissioners court, obligate the county by contract or by the creation of new positions that cause an increase in expenditure of county funds.

(i) Subject to Subsection (f), a court or the courts' designee required under Subsection (c) to appoint an attorney to represent a defendant accused or convicted of a felony may appoint an attorney from any county located in the court's administrative judicial region.

(j) An attorney appointed under this article shall:

(1) make every reasonable effort to contact the defendant not later than the end of the first working day after the date on which the attorney is appointed and to interview the defendant as soon as practicable after the attorney is appointed;

(2) represent the defendant until charges are dismissed, the defendant is acquitted, appeals are exhausted, or the attorney is permitted or ordered by the court to withdraw as counsel for the defendant after a finding of good cause is entered on the record;

(3) with respect to a defendant not represented by other counsel, before withdrawing as counsel for the defendant after a trial or the entry of a plea of guilty:

(A) advise the defendant of the defendant's right to file a motion for new trial and a notice of appeal;

(B) if the defendant wishes to pursue either or both remedies described by Paragraph (A), assist the defendant in requesting the prompt appointment of replacement counsel; and

(C) if replacement counsel is not appointed promptly and the defendant wishes to pursue an appeal, file a timely notice of appeal; and

(4) not later than October 15 of each year and on a form prescribed by the Texas Indigent Defense Com-

mission, submit to the county information, for the preceding fiscal year, that describes the percentage of the attorney's practice time that was dedicated to work based on appointments accepted in the county under this article and Title 3, Family Code.

(k) A court may replace an attorney who violates Subsection (j)(1) with other counsel. A majority of the judges of the county courts and statutory county courts or the district courts, as appropriate, trying criminal cases in the county may remove from consideration for appointment an attorney who intentionally or repeatedly violates Subsection (j)(1).

(*l*) Procedures adopted under Subsection (a) must include procedures and financial standards for determining whether a defendant is indigent. The procedures and standards shall apply to each defendant in the county equally, regardless of whether the defendant is in custody or has been released on bail.

(m) In determining whether a defendant is indigent, the court or the courts' designee may consider the defendant's income, source of income, assets, property owned, outstanding obligations, necessary expenses, the number and ages of dependents, and spousal income that is available to the defendant. The court or the courts' designee may not consider whether the defendant has posted or is capable of posting bail, except to the extent that it reflects the defendant's financial circumstances as measured by the considerations listed in this subsection.

(n) A defendant who requests a determination of indigency and appointment of counsel shall:

(1) complete under oath a questionnaire concerning his financial resources;

(2) respond under oath to an examination regarding his financial resources by the judge or magistrate responsible for determining whether the defendant is indigent; or

(3) complete the questionnaire and respond to examination by the judge or magistrate.

(*o*) Before making a determination of whether a defendant is indigent, the court shall request the defendant to sign under oath a statement substantially in the following form:

"On this _____ day of _____, 20 _____, I have been advised by the (name of the court) Court of my right to representation by counsel in connection with the charge pending against me. I am without means to employ counsel of my own choosing and I hereby request the court to appoint counsel for me. (signature of the defendant)"

(p) A defendant who is determined by the court to be indigent is presumed to remain indigent for the remainder of the proceedings in the case unless a material change in the defendant's financial circumstances occurs. If there is a material change in financial circumstances after a determination of indigency or nonindigency is made, the defendant, the defendant's counsel, or the attorney representing the state may move for reconsideration of the determination.

(q) A written or oral statement elicited under this article or evidence derived from the statement may not be used for any purpose, except to determine the defendant's indigency or to impeach the direct testimony of the defendant. This subsection does not prohibit prosecution of the defendant under Chapter 37, Penal Code.

(r) A court may not threaten to arrest or incarcerate a person solely because the person requests the assistance of counsel.

Acts 1965, 59th Leg., p. 317, ch. 722, § 1, eff. Jan. 1, 1966. Amended by Acts 1987, 70th Leg., ch. 979, § 2, eff. Sept. 1, 1987; Acts 2001, 77th Leg., ch. 906, § 6, eff. Jan. 1, 2002; Acts 2009, 81st Leg., ch. 781, § 6, eff. Sept. 1, 2009; Acts 2011, 82nd Leg., ch. 671 (S.B. 1681), § 1, eff. Sept. 1, 2011; Acts 2011, 82nd Leg., ch. 984 (H.B. 1754), § 7, eff. Sept. 1, 2011; Acts 2013, 83rd Leg., ch. 912 (H.B. 1318), § 1(a), eff. Sept. 1, 2014; Acts 2015, 84th Leg., ch. 595 (S.B. 316), § 1, eff. Sept. 1, 2015; Acts 2015, 84th Leg., ch. 858 (S.B. 1517), § 4, eff. Sept. 1, 2015.

Section 5 of Acts 2015, 84th Leg., ch. 858 (S.B. 1517) provides:

"The change in law made by this Act applies only to a person who is arrested on or after the effective date [Sept. 1, 2015] of this Act. A person arrested before the effective date of this Act is governed by the law in effect on the date the person was arrested, and the former law is continued in effect for that purpose."

Art. 26.041. Procedures Related to Guardianships

(a) In this article:

(1) "Guardian" has the meaning assigned by Section 1002.012, Estates Code.

(2) "Letters of guardianship" means a certificate issued under Section 1106.001(a), Estates Code.

(b) A guardian who provides a court with letters of guardianship for a defendant may:

(1) provide information relevant to the determination of indigency; and

(2) request that counsel be appointed in accordance with this chapter.

Added by Acts 2015, 84th Leg., ch. 688 (H.B. 634), § 1, eff. Sept. 1, 2015.

Section 6 of Acts 2015, 84th Leg., ch. 688 (H.B. 634) provides:

"Article 26.041, Code of Criminal Procedure, as added by this Act, applies to a defendant for whom indigency is at issue, regardless of whether the defendant is arrested before, on, or after the effective date of this Act."

Arts. 26.042, 26.043. Repealed by Acts 2001, 77th Leg., ch. 906, § 15, eff. Jan. 1, 2002

Art. 26.044. Public Defender's Office

(a) In this chapter:

(1) "Governmental entity" includes a county, a group of counties, a department of a county, an administrative judicial region created by Section 74.042, Government Code, and any entity created under the Interlocal Cooperation Act as permitted by Chapter 791, Government Code.

(2) "Office of capital and forensic writs" means the office of capital and forensic writs established under Subchapter B, Chapter 78, Government Code.

(3) "Oversight board" means an oversight board established in accordance with Article 26.045.

(4) "Public defender's office" means an entity that:

(A) is either:

(i) a governmental entity; or

(ii) a nonprofit corporation operating under a written agreement with a governmental entity, other than an individual judge or court; and

(B) uses public funds to provide legal representation and services to indigent defendants accused of a crime or juvenile offense, as those terms are defined by Section 79.001, Government Code.

(b) The commissioners court of any county, on written approval of a judge of a county court, statutory county court, or district court trying criminal cases or cases under Title 3, Family Code, in the county, may create a department of the county or by contract may designate a nonprofit corporation to serve as a public defender's office. The commissioners courts of two or more counties may enter into a written agreement to jointly create or designate and jointly fund a regional public defender's office. In creating or designating a public defender's office under this subsection, the commissioners court shall specify or the commissioners courts shall jointly specify, if creating or designating a regional public defender's office:

(1) the duties of the public defender's office;

(2) the types of cases to which the public defender's office may be appointed under Article 26.04(f) and the courts in which an attorney employed by the public defender's office may be required to appear;

(3) if the public defender's office is a nonprofit corporation, the term during which the contract designating the public defender's office is effective and how that contract may be renewed on expiration of the term; and

(4) if an oversight board is established under Article 26.045 for the public defender's office, the powers and duties that have been delegated to the oversight board.

(b–1) The applicable commissioners court or commissioners courts shall require a written plan from a governmental entity serving as a public defender's office.

(c) Before contracting with a nonprofit corporation to serve as a public defender's office under Subsection (b), the commissioners court or commissioners courts shall solicit proposals for the public defender's office.

(c–1) A written plan under Subsection (b–1) or a proposal under Subsection (c) must include:

(1) a budget for the public defender's office, including salaries;

(2) a description of each personnel position, including the chief public defender position;

(3) the maximum allowable caseloads for each attorney employed by the public defender's office;

(4) provisions for personnel training;

(5) a description of anticipated overhead costs for the public defender's office;

(6) policies regarding the use of licensed investigators and expert witnesses by the public defender's office; and

(7) a policy to ensure that the chief public defender and other attorneys employed by the public defender's office do not provide representation to a defendant if doing so would create a conflict of interest that has not been waived by the client.

(d) After considering each proposal for the public defender's office submitted by a nonprofit corporation under Subsection (c), the commissioners court or commissioners courts shall select a proposal that reasonably demonstrates that the public defender's office will provide adequate quality representation for indigent defendants in the county or counties.

(e) The total cost of the proposal under Subsection (c) may not be the sole consideration in selecting a proposal.

(f) A public defender's office must be directed by a chief public defender who:

(1) is a member of the State Bar of Texas;

(2) has practiced law for at least three years; and

(3) has substantial experience in the practice of criminal law.

(g) A public defender's office is entitled to receive funds for personnel costs and expenses incurred in operating as a public defender's office in amounts fixed by the commissioners court and paid out of the appropriate county fund, or jointly fixed by the commissioners courts and proportionately paid out of each appropriate county fund if the public defender's office serves more than one county.

(h) A public defender's office may employ attorneys, licensed investigators, and other personnel necessary to perform the duties of the public defender's office as specified by the commissioners court or commissioners courts under Subsection (b)(1).

(i) Except as authorized by this article, the chief public defender and other attorneys employed by a public defender's office may not:

(1) engage in the private practice of criminal law; or

(2) accept anything of value not authorized by this article for services rendered under this article.

(j) A public defender's office may not accept an appointment under Article 26.04(f) if:

(1) a conflict of interest exists that has not been waived by the client;

(2) the public defender's office has insufficient resources to provide adequate representation for the defendant;

(3) the public defender's office is incapable of providing representation for the defendant in accordance with the rules of professional conduct;

(4) the acceptance of the appointment would violate the maximum allowable caseloads established at the public defender's office; or

(5) the public defender's office shows other good cause for not accepting the appointment.

(j–1) On refusing an appointment under Subsection (j), a chief public defender shall file with the court a written statement that identifies any reason for refusing the appointment. The court shall determine whether the chief public defender has demonstrated adequate good cause for refusing the appointment and shall include the statement with the papers in the case.

(j–2) A chief public defender may not be terminated, removed, or sanctioned for refusing in good faith to accept an appointment under Subsection (j).

(k) The judge may remove from a case a person who violates a provision of Subsection (i).

(*l*) A public defender's office may investigate the financial condition of any person the public defender's office is appointed to represent. The public defender's office shall report the results of the investigation to the appointing judge. The judge may hold a hearing to determine if the person is indigent and entitled to representation under this article.

(m) If it is necessary that an attorney who is not employed by a public defender's office be appointed, the attorney is entitled to the compensation provided by Article 26.05 of this code.

(n) An attorney employed by a public defender's office may be appointed with respect to an application for a writ of habeas corpus filed under Article 11.071 only if:

(1) an attorney employed by the office of capital writs is not appointed in the case; and

(2) the attorney employed by the public defender's office is on the list of competent counsel maintained under Section 78.056, Government Code.

Added by Acts 1985, 69th Leg., ch. 480, § 17, eff. Sept. 1, 1985. Amended by Acts 1987, 70th Leg., ch. 167, § 4.03(a), eff. Sept. 1, 1987; Acts 2001, 77th Leg., ch. 906, § 7, eff. Jan. 1, 2002; Acts 2005, 79th Leg., ch. 965, § 6, eff. Sept. 1, 2005; Acts 2009, 81st Leg., ch. 781, §§ 7, 8, eff. Sept. 1, 2009; Acts 2011, 82nd Leg., ch. 984 (H.B. 1754), §§ 8, 9, eff. Sept. 1, 2011; Acts 2013, 83rd Leg., ch. 866 (H.B. 577), § 1, eff. June 14, 2013; Acts 2013, 83rd Leg., ch. 912 (H.B. 1318), § 2, eff. Sept. 1, 2013; Acts 2015, 84th Leg., ch. 1215 (S.B. 1743), § 6, eff. Sept. 1, 2015.

Art. 26.045. Public Defender Oversight Board

(a) The commissioners court of a county or the commissioners courts of two or more counties may establish an oversight board for a public defender's office created or designated in accordance with this chapter.

(b) The commissioners court or courts that establish an oversight board under this article shall appoint members of the board. Members may include one or more of the following:

(1) an attorney;

(2) the judge of a trial court in this state;

(3) a county commissioner;

(4) a county judge;

(5) a community representative; and

(6) a former client or a family member of a former client of the public defender's office for which the oversight board was established under this article.

(c) The commissioners court or courts may delegate to the board any power or duty of the commissioners court to provide oversight of the office under Article 26.044, including:

(1) recommending selection and removal of a chief public defender;

(2) setting policy for the office; and

(3) developing a budget proposal for the office.

(d) An oversight board established under this article may not gain access to privileged or confidential information.

Added by Acts 2011, 82nd Leg., ch. 984 (H.B. 1754), § 10, eff. Sept. 1, 2011.

Art. 26.046.   Repealed by Acts 2001, 77th Leg., ch. 906 § 15, eff. Jan. 1, 2002

Art. 26.047.   Managed Assigned Counsel Program

(a) In this article:

(1) "Governmental entity" has the meaning assigned by Article 26.044.

(2) "Managed assigned counsel program" or "program" means a program operated with public funds:

(A) by a governmental entity, nonprofit corporation, or bar association under a written agreement with a governmental entity, other than an individual judge or court; and

(B) for the purpose of appointing counsel under Article 26.04 of this code or Section 51.10, Family Code.

(b) The commissioners court of any county, on written approval of a judge of the juvenile court of a county or a county court, statutory county court, or district court trying criminal cases in the county, may appoint a governmental entity, nonprofit corporation, or bar association to operate a managed assigned counsel program. The commissioners courts of two or more counties may enter into a written agreement to jointly appoint and fund a governmental entity, non-

profit corporation, or bar association to operate a managed assigned counsel program. In appointing an entity to operate a managed assigned counsel program under this subsection, the commissioners court shall specify or the commissioners courts shall jointly specify:

(1) the types of cases in which the program may appoint counsel under Article 26.04 of this code or Section 51.10, Family Code, and the courts in which the counsel appointed by the program may be required to appear; and

(2) the term of any agreement establishing a program and how the agreement may be terminated or renewed.

(c) The commissioners court or commissioners courts shall require a written plan of operation from an entity operating a program under this article. The plan of operation must include:

(1) a budget for the program, including salaries;

(2) a description of each personnel position, including the program's director;

(3) the maximum allowable caseload for each attorney appointed by the program;

(4) provisions for training personnel of the program and attorneys appointed under the program;

(5) a description of anticipated overhead costs for the program;

(6) a policy regarding licensed investigators and expert witnesses used by attorneys appointed under the program;

(7) a policy to ensure that appointments are reasonably and impartially allocated among qualified attorneys; and

(8) a policy to ensure that an attorney appointed under the program does not accept appointment in a case that involves a conflict of interest for the attorney that has not been waived by all affected clients.

(d) A program under this article must have a director. Unless the program uses a review committee appointed under Subsection (e), a program under this article must be directed by a person who:

(1) is a member of the State Bar of Texas;

(2) has practiced law for at least three years; and

(3) has substantial experience in the practice of criminal law.

(e) The governmental entity, nonprofit corporation, or bar association operating the program may appoint a review committee of three or more individuals to approve attorneys for inclusion on the program's public appointment list described by Subsection (f). Each member of the committee:

(1) must meet the requirements described by Subsection (d);

(2) may not be employed as a prosecutor; and

(3) may not be included on or apply for inclusion on the public appointment list described by Subsection (f).

(f) The program's public appointment list from which an attorney is appointed must contain the names of qualified attorneys, each of whom:

(1) applies to be included on the list;

(2) meets any applicable requirements specified by the procedure for appointing counsel adopted under Article 26.04(a) and the Texas Indigent Defense Commission; and

(3) is approved by the program director or review committee, as applicable.

(g) A court may replace an attorney appointed by the program for the same reasons and in the same manner described by Article 26.04(k).

(h) A managed assigned counsel program is entitled to receive funds for personnel costs and expenses incurred in amounts fixed by the commissioners court and paid out of the appropriate county fund, or jointly fixed by the commissioners courts and proportionately paid out of each appropriate county fund if the program serves more than one county.

(i) A managed assigned counsel program may employ personnel and enter into contracts necessary to perform the program's duties as specified by the commissioners court or commissioners courts under this article.

Added by Acts 2011, 82nd Leg., ch. 984 (H.B. 1754), § 11, eff. Sept. 1, 2011.

Arts. 26.048, 26.049. Repealed by Acts 2001, 77th Leg., ch. 906, § 15, eff. Jan. 1, 2002

Art. 26.05. Compensation of Counsel Appointed to Defend

(a) A counsel, other than an attorney with a public defender's office or an attorney employed by the office of capital and forensic writs, appointed to represent a defendant in a criminal proceeding, including a habeas corpus hearing, shall be paid a reasonable attorney's fee for performing the following services, based on the time and labor required, the complexity of the case, and the experience and ability of the appointed counsel:

(1) time spent in court making an appearance on behalf of the defendant as evidenced by a docket entry, time spent in trial, and time spent in a proceeding in which sworn oral testimony is elicited;

(2) reasonable and necessary time spent out of court on the case, supported by any documentation that the court requires;

(3) preparation of an appellate brief and preparation and presentation of oral argument to a court of appeals or the Court of Criminal Appeals; and

(4) preparation of a motion for rehearing.

(b) All payments made under this article shall be paid in accordance with a schedule of fees adopted by formal action of the judges of the county courts, statutory county courts, and district courts trying criminal cases in each county. On adoption of a schedule of fees as provided by this subsection, a copy of the schedule shall be sent to the commissioners court of the county.

(c) Each fee schedule adopted shall state reasonable fixed rates or minimum and maximum hourly rates, taking into consideration reasonable and necessary overhead costs and the availability of qualified attorneys willing to accept the stated rates, and shall provide a form for the appointed counsel to itemize the types of services performed. No payment shall be made under this article until the form for itemizing the services performed is submitted to the judge presiding over the proceedings or, if the county operates a managed assigned counsel program under Article 26.047, to the director of the program, and until the judge or director, as applicable, approves the payment. If the judge or director disapproves the requested amount of payment, the judge or director shall make written findings stating the amount of payment that the judge or director approves and each reason for approving an amount different from the requested amount. An attorney whose request for payment is disapproved or is not otherwise acted on by the 60th day after the date the request for payment is submitted may appeal the disapproval or failure to act by filing a motion with the presiding judge of the administrative judicial region. On the filing of a motion, the presiding judge of the administrative judicial region shall review the disapproval of payment or failure to act and determine the appropriate amount of payment. In reviewing the disapproval or failure to act, the presiding judge of the administrative judicial region may conduct a hearing. Not later than the 45th day after the date an application for payment of a fee is submitted under this article, the commissioners court shall pay to the appointed counsel the amount that is approved by the presiding judge of the administrative judicial region and that is in accordance with the fee schedule for that county.

(d) A counsel in a noncapital case, other than an attorney with a public defender's office, appointed to represent a defendant under this code shall be reimbursed for reasonable and necessary expenses, including expenses for investigation and for mental health and other experts. Expenses incurred with prior court approval shall be reimbursed in the same manner provided for capital cases by Articles 26.052(f) and (g), and expenses incurred without prior court approval shall be reimbursed in the manner provided for capital cases by Article 26.052(h).

(e) A majority of the judges of the county courts and statutory county courts or the district courts, as appropriate, trying criminal cases in the county may remove an attorney from consideration for appointment if, after a hearing, it is shown that the attorney submitted a claim for legal services not performed by the attorney.

(f) All payments made under this article shall be paid from the general fund of the county in which the prosecution was instituted or habeas corpus hearing held and may be included as costs of court.

(g) If the judge determines that a defendant has financial resources that enable the defendant to offset in part or in whole the costs of the legal services provided to the defendant in accordance with Article 1.051(c) or (d), including any expenses and costs, the judge shall order the defendant to pay during the pendency of the charges or, if convicted, as court costs the amount that the judge finds the defendant is able to pay. The defendant may not be ordered to pay an amount that exceeds:

(1) the actual costs, including any expenses and costs, paid by the county for the legal services provided by an appointed attorney; or

(2) if the defendant was represented by a public defender's office, the actual amount, including any expenses and costs, that would have otherwise been paid to an appointed attorney had the county not had a public defender's office.

(g–1)(1) This subsection applies only to a defendant who at the time of sentencing to confinement or

placement on community supervision, including deferred adjudication community supervision, did not have the financial resources to pay the maximum amount described by Subsection (g)(1) or (2), as applicable, for legal services provided to the defendant.

(2) At any time during a defendant's sentence of confinement or period of community supervision, the judge, after providing written notice to the defendant and an opportunity for the defendant to present information relevant to the defendant's ability to pay, may order a defendant to whom this subsection applies to pay any unpaid portion of the amount described by Subsection (g)(1) or (2), as applicable, if the judge determines that the defendant has the financial resources to pay the additional portion.

(3) The judge may amend an order entered under Subdivision (2) if, subsequent to the judge's determination under that subdivision, the judge determines that the defendant is indigent or demonstrates an inability to pay the amount ordered.

(4) In making a determination under this subsection, the judge may only consider the information a court or courts' designee is authorized to consider in making an indigency determination under Article 26.04(m).

(5) Notwithstanding any other law, the judge may not revoke or extend the defendant's period of community supervision solely to collect the amount the defendant has been ordered to pay under this subsection.

(h) Reimbursement of expenses incurred for purposes of investigation or expert testimony may be paid directly to a private investigator licensed under Chapter 1702, Occupations Code, or to an expert witness in the manner designated by appointed counsel and approved by the court.

(i) Repealed by Acts 2011, 82nd Leg., ch. 984 (H.B. 1754), § 15(1).

Acts 1965, 59th Leg., p. 317, ch. 722, § 1, eff. Jan. 1, 1966. Amended by Acts 1969, 61st Leg., p. 1054, ch. 347, § 1, eff. May 27, 1969; Acts 1971, 62nd Leg., p. 1777, ch. 520, § 1, eff. Aug. 30, 1971; Acts 1973, 63rd Leg., p. 1126, ch. 426, art. 3, § 3, eff. June 14, 1973; Acts 1981, 67th Leg., p. 803, ch. 291, § 106, eff. Sept. 1, 1981; Acts 1987, 70th Leg., ch. 979, § 3, eff. Sept. 1, 1987; Acts 1999, 76th Leg., ch. 837, § 1, eff. Sept. 1, 1999; Acts 2001, 77th Leg., ch. 906, § 8, eff. Jan. 1, 2002; Acts 2001, 77th Leg., ch. 1420, § 14.734, eff. Sept. 1, 2001; Acts 2007, 80th Leg., ch. 1014, § 1, eff. Sept. 1, 2007; Acts 2009, 81st Leg., ch. 781, § 9, eff. Sept. 1, 2009; Acts 2011, 82nd Leg., ch. 984 (H.B. 1754), §§ 12, 15(1), eff. Sept. 1, 2011; Acts 2015, 84th Leg., ch. 106 (H.B. 3633), § 1, eff. Sept. 1, 2015; Acts 2015, 84th Leg., ch. 1215 (S.B. 1743), § 7, eff. Sept. 1, 2015; Acts 2017, 85th Leg., ch. 554 (S.B. 527), § 1, eff. Sept. 1, 2017.

Section 4 of Acts 2015, 84th Leg., ch. 106 (H.B. 3633) provides:

"The change in law made by this Act applies only to a criminal hearing or proceeding that commences on or after the effective date [Sept. 1, 2015] of this Act, regardless of when the defendant committed the underlying offense for which the defendant became subject to the hearing or proceeding. A criminal hearing or proceeding that commences before the effective date of this Act is governed by the law in effect on the date the hearing or proceeding commenced, and the former law is continued in effect for that purpose."

Art. 26.050. Repealed by Acts 2001, 77th Leg., ch. 906, § 15, eff. Jan. 1, 2002

Art. 26.051. Indigent inmate defense

(a) In this article:

(1) "Board" means the Texas Board of Criminal Justice.

(2) "Correctional institutions division" means the correctional institutions division of the Texas Department of Criminal Justice.

(b), (c) Repealed by Acts 2007, 80th Leg., ch. 1014, § 7.

(d) A court shall:

(1) notify the board if it determines that a defendant before the court is indigent and is an inmate charged with an offense committed while in the custody of the correctional institutions division or a correctional facility authorized by Section 495.001, Government Code; and

(2) request that the board provide legal representation for the inmate.

(e) The board shall provide legal representation for inmates described by Subsection (d) of this section. The board may employ attorneys, support staff, and any other personnel required to provide legal representation for those inmates. All personnel employed under this article are directly responsible to the board in the performance of their duties. The board shall pay all fees and costs associated with providing legal representation for those inmates.

(f) Repealed by Acts 1993, 73rd Leg., ch. 988, § 7.02, eff. Sept. 1, 1993.

(g) The court shall appoint an attorney other than an attorney provided by the board if the court determines for any of the following reasons that a conflict of interest could arise from the use of an attorney provided by the board under Subsection (e) of this article:

(1) the case involves more than one inmate and the representation of more than one inmate could impair the attorney's effectiveness;

(2) the case is appealed and the court is satisfied that conflict of interest would prevent the presentation of a good faith allegation of ineffective assistance of counsel by a trial attorney provided by the board; or

(3) any conflict of interest exists under the Texas Disciplinary Rules of Professional Conduct of the State Bar of Texas that precludes representation by an attorney appointed by the board.

(h) When the court appoints an attorney other than an attorney provided by the board:

(1) except as otherwise provided by this article, the inmate's legal defense is subject to Articles 1.051, 26.04, 26.05, and 26.052, as applicable; and

(2) the county in which a facility of the correctional institutions division or a correctional facility authorized by Section 495.001, Government Code, is located shall pay from its general fund the total costs of the aggregate amount allowed and awarded by the court for attorney compensation and expenses under Article 26.05 or 26.052, as applicable.

(i) The state shall reimburse a county for attorney compensation and expenses awarded under Subsection (h). A court seeking reimbursement for a county shall certify to the comptroller of public accounts the amount of compensation and expenses for which the county is entitled to be reimbursed under this article. Not later than the 60th day after the date the comptroller receives from the court the request for reimbursement, the comptroller shall issue a warrant to the county in the amount certified by the court.

Added by Acts 1990, 71st Leg., 6th C.S., ch. 15, § 2, eff. June 14, 1990. Amended by Acts 1991, 72nd Leg., ch. 719, § 1, eff. Sept. 1, 1991; Acts 1993, 73rd Leg., ch. 988, §§ 7.01, 7.02, eff. Sept. 1, 1993; Acts 2007, 80th Leg., ch. 1014, §§ 2, 3, 7, eff. Sept. 1, 2007.

Art. 26.052. Appointment of counsel in death penalty case; reimbursement of investigative expenses

(a) Notwithstanding any other provision of this chapter, this article establishes procedures in death penalty cases for appointment and payment of counsel to represent indigent defendants at trial and on direct appeal and to apply for writ of certiorari in the United States Supreme Court.

(b) If a county is served by a public defender's office, trial counsel and counsel for direct appeal or to apply for a writ of certiorari may be appointed as provided by the guidelines established by the public defender's office. In all other cases in which the death penalty is sought, counsel shall be appointed as provided by this article.

(c) A local selection committee is created in each administrative judicial region created under Section 74.042, Government Code. The administrative judge of the judicial region shall appoint the members of the committee. A committee shall have not less than four members, including:

(1) the administrative judge of the judicial region;

(2) at least one district judge;

(3) a representative from the local bar association; and

(4) at least one practitioner who is board certified by the State Bar of Texas in criminal law.

(d)(1) The committee shall adopt standards for the qualification of attorneys to be appointed to represent indigent defendants in capital cases in which the death penalty is sought.

(2) The standards must require that a trial attorney appointed as lead counsel to a capital case:

(A) be a member of the State Bar of Texas;

(B) exhibit proficiency and commitment to providing quality representation to defendants in death penalty cases;

(C) have not been found by a federal or state court to have rendered ineffective assistance of counsel during the trial or appeal of any capital case, unless the local selection committee determines under Subsection (n) that the conduct underlying the finding no longer accurately reflects the attorney's ability to provide effective representation;

(D) have at least five years of criminal law experience;

(E) have tried to a verdict as lead defense counsel a significant number of felony cases, including homicide trials and other trials for offenses punishable as second or first degree felonies or capital felonies;

(F) have trial experience in:

(i) the use of and challenges to mental health or forensic expert witnesses; and

(ii) investigating and presenting mitigating evidence at the penalty phase of a death penalty trial; and

(G) have participated in continuing legal education courses or other training relating to criminal defense in death penalty cases.

(3) The standards must require that an attorney appointed as lead appellate counsel in the direct appeal of a capital case:

(A) be a member of the State Bar of Texas;

(B) exhibit proficiency and commitment to providing quality representation to defendants in death penalty cases;

(C) have not been found by a federal or state court to have rendered ineffective assistance of counsel during the trial or appeal of any capital case, unless the local selection committee determines under Subsection (n) that the conduct underlying the finding no longer accurately reflects the attorney's ability to provide effective representation;

(D) have at least five years of criminal law experience;

(E) have authored a significant number of appellate briefs, including appellate briefs for homicide cases and other cases involving an offense punishable as a capital felony or a felony of the first degree or an offense described by Article 42A.054(a);

(F) have trial or appellate experience in:

(i) the use of and challenges to mental health or forensic expert witnesses; and

(ii) the use of mitigating evidence at the penalty phase of a death penalty trial; and

(G) have participated in continuing legal education courses or other training relating to criminal defense in appealing death penalty cases.

(4) The committee shall prominently post the standards in each district clerk's office in the region with a list of attorneys qualified for appointment.

(5) Not later than the second anniversary of the date an attorney is placed on the list of attorneys qualified for appointment in death penalty cases and each year following the second anniversary, the attorney must present proof to the committee that the attorney has successfully completed the minimum continuing legal education requirements of the State Bar of Texas, including a course or other form of training relating to criminal defense in death penalty cases or in appealing death penalty cases, as applicable. The committee shall remove the attorney's name from the list of qualified attorneys if the attorney fails to provide the committee with proof of completion of the continuing legal education requirements.

(e) The presiding judge of the district court in which a capital felony case is filed shall appoint two attorneys, at least one of whom must be qualified under this chapter, to represent an indigent defendant as soon as practicable after charges are filed, unless the state gives notice in writing that the state will not seek the death penalty.

(f) Appointed counsel may file with the trial court a pretrial ex parte confidential request for advance payment of expenses to investigate potential defenses. The request for expenses must state:

(1) the type of investigation to be conducted;

(2) specific facts that suggest the investigation will result in admissible evidence; and

(3) an itemized list of anticipated expenses for each investigation.

(g) The court shall grant the request for advance payment of expenses in whole or in part if the request is reasonable. If the court denies in whole or in part the request for expenses, the court shall:

(1) state the reasons for the denial in writing;

(2) attach the denial to the confidential request; and

(3) submit the request and denial as a sealed exhibit to the record.

(h) Counsel may incur expenses without prior approval of the court. On presentation of a claim for reimbursement, the court shall order reimbursement of counsel for the expenses, if the expenses are reasonably necessary and reasonably incurred.

(i) If the indigent defendant is convicted of a capital felony and sentenced to death, the defendant is entitled to be represented by competent counsel on appeal and to apply for a writ of certiorari to the United States Supreme Court.

(j) As soon as practicable after a death sentence is imposed in a capital felony case, the presiding judge of the convicting court shall appoint counsel to represent an indigent defendant on appeal and to apply for a writ of certiorari, if appropriate.

(k) The court may not appoint an attorney as counsel on appeal if the attorney represented the defendant at trial, unless:

(1) the defendant and the attorney request the appointment on the record; and

(2) the court finds good cause to make the appointment.

(l) An attorney appointed under this article to represent a defendant at trial or on direct appeal is compensated as provided by Article 26.05 from county funds. Advance payment of expenses anticipated or reimbursement of expenses incurred for purposes of investigation or expert testimony may be paid directly to a private investigator licensed under Chapter 1702, Occupations Code, or to an expert witness in the manner designated by appointed counsel and approved by the court.

(m) The local selection committee shall annually review the list of attorneys posted under Subsection (d) to ensure that each listed attorney satisfies the requirements under this chapter.

(n) At the request of an attorney, the local selection committee shall make a determination under Subsection (d)(2)(C) or (3)(C), as applicable, regarding an attorney's current ability to provide effective representation following a judicial finding that the attorney previously rendered ineffective assistance of counsel in a capital case.

Added by Acts 1995, 74th Leg., ch. 319, § 2, eff. Sept. 1, 1995. Amended by Acts 1999, 76th Leg., ch. 837, § 2, eff. Sept. 1, 1999; Acts 2001, 77th Leg., ch. 906, § 9, eff. Jan. 1, 2002; Acts 2001, 77th Leg., ch. 1420, § 14.735, eff. Sept. 1, 2001; Acts 2005, 79th Leg., ch. 787, § 14, eff. Sept. 1, 2005; Acts 2005, 79th Leg., ch. 965, § 7, eff. Sept. 1, 2005; Acts 2009, 81st Leg., ch. 32, § 1, eff. Sept. 1, 2009; Acts 2011, 82nd Leg., ch. 1343 (S.B. 1308), § 1, eff. Sept. 1, 2011; Acts 2015, 84th Leg., ch. 770 (H.B. 2299), § 2.06, eff. Jan. 1, 2017.

Art. 26.053.   Repealed by Acts 2015, 84th Leg., ch. 361 (H.B. 2193), § 1, eff. June 9, 2015

Art. 26.054.   Repealed by Acts 2001, 77th Leg., ch. 906, § 15, eff. Jan. 1, 2002

Art. 26.055.   Repealed by Acts 2007, 80th Leg., ch. 1014, § 7, eff. Sept. 1, 2007.

Art. 26.056.   Contribution from state in certain counties

Sec. 1.   A county in which a state training school for delinquent children is located shall pay from its general fund the first $250 of fees awarded for court-appointed counsel under Article 26.05 toward defending a child committed to the school from another county who is being prosecuted for a felony or misdemeanor in the county where the training school is located.

Sec. 2.   If the fees awarded for counsel compensation are in excess of $250, the court shall certify the amount in excess of $250 to the Comptroller of Public Accounts of the State of Texas. The Comptroller shall issue a warrant to the court-appointed counsel in the amount certified to the comptroller by the court.

Acts 1967, 60th Leg., p. 733, ch. 307, § 1, eff. Aug. 28, 1967. Renumbered from art. 26.05–1 by Acts 1987, 70th Leg., ch. 167, § 5.02(2), eff. Sept. 1, 1987.

Art. 26.057. Cost of employment of counsel for certain minors

If a juvenile has been transferred to a criminal court under Section 54.02, Family Code, and if a court appoints counsel for the juvenile under Article 26.04 of this code, the county that pays for the counsel has a cause of action against a parent or other person who is responsible for the support of the juvenile and is financially able to employ counsel for the juvenile but refuses to do so. The county may recover its cost of payment to the appointed counsel and may recover attorney's fees necessary to prosecute the cause of action against the parent or other person.

Acts 1987, 70th Leg., ch. 979, § 4, eff. Sept. 1, 1987. Renumbered from Vernon's Ann.C.C.P. art. 26.056 by Acts 1989, 71st Leg., ch. 2, § 16.01(8), eff. Aug. 28, 1989.

Art. 26.058. Repealed by Acts 2001, 77th Leg., ch. 906, § 15, eff. Jan. 1, 2002

Art. 26.05–1. Renumbered as Vernon's Ann.C.C.P. art. 26.056 by Acts 1987, 70th Leg., ch. 167, § 5.02(2), eff. Sept. 1, 1987

Art. 26.06. Elected officials not to be appointed

No court may appoint an elected county, district or state official to represent a person accused of crime, unless the official has notified the court of his availability for appointment. If an official has notified the court of his availability and is appointed as counsel, he may decline the appointment if he determines that it is in the best interest of his office to do so. Nothing in this Code shall modify any statutory provision for legislative continuance.

Acts 1965, 59th Leg., p. 317, ch. 722, § 1, eff. Jan. 1, 1966.

Art. 26.07. Name as stated in indictment

When the defendant is arraigned, his name, as stated in the indictment, shall be distinctly called; and unless he suggest by himself or counsel that he is not indicted by his true name, it shall be taken that his name is truly set forth, and he shall not thereafter be allowed to deny the same by way of defense.

Acts 1965, 59th Leg., p. 317, ch. 722, § 1, eff. Jan. 1, 1966.

Art. 26.08. If defendant suggests different name

If the defendant, or his counsel for him, suggests that he bears some name different from that stated in the indictment, the same shall be noted upon the minutes of the court, the indictment corrected by inserting therein the name of the defendant as suggested by himself or his counsel for him, the style of the case changed so as to give his true name, and the cause proceed as if the true name had been first recited in the indictment.

Acts 1965, 59th Leg., p. 317, ch. 722, § 1, eff. Jan. 1, 1966.

Art. 26.09. If accused refuses to give his real name

If the defendant alleges that he is not indicted by his true name, and refuses to say what his real name is, the cause shall proceed as if the name stated in the indictment were true; and the defendant shall not be allowed to contradict the same by way of defense.

Acts 1965, 59th Leg., p. 317, ch. 722, § 1, eff. Jan. 1, 1966.

Art. 26.10. Where name is unknown

A defendant described as a person whose name is unknown may have the indictment so corrected as to give therein his true name.

Acts 1965, 59th Leg., p. 317, ch. 722, § 1, eff. Jan. 1, 1966.

Art. 26.11. Indictment read

The name of the accused having been called, if no suggestion, such as is spoken of in the four preceding Articles, be made, or being made is disposed of as before directed, the indictment shall be read, and the defendant asked whether he is guilty or not, as therein charged.

Acts 1965, 59th Leg., p. 317, ch. 722, § 1, eff. Jan. 1, 1966.

Art. 26.12. Plea of not guilty entered

If the defendant answers that he is not guilty, such plea shall be entered upon the minutes of the court; if he refuses to answer, the plea of not guilty shall in like manner be entered.

Acts 1965, 59th Leg., p. 317, ch. 722, § 1, eff. Jan. 1, 1966.

Art. 26.13. Plea of guilty

(a) Prior to accepting a plea of guilty or a plea of nolo contendere, the court shall admonish the defendant of:

(1) the range of the punishment attached to the offense;

(2) the fact that the recommendation of the prosecuting attorney as to punishment is not binding on the

court. Provided that the court shall inquire as to the existence of a plea bargain agreement between the state and the defendant and, if an agreement exists, the court shall inform the defendant whether it will follow or reject the agreement in open court and before any finding on the plea. Should the court reject the agreement, the defendant shall be permitted to withdraw the defendant's plea of guilty or nolo contendere;

(3) the fact that if the punishment assessed does not exceed the punishment recommended by the prosecutor and agreed to by the defendant and the defendant's attorney, the trial court must give its permission to the defendant before the defendant may prosecute an appeal on any matter in the case except for those matters raised by written motions filed prior to trial;

(4) the fact that if the defendant is not a citizen of the United States of America, a plea of guilty or nolo contendere for the offense charged may result in deportation, the exclusion from admission to this country, or the denial of naturalization under federal law;

(5) the fact that the defendant will be required to meet the registration requirements of Chapter 62, if the defendant is convicted of or placed on deferred adjudication for an offense for which a person is subject to registration under that chapter; and

(6) the fact that if the defendant is placed on community supervision, after satisfactorily fulfilling the conditions of community supervision and on expiration of the period of community supervision, the court is authorized to release the defendant from the penalties and disabilities resulting from the offense as provided by Article 42A.701(f).

(b) No plea of guilty or plea of nolo contendere shall be accepted by the court unless it appears that the defendant is mentally competent and the plea is free and voluntary.

(c) In admonishing the defendant as herein provided, substantial compliance by the court is sufficient, unless the defendant affirmatively shows that he was not aware of the consequences of his plea and that he was misled or harmed by the admonishment of the court.

(d) The court may make the admonitions required by this article either orally or in writing. If the court makes the admonitions in writing, it must receive a statement signed by the defendant and the defendant's attorney that he understands the admonitions and is aware of the consequences of his plea. If the defendant is unable or refuses to sign the statement, the court shall make the admonitions orally.

(e) Before accepting a plea of guilty or a plea of nolo contendere, the court shall, as applicable in the case:

(1) inquire as to whether a victim impact statement has been returned to the attorney representing the state and ask for a copy of the statement if one has been returned; and

(2) inquire as to whether the attorney representing the state has given notice of the existence and terms of any plea bargain agreement to the victim, guardian of a victim, or close relative of a deceased victim, as those terms are defined by Article 56.01.

(f) The court must substantially comply with Subsection (e) of this article. The failure of the court to comply with Subsection (e) of this article is not grounds for the defendant to set aside the conviction, sentence, or plea.

(g) Before accepting a plea of guilty or a plea of nolo contendere and on the request of a victim of the offense, the court may assist the victim and the defendant in participating in a victim-offender mediation program.

(h) The court must substantially comply with Subsection (a)(5). The failure of the court to comply with Subsection (a)(5) is not a ground for the defendant to set aside the conviction, sentence, or plea.

(h–1) The court must substantially comply with Subsection (a)(6). The failure of the court to comply with Subsection (a)(6) is not a ground for the defendant to set aside the conviction, sentence, or plea.

(i) Notwithstanding this article, a court shall not order the state or any of its prosecuting attorneys to participate in mediation, dispute resolution, arbitration, or other similar procedures in relation to a criminal prosecution unless upon written consent of the state.

Acts 1965, 59th Leg., p. 317, ch. 722, § 1, eff. Jan. 1, 1966. Amended by Acts 1973, 63rd Leg., p. 969, ch. 399, § 2(A), eff. Jan. 1, 1974; Acts 1975, 64th Leg., p. 909, ch. 341, § 3, eff. June 19, 1975; Acts 1977, 65th Leg., p. 748, ch. 280, § 1, eff. Aug. 29, 1977; Acts 1979, 66th Leg., p. 1108, ch. 524, § 1, eff. Sept. 1, 1979; Acts 1979, 66th Leg., p. 1160, ch. 561, § 1, eff. Sept. 1, 1979; Acts 1985, 69th Leg., p. 5065, ch. 671, § 1, eff. June 14, 1985; Acts 1985, 69th Leg., ch. 685, § 8(a), eff. Aug. 26, 1985; Acts 1987, 70th Leg., ch. 443, § 1, eff. Aug. 1, 1987; Acts 1991, 72nd Leg., ch. 202, § 1, eff. Sept. 1, 1991; Acts 1997, 75th Leg., ch. 670, § 4, eff. Sept. 1, 1997; Acts 1999, 76th Leg., ch. 425, § 1, eff. Aug. 30, 1999; Acts 1999, 76th Leg., ch. 1415, § 1, eff. Sept. 1, 1999; Acts 2001, 77th Leg., ch. 1420, § 21.001(8), eff. Sept. 1, 2001; Acts 2005, 79th Leg., ch. 1008, § 1.03, eff. Sept. 1, 2005; Acts 2007, 80th Leg., ch. 125, § 1, eff. Sept. 1, 2007; Acts 2009, 81st Leg., ch. 1379, § 2, eff. Sept. 1, 2009; Acts 2011, 82nd Leg., ch. 1073 (S.B. 1010), § 1, eff. Sept. 1, 2011; Acts 2017, 85th Leg., ch. 1017 (H.B. 1507), § 1, eff. Sept. 1, 2017.

Section 4(b) of Acts 2017, 85th Leg., ch. 1017 (H.B. 1507) provides: "Article 26.13(a), Code of Criminal Procedure, as amended by this Act, applies only to a plea of guilty or a plea of nolo contendere accepted by a court on or after January 1, 2018, regardless of whether the offense for which the plea was submitted was committed before, on, or after that date."

Art. 26.14.   Jury on plea of guilty

Where a defendant in a case of felony persists in pleading guilty or in entering a plea of nolo contendere, if the punishment is not absolutely fixed by law, a jury shall be impaneled to assess the punishment and evidence may be heard to enable them to decide thereupon, unless the defendant in accordance with Articles 1.13 or 37.07 shall have waived his right to trial by jury.

Acts 1965, 59th Leg., p. 317, ch. 722, § 1, eff. Jan. 1, 1966.

Art. 26.15   Correcting name

In any case, the same proceedings shall be had with respect to the name of the defendant and the correction of the indictment or information as provided with respect to the same in capital cases.

Acts 1965, 59th Leg., p. 317, ch. 722, § 1, eff. Jan. 1, 1966.

CHAPTER TWENTY–SEVEN. THE PLEADING IN CRIMINAL ACTIONS

Art. 27.01.   Indictment or information

The primary pleading in a criminal action on the part of the State is the indictment or information.

Acts 1965, 59th Leg., p. 317, ch. 722, § 1, eff. Jan. 1, 1966.

Art. 27.02.   Defendant's pleadings

The pleadings and motions of the defendant shall be:

(1) A motion to set aside or an exception to an indictment or information for some matter of form or substance;

(2) A special plea as provided in Article 27.05 of this code;

(3) A plea of guilty;

(4) A plea of not guilty;

(5) A plea of nolo contendere, the legal effect of which shall be the same as that of a plea of guilty, except that such plea may not be used against the defendant as an admission in any civil suit based upon or growing out of the act upon which the criminal prosecution is based;

(6) An application for probation,[1] if any;

(7) An election, if any, to have the jury assess the punishment if he is found guilty; and

(8) Any other motions or pleadings that are by law permitted to be filed.

Acts 1965, 59th Leg., p. 317, ch. 722, § 1, eff. Jan. 1, 1966. Amended by Acts 1967, 60th Leg., p. 1738, ch. 659, § 17, eff. Aug. 28, 1967; Acts 1973, 63rd Leg., p. 968, ch. 399, § 2(A), eff. Jan. 1, 1974.

[1] A reference to "probation" or "deferred adjudication" means "community supervision", pursuant to Acts 1993, 73rd Leg., ch. 900, § 4.04(a).

Art. 27.03.   Motion to set aside indictment

In addition to any other grounds authorized by law, a motion to set aside an indictment or information may be based on the following:

1. That it appears by the records of the court that the indictment was not found by at least nine grand jurors, or that the information was not based upon a valid complaint;

2. That some person not authorized by law was present when the grand jury was deliberating upon the accusation against the defendant, or was voting upon the same; and

3. That the grand jury was illegally impaneled; provided, however, in order to raise such question on motion to set aside the indictment, the defendant must show that he did not have an opportunity to challenge the array at the time the grand jury was impaneled.

Acts 1965, 59th Leg., p. 317, ch. 722, § 1, eff. Jan. 1, 1966.

Art. 27.04.   Motion tried by judge

An issue of fact arising upon a motion to set aside an indictment or information shall be tried by the judge without a jury.

Acts 1965, 59th Leg., p. 317, ch. 722, § 1, eff. Jan. 1, 1966.

Art. 27.05. Defendant's special plea

A defendant's only special plea is that he has already been prosecuted for the same or a different offense arising out of the same criminal episode that was or should have been consolidated into one trial, and that the former prosecution:

(1) resulted in acquittal;

(2) resulted in conviction;

(3) was improperly terminated; or

(4) was terminated by a final order or judgment for the defendant that has not been reversed, set aside, or vacated and that necessarily required a determination inconsistent with a fact that must be established to secure conviction in the subsequent prosecution.

Acts 1965, 59th Leg., p. 317, ch. 722, § 1, eff. Jan. 1, 1966. Amended by Acts 1973, 63rd Leg., p. 969, ch. 399, § 2(A), eff. Jan. 1, 1974.

Art. 27.06. Special plea verified

Every special plea shall be verified by the affidavit of the defendant.

Acts 1965, 59th Leg., p. 317, ch. 722, § 1, eff. Jan. 1, 1966.

Art. 27.07. Special plea tried

All issues of fact presented by a special plea shall be tried by the trier of the facts on the trial on the merits.

Acts 1965, 59th Leg., p. 317, ch. 722, § 1, eff. Jan. 1, 1966.

Art. 27.08. Exception to substance of indictment

There is no exception to the substance of an indictment or information except:

1. That it does not appear therefrom that an offense against the law was committed by the defendant;

2. That it appears from the face thereof that a prosecution for the offense is barred by a lapse of time, or that the offense was committed after the finding of the indictment;

3. That it contains matter which is a legal defense or bar to the prosecution; and

4. That it shows upon its face that the court trying the case has no jurisdiction thereof.

Acts 1965, 59th Leg., p. 317, ch. 722, § 1, eff. Jan. 1, 1966.

Art. 27.09. Exception to form of indictment

Exceptions to the form of an indictment or information may be taken for the following causes only:

1. That it does not appear to have been presented in the proper court as required by law;

2. The want of any requisite prescribed by Articles 21.02 and 21.21.

3. That it was not returned by a lawfully chosen or empaneled grand jury.

Acts 1965, 59th Leg., p. 317, ch. 722, § 1, eff. Jan. 1, 1966.

Art. 27.10. Written pleadings

All motions to set aside an indictment or information and all special pleas and exceptions shall be in writing.

Acts 1965, 59th Leg., p. 317, ch. 722, § 1, eff. Jan. 1, 1966.

Art. 27.11. Ten days allowed for filing pleadings

In all cases the defendant shall be allowed ten entire days, exclusive of all fractions of a day after his arrest, and during the term of the court, to file written pleadings.

Acts 1965, 59th Leg., p. 317, ch. 722, § 1, eff. Jan. 1, 1966.

Art. 27.12. Time after service

In cases where the defendant is entitled to be served with a copy of the indictment, he shall be allowed the ten days time mentioned in the preceding Article to file written pleadings after such service.

Acts 1965, 59th Leg., p. 317, ch. 722, § 1, eff. Jan. 1, 1966.

Art. 27.13. Plea of guilty or nolo contendere in felony

A plea of "guilty" or a plea of "nolo contendere" in a felony case must be made in open court by the defendant in person; and the proceedings shall be as provided in Articles 26.13, 26.14 and 27.02. If the plea is before the judge alone, same may be made in the same manner as is provided for by Articles 1.13 and 1.15.

Acts 1965, 59th Leg., p. 317, ch. 722, § 1, eff. Jan. 1, 1966.

Art. 27.14. Plea of guilty or nolo contendere in misdemeanor

(a) A plea of "guilty" or a plea of "nolo contendere" in a misdemeanor case may be made either by the defendant or his counsel in open court; in such case, the defendant or his counsel may waive a jury, and the punishment may be assessed by the court either upon or without evidence, at the discretion of the court.

(b) A defendant charged with a misdemeanor for which the maximum possible punishment is by fine only may, in lieu of the method provided in Subsection (a), mail or deliver in person to the court a plea of "guilty" or a plea of "nolo contendere" and a waiver of jury trial. The defendant may also request in writing that the court notify the defendant, at the address stated in the request, of the amount of an appeal bond that the court will approve. If the court receives a plea and waiver before the time the defendant is scheduled to appear in court, the court shall dispose of the case without requiring a court appearance by the defendant. If the court receives a plea and waiver after the time the defendant is scheduled to appear in court but at least five business days before a scheduled trial date, the court shall dispose of the case without requiring a court appearance by the defendant. The court shall notify the defendant either in person or by regular mail of the amount of any fine or costs assessed in the case, information regarding the alternatives to the full payment of any fine or costs assessed against the defendant, if the defendant is unable to pay that amount, and, if requested by the defendant, the amount of an appeal bond that the court will approve. Except as otherwise provided by this code, the defendant shall pay any fine or costs assessed or give an appeal bond in the amount stated in the notice before the 31st day after receiving the notice.

(c) In a misdemeanor case for which the maximum possible punishment is by fine only, payment of a fine or an amount accepted by the court constitutes a finding of guilty in open court as though a plea of nolo contendere had been entered by the defendant and constitutes a waiver of a jury trial in writing.

(d) If written notice of an offense for which maximum possible punishment is by fine only or of a violation relating to the manner, time, and place of parking has been prepared, delivered, and filed with the court and a legible duplicate copy has been given to the defendant, the written notice serves as a complaint to which the defendant may plead "guilty," "not guilty," or "nolo contendere." If the defendant pleads "not guilty" to the offense or fails to appear based on the written notice, a complaint shall be filed that conforms to the requirements of Chapter 45 of this code, and that complaint serves as an original complaint. A defendant may waive the filing of a sworn complaint and elect that the prosecution proceed on the written notice of the charged offense if the defendant agrees in writing with the prosecution, signs the agreement, and files it with the court.

(e)(1) [1] Before accepting a plea of guilty or a plea of nolo contendere by a defendant charged with a misdemeanor involving family violence, as defined by Section 71.004, Family Code, the court shall admonish the defendant by using the following statement:

"If you are convicted of a misdemeanor offense involving violence where you are or were a spouse, intimate partner, parent, or guardian of the victim or are or were involved in another, similar relationship with the victim, it may be unlawful for you to possess or purchase a firearm, including a handgun or long gun, or ammunition, pursuant to federal law under 18 U.S.C. Section 922(g)(9) or Section 46.04(b), Texas Penal Code. If you have any questions whether these laws make it illegal for you to possess or purchase a firearm, you should consult an attorney."

(2) The court may provide the admonishment under Subdivision (1) orally or in writing, except that if the defendant is charged with a misdemeanor punishable by fine only, the statement printed on a citation issued under Article 14.06(b) may serve as the court admonishment required by this subsection.

Acts 1965, 59th Leg., p. 317, ch. 722, § 1, eff. Jan. 1, 1966. Amended by Acts 1967, 60th Leg., p. 1738, ch. 659, § 18, eff. Aug. 28, 1967; Acts 1977, 65th Leg., p. 2143, ch. 858, § 1, eff. June 16, 1977; Acts 1979, 66th Leg., p. 450, ch. 207, § 1, eff. Sept. 1, 1979; Acts 1983, 68th Leg., p. 1257, ch. 273, § 1, eff. Sept. 1, 1983; Acts 1985, 69th Leg., ch. 87, § 1, eff. Sept. 1, 1985; Acts 1993, 73rd Leg., ch. 76, § 1, eff. Sept. 1, 1993; Acts 2001, 77th Leg., ch. 285, § 1, eff. Sept. 1, 2001; Acts 2009, 81st Leg., ch. 473, § 1, eff. Sept. 1, 2009; Acts 2009, 81st Leg., ch. 1121, § 1, eff. Sept. 1, 2009; Acts 2009, 81st Leg., ch. 1379, § 3, eff. Sept. 1, 2009; Acts 2017, 85th Leg., ch. 977 (H.B. 351), § 3, eff. Sept. 1, 2017; Acts 2017, 85th Leg., ch. 1127 (S.B. 1913), § 3, eff. Sept. 1, 2017.

[1] So in enrolled bill.

Section 32 of Acts 2017, 85th Leg., ch. 977 (H.B. 351) provides:

"The changes in law made by this Act to Articles 14.06 and 27.14, Code of Criminal Procedure, and Section 502.010 and Chapter 706, Transportation Code, apply only to an offense committed on or after the effective date [Sept. 1, 2017] of this Act. An offense committed before the effective date of this Act is governed by the law in effect on the date the offense was committed, and the former law is continued in effect for that purpose. For purposes of this section, an offense was committed before the effective date of this Act if any element of the offense occurred before that date."

Section 28 of Acts 2017, 85th Leg., ch. 1127 (S.B. 1913) provides:

"The changes in law made by this Act to Articles 14.06 and 27.14, Code of Criminal Procedure, and Section 502.010 and Chapter 706, Transportation Code, apply only to an offense committed on or after the effective date [Sept. 1, 2017] of this Act. An offense committed before the effective date of this Act is governed by the law in effect on the date the offense was committed, and the former law is continued in effect for that purpose. For purposes of this section, an offense was committed before the effective date of this Act if any element of the offense occurred before that date."

Art. 27.15. Change of venue to plead guilty

When in any county which is located in a judicial district composed of more than one county, a party is charged with a felony and the maximum punishment therefor shall not exceed fifteen years, and the district court of said county is not in session, such party may, if he desires to plead guilty, or enter a plea of nolo contendere, make application to the district judge of such district for a change of venue to the county in which said court is in session, and said district judge may enter an order changing the venue of said cause to the county in which the court is then in session, and the defendant may plead guilty or enter a plea of nolo contendere to said charge in said court to which the venue has been changed.

Acts 1965, 59th Leg., p. 317, ch. 722, § 1, eff. Jan. 1, 1966.

Art. 27.16.   Plea of not guilty, how made

(a) The plea of not guilty may be made orally by the defendant or by his counsel in open court. If the defendant refuses to plead, the plea of not guilty shall be entered for him by the court.

(b) A defendant charged with a misdemeanor for which the maximum possible punishment is by fine only may, in lieu of the method provided in Subsection (a) of this article, mail to the court a plea of not guilty.

Acts 1965, 59th Leg., p. 317, ch. 722, § 1, eff. Jan. 1, 1966. Amended by Acts 1977, 65th Leg., p. 2143, ch. 858, § 2, eff. June 16, 1977.

Art. 27.17.   Plea of not guilty construed

The plea of not guilty shall be construed to be a denial of every material allegation in the indictment or information. Under this plea, evidence to establish the insanity of defendant, and every fact whatever tending to acquit him of the accusation may be introduced, except such facts as are proper for a special plea under Article 27.05.

Acts 1965, 59th Leg., p. 317, ch. 722, § 1, eff. Jan. 1, 1966.

Art. 27.18.   Plea or Waiver of Rights by Videoconference

(a) Notwithstanding any provision of this code requiring that a plea or a waiver of a defendant's right be made in open court, a court may accept the plea or waiver by videoconference to the court if:

(1) the defendant and the attorney representing the state file with the court written consent to the use of videoconference;

(2) the videoconference provides for a simultaneous, compressed full motion video, and interactive communication of image and sound between the judge, the attorney representing the state, the defendant, and the defendant's attorney; and

(3) on request of the defendant, the defendant and the defendant's attorney are able to communicate privately without being recorded or heard by the judge or the attorney representing the state.

(b) On motion of the defendant or the attorney representing the state or in the court's discretion, the court may terminate an appearance by videoconference at any time during the appearance and require an appearance by the defendant in open court.

(c) A record of the communication shall be made by a court reporter or by electronic recording and preserved by the court reporter or by electronic recording until all appellate proceedings have been disposed of. A court reporter or court recorder is not required to transcribe or make a duplicate electronic recording of a plea taken under this article unless an appeal is taken in the case and a party requests a transcript.

(c–1) The defendant may obtain a copy of the record, including any electronic recording, on payment of a reasonable amount to cover the costs of reproduction or, if the defendant is indigent, the court shall provide a copy to the defendant without charging a cost for the copy.

(c–2) The loss or destruction of or failure to create a court record or an electronic recording of a plea entered under this article is not alone sufficient grounds for a defendant to withdraw the defendant's plea or to request the court to set aside a conviction, sentence, or plea.

(d) A defendant who is confined in a county other than the county in which charges against the defendant are pending may use the videoconference method provided by this article or by Article 15.17 to enter a plea or waive a right in the court with jurisdiction over the case.

(e) A defendant who enters a plea or waiver under Subsection (d):

(1) consents to venue in the county in which the court receiving the plea or waiver is located; and

(2) waives any claim of error related to venue.

(f) Subsection (e) does not prohibit a court from granting a defendant's motion for a change of venue during the trial of the defendant.

(g) If a defendant enters a plea of guilty or nolo contendere under Subsection (d), the attorney representing the state may request at the time the plea is entered that the defendant submit a fingerprint of the defendant suitable for attachment to the judgment. On request for a fingerprint under this subsection, the county in which the defendant is confined shall obtain a fingerprint of the defendant and use first-class mail or other means acceptable to the attorney representing the state and the county to forward the fingerprint to the court accepting the plea.

Added by Acts 1997, 75th Leg., ch. 1014, § 1, eff. Sept. 1, 1997. Amended by Acts 2005, 79th Leg., ch. 1094, § 6, eff. Sept. 1, 2005. Amended by Acts 2011, 82nd Leg., ch. 1031 (H.B. 2847), § 5, eff. Sept. 1, 2011; Acts 2011, 82nd Leg., ch. 1341 (S.B. 1233), § 6, eff. June 17, 2011; Acts 2017, 85th Leg., ch. 1064 (H.B. 3165), §§ 5 to 10, eff. Sept. 1, 2017.

Section 13 of Acts 2017, 85th Leg., ch. 1064 (H.B. 3165) provides:

"Article 27.18, Code of Criminal Procedure, as amended by this Act, applies to a plea of guilty or nolo contendere entered on or after the effective date [Sept. 1, 2017] of this Act, regardless of whether the offense with reference to which the plea is entered is committed before, on, or after that date."

Art. 27.19.   Plea by Certain Defendants

(a) Notwithstanding any other provision of this code, a court shall accept a plea of guilty or nolo contendere from a defendant who is confined in a penal institution if the plea is made:

(1) in accordance with the procedure established by Article 27.18; or

(2) in writing, including a writing delivered by United States mail or secure electronic or facsimile transmission, before the appropriate court having jurisdiction in the county in which the penal institution is located, provided that:

(A) the defendant is notified by the court of original jurisdiction of the right to counsel and the procedures for requesting appointment of counsel, and is provided a reasonable opportunity to request a court-appointed lawyer;

(B) if the defendant elects to proceed without counsel, the defendant must waive the right to counsel in accordance with Article 1.051;

(C) the defendant must waive the right to be present at the taking of the plea or to have counsel present, if the defendant has counsel; and

(D) if the defendant is charged with a felony, judgment and sentence are rendered in accordance with the conditions and the procedure established by Article 42.14(b).

(b) In this article, "penal institution" has the meaning assigned by Section 1.07, Penal Code.

(c) Before accepting a plea submitted under Subsection (a)(2), the court shall verify that the person submitting the plea is:

(1) the defendant named in the information or indictment; or

(2) a person with legal authority to act for the defendant named in the information or indictment.

Added by Acts 2009, 81st Leg., ch. 291, § 1, eff. Sept. 1, 2009. Amended by Acts 2011, 82nd Leg., ch. 665 (S.B. 1522), § 1, eff. Sept. 1, 2011.

CHAPTER TWENTY–EIGHT. MOTIONS, PLEADINGS AND EXCEPTIONS

Article

Art. 28.01.   Pre-trial

Sec. 1.   The court may set any criminal case for a pre-trial hearing before it is set for trial upon its merits, and direct the defendant and his attorney, if any of record, and the State's attorney, to appear before the court at the time and place stated in the court's order for a conference and hearing. The defendant must be present at the arraignment, and his presence is required during any pre-trial proceeding. The pre-trial hearing shall be to determine any of the following matters:

(1) Arraignment of the defendant, if such be necessary; and appointment of counsel to represent the defendant, if such be necessary;

(2) Pleadings of the defendant;

(3) Special pleas, if any;

(4) Exceptions to the form or substance of the indictment or information;

(5) Motions for continuance either by the State or defendant; provided that grounds for continuance not existing or not known at the time may be presented and considered at any time before the defendant announces ready for trial;

(6) Motions to suppress evidence—When a hearing on the motion to suppress evidence is granted, the

court may determine the merits of said motion on the motions themselves, or upon opposing affidavits, or upon oral testimony, subject to the discretion of the court;

(7) Motions for change of venue by the State or the defendant; provided, however, that such motions for change of venue, if overruled at the pre-trial hearing, may be renewed by the State or the defendant during the voir dire examination of the jury;

(8) Discovery;

(9) Entrapment; and

(10) Motion for appointment of interpreter.

Sec. 2. When a criminal case is set for such pre-trial hearing, any such preliminary matters not raised or filed seven days before the hearing will not thereafter be allowed to be raised or filed, except by permission of the court for good cause shown; provided that the defendant shall have sufficient notice of such hearing to allow him not less than 10 days in which to raise or file such preliminary matters. The record made at such pre-trial hearing, the rulings of the court and the exceptions and objections thereto shall become a part of the trial record of the case upon its merits.

Sec. 3. The notice mentioned in Section 2 above shall be sufficient if given in any one of the following ways:

(1) By announcement made by the court in open court in the presence of the defendant or his attorney of record;

(2) By personal service upon the defendant or his attorney of record;

(3) By mail to either the defendant or his attorney of record deposited by the clerk in the mail at least six days prior to the date set for hearing. If the defendant has no attorney of record such notice shall be addressed to defendant at the address shown on his bond, if the bond shows such an address, and if not, it may be addressed to one of the sureties on his bond. If the envelope containing the notice is properly addressed, stamped and mailed, the state will not be required to show that it was received.

Acts 1965, 59th Leg., p. 317, ch. 722, § 1, eff. Jan. 1, 1966. Amended by Acts 1967, 60th Leg., p. 1738, ch. 659, § 19, eff. Aug. 28, 1967; Acts 1973, 63rd Leg., p. 969, ch. 399, § 2(A), eff. Jan. 1, 1974; Acts 1979, 66th Leg., p. 204, ch. 113, § 1, eff. Aug. 27, 1979; Acts 1979, 66th Leg., p. 453, ch. 209, § 2, eff. Aug. 27, 1979.

Art. 28.02. Order of argument

The counsel of the defendant has the right to open and conclude the argument upon all pleadings of the defendant presented for the decision of the judge.

Acts 1965, 59th Leg., p. 317, ch. 722, § 1, eff. Jan. 1, 1966.

Art. 28.03. Process for testimony on pleadings

When the matters involved in any written pleading depend in whole or in part upon testimony, and not altogether upon the record of the court, every process known to the law may be obtained on behalf of either party to procure such testimony; but there shall be no delay on account of the want of the testimony, unless it be shown to the satisfaction of the court that all the means given by the law have been used to procure the same.

Acts 1965, 59th Leg., p. 317, ch. 722, § 1, eff. Jan. 1, 1966.

Art. 28.04. Quashing charge in misdemeanor

If the motion to set aside or the exception to an indictment or information is sustained, the defendant in a misdemeanor case shall be discharged, but may be again prosecuted within the time allowed by law.

Acts 1965, 59th Leg., p. 317, ch. 722, § 1, eff. Jan. 1, 1966.

Art. 28.05. Quashing indictment in felony

If the motion to set aside or the exception to the indictment in cases of felony be sustained, the defendant shall not therefor be discharged, but may immediately be recommitted by order of the court, upon motion of the State's attorney or without motion; and proceedings may afterward be had against him as if no prosecution had ever been commenced.

Acts 1965, 59th Leg., p. 317, ch. 722, § 1, eff. Jan. 1, 1966.

Art. 28.06. Shall be fully discharged, when

Where, after the motion or exception is sustained, it is made known to the court by sufficient testimony that the offense of which the defendant is accused will be barred by limitation before another indictment can be presented, he shall be fully discharged.

Acts 1965, 59th Leg., p. 317, ch. 722, § 1, eff. Jan. 1, 1966.

Art. 28.061. Discharge for Delay

If a motion to set aside an indictment, information, or complaint for failure to provide a speedy trial is sustained, the court shall discharge the defendant. A discharge under this article is a bar to any further prosecution for the offense discharged and for any other offense arising out of the same transaction, other than an offense of a higher grade that the attorney representing the state and prosecuting the offense that was discharged does not have the primary duty to prosecute.

Acts 1977, 65th Leg., p. 1972, ch. 787, § 4, eff. July 1, 1978. Amended by Acts 1987, 70th Leg., ch. 383, § 1, eff. Sept. 1, 1987; Acts 1997, 75th Leg., ch. 289, § 1, eff. May 26, 1997.

Art. 28.07. If exception is that no offense is charged

If an exception to an indictment or information is taken and sustained upon the ground that there is no offense against the law charged therein, the defendant shall be discharged, unless an affidavit be filed accusing him of the commission of a penal offense.

Acts 1965, 59th Leg., p. 317, ch. 722, § 1, eff. Jan. 1, 1966.

Art. 28.08. When defendant is held by order of court

If the motion to set aside the indictment or any exception thereto is sustained, but the court refuses to discharge the defendant, then at the expiration of ten days from the order sustaining such motions or exceptions, the defendant shall be discharged, unless in the meanwhile complaint has been made before a magistrate charging him with an offense, or unless another indictment has been presented against him for such offense.

Acts 1965, 59th Leg., p. 317, ch. 722, § 1, eff. Jan. 1, 1966.

Art. 28.09. Exception on account of form or substance

If the exception to an indictment or information is sustained, the information or indictment may be amended if permitted by Article 28.10 of this code, and the cause may proceed upon the amended indictment or information.

Acts 1965, 59th Leg., p. 317, ch. 722, § 1, eff. Jan. 1, 1966. Amended by Acts 1985, 69th Leg., ch. 577, § 1, eff. Dec. 1, 1985.

Art. 28.10. Amendment of indictment or information

(a) After notice to the defendant, a matter of form or substance in an indictment or information may be amended at any time before the date the trial on the merits commences. On the request of the defendant, the court shall allow the defendant not less than 10 days, or a shorter period if requested by the defendant, to respond to the amended indictment or information.

(b) A matter of form or substance in an indictment or information may also be amended after the trial on the merits commences if the defendant does not object.

(c) An indictment or information may not be amended over the defendant's objection as to form or substance if the amended indictment or information charges the defendant with an additional or different offense or if the substantial rights of the defendant are prejudiced.

Acts 1965, 59th Leg., p. 317, ch. 722, § 1, eff. Jan. 1, 1966. Amended by Acts 1985, 69th Leg., ch. 577, § 1, eff. Dec. 1, 1985.

Art. 28.11. How amended

All amendments of an indictment or information shall be made with the leave of the court and under its direction.

Acts 1965, 59th Leg., p. 317, ch. 722, § 1, eff. Jan. 1, 1966.

Art. 28.12. Exception and trial of special pleas

When a special plea is filed by the defendant, the State may except to it for substantial defects. If the exception be sustained, the plea may be amended. If the plea be not excepted to, it shall be considered that issue has been taken upon the same. Such special pleas as set forth matter of fact proper to be tried by a jury shall be submitted and tried with a plea of not guilty.

Acts 1965, 59th Leg., p. 317, ch. 722, § 1, eff. Jan. 1, 1966.

Art. 28.13. Former acquittal or conviction

A former judgment of acquittal or conviction in a court of competent jurisdiction shall be a bar to any further prosecution for the same offense, but shall not bar a prosecution for any higher grade of offense over which said court had not jurisdiction, unless such judgment was had upon indictment or information, in which case the prosecution shall be barred for all grades of the offense.

Acts 1965, 59th Leg., p. 317, ch. 722, § 1, eff. Jan. 1, 1966.

Art. 28.14. Plea allowed

Judgment shall, in no case, be given against the defendant where his motion, exception or plea is overruled; but in all cases the plea of not guilty may be made by or for him.

Acts 1965, 59th Leg., p. 317, ch. 722, § 1, eff. Jan. 1, 1966.

CHAPTER TWENTY–NINE.   CONTINUANCE

Art. 29.01.   By operation of law

Criminal actions are continued by operation of law if:

(1) The individual defendant has not been arrested;

(2) A defendant corporation or association has not been served with summons; or

(3) There is not sufficient time for trial at that term of court.

Acts 1965, 59th Leg., p. 317, ch. 722, § 1, eff. Jan. 1, 1966. Amended by Acts 1973, 63rd Leg., p. 970, ch. 399, § 2(A), eff. Jan. 1, 1974.

Art. 29.011.   Religious holy day

(a) In this article:

(1) "Religious organization" means an organization that meets the standards for qualifying as a religious organization under Section 11.20, Tax Code.

(2) "Religious holy day" means a day on which the tenets of a religious organization prohibit its members from participating in secular activities, such as court proceedings.

(b) If a defendant, an attorney representing the defendant, or an attorney representing the state in a criminal action is required to appear at a court proceeding on a religious holy day observed by the person, the court shall continue the action.

(c) A defendant or attorney seeking a continuance must file with the court an affidavit stating:

(1) the grounds for the continuance; and

(2) that the person holds religious beliefs that prohibit him from taking part in a court proceeding on the day for which the continuance is sought.

(d) An affidavit filed under Subsection (c) of this article is proof of the facts stated and need not be corroborated.

Acts 1987, 70th Leg., ch. 825, § 1, eff. Sept. 1, 1987; Amended by Acts 1991, 72nd Leg., ch. 815, § 1, eff. Sept. 1, 1991.

Art. 29.012.   Religious holy day

(a) In this article:

(1) "Religious organization" means an organization that meets the standards for qualification as a religious organization under Section 11.20, Tax Code.

(2) "Religious holy day" means a day on which the tenets of a religious organization prohibit its members from participating in secular activities, such as court proceedings.

(b) If a juror in a criminal action is required to appear at a court proceeding on a religious holy day observed by the juror, the court or the court's designee[1] shall recess the criminal action until the next day the court is in session after the conclusion of the holy day.

(c) A juror seeking a recess must file with the court before the final selection of the jury an affidavit stating:

(1) the grounds for the recess; and

(2) that the juror holds religious beliefs that prohibit him from taking part in a court proceeding on the day for which the recess is sought.

(d) An affidavit filed under Subsection (c) of this section is proof of the facts stated and need not be corroborated.

Acts 1987, 70th Leg., ch. 589, § 1, eff. Aug. 31, 1987; Acts 1987, 70th Leg., ch. 825, § 4, eff. Sept. 1, 1987.

[1] Chapter 825 did not contain "or the court's designee".

Art. 29.02.   By agreement

A criminal action may be continued by consent of the parties thereto, in open court, at any time on a showing of good cause, but a continuance may be only for as long as is necessary.

Acts 1965, 59th Leg., p. 317, ch. 722, § 1, eff. Jan. 1, 1966. Amended by Acts 1977, 65th Leg., p. 1972, ch. 787, § 3, eff. July 1, 1978.

Art. 29.03.   For sufficient cause shown

A criminal action may be continued on the written motion of the State or of the defendant, upon sufficient cause shown; which cause shall be fully set forth in the motion. A continuance may be only for as long as is necessary.

Acts 1965, 59th Leg., p. 317, ch. 722, § 1, eff. Jan. 1, 1966. Amended by Acts 1977, 65th Leg., p. 1972, ch. 787, § 3, eff. July 1, 1978.

Art. 29.035.　For Insufficient Notice of Hearing or Trial

(a) Notwithstanding Article 28.01 or any other provision of this chapter, and except as otherwise provided by this article, a trial court shall grant a continuance of a criminal action on oral or written motion of the state or the defendant if the trial court sets a hearing or trial without providing to the attorney for the state and the defendant, or the defendant's attorney, notice of the hearing or trial at least three business days before the date of the hearing or trial.

(b) This article does not apply during the period between:

(1) the date the trial begins; and

(2) the date the judgment is entered.

Added by Acts 2017, 85th Leg., ch. 1005 (H.B. 1266), § 1, eff. Sept. 1, 2017.

Section 2 of Acts 2017, 85th Leg., ch. 1005 (H.B. 1266) provides:

"Article 29.035, Code of Criminal Procedure, as added by this Act, applies to a criminal action pending before a trial court on or after the effective date [Sept. 1, 2017] of this Act, regardless of whether the offense that is the subject of the action was committed before, on, or after the effective date of this Act."

Art. 29.04.　First motion by state

It shall be sufficient, upon the first motion by the State for a continuance, if the same be for the want of a witness, to state:

1. The name of the witness and his residence, if known, or that his residence is unknown;

2. The diligence which has been used to procure his attendance; and it shall not be considered sufficient diligence to have caused to be issued, or to have applied for, a subpoena, in cases where the law authorized an attachment to issue; and

3. That the testimony of the witness is believed by the applicant to be material for the State.

Acts 1965, 59th Leg., p. 317, ch. 722, § 1, eff. Jan. 1, 1966.

Art. 29.05.　Subsequent motion by state

On any subsequent motion for a continuance by the State, for the want of a witness, the motion, in addition to the requisites in the preceding Article, must show:

1. The facts which the applicant expects to establish by the witness, and it must appear to the court that they are material;

2. That the applicant expects to be able to procure the attendance of the witness at the next term of the court; and

3. That the testimony cannot be procured from any other source during the present term of the court.

Acts 1965, 59th Leg., p. 317, ch. 722, § 1, eff. Jan. 1, 1966.

Art. 29.06.　First motion by defendant

In the first motion by the defendant for a continuance, it shall be necessary, if the same be on account of the absence of a witness, to state:

1. The name of the witness and his residence, if known, or that his residence is not known.

2. The diligence which has been used to procure his attendance; and it shall not be considered sufficient diligence to have caused to be issued, or to have applied for, a subpoena, in cases where the law authorized an attachment to issue.

3. The facts which are expected to be proved by the witness, and it must appear to the court that they are material.

4. That the witness is not absent by the procurement or consent of the defendant.

5. That the motion is not made for delay.

6. That there is no reasonable expectation that attendance of the witness can be secured during the present term of court by a postponement of the trial to some future day of said term. The truth of the first, or any subsequent motion, as well as the merit of the ground set forth therein and its sufficiency shall be addressed to the sound discretion of the court called to pass upon the same, and shall not be granted as a matter of right. If a motion for continuance be overruled, and the defendant convicted, if it appear upon the trial that the evidence of the witness or witnesses named in the motion was of a material character, and that the facts set forth in said motion were probably true, a new trial should be granted, and the cause continued or postponed to a future day of the same term.

Acts 1965, 59th Leg., p. 317, ch. 722, § 1, eff. Jan. 1, 1966.

Art. 29.07.　Subsequent motion by defendant

Subsequent motions for continuance on the part of the defendant shall, in addition to the requisites in the preceding Article, state also:

1. That the testimony cannot be procured from any other source known to the defendant; and

2. That the defendant has reasonable expectation of procuring the same at the next term of the court.

Acts 1965, 59th Leg., p. 317, ch. 722, § 1, eff. Jan. 1, 1966.

Art. 29.08. Motion sworn to

All motions for continuance must be sworn to by a person having personal knowledge of the facts relied on for the continuance.

Acts 1965, 59th Leg., p. 317, ch. 722, § 1, eff. Jan. 1, 1966. Amended by Acts 1981, 67th Leg., p. 504, ch. 210, § 1, eff. Sept. 1, 1981.

Art. 29.09. Controverting motion

Any material fact stated, affecting diligence, in a motion for a continuance, may be denied in writing by the adverse party. The denial shall be supported by the oath of some credible person, and filed as soon as practicable after the filing of such motion.

Acts 1965, 59th Leg., p. 317, ch. 722, § 1, eff. Jan. 1, 1966.

Art. 29.10. When denial is filed

When such denial is filed, the issue shall be tried by the judge; and he shall hear testimony by affidavits, and grant or refuse continuance, according to the law and facts of the case.

Acts 1965, 59th Leg., p. 317, ch. 722, § 1, eff. Jan. 1, 1966.

Art. 29.11. Argument

No argument shall be heard on a motion for a continuance, unless requested by the judge; and when argument is heard, the applicant shall have the right to open and conclude it.

Acts 1965, 59th Leg., p. 317, ch. 722, § 1, eff. Jan. 1, 1966.

Art. 29.12. Bail resulting from continuance

If a defendant in a capital case demand a trial, and it appears that more than one continuance has been granted to the State, and that the defendant has not before applied for a continuance, he shall be entitled to be admitted to bail, unless it be made to appear to the satisfaction of the court that a material witness of the State had been prevented from attendance by the procurement of the defendant or some person acting in his behalf.

Acts 1965, 59th Leg., p. 317, ch. 722, § 1, eff. Jan. 1, 1966.

Art. 29.13. Continuance after trial is begun

A continuance or postponement may be granted on the motion of the State or defendant after the trial has begun, when it is made to appear to the satisfaction of the court that by some unexpected occurrence since the trial began, which no reasonable diligence could have anticipated, the applicant is so taken by surprise that a fair trial cannot be had.

Acts 1965, 59th Leg., p. 317, ch. 722, § 1, eff. Jan. 1, 1966.

Art. 29.14. Consideration of Impact on Certain Victims

(a) In this article, "victim" means the victim of an assault or sexual assault who is younger than 17 years of age or whose case involves family violence as defined by Section 71.004, Family Code.

(b) On request by the attorney representing the state, a court that considers a motion for continuance on the part of the defendant shall also consider the impact of the continuance on the victim. On request by the attorney representing the state or by counsel for the defendant, the court shall state on the record the reason for granting or denying the continuance.

Added by Acts 2009, 81st Leg., ch. 664, § 2, eff. Sept. 1, 2009.

CHAPTER THIRTY. DISQUALIFICATION OF THE JUDGE

Art. 30.01. Causes which disqualify

No judge or justice of the peace shall sit in any case where he may be the party injured, or where he has been of counsel for the State or the accused, or where the accused or the party injured may be connected with him by consanguinity or affinity within the third degree, as determined under Chapter 573, Government Code.

Acts 1965, 59th Leg., p. 317, ch. 722, § 1, eff. Jan. 1, 1966. Amended by Acts 1991, 72nd Leg., ch. 561, § 9, eff. Aug. 26, 1991; Acts 1995, 74th Leg., ch. 76, § 5.95(27), eff. Sept. 1, 1995.

Art. 30.02. District judge disqualified

Whenever any case is pending in which the district judge or criminal district judge is disqualified from trying the case, no change of venue shall be made necessary thereby; but the judge presiding shall certify that fact to the presiding judge of the administrative judicial district in which the case is pending and the presiding judge of such administrative judicial district shall assign a judge to try such case in accordance with the provisions of Article 200a, V.A.C.S.[1]

Acts 1965, 59th Leg., p. 317, ch. 722, § 1, eff. Jan. 1, 1966.

[1] Repealed; see, now, V.T.C.A. Government Code, § 74.042 et seq.

Arts. 30.03 to 30.06.　Repealed by Acts 1999, 76th Leg., ch. 1388, § 14, eff. Sept. 1, 1999

Art. 30.07.　Justice disqualified

If a justice of the peace be disqualified from sitting in any criminal action pending before him, he shall transfer the same to any justice of the peace in the county who is not disqualified to try the case.

Acts 1965, 59th Leg., p. 317, ch. 722, § 1, eff. Jan. 1, 1966.

Art. 30.08.　Order of transfer

In cases provided for in the preceding Article, the order of transfer shall state the cause of the transfer, and name the court to which the transfer is made, and the time and place, when and where, the parties and witnesses shall appear before such court. The rules governing the transfer of cases from the district to inferior courts shall govern in the transfer of cases under the preceding Article.

Acts 1965, 59th Leg., p. 317, ch. 722, § 1, eff. Jan. 1, 1966.

CHAPTER THIRTY–ONE.
CHANGE OF VENUE

Art. 31.01.　On court's own motion

Whenever in any case of felony or misdemeanor punishable by confinement, the judge presiding shall be satisfied that a trial, alike fair and impartial to the accused and to the State, cannot, from any cause, be had in the county in which the case is pending, he may, upon his own motion, after due notice to accused and the State, and after hearing evidence thereon, order a change of venue to any county in the judicial district in which such county is located or in an adjoining district, stating in his order the grounds for such change of venue. The judge, upon his own motion, after ten days notice to the parties or their counsel, may order a change of venue to any county beyond an adjoining district; provided, however, an order changing venue to a county beyond an adjoining district shall be grounds for reversal if, upon timely contest by the defendant, the record of the contest affirmatively shows that any county in his own and the adjoining district is not subject to the same conditions which required the transfer.

Acts 1965, 59th Leg., p. 317, ch. 722, § 1, eff. Jan. 1, 1966.

Art. 31.02.　State may have

Whenever the district or county attorney shall represent in writing to the court before which any felony or misdemeanor case punishable by confinement, is pending, that, by reason of existing combinations or influences in favor of the accused, or on account of the lawless condition of affairs in the county, a fair and impartial trial as between the accused and the State cannot be safely and speedily had; or whenever he shall represent that the life of the prisoner, or of any witness, would be jeopardized by a trial in the county in which the case is pending, the judge shall hear proof in relation thereto, and if satisfied that such representation is well-founded and that the ends of public justice will be subserved thereby, he shall order a change of venue to any county in the judicial district in which such county is located or in an adjoining district.

Acts 1965, 59th Leg., p. 317, ch. 722, § 1, eff. Jan. 1, 1966.

Art. 31.03.　Granted on motion of defendant

(a) A change of venue may be granted in any felony or misdemeanor case punishable by confinement on the written motion of the defendant, supported by his own affidavit and the affidavit of at least two credible persons, residents of the county where the prosecution is instituted, for either of the following causes, the truth and sufficiency of which the court shall determine:

1.　That there exists in the county where the prosecution is commenced so great a prejudice against him that he cannot obtain a fair and impartial trial; and

2.　That there is a dangerous combination against him instigated by influential persons, by reason of which he cannot expect a fair trial.

An order changing venue to a county beyond an adjoining district shall be grounds for reversal, if upon timely contest by defendant, the record of the contest affirmatively shows that any county in his own and the adjoining district is not subject to the same conditions which required the transfer.

(b) For the convenience of parties and witnesses, and in the interest of justice, the court upon motion of the defendant and with the consent of the attorney for the state may transfer the proceeding as to him to another district.

(c) The court upon motion of the defendant and with the consent of the attorney for the state may transfer the proceedings to another district in those cases wherein the defendant stipulates that a plea of guilty will be entered.

Acts 1965, 59th Leg., p. 317, ch. 722, § 1, eff. Jan. 1, 1966. Amended by Acts 1979, 66th Leg., p. 266, ch. 140, § 1, eff. Aug. 27, 1979.

Art. 31.04. Motion may be controverted

The credibility of the persons making affidavit for change of venue, or their means of knowledge, may be attacked by the affidavit of a credible person. The issue thus formed shall be tried by the judge, and the motion granted or refused, as the law and facts shall warrant.

Acts 1965, 59th Leg., p. 317, ch. 722, § 1, eff. Jan. 1, 1966.

Art. 31.05. Clerk's duties on change of venue

Where an order for a change of venue of any court in any criminal cause in this State has been made the clerk of the court where the prosecution is pending shall make out a certified copy of the court's order directing such change of venue, together with a certified copy of the defendant's bail bond or personal bond, together with all the original papers in said cause and also a certificate of the said clerk under his official seal that such papers are the papers and all the papers on file in said court in said cause; and he shall transmit the same to the clerk of the court to which the venue has been changed.

Acts 1965, 59th Leg., p. 317, ch. 722, § 1, eff. Jan. 1, 1966.

Art. 31.06. If defendant be in custody

When the venue is changed in any criminal action if the defendant be in custody, an order shall be made for his removal to the proper county, and his delivery to the sheriff thereof before the next succeeding term of the court of the county to which the case is to be taken, and he shall be delivered by the sheriff as directed in the order.

Acts 1965, 59th Leg., p. 317, ch. 722, § 1, eff. Jan. 1, 1966.

Art. 31.07. Witness need not again be summoned

When the venue in a criminal action has been changed, it shall not be necessary to have the witnesses therein again subpoenaed, attached or bailed, but all the witnesses who have been subpoenaed, attached or bailed to appear and testify in the cause shall be held bound to appear before the court to which the cause has been transferred, as if there had been no such transfer.

Acts 1965, 59th Leg., p. 317, ch. 722, § 1, eff. Jan. 1, 1966.

Art. 31.08. Return to county of original venue

Sec. 1. (a) On the completion of a trial in which a change of venue has been ordered and after the jury has been discharged, the court, with the consent of counsel for the state and the defendant, may return the cause to the original county in which the indictment or information was filed. Except as provided by Subsection (b) of this section, all subsequent and ancillary proceedings, including the pronouncement of sentence after appeals have been exhausted, must be heard in the county in which the indictment or information was filed.

(b) A motion for new trial alleging jury misconduct must be heard in the county in which the cause was tried. The county in which the indictment or information was filed must pay the costs of the prosecution of the motion for new trial.

Sec. 2. (a) Except as provided by Subsection (b), on an order returning venue to the original county in which the indictment or information was filed, the clerk of the county in which the cause was tried shall:

(1) make a certified copy of the court's order directing the return to the original county;

(2) make a certified copy of the defendant's bail bond, personal bond, or appeal bond;

(3) gather all the original papers in the cause and certify under official seal that the papers are all the original papers on file in the court; and

(4) transmit the items listed in this section to the clerk of the court of original venue.

(b) This article does not apply to a proceeding in which the clerk of the court of original venue was present and performed the duties as clerk for the court under Article 31.09.

Sec. 3. Except for the review of a death sentence under Section 2(h), Article 37.071, or under Section 2(h), Article 37.072, an appeal taken in a cause returned to the original county under this article must be docketed in the appellate district in which the county of original venue is located.

Added by Acts 1989, 71st Leg., ch. 824, § 1, eff. Sept. 1, 1989. Amended by Acts 1995, 74th Leg., ch. 651, § 1, eff. Sept. 1, 1995; Acts 2007, 80th Leg., ch. 593, § 3.13, eff. Sept. 1, 2007.

Art. 31.09. Change of venue; use of existing services

(a) If a change of venue in a criminal case is ordered under this chapter, the judge ordering the change of venue may, with the written consent of the prosecuting attorney, the defense attorney, and the defendant, maintain the original case number on its own docket, preside over the case, and use the services of the court reporter, the court coordinator, and the clerk of the court of original venue. The court shall use the courtroom facilities and any other services or facilities of the district or county to which venue is changed. A jury, if required, must consist of residents of the district or county to which venue is changed.

(b) Notwithstanding Article 31.05, the clerk of the court of original venue shall:

(1) maintain the original papers of the case, including the defendant's bail bond or personal bond;

(2) make the papers available for trial; and

(3) act as the clerk in the case.

Added by Acts 1995, 74th Leg., ch. 651, § 2, eff. Sept. 1, 1995.

TRIAL AND ITS INCIDENTS

CHAPTER THIRTY–TWO. DISMISSING PROSECUTIONS

Article
32.01.   Defendant in Custody and No Indictment Presented.
32.02.   Dismissal by state's attorney.

Art. 32.01. Defendant in Custody and No Indictment Presented

(a) When a defendant has been detained in custody or held to bail for the defendant's appearance to answer any criminal accusation, the prosecution, unless otherwise ordered by the court, for good cause shown, supported by affidavit, shall be dismissed and the bail discharged, if indictment or information be not presented against the defendant on or before the last day of the next term of the court which is held after the defendant's commitment or admission to bail or on or before the 180th day after the date of

commitment or admission to bail, whichever date is later.

(b) A surety may file a motion under Subsection (a) for the purpose of discharging the defendant's bail only.

Acts 1965, 59th Leg., p. 317, ch. 722, § 1, eff. Jan. 1, 1966. Amended by Acts 1997, 75th Leg., ch. 289, § 2, eff. May 26, 1997; Acts 2005, 79th Leg., ch. 743, § 6, eff. Sept. 1, 2005; Acts 2015, 84th Leg., ch. 152 (H.B. 643), § 1, eff. Sept. 1, 2015.

Art. 32.02. Dismissal by state's attorney

The attorney representing the State may, by permission of the court, dismiss a criminal action at any time upon filing a written statement with the papers in the case setting out his reasons for such dismissal, which shall be incorporated in the judgment of dismissal. No case shall be dismissed without the consent of the presiding judge.

Acts 1965, 59th Leg., p. 317, ch. 722, § 1, eff. Jan. 1, 1966.

CHAPTER THIRTY–TWO A. SPEEDY TRIAL

Article
32A.01.   Trial Priorities.
32A.02.   Repealed.

Art. 32A.01.   Trial Priorities

(a) Insofar as is practicable, the trial of a criminal action shall be given preference over trials of civil cases, and the trial of a criminal action against a defendant who is detained in jail pending trial of the action shall be given preference over trials of other criminal actions not described by Subsection (b) or (c).

(b) Unless extraordinary circumstances require otherwise, the trial of a criminal action in which the alleged victim is younger than 14 years of age shall be given preference over other matters before the court, whether civil or criminal.

(c) Except as provided by Subsection (b), the trial of a criminal action against a defendant who has been determined to be restored to competency under Article 46B.084 shall be given preference over other matters before the court, whether civil or criminal.

Acts 1977, 65th Leg., p. 1970, ch. 787, § 1, eff. July 1, 1978. Amended by Acts 2015, 84th Leg., ch. 1251 (H.B. 1396), § 3, eff. Sept. 1, 2015; Acts 2017, 85th Leg., ch. 748 (S.B. 1326), § 4, eff. Sept. 1, 2017.

Section 37 of Acts 2017, 85th Leg., ch. 748 (S.B. 1326) provides:

"The changes in law made by this Act apply only to a defendant charged with an offense committed on or after the effective date [Sept. 1, 2017] of this Act. A defendant charged with an offense committed before the effective date of this Act is governed by the law in effect on the date the offense was committed, and the former law is continued in effect for that purpose. For purposes of this section, an offense was committed before the effective date of this Act if any element of the offense occurred before that date."

Art. 32A.02. Repealed by Acts 2005, 79th Leg., ch. 1019, § 2, eff. June 18, 2005

CHAPTER THIRTY-THREE.
THE MODE OF TRIAL

Art. 33.01. Jury Size

(a) Except as provided by Subsection (b), in the district court, the jury shall consist of twelve qualified jurors. In the county court and inferior courts, the jury shall consist of six qualified jurors.

(b) In a trial involving a misdemeanor offense, a district court jury shall consist of six qualified jurors.

Acts 1965, 59th Leg., p. 317, ch. 722, § 1, eff. Jan. 1, 1966. Amended by Acts 2003, 78th Leg., ch. 466, § 1, eff. Jan. 1, 2004.

Art. 33.011. Alternate jurors

(a) In district courts, the judge may direct that not more than four jurors in addition to the regular jury be called and impaneled to sit as alternate jurors. In county courts, the judge may direct that not more than two jurors in addition to the regular jury be called and impaneled to sit as alternate jurors.

(b) Alternate jurors in the order in which they are called shall replace jurors who, prior to the time the jury renders a verdict on the guilt or innocence of the defendant and, if applicable, the amount of punishment, become or are found to be unable or disqualified to perform their duties or are found by the court on agreement of the parties to have good cause for not performing their duties. Alternate jurors shall be drawn and selected in the same manner, shall have the same qualifications, shall be subject to the same examination and challenges, shall take the same oath, and shall have the same functions, powers, facilities, security, and privileges as regular jurors. An alternate juror who does not replace a regular juror shall

be discharged after the jury has rendered a verdict on the guilt or innocence of the defendant and, if applicable, the amount of punishment.

Acts 1983, 68th Leg., p. 4594, ch. 775, § 2, eff. Aug. 29, 1983. Amended by Acts 2007, 80th Leg., ch. 846, § 1, eff. Sept. 1, 2007.

Art. 33.02. Failure to register

Failure to register to vote shall not disqualify any person from jury service.

Acts 1965, 59th Leg., p. 317, ch. 722, § 1, eff. Jan. 1, 1966. Amended by Acts 1981, 67th Leg., p. 3143, ch. 827, § 6, eff. Aug. 31, 1981.

Art. 33.03. Presence of defendant

In all prosecutions for felonies, the defendant must be personally present at the trial, and he must likewise be present in all cases of misdemeanor when the punishment or any part thereof is imprisonment in jail; provided, however, that in all cases, when the defendant voluntarily absents himself after pleading to the indictment or information, or after the jury has been selected when trial is before a jury, the trial may proceed to its conclusion. When the record in the appellate court shows that the defendant was present at the commencement, or any portion of the trial, it shall be presumed in the absence of all evidence in the record to the contrary that he was present during the whole trial. Provided, however, that the presence of the defendant shall not be required at the hearing on the motion for new trial in any misdemeanor case.

Acts 1965, 59th Leg., p. 317, ch. 722, § 1, eff. Jan. 1, 1966. Amended by Acts 1979, 66th Leg., p. 1832, ch. 745, § 1, eff. Aug. 27, 1979.

Art. 33.04. May appear by counsel

In other misdemeanor cases, the defendant may, by consent of the State's attorney, appear by counsel, and the trial may proceed without his personal presence.

Acts 1965, 59th Leg., p. 317, ch. 722, § 1, eff. Jan. 1, 1966.

Art. 33.05. On bail during trial

If the defendant is on bail when the trial commences, such bail shall be considered as discharged if he is acquitted. If a verdict of guilty is returned against him, the discharge of his bail shall be governed by other provisions of this Code.

Acts 1965, 59th Leg., p. 317, ch. 722, § 1, eff. Jan. 1, 1966.

Art. 33.06. Sureties bound in case of mistrial

If there be a mistrial in a felony case, the original sureties, if any, of the defendant shall be still held bound for his appearance until they surrender him in accordance with the provisions of this Code.

Acts 1965, 59th Leg., p. 317, ch. 722, § 1, eff. Jan. 1, 1966.

Art. 33.07. Record of criminal actions

Each clerk of a court of record having criminal jurisdiction shall keep a record in which shall be set down the style and file number of each criminal action, the nature of the offense, the names of counsel, the proceedings had therein, and the date of each proceeding.

Acts 1965, 59th Leg., p. 317, ch. 722, § 1, eff. Jan. 1, 1966. Amended by Acts 2007, 80th Leg., ch. 628, § 3, eff. Sept. 1, 2007.

Art. 33.08. To fix day for criminal docket

The district courts and county courts shall have control of their respective dockets as to the settings of criminal cases.

Acts 1965, 59th Leg., p. 317, ch. 722, § 1, eff. Jan. 1, 1966.

Art. 33.09. Jury drawn

Jury panels, including special venires, for the trial of criminal cases shall be selected and summoned (with return on summons) in the same manner as the selection of panels for the trial of civil cases except as otherwise provided in this Code.

Acts 1965, 59th Leg., p. 317, ch. 722, § 1, eff. Jan. 1, 1966.

CHAPTER THIRTY–FOUR. SPECIAL VENIRE IN CAPITAL CASES

Art. 34.01. Special venire

A "special venire" is a writ issued in a capital case by order of the district court, commanding the sheriff to summon either verbally or by mail such a number of persons, not less than 50, as the court may order, to appear before the court on a day named in the writ from whom the jury for the trial of such case is to be selected. Where as many as one hundred jurors have been summoned in such county for regular service for the week in which such capital case is set for trial, the judge of the court having jurisdiction of a capital case in which a motion for a special venire has been made, shall grant or refuse such motion for a special venire, and upon such refusal require the case to be tried by

regular jurors summoned for service in such county for the week in which such capital case is set for trial and such additional talesmen as may be summoned by the sheriff upon order of the court as provided in Article 34.02 of this Code, but the clerk of such court shall furnish the defendant or his counsel a list of the persons summoned as provided in Article 34.04.

Acts 1965, 59th Leg., p. 317, ch. 722, § 1, eff. Jan. 1, 1966.

Art. 34.02. Additional names drawn

In any criminal case in which the court deems that the veniremen theretofore drawn will be insufficient for the trial of the case, or in any criminal case in which the venire has been exhausted by challenge or otherwise, the court shall order additional veniremen in such numbers as the court may deem advisable, to be summoned as follows:

(a) In a jury wheel county, the names of those to be summoned shall be drawn from the jury wheel.

(b) In counties not using the jury wheel, the veniremen shall be summoned by the sheriff.

Acts 1965, 59th Leg., p. 317, ch. 722, § 1, eff. Jan. 1, 1966.

Art. 34.03. Instructions to sheriff

When the sheriff is ordered by the court to summon persons upon a special venire whose names have not been selected under the Jury Wheel Law, the court shall, in every case, caution and direct the sheriff to summon such persons as have legal qualifications to serve on juries, informing him of what those qualifications are, and shall direct him, as far as he may be able to summon persons of good character who can read and write, and such as are not prejudiced against the defendant or biased in his favor, if he knows of such bias or prejudice.

Acts 1965, 59th Leg., p. 317, ch. 722, § 1, eff. Jan. 1, 1966.

Art. 34.04. Notice of list

No defendant in a capital case in which the state seeks the death penalty shall be brought to trial until he shall have had at least two days (including holidays) a copy of the names of the persons summoned as veniremen, for the week for which his case is set for trial except where he waives the right or is on bail. When such defendant is on bail, the clerk of the court in which the case is pending shall furnish such a list to the defendant or his counsel at least two days prior to the trial (including holidays) upon timely motion by the defendant or his counsel therefor at the office of such clerk, and the defendant shall not be brought to trial until such list has been furnished defendant or his counsel for at least two days (including holidays). Where the venire is exhausted, by challenges or otherwise, and additional names are drawn, the defendant shall not be entitled to two days service of the names additionally drawn, but the clerk shall compile a list of such names promptly after they are drawn and if the defendant is not on bail, the sheriff shall serve a copy of such list promptly upon the defendant, and if on bail, the clerk shall furnish a copy of such list to the defendant or his counsel upon request, but the proceedings shall not be delayed thereby.

Acts 1965, 59th Leg., p. 317, ch. 722, § 1, eff. Jan. 1, 1966. Amended by Acts 1991, 72nd Leg., ch. 652, § 4, eff. Sept. 1, 1991.

Art. 34.05. Mechanical or Electronic Selection Method

A mechanical or electronic method of jury selection as provided by Chapter 62, Government Code, may be used under this chapter.

Added by Acts 1995, 74th Leg., ch. 694, § 1, eff. Sept. 1, 1995.

CHAPTER THIRTY–FIVE. FORMATION OF THE JURY

Art. 35.01. Jurors called

When a case is called for trial and the parties have announced ready for trial, the names of those summoned as jurors in the case shall be called. Those not present may be fined not less than $100 nor more than $500. An attachment may issue on request of either party for any absent summoned juror, to have him brought forthwith before the court. A person who is summoned but not present, may upon an appearance, before the jury is qualified, be tried as to his qualifications and impaneled as a juror unless challenged, but no cause shall be unreasonably delayed on account of his absence.

Acts 1965, 59th Leg., p. 317, ch. 722, § 1, eff. Jan. 1, 1966. Amended by Acts 2009, 81st Leg., ch. 640, § 3, eff. Sept. 1, 2009.

Art. 35.02. Sworn to answer questions

To those present the court shall cause to be administered this oath: "You, and each of you, solemnly swear that you will make true answers to such questions as may be propounded to you by the court, or under its directions, touching your service and qualifications as a juror, so help you God."

Acts 1965, 59th Leg., p. 317, ch. 722, § 1, eff. Jan. 1, 1966.

Art. 35.03. Excuses

Sec. 1. Except as provided by Sections 2 and 3 of this article, the court shall then hear and determine excuses offered for not serving as a juror, including any claim of an exemption or a lack of qualification, and if the court considers the excuse sufficient, the court shall discharge the prospective juror or postpone the prospective juror's service to a date specified by the court, as appropriate.

Sec. 2. Under a plan approved by the commissioners court of the county in the same manner as a plan is approved for jury selection under Section 62.011, Government Code, in a case other than a capital felony case, the court's designee may hear and determine an excuse offered for not serving as a juror, including any claim of an exemption or a lack of qualification. The court's designee may discharge the prospective juror or postpone the prospective juror's service to a date specified by the court's designee, as appropriate, if:

(1) the court's designee considers the excuse sufficient; and

(2) the juror submits to the court's designee a statement of the ground of the exemption or lack of qualification or other excuse.

Sec. 3. A court or a court's designee may discharge a juror or postpone the juror's service on the basis of the juror's observation of a religious holy day or religious beliefs only if the juror provides an affidavit as required by Article 29.012(c) of this code.

Acts 1965, 59th Leg., p. 317, ch. 722, § 1, eff. Jan. 1, 1966. Amended by Acts 1987, 70th Leg., ch. 589, § 2, eff. Aug. 31, 1987; Acts 1987, 70th Leg., 2nd C.S., ch. 43, § 2, eff. Oct. 20, 1987; Acts 2005, 79th Leg., ch. 905, § 1, eff. Sept. 1, 2005.

Art. 35.04. Claiming exemption

Any person summoned as a juror who is exempt by law from jury service may establish his exemption without appearing in person by filing a signed statement of the ground of his exemption with the clerk of the court at any time before the date upon which he is summoned to appear.

Acts 1965, 59th Leg., p. 317, ch. 722, § 1, eff. Jan. 1, 1966. Amended by Acts 1971, 62nd Leg., p. 1560, ch. 421, § 3, eff. May 26, 1971.

Art. 35.05. Excused by consent

One summoned upon a special venire may by consent of both parties be excused from attendance by the court at any time before he is impaneled.

Acts 1965, 59th Leg., p. 317, ch. 722, § 1, eff. Jan. 1, 1966.

Art. 35.06. Challenge to array first heard

The court shall hear and determine a challenge to the array before interrogating those summoned as to their qualifications.

Acts 1965, 59th Leg., p. 317, ch. 722, § 1, eff. Jan. 1, 1966.

Art. 35.07. Challenge to the array

Each party may challenge the array only on the ground that the officer summoning the jury has wilfully summoned jurors with a view to securing a conviction or an acquittal. All such challenges must be in writing setting forth distinctly the grounds of such challenge. When made by the defendant, it must be supported by his affidavit or the affidavit of any credible person. When such challenge is made, the judge shall hear evidence and decide without delay whether or not the challenge shall be sustained.

Acts 1965, 59th Leg., p. 317, ch. 722, § 1, eff. Jan. 1, 1966.

Art. 35.08. When challenge is sustained

The array of jurors summoned shall be discharged if the challenge be sustained, and the court shall order other jurors to be summoned in their stead, and direct that the officer who summoned those so discharged, and on account of whose misconduct the challenge has been sustained shall not summon any other jurors in the case.

Acts 1965, 59th Leg., p. 317, ch. 722, § 1, eff. Jan. 1, 1966.

Art. 35.09. List of new venire

When a challenge to the array has been sustained, the defendant shall be entitled, as in the first instance, to service of a copy of the list of names of those summoned by order of the court.

Acts 1965, 59th Leg., p. 317, ch. 722, § 1, eff. Jan. 1, 1966.

Art. 35.10. Court to try qualifications

When no challenge to the array has been made, or if made, has been over-ruled, the court shall proceed to try the qualifications of those present who have been summoned to serve as jurors.

Acts 1965, 59th Leg., p. 317, ch. 722, § 1, eff. Jan. 1, 1966.

Art. 35.11. Preparation of list

The trial judge, on the demand of the defendant or his attorney, or of the State's counsel, shall cause a sufficient number of jurors from which a jury may be selected to try the case to be randomly selected from the members of the general panel drawn or assigned as jurors in the case. The clerk shall randomly select the jurors by a computer or other process of random selection and shall write or print the names, in the order selected, on the jury list from which the jury is to be selected to try the case. The clerk shall deliver a copy of the list to the State's counsel and to the defendant or his attorney.

Acts 1965, 59th Leg., p. 317, ch. 722, § 1, eff. Jan. 1, 1966. Amended by Acts 1991, 72nd Leg., ch. 337, § 1, eff. Sept. 1, 1991.

Art. 35.12. Mode of Testing

(a) In testing the qualification of a prospective juror after the juror has been sworn, the juror shall be asked by the court, or under its direction:

1. Except for failure to register, are you a qualified voter in this county and state under the Constitution and laws of this state?

2. Have you ever been convicted of theft or any felony?

3. Are you under indictment or legal accusation for theft or any felony?

(b) In testing the qualifications of a prospective juror, with respect to whether the juror has been the subject of an order of nondisclosure or has a criminal history that includes information subject to that order, the juror may state only that the matter in question has been sealed.

Acts 1965, 59th Leg., p. 317, ch. 722, § 1, eff. Jan. 1, 1966. Amended by Acts 1969, 61st Leg., p. 1364, ch. 412, § 2, eff. Sept. 1, 1969; Acts 1981, 67th Leg., p. 3143, ch. 827, § 7, eff. Aug. 31, 1981; Acts 2005, 79th Leg., ch. 1309, § 4, eff. Sept. 1, 2005.

Art. 35.13. Passing juror for challenge

A juror in a capital case in which the state has made it known it will seek the death penalty, held to be qualified, shall be passed for acceptance or challenge first to the state and then to the defendant. Challenges to jurors are either peremptory or for cause.

Acts 1965, 59th Leg., p. 317, ch. 722, § 1, eff. Jan. 1, 1966. Amended by Acts 1967, 60th Leg., p. 1739, ch. 659, § 20, eff. Aug. 28, 1967.

Art. 35.14. A peremptory challenge

A peremptory challenge is made to a juror without assigning any reason therefor.

Acts 1965, 59th Leg., p. 317, ch. 722, § 1, eff. Jan. 1, 1966.

Art. 35.15. Number of challenges

(a) In capital cases in which the State seeks the death penalty both the State and defendant shall be entitled to fifteen peremptory challenges. Where two or more defendants are tried together, the State shall be entitled to eight peremptory challenges for each defendant; and each defendant shall be entitled to eight peremptory challenges.

(b) In non-capital felony cases and in capital cases in which the State does not seek the death penalty, the State and defendant shall each be entitled to ten peremptory challenges. If two or more defendants are tried together each defendant shall be entitled to six peremptory challenges and the State to six for each defendant.

(c) The State and the defendant shall each be entitled to five peremptory challenges in a misdemeanor tried in the district court and to three in the county court, or county court at law. If two or more defendants are tried together, each defendant shall be entitled to three such challenges and the State to three for each defendant in either court.

(d) The State and the defendant shall each be entitled to one peremptory challenge in addition to those otherwise allowed by law if one or two alternate jurors are to be impaneled and two peremptory challenges if three or four alternate jurors are to be impaneled. The additional peremptory challenges provided by this subsection may be used against an alternate juror only, and the other peremptory challenges allowed by law may not be used against an alternate juror.

Acts 1965, 59th Leg., p. 317, ch. 722, § 1, eff. Jan. 1, 1966. Amended by Acts 1973, 63rd Leg., p. 1127, ch. 426, art. 3, § 4, eff. June 14, 1973; Acts 1983, 68th Leg., p. 4594, ch. 775, § 3, eff. Aug. 29, 1983; Acts 1991, 72nd Leg., ch. 652, § 5, eff. Sept. 1, 1991.

Art. 35.16. Reasons for challenge for cause

(a) A challenge for cause is an objection made to a particular juror, alleging some fact which renders the juror incapable or unfit to serve on the jury. A challenge for cause may be made by either the state or the defense for any one of the following reasons:

1. That the juror is not a qualified voter in the state and county under the Constitution and laws of the state; provided, however, the failure to register to vote shall not be a disqualification;

2. That the juror has been convicted of misdemeanor theft or a felony;

3. That the juror is under indictment or other legal accusation for misdemeanor theft or a felony;

4. That the juror is insane;

5. That the juror has such defect in the organs of feeling or hearing, or such bodily or mental defect or disease as to render the juror unfit for jury service, or that the juror is legally blind and the court in its discretion is not satisfied that the juror is fit for jury service in that particular case;

6. That the juror is a witness in the case;

7. That the juror served on the grand jury which found the indictment;

8. That the juror served on a petit jury in a former trial of the same case;

9. That the juror has a bias or prejudice in favor of or against the defendant;

10. That from hearsay, or otherwise, there is established in the mind of the juror such a conclusion as to the guilt or innocence of the defendant as would influence the juror in finding a verdict. To ascertain whether this cause of challenge exists, the juror shall first be asked whether, in the juror's opinion, the conclusion so established will influence the juror's verdict. If the juror answers in the affirmative, the juror shall be discharged without further interrogation by either party or the court. If the juror answers in the negative, the juror shall be further examined as to how the juror's conclusion was formed, and the extent

to which it will affect the juror's action; and, if it appears to have been formed from reading newspaper accounts, communications, statements or reports or mere rumor or hearsay, and if the juror states that the juror feels able, notwithstanding such opinion, to render an impartial verdict upon the law and the evidence, the court, if satisfied that the juror is impartial and will render such verdict, may, in its discretion, admit the juror as competent to serve in such case. If the court, in its discretion, is not satisfied that the juror is impartial, the juror shall be discharged;

11. That the juror cannot read or write.

No juror shall be impaneled when it appears that the juror is subject to the second, third or fourth grounds of challenge for cause set forth above, although both parties may consent. All other grounds for challenge may be waived by the party or parties in whose favor such grounds of challenge exist.

In this subsection "legally blind" shall mean having not more than 20/200 of visual acuity in the better eye with correcting lenses, or visual acuity greater than 20/200 but with a limitation in the field of vision such that the widest diameter of the visual field subtends an angle no greater than 20 degrees.

(b) A challenge for cause may be made by the State for any of the following reasons:

1. That the juror has conscientious scruples in regard to the infliction of the punishment of death for crime, in a capital case, where the State is seeking the death penalty;

2. That he is related within the third degree of consanguinity or affinity, as determined under Chapter 573, Government Code, to the defendant; and

3. That he has a bias or prejudice against any phase of the law upon which the State is entitled to rely for conviction or punishment.

(c) A challenge for cause may be made by the defense for any of the following reasons:

1. That he is related within the third degree of consanguinity or affinity, as determined under Chapter 573, Government Code, to the person injured by the commission of the offense, or to any prosecutor in the case; and

2. That he has a bias or prejudice against any of the law applicable to the case upon which the defense is entitled to rely, either as a defense to some phase of the offense for which the defendant is being prosecut-

ed or as a mitigation thereof or of the punishment therefor.

Acts 1965, 59th Leg., p. 317, ch. 722, § 1, eff. Jan. 1, 1966. Amended by Acts 1969, 61st Leg., p. 1364, ch. 412, § 3, eff. Sept. 1, 1969; Acts 1975, 64th Leg., p. 475, ch. 202, § 2, eff. Sept. 1, 1975; Acts 1981, 67th Leg., p. 3143, ch. 827, § 8, eff. Aug. 31, 1981; Acts 1983, 68th Leg., p. 619, ch. 134, § 2, eff. Sept. 1, 1983; Acts 1991, 72nd Leg., ch. 561, § 10, eff. Aug. 26, 1991; Acts 1995, 74th Leg., ch. 76, § 5.95(27), eff. Sept. 1, 1995; Acts 2005 79th Leg., ch. 801, § 3, eff. Sept. 1, 2005.

Art. 35.17. Voir dire examination

1. When the court in its discretion so directs, except as provided in Section 2, the state and defendant shall conduct the voir dire examination of prospective jurors in the presence of the entire panel.

2. In a capital felony case in which the State seeks the death penalty, the court shall propound to the entire panel of prospective jurors questions concerning the principles, as applicable to the case on trial, of reasonable doubt, burden of proof, return of indictment by grand jury, presumption of innocence, and opinion. Then, on demand of the State or defendant, either is entitled to examine each juror on voir dire individually and apart from the entire panel, and may further question the juror on the principles propounded by the court.

Acts 1965, 59th Leg., p. 317, ch. 722, § 1, eff. Jan. 1, 1966. Amended by Acts 1973, 63rd Leg., p. 1127, ch. 426, art. 3, § 5, eff. June 14, 1973; Acts 1991, 72nd Leg., ch. 652, § 6, eff. Sept. 1, 1991.

Art. 35.18. Other evidence on challenge

Upon a challenge for cause, the examination is not confined to the answers of the juror, but other evidence may be heard for or against the challenge.

Acts 1965, 59th Leg., p. 317, ch. 722, § 1, eff. Jan. 1, 1966.

Art. 35.19. Absolute disqualification

No juror shall be impaneled when it appears that he is subject to the second, third or fourth cause of challenge in Article 35.16, though both parties may consent.

Acts 1965, 59th Leg., p. 317, ch. 722, § 1, eff. Jan. 1, 1966. Amended by Acts 1969, 61st Leg., p. 1364, ch. 412, § 4, eff. Sept. 1, 1969.

Art. 35.20. Names called in order

In selecting the jury from the persons summoned, the names of such persons shall be called in the order in which they appear upon the list furnished the defendant. Each juror shall be tried and passed upon separately. A person who has been summoned, but who is not present, may, upon his appearance before the jury is completed, be tried as to his qualifications and impaneled as a juror, unless challenged, but no cause shall be unreasonably delayed on account of such absence.

Acts 1965, 59th Leg., p. 317, ch. 722, § 1, eff. Jan. 1, 1966.

Art. 35.21. Judge to decide qualifications

The court is the judge, after proper examination, of the qualifications of a juror, and shall decide all challenges without delay and without argument thereupon.

Acts 1965, 59th Leg., p. 317, ch. 722, § 1, eff. Jan. 1, 1966.

Art. 35.22. Oath to jury

When the jury has been selected, the following oath shall be administered them by the court or under its direction: "You and each of you do solemnly swear that in the case of the State of Texas against the defendant, you will a true verdict render according to the law and the evidence, so help you God".

Acts 1965, 59th Leg., p. 317, ch. 722, § 1, eff. Jan. 1, 1966.

Art. 35.23. Jurors may separate

The court may adjourn veniremen to any day of the term. When jurors have been sworn in a felony case, the court may, at its discretion, permit the jurors to separate until the court has given its charge to the jury. The court on its own motion may and on the motion of either party shall, after having given its charge to the jury, order that the jury not be allowed to separate, after which the jury shall be kept together, and not permitted to separate except to the extent of housing female jurors separate and apart from male jurors, until a verdict has been rendered or the jury finally discharged. Any person who makes known to the jury which party made the motion not to allow separation of the jury shall be punished for contempt of court. If such jurors are kept overnight, facilities shall be provided for female jurors separate and apart from the facilities provided for male jurors. In misdemeanor cases the court may, at its discretion, permit the jurors to separate at any time before the verdict. In any case in which the jury is permitted to separate, the court shall first give the jurors proper instructions with regard to their conduct as jurors when so separated.

Acts 1965, 59th Leg., p. 317, ch. 722, § 1, eff. Jan. 1, 1966. Amended by Acts 1989, 71st Leg., ch. 825, § 1, eff. Sept. 1, 1989.

Art. 35.24. Repealed by Acts 1975, 64th Leg., p. 1353, ch. 510, § 2, eff. Sept. 1, 1975

Art. 35.25. Making peremptory challenge

In non-capital cases and in capital cases in which the State's attorney has announced that he will not qualify the jury for, or seek the death penalty, the party desiring to challenge any juror peremptorily shall strike the name of such juror from the list furnished him by the clerk.

Acts 1965, 59th Leg., p. 317, ch. 722, § 1, eff. Jan. 1, 1966.

Art. 35.26. Lists returned to clerk

(a) When the parties have made or declined to make their peremptory challenges, they shall deliver their lists to the clerk. Except as provided in Subsection (b) of this section, the clerk shall, if the case be in the district court, call off the first twelve names on the lists that have not been stricken. If the case be in the county court, he shall call off the first six names on the lists that have not been stricken. Those whose names are called shall be the jury.

(b) In a capital case in which the state seeks the death penalty, the court may direct that two alternate jurors be selected and that the first fourteen names not stricken be called off by the clerk. The last two names to be called are the alternate jurors.

Acts 1965, 59th Leg., p. 317, ch. 722, § 1, eff. Jan. 1, 1966. Amended by Acts 1981, 67th Leg., p. 2264, ch. 545, § 1, eff. June 12, 1981; Acts 1991, 72nd Leg., ch. 652, § 7, eff. Sept. 1, 1991.

Art. 35.261. Peremptory challenges based on race prohibited

(a) After the parties have delivered their lists to the clerk under Article 35.26 of this code and before the court has impanelled the jury, the defendant may request the court to dismiss the array and call a new array in the case. The court shall grant the motion of a defendant for dismissal of the array if the court determines that the defendant is a member of an identifiable racial group, that the attorney representing the state exercised peremptory challenges for the purpose of excluding persons from the jury on the basis of their race, and that the defendant has offered evidence of relevant facts that tend to show that challenges made by the attorney representing the state were made for reasons based on race. If the defendant establishes a prima facie case, the burden then shifts to the attorney representing the state to give a racially neutral explanation for the challenges. The burden of persuasion remains with the defendant to establish purposeful discrimination.

(b) If the court determines that the attorney representing the state challenged prospective jurors on the basis of race, the court shall call a new array in the case.

Acts 1987, 70th Leg., ch. 751, § 1, eff. Aug. 31, 1987.

Art. 35.27. Reimbursement of nonresident witnesses

Expenses for Nonresident Witnesses

Sec. 1. (a) Every person subpoenaed by either party or otherwise required or requested in writing by the prosecuting attorney or the court to appear for the purpose of giving testimony in a criminal proceeding who resides outside the state or the county in which the prosecution is pending shall be reimbursed by the state for the reasonable and necessary transportation, meal, and lodging expenses he incurs by reason of his attendance as a witness at such proceeding.

(b) The state may reimburse a witness for transportation only if the transportation is provided by a commercial transportation company or the witness uses the witness's personally owned or leased motor vehicle. In this article, "commercial transportation company" means an entity that offers transportation of people or goods to the public in exchange for compensation.

(c) The state may reimburse a witness for lodging only if the lodging is provided by a commercial lodging establishment. In this article, "commercial lodging establishment" means a motel, hotel, inn, apartment, or similar entity that offers lodging to the public in exchange for compensation.

Amount of Reimbursement for Expenses

Sec. 2. Any person seeking reimbursement as a witness shall make an affidavit setting out the transportation, meal, and lodging expenses necessitated by his travel to and from and attendance at the place he appeared to give testimony, together with the number of days that such travel and attendance made him absent from his place of residence. A reimbursement paid by the state to a witness for transportation, meal, or lodging expenses may not be paid at a rate that exceeds the maximum rates provided by law for state employees.

Direct Payment of Transportation or Lodging Expenses

Sec. 2A. If this article requires the state to reimburse a witness for transportation or lodging expenses, the state may instead directly pay a commercial transportation company or commercial lodging establishment for those expenses.

Other Expenses

Sec. 3. In addition to reimbursement or payment for transportation, meal, and lodging expenses, the comptroller, upon proper application by the attorney for the state, shall reimburse or pay the other expenses required by the laws of this state or the state from which the attendance of the witness is sought.

Application and Approval by Judge

Sec. 4. A reimbursement to a witness as provided by this article shall be paid by the state to the witness or his assignee. Claim shall be made by sworn application to the comptroller, a copy of which shall be filed with the clerk of the court, setting out the facts showing entitlement as provided in this article to the reimbursement, which application shall be presented for approval by the judge who presided over the court or empaneled the grand jury before whom the criminal proceeding was pending. No fee shall be required of any witness for the processing of his claim for reimbursement.

Payment by State

Sec. 5. The Comptroller of Public Accounts, upon receipt of a claim approved by the judge, shall examine it and, if he deems the claim in compliance with and authorized by this Article, draw his warrant on the State Treasury for the amount due the witness, or to any person to which the certificate has been assigned by the witness, but no warrant may issue to any assignee of a witness claim unless the assignment is made under oath and acknowledged before some person authorized to administer oaths, certified to by the officer, and under seal. If the appropriation for paying the account is exhausted, the Comptroller of Public Accounts shall file it away and issue a certificate in the name of the witness entitled to it, stating therein the amount of the claim. Each claim not filed in the office of the Comptroller of Public Accounts within twelve months from the date it became due and payable shall be forever barred.

Advance by State

Sec. 6. Funds required to be tendered to an out-of-state witness pursuant to Article 24.28 of this Code shall be paid by the Comptroller of Public Accounts into the registry of the Court in which the case is to be tried upon certification by the Court such funds are necessary to obtain attendance of said witness. The court shall then cause to be issued checks drawn upon the registry of the Court to secure the attendance of such witness. In the event that such funds are not used pursuant to this Act, the Court shall return the funds to the Comptroller of Public Accounts.

Advance by County

Sec. 7. The county in which a criminal proceeding is pending, upon request of the district attorney or other prosecutor charged with the duty of prosecution in the proceeding, may advance funds from its treasury to any witness who will be entitled to reimbursement under this article. The amount advanced may not exceed the amount that is reasonably necessary to enable the witness to attend as required or requested. However, the amount advanced may include sums in excess of the reimbursement provided for by this article if the excess is required for compliance with Section 4 of Article 24.28 in securing the attendance of a witness from another state under the Uniform Act. A county that advances funds to a witness under this section is entitled to reimbursement by the state as an assignee of the witness.

Advance for Expenses for Witnesses of Indigent Defendant

Sec. 8. Upon application by a defendant shown to be indigent and a showing to the court of reasonable necessity and materiality for the testimony of a witness residing outside the State, the court shall act pursuant to Section 6 hereof to secure advance of funds necessary for the attendance of such witness.

Limitations

Sec. 9. A witness, when attached and conveyed by a sheriff or other officer, is not eligible to receive reimbursement of transportation, meal, or lodging expenses incurred while in the custody of the officer. A court, in its discretion, may limit the number of character witnesses allowed reimbursement under this article to not fewer than two for each defendant and two per defendant for the state.

Acts 1965, 59th Leg., p. 317, ch. 722, § 1, eff. Jan. 1, 1966. Amended by Acts 1973, 63rd Leg., p. 1287, ch. 477, § 2, eff. Aug. 27, 1973; Acts 1979, 66th Leg., p. 1039, ch. 469, § 1, eff. Sept. 1, 1979; Acts 1993, 73rd Leg., ch. 449, § 18, eff. Sept. 1, 1993.

Art. 35.28. When no clerk

In each instance in Article 35.27 in which the clerk of the court is authorized or directed to perform any act, the judge of such court shall perform the same if there is no clerk of the court.

Acts 1965, 59th Leg., p. 317, ch. 722, § 1, eff. Jan. 1, 1966.

Art. 35.29. Personal Information About Jurors

(a) Except as provided by Subsections (b) and (c), information collected by the court or by a prosecuting attorney during the jury selection process about a person who serves as a juror, including the juror's home address, home telephone number, social security number, driver's license number, and other personal information, is confidential and may not be disclosed by the court, the prosecuting attorney, the defense counsel, or any court personnel.

(b) On application by a party in the trial, or on application by a bona fide member of the news media acting in such capacity, to the court for the disclosure of information described by Subsection (a), the court shall, on a showing of good cause, permit disclosure of the information sought.

(c) The defense counsel may disclose information described by Subsection (a) to successor counsel representing the same defendant in a proceeding under Article 11.071 without application to the court or a showing of good cause.

Added by Acts 1993, 73rd Leg., ch. 371, § 1, eff. Sept. 1, 1993. Amended by Acts 2013, 83rd Leg., ch. 1318 (S.B. 270), § 1, eff. Sept. 1, 2013.

CHAPTER THIRTY–SIX. THE TRIAL BEFORE THE JURY

Art. 36.01. Order of proceeding in trial

(a) A jury being impaneled in any criminal action, except as provided by Subsection (b) of this article, the cause shall proceed in the following order:

1. The indictment or information shall be read to the jury by the attorney prosecuting. When prior convictions are alleged for purposes of enhancement only and are not jurisdictional, that portion of the indictment or information reciting such convictions shall not be read until the hearing on punishment is held as provided in Article 37.07.

2. The special pleas, if any, shall be read by the defendant's counsel, and if the plea of not guilty is also relied upon, it shall also be stated.

3. The State's attorney shall state to the jury the nature of the accusation and the facts which are expected to be proved by the State in support thereof.

4. The testimony on the part of the State shall be offered.

5. The nature of the defenses relied upon and the facts expected to be proved in their support shall be stated by defendant's counsel.

6. The testimony on the part of the defendant shall be offered.

7. Rebutting testimony may be offered on the part of each party.

8. In the event of a finding of guilty, the trial shall then proceed as set forth in Article 37.07.

(b) The defendant's counsel may make the opening statement for the defendant immediately after the attorney representing the State makes the opening statement for the State. After the defendant's attorney concludes the defendant's opening statement, the State's testimony shall be offered. At the conclusion of the presentation of the State's testimony, the defendant's testimony shall be offered, and the order of proceedings shall continue in the manner described by Subsection (a) of this article.

Acts 1965, 59th Leg., vol. 2, p. 317, ch. 722. Amended by Acts 1987, 70th Leg., ch. 519, § 1, eff. Sept. 1, 1987.

Art. 36.02. Testimony at any time

The court shall allow testimony to be introduced at any time before the argument of a cause is concluded, if it appears that it is necessary to a due administration of justice.

Acts 1965, 59th Leg., vol. 2, p. 317, ch. 722.

Art. 36.03. Invocation of Rule

(a) Notwithstanding Rule 614, Texas Rules of Evidence, a court at the request of a party may order the exclusion of a witness who for the purposes of the prosecution is a victim, close relative of a deceased victim, or guardian of a victim only if the witness is to testify and the court determines that the testimony of the witness would be materially affected if the witness hears other testimony at the trial.

(b) On the objection of the opposing party, the court may require the party requesting exclusion of a witness under Subsection (a) to make an offer of proof to justify the exclusion.

(c) Subsection (a) does not limit the authority of the court on its own motion to exclude a witness or other person to maintain decorum in the courtroom.

(d) In this article:

(1) "Close relative of a deceased victim" and "guardian of a victim" have the meanings assigned by Article 56.01.

(2) "Victim" means a victim of any criminal offense.

(e) At the commencement of a trial, the court shall admonish each witness who is to testify as to those persons whom the court determines the witness may talk to about the case before the trial ends and those persons whom the witness may not talk to about the case. The court may punish as contempt a witness who violates the admonishment provided by the court.

Added by Acts 2001, 77th Leg., ch. 1034, § 1, eff. Sept. 1, 2001.

Art. 36.04. Repealed by Texas Rules of Criminal Evidence effective September 1, 1986 [Acts 1985, 69th Leg., ch. 685, § 9(b)]

Art. 36.05. Not to hear testimony

Witnesses under rule shall be attended by an officer, and all their reasonable wants provided for, unless the court, in its discretion, directs that they be allowed to go at large; but in no case where the witnesses are under rule shall they be allowed to hear any testimony in the case.

Acts 1965, 59th Leg., vol. 2, p. 317, ch. 722.

Art. 36.06.   Instructed by the court

Witnesses, when placed under rule, shall be instructed by the court that they are not to converse with each other or with any other person about the case, except by permission of the court, and that they are not to read any report of or comment upon the testimony in the case while under rule. The officer who attends the witnesses shall report to the court at once any violation of its instructions, and the party violating the same shall be punished for contempt of court.

Acts 1965, 59th Leg., vol. 2, p. 317, ch. 722.

Art. 36.07.   Order of argument

The order of argument may be regulated by the presiding judge; but the State's counsel shall have the right to make the concluding address to the jury.

Acts 1965, 59th Leg., vol. 2, p. 317, ch. 722.

Art. 36.08.   Number of arguments

The court shall never restrict the argument in felony cases to a number of addresses less than two on each side.

Acts 1965, 59th Leg., vol. 2, p. 317, ch. 722.

Art. 36.09.   Severance on separate indictments

Two or more defendants who are jointly or separately indicted or complained against for the same offense or any offense growing out of the same transaction may be, in the discretion of the court, tried jointly or separately as to one or more defendants; provided that in any event either defendant may testify for the other or on behalf of the state; and provided further, that in cases in which, upon timely motion to sever, and evidence introduced thereon, it is made known to the court that there is a previous admissible conviction against one defendant or that a joint trial would be prejudicial to any defendant, the court shall order a severance as to the defendant whose joint trial would prejudice the other defendant or defendants.

Acts 1965, 59th Leg., vol. 2, p. 317, ch. 722. Amended by Acts 1967, 60th Leg., p. 1739, ch. 659, § 21, eff. Aug. 28, 1967.

Art. 36.10.   Order of trial

If a severance is granted, the defendants may agree upon the order in which they are to be tried, but if they fail to agree, the court shall direct the order of the trial.

Acts 1965, 59th Leg., vol. 2, p. 317, ch. 722.

Art. 36.11.   Discharge before verdict

If it appears during a trial that the court has no jurisdiction of the offense, or that the facts charged in the indictment do not constitute an offense, the jury shall be discharged. The accused shall also be discharged, but such discharge shall be no bar in any case to a prosecution before the proper court for any offense unless termination of the former prosecution was improper.

Acts 1965, 59th Leg., vol. 2, p. 317, ch. 722. Amended by Acts 1973, 63rd Leg., p. 971, ch. 399, § 2(A), eff. Jan. 1, 1974.

Art. 36.12.   Court may commit

If the want of jurisdiction arises from the fact that the defendant is not liable to prosecution in the county where the indictment was presented, the court may in felony cases order the accused into custody for a reasonable length of time to await a warrant for his arrest from the proper county; or if the offense be bailable, may require him to enter into recognizance to answer before the proper court; in which case a certified copy of the recognizance shall be sent forthwith to the clerk of the proper court, to be enforced by that court in case of forfeiture.

Acts 1965, 59th Leg., vol. 2, p. 317, ch. 722.

Art. 36.13.   Jury is judge of facts

Unless otherwise provided in this Code, the jury is the exclusive judge of the facts, but it is bound to receive the law from the court and be governed thereby.

Acts 1965, 59th Leg., vol. 2, p. 317, ch. 722.

Art. 36.14.   Charge of court

Subject to the provisions of Article 36.07 in each felony case and in each misdemeanor case tried in a court of record, the judge shall, before the argument begins, deliver to the jury, except in pleas of guilty, where a jury has been waived, a written charge distinctly setting forth the law applicable to the case; not expressing any opinion as to the weight of the evidence, not summing up the testimony, discussing the facts or using any argument in his charge calculated to arouse the sympathy or excite the passions of the jury. Before said charge is read to the jury, the defendant or his counsel shall have a reasonable time to examine the same and he shall present his objections thereto in writing, distinctly specifying each ground of objection. Said objections may embody errors claimed to have been committed in the charge, as well as errors claimed to have been committed by omissions therefrom or in failing to charge upon issues arising from the facts, and in no event shall it be necessary for the defendant or his counsel to present special requested charges to preserve or maintain any error assigned to the charge, as herein provided. The requirement that the objections to the court's charge be in writing will be complied with if the objections are dictated to the court reporter in the presence of the court and the state's counsel, before the reading of the court's charge to the jury. Compliance with the provisions of this Article is all that is necessary to preserve, for review, the exceptions and objections presented to the charge and any amendment or modification thereof. In no event shall it be necessary for the defendant to except to the action of the court in over-ruling defendant's exceptions or objections to the charge.

Acts 1965, 59th Leg., vol. 2, p. 317, ch. 722. Amended by Acts 1975, 64th Leg., p. 617, ch. 253, § 1, eff. Sept. 1, 1975; Acts 1981, 67th Leg., p. 2244, ch. 537, § 1, eff. June 12, 1981.

Art. 36.15.   Requested special charges

Before the court reads his charge to the jury, counsel on both sides shall have a reasonable time to present written instructions and ask that they be given to the jury. The requirement that the instructions be in writing is complied with if the instructions are dictated to the court reporter in the presence of the court and the state's counsel, before the reading of the court's charge to the jury. The court shall give or refuse these charges. The defendant may, by a special requested instruction, call the trial court's attention to error in the charge, as well as omissions therefrom, and no other exception or objection to the court's charge shall be necessary to preserve any error reflected by any special requested instruction which the trial court refuses.

Any special requested charge which is granted shall be incorporated in the main charge and shall be treated as a part thereof, and the jury shall not be advised that it is a special requested charge of either party. The judge shall read to the jury only such special charges as he gives.

When the defendant has leveled objections to the charge or has requested instructions or both, and the court thereafter modifies his charge and rewrites the same and in so doing does not respond to objections or requested charges, or any of them, then the objections or requested charges shall not be deemed to have been waived by the party making or requesting the same, but shall be deemed to continue to have been urged by the party making or requesting the same

unless the contrary is shown by the record; no exception by the defendant to the action of the court shall be necessary or required in order to preserve for review the error claimed in the charge.

Acts 1965, 59th Leg., vol. 2, p. 317, ch. 722. Amended by Acts 1979, 36th Leg., p. 1109, ch. 525, § 1, eff. Sept. 1, 1979; Acts 1981, 67th Leg., p. 2245, ch. 537, § 1, eff. June 12, 1981.

Art. 36.16.   Final charge

After the judge shall have received the objections to his main charge, together with any special charges offered, he may make such changes in his main charge as he may deem proper, and the defendant or his counsel shall have the opportunity to present their objections thereto and in the same manner as is provided in Article 36.15, and thereupon the judge shall read his charge to the jury as finally written, together with any special charges given, and no further exception or objection shall be required of the defendant in order to preserve any objections or exceptions theretofore made. After the argument begins no further charge shall be given to the jury unless required by the improper argument of counsel or the request of the jury, or unless the judge shall, in his discretion, permit the introduction of other testimony, and in the event of such further charge, the defendant or his counsel shall have the right to present objections in the same manner as is prescribed in Article 36.15. The failure of the court to give the defendant or his counsel a reasonable time to examine the charge and specify the ground of objection shall be subject to review either in the trial court or in the appellate court.

Acts 1965, 56th Leg., vol. 2, p. 317, ch. 722.

Art. 36.17.   Charge certified by judge

The general charge given by the court and all special charges given or refused shall be certified by the judge and filed among the papers in the cause.

Acts 1965, 59th Leg., vol. 2, p. 317, ch. 722.

Art. 36.18.   Jury may take charge

The jury may take to their jury room the charges given by the court after the same have been filed. They shall not be permitted to take with them any charge or part thereof which the court has refused to give.

Acts 1965, 59th Leg., vol. 2, p. 317, ch. 722.

Art. 36.19.　Review of charge on appeal

Whenever it appears by the record in any criminal action upon appeal that any requirement of Articles 36.14, 36.15, 36.16, 36.17 and 36.18 has been disregarded, the judgment shall not be reversed unless the error appearing from the record was calculated to injure the rights of defendant, or unless it appears from the record that the defendant has not had a fair and impartial trial. All objections to the charge and to the refusal of special charges shall be made at the time of the trial.

Acts 1965, 59th Leg., vol. 2, p. 317, ch. 722.

Art. 36.20.　Repealed by Texas Rules of Appellate Procedure effective September 1, 1986 (Acts 1985, 69th Leg., ch. 685, § 4)

Art. 36.21.　To provide jury room

The sheriff shall provide a suitable room for the deliberation of the jury and supply them with such necessary food and lodging as he can obtain. No intoxicating liquor shall be furnished them. In all cases wherein a jury consists partly of male jurors and partly of female jurors, the sheriff shall provide facilities for the female jurors separate and apart from the facilities provided for the male jurors.

Acts 1965, 59th Leg., vol. 2, p. 317, ch. 722.

Art. 36.215.　Recording of Jury Deliberations

A person may not use any device to produce or make an audio, visual, or audio-visual broadcast, recording, or photograph of a jury while the jury is deliberating.

Added by Acts 2003, 78th Leg., ch. 54, § 1, eff. Sept. 1, 2003.

Art. 36.22.　Conversing with jury

No person shall be permitted to be with a jury while it is deliberating. No person shall be permitted to converse with a juror about the case on trial except in the presence and by the permission of the court.

Acts 1965, 59th Leg., vol. 2, p. 317, ch. 722.

Art. 36.23.　Violation of preceding article

Any juror or other person violating the preceding Article shall be punished for contempt of court by confinement in jail not to exceed three days or by fine not to exceed one hundred dollars, or by both such fine and imprisonment.

Acts 1965, 59th Leg., vol. 2, p. 317, ch. 722.

Art. 36.24.　Officer shall attend jury

The sheriff of the county shall furnish the court with a bailiff during the trial of any case to attend the wants of the jury and to act under the direction of the court. If the person furnished by the sheriff is to be called as a witness in the case he may not serve as bailiff.

Acts 1965, 59th Leg., vol. 2, p. 317, ch. 722.

Art. 36.25.　Written evidence

There shall be furnished to the jury upon its request any exhibits admitted as evidence in the case.

Acts 1965, 59th Leg., vol. 2, p. 317, ch. 722.

Art. 36.26.　Foreman of jury

Each jury shall appoint one of its members foreman.

Acts 1965, 59th Leg., vol. 2, p. 317, ch. 722.

Art. 36.27.　Jury may communicate with court

When the jury wishes to communicate with the court, it shall so notify the sheriff, who shall inform the court thereof. Any communication relative to the cause must be written, prepared by the foreman and shall be submitted to the court through the bailiff. The court shall answer any such communication in writing, and before giving such answer to the jury shall use reasonable diligence to secure the presence of the defendant and his counsel, and shall first submit the question and also submit his answer to the same to the defendant or his counsel or objections and exceptions, in the same manner as any other written instructions are submitted to such counsel, before the court gives such answer to the jury, but if he is unable to secure the presence of the defendant and his counsel, then he shall proceed to answer the same as he deems proper. The written instruction or answer to the communication shall be read in open court unless expressly waived by the defendant.

All such proceedings in felony cases shall be a part of the record and recorded by the court reporter.

Acts 1965, 59th Leg., vol. 2, p. 317, ch. 722.

Art. 36.28.　Jury may have witness re-examined or testimony read

In the trial of a criminal case in a court of record, if the jury disagree as to the statement of any witness they may, upon applying to the court, have read to them from the court reporter's notes that part of such witness testimony or the particular point in dispute, and no other; but if there be no such reporter, or if his notes cannot be read to the jury, the court may cause such witness to be again brought upon the stand and the judge shall direct him to repeat his testimony as to the point in dispute, and no other, as nearly as he can in the language used on the trial.

Acts 1965, 59th Leg., vol. 2, p. 317, ch. 722.

Art. 36.29. If a Juror Dies or Becomes Disabled

(a) Not less than twelve jurors can render and return a verdict in a felony case. It must be concurred in by each juror and signed by the foreman. Except as provided in Subsection (b), however, after the trial of any felony case begins and a juror dies or, as determined by the judge, becomes disabled from sitting at any time before the charge of the court is read to the jury, the remainder of the jury shall have the power to render the verdict; but when the verdict shall be rendered by less than the whole number, it shall be signed by every member of the jury concurring in it.

(b) If alternate jurors have been selected in a capital case in which the state seeks the death penalty and a juror dies or becomes disabled from sitting at any time before the charge of the court is read to the jury, the alternate juror whose name was called first under Article 35.26 of this code shall replace the dead or disabled juror. Likewise, if another juror dies or becomes disabled from sitting before the charge of the court is read to the jury, the other alternate juror shall replace the second juror to die or become disabled.

(c) After the charge of the court is read to the jury, if a juror becomes so sick as to prevent the continuance of the juror's duty and an alternate juror is not available, or if any accident of circumstance occurs to prevent the jury from being kept together under circumstances under which the law or the instructions of the court requires that the jury be kept together, the jury shall be discharged, except that on agreement on the record by the defendant, the defendant's counsel, and the attorney representing the state 11 members of a jury may render a verdict and, if punishment is to be assessed by the jury, assess punishment. If a verdict is rendered by less than the whole number of the jury, each member of the jury shall sign the verdict.

(d) After the jury has rendered a verdict on the guilt or innocence of the defendant and, if applicable, the amount of punishment, the court shall discharge an alternate juror who has not replaced a juror.

Acts 1965, 59th Leg., vol. 2, p. 317, ch. 722. Amended by Acts 1981, 67th Leg., p. 2264, ch. 545, § 2, eff. June 12, 1981; Acts 1991, 72nd Leg., ch. 652, § 8, eff. Sept. 1, 1991; Acts 1997, 75th Leg., ch. 866, § 1, eff. Sept. 1, 1997; Acts 2001, 77th Leg., ch. 1000, § 1, eff. Sept. 1, 2001; Acts 2001, 77th Leg., ch. 1000, § 2, eff. Sept. 1, 2001; Acts 2007, 80th Leg., ch. 846, § 2, eff. Sept. 1, 2007; Acts 2009, 81st Leg., ch. 627, § 1, eff. Sept. 1, 2009.

Art. 36.30. Discharging jury in misdemeanor

If nine of the jury can be kept together in a misdemeanor case in the district court, they shall not be discharged. If more than three of the twelve are discharged, the entire jury shall be discharged.

Acts 1965, 59th Leg., vol. 2, p. 317, ch. 722.

Art. 36.31. Disagreement of jury

After the cause is submitted to the jury, it may be discharged when it cannot agree and both parties consent to its discharge; or the court may in its discretion discharge it where it has been kept together for such time as to render it altogether improbable that it can agree.

Acts 1965, 59th Leg., vol. 2, p. 317, ch. 722.

Art. 36.32. Receipt of verdict and final adjournment

During the trial of any case, the term shall be deemed to have been extended until such time as the jury has rendered its verdict or been discharged according to law.

Acts 1965, 59th Leg., vol. 2, p. 317, ch. 722.

Art. 36.33. Discharge without verdict

When a jury has been discharged, as provided in the four preceding Articles, without having rendered a verdict, the cause may be again tried at the same or another term.

Acts 1965, 59th Leg., vol. 2, p. 317, ch. 722.

CHAPTER THIRTY–SEVEN. THE VERDICT

Art. 37.01. Verdict

A "verdict" is a written declaration by a jury of its decision of the issue submitted to it in the case.

Acts 1965, 59th Leg., vol. 2, p. 317, ch. 722.

Art. 37.02. Verdict by nine jurors

In misdemeanor cases in the district court, where one or more jurors have been discharged from serving after the cause has been submitted to them, if all the alternate jurors selected under Article 33.011 of this code have either been seated or discharged, and there be as many as nine of the jurors remaining, those remaining may render and return a verdict; but in such case, the verdict must be signed by each juror rendering it.

Acts 1965, 59th Leg., vol. 2, p. 317, ch. 722. Amended by Acts 1983, 68th Leg., p. 4594, ch. 775, § 4, eff. Aug. 29, 1983.

Art. 37.03. In county court

In the county court the verdict must be concurred in by each juror.

Acts 1965, 59th Leg., vol. 2, p. 317, ch. 722.

Art. 37.04. When jury has agreed

When the jury agrees upon a verdict, it shall be brought into court by the proper officer; and if it states that it has agreed, the verdict shall be read aloud by the judge, the foreman, or the clerk. If in proper form and no juror dissents therefrom, and neither party requests a poll of the jury, the verdict shall be entered upon the minutes of the court.

Acts 1965, 59th Leg., vol. 2, p. 317, ch. 722. Amended by Acts 1981, 67th Leg., p. 171, ch. 78, § 1, eff. April 30, 1981.

Art. 37.05. Polling the Jury

(a) The State and the defendant each have the right to have the jury polled, which is done by calling separately the name or identification number of each juror and asking the juror if the verdict is the juror's. If all jurors, when asked, answer in the affirmative, the verdict shall be entered upon the minutes; but if any juror answers in the negative, the jury shall retire again to consider its verdict.

(b) For the purposes of polling the jury in Subsection (a), the judge may assign each juror an identification number to use in place of the juror's name.

Acts 1965, 59th Leg., vol. 2, p. 317, ch. 722. Amended by Acts 2017, 85th Leg., ch. 287 (S.B. 46), § 1, eff. Sept. 1, 2017.

Art. 37.06. Presence of defendant

In felony cases the defendant must be present when the verdict is read unless his absence is wilful or voluntary. A verdict in a misdemeanor case may be received and read in the absence of the defendant.

Acts 1965, 59th Leg., vol. 2, p. 317, ch. 722.

Art. 37.07. Verdict must be general; separate hearing on proper punishment

Sec. 1. (a) The verdict in every criminal action must be general. When there are special pleas on which a jury is to find they must say in their verdict that the allegations in such pleas are true or untrue.

(b) If the plea is not guilty, they must find that the defendant is either guilty or not guilty, and, except as provided in Section 2, they shall assess the punishment in all cases where the same is not absolutely fixed by law to some particular penalty.

(c) If the charging instrument contains more than one count or if two or more offenses are consolidated for trial pursuant to Chapter 3 of the Penal Code, the jury shall be instructed to return a finding of guilty or not guilty in a separate verdict as to each count and offense submitted to them.

Sec. 2. (a) In all criminal cases, other than misdemeanor cases of which the justice court or municipal court has jurisdiction, which are tried before a jury on a plea of not guilty, the judge shall, before argument begins, first submit to the jury the issue of guilt or innocence of the defendant of the offense or offenses charged, without authorizing the jury to pass upon the punishment to be imposed. If the jury fails to agree on the issue of guilt or innocence, the judge shall declare a mistrial and discharge the jury, and jeopardy does not attach in the case.

(b) Except as provided by Article 37.071 or 37.072, if a finding of guilty is returned, it shall then be the responsibility of the judge to assess the punishment applicable to the offense; provided, however, that (1) in any criminal action where the jury may recommend community supervision and the defendant filed his sworn motion for community supervision before the trial began, and (2) in other cases where the defendant so elects in writing before the commencement of the voir dire examination of the jury panel, the punishment shall be assessed by the same jury, except as provided in Section 3(c) of this article and in Article 44.29. If a finding of guilty is returned, the defendant may, with the consent of the attorney for the state, change his election of one who assesses the punishment.

(c) Punishment shall be assessed on each count on which a finding of guilty has been returned.

Sec. 3. Evidence of prior criminal record in all criminal cases after a finding of guilty.

(a)(1) Regardless of the plea and whether the punishment be assessed by the judge or the jury, evidence may be offered by the state and the defendant as to any matter the court deems relevant to sentencing, including but not limited to the prior criminal record of the defendant, his general reputation, his character, an opinion regarding his character, the circumstances of the offense for which he is being tried, and, notwithstanding Rules 404 and 405, Texas Rules of Evidence, any other evidence of an extraneous crime or bad act that is shown beyond a reasonable doubt by evidence to have been committed by the defendant or for which he could be held criminally responsible, regardless of whether he has previously been charged with or finally convicted of the crime or act. A court may consider as a factor in mitigating punishment the conduct of a defendant while participating in a program under Chapter 17 as a condition of release on bail. Additionally, notwithstanding Rule 609(d), Texas Rules of Evidence, and subject to Subsection (h), evidence may be offered by the state and the defendant of an adjudication of delinquency based on a violation by the defendant of a penal law of the grade of:

(A) a felony; or

(B) a misdemeanor punishable by confinement in jail.

(2) Notwithstanding Subdivision (1), evidence may not be offered by the state to establish that the race or ethnicity of the defendant makes it likely that the defendant will engage in future criminal conduct.

(3) Regardless of the plea and whether the punishment is assessed by the judge or the jury, during the punishment phase of the trial of an offense under Section 35A.02, Penal Code, subject to the applicable rules of evidence, the state and the defendant may offer evidence not offered during the guilt or innocence phase of the trial concerning the total pecuniary loss to the Medicaid program caused by the defendant's conduct or, if applicable, the scheme or continuing course of conduct of which the defendant's conduct is part. Subject to the applicable rules of evidence, an employee of the Health and Human Services Commission's office of inspector general or the office of attorney general's Medicaid fraud control unit may testify concerning the total pecuniary loss to the Medicaid program. An employee who testifies under this subdivision is subject to cross-examination. Evidence offered under this subdivision may be considered by the judge or jury in ordering or recommending the amount of any restitution to be made to the Medicaid program or the appropriate punishment for the defendant.

(b) After the introduction of such evidence has been concluded, and if the jury has the responsibility of assessing the punishment, the court shall give such additional written instructions as may be necessary and the order of procedure and the rules governing the conduct of the trial shall be the same as are applicable on the issue of guilt or innocence.

(c) If the jury finds the defendant guilty and the matter of punishment is referred to the jury, the verdict shall not be complete until a jury verdict has been rendered on both the guilt or innocence of the defendant and the amount of punishment. In the event the jury shall fail to agree on the issue of punishment, a mistrial shall be declared only in the punishment phase of the trial, the jury shall be discharged, and no jeopardy shall attach. The court shall impanel another jury as soon as practicable to determine the issue of punishment.

(d) When the judge assesses the punishment, the judge may order a presentence report as contemplated in Subchapter F, Chapter 42A, and after considering the report, and after the hearing of the evidence hereinabove provided for, the judge shall forthwith announce the judge's decision in open court as to the punishment to be assessed.

(e) Nothing herein contained shall be construed as affecting the admissibility of extraneous offenses on the question of guilt or innocence.

(f) In cases in which the matter of punishment is referred to a jury, either party may offer into evidence the availability of community corrections facilities serving the jurisdiction in which the offense was committed.

(g) On timely request of the defendant, notice of intent to introduce evidence under this article shall be given in the same manner required by Rule 404(b), Texas Rules of Evidence. If the attorney representing the state intends to introduce an extraneous crime or bad act that has not resulted in a final conviction in a court of record or a probated or suspended sentence, notice of that intent is reasonable only if the notice includes the date on which and the county in which the alleged crime or bad act occurred and the name of the alleged victim of the crime or bad act. The requirement under this subsection that the attorney representing the state give notice applies only if the defendant makes a timely request to the attorney representing the state for the notice.

(h) Regardless of whether the punishment will be assessed by the judge or the jury, neither the state nor the defendant may offer before sentencing evidence that the defendant plans to undergo an orchiectomy.

(i) Evidence of an adjudication for conduct that is a violation of a penal law of the grade of misdemeanor punishable by confinement in jail is admissible only if the conduct upon which the adjudication is based occurred on or after January 1, 1996.

Sec. 4. (a) In the penalty phase of the trial of a felony case in which the punishment is to be assessed by the jury rather than the court, if the offense of which the jury has found the defendant guilty is an offense under Section 71.02, Penal Code, other than an offense punishable as a state jail felony under that section, an offense under Section 71.023, Penal Code, or an offense listed in Article 42A.054(a), or if the judgment contains an affirmative finding under Article 42A.054(c) or (d), unless the defendant has been convicted of an offense under Section 21.02, Penal Code, an offense under Section 22.021, Penal Code, that is punishable under Subsection (f) of that section, or a capital felony, the court shall charge the jury in writing as follows:

"Under the law applicable in this case, the defendant, if sentenced to a term of imprisonment, may earn time off the period of incarceration imposed through the award of good conduct time. Prison authorities may award good conduct time to a prisoner who exhibits good behavior, diligence in carrying out prison work assignments, and attempts at rehabilitation. If a prisoner engages in misconduct, prison authorities may also take away all or part of any good conduct time earned by the prisoner.

"It is also possible that the length of time for which the defendant will be imprisoned might be reduced by the award of parole.

"Under the law applicable in this case, if the defendant is sentenced to a term of imprisonment, the defendant will not become eligible for parole until the actual time served equals one-half of the sentence imposed or 30 years, whichever is less, without consideration of any good conduct time the defendant may earn. If the defendant is sentenced to a term of less than four years, the defendant must serve at least two years before the defendant is eligible for parole. Eligibility for parole does not guarantee that parole will be granted.

"It cannot accurately be predicted how the parole law and good conduct time might be applied to this defendant if sentenced to a term of imprisonment, because the application of these laws will depend on decisions made by prison and parole authorities.

"You may consider the existence of the parole law and good conduct time. However, you are not to consider the extent to which good conduct time may be awarded to or forfeited by this particular defendant. You are not to consider the manner in which the parole law may be applied to this particular defendant."

(b) In the penalty phase of the trial of a felony case in which the punishment is to be assessed by the jury rather than the court, if the offense is punishable as a felony of the first degree, if a prior conviction has been alleged for enhancement of punishment as provided by Section 12.42(b), (c)(1) or (2), or (d), Penal Code, or if the offense is a felony not designated as a capital felony or a felony of the first, second, or third degree and the maximum term of imprisonment that may be imposed for the offense is longer than 60 years, unless the offense of which the jury has found the defendant guilty is an offense that is punishable under Section 21.02(h), Penal Code, or is listed in Article 42A.054(a) or the judgment contains an affirmative finding under Article 42A.054(c) or (d), the court shall charge the jury in writing as follows:

"Under the law applicable in this case, the defendant, if sentenced to a term of imprisonment, may earn time off the period of incarceration imposed through the award of good conduct time. Prison authorities may award good conduct time to a prisoner who exhibits good behavior, diligence in carrying out prison work assignments, and attempts at rehabilitation. If a prisoner engages in misconduct, prison authorities may also take away all or part of any good conduct time earned by the prisoner.

"It is also possible that the length of time for which the defendant will be imprisoned might be reduced by the award of parole.

"Under the law applicable in this case, if the defendant is sentenced to a term of imprisonment, he will not become eligible for parole until the actual time served plus any good conduct time earned equals one-fourth of the sentence imposed or 15 years, whichever is less. Eligibility for parole does not guarantee that parole will be granted.

"It cannot accurately be predicted how the parole law and good conduct time might be applied to this defendant if he is sentenced to a term of imprisonment, because the application of these laws will depend on decisions made by prison and parole authorities.

"You may consider the existence of the parole law and good conduct time. However, you are not to consider the extent to which good conduct time may be awarded to or forfeited by this particular defendant. You are not to consider the manner in which the parole law may be applied to this particular defendant."

(c) In the penalty phase of the trial of a felony case in which the punishment is to be assessed by the jury rather than the court, if the offense is punishable as a felony of the second or third degree, if a prior conviction has been alleged for enhancement as provided by Section 12.42(a), Penal Code, or if the offense is a felony not designated as a capital felony or a felony of the first, second, or third degree and the maximum term of imprisonment that may be imposed for the offense is 60 years or less, unless the offense of which the jury has found the defendant guilty is listed in Article 42A.054(a) or the judgment contains an affirmative finding under Article 42A.054(c) or (d), the court shall charge the jury in writing as follows:

"Under the law applicable in this case, the defendant, if sentenced to a term of imprisonment, may earn time off the period of incarceration imposed through the award of good conduct time. Prison authorities may award good conduct time to a prisoner who exhibits good behavior, diligence in carrying out prison work assignments, and attempts at rehabilitation. If a prisoner engages in misconduct, prison authorities may also take away all or part of any good conduct time earned by the prisoner.

"It is also possible that the length of time for which the defendant will be imprisoned might be reduced by the award of parole.

"Under the law applicable in this case, if the defendant is sentenced to a term of imprisonment, he will not become eligible for parole until the actual time served plus any good conduct time earned equals one-fourth of the sentence imposed. Eligibility for parole does not guarantee that parole will be granted.

"It cannot accurately be predicted how the parole law and good conduct time might be applied to this defendant if he is sentenced to a term of imprisonment, because the application of these laws will depend on decisions made by prison and parole authorities.

"You may consider the existence of the parole law and good conduct time. However, you are not to consider the extent to which good conduct time may be awarded to or forfeited by this particular defendant. You are not to consider the manner in which the parole law may be applied to this particular defendant."

(d) This section does not permit the introduction of evidence on the operation of parole and good conduct time laws.

Acts 1965, 59th Leg., vol. 2, p. 317, ch. 722. Amended by Acts 1967, 60th Leg., p. 1739, ch. 659, § 22, eff. Aug. 28, 1967; Acts 1973, 63rd Leg., p. 971, ch. 399, § 2(A), eff. Jan. 1, 1974; Acts 1973, 63rd Leg., p. 1126, ch. 426, art. 3, § 2, eff. June 14, 1973; Acts 1981, 67th Leg., p. 2466, ch. 639, § 1, eff. Sept. 1, 1981; Acts 1985, 69th Leg., ch. 291, § 1, eff. Sept. 1, 1985; 1985, 69th Leg., ch. 685, § 8(b), eff. Aug. 26, 1985; Acts 1985, 69th Leg., ch. 576, § 1, eff. Sept. 1, 1985; Acts 1987, 70th Leg., ch. 179, § 2, eff. Aug. 31, 1987; Acts 1987, 70th Leg., ch. 385, § 19, eff. Sept. 1, 1987; Acts 1987, 70th Leg., ch. 386, § 1, eff. Sept. 1, 1987; Acts 1987, 70th Leg., ch. 66, § 1, eff. May 6, 1987; Acts 1987, 70th Leg., ch. 1101, § 15, eff. Sept. 1, 1987; Acts 1989, 71st Leg., ch. 103, § 1; Acts 1989, 71st Leg., ch. 785, § 4.04, eff. Sept. 1, 1989; Acts 1990, 71st Leg., 6th C.S., ch. 25, § 30, eff. June 18, 1990; Acts 1993, 73rd Leg., ch. 900, § 5.05, eff. Sept. 1, 1993; Acts 1993, 73rd Leg., ch. 900, § 5.01, eff. Sept. 1, 1993; Acts 1993, 73rd Leg., ch. 900, § 5.06, eff. Sept. 1, 1993; Acts 1993, 73rd Leg., ch. 900, § 5.02, eff. Sept. 1, 1993; by Acts 1995, 74th Leg., ch. 262, § 82, eff. Jan. 1, 1996; Acts 1997, 75th Leg., ch. 1086, § 31, eff. Sept. 1, 1997; Acts 1997, 75th Leg., ch. 144, § 2, eff. May 20, 1997; Acts 1997, 75th Leg., ch. 1086, § 31, eff. Sept. 1, 1997; Acts 1999, 76th Leg., ch. 62, § 19.01(7), eff. Sept. 1, 1999; Acts 2001, 77th Leg., ch. 585, § 1, eff. Sept. 1, 2001; Acts 2005, 79th Leg., ch. 660, § 1, eff. Sept. 1, 2005; Acts 2005, 79th Leg., ch. 660, § 1 eff. Sept. 1, 2005; Acts 2005, 79th Leg., ch. 660, § 2, eff. Sept. 1, 2005; Acts 2005, 79th Leg., ch. 728, § 4.003, eff. Sept. 1, 2005; Acts 2007, 80th Leg., ch. 593, §§ 3.14, 3.15 eff. Sept. 1, 2007; Acts 2011, 82nd Leg., ch. 620 (S.B. 688), § 3, eff. Sept. 1, 2011; Acts 2013, 83rd Leg., ch. 1325 (S.B. 549), § 1, eff. Sept. 1, 2013; Acts 2015, 84th Leg., ch. 770 (H.B. 2299), §§ 2.07, 2.08, eff. Jan. 1, 2017.

Art. 37.071.   Procedure in capital case

Sec. 1.   If a defendant is found guilty in a capital felony case in which the state does not seek the death penalty, the judge shall sentence the defendant to life imprisonment or to life imprisonment without parole as required by Section 12.31, Penal Code.

Sec. 2.   (a)(1) If a defendant is tried for a capital offense in which the state seeks the death penalty, on a finding that the defendant is guilty of a capital offense, the court shall conduct a separate sentencing proceeding to determine whether the defendant shall be sentenced to death or life imprisonment without parole. The proceeding shall be conducted in the trial court and, except as provided by Article 44.29(c) of this code, before the trial jury as soon as practicable. In the proceeding, evidence may be presented by the state and the defendant or the defendant's counsel as to any matter that the court deems relevant to sentence, including evidence of the defendant's background or character or the circumstances of the offense that mitigates against the imposition of the death penalty. This subdivision shall not be construed to authorize the introduction of any evidence secured in violation of the Constitution of the United States or of the State of Texas. The state and the defendant or the defendant's counsel shall be permitted to present argument for or against sentence of death. The introduction of evidence of extraneous conduct is governed by the notice requirements of Section 3(g), Article 37.07. The court, the attorney representing the state, the defendant, or the defendant's counsel may not inform a juror or a prospective juror of the effect of a failure of a jury to agree on issues submitted under Subsection (c) or (e).

(2) Notwithstanding Subdivision (1), evidence may not be offered by the state to establish that the race or ethnicity of the defendant makes it likely that the defendant will engage in future criminal conduct.

(b) On conclusion of the presentation of the evidence, the court shall submit the following issues to the jury:

(1) whether there is a probability that the defendant would commit criminal acts of violence that would constitute a continuing threat to society; and

(2) in cases in which the jury charge at the guilt or innocence stage permitted the jury to find the defendant guilty as a party under Sections 7.01 and 7.02, Penal Code, whether the defendant actually caused the death of the deceased or did not actually cause the death of the deceased but intended to kill the deceased or another or anticipated that a human life would be taken.

(c) The state must prove each issue submitted under Subsection (b) of this article beyond a reasonable doubt, and the jury shall return a special verdict of "yes" or "no" on each issue submitted under Subsection (b) of this Article.

(d) The court shall charge the jury that:

(1) in deliberating on the issues submitted under Subsection (b) of this article, it shall consider all evidence admitted at the guilt or innocence stage and the punishment stage, including evidence of the defendant's background or character or the circumstances of the offense that militates for or mitigates against the imposition of the death penalty;

(2) it may not answer any issue submitted under Subsection (b) of this article "yes" unless it agrees unanimously and it may not answer any issue "no" unless 10 or more jurors agree; and

(3) members of the jury need not agree on what particular evidence supports a negative answer to any issue submitted under Subsection (b) of this article.

(e)(1) The court shall instruct the jury that if the jury returns an affirmative finding to each issue submitted under Subsection (b), it shall answer the following issue:

Whether, taking into consideration all of the evidence, including the circumstances of the offense, the defendant's character and background, and the personal moral culpability of the defendant, there is a sufficient mitigating circumstance or circumstances to warrant that a sentence of life imprisonment without parole rather than a death sentence be imposed.

(2) The court shall:

(A) instruct the jury that if the jury answers that a circumstance or circumstances warrant that a sentence of life imprisonment without parole rather than a death sentence be imposed, the court will sentence the defendant to imprisonment in the Texas Department of Criminal Justice for life without parole; and

(B) charge the jury that a defendant sentenced to confinement for life without parole under this article is ineligible for release from the department on parole.

(f) The court shall charge the jury that in answering the issue submitted under Subsection (e) of this article, the jury:

(1) shall answer the issue "yes" or "no";

(2) may not answer the issue "no" unless it agrees unanimously and may not answer the issue "yes" unless 10 or more jurors agree;

(3) need not agree on what particular evidence supports an affirmative finding on the issue; and

(4) shall consider mitigating evidence to be evidence that a juror might regard as reducing the defendant's moral blameworthiness.

(g) If the jury returns an affirmative finding on each issue submitted under Subsection (b) and a negative finding on an issue submitted under Subsection (e)(1), the court shall sentence the defendant to death. If the jury returns a negative finding on any issue submitted under Subsection (b) or an affirmative finding on an issue submitted under Subsection (e)(1) or is unable to answer any issue submitted under Subsection (b) or (e), the court shall sentence the defendant to confinement in the Texas Department of Criminal Justice for life imprisonment without parole.

(h) The judgment of conviction and sentence of death shall be subject to automatic review by the Court of Criminal Appeals.

(i) This article applies to the sentencing procedure in a capital case for an offense that is committed on or after September 1, 1991. For the purposes of this section, an offense is committed on or after September 1, 1991, if any element of that offense occurs on or after that date.

Added by Acts 1973, 63rd Leg., p. 1125, ch. 426, art. 3, § 1, eff. June 14, 1973. Amended by Acts 1981, 67th Leg., p. 2673, ch. 725, § 1, eff. Aug. 31, 1981; Acts 1985, 69th Leg., ch. 44, § 2, eff. Sept. 1, 1985; Acts 1991, 72nd Leg., ch. 652, § 9, eff. Sept. 1, 1991; Acts 1991, 72nd Leg., ch. 838, § 1, eff. Sept. 1, 1991; Acts 1993, 73rd Leg., ch. 781, § 1, eff. Aug. 30, 1993; Acts 1999, 76th Leg., ch. 140, § 1, eff. Sept. 1, 1999; Acts 2001, 77th Leg., ch. 585, § 2, eff. Sept. 1, 2001; Acts 2005, 79th Leg., ch. 787, § 6, eff. Sept. 1, 2005; Acts 2005, 79th Leg., ch. 399, § 1, eff. Sept. 1, 2005; Acts 2005, 79th Leg., ch. 787, § 7, eff. Sept. 1, 2005; Acts 2005, 79th Leg., ch. 787, § 8, eff. Sept. 1, 2005; Acts 2005, 79th Leg., ch. 787, § 9, eff. Sept. 1, 2005; Acts 2009, 81st Leg., ch. 87, §§ 25.015, 25.016, eff. Sept. 1, 2009; Acts 2013, 83rd Leg., 2nd C.S., ch. 2 (S.B. 2), § 2, eff. July 22, 2013.

Art. 37.0711. Procedure in capital case for offense committed before September 1, 1991

Sec. 1. This article applies to the sentencing procedure in a capital case for an offense that is committed before September 1, 1991, whether the sentencing procedure is part of the original trial of the offense, an award of a new trial for both the guilt or innocence stage and the punishment stage of the trial, or an award of a new trial only for the punishment stage of the trial. For the purposes of this section, an offense is committed before September 1, 1991, if every element of the offense occurs before that date.

Sec. 2. If a defendant is found guilty in a case in which the state does not seek the death penalty, the judge shall sentence the defendant to life imprisonment.

Sec. 3. (a)(1) If a defendant is tried for a capital offense in which the state seeks the death penalty, on a finding that the defendant is guilty of a capital offense, the court shall conduct a separate sentencing proceeding to determine whether the defendant shall be sentenced to death or life imprisonment. The proceeding shall be conducted in the trial court and, except as provided by Article 44.29(c) of this code, before the trial jury as soon as practicable. In the proceeding, evidence may be presented as to any matter that the court deems relevant to sentence. This subdivision shall not be construed to authorize the introduction of any evidence secured in violation of the Constitution of the United States or of this state. The state and the defendant or the defendant's counsel shall be permitted to present argument for or against sentence of death.

(2) Notwithstanding Subdivision (1), evidence may not be offered by the state to establish that the race or ethnicity of the defendant makes it likely that the defendant will engage in future criminal conduct.

(b) On conclusion of the presentation of the evidence, the court shall submit the following three issues to the jury:

(1) whether the conduct of the defendant that caused the death of the deceased was committed deliberately and with the reasonable expectation that the death of the deceased or another would result;

(2) whether there is a probability that the defendant would commit criminal acts of violence that would constitute a continuing threat to society; and

(3) if raised by the evidence, whether the conduct of the defendant in killing the deceased was unreasonable in response to the provocation, if any, by the deceased.

(c) The state must prove each issue submitted under Subsection (b) of this section beyond a reasonable doubt, and the jury shall return a special verdict of "yes" or "no" on each issue submitted.

(d) The court shall charge the jury that:

(1) it may not answer any issue submitted under Subsection (b) of this section "yes" unless it agrees unanimously; and

(2) it may not answer any issue submitted under Subsection (b) of this section "no" unless 10 or more jurors agree.

(e) The court shall instruct the jury that if the jury returns an affirmative finding on each issue submitted under Subsection (b) of this section, it shall answer the following issue:

Whether, taking into consideration all of the evidence, including the circumstances of the offense, the defendant's character and background, and the personal moral culpability of the defendant, there is a sufficient mitigating circumstance or circumstances to warrant that a sentence of life imprisonment rather than a death sentence be imposed.

(f) The court shall charge the jury that, in answering the issue submitted under Subsection (e) of this section, the jury:

(1) shall answer the issue "yes" or "no";

(2) may not answer the issue "no" unless it agrees unanimously and may not answer the issue "yes" unless 10 or more jurors agree; and

(3) shall consider mitigating evidence that a juror might regard as reducing the defendant's moral blameworthiness.

(g) If the jury returns an affirmative finding on each issue submitted under Subsection (b) and a negative finding on the issue submitted under Subsection (e), the court shall sentence the defendant to death. If the jury returns a negative finding on any issue submitted under Subsection (b) or an affirmative finding on the issue submitted under Subsection (e) or is unable to answer any issue submitted under Subsection (b) or (e), the court shall sentence the defendant to confinement in the Texas Department of Criminal Justice for life.

(h) If a defendant is convicted of an offense under Section 19.03(a)(7), Penal Code, the court shall submit the issues under Subsections (b) and (e) of this section only with regard to the conduct of the defendant in murdering the deceased individual first named in the indictment.

(i) The court, the attorney for the state, or the attorney for the defendant may not inform a juror or prospective juror of the effect of failure of the jury to agree on an issue submitted under this article.

(j) The Court of Criminal Appeals shall automatically review a judgment of conviction and sentence of death not later than the 60th day after the date of certification by the sentencing court of the entire record, unless the Court of Criminal Appeals extends the time for an additional period not to exceed 30 days for good cause shown. Automatic review under this subsection has priority over all other cases before the Court of Criminal Appeals, and the court shall hear automatic reviews under rules adopted by the court for that purpose.

Added by Acts 1993, 73rd Leg., ch. 781, § 2, eff. Aug. 30, 1993. Amended by Acts 1995, 74th Leg., ch. 76, § 14.22, eff. Sept. 1, 1995; Acts 2001, 77th Leg., ch. 585, § 3, eff. Sept. 1, 2001; Acts 2009, 81st Leg., ch. 87, § 25.017, eff. Sept. 1, 2009.

Art. 37.072. Procedure in Repeat Sex Offender Capital Case

Sec. 1. If a defendant is found guilty in a capital felony case punishable under Section 12.42(c)(3), Penal Code, in which the state does not seek the death penalty, the judge shall sentence the defendant to life imprisonment without parole.

Sec. 2. (a)(1) If a defendant is tried for an offense punishable under Section 12.42(c)(3), Penal Code, in which the state seeks the death penalty, on a finding that the defendant is guilty of a capital offense, the court shall conduct a separate sentencing proceeding to determine whether the defendant shall be sentenced to death or life imprisonment without parole. The proceeding shall be conducted in the trial court and, except as provided by Article 44.29(d) of this code, before the trial jury as soon as practicable. In the proceeding, evidence may be presented by the state and the defendant or the defendant's counsel as to any matter that the court considers relevant to sentence, including evidence of the defendant's background or character or the circumstances of the offense that mitigates against the imposition of the death penalty. This subdivision may not be construed to authorize the introduction of any evidence secured in violation of the Constitution of the United States or of the State of Texas. The state and the defendant or the defendant's counsel shall be permitted to present argument for or against sentence of death. The introduction of evidence of extraneous conduct is governed by the notice requirements of Section 3(g), Article 37.07. The court, the attorney representing the state, the defendant, or the defendant's counsel may not inform a juror or a prospective juror of the effect of a failure of a jury to agree on issues submitted under Subsection (b) or (e).

(2) Notwithstanding Subdivision (1), evidence may not be offered by the state to establish that the race or ethnicity of the defendant makes it likely that the defendant will engage in future criminal conduct.

(b) On conclusion of the presentation of the evidence, the court shall submit the following issues to the jury:

(1) whether there is a probability that the defendant would commit criminal acts of violence that would constitute a continuing threat to society; and

(2) in cases in which the jury charge at the guilt or innocence stage permitted the jury to find the defendant guilty as a party under Sections 7.01 and 7.02, Penal Code, whether the defendant actually engaged in the conduct prohibited by Section 22.021, Penal Code, or did not actually engage in the conduct prohibited by Section 22.021, Penal Code, but intended that the offense be committed against the victim or another intended victim.

(c) The state must prove beyond a reasonable doubt each issue submitted under Subsection (b) of this section, and the jury shall return a special verdict of "yes" or "no" on each issue submitted under Subsection (b) of this section.

(d) The court shall charge the jury that:

(1) in deliberating on the issues submitted under Subsection (b) of this section, it shall consider all evidence admitted at the guilt or innocence stage and the punishment stage, including evidence of the defendant's background or character or the circumstances of the offense that militates for or mitigates against the imposition of the death penalty;

(2) it may not answer any issue submitted under Subsection (b) of this section "yes" unless it agrees unanimously and it may not answer any issue "no" unless 10 or more jurors agree; and

(3) members of the jury need not agree on what particular evidence supports a negative answer to any issue submitted under Subsection (b) of this section.

(e)(1) The court shall instruct the jury that if the jury returns an affirmative finding to each issue submitted under Subsection (b), it shall answer the following issue:

Whether, taking into consideration all of the evidence, including the circumstances of the offense, the defendant's character and background, and the personal moral culpability of the defendant, there is a sufficient mitigating circumstance or circumstances to

warrant that a sentence of life imprisonment without parole rather than a death sentence be imposed.

(2) The court shall:

(A) instruct the jury that if the jury answers that a circumstance or circumstances warrant that a sentence of life imprisonment without parole rather than a death sentence be imposed, the court will sentence the defendant to imprisonment in the Texas Department of Criminal Justice for life without parole; and

(B) charge the jury that a defendant sentenced to confinement for life without parole under this article is ineligible for release from the department on parole.

(f) The court shall charge the jury that in answering the issue submitted under Subsection (e) of this section, the jury:

(1) shall answer the issue "yes" or "no";

(2) may not answer the issue "no" unless it agrees unanimously and may not answer the issue "yes" unless 10 or more jurors agree;

(3) need not agree on what particular evidence supports an affirmative finding on the issue; and

(4) shall consider mitigating evidence to be evidence that a juror might regard as reducing the defendant's moral blameworthiness.

(g) If the jury returns an affirmative finding on each issue submitted under Subsection (b) and a negative finding on an issue submitted under Subsection (e)(1), the court shall sentence the defendant to death. If the jury returns a negative finding on any issue submitted under Subsection (b) or an affirmative finding on an issue submitted under Subsection (e)(1) or is unable to answer any issue submitted under Subsection (b) or (e), the court shall sentence the defendant to imprisonment in the Texas Department of Criminal Justice for life without parole.

(h) The judgment of conviction and sentence of death shall be subject to automatic review by the Court of Criminal Appeals.

Added by Acts 2007, 80th Leg., ch. 593, § 1.04, eff. Sept. 1, 2007.

Art. 37.073. Repayment of Rewards

(a) After a defendant has been convicted of a felony offense, the judge may order a defendant to repay all or part of a reward paid by a crime stoppers organization.

(b) In determining whether the defendant must repay the reward or part of the reward, the court shall consider:

(1) the ability of the defendant to make the payment and the financial hardship on the defendant to make the required payment; and

(2) the importance of the information to the prosecution of the defendant as provided by the arresting officer or the attorney for the state with due regard for the confidentiality of the crime stoppers organization records.

(c) In this article, "crime stoppers organization" means a crime stoppers organization, as defined by Subdivision (2), Section 414.001, Government Code, that is approved by the Texas Crime Stoppers Council to receive payments of rewards under this article and Article 42.152.

Added by Acts 1989, 71st Leg., ch. 611, § 1, eff. Sept. 1, 1989. Renumbered from art. 37.072 by Acts 1991, 72nd Leg., ch. 16, § 19.01(5), eff. Aug. 26, 1991. Amended by Acts 1997, 75th Leg., ch. 700, § 10, eff. Sept. 1, 1997; Acts 2009, 81st Leg., ch. 168, § 4, eff. May 27, 2009.

Art. 37.08. Conviction of lesser included offense

In a prosecution for an offense with lesser included offenses, the jury may find the defendant not guilty of the greater offense, but guilty of any lesser included offense.

Acts 1965, 59th Leg., vol. 2, p. 317, ch. 722. Amended by Acts 1973, 63rd Leg., p. 972, ch. 399, § 2(A), eff. Jan. 1, 1974.

Art. 37.09. Lesser included offense

An offense is a lesser included offense if:

(1) it is established by proof of the same or less than all the facts required to establish the commission of the offense charged;

(2) it differs from the offense charged only in the respect that a less serious injury or risk of injury to the same person, property, or public interest suffices to establish its commission;

(3) it differs from the offense charged only in the respect that a less culpable mental state suffices to establish its commission; or

(4) it consists of an attempt to commit the offense charged or an otherwise included offense.

Acts 1965, 59th Leg., vol. 2, p. 317, ch. 722. Amended by Acts 1973, 63rd Leg., p. 972, ch. 399, § 2(A), eff. Jan. 1, 1974.

Art. 37.10. Informal verdict

(a) If the verdict of the jury is informal, its attention shall be called to it, and with its consent the verdict may, under the direction of the court, be reduced to the proper form. If the jury refuses to have the verdict altered, it shall again retire to its room to deliberate, unless it manifestly appear that the verdict is intended as an acquittal; and in that case, the judgment shall be rendered accordingly, discharging the defendant.

(b) If the jury assesses punishment in a case and in the verdict assesses both punishment that is authorized by law for the offense and punishment that is not authorized by law for the offense, the court shall reform the verdict to show the punishment authorized by law and to omit the punishment not authorized by law. If the trial court is required to reform a verdict under this subsection and fails to do so, the appellate court shall reform the verdict as provided by this subsection.

Acts 1965, 59th Leg., vol. 2, p. 317, ch. 722. Amended by Acts 1985, 69th Leg., ch. 442, § 1, eff. June 11, 1985.

Art. 37.11. Defendants tried jointly

Where several defendants are tried together, the jury may convict each defendant it finds guilty and acquit others. If it agrees to a verdict as to one or more, it may find a verdict in accordance with such agreement, and if it cannot agree as to others, a mistrial may be entered as to them.

Acts 1965, 59th Leg., vol. 2, p. 317, ch. 722.

Art. 37.12. Judgment on verdict

On each verdict of acquittal or conviction, the proper judgment shall be entered immediately. If acquitted, the defendant shall be at once discharged from all further liability upon the charge for which he was tried; provided that, in misdemeanor cases where there is returned a verdict, or a plea of guilty is entered and the punishment assessed is by fine only, the court may, on written request of the defendant and for good cause shown, defer judgment until some other day fixed by order of the court; but in no event shall the judgment be deferred for a longer period of time than six months. On expiration of the time fixed by the order of the court, the court or judge thereof, shall enter judgment on the verdict or plea and the same shall be executed as provided by Chapter 43 of this Code. Provided further, that the court or judge thereof, in the exercise of sound discretion may permit the defendant where judgment is deferred, to remain at large on his personal bond, or may require him to enter into bail bond in a sum at least double the amount of the assessed fine and costs, conditioned that the defendant and sureties, jointly and severally, will pay such fine and costs unless the defendant personally appears on the day, set in the order and discharges the judgment in the manner provided by Chapter 43 of this Code; and for the enforcement of any judgment entered, all writs, processes and remedies of this Code are made applicable so far as necessary to carry out the provisions of this Article.

Acts 1965, 59th Leg., vol. 2, p. 317, ch. 722.

Art. 37.13. If jury believes accused insane

When a jury has been impaneled to assess the punishment upon a plea of guilty, it shall say in its verdict what the punishment is which it assesses; but if it is of the opinion that a person pleading guilty is insane, it shall so report to the court, and an issue as to that fact shall be tried before another jury; and if, upon such trial, it be found that the defendant is insane, such proceedings shall be had as directed in cases where a defendant becomes insane after conviction.

Acts 1965, 59th Leg., vol. 2, p. 317, ch. 722.

Art. 37.14. Acquittal of higher offense as jeopardy

If a defendant, prosecuted for an offense which includes within it lesser offenses, be convicted of an offense lower than that for which he is indicted, and a new trial be granted him, or the judgment be arrested for any cause other than the want of jurisdiction, the verdict upon the first trial shall be considered an acquittal of the higher offense; but he may, upon a second trial, be convicted of the same offense of which he was before convicted, or any other inferior thereto.

Acts 1965, 59th Leg., vol. 2, p. 317, ch. 722.

Art. 37.15. Expired

CHAPTER THIRTY–EIGHT. EVIDENCE IN CRIMINAL ACTIONS

Article
38.50. Retention and preservation of toxicological evidence of certain intoxication offenses.

Art. 38.01. Texas Forensic Science Commission

Creation

Sec. 1. The Texas Forensic Science Commission is created.

Definitions

Sec. 2. In this article:

(1) "Accredited field of forensic science" means a specific forensic method or methodology validated or approved by the commission under this article.

(2) "Commission" means the Texas Forensic Science Commission.

(3) "Crime laboratory" has the meaning assigned by Article 38.35.

(4) "Forensic analysis" means a medical, chemical, toxicologic, ballistic, or other expert examination or test performed on physical evidence, including DNA evidence, for the purpose of determining the connection of the evidence to a criminal action, except that the term does not include the portion of an autopsy conducted by a medical examiner or other forensic pathologist who is a licensed physician.

(5) "Office of capital and forensic writs" means the office of capital and forensic writs established under Subchapter B, Chapter 78, Government Code.[1]

(6) "Physical evidence" has the meaning assigned by Article 38.35.

Composition

Sec. 3. (a) The commission is composed of nine members appointed by the governor as follows:

(1) two members who must have expertise in the field of forensic science;

(2) one member who must be a prosecuting attorney that the governor selects from a list of 10 names submitted by the Texas District and County Attorneys Association;

(3) one member who must be a defense attorney that the governor selects from a list of 10 names submitted by the Texas Criminal Defense Lawyers Association;

(4) one member who must be a faculty member or staff member of The University of Texas who specializes in clinical laboratory medicine that the governor selects from a list of five names submitted by the chancellor of The University of Texas System;

(5) one member who must be a faculty member or staff member of Texas A&M University who specializes in clinical laboratory medicine that the governor selects from a list of five names submitted by the chancellor of The Texas A&M University System;

(6) one member who must be a faculty member or staff member of Texas Southern University that the governor selects from a list of five names submitted by the chancellor of Texas Southern University;

(7) one member who must be a director or division head of the University of North Texas Health Science Center at Fort Worth Missing Persons DNA Database; and

(8) one member who must be a faculty or staff member of the Sam Houston State University College of Criminal Justice and have expertise in the field of forensic science or statistical analyses that the governor selects from a list of five names submitted by the chancellor of the Texas State University System.

(b) Each member of the commission serves a two-year term. The terms expire on September 1 of:

(1) each odd-numbered year, for a member appointed under Subsection (a)(1), (2), (3), or (4); and

(2) each even-numbered year, for a member appointed under Subsection (a)(5), (6), (7), or (8).

(c) The governor shall designate a member of the commission to serve as the presiding officer.

Rules

Sec. 3–a. The commission shall adopt rules necessary to implement this article.

Duties

Sec. 4. (a) The commission shall:

(1) develop and implement a reporting system through which a crime laboratory may report professional negligence or professional misconduct;

(2) require a crime laboratory that conducts forensic analyses to report professional negligence or professional misconduct to the commission; and

(3) investigate, in a timely manner, any allegation of professional negligence or professional misconduct that would substantially affect the integrity of the results of a forensic analysis conducted by a crime laboratory.

(a–1) The commission may initiate for educational purposes an investigation of a forensic analysis without receiving a complaint, submitted through the reporting system implemented under Subsection (a)(1), that contains an allegation of professional negligence or professional misconduct involving the forensic analysis conducted if the commission determines by a majority vote of a quorum of the members of the commission that an investigation of the forensic analysis would advance the integrity and reliability of forensic science in this state.

(b) If the commission conducts an investigation under Subsection (a)(3) of a crime laboratory that is accredited under this article pursuant to an allegation of professional negligence or professional misconduct involving an accredited field of forensic science, the investigation:

(1) must include the preparation of a written report that identifies and also describes the methods and procedures used to identify:

(A) the alleged negligence or misconduct;

(B) whether negligence or misconduct occurred;

(C) any corrective action required of the laboratory, facility, or entity;

(D) observations of the commission regarding the integrity and reliability of the forensic analysis conducted;

(E) best practices identified by the commission during the course of the investigation; and

(F) other recommendations that are relevant, as determined by the commission; and

(2) may include one or more:

(A) retrospective reexaminations of other forensic analyses conducted by the laboratory, facility, or entity that may involve the same kind of negligence or misconduct; and

(B) follow-up evaluations of the laboratory, facility, or entity to review:

(i) the implementation of any corrective action required under Subdivision (1)(C); or

(ii) the conclusion of any retrospective reexamination under Paragraph (A).

(b–1) If the commission conducts an investigation under Subsection (a)(3) of a crime laboratory that is not accredited under this article or the investigation is conducted pursuant to an allegation involving a forensic method or methodology that is not an accredited field of forensic science, the investigation may include the preparation of a written report that contains:

(1) observations of the commission regarding the integrity and reliability of the forensic analysis conducted;

(2) best practices identified by the commission during the course of the investigation; or

(3) other recommendations that are relevant, as determined by the commission.

(b–2) If the commission conducts an investigation of a forensic analysis under Subsection (a–1), the investigation must include the preparation of a written report that contains:

(1) observations of the commission regarding the integrity and reliability of the forensic analysis conducted;

(2) best practices identified by the commission during the course of the investigation; and

(3) other recommendations that are relevant, as determined by the commission.

(c) The commission by contract may delegate the duties described by Subsections (a)(1) and (3) to any person the commission determines to be qualified to assume those duties.

(d) The commission may require that a crime laboratory investigated under this section pay any costs incurred to ensure compliance with Subsection (b), (b–1), or (b–2).

(e) The commission shall make all investigation reports completed under Subsection (b), (b–1), or (b–2) available to the public. A report completed under Subsection (b), (b–1), or (b–2), in a subsequent civil or criminal proceeding, is not prima facie evidence of the information or findings contained in the report.

(f) The commission may not make a determination of whether professional negligence or professional misconduct occurred or issue a finding on that question in an investigation initiated under Subsection (a–1) or for which an investigation report may be prepared under Subsection (b–1).

(g) The commission may not issue a finding related to the guilt or innocence of a party in an underlying civil or criminal trial involving conduct investigated by the commission under this article.

(h) The commission may review and refer cases that are the subject of an investigation under Subsection (a)(3) or (a–1) to the office of capital and forensic writs in accordance with Section 78.054(b), Government Code.

Forensic analyst licensing

Sec. 4–a. (a) Notwithstanding Section 2, in this section:

(1) "Forensic analysis" has the meaning assigned by Article 38.35.

(2) "Forensic analyst" means a person who on behalf of a crime laboratory accredited under this article technically reviews or performs a forensic analysis or draws conclusions from or interprets a forensic analysis for a court or crime laboratory. The term does not include a medical examiner or other forensic pathologist who is a licensed physician.

Text of Sec. 4–a(b) effective January 1, 2019

(b) A person may not act or offer to act as a forensic analyst unless the person holds a forensic analyst license. The commission by rule may establish classifications of forensic analyst licenses if the commission determines that it is necessary to ensure the availability of properly trained and qualified forensic analysts to perform activities regulated by the commission.

(c) The commission by rule may establish voluntary licensing programs for forensic disciplines that are not subject to accreditation under this article.

(d) The commission by rule shall:

(1) establish the qualifications for a license that include:

(A) successful completion of the education requirements established by the commission;

(B) specific course work and experience, including instruction in courtroom testimony and ethics in a crime laboratory;

(C) successful completion of an examination required or recognized by the commission; and

(D) successful completion of proficiency testing to the extent required for crime laboratory accreditation;

(2) set fees for the issuance and renewal of a license; and

(3) establish the term of a forensic analyst license.

(e) The commission by rule may recognize a certification issued by a national organization in an accredited field of forensic science as satisfying the requirements established under Subsection (d)(1)(C) to the extent the commission determines the content required to receive the certification is substantially equivalent to the content of the requirements under that subsection.

(f) The commission shall issue a license to an applicant who:

(1) submits an application on a form prescribed by the commission;

(2) meets the qualifications established by commission rule; and

(3) pays the required fee.

Advisory committee

Sec. 4–b. (a) The commission shall establish an advisory committee to advise the commission and make recommendations on matters related to the licensing of forensic analysts under Section 4–a.

(b) The advisory committee consists of nine members as follows:

(1) one prosecuting attorney recommended by the Texas District and County Attorneys Association;

(2) one defense attorney recommended by the Texas Criminal Defense Lawyers Association; and

(3) seven members who are forensic scientists, crime laboratory directors, or crime laboratory quality managers, selected by the commission from a list of 20 names submitted by the Texas Association of Crime Laboratory Directors.

(c) The commission shall ensure that appointments under Subsection (b)(3) include representation from municipal, county, state, and private crime laboratories that are accredited under this article.

(d) The advisory committee members serve staggered two-year terms, with the terms of four or five members, as appropriate, expiring on August 31 of each year. An advisory committee member may not serve more than two consecutive terms. A vacancy on the advisory committee is filled by appointing a member in the same manner as the original appointment to serve for the unexpired portion of the term.

(e) The advisory committee shall elect a presiding officer from among its members to serve a one-year term. A member may serve more than one term as presiding officer.

(f) The advisory committee shall meet annually and at the call of the presiding officer or the commission.

(g) An advisory committee member is not entitled to compensation. A member is entitled to reimbursement for actual and necessary expenses incurred in performing duties as a member of the advisory committee subject to the General Appropriations Act.

(h) Chapter 2110, Government Code, does not apply to the advisory committee.

Disciplinary action

Sec. 4–c. (a) On a determination by the commission that a license holder has committed professional misconduct under this article or violated this article or a rule or order of the commission under this article, the commission may:

(1) revoke or suspend the person's license;

(2) refuse to renew the person's license; or

(3) reprimand the license holder.

(b) The commission may place on probation a person whose license is suspended. If a license suspension is probated, the commission may require the license holder to:

(1) report regularly to the commission on matters that are the basis of the probation; or

(2) continue or review continuing professional education until the license holder attains a degree of skill satisfactory to the commission in those areas that are the basis of the probation.

(c) Disciplinary proceedings of the commission are governed by Chapter 2001, Government Code. A hearing under this section shall be conducted by an administrative law judge of the State Office of Administrative Hearings.

Crime laboratory accreditation process

Sec. 4–d. (a) Notwithstanding Section 2, in this section "forensic analysis" has the meaning assigned by Article 38.35.

(b) The commission by rule:

(1) shall establish an accreditation process for crime laboratories and other entities conducting forensic analyses of physical evidence for use in criminal proceedings; and

(2) may modify or remove a crime laboratory exemption under this section if the commission determines that the underlying reason for the exemption no longer applies.

(b–1) As part of the accreditation process established and implemented under Subsection (b), the commission may:

(1) establish minimum standards that relate to the timely production of a forensic analysis to the agency requesting the analysis and that are consistent with this article and applicable laws;

(2) validate or approve specific forensic methods or methodologies; and

(3) establish procedures, policies, and practices to improve the quality of forensic analyses conducted in this state.

(b–2) The commission may require that a laboratory, facility, or entity required to be accredited under this section pay any costs incurred to ensure compliance with the accreditation process.

(b–3) A laboratory, facility, or entity that must be accredited under this section shall, as part of the accreditation process, agree to consent to any request for cooperation by the commission that is made as part of the exercise of the commission's duties under this article.

(c) The commission by rule may exempt from the accreditation process established under Subsection (b) a crime laboratory conducting a forensic analysis or a type of analysis, examination, or test if the commission determines that:

(1) independent accreditation is unavailable or inappropriate for the laboratory or the type of analysis, examination, or test performed by the laboratory;

(2) the type of analysis, examination, or test performed by the laboratory is admissible under a well-established rule of evidence or a statute other than Article 38.35;

(3) the type of analysis, examination, or test performed by the laboratory is routinely conducted outside of a crime laboratory by a person other than an employee of the crime laboratory; or

(4) the laboratory:

(A) is located outside this state or, if located in this state, is operated by a governmental entity other than the state or a political subdivision of the state; and

(B) was accredited at the time of the analysis under an accreditation process with standards that meet or exceed the relevant standards of the process established under Subsection (b).

(d) The commission may at any reasonable time enter and inspect the premises or audit the records, reports, procedures, or other quality assurance matters of a crime laboratory that is accredited or seeking accreditation under this section.

(e) The commission may collect costs incurred under this section for accrediting, inspecting, or auditing a crime laboratory.

(f) If the commission provides a copy of an audit or other report made under this section, the commission may charge $6 for the copy, in addition to any other cost permitted under Chapter 552, Government Code, or a rule adopted under that chapter.

Reimbursement

Sec. 5. A member of the commission may not receive compensation but is entitled to reimbursement for the member's travel expenses as provided by Chapter 660, Government Code, and the General Appropriations Act.

Assistance

Sec. 6. The Texas Legislative Council, the Legislative Budget Board, and The University of Texas at Austin shall assist the commission in performing the commission's duties.

Submission

Sec. 7. The commission shall submit any report received under Section 4(a)(2) and any report prepared under Section 4(b)(1) to the governor, the lieutenant governor, and the speaker of the house of representatives not later than December 1 of each even-numbered year.

Annual Report

Sec. 8. Not later than December 1 of each year, the commission shall prepare and publish a report that includes:

(1) a description of each complaint filed with the commission during the preceding 12–month period, the disposition of each complaint, and the status of any complaint still pending on December 31;

(2) a description of any specific forensic method or methodology the commission designates as part of the accreditation process for crime laboratories established by rule under this article;

(3) recommendations for best practices concerning the definition of "forensic analysis" provided by statute or by rule;

(4) developments in forensic science made or used in other state or federal investigations and the activities of the commission, if any, with respect to those developments; and

(5) other information that is relevant to investigations involving forensic science, as determined by the presiding officer of the commission.

Administrative attachment to Office of Court Administration

Sec. 9. (a) The commission is administratively attached to the Office of Court Administration of the Texas Judicial System.

(b) The Office of Court Administration of the Texas Judicial System shall provide administrative support to the commission as necessary to enable the commission to carry out the purposes of this article.

(c) Only the commission may exercise the duties of the commission under this article. Except as provided by Subsection (b), the Office of Court Administration of the Texas Judicial System does not have any authority or responsibility with respect to the duties of the commission under this article.

Open records limitation

Sec. 10. Information that is filed as part of an allegation of professional misconduct or professional negligence or that is obtained during an investigation of an allegation of professional misconduct or professional negligence is not subject to release under Chapter 552, Government Code, until the conclusion of an investigation by the commission under Section 4.

Report inadmissible as evidence

Sec. 11. A written report prepared by the commission under this article is not admissible in a civil or criminal action.

Collection of certain forensic evidence

Sec. 12. The commission shall establish a method for collecting DNA and other forensic evidence related to unidentified bodies located less than 120 miles from the Rio Grande River.

Texas Forensic Science Commission operating account

Sec. 13. The Texas Forensic Science Commission operating account is an account in the general revenue fund. The commission shall deposit fees collected under Section 4-a for the issuance or renewal of a forensic analyst license to the credit of the account. Money in the account may be appropriated only to the commission for the administration and enforcement of this article.

Added by Acts 2003, 78th Leg., ch. 698, § 4, eff. June 20, 2003; Acts 2005, 79th Leg., ch. 1224, § 1, eff. Sept. 1, 2005. Amended by Acts 2005, 79th Leg., ch. 1224, § 3, eff. Sept. 1, 2005; Acts 2013, 83rd Leg., ch. 782 (S.B.1238), §§ 1 to 4, 6, eff. June 14, 2013; Acts 2015, 84th Leg., ch. 1215 (S.B. 1743), §§ 8, 9, eff. Sept. 1, 2015; Acts 2015, 84th Leg., ch. 1276 (S.B. 1287), §§ 1 to 3, 5 to 7, eff. Sept. 1, 2015; Acts 2015, 84th Leg., ch. 1276 (S.B. 1287), § 4. Redesignated Sec. 4–d from V.T.C.A., Government Code § 411.0205 by Acts 2015, 84th Leg., ch. 1276 (S.B. 1287), § 5, eff. Sept. 1, 2015. Amended by Acts 2017, 85th Leg., ch. 212 (S.B. 1124), § 1, eff. Sept. 1, 2017; Acts 2017, 85th Leg., ch. 324 (S.B. 1488), § 24.001(4), eff. Sept.1, 2017; Acts 2017, 85th Leg., ch. 1115 (S.B. 298), § 1, eff. Sept. 1, 2017.

[1] V.T.C.A., Government Code § 78.051 et seq.

Sections 14 and 17 of Acts 2015, 84th Leg., ch. 1276 (S.B. 1287) provide:

"Sec. 14. On the effective date of this Act:

"(1) a certificate of accreditation issued by the Department of Public Safety under former Section 411.0205, Government Code, is continued in effect as a certificate of accreditation of the Texas Forensic Science Commission; and

"(2) an application or proceeding before the Department of Public Safety under former Section 411.0205, Government Code, that is pending on the effective date of this Act is transferred without change in status to the Texas Forensic Science Commission."

"Sec. 17. (a) Except as provided by Subsection (b) of this section, this Act takes effect September 1, 2015.

"(b) Section 4–a(b), Article 38.01, Code of Criminal Procedure, as added by this Act, takes effect January 1, 2019."

Art. 38.02. Effect Under Public Information Law of Release of Certain Information

A release of information by an attorney representing the state to defense counsel for a purpose relating to the pending or reasonably anticipated prosecution of a criminal case is not considered a voluntary release of information to the public for purposes of Section 552.007, Government Code, and does not waive the right to assert in the future that the information is excepted from required disclosure under Chapter 552, Government Code.

Added by Acts 2009, 81st Leg., ch. 630, § 1, eff. June 19, 2009.

Art. 38.03. Presumption of innocence

All persons are presumed to be innocent and no person may be convicted of an offense unless each element of the offense is proved beyond a reasonable doubt. The fact that he has been arrested, confined, or indicted for, or otherwise charged with, the offense gives rise to no inference of guilt at his trial.

Acts 1965, 59th Leg., vol. 2, p. 317, ch. 722. Amended by Acts 1981, 67th Leg., p. 2247, ch. 539, § 1, eff. June 12, 1981.

Art. 38.04. Jury are judges of facts

The jury, in all cases, is the exclusive judge of the facts proved, and of the weight to be given to the testimony, except where it is provided by law that proof of any particular fact is to be taken as either conclusive or presumptive proof of the existence of another fact, or where the law directs that a certain degree of weight is to be attached to a certain species of evidence.

Acts 1965, 59th Leg., vol. 2, p. 317, ch. 722.

Art. 38.05. Judge shall not discuss evidence

In ruling upon the admissibility of evidence, the judge shall not discuss or comment upon the weight of the same or its bearing in the case, but shall simply decide whether or not it is admissible; nor shall he, at any stage of the proceeding previous to the return of the verdict, make any remark calculated to convey to the jury his opinion of the case.

Acts 1965, 59th Leg., vol. 2, p. 317, ch. 722.

Art. 38.06. Repealed by Texas Rules of Criminal Evidence effective September 1, 1986 [Acts 1985, 69th Leg., ch. 685, § 9(b)]

Art. 38.07. Testimony in Corroboration of Victim of Sexual Offense

(a) A conviction under Chapter 21, Section 20A.02(a)(3), (4), (7), or (8), Section 22.011, or Section 22.021, Penal Code, is supportable on the uncorroborated testimony of the victim of the sexual offense if the victim informed any person, other than the defendant, of the alleged offense within one year after the date on which the offense is alleged to have occurred.

(b) The requirement that the victim inform another person of an alleged offense does not apply if at the time of the alleged offense the victim was a person:

(1) 17 years of age or younger;

(2) 65 years of age or older; or

(3) 18 years of age or older who by reason of age or physical or mental disease, defect, or injury was substantially unable to satisfy the person's need for food, shelter, medical care, or protection from harm.

Added by Acts 1975, 64th Leg., p. 479, ch. 203, § 6, eff. Sept. 1, 1975. Amended by Acts 1983, 68th Leg., p. 2090, ch. 382, § 1, eff. Sept. 1, 1983; Acts 1983, 68th Leg., p. 5317, ch. 977, § 7, eff. Sept. 1, 1983; Acts 1993, 73rd Leg., ch. 200, § 1, eff. May 19, 1993; Acts 1993, 73rd Leg., ch. 900, § 12.01, eff. Sept. 1, 1993; Acts 2001, 77th Leg., ch. 1018, § 1, eff. Sept. 1, 2001; Acts 2011, 82nd Leg., ch. 1 (S.B. 24), § 2.05, eff. Sept. 1, 2011.

Art. 38.071. Testimony of child who is victim of offense

Sec. 1. This article applies only to a hearing or proceeding in which the court determines that a child younger than 13 years of age would be unavailable to testify in the presence of the defendant about an offense defined by any of the following sections of the Penal Code:

(1) Section 19.02 (Murder);

(2) Section 19.03 (Capital Murder);

(3) Section 19.04 (Manslaughter);

(4) Section 20.04 (Aggravated Kidnapping);

(5) Section 21.11 (Indecency with a Child);

(6) Section 22.011 (Sexual Assault);

(7) Section 22.02 (Aggravated Assault);

(8) Section 22.021 (Aggravated Sexual Assault);

(9) Section 22.04(e) (Injury to a Child, Elderly Individual, or Disabled Individual);

(10) Section 22.04(f) (Injury to a Child, Elderly Individual, or Disabled Individual), if the conduct is committed intentionally or knowingly;

(11) Section 25.02 (Prohibited Sexual Conduct);

(12) Section 29.03 (Aggravated Robbery);

(13) Section 43.25 (Sexual Performance by a Child);

(14) Section 21.02 (Continuous Sexual Abuse of Young Child or Children);

(15) Section 43.05(a)(2) (Compelling Prostitution); or

(16) Section 20A.02(a)(7) or (8) (Trafficking of Persons).

Sec. 2. (a) The recording of an oral statement of the child made before the indictment is returned or the complaint has been filed is admissible into evidence if the court makes a determination that the factual issues of identity or actual occurrence were fully and fairly inquired into in a detached manner by a neutral individual experienced in child abuse cases that seeks to find the truth of the matter.

(b) If a recording is made under Subsection (a) of this section and after an indictment is returned or a complaint has been filed, by motion of the attorney representing the state or the attorney representing the defendant and on the approval of the court, both attorneys may propound written interrogatories that shall be presented by the same neutral individual who made the initial inquiries, if possible, and recorded under the same or similar circumstances of the original recording with the time and date of the inquiry clearly indicated in the recording.

(c) A recording made under Subsection (a) of this section is not admissible into evidence unless a recording made under Subsection (b) is admitted at the same time if a recording under Subsection (b) was requested prior to the time of the hearing or proceeding.

Sec. 3. (a) On its own motion or on the motion of the attorney representing the state or the attorney representing the defendant, the court may order that the testimony of the child be taken in a room other than the courtroom and be televised by closed circuit equipment in the courtroom to be viewed by the court and the finder of fact. To the extent practicable, only the judge, the court reporter, the attorneys for the defendant and for the state, persons necessary to operate the equipment, and any person whose presence would contribute to the welfare and well-being of the child may be present in the room with the child during his testimony. Only the attorneys and the judge may question the child. To the extent practicable, the persons necessary to operate the equipment shall be confined to an adjacent room or behind a screen or mirror that permits them to see and hear the child during his testimony, but does not permit the child to see or hear them. The court shall permit the defendant to observe and hear the testimony of the child and to communicate contemporaneously with his attorney during periods of recess or by audio contact, but the court shall attempt to ensure that the child cannot hear or see the defendant. The court shall permit the attorney for the defendant adequate opportunity to confer with the defendant during cross-examination of the child. On application of the attorney for the defendant, the court may recess the proceeding before or during cross-examination of the child for a reasonable time to allow the attorney for the defendant to confer with defendant.

(b) The court may set any other conditions and limitations on the taking of the testimony that it finds just and appropriate, taking into consideration the interests of the child, the rights of the defendant, and any other relevant factors.

Sec. 4. (a) After an indictment has been returned or a complaint filed, on its own motion or on the motion of the attorney representing the state or the attorney representing the defendant, the court may order that the testimony of the child be taken outside the courtroom and be recorded for showing in the courtroom before the court and the finder of fact. To the extent practicable, only those persons permitted to be present at the taking of testimony under Section 3 of this article may be present during the taking of the child's testimony, and the persons operating the equipment shall be confined from the child's sight and hearing as provided by Section 3. The court shall permit the defendant to observe and hear the testimony of the child and to communicate contemporaneously with his attorney during periods of recess or by audio contact but shall attempt to ensure that the child cannot hear or see the defendant.

(b) The court may set any other conditions and limitations on the taking of the testimony that it finds just and appropriate, taking into consideration the interests of the child, the rights of the defendant, and any other relevant factors. The court shall also ensure that:

(1) the recording is both visual and aural and is recorded on film or videotape or by other electronic means;

(2) the recording equipment was capable of making an accurate recording, the operator was competent, the quality of the recording is sufficient to allow the court and the finder of fact to assess the demeanor of the child and the interviewer, and the recording is accurate and is not altered;

(3) each voice on the recording is identified;

(4) the defendant, the attorneys for each party, and the expert witnesses for each party are afforded an opportunity to view the recording before it is shown in the courtroom;

(5) before giving his testimony, the child was placed under oath or was otherwise admonished in a manner appropriate to the child's age and maturity to testify truthfully;

(6) the court finds from the recording or through an in camera examination of the child that the child was competent to testify at the time the recording was made; and

(7) only one continuous recording of the child was made or the necessity for pauses in the recordings or for multiple recordings is established at the hearing or proceeding.

(c) After a complaint has been filed or an indictment returned charging the defendant, on the motion of the attorney representing the state, the court may order that the deposition of the child be taken outside of the courtroom in the same manner as a deposition may be taken in a civil matter. A deposition taken under this subsection is admissible into evidence.

Sec. 5. (a) On the motion of the attorney representing the state or the attorney representing the defendant and on a finding by the court that the following requirements have been substantially satisfied, the recording of an oral statement of the child made before a complaint has been filed or an indictment returned is admissible into evidence if:

(1) no attorney or peace officer was present when the statement was made;

(2) the recording is both visual and aural and is recorded on film or videotape or by other electronic means;

(3) the recording equipment was capable of making an accurate recording, the operator of the equipment was competent, the quality of the recording is sufficient to allow the court and the finder of fact to assess the demeanor of the child and the interviewer, and the recording is accurate and has not been altered;

(4) the statement was not made in response to questioning calculated to lead the child to make a particular statement;

(5) every voice on the recording is identified;

(6) the person conducting the interview of the child in the recording is expert in the handling, treatment, and investigation of child abuse cases, present at the hearing or proceeding, called by the state, and subject to cross-examination;

(7) immediately after a complaint was filed or an indictment returned, the attorney representing the state notified the court, the defendant, and the attorney representing the defendant of the existence of the recording;

(8) the defendant, the attorney for the defendant, and the expert witnesses for the defendant were afforded an opportunity to view the recording before it is offered into evidence and, if a proceeding was requested as provided by Subsection (b) of this section, in a proceeding conducted before a district court judge but outside the presence of the jury were afforded an opportunity to cross-examine the child as provided by Subsection (b) of this section from any time immediately following the filing of the complaint or the returning of an indictment charging the defendant until the date the hearing or proceeding begins;

(9) the recording of the cross-examination, if there is one, is admissible under Subsection (b) of this section;

(10) before giving his testimony, the child was placed under oath or was otherwise admonished in a manner appropriate to the child's age and maturity to testify truthfully;

(11) the court finds from the recording or through an in camera examination of the child that the child was competent to testify at the time that the recording was made; and

(12) only one continuous recording of the child was made or the necessity for pauses in the recordings or for multiple recordings has been established at the hearing or proceeding.

(b) On the motion of the attorney representing the defendant, a district court may order that the cross-examination of the child be taken and be recorded before the judge of that court at any time until a recording made in accordance with Subsection (a) of this section has been introduced into evidence at the hearing or proceeding. On a finding by the court that the following requirements were satisfied, the recording of the cross-examination of the child is admissible into evidence and shall be viewed by the finder of fact only after the finder of fact has viewed the recording authorized by Subsection (a) of this section if:

(1) the recording is both visual and aural and is recorded on film or videotape or by other electronic means;

(2) the recording equipment was capable of making an accurate recording, the operator of the equipment was competent, the quality of the recording is sufficient to allow the court and the finder of fact to assess the demeanor of the child and the attorney representing the defendant, and the recording is accurate and has not been altered;

(3) every voice on the recording is identified;

(4) the defendant, the attorney representing the defendant, the attorney representing the state, and the expert witnesses for the defendant and the state were afforded an opportunity to view the recording before the hearing or proceeding began;

(5) the child was placed under oath before the cross-examination began or was otherwise admonished in a manner appropriate to the child's age and maturity to testify truthfully; and

(6) only one continuous recording of the child was made or the necessity for pauses in the recordings or for multiple recordings was established at the hearing or proceeding.

(c) During cross-examination under Subsection (b) of this section, to the extent practicable, only a district court judge, the attorney representing the defendant, the attorney representing the state, persons necessary to operate the equipment, and any other person whose presence would contribute to the welfare and well-being of the child may be present in the room with the child during his testimony. Only the attorneys and the judge may question the child. To the extent practicable, the persons operating the equipment shall be confined to an adjacent room or behind a screen or mirror that permits them to see and hear the child during his testimony but does not permit the child to see or hear them. The court shall permit the defendant to observe and hear the testimony of the child and to communicate contemporaneously with his attorney during periods of recess or by audio contact, but shall attempt to ensure that the child cannot hear or see the defendant.

(d) Under Subsection (b) of this section the district court may set any other conditions and limitations on the taking of the cross-examination of a child that it finds just and appropriate, taking into consideration the interests of the child, the rights of the defendant, and any other relevant factors.

Sec. 6. If the court orders the testimony of a child to be taken under Section 3 or 4 of this article or if the court finds the testimony of the child taken under Section 2 or 5 of this article is admissible into evidence, the child may not be required to testify in court at the proceeding for which the testimony was taken, unless the court finds there is good cause.

Sec. 7. In making any determination of good cause under this article, the court shall consider the rights of the defendant, the interests of the child, the relationship of the defendant to the child, the character and duration of the alleged offense, any court finding related to the availability of the child to testify, the age, maturity, and emotional stability of the child, the time elapsed since the alleged offense, and any other relevant factors.

Sec. 8. (a) In making a determination of unavailability under this article, the court shall consider relevant factors including the relationship of the defendant to the child, the character and duration of the alleged offense, the age, maturity, and emotional stability of the child, and the time elapsed since the alleged offense, and whether the child is more likely than not to be unavailable to testify because:

(1) of emotional or physical causes, including the confrontation with the defendant; or

(2) the child would suffer undue psychological or physical harm through his involvement at the hearing or proceeding.

(b) A determination of unavailability under this article can be made after an earlier determination of availability. A determination of availability under this article can be made after an earlier determination of unavailability.

Sec. 9. If the court finds the testimony taken under Section 2 or 5 of this article is admissible into evidence or if the court orders the testimony to be taken under Section 3 or 4 of this article and if the identity of the perpetrator is a contested issue, the child additionally must make an in-person identification of the defendant either at or before the hearing or proceeding.

Sec. 10. In ordering a child to testify under this article, the court shall take all reasonable steps necessary and available to minimize undue psychological trauma to the child and to minimize the emotional and physical stress to the child caused by relevant factors, including the confrontation with the defendant and the ordinary participation of the witness in the courtroom.

Sec. 11. In a proceeding under Section 2, 3, or 4 or Subsection (b) of Section 5 of this article, if the defendant is not represented by counsel and the court finds that the defendant is not able to obtain counsel for the purposes of the proceeding, the court shall appoint counsel to represent the defendant at the proceeding.

Sec. 12. In this article, "cross-examination" has the same meaning as in other legal proceedings in the state.

Sec. 13. The attorney representing the state shall determine whether to use the procedure provided in Section 2 of this article or the procedure provided in Section 5 of this article.

Added by Acts 1983, 68th Leg., p. 3828, ch. 599, § 1, eff. Aug. 29, 1983. Amended by Acts 1987, 70th Leg., ch. 998, § 1, eff. Aug. 31, 1987; Acts 1987, 70th Leg., 2nd C.S., ch. 55, § 1, eff. Oct. 20, 1987; Acts 1991, 72nd Leg., ch. 266, § 1, eff. Sept. 1, 1991; Acts 1995, 74th Leg., ch. 76, § 14.24, eff. Sept. 1, 1995; Acts 2001, 77th Leg., ch. 338, §§ 1 to 8, eff. Sept. 1, 2001; Acts 2007, 80th Leg., ch. 593, § 3.16, eff. Sept. 1, 2007; Acts 2011, 82nd Leg., ch. 1 (S.B. 24), § 2.06, eff. Sept. 1, 2011.

For validity of Sec. 2 of this article see Coronado v. State (Cr.App. 2011) 351 S.W.3rd 315.

Art. 38.072. Hearsay Statement of Certain Abuse Victims

Sec. 1. This article applies to a proceeding in the prosecution of an offense under any of the following provisions of the Penal Code, if committed against a child younger than 14 years of age or a person with a disability:

(1) Chapter 21 (Sexual Offenses) or 22 (Assaultive Offenses);

(2) Section 25.02 (Prohibited Sexual Conduct);

(3) Section 43.25 (Sexual Performance by a Child);

(4) Section 43.05(a)(2) (Compelling Prostitution);

(5) Section 20A.02(a)(7) or (8) (Trafficking of Persons); or

(6) Section 15.01 (Criminal Attempt), if the offense attempted is described by Subdivision (1), (2), (3), (4), or (5) of this section.

Sec. 2. (a) This article applies only to statements that:

(1) describe:

(A) the alleged offense; or

(B) if the statement is offered during the punishment phase of the proceeding, a crime, wrong, or act other than the alleged offense that is:

(i) described by Section 1;

(ii) allegedly committed by the defendant against the child who is the victim of the offense or another child younger than 14 years of age; and

(iii) otherwise admissible as evidence under Article 38.37, Rule 404 or 405, Texas Rules of Evidence, or another law or rule of evidence of this state;

(2) were made by the child or person with a disability against whom the charged offense or extraneous crime, wrong, or act was allegedly committed; and

(3) were made to the first person, 18 years of age or older, other than the defendant, to whom the child or person with a disability made a statement about the offense or extraneous crime, wrong, or act.

(b) A statement that meets the requirements of Subsection (a) is not inadmissible because of the hearsay rule if:

(1) on or before the 14th day before the date the proceeding begins, the party intending to offer the statement:

(A) notifies the adverse party of its intention to do so;

(B) provides the adverse party with the name of the witness through whom it intends to offer the statement; and

(C) provides the adverse party with a written summary of the statement;

(2) the trial court finds, in a hearing conducted outside the presence of the jury, that the statement is reliable based on the time, content, and circumstances of the statement; and

(3) the child or person with a disability testifies or is available to testify at the proceeding in court or in any other manner provided by law.

Sec. 3. In this article, "person with a disability" means a person 13 years of age or older who because of age or physical or mental disease, disability, or injury is substantially unable to protect the person's self from harm or to provide food, shelter, or medical care for the person's self.

Added by Acts 1985, 69th Leg., ch. 590, § 1, eff. Sept. 1, 1985. Amended by Acts 1995, 74th Leg., ch. 76, § 14.25, eff. Sept. 1, 1995; Acts 2009, 81st Leg., ch. 284, § 1, eff. June 11, 2009; Acts 2009, 81st Leg., ch. 710, §§ 1, 2, eff. Sept. 1, 2009; Acts 2011, 82nd Leg., ch. 1 (S.B. 24), § 2.07, eff. Sept. 1, 2011.

Art. 38.073. Testimony of Inmate Witnesses

In a proceeding in the prosecution of a criminal offense in which an inmate in the custody of the Texas Department of Criminal Justice is required to testify as a witness, any deposition or testimony of the inmate witness may be conducted by a video teleconferencing system in the manner described by Article 27.18.

Added by Acts 2001, 77th Leg., ch. 788, § 2, eff. June 14, 2001. Amended by Acts 2011, 82nd Leg., ch. 1031 (H.B. 2847), § 6, eff. Sept. 1, 2011; Acts 2011, 82nd Leg., ch. 1341 (S.B. 1233), § 7, eff. June 17, 2011.

Art. 38.074. Testimony of child in prosecution of offense

Sec. 1. In this article:

(1) "Child" has the meaning assigned by Section 22.011(c), Penal Code.

(2) "Support person" means any person whose presence would contribute to the welfare and well-being of a child.

Sec. 2. This article applies to the testimony of a child in any hearing or proceeding in the prosecution of any offense, other than the testimony of a child in a hearing or proceeding in a criminal case in which that child is the defendant.

Sec. 3. (a) A court shall:

(1) administer an oath to a child in a manner that allows the child to fully understand the child's duty to tell the truth;

(2) ensure that questions asked of the child are stated in language appropriate to the child's age;

(3) explain to the child that the child has the right to have the court notified if the child is unable to understand any question and to have a question restated in a form that the child does understand;

(4) ensure that a child testifies only at a time of day when the child is best able to understand the ques-

tions and to undergo the proceedings without being traumatized, including:

(A) limiting the duration of the child's testimony;

(B) limiting the timing of the child's testimony to the child's normal school hours; or

(C) ordering a recess during the child's testimony when necessary for the energy, comfort, or attention span of the child; and

(5) prevent intimidation or harassment of the child by any party and, for that purpose, rephrase as appropriate any question asked of the child.

(b) On the motion of any party, or a parent, managing conservator, guardian, or guardian ad litem of a child or special advocate for a child, the court shall allow the child to have a toy, blanket, or similar comforting item in the child's possession while testifying or allow a support person to be present in close proximity to the child during the child's testimony if the court finds by a preponderance of the evidence that:

(1) the child cannot reliably testify without the possession of the item or presence of the support person, as applicable; and

(2) granting the motion is not likely to prejudice the trier of fact in evaluating the child's testimony.

(c) A support person who is present during a child's testimony may not:

(1) obscure the child from the view of the defendant or the trier of fact;

(2) provide the child with an answer to any question asked of the child; or

(3) assist or influence the testimony of the child.

(d) The court may set any other conditions and limitations on the taking of the testimony of a child that it finds just and appropriate, considering the interests of the child, the rights of the defendant, and any other relevant factors.

Added by Acts 2011, 82nd Leg., ch. 1227 (S.B. 578), § 1, eff. Sept. 1, 2011.

Art. 38.075. Corroboration of Certain Testimony Required

(a) A defendant may not be convicted of an offense on the testimony of a person to whom the defendant made a statement against the defendant's interest during a time when the person was imprisoned or confined in the same correctional facility as the defendant unless the testimony is corroborated by other evidence tending to connect the defendant with the offense committed. In this subsection, "correctional facility" has the meaning assigned by Section 1.07, Penal Code.

(b) Corroboration is not sufficient for the purposes of this article if the corroboration only shows that the offense was committed.

(c) Evidence of a prior offense committed by a person who gives testimony described by Subsection (a) may be admitted for the purpose of impeachment if the person received a benefit described by Article 39.14(h–1)(2) with respect to the offense, regardless of whether the person was convicted of the offense.

Added by Acts 2009, 81st Leg., ch. 1422, § 1, eff. Sept. 1, 2009. Amended by Acts 2017, 85th Leg., ch. 686 (H.B. 34), § 3, eff. Sept. 1, 2017.

Section 12 of Acts 2017, 85th Leg., ch. 686 (H.B. 34) provides:

"Article 38.075(c), Code of Criminal Procedure, as added by this Act, applies to the admissibility of evidence in a criminal proceeding that commences on or after the effective date [Sept. 1, 2017] of this Act. The admissibility of evidence in a criminal proceeding that commences before the effective date of this Act is governed by the law in effect on the date the proceeding commenced, and the former law is continued in effect for that purpose."

Art. 38.08.   Defendant may testify

Any defendant in a criminal action shall be permitted to testify in his own behalf therein, but the failure of any defendant to so testify shall not be taken as a circumstance against him, nor shall the same be alluded to or commented on by counsel in the cause.

Acts 1965, 59th Leg., vol. 2, p. 317, ch. 722, eff. Jan. 1, 1966.

Art. 38.09.   Repealed by Texas Rules of Criminal Evidence effective September 1, 1986 [Acts 1985, 69th Leg., ch. 685, § 9(b)]

Art. 38.10.   Exceptions to the Spousal Adverse Testimony Privilege

The privilege of a person's spouse not to be called as a witness for the state does not apply in any proceeding in which the person is charged with:

(1) a crime committed against the person's spouse, a minor child, or a member of the household of either spouse; or

(2) an offense under Section 25.01, Penal Code (Bigamy).

Added by Acts 1995, 74th Leg., ch. 67, § 2, eff. Sept. 1, 1995. Amended by Acts 2005, 79th Leg., ch. 268, § 4.01, eff. Sept. 1, 2005.

Art. 38.101.   Communications by drug abusers

A communication to any person involved in the treatment or examination of drug abusers by a person being treated voluntarily or being examined for admission to voluntary treatment for drug abuse is not admissible. However, information derived from the treatment or examination of drug abusers may be used for statistical and research purposes if the names of the patients are not revealed.

Added by Acts 1971, 62nd Leg., p. 2984, ch. 983, § 2, eff. June 15, 1971.

Art.   38.11.   Journalist's Qualified Testimonial Privilege in Criminal Proceedings
Definitions

Sec. 1.   In this article:

(1) "Communication service provider" means a person or the parent, subsidiary, division, or affiliate of a person who transmits information chosen by a customer by electronic means, including:

(A) a telecommunications carrier, as defined by Section 3, Communications Act of 1934 (47 U.S.C. Section 153);

(B) a provider of information service, as defined by Section 3, Communications Act of 1934 (47 U.S.C. Section 153);

(C) a provider of interactive computer service, as defined by Section 230, Communications Act of 1934 (47 U.S.C. Section 230); and

(D) an information content provider, as defined by Section 230, Communications Act of 1934 (47 U.S.C. Section 230).

(2) "Journalist" means a person, including a parent, subsidiary, division, or affiliate of a person, who for a substantial portion of the person's livelihood or for substantial financial gain, gathers, compiles, prepares, collects, photographs, records, writes, edits, reports, investigates, processes, or publishes news or information that is disseminated by a news medium or communication service provider and includes:

(A) a person who supervises or assists in gathering, preparing, and disseminating the news or information; or

(B) notwithstanding the foregoing, a person who is or was a journalist, scholar, or researcher employed by an institution of higher education at the time the person obtained or prepared the requested information, or a person who at the time the person obtained or prepared the requested information:

(i) is earning a significant portion of the person's livelihood by obtaining or preparing information for dissemination by a news medium or communication service provider; or

(ii) was serving as an agent, assistant, employee, or supervisor of a news medium or communication service provider.

(3) "News medium" means a newspaper, magazine or periodical, book publisher, news agency, wire service, radio or television station or network, cable, satellite, or other transmission system or carrier or channel, or a channel or programming service for a station, network, system, or carrier, or an audio or audiovisual production company or Internet company or provider, or the parent, subsidiary, division, or affiliate of that entity, that disseminates news or information to the public by any means, including:

(A) print;

(B) television;

(C) radio;

(D) photographic;

(E) mechanical;

(F) electronic; and

(G) other means, known or unknown, that are accessible to the public.

(4) "Official proceeding" means any type of administrative, executive, legislative, or judicial proceeding that may be conducted before a public servant.

(5) "Public servant" means a person elected, selected, appointed, employed, or otherwise designated as one of the following, even if the person has not yet qualified for office or assumed the person's duties:

(A) an officer, employee, or agent of government;

(B) a juror or grand juror;

(C) an arbitrator, referee, or other person who is authorized by law or private written agreement to hear or determine a cause or controversy;

(D) an attorney or notary public when participating in the performance of a governmental function; or

(E) a person who is performing a governmental function under a claim of right, although the person is not legally qualified to do so.

Purpose

Sec. 2. The purpose of this article is to increase the free flow of information and preserve a free and active press and, at the same time, protect the right of the public to effective law enforcement and the fair administration of justice.

Privilege

Sec. 3. (a) Except as otherwise provided by this article, a judicial, legislative, administrative, or other body with the authority to issue a subpoena or other compulsory process may not compel a journalist to testify regarding or to produce or disclose in an official proceeding:

(1) any confidential or nonconfidential unpublished information, document, or item obtained or prepared while acting as a journalist; or

(2) the source of any information, document, or item described by Subdivision (1).

(b) A subpoena or other compulsory process may not compel the parent, subsidiary, division, or affiliate of a communication service provider or news medium to disclose the unpublished information, documents, or items or the source of any information, documents, or items that are privileged from disclosure under Subsection (a).

Privilege Concerning Confidential Sources

Sec. 4. (a) A journalist may be compelled to testify regarding or to disclose the confidential source of any information, document, or item obtained while acting as a journalist if the person seeking the testimony, production, or disclosure makes a clear and specific showing that the source of any information, document, or item:

(1) was observed by the journalist committing a felony criminal offense and the subpoenaing party has exhausted reasonable efforts to obtain from alternative sources the confidential source of any information, document, or item obtained or prepared while acting as a journalist;

(2) is a person who confessed or admitted to the journalist the commission of a felony criminal offense and the subpoenaing party has exhausted reasonable efforts to obtain from alternative sources the confidential source of any information, document, or item obtained or prepared while acting as a journalist;

(3) is a person for whom probable cause exists that the person participated in a felony criminal offense and the subpoenaing party has exhausted reasonable efforts to obtain from alternative sources the confidential source of any information, document, or item obtained or prepared while acting as a journalist; or

(4) disclosure of the confidential source is reasonably necessary to stop or prevent reasonably certain death or substantial bodily harm.

(b) If the alleged criminal conduct is the act of communicating, receiving, or possessing the information, document, or item, this section does not apply, and Section 5 governs the act.

(c) Notwithstanding Subsection (b), if the information, document, or item was disclosed or received in violation of a grand jury oath given to either a juror or a witness under Article 19.34 or 20.16, a journalist may be compelled to testify if the person seeking the testimony, production, or disclosure makes a clear and specific showing that the subpoenaing party has exhausted reasonable efforts to obtain from alternative sources the confidential source of any information, document, or item obtained. In this context, the court has the discretion to conduct an in camera hearing. The court may not order the production of the confidential source until a ruling has been made on the motion.

(d) An application for a subpoena of a journalist under Article 24.03, or a subpoena of a journalist issued by an attorney representing the state under Article 20.10 or 20.11, must be signed by the elected district attorney, elected criminal district attorney, or elected county attorney, as applicable. If the elected district attorney, elected criminal district attorney, or elected county attorney has been disqualified or recused or has resigned, the application for the subpoena or the subpoena must be signed by the person succeeding the elected attorney. If the elected officer is not in the jurisdiction, the highest ranking assistant to the elected officer must sign the subpoena.

Privilege Concerning Unpublished Information, Document, or Item and Nonconfidential Sources

Sec. 5. (a) After service of subpoena and an opportunity to be heard, a court may compel a journalist, a journalist's employer, or a person with an independent contract with a journalist to testify regarding or to produce or disclose any unpublished information, document, or item or the source of any information, document, or item obtained while acting as a journalist, other than as described by Section 4, if the person seeking the unpublished information, document, or item or the source of any information, document, or item makes a clear and specific showing that:

(1) all reasonable efforts have been exhausted to obtain the information from alternative sources; and

(2) the unpublished information, document, or item:

(A) is relevant and material to the proper administration of the official proceeding for which the testimony, production, or disclosure is sought and is essential to the maintenance of a claim or defense of the person seeking the testimony, production, or disclosure; or

(B) is central to the investigation or prosecution of a criminal case and based on something other than the assertion of the person requesting the subpoena, reasonable grounds exist to believe that a crime has occurred.

(b) The court, when considering an order to compel testimony regarding or to produce or disclose any unpublished information, document, or item or the source of any information, document, or item obtained while acting as a journalist, should consider the following factors, including but not limited to whether:

(1) the subpoena is overbroad, unreasonable, or oppressive;

(2) reasonable and timely notice was given of the demand for the information, document, or item;

(3) in this instance, the interest of the party subpoenaing the information outweighs the public interest in gathering and dissemination of news, including the concerns of the journalist; and

(4) the subpoena or compulsory process is being used to obtain peripheral, nonessential, or speculative information.

(c) A court may not consider a single factor under Subsection (b) as outcome-determinative in the decision whether to compel the testimony or the production or disclosure of the unpublished information, document, or item, or the source of any information, document, or item.

Notice

Sec. 6. An order to compel testimony, production, or disclosure to which a journalist has asserted a privilege under this article may be issued only after timely notice to the journalist, the journalist's employer, or a person who has an independent contract with the journalist and a hearing. The order must include clear and specific findings as to the showing made by the person seeking the testimony, production, or disclosure and the clear and specific evidence on which the court relied in issuing the court's order.

Publication of Privilege Information

Sec. 7. Publication or dissemination by a news medium or communication service provider of information, documents, or items privileged under this article is not a waiver of the journalist's privilege regarding sources and unpublished information, documents, or items.

Published Information

Sec. 8. This article does not apply to any information, document, or item that has at any time been published or broadcast by the journalist.

Reimbursement of Costs

Sec. 9. The subpoenaing party shall pay a journalist a reasonable fee for the journalist's time and costs incurred in providing the information, item, or document subpoenaed, based on the fee structure provided by Subchapter F, Chapter 552, Government Code.

Added by Acts 2009, 81st Leg., ch. 29, § 2, eff. May 13, 2009.

Art. 38.111.   News Media Recordings

Extrinsic evidence of the authenticity of evidence as a condition precedent to the admissibility of the evidence in a criminal proceeding is not required with respect to a recording that purports to be a broadcast by a radio or television station that holds a license issued by the Federal Communications Commission at the time of the recording.   The court may take judicial notice of the recording license as provided by Rule 201, Texas Rules of Evidence.

Added by Acts 2009, 81st Leg., ch. 29, § 2, eff. May 13, 2009.

Art. 38.12.   Religious opinion

No person is incompetent to testify on account of his religious opinion or for the want of any religious belief.

Acts 1965, 59th Leg., vol. 2, p. 317, ch. 722, eff. Jan. 1, 1966.

Art. 38.13.   Repealed by Texas Rules of Criminal Evidence effective September 1, 1986 [Acts 1985, 69th Leg., ch. 685, § 9(b)]

Art. 38.14.   Testimony of accomplice

A conviction cannot be had upon the testimony of an accomplice unless corroborated by other evidence tending to connect the defendant with the offense committed; and the corroboration is not sufficient if it merely shows the commission of the offense.

Acts 1965, 59th Leg., vol. 2, p. 317, ch. 722, eff. Jan. 1, 1966.

Art. 38.141.   Testimony of Undercover Peace Officer or Special Investigator

(a) A defendant may not be convicted of an offense under Chapter 481, Health and Safety Code, on the testimony of a person who is not a licensed peace officer or a special investigator but who is acting covertly on behalf of a law enforcement agency or under the color of law enforcement unless the testimony is corroborated by other evidence tending to connect the defendant with the offense committed.

(b) Corroboration is not sufficient for the purposes of this article if the corroboration only shows the commission of the offense.

(c) In this article, "peace officer" means a person listed in Article 2.12, and "special investigator" means a person listed in Article 2.122.

Added by Acts 2001, 77th Leg., ch. 1102, § 1, eff. Sept. 1, 2001.

Art. 38.15.   Two witnesses in treason

No person can be convicted of treason except upon the testimony of at least two witnesses to the same overt act, or upon his own confession in open court.

Acts 1965, 59th Leg., vol. 2, p. 317, ch. 722, eff. Jan. 1, 1966.

Art. 38.16.   Evidence in treason

Evidence shall not be admitted in a prosecution for treason as to an overt act not expressly charged in the indictment; nor shall any person be convicted under an indictment for treason unless one or more overt acts are expressly charged therein.

Acts 1965, 59th Leg., vol. 2, p. 317, ch. 722, eff. Jan. 1, 1966.

Art. 38.17.   Two witnesses required

In all cases where, by law, two witnesses, or one with corroborating circumstances, are required to authorize a conviction, if the requirement be not fulfilled, the court shall instruct the jury to render a verdict of acquittal, and they are bound by the instruction.

Acts 1965, 59th Leg., vol. 2, p. 317, ch. 722, eff. Jan. 1, 1966.

Art. 38.18.   Perjury and aggravated perjury

(a) No person may be convicted of perjury or aggravated perjury if proof that his statement is false rests solely upon the testimony of one witness other than the defendant.

(b) Paragraph (a) of this article does not apply to prosecutions for perjury or aggravated perjury involving inconsistent statements.

Acts 1965, 59th Leg., vol. 2, p. 317, ch. 722, eff. Jan. 1, 1966. Amended by Acts 1973, 63rd Leg., p. 973, ch. 399, § 2(A), eff. Jan. 1, 1974.

Art. 38.19.   Intent to defraud in forgery

In trials of forgery, it need not be proved that the defendant committed the act with intent to defraud any particular person. It shall be sufficient to prove that the forgery was, in its nature, calculated to injure or defraud any of the sovereignties, bodies corporate or politic, officers or persons, named in the definition of forgery in the Penal Code.

Acts 1965, 59th Leg., vol. 2, p. 317, ch. 722, eff. Jan. 1, 1966.

Art. 38.20.   Photograph and Live Lineup Identification Procedures

Sec. 1. In this article, "institute" means the Bill Blackwood Law Enforcement Management Institute of Texas located at Sam Houston State University.

Sec. 2. This article applies only to a law enforcement agency of this state or of a county, municipality, or other political subdivision of this state that employs peace officers who conduct photograph or live lineup identification procedures in the routine performance of the officers' official duties.

Sec. 3. (a) Each law enforcement agency shall adopt, implement, and as necessary amend a detailed written policy regarding the administration of photograph and live lineup identification procedures in accordance with this article. A law enforcement agency may adopt:

(1) the model policy adopted under Subsection (b); or

(2) the agency's own policy that, at a minimum, conforms to the requirements of Subsection (c).

(b) The institute, in consultation with large, medium, and small law enforcement agencies and with law enforcement associations, scientific experts in eyewitness memory research, and appropriate organizations engaged in the development of law enforcement policy, shall develop, adopt, and disseminate to all law enforcement agencies in this state a model policy and associated training materials regarding the administration of photograph and live lineup identification procedures. The institute shall provide for a period of public comment before adopting the policy and materials.

(c) The model policy or any other policy adopted by a law enforcement agency under Subsection (a) must:

(1) be based on:

(A) credible field, academic, or laboratory research on eyewitness memory;

(B) relevant policies, guidelines, and best practices designed to reduce erroneous eyewitness identifications and to enhance the reliability and objectivity of eyewitness identifications; and

(C) other relevant information as appropriate; and

(2) include the following information regarding evidence-based practices:

(A) procedures for selecting photograph and live lineup filler photographs or participants to ensure that the photographs or participants:

(i) are consistent in appearance with the description of the alleged perpetrator; and

(ii) do not make the suspect noticeably stand out;

(B) instructions given to a witness before conducting a photograph or live lineup identification procedure that must include a statement that the person who committed the offense may or may not be present in the procedure;

(C) procedures for documenting and preserving the results of a photograph or live lineup identification procedure, including the documentation of witness statements, regardless of the outcome of the procedure;

(D) procedures for administering a photograph or live lineup identification procedure to an illiterate person or a person with limited English language proficiency;

(E) for a live lineup identification procedure, if practicable, procedures for assigning an administrator who is unaware of which member of the live lineup is the suspect in the case or alternative procedures designed to prevent opportunities to influence the witness;

(F) for a photograph identification procedure, procedures for assigning an administrator who is capable of administering a photograph array in a blind manner or in a manner consistent with other proven or supported best practices designed to prevent opportunities to influence the witness; and

(G) any other procedures or best practices supported by credible research or commonly accepted as a means to reduce erroneous eyewitness identifications and to enhance the objectivity and reliability of eyewitness identifications.

(d) A witness who makes an identification based on a photograph or live lineup identification procedure shall be asked immediately after the procedure to state, in the witness's own words, how confident the witness is in making the identification. A law enforcement agency shall document in accordance with Subsection (c)(2)(C) any statement made under this subsection.

Sec. 4. (a) Not later than December 31 of each odd-numbered year, the institute shall review the model policy and training materials adopted under this article and shall modify the policy and materials as appropriate.

(b) Not later than September 1 of each even-numbered year, each law enforcement agency shall review its policy adopted under this article and shall modify that policy as appropriate.

Sec. 5. (a) Any evidence or expert testimony presented by the state or the defendant on the subject of eyewitness identification is admissible only subject to compliance with the Texas Rules of Evidence. Except as provided by Subsection (c), evidence of compliance with the model policy or any other policy adopted under this article is not a condition precedent to the admissibility of an out-of-court eyewitness identification.

(b) Notwithstanding Article 38.23 as that article relates to a violation of a state statute and except as provided by Subsection (c), a failure to conduct a photograph or live lineup identification procedure in substantial compliance with the model policy or any other policy adopted under this article does not bar the admission of eyewitness identification testimony in the courts of this state.

(c) If a witness who has previously made an out-of-court photograph or live lineup identification of the accused makes an in-court identification of the accused, the eyewitness identification is admissible into evidence against the accused only if the evidence is accompanied by the details of each prior photograph or live lineup identification made of the accused by the witness, including the manner in which the identification procedure was conducted.

Added by Acts 2011, 82nd Leg., ch. 219 (H.B. 215), § 1, eff. Sept. 1, 2011. Amended by Acts 2017, 85th Leg., ch. 686 (H.B. 34), §§ 4, 5, eff. Sept. 1, 2017.

Section 13 of Acts 2017, 85th Leg., ch. 686 (H.B. 34) provides:

"(a) Section 3(d), Article 38.20, Code of Criminal Procedure, as added by this Act, applies only to a photograph or live lineup identification procedure conducted on or after the effective date [Sept. 1, 2017] of this Act, regardless of whether the offense to which the procedure is related was committed before, on, or after the effective date of this Act.

"(b) Section 5, Article 38.20, Code of Criminal Procedure, as amended by this Act, applies only to the trial of an offense with respect to which a prior photograph or live lineup identification of the accused occurred on or after the effective date of this Act, regardless of whether the offense that is the subject of the trial was committed before, on, or after the effective date of this Act."

Art. 38.21. Statement

A statement of an accused may be used in evidence against him if it appears that the same was freely and voluntarily made without compulsion or persuasion, under the rules hereafter prescribed.

Acts 1965, 59th Leg., vol. 2, p. 317, ch. 722, eff. Jan. 1, 1966. Amended by Acts 1977, 65th Leg., p. 935, ch. 348, § 1, eff. Aug. 29, 1977.

Art. 38.22. When statements may be used

Sec. 1. In this article, a written statement of an accused means:

(1) a statement made by the accused in his own handwriting; or

(2) a statement made in a language the accused can read or understand that:

(A) is signed by the accused; or

(B) bears the mark of the accused, if the accused is unable to write and the mark is witnessed by a person other than a peace officer.

Sec. 2. No written statement made by an accused as a result of custodial interrogation is admissible as evidence against him in any criminal proceeding unless it is shown on the face of the statement that:

(a) the accused, prior to making the statement, either received from a magistrate the warning provided in Article 15.17 of this code or received from the person to whom the statement is made a warning that:

(1) he has the right to remain silent and not make any statement at all and that any statement he makes may be used against him at his trial;

(2) any statement he makes may be used as evidence against him in court;

(3) he has the right to have a lawyer present to advise him prior to and during any questioning;

(4) if he is unable to employ a lawyer, he has the right to have a lawyer appointed to advise him prior to and during any questioning; and

(5) he has the right to terminate the interview at any time; and

(b) the accused, prior to and during the making of the statement, knowingly, intelligently, and voluntarily waived the rights set out in the warning prescribed by Subsection (a) of this section.

Sec. 3.   (a) No oral or sign language statement of an accused made as a result of custodial interrogation shall be admissible against the accused in a criminal proceeding unless:

(1) an electronic recording, which may include motion picture, video tape, or other visual recording, is made of the statement;

(2) prior to the statement but during the recording the accused is given the warning in Subsection (a) of Section 2 above and the accused knowingly, intelligently, and voluntarily waives any rights set out in the warning;

(3) the recording device was capable of making an accurate recording, the operator was competent, and the recording is accurate and has not been altered;

(4) all voices on the recording are identified; and

(5) not later than the 20th day before the date of the proceeding, the attorney representing the defendant is provided with a true, complete, and accurate copy of all recordings of the defendant made under this article.

(b) Every electronic recording of any statement made by an accused during a custodial interrogation must be preserved until such time as the defendant's conviction for any offense relating thereto is final, all direct appeals therefrom are exhausted, or the prosecution of such offenses is barred by law.

(c) Subsection (a) of this section shall not apply to any statement which contains assertions of facts or circumstances that are found to be true and which conduce to establish the guilt of the accused, such as the finding of secreted or stolen property or the instrument with which he states the offense was committed.

(d) If the accused is a deaf person, the accused's statement under Section 2 or Section 3(a) of this article is not admissible against the accused unless the warning in Section 2 of this article is interpreted to the deaf person by an interpreter who is qualified and sworn as provided in Article 38.31 of this code.

(e) The courts of this state shall strictly construe Subsection (a) of this section and may not interpret Subsection (a) as making admissible a statement unless all requirements of the subsection have been satisfied by the state, except that:

(1) only voices that are material are identified; and

(2) the accused was given the warning in Subsection (a) of Section 2 above or its fully effective equivalent.

Sec. 4.   When any statement, the admissibility of which is covered by this article, is sought to be used in connection with an official proceeding, any person who swears falsely to facts and circumstances which, if true, would render the statement admissible under this article is presumed to have acted with intent to deceive and with knowledge of the statement's meaning for the purpose of prosecution for aggravated perjury under Section 37.03 of the Penal Code. No person prosecuted under this subsection shall be eligible for probation.

Sec. 5.   Nothing in this article precludes the admission of a statement made by the accused in open court at his trial, before a grand jury, or at an examining trial in compliance with Articles 16.03 and 16.04 of this code, or of a statement that is the res gestae of the arrest or of the offense, or of a statement that does not stem from custodial interrogation, or of a voluntary statement, whether or not the result of custodial interrogation, that has a bearing upon the credibility of the accused as a witness, or of any other statement that may be admissible under law.

Sec. 6.   In all cases where a question is raised as to the voluntariness of a statement of an accused, the court must make an independent finding in the absence of the jury as to whether the statement was made under voluntary conditions. If the statement has been found to have been voluntarily made and held admissible as a matter of law and fact by the court in a hearing in the absence of the jury, the court must enter an order stating its conclusion as to whether or not the statement was voluntarily made, along with the specific finding of facts upon which the conclusion was based, which order shall be filed among the papers of the cause. Such order shall not be exhibited to the jury nor the finding thereof made known to the jury in any manner. Upon the finding by the judge as a matter of law and fact that the statement was voluntarily made, evidence pertaining to such matter may be submitted to the jury and it shall be instructed that unless the jury believes beyond a reasonable doubt that the statement was voluntarily made, the jury shall not consider such statement for any purpose nor any evidence obtained as a result thereof. In any case where a motion to suppress the statement has been filed and evidence has been submitted to the court on this issue, the court within its discretion may reconsider such evidence in his finding that the statement was voluntarily made and the same evidence submitted to the court at the hearing on the motion to suppress shall be made a part of the record the same as if it were being presented at the time of trial. However, the state or the defendant shall be entitled to present any new evidence on the issue of the voluntariness of the statement prior to the court's final ruling and order stating its findings.

Sec. 7. When the issue is raised by the evidence, the trial judge shall appropriately instruct the jury, generally, on the law pertaining to such statement.

Sec. 8. Notwithstanding any other provision of this article, a written, oral, or sign language statement of an accused made as a result of a custodial interrogation is admissible against the accused in a criminal proceeding in this state if:

(1) the statement was obtained in another state and was obtained in compliance with the laws of that state or this state; or

(2) the statement was obtained by a federal law enforcement officer in this state or another state and was obtained in compliance with the laws of the United States.

Sec. 9. Notwithstanding any other provision of this article, no oral, sign language, or written statement that is made by a person accused of an offense listed in Article 2.32(b) and made as a result of a custodial interrogation occurring in a place of detention, as that term is defined by Article 2.32, is admissible against the accused in a criminal proceeding unless:

(1) an electronic recording was made of the statement, as required by Article 2.32(b); or

(2) the attorney representing the state offers proof satisfactory to the court that good cause, as described by Article 2.32(d), existed that made electronic recording of the custodial interrogation infeasible.

Acts 1965, 59th Leg., vol. 2, p. 317, ch. 722, eff. Jan. 1, 1966. Amended by Acts 1967, 60th Leg., p. 1740, ch. 659, § 23, eff. Aug. 28, 1967; Acts 1977, 65th Leg., p. 935, ch. 348, § 2, eff. Aug. 29, 1977; 1979, 66th Leg., p. 398, ch. 186, § 4, eff. May 15, 1979; Acts 1979, 66th Leg., p. 398, ch. 186, § 5, eff. May 15, 1979; Acts 1981, 67th Leg., p. 711, ch. 271, § 1, eff. Sept. 1, 1981; Acts 1989, 71st Leg., ch. 777, §§ 1, 2, eff. Sept. 1, 1989; Acts 2001, 77th Leg., ch. 990, § 1, eff. Sept. 1, 2001; Acts 2013, 83rd Leg., ch. 679 (H.B. 2090), § 1, eff. Sept. 1, 2013; Acts 2017, 85th Leg., ch. 686 (H.B. 34), § 6, eff. Sept. 1, 2017; Acts 2017, 85th Leg., ch. 1122 (S.B. 1253), § 2, eff. Sept. 1, 2017.

Section 11 of Acts 2017, 85th Leg., ch. 686 (H.B. 34) provides:

"Article 2.32 and Section 9, Article 38.22, Code of Criminal Procedure, as added by this Act, apply to the use of a statement resulting from a custodial interrogation that occurs on or after March 1, 2018, regardless of whether the criminal offense giving rise to that interrogation is committed before, on, or after that date."

Section 3 of Acts 2017, 85th Leg., ch. 1122 (S.B. 1253) provides:

"Section 9, Article 38.22, Code of Criminal Procedure, as added by this Act, applies to the use of a statement resulting from a custodial interrogation that occurs on or after March 1, 2018, regardless of whether the criminal offense giving rise to that interrogation is committed before, on, or after that date."

Art. 38.23. Evidence not to be used

(a) No evidence obtained by an officer or other person in violation of any provisions of the Constitution or laws of the State of Texas, or of the Constitution or laws of the United States of America, shall be admitted in evidence against the accused on the trial of any criminal case.

In any case where the legal evidence raises an issue hereunder, the jury shall be instructed that if it believes, or has a reasonable doubt, that the evidence was obtained in violation of the provisions of this Article, then and in such event, the jury shall disregard any such evidence so obtained.

(b) It is an exception to the provisions of Subsection (a) of this Article that the evidence was obtained by a law enforcement officer acting in objective good faith reliance upon a warrant issued by a neutral magistrate based on probable cause.

Acts 1965, 59th Leg., vol. 2, p. 317, ch. 722, eff. Jan. 1, 1966. Amended by Acts 1987, 70th Leg., ch. 546, § 1, eff. Sept. 1, 1987.

Art. 38.24. Repealed by Texas Rules of Criminal Evidence effective September 1, 1986 [Acts 1985, 69th Leg., ch. 685, § 9(b)]

Art. 38.25. Written part of instrument controls

When an instrument is partly written and partly printed, the written shall control the printed portion when the two are inconsistent.

Acts 1965, 59th Leg., vol. 2, p. 317, ch. 722, eff. Jan. 1, 1966.

Art. 38.26. Repealed by Texas Rules of Criminal Evidence effective September 1, 1986 [Acts 1985, 69th Leg., ch. 685, § 9(b)]

Art. 38.27. Evidence of handwriting

It is competent to give evidence of handwriting by comparison, made by experts or by the jury. Proof by comparison only shall not be sufficient to establish the handwriting of a witness who denies his signature under oath.

Acts 1965, 59th Leg., vol. 2, p. 317, ch. 722, eff. Jan. 1, 1966.

Arts. 38.28, 38.29. Repealed by Texas Rules of Criminal Evidence effective September 1, 1986 [Acts 1985, 69th Leg., ch. 685, § 9(b)]

Art. 38.30. Interpreter

(a) When a motion for appointment of an interpreter is filed by any party or on motion of the court, in any criminal proceeding, it is determined that a person charged or a witness does not understand and speak the English language, an interpreter must be sworn to interpret for the person charged or the witness. Any person may be subpoenaed, attached or recognized in any criminal action or proceeding, to appear before the proper judge or court to act as interpreter therein, under the same rules and penalties as are provided for witnesses. In the event that the only available interpreter is not considered to possess adequate interpreting skills for the particular situation or the interpreter is not familiar with use of slang, the person charged or witness may be permitted by the court to nominate another person to act as intermediary between the person charged or witness and the appointed interpreter during the proceedings.

(a–1) A qualified telephone interpreter may be sworn to interpret for the person in any criminal proceeding before a judge or magistrate if an interpreter is not available to appear in person at the proceeding or if the only available interpreter is not considered to possess adequate interpreting skills for the particular situation or is unfamiliar with the use of slang. In this subsection, "qualified telephone interpreter" means a telephone service that employs:

(1) licensed court interpreters as defined by Section 157.001, Government Code; or

(2) federally certified court interpreters.

(b) Except as provided by Subsection (c) of this article, interpreters appointed under the terms of this article will receive from the general fund of the county for their services a sum not to exceed $100 a day as follows: interpreters shall be paid not less than $15 nor more than $100 a day at the discretion of the judge presiding, and when travel of the interpreter is involved all the actual expenses of travel, lodging, and meals incurred by the interpreter pertaining to the case the interpreter is appointed to serve shall be paid at the same rate applicable to state employees.

(c) A county commissioners court may set a payment schedule and expend funds for the services of interpreters in excess of the daily amount of not less than $15 or more than $100 established by Subsection (b) of this article.

Acts 1965, 59th Leg., vol. 2, p. 317, ch. 722, eff. Jan. 1, 1966. Amended by Acts 1979, 66th Leg., p. 453, ch. 209, § 1, eff. Aug. 27, 1979; Acts 1991, 72nd Leg., ch. 700, § 1, eff. June 16, 1991; Acts 2005, 79th Leg., ch. 956, § 1, eff. Sept. 1, 2005; Acts 2013, 83rd Leg., ch. 42 (S.B. 966), § 2.01, eff. Sept. 1, 2014; Acts 2015, 84th Leg., ch. 1182 (S.B. 1139), § 8.01, eff. Sept. 1, 2015.

Art. 38.31. Interpreters for deaf persons

(a) If the court is notified by a party that the defendant is deaf and will be present at an arraignment, hearing, examining trial, or trial, or that a witness is deaf and will be called at a hearing, examining trial, or trial, the court shall appoint a qualified interpreter to interpret the proceedings in any language that the deaf person can understand, including but not limited to sign language. On the court's motion or the motion of a party, the court may order testimony of a deaf witness and the interpretation of that testimony by the interpreter visually, electronically recorded for use in verification of the transcription of the reporter's notes. The clerk of the court shall include that recording in the appellate record if requested by a party under Article 40.09 of this Code.

(b) Following the filing of an indictment, information, or complaint against a deaf defendant, the court on the motion of the defendant shall appoint a qualified interpreter to interpret in a language that the defendant can understand, including but not limited to sign language, communications concerning the case between the defendant and defense counsel. The interpreter may not disclose a communication between the defendant and defense counsel or a fact that came to the attention of the interpreter while interpreting those communications if defense counsel may not disclose that communication or fact.

(c) In all cases where the mental condition of a person is being considered and where such person may be committed to a mental institution, and where such person is deaf, all of the court proceedings pertaining to him shall be interpreted by a qualified interpreter appointed by the court.

(d) A proceeding for which an interpreter is required to be appointed under this Article may not commence until the appointed interpreter is in a position not exceeding ten feet from and in full view of the deaf person.

(e) The interpreter appointed under the terms of this Article shall be required to take an oath that he will make a true interpretation to the person accused or being examined, which person is deaf, of all the proceedings of his case in a language that he understands; and that he will repeat said deaf person's answer to questions to counsel, court, or jury, in the English language, in his best skill and judgment.

(f) Interpreters appointed under this Article are entitled to a reasonable fee determined by the court after considering the recommendations of the Texas

Commission for the Deaf and Hard of Hearing. When travel of the interpreter is involved all the actual expenses of travel, lodging, and meals incurred by the interpreter pertaining to the case he is appointed to serve shall be paid at the same rate applicable to state employees.

(g) In this Code:

(1) "Deaf person" means a person who has a hearing impairment, regardless of whether the person also has a speech impairment, that inhibits the person's comprehension of the proceedings or communication with others.

(2) "Qualified interpreter" means an interpreter for the deaf who holds a current legal certificate issued by the National Registry of Interpreters for the Deaf or a current court interpreter certificate issued by the Board for Evaluation of Interpreters at the Department of Assistive and Rehabilitative Services.

Acts 1965, 59th Leg., vol. 2, p. 317, ch. 722, eff. Jan. 1, 1966. Amended by Acts 1967, 60th Leg., p. 195, ch. 105, § 2, eff. Aug. 28, 1967; Acts 1979, 66th Leg., p. 396, ch. 186, § 1, eff. May 15, 1979; Acts 1987, 70th Leg., ch. 434, § 1, eff. June 17, 1987; Acts 1995, 74th Leg., ch. 835, § 14, eff. Sept. 1, 1995; Acts 2005, 79th Leg., ch. 614, § 11, eff. Sept. 1, 2006; Acts 2013, 83rd Leg., ch. 161 (S.B. 1093), § 3.006, eff. Sept. 1, 2013.

Art. 38.32. Presumption of death

(a) Upon introduction and admission into evidence of a valid certificate of death wherein the time of death of the decedent has been entered by a licensed physician, a presumption exists that death occurred at the time stated in the certificate of death.

(b) A presumption existing pursuant to Section (a) of this Article is sufficient to support a finding as to time of death but may be rebutted through a showing by a preponderance of the evidence that death occurred at some other time.

Added by Acts 1969, 61st Leg., p. 1034, ch. 337, § 1, eff. May 27, 1969.

Art. 38.33. Preservation and use of evidence of certain misdemeanor convictions[1]

Sec. 1.   The court shall order that a defendant who is convicted of a felony or a misdemeanor offense that is punishable by confinement in jail have a thumbprint of the defendant's right thumb rolled legibly on the judgment or the docket sheet in the case. The court shall order a defendant who is placed on deferred adjudication community supervision under Subchapter C, Chapter 42A, for an offense described by this section to have a thumbprint of the defendant's right

thumb rolled legibly on the order placing the defendant on deferred adjudication community supervision. If the defendant does not have a right thumb, the defendant must have a thumbprint of the defendant's left thumb rolled legibly on the judgment, order, or docket sheet. The defendant must have a fingerprint of the defendant's index finger rolled legibly on the judgment, order, or docket sheet if the defendant does not have a right thumb or a left thumb. The judgment, order, or docket sheet must contain a statement that describes from which thumb or finger the print was taken, unless a rolled 10–finger print set was taken. A clerk or bailiff of the court or other person qualified to take fingerprints shall take the thumbprint or fingerprint, either by use of the ink-rolled print method or by use of a live-scanning device that prints the thumbprint or fingerprint image on the judgment, order, or docket sheet.

Sec. 2.   This article does not prohibit a court from including in the records of the case additional information to identify the defendant.

Added by Acts 1979, 66th Leg., p. 1851, ch. 751, § 1, eff. Sept. 1, 1979. Amended by Acts 1983, 68th Leg., p. 1586, ch. 303, § 7, eff. Jan. 1, 1984; Acts 1987, 70th Leg., ch. 721, § 1, eff. Sept. 1, 1987; Acts 1989, 71st Leg., ch. 603, § 1, eff. Sept. 1, 1989; Acts 1991, 72nd Leg., 2nd C.S., ch. 10, § 7.01, eff. Dec. 1, 1991; Acts 2015, 84th Leg., ch. 770 (H.B. 2299), § 2.09, eff. Jan. 1, 2017.

[1] So in enrolled bill; article relates to identification by fingerprinting of defendants convicted of involuntary manslaughter while intoxicated and other felony or misdemeanor offenses.

Art. 38.34. Photographic Evidence in Theft Cases

(a) In this article, "property" means any tangible personal property.

(b) A photograph of property that a person is alleged to have unlawfully appropriated with the intent to deprive the owner of the property is admissible into evidence under rules of law governing the admissibility of photographs. The photograph is as admissible in evidence as is the property itself.

(c) The provisions of Article 18.16 concerning the bringing of stolen property before a magistrate for examination are complied with if a photograph of the stolen property is brought before the magistrate.

(d) The defendant's rights of discovery and inspection of tangible physical evidence are satisfied if a photograph of the property is made available to the defendant by the state on order of any court having jurisdiction over the cause.

Added by Acts 1985, 69th Leg., ch. 144, § 1, eff. Sept. 1, 1985. Amended by Acts 2009, 81st Leg., ch. 613, § 1, eff. Sept. 1, 2009.

Art. 38.35. Forensic Analysis of Evidence; Admissibility

(a) In this article:

(1) "Crime laboratory'" includes a public or private laboratory or other entity that conducts a forensic analysis subject to this article.

(2) "Criminal action" includes an investigation, complaint, arrest, bail, bond, trial, appeal, punishment, or other matter related to conduct proscribed by a criminal offense.

(3) "Commission" means the Texas Forensic Science Commission established under Article 38.01.

(4) "Forensic analysis" means a medical, chemical, toxicologic, ballistic, or other expert examination or test performed on physical evidence, including DNA evidence, for the purpose of determining the connection of the evidence to a criminal action. The term includes an examination or test requested by a law enforcement agency, prosecutor, criminal suspect or defendant, or court. The term does not include:

(A) latent print examination;

(B) a test of a specimen of breath under Chapter 724, Transportation Code;

(C) digital evidence;

(D) an examination or test excluded by rule under Article 38.01;

(E) a presumptive test performed for the purpose of determining compliance with a term or condition of community supervision or parole and conducted by or under contract with a community supervision and corrections department, the parole division of the Texas Department of Criminal Justice, or the Board of Pardons and Paroles; or

(F) an expert examination or test conducted principally for the purpose of scientific research, medical practice, civil or administrative litigation, or other purpose unrelated to determining the connection of physical evidence to a criminal action.

(5) "Physical evidence" means any tangible object, thing, or substance relating to a criminal action.

(b) A law enforcement agency, prosecutor, or court may request a forensic analysis by a crime laboratory of physical evidence if the evidence was obtained in connection with the requesting entity's investigation or disposition of a criminal action and the requesting entity:

(1) controls the evidence;

(2) submits the evidence to the laboratory; or

(3) consents to the analysis.

(c) A law enforcement agency, other governmental agency, or private entity performing a forensic analysis of physical evidence may require the requesting law enforcement agency to pay a fee for such analysis.

(d)(1) Except as provided by Subsection (e), a forensic analysis of physical evidence under this article and expert testimony relating to the evidence are not admissible in a criminal action if, at the time of the analysis, the crime laboratory conducting the analysis was not accredited by the commission under Article 38.01.

(2) If before the date of the analysis the commission issues a certificate of accreditation under Article 38.01 to a crime laboratory conducting the analysis, the certificate is prima facie evidence that the laboratory was accredited by the commission at the time of the analysis.

(e) A forensic analysis of physical evidence under this article and expert testimony relating to the evidence are not inadmissible in a criminal action based solely on the accreditation status of the crime laboratory conducting the analysis if the laboratory:

(A) except for making proper application, was eligible for accreditation by the commission at the time of the examination or test; and

(B) obtains accreditation from the commission before the time of testimony about the examination or test.

(f) This article does not apply to the portion of an autopsy conducted by a medical examiner or other forensic pathologist who is a licensed physician.

Added by Acts 1991, 72nd Leg., ch. 298, § 1, eff. Sept. 1, 1991. Amended by Acts 2003, 78th Leg., ch. 698, § 1, eff. June 20, 2003; Acts 2003, 78th Leg., ch. 698, § 2, eff. June 20, 2003; Acts 2003, 78th Leg., ch. 698, § 3, eff. June 20, 2003; Acts 2005, 79th Leg., ch. 1224, § 2, eff. Sept. 1, 2005; Acts 2015, 84th Leg., ch. 1276 (S.B. 1287), §§ 8, 9, eff. Sept. 1, 2015.

Art. 38.36. Evidence in Prosecutions for Murder

(a) In all prosecutions for murder, the state or the defendant shall be permitted to offer testimony as to all relevant facts and circumstances surrounding the killing and the previous relationship existing between the accused and the deceased, together with all relevant facts and circumstances going to show the condition of the mind of the accused at the time of the offense.

(b) In a prosecution for murder, if a defendant raises as a defense a justification provided by Section 9.31, 9.32, or 9.33, Penal Code, the defendant, in order to establish the defendant's reasonable belief that use of force or deadly force was immediately necessary, shall be permitted to offer:

(1) relevant evidence that the defendant had been the victim of acts of family violence committed by the deceased, as family violence is defined by Section 71.004, Family Code; and

(2) relevant expert testimony regarding the condition of the mind of the defendant at the time of the offense, including those relevant facts and circumstances relating to family violence that are the basis of the expert's opinion.

Added by Acts 1993, 73rd Leg., ch. 900, § 7.03, eff. Sept. 1, 1994. Amended by Acts 2003, 78th Leg., ch. 1276, § 7.002(g), eff. Sept. 1, 2003.

Art. 38.37. Evidence of extraneous offenses or acts

Sec. 1. (a) Subsection (b) applies to a proceeding in the prosecution of a defendant for an offense, or an attempt or conspiracy to commit an offense, under the following provisions of the Penal Code:

(1) if committed against a child under 17 years of age:

(A) Chapter 21 (Sexual Offenses);

(B) Chapter 22 (Assaultive Offenses); or

(C) Section 25.02 (Prohibited Sexual Conduct); or

(2) if committed against a person younger than 18 years of age:

(A) Section 43.25 (Sexual Performance by a Child);

(B) Section 20A.02(a)(7) or (8); or

(C) Section 43.05(a)(2) (Compelling Prostitution).

(b) Notwithstanding Rules 404 and 405, Texas Rules of Evidence, evidence of other crimes, wrongs, or acts committed by the defendant against the child who is the victim of the alleged offense shall be admitted for its bearing on relevant matters, including:

(1) the state of mind of the defendant and the child; and

(2) the previous and subsequent relationship between the defendant and the child.

Sec. 2. (a) Subsection (b) applies only to the trial of a defendant for:

(1) an offense under any of the following provisions of the Penal Code:

(A) Section 20A.02, if punishable as a felony of the first degree under Section 20A.02(b)(1) (Sex Trafficking of a Child);

(B) Section 21.02 (Continuous Sexual Abuse of Young Child or Children);

(C) Section 21.11 (Indecency With a Child);

(D) Section 22.011(a)(2) (Sexual Assault of a Child);

(E) Sections 22.021(a)(1)(B) and (2) (Aggravated Sexual Assault of a Child);

(F) Section 33.021 (Online Solicitation of a Minor);

(G) Section 43.25 (Sexual Performance by a Child); or

(H) Section 43.26 (Possession or Promotion of Child Pornography), Penal Code; or

(2) an attempt or conspiracy to commit an offense described by Subdivision (1).

(b) Notwithstanding Rules 404 and 405, Texas Rules of Evidence, and subject to Section 2-a, evidence that the defendant has committed a separate offense described by Subsection (a)(1) or (2) may be admitted in the trial of an alleged offense described by Subsection (a)(1) or (2) for any bearing the evidence has on relevant matters, including the character of the defendant and acts performed in conformity with the character of the defendant.

Sec. 2-a. Before evidence described by Section 2 may be introduced, the trial judge must:

(1) determine that the evidence likely to be admitted at trial will be adequate to support a finding by the jury that the defendant committed the separate offense beyond a reasonable doubt; and

(2) conduct a hearing out of the presence of the jury for that purpose.

Sec. 3. The state shall give the defendant notice of the state's intent to introduce in the case in chief evidence described by Section 1 or 2 not later than the 30th day before the date of the defendant's trial.

Sec. 4. This article does not limit the admissibility of evidence of extraneous crimes, wrongs, or acts under any other applicable law.

Added by Acts 1995, 74th Leg., ch. 318, § 48(a), eff. Sept. 1, 1995. Amended by Acts 2005, 79th Leg., ch. 728, § 4.004, eff. Sept. 1, 2005. Amended by Acts 2011, 82nd Leg., ch. 1 (S.B. 24), § 2.08, eff. Sept. 1, 2011; Acts 2013, 83rd Leg., ch. 387 (S.B. 12), § 1, eff. Sept. 1, 2013.

Art. 38.371. Evidence in Prosecutions of Certain Offenses Involving Family Violence

(a) This article applies to a proceeding in the prosecution of a defendant for an offense, or for an attempt or conspiracy to commit an offense, that is committed under:

(1) Section 22.01, 22.02, or 22.04, Penal Code, against a person whose relationship to or association with the defendant is described by Section 71.0021(b), 71.003, or 71.005, Family Code; or

(2) Section 25.07 or 25.072, Penal Code, if the offense is based on a violation of an order or a condition of bond in a case involving family violence.

(b) In the prosecution of an offense described by Subsection (a), subject to the Texas Rules of Evidence or other applicable law, each party may offer testimony or other evidence of all relevant facts and circumstances that would assist the trier of fact in determining whether the actor committed the offense described by Subsection (a), including testimony or evidence regarding the nature of the relationship between the actor and the alleged victim.

(c) This article does not permit the presentation of character evidence that would otherwise be inadmissible under the Texas Rules of Evidence or other applicable law.

Added by Acts 2015, 84th Leg., ch. 1086 (H.B. 2645), § 1, eff. Sept. 1, 2015. Amended by Acts 2017, 85th Leg., ch. 743 (S.B. 1250), § 1, eff. Sept. 1, 2017.

Section 4(a) of Acts 2015, 84th Leg., ch. 1086 (H.B. 2645) provides:

"(a) The change in law made by this Act in adding Article 38.371, Code of Criminal Procedure, applies to the admissibility of evidence in a criminal proceeding that commences on or after the effective date [Sept. 1, 2015] of this Act. The admissibility of evidence in a criminal proceeding that commences before the effective date of this Act is governed by the law in effect on the date the proceeding commenced, and the former law is continued in effect for that purpose."

Section 2 of Acts 2017, 85th Leg., ch. 743 (S.B. 1250) provides:

"The change in law made by this Act applies to the admissibility of evidence in a criminal proceeding that commences on or after the effective date [Sept. 1, 2017] of this Act. The admissibility of evidence in a criminal proceeding that commences before the effective date of this Act is governed by the law in effect on the date the proceeding commenced, and the former law is continued in effect for that purpose."

Art. 38.38. Evidence relating to retaining attorney

Evidence that a person has contacted or retained an attorney is not admissible on the issue of whether the person committed a criminal offense. In a criminal case, neither the judge nor the attorney representing the state may comment on the fact that the defendant has contacted or retained an attorney in the case.

Added by Acts 1995, 74th Leg., ch. 318, § 49, eff. Sept. 1, 1995.

Art. 38.39. Evidence in an Aggregation Prosecution With Numerous Victims

In trials involving an allegation of a continuing scheme of fraud or theft alleged to have been committed against a large class of victims in an aggregate amount or value, it need not be proved by direct evidence that each alleged victim did not consent or did not effectively consent to the transaction in question. It shall be sufficient if the lack of consent or effective consent to a particular transaction or transactions is proven by either direct or circumstantial evidence.

Added by Acts 2001, 77th Leg., ch. 1411, § 2, eff. Sept. 1, 2001.

Art. 38.40.[1] Evidence of Pregnancy

(a) In a prosecution for the death of or injury to an individual who is an unborn child, the prosecution shall provide medical or other evidence that the mother of the individual was pregnant at the time of the alleged offense.

(b) For the purpose of this section, "individual" has the meaning assigned by Section 1.07, Penal Code.

Added by Acts 2003, 78th Leg., ch. 822, § 2.06, eff. Sept. 1, 2003.

[1] This article was enacted as § 38.40 and was editorially redesignated as Art. 38.40

Art. 38.41. Certificate of Analysis

Sec. 1. A certificate of analysis that complies with this article is admissible in evidence on behalf of the state or the defendant to establish the results of a laboratory analysis of physical evidence conducted by or for a law enforcement agency without the necessity of the analyst personally appearing in court.

Sec. 2. This article does not limit the right of a party to summon a witness or to introduce admissible evidence relevant to the results of the analysis.

Sec. 3. A certificate of analysis under this article must contain the following information certified under oath:

(1) the names of the analyst and the laboratory employing the analyst;

(2) a statement that the laboratory employing the analyst is accredited by a nationally recognized board or association that accredits crime laboratories;

(3) a description of the analyst's educational background, training, and experience;

(4) a statement that the analyst's duties of employment included the analysis of physical evidence for one or more law enforcement agencies;

(5) a description of the tests or procedures conducted by the analyst;

(6) a statement that the tests or procedures used were reliable and approved by the laboratory employing the analyst; and

(7) the results of the analysis.

Sec. 4. Not later than the 20th day before the trial begins in a proceeding in which a certificate of analysis under this article is to be introduced, the certificate must be filed with the clerk of the court and a copy must be provided by fax, secure electronic mail, hand delivery, or certified mail, return receipt requested, to the opposing party. The certificate is not admissible under Section 1 if, not later than the 10th day before the trial begins, the opposing party files a written objection to the use of the certificate with the clerk of the court and provides a copy of the objection by fax, secure electronic mail, hand delivery, or certified mail, return receipt requested, to the offering party.

Sec. 5. A certificate of analysis is sufficient for purposes of this article if it uses the following form or if it otherwise substantially complies with this article:

BEFORE ME, the undersigned authority, personally appeared _____, who being duly sworn, stated as follows:

CERTIFICATE OF ANALYSIS

My name is _____. I am of sound mind, over the age of 18 years, capable of making this affidavit, and personally acquainted with the facts stated in this affidavit.

I am employed by the _____, which was authorized to conduct the analysis referenced in this affidavit. Part of my duties for this laboratory involved the analysis of physical evidence for one or more law enforcement agencies. This laboratory is accredited by _____.

My educational background is as follows: (description of educational background)

My training and experience that qualify me to perform the tests or procedures referred to in this affidavit and determine the results of those tests or procedures are as follows: (description of training and experience)

I received the physical evidence listed on laboratory report no. _____ (attached) on the ___ day of _____, 20___. On the date indicated in the laboratory report, I conducted the following tests or procedures on the physical evidence: (description of tests and procedures)

The tests and procedures used were reliable and approved by the laboratory. The results are as indicated on the lab report.

_____

Affiant

SWORN TO AND SUBSCRIBED before me on the ___ day of _____, 20___.

_____

Notary Public, State of Texas

Added by Acts 2003, 78th Leg., ch. 923, § 1, eff. Sept. 1, 2003. Amended by Acts 2013, 83rd Leg., ch. 78 (S.B. 354), § 4, eff. May 18, 2013.

Art. 38.42. Chain of Custody Affidavit

Sec. 1. A chain of custody affidavit that complies with this article is admissible in evidence on behalf of the state or the defendant to establish the chain of custody of physical evidence without the necessity of any person in the chain of custody personally appearing in court.

Sec. 2. This article does not limit the right of a party to summon a witness or to introduce admissible evidence relevant to the chain of custody.

Sec. 3. A chain of custody affidavit under this article must contain the following information stated under oath:

(1) the affiant's name and address;

(2) a description of the item of evidence and its container, if any, obtained by the affiant;

(3) the name of the affiant's employer on the date the affiant obtained custody of the physical evidence;

(4) the date and method of receipt and the name of the person from whom or location from which the item of physical evidence was received;

(5) the date and method of transfer and the name of the person to whom or location to which the item of physical evidence was transferred; and

(6) a statement that the item of evidence was transferred in essentially the same condition as received except for any minor change resulting from field or laboratory testing procedures.

Sec. 4. Not later than the 20th day before the trial begins in a proceeding in which a chain of custody affidavit under this article is to be introduced, the affidavit must be filed with the clerk of the court and a copy must be provided by fax, secure electronic mail, hand delivery, or certified mail, return receipt requested, to the opposing party. The affidavit is not admissible under Section 1 if, not later than the 10th day before the trial begins, the opposing party files a written objection to the use of the affidavit with the clerk of the court and provides a copy of the objection by fax, secure electronic mail, hand delivery, or certified mail, return receipt requested, to the offering party.

Sec. 5. A chain of custody affidavit is sufficient for purposes of this article if it uses the following form or if it otherwise substantially complies with this article:

BEFORE ME, the undersigned authority, personally appeared _____, who being by me duly sworn, stated as follows:

CHAIN OF CUSTODY AFFIDAVIT

My name is _____. I am of sound mind, over the age of 18 years, capable of making this affidavit, and personally acquainted with the facts stated in this affidavit.

My address is _____.

On the ___ day of _____, 20___, I was employed by _____.

On that date, I came into possession of the physical evidence described as follows: (description of evidence)

I received the physical evidence from _____ (name of person or description of location) on the ___ day of _____, 20___, by (method of receipt).

This physical evidence was in a container described and marked as follows: (description of container)

I transferred the physical evidence to _____ (name of person or description of location) on the ___ day of _____, 20___, by (method of delivery).

During the time that the physical evidence was in my custody, I did not make any changes or alterations to the condition of the physical evidence except for those resulting from field or laboratory testing procedures, and the physical evidence or a representative sample of the physical evidence was transferred in essentially the same condition as received.

_____

Affiant

SWORN TO AND SUBSCRIBED before me on the ___ day of _____, 20___.

_____

Notary Public, State of Texas

Added by Acts 2003, 78th Leg., ch. 923, § 1, eff. Sept. 1, 2003. Amended by Acts 2013, 83rd Leg., ch. 78 (S.B. 354), § 5, eff. May 18, 2013.

Art. 38.43. Evidence Containing Biological Material

(a) In this article, "biological evidence" means:

(1) the contents of a sexual assault examination kit; or

(2) any item that contains blood, semen, hair, saliva, skin tissue, fingernail scrapings, bone, bodily fluids, or any other identifiable biological material that was collected as part of an investigation of an alleged felony offense or conduct constituting a felony offense that might reasonably be used to:

(A) establish the identity of the person committing the offense or engaging in the conduct constituting the offense; or

(B) exclude a person from the group of persons who could have committed the offense or engaged in the conduct constituting the offense.

(b) This article applies to a governmental or public entity or an individual, including a law enforcement agency, prosecutor's office, court, public hospital, or crime laboratory, that is charged with the collection, storage, preservation, analysis, or retrieval of biological evidence.

(c) An entity or individual described by Subsection (b) shall ensure that biological evidence collected pursuant to an investigation or prosecution of a felony offense or conduct constituting a felony offense is retained and preserved:

(1) for not less than 40 years, or until the applicable statute of limitations has expired, if there is an unapprehended actor associated with the offense; or

(2) in a case in which a defendant has been convicted, placed on deferred adjudication community supervision, or adjudicated as having engaged in delinquent conduct and there are no additional unapprehended actors associated with the offense:

(A) until the inmate is executed, dies, or is released on parole, if the defendant is convicted of a capital felony;

(B) until the defendant dies, completes the defendant's sentence, or is released on parole or mandatory supervision, if the defendant is sentenced to a term of confinement or imprisonment in the Texas Department of Criminal Justice;

(C) until the defendant completes the defendant's term of community supervision, including deferred adjudication community supervision, if the defendant is placed on community supervision;

(D) until the defendant dies, completes the defendant's sentence, or is released on parole, mandatory supervision, or juvenile probation, if the defendant is committed to the Texas Juvenile Justice Department; or

(E) until the defendant completes the defendant's term of juvenile probation, including a term of community supervision upon transfer of supervision to a criminal court, if the defendant is placed on juvenile probation.

(d) The attorney representing the state, clerk, or other officer in possession of biological evidence described by Subsection (a) may destroy the evidence, but only if the attorney, clerk, or officer by mail notifies the defendant, the last attorney of record for the defendant, and the convicting court of the decision to destroy the evidence and a written objection is not received by the attorney, clerk, or officer from the defendant, attorney of record, or court before the 91st day after the later of the following dates:

(1) the date on which the attorney representing the state, clerk, or other officer receives proof that the defendant received notice of the planned destruction of evidence; or

(2) the date on which notice of the planned destruction of evidence is mailed to the last attorney of record for the defendant.

(e) To the extent of any conflict, this article controls over Article 2.21.

(f) The Department of Public Safety shall adopt standards and rules authorizing a county with a population less than 100,000 to ensure the preservation of biological evidence by promptly delivering the evidence to the Department of Public Safety for storage in accordance with Section 411.053, Government Code, and department rules.

(g) The Department of Public Safety shall adopt standards and rules, consistent with best practices, relating to a person described by Subsection (b), that specify the manner of collection, storage, preservation, and retrieval of biological evidence.

(h) A person described by Subsection (b) may solicit and accept gifts, grants, donations, and contributions to support the collection, storage, preservation, retrieval, and destruction of biological evidence.

(i) Before a defendant is tried for a capital offense in which the state is seeking the death penalty, subject to Subsection (j), the state shall require either the Department of Public Safety through one of its laboratories or a laboratory accredited under Article 38.01 to perform DNA testing, in accordance with the laboratory's capabilities at the time the testing is performed, on any biological evidence that was collected as part of an investigation of the offense and is in the possession of the state. The laboratory that performs the DNA testing shall pay for all DNA testing performed in accordance with this subsection.

(j) As soon as practicable after the defendant is charged with a capital offense, or on a motion by the state or the defendant in a capital case, unless the state has affirmatively waived the death penalty in writing, the court shall order the state and the defendant to meet and confer about which biological materials collected as part of an investigation of the offense qualify as biological evidence that is required to be tested under Subsection (i). If the state and the defendant agree on which biological materials constitute biological evidence, the biological evidence shall be tested in accordance with Subsection (i). If the state and the defendant do not agree on which biological materials qualify as biological evidence, the state or the defendant may request the court to hold a hearing to determine the issue. On receipt of a request for a hearing under this subsection, the court shall set a date for the hearing and provide written notice of the hearing date to the state and the defendant. At the hearing, there is a rebuttable presumption that the biological material that the defendant requests to be tested constitutes biological evidence that is required to be tested under Subsection (i). This subsection does not in any way prohibit the state from testing biological evidence in the state's possession.

(k) If an item of biological evidence is destroyed or lost as a result of DNA testing performed under Subsection (i), the laboratory that tested the evidence must provide to the defendant any bench notes prepared by the laboratory that are related to the testing of the evidence and the results of that testing.

(*l*) The defendant's exclusive remedy for testing that was not performed as required under Subsection (i) or (j) is to seek a writ of mandamus from the court of criminal appeals at any time on or before the date an application for a writ of habeas corpus is due to be filed in the defendant's case under Section 4(a), Article 11.071. An application for a writ of mandamus under this subsection does not toll any period of limitations applicable to a habeas petition under state or federal law. The defendant is entitled to only one application for a writ of mandamus under this subsection. At any time after the date an application for a writ of habeas corpus is filed in the defendant's case under Section 4(a), Article 11.071, the defendant may file one additional motion for forensic testing under Chapter 64.

(m) A defendant may have another laboratory accredited under Article 38.01 perform additional testing of any biological evidence required to be tested under Subsection (i). On an ex parte showing of good cause to the court, a defendant may have a laboratory accredited under Article 38.01 perform testing of any biological material that is not required to be tested under Subsection (i). The defendant is responsible for the cost of any testing performed under this subsection.

Added by Acts 2001, 77th Leg., ch. 2, § 1, eff. April 5, 2001. Renumbered from Vernon's Ann.C.C.P. art. 38.39 by Acts 2005, 79th Leg., ch. 728, § 23.001(8), eff. Sept. 1, 2005. Amended by Acts 2009, 81st Leg., ch. 1179, § 1, eff. Sept. 1, 2009; Acts 2011, 82nd Leg., ch. 91 (S.B. 1303), § 27.002(1), eff. Sept. 1, 2011; Acts 2011, 82nd Leg., ch. 1248 (S.B. 1616), § 1, eff. June 17, 2011; Acts 2013, 83rd Leg., ch. 1349 (S.B. 1292), § 1, eff. Sept. 1, 2013; Acts 2015, 84th Leg., ch. 734 (H.B. 1549), § 4, eff. Sept. 1, 2015; Acts 2015, 84th Leg., ch. 1276 (S.B. 1287), § 10, eff. Sept. 1, 2015.

Section 150 of Acts 2015, 84th Leg., ch. 734 (H.B. 1549) provides:

"If any provision of this Act conflicts with a provision of another Act of the 84th Legislature, Regular Session, 2015, the provision of the other Act controls to the extent of the conflict, regardless of the date of enactment."

Art. 38.44. Admissibility of Electronically Preserved Document

An electronically preserved document has the same legal significance and admissibility as if the document had been maintained in hard-copy form. If a party opposes admission of the document on the grounds that the document has been materially altered, the proponent of the document must disprove the allegation by a preponderance of the evidence.

Added by Acts 2005, 79th Leg., ch. 312, § 5, eff. June 17, 2005.

Art. 38.45. Evidence Depicting or Describing Abuse of or Sexual Conduct By Child or Minor

(a) During the course of a criminal hearing or proceeding, the court may not make available or allow to be made available for copying or dissemination to the public property or material:

(1) that constitutes child pornography, as described by Section 43.26(a)(1), Penal Code;

(2) the promotion or possession of which is prohibited under Section 43.261, Penal Code; or

(3) that is described by Section 2 or 5, Article 38.071, of this code.

(b) The court shall place property or material described by Subsection (a) under seal of the court on conclusion of the criminal hearing or proceeding.

(c) The attorney representing the state shall be provided access to property or material described by Subsection (a). In the manner provided by Article 39.15, the defendant, the defendant's attorney, and any individual the defendant seeks to qualify to provide expert testimony at trial shall be provided access to property or material described by Subsection (a).

(d) A court that places property or material described by Subsection (a) under seal may issue an order lifting the seal on a finding that the order is in the best interest of the public.

Added by Acts 2009, 81st Leg., ch. 276, § 1, eff. Sept. 1, 2009. Amended by Acts 2011, 82nd Leg., ch. 1322 (S.B. 407), §§ 7, 8, eff. Sept. 1, 2011.

Art. 38.451. Evidence Depicting Invasive Visual Recording of Child

(a) During the course of a criminal hearing or proceeding concerning an offense under Section 21.15, Penal Code, that was committed against a child younger than 14 years of age, the court shall not make available or allow to be made available the copying or dissemination to the public property or material that constitutes or contains a visual image, as described by Section 21.15(b), Penal Code, of a child younger than 14 years of age and that was seized by law enforcement based on a reasonable suspicion that an offense under that subsection has been committed.

(b) The court shall place property or material described by Subsection (a) under seal of the court on the conclusion of the hearing or proceeding.

(c) The attorney representing the state shall be provided access to the property or material described by Subsection (a). In the manner provided by Article 39.151, the defendant, the defendant's attorney, and any individual the defendant seeks to qualify to provide expert testimony at trial shall be provided access to the property or material provided by Subsection (a).

(d) A court that places property or material described by Subsection (a) under seal may issue an order lifting the seal on a finding that the order is in the best interest of the public.

Added by Acts 2015, 84th Leg., ch. 955 (S.B. 1317), § 3, eff. June 18, 2015.

Section 5 of Acts 2015, 84th Leg., ch. 955 (S.B. 1317) provides:

"The change in law made by this Act applies only to an offense committed on or after the effective date of this Act. An offense committed before the effective date of this Act is governed by the law in effect on the date the offense was committed, and the former law is continued in effect for that purpose. For purposes of this section, an offense was committed before the effective date of this Act if any element of the offense occurred before that date."

Art. 38.46. Evidence in Prosecutions for Stalking

(a) In a prosecution for stalking, each party may offer testimony as to all relevant facts and circumstances that would aid the trier of fact in determining whether the actor's conduct would cause a reasonable person to experience a fear described by Section 42.072(a)(3)(A), (B), or (C), Penal Code, including the facts and circumstances surrounding any existing or previous relationship between the actor and the alleged victim, a member of the alleged victim's family or household, or an individual with whom the alleged victim has a dating relationship.

(b) This article does not permit the presentation of character evidence that would otherwise be inadmissible under the Texas Rules of Evidence or other applicable law.

Added by Acts 2011, 82nd Leg., ch. 591 (S.B. 82), § 3, eff. Sept. 1, 2011.

Art. 38.47. Evidence in Aggregation Prosecution for Fraud or Theft Committed With Respect to Numerous Medicaid or Medicare Recipients

In trials involving an allegation of a continuing scheme of fraud or theft that involves Medicaid or Medicare benefits and is alleged to have been committed with respect to a large class of Medicaid or Medicare recipients in an aggregate amount or value, the attorney representing the state is not required to prove by direct evidence that each Medicaid or Medicare recipient did not consent or effectively consent to a transaction in question. It is sufficient if the lack of consent or effective consent to a particular transaction or transactions is proven by either direct or circumstantial evidence.

Added by Acts 2011, 82nd Leg., ch. 104 (S.B. 1680), § 1, eff. Sept. 1, 2011. Redesignated from Vernon's C.C.P. art. 38.46 by Acts 2013, 83rd Leg., ch. 161 (S.B. 1093), § 22.001(6), eff. Sept. 1, 2013.

Art. 38.48. Evidence in Prosecution for Tampering With Witness or Prospective Witness Involving Family Violence

(a) This article applies to the prosecution of an offense under Section 36.05, Penal Code, in which:

(1) the underlying official proceeding involved family violence, as defined by Section 71.004, Family Code; or

(2) the actor is alleged to have violated Section 36.05, Penal Code, by committing an act of family violence against a witness or prospective witness.

(b) In the prosecution of an offense described by Subsection (a), subject to the Texas Rules of Evidence or other applicable law, each party may offer testimony or other evidence of all relevant facts and circumstances that would assist the trier of fact in determining whether the actor's conduct coerced the witness or prospective witness, including the nature of the relationship between the actor and the witness or prospective witness.

Added by Acts 2013, 83rd Leg., ch. 165 (S.B. 1360), § 3, eff. Sept. 1, 2013.

Art. 38.49. Forfeiture by Wrongdoing

(a) A party to a criminal case who wrongfully procures the unavailability of a witness or prospective witness:

(1) may not benefit from the wrongdoing by depriving the trier of fact of relevant evidence and testimony; and

(2) forfeits the party's right to object to the admissibility of evidence or statements based on the unavailability of the witness as provided by this article through forfeiture by wrongdoing.

(b) Evidence and statements related to a party that has engaged or acquiesced in wrongdoing that was intended to, and did, procure the unavailability of a witness or prospective witness are admissible and may be used by the offering party to make a showing of forfeiture by wrongdoing under this article, subject to Subsection (c).

(c) In determining the admissibility of the evidence or statements described by Subsection (b), the court shall determine, out of the presence of the jury, whether forfeiture by wrongdoing occurred by a preponderance of the evidence. If practicable, the court shall make the determination under this subsection before trial using the procedures under Article 28.01 of this code and Rule 104, Texas Rules of Evidence.

(d) The party offering the evidence or statements described by Subsection (b) is not required to show that:

(1) the actor's sole intent was to wrongfully cause the witness's or prospective witness's unavailability;

(2) the actions of the actor constituted a criminal offense; or

(3) any statements offered are reliable.

(e) A conviction for an offense under Section 36.05 or 36.06(a), Penal Code, creates a presumption of forfeiture by wrongdoing under this article.

(f) Rule 403, Texas Rules of Evidence, applies to this article. This article does not permit the presentation of character evidence that would otherwise be inadmissible under the Texas Rules of Evidence or other applicable law.

Added by Acts 2013, 83rd Leg., ch. 165 (S.B. 1360), § 3, eff. Sept. 1, 2013. Amended by Acts 2015, 84th Leg., ch. 848 (S.B. 923), § 1, eff. Sept. 1, 2015.

Section 3 of Acts 2015, 84th Leg., ch. 848 (S.B. 923) provides:

"The change in law made by this Act applies only to an offense committed on or after the effective date [Sept. 1, 2015] of this Act. An offense committed before the effective date of this Act is governed by the law in effect on the date the offense was committed, and the former law is continued in effect for that purpose. For purposes of this section, an offense was committed before the effective date of this Act if any element of the offense occurred before that date."

Art. 38.50. Retention and preservation of toxicological evidence of certain intoxication offenses

(a) In this article, "toxicological evidence" means a blood or urine specimen that was collected as part of an investigation of an alleged offense under Chapter 49, Penal Code.

(b) This article applies to a governmental or public entity or an individual, including a law enforcement agency, prosecutor's office, or crime laboratory, that is charged with the collection, storage, preservation, analysis, or retrieval of toxicological evidence.

(c) An entity or individual described by Subsection (b) shall ensure that toxicological evidence collected pursuant to an investigation or prosecution of an offense under Chapter 49, Penal Code, is retained and preserved, as applicable:

(1) for the greater of two years or the period of the statute of limitations for the offense, if the indictment or information charging the defendant, or the petition in a juvenile proceeding, has not been presented;

(2) for the duration of a defendant's sentence or term of community supervision, as applicable, if the defendant is convicted or placed on community supervision, or for the duration of the commitment or supervision period applicable to the disposition of a juvenile adjudicated as having engaged in delinquent conduct or conduct indicating a need for supervision; or

(3) until the defendant is acquitted or the indictment or information is dismissed with prejudice, or, in a juvenile proceeding, until a hearing is held and the court does not find the child engaged in delinquent conduct or conduct indicating a need for supervision.

(d) For each offense subject to this article, the court shall determine as soon as practicable the appropriate retention and preservation period for the toxicological evidence under Subsection (c) and notify the defendant or the child or child's guardian and the entity or individual charged with storage of the toxicological evidence of the period for which the evidence is to be retained and preserved. If an action of the prosecutor or the court changes the applicable period under Subsection (c), the court shall notify the persons described by this subsection about the change.

(e) The entity or individual charged with storing toxicological evidence may destroy the evidence on expiration of the period provided by the notice most recently issued by the court under Subsection (d).

(f) To the extent of any conflict between this article and Article 2.21 or 38.43, this article controls.

Added by Acts 2015, 84th Leg., ch. 286 (H.B. 1264), § 1, eff. Sept. 1, 2015.

Section 2 of Acts 2015, 84th Leg., ch. 286 (H.B. 1264) provides:

"Article 38.50, Code of Criminal Procedure, as added by this Act, applies to all toxicological evidence stored by an entity or individual on or after the effective date [Sept. 1, 2015] of this Act, regardless of whether the evidence was collected before, on, or after the effective date of this Act."

CHAPTER THIRTY–NINE. DEPOSITIONS AND DISCOVERY

Art. 39.01.   In Examining Trial

When an examination takes place in a criminal action before a magistrate, the state or the defendant may have the deposition of any witness taken by any officer authorized by this chapter. The state or the defendant may not use the deposition for any purpose unless that party first acknowledges that the entire evidence or statement of the witness may be used for or against the defendant on the trial of the case, subject to all legal objections. The deposition of a witness duly taken before an examining trial or a jury of inquest and reduced to writing or recorded and then certified according to law, provided that the defendant and the defendant's attorney were present when that testimony was taken and that the defendant had the privilege afforded of cross-examining the witness, or taken at any prior trial of the defendant for the same offense, may be used by either the state or the defendant in the trial of the defendant's criminal case under the following circumstances:

When oath is made by the party using the deposition that the witness resides outside the state; or that since the witness's testimony was taken, the witness has died, or has removed beyond the limits of the state, or has been prevented from attending the court through the act or agency of the other party, or by the act or agency of any person whose object was to deprive the state or the defendant of the benefit of the testimony; or that by reason of age or bodily infirmity, that witness cannot attend; or that the witness is a Medicaid or Medicare recipient or a caregiver or guardian of the recipient, and the recipient's Medicaid or Medicare account was charged for a product or service that was not provided or rendered to the recipient. When the testimony is sought to be used by the state, the oath may be made by any credible person. When sought to be used by the defendant, the oath must be made by the defendant in person.

Acts 1965, 59th Leg., vol. 2, p. 317, ch. 722, eff. Jan. 1, 1966. Amended by Acts 2005, 79th Leg., ch. 1021, § 1, eff. Sept. 1, 2005; Acts 2011, 82nd Leg., ch. 104 (S.B. 1680), § 2, eff. Sept. 1, 2011.

Art. 39.02.   Witness Depositions

Depositions of witnesses may be taken by either the state or the defendant. When a party desires to take the deposition of a witness, the party shall file with the clerk of the court in which the case is pending an affidavit stating the facts necessary to constitute a good reason for taking the witness's deposition and an application to take the deposition. On the filing of the affidavit and application, and after notice to the opposing party, the court shall hear the application and determine if good reason exists for taking the deposition. The court shall base its determination and shall grant or deny the application on the facts made known at the hearing. This provision is limited to the purposes stated in Article 39.01.

Acts 1965, 59th Leg., vol. 2, p. 317, ch. 722, eff. Jan. 1, 1966. Amended by Acts 1967, 60th Leg., p. 1741, ch. 659, § 24, eff. Aug. 28, 1967; Acts 2005, 79th Leg., ch. 1021, § 1, eff. Sept. 1, 2005.

Art. 39.025.   Depositions of Elderly or Disabled Persons

(a) In this article:

(1) "Disabled person" means a person with a disability as defined by Section 3, Americans with Disabilities Act (42 U.S.C. 12102).

(2) "Elderly person" means a person 65 years of age or older.

(b) The court shall order the attorney representing the state to take the deposition of an elderly or disabled person who is the alleged victim of or witness to an offense not later than the 60th day after the date on which the state files an application to take the deposition under Article 39.02.

(c) The attorney representing the state and the defendant or the defendant's attorney may, by written agreement filed with the court, extend the deadline for the taking of the deposition.

(d) The court shall grant any request by the attorney representing the state to extend the deadline for the taking of the deposition if a reason for the request is the unavailability, health, or well-being of the victim or witness.

(e) The Texas Rules of Civil Procedure govern the taking of the deposition, except to the extent of any conflict with this code or applicable court rules adopted for criminal proceedings, in which event this code and the rules for criminal proceedings govern. The attorney representing the state and the defendant or defendant's attorney may agree to modify the rules applicable to the deposition by written agreement filed with the court before the taking of the deposition.

(f) If a defendant is unavailable to attend a deposition because the defendant is confined in a correctional facility, the court shall issue any orders or warrants necessary to secure the defendant's presence at the deposition. The sheriff of the county in which a deposition under this subsection is to be taken shall provide a secure location for the taking of the deposition and sufficient law enforcement personnel to ensure the deposition is taken safely. The state's application to take a deposition or notice of deposition is not required to include the identity of any law enforcement agents the sheriff assigns to the deposition and may not serve as a basis for the defendant to object to the taking of the deposition.

(g) If a defendant is unavailable to attend a deposition for any reason other than confinement in a correctional facility, the defendant or defendant's attorney shall request a continuance from the court. The court may grant the continuance if the defendant or defendant's attorney demonstrates good cause for the continuance and that the request is not brought for the purpose of delay or avoidance. A defendant's failure to attend a deposition or request a continuance in accordance with this subsection constitutes a waiver of the defendant's right to be present at the deposition.

Added by Acts 2009, 81st Leg., ch. 678, § 1, eff. Sept. 1, 2009.

Art. 39.026. Depositions of Medicaid or Medicare Recipients or Caregivers

(a) In this article:

(1) "Caregiver" means a person, including a guardian, who is authorized by law, contract, or familial relationship to care for a recipient.

(2) "Medicaid" means the state Medicaid program.

(3) "Medicaid recipient" has the meaning assigned by Section 36.001, Human Resources Code.

(4) "Medicare" means the federal health insurance program that is operated under the Health Insurance for the Aged Act (42 U.S. C. Section 1395 et seq.).

(5) "Medicare recipient" means an individual on whose behalf a person claims or receives a payment under Medicare, without regard to whether the individual was eligible for benefits under Medicare.

(6) "Recipient" means a Medicaid recipient or a Medicare recipient.

(b) The court may order the attorney representing the state to take the deposition of a recipient or caregiver who is the alleged victim of or witness to an offense constituting fraud or theft that involves Medicaid or Medicare benefits. Any order under this subsection must be issued not later than the 180th day after the date on which the state files an application to take the deposition under Article 39.02.

(c) On the motion of either party, the court may order the attorney representing the state to take the deposition of a recipient or caregiver by video recording. The person operating the video recording device must be available to testify regarding the authenticity of the video recording and the taking of the deposition in order for the video recording to be admissible.

(d) If the court finds that the video recording of the deposition is properly authenticated and that requiring the jury to view the entire recording would unnecessarily prolong the trial, the court may allow a party to offer the entire video recording into evidence without requiring the jury to view the entire video recording during the trial. This subsection does not preclude the attorney representing the state, the defendant, or the defendant's attorney from offering into evidence and playing for the jury a portion of a video-recorded deposition.

(e) The attorney representing the state and the defendant or the defendant's attorney, by written agreement filed with the court, may extend the deadline for the taking of the deposition.

(f) The court shall grant any request by the attorney representing the state to extend the deadline for the taking of the deposition if a reason for the request is the unavailability, health, or well-being of the recipient or caregiver.

(g) The Texas Rules of Civil Procedure govern the taking of the deposition, except that, to the extent of any conflict with this code or applicable court rules adopted for criminal proceedings, this code and the rules for criminal proceedings govern. The attorney representing the state and the defendant or the defendant's attorney may agree to modify the rules applicable to the deposition by written agreement filed with the court before the taking of the deposition.

(h) If a defendant is unavailable to attend a deposition because the defendant is confined in a correctional facility, the court shall issue any orders or warrants necessary to secure the defendant's presence at the deposition. The sheriff of the county in which a deposition is to be taken under this subsection shall provide a secure location for the taking of the deposition and sufficient law enforcement personnel to ensure that the deposition is taken safely. The state's application to take a deposition or notice of deposition is not required to include the identity of any law enforcement agent the sheriff assigns to the deposition under this subsection, and the defendant may not object to the taking of the deposition based solely on the state's omission of the identity of that agent.

(i) If a defendant is unavailable to attend a deposition for any reason other than confinement in a correctional facility, the defendant or the defendant's attorney shall request a continuance from the court. The court may grant the continuance if the defendant or the defendant's attorney demonstrates good cause for the continuance and that the request is not brought for the purpose of delay or avoidance. A defendant's failure to attend a deposition or request a continuance in accordance with this subsection constitutes a waiver of the defendant's right to be present at the deposition.

Added by Acts 2011, 82nd Leg., ch. 104 (S.B. 1680), § 3, eff. Sept. 1, 2011.

Art. 39.03. Officers who may take the deposition

Upon the filing of such an affidavit and application, the court shall appoint, order or designate one of the following persons before whom such deposition shall be taken:

1. A district judge.

2. A county judge.

3. A notary public.

4. A district clerk.

5. A county clerk.

Such order shall specifically name such person and the time when and place where such deposition shall be taken. Failure of a witness to respond thereto, shall be punishable by contempt by the court. Such deposition shall be oral or written, as the court shall direct.

Acts 1965, 59th Leg., vol. 2, p. 317, ch. 722, eff. Jan. 1, 1966. Amended by Acts 1967, 60th Leg., p. 1741, ch. 659, § 25, eff. Aug. 28, 1967.

Art. 39.04. Applicability of civil rules

The rules prescribed in civil cases for issuance of commissions, subpoenaing witnesses, taking the depositions of witnesses and all other formalities governing depositions shall, as to the manner and form of taking and returning the same and other formalities to the taking of the same, govern in criminal actions, when not in conflict with this Code.

Acts 1965, 59th Leg., vol. 2, p. 317, ch. 722, eff. Jan. 1, 1966.

Art. 39.05. Objections

The rules of procedure as to objections in depositions in civil actions shall govern in criminal actions when not in conflict with this Code.

Acts 1965, 59th Leg., vol. 2, p. 317, ch. 722, eff. Jan. 1, 1966.

Art. 39.06. Written interrogatories

When any such deposition is to be taken by written interrogatories, such written interrogatories shall be filed with the clerk of the court, and a copy of the same served on all other parties or their counsel for the length of time and in the manner required for service of interrogatories in civil action, and the same procedure shall also be followed with reference to cross-interrogatories as that prescribed in civil actions.

Acts 1965, 59th Leg., vol. 2, p. 317, ch. 722, eff. Jan. 1, 1966.

Art. 39.07. Certificate

Where depositions are taken under commission in criminal actions, the officer or officers taking the same shall certify that the person deposing is the identical person named in the commission; or, if they cannot certify to the identity of the witness, there shall be an affidavit of some person attached to the deposition proving the identity of such witness, and the officer or officers shall certify that the person making the affidavit is known to them.

Acts 1965, 59th Leg., vol. 2, p. 317, ch. 722, eff. Jan. 1, 1966. Amended by Acts 1967, 60th Leg., p. 1742, ch. 659, § 26, eff. Aug. 28, 1967.

Art. 39.08. Authenticating the deposition

The official seal and signature of the officer taking the deposition shall be attached to the certificate authenticating the deposition.

Acts 1965, 59th Leg., vol. 2, p. 317, ch. 722, eff. Jan. 1, 1966.

Art. 39.09. Non-resident witnesses

Depositions of a witness residing out of the State may be taken before a judge or before a commissioner of deeds and depositions for this State, who resides within the State where the deposition is to be taken, or before a notary public of the place where such deposition is to be taken, or before any commissioned officer of the armed services or before any diplomatic or consular officer. The deposition of a non-resident witness who may be temporarily within the State, may be taken under the same rules which apply to the taking of depositions of other witnesses in the State.

Acts 1965, 59th Leg., vol. 2, p. 317, ch. 722, eff. Jan. 1, 1966.

Art. 39.10. Return

In all cases the return of depositions may be made as provided in civil actions.

Acts 1965, 59th Leg., vol. 2, p. 317, ch. 722, eff. Jan. 1, 1966.

Art. 39.11. Waiver

The State and defense may agree upon a waiver of any formalities in the taking of a deposition other than that the taking of such deposition must be under oath.

Acts 1965, 59th Leg., vol. 2, p. 317, ch. 722, eff. Jan. 1, 1966.

Art. 39.12. Predicate to Read

Depositions taken in criminal actions shall not be read unless oath be made that the witness resides out of the state; or that since the deposition was taken, the witness has died; or that the witness has removed beyond the limits of the state; or that the witness has been prevented from attending the court through the act or agency of the defendant; or by the act or agency of any person whose object was to deprive the state or the defendant of the benefit of the testimony; or that by reason of age or bodily infirmity, the witness cannot attend; or that the witness is a Medicaid or Medicare recipient or a caregiver or guardian of the recipient, and the recipient's Medicaid or Medicare account was charged for a product or service that was not provided or rendered to the recipient. When the deposition is sought to be used by the state, the oath may be made by any credible person. When sought to be used by the defendant, the oath shall be made by the defendant in person.

Acts 1965, 59th Leg., vol. 2, p. 317, ch. 722, eff. Jan. 1, 1966. Amended by Acts 2011, 82nd Leg., ch. 104 (S.B. 1680), § 4, eff. Sept. 1, 2011.

Art. 39.13. Impeachment

Nothing contained in the preceding Articles shall be construed as prohibiting the use of any such evidence for impeachment purposes under the rules of evidence heretofore existing at common law.

Acts 1965, 59th Leg., vol. 2, p. 317, ch. 722, eff. Jan. 1, 1966.

Art. 39.14. Discovery

(a) Subject to the restrictions provided by Section 264.408, Family Code, and Article 39.15 of this code, as soon as practicable after receiving a timely request from the defendant the state shall produce and permit the inspection and the electronic duplication, copying, and photographing, by or on behalf of the defendant, of any offense reports, any designated documents, papers, written or recorded statements of the defendant or a witness, including witness statements of law enforcement officers but not including the work product of counsel for the state in the case and their investigators and their notes or report, or any designated books, accounts, letters, photographs, or objects or other tangible things not otherwise privileged that constitute or contain evidence material to any matter involved in the action and that are in the possession, custody, or control of the state or any person under contract with the state. The state may provide to the defendant electronic duplicates of any documents or other information described by this article. The rights granted to the defendant under this article do not extend to written communications between the state and an agent, representative, or employee of the state. This article does not authorize the removal of the documents, items, or information from the possession of the state, and any inspection shall be in the presence of a representative of the state.

(b) On a party's request made not later than the 30th day before the date that jury selection in the trial is scheduled to begin or, in a trial without a jury, the presentation of evidence is scheduled to begin, the party receiving the request shall disclose to the requesting party the name and address of each person the disclosing party may use at trial to present evidence under Rules 702, 703, and 705, Texas Rules of Evidence. Except as otherwise provided by this subsection, the disclosure must be made in writing in hard copy form or by electronic means not later than the 20th day before the date that jury selection in the trial is scheduled to begin or, in a trial without a jury, the presentation of evidence is scheduled to begin. On motion of a party and on notice to the other parties, the court may order an earlier time at which one or more of the other parties must make the disclosure to the requesting party.

(c) If only a portion of the applicable document, item, or information is subject to discovery under this article, the state is not required to produce or permit the inspection of the remaining portion that is not subject to discovery and may withhold or redact that portion. The state shall inform the defendant that a portion of the document, item, or information has been withheld or redacted. On request of the defendant, the court shall conduct a hearing to determine whether withholding or redaction is justified under this article or other law.

(d) In the case of a pro se defendant, if the court orders the state to produce and permit the inspection of a document, item, or information under this subsection, the state shall permit the pro se defendant to inspect and review the document, item, or information but is not required to allow electronic duplication as described by Subsection (a).

(e) Except as provided by Subsection (f), the defendant, the attorney representing the defendant, or an investigator, expert, consulting legal counsel, or other agent of the attorney representing the defendant may not disclose to a third party any documents, evidence, materials, or witness statements received from the state under this article unless:

(1) a court orders the disclosure upon a showing of good cause after notice and hearing after considering the security and privacy interests of any victim or witness; or

(2) the documents, evidence, materials, or witness statements have already been publicly disclosed.

(f) The attorney representing the defendant, or an investigator, expert, consulting legal counsel, or agent for the attorney representing the defendant, may allow a defendant, witness, or prospective witness to view the information provided under this article, but may not allow that person to have copies of the information provided, other than a copy of the witness's own statement. Before allowing that person to view a document or the witness statement of another under this subsection, the person possessing the information shall redact the address, telephone number, driver's license number, social security number, date of birth, and any bank account or other identifying numbers contained in the document or witness statement. For purposes of this article, the defendant may not be the agent for the attorney representing the defendant.

(g) Nothing in this article shall be interpreted to limit an attorney's ability to communicate regarding his or her case within the Texas Disciplinary Rules of Professional Conduct, except for the communication of information identifying any victim or witness, including name, except as provided in Subsections (e) and (f), address, telephone number, driver's license number, social security number, date of birth, and bank account information or any information that by reference would make it possible to identify a victim or a witness. Nothing in this subsection shall prohibit the disclosure of identifying information to an administrative, law enforcement, regulatory, or licensing agency for the purposes of making a good faith complaint.

(h) Notwithstanding any other provision of this article, the state shall disclose to the defendant any exculpatory, impeachment, or mitigating document, item, or information in the possession, custody, or control of the state that tends to negate the guilt of the defendant or would tend to reduce the punishment for the offense charged.

(h-1) In this subsection, "correctional facility" has the meaning assigned by Section 1.07, Penal Code. Notwithstanding any other provision of this article, if the state intends to use at a defendant's trial testimony of a person to whom the defendant made a statement against the defendant's interest while the person was imprisoned or confined in the same correctional facility as the defendant, the state shall disclose to the defendant any information in the possession, custody, or control of the state that is relevant to the person's credibility, including:

(1) the person's complete criminal history, including any charges that were dismissed or reduced as part of a plea bargain;

(2) any grant, promise, or offer of immunity from prosecution, reduction of sentence, or other leniency or special treatment, given by the state in exchange for the person's testimony; and

(3) information concerning other criminal cases in which the person has testified, or offered to testify, against a defendant with whom the person was imprisoned or confined, including any grant, promise, or offer as described by Subdivision (2) given by the state in exchange for the testimony.

(i) The state shall electronically record or otherwise document any document, item, or other information provided to the defendant under this article.

(j) Before accepting a plea of guilty or nolo contendere, or before trial, each party shall acknowledge in writing or on the record in open court the disclosure, receipt, and list of all documents, items, and information provided to the defendant under this article.

(k) If at any time before, during, or after trial the state discovers any additional document, item, or information required to be disclosed under Subsection (h), the state shall promptly disclose the existence of the document, item, or information to the defendant or the court.

(*l*) A court may order the defendant to pay costs related to discovery under this article, provided that costs may not exceed the charges prescribed by Subchapter F, Chapter 552, Government Code.

(m) To the extent of any conflict, this article prevails over Chapter 552, Government Code.

(n) This article does not prohibit the parties from agreeing to discovery and documentation requirements equal to or greater than those required under this article.

Acts 1965, 59th Leg., vol. 2, p. 317, ch. 722, eff. Jan. 1, 1966. Amended by Acts 1999, 76th Leg., ch. 578, § 1, eff. Sept. 1, 1999; Acts 2005, 79th Leg., ch. 1019, § 1, eff. June 18, 2005; Acts 2009, 81st Leg., ch. 276, § 2, eff. Sept. 1, 2009; Acts 2013, 83rd Leg., ch. 49 (S.B. 1611), § 2, eff. Jan. 1, 2014; Acts 2015, 84th Leg., ch. 459 (H.B. 510), § 1, eff. Sept. 1, 2015; Acts 2015, 84th Leg., ch. 1236 (S.B. 1296), § 4.001, eff. Sept. 1, 2015; Acts 2017, 85th Leg., ch. 686 (H.B. 34), § 7, eff. Sept. 1, 2017.

Section 2 of Acts 2015, 84th Leg., ch. 459 (H.B. 510) provides:

"The change in law made by this Act applies to the prosecution of an offense committed on or after the effective date [Sept. 1, 2015] of this Act. The prosecution of an offense committed before the effective date of this Act is governed by the law in effect on the date the offense was committed, and the former law is continued in effect for that purpose. For purposes of this section, an offense is committed before the effective date of this Act if any element of the offense occurs before the effective date."

Section 14 of Acts 2017, 85th Leg., ch. 686 (H.B. 34) provides:

"Article 39.14(h–1), Code of Criminal Procedure, as added by this Act, applies to the prosecution of an offense committed on or after the effective date [Sept. 1, 2017] of this Act. The prosecution of an offense committed before the effective date of this Act is governed by the law in effect on the date the offense was committed, and the former law is continued in effect for that purpose. For purposes of this section, an offense is committed before the effective date of this Act if any element of the offense occurs before the effective date."

Art. 39.15. Discovery of Evidence Depicting or Describing Abuse of or Sexual Conduct By Child or Minor

(a) In the manner provided by this article, a court shall allow discovery under Article 39.14 of property or material:

(1) that constitutes child pornography, as described by Section 43.26(a)(1), Penal Code;

(2) the promotion or possession of which is prohibited under Section 43.261, Penal Code; or

(3) that is described by Section 2 or 5, Article 38.071, of this code.

(b) Property or material described by Subsection (a) must remain in the care, custody, or control of the court or the state as provided by Article 38.45.

(c) A court shall deny any request by a defendant to copy, photograph, duplicate, or otherwise reproduce any property or material described by Subsection (a), provided that the state makes the property or material reasonably available to the defendant.

(d) For purposes of Subsection (c), property or material is considered to be reasonably available to the defendant if, at a facility under the control of the state, the state provides ample opportunity for the inspection, viewing, and examination of the property or material by the defendant, the defendant's attorney, and any individual the defendant seeks to qualify to provide expert testimony at trial.

Added by Acts 2009, 81st Leg., ch. 276, § 3, eff. Sept. 1, 2009. Amended by Acts 2011, 82nd Leg., ch. 1322 (S.B. 407), §§ 9, 10, eff. Sept. 1, 2011.

Art. 39.151. Discovery of Evidence Depicting Invasive Visual Recording of Child

(a) In the manner provided by this article, a court shall allow discovery of property or material that constitutes or contains a visual image, as described by Section 21.15(b), Penal Code, of a child younger than 14 years of age and that was seized by law enforcement based on a reasonable suspicion that an offense under that subsection has been committed.

(b) Property or material described by Subsection (a) must remain in the care, custody, or control of the court or the state as provided by Article 38.451.

(c) A court shall deny any request by a defendant to copy, photograph, duplicate, or otherwise reproduce any property or material described by Subsection (a), provided that the state makes the property or material reasonably available to the defendant.

(d) For purposes of Subsection (c), property or material is considered to be reasonably available to the defendant if, at a facility under the control of the state, the state provides ample opportunity for the inspection, viewing, and examination of the property or material by the defendant, the defendant's attorney, and any individual the defendant seeks to qualify to provide expert testimony at trial.

Added by Acts 2015, 84th Leg., ch. 955 (S.B. 1317), § 4, eff. June 18, 2015.

Section 5 of Acts 2015, 84th Leg., ch. 955 (S.B. 1317) provides:

"The change in law made by this Act applies only to an offense committed on or after the effective date of this Act. An offense committed before the effective date of this Act is governed by the law in effect on the date the offense was committed, and the former law is continued in effect for that purpose. For purposes of this section, an offense was committed before the effective date of this Act if any element of the offense occurred before that date."

PROCEEDINGS AFTER VERDICT

CHAPTER 40. NEW TRIALS

Art. 40.001. New Trial on Material Evidence

A new trial shall be granted an accused where material evidence favorable to the accused has been discovered since trial.

Added by Acts 1993, 73rd Leg., ch. 900, § 11.01, eff. Sept. 1, 1993.

Arts. 40.01 to 40.11. Repealed by Texas Rules of Appellate Procedure effective September 1, 1986 (Acts 1985, 69th Leg., ch. 685, § 4)

CHAPTER 41. ARREST OF JUDGMENT [REPEALED]

Arts. 41.01 to 41.05. Repealed by Texas Rules of Appellate Procedure effective September 1, 1986 (Acts 1985, 69th Leg., ch. 685, § 4)

CHAPTER 42. JUDGMENT AND SENTENCE

Art. 42.01. Judgment

Text of Sec. 1 effective until January 1, 2019

Sec. 1. A judgment is the written declaration of the court signed by the trial judge and entered of record showing the conviction or acquittal of the defendant. The sentence served shall be based on the information contained in the judgment. The judgment shall reflect:

1. The title and number of the case;

2. That the case was called and the parties appeared, naming the attorney for the state, the defendant, and the attorney for the defendant, or, where a defendant is not represented by counsel, that the defendant knowingly, intelligently, and voluntarily waived the right to representation by counsel;

3. The plea or pleas of the defendant to the offense charged;

4. Whether the case was tried before a jury or a jury was waived;

5. The submission of the evidence, if any;

6. In cases tried before a jury that the jury was charged by the court;

7. The verdict or verdicts of the jury or the finding or findings of the court;

8. In the event of a conviction that the defendant is adjudged guilty of the offense as found by the verdict of the jury or the finding of the court, and that the defendant be punished in accordance with the jury's verdict or the court's finding as to the proper punishment;

9. In the event of conviction where death or any punishment is assessed that the defendant be sentenced to death, a term of confinement or community supervision, or to pay a fine, as the case may be;

10. In the event of conviction where the imposition of sentence is suspended and the defendant is placed on community supervision, setting forth the punishment assessed, the length of community supervision, and the conditions of community supervision;

11. In the event of acquittal that the defendant be discharged;

12. The county and court in which the case was tried and, if there was a change of venue in the case, the name of the county in which the prosecution was originated;

13. The offense or offenses for which the defendant was convicted;

14. The date of the offense or offenses and degree of offense for which the defendant was convicted;

15. The term of sentence;

16. The date judgment is entered;

17. The date sentence is imposed;

18. The date sentence is to commence and any credit for time served;

19. The terms of any order entered pursuant to Article 42.08 that the defendant's sentence is to run cumulatively or concurrently with another sentence or sentences;

20. The terms of any plea bargain;

21. Affirmative findings entered pursuant to Article 42A.054(c) or (d);

22. The terms of any fee payment ordered under Article 42.151;

23. The defendant's thumbprint taken in accordance with Article 38.33;

24. In the event that the judge orders the defendant to repay a reward or part of a reward under Articles 37.073 and 42.152, a statement of the amount of the payment or payments required to be made;

25. In the event that the court orders restitution to be paid to the victim, a statement of the amount of restitution ordered and:

(A) the name and address of a person or agency that will accept and forward restitution payments to the victim; or

(B) if the court specifically elects to have payments made directly to the crime victim, the name and permanent address of the victim at the time of judgment;

26. In the event that a presentence investigation is required by Subchapter F, Chapter 42A, a statement that the presentence investigation was done according to the applicable provision;

27. In the event of conviction of an offense for which registration as a sex offender is required under Chapter 62, a statement that the registration requirement of that chapter applies to the defendant and a statement of the age of the victim of the offense;

28. The defendant's state identification number required by Section 60.052(a)(2),[1] if that number has been assigned at the time of the judgment; and

29. The incident number required by Section 60.052(a)(4), if that number has been assigned at the time of the judgment.

Text of Sec. 1 effective January 1, 2019

Sec. 1. A judgment is the written declaration of the court signed by the trial judge and entered of record showing the conviction or acquittal of the defendant. The sentence served shall be based on the information contained in the judgment. The judgment shall reflect:

1. The title and number of the case;

2. That the case was called and the parties appeared, naming the attorney for the state, the defendant, and the attorney for the defendant, or, where a defendant is not represented by counsel, that the defendant knowingly, intelligently, and voluntarily waived the right to representation by counsel;

3. The plea or pleas of the defendant to the offense charged;

4. Whether the case was tried before a jury or a jury was waived;

5. The submission of the evidence, if any;

6. In cases tried before a jury that the jury was charged by the court;

7. The verdict or verdicts of the jury or the finding or findings of the court;

8. In the event of a conviction that the defendant is adjudged guilty of the offense as found by the verdict of the jury or the finding of the court, and that the defendant be punished in accordance with the jury's verdict or the court's finding as to the proper punishment;

9. In the event of conviction where death or any punishment is assessed that the defendant be sentenced to death, a term of confinement or community supervision, or to pay a fine, as the case may be;

10. In the event of conviction where the imposition of sentence is suspended and the defendant is placed on community supervision, setting forth the punishment assessed, the length of community supervision, and the conditions of community supervision;

11. In the event of acquittal that the defendant be discharged;

12. The county and court in which the case was tried and, if there was a change of venue in the case, the name of the county in which the prosecution was originated;

13. The offense or offenses for which the defendant was convicted;

14. The date of the offense or offenses and degree of offense for which the defendant was convicted;

15. The term of sentence;

16. The date judgment is entered;

17. The date sentence is imposed;

18. The date sentence is to commence and any credit for time served;

19. The terms of any order entered pursuant to Article 42.08 that the defendant's sentence is to run cumulatively or concurrently with another sentence or sentences;

20. The terms of any plea bargain;

21. Affirmative findings entered pursuant to Article 42A.054(c) or (d);

22. The terms of any fee payment ordered under Article 42.151;

23. The defendant's thumbprint taken in accordance with Article 38.33;

24. In the event that the judge orders the defendant to repay a reward or part of a reward under Articles 37.073 and 42.152, a statement of the amount of the payment or payments required to be made;

25. In the event that the court orders restitution to be paid to the victim, a statement of the amount of restitution ordered and:

(A) the name and address of a person or agency that will accept and forward restitution payments to the victim; or

(B) if the court specifically elects to have payments made directly to the crime victim, the name and permanent address of the victim at the time of judgment;

26. In the event that a presentence investigation is required by Subchapter F, Chapter 42A, a statement that the presentence investigation was done according to the applicable provision;

27. In the event of conviction of an offense for which registration as a sex offender is required under Chapter 62, a statement that the registration requirement of that chapter applies to the defendant and a statement of the age of the victim of the offense;

28. The defendant's state identification number required by Article 66.152(a)(2), if that number has been assigned at the time of the judgment; and

29. The incident number required by Article 66.152(a)(4), if that number has been assigned at the time of the judgment.

Sec. 2. The judge may order the prosecuting attorney, or the attorney or attorneys representing any defendant, or the court clerk under the supervision of an attorney, to prepare the judgment, or the court may prepare the same.

Sec. 3. The provisions of this article shall apply to both felony and misdemeanor cases.

Sec. 4. The Office of Court Administration of the Texas Judicial System shall promulgate a standardized felony judgment form that conforms to the requirements of Section 1 of this article. A court entering a felony judgement[2] shall use the form promulgated under this section.

Sec. 5. In addition to the information described by Section 1 of this article, the judgment should reflect affirmative findings entered pursuant to Article 42.013 of this code.

Sec. 6. In addition to the information described by Section 1 of this article, the judgment should reflect affirmative findings entered pursuant to Article 42.014 of this code.

Sec. 7. In addition to the information described by Section 1, the judgment should reflect affirmative findings entered pursuant to Article 42.015.

Sec. 8. In addition to the information described by Section 1, the judgment should reflect affirmative findings entered pursuant to Article 42.017.

Sec. 9. In addition to the information described by Section 1, the judgment should reflect affirmative findings entered pursuant to Article 42.0197.

Sec. 10. In addition to the information described by Section 1, the judgment should reflect affirmative findings entered pursuant to Article 42.0198.

Sec. 11. In addition to the information described by Section 1, the judgment should reflect whether a victim impact statement was returned to the attorney representing the state pursuant to Article 56.03(e).

Text of sec. 12, as added by Acts 2017, 85th Leg., ch. 178 (S.B. 7), § 2

Sec. 12. In addition to the information described by Section 1, the judgment should reflect affirmative findings entered pursuant to Article 42.0192.

Text of sec. 12, as added by Acts 2017, 85th Leg., ch. 443 (S.B. 500), § 3

Sec. 12. In addition to the information described by Section 1, the judgment should reflect affirmative findings entered pursuant to Article 42.0196.

Acts 1965, 59th Leg., vol. 2, p. 317, ch. 722. Amended by Acts 1975, 64th Leg., p. 245, ch. 95, § 1, eff. Sept. 1, 1975; Acts 1981, 67th Leg., p. 809, ch. 291, § 111, eff. Sept. 1, 1981; Acts 1985, 69th Leg., ch. 344, § 1, eff. Jan. 1, 1986; Acts 1985, 69th Leg., ch. 344, § 2, eff. June 10, 1985; Acts 1987, 70th Leg., ch. 110, § 2, eff. Aug. 31, 1987; Acts 1989, 71st Leg., ch. 360, § 2, eff. Sept. 1, 1989; Acts 1989, 71st Leg., ch. 603, § 2, eff. Sept. 1, 1989; Acts 1989, 71st Leg., ch. 611, § 2, eff. Sept. 1, 1989; Acts 1989, 71st Leg., ch. 806, § 1, eff. Sept. 1, 1989; Acts 1991, 72nd Leg., ch. 16, § 4.04, eff. Aug. 26, 1991; Acts 1991, 72nd Leg., 2nd C.S., ch. 10, § 7.02, eff. Dec. 1, 1991; Acts 1993, 73rd Leg., ch. 900, §§ 5.03, 9.02 eff. Sept. 1, 1993; Acts 1993, 73rd Leg., ch. 987, § 4, eff. Sept. 1, 1993; Acts 1995, 74th Leg., ch. 258, § 9, eff. Sept. 1, 1995; Acts 1997, 75th Leg., ch. 668, § 2, eff. Sept. 1, 1997; Acts 1999, 76th Leg., ch. 580, § 6, eff. Sept. 1, 1999; Acts 1999, 76th Leg., ch. 1193, § 1, eff. Sept. 1, 1999; Acts 1999, 76th Leg., ch. 1415, § 2, eff. Sept. 1, 1999; Acts 2001, 77th Leg., ch. 1159, § 1, eff. Sept. 1, 2001; Acts 2005, 79th Leg., ch. 1218, § 1, eff. Sept. 1, 2005; Acts 2009, 81st Leg., ch. 1040, § 1, eff. Sept. 1, 2009; Acts 2009, 81st Leg., ch. 1130, § 15, eff. Sept. 1, 2009; Acts 2009, 81st Leg., ch. 1400, § 1, eff. Sept. 1, 2009; Acts 2011, 82nd Leg., ch. 91 (S.B. 1303), § 27.001(2), eff. Sept. 1, 2011; Acts 2013, 83rd Leg., ch. 1154 (S.B. 213), § 24, eff. Sept. 1, 2013; Acts 2015, 84th Leg., ch. 770 (H.B. 2299), § 2.10, eff. Jan. 1, 2017; Acts 2017, 85th Leg., ch. 178 (S.B. 7), § 2, eff. Sept. 1, 2017; Acts 2017, 85th Leg., ch. 443 (S.B. 500), § 3, eff. June 6, 2017; Acts 2017, 85th Leg., ch. 1058 (H.B. 2931), § 4.02, eff. Jan. 1, 2019.

[1] Vernon's Ann. C.C.P. art. 60.052.

[2] So in enrolled bill; probably should read "judgment".

Section 19 of Acts 2017, 85th Leg., ch. 178 (S.B. 7) provides:

"Section 12, Article 42.01, Code of Criminal Procedure, and Article 42.0192, Code of Criminal Procedure, as added by this Act, apply only to a judgment of conviction entered on or after the effective date [Sept. 1, 2017] of this Act."

Art. 42.011. Judgment Affecting an Officer or Jailer

If a person licensed under Chapter 1701, Occupations Code, is charged with the commission of a felony and a court that knows the person is licensed under that chapter convicts the person or places the person on community supervision, the clerk of the court shall send the Texas Commission on Law Enforcement, by mail or electronically, the license number of the person and a certified copy of the court's judgment reflecting that the person has been convicted or placed on community supervision.

Added by Acts 1995, 74th Leg., ch. 538, § 10, eff. Sept. 1, 1995. Amended by Acts 2013, 83rd Leg., ch. 93 (S.B. 686), § 2.09, eff. May 18, 2013.

Art. 42.012. Finding That Controlled Substance Used to Commit Offense

In the punishment phase of the trial of an offense under Chapter 29[1], Chapter 31[2], or Title 5[3], Penal Code, if the court determines beyond a reasonable doubt that the defendant administered or provided a controlled substance to the victim of the offense with the intent of facilitating the commission of the offense, the court shall make an affirmative finding of that fact and enter the affirmative finding in the judgment of that case.

Added by Acts 1999, 76th Leg., ch. 417, § 2(b), eff. Sept. 1, 1999. Renumbered from Vernon's Ann. C.C.P. art. 42.015 by Acts 2001, 77th Leg., ch. 1420, § 21.001(9), eff. Sept. 1, 2001.

[1] V.T.C.A., Penal Code § 29.01 et. seq.

[2] V.T.C.A., Penal Code § 31.01 et seq.

[3] V.T.C.A., Penal Code § 19.01 et seq.

Art. 42.013. Finding of family violence
Finding of family violence

Art. 42.013. In the trial of an offense under Title 5[1], Penal Code, if the court determines that the offense involved family violence, as defined by Section 71.004, Family Code, the court shall make an affirmative finding of that fact and enter the affirmative finding in the judgment of the case.

Added by Acts 1993, 73rd Leg., ch. 900, § 9.01, eff. Sept. 1, 1993. Amended by Acts 2003, 78th Leg., ch. 1276, § 7.002(h), eff. Sept. 1, 2003.

[1] V.T.C.A., Penal Code § 19.01 et seq.

Art. 42.0131. Required Notice for Persons Convicted of Misdemeanors Involving Family Violence

If a person is convicted of a misdemeanor involving family violence, as defined by Section 71.004, Family Code, the court shall notify the person of the fact that it is unlawful for the person to possess or transfer a firearm or ammunition.

Added by Acts 2007, 80th Leg., ch. 125, § 2, eff. Sept. 1, 2007.

Art. 42.014. Finding That Offense Was Committed Because of Bias or Prejudice

(a) In the trial of an offense under Title 5[1], Penal Code, or Section 28.02, 28.03, or 28.08, Penal Code, the judge shall make an affirmative finding of fact and enter the affirmative finding in the judgment of the case if at the guilt or innocence phase of the trial, the judge or the jury, whichever is the trier of fact, determines beyond a reasonable doubt that the defendant intentionally selected the person against whom the offense was committed, or intentionally selected the person's property that was damaged or affected as a result of the offense, because of the defendant's bias or prejudice against a group identified by race, color, disability, religion, national origin or ancestry, age, gender, or sexual preference or by status as a peace officer or judge.

(b) The sentencing judge may, as a condition of punishment, require attendance in an educational program to further tolerance and acceptance of others.

(c) In this article, "sexual preference" has the following meaning only: a preference for heterosexuality, homosexuality, or bisexuality.

Added by Acts 1993, 73rd Leg., ch. 987, § 5, eff. Sept. 1, 1993. Amended by Acts 1995, 74th Leg., ch. 318, § 50, eff. Sept. 1, 1995; Acts 2001, 77th Leg., ch. 85, § 1.02, eff. Sept. 1, 2001; Acts 2017, 85th Leg., ch. 440 (H.B. 2908), § 1, eff. Sept. 1, 2017.

[1] V.T.C.A., Penal Code § 19.01 et seq.

Section 6 of Acts 2017, 85th Leg., ch. 440 (H.B. 2908) provides:

"The changes in law made by this Act apply only to an offense committed on or after the effective date [Sept. 1, 2017] of this Act. An offense committed before the effective date of this Act is governed by the law in effect on the date the offense was committed, and the former law is continued in effect for that purpose. For purposes of this section, an offense was committed before the effective date of this Act if any element of the offense occurred before that date."

Art. 42.015. Finding of Age of Victim

(a) In the trial of an offense under Section 20.02, 20.03, or 20.04, Penal Code, or an attempt, conspiracy, or solicitation to commit one of those offenses, the judge shall make an affirmative finding of fact and enter the affirmative finding in the judgment in the case if the judge determines that the victim or intended victim was younger than 17 years of age at the time of the offense.

(b) In the trial of a sexually violent offense, as defined by Article 62.001, the judge shall make an affirmative finding of fact and enter the affirmative finding in the judgment in the case if the judge determines that the victim or intended victim was younger than 14 years of age at the time of the offense.

Added by Acts 1999, 76th Leg., ch. 1193, § 2, eff. Sept. 1, 1999; Acts 1999, 76th Leg., ch. 1415, § 3, eff. Sept. 1, 1999. Amended by Acts 2013, 83rd Leg., ch. 663 (H.B. 1302), § 2, eff. Sept. 1, 2013.

Art. 42.016. Special Driver's License or Identification Requirements for Certain Sex Offenders

If a person is convicted of, receives a grant of deferred adjudication for, or is adjudicated as having engaged in delinquent conduct based on a violation of an offense for which a conviction or adjudication requires registration as a sex offender under Chapter 62, the court shall:

(1) issue an order requiring the Texas Department of Public Safety to include in any driver's license record or personal identification certificate record maintained by the department for the person an indication that the person is subject to the registration requirements of Chapter 62;

(2) require the person to apply to the Texas Department of Public Safety in person for an original or renewal driver's license or personal identification certificate not later than the 30th day after the date the person is released or the date the department sends written notice to the person of the requirements of Article 62.060, as applicable, and to annually renew the license or certificate;

(3) notify the person of the consequence of the conviction or order of deferred adjudication as it relates to the order issued under this article; and

(4) send to the Texas Department of Public Safety a copy of the record of conviction, a copy of the order granting deferred adjudication, or a copy of the juvenile adjudication, as applicable, and a copy of the order issued under this article.

Added by Acts 1999, 76th Leg., ch. 1401, § 1, eff. Sept. 1, 2000. Amended by Acts 2005, 79th Leg., ch. 1008, § 2.01, eff. Sept. 1, 2005.

Art. 42.017. Finding Regarding Age–Based Offense

In the trial of an offense under Section 21.11 or 22.011, Penal Code, the judge shall make an affirmative finding of fact and enter the affirmative finding in the judgment in the case if the judge determines that:

(1) at the time of the offense, the defendant was not more than four years older than the victim or intended victim and the victim or intended victim was at least 15 years of age; and

(2) the conviction is based solely on the ages of the defendant and the victim or intended victim at the time of the offense.

Added by Acts 2001, 77th Leg., ch. 1159, § 2, eff. Sept. 1, 2001. Amended by Acts 2007, 80th Leg., ch. 593, § 3.17, eff. Sept. 1, 2007; Acts 2011, 82nd Leg., ch. 134 (S.B. 198), § 1, eff. Sept. 1, 2011.

Art. 42.018. Notice Provided by Clerk of Court

(a) This article applies only to:

(1) conviction or deferred adjudication community supervision granted on the basis of an offense for which a conviction or grant of deferred adjudication community supervision requires the defendant to register as a sex offender under Chapter 62; or

(2) conviction of an offense under Title 5 [1], Penal Code, if the victim of the offense was under 18 years of age at the time the offense was committed.

(b) Not later than the fifth day after the date a person who holds a certificate issued under Subchapter B [2], Chapter 21, Education Code, is convicted or granted deferred adjudication on the basis of an offense, the clerk of the court in which the conviction or deferred adjudication is entered shall provide to the State Board for Educator Certification written notice of the person's conviction or deferred adjudication, including the offense on which the conviction or deferred adjudication was based.

Added by Acts 2003, 78th Leg., ch. 920, § 2, eff. June 20, 2003. Amended by Acts 2017, 85th Leg., ch. 178 (S.B. 7), § 3, eff. Sept. 1, 2017.

[1] V.T.C.A., Penal Code § 19.01 et seq.
[2] V.T.C.A., Education Code § 21.031 et seq.

Art. 42.0181. Notice of Theft, Fraud, Money Laundering, or Insurance Fraud Provided by Clerk of Court

Not later than the fifth day after the date a person who holds a certificate of authority, license, or other authority issued by the Texas Department of Insurance is convicted of or granted deferred adjudication for an offense under Chapter 31, 32, 34, or 35, Penal Code, the clerk of the court in which the conviction or order of deferred adjudication is entered shall provide to the Texas Department of Insurance written notice of the person's conviction or deferred adjudication, including the offense on which the conviction or deferred adjudication was based.

Added by Acts 2005, 79th Leg., ch. 1162, § 7, eff. Sept. 1, 2005.

Art. 42.0182. Findings Regarding Tax Fraud

(a) In the trial of an offense under the Tax Code or an offense under the Penal Code related to the administration of taxes, the state may file a written request with the court in which the indictment or information is pending for the court to make affirmative findings regarding the commission of tax fraud as described by Subsection (b). The state must provide a copy of the written request to the defendant before the date the trial begins.

(b) If the state requests affirmative findings in the manner required by Subsection (a), the court shall make the requested affirmative findings and enter the findings in the papers in the case if the court finds by clear and convincing evidence that:

(1) the defendant's failure to pay a tax or file a report when due, as required by Title 2 or 3, Tax Code, was a result of fraud or an intent to evade the tax;

(2) the defendant altered, destroyed, or concealed any record, document, or thing, or presented to the comptroller any altered or fraudulent record, document, or thing, or otherwise engaged in fraudulent conduct for the apparent purpose of affecting the course or outcome of an audit, investigation, redetermination, or other proceeding before the comptroller; or

(3) the defendant's failure to file a report under Chapter 162, Tax Code, or to pay a tax under that chapter when the tax became due is attributable to fraud or an intent to evade the application of Chapter 162, Tax Code, or a rule adopted under Chapter 111 or 162, Tax Code.

Added by Acts 2011, 82nd Leg., ch. 68 (S.B. 934), § 4, eff. Sept. 1, 2011.

Art. 42.0183. Notice of Family Violence Offenses Provided by Clerk of Court

(a) This article applies only:

(1) to conviction or deferred adjudication granted on the basis of:

(A) an offense that constitutes family violence, as defined by Section 71.004, Family Code; or

(B) an offense under Title 5, Penal Code; and

(2) if the defendant is a member of the state military forces or is serving in the armed forces of the United States in an active-duty status.

(b) As soon as possible after the date on which the defendant is convicted or granted deferred adjudication on the basis of an offense, the clerk of the court in which the conviction or deferred adjudication is entered shall provide written notice of the conviction or deferred adjudication to the staff judge advocate general or the provost marshal of the military installation to which the defendant is assigned with the intent that the commanding officer will be notified, as applicable.

Added by Acts 2011, 82nd Leg., ch. 327 (H.B. 2624), § 3, eff. Sept. 1, 2011. Redesignated from Vernon's Ann.C.C.P. art. 42.0182 by Acts 2013, 83rd Leg., ch. 161 (S.B. 1093), § 22.001(7), eff. Sept. 1, 2013. Amended by Acts 2017, 85th Leg., ch. 147 (H.B. 1655), § 1, eff. Sept. 1, 2017.

Section 2 of Acts 2017, 85th Leg., ch. 147 (H.B. 1655) provides:

"The change in law made by this Act to Article 42.0183(b), Code of Criminal Procedure, applies only to a judgment of conviction entered on or after the effective date [Sept. 1, 2017] of this Act or a grant of deferred adjudication made on or after the effective date of this Act."

Art. 42.019. Motor Fuel Theft

(a) A judge shall enter an affirmative finding in the judgment in a case if the judge or jury, whichever is the finder of fact, determines beyond a reasonable doubt in the guilt or innocence phase of the trial of an offense under Section 31.03, Penal Code, that the defendant, in committing the offense:

(1) dispensed motor fuel into the fuel tank of a motor vehicle on the premises of an establishment at which motor fuel is offered for retail sale; and

(2) after dispensing the motor fuel, left the premises of the establishment without paying the establishment for the motor fuel.

(b) If a judge enters an affirmative finding as required by Subsection (a) and determines that the defendant has previously been convicted of an offense the judgment for which contains an affirmative finding under Subsection (a), the judge shall enter a special affirmative finding in the judgment in the case.

Added by Acts 2001, 77th Leg., ch. 359, § 1, eff. Sept. 1, 2001.

Art. 42.0191. Finding Regarding Victims of Trafficking or Other Abuse

(a) In the trial of an offense, on the motion of the attorney representing the state the judge shall make an affirmative finding of fact and enter the affirmative finding in the papers in the case if the judge determines that, regardless of whether the conduct at issue is the subject of the prosecution or part of the same criminal episode as the conduct that is the subject of the prosecution, a victim in the trial:

(1) is or has been a victim of a severe form of trafficking in persons, as defined by 22 U.S.C. Section 7102(8); or

(2) has suffered substantial physical or mental abuse as a result of having been a victim of criminal activity described by 8 U.S.C. Section 1101(a)(15)(U)(iii).

(b) That part of the papers in the case containing an affirmative finding under this article:

(1) must include specific information identifying the victim, as available;

(2) may not include information identifying the victim's location; and

(3) is confidential, unless written consent for the release of the affirmative finding is obtained from the victim or, if the victim is younger than 18 years of age, the victim's parent or guardian.

Added by Acts 2007, 80th Leg., ch. 849, § 1, eff. June 15, 2007.

Art. 42.0192. Finding Regarding Offense Related to Performance of Public Service

(a) In the trial of an offense described by Section 824.009, Government Code, the judge shall make an affirmative finding of fact and enter the affirmative finding in the judgment in the case if the judge determines that the offense committed was related to the defendant's employment described by Section 824.009(b), Government Code, while a member of the Teacher Retirement System of Texas.

(b) A judge who makes the affirmative finding described by this article shall make the determination and provide the notice required by Section 824.009(l), Government Code, as applicable.

Added by Acts 2017, 85th Leg., ch. 178 (S.B. 7), § 4, eff. Sept. 1, 2017.

Section 19 of Acts 2017, 85th Leg., ch. 178 (S.B. 7) provides:

"Section 12, Article 42.01, Code of Criminal Procedure, and Article 42.0192, Code of Criminal Procedure, as added by this Act, apply only to a judgment of conviction entered on or after the effective date [Sept. 1, 2017] of this Act."

Art. 42.0196. Finding regarding offense related to performance of public service

(a) In the trial of an offense described by Section 810.002, Government Code, the judge shall make an affirmative finding of fact and enter the affirmative finding in the judgment in the case if the judge determines that the defendant is:

(1) a member of the elected class described by Section 810.002(b)(1), Government Code, while a member of the Employees Retirement System of Texas; or

(2) a holder of an elected office for which the defendant wholly or partly became eligible for membership in a public retirement system.

(b) A judge who makes the affirmative finding described by this article shall make the determination and provide the notice required by Section 810.002(k), Government Code.

Added by Acts 2017, 85th Leg., ch. 443 (S.B. 500), § 4, eff. June 6, 2017.

Art. 42.0197. Finding Regarding Gang-Related Conduct

In the trial of an offense, on the motion of the attorney representing the state the judge shall make an affirmative finding of fact and enter the affirmative finding in the judgment in the case if the judge determines that the applicable conduct was engaged in as part of the activities of a criminal street gang as defined by Section 71.01, Penal Code.

Added by Acts 2009, 81st Leg., ch. 1130, § 16, eff. Sept. 1, 2009.

Art. 42.0198. Finding Regarding Delay in Arrest of Defendant

In the trial of an offense under Section 19.02, 22.011, or 22.021, Penal Code, on the motion of the attorney representing the state the judge shall make an affirmative finding of fact regarding the number of months that elapsed, if any, between the date an arrest warrant was issued for the defendant following an indictment for the offense and the date the defendant was arrested for the offense. The judge shall enter the affirmative finding in the judgment in the case.

Added by Acts 2009, 81st Leg., ch. 1400, § 2, eff. Sept. 1, 2009.

Art. 42.0199. Finding Regarding Diligent Participation Credit

If a person is convicted of a state jail felony, the judge shall make a finding and enter the finding in the judgment of the case regarding whether the person is presumptively entitled to diligent participation credit in accordance with Article 42A.559.

Added by Acts 2015, 84th Leg., ch. 225 (H.B. 1546), § 1, eff. Sept. 1, 2015. Amended by Acts 2017, 85th Leg., ch. 324 (S.B. 1488), § 23.001, eff. Sept. 1, 2017.

Section 3 of Acts 2015, 84th Leg., ch. 225 (H.B. 1546) provides:

"The change in law made by this Act applies only to a person confined in a state jail felony facility for an offense committed on or after the effective date [Sept. 1, 2015] of this Act. A person confined in a state jail felony facility for an offense committed before the effective date of this Act is covered by the law in effect when the offense was committed, and the former law is continued in effect for that purpose. For purposes of this section, an offense was committed before the effective date of this Act if any element of the offense occurred before that date."

Art. 42.02. Sentence

The sentence is that part of the judgment, or order revoking a suspension of the imposition of a sentence, that orders that the punishment be carried into execution in the manner prescribed by law.

Acts 1965, 59th Leg., vol. 2, p. 317, ch. 722; Amended by Acts 1981, 67th Leg., p. 809, ch. 291, § 112, eff. Sept. 1, 1981; Acts 1993, 73rd Leg., ch. 900, § 5.03, eff. Sept. 1, 1993.

Art. 42.023. Judge may consider alternative sentencing

Before pronouncing sentence on a defendant convicted of a criminal offense, the judge may consider whether the defendant should be committed for care and treatment under Section 462.081, Health and Safety Code.

Added by Acts 1993, 73rd Leg., ch. 900, § 5.03, eff. Sept. 1, 1993.

Art. 42.025. Sentencing Hearing at Secondary School

(a) A judge may order the sentencing hearing of a defendant convicted of an offense involving possession, manufacture, or delivery of a controlled substance under Chapter 481, Health and Safety Code, to be held at a secondary school if:

(1) the judge determines that the sentencing hearing would have educational value to students due to the nature of the offense and its consequences;

(2) the defendant agrees;

(3) the school administration agrees; and

(4) appropriate measures are taken to ensure:

(A) the safety of the students; and

(B) a fair hearing for the defendant that complies with all applicable laws and rules.

(b) A judge may, at a secondary school, receive a plea of guilty or nolo contendere from a defendant charged with an offense described by Subsection (a) and place the defendant on deferred adjudication under Subchapter C, Chapter 42A, if:

(1) the judge makes the determination that the proceeding would have educational value, as provided by Subsection (a)(1);

(2) the defendant and the school agree to the location of the proceeding, as provided by Subsections (a)(2) and (3); and

(3) appropriate measures are taken in regard to the safety of students and the rights of the defendant, as described by Subsection (a)(4).

Added by Acts 2011, 82nd Leg., ch. 1280 (H.B. 1113), § 1, eff. Sept. 1, 2011. Amended by Acts 2015, 84th Leg., ch. 770 (H.B. 2299), § 2.11, eff. Jan. 1, 2017.

Art. 42.03. Pronouncing sentence; time; credit for time spent in jail between arrest and sentence or pending appeal

Sec. 1. (a) Except as provided in Article 42.14, sentence shall be pronounced in the defendant's presence.

(b) The court shall permit a victim, close relative of a deceased victim, or guardian of a victim, as defined by Article 56.01 of this code, to appear in person to present to the court and to the defendant a statement of the person's views about the offense, the defendant, and the effect of the offense on the victim. The victim, relative, or guardian may not direct questions to the defendant while making the statement. The court reporter may not transcribe the statement. The statement must be made:

(1) after punishment has been assessed and the court has determined whether or not to grant community supervision in the case;

(2) after the court has announced the terms and conditions of the sentence; and

(3) after sentence is pronounced.

Sec. 2. (a) In all criminal cases the judge of the court in which the defendant is convicted shall give the defendant credit on the defendant's sentence for the time that the defendant has spent:

(1) in jail for the case, including confinement served as described by Article 46B.009 and excluding confinement served as a condition of community supervision, from the time of his arrest and confinement until his sentence by the trial court;

(2) in a substance abuse treatment facility operated by the Texas Department of Criminal Justice under Section 493.009, Government Code, or another court-ordered residential program or facility as a condition of deferred adjudication community supervision granted in the case if the defendant successfully completes the treatment program at that facility; or

(3) confined in a mental health facility or residential care facility as described by Article 46B.009.

(b) In all revocations of a suspension of the imposition of a sentence the judge shall enter the restitution due and owing on the date of the revocation.

Sec. 3. If a defendant appeals his conviction, is not released on bail, and is retained in a jail as provided in Section 7, Article 42.09, pending his appeal, the judge of the court in which the defendant was convicted shall give the defendant credit on his sentence for the time that the defendant has spent in jail pending disposition of his appeal. The court shall endorse on both the commitment and the mandate from the appellate court all credit given the defendant under this section, and the Texas Department of Criminal Justice shall grant the credit in computing the defendant's eligibility for parole and discharge.

Sec. 4. When a defendant who has been sentenced to imprisonment in the Texas Department of Criminal Justice has spent time in jail pending trial and sentence or pending appeal, the judge of the sentencing court shall direct the sheriff to attach to the commitment papers a statement assessing the defendant's conduct while in jail.

Sec. 5. Except as otherwise provided by Article 42A.106(b), the court after pronouncing the sentence shall inform the defendant of the defendant's right to petition the court for an order of nondisclosure of criminal history record information under Subchapter E–1, Chapter 411, Government Code, unless the defendant is ineligible to pursue that right because of the requirements that apply to obtaining the order in the defendant's circumstances, such as:

(1) the nature of the offense for which the defendant is convicted; or

(2) the defendant's criminal history.

Sec. 6. Repealed by Acts 1989, 71st Leg., ch. 785, § 4.24, eff. Sept. 1, 1989.

Sec. 7, 8. Deleted by Acts 1993, 73rd Leg., ch. 900, § 5.03, eff. Sept. 1, 1993.

Acts 1965, 59th Leg., vol. 2, p. 317, ch. 722. Amended by Acts 1967, 60th Leg., p. 1743, ch. 659, § 28, eff. Aug. 28, 1967; Acts 1973, 63rd Leg., p. 205, ch. 91, § 1, eff. Aug. 27, 1973; Acts 1977, 65th Leg., p. 1036, ch. 382, § 1, eff. Aug. 29, 1977; Acts 1977, 65th Leg., p. 2076, ch. 827, § 1, eff. Aug. 29, 1977; Acts 1981, 67th Leg., p. 353, ch. 141, § 1, eff. Sept. 1, 1981; Acts 1981, 67th Leg., p. 809, ch. 291, § 113, eff. Sept. 1, 1981; Acts 1981, 67th Leg., p. 2418, ch. 616, § 1, eff. Aug. 31, 1981; Acts 1983, 68th Leg., p. 3792, ch. 586, § 4, eff. Aug. 29, 1983; Acts 1983, 68th Leg., p. 4666, ch. 809, § 1, eff. Aug. 29, 1983; Acts 1985, 69th Leg., ch. 232, § 13, eff. Sept. 1, 1985; Acts 1989, 71st Leg., ch. 785, § 4.06, eff. June 15, 1989; Acts 1989, 71st Leg., ch. 848, § 1, eff. June 14, 1989; Acts 1989, 71st Leg., ch. 1040, §§ 1, 2 eff. Aug. 28, 1989; Acts 1991, 72nd Leg., ch. 16, § 4.05, eff. Aug. 26, 1991; Acts 1991, 72nd Leg., ch. 278, § 1, eff. June 5, 1991; Acts 1991, 72nd Leg., 2nd C.S., ch. 10, §§ 14.01, 14.02, 14.03, 14.04, 15.03 eff. Oct. 1, 1991; Acts 1991, 72nd Leg., 2nd C.S., ch. 10, § 8.02, eff. Dec. 1, 1991; Acts 1993, 73rd Leg., ch. 900, § 5.03, eff. Sept. 1, 1993; Acts 1995, 74th Leg., ch. 556, § 1, eff. Sept. 1, 1995; Acts 2003, 78th Leg., ch. 406, § 2, eff. Sept. 1, 2003; Acts 2007, 80th Leg., ch. 1205, § 1, eff. Sept. 1, 2007; Acts 2009, 81st Leg., ch. 87, § 25.018, eff. Sept. 1, 2009; Acts 2011, 82nd Leg., ch. 718 (H.B. 748), § 1, eff. Sept. 1, 2011; Acts 2011, 82nd Leg., ch. 822 (H.B. 2725), § 1, eff. Sept. 1, 2011; Acts 2015, 84th Leg., ch. 770 (H.B. 2299), § 2.12, eff. Jan. 1, 2017; Acts 2015, 84th Leg., ch. 1279 (S.B. 1902), § 15, eff. Sept. 1, 2015; Acts 2017, 85th Leg., ch. 324 (S.B. 1488), § 23.002, eff. Sept. 1, 2017.

Section 32 of Acts 2015, 84th Leg., ch. 1279 (S.B. 1902) provides:

"Sec. 32. The changes in law made by this Act apply only to the issuance of an order of nondisclosure of criminal history record information for an offense committed on or after the effective date [Sept. 1, 2015] of this Act. The issuance of an order of nondisclosure of criminal history record information for an offense committed before the effective date of this Act is governed by the law in effect on the date the offense was committed, and the former law is continued in effect for that purpose. For purposes of this section, an offense is committed before the effective date of this Act if any element of the offense occurs before the effective date."

Art. 42.031.   Work release program

Sec. 1. (a) The sheriff of each county may attempt to secure employment for each defendant sentenced to the county jail work release program under Article 42.034 and each defendant confined in the county jail awaiting transfer to the Texas Department of Criminal Justice.

(b) The employer of a defendant participating in a program under this article shall pay the defendant's salary to the sheriff. The sheriff shall deposit the salary into a special fund to be given to the defendant on his release after deducting:

(1) the cost to the county for the defendant's confinement during the pay period based on the average daily cost of confining defendants in the county jail, as determined by the commissioners court of the county;

(2) support of the defendant's dependents; and

(3) restitution to the victims of an offense committed by the defendant.

(c) At the time of sentencing or at a later date, the court sentencing a defendant may direct the sheriff not to deduct the cost described under Subdivision (1) of Subsection (b) of this section or to deduct only a specified portion of the cost if the court determines that the full deduction would cause a significant financial hardship to the defendant's dependents.

(d) If the sheriff does not find employment for a defendant who would otherwise be sentenced to imprisonment in the department, the sheriff shall:

(1) transfer the defendant to the sheriff of a county who agrees to accept the defendant as a participant in the county jail work release program; or

(2) retain the defendant in the county jail for employment as soon as possible in a jail work release program.

Sec. 2. A defendant participating in a program under this article shall be confined in the county jail or in another facility designated by the sheriff at all times except for:

(1) time spent at work and traveling to or from work; and

(2) time spent attending or traveling to or from an education or rehabilitation program approved by the sheriff.

Sec. 3. (a) The sheriff of each county shall classify each felon serving a sentence in the county jail work release program for the purpose of awarding good conduct time credit in the same manner as inmates of the Texas Department of Criminal Justice are classified under Chapter 498, Government Code, and shall award good conduct time in the same manner as the director of the department does in that chapter.

(b) If the sheriff determines that the defendant is conducting himself in a manner that is dangerous to inmates in the county jail or to society as a whole, the sheriff may remove the defendant from participation in the program pending a hearing before the sentencing court. At the hearing, if the court determines that the sheriff's assessment of the defendant's conduct is correct, the court may terminate the defendant's participation in the program and order the defendant to the term of imprisonment that the defendant would have received had he not entered the program. If the court determines that the sheriff's assessment is incorrect, the court shall order the sheriff to readmit the defendant to the program. A defendant shall receive as credit toward his sentence any time served as a participant in the program.

Added by Acts 1989, 71st Leg., ch. 2, § 5.03(a), eff. Aug. 28, 1989. Amended by Acts 1991, 72nd Leg., 2nd C.S., ch. 10, § 14.10, eff. Oct. 1, 1991; Acts 1991, 72nd Leg., 2nd C.S., ch. 10, § 14.11, eff. Oct. 1, 1991; Acts 1993, 73rd Leg., ch. 900, § 5.03, eff. Sept. 1, 1993; Acts 2009, 81st Leg., ch. 87, §§ 25.019, 25.020, eff. Sept. 1, 2009.

Art. 42.032. Good conduct

Sec. 1. To encourage county jail discipline, a distinction may be made to give orderly, industrious, and obedient defendants the comforts and privileges they deserve. The reward for good conduct may consist of a relaxation of strict county jail rules and extension of social privileges consistent with proper discipline.

Sec. 2. The sheriff in charge of each county jail may grant commutation of time for good conduct, industry, and obedience. A deduction not to exceed one day for each day of the original sentence actually served may be made for the term or terms of sentences if a charge of misconduct has not been sustained against the defendant.

Sec. 3. This article applies whether or not the judgment of conviction is a fine or jail sentence or both, but the deduction in time may not exceed one-third of the original sentence as to fines and court costs assessed in the judgment of conviction.

Sec. 4. A defendant serving two or more cumulative sentences shall be allowed commutation as if the sentences were one sentence.

Sec. 5. Any part or all of the commutation accrued under this article may be forfeited and taken away by the sheriff:

(1) for a sustained charge of misconduct in violation of any rule known to the defendant, including escape or attempt to escape, if the sheriff has complied with discipline proceedings as approved by the Commission on Jail Standards;

(2) on receipt by the sheriff of a certified copy of a final order of a state or federal court that dismisses as frivolous or malicious a lawsuit brought by a defendant while the defendant was in the custody of the sheriff; or

(3) if the defendant, in violation of an order entered under Article 42.24, contacts the victim of the offense for which the defendant is serving a sentence or a member of the victim's family.

Sec. 6. Repealed by Acts 2009, 81st Leg., ch. 854, § 7.

Sec. 7. The sheriff shall keep a conduct record in card or ledger form and a calendar card on each defendant showing all forfeitures of commutation time and the reasons for the forfeitures.

Added by Acts 1989, 71st Leg., ch. 2, § 5.04(a), eff. Aug. 28, 1989. Amended by Acts 1991, 72nd Leg., 2nd C.S., ch. 10, § 14.05, eff. Oct. 1, 1991; Acts 1993, 73rd Leg., ch. 900, § 5.03, eff. Sept. 1, 1993; Acts 1999, 76th Leg., ch. 655, § 2(a), eff. June 18, 1999; Acts 2009, 81st Leg., ch. 854, § 7, eff. June 19, 2009; Acts 2011, 82nd Leg., ch. 491 (H.B. 1028), § 2, eff. Sept. 1, 2011.

Art. 42.033. Sentence to serve time during off-work hours

(a) Where jail time has been awarded to a person sentenced for a misdemeanor or sentenced to confinement in the county jail for a felony or when a defendant is serving a period of confinement as a condition of community supervision, the trial judge, at the time of the pronouncement of sentence or at any time while the defendant is serving the sentence or period of confinement, when in the judge's discretion the ends of justice would best be served, may permit the defendant to serve the defendant's sentence or period of confinement intermittently during his off-work hours or on weekends. The judge may require bail of the defendant to ensure the faithful performance of the sentence or period of confinement. The judge may attach conditions regarding the employment, travel, and other conduct of the defendant during the performance of such a sentence or period of confinement.

(b) The court may impose as a condition to permitting a defendant to serve the jail time assessed or period of confinement intermittently an additional requirement that the defendant make any of the following payments to the court, agencies, or persons, or that the defendant execute a letter and direct it to the defendant's employer directing the employer to deduct from the defendant's salary an amount directed by the court, which is to be sent by the employer to the clerk of the court. The money received by the court under this section may be used to pay the following expenses as directed by the court:

(1) the support of the defendant's dependents, if necessary;

(2) the defendant's documented personal, business, and travel expenses;

(3) reimbursement of the general fund of the county for the maintenance of the defendant in jail; and

(4) installment payments on restitution, fines, and court costs ordered by the court.

(c) The condition imposed under Subsection (b) of this article is not binding on an employer, except that income withheld for child support is governed by Chapter 158, Family Code.

(d) The court may permit the defendant to serve the defendant's sentence or period of confinement intermittently in order for the defendant to continue employment if the court imposes confinement for failure to pay a fine or court costs, as punishment for criminal nonsupport under Section 25.05, Penal Code, or for contempt of a court order for periodic payments for the support of a child.

(e) The court may permit the defendant to seek employment or obtain medical, psychological, or substance abuse treatment or counseling or obtain training or needed education under the same terms and conditions that apply to employment under this article.

Added by Acts 1989, 71st Leg., ch. 785, § 4.07, eff. Sept. 1, 1989. Amended by Acts 1991, 72nd Leg., 2nd C.S., ch. 10, § 14.06, eff. Oct. 1, 1991; Acts 1993, 73rd Leg., ch. 900, § 5.03, eff. Sept. 1, 1993; Acts 1997, 75th Leg., ch. 165, § 7.03, eff. Sept. 1, 1997.

Art. 42.034.   County jail work release program

(a) If jail time has been awarded to a person sentenced for a misdemeanor or sentenced to confinement in the county jail for a felony, the trial judge at the time of pronouncement of sentence or at any time while the defendant is serving the sentence, when in the judge's discretion the ends of justice would best be served, may require the defendant to serve an alternate term for the same period of time in the county jail work release program of the county in which the offense occurred, if the person is classified by the sheriff as a low-risk offender under the classification system developed by the Commission on Jail Standards under Section 511.009, Government Code.

(b) The sheriff shall provide a classification report for a defendant to a judge as necessary so that the judge can determine whether to require the defendant to participate in the work release program under this article.

(c) A defendant sentenced under this article who would otherwise be sentenced to confinement in jail may earn good conduct credit in the same manner as provided by Article 42.032 of this code, but only while actually confined.

Added by Acts 1989, 71st Leg., ch. 785, § 4.08, eff. Sept. 1, 1989. Amended by Acts 1991, 72nd Leg., 2nd C.S., ch. 10, § 14.07, eff. Oct. 1, 1991; Acts 1993, 73rd Leg., ch. 900, § 5.03, eff. Sept. 1, 1993; Acts 1995, 74th Leg., ch. 722, § 1, eff. Sept. 1, 1995.

Art. 42.035.   Electronic monitoring; house arrest

(a) A court may require a defendant to serve all or part of a sentence of confinement in county jail by participating in an electronic monitoring program rather than being confined in the county jail, if the program:

(1) is operated by a community supervision and corrections department that serves the county in which the court is located and has been approved by the community justice assistance division of the Texas Department of Criminal Justice; or

(2) is operated by the commissioners court of the county, or by a private vendor under contract with the commissioners court, under Section 351.904, Local Government Code, if the defendant has not been placed on community supervision.

(b) A judge, at the time of the pronouncement of a sentence of confinement or at any time while the defendant is serving the sentence, on the judge's own motion or on the written motion of the defendant, may permit the defendant to serve the sentence under house arrest, including electronic monitoring and any other conditions the court chooses to impose, during the person's off-work hours. The judge may require bail of the defendant to ensure the faithful performance of the sentence.

(c) The court may require the defendant to pay to the community supervision and corrections department or the county any reasonable cost incurred because of the defendant's participation in the house arrest program, including the cost of electronic monitoring.

(d) A defendant who submits to electronic monitoring or participates in the house arrest program under this article discharges a sentence of confinement in the same manner as if the defendant were confined in county jail.

(e) A court may revoke a defendant's participation in an electronic monitoring program and require the defendant to serve the remainder of the defendant's sentence of confinement in county jail if the defendant violates a condition imposed by a court under this article, including a condition requiring the defendant to pay for participating in the program under Subsection (c).

Added by Acts 1989, 71st Leg., ch. 785, § 4.09, eff. Sept. 1, 1989. Amended by Acts 1993, 73rd Leg., ch. 900, § 5.03, eff. Sept. 1, 1993; Acts 2009, 81st Leg., ch. 854, § 1, eff. June 19, 2009.

Art. 42.036. Community service

(a) A court may require a defendant, other than a defendant convicted of an offense under Sections 49.04–49.08, Penal Code, to serve all or part of a sentence of confinement or period of confinement required as a condition of community supervision in county jail by performing community service rather than by being confined in county jail unless the sentence of confinement was imposed by the jury in the case.

(b) In its order requiring a defendant to participate in community service work, the court must specify:

(1) the number of hours the defendant is required to work; and

(2) the entity or organization for which the defendant is required to work.

(c) The court may order the defendant to perform community service work under this article only for a governmental entity or a nonprofit organization that provides services to the general public that enhance social welfare and the general well-being of the community. A governmental entity or nonprofit organization that accepts a defendant under this section to perform community service must agree to supervise the defendant in the performance of the defendant's work and report on the defendant's work to the community supervision and corrections department or court-related services office.

(d) The court may require bail of a defendant to ensure the defendant's faithful performance of community service and may attach conditions to the bail as it determines are proper.

(e) A court may not order a defendant who is employed to perform more than 16 hours per week of community service under this article unless the court determines that requiring the defendant to work additional hours does not work a hardship on the defendant or the defendant's dependents. A court may not order a defendant who is unemployed to perform more than 32 hours per week of community service under this article, but may direct the defendant to use the remaining hours of the week to seek employment.

(f) A defendant is considered to have served one day in jail for each eight hours of community service performed under this article.

(g) Deleted by Acts 1993, 73rd Leg., ch. 900, § 5.03, eff. Sept. 1, 1993.

(h) Repealed by Acts 1995, 74th Leg., ch. 76, § 3.14, eff. Sept. 1, 1995.

Added by Acts 1989, 71st Leg., ch. 785, § 4.10, eff. Sept. 1, 1989. Amended by Acts 1990, 71st Leg., 6th C.S., ch. 25, § 27, eff. June 18, 1990; Acts 1991, 72nd Leg., 2nd C.S., ch. 10, §§ 14.08, 15.01, eff. Oct. 1, 1991; Acts 1993, 73rd Leg., ch. 201, § 2, eff. Aug. 30, 1993; Acts 1993, 73rd Leg., ch. 900, § 5.03, eff. Sept. 1, 1993; Acts 1995, 74th Leg., ch. 76, § 3.14, eff. Sept. 1, 1995.

Art. 42.037. Restitution

(a) In addition to any fine authorized by law, the court that sentences a defendant convicted of an offense may order the defendant to make restitution to any victim of the offense or to the compensation to victims of crime fund established under Subchapter B, Chapter 56, to the extent that fund has paid compensation to or on behalf of the victim. If the court does not order restitution or orders partial restitution under this subsection, the court shall state on the record the reasons for not making the order or for the limited order.

(b)(1) If the offense results in damage to or loss or destruction of property of a victim of the offense, the court may order the defendant:

(A) to return the property to the owner of the property or someone designated by the owner; or

(B) if return of the property is impossible or impractical or is an inadequate remedy, to pay an amount equal to the greater of:

(i) the value of the property on the date of the damage, loss, or destruction; or

(ii) the value of the property on the date of sentencing, less the value of any part of the property that is returned on the date the property is returned.

(2) If the offense results in personal injury to a victim, the court may order the defendant to make restitution to:

(A) the victim for any expenses incurred by the victim as a result of the offense; or

(B) the compensation to victims of crime fund to the extent that fund has paid compensation to or on behalf of the victim.

(3) If the victim or the victim's estate consents, the court may, in addition to an order under Subdivision (2), order the defendant to make restitution by performing services instead of by paying money or make restitution to a person or organization, other than the compensation to victims of crime fund, designated by the victim or the estate.

(c) The court, in determining whether to order restitution and the amount of restitution, shall consider:

(1) the amount of the loss sustained by any victim and the amount paid to or on behalf of the victim by the compensation to victims of crime fund as a result of the offense; and

(2) other factors the court deems appropriate.

(d) If the court orders restitution under this article and the victim is deceased the court shall order the defendant to make restitution to the victim's estate.

(e) The court shall impose an order of restitution that is as fair as possible to the victim or to the compensation to victims of crime fund, as applicable. The imposition of the order may not unduly complicate or prolong the sentencing process.

(f)(1) The court may not order restitution for a loss for which the victim has received or will receive compensation only from a source other than the compensation to victims of crime fund. The court may, in the interest of justice, order restitution to any person who has compensated the victim for the loss to the extent the person paid compensation. An order of restitution shall require that all restitution to a victim or to the compensation to victims of crime fund be made before any restitution to any other person is made under the order.

(2) Any amount recovered by a victim from a person ordered to pay restitution in a federal or state civil proceeding is reduced by any amount previously paid to the victim by the person under an order of restitution.

(g)(1) The court may require a defendant to make restitution under this article within a specified period or in specified installments. If the court requires the defendant to make restitution in specified installments, in addition to the installment payments, the court may require the defendant to pay a one-time restitution fee of $12, $6 of which the court shall retain for costs incurred in collecting the specified installments and $6 of which the court shall order to be paid to the compensation to victims of crime fund.

(2) The end of the period or the last installment may not be later than:

(A) the end of the period of probation, if probation is ordered;

(B) five years after the end of the term of imprisonment imposed, if the court does not order probation; or

(C) five years after the date of sentencing in any other case.

(3) If the court does not provide otherwise, the defendant shall make restitution immediately.

(4) Except as provided by Subsection (n), the order of restitution must require the defendant to: (i) make restitution directly to the person or agency that will accept and forward restitution payments to the victim or other person eligible for restitution under this article, including the compensation to victims of crime fund; (ii) make restitution directly to the victim or other person eligible for restitution under this article, including the compensation to victims of crime fund; or (iii) deliver the amount or property due as restitution to a community supervision and corrections department for transfer to the victim or person.

(h) If a defendant is placed on community supervision or is paroled or released on mandatory supervision, the court or the parole panel shall order the payment of restitution ordered under this article as a condition of community supervision, parole, or mandatory supervision. The court may revoke community supervision and the parole panel may revoke parole or mandatory supervision if the defendant fails to comply with the order. In determining whether to revoke community supervision, parole, or mandatory supervision, the court or parole panel shall consider:

(1) the defendant's employment status;

(2) the defendant's current and future earning ability;

(3) the defendant's current and future financial resources;

(4) the willfulness of the defendant's failure to pay;

(5) any other special circumstances that may affect the defendant's ability to pay; and

(6) the victim's financial resources or ability to pay expenses incurred by the victim as a result of the offense.

(i) In addition to any other terms and conditions of community supervision imposed under Chapter 42A, the court may require a defendant to reimburse the compensation to victims of crime fund created under Subchapter B, Chapter 56,[1] for any amounts paid from that fund to or on behalf of a victim of the defendant's offense. In this subsection, "victim" has the meaning assigned by Article 56.32.

(j) The court may order a community supervision and corrections department to obtain information pertaining to the factors listed in Subsection (c). The supervision officer shall include the information in the report required under Article 42A.252(a) or a separate report, as the court directs. The court shall permit the defendant and the prosecuting attorney to read the report.

(k) The court shall resolve any dispute relating to the proper amount or type of restitution. The standard of proof is a preponderance of the evidence. The burden of demonstrating the amount of the loss sustained by a victim as a result of the offense is on the prosecuting attorney. The burden of demonstrating the financial resources of the defendant and the financial needs of the defendant and the defendant's dependents is on the defendant. The burden of demonstrating other matters as the court deems appropriate is on the party designated by the court as justice requires.

(l) Conviction of a defendant for an offense involving the act giving rise to restitution under this article estops the defendant from denying the essential allegations of that offense in any subsequent federal civil proceeding or state civil proceeding brought by the victim, to the extent consistent with state law.

(m) An order of restitution may be enforced by the state or a victim named in the order to receive the restitution in the same manner as a judgment in a civil action.

(n) If a defendant is convicted of or receives deferred adjudication for an offense under Section 25.05, Penal Code, if the child support order on which prosecution of the offense was based required the defendant to pay the support to a local registry or the Title IV-D agency, and if the court orders restitution under this article, the order of restitution must require the defendant to pay the child support in the following manner:

(1) during any period in which the defendant is under the supervision of a community supervision and corrections department, to the department for transfer to the local registry or Title IV-D agency designated as the place of payment in the child support order; and

(2) during any period in which the defendant is not under the supervision of a department, directly to the registry or agency described by Subdivision (1).

(o) The department may waive a supervision fee or an administrative fee imposed on an inmate under Section 508.182, Government Code, during any period in which the inmate is required to pay restitution under this article.

(p)(1) A court shall order a defendant convicted of an offense under Section 28.03(f), Penal Code, involving damage or destruction inflicted on a place of human burial or under Section 42.08, Penal Code, to make restitution in the amount described by Subsection (b)(1)(B) to a cemetery organization operating a cemetery affected by the commission of the offense.

(2) If a court orders an unemancipated minor to make restitution under Subsection (a) and the minor is financially unable to make the restitution, the court may order:

(A) the minor to perform a specific number of hours of community service to satisfy the restitution; or

(B) the parents or other person responsible for the minor's support to make the restitution in the amount described by Subsection (b)(1)(B).

(3) In this subsection, "cemetery" and "cemetery organization" have the meanings assigned by Section 711.001, Health and Safety Code.

(q) The court shall order a defendant convicted of an offense under Section 22.11, Penal Code, to make restitution to the victim of the offense or the victim's employer in an amount equal to the sum of any expenses incurred by the victim or employer to:

(1) test the victim for HIV, hepatitis A, hepatitis B, tuberculosis, or any other disease designated as a reportable disease under Section 81.048, Health and Safety Code; or

(2) treat the victim for HIV, hepatitis A, hepatitis B, tuberculosis, or any other disease designated as a reportable disease under Section 81.048, Health and Safety Code, the victim contracts as a result of the offense.

(r) The court may order a defendant convicted of an offense under Section 43.26, Penal Code, to make restitution to an individual who as a child younger than 18 years of age was depicted in the visual material, in an amount equal to the expenses incurred by the individual as a result of the offense, including:

(1) medical services relating to physical, psychiatric, or psychological care;

(2) physical and occupational therapy or rehabilitation;

(3) necessary transportation, temporary housing, and child care expenses;

(4) lost income; and

(5) attorney's fees.

(s)(1) A court shall order a defendant convicted of an offense under Section 28.08, Penal Code, to make restitution by:

(A) reimbursing the owner of the property for the cost of restoring the property; or

(B) with the consent of the owner of the property, personally restoring the property by removing or painting over any markings the defendant made.

(2) A court shall order a defendant convicted of an offense under Section 28.08, Penal Code, to make restitution to a political subdivision that owns public property or erects a street sign or official traffic-control device on which the defendant makes markings in violation of Section 28.08, Penal Code, by:

(A) paying an amount equal to the lesser of the cost to the political subdivision of replacing or restoring the public property, street sign, or official traffic-control device; or

(B) with the consent of the political subdivision, restoring the public property, street sign, or official traffic-control device by removing or painting over any markings made by the defendant on the property, sign, or device.

(3) If the court orders a defendant to make restitution under this subsection and the defendant is financially unable to make the restitution, the court may order the defendant to perform a specific number of hours of community service to satisfy the restitution.

(4) Notwithstanding Subsection (g)(4), a court shall direct a defendant ordered to make restitution under this subsection as a condition of community supervision to deliver the amount or property due as restitution to the defendant's supervising officer for transfer to the owner. A parole panel shall direct a defendant ordered to make restitution under this subsection as a condition of parole or mandatory supervision to deliver the amount or property due as restitution to the defendant's supervising officer. The defendant's supervising officer shall notify the court when the defendant has delivered the full amount of restitution ordered.

(5) For purposes of this subsection, "official traffic-control device" has the meaning assigned by Section 541.304, Transportation Code.

(t) If a person is convicted of an offense under Section 641.054, Business & Commerce Code, the court shall order the person to make restitution to an owner or lawful producer of a master recording that has suffered financial loss as a result of the offense or to a trade association that represents that owner or lawful producer. The amount of restitution ordered shall be:

(1) the greater of:

(A) the aggregate wholesale value of the lawfully manufactured and authorized recordings corresponding to the number of nonconforming recordings involved in the offense; or

(B) the actual financial loss to the owner, lawful producer, or trade association; and

(2) the costs associated with investigating the offense.

(u) For purposes of Subsection (t)(1)(A):

(1) the calculation of the aggregate wholesale value is based on the average wholesale value of the lawfully manufactured and authorized recordings; and

(2) the specific wholesale value of each nonconforming recording is not relevant to the calculation.

(v) For purposes of Subsection (t)(1)(B), the possession of a nonconforming recording intended for sale constitutes an actual financial loss to an owner or lawful producer equal to the actual value of the legitimate wholesale purchases displaced by the nonconforming recordings.

Added by Acts 1993, 73rd Leg., ch. 806, § 1, eff. Sept. 1, 1993. Amended by Acts 1995, 74th Leg., ch. 76, § 5.95(111), eff. Sept. 1, 1995; Acts 1995, 74th Leg., ch. 318, § 51, eff. Sept. 1, 1995; Acts 1999, 76th Leg., ch. 40, §§ 2, 3, eff. Sept. 1, 1999; Acts 2001, 77th Leg., ch. 856, § 10, eff. Sept. 1, 2001; Acts 2001, 77th Leg., ch. 1034, § 2, eff. Sept. 1, 2001; Acts 2005, 79th Leg., ch. 543, § 4, eff. Sept. 1, 2005; Acts 2005, 79th Leg., ch. 969, § 1, eff. Sept. 1, 2005; Sept. 1, 2005; Acts 2005, 79th Leg., ch. 1025, § 2, eff. June 18, 2005; Acts 2007, 80th Leg., ch. 921, § 17.001(10), eff. Sept. 1, 2007; Acts 2007, 80th Leg., ch. 1053, § 2, eff. Sept. 1, 2007; Acts 2009, 81st Leg., ch. 87, § 25.021, eff. Sept. 1, 2009; Acts 2009, 81st Leg., ch. 639, § 1, eff. Sept. 1, 2009; Acts 2009, 81st Leg., ch. 1040, § 2, eff. Sept. 1, 2009; Acts 2015, 84th Leg., ch. 770 (H.B. 2299), § 2.13, eff. Jan. 1, 2017; Acts 2015, 84th Leg., ch. 933 (H.B. 2291), § 1, eff. Sept. 1, 2015; Acts 2017, 85th Leg., ch. 913 (S.B. 1343), § 4, eff. Sept. 1, 2017.

[1] Vernon's Ann.C.C.P. art. 56.31 et seq.

Section 3 of Acts 2015, 84th Leg., ch. 933 (H.B. 2291) provides:

"The change in law made by this Act applies only to an offense committed on or after the effective date [Sept. 1, 2015] of this Act. An offense committed before the effective date of this Act is governed by the law in effect on the date the offense was committed, and the former law is continued in effect for that purpose. For purposes of this section, an offense was committed before the effective date of this Act if any element of the offense occurred before that date."

Section 5(a) of Acts 2017, 85th Leg., ch. 913 (S.B. 1343) provides:

"(a) Except as provided by Subsection (b) of this section, the changes in law made by this Act apply only to an offense committed on or after the effective date [Sept. 1, 2017] of this Act. An offense committed before the effective date of this Act is governed by the law in effect on the date the offense was committed, and the former law is continued in effect for that purpose. For purposes of this subsection, an offense was committed before the effective date of this Act if any element of the offense occurred before that date."

Art. 42.0371. Mandatory Restitution for Kidnapped or Abducted Children

(a) The court shall order a defendant convicted of an offense under Chapter 20, Penal Code, or Section 25.03, 25.031, or 25.04, Penal Code, to pay restitution in an amount equal to the cost of necessary rehabilitation, including medical, psychiatric, and psychological care and treatment, for the victim of the offense if the victim is younger than 17 years of age.

(b) The court shall, after considering the financial circumstances of the defendant, specify in a restitution order issued under Subsection (a) the manner in which the defendant must pay the restitution.

(c) A restitution order issued under Subsection (a) may be enforced by the state or a victim named in the order to receive the restitution in the same manner as a judgment in a civil action.

(d) The court may hold a hearing, make findings of fact, and amend a restitution order issued under Subsection (a) if the defendant fails to pay the victim named in the order in the manner specified by the court.

Added by Acts 1999, 76th Leg., ch. 657, § 1, eff. Sept. 1, 1999.

Art. 42.0372. Mandatory Restitution for Child Victims of Trafficking of Persons or Compelling Prostitution

(a) The court shall order a defendant convicted of an offense under Section 20A.02 or 43.05(a)(2), Penal Code, to pay restitution in an amount equal to the cost of necessary rehabilitation, including medical, psychiatric, and psychological care and treatment, for any victim of the offense who is younger than 18 years of age.

(b) The court shall, after considering the financial circumstances of the defendant, specify in a restitution order issued under Subsection (a) the manner in which the defendant must pay the restitution.

(c) A restitution order issued under Subsection (a) may be enforced by the state, or by a victim named in the order to receive the restitution, in the same manner as a judgment in a civil action.

(d) The court may hold a hearing, make findings of fact, and amend a restitution order issued under Subsection (a) if the defendant fails to pay the victim named in the order in the manner specified by the court.

Added by Acts 2011, 82nd Leg., ch. 515 (H.B. 2014), § 2.02, eff. Sept. 1, 2011.

Art. 42.0373. Mandatory Restitution for Child Witness of Family Violence

(a) If after a conviction or a grant of deferred adjudication a court places a defendant on community supervision for an offense involving family violence, as defined by Section 71.004, Family Code, the court shall determine from the complaint, information, indictment, or other charging instrument, the presentence report, or other evidence before the court whether:

(1) the offense was committed in the physical presence of, or in the same habitation or vehicle occupied by, a person younger than 15 years of age; and

(2) at the time of the offense, the defendant had knowledge or reason to know that the person younger

than 15 years of age was physically present or occupied the same habitation or vehicle.

(b) If the court determines both issues described by Subsection (a) in the affirmative, the court shall order the defendant to pay restitution in an amount equal to the cost of necessary rehabilitation, including medical, psychiatric, and psychological care and treatment, for a person described by Subsection (a)(1).

(c) The court shall, after considering the financial circumstances of the defendant, specify in a restitution order issued under Subsection (b) the manner in which the defendant must pay the restitution. The order must require restitution payments to be delivered in the manner described by Article 42.037(g)(4)(iii).

(d) A restitution order issued under Subsection (b) may be enforced by the state, or by a person or a parent or guardian of the person named in the order to receive the restitution, in the same manner as a judgment in a civil action.

(e) The court may hold a hearing, make findings of fact, and amend a restitution order issued under Subsection (b) if the defendant fails to pay the person named in the order in the manner specified by the court.

(f) A determination under this article may not be entered as an affirmative finding in the judgment for the offense for which the defendant was placed on community supervision.

Added by Acts 2015, 84th Leg., ch. 1061 (H.B. 2159), § 1, eff. Sept. 1, 2015.

Section 2 of Acts 2015, 84th Leg., ch. 1061 (H.B. 2159) provides:

"The changes in law made by this Act apply only to an offense committed on or after the effective date [Sept. 1, 2015] of this Act. An offense committed before the effective date of this Act is governed by the law in effect on the date the offense was committed, and the former law is continued in effect for that purpose. For purposes of this section, an offense was committed before the effective date of this Act if any element of the offense occurred before that date."

Art. 42.038. Reimbursement for Confinement Expenses

(a) In addition to any fine, cost, or fee authorized by law, a court that sentences a defendant convicted of a misdemeanor to serve a term of confinement in county jail and orders execution of the sentence may require the defendant to reimburse the county for the defendant's confinement at a rate of $25 a day.

(b) A court that requires a defendant convicted of a misdemeanor or placed on deferred adjudication for a misdemeanor to submit to a period of confinement in county jail as a condition of community supervision may also require as a condition of community supervision that the defendant reimburse the county for the defendant's confinement, with the amount of reimbursement determined as if the defendant were serving an executed sentence.

(c) A judge may not require reimbursement under this article if the judge determines the defendant is indigent based on the defendant's sworn statement or affidavit filed with the court. A court that requires reimbursement under this article may require the defendant to reimburse the county only for those days the defendant is confined after the date of conviction or on which a plea of guilty or nolo contendere was entered. The court may not require a defendant to reimburse the county for those days the defendant was confined after arrest and before the date of conviction or on which the plea of guilty or nolo contendere was entered.

(d) The court, in determining whether to order reimbursement under this article, shall consider:

(1) the defendant's employment status, earning ability, and financial resources; and

(2) any other special circumstances that may affect the defendant's ability to pay, including child support obligations and including any financial responsibilities owed by the defendant to dependents or restitution payments owed by the defendant to a victim.

(e) On the day on which a defendant who is required to reimburse the county under this article discharges an executed sentence of confinement or completes the period of confinement required as a condition of community supervision, the sheriff shall present to the defendant a bill computed by multiplying the daily rate of $25 times the number of days the defendant was confined in the county jail, not counting the day on which the execution of the sentence or the period of confinement began. For purposes of this subsection, a defendant who is confined in county jail for only a portion of a day is nonetheless considered to have been confined for the whole day.

(f) The court may require a defendant to reimburse the county under this article by paying to the sheriff the bill presented by the sheriff within a specified period or in specified installments. The end of the period or the last installment may not be later than:

(1) the end of the period of community supervision, if community supervision is ordered; or

(2) the fifth anniversary of the last day of the term of confinement, if the court does not order community supervision.

Added by Acts 1999, 76th Leg., ch. 295, § 1, eff. Sept. 1, 1999.

Art. 42.039. Completion of Sentence in Federal Custody

(a) This article applies only to a criminal case in which:

(1) the judgment requires the defendant to be confined in a secure correctional facility; and

(2) the defendant is subject to an immigration detainer request.

(b) In a criminal case described by Subsection (a), the judge shall, at the time of pronouncement of a sentence of confinement, issue an order requiring the secure correctional facility in which the defendant is to be confined and all appropriate government officers, including a sheriff, a warden, or members of the Board of Pardons and Paroles, as appropriate, to require the defendant to serve in federal custody the final portion of the defendant's sentence, not to exceed a period of seven days, following the facility's or officer's determination that the change in the place of confinement will facilitate the seamless transfer of the defendant into federal custody. In the absence of an order issued under this subsection, a facility or officer acting under exigent circumstances may perform the transfer after making the determination described by this subsection. This subsection applies only if appropriate officers of the federal government consent to the transfer of the defendant into federal custody under the circumstances described by this subsection.

(c) If the applicable information described by Subsection (a)(2) is not available at the time sentence is pronounced in the case, the judge shall issue the order described by Subsection (b) as soon as the information becomes available. The judge retains jurisdiction for the purpose of issuing an order under this article.

(d) For purposes of this article, "secure correctional facility" has the meaning assigned by Section 1.07, Penal Code.

Added by Acts 2017, 85th Leg., ch. 4 (S.B. 4), § 2.02, eff. Sept. 1, 2017.

Section 7.01 of Acts 2017, 85th Leg., ch. 4 (S.B. 4) provides:

"It is the intent of the legislature that every provision, section, subsection, sentence, clause, phrase, or word in this Act, and every application of the provisions in this Act to each person or entity, are severable from each other. If any application of any provision in this Act to any person, group of persons, or circumstances is found by a court to be invalid for any reason, the remaining applications of that provision to all other persons and circumstances shall be severed and may not be affected."

Art. 42.04. Sentence when appeal is taken

When a defendant is sentenced to death, no date shall be set for the execution of sentence until after the receipt by the clerk of the trial court of the mandate of affirmance of the court of criminal appeals.

Acts 1965, 59th Leg., vol. 2, p. 317, ch. 722. Amended by Acts 1981, 67th Leg., p. 809, ch. 291, § 114, eff. Sept. 1, 1981.

Art. 42.04a. Repealed by Texas Rules of Appellate Procedure effective September 1, 1986 (Acts 1985, 69th Leg., ch. 685, § 4)

Art. 42.045. [Blank]

Art. 42.05. If court is about to adjourn

The time limit within which any act is to be done within the meaning of this Code shall not be affected by the expiration of the term of the court.

Acts 1965, 59th Leg., vol. 2, p. 317, ch. 722.

Art. 42.06. Repealed by Texas Rules of Appellate Procedure effective September 1, 1986 (Acts 1985, 69th Leg., ch. 685, § 4)

Art. 42.07. Reasons to prevent sentence

Before pronouncing sentence, the defendant shall be asked whether he has anything to say why the sentence should not be pronounced against him. The only reasons which can be shown, on account of which sentence cannot be pronounced, are:

1. That the defendant has received a pardon from the proper authority, on the presentation of which, legally authenticated, he shall be discharged.

2. That the defendant is incompetent to stand trial; and if evidence be shown to support a finding of incompetency to stand trial, no sentence shall be pronounced, and the court shall proceed under Chapter 46B; and

3. When a person who has been convicted escapes after conviction and before sentence and an individual supposed to be the same has been arrested he may before sentence is pronounced, deny that he is the person convicted, and an issue be accordingly tried

before a jury, or before the court if a jury is waived, as to his identity.

Acts 1965, 59th Leg., vol. 2, p. 317, ch. 722. Amended by Acts 1975, 64th Leg., p. 1102, ch. 415, § 3, eff. June 19, 1975; Acts 1981, 67th Leg., p. 810, ch. 291, § 115, eff. Sept. 1, 1981; Acts 2003, 78th Leg., ch. 35, § 3, eff. Jan. 1, 2004.

Art. 42.08. Cumulative or concurrent sentence

(a) When the same defendant has been convicted in two or more cases, judgment and sentence shall be pronounced in each case in the same manner as if there had been but one conviction. Except as provided by Subsections (b) and (c), in the discretion of the court, the judgment in the second and subsequent convictions may either be that the sentence imposed or suspended shall begin when the judgment and the sentence imposed or suspended in the preceding conviction has ceased to operate, or that the sentence imposed or suspended shall run concurrently with the other case or cases, and sentence and execution shall be accordingly; provided, however, that the cumulative total of suspended sentences in felony cases shall not exceed 10 years, and the cumulative total of suspended sentences in misdemeanor cases shall not exceed the maximum period of confinement in jail applicable to the misdemeanor offenses, though in no event more than three years, including extensions of periods of community supervision under Article 42A.752(a)(2), if none of the offenses are offenses under Chapter 49, Penal Code, or four years, including extensions, if any of the offenses are offenses under Chapter 49, Penal Code.

(b) If a defendant is sentenced for an offense committed while the defendant was an inmate in the Texas Department of Criminal Justice and serving a sentence for an offense other than a state jail felony and the defendant has not completed the sentence he was serving at the time of the offense, the judge shall order the sentence for the subsequent offense to commence immediately on completion of the sentence for the original offense.

(c) If a defendant has been convicted in two or more cases and the court suspends the imposition of the sentence in one of the cases, the court may not order a sentence of confinement to commence on the completion of a suspended sentence for an offense.

Acts 1965, 59th Leg., vol. 2, p. 317, ch. 722. Amended by Acts 1985, 69th Leg., ch. 29, § 1, eff. Sept. 1, 1985; Acts 1987, 70th Leg., ch. 513, § 1, eff. Aug. 31, 1987; Acts 1989, 71st Leg., ch. 785, § 4.11, eff. Sept. 1, 1989. Acts 1993, 73rd Leg., ch. 900, § 5.03, eff. Sept. 1, 1993; Acts 2009, 81st Leg., ch. 87, § 25.022, eff. Sept. 1, 2009; Acts 2015, 84th Leg., ch. 770 (H.B. 2299), § 2.14, eff. Jan. 1, 2017.

Art. 42.09. Commencement of sentence; status during appeal; pen packet

Sec. 1. Except as provided in Sections 2 and 3, a defendant shall be delivered to a jail or to the Texas Department of Criminal Justice when his sentence is pronounced, or his sentence to death is announced, by the court. The defendant's sentence begins to run on the day it is pronounced, but with all credits, if any, allowed by Article 42.03.

Sec. 2. If a defendant appeals his conviction and is released on bail pending disposition of his appeal, when his conviction is affirmed, the clerk of the trial court, on receipt of the mandate from the appellate court, shall issue a commitment against the defendant. The officer executing the commitment shall endorse thereon the date he takes the defendant into custody and the defendant's sentence begins to run from the date endorsed on the commitment. The Texas Department of Criminal Justice shall admit the defendant named in the commitment on the basis of the commitment.

Sec. 3. If a defendant convicted of a felony is sentenced to death or to life in the Texas Department of Criminal Justice or is ineligible for release on bail pending appeal under Article 44.04(b) and gives notice of appeal, the defendant shall be transferred to the department on a commitment pending a mandate from the court of appeals or the Court of Criminal Appeals.

Sec. 4. If a defendant is convicted of a felony, is eligible for release on bail pending appeal under Article 44.04(b), and gives notice of appeal, he shall be transferred to the Texas Department of Criminal Justice on a commitment pending a mandate from the Court of Appeals or the Court of Criminal Appeals upon request in open court or upon written request to the sentencing court. Upon a valid transfer to the department under this section, the defendant may not thereafter be released on bail pending his appeal.

Sec. 5. If a defendant is transferred to the Texas Department of Criminal Justice pending appeal under Section 3 or 4, his sentence shall be computed as if no appeal had been taken if the appeal is affirmed.

Sec. 6. All defendants who have been transferred to the Texas Department of Criminal Justice pending the appeal of their convictions under this article shall be under the control and authority of the department for all purposes as if no appeal were pending.

Sec. 7. If a defendant is sentenced to a term of imprisonment in the Texas Department of Criminal Justice but is not transferred to the department under

Section 3 or 4, the court, before the date on which it would lose jurisdiction under Article 42A.202(a), shall send to the department a document containing a statement of the date on which the defendant's sentence was pronounced and credits earned by the defendant under Article 42.03 as of the date of the statement.

Sec. 8. (a) A county that transfers a defendant to the Texas Department of Criminal Justice under this article shall deliver to an officer designated by the department:

(1) a copy of the judgment entered pursuant to Article 42.01, completed on a standardized felony judgment form described by Section 4 of that article;

(2) a copy of any order revoking community supervision and imposing sentence pursuant to Article 42A.755, including:

(A) any amounts owed for restitution, fines, and court costs, completed on a standardized felony judgment form described by Section 4, Article 42.01; and

(B) a copy of the client supervision plan prepared for the defendant by the community supervision and corrections department supervising the defendant, if such a plan was prepared;

(3) a written report that states the nature and the seriousness of each offense and that states the citation to the provision or provisions of the Penal Code or other law under which the defendant was convicted;

(4) a copy of the victim impact statement, if one has been prepared in the case under Article 56.03;

(5) a statement as to whether there was a change in venue in the case and, if so, the names of the county prosecuting the offense and the county in which the case was tried;

(6) if requested, information regarding the criminal history of the defendant, including the defendant's state identification number if the number has been issued;

(7) a copy of the indictment or information for each offense;

(8) a checklist sent by the department to the county and completed by the county in a manner indicating that the documents required by this subsection and Subsection (c) accompany the defendant;

(9) if prepared, a copy of a presentence or postsentence report prepared under Subchapter F, Chapter 42A;

(10) a copy of any detainer, issued by an agency of the federal government, that is in the possession of the county and that has been placed on the defendant;

(11) if prepared, a copy of the defendant's Texas Uniform Health Status Update Form; and

(12) a written description of a hold or warrant, issued by any other jurisdiction, that the county is aware of and that has been placed on or issued for the defendant.

(b) The Texas Department of Criminal Justice shall not take a defendant into custody under this article until the designated officer receives the documents required by Subsections (a) and (c) of this section. The designated officer shall certify under the seal of the department the documents received under Subsections (a) and (c) of this section. A document certified under this subsection is self-authenticated for the purposes of Rules 901 and 902, Texas Rules of Evidence.

(c) A county that transfers a defendant to the Texas Department of Criminal Justice under this article shall also deliver to the designated officer any presentence or postsentence investigation report, revocation report, psychological or psychiatric evaluation of the defendant, including an evaluation prepared for the juvenile court before transferring the defendant to criminal court and contained in the criminal prosecutor's file, and available social or psychological background information relating to the defendant and may deliver to the designated officer any additional information upon which the judge or jury bases the punishment decision.

(d) The correctional institutions division of the Texas Department of Criminal Justice shall make documents received under Subsections (a) and (c) available to the parole division on the request of the parole division and shall, on release of a defendant on parole or to mandatory supervision, immediately provide the parole division with copies of documents received under Subsection (a). The parole division shall provide to the parole officer appointed to supervise the defendant a comprehensive summary of the information contained in the documents referenced in this section not later than the 14th day after the date of the defendant's release. The summary shall include a current photograph of the defendant and a complete set of the defendant's fingerprints. Upon written request from the county sheriff, the photograph and fingerprints shall be filed with the sheriff of the county to which the parolee is assigned if that county is not the county from which the parolee was sentenced.

(e) A county is not required to deliver separate documents containing information relating to citations to provisions of the Penal Code or other law and to changes of venue, as otherwise required by Subsections (a)(3) and (a)(5) of this article, if the standardized felony judgment form described by Section 4, Article 42.01, of this code is modified to require that information.

(f) Except as provided by Subsection (g) of this section, the county sheriff is responsible for ensuring that documents and information required by this section accompany defendants sentenced by district courts in the county to the Texas Department of Criminal Justice.

(g) If the presiding judge of the administrative judicial region in which the county is located determines that the county sheriff is unable to perform the duties required by Subsection (f) of this section, the presiding judge may impose those duties on:

(1) the district clerk; or

(2) the prosecutor of each district court in the county.

(h) If a parole panel releases on parole a person who is confined in a jail in this state, a federal correctional institution, or a correctional institution in another state, the Texas Department of Criminal Justice shall request the sheriff who would otherwise be required to transfer the person to the department to forward to the department the information described by Subsections (a) and (c) of this section. The sheriff shall comply with the request of the department. The department shall determine whether the information forwarded by the sheriff under this subsection contains a thumbprint taken from the person in the manner provided by Article 38.33 of this code and, if not, the department shall obtain a thumbprint taken in the manner provided by that article and shall forward the thumbprint to the department for inclusion with the information sent by the sheriff.

(i) A county may deliver the documents required under Subsections (a) and (c) of this section to the Texas Department of Criminal Justice by electronic means. For purposes of this subsection, "electronic means" means the transmission of data between word processors, data processors, or similar automated information equipment over dedicated cables, commercial lines, or other similar methods of transmission.

(j) If after a county transfers a defendant or inmate to the Texas Department of Criminal Justice the charges on which the defendant or inmate was convicted and for which the defendant or inmate was transferred are dismissed, the county shall immediately notify an officer designated by the department of the dismissal.

Sec. 9. A county that transfers a defendant to the Texas Department of Criminal Justice under this article may deliver to an officer designated by the department a certified copy of a final order of a state or federal court that dismisses as frivolous or malicious a lawsuit brought by the inmate while the inmate was confined in the county jail awaiting transfer to the department following conviction of a felony or revocation of community supervision, parole, or mandatory supervision. The county may deliver the copy to the department at the time of the transfer of the inmate or at any time after the transfer of the inmate.

Acts 1965, 59th Leg., vol. 2, p. 317, ch. 722. Amended by Acts 1973, 63rd Leg., p. 206, ch. 91, § 2, eff. Aug. 27, 1973; Acts 1977, 65th Leg., p. 2018, ch. 806, § 1, eff. Aug. 29, 1977; Acts 1981, 67th Leg., p. 810, ch. 291, § 117, eff. Sept. 1, 1981. Acts 1983, 68th Leg., p. 148, ch. 40, § 1, eff. April 26, 1983; Acts 1983, 68th Leg., p. 4668, ch. 810, § 1, eff. Sept. 1, 1983; Acts 1985, 69th Leg., ch. 344, § 3, eff. Jan. 1, 1986; Acts 1987, 70th Leg., ch. 1049, § 53, eff. Sept. 1, 1987; Acts 1989, 71st Leg., ch. 33, § 2, eff. April 26, 1989; Acts 1989, 71st Leg., ch. 785, § 4.12, eff. Sept. 1, 1989; Acts 1991, 72nd Leg., 2nd C.S., ch. 10, § 11.05, eff. Aug. 29, 1991; Acts 1993, 73rd Leg., ch. 900, § 5.03, eff. Sept. 1, 1993; Acts 1995, 74th Leg., ch. 321, § 3.001, eff. Sept. 1, 1995; Acts 1995, 74th Leg., ch. 723, § 1, eff. Sept. 1, 1995; Acts 1999, 76th Leg., ch. 655, § 1, eff. June 18, 1999; Acts 1999, 76th Leg., ch. 1188, § 1.42, eff. Sept. 1, 1999; Acts 1999, 76th Leg., ch. 1477, § 29, eff. Sept. 1, 1999; Acts 2001, 77th Leg., ch. 214, § 1, eff. May 22, 2001; Acts 2001, 77th Leg., ch. 453, § 1, eff. June 8, 2001; Acts 2003, 78th Leg., ch. 14, § 1, eff. Sept. 1, 2003; Acts 2005, 79th Leg., ch. 728, § 4.005, eff. Sept. 1, 2005; Acts 2007, 80th Leg., ch. 1308, § 4, eff. June 15, 2007; Acts 2009, 81st Leg., ch. 87, §§ 25.023, 25.024, eff. Sept. 1, 2009; Acts 2009, 81st Leg., ch. 980, § 1, eff. Sept. 1, 2009; Acts 2015, 84th Leg., ch. 282 (H.B. 904), § 1, eff. Sept. 1, 2015; Acts 2015, 84th Leg., ch. 770 (H.B. 2299), §§ 2.15, 2.16, eff. Jan. 1, 2017.

Art. 42.10. Satisfaction of judgment as in misdemeanor convictions

When a person is convicted of a felony, and the punishment assessed is only a fine or a term in jail, or both, the judgment may be satisfied in the same manner as a conviction for a misdemeanor is by law satisfied.

Acts 1965, 59th Leg., vol. 2, p. 317, ch. 722.

Art. 42.11. Repealed, upon the first anniversary of the Interstate Compact for Adult Of-

fender Supervision, effective June 19, 2003 [Acts 2001, 77th Leg., ch. 543, § 2]

Art. 42.111. Deferral of Proceedings in Cases Appealed to County Court

If a defendant convicted of a misdemeanor punishable by fine only appeals the conviction to a county court, on the trial in county court the defendant may enter a plea of guilty or nolo contendere to the offense. If the defendant enters a plea of guilty or nolo contendere, the court may defer further proceedings without entering an adjudication of guilt in the same manner as provided for the deferral of proceedings in justice court or municipal court under Article 45.051 of this code. This article does not apply to a misdemeanor case disposed of under Subchapter B[1], Chapter 543, Transportation Code, or a serious traffic violation as defined by Section 522.003, Transportation Code.

Added by Acts 1989, 71st Leg., ch. 399, § 2, eff. June 14, 1989. Amended by Acts 1991, 72nd Leg., ch. 775, § 18, eff. Sept. 1, 1991; Acts 1999, 76th Leg., ch. 62, § 3.03, eff. Sept. 1, 1999; Acts 1999, 76th Leg., ch. 1545, § 62, eff. Sept. 1, 1999.

[1] V.T.C.A., Transportation Code § 543.101.

Art. 42.12. Repealed by Acts 2015, 84th Leg., ch. 770 (H.B. 2299), § 3.01, eff. Jan. 1, 2017; Acts 2017, 85th Leg., ch. 324 (S.B. 1488), §§ 23.012(d), 23.013(d), 23.014(b), 23.015(b), 23.016(h), 23.017(b), 23.018(b), 23.019(b), 23.020(b), 23.021(b), eff. Sept. 1, 2017; Acts 2017, 85th Leg., ch. 877 (H.B. 3016), § 11, eff. Sept. 1, 2017

Art. 42.121. Repealed by Acts 1989, 71st Leg., 785, § 3.10, eff. Sept. 1, 1989; Acts 1995, 74th Leg., ch. 321, § 3.020(b), (c), eff. Sept. 1, 1995

Art. 42.122. Adult probation officers of the 222nd Judicial District; salary and allowances [1]

The adult probation officer of the 222nd Judicial District receives a salary of not less than $15,000 per annum. Also, the probation officer receives allowances, not to exceed the amount allowed by the federal government for traveling the most practical route to and from the place where the duties are discharged, for his necessary travel and hotel expenses. Upon the sworn statement of the officer, approved by the judge,

the respective counties of the judicial district pay the expenses incurred for their regular or special term of court out of the general county fund. In lieu of travel allowances the commissioners court of each county, by agreement, may provide transportation under the same terms and conditions as provided for sheriffs.

Added by Acts 1985, 69th Leg., ch. 480, § 18, eff. Sept. 1, 1985.

[1] Article heading editorially supplied.

Art. 42.13. Repealed by Acts 1995, 74th Leg., ch. 76, § 7.10, eff. Sept. 1, 1995

Art. 42.131. Repealed by Acts 1995, 74th Leg., ch. 76, § 7.12, eff. Sept. 1, 1995

Art. 42.14. In Absence of Defendant

(a) In a misdemeanor case, the judgment and sentence may be rendered in the absence of the defendant.

(b) In a felony case, the judgment and sentence may be rendered in the absence of the defendant only if:

(1) the defendant is confined in a penal institution;

(2) the defendant is not charged with a felony offense:

(A) that is listed in Article 42A.054(a); or

(B) for which it is alleged that:

(i) a deadly weapon was used or exhibited during the commission of the offense or during immediate flight from the commission of the offense; and

(ii) the defendant used or exhibited the deadly weapon or was a party to the offense and knew that a deadly weapon would be used or exhibited;

(3) the defendant in writing before the appropriate court having jurisdiction in the county in which the penal institution is located:

(A) waives the right to be present at the rendering of the judgment and sentence or to have counsel present;

(B) affirms that the defendant does not have anything to say as to why the sentence should not be pronounced and that there is no reason to prevent the sentence under Article 42.07;

(C) states that the defendant has entered into a written plea agreement with the attorney representing the state in the prosecution of the case; and

(D) requests the court to pronounce sentence in the case in accordance with the plea agreement;

(4) the defendant and the attorney representing the state in the prosecution of the case have entered into a written plea agreement that is made a part of the record in the case; and

(5) sentence is pronounced in accordance with the plea agreement.

(c) A judgment and sentence may be rendered under this article in the absence of the defendant only after the defendant is notified by the court of original jurisdiction of the right to counsel and the defendant requests counsel or waives the right to counsel in accordance with Article 1.051.

(d) In this article, "deadly weapon" and "penal institution" have the meanings assigned by Section 1.07, Penal Code.

(e) If a defendant enters a plea of guilty or nolo contendere under Article 27.19, the attorney representing the state may request at the time the plea is entered that the defendant submit a fingerprint of the defendant suitable for attachment to the judgment. On request for a fingerprint under this subsection, the county in which the defendant is confined shall obtain a fingerprint of the defendant and use first-class mail or other means acceptable to the attorney representing the state and the county to forward the fingerprint to the court accepting the plea.

Acts 1965, 59th Leg., vol. 2, p. 317, ch. 722. Amended by Acts 2009, 81st Leg., ch. 291, § 2, eff. Sept. 1, 2009; Acts 2015, 84th Leg., ch. 770 (H.B. 2299), § 2.17, eff. Jan. 1, 2017.

Art. 42.141. Battering intervention and prevention program

Definitions

Sec. 1. In this article:

(1) "Batterer" means a person who commits repeated acts of violence or who repeatedly threatens violence against another who is:

(A) related to the actor by affinity or consanguinity, as determined under Chapter 573, Government Code;

(B) is a former spouse of the actor; or

(C) resides or has resided in the same household with the actor.

(2) "Division" means the community justice assistance division of the Texas Department of Criminal Justice.

(3) "Family" has the meaning assigned by Section 71.003, Family Code.

(4) "Family violence" has the meaning assigned by Section 71.004, Family Code.

(5) "Shelter center" has the meaning assigned by Section 51.002, Human Resources Code.

(6) "Household" has the meaning assigned by Section 71.005, Family Code.

(7) 'Program' means a battering intervention and prevention program that:

(A) meets:

(i) the guidelines adopted by the community justice assistance division of the Texas Department of Criminal Justice with the assistance of the statewide nonprofit organization described by Section 3(1); and

(ii) any other eligibility requirements adopted by the Texas Department of Criminal Justice; and

(B) provides, on a local basis to batterers referred by the courts for intervention, educational services and intervention designed to help the batterers stop their abusive behavior.

(8) "Project" means the statewide activities for the funding of battering intervention and prevention programs, the related community educational campaign, and education and research regarding such programs.

(9) "Responsive law enforcement climate" means an area where, in cases of family violence:

(A) the local law enforcement agency has a policy or record of arresting batterers; and

(B) the local criminal justice system:

(i) cooperates with the victim in filing protective orders; and

(ii) takes appropriate action against a person who violates protective orders.

Establishment

Sec. 2. The battering intervention and prevention program is established in the division.

Duties of the Division

Sec. 3. The division shall:

(1) contract with a nonprofit organization that for the five-year period before the date on which a contract is to be signed has been involved in providing to shelter centers, law enforcement agencies, and the legal community statewide advocacy and technical assistance relating to family violence, with the contract

requiring the nonprofit organization to perform the duties described in Section (4) of this article;

(2) seek the input of the statewide nonprofit organization described in Subdivision (1) in the development of standards for selection of programs for inclusion in the project and the review of proposals submitted by programs;

(3) issue requests for proposals for the programs and an educational campaign not later than January 1, 1990;

(4) award contracts for programs that are operated by nonprofit organizations and that take into consideration:

(A) a balanced geographical distribution of urban, rural, and suburban models; and

(B) the presence of a responsive law enforcement climate in the community;

(5) develop and monitor the project in cooperation with the nonprofit organization described by Subdivision (1);

(6) monitor the development of a community educational campaign in cooperation with the nonprofit organization described by Subdivision (1);

(7) assist the nonprofit organization described by Subdivision (1) in designing program evaluations and research activities;

(8) facilitate training of probation officers and other criminal justice professionals by the nonprofit organization described by Subdivision (1) and by programs;

(9) seek the assistance of the nonprofit organization described by Subdivision (1) in developing program guidelines and in accrediting programs and providers providing battering intervention and prevention services as conforming to those guidelines; and

(10) before adopting program guidelines under Section 4A:

(A) notify the licensing authorities described by Chapters 152, 501, 502, 503, and 505, Occupations Code, that the division is considering adopting program guidelines; and

(B) invite the licensing authorities to comment on the program guidelines.

Duties of the Nonprofit Organization

Sec. 4. The nonprofit organization with which the division contracts under Section 3(1) shall:

(1) assist the division in developing and issuing requests for proposals for the programs and the educational campaign;

(2) assist the division in reviewing the submitted proposals and making recommendations for proposals to be selected for funding;

(3) develop and monitor the project in cooperation with the division;

(4) provide technical assistance to programs to:

(A) develop appropriate services for batterers;

(B) train staff;

(C) improve coordination with shelter centers, the criminal justice system, the judiciary, law enforcement agencies, prosecutors, and other appropriate officials and support services;

(D) implement the community educational campaign; and

(E) participate in project administered program evaluation and research activities;

(5) provide technical assistance to the division to:

(A) develop and implement standards for selection of programs for inclusion in the project; and

(B) develop standards for selection of the community educational campaign described in Section 6 of this article;

(6) submit an annual written report to the division and to the legislature with recommendations for continuation, elimination, or changes in the project;

(7) evaluate the programs and the community educational campaign, including an analysis of the effectiveness of the project and the level of public awareness relating to family violence; and

(8) assist the division in developing program guidelines and in accrediting programs and providers providing battering intervention and prevention services as conforming to those guidelines.

Adoption of Program Guidelines; Accreditation Process

Sec. 4A. With the assistance of the statewide nonprofit organization described by Section 3(1) and after notifying the licensing authorities described by Section 3(10), the division shall adopt guidelines for programs and shall accredit programs and providers providing battering intervention and prevention services as conforming to those guidelines. The division shall collect from each program or provider that applies for accreditation under this section a one-time application fee in an amount set by the Texas Department of Criminal Justice.

Programs

Sec. 5.   (a) A program proposal must:

(1) describe the counseling or treatment the program will offer;

(2) include letters from a local law enforcement agency or agencies, courts, probation officers, and other community resources describing the community's commitment to improve the criminal justice system's response to victims and batterers and to cooperate with and interact in the programs' activities;

(3) include a letter from the local shelter center describing the support services available to victims of family violence in the community and the shelter's commitment to cooperate and work with the program; and

(4) describe the public education and local community outreach activities relating to family violence currently available in the community and a statement of commitment to participate on the local level in the public educational campaign described in Section 6 of this article.

(b) A program must:

(1) be situated in a county in which a shelter center is located;

(2) offer counseling or treatment in which the primary approach is direct intervention with the batterer, on an individual or group basis, but that does not require the victim of the family violence to participate in the counseling or treatment;

(3) offer training to law enforcement prosecutors, judges, probation officers, and others on the dynamics of family violence, treatment options, and program activities; and

(4) have a system for receiving referrals from the courts and for reporting to the court regarding batterers' compliance with the treatment program.

(c) This section does not preclude a program from serving a batterer other than one who was ordered by a court to participate in the program established under this subchapter.

Community Educational Campaign

Sec. 6.   (a) The division, with assistance from the nonprofit organization, shall select the community educational campaign relating to family violence after the commission has selected the programs. The campaign is to be implemented in the areas covered by the programs.

(b) The campaign shall use a variety of media, including newspapers, radio, television, and billboards, and shall focus on:

(1) the criminality of acts of violence toward family members;

(2) the consequences of family violence crimes to the batterer; and

(3) eradicating public misconceptions of family violence.

Use of Legislative Appropriation

Sec. 7.   Of a legislative appropriation for the project established under this article:

(1) not more than six percent may be used by the division for management and administration of the project;

(2) not more than 14 percent may be applied to the contract between the division and the nonprofit organization; and

(3) not more than three percent may be applied to the contract for the community educational campaign.

Contract Date

Sec. 8.   The contract required under Section 3(a) of this article shall be signed not later than November 1, 1989.

Added by Acts 1989, 71st Leg., ch. 785, § 3.05, eff. Sept. 1, 1989. Amended by Acts 1991, 72nd Leg., ch. 561, § 11, eff. Aug. 26, 1991; Acts 1995, 74th Leg., ch. 76, § 5.95(27), eff. Sept. 1, 1995; Acts 2003, 78th Leg., ch. 1276, § 7.002(i), eff. Sept. 1, 2003; Acts 2007, 80th Leg., ch. 113, §§ 2, 3, eff. Sept. 1, 2007.

Art. 42.15.   Fines and Costs

(a) When the defendant is fined, the judgment shall be that the defendant pay the amount of the fine and all costs to the state.

(a–1) Notwithstanding any other provision of this article, during or immediately after imposing a sentence in a case in which the defendant entered a plea in open court as provided by Article 27.13, 27.14(a), or 27.16(a), a court shall inquire whether the defendant has sufficient resources or income to immediately pay all or part of the fine and costs. If the court determines that the defendant does not have sufficient resources or income to immediately pay all or part of the fine and costs, the court shall determine whether the fine and costs should be:

Text of (a–1)(1), as added by Acts 2017, 85th Leg., ch. 977 (H.B. 351), § 4

(1) required to be paid at some later date or in a specified portion at designated intervals;

Text of (a–1)(1), as added by Acts 2017, 85th Leg., ch. 1127 (S.B. 1913), § 4

(1) subject to Subsection (c), required to be paid at some later date or in a specified portion at designated intervals;

(2) discharged by performing community service under, as applicable, Article 43.09(f), Article 45.049, Article 45.0492, as added by Chapter 227 (H.B. 350), Acts of the 82nd Legislature, Regular Session, 2011, or Article 45.0492, as added by Chapter 777 (H.B. 1964), Acts of the 82nd Legislature, Regular Session, 2011;

(3) waived in full or in part under Article 43.091 or 45.0491; or

(4) satisfied through any combination of methods under Subdivisions (1)–(3).

(b) Subject to Subsections (c) and (d) and Article 43.091, when imposing a fine and costs, a court may direct a defendant:

(1) to pay the entire fine and costs when sentence is pronounced;

(2) to pay the entire fine and costs at some later date; or

(3) to pay a specified portion of the fine and costs at designated intervals.

(c) When imposing a fine and costs in a misdemeanor case, if the court determines that the defendant is unable to immediately pay the fine and costs, the court shall allow the defendant to pay the fine and costs in specified portions at designated intervals.

(d) A judge may allow a defendant who is a child, as defined by Article 45.058(h), to elect at the time of conviction, as defined by Section 133.101, Local Government Code, to discharge the fine and costs by:

(1) performing community service or receiving tutoring under Article 45.0492, as added by Chapter 227 (H.B. 350), Acts of the 82nd Legislature, Regular Session, 2011; or

(2) paying the fine and costs in a manner described by Subsection (b).

(e) The election under Subsection (d) must be made in writing, signed by the defendant, and, if present, signed by the defendant's parent, guardian, or managing conservator. The court shall maintain the written election as a record of the court and provide a copy to the defendant.

(f) The requirement under Article 45.0492(a), as added by Chapter 227 (H.B. 350), Acts of the 82nd Legislature, Regular Session, 2011, that an offense occur in a building or on the grounds of the primary or secondary school at which the defendant was enrolled at the time of the offense does not apply to the performance of community service or the receipt of tutoring to discharge a fine or costs under Subsection (d)(1).

Acts 1965, 59th Leg., vol. 2, p. 317, ch. 722. Amended by Acts 1971, 62nd Leg., p. 2990, ch. 987, § 1, eff. June 15, 1971; Acts 2011, 82nd Leg., ch. 464 (H.B. 27), § 2, eff. Sept. 1, 2011; Acts 2013, 83rd Leg., ch. 1320 (S.B. 395), § 1, eff. Sept. 1, 2013; Acts 2013, 83rd Leg., ch. 1407 (S.B. 393), § 1, eff. Sept. 1, 2013; Acts 2017, 85th Leg., ch. 977 (H.B. 351), § 4, eff. Sept. 1, 2017; Acts 2017, 85th Leg., ch. 1127 (S.B. 1913), § 4, eff. Sept. 1, 2017.

Section 33 of Acts 2017, 85th Leg., ch. 977 (H.B. 351) provides:

"The changes in law made by this Act to Articles 42.15, 43.09, 43.091, 45.014, 45.041, 45.046, 45.049, and 45.0491, Code of Criminal Procedure, and Articles 45.0492, Code of Criminal Procedure, as added by Chapter 227 (H.B. 350), Acts of the 82nd Legislature, Regular Session, 2011, and 45.0492, Code of Criminal Procedure, as added by Chapter 777 (H.B. 1964), Acts of the 82nd Legislature, Regular Session, 2011, apply to a sentencing proceeding that commences before, on, or after the effective date [Sept. 1, 2017] of this Act."

Section 29 of Acts 2017, 85th Leg., ch. 1127 (S.B. 1913) provides:

"The changes in law made by this Act to Articles 42.15, 43.09, 43.091, 45.014, 45.041, 45.046, 45.049, and 45.0491, Code of Criminal Procedure, and Articles 45.0492, Code of Criminal Procedure, as added by Chapter 227 (H.B. 350), Acts of the 82nd Legislature, Regular Session, 2011, and 45.0492, Code of Criminal Procedure, as added by Chapter 777 (H.B. 1964), Acts of the 82nd Legislature, Regular Session, 2011, apply to a sentencing proceeding that commences before, on, or after the effective date [Sept. 1, 2017] of this Act."

Art. 42.151. Fees for abused children's counseling

If a court orders a defendant to pay a fee under Article 37.072 of this code, the court shall assess the fee against the defendant in the same manner as other costs of prosecution are assessed against a defendant. The court may direct a defendant:

(1) to pay the entire fee when sentence is pronounced;

(2) to pay the entire fee at some later date; or

(3) to pay a specified portion of the fee at designated intervals.

Added by Acts 1989, 71st Leg., ch. 360, § 3, eff. Sept. 1, 1989.

Art. 42.152.   Repayment of Reward

(a) If a judge orders a defendant to repay a reward or part of a reward under Article 37.073 of this code, the court shall assess this cost against the defendant in the same manner as other costs of prosecution are assessed against a defendant. The court may order the defendant to:

(1) pay the entire amount required when sentence is pronounced;

(2) pay the entire amount required at a later date specified by the court; or

(3) pay specified portions of the required amount at designated intervals.

(b) After receiving a payment from a person ordered to make the payment under this article, the clerk of the court or fee officer shall:

(1) make a record of the payment;

(2) deduct a one-time $7 processing fee from the reward repayment;

(3) forward the payment to the designated crime stoppers organization; and

(4) make a record of the forwarding of the payment.

Added by Acts 1989, 71st Leg., ch. 611, § 3, eff. Sept. 1, 1989. Renumbered from art. 42.151 by Acts 1991, 72nd Leg., ch. 16, § 19.01(6), eff. Aug. 26, 1991. Amended by Acts 1997, 75th Leg., ch. 700, § 12, eff. Sept. 1, 1997.

Art. 42.16.   On other judgment

If the punishment is any other than a fine, the judgment shall specify it, and order it enforced by the proper process. It shall also adjudge the costs against the defendant, and order the collection thereof as in other cases.

Acts 1965, 59th Leg., vol. 2, p. 317, ch. 722.

Art. 42.17.   Transfer under treaty

When a treaty is in effect between the United States and a foreign country providing for the transfer of convicted offenders who are citizens or nationals of foreign countries to the foreign countries of which they are citizens or nationals, the governor is authorized, subject to the terms of such treaty, to act on behalf of the State of Texas and to consent to the transfer of such convicted offenders under the provisions of Article IV, Section 11 of the Constitution of the State of Texas.

Added by Acts 1977, 65th Leg., p. 1266, ch. 489, § 1, eff. June 15, 1977.

Art. 42.18.   Repealed by Acts 1997, 75th Leg., ch. 165, § 12.22, eff. Sept. 1, 1997

Art. 42.19.   Interstate corrections compact

Article I.   Purpose and Policy

The party states, desiring by common action to fully utilize and improve their institutional facilities and provide adequate programs for the confinement, treatment, and rehabilitation of various types of offenders, declare that it is the policy of each of the party states to provide such facilities and programs on a basis of cooperation with one another, thereby serving the best interests of such offenders and of society and effecting economies in capital expenditures and operational costs. The purpose of this compact is to provide for the mutual development and execution of such programs of cooperation for the confinement, treatment, and rehabilitation of offenders with the most economical use of human and material resources.

Article II.   Definitions

As used in this compact, unless the context clearly requires otherwise:

(a) "State" means a state of the United States; the United States of America; a territory or possession of the United States; the District of Columbia; the commonwealth of Puerto Rico.

(b) "Sending state" means a state party to this compact in which conviction or court commitment was had.

(c) "Receiving state" means a state party to this compact to which an inmate is sent for confinement other than a state in which conviction or court commitment was had.

(d) "Inmate" means a male or female offender who is committed, under sentence to or confined in a penal or correctional institution.

(e) "Institution" means any penal or correctional facility, including but not limited to a facility for the mentally ill or mentally defective, in which inmates as defined in (d) above may lawfully be confined.

Article III.   Contracts

(a) Each party state may make one or more contracts with any one or more of the other party states for the confinement of inmates on behalf of a sending state in institutions situated within receiving states. Any such contract shall provide for:

1. Its duration.

2. Payments to be made to the receiving state by the sending state for inmate maintenance, extraordinary medical and dental expenses, and any participation in or receipt by inmates of rehabilitative or correctional services, facilities, programs, or treatment not reasonably included as part of normal maintenance.

3. Participation in programs of inmate employment, if any; the disposition or crediting of any payments received by inmates on account thereof; and the crediting of proceeds from or disposal of any products resulting therefrom.

4. Delivery and retaking of inmates.

5. Such other matters as may be necessary and appropriate to fix the obligations, responsibilities, and rights of the sending and receiving states.

(b) The terms and provisions of this compact shall be a part of any contract entered into by the authority of or pursuant thereto, and nothing in any such contract shall be inconsistent therewith.

Article IV. Procedures and Rights

(a) Whenever the duly constituted authorities in a state party to this compact, and which has entered into a contract pursuant to Article III, shall decide that confinement in, or transfer of an inmate to, an institution within the territory of another party state is necessary or desirable in order to provide adequate quarters and care or an appropriate program of rehabilitation or treatment, such official may direct that the confinement be within an institution within the territory of such other party state, the receiving state to act in that regard solely as agent for the sending state.

(b) The appropriate officials of any state party to this compact shall have access, at all reasonable times, to any institution in which it has a contractual right to confine inmates for the purpose of inspecting the facilities thereof and visiting such of its inmates as may be confined in the institution.

(c) Inmates confined in an institution pursuant to this compact shall at all times be subject to the jurisdiction of the sending state and may at any time be removed therefrom for transfer to a prison or other institution within the sending state, for transfer to another institution in which the sending state may have a contractual or other right to confine inmates, for release on probation or parole, for discharge, or for any other purpose permitted by the laws of the sending state. However, the sending state shall continue to be obligated to such payments as may be required pursuant to the terms of any contract entered into under the terms of Article III.

(d) Each receiving state shall provide regular reports to each sending state on the inmates of that sending state who are in institutions pursuant to this compact including a conduct record of each inmate and shall certify such record to the official designated by the sending state, in order that each inmate may have official review of his or her record in determining and altering the disposition of the inmate in accordance with the law which may obtain in the sending state and in order that the same may be a source of information for the sending state.

(e) All inmates who may be confined in an institution pursuant to this compact shall be treated in a reasonable and humane manner and shall be treated equally with such similar inmates of the receiving state as may be confined in the same institution. The fact of confinement in a receiving state shall not deprive any inmate so confined of any legal rights which the inmate would have had if confined in an appropriate institution of the sending state.

(f) Any hearing or hearings to which an inmate confined pursuant to this compact may be entitled by the laws of the sending state may be had before the appropriate authorities of the sending state, or of the receiving state if authorized by the sending state. The receiving state shall provide adequate facilities for such hearing as may be conducted by the appropriate officials of a sending state. In the event such hearing or hearings are had before officials of the receiving state, the governing law shall be that of the sending state and a record of the hearing or hearings as prescribed by the sending state shall be made. The record together with any recommendations of the hearing officials shall be transmitted forthwith to the official or officials before whom the hearing would have been had if it had taken place in the sending state. In any and all proceedings had pursuant to the provisions of this paragraph (f), the officials of the receiving state shall act solely as agents of the sending state and no final determination shall be made in any matter except by the appropriate officials of the sending state.

(g) Any inmate confined pursuant to this compact shall be released within the territory of the sending state unless the inmate and the sending and receiving states shall agree upon release in some other place. The sending state shall bear the cost of such return to its territory.

(h) Any inmate confined pursuant to this compact shall have any rights and all rights to participate in and derive any benefits or incur or be relieved of any obligations or have such obligations modified or his status changed on account of any action or proceeding in which he could have participated if confined in any appropriate institution of the sending state located within such state.

(i) The parent, guardian, trustee, or other person or persons entitled under the laws of the sending state to act for, advise, or otherwise function with respect to any inmate shall not be deprived of or restricted in his exercise of any power in respect of any inmate confined pursuant to the terms of this compact.

Article V.   Act Not Reviewable in Receiving State: Extradition

(a) Any decision of the sending state in respect of any matter over which it retains jurisdiction pursuant to this compact shall be conclusive upon and not reviewable within the receiving state, but if at the time the sending state seeks to remove an inmate from an institution in the receiving state there is pending against the inmate within such state any criminal charge or if the inmate is formally accused of having committed within such state a criminal offense, the inmate shall not be returned without the consent of the receiving state until discharged from prosecution or other form of proceeding, imprisonment, or detention for such offense. The duly accredited officer of the sending state shall be permitted to transport inmates pursuant to this compact through any and all states party to this compact without interference.

(b) An inmate who escapes from an institution in which he is confined pursuant to this compact shall be deemed a fugitive from the sending state and from the state in which the institution escaped from is situated. In the case of an escape to a jurisdiction other than the sending or receiving state, the responsibility for institution of extradition or rendition proceedings shall be that of the sending state, but nothing contained herein shall be construed to prevent or affect the activities of officers and agencies of any jurisdiction directed toward the apprehension and return of an escapee.

Article VI.   Federal Aid

Any state party to this compact may accept federal aid for use in connection with any institution or program, the use of which is or may be affected by this compact or any contract pursuant thereto. Any inmate in a receiving state pursuant to this compact may participate in any such federally aided program or activity for which the sending and receiving states have made contractual provision. However, if such program or activity is not part of the customary correctional regimen, the express consent of the appropriate official of the sending state shall be required therefor.

Article VII.   Entry Into Force

This compact shall enter into force and become effective and binding upon the states so acting when it has been enacted into law by any two states. Thereafter, this compact shall enter into force and become effective and binding as to any other of such states upon similar action by such state.

Article VIII.   Withdrawal and Termination

This compact shall continue in force and remain binding upon a party state until it shall have enacted a statute repealing the compact and providing for the sending of formal written notice of withdrawal from the compact to the appropriate officials of all other party states. An actual withdrawal shall not take effect until one year after the notices provided in the statute have been sent. Such withdrawal shall not relieve the withdrawing state from its obligations assumed hereunder prior to the effective date of withdrawal. Before the effective date of withdrawal, a withdrawal state shall remove to its territory, at its own expense, such inmates as it may have confined pursuant to the provisions of this compact.

Article IX.   Other Arrangements Unaffected

Nothing contained in this compact shall be construed to abrogate or impair an agreement or other arrangement which a party state may have with a nonparty state for the confinement, rehabilitation, or treatment of inmates, nor to repeal any other laws of a party state authorizing the making of cooperative institutional arrangements.

Article X.   Construction and Severability

(a) The provisions of this compact shall be liberally construed and shall be severable. If any phrase, clause, sentence, or provision of this compact is declared to be contrary to the constitution of any participating state or of the United States or the applicability thereof to any government, agency, person, or circumstance is held invalid, the validity of the remainder of this compact and the applicability thereof to any government, agency, person, or circumstance shall not be affected thereby. If this compact shall be held contrary to the constitution of any state participating therein, the compact shall remain in full force and effect as to the remaining states and in full force and effect as to the state affected as to all severable matters.

(b) Powers. The director of the Texas Department of Criminal Justice is authorized and directed to do all things necessary or incidental to the carrying out of the compact in every particular.

Added by Acts 1985, 69th Leg., ch. 24, § 1, eff. Jan. 1, 1986. Renumbered from art. 42.18 by Acts 1987, 70th Leg., ch. 167, § 5.01(a)(9), eff. Sept. 1, 1987. Amended by Acts 2009, 81st Leg., ch. 87, § 25.031, eff. Sept. 1, 2009.

Art. 42.20. Immunities

(a) An individual listed in Subsection (c) of this article and the governmental entity that the individual serves as an officer or employee are not liable for damages arising from an act or failure to act by the individual or governmental entity in connection with a community service program or work program established under this chapter or in connection with an inmate, offender, or releasee programmatic or nonprogrammatic activity, including work, educational, and treatment activities, if the act or failure to act:

(1) was performed pursuant to a court order or was otherwise performed in an official capacity; and

(2) was not performed with conscious indifference for the safety of others.

(b) Chapter 101, Civil Practice and Remedies Code, does not apply to a claim based on an act or a failure to act of an individual listed in Subsection (c) of this article or a governmental entity the officer serves as an officer or employee if the act or failure to act is in connection with a program described by Subsection (a) of this article.

(c) This article applies to:

(1) a director or employee of a community supervision and corrections department or a community corrections facility;

(2) a sheriff or employee of a sheriff's department;

(3) a county judge, county attorney, county commissioner, or county employee;

(4) a district judge, district attorney, or criminal district attorney;

(5) an officer or employee of a state agency; or

(6) an officer or employee of a political subdivision other than a county.

Added by Acts 1993, 73rd Leg., ch. 900, § 5.03, eff. Sept. 1, 1993. Amended by Acts 1995, 74th Leg., ch. 76, § 3.13, eff. Sept. 1, 1995; Acts 2003, 78th Leg., ch. 406, § 1, eff. Sept. 1, 2003.

Art. 42.21. Notice of release of family violence offenders

(a) Before releasing a person convicted of a family violence offense, the entity holding the person shall make a reasonable attempt to give personal notice of the imminent release to the victim of the offense or to another person designated by the victim to receive the notice. An attempt by an entity to give notice to the victim or person designated by the victim at the victim's or person's last known telephone number or address, as shown on the records of the entity, constitutes a reasonable attempt to give notice under this subsection.

(b) An entity or an employee of an entity is not liable for damages arising from complying or failing to comply with Subsection (a) of this article.

(c) In this article, "family violence" has the meaning assigned by Section 71.004, Family Code.

Added by Acts 1995, 74th Leg., ch. 661, § 2, eff. Aug. 28, 1995. Amended by Acts 2003, 78th Leg., ch. 1276, § 7.002(j), eff. Sept. 1, 2003.

Art. 42.22. Restitution Liens
Definitions

Sec. 1. In this article:

(1) "Department" means the Texas Department of Motor Vehicles.

(2) "Motor vehicle" has the meaning assigned by Chapter 501, Transportation Code.

(3) "State" means the State of Texas and all political subdivisions thereof.

(4) "Victim" means:

(A) a "close relative of a deceased victim," "guardian of a victim," or "victim," as those terms are defined by Article 56.01 of this code; or

(B) an individual who suffers damages as a result of another committing an offense under Section 38.04, Penal Code, in which the defendant used a motor vehicle while the defendant was in flight.

(5) "Personal property" means any property other than real property including all tangible and intangible types of property and including but not limited to

copyrights, book rights, movie rights, patents, and trademarks acquired by the defendant prior to, during, and after conviction.

Lien Established

Sec. 2. (a) The victim of a criminal offense has a restitution lien to secure the amount of restitution to which the victim is entitled under the order of a court in a criminal case.

(b) The state also has a restitution lien to secure the:

(1) amount of fines or costs entered against a defendant in the judgment in a felony criminal case;

(2) amount of reimbursement for costs of:

(A) confinement ordered under Article 42.038; or

(B) notice provided under Article 62.056 or 62.201; and

(3) amount of damages incurred by the state as a result of the commission of an offense under Section 38.04, Penal Code, in which the defendant used a motor vehicle while the defendant was in flight.

Perfection

Sec. 3. (a) Except as provided by this section, a restitution lien attaches and is perfected when an affidavit to perfect the lien is filed in accordance with this article.

(b) If a lien established under this article is attached to a motor vehicle, the lien must be perfected in the manner provided by Chapter 501, Transportation Code, and the court that entered the order of restitution giving rise to the lien shall include in the order a requirement that the defendant surrender to the court evidence of current legal ownership of the motor vehicle and the title, if applicable, against which the lien attaches. A lien against a motor vehicle as provided by this article is not perfected until the defendant's title to the vehicle has been surrendered to the court and the department has issued a subsequent title that discloses on its face the fact that the vehicle is subject to a restitution lien established as provided by this article.

Judgment Required

Sec. 4. An affidavit to perfect a restitution lien may not be filed under this article until a court has ordered restitution or entered a judgment requiring the defendant to pay a fine or costs.

Persons Who May File

Sec. 5. The following persons may file an affidavit to perfect a restitution lien:

(1) the attorney representing the state in a criminal case in which a victim is determined by the court to be entitled to restitution or in which a defendant is ordered to pay fines or costs; or

(2) a victim in a criminal case determined by the court to be entitled to restitution.

Affidavit

Sec. 6. An affidavit to perfect a restitution lien must be signed by the attorney representing the state or a magistrate and must contain:

(1) the name and date of birth of the defendant whose property or other interests are subject to the lien;

(2) the residence or principal place of business of the person named in the lien, if known;

(3) the criminal proceeding giving rise to the lien, including the name of the court, the name of the case, and the court's file number for the case;

(4) the name and address of the attorney representing the state and the name of the person entitled to restitution;

(5) a statement that the notice is being filed under this article;

(6) the amount of restitution and the amount of fines and costs the defendant has been ordered to pay by the court;

(7) a statement that the amount of restitution owed at any one time may be less than the original balance and that the outstanding balance is reflected in the records of the clerk of the court hearing the criminal proceeding giving rise to the lien; and

(8) the vehicle description and vehicle identification number.

Filing

Sec. 7. (a) An affidavit to perfect a restitution lien may be filed with:

(1) the secretary of state;

(2) the department in the manner provided by Chapter 501, Transportation Code; or

(3) the county clerk of the county in which:

(A) the crime was committed;

(B) the defendant resides; or

(C) the property is located.

(b) The uniform fee for filing and indexing and for stamping a copy furnished by the state or victim to show the date and place of filing is $5.

(c) The secretary of state shall deposit the filing fee in the state treasury to the credit of the statutory filing fund solely to defray the costs of administration of this section. The department shall deposit the filing fee in the state treasury to the credit of the state highway fund to be used solely to defray the costs of administering this section.

(d) The county clerk shall immediately record the restitution lien in the judgment records of the county. The clerk shall note in the records the date and hour the lien is received.

(e) The secretary of state shall immediately file the restitution lien in the security interest and financing statement records of the secretary of state. The secretary of state shall note in the records the date and hour the lien is received.

(f) The department shall immediately file the restitution lien in the motor vehicle records of the department. The department shall note in the records the date and hour the lien is received.

(g) When a restitution lien is filed, the county clerk or secretary of state shall enter the restitution lien in an alphabetical index to the records in which the lien is filed showing:

(1) the name of the person entitled to restitution;

(2) the name of the defendant obligated to pay restitution, fines, or costs;

(3) the amount of the lien; and

(4) the name of the court that ordered restitution.

(h) A person who files an affidavit to perfect a restitution lien under this article shall notify in writing the clerk of the court entering the judgment creating the lien of all officers or entities with which the affidavit was filed.

Subject Property

Sec. 8. A restitution lien extends to:

(1) any interest of the defendant in real property whether then owned or after-acquired located in a county in which the lien is perfected by the filing of an affidavit with the county clerk;

(2) any interest of the defendant in tangible or intangible personal property whether then owned or after-acquired other than a motor vehicle if the lien is

perfected by the filing of the affidavit with the secretary of state; or

(3) any interest of the defendant in a motor vehicle whether then owned or after-acquired if the lien is perfected by the filing of the affidavit with the department.

Priority

Sec. 9. The perfection of a restitution lien under this article is notice of the claim to all persons dealing with the defendant or the property identified in the affidavit perfecting the lien. Without regard to whether perfected before or after the perfection of a restitution lien filed and perfected under this article, a perfected real estate mortgage lien, a vendor's lien, a purchase money security interest, a chattel paper security interest, a lien on a motor vehicle perfected as provided by Chapter 501, Transportation Code, or a worker's lien perfected in the manner provided by law is superior and prior to a restitution lien filed and perfected under this article. Except as provided by this article, a perfected lien in favor of a victim is superior and prior to a lien perfected by the state under this article, and the perfected lien in favor of the state is superior and prior to the claim or interest of any other person, other than:

(1) a person who acquires a valid lien or security interest perfected before the perfection of the restitution lien;

(2) a bona fide purchaser who acquires an interest in the property, if personal property, before the filing of the restitution lien, to the extent that the purchaser gives value; or

(3) a bona fide purchaser for value who acquires and files for record an interest in the property, if real property, before the perfection of the restitution lien.

Payment

Sec. 10. The clerk receiving a payment from a defendant ordered to pay restitution shall make payments to the person having an interest in the restitution lien on a schedule of not less than quarterly payments as determined by the clerk or agency.

Foreclosure

Sec. 11. If a defendant fails to timely make a payment required by the order of the court entering the judgment creating the restitution lien, the person having an interest in the lien may file suit in a court of competent jurisdiction to foreclose the lien. If the defendant cures the default on or before the 20th day after the date the suit is filed and pays the person who files the suit costs of court and reasonable attorney's fees, the court may dismiss the suit without prejudice to the person. The person may refile the suit against the defendant if the defendant subsequently defaults.

Expiration; Records

Sec. 12.　(a) A restitution lien expires on the 10th anniversary of the date the lien was filed or on the date the defendant satisfies the judgment creating the lien, whichever occurs first. The person having an interest in the lien may refile the lien before the date the lien expires. A lien that is refiled expires on the 10th anniversary of the date the lien was refiled or the date the defendant satisfies the judgment creating the lien, whichever occurs first.

(b) Failure to execute or foreclose the restitution lien does not cause dormancy of the lien.

(c) The clerk of the court entering the judgment creating the restitution lien shall maintain a record of the outstanding balance of restitution, fines, or costs owed. If the defendant satisfies the judgment, the clerk shall immediately execute and file for record a release of the restitution lien with all officers or entities with which the affidavit perfecting the lien was filed, as indicated by the notice received by the clerk under Section 7(h) of this article, unless a release was executed and filed by the person who filed the affidavit to perfect the lien.

(d) A partial release of a lien as to specific property may be executed by the attorney representing the state or a magistrate who signs an affidavit described by Section 6 of this article on payment of a sum determined to represent the defendant's interest in any property to which the lien may attach.

Added by Acts 1995, 74th Leg., ch. 997, § 1, eff. Sept. 1, 1996. Amended by Acts 1997, 75th Leg., ch. 1118, § 1, eff. Sept. 1, 1997. Renumbered from Vernon's Ann.C.C.P. art. 42.21 by Acts 1997, 75th Leg., ch. 165, § 31.01(12), eff. Sept. 1, 1997. Amended by Acts 1999, 76th Leg., ch. 295, § 2, eff. Sept. 1, 1999; Acts 2001, 77th Leg., ch. 1334, § 1, eff. Sept. 1, 2001; Acts 2001, 77th Leg., ch. 1334, § 2, eff. Sept. 1, 2001; Acts 2003, 78th Leg., ch. 1300, § 2, eff. Sept. 1, 2003; Acts 2005, 79th Leg., ch. 1008, § 2.02, eff. Sept. 1, 2005; Acts 2009, 81st Leg., ch. 933, § 3B.01, eff. Sept. 1, 2009.

Art. 42.23.　Notification of Court of Family Violence Conviction

(a) In this article, "family violence" has the meaning assigned by Section 71.004, Family Code.

(b) If the attorney representing the state in a criminal case involving family violence learns that the defendant is subject to the jurisdiction of another court relating to an order that provides for the appointment of a conservator or that sets the terms and conditions of conservatorship or for possession of or access to a child, the attorney representing the state shall notify the court in which the defendant is being tried of the existence of the order and the identity of the court of continuing jurisdiction.

(c) On the conviction or entry of an order deferring adjudication of a defendant for an offense involving family violence, the convicting court or the court entering the order shall notify the court of continuing jurisdiction of the conviction or deferred adjudication.

Added by Acts 2001, 77th Leg., ch. 1289, § 11, eff. Sept. 1, 2001.

Art. 42.24.　Prohibiting Contact With Victim

If a defendant's sentence includes a term of confinement or imprisonment, the convicting court may, as part of the sentence, prohibit the defendant from contacting, during the term of the defendant's confinement or imprisonment, the victim of the offense of which the defendant is convicted or a member of the victim's family.

Added by Acts 2011, 82nd Leg., ch. 491 (H.B. 1028), § 1, eff. Sept. 1, 2011.

CHAPTER 42A.　COMMUNITY SUPERVISION

SUBCHAPTER A.　GENERAL PROVISIONS

SUBCHAPTER B.　PLACEMENT ON COMMUNITY SUPERVISION

PROCEEDINGS AFTER VERDICT

SUBCHAPTER A. GENERAL PROVISIONS

Art. 42A.001. Definitions

In this chapter:

(1) "Community supervision" means the placement of a defendant by a court under a continuum of programs and sanctions, with conditions imposed by the court for a specified period during which:

(A) criminal proceedings are deferred without an adjudication of guilt; or

(B) a sentence of imprisonment or confinement, imprisonment and fine, or confinement and fine, is probated and the imposition of sentence is suspended in whole or in part.

(2) "Court" means a court of record having original criminal jurisdiction.

(3) "Electronic monitoring" includes voice tracking systems, position tracking systems, position location systems, biometric tracking systems, and any other electronic or telecommunications system that may be used to assist in the supervision of defendants under this chapter.

(4) "Supervision officer" means a person appointed or employed under Section 76.004, Government Code, to supervise defendants placed on community supervision.

Added by Acts 2015, 84th Leg., ch. 770 (H.B. 2299), § 1.01, eff. Jan. 1, 2017.

Art. 42A.002. Reference in Law

A reference in a law to a statute or a part of a statute revised in this chapter by Chapter 770 (H.B. 2299), Acts of the 84th Legislature, Regular Session, 2015, is considered to be a reference to the part of this chapter that revises that statute or part of that statute.

Added by Acts 2017, 85th Leg., ch. 877 (H.B. 3016), § 9, eff. Sept. 1, 2017.

SUBCHAPTER B. PLACEMENT ON COMMUNITY SUPERVISION

Art. 42A.051. Authority to Grant Community Supervision, Impose or Modify Conditions, or Discharge Defendant

(a) Unless the judge has transferred jurisdiction of the case to another court under Article 42A.151, only the court in which the defendant was tried may:

(1) grant community supervision;

(2) impose conditions; or

(3) discharge the defendant.

(b) The judge of the court having jurisdiction of the case may, at any time during the period of community supervision, modify the conditions of community supervision. Except as provided by Article 42A.052(a), only the judge may modify the conditions.

Added by Acts 2015, 84th Leg., ch. 770 (H.B. 2299), § 1.01, eff. Jan. 1, 2017.

Art. 42A.052. Modification of Conditions by Supervision Officer or Magistrate

(a) A judge who places a defendant on community supervision may authorize the supervision officer supervising the defendant or a magistrate appointed by the district courts in the county that give preference to criminal cases to modify the conditions of community supervision for the limited purpose of transferring the defendant to different programs within the community supervision continuum of programs and sanctions.

(b) A supervision officer or magistrate who modifies the conditions of community supervision shall:

(1) deliver a copy of the modified conditions to the defendant;

(2) file a copy of the modified conditions with the sentencing court; and

(3) note the date of delivery of the copy in the defendant's file.

(c) If the defendant agrees to the modification in writing, the officer or magistrate shall file a copy of the modified conditions with the district clerk and the conditions shall be enforced as modified. If the defendant does not agree to the modification in writing, the supervision officer or magistrate shall refer the case to the judge for modification in the manner provided by Article 42A.752.

Added by Acts 2015, 84th Leg., ch. 770 (H.B. 2299), § 1.01, eff. Jan. 1, 2017.

Art. 42A.053. Judge–Ordered Community Supervision

(a) A judge, in the best interest of justice, the public, and the defendant, after conviction or a plea of guilty or nolo contendere, may:

(1) suspend the imposition of the sentence and place the defendant on community supervision; or

(2) impose a fine applicable to the offense and place the defendant on community supervision.

(b) A judge may not deny community supervision to a defendant based solely on the defendant's inability to speak, read, write, hear, or understand English.

(c) A defendant is not eligible for community supervision under this article if the defendant is sentenced to serve:

(1) a term of imprisonment that exceeds 10 years; or

(2) a term of confinement under Section 12.35, Penal Code.

(d) In a felony case:

(1) the minimum period of community supervision is the same as the minimum term of imprisonment applicable to the offense; and

(2) the maximum period of community supervision is:

(A) 10 years, for a felony other than a third degree felony described by Paragraph (B); and

(B) five years, for any of the following third degree felonies:

(i) a third degree felony under Title 7, Penal Code; and

(ii) a third degree felony under Chapter 481, Health and Safety Code.

(e) Notwithstanding Subsection (d), the minimum period of community supervision under this article for a felony described by Article 42A.453(b) is five years.

(f) The maximum period of community supervision in a misdemeanor case is two years.

(g) Notwithstanding Subsection (d)(2) or (f), a judge may extend the maximum period of community supervision in the manner provided by Article 42A.753 or 42A.757.

Added by Acts 2015, 84th Leg., ch. 770 (H.B. 2299), § 1.01, eff. Jan. 1, 2017.

Art. 42A.054. Limitation on Judge–Ordered Community Supervision

(a) Article 42A.053 does not apply to a defendant adjudged guilty of an offense under:

(1) Section 15.03, Penal Code, if the offense is punishable as a felony of the first degree;

(2) Section 19.02, Penal Code (Murder);

(3) Section 19.03, Penal Code (Capital Murder);

(4) Section 20.04, Penal Code (Aggravated Kidnapping);

(5) Section 20A.02, Penal Code (Trafficking of Persons);

(6) Section 21.11(a)(1), Penal Code (Indecency with a Child);

(7) Section 22.011, Penal Code (Sexual Assault);

(8) Section 22.021, Penal Code (Aggravated Sexual Assault);

(9) Section 22.04(a)(1), Penal Code (Injury to a Child, Elderly Individual, or Disabled Individual), if:

(A) the offense is punishable as a felony of the first degree; and

(B) the victim of the offense is a child;

(10) Section 29.03, Penal Code (Aggravated Robbery);

(11) Section 30.02, Penal Code (Burglary), if:

(A) the offense is punishable under Subsection (d) of that section; and

(B) the actor committed the offense with the intent to commit a felony under Section 21.02, 21.11, 22.011, 22.021, or 25.02, Penal Code;

(12) Section 43.05, Penal Code (Compelling Prostitution);

(13) Section 43.25, Penal Code (Sexual Performance by a Child); or

(14) Chapter 481, Health and Safety Code, for which punishment is increased under:

(A) Section 481.140 of that code (Use of Child in Commission of Offense); or

(B) Section 481.134(c), (d), (e), or (f) of that code (Drug-free Zones) if it is shown that the defendant has been previously convicted of an offense for which punishment was increased under any of those subsections.

(b) Article 42A.053 does not apply to a defendant when it is shown that:

(1) a deadly weapon as defined by Section 1.07, Penal Code, was used or exhibited during the:

(A) commission of a felony offense; or

(B) immediate flight from the commission of a felony offense; and

(2) the defendant:

(A) used or exhibited the deadly weapon; or

(B) was a party to the offense and knew that a deadly weapon would be used or exhibited.

(c) On an affirmative finding regarding the use or exhibition of a deadly weapon as described by Subsection (b), the trial court shall enter the finding in the judgment of the court.

(d) On an affirmative finding that the deadly weapon under Subsection (c) was a firearm, the court shall enter that finding in its judgment.

Added by Acts 2015, 84th Leg., ch. 770 (H.B. 2299), § 1.01, eff. Jan. 1, 2017.

Art. 42A.055. Jury–Recommended Community Supervision

(a) A jury that imposes confinement as punishment for an offense may recommend to the judge that the judge suspend the imposition of the sentence and place the defendant on community supervision. A judge shall suspend the imposition of the sentence and place the defendant on community supervision if the jury makes that recommendation in the verdict.

(b) A defendant is eligible for community supervision under this article only if:

(1) before the trial begins, the defendant files a written sworn motion with the judge that the defendant has not previously been convicted of a felony in this or any other state; and

(2) the jury enters in the verdict a finding that the information contained in the defendant's motion is true.

(c) If the jury recommends to the judge that the judge place the defendant on community supervision, the judge shall place the defendant on community supervision for any period permitted under Articles 42A.053(d) and (f), as appropriate.

(d) A judge may extend the maximum period of community supervision in the manner provided by Article 42A.753 or 42A.757.

Added by Acts 2015, 84th Leg., ch. 770 (H.B. 2299), § 1.01, eff. Jan. 1, 2017.

Art. 42A.056. Limitation on Jury–Recommended Community Supervision

A defendant is not eligible for community supervision under Article 42A.055 if the defendant:

(1) is sentenced to a term of imprisonment that exceeds 10 years;

(2) is convicted of a state jail felony for which suspension of the imposition of the sentence occurs automatically under Article 42A.551;

(3) is adjudged guilty of an offense under Section 19.02, Penal Code;

(4) is convicted of an offense under Section 21.11(a)(1), 22.011, or 22.021, Penal Code, if the victim of the offense was younger than 14 years of age at the time the offense was committed;

(5) is convicted of an offense under Section 20.04, Penal Code, if:

(A) the victim of the offense was younger than 14 years of age at the time the offense was committed; and

(B) the actor committed the offense with the intent to violate or abuse the victim sexually;

(6) is convicted of an offense under Section 20A.02, 43.05, or 43.25, Penal Code; or

(7) is convicted of an offense for which punishment is increased under Section 481.134(c), (d), (e), or (f), Health and Safety Code, if it is shown that the defendant has been previously convicted of an offense for which punishment was increased under any of those subsections.

Added by Acts 2015, 84th Leg., ch. 770 (H.B. 2299), § 1.01, eff. Jan. 1, 2017.

Art. 42A.057. Minimum Period of Community Supervision for Certain Burglaries of Vehicles

The minimum period of community supervision for an offense under Section 30.04, Penal Code, punishable as a Class A misdemeanor with a minimum term of confinement of six months is one year.

Added by Acts 2015, 84th Leg., ch. 770 (H.B. 2299), § 1.01, eff. Jan. 1, 2017.

Art. 42A.058. Information provided to defendant placed on community supervision

A judge placing a defendant on community supervision shall inform the defendant in writing and on a form prescribed by the Office of Court Administration of the Texas Judicial System that, after satisfactorily fulfilling the conditions of community supervision and on expiration of the period of community supervision, the judge is authorized to release the defendant from the penalties and disabilities resulting from the offense as provided by Article 42A.701(f).

Added by Acts 2017, 85th Leg., ch. 1017 (H.B. 1507), § 2, eff. Sept. 1, 2017.

Section 4(c) of Acts 2017, 85th Leg., ch. 1017 (H.B. 1507) provides:

"(c) Article 42A.058, Code of Criminal Procedure, as added by this Act, applies only to a defendant placed on community supervision on or after January 1, 2018, regardless of whether the offense for which the defendant was placed on community supervision was committed before, on, or after that date."

SUBCHAPTER C. DEFERRED ADJUDICATION COMMUNITY SUPERVISION

Art. 42A.101. Placement on Deferred Adjudication Community Supervision

(a) Except as provided by Article 42A.102(b), if in the judge's opinion the best interest of society and the defendant will be served, the judge may, after receiving a plea of guilty or nolo contendere, hearing the evidence, and finding that it substantiates the defendant's guilt, defer further proceedings without entering an adjudication of guilt and place the defendant on deferred adjudication community supervision.

(b) After placing the defendant on deferred adjudication community supervision under Subsection (a), the judge shall inform the defendant orally or in writing of the possible consequences under Articles 42A.108 and 42A.110 of a violation of a condition of deferred adjudication community supervision. If the information is provided orally, the judge must record and maintain the judge's statement to the defendant. The failure of a judge to inform a defendant of possible consequences under Articles 42A.108 and 42A.110 is not a ground for reversal unless the defendant shows that the defendant was harmed by the failure of the judge to provide the information.

Added by Acts 2015, 84th Leg., ch. 770 (H.B. 2299), § 1.01, eff. Jan. 1, 2017.

Art. 42A.102. Eligibility for Deferred Adjudication Community Supervision

(a) A judge may place on deferred adjudication community supervision a defendant charged with an offense under Section 21.11, 22.011, or 22.021, Penal Code, regardless of the age of the victim, or a defendant charged with a felony described by Article 42A.453(b) only if the judge makes a finding in open court that placing the defendant on deferred adjudication community supervision is in the best interest of the victim. The failure of the judge to make a finding under this subsection is not grounds for the defendant to set aside the plea, deferred adjudication, or any subsequent conviction or sentence.

(b) In all other cases, the judge may grant deferred adjudication community supervision unless:

(1) the defendant is charged with an offense:

(A) under Sections 49.04–49.08, Penal Code; or

(B) for which punishment may be increased under Section 481.134(c), (d), (e), or (f), Health and Safety Code, if it is shown that the defendant has been previously convicted of an offense for which punishment was increased under any one of those subsections;

(2) the defendant:

(A) is charged with an offense under Section 21.11, 22.011, or 22.021, Penal Code, regardless of the age of the victim, or a felony described by Article 42A.453(b); and

(B) has previously been placed on community supervision for an offense under Paragraph (A);

(3) the defendant is charged with an offense under:

(A) Section 21.02, Penal Code; or

(B) Section 22.021, Penal Code, that is punishable under Subsection (f) of that section or under Section 12.42(c)(3) or (4), Penal Code; or

(4) the defendant is charged with an offense under Section 19.02, Penal Code, except that the judge may grant deferred adjudication community supervision on determining that the defendant did not cause the death of the deceased, did not intend to kill the deceased or another, and did not anticipate that a human life would be taken.

Added by Acts 2015, 84th Leg., ch. 770 (H.B. 2299), § 1.01, eff. Jan. 1, 2017.

Art. 42A.103. Period of Deferred Adjudication Community Supervision

(a) In a felony case, the period of deferred adjudication community supervision may not exceed 10 years. For a defendant charged with a felony under Section 21.11, 22.011, or 22.021, Penal Code, regardless of the age of the victim, and for a defendant charged with a felony described by Article 42A.453(b), the period of deferred adjudication community supervision may not be less than five years.

(b) In a misdemeanor case, the period of deferred adjudication community supervision may not exceed two years.

(c) A judge may extend the maximum period of deferred adjudication community supervision in the manner provided by Article 42A.753 or 42A.757.

Added by Acts 2015, 84th Leg., ch. 770 (H.B. 2299), § 1.01, eff. Jan. 1, 2017.

Art. 42A.104. Conditions of Deferred Adjudication Community Supervision; Imposition of Fine

(a) The judge may impose a fine applicable to the offense and require any reasonable condition of deferred adjudication community supervision that a judge could impose on a defendant placed on community supervision for a conviction that was probated and suspended, including:

(1) confinement; and

(2) mental health treatment under Article 42A.506.

(b) The provisions of Subchapter L specifying whether a defendant convicted of a state jail felony is to be confined in a county jail or state jail felony facility and establishing the minimum and maximum terms of confinement as a condition of community supervision apply in the same manner to a defendant placed on deferred adjudication community supervision after pleading guilty or nolo contendere to a state jail felony.

Added by Acts 2015, 84th Leg., ch. 770 (H.B. 2299), § 1.01, eff. Jan. 1, 2017.

Art. 42A.105. Affirmative Findings

(a) If a judge places on deferred adjudication community supervision a defendant charged with a sexually violent offense, as defined by Article 62.001, the judge shall make an affirmative finding of fact and file a statement of that affirmative finding with the papers in the case if the judge determines that the victim or intended victim was younger than 14 years of age at the time of the offense.

(b) If a judge places on deferred adjudication community supervision a defendant charged with an offense under Section 20.02, 20.03, or 20.04, Penal Code, or an attempt, conspiracy, or solicitation to commit one of those offenses, the judge shall make an affirmative finding of fact and file a statement of that affirmative finding with the papers in the case if the judge determines that the victim or intended victim was younger than 17 years of age at the time of the offense.

(c) If a judge places on deferred adjudication community supervision a defendant charged with an offense under Section 21.11 or 22.011, Penal Code, the judge shall make an affirmative finding of fact and file a statement of that affirmative finding with the papers in the case if the judge determines that:

(1) at the time of the offense, the defendant was not more than four years older than the victim or intended victim and the victim or intended victim was at least 15 years of age; and

(2) the charge to which the plea is entered under this subchapter is based solely on the ages of the defendant and the victim or intended victim at the time of the offense.

(d) If a judge places a defendant on deferred adjudication community supervision, on the motion of the attorney representing the state the judge shall make an affirmative finding of fact and file a statement of that affirmative finding with the papers in the case if the judge determines that, regardless of whether the conduct at issue is the subject of the prosecution or part of the same criminal episode as the conduct that is the subject of the prosecution, a victim in the trial:

(1) is or has been a victim of a severe form of trafficking in persons, as defined by 22 U.S.C. Section 7102(9); or

(2) has suffered substantial physical or mental abuse as a result of having been a victim of criminal activity described by 8 U.S.C. Section 1101(a)(15)(U)(iii).

(e) The part of the papers in the case containing an affirmative finding under Subsection (d):

(1) must include specific information identifying the victim, as available;

(2) may not include information identifying the victim's location; and

(3) is confidential, unless written consent for the release of the affirmative finding is obtained from the victim or, if the victim is younger than 18 years of age, the victim's parent or guardian. (Code Crim. Proc., Art. 42.12, Secs. 5(e), (g), (i), (j).)

(f) If a judge places on deferred adjudication community supervision a defendant charged with a misdemeanor other than a misdemeanor under Chapter 20, 21, 22, 25, 42, 43, 46, or 71, Penal Code, the judge shall make an affirmative finding of fact and file a statement of that affirmative finding with the papers in the

case if the judge determines that it is not in the best interest of justice that the defendant receive an automatic order of nondisclosure under Section 411.072, Government Code.

Added by Acts 2015, 84th Leg., ch. 770 (H.B. 2299), § 1.01, eff. Jan. 1, 2017. Amended by Acts 2017, 85th Leg., ch. 324 (S.B. 1488), § 23.012(a), eff. Sept. 1, 2017; Acts 2017, 85th Leg., ch. 877 (H.B. 3016), § 10, eff. Sept. 1, 2017.

Art. 42A.106. Record Not Confidential; Right to Petition for Order of Nondisclosure

(a) Except as provided by Section 552.142, Government Code, a record in the custody of the court clerk regarding a case in which a defendant is granted deferred adjudication community supervision is not confidential.

(b) Before placing a defendant on deferred adjudication community supervision, the court shall inform the defendant of the defendant's right to receive or petition the court for an order of nondisclosure of criminal history record information under Subchapter E-1, Chapter 411, Government Code, as applicable, unless the defendant is ineligible for an order because of:

(1) the nature of the offense for which the defendant is placed on deferred adjudication community supervision; or

(2) the defendant's criminal history.

Added by Acts 2015, 84th Leg., ch. 770 (H.B. 2299), § 1.01, eff. Jan. 1, 2017. Amended by Acts 2017, 85th Leg., ch. 324 (S.B. 1488), § 23.012(b), eff. Sept. 1, 2017.

Art. 42A.107. Request for Final Adjudication

On written motion of the defendant requesting final adjudication that is filed within 30 days after the entry of the defendant's plea and the deferment of adjudication, the judge shall proceed to final adjudication as in all other cases.

Added by Acts 2015, 84th Leg., ch. 770 (H.B. 2299), § 1.01, eff. Jan. 1, 2017.

Art. 42A.108. Violation of Condition of Deferred Adjudication Community Supervision; Hearing

(a) On violation of a condition of deferred adjudication community supervision imposed under Article 42A.104, the defendant may be arrested and detained as provided in Article 42A.751.

(b) The defendant is entitled to a hearing limited to a determination by the court of whether the court will proceed with an adjudication of guilt on the original charge. The court may not proceed with an adjudication of guilt on the original charge if the court finds that the only evidence supporting the alleged violation of a condition of deferred adjudication community supervision is the uncorroborated results of a polygraph examination. The determination to proceed with an adjudication of guilt on the original charge is reviewable in the same manner as a revocation hearing conducted under Article 42A.751(d) in a case in which the adjudication of guilt was not deferred.

(c) A court retains jurisdiction to hold a hearing under Subsection (b) and to proceed with an adjudication of guilt, regardless of whether the period of deferred adjudication community supervision imposed on the defendant has expired, if before the expiration of the supervision period:

(1) the attorney representing the state files a motion to proceed with the adjudication; and

(2) a capias is issued for the arrest of the defendant.

Added by Acts 2015, 84th Leg., ch. 770 (H.B. 2299), § 1.01, eff. Jan. 1, 2017.

Art. 42A.109. Due Diligence Defense

For the purposes of a hearing under Article 42A.108, it is an affirmative defense to revocation for an alleged violation based on a failure to report to a supervision officer as directed or to remain within a specified place that no supervision officer, peace officer, or other officer with the power of arrest under a warrant issued by a judge for that alleged violation contacted or attempted to contact the defendant in person at the defendant's last known residence address or last known employment address, as reflected in the files of the department serving the county in which the order of deferred adjudication community supervision was entered.

Added by Acts 2015, 84th Leg., ch. 770 (H.B. 2299), § 1.01, eff. Jan. 1, 2017.

Art. 42A.110. Proceedings After Adjudication

(a) After an adjudication of guilt, all proceedings, including assessment of punishment, pronouncement of sentence, granting of community supervision, and defendant's appeal, continue as if the adjudication of guilt had not been deferred.

(b) A court assessing punishment after an adjudication of guilt of a defendant charged with a state jail felony may suspend the imposition of the sentence and place the defendant on community supervision or may order the sentence to be executed, regardless of whether the defendant has previously been convicted of a felony.

Added by Acts 2015, 84th Leg., ch. 770 (H.B. 2299), § 1.01, eff. Jan. 1, 2017.

Art. 42A.111. Dismissal and Discharge

(a) On expiration of a period of deferred adjudication community supervision imposed under this subchapter, if the judge has not proceeded to an adjudication of guilt, the judge shall dismiss the proceedings against the defendant and discharge the defendant.

(b) The judge may dismiss the proceedings and discharge a defendant before the expiration of the period of deferred adjudication community supervision if, in the judge's opinion, the best interest of society and the defendant will be served, except that the judge may not dismiss the proceedings and discharge a defendant charged with an offense requiring the defendant to register as a sex offender under Chapter 62.

(c) Except as provided by Section 12.42(g), Penal Code, a dismissal and discharge under this article may not be considered a conviction for the purposes of disqualifications or disabilities imposed by law for conviction of an offense.

(d) For any defendant who receives a dismissal and discharge under this article:

(1) on conviction of a subsequent offense, the fact that the defendant previously has received deferred adjudication community supervision is admissible before the court or jury for consideration on the issue of penalty;

(2) if the defendant is an applicant for or the holder of a license under Chapter 42, Human Resources Code, the Department of Family and Protective Services may consider the fact that the defendant previously has received deferred adjudication community supervision in issuing, renewing, denying, or revoking a license under that chapter; and

(3) if the defendant is an applicant for or the holder of a license to provide mental health or medical services for the rehabilitation of sex offenders, the Council on Sex Offender Treatment may consider the fact that the defendant previously has received deferred adjudication community supervision in issuing, renewing, denying, or revoking a license issued by that council.

(e) A judge who dismisses the proceedings against a defendant and discharges the defendant under this article:

(1) shall

provide the defendant with a copy of the order of dismissal and discharge; and

(2) if the judge determines that the defendant is or may become eligible for an order of nondisclosure of criminal history record information under Subchapter E–1, Chapter 411, Government Code, shall, as applicable:

(A) grant an order of nondisclosure of criminal history record information to the defendant;

(B) inform the defendant of the defendant's eligibility to receive an order of nondisclosure of criminal history record information without a petition and the earliest date on which the defendant is eligible to receive the order; or

(C) inform the defendant of the defendant's eligibility to petition the court for an order of nondisclosure of criminal history record information and the earliest date the defendant is eligible to file the petition for the order.

Added by Acts 2015, 84th Leg., ch. 770 (H.B. 2299), § 1.01, eff. Jan. 1, 2017. Amended by Acts 2017, 85th Leg., ch. 324 (S.B. 1488), § 23.012(c), eff. Sept. 1, 2017.

SUBCHAPTER D. JURISDICTION OVER CASE; GEOGRAPHICAL JURISDICTION

Art. 42A.151. Transfer of Jurisdiction

(a) After a defendant has been placed on community supervision, jurisdiction of the case may be transferred to a court of the same rank in this state that:

(1) has geographical jurisdiction where the defendant:

(A) resides; or

(B) violates a condition of community supervision; and

(2) consents to the transfer.

(b) On transfer, the clerk of the court of original jurisdiction shall forward to the court accepting jurisdiction a transcript of any portion of the record as the transferring judge shall direct. The court accepting jurisdiction subsequently shall proceed as if the defendant's trial and conviction had occurred in that court.

Added by Acts 2015, 84th Leg., ch. 770 (H.B. 2299), § 1.01, eff. Jan. 1, 2017.

Art. 42A.152. Issuance of Warrant by Court Having Geographical Jurisdiction

(a) A judge of a court having geographical jurisdiction where a defendant resides or where the defendant violates a condition of community supervision may issue a warrant for the defendant's arrest.

(b) Notwithstanding Subsection (a), the determination of the action to be taken after the defendant's arrest may be made only by the judge of the court having jurisdiction of the case at the time the action is taken.

Added by Acts 2015, 84th Leg., ch. 770 (H.B. 2299), § 1.01, eff. Jan. 1, 2017.

Art. 42A.153. Change of Residence Within the State

(a) If, for good and sufficient reasons, a defendant desires to change the defendant's residence within the state, the change may be effected by application to the supervising supervision officer.

(b) The change of residence is subject to:

(1) the judge's consent; and

(2) any regulations the judge may require in the absence of a supervision officer in the locality to which the defendant is transferred.

Added by Acts 2015, 84th Leg., ch. 770 (H.B. 2299), § 1.01, eff. Jan. 1, 2017.

Art. 42A.154. Leaving the State

A defendant who leaves the state without permission of the judge having jurisdiction of the case is:

(1) considered a fugitive from justice; and

(2) subject to extradition as provided by law.

Added by Acts 2015, 84th Leg., ch. 770 (H.B. 2299), § 1.01, eff. Jan. 1, 2017.

SUBCHAPTER E. PARTIAL EXECUTION OF SENTENCE; CONTINUING JURISDICTION

Art. 42A.201. Continuing Jurisdiction in Misdemeanor Cases

(a) For the purposes of this article, the jurisdiction of the courts in this state in which a sentence requiring confinement in a jail is imposed for conviction of a misdemeanor continues for 180 days from the date the execution of the sentence actually begins.

(b) The judge of a court that imposed a sentence requiring confinement in a jail for conviction of a misdemeanor may, on the judge's own motion, on the motion of the attorney representing the state, or on the written motion of the defendant, suspend further execution of the sentence and place the defendant on community supervision under the terms and conditions of this chapter if, in the opinion of the judge, the defendant would not benefit from further confinement.

(c) When the defendant files a written motion with the court requesting suspension of further execution of the sentence and placement on community supervision or when requested to do so by the judge, the clerk of the court shall request a copy of the defendant's record while confined from the agency operating the jail in which the defendant is confined. On receipt of the request, the agency shall forward a copy of the record to the court as soon as possible.

(d) The judge may deny the motion without holding a hearing but may not grant a motion without holding a hearing and allowing the attorney representing the state and the defendant to present evidence in the case.

Added by Acts 2015, 84th Leg., ch. 770 (H.B. 2299), § 1.01, eff. Jan. 1, 2017.

Art. 42A.202. Continuing Jurisdiction in Felony Cases

(a) For the purposes of this article, the jurisdiction of a court imposing a sentence requiring imprisonment in the Texas Department of Criminal Justice for an offense other than a state jail felony continues for 180 days from the date the execution of the sentence actually begins.

(b) Before the expiration of the 180–day period described by Subsection (a), the judge of the court that imposed the sentence described by that subsection may, on the judge's own motion, on the motion of the attorney representing the state, or on the written motion of the defendant, suspend further execution of the sentence and place the defendant on community supervision under the terms and conditions of this chapter if:

(1) in the opinion of the judge, the defendant would not benefit from further imprisonment;

(2) the defendant is otherwise eligible for community supervision under this chapter; and

(3) the defendant had never before been incarcerated in a penitentiary serving a sentence for a felony.

(c) When the defendant files a written motion requesting the judge to suspend further execution of the sentence and place the defendant on community supervision, the defendant shall immediately deliver or cause to be delivered a copy of the motion to the office of the attorney representing the state.

(d) When the defendant or the attorney representing the state files a written motion requesting the judge to suspend further execution of the sentence and place the defendant on community supervision, and when requested to do so by the judge, the clerk of the court shall request a copy of the defendant's record while imprisoned from the Texas Department of Criminal Justice or, if the defendant is confined in county jail, from the sheriff. On receipt of the request, the Texas Department of Criminal Justice or the sheriff shall forward a copy of the record to the judge as soon as possible.

(e) The judge may deny the motion without holding a hearing but may not grant the motion without holding a hearing and providing the attorney representing the state and the defendant the opportunity to present evidence on the motion.

Added by Acts 2015, 84th Leg., ch. 770 (H.B. 2299), § 1.01, eff. Jan. 1, 2017.

Art. 42A.203. Authority to Suspend Execution of Sentence in Felony Cases

(a) Except as otherwise provided by Subsection (b), only the judge who originally sentenced the defendant may suspend execution of the sentence and place the defendant on community supervision under Article 42A.202.

(b) If the judge who originally sentenced the defendant is deceased or disabled or the office is vacant, and if a motion is filed in accordance with Article 42A.202, the clerk of the court shall promptly forward a copy of the motion to the presiding judge of the administrative judicial district for that court. The presiding judge may deny the motion without holding a hearing or may appoint a judge to hold a hearing on the motion.

Added by Acts 2015, 84th Leg., ch. 770 (H.B. 2299), § 1.01, eff. Jan. 1, 2017.

Art. 42A.204. Partial Execution of Sentence: Firearm Used or Exhibited

(a) If in the trial of a felony of the second degree or higher there is an affirmative finding described by

Article 42A.054(d) and the jury recommends that the court place the defendant on community supervision, the court may order the defendant imprisoned in the Texas Department of Criminal Justice for not less than 60 and not more than 120 days.

(b) At any time after the defendant has served 60 days in the custody of the Texas Department of Criminal Justice, the sentencing judge, on the judge's own motion or on motion of the defendant, may order the defendant released to community supervision.

(c) The department shall release the defendant to community supervision after the defendant has served 120 days.

Added by Acts 2015, 84th Leg., ch. 770 (H.B. 2299), § 1.01, eff. Jan. 1, 2017.

SUBCHAPTER F. PRESENTENCE AND POSTSENTENCE REPORTS AND EVALUATIONS

Art. 42A.251. Definitions

In this subchapter:

(1) "Council" means the Council on Sex Offender Treatment.

(2) "Sex offender" means a person who has been convicted of, or has entered a plea of guilty or nolo contendere for, an offense under any one of the following provisions of the Penal Code:

(A) Section 20.04(a)(4) (Aggravated Kidnapping), if the person committed the offense with the intent to violate or abuse the victim sexually;

(B) Section 21.08 (Indecent Exposure);

(C) Section 21.11 (Indecency with a Child);

(D) Section 22.011 (Sexual Assault);

(E) Section 22.021 (Aggravated Sexual Assault);

(F) Section 25.02 (Prohibited Sexual Conduct);

(G) Section 30.02 (Burglary), if:

(i) the offense is punishable under Subsection (d) of that section; and

(ii) the person committed the offense with the intent to commit a felony listed in this subdivision;

(H) Section 43.25 (Sexual Performance by a Child); or

(I) Section 43.26 (Possession or Promotion of Child Pornography).

Added by Acts 2015, 84th Leg., ch. 770 (H.B. 2299), § 1.01, eff. Jan. 1, 2017.

Art. 42A.252. Presentence Report Required

(a) Except as provided by Subsections (b) and (c), before the imposition of the sentence by a judge, the judge shall direct a supervision officer to prepare a presentence report for the judge.

(b) The judge is not required to direct a supervision officer to prepare a presentence report in a misdemeanor case if:

(1) the defendant requests that a report not be made and the judge agrees to the request; or

(2) the judge:

(A) finds that there is sufficient information in the record to permit the meaningful exercise of sentencing discretion; and

(B) explains that finding on the record.

(c) The judge is not required to direct a supervision officer to prepare a presentence report in a felony case if:

(1) punishment is to be assessed by a jury;

(2) the defendant is convicted of or enters a plea of guilty or nolo contendere to capital murder;

(3) the only available punishment is imprisonment; or

(4) the judge is informed that a plea bargain agreement exists, under which the defendant agrees to a punishment of imprisonment, and the judge intends to follow that agreement.

Added by Acts 2015, 84th Leg., ch. 770 (H.B. 2299), § 1.01, eff. Jan. 1, 2017.

Art. 42A.253. Contents of Presentence Report

(a) A presentence report must be in writing and include:

(1) the circumstances of the offense with which the defendant is charged;

(2) the amount of restitution necessary to adequately compensate a victim of the offense;

(3) the criminal and social history of the defendant;

(4) a proposed supervision plan describing programs and sanctions that the community supervision and corrections department will provide the defendant if the judge suspends the imposition of the sentence or grants deferred adjudication community supervision;

(5) if the defendant is charged with a state jail felony, recommendations for conditions of community supervision that the community supervision and corrections department considers advisable or appropri-

ate based on the circumstances of the offense and other factors addressed in the report;

(6) the results of a psychological evaluation of the defendant that determines, at a minimum, the defendant's IQ and adaptive behavior score if the defendant:

(A) is convicted of a felony offense; and

(B) appears to the judge, through the judge's own observation or on the suggestion of a party, to have a mental impairment;

(7) information regarding whether the defendant is a current or former member of the state military forces or whether the defendant currently serves or has previously served in the armed forces of the United States in an active-duty status and, if available, a copy of the defendant's military discharge papers and military records;

(8) if the defendant has served in the armed forces of the United States in an active-duty status, a determination as to whether the defendant was deployed to a combat zone and whether the defendant may suffer from post-traumatic stress disorder or a traumatic brain injury; and

(9) any other information relating to the defendant or the offense as requested by the judge.

(b) A presentence report is not required to contain a sentencing recommendation.

Added by Acts 2015, 84th Leg., ch. 770 (H.B. 2299), § 1.01, eff. Jan. 1, 2017.

Art. 42A.254. Inspection by Judge; Disclosure of Contents

The judge may not inspect a presentence report and the contents of the report may not be disclosed to any person unless:

(1) the defendant pleads guilty or nolo contendere or is convicted of the offense; or

(2) the defendant, in writing, authorizes the judge to inspect the report.

Added by Acts 2015, 84th Leg., ch. 770 (H.B. 2299), § 1.01, eff. Jan. 1, 2017.

Art. 42A.255. Inspection and Comment by Defendant; Access to Information by State

(a) Unless waived by the defendant, at least 48 hours before sentencing a defendant, the judge shall permit the defendant or the defendant's attorney to read the presentence report.

(b) The judge shall allow the defendant or the defendant's attorney to comment on a presentence investigation or a postsentence report and, with the approval of the judge, introduce testimony or other information alleging a factual inaccuracy in the investigation or report.

(c) The judge shall allow the attorney representing the state access to any information made available to the defendant under this article.

Added by Acts 2015, 84th Leg., ch. 770 (H.B. 2299), § 1.01, eff. Jan. 1, 2017.

Art. 42A.256. Release of Information to Supervision Officer; Confidentiality of Report

(a) The judge by order may direct that any information and records that are not privileged and that are relevant to a presentence or postsentence report be released to a supervision officer conducting a presentence investigation under this subchapter or preparing a postsentence report under Article 42A.259. The judge may also issue a subpoena to obtain that information.

(b) A presentence or postsentence report and all information obtained in connection with a presentence investigation or postsentence report are confidential and may be released only as:

(1) provided by:

(A) Subsection (c);

(B) Article 42A.255;

(C) Article 42A.257;

(D) Article 42A.259; or

(E) Section 614.017, Health and Safety Code; or

(2) directed by the judge for the effective supervision of the defendant.

(c) If the defendant is a sex offender, a supervision officer may release information in a presentence or postsentence report concerning the social and criminal history of the defendant to a person who:

(1) is licensed or certified in this state to provide mental health or medical services, including a:

(A) physician;

(B) psychiatrist;

(C) psychologist;

(D) licensed professional counselor;

(E) licensed marriage and family therapist; or

(F) certified social worker; and

(2) provides mental health or medical services for the rehabilitation of the defendant.

Added by Acts 2015, 84th Leg., ch. 770 (H.B. 2299), § 1.01, eff. Jan. 1, 2017.

Art. 42A.257.   Evaluation for Purposes of Alcohol or Drug Rehabilitation

(a) The judge shall direct a supervision officer approved by the community supervision and corrections department or the judge, or a person, program, or other agency approved by the Department of State Health Services, to conduct an evaluation to determine the appropriateness of, and a course of conduct necessary for, alcohol or drug rehabilitation for a defendant and to report the results of that evaluation to the judge, if:

(1) the judge determines that alcohol or drug abuse may have contributed to the commission of the offense; or

(2) the case involves a second or subsequent offense under:

(A) Section 49.04, Penal Code, if the offense was committed within five years of the date on which the most recent preceding offense was committed; or

(B) Section 49.07 or 49.08, Penal Code, if the offense involved the operation of a motor vehicle and was committed within five years of the date on which the most recent preceding offense was committed.

(b) The evaluation must be made:

(1) after arrest and before conviction, if requested by the defendant;

(2) after conviction and before sentencing, if the judge assesses punishment in the case;

(3) after sentencing and before the entry of a final judgment, if the jury assesses punishment in the case; or

(4) after community supervision is granted, if the evaluation is required as a condition of community supervision under Article 42A.402.

Added by Acts 2015, 84th Leg., ch. 770 (H.B. 2299), § 1.01, eff. Jan. 1, 2017.

Art. 42A.258.   Evaluation for Purposes of Sex Offender Treatment, Specialized Supervision, or Rehabilitation

(a) If the defendant is a sex offender, the judge shall direct a supervision officer approved by the community supervision and corrections department or the judge, or a person, program, or other agency approved by the council, to:

(1) evaluate the appropriateness of, and a course of conduct necessary for, treatment, specialized supervision, or rehabilitation of the defendant; and

(2) report the results of the evaluation to the judge.

(b) The judge may require the evaluation to use offense-specific standards of practice adopted by the council and may require the report to reflect those standards.

(c) The evaluation must be made:

(1) after arrest and before conviction, if requested by the defendant; or

(2) after conviction and before the entry of a final judgment.

Added by Acts 2015, 84th Leg., ch. 770 (H.B. 2299), § 1.01, eff. Jan. 1, 2017.

Art. 42A.259.   Postsentence Report

(a) If a presentence report in a felony case is not required under Article 42A.252(c), the judge may direct a supervision officer to prepare a postsentence report containing the same information that would have been required for the presentence report, other than a proposed supervision plan and any information that is reflected in the judgment.

(b) If a postsentence report is ordered, the supervision officer shall send the report to the clerk of the court not later than the 30th day after the date on which sentence is pronounced or deferred adjudication community supervision is granted. The clerk shall deliver the postsentence report with the papers in the case to a designated officer of the Texas Department of Criminal Justice, to the extent required by Section 8(a), Article 42.09.

Added by Acts 2015, 84th Leg., ch. 770 (H.B. 2299), § 1.01, eff. Jan. 1, 2017.

SUBCHAPTER G.   DISCRETIONARY CONDITIONS GENERALLY

Art. 42A.301.   Basic Discretionary Conditions

(a) The judge of the court having jurisdiction of the case shall determine the conditions of community supervision after considering the results of a risk and needs assessment conducted with respect to the defendant. The assessment must be conducted using an instrument that is validated for the purpose of assessing the risks and needs of a defendant placed on community supervision. The judge may impose any reasonable condition that is not duplicative of another condition and that is designed to protect or restore the community, protect or restore the victim, or punish, rehabilitate, or reform the defendant. In determining the conditions, the judge shall consider the extent to which the conditions impact the defendant's:

(1) work, education, and community service schedule or obligations; and

(2) ability to meet financial obligations.

(b) Conditions of community supervision may include conditions requiring the defendant to:

(1) commit no offense against the laws of this state or of any other state or of the United States;

(2) avoid injurious or vicious habits;

(3) avoid persons or places of disreputable or harmful character, including any person, other than a family member of the defendant, who is an active member of a criminal street gang;

(4) report to the supervision officer as directed by the judge or supervision officer and obey all rules and regulations of the community supervision and corrections department;

(5) permit the supervision officer to visit the defendant at the defendant's home or elsewhere;

(6) work faithfully at suitable employment to the extent possible;

(7) remain within a specified place;

(8) pay in one or more amounts:

(A) the defendant's fine, if one is assessed; and

(B) all court costs, regardless of whether a fine is assessed;

(9) support the defendant's dependents;

(10) participate, for a period specified by the judge, in any community-based program, including a community service project under Article 42A.304;

(11) if the judge determines that the defendant has financial resources that enable the defendant to offset in part or in whole the costs of the legal services provided to the defendant in accordance with Article 1.051(c) or (d), including any expenses and costs, reimburse the county in which the prosecution was instituted for the costs of the legal services in an amount that the judge finds the defendant is able to pay, except that the defendant may not be ordered to pay an amount that exceeds:

(A) the actual costs, including any expenses and costs, paid by the county for the legal services provided by an appointed attorney; or

(B) if the defendant was represented by a public defender's office, the actual amount, including any expenses and costs, that would have otherwise been paid to an appointed attorney had the county not had a public defender's office;

(12) if under custodial supervision in a community corrections facility:

(A) remain under that supervision;

(B) obey all rules and regulations of the facility; and

(C) pay a percentage of the defendant's income to:

(i) the facility for room and board; and

(ii) the defendant's dependents for their support during the period of custodial supervision;

(13) submit to testing for alcohol or controlled substances;

(14) attend counseling sessions for substance abusers or participate in substance abuse treatment services in a program or facility approved or licensed by the Department of State Health Services;

(15) with the consent of the victim of a misdemeanor offense or of any offense under Title 7, Penal Code, participate in victim-defendant mediation;

(16) submit to electronic monitoring;

(17) reimburse the compensation to victims of crime fund for any amounts paid from that fund to or on behalf of a victim, as defined by Article 56.32, of the offense or if no reimbursement is required, make one payment to the compensation to victims of crime fund in an amount not to exceed $50 if the offense is a misdemeanor or not to exceed $100 if the offense is a felony;

(18) reimburse a law enforcement agency for the analysis, storage, or disposal of raw materials, controlled substances, chemical precursors, drug paraphernalia, or other materials seized in connection with the offense;

(19) pay all or part of the reasonable and necessary costs incurred by the victim for psychological counseling made necessary by the offense or for counseling and education relating to acquired immune deficiency syndrome or human immunodeficiency virus made necessary by the offense;

(20) make one payment in an amount not to exceed $50 to a crime stoppers organization, as defined by Section 414.001, Government Code, and as certified by the Texas Crime Stoppers Council;

(21) submit a DNA sample to the Department of Public Safety under Subchapter G, Chapter 411, Government Code, for the purpose of creating a DNA record of the defendant;

(22) in any manner required by the judge, provide in the county in which the offense was committed public notice of the offense for which the defendant was placed on community supervision; and

(23) reimburse the county in which the prosecution was instituted for compensation paid to any interpreter in the case.

(c) Before the judge may require as a condition of community supervision that the defendant receive treatment in a state-funded substance abuse treatment program, including an inpatient or outpatient program, a substance abuse felony program under Article 42A.303, or a program provided to the defendant while confined in a community corrections facility as defined by Article 42A.601, the judge must consider the results of an evaluation conducted to determine the appropriate type and level of treatment necessary to address the defendant's alcohol or drug dependency.

Added by Acts 2015, 84th Leg., ch. 770 (H.B. 2299), § 1.01, eff. Jan. 1, 2017. Amended by Acts 2017, 85th Leg., ch. 109 (S.B. 1584), § 1, eff. Sept. 1, 2017; Acts 2017, 85th Leg., ch. 324 (S.B. 1488), § 23.013(a), eff. Sept. 1, 2017.

Section 2 of Acts 2017, 85th Leg., ch. 109 (S.B. 1584) provides:

"The change in law made by this Act applies to a defendant placed on community supervision on or after the effective date [Sept. 1, 2017] of this Act, regardless of whether the offense for which the defendant was placed on community supervision was committed before, on, or after the effective date of this Act."

Art. 42A.302. Confinement

(a) If a judge having jurisdiction of a case requires as a condition of community supervision that the defendant submit to a term of confinement in a county jail, the term of confinement may not exceed:

(1) 30 days, in a misdemeanor case; or

(2) 180 days, in a felony case.

(b) A judge who requires as a condition of community supervision that the defendant serve a term of confinement in a community corrections facility under Subchapter M may not impose a term of confinement under this article that, if added to the term imposed under Subchapter M, exceeds 24 months.

(c) A judge may impose a term of confinement as a condition of community supervision under this article on placing the defendant on supervision or at any time during the supervision period. The judge may impose terms of confinement as a condition of community supervision in increments smaller than the maximum terms provided by Subsection (a), except that the judge may not impose terms of confinement that, if added together, exceed the maximum terms provided by Subsection (a).

Added by Acts 2015, 84th Leg., ch. 770 (H.B. 2299), § 1.01, eff. Jan. 1, 2017.

Art. 42A.303. Substance Abuse Felony Program

(a) If a court places a defendant on community supervision under any provision of this chapter as an alternative to imprisonment, the judge may require as a condition of community supervision that the defendant serve a term of confinement and treatment in a substance abuse felony punishment facility operated by the Texas Department of Criminal Justice under Section 493.009, Government Code.

(b) A term of confinement and treatment imposed under this article must be an indeterminate term of not more than one year or less than 90 days.

(c) The judge may impose the condition of community supervision described by this article if:

(1) the defendant is charged with or convicted of a felony other than:

(A) a felony under Section 21.11, 22.011, or 22.021, Penal Code; or

(B) criminal attempt of a felony under Section 21.11, 22.011, or 22.021, Penal Code; and

(2) the judge makes an affirmative finding that:

(A) drug or alcohol abuse significantly contributed to the commission of the offense or violation of a condition of community supervision, as applicable; and

(B) the defendant is a suitable candidate for treatment, as determined by the suitability criteria established by the Texas Board of Criminal Justice under Section 493.009(b), Government Code.

(d) If a judge requires as a condition of community supervision that the defendant serve a term of confinement and treatment in a substance abuse felony punishment facility under this article, the judge shall also require as a condition of community supervision that on release from the facility the defendant:

(1) participate in a drug or alcohol abuse continuum of care treatment plan; and

(2) pay a fee in an amount established by the judge for residential aftercare required as part of the treatment plan.

(e) The Department of State Health Services shall develop the continuum of care treatment plan described by Subsection (d)(1).

(f) The clerk of a court that collects a fee imposed under Subsection (d)(2) shall deposit the fee to be sent to the comptroller as provided by Subchapter B, Chapter 133, Local Government Code, and the comptroller shall deposit the fee into the general revenue fund. If the clerk does not collect a fee imposed under Subsection (d)(2), the clerk is not required to file any report required by the comptroller that relates to the collection of the fee. In establishing the amount of a fee under Subsection (d)(2), the judge shall consider fines, fees, and other necessary expenses for which the defendant is obligated. The judge may not:

(1) establish the fee in an amount that is greater than 25 percent of the defendant's gross income while the defendant is a participant in residential aftercare; or

(2) require the defendant to pay the fee at any time other than a time at which the defendant is both employed and a participant in residential aftercare.

Added by Acts 2015, 84th Leg., ch. 770 (H.B. 2299), § 1.01, eff. Jan. 1, 2017.

Art. 42A.304. Community Service

(a) A judge may require as a condition of community supervision that the defendant work a specified number of hours at one or more community service projects for one or more organizations approved by the judge and designated by the department. The judge may not require the defendant to work at a community service project if, as determined and noted on the community supervision order by the judge:

(1) the defendant is physically or mentally incapable of participating in the project;

(2) participating in the project will cause a hardship to the defendant or to the defendant's dependents;

(3) the defendant is to be confined in a substance abuse felony punishment facility as a condition of community supervision; or

(4) there is other good cause shown.

(b) The amount of community service work ordered by the judge may not exceed:

(1) 1,000 hours for an offense classified as a first degree felony;

(2) 800 hours for an offense classified as a second degree felony;

(3) 600 hours for:

(A) an offense classified as a third degree felony; or

(B) an offense under Section 30.04, Penal Code, classified as a Class A misdemeanor;

(4) 400 hours for an offense classified as a state jail felony;

(5) 200 hours for:

(A) an offense classified as a Class A misdemeanor, other than an offense described by Subdivision (3)(B); or

(B) a misdemeanor for which the maximum permissible confinement, if any, exceeds six months or the maximum permissible fine, if any, exceeds $4,000; and

(6) 100 hours for:

(A) an offense classified as a Class B misdemeanor; or

(B) a misdemeanor for which the maximum permissible confinement, if any, does not exceed six months and the maximum permissible fine, if any, does not exceed $4,000.

(c) A defendant required to perform community service under this article is not a state employee for the purposes of Chapter 501 or 504, Labor Code.

(d) If the court makes an affirmative finding under Article 42.014, the judge may order the defendant to perform community service under this article at a project designated by the judge that primarily serves the person or group who was the target of the defendant. If the judge orders community service under this subsection, the judge shall order the defendant to perform not less than:

(1) 300 hours of service if the offense is classified as a felony; or

(2) 100 hours of service if the offense is classified as a misdemeanor.

(e) A defendant required to perform community service under this article after conviction of an offense under Section 352.082, Local Government Code, or Section 365.012, 365.013, or 365.016, Health and Safety Code, shall perform the amount of service ordered by the court, which may not exceed 60 hours. The community service must consist of picking up litter in the county in which the defendant resides or working at a recycling facility if a program for performing that type of service is available in the community in which the court is located. A court may credit the amount of community service performed by a defendant under this subsection toward any amount of community service the defendant is ordered to perform under another provision of this code as a result of the defendant's inability to pay a fine or cost imposed in the judgment for the applicable offense.

(f) Instead of requiring the defendant to work a specified number of hours at one or more community service projects under Subsection (a), the judge may order a defendant to make a specified donation to:

(1) a nonprofit food bank or food pantry in the community in which the defendant resides;

(2) a charitable organization engaged primarily in performing charitable functions for veterans in the community in which the defendant resides; or

(3) in a county with a population of less than 50,000, another nonprofit organization that:

(A) is exempt from taxation under Section 501(a) of the Internal Revenue Code of 1986 because it is listed in Section 501(c)(3) of that code; and

(B) provides services or assistance to needy individuals and families in the community in which the defendant resides.

(g) In this article:

(1) "Charitable organization" has the meaning assigned by Section 2252.906, Government Code.

(2) "Veteran" has the meaning assigned by Section 434.022, Government Code.

Added by Acts 2015, 84th Leg., ch. 770 (H.B. 2299), § 1.01, eff. Jan. 1, 2017. Amended by Acts 2017, 85th Leg., ch. 829 (H.B. 1884), § 1, eff. Sept. 1, 2017; Acts 2017, 85th Leg., ch. 324 (S.B. 1488), § 23.015(a), eff. Sept. 1, 2017.

Section 5 of Acts 2017, 85th Leg., ch. 829 (H.B. 1884) provides:

"The changes in law made by this Act apply only to an offense committed on or after the effective date [Sept. 1, 2017] of this Act. An offense committed before the effective date of this Act is governed by the law in effect on the date the offense was committed, and the former law is continued in effect for that purpose. For purposes of this section, an offense was committed before the effective date of this Act if any element of the offense occurred before that date."

Art. 42A.305. Community Outreach

(a) This article applies only to a defendant placed on community supervision for an offense involving the possession, manufacture, or delivery of a controlled substance under Chapter 481, Health and Safety Code.

(b) If a judge orders a defendant to whom this article applies to perform community service, the judge may authorize the defendant to perform not more than 30 hours of community outreach under this article instead of performing hours of community service.

(c) Community outreach under this article must consist of working with a secondary school at the direction of the judge to educate students on the dangers and legal consequences of possessing, manufacturing, or delivering a controlled substance.

(d) A secondary school is not required to allow a defendant to perform community outreach at that school.

(e) The judge may not authorize the defendant to perform hours of community outreach under this article instead of performing hours of community service if:

(1) the defendant is physically or mentally incapable of participating in community outreach; or

(2) the defendant is subject to registration as a sex offender under Chapter 62.

Added by Acts 2015, 84th Leg., ch. 770 (H.B. 2299), § 1.01, eff. Jan. 1, 2017.

Art. 42A.306. Supervision of Defendant from Out of State

A judge who receives a defendant for supervision as authorized by Section 510.017, Government Code, may impose on the defendant any term of community supervision authorized by this chapter.

Added by Acts 2015, 84th Leg., ch. 770 (H.B. 2299), § 1.01, eff. Jan. 1, 2017.

Art. 42A.307. Orchiectomy Prohibited

A judge may not require a defendant to undergo an orchiectomy as a condition of community supervision.

Added by Acts 2015, 84th Leg., ch. 770 (H.B. 2299), § 1.01, eff. Jan. 1, 2017.

SUBCHAPTER H. MANDATORY CONDITIONS GENERALLY

Art. 42A.351. Educational Skill Level

(a) If the judge or jury places a defendant on community supervision, the judge shall require the defendant to demonstrate to the court whether the defendant has an educational skill level that is equal to or greater than the average educational skill level of students who have completed the sixth grade in public schools in this state.

(b) If the judge determines that the defendant has not attained the educational skill level described by Subsection (a), the judge shall require as a condition of community supervision that the defendant attain that level of educational skill, unless the judge also determines that the defendant lacks the intellectual capacity or the learning ability to ever achieve that level of educational skill.

Added by Acts 2015, 84th Leg., ch. 770 (H.B. 2299), § 1.01, eff. Jan. 1, 2017.

Art. 42A.352.　DNA sample

A judge granting community supervision to a defendant convicted of a felony shall require as a condition of community supervision that the defendant provide a DNA sample under Subchapter G, Chapter 411, Government Code, for the purpose of creating a DNA record of the defendant, unless the defendant has already submitted the required sample under other state law.

Added by Acts 2015, 84th Leg., ch. 770 (H.B. 2299), § 1.01, eff. Jan. 1, 2017.

SUBCHAPTER I.　CONDITIONS APPLICABLE TO CERTAIN INTOXICATION OFFENSES

Art. 42A.401.　Confinement as Condition of Community Supervision for Certain Intoxication Offenses

(a) A judge granting community supervision to a defendant convicted of an offense under Chapter 49, Penal Code, shall require as a condition of community supervision that the defendant submit to:

(1) not less than 72 hours of continuous confinement in county jail if the defendant was punished under Section 49.09(a), Penal Code;

(2) not less than five days of confinement in county jail if the defendant was punished under Section 49.09(a), Penal Code, and was subject to Section 49.09(h), Penal Code;

(3) not less than 10 days of confinement in county jail if the defendant was punished under Section 49.09(b), Penal Code;

(4) not less than 30 days of confinement in county jail if the defendant was convicted of an offense under Section 49.07, Penal Code; or

(5) a term of confinement of not less than 120 days if the defendant was convicted of an offense under Section 49.08, Penal Code.

(b) If a sentence of confinement is imposed on the revocation of community supervision, the term of confinement served under Subsection (a) may not be credited toward completion of the sentence imposed.

Added by Acts 2015, 84th Leg., ch. 770 (H.B. 2299), § 1.01, eff. Jan. 1, 2017.

Art. 42A.402.　Drug or Alcohol Dependence Evaluation and Rehabilitation

(a) A judge granting community supervision to a defendant convicted of an offense under Chapter 49, Penal Code, shall require as a condition of community supervision that the defendant submit to an evaluation by a supervision officer or by a person, program, or facility approved by the Department of State Health Services for the purpose of having the facility prescribe and carry out a course of conduct necessary for the rehabilitation of the defendant's drug or alcohol dependence condition.

(b) If the director of a facility to which a defendant is referred under Subsection (a) determines that the defendant is not making a good faith effort to participate in a program of rehabilitation, the director shall notify the judge who referred the defendant to the facility of that determination.

(c) If a judge requires as a condition of community supervision that the defendant participate in a prescribed course of conduct necessary for the rehabilitation of the defendant's drug or alcohol dependence condition, the judge shall require that the defendant pay for all or part of the cost of the rehabilitation based on the defendant's ability to pay. The judge, in the judge's discretion, may credit against the fine assessed the cost paid by the defendant. In determining a defendant's ability to pay the cost of rehabilitation under this subsection, the judge shall consider whether the defendant has insurance coverage that will pay for rehabilitation.

(d) A judge who grants community supervision to a defendant convicted of an offense under Sections 49.04–49.08, Penal Code, shall require, if the defendant has not submitted to an evaluation under Article 42A.257 before receiving community supervision, that the defendant submit to the evaluation as a condition of community supervision. If the evaluation indicates to the judge that the defendant needs treatment for drug or alcohol dependency, the judge shall require the defendant to submit to that treatment as a condition of community supervision in a program or facility that:

(1) is approved or licensed by the Department of State Health Services; or

(2) complies with standards established by the community justice assistance division of the Texas Department of Criminal Justice, after consultation by the division with the Department of State Health Services.

Added by Acts 2015, 84th Leg., ch. 770 (H.B. 2299), § 1.01, eff. Jan. 1, 2017.

Art. 42A.403. Educational Program for Certain Intoxication Offenders; Waiver or Extension of Time

(a) A judge who places on community supervision a defendant convicted of an offense under Sections 49.04–49.08, Penal Code, shall require as a condition of community supervision that the defendant attend and successfully complete, before the 181st day after the date community supervision is granted, an educational program designed to rehabilitate persons who have driven while intoxicated that is jointly approved by:

(1) the Texas Department of Licensing and Regulation;

(2) the Department of Public Safety;

(3) the traffic safety section of the traffic operations division of the Texas Department of Transportation; and

(4) the community justice assistance division of the Texas Department of Criminal Justice.

(b) This article does not apply to a defendant if a jury recommends community supervision for the defendant and also recommends that the defendant's driver's license not be suspended.

(c) If the defendant by a motion in writing shows good cause, the judge may:

(1) waive the educational program requirement; or

(2) to enable the defendant to successfully complete the program, grant an extension of time that expires not later than the first anniversary of the beginning date of the defendant's community supervision.

(d) In determining good cause, the judge may consider but is not limited to:

(1) the defendant's school and work schedule;

(2) the defendant's health;

(3) the distance that the defendant must travel to attend an educational program; and

(4) the fact that the defendant resides out of state, does not have a valid driver's license, or does not have access to transportation.

(d–1) The judge shall waive the educational program requirement if the defendant successfully completes equivalent education at a residential treatment facility under Article 42A.4045.

(e) The judge shall set out in the judgment, as applicable:

(1) the finding of good cause for waiver; or

(2) the finding that the defendant has successfully completed equivalent education as provided by Article 42A.4045.

Added by Acts 2015, 84th Leg., ch. 770 (H.B. 2299), § 1.01, eff. Jan. 1, 2017. Amended by Acts 2017, 85th Leg., ch. 324 (S.B. 1488), § 23.016(a), (b), eff. Sept. 1, 2017.

Art. 42A.404. Educational Program for Certain Repeat Intoxication Offenders; Waiver

(a) The judge shall require a defendant who is punished under Section 49.09, Penal Code, to attend and successfully complete as a condition of community supervision an educational program for repeat offenders that is approved by the Texas Department of Licensing and Regulation.

(b) The judge may waive the educational program requirement if the defendant by a motion in writing shows good cause. In determining good cause, the judge may consider:

(1) the defendant's school and work schedule;

(2) the defendant's health;

(3) the distance that the defendant must travel to attend an educational program; and

(4) whether the defendant resides out of state or does not have access to transportation.

(b–1) The judge shall waive the educational program requirement if the defendant successfully completes equivalent education at a residential treatment facility under Article 42A.4045.

(c) The judge shall set out in the judgment, as applicable:

(1) the finding of good cause for waiver; or

(2) the finding that the defendant has successfully completed equivalent education as provided by Article 42A.4045.

Added by Acts 2015, 84th Leg., ch. 770 (H.B. 2299), § 1.01, eff. Jan. 1, 2017. Amended by Acts 2017, 85th Leg., ch. 324 (S.B. 1488), § 23.016(c), (d), eff. Sept. 1, 2017.

Art. 42A.4045. Alternative to Educational Program: Substance Abuse Treatment Facility

(a) A judge shall waive the educational requirement under Article 42A.403 or 42A.404 for a defendant who is required to receive treatment as a resident of a substance abuse treatment facility as a condition of community supervision if the defendant successfully completes equivalent education while the defendant is confined to the residential treatment facility.

(b) The Department of State Health Services shall approve equivalent education provided at substance abuse treatment facilities.

(c) The executive commissioner of the Health and Human Services Commission shall adopt rules to implement this article.

(d) For purposes of this article, a substance abuse treatment facility includes:

(1) a substance abuse felony punishment facility operated by the Texas Department of Criminal Justice under Section 493.009, Government Code;

(2) a community corrections facility, as defined by Section 509.001, Government Code; or

(3) a chemical dependency treatment facility licensed under Chapter 464, Health and Safety Code.

Added by Acts 2017, 85th Leg., ch. 324 (S.B. 1488), § 23.016(e), eff. Sept. 1, 2017.

Art. 42A.405. Rules for and Administration of Educational Programs

(a) The Texas Department of Licensing and Regulation shall adopt rules for the educational program under Article 42A.404.

(b) The Texas Department of Licensing and Regulation shall:

(1) publish the jointly approved rules for the educational program under Article 42A.403; and

(2) monitor, coordinate, and provide training to persons providing the educational programs under this subchapter.

(c) The Texas Department of Licensing and Regulation is responsible for the administration of the certification of approved educational programs.

(d) The Texas Department of Licensing and Regulation may charge a nonrefundable application fee for the initial certification of approval or for a renewal of the certification.

Added by Acts 2015, 84th Leg., ch. 770 (H.B. 2299), § 1.01, eff. Jan. 1, 2017. Amended by Acts 2017, 85th Leg., ch. 324 (S.B. 1488), § 23.016(f), eff. Sept. 1, 2017.

Art. 42A.406. Effect of Educational Program Requirements on Driving Record and License

(a) If a defendant is required as a condition of community supervision to attend an educational program under Article 42A.403 or 42A.404, or if the court waives the educational program requirement under Article 42A.403 or the defendant successfully completes equivalent education under Article 42A.4045, the court clerk shall immediately report that fact to the Department of Public Safety, on a form prescribed by the department, for inclusion in the defendant's driving record. If the court grants an extension of time in which the defendant may complete the educational program under Article 42A.403, the court clerk shall immediately report that fact to the Department of Public Safety on a form prescribed by the department. The clerk's report under this subsection must include the beginning date of the defendant's community supervision.

(b) On the defendant's successful completion of an educational program under Article 42A.403 or 42A.404, the defendant's instructor shall give notice to the Department of Public Safety for inclusion in the defendant's driving record and to the community supervision and corrections department. The community supervision and corrections department shall forward the notice to the court clerk for filing.

(b-1) Upon release from a residential treatment facility at which the person successfully completed equivalent education under Article 42A.4045, at the request of the court clerk, the director of the residential treatment facility shall give notice to the Department of Public Safety for inclusion in the person's driving record.

(c) If the Department of Public Safety does not receive notice that a defendant required to complete an educational program has successfully completed the program within the period required by the judge under this subchapter, as shown on department records, the department, as provided by Sections 521.344(e) and (f), Transportation Code, shall:

(1) revoke the defendant's driver's license; or

(2) prohibit the defendant from obtaining a license.

(d) The Department of Public Safety may not reinstate a license revoked under Subsection (c) as the result of an educational program requirement imposed under Article 42A.403 unless the defendant whose license was revoked applies to the department for reinstatement of the license and pays to the department a reinstatement fee of $100. The Department of Public Safety shall remit all fees collected under this subsection to the comptroller for deposit in the general revenue fund.

Added by Acts 2015, 84th Leg., ch. 770 (H.B. 2299), § 1.01, eff. Jan. 1, 2017. Amended by Acts 2017, 85th Leg., ch. 324 (S.B. 1488), § 23.016(g), eff. Sept. 1, 2017.

Art. 42A.407. Suspension of Driver's License

(a) A jury that recommends community supervision for a defendant convicted of an offense under Sections 49.04–49.08, Penal Code, may recommend that any driver's license issued to the defendant under Chapter 521, Transportation Code, not be suspended. This subsection does not apply to a defendant punished under Section 49.09(a) or (b), Penal Code, and subject to Section 49.09(h), Penal Code.

(b) Notwithstanding Sections 521.344(d)–(i), Transportation Code, if under Article 42A.404 the judge requires a defendant punished under Section 49.09, Penal Code, to attend an educational program as a condition of community supervision, or waives the required attendance for the program, and the defendant has previously been required to attend such an educational program, or the required attendance at the program had been waived, the judge shall order the suspension of the defendant's driver's license for a period determined by the judge according to the following schedule:

(1) not less than 90 days or more than one year, if the defendant is convicted under Sections 49.04–49.08, Penal Code;

(2) not less than 180 days or more than two years, if the defendant is punished under Section 49.09(a) or (b), Penal Code; or

(3) not less than one year or more than two years, if the defendant is convicted of a second or subsequent offense under Sections 49.04–49.08, Penal Code, committed within five years of the date on which the most recent preceding offense was committed.

(c) If the Department of Public Safety receives notice that a defendant has been required to attend a subsequent educational program under Article 42A.403 or 42A.404, although the previously required attendance had been waived, but the judge has not ordered a period of suspension, the department shall:

(1) suspend the defendant's driver's license; or

(2) issue an order prohibiting the defendant from obtaining a license for a period of one year.

(d) The judge shall suspend the defendant's driver's license for a period provided under Subchapter O, Chapter 521, Transportation Code, if:

(1) a judge revokes the community supervision of the defendant for:

(A) an offense under Section 49.04, Penal Code; or

(B) an offense involving the operation of a motor vehicle under Section 49.07, Penal Code; and

(2) the license has not previously been ordered by the judge to be suspended, or the suspension was previously probated.

(e) The suspension of a defendant's driver's license under Subsection (d) shall be reported to the Department of Public Safety as provided under Section 521.347, Transportation Code.

(f) Notwithstanding any other provision of this subchapter or other law, a judge who places on community supervision a defendant who was younger than 21 years of age at the time of the offense and was convicted for an offense under Sections 49.04–49.08, Penal Code, shall order that the defendant's driver's license be suspended for 90 days beginning on the date the defendant is placed on community supervision. (Code Crim. Proc., Art. 42.12, Secs. 13(g), (k), (l), (m), (n) (part).)

(g) Notwithstanding any other provision of this subchapter, a defendant whose license is suspended for an offense under Sections 49.04–49.08, Penal Code, may operate a motor vehicle during the period of suspension if the defendant:

(1) obtains and uses an ignition interlock device as provided by Article 42A.408 for the entire period of the suspension; and

(2) applies for and receives an occupational driver's license with an ignition interlock designation under Section 521.2465, Transportation Code.

Added by Acts 2015, 84th Leg., ch. 770 (H.B. 2299), § 1.01, eff. Jan. 1, 2017. Amended by Acts 2017, 85th Leg., ch. 324 (S.B. 1488), § 23.017(a), eff. Sept. 1, 2017.

Art. 42A.408.   Use of Ignition Interlock Device

(a) In this article, "ignition interlock device" means a device that uses a deep-lung breath analysis mechanism to make impractical the operation of the motor vehicle if ethyl alcohol is detected in the breath of the operator.

(b) The court may require as a condition of community supervision that a defendant placed on community supervision after conviction of an offense under Sections 49.04–49.08, Penal Code, have an ignition interlock device installed on the motor vehicle owned by the defendant or on the vehicle most regularly driven by the defendant and that the defendant not operate any motor vehicle that is not equipped with that device.

(c) The court shall require as a condition of community supervision that a defendant described by Subsection (b) have an ignition interlock device installed on the motor vehicle owned by the defendant or on the vehicle most regularly driven by the defendant and that the defendant not operate any motor vehicle unless the vehicle is equipped with that device if:

(1) it is shown on the trial of the offense that an analysis of a specimen of the defendant's blood, breath, or urine showed an alcohol concentration level of 0.15 or more at the time the analysis was performed;

(2) the defendant is placed on community supervision after conviction of an offense under Sections 49.04–49.06, Penal Code, for which the defendant is punished under Section 49.09(a) or (b), Penal Code; or

(3) the court determines under Subsection (d) that the defendant has one or more previous convictions under Sections 49.04–49.08, Penal Code.

(d) Before placing on community supervision a defendant convicted of an offense under Sections 49.04–49.08, Penal Code, the court shall determine from criminal history record information maintained by the Department of Public Safety whether the defendant has one or more previous convictions under any of those sections. A previous conviction may not be used for purposes of restricting a defendant to the operation of a motor vehicle equipped with an ignition interlock device under Subsection (c) if:

(1) the previous conviction was a final conviction under Section 49.04, 49.045, 49.05, 49.06, 49.07, or 49.08, Penal Code, and was for an offense committed before the beginning of the 10–year period preceding the date of the instant offense for which the defendant was convicted and placed on community supervision; and

(2) the defendant has not been convicted of an offense under Section 49.04, 49.045, 49.05, 49.06, 49.07, or 49.08, Penal Code, committed within the 10–year period preceding the date of the instant offense for which the defendant was convicted and placed on community supervision.

(e) Notwithstanding any other provision of this subchapter or other law, a judge who places on community supervision a defendant who was younger than 21 years of age at the time of the offense and was convicted for an offense under Sections 49.04–49.08, Penal Code, shall require as a condition of community supervision that the defendant not operate any motor vehicle unless the vehicle is equipped with an ignition interlock device.

(f) The court shall require the defendant to obtain an ignition interlock device at the defendant's own cost before the 30th day after the date of conviction unless the court finds that to do so would not be in the best interest of justice and enters its findings on record. The court shall require the defendant to provide evidence to the court within the 30–day period that the device has been installed on the appropriate vehicle and order the device to remain installed on that vehicle for a period the length of which is not less than 50 percent of the supervision period. If the court determines the defendant is unable to pay for the ignition interlock device, the court may impose a reasonable payment schedule not to exceed twice the length of the period of the court's order.

(g) The Department of Public Safety shall approve ignition interlock devices for use under this article. Section 521.247, Transportation Code, applies to the approval of a device under this article and the consequences of that approval.

(h) Notwithstanding any other provision of this subchapter, if a defendant is required to operate a motor vehicle in the course and scope of the defendant's employment and if the vehicle is owned by the employer, the defendant may operate that vehicle without installation of an approved ignition interlock device if the employer has been notified of that driving privilege restriction and if proof of that notification is with the vehicle. The employment exemption does not apply if the business entity that owns the vehicle is owned or controlled by the defendant.

Added by Acts 2015, 84th Leg., ch. 770 (H.B. 2299), § 1.01, eff. Jan. 1, 2017.

Art. 42A.409. Community Supervision for Enhanced Public Intoxication Offense

(a) On conviction of an offense punishable as a Class C misdemeanor under Section 49.02, Penal Code, for which punishment is enhanced under Section 12.43(c), Penal Code, based on previous convictions under Section 49.02 or 42.01, Penal Code, the court may suspend the imposition of the sentence and place the defendant on community supervision if the court finds that the defendant would benefit from community supervision and enters its finding on the record. The judge may suspend in whole or in part the imposition of any fine imposed on conviction.

(b) All provisions of this chapter applying to a defendant placed on community supervision for a misdemeanor apply to a defendant placed on community supervision under Subsection (a), except that the court shall require the defendant as a condition of community supervision to:

(1) submit to diagnostic testing for addiction to alcohol or a controlled substance or drug;

(2) submit to a psychological assessment;

(3) if indicated as necessary by testing and assessment, participate in an alcohol or drug abuse treatment or education program; and

(4) pay the costs of testing, assessment, and treatment or education, either directly or as a court cost.

Added by Acts 2015, 84th Leg., ch. 770 (H.B. 2299), § 1.01, eff. Jan. 1, 2017.

SUBCHAPTER J. CONDITIONS APPLICABLE TO SEX OFFENDERS

Art. 42A.451. Sex Offender Registration; Dna Sample

A judge granting community supervision to a defendant required to register as a sex offender under Chapter 62 shall require that the defendant, as a condition of community supervision:

(1) register under that chapter; and

(2) submit a DNA sample to the Department of Public Safety under Subchapter G, Chapter 411, Government Code, for the purpose of creating a DNA record of the defendant, unless the defendant has already submitted the required sample under other state law.

Added by Acts 2015, 84th Leg., ch. 770 (H.B. 2299), § 1.01, eff. Jan. 1, 2017.

Art. 42A.452. Treatment, Specialized Supervision, or Rehabilitation

A judge who grants community supervision to a sex offender evaluated under Article 42A.258 may require the sex offender as a condition of community supervision to submit to treatment, specialized supervision, or rehabilitation according to offense-specific standards of practice adopted by the Council on Sex Offender Treatment. On a finding that the defendant is financially able to make payment, the judge shall require the defendant to pay all or part of the reasonable and necessary costs of the treatment, supervision, or rehabilitation.

Added by Acts 2015, 84th Leg., ch. 770 (H.B. 2299), § 1.01, eff. Jan. 1, 2017.

Art. 42A.453. Child Safety Zone

(a) In this article, "playground," "premises," "school," "video arcade facility," and "youth center" have the meanings assigned by Section 481.134, Health and Safety Code.

(b) This article applies to a defendant placed on community supervision for an offense under:

(1) Section 20.04(a)(4), Penal Code, if the defendant committed the offense with the intent to violate or abuse the victim sexually;

(2) Section 20A.02, Penal Code, if the defendant:

(A) trafficked the victim with the intent or knowledge that the victim would engage in sexual conduct, as defined by Section 43.25, Penal Code; or

(B) benefited from participating in a venture that involved a trafficked victim engaging in sexual conduct, as defined by Section 43.25, Penal Code;

(3) Section 21.08, 21.11, 22.011, 22.021, or 25.02, Penal Code;

(4) Section 30.02, Penal Code, punishable under Subsection (d) of that section, if the defendant committed the offense with the intent to commit a felony listed in Subdivision (1) or (3); or

(5) Section 43.05(a)(2), 43.25, or 43.26, Penal Code.

(c) If a judge grants community supervision to a defendant described by Subsection (b) and the judge determines that a child as defined by Section 22.011(c), Penal Code, was the victim of the offense, the judge shall establish a child safety zone applicable to the defendant by requiring as a condition of community supervision that the defendant:

(1) not:

(A) supervise or participate in any program that:

(i) includes as participants or recipients persons who are 17 years of age or younger; and

(ii) regularly provides athletic, civic, or cultural activities; or

(B) go in, on, or within 1,000 feet of a premises where children commonly gather, including a school, day-care facility, playground, public or private youth center, public swimming pool, or video arcade facility; and

(2) attend psychological counseling sessions for sex offenders with an individual or organization that provides sex offender treatment or counseling as specified or approved by the judge or the defendant's supervision officer.

(d) Notwithstanding Subsection (c)(1), a judge is not required to impose the conditions described by Subsection (c)(1) if the defendant is a student at a primary or secondary school.

(e) At any time after the imposition of a condition under Subsection (c)(1), the defendant may request the court to modify the child safety zone applicable to the defendant because the zone as created by the court:

(1) interferes with the defendant's ability to attend school or hold a job and consequently constitutes an undue hardship for the defendant; or

(2) is broader than is necessary to protect the public, given the nature and circumstances of the offense.

(f) A supervision officer for a defendant described by Subsection (b) may permit the defendant to enter on an event-by-event basis into the child safety zone from which the defendant is otherwise prohibited from entering if:

(1) the defendant has served at least two years of the period of community supervision;

(2) the defendant enters the zone as part of a program to reunite with the defendant's family;

(3) the defendant presents to the supervision officer a written proposal specifying where the defendant intends to go within the zone, why and with whom the defendant is going, and how the defendant intends to cope with any stressful situations that occur;

(4) the sex offender treatment provider treating the defendant agrees with the supervision officer that the defendant should be allowed to attend the event; and

(5) the supervision officer and the treatment provider agree on a chaperon to accompany the defendant and the chaperon agrees to perform that duty.

(g) Article 42A.051(b) does not prohibit a supervision officer from modifying a condition of community supervision by permitting a defendant to enter a child safety zone under Subsection (f).

(h) Notwithstanding Subsection (c)(1)(B), a requirement that a defendant not go in, on, or within 1,000 feet of certain premises does not apply to a defendant while the defendant is in or going immediately to or from a:

(1) community supervision and corrections department office;

(2) premises at which the defendant is participating in a program or activity required as a condition of community supervision;

(3) residential facility in which the defendant is required to reside as a condition of community supervision, if the facility was in operation as a residence for defendants on community supervision on June 1, 2003; or

(4) private residence at which the defendant is required to reside as a condition of community supervision.

(i) A supervision officer who under Subsection (c)(2) specifies a sex offender treatment provider to provide counseling to a defendant shall:

(1) contact the provider before the defendant is released;

(2) establish the date, time, and place of the first session between the defendant and the provider; and

(3) request the provider to immediately notify the supervision officer if the defendant fails to attend the first session or any subsequent scheduled session.

Added by Acts 2015, 84th Leg., ch. 770 (H.B. 2299), § 1.01, eff. Jan. 1, 2017.

Art. 42A.454.   Certain Internet Activity Prohibited

(a) This article applies only to a defendant who is required to register as a sex offender under Chapter 62, by court order or otherwise, and:

(1) is convicted of or receives a grant of deferred adjudication community supervision for a violation of Section 21.11, 22.011(a)(2), 22.021(a)(1)(B), 33.021, or 43.25, Penal Code;

(2) used the Internet or any other type of electronic device used for Internet access to commit the offense

or engage in the conduct for which the person is required to register under Chapter 62; or

(3) is assigned a numeric risk level of two or three based on an assessment conducted under Article 62.007.

(b) If the court grants community supervision to a defendant described by Subsection (a), the court as a condition of community supervision shall:

(1) prohibit the defendant from using the Internet to:

(A) access material that is obscene, as defined by Section 43.21, Penal Code;

(B) access a commercial social networking site, as defined by Article 62.0061(f);

(C) communicate with any individual concerning sexual relations with an individual who is younger than 17 years of age; or

(D) communicate with another individual the defendant knows is younger than 17 years of age; and

(2) to ensure the defendant's compliance with Subdivision (1), require the defendant to submit to regular inspection or monitoring of each electronic device used by the defendant to access the Internet.

(c) The court may modify at any time the condition described by Subsection (b)(1)(D) if:

(1) the condition interferes with the defendant's ability to attend school or become or remain employed and consequently constitutes an undue hardship for the defendant; or

(2) the defendant is the parent or guardian of an individual who is younger than 17 years of age and the defendant is not otherwise prohibited from communicating with that individual.

Added by Acts 2015, 84th Leg., ch. 770 (H.B. 2299), § 1.01, eff. Jan. 1, 2017. Amended by Acts 2017, 85th Leg., ch. 324 (S.B. 1488), § 23.018(a), eff. Sept. 1, 2017.

Art. 42A.455. Payment to Children's Advocacy Center

A judge who grants community supervision to a defendant charged with or convicted of an offense under Section 21.11 or 22.011(a)(2), Penal Code, may require the defendant to make one payment in an amount not to exceed $50 to a children's advocacy center established under Subchapter E, Chapter 264, Family Code.

Added by Acts 2015, 84th Leg., ch. 770 (H.B. 2299), § 1.01, eff. Jan. 1, 2017.

SUBCHAPTER K. CONDITIONS APPLICABLE TO CERTAIN OTHER OFFENSES AND OFFENDERS

Art. 42A.501. Community Supervision for Offense Committed Because of Bias or Prejudice

(a) A court granting community supervision to a defendant convicted of an offense for which the court has made an affirmative finding under Article 42.014 shall require as a term of community supervision that the defendant:

(1) serve a term of not more than one year imprisonment in the Texas Department of Criminal Justice if the offense is a felony other than an offense under Section 19.02, Penal Code; or

(2) serve a term of not more than 90 days confinement in jail if the offense is a misdemeanor.

(b) The court may not grant community supervision on its own motion or on the recommendation of the jury to a defendant convicted of an offense for which the court has made an affirmative finding under Article 42.014 if:

(1) the offense for which the court has made the affirmative finding is an offense under Section 19.02, Penal Code; or

(2) the defendant has been previously convicted of an offense for which the court made an affirmative finding under Article 42.014.

Added by Acts 2015, 84th Leg., ch. 770 (H.B. 2299), § 1.01, eff. Jan. 1, 2017.

Art. 42A.502. Community Supervision for Certain Violent Offenses; Child Safety Zone

(a) In this article, "playground," "premises," "school," "video arcade facility," and "youth center" have the meanings assigned by Section 481.134, Health and Safety Code.

(b) A judge granting community supervision to a defendant convicted of an offense listed in Article 42A.054(a) or for which the judgment contains an affirmative finding under Article 42A.054(c) or (d) may establish a child safety zone applicable to the defendant, if the nature of the offense for which the defendant is convicted warrants the establishment of a child safety zone, by requiring as a condition of community supervision that the defendant not:

(1) supervise or participate in any program that:

(A) includes as participants or recipients persons who are 17 years of age or younger; and

(B) regularly provides athletic, civic, or cultural activities; or

(2) go in or on, or within a distance specified by the judge of, a premises where children commonly gather, including a school, day-care facility, playground, public or private youth center, public swimming pool, or video arcade facility.

(c) At any time after the imposition of a condition under Subsection (b), the defendant may request the judge to modify the child safety zone applicable to the defendant because the zone as created by the judge:

(1) interferes with the defendant's ability to attend school or hold a job and consequently constitutes an undue hardship for the defendant; or

(2) is broader than is necessary to protect the public, given the nature and circumstances of the offense.

(d) This article does not apply to a defendant described by Article 42A.453.

Added by Acts 2015, 84th Leg., ch. 770 (H.B. 2299), § 1.01, eff. Jan. 1, 2017.

Art. 42A.503.   Community Supervision for Certain Child Abuse Offenses; Prohibited Contact With Victim

(a) If the court grants community supervision to a defendant convicted of an offense described by Article 17.41(a), the court may require as a condition of community supervision that the defendant not:

(1) directly communicate with the victim of the offense; or

(2) go near a residence, school, or other location, as specifically described in the copy of terms and conditions, that is frequented by the victim.

(b) In imposing the condition under Subsection (a), the court may grant the defendant supervised access to the victim.

(c) To the extent that a condition imposed under this article conflicts with an existing court order granting possession of or access to a child, the condition imposed under this article prevails for a period specified by the court granting community supervision, not to exceed 90 days.

Added by Acts 2015, 84th Leg., ch. 770 (H.B. 2299), § 1.01, eff. Jan. 1, 2017.

Art. 42A.504.   Community Supervision for Certain Offenses Involving Family Violence; Special Conditions

(a) In this article:

(1) "Family violence" has the meaning assigned by Section 71.004, Family Code.

(2) "Family violence center" has the meaning assigned by Section 51.002, Human Resources Code.

(b) If a judge grants community supervision to a defendant convicted of an offense under Title 5, Penal Code, that the court determines involves family violence, the judge shall require the defendant to pay $100 to a family violence center that:

(1) receives state or federal funds; and

(2) serves the county in which the court is located.

(c) If the court grants community supervision to a defendant convicted of an offense involving family violence, the court may require the defendant, at the direction of the supervision officer, to:

(1) attend a battering intervention and prevention program or counsel with a provider of battering intervention and prevention services if the program or provider has been accredited under Section 4A, Article 42.141, as conforming to program guidelines under that article; or

(2) if the referral option under Subdivision (1) is not available, attend counseling sessions for the elimination of violent behavior with a licensed counselor, social worker, or other professional who has completed family violence intervention training that the community justice assistance division of the Texas Department of Criminal Justice has approved, after consultation with the licensing authorities described by Chapters 152, 501, 502, 503, and 505, Occupations Code, and experts in the field of family violence.

(d) If the court requires the defendant to attend counseling or a program, the court shall require the defendant to begin attendance not later than the 60th day after the date the court grants community supervision, notify the supervision officer of the name, address, and phone number of the counselor or program, and report the defendant's attendance to the supervision officer. The court shall require the defendant to pay all the reasonable costs of the counseling sessions or attendance in the program on a finding that the defendant is financially able to make payment. If the court finds the defendant is unable to make payment, the court shall make the counseling sessions or enrollment in the program available without cost to the defendant. The court may also require the defendant to pay all or a part of the reasonable costs incurred by the victim for counseling made necessary by the offense, on a finding that the defendant is financially able to make payment. The court may order the defendant to make payments under this subsection for a period not to exceed one year after the date on which the order is entered.

Added by Acts 2015, 84th Leg., ch. 770 (H.B. 2299), § 1.01, eff. Jan. 1, 2017.

Art. 42A.505. Community Supervision for Stalking Offense; Prohibited Contact With Victim

(a) If the court grants community supervision to a defendant convicted of an offense under Section 42.072, Penal Code, the court may require as a condition of community supervision that the defendant not:

(1) communicate directly or indirectly with the victim; or

(2) go to or near:

(A) the residence, place of employment, or business of the victim; or

(B) a school, day-care facility, or similar facility where a dependent child of the victim is in attendance.

(b) If the court requires the prohibition contained in Subsection (a)(2) as a condition of community supervision, the court shall specifically describe the prohibited locations and the minimum distances, if any, that the defendant must maintain from the locations.

Added by Acts 2015, 84th Leg., ch. 770 (H.B. 2299), § 1.01, eff. Jan. 1, 2017.

Art. 42A.506. Community Supervision for Defendant With Mental Impairment

If the judge places a defendant on community supervision and the defendant is determined to be a person with mental illness or a person with an intellectual disability, as provided by Article 16.22 or Chapter 46B or in a psychological evaluation conducted under Article 42A.253(a)(6), the judge may require the defendant as a condition of community supervision to submit to outpatient or inpatient mental health or intellectual disability treatment if:

(1) the defendant's:

(A) mental impairment is chronic in nature; or

(B) ability to function independently will continue to deteriorate if the defendant does not receive mental health or intellectual disability services; and

(2) the judge determines, in consultation with a local mental health or intellectual disability services provider, that mental health or intellectual disability services, as appropriate, are available for the defendant through:

(A) the Department of State Health Services or the Department of Aging and Disability Services under Section 534.053, Health and Safety Code; or

(B) another mental health or intellectual disability services provider.

Added by Acts 2015, 84th Leg., ch. 770 (H.B. 2299), § 1.01, eff. Jan. 1, 2017.

Art. 42A.507. Community Supervision for Certain Defendants Identified as Members of Criminal Street Gangs; Electronic Monitoring

Text of (a) effective until January 1, 2019

(a) This article applies only to a defendant who:

(1) is identified as a member of a criminal street gang in an intelligence database established under Chapter 61; and

(2) has two or more times been previously convicted of, or received a grant of deferred adjudication community supervision or another functionally equivalent form of community supervision or probation for, a felony offense under the laws of this state, another state, or the United States.

Text of (a) effective January 1, 2019

(a) This article applies only to a defendant who:

(1) is identified as a member of a criminal street gang in an intelligence database established under Chapter 67; and

(2) has two or more times been previously convicted of, or received a grant of deferred adjudication community supervision or another functionally equivalent form of community supervision or probation for, a felony offense under the laws of this state, another state, or the United States.

(b) A court granting community supervision to a defendant described by Subsection (a) may, on the defendant's conviction of a felony offense, require as a condition of community supervision that the defendant submit to tracking under an electronic monitoring service or other appropriate technological service designed to track a person's location.

Added by Acts 2015, 84th Leg., ch. 770 (H.B. 2299), § 1.01, eff. Jan. 1, 2017. Amended by Acts 2017, 85th Leg., ch. 1058 (H.B. 2931), § 4.03, eff. Jan. 1, 2019.

Art. 42A.508. Community Supervision for Certain Organized Crime Offenses; Restrictions on Operation of Motor Vehicle

A court granting community supervision to a defendant convicted of an offense under Chapter 71, Penal Code, may impose as a condition of community supervision restrictions on the defendant's operation of a motor vehicle, including specifying:

(1) hours during which the defendant may not operate a motor vehicle; and

(2) locations at or in which the defendant may not operate a motor vehicle.

Added by Acts 2015, 84th Leg., ch. 770 (H.B. 2299), § 1.01, eff. Jan. 1, 2017.

Art. 42A.509. Community Supervision for Graffiti Offense

A court granting community supervision to a defendant convicted of an offense under Section 28.08, Penal Code, shall require as a condition of community supervision that the defendant perform:

(1) at least 15 hours of community service if the amount of pecuniary loss resulting from the commission of the offense is $50 or more but less than $500; or

(2) at least 30 hours of community service if the amount of pecuniary loss resulting from the commission of the offense is $500 or more.

Added by Acts 2015, 84th Leg., ch. 770 (H.B. 2299), § 1.01, eff. Jan. 1, 2017.

Art. 42A.510. Community Supervision for Enhanced Disorderly Conduct Offense

(a) On conviction of an offense punishable as a Class C misdemeanor under Section 42.01, Penal Code, for which punishment is enhanced under Section 12.43(c), Penal Code, based on previous convictions under Section 42.01 or 49.02, Penal Code, the court may suspend the imposition of the sentence and place the defendant on community supervision if the court finds that the defendant would benefit from community supervision and enters its finding on the record. The judge may suspend in whole or in part the imposition of any fine imposed on conviction.

(b) All provisions of this chapter applying to a defendant placed on community supervision for a misdemeanor apply to a defendant placed on community supervision under this article, except that the court shall require the defendant as a condition of community supervision to:

(1) submit to diagnostic testing for addiction to alcohol or a controlled substance or drug;

(2) submit to a psychological assessment;

(3) if indicated as necessary by testing and assessment, participate in an alcohol or drug abuse treatment or education program; and

(4) pay the costs of testing, assessment, and treatment or education, either directly or as a court cost.

Added by Acts 2015, 84th Leg., ch. 770 (H.B. 2299), § 1.01, eff. Jan. 1, 2017.

Art. 42A.511. Community Supervision for Certain Offenses Involving Animals

(a) If a judge grants community supervision to a defendant convicted of an offense under Section 42.09, 42.091, 42.092, or 42.10, Penal Code, the judge may require the defendant to:

(1) complete an online responsible pet owner course approved and certified by the Texas Department of Licensing and Regulation; or

(2) attend a responsible pet owner course sponsored by a municipal animal shelter, as defined by Section 823.001, Health and Safety Code, that:

(A) receives federal, state, county, or municipal funds; and

(B) serves the county in which the court is located.

Text of (b), as added by Acts 2017, 85th Leg., ch. 739 (S.B. 1232), § 4

(b) If a judge grants community supervision to a defendant convicted of an offense under Section 21.09, Penal Code, the judge may:

(1) require the defendant to relinquish custody of any animals in the defendant's possession;

(2) prohibit the defendant from possessing or exercising control over any animals or residing in a household where animals are present; or

(3) require the defendant to participate in a psychological counseling or other appropriate treatment program for a period to be determined by the court.

Text of (b), as added by Acts 2017, 85th Leg., ch. 1132 (H.B. 162), § 1

(b) For purposes of the online responsible pet owner course described by Subsection (a)(1), the Texas Department of Licensing and Regulation or the Texas Commission of Licensing and Regulation, as appropriate:

(1) is responsible for the approval, certification, and administration of the course and course providers;

(2) may charge fees for:

(A) initial and renewal course certifications;

(B) initial and renewal course provider certifications;

(C) course participant completion certificates; and

(D) other fees necessary for the administration of the course and course providers;

(3) shall adopt rules regarding the administration of the course and course providers, including rules regarding:

(A) the criteria for course approval and certification;

(B) the criteria for course provider approval and certification;

(C) curriculum development;

(D) course length and content;

(E) criteria for a participant to complete the course; and

(F) a course completion certificate that is acceptable to a court;

(4) is authorized to monitor and audit the provision of the course by the course providers; and

(5) may take enforcement actions as appropriate to enforce this subsection.

Added by Acts 2015, 84th Leg., ch. 770 (H.B. 2299), § 1.01, eff. Jan. 1, 2017. Amended by Acts 2017, 85th Leg., ch. 739 (S.B. 1232), § 4, eff. Sept. 1, 2017; Acts 2017, 85th Leg., ch. 1132 (H.B. 162), § 1, eff. Sept. 1, 2017.

Section 9 of Acts 2017, 85th Leg., ch. 739 (S.B. 1232) provides:

"The change in law made by this Act applies only to an offense committed on or after the effective date [Sept. 1, 2017] of this Act. An offense committed before the effective date of this Act is governed by the law in effect on the date the offense was committed, and the former law is continued in effect for that purpose. For purposes of this section, an offense was committed before the effective date of this Act if any element of the offense occurred before that date."

Art. 42A.512. Community Supervision for Electronic Transmission of Certain Visual Material

(a) In this article, "parent" means a natural or adoptive parent, managing or possessory conservator, or legal guardian. The term does not include a parent whose parental rights have been terminated.

(b) If a judge grants community supervision to a defendant who is convicted of or charged with an offense under Section 43.261, Penal Code, the judge may require as a condition of community supervision that the defendant attend and successfully complete an educational program described by Section 37.218, Education Code, or another equivalent educational program.

(c) The court shall require the defendant or the defendant's parent to pay the cost of attending an educational program under Subsection (b) if the court determines that the defendant or the defendant's parent is financially able to make payment.

Added by Acts 2015, 84th Leg., ch. 770 (H.B. 2299), § 1.01, eff. Jan. 1, 2017.

Art. 42A.513. Community Supervision for Making Firearm Accessible to Child

(a) A court granting community supervision to a defendant convicted of an offense under Section 46.13, Penal Code, may require as a condition of community supervision that the defendant:

(1) provide an appropriate public service activity designated by the court; or

(2) attend a firearms safety course that meets or exceeds the requirements set by the National Rifle Association as of January 1, 1995, for a firearms safety course that requires not more than 17 hours of instruction.

(b) The court shall require the defendant to pay the cost of attending the firearms safety course under Subsection (a)(2).

Added by Acts 2015, 84th Leg., ch. 770 (H.B. 2299), § 1.01, eff. Jan. 1, 2017.

Art. 42A.514. Community Supervision for Certain Alcohol or Drug Related Offenses

(a) If a judge grants community supervision to a defendant younger than 18 years of age convicted of an alcohol-related offense under Section 106.02, 106.025, 106.04, 106.041, 106.05, or 106.07, Alcoholic Beverage Code, or Section 49.02, Penal Code, or an offense involving possession of a controlled substance or marihuana under Section 481.115, 481.1151, 481.116, 481.1161, 481.117, 481.118, or 481.121, Health and Safety Code, the judge may require the defendant as a condition of community supervision to attend, as appropriate:

(1) an alcohol awareness program approved under Section 106.115, Alcoholic Beverage Code; or

(2) a drug education program that is designed to educate persons on the dangers of drug abuse and is approved by the Department of State Health Services in accordance with Section 521.374, Transportation Code.

(b) If a judge requires a defendant as a condition of community supervision to attend an alcohol awareness program or drug education program described by Subsection (a), unless the judge determines that the defendant is indigent and unable to pay the cost, the judge shall require the defendant to pay the cost of attending the program. The judge may allow the defendant to pay the cost of attending the program in installments during the term of community supervision.

Added by Acts 2017, 85th Leg., ch. 324 (S.B. 1488), § 23.019(a), eff. Sept. 1, 2017.

SUBCHAPTER L. STATE JAIL FELONY COMMUNITY SUPERVISION

Art. 42A.551. Placement on Community Supervision; Execution of Sentence

(a) Except as otherwise provided by Subsection (b) or (c), on conviction of a state jail felony under Section 481.115(b), 481.1151(b)(1), 481.116(b), 481.1161(b)(3), 481.121(b)(3), or 481.129(g)(1), Health and Safety Code, that is punished under Section 12.35(a), Penal Code, the judge shall suspend the imposition of the sentence and place the defendant on community supervision.

(b) If the defendant has been previously convicted of a felony, other than a felony punished under Section 12.44(a), Penal Code, or if the conviction resulted from an adjudication of the guilt of a defendant previously placed on deferred adjudication community supervision for the offense, the judge may:

(1) suspend the imposition of the sentence and place the defendant on community supervision; or

(2) order the sentence to be executed.

(c) Subsection (a) does not apply to a defendant who:

(1) under Section 481.1151(b)(1), Health and Safety Code, possessed more than five abuse units of the controlled substance;

(2) under Section 481.1161(b)(3), Health and Safety Code, possessed more than one pound, by aggregate weight, including adulterants or dilutants, of the controlled substance; or

(3) under Section 481.121(b)(3), Health and Safety Code, possessed more than one pound of marihuana.

(d) On conviction of a state jail felony punished under Section 12.35(a), Penal Code, other than a state jail felony listed in Subsection (a), subject to Subsection (e), the judge may:

(1) suspend the imposition of the sentence and place the defendant on community supervision; or

(2) order the sentence to be executed:

(A) in whole; or

(B) in part, with a period of community supervision to begin immediately on release of the defendant from confinement.

(e) In any case in which the jury assesses punishment, the judge must follow the recommendations of the jury in suspending the imposition of a sentence or ordering a sentence to be executed. If a jury assessing punishment does not recommend community supervision, the judge must order the sentence to be executed in whole.

(f) A defendant is considered to be finally convicted if the judge orders the sentence to be executed under Subsection (d)(2), regardless of whether the judge orders the sentence to be executed in whole or only in part.

(g) The judge may suspend in whole or in part the imposition of any fine imposed on conviction.

Added by Acts 2015, 84th Leg., ch. 770 (H.B. 2299), § 1.01, eff. Jan. 1, 2017.

Art. 42A.552. Review of Presentence Report

Before imposing a sentence in a state jail felony case in which the judge assesses punishment, the judge shall:

(1) review the presentence report prepared for the defendant under Subchapter F; and

(2) determine whether the best interests of justice require the judge to:

(A) suspend the imposition of the sentence and place the defendant on community supervision; or

(B) order the sentence to be executed in whole or in part as provided by Article 42A.551(d).

Added by Acts 2015, 84th Leg., ch. 770 (H.B. 2299), § 1.01, eff. Jan. 1, 2017.

Art. 42A.553. Minimum and Maximum Periods of Community Supervision; Extension

(a) The minimum period of community supervision a judge may impose under this subchapter is two years. The maximum period of community supervision a judge may impose under this subchapter is five years, except that the judge may extend the maximum period of community supervision under this subchapter to not more than 10 years.

(b) A judge may extend a period of community supervision under this subchapter:

(1) at any time during the period of community supervision; or

(2) before the first anniversary of the date the period of community supervision ends, if a motion for revocation of community supervision is filed before the date the period of community supervision ends.

Added by Acts 2015, 84th Leg., ch. 770 (H.B. 2299), § 1.01, eff. Jan. 1, 2017.

Art. 42A.554. Conditions of Community Supervision

(a) A judge assessing punishment in a state jail felony case may impose any condition of community supervision on the defendant that the judge could impose on a defendant placed on supervision for an offense other than a state jail felony.

(b) If the judge suspends the execution of the sentence or orders the execution of the sentence only in part as provided by Article 42A.551(d), the judge shall impose conditions of community supervision consistent with the recommendations contained in the presentence report prepared for the defendant under Subchapter F.

(c) Except as otherwise provided by this subsection, a judge who places a defendant on community supervision for an offense listed in Article 42A.551(a) shall require the defendant to comply with substance abuse treatment conditions that are consistent with standards adopted by the Texas Board of Criminal Justice under Section 509.015, Government Code. A judge is not required to impose the substance abuse treatment conditions if the judge makes an affirmative finding that the defendant does not require imposition of the

conditions to successfully complete the period of community supervision.

Added by Acts 2015, 84th Leg., ch. 770 (H.B. 2299), § 1.01, eff. Jan. 1, 2017.

Art. 42A.555. Confinement as a Condition of Community Supervision

(a) A judge assessing punishment in a state jail felony case may impose as a condition of community supervision that a defendant submit at the beginning of the period of community supervision to a term of confinement in a state jail felony facility for a term of:

(1) not less than 90 days or more than 180 days; or

(2) not less than 90 days or more than one year, if the defendant is convicted of an offense punishable as a state jail felony under Section 481.112, 481.1121, 481.113, or 481.120, Health and Safety Code.

(b) A judge may not require a defendant to submit to both the term of confinement authorized by this article and a term of confinement under Subchapter C or Article 42A.302. (Code Crim. Proc., Art. 42.12, Secs. 15(c)(1) (part), (d) (part).)

Added by Acts 2015, 84th Leg., ch. 770 (H.B. 2299), § 1.01, eff. Jan. 1, 2017.

Art. 42A.556. Sanctions Imposed on Modification of Community Supervision

If in a state jail felony case a defendant violates a condition of community supervision imposed under this chapter and after a hearing under Article 42A.751(d) the judge modifies the defendant's community supervision, the judge may impose any sanction permitted by Article 42A.752, except that if the judge requires a defendant to serve a term of confinement in a state jail felony facility as a modification of the defendant's community supervision, the minimum term of confinement is 90 days and the maximum term of confinement is 180 days.

Added by Acts 2015, 84th Leg., ch. 770 (H.B. 2299), § 1.01, eff. Jan. 1, 2017.

Art. 42A.557. Report by Director of Facility

The facility director of a state jail felony facility shall report to a judge who orders a defendant confined in the facility as a condition of community supervision or as a sanction imposed on a modification of community supervision under Article 42A.556 not less than every 90 days on the defendant's programmatic progress, conduct, and conformity to the rules of the facility.

Added by Acts 2015, 84th Leg., ch. 770 (H.B. 2299), § 1.01, eff. Jan. 1, 2017.

Art. 42A.558. Revocation; Options Regarding Execution of Sentence

(a) If in a state jail felony case a defendant violates a condition of community supervision imposed under this chapter and after a hearing under Article 42A.751(d) the judge revokes the defendant's community supervision, the judge shall dispose of the case in the manner provided by Article 42A.755.

(b) The court retains jurisdiction over the defendant for the period during which the defendant is confined in a state jail felony facility. At any time after the 75th day after the date the defendant is received into the custody of a state jail felony facility, the judge on the judge's own motion, on the motion of the attorney representing the state, or on the motion of the defendant may suspend further execution of the sentence and place the defendant on community supervision under the conditions of this subchapter.

(c) When the defendant or the attorney representing the state files a written motion requesting the judge to suspend further execution of the sentence and place the defendant on community supervision, the clerk of the court, if requested to do so by the judge, shall request a copy of the defendant's record while confined from the facility director of the state jail felony facility in which the defendant is confined or, if the defendant is confined in county jail, from the sheriff. On receipt of the request, the facility director or the sheriff shall forward a copy of the record to the judge as soon as possible.

(d) When the defendant files a written motion requesting the judge to suspend further execution of the sentence and place the defendant on community supervision, the defendant shall immediately deliver or cause to be delivered a copy of the motion to the office of the attorney representing the state. The judge may deny the motion without holding a hearing but may not grant the motion without holding a hearing and providing the attorney representing the state and the defendant the opportunity to present evidence on the motion.

Added by Acts 2015, 84th Leg., ch. 770 (H.B. 2299), § 1.01, eff. Jan. 1, 2017.

Art. 42A.559. Credits for Time Served

(a) For purposes of this article, "diligent participation" includes:

(1) successful completion of an educational, vocational, or treatment program;

(2) progress toward successful completion of an educational, vocational, or treatment program that was interrupted by illness, injury, or another circumstance outside the control of the defendant; and

(3) active involvement in a work program.

(b) A defendant confined in a state jail felony facility does not earn good conduct time for time served in the facility but may be awarded diligent participation credit in accordance with Subsection (f) or (g).

(c) A judge:

(1) may credit against any time a defendant is required to serve in a state jail felony facility time served in a county jail from the time of the defendant's arrest and confinement until sentencing by the trial court; and

(2) shall credit against any time a defendant is required to serve in a state jail felony facility time served before sentencing in a substance abuse felony punishment facility operated by the Texas Department of Criminal Justice under Section 493.009, Government Code, or other court-ordered residential program or facility as a condition of deferred adjudication community supervision, but only if the defendant successfully completes the treatment program in that facility.

(d) A judge shall credit against any time a defendant is subsequently required to serve in a state jail felony facility after revocation of community supervision time served after sentencing:

(1) in a state jail felony facility; or

(2) in a substance abuse felony punishment facility operated by the Texas Department of Criminal Justice under Section 493.009, Government Code, or other court-ordered residential program or facility if the defendant successfully completes the treatment program in that facility.

(e) For a defendant who has participated in an educational, vocational, treatment, or work program while confined in a state jail felony facility, the Texas Department of Criminal Justice shall record the number of days during which the defendant diligently participated in any educational, vocational, treatment, or work program.

(f) For a defendant with a judgment that contains a finding under Article 42.0199 that the defendant is presumptively entitled to diligent participation credit and who has not been the subject of disciplinary action while confined in the state jail felony facility, the department shall credit against any time the defendant is required to serve in a state jail felony facility additional time for each day the defendant actually served in the facility while diligently participating in an educational, vocational, treatment, or work program.

(g) For a defendant with a judgment that contains a finding under Article 42.0199 that the defendant is not presumptively entitled to diligent participation credit or who has been the subject of disciplinary action while confined in the state jail felony facility, the department shall, not later than the 30th day before the date on which the defendant will have served 80 percent of the defendant's sentence, report to the sentencing court the record of the number of days under Subsection (e). The contents of a report submitted under this subsection are not subject to challenge by a defendant. A judge, based on the report, may credit against any time a defendant is required to serve in a state jail felony facility additional time for each day the defendant actually served in the facility while diligently participating in an educational, vocational, treatment, or work program.

(h) A time credit under Subsection (f) or (g) may not exceed one-fifth of the amount of time the defendant is originally required to serve in the facility. A defendant may not be awarded a time credit under Subsection (f) or (g) for any period during which the defendant is subject to disciplinary status. A time credit under Subsection (f) or (g) is a privilege and not a right.

Added by Acts 2015, 84th Leg., ch. 770 (H.B. 2299), § 1.01, eff. Jan. 1, 2017. Amended by Acts 2017, 85th Leg., ch. 324 (S.B. 1488), § 23.020(a), eff. Sept. 1, 2017.

Art. 42A.560. Medical Release

(a) If a defendant is convicted of a state jail felony and the sentence is executed, the judge sentencing the defendant may release the defendant to a medically suitable placement if the judge determines that the defendant does not constitute a threat to public safety and the Texas Correctional Office on Offenders with Medical or Mental Impairments:

(1) in coordination with the Correctional Managed Health Care Committee, prepares a case summary and medical report that identifies the defendant as:

(A) being a person who is elderly or terminally ill or a person with a physical disability;

(B) being a person with mental illness or an intellectual disability; or

(C) having a condition requiring long-term care; and

(2) in cooperation with the community supervision and corrections department serving the sentencing court, prepares for the defendant a medically recommended intensive supervision and continuity of care plan that:

(A) ensures appropriate supervision of the defendant by the community supervision and corrections department; and

(B) requires the defendant to remain under the care of a physician at and reside in a medically suitable placement.

(b) The Texas Correctional Office on Offenders with Medical or Mental Impairments shall submit to a judge who releases a defendant to an appropriate medical care facility under Subsection (a) a quarterly status report concerning the defendant's medical and treatment status.

(c) If a defendant released to a medically suitable placement under Subsection (a) violates the terms of that release, the judge may dispose of the matter as provided by Articles 42A.556 and 42A.558(a).

Added by Acts 2015, 84th Leg., ch. 770 (H.B. 2299), § 1.01, eff. Jan. 1, 2017.

Art. 42A.561. Medical Release

(a) If a defendant is convicted of a state jail felony and the sentence is executed, the judge sentencing the defendant may release the defendant to a medical care facility or medical treatment program if the Texas Correctional Office on Offenders with Medical or Mental Impairments:

(1) identifies the defendant as:

(A) being a person who is elderly or terminally ill or a person with a physical disability;

(B) being a person with mental illness or an intellectual disability; or

(C) having a condition requiring long-term care; and

(2) in cooperation with the community supervision and corrections department serving the sentencing court, prepares for the defendant a medically recommended intensive supervision plan that:

(A) ensures appropriate supervision of the defendant; and

(B) requires the defendant to remain under the care of a physician at the facility or in the program.

(b) If a defendant released to a medical care facility or medical treatment program under Subsection (a) violates the terms of that release, the judge may dispose of the matter as provided by Articles 42A.556 and 42A.558(a).

Added by Acts 2015, 84th Leg., ch. 770 (H.B. 2299), § 1.01, eff. Jan. 1, 2017.

Art. 42A.562.   Placement on Community Supervision; Educational and Vocational Training Pilot Program

(a) Except as provided by Subsection (b), a judge assessing punishment in a state jail felony case may suspend the imposition of the sentence and place the defendant on community supervision with the conditions that the defendant:

(1) submit at the beginning of the term of community supervision to confinement in a state jail felony facility for a term not to exceed 90 days; and

(2) participate in a program operated under Section 507.007, Government Code.

(b) A judge may not place a defendant on community supervision under this article if the defendant is or has previously been convicted of an offense under Title 5, Penal Code.

(c) Before a judge may place a defendant on community supervision under this article, the defendant must be assessed using the risk and needs assessment instrument adopted under Section 501.0921, Government Code, or a similar instrument that takes into consideration the defendant's prior criminal history.

(d) Notwithstanding Article 42A.559(c), the judge shall credit against the time the defendant is required to serve under Subsection (a)(1) time the defendant served in a county jail from the time of the defendant's arrest until sentencing.

(e) Notwithstanding the minimum period of community supervision provided by Article 42A.553(a), a judge placing a defendant on community supervision under this article shall impose a period of community supervision not to exceed 270 days.

(f) A defendant placed on community supervision under this article must participate fully in the program described by Subsection (a)(2). The provisions of Subchapter P authorizing the judge to revoke a

defendant's community supervision or otherwise sanction the defendant apply with respect to a defendant who violates the requirement of this subsection.

Added by Acts 2017, 85th Leg., ch. 1060 (H.B. 3130), § 1, eff. Sept. 1, 2017.

Section 4 of Acts 2017, 85th Leg., ch. 1060 (H.B. 3130) provides:

"Article 42A.562, Code of Criminal Procedure, as added by this Act, applies only to a defendant who receives a sentence of confinement in a state jail on or after September 1, 2019. A defendant who receives a sentence of confinement in a state jail before September 1, 2019, is governed by the law in effect immediately before the effective date of this Act, and the former law is continued in effect for that purpose."

SUBCHAPTER M. COMMUNITY CORRECTIONS FACILITIES

Art. 42A.601.   Definition

In this subchapter, "community corrections facility" has the meaning assigned by Section 509.001, Government Code.

Added by Acts 2015, 84th Leg., ch. 770 (H.B. 2299), § 1.01, eff. Jan. 1, 2017.

Art. 42A.602.   Maximum Term or Terms of Confinement

(a) If a judge requires as a condition of community supervision or participation in a pretrial intervention program operated under Section 76.011, Government Code, or a drug court program established under Chapter 123, Government Code, or former law that the defendant serve a term of confinement in a community corrections facility, the term may not exceed 24 months.

(b) A judge who requires as a condition of community supervision that the defendant serve a term of confinement in a community corrections facility may not impose a subsequent term of confinement in a community corrections facility or jail during the same supervision period that, if added to the terms previously imposed, exceeds 36 months.

Added by Acts 2015, 84th Leg., ch. 770 (H.B. 2299), § 1.01, eff. Jan. 1, 2017. Amended by Acts 2017, 85th Leg., ch. 977 (H.B. 351), § 5(a), eff. Sept. 1, 2017.

Section 5(d) of Acts 2017, 85th Leg., ch. 977 (H.B. 351) provides:

"(d) The change in law made by this section applies only to a person placed in a pretrial intervention program operated under Section 76.011, Government Code, for an offense committed on or after the effective date [Sept. 1, 2017] of this Act. A person placed in a pretrial intervention program operated under Section 76.011, Government Code, for an offense committed before the effective date of this Act is governed by the law in effect on the date the offense was committed, and the former law is continued in effect for that purpose. For purposes of this subsection, an offense was committed before the effective date of this Act if any element of the offense was committed before that date."

Art. 42A.603. Effect of Revocation on Credit for Time Spent in Facility

A defendant granted community supervision under this chapter and required as a condition of community supervision to serve a term of confinement under this subchapter may not earn good conduct credit for time spent in a community corrections facility or apply time spent in the facility toward completion of a prison sentence if the community supervision is revoked.

Added by Acts 2015, 84th Leg., ch. 770 (H.B. 2299), § 1.01, eff. Jan. 1, 2017.

Art. 42A.604. Evaluation of Defendant's Behavior and Attitude

(a) As directed by the judge, the community corrections facility director shall file with the community supervision and corrections department director or administrator of a drug court program, as applicable, a copy of an evaluation made by the facility director of the defendant's behavior and attitude at the facility. The community supervision and corrections department director or program administrator shall examine the evaluation, make written comments on the evaluation that the director or administrator considers relevant, and file the evaluation and comments with the judge who granted community supervision to the defendant or placed the defendant in a pretrial intervention program or drug court program. If the evaluation indicates that the defendant has made significant progress toward compliance with court-ordered conditions of community supervision or objectives of placement in the program, as applicable, the judge may release the defendant from the community corrections facility. A defendant who served a term in the facility as a condition of community supervision shall serve the remainder of the defendant's community supervision under any terms and conditions the court imposes under this chapter.

(b) Not later than 18 months after the date on which a defendant is granted community supervision under this chapter and required as a condition of community supervision to serve a term of confinement under this subchapter, the community corrections facility director shall file with the community supervision and corrections department director a copy of an evaluation made by the facility director of the defendant's behavior and attitude at the facility. The community supervision and corrections department director shall examine the evaluation, make written comments on the evaluation that the director considers relevant, and file the evaluation and comments with the judge who granted community supervision to

the defendant. If the report indicates that the defendant has made significant progress toward court-ordered conditions of community supervision, the judge shall modify the judge's sentence and release the defendant in the same manner as provided by Subsection (a). If the report indicates that the defendant would benefit from continued participation in the community corrections facility program, the judge may order the defendant to remain at the community corrections facility for a period determined by the judge. If the report indicates that the defendant has not made significant progress toward rehabilitation, the judge may revoke community supervision and order the defendant to serve the term of confinement specified in the defendant's sentence.

Added by Acts 2015, 84th Leg., ch. 770 (H.B. 2299), § 1.01, eff. Jan. 1, 2017. Amended by Acts 2017, 85th Leg., ch. 977 (H.B. 351), § 5(b), eff. Sept. 1, 2017.

Section 5(d) of Acts 2017, 85th Leg., ch. 977 (H.B. 351) provides:

"(d) The change in law made by this section applies only to a person placed in a pretrial intervention program operated under Section 76.011, Government Code, for an offense committed on or after the effective date [Sept. 1, 2017] of this Act. A person placed in a pretrial intervention program operated under Section 76.011, Government Code, for an offense committed before the effective date of this Act is governed by the law in effect on the date the offense was committed, and the former law is continued in effect for that purpose. For purposes of this subsection, an offense was committed before the effective date of this Act if any element of the offense was committed before that date."

Art. 42A.605. Placement in Community Service Project

If ordered by the judge who placed the defendant on community supervision, a community corrections facility director shall attempt to place a defendant as a worker in a community service project of a type described by Article 42A.304.

Added by Acts 2015, 84th Leg., ch. 770 (H.B. 2299), § 1.01, eff. Jan. 1, 2017.

Art. 42A.606. Confinement Required; Exceptions

A defendant participating in a program under this subchapter must be confined in the community corrections facility at all times except for time spent:

(1) attending and traveling to and from:

(A) an education or rehabilitation program as ordered by the court; or

(B) a community service project;

(2) away from the facility for purposes described by this subchapter; and

(3) traveling to and from work, if applicable.

Added by Acts 2015, 84th Leg., ch. 770 (H.B. 2299), § 1.01, eff. Jan. 1, 2017.

Art. 42A.607. Disposition of Salary

If a defendant who is required as a condition of community supervision to serve a term of confinement under this subchapter is not required by the judge to deliver the defendant's salary to the restitution center director, the employer of the defendant shall deliver the salary to the director. The director shall deposit the salary into a fund to be given to the defendant on release after the director deducts:

(1) the cost to the center for the defendant's food, housing, and supervision;

(2) the necessary expense for the defendant's travel to and from work and community service projects, and other incidental expenses of the defendant;

(3) support of the defendant's dependents; and

(4) restitution to the victims of an offense committed by the defendant.

Added by Acts 2015, 84th Leg., ch. 770 (H.B. 2299), § 1.01, eff. Jan. 1, 2017.

SUBCHAPTER N. PAYMENTS; FEES

Art. 42A.651. Payment as Condition of Community Supervision

(a) A judge may not order a defendant to make a payment as a term or condition of community supervision, except for:

(1) the payment of fines, court costs, or restitution to the victim;

(2) reimbursement of a county as described by Article 42A.301(11); or

(3) a payment ordered as a condition that relates personally to the rehabilitation of the defendant or that is otherwise expressly authorized by law.

(b) A defendant's obligation to pay a fine or court cost as ordered by a judge is independent of any requirement to pay the fine or court cost as a condition of the defendant's community supervision. A defendant remains obligated to pay any unpaid fine or court cost after the expiration of the defendant's period of community supervision.

(c) A judge may not impose a condition of community supervision requiring a defendant to reimburse a county for the costs of legal services as described by

Article 42A.301(11) if the defendant has already satisfied that obligation under Article 26.05(g).

Added by Acts 2015, 84th Leg., ch. 770 (H.B. 2299), § 1.01, eff. Jan. 1, 2017. Amended by Acts 2017, 85th Leg., ch. 324 (S.B. 1488), § 23.013(b), eff. Sept. 1, 2017.

Art. 42A.652. Monthly Fee

(a) Except as otherwise provided by this article, a judge who grants community supervision to a defendant shall set a fee of not less than $25 and not more than $60 to be paid each month during the period of community supervision by the defendant to:

(1) the court of original jurisdiction; or

(2) the court accepting jurisdiction of the defendant's case, if jurisdiction is transferred under Article 42A.151.

(b) The judge may make payment of the monthly fee a condition of granting or continuing the community supervision. The judge may waive or reduce the fee or suspend a monthly payment of the fee if the judge determines that payment of the fee would cause the defendant a significant financial hardship.

(c) A court accepting jurisdiction of a defendant's case under Article 42A.151 shall enter an order directing the defendant to pay the monthly fee to that court instead of to the court of original jurisdiction. To the extent of any conflict between an order issued under this subsection and an order issued by a court of original jurisdiction, the order entered under this subsection prevails.

(d) A judge who receives a defendant for supervision as authorized by Section 510.017, Government Code, may require the defendant to pay the fee authorized by this article.

(e) A judge may not require a defendant to pay the fee under this article for any month after the period of community supervision has been terminated by the judge under Article 42A.701.

(f) A judge shall deposit any fee received under this article in the special fund of the county treasury, to be used for the same purposes for which state aid may be used under Chapter 76, Government Code.

Added by Acts 2015, 84th Leg., ch. 770 (H.B. 2299), § 1.01, eff. Jan. 1, 2017.

Art. 42A.653. Additional Monthly Fee for Certain Sex Offenders

(a) A judge who grants community supervision to a defendant convicted of an offense under Section 21.08, 21.11, 22.011, 22.021, 25.02, 43.25, or 43.26, Penal

Code, shall require as a condition of community supervision that the defendant pay to the defendant's supervision officer a community supervision fee of $5 each month during the period of community supervision.

(b) A fee imposed under this article is in addition to court costs or any other fee imposed on the defendant.

(c) A community supervision and corrections department shall deposit a fee collected under this article to be sent to the comptroller as provided by Subchapter B, Chapter 133, Local Government Code. The comptroller shall deposit the fee in the sexual assault program fund under Section 420.008, Government Code.

(d) If a community supervision and corrections department does not collect a fee imposed under this article, the department is not required to file any report required by the comptroller that relates to the collection of the fee.

Added by Acts 2015, 84th Leg., ch. 770 (H.B. 2299), § 1.01, eff. Jan. 1, 2017.

Art. 42A.654.   Fees Due on Conviction

For the purpose of determining when fees due on conviction are to be paid to any officer, the placement of a defendant on community supervision is considered a final disposition of the case, without the necessity of waiting for the termination of the period of community supervision.

Added by Acts 2015, 84th Leg., ch. 770 (H.B. 2299), § 1.01, eff. Jan. 1, 2017.

Art. 42A.655.   Ability to Pay

The court shall consider the defendant's ability to pay before ordering the defendant to make any payments under this chapter.

Added by Acts 2015, 84th Leg., ch. 770 (H.B. 2299), § 1.01, eff. Jan. 1, 2017.   Amended by Acts 2017, 85th Leg., ch. 324 (S.B. 1488), § 23.013(c), eff. Sept. 1, 2017.

SUBCHAPTER O.   REDUCTION OR TERMINATION OF COMMUNITY SUPERVISION PERIOD

Art. 42A.701.   Reduction or Termination of Community Supervision Period

(a) At any time after the defendant has satisfactorily completed one-third of the original community supervision period or two years of community supervision, whichever is less, the judge may reduce or terminate the period of community supervision.

(b) On completion of one-half of the original community supervision period or two years of community supervision, whichever is more, the judge shall review the defendant's record and consider whether to reduce or terminate the period of community supervision, unless the defendant:

(1) is delinquent in paying required costs, fines, fees, or restitution that the defendant has the ability to pay; or

(2) has not completed court-ordered counseling or treatment.

(c) Before reducing or terminating a period of community supervision or conducting a review under this article, the judge shall notify the attorney representing the state and the defendant or, if the defendant has an attorney, the defendant's attorney.

(d) If the judge determines that the defendant has failed to satisfactorily fulfill the conditions of community supervision, the judge shall advise the defendant in writing of the requirements for satisfactorily fulfilling those conditions.

(e) On the satisfactory fulfillment of the conditions of community supervision and the expiration of the period of community supervision, the judge by order shall:

(1) amend or modify the original sentence imposed, if necessary, to conform to the community supervision period; and

(2) discharge the defendant.

(f) If the judge discharges the defendant under this article, the judge may set aside the verdict or permit the defendant to withdraw the defendant's plea. A judge acting under this subsection shall dismiss the accusation, complaint, information, or indictment against the defendant. A defendant who receives a discharge and dismissal under this subsection is released from all penalties and disabilities resulting from the offense of which the defendant has been convicted or to which the defendant has pleaded guilty, except that:

(1) proof of the conviction or plea of guilty shall be made known to the judge if the defendant is convicted of any subsequent offense; and

(2) if the defendant is an applicant for or the holder of a license under Chapter 42, Human Resources Code, the Department of Family and Protective Services may consider the fact that the defendant previously has received community supervision under this

chapter in issuing, renewing, denying, or revoking a license under Chapter 42, Human Resources Code.

(f–1) The Office of Court Administration of the Texas Judicial System shall adopt a standardized form for use in discharging a defendant under this article. A judge discharging a defendant under this article must use the form adopted under this subsection. The form must provide for the judge to:

(1) discharge the defendant; or

(2) discharge the defendant, set aside the verdict or permit the defendant to withdraw the defendant's plea, and dismiss the accusation, complaint, information, or indictment against the defendant.

(f–2) The form adopted under Subsection (f–1) must state that a defendant who receives a discharge described by Subsection (f–1)(2) is released from the penalties and disabilities resulting from the offense as provided by Subsection (f).

(g) This article does not apply to a defendant convicted of:

(1) an offense under Sections 49.04–49.08, Penal Code;

(2) an offense the conviction of which requires registration as a sex offender under Chapter 62; or

(3) a felony described by Article 42A.054.

Added by Acts 2015, 84th Leg., ch. 770 (H.B. 2299), § 1.01, eff. Jan. 1, 2017. Amended by Acts 2017, 85th Leg., ch. 1017 (H.B. 1507), § 3, eff. Sept. 1, 2017.

Section 4(d) of Acts 2017, 85th Leg., ch. 1017 (H.B. 1507) provides:

"(d) Articles 42A.701(f–1) and (f–2), Code of Criminal Procedure, as added by this Act, apply only to a discharge from community supervision that occurs on or after January 1, 2018. A discharge from community supervision that occurs before January 1, 2018, is governed by the law in effect on the date the discharge occurs, and the former law is continued in effect for that purpose."

Art. 42A.702. Time Credits for Completion of Certain Conditions of Community Supervision

(a) This article applies only to a defendant who:

(1) is granted community supervision, including deferred adjudication community supervision, for an offense punishable as a state jail felony or a felony of the third degree, other than an offense:

(A) included as a "reportable conviction or adjudication" under Article 62.001(5);

(B) involving family violence as defined by Section 71.004, Family Code;

(C) under Section 20.03 or 28.02, Penal Code; or

(D) under Chapter 49, Penal Code;

(2) is not delinquent in paying required costs, fines, or fees; and

(3) has fully satisfied any order to pay restitution to a victim.

(b) A defendant described by Subsection (a) is entitled to receive any combination of time credits toward the completion of the defendant's period of community supervision in accordance with this article if the court ordered the defendant as a condition of community supervision to:

(1) make a payment described by Subsection (c);

(2) complete a treatment or rehabilitation program described by Subsection (d); or

(3) earn a diploma, certificate, or degree described by Subsection (e).

(c) A defendant is entitled to time credits toward the completion of the defendant's period of community supervision for the full payment of court costs, fines, attorney's fees, and restitution as follows:

(1) court costs: 15 days;

(2) fines: 30 days;

(3) attorney's fees: 30 days; and

(4) restitution: 60 days.

(d) A defendant is entitled to time credits toward the completion of the defendant's period of community supervision for the successful completion of treatment or rehabilitation programs as follows:

(1) parenting class or parental responsibility program: 30 days;

(2) anger management program: 30 days;

(3) life skills training program: 30 days;

(4) vocational, technical, or career education or training program: 60 days; and

(5) alcohol or substance abuse counseling or treatment: 90 days.

(e) A defendant is entitled to time credits toward the completion of the defendant's period of community supervision for earning the following diplomas, certificates, or degrees:

(1) a high school diploma or high school equivalency certificate: 90 days; and

(2) an associate's degree: 120 days.

(f) A defendant's supervision officer shall notify the court if one or more time credits under this article, cumulated with the amount of the original community supervision period the defendant has completed, allow or require the court to conduct a review of the defendant's community supervision under Article 42A.701. On receipt of the notice from the supervision officer, the court shall conduct the review of the defendant's community supervision to determine if the defendant is eligible for a reduction or termination of community supervision under Article 42A.701, taking into account any time credits to which the defendant is entitled under this article in determining if the defendant has completed, as applicable:

(1) the lesser of one-third of the original community supervision period or two years of community supervision; or

(2) the greater of one-half of the original community supervision period or two years of community supervision.

(g) A court may order that some or all of the time credits to which a defendant is entitled under this article be forfeited if, before the expiration of the original period or a reduced period of community supervision, the court:

(1) after a hearing under Article 42A.751(d), finds that a defendant violated one or more conditions of community supervision; and

(2) modifies or continues the defendant's period of community supervision under Article 42A.752 or revokes the defendant's community supervision under Article 42A.755.

Added by Acts 2015, 84th Leg., ch. 770 (H.B. 2299), § 1.01, eff. Jan. 1, 2017.

SUBCHAPTER P. REVOCATION AND OTHER SANCTIONS

Art. 42A.751. Violation of Conditions of Community Supervision; Detention and Hearing

(a) At any time during the period of community supervision, the judge may issue a warrant for a violation of any condition of community supervision and cause a defendant convicted under Section 43.02, Penal Code, Chapter 481, Health and Safety Code, or Sections 485.031 through 485.035, Health and Safety Code, or placed on deferred adjudication community supervision after being charged with one of those offenses, to be subject to:

(1) the control measures of Section 81.083, Health and Safety Code; and

(2) the court-ordered-management provisions of Subchapter G, Chapter 81, Health and Safety Code.

(b) At any time during the period of community supervision, the judge may issue a warrant for a violation of any condition of community supervision and cause the defendant to be arrested. Any supervision officer, police officer, or other officer with the power of arrest may arrest the defendant with or without a warrant on the order of the judge to be noted on the docket of the court. Subject to Subsection (c), a defendant arrested under this subsection may be detained in the county jail or other appropriate place of confinement until the defendant can be taken before the judge for a determination regarding the alleged violation. The arresting officer shall immediately report the arrest and detention to the judge.

(c) Without any unnecessary delay, but not later than 48 hours after the defendant is arrested, the arresting officer or the person with custody of the defendant shall take the defendant before the judge who ordered the arrest for the alleged violation of a condition of community supervision or, if the judge is unavailable, before a magistrate of the county in which the defendant was arrested. The judge or magistrate shall perform all appropriate duties and may exercise all appropriate powers as provided by Article 15.17 with respect to an arrest for a new offense, except that only the judge who ordered the arrest for the alleged violation may authorize the defendant's release on bail. The defendant may be taken before the judge or magistrate under this subsection by means of an electronic broadcast system as provided by and subject to the requirements of Article 15.17.

(d) If the defendant has not been released on bail as permitted under Subsection (c), on motion by the defendant, the judge who ordered the arrest for the alleged violation of a condition of community supervision shall cause the defendant to be brought before the judge for a hearing on the alleged violation within 20 days of the date the motion is filed. After a hearing without a jury, the judge may continue, extend, modify, or revoke the community supervision.

(e) A judge may revoke without a hearing the community supervision of a defendant who is imprisoned in a penal institution if the defendant in writing before a court of record or a notary public in the jurisdiction where the defendant is imprisoned:

(1) waives the defendant's right to a hearing and to counsel;

(2) affirms that the defendant has nothing to say as to why sentence should not be pronounced against the defendant; and

(3) requests the judge to revoke community supervision and to pronounce sentence.

(f) In a felony case, the state may amend the motion to revoke community supervision at any time before the seventh day before the date of the revocation hearing, after which time the motion may not be amended except for good cause shown. The state may not amend the motion after the commencement of taking evidence at the revocation hearing.

(g) The judge may continue the revocation hearing for good cause shown by either the defendant or the state.

(h) The court may not revoke the community supervision of a defendant if, at the revocation hearing, the court finds that the only evidence supporting the alleged violation of a condition of community supervision is the uncorroborated results of a polygraph examination.

(i) In a revocation hearing at which it is alleged only that the defendant violated the conditions of community supervision by failing to pay community supervision fees or court costs or by failing to pay the costs of legal services as described by Article 42A.301(11), the state must prove by a preponderance of the evidence that the defendant was able to pay and did not pay as ordered by the judge.

(j) The court may order a community supervision and corrections department to obtain information pertaining to the factors listed under Article 42.037(h) and include that information in the presentence report required under Article 42A.252(a) or a separate report, as the court directs.

(k) A defendant has a right to counsel at a hearing under this article. The court shall appoint counsel for an indigent defendant in accordance with the procedures adopted under Article 26.04.

(*l*) A court retains jurisdiction to hold a hearing under Subsection (d) and to revoke, continue, or modify community supervision, regardless of whether the period of community supervision imposed on the defendant has expired, if before the expiration of the supervision period:

(1) the attorney representing the state files a motion to revoke, continue, or modify community supervision; and

(2) a capias is issued for the arrest of the defendant.

Added by Acts 2015, 84th Leg., ch. 770 (H.B. 2299), § 1.01, eff. Jan. 1, 2017. Amended by Acts 2017, 85th Leg., ch. 324 (S.B. 1488), §§ 23.014(a), 23.021(a), eff. Sept. 1, 2017.

Art. 42A.752. Continuation or Modification of Community Supervision After Violation

(a) If after a hearing under Article 42A.751(d) a judge continues or modifies community supervision after determining that the defendant violated a condition of community supervision, the judge may impose any other conditions the judge determines are appropriate, including:

(1) a requirement that the defendant perform community service for a number of hours specified by the court under Article 42A.304, or an increase in the number of hours that the defendant has previously been required to perform under that article in an amount not to exceed double the number of hours permitted by that article;

(2) an extension of the period of community supervision, in the manner described by Article 42A.753;

(3) an increase in the defendant's fine, in the manner described by Subsection (b); or

(4) the placement of the defendant in a substance abuse felony punishment program operated under Section 493.009, Government Code, if:

(A) the defendant is convicted of a felony other than:

(i) a felony under Section 21.11, 22.011, or 22.021, Penal Code; or

(ii) criminal attempt of a felony under Section 21.11, 22.011, or 22.021, Penal Code; and

(B) the judge makes an affirmative finding that:

(i) drug or alcohol abuse significantly contributed to the commission of the offense or violation of a condition of community supervision, as applicable; and

(ii) the defendant is a suitable candidate for treatment, as determined by the suitability criteria established by the Texas Board of Criminal Justice under Section 493.009(b), Government Code.

(b) A judge may impose a sanction on a defendant described by Subsection (a)(3) by increasing the fine imposed on the defendant. The original fine imposed on the defendant and an increase in the fine imposed under this subsection may not exceed the maximum fine for the offense for which the defendant was sentenced. The judge shall deposit money received from an increase in the defendant's fine under this subsection in the special fund of the county treasury to be used for the same purposes for which state aid may be used under Chapter 76, Government Code.

(c) If the judge imposes a sanction under Subsection (a)(4), the judge shall also impose a condition requiring the defendant on successful completion of the program to participate in a drug or alcohol abuse continuum of care treatment plan.

Added by Acts 2015, 84th Leg., ch. 770 (H.B. 2299), § 1.01, eff. Jan. 1, 2017.

Art. 42A.753. Extension of Community Supervision After Violation

(a) On a showing of good cause, the judge may extend a period of community supervision under Article 42A.752(a)(2) as frequently as the judge determines is necessary, but the period of community supervision in a first, second, or third degree felony case may not exceed 10 years and, except as otherwise provided by Subsection (b), the period of community supervision in a misdemeanor case may not exceed three years.

(b) The judge may extend the period of community supervision in a misdemeanor case for any period the judge determines is necessary, not to exceed an additional two years beyond the three-year limit provided by Subsection (a), if:

(1) the defendant fails to pay a previously assessed fine, cost, or restitution; and

(2) the judge determines that extending the supervision period increases the likelihood that the defendant will fully pay the fine, cost, or restitution.

(c) A court may extend a period of community supervision under Article 42A.752(a)(2):

(1) at any time during the supervision period; or

(2) before the first anniversary of the date the supervision period ends, if a motion for revocation of community supervision is filed before the date the supervision period ends. (Code Crim. Proc., Art. 42.12, Sec. 22(c).)

Added by Acts 2015, 84th Leg., ch. 770 (H.B. 2299), § 1.01, eff. Jan. 1, 2017.

Art. 42A.754. Authority to Revoke Community Supervision

Only the court in which the defendant was tried may revoke the defendant's community supervision

unless the judge has transferred jurisdiction of the case to another court under Article 42A.151.

Added by Acts 2015, 84th Leg., ch. 770 (H.B. 2299), § 1.01, eff. Jan. 1, 2017.

Art. 42A.755. Revocation of Community Supervision

(a) If community supervision is revoked after a hearing under Article 42A.751(d), the judge may:

(1) proceed to dispose of the case as if there had been no community supervision; or

(2) if the judge determines that the best interests of society and the defendant would be served by a shorter term of confinement, reduce the term of confinement originally assessed to any term of confinement not less than the minimum prescribed for the offense of which the defendant was convicted.

(b) The judge shall enter in the judgment in the case the amount of restitution owed by the defendant on the date of revocation.

(c) Except as otherwise provided by Subsection (d), no part of the period that the defendant is on community supervision may be considered as any part of the term that the defendant is sentenced to serve.

(d) On revocation, the judge shall credit to the defendant time served as a condition of community supervision in a substance abuse felony punishment facility operated by the Texas Department of Criminal Justice under Section 493.009, Government Code, or other court-ordered residential program or facility, but only if the defendant successfully completes the treatment program in that facility.

(e) The right of the defendant to appeal for a review of the conviction and punishment, as provided by law, shall be accorded the defendant at the time the defendant is placed on community supervision. When the defendant is notified that the defendant's community supervision is revoked for a violation of the conditions of community supervision and the defendant is called on to serve a sentence in a jail or in the Texas Department of Criminal Justice, the defendant may appeal the revocation.

Added by Acts 2015, 84th Leg., ch. 770 (H.B. 2299), § 1.01, eff. Jan. 1, 2017.

Art. 42A.756. Due Diligence Defense

For the purposes of a hearing under Article 42A.751(d), it is an affirmative defense to revocation for an alleged violation based on a failure to report to a supervision officer as directed or to remain within a specified place that no supervision officer, peace officer, or other officer with the power of arrest under a warrant issued by a judge for that alleged violation contacted or attempted to contact the defendant in person at the defendant's last known residence address or last known employment address, as reflected in the files of the department serving the county in which the order of deferred adjudication community supervision was entered.

Added by Acts 2015, 84th Leg., ch. 770 (H.B. 2299), § 1.01, eff. Jan. 1, 2017.

Art. 42A.757.　Extension of Community Supervision for Certain Sex Offenders

(a) If a defendant is placed on deferred adjudication community supervision after being convicted of an offense under Section 21.11, 22.011, or 22.021, Penal Code, at any time during the period of community supervision, the judge may extend the period of community supervision as provided by this article.

(b) At a hearing at which the defendant is provided the same rights as are provided to a defendant at a hearing under Article 42A.751(d), the judge may extend the defendant's supervision period for a period not to exceed 10 additional years if the judge determines that:

(1) the defendant has not sufficiently demonstrated a commitment to avoid future criminal behavior; and

(2) the release of the defendant from supervision would endanger the public.

(c) A judge may extend a period of community supervision under this article only once.

(d) A judge may extend a period of community supervision for a defendant under both Article 42A.752(a)(2) and this article.

(e) The prohibition in Article 42A.753(a) against a period of community supervision in a felony case exceeding 10 years does not apply to a defendant for whom community supervision is increased under this article or under both Article 42A.752(a)(2) and this article.

Added by Acts 2015, 84th Leg., ch. 770 (H.B. 2299), § 1.01, eff. Jan. 1, 2017.

CHAPTER 43.　EXECUTION OF JUDGMENT

Art. 43.01.　Discharging judgment for fine

(a) When the sentence against an individual defendant is for fine and costs, he shall be discharged from the same:

(1) when the amount thereof has been fully paid;

(2) when remitted by the proper authority;

(3) when he has remained in custody for the time required by law to satisfy the amount thereof; or

(4) when the defendant has discharged the amount of fines and costs in any other manner permitted by this code.

(b) When the sentence against a defendant corporation or association is for fine and costs, it shall be discharged from same:

(1) when the amount thereof has been fully paid;

(2) when the execution against the corporation or association has been fully satisfied; or

(3) when the judgment has been fully satisfied in any other manner.

Acts 1965, 59th Leg., vol. 2, p. 317, ch. 722. Amended by Acts 1973, 63rd Leg., p. 974, ch. 399, § 2(A), eff. Jan. 1, 1974; Acts 1993, 73rd Leg., ch. 900, § 5.04, eff. Sept. 1, 1993.

Art. 43.015. Definitions

In this chapter:

(1) "Capias" means a writ that is:

(A) issued by a court having jurisdiction of a case after judgment and sentence; and

(B) directed "To any peace officer of the State of Texas" and commanding the officer to arrest a person convicted of an offense and bring the arrested person before that court immediately or on a day or at a term stated in the writ.

(2) "Capias pro fine" means a writ that is:

(A) issued by a court having jurisdiction of a case after judgment and sentence for unpaid fines and costs; and

(B) directed "To any peace officer of the State of Texas" and commanding the officer to arrest a person convicted of an offense and bring the arrested person before that court immediately.

Added by Acts 2007, 80th Leg., ch. 1263, § 7, eff. Sept. 1, 2007.

Art. 43.02. Payable in money

All recognizances, bail bonds, and undertakings of any kind, whereby a party becomes bound to pay money to the State, and all fines and forfeitures of a pecuniary character, shall be collected in the lawful money of the United States only.

Acts 1965, 59th Leg., vol. 2, p. 317, ch. 722.

Art. 43.021. Capias or Capias Pro Fine in Electronic Form

A capias or capias pro fine may be issued in electronic form.

Added by Acts 2007, 80th Leg., ch. 1263, § 8, eff. Sept. 1, 2007.

Art. 43.03. Payment of fine

(a) If a defendant is sentenced to pay a fine or costs or both and the defendant defaults in payment, the court after a hearing under Subsection (d) of this article may order the defendant confined in jail until discharged as provided by law, may order the defendant to discharge the fines and costs in any other manner provided by Article 43.09 of this code, or may waive payment of the fines and costs as provided by Article 43.091. A certified copy of the judgment, sentence, and order is sufficient to authorize confinement under this subsection.

(b) A term of confinement for default in payment of fine or costs or both may not exceed the maximum term of confinement authorized for the offense for which the defendant was sentenced to pay the fine or costs or both. If a court orders a term of confinement for default in payment of fines or costs under this article at a time during which a defendant is serving another term of confinement for default or is serving a term of confinement for conviction of an offense, the term of confinement for default runs concurrently with the other term of confinement, unless the court orders the terms to run consecutively under Article 42.08 of this code.

(c) If a defendant is sentenced both to confinement and to pay a fine or costs or both, and he defaults in payment of either, a term of confinement for the default, when combined with the term of confinement already assessed, may not exceed the maximum term of confinement authorized for the offense for which the defendant was sentenced.

(d) A court may not order a defendant confined under Subsection (a) of this article unless the court at a hearing makes a written determination that:

(1) the defendant is not indigent and has failed to make a good faith effort to discharge the fines and costs; or

(2) the defendant is indigent and:

(A) has failed to make a good faith effort to discharge the fines and costs under Article 43.09(f); and

(B) could have discharged the fines and costs under Article 43.09 without experiencing any undue hardship.

(e) This article does not apply to a court governed by Chapter 45.

(f) For purposes of a hearing described by Subsection (d), a defendant may be brought before the court in person or by means of an electronic broadcast system through which an image of the defendant is presented to the court. For purposes of this subsection, "electronic broadcast system" means a two-way electronic communication of image and sound between the defendant and the court and includes secure Internet videoconferencing.

Acts 1965, 59th Leg., vol. 2, p. 317, ch. 722. Amended by Acts 1971, 62nd Leg., p. 2990, ch. 987, § 2, eff. June 15, 1971; Acts 1973, 63rd Leg., p. 974, ch. 399, § 2(A), eff. Jan. 1, 1974; Acts 1993, 73rd Leg., ch. 900, § 5.04, eff. Sept. 1, 1993; Acts 2001, 77th Leg., ch. 1111, § 1, eff. Sept. 1, 2001; Acts 2007, 80th Leg., ch. 1263, § 9, eff. Sept. 1, 2007; Acts 2009, 81st Leg., ch. 474, § 1, eff. Sept. 1, 2009.

Art. 43.04. If Defendant is Absent

When a judgment and sentence have been rendered against a defendant in the defendant's absence, the court may order a capias issued for the defendant's arrest. The sheriff shall execute the capias by bringing the defendant before the court or by placing the defendant in jail until the defendant can be brought before the court.

Acts 1965, 59th Leg., vol. 2, p. 317, ch. 722. Amended by Acts 1971, 62nd Leg., p. 2990, ch. 987, § 3, eff. June 15, 1971; Acts 2007, 80th Leg., ch. 1263, § 10, eff. Sept. 1, 2007.

Art. 43.05. Capias Pro Fine Shall Recite

(a) A capias pro fine issued for the arrest and commitment of a defendant convicted of a misdemeanor or felony, or found in contempt, the penalty for which includes a fine, shall recite the judgment and sentence and command a peace officer to immediately bring the defendant before the court.

Text of (a–1), as added by Acts 2017, 85th Leg., ch. 977 (H.B. 351), § 6

(a–1) Before a court may issue a capias pro fine for the defendant's failure to satisfy the judgment according to its terms:

(1) the court must provide by regular mail to the defendant notice that includes:

(A) a statement that the defendant has failed to satisfy the judgment according to its terms; and

(B) a date and time when the court will hold a hearing on the defendant's failure to satisfy the judgment according to its terms; and

(2) either:

(A) the defendant fails to appear at the hearing; or

(B) based on evidence presented at the hearing, the court determines that the capias pro fine should be issued.

Text of (a–1), as added by Acts 2017, 85th Leg., ch. 1127 (S.B. 1913), § 5

(a–1) A court may not issue a capias pro fine for the defendant's failure to satisfy the judgment according to its terms unless the court holds a hearing on the defendant's ability to satisfy the judgment and:

(1) the defendant fails to appear at the hearing; or

(2) based on evidence presented at the hearing, the court determines that the capias pro fine should be issued.

(a–2) The court shall recall a capias pro fine if, before the capias pro fine is executed:

(1) the defendant voluntarily appears to resolve the amount owed; and

(2) the amount owed is resolved in any manner authorized by this code.

(b) A capias pro fine authorizes a peace officer to place the defendant in jail until the business day following the date of the defendant's arrest if the defendant cannot be brought before the court immediately.

Text of (c), as added by Acts 2015, 84th Leg., ch. 1171 (S.B. 873), § 1

(c) If the court that issued the capias pro fine is unavailable, the arresting officer may, in lieu of placing the defendant in jail, take the defendant to:

(1) another court in the same county with jurisdiction over Class A and Class B misdemeanors or a county criminal law magistrate court in the same county, if the court that issued the capias pro fine was a county court or a statutory county court with Class A and Class B misdemeanor jurisdiction; or

(2) another court in the same county with jurisdiction over felony cases or a county criminal law magistrate court in the same county, if the court that issued the capias pro fine was a district court with felony jurisdiction.

Text of (c), as added by Acts 2015, 84th Leg., ch. 1182 (S.B. 1139), § 9.01

(c) If the court that issued the capias pro fine is unavailable, the arresting officer may take the defendant to one of the following locations in lieu of placing the defendant in jail:

(1) if the court that issued the capias pro fine was a county court or a statutory county court with Class A and Class B misdemeanor jurisdiction, to another court in the same county with concurrent jurisdiction over Class A and Class B misdemeanors or to a county criminal law magistrate in the same county; or

(2) if the court that issued the capias pro fine was a district court with felony jurisdiction, to another court in the same county with concurrent jurisdiction over felony cases or to a county criminal law magistrate in the same county.

Acts 1965, 59th Leg., vol. 2, p. 317, ch. 722. Amended by Acts 1971, 62nd Leg., p. 2990, ch. 987, § 4, eff. June 15, 1971; Acts 2007, 80th Leg., ch. 1263, § 11, eff. Sept. 1, 2007; Acts 2015, 84th Leg., ch. 1171 (S.B. 873), § 1, eff. Sept. 1, 2015; Acts 2015, 84th Leg., ch. 1182 (S.B. 1139), § 9.01, eff. Sept. 1, 2015; Acts 2017, 85th Leg., ch. 977 (H.B. 351), § 6, eff. Sept. 1, 2017; Acts 2017, 85th Leg., ch. 1127 (S.B. 1913), § 5, eff. Sept. 1, 2017.

Section 34 of Acts 2017, 85th Leg., ch. 977 (H.B. 351) provides:

"The change in law made by this Act to Articles 43.05 and 45.045, Code of Criminal Procedure, applies only to a capias pro fine issued on or after the effective date [Sept. 1, 2017] of this Act. A capias pro fine issued before the effective date of this Act is governed by the law in effect on the date the capias pro fine was issued, and the former law is continued in effect for that purpose."

Section 30 of Acts 2017, 85th Leg., ch. 1127 (S.B. 1913) provides:

"The change in law made by this Act to Articles 43.05 and 45.045, Code of Criminal Procedure, applies only to a capias pro fine issued on or after the effective date [Sept. 1, 2017] of this Act. A capias pro fine issued before the effective date of this Act is governed by the law in effect on the date the capias pro fine was issued, and the former law is continued in effect for that purpose."

Art. 43.06. Capias or Capias Pro Fine May Issue to Any County

A capias or capias pro fine may be issued to any county in the State, and shall be executed and returned as in other cases, but no bail shall be taken in such cases.

Acts 1965, 59th Leg., vol. 2, p. 317, ch. 722. Amended by Acts 2007, 80th Leg., ch. 1263, § 12, eff. Sept. 1, 2007.

Art. 43.07. Execution for Fine and Costs

In each case of pecuniary fine, an execution may issue for the fine and costs, though a capias pro fine was issued for the defendant; and a capias pro fine may issue for the defendant though an execution was issued against the defendant's property. The execution shall be collected and returned as in civil actions. When the execution has been collected, the defendant shall be at once discharged; and whenever the fine and costs have been legally discharged in any way, the execution shall be returned satisfied.

Acts 1965, 59th Leg., vol. 2, p. 317, ch. 722. Amended by Acts 2007, 80th Leg., ch. 1263, § 13, eff. Sept. 1, 2007.

Art. 43.08. Further enforcement of judgment

When a defendant has been committed to jail in default of the fine and costs adjudged against him, the further enforcement of such judgment and sentence shall be in accordance with the provisions of this Code.

Acts 1965, 59th Leg., vol. 2, p. 317, ch. 722.

Art. 43.09. Fine discharged

(a) When a defendant is convicted of a misdemeanor and the defendant's punishment is assessed at a pecuniary fine or is confined in a jail after conviction of a felony for which a fine is imposed, if the defendant is unable to pay the fine and costs adjudged against the defendant, the defendant may for such time as will satisfy the judgment be put to work in the county jail industries program, in the workhouse, or on the county farm, or public improvements and maintenance projects of the county or a political subdivision located in whole or in part in the county, as provided in Article 43.10; or if there is no such county jail industries program, workhouse, farm, or improvements and maintenance projects, the defendant shall be confined in jail for a sufficient length of time to discharge the full amount of fine and costs adjudged against the defendant; rating such confinement at $100 for each day and rating such labor at $100 for each day; provided, however, that the defendant may pay the pecuniary fine assessed against the defendant at any time while the defendant is serving at work in the county jail industries program, in the workhouse, or on the county farm, or on the public improvements and maintenance projects of the county or a political subdivision located in whole or in part in the county, or while the defendant is serving the defendant's jail sentence, and in such instances the defendant is entitled to the credit earned under this subsection during the time that the defendant has served and the defendant shall only be required to pay the balance of the pecuniary fine assessed against the defendant. A defendant who performs labor under this article during a day in which the defendant is confined is entitled to both the credit for confinement and the credit for labor provided by this article.

(b) In its discretion, the court may order that for each day's confinement served by a defendant under this article, the defendant receive credit toward payment of the pecuniary fine and credit toward payment of costs adjudged against the defendant. Additionally, the court may order that the defendant receive credit under this article for each day's confinement served by the defendant as punishment for the offense.

(c) In its discretion, the court may order that a defendant serving concurrent, but not consecutive, sentences for two or more misdemeanors may, for each day served, receive credit toward the satisfaction of costs and fines imposed for each separate offense.

(d) Notwithstanding any other provision of this article, in its discretion, the court or the sheriff of the county may grant an additional two days credit for each day served to any inmate participating in an approved work program under this article or a rehabilitation, restitution, or education program.

(e) A court in a county that operates an electronic monitoring program or contracts with a private vendor to operate an electronic monitoring program under Section 351.904, Local Government Code, or that is served by a community supervision and corrections department that operates an electronic monitoring program approved by the community justice assistance division of the Texas Department of Criminal Justice, may require a defendant who is unable to pay a fine or costs to discharge all or part of the fine or costs by participating in the program. A defendant who participates in an electronic monitoring program under this subsection discharges fines and costs in the same manner as if the defendant were confined in county jail.

(f) A court may require a defendant who is unable to pay a fine or costs to discharge all or part of the fine or costs by performing community service.

(g) In the court's order requiring a defendant to perform community service under Subsection (f), the court must specify:

(1) the number of hours of community service the defendant is required to perform;

(2) whether the community supervision and corrections department or a court-related services office will perform the administrative duties required by the placement of the defendant in the community service program; and

(3) the date by which the defendant must submit to the court documentation verifying the defendant's completion of the community service.

Text of (h), as amended by Acts 2017,
85th Leg., ch. 977 (H.B. 351), § 7

(h) The court may order the defendant to perform community service under Subsection (f):

(1) by attending:

(A) a work and job skills training program;

(B) a preparatory class for the high school equivalency examination administered under Section 7.111, Education Code;

(C) an alcohol or drug abuse program;

(D) a rehabilitation program;

(E) a counseling program, including a self-improvement program;

(F) a mentoring program; or

(G) any similar activity; or

(2) for:

(A) a governmental entity;

(B) a nonprofit organization or another organization that provides services to the general public that

enhance social welfare and the general well-being of the community, as determined by the court; or

(C) an educational institution.

Text of (h), as amended by Acts 2017, 85th
Leg., ch. 1127 (S.B. 1913), § 6

(h) The court may order the defendant to perform community service under Subsection (f):

(1) by attending a work and job skills training program, preparatory class for the high school equivalency examination administered under Section 7.111, Education Code, or similar activity; or

(2) for:

(A) a governmental entity;

(B) a nonprofit organization or another organization that provides services to the general public that enhance social welfare and the general well-being of the community, as determined by the court; or

(C) an educational institution.

(h–1) An entity that accepts a defendant under Subsection (f) to perform community service must agree to supervise, either on-site or remotely, the defendant in the performance of the defendant's community service and report on the defendant's community service to the district probation department or court-related services office.

(i) The court may require bail of a defendant to ensure the defendant's faithful performance of community service under Subsection (f) of this article and may attach conditions to the bail as it determines are proper.

(j) A court may not order a defendant to perform more than 16 hours per week of community service under Subsection (f) unless the court determines that requiring the defendant to perform additional hours does not impose an undue hardship on the defendant or the defendant's dependents.

(k) A defendant is considered to have discharged $100 of fines or costs for each eight hours of community service performed under Subsection (f) of this article.

(*l*) A sheriff, employee of a sheriff's department, county commissioner, county employee, county judge, an employee of a community corrections and supervision department, restitution center, or officer or employee of a political subdivision other than a county or an entity that accepts a defendant under this article to perform community service is not liable for damages arising from an act or failure to act in connection with manual labor performed by an inmate or community service performed by a defendant under this article if the act or failure to act:

(1) was performed pursuant to confinement or other court order; and

(2) was not intentional, wilfully or wantonly negligent, or performed with conscious indifference or reckless disregard for the safety of others.

(m) Repealed by Acts 2007, 80th Leg., ch. 1263, § 22.

(n) This article does not apply to a court governed by Chapter 45.

Acts 1965, 59th Leg., vol. 2, p. 317, ch. 722. Amended by Acts 1981, 67th Leg., p. 360, ch. 143, § 1, eff. May 14, 1981; Acts 1987, 70th Leg., ch. 347, § 1, eff. Sept. 1, 1987; Acts 1989, 71st Leg., ch. 785, § 4.13, eff. Sept. 1, 1989; Acts 1989, 71st Leg., ch. 753, § 1, eff. Sept. 1, 1989; Acts 1989, 71st Leg., ch. 1040, § 3, eff. Aug. 28, 1989; Acts 1989, 71st Leg., ch. 1040, § 4, eff. Aug. 28, 1989; Acts 1991, 72nd Leg., ch. 16, § 4.06, eff. Aug. 26, 1991; Acts 1991, 72nd Leg., ch. 900, § 1, eff. Aug. 26, 1991; Acts 1993, 73rd Leg., ch. 578, § 2, eff. June 11, 1993; Acts 1993, 73rd Leg., ch. 578, § 2, eff. June 11, 1993; Acts 1993, 73rd Leg., ch. 414, § 1, eff. June 6, 1993A; Acts 1993, 73rd Leg., ch. 900, § 5.04, eff. Sept. 1, 1993; Acts 1999, 76th Leg., ch. 1545, § 3, eff. Sept. 1, 1999; Acts 2007, 80th Leg., ch. 1263, §§ 14, 22, eff. Sept. 1, 2007; Acts 2009, 81st Leg., ch. 854, § 2, eff. June 19, 2009; Acts 2017, 85th Leg., ch. 977 (H.B. 351), § 7, eff. Sept. 1, 2017; Acts 2017, 85th Leg., ch. 1127 (S.B. 1913), § 6, eff. Sept. 1, 2017.

Without reference to the amendment of subsec. (l) by Acts 1993, 73rd Leg., ch. 578, § 2, subsec. (l) was deleted by Acts 1993, 73rd Leg., ch. 900, § 5.04.

Section 33 of Acts 2017, 85th Leg., ch. 977 (H.B. 351) provides:

"The changes in law made by this Act to Articles 42.15, 43.09, 43.091, 45.014, 45.041, 45.046, 45.049, and 45.0491, Code of Criminal Procedure, and Articles 45.0492, Code of Criminal Procedure, as added by Chapter 227 (H.B. 350), Acts of the 82nd Legislature, Regular Session, 2011, and 45.0492, Code of Criminal Procedure, as added by Chapter 777 (H.B. 1964), Acts of the 82nd Legislature, Regular Session, 2011, apply to a sentencing proceeding that commences before, on, or after the effective date [Sept. 1, 2017] of this Act."

Section 29 of Acts 2017, 85th Leg., ch. 1127 (S.B. 1913) provides:

"The changes in law made by this Act to Articles 42.15, 43.09, 43.091, 45.014, 45.041, 45.046, 45.049, and 45.0491, Code of Criminal Procedure, and Articles 45.0492, Code of Criminal Procedure, as added by Chapter 227 (H.B. 350), Acts of the 82nd Legislature, Regular Session, 2011, and 45.0492, Code of Criminal Procedure, as added by Chapter 777 (H.B. 1964), Acts of the 82nd Legislature, Regular Session, 2011, apply to a sentencing proceeding that commences before, on, or after the effective date [Sept. 1, 2017] of this Act."

Art. 43.091. Waiver of payment of fines and costs for certain defendants and for children

A court may waive payment of all or part of a fine or costs imposed on a defendant if the court determines that:

(1) the defendant is indigent or does not have sufficient resources or income to pay all or part of the fine or costs or was, at the time the offense was committed, a child as defined by Article 45.058(h); and

(2) each alternative method of discharging the fine or cost under Article 43.09 or 42.15 would impose an undue hardship on the defendant.

Added by Acts 2001, 77th Leg., ch. 1111, § 2, eff. Sept. 1, 2001. Amended by Acts 2007, 80th Leg., ch. 1263, § 15, eff. Sept. 1, 2007; Acts 2013, 83rd Leg., ch. 1320 (S.B. 395), § 2, eff. Sept. 1, 2013; Acts 2013, 83rd Leg., ch. 1407 (S.B. 393), § 2, eff. Sept. 1, 2013; Acts 2017, 85th Leg., ch. 977 (H.B. 351), § 8, eff. Sept. 1, 2017; Acts 2017, 85th Leg., ch. 1127 (S.B. 1913), § 7, eff. Sept. 1, 2017.

Section 33 of Acts 2017, 85th Leg., ch. 977 (H.B. 351) provides:

"The changes in law made by this Act to Articles 42.15, 43.09, 43.091, 45.014, 45.041, 45.046, 45.049, and 45.0491, Code of Criminal Procedure, and Articles 45.0492, Code of Criminal Procedure, as added by Chapter 227 (H.B. 350), Acts of the 82nd Legislature, Regular Session, 2011, and 45.0492, Code of Criminal Procedure, as added by Chapter 777 (H.B. 1964), Acts of the 82nd Legislature, Regular Session, 2011, apply to a sentencing proceeding that commences before, on, or after the effective date [Sept. 1, 2017] of this Act."

Section 29 of Acts 2017, 85th Leg., ch. 1127 (S.B. 1913) provides:

"The changes in law made by this Act to Articles 42.15, 43.09, 43.091, 45.014, 45.041, 45.046, 45.049, and 45.0491, Code of Criminal Procedure, and Articles 45.0492, Code of Criminal Procedure, as added by Chapter 227 (H.B. 350), Acts of the 82nd Legislature, Regular Session, 2011, and 45.0492, Code of Criminal Procedure, as added by Chapter 777 (H.B. 1964), Acts of the 82nd Legislature, Regular Session, 2011, apply to a sentencing proceeding that commences before, on, or after the effective date [Sept. 1, 2017] of this Act."

Art. 43.10. Manual Labor

Where the punishment assessed in a conviction for a misdemeanor is confinement in jail for more than one day or is only a pecuniary fine and the defendant is unable to pay the fine and costs adjudged against the defendant, or where the defendant is sentenced to jail for a felony or is confined in jail after conviction of a felony, the defendant shall be required to work in the county jail industries program or shall be required to do manual labor in accordance with the following rules and regulations:

1. Each commissioners court may provide for the erection of a workhouse and the establishment of a county farm in connection therewith for the purpose of utilizing the labor of defendants under this article;

2. Such farms and workhouses shall be under the control and management of the sheriff, and the sheriff

may adopt such rules and regulations not inconsistent with the rules and regulations of the Commission on Jail Standards and with the laws as the sheriff deems necessary;

3. Such overseers and guards may be employed by the sheriff under the authority of the commissioners court as may be necessary to prevent escapes and to enforce such labor, and they shall be paid out of the county treasury such compensation as the commissioners court may prescribe;

4. They shall be put to labor upon public works and maintenance projects, including public works and maintenance projects for a political subdivision located in whole or in part in the county. They may be put to labor upon maintenance projects for a cemetery that the commissioners court uses public funds, county employees, or county equipment to maintain under Section 713.028, Health and Safety Code. They may also be put to labor providing maintenance and related services to a nonprofit organization that qualifies for a tax exemption under Section 501(a), Internal Revenue Code of 1986, as an organization described by Section 501(c)(3) of that code, and is organized as a nonprofit corporation under the Texas Non–Profit Corporation Act (Article 1396–1.01 et seq., Vernon's Texas Civil Statutes), provided that, at the sheriff's request, the commissioners court determines that the nonprofit organization provides a public service to the county or to a political subdivision located in whole or in part in the county;

5. A defendant who from age, disease, or other physical or mental disability is unable to do manual labor shall not be required to work. The defendant's inability to do manual labor may be determined by a physician appointed for that purpose by the county judge or the commissioners court, who shall be paid for such service such compensation as said court may allow; and

6. For each day of manual labor, in addition to any other credits allowed by law, a defendant is entitled to have one day deducted from each sentence the defendant is serving.

Amended by Acts 1981, 67th Leg., p. 2647, ch. 708, § 1, eff. Aug. 31, 1981; Acts 1989, 71st Leg., ch. 753, § 2, eff. Sept. 1, 1989; Acts 1989, 71st Leg., ch. 785, § 4.14, eff. Sept. 1, 1989; Acts 1991, 72nd Leg., ch. 900, § 2, eff. Aug. 26, 1991; Acts 1991, 72nd Leg., 2nd C.S., ch. 10, § 14.09, eff. Oct. 1, 1991; Acts 1993, 73rd Leg., ch. 578, § 3, eff. June 11, 1993; Acts 1993, 73rd Leg., ch. 900, § 5.04, eff. Sept. 1, 1993; Acts 1995, 74th Leg., ch. 76, § 3.19, eff. Sept. 1, 1995; Acts 1995, 74th Leg., ch. 321, § 3.015, eff. Sept. 1, 1995; Acts 2005, 79th Leg., ch. 853, § 2, eff. Sept. 1, 2005; Acts 2005, 79th Leg., ch. 1187, § 1, eff. June 18, 2005; Acts 2009, 81st Leg., ch. 854, § 3, eff. June 19, 2009.

Art. 43.101. Voluntary work

(a) A defendant who is confined in county jail before trial, after conviction of a misdemeanor, or after conviction of a felony or revocation of community supervision, parole, or mandatory supervision and awaiting transfer to the Texas Department of Criminal Justice may volunteer to participate in any work program operated by the sheriff that uses the labor of convicted defendants.

(b) The sheriff may accept a defendant as a volunteer under Subsection (a) if the defendant is not awaiting trial for an offense involving violence or is not awaiting transfer to the Texas Department of Criminal Justice after conviction of a felony involving violence, and if the sheriff determines that the inmate has not engaged previously in violent conduct and does not pose a security risk to the general public if allowed to participate in the work program.

(c) A defendant participating in a work program under this section is not an employee for the purposes of Chapter 501 or 504, Labor Code.

(d) For each day of volunteer work, in addition to any other credits allowed by law, the court or sheriff may deduct one day from each sentence imposed on the defendant in relation to the offense or violation of the terms of release for which the defendant was confined in county jail.

Added by Acts 1989, 71st Leg., ch. 753, § 3, eff. Sept. 1, 1989. Amended by Acts 1993, 73rd Leg., ch. 86, § 1, eff. Aug. 30, 1993; Acts 1993, 73rd Leg., ch. 900, § 5.04, eff. Sept. 1, 1993; Acts 1995, 74th Leg., ch. 76, § 3.20, eff. Sept. 1, 1995; Acts 2009, 81st Leg., ch. 87, § 25.032, eff. Sept. 1, 2009; Acts 2009, 81st Leg., ch. 854, § 4, eff. June 19, 2009.

Art. 43.11. Authority for confinement

When, by the judgment and sentence of the court, a defendant is to be confined in jail, a certified copy of such judgment and sentence shall be sufficient authority for the sheriff to place such defendant in jail.

Acts 1965, 59th Leg., vol. 2, p. 317, ch. 722. Amended by Acts 1993, 73rd Leg., ch. 900, § 5.04, eff. Sept. 1, 1993.

Art. 43.12. Repealed by Acts 2007, 80th Leg., ch. 1263, § 22, eff. Sept. 1, 2007

Art. 43.13. Discharge of Defendant

(a) A defendant who has remained in jail the length of time required by the judgment and sentence shall be discharged. The sheriff shall return the copy of the judgment and sentence, or the capias under which the defendant was imprisoned, to the proper court, stating how it was executed.

(b) A defendant convicted of a misdemeanor and sentenced to a term of confinement of more than 30 days discharges the defendant's sentence at any time between the hours of 6 a.m. and 7 p.m. on the day of discharge.

Acts 1965, 59th Leg., vol. 2, p. 317, ch. 722. Amended by Acts 1997, 75th Leg., ch. 714, § 1, eff. Sept. 1, 1997.

Art. 43.131. Immunities

(a) An individual listed in Subsection (c) of this article and the governmental entity that the individual serves as an officer or employee are not liable for damages arising from an act or failure to act by the individual or governmental entity in connection with a community service program or work program established under this chapter if the act or failure to act:

(1) was performed pursuant to a court order or was otherwise performed in an official capacity; and

(2) was not performed with conscious indifference for the safety of others.

(b) Chapter 101, Civil Practice and Remedies Code, does not apply to a claim based on an act or a failure to act of an individual listed in Subsection (c) of this article or a governmental entity the officer serves as an officer or employee if the act or failure to act is in connection with a program described by Subsection (a) of this article.

(c) This article applies to:

(1) a director or employee of a community supervision and corrections department or a community corrections facility;

(2) a sheriff or employee of a sheriff's department;

(3) a county judge, county commissioner, or county employee;

(4) an officer or employee of a state agency; or

(5) an officer or employee of a political subdivision other than a county.

Added by Acts 1993, 73rd Leg., ch. 900, § 5.04, eff. Sept. 1, 1993.

Art. 43.14. Execution of Convict: Confidential Information

(a) Whenever the sentence of death is pronounced against a convict, the sentence shall be executed at any time after the hour of 6 p.m. on the day set for the execution, by intravenous injection of a substance or substances in a lethal quantity sufficient to cause death and until such convict is dead, such execution procedure to be determined and supervised by the director of the correctional institutions division of the Texas Department of Criminal Justice.

(b) The name, address, and other identifying information of the following is confidential and excepted from disclosure under Section 552.021, Government Code:

(1) any person who participates in an execution procedure described by Subsection (a), including a person who uses, supplies, or administers a substance during the execution; and

(2) any person or entity that manufactures, transports, tests, procures, compounds, prescribes, dispenses, or provides a substance or supplies used in an execution.

Acts 1965, 59th Leg., vol. 2, p. 317, ch. 722. Amended by Acts 1977, 65th Leg., p. 287, ch. 138, § 1, eff. Aug. 29, 1977; Acts 1981, 67th Leg., p. 812, ch. 291, § 120, eff. Sept. 1, 1981; Acts 1991, 72nd Leg., ch. 652, § 11, eff. Sept. 1, 1991; Acts 1995, 74th Leg., ch. 319, § 3, eff. Sept. 1, 1995; Acts 2009, 81st Leg., ch. 87, § 25.033, eff. Sept. 1, 2009; Acts 2015, 84th Leg., ch. 209 (S.B. 1697), § 2, eff. Sept. 1, 2015.

Section 3 of Acts 2015, 84th Leg., ch. 209 (S.B. 1697) provides:

"The changes in law made by this Act apply only to a request for information that is received by a governmental body or an officer for public information on or after the effective date [Sept. 1, 2015] of this Act. A request for information that was received before the effective date of this Act is governed by the law in effect on the date the request was received, and the former law is continued in effect for that purpose."

Art. 43.141. Scheduling of execution date; withdrawal; modification

(a) If an initial application under Article 11.071 is timely filed, the convicting court may not set an execution date before:

(1) the court of criminal appeals denies relief; or

(2) if the case is filed and set for submission, the court of criminal appeals issues a mandate.

(b) If an original application is not timely filed under Article 11.071 or good cause is not shown for an untimely application under Article 11.071, the convicting court may set an execution date.

(b–1) Not later than the second business day after the date on which the convicting court enters an order setting the execution date, a copy of the order must be sent by first-class mail, e-mail, or fax to:

(1) the attorney who represented the condemned person in the most recently concluded stage of a state or federal postconviction proceeding; and

(2) the office of capital writs established under Subchapter B, Chapter 78, Government Code [1].

(b–2) The exclusive remedy for a failure to comply with Subsection (b–1) is the resetting of the execution date under this article.

(c) An execution date may not be earlier than the 91st day after the date the convicting court enters the order setting the execution date.

(d) The convicting court may modify or withdraw the order of the court setting a date for execution in a death penalty case if the court determines that additional proceedings are necessary on:

(1) a subsequent or untimely application for a writ of habeas corpus filed under Article 11.071; or

(2) a motion for forensic testing of DNA evidence submitted under Chapter 64.

(e) If the convicting court withdraws the order of the court setting the execution date, the court shall recall the warrant of execution. If the court modifies the order of the court setting the execution date, the court shall recall the previous warrant of execution, and the clerk of the court shall issue a new warrant.

Added by Acts 1995, 74th Leg., ch. 319, § 4, eff. Sept. 1, 1995. Amended by Acts 2003, 78th Leg., ch. 13, § 6, eff. Sept. 1, 2003. Amended by Acts 2015, 84th Leg., ch. 951 (S.B. 1071), § 1, eff. Sept. 1, 2015.

[1] V.T.C.A, Government Code § 78.051 et seq.

Section 3(a) of Acts 2015, 84th Leg., ch. 951 (S.B. 1071) provides:

"(a) Article 43.141, Code of Criminal Procedure, as amended by this Act, applies only to an order entered on or after the effective date [Sept. 1, 2015] of this Act. An order entered before the effective date of this Act is governed by the law in effect on the date the order was entered, and the former law is continued in effect for that purpose."

Art. 43.15. Warrant of Execution

(a) Whenever any person is sentenced to death, the clerk of the court in which the sentence is pronounced shall, not later than the 10th day after the court enters its order setting the date for execution, issue a warrant under the seal of the court for the execution of the sentence of death, which shall recite the fact of conviction, setting forth specifically the offense, the judgment of the court, and the time fixed for the execution, and which shall be directed to the director of the correctional institutions division of the Texas Department of Criminal Justice at Huntsville, Texas, commanding the director to proceed, at the time and place named in the order of execution, to carry the same into execution, as provided in Article 43.14, and shall deliver such warrant to the sheriff of the county in which such judgment of conviction was had, to be delivered by the sheriff to the director, together with the condemned person if the person has not previously been so delivered.

(b) At the time the warrant is issued under Subsection (a), the clerk of the court shall send a copy of the warrant to:

(1) the attorney who represented the condemned person in the most recently concluded stage of a state or federal postconviction proceeding;

(2) the attorney representing the state; and

(3) the office of capital writs established under Subchapter B, Chapter 78, Government Code.[1]

Acts 1965, 59th Leg., vol. 2, p. 317, ch. 722. Amended by Acts 1981, 67th Leg., p. 812, ch. 291, § 121, eff. Sept. 1, 1981; Acts 2015, 84th Leg., ch. 951 (S.B. 1071), § 2, eff. Sept. 1, 2015.

[1] V.T.C.A, Government Code § 78.051 et seq.

Section 3(b) of Acts 2015, 84th Leg., ch. 951 (S.B. 1071) provides:

"(b) Article 43.15, Code of Criminal Procedure, as amended by this Act, applies only to a warrant issued on or after the effective date [Sept. 1, 2015] of this Act. A warrant issued before the effective date of this Act is governed by the law in effect on the date the warrant was issued, and the former law is continued in effect for that purpose."

Art. 43.16. Taken to department of corrections

Immediately upon the receipt of such warrant, the sheriff shall transport such condemned person to the Director of the Department of Corrections, if he has not already been so delivered, and shall deliver him and the warrant aforesaid into the hands of the Director of the Department of Corrections and shall take from the Director of the Department of Corrections his receipt for such person and such warrant, which receipt the sheriff shall return to the office of the clerk of the court where the judgment of death was rendered. For his services, the sheriff shall be entitled to the same compensation as is now allowed by law to sheriffs for removing or conveying prisoners under the provisions of Section 4 of Article 1029 or 1030 of the Code of Criminal Procedure of 1925, as amended.

Acts 1965, 59th Leg., vol. 2, p. 317, ch. 722. Amended by Acts 1981, 67th Leg., p. 812, ch. 291, § 122, eff. Sept. 1, 1981.

Art. 43.17. Visitors

Upon the receipt of such condemned person by the Director of the Department of Corrections, the condemned person shall be confined therein until the time for his or her execution arrives, and while so confined, all persons outside of said prison shall be denied access to him or her, except his or her physician, lawyer, and clergyperson, who shall be admitted to see him or her when necessary for his or her health or for the transaction of business, and the relatives and friends of the condemned person, who shall be admitted to see and converse with him or her at all proper times, under such reasonable rules and regulations as may be made by the Board of Directors of the Department of Corrections.

Acts 1965, 59th Leg., vol. 2, p. 317, ch. 722. Amended by Acts 1979, 66th Leg., p. 1181; ch. 572, § 1, eff. Aug. 27, 1979.

Art. 43.18.   Executioner

The director of the Texas Department of Criminal Justice shall designate an executioner to carry out the death penalty provided by law.

Acts 1965, 59th Leg., vol. 2, p. 317, ch. 722. Amended by Acts 1975, 64th Leg., p. 911, ch. 341, § 6, eff. June 19, 1975; Acts 1977, 65th Leg., p. 288, ch. 138, § 2, eff. Aug. 29, 1977; Acts 2009, 81st Leg., ch. 87, § 25.034, eff. Sept. 1, 2009.

Art. 43.19.   Place of execution

The execution shall take place at a location designated by the Texas Department of Criminal Justice in a room arranged for that purpose.

Acts 1965, 59th Leg., vol. 2, p. 317, ch. 722. Amended by Acts 1985, 69th Leg., ch. 250, § 1, eff. Aug. 26, 1985; Acts 2009, 81st Leg., ch. 87, § 25.035, eff. Sept. 1, 2009.

Art. 43.20.   Present at execution

The following persons may be present at the execution: the executioner, and such persons as may be necessary to assist him in conducting the execution; the Board of Directors of the Department of Corrections, two physicians, including the prison physician, the spiritual advisor of the condemned, the chaplains of the Department of Corrections, the county judge and sheriff of the county in which the Department of Corrections is situated, and any of the relatives or friends of the condemned person that he may request, not exceeding five in number, shall be admitted. No convict shall be permitted by the prison authorities to witness the execution.

Acts 1965, 59th Leg., vol. 2, p. 317, ch. 722.

Art. 43.21.   Escape after sentence

If the condemned escape after sentence and before his delivery to the Director of the Department of Corrections, and be not rearrested until after the time fixed for execution, any person may arrest and commit him to the jail of the county in which he was sentenced; and thereupon the court by whom the condemned was sentenced; either in term-time or vacation, on notice of such arrest being given by the sheriff, shall again appoint a time for the execution, not less than thirty days from such appointment, which appointment shall be by the clerk of said court

immediately certified to the Director of the Department of Corrections and such clerk shall place such certificate in the hands of the sheriff, who shall deliver the same, together with the warrant aforesaid and the condemned person to the Director of the Department of Corrections, who shall receipt to the sheriff for the same and proceed at the appointed time to carry the sentence of death into execution as hereinabove provided.

Acts 1965, 59th Leg., vol. 2, p. 317, ch. 722.

Art. 43.22.   Escape from Department of Corrections

If the condemned person escapes after his delivery to the Director of the Department of Corrections, and is not retaken before the time appointed for his execution, any person may arrest and commit him to the Director of the Department of Corrections whereupon the Director of the Department of Corrections shall certify the fact of his escape and recapture to the court in which sentence was passed; and the court, either in term-time or vacation, shall again appoint a time for the execution which shall not be less than thirty days from the date of such appointment; and thereupon the clerk of such court shall certify such appointment to the Director of the Department of Corrections, who shall proceed at the time so appointed to execute the condemned, as hereinabove provided. The sheriff or other officer or other person performing any service under this and the preceding Article shall receive the same compensation as is provided for similar services under the provisions of Articles 1029 or 1030 of the Code of Criminal Procedure of 1925, as amended. If for any reason execution is delayed beyond the date set, then the court which originally sentenced the defendant may set a later date for execution.

Acts 1965, 59th Leg., vol. 2, p. 317, ch. 722.

Art. 43.23.   Return of Director

When the execution of sentence is suspended or respited to another date, same shall be noted on the warrant and on the arrival of such date, the Director of the Department of Corrections shall proceed with such execution; and in case of death of any condemned person before the time for his execution arrives, or if he should be pardoned or his sentence commuted by the Governor, no execution shall be had; but in such cases, as well as when the sentence is executed, the Director of the Department of Corrections shall return the warrant and certificate with a statement of any such act and his proceedings endorsed thereon, together with a statement showing what disposition was made of the dead body of the convict, to the clerk of the court in which the sentence was passed, who shall record the warrant and return in the minutes of the court.

Acts 1965, 59th Leg., vol. 2, p. 317, ch. 722.

Art. 43.24. Treatment of condemned

No torture, or ill treatment, or unnecessary pain, shall be inflicted upon a prisoner to be executed under the sentence of the law.

Acts 1965, 59th Leg., vol. 2, p. 317, ch. 722.

Art. 43.25. Body of convict

The body of a convict who has been legally executed shall be embalmed immediately and so directed by the Director of the Department of Corrections. If the body is not demanded or requested by a relative or bona fide friend within forty-eight hours after execution then it shall be delivered to the Anatomical Board of the State of Texas, if requested by the Board. If the body is requested by a relative, bona fide friend, or the Anatomical Board of the State of Texas, such recipient shall pay a fee of not to exceed twenty-five dollars to the mortician for his services in embalming the body for which the mortician shall issue to the recipient a written receipt. When such receipt is delivered to the Director of the Department of Corrections, the body of the deceased shall be delivered to the party named in the receipt or his authorized agent. If the body is not delivered to a relative, bona fide friend, or the Anatomical Board of the State of Texas, the Director of the Department of Corrections shall cause the body to be decently buried, and the fee for embalming shall be paid by the county in which the indictment which resulted in conviction was found.

Acts 1965, 59th Leg., vol. 2, p. 317, ch. 722.

Art. 43.26. Preventing rescue

The sheriff may, when he supposes there will be a necessity, order such number of citizens of his county, or request any military or militia company, to aid in preventing the rescue of a prisoner.

Acts 1965, 59th Leg., vol. 2, p. 317, ch. 722.

Art. 43.27. Expired

APPEAL AND WRIT OF ERROR

CHAPTER 44. APPEAL AND WRIT OF ERROR

Art. 44.01. Appeal by state

(a) The state is entitled to appeal an order of a court in a criminal case if the order:

(1) dismisses an indictment, information, or complaint or any portion of an indictment, information, or complaint;

(2) arrests or modifies a judgment;

(3) grants a new trial;

APPEAL AND WRIT OF ERROR

(4) sustains a claim of former jeopardy;

(5) grants a motion to suppress evidence, a confession, or an admission, if jeopardy has not attached in the case and if the prosecuting attorney certifies to the trial court that the appeal is not taken for the purpose of delay and that the evidence, confession, or admission is of substantial importance in the case; or

(6) is issued under Chapter 64.

(b) The state is entitled to appeal a sentence in a case on the ground that the sentence is illegal.

(c) The state is entitled to appeal a ruling on a question of law if the defendant is convicted in the case and appeals the judgment.

(d) The prosecuting attorney may not make an appeal under Subsection (a) or (b) of this article later than the 20th day after the date on which the order, ruling, or sentence to be appealed is entered by the court.

(e) The state is entitled to a stay in the proceedings pending the disposition of an appeal under Subsection (a) or (b) of this article.

(f) The court of appeals shall give precedence in its docket to an appeal filed under Subsection (a) or (b) of this article. The state shall pay all costs of appeal under Subsection (a) or (b) of this article, other than the cost of attorney's fees for the defendant.

(g) If the state appeals pursuant to this article and the defendant is on bail, he shall be permitted to remain at large on the existing bail. If the defendant is in custody, he is entitled to reasonable bail, as provided by law, unless the appeal is from an order which would terminate the prosecution, in which event the defendant is entitled to release on personal bond.

(h) The Texas Rules of Appellate Procedure apply to a petition by the state to the Court of Criminal Appeals for review of a decision of a court of appeals in a criminal case.

(i) In this article, "prosecuting attorney" means the county attorney, district attorney, or criminal district attorney who has the primary responsibility of prosecuting cases in the court hearing the case and does not include an assistant prosecuting attorney.

(j) Nothing in this article is to interfere with the defendant's right to appeal under the procedures of Article 44.02. The defendant's right to appeal under Article 44.02 may be prosecuted by the defendant where the punishment assessed is in accordance with Subchapter C, Chapter 42A, as well as any other punishment assessed in compliance with Article 44.02.

(k) The state is entitled to appeal an order granting relief to an applicant for a writ of habeas corpus under Article 11.072.

(l) The state is entitled to appeal an order entered under:

(1) Subchapter G or H, Chapter 62, that exempts a person from complying with the requirements of Chapter 62; and

(2) Subchapter I, Chapter 62, that terminates a person's obligation to register under Chapter 62.

Acts 1965, 59th Leg., vol. 2, p. 317, ch. 722. Amended by Acts 1981, 67th Leg., p. 812, ch. 291, § 123, eff. Sept. 1, 1981; Acts 1987, 70th Leg., ch. 382, § 1, Nov. 3, 1987; Acts 2003, 78th Leg., ch. 13, § 7, eff. Sept. 1, 2003. Acts 2003, 78th Leg., ch. 587, § 2, eff. June 20, 2003; Acts 2005, 79th Leg., ch. 1008, § 1.04, eff. Sept. 1, 2005; Acts 2007, 80th Leg., ch. 1038, § 2, eff. Sept. 1, 2007; Acts 2015, 84th Leg., ch. 770 (H.B. 2299), § 2.18, eff. Jan. 1, 2017.

Art. 44.02. Defendant may appeal

A defendant in any criminal action has the right of appeal under the rules hereinafter prescribed, provided, however, before the defendant who has been convicted upon either his plea of guilty or plea of nolo contendere before the court and the court, upon the election of the defendant, assesses punishment and the punishment does not exceed the punishment recommended by the prosecutor and agreed to by the defendant and his attorney may prosecute his appeal, he must have permission of the trial court, except on those matters which have been raised by written motion filed prior to trial. This article in no way affects appeals pursuant to Article 44.17 of this chapter.

Acts 1965, 59th Leg., vol. 2, p. 317, ch. 722. Amended by Acts 1977, 65th Leg., p. 940, ch. 351, § 1, eff. Aug. 29, 1977.

Partial Repeal by Texas Rules of Appellate Procedure

By orders of the Texas Court of Criminal Appeals dated December 18, 1985, effective September 1, 1986, and April 10, 1986, effective September 1, 1986, adopting the Texas Rules of Appellate Procedure, pursuant to Acts 1985, 69th Leg., ch. 685, § 4, the court repealed the proviso in this article. See, now, Vernon's Ann.Texas Rules App.Proc., rule 25.2.

Art. 44.03. Repealed by Texas Rules of Appellate Procedure effective September 1, 1986 (Acts 1985, 69th Leg., ch. 685, § 4)

Art. 44.04. Bond pending appeal

(a) Pending the determination of any motion for new trial or the appeal from any misdemeanor conviction, the defendant is entitled to be released on reasonable bail.

(b) The defendant may not be released on bail pending the appeal from any felony conviction where the punishment equals or exceeds 10 years confinement or where the defendant has been convicted of an offense listed under Article 42A.054(a), but shall immediately be placed in custody and the bail discharged.

(c) Pending the appeal from any felony conviction other than a conviction described in Subsection (b) of this section, the trial court may deny bail and commit the defendant to custody if there then exists good cause to believe that the defendant would not appear when his conviction became final or is likely to commit another offense while on bail, permit the defendant to remain at large on the existing bail, or, if not then on bail, admit him to reasonable bail until his conviction becomes final. The court may impose reasonable conditions on bail pending the finality of his conviction. On a finding by the court on a preponderance of the evidence of a violation of a condition, the court may revoke the bail.

(d) After conviction, either pending determination of any motion for new trial or pending final determination of the appeal, the court in which trial was had may increase or decrease the amount of bail, as it deems proper, either upon its own motion or the motion of the State or of the defendant.

(e) Any bail entered into after conviction and the sureties on the bail must be approved by the court where trial was had. Bail is sufficient if it substantially meets the requirements of this code and may be entered into and given at any term of court.

(f) In no event shall the defendant and the sureties on his bond be released from their liability on such bond or bonds until the defendant is placed in the custody of the sheriff.

(g) The right of appeal to the Court of Appeals of this state is expressly accorded the defendant for a review of any judgment or order made hereunder, and said appeal shall be given preference by the appellate court.

(h) If a conviction is reversed by a decision of a Court of Appeals, the defendant, if in custody, is entitled to release on reasonable bail, regardless of the length of term of imprisonment, pending final determination of an appeal by the state or the defendant on a motion for discretionary review. If the defendant requests bail before a petition for discretionary review has been filed, the Court of Appeals shall determine the amount of bail. If the defendant requests bail after a petition for discretionary review has been filed, the Court of Criminal Appeals shall determine the amount of bail. The sureties on the bail must be approved by the court where the trial was had. The defendant's right to release under this subsection attaches immediately on the issuance of the Court of Appeals' final ruling as defined by Tex.Cr. App.R. 209(c).

(i) Notwithstanding any other law, pending the determination of a defendant's motion for new trial or the defendant's appeal from a misdemeanor conviction, the defendant is entitled to be released after completion of a sentence of confinement imposed for the conviction. The trial court may require the defendant to give a personal bond but may not, either instead of or in addition to the personal bond, require:

(1) any condition of the personal bond;

(2) another type of bail bond; or

(3) a surety or other security.

Acts 1965, 59th Leg., vol. 2, p. 317, ch. 722. Amended by Acts 1977, 65th Leg., p. 636, ch. 234, § 1, eff. Aug. 29, 1977; Acts 1981, 67th Leg., p. 707, ch. 268, § 17, eff. Sept. 1, 1981; Acts 1981, 67th Leg., p. 813, ch. 291, § 125, eff. Sept. 1, 1981; Acts 1983, 68th Leg., p. 1104, ch. 249, § 2, eff. Aug. 29, 1983; Acts 1983, 68th Leg., p. 2416, ch. 425, § 26, eff. Aug. 29, 1983; Acts 1985, 69th Leg., ch. 968, § 1, eff. Aug. 26, 1985; Acts 1991, 72nd Leg., ch. 14, § 284(50), eff. Sept. 1, 1991; Acts 1999, 76th Leg., ch. 546, § 1, eff. Sept. 1, 1999; Acts 2003, 78th Leg., ch. 942, § 3, eff. June 20, 2003; Acts 2015, 84th Leg., ch. 770 (H.B. 2299), § 2.19, eff. Jan. 1, 2017; Acts 2017, 85th Leg., ch. 1011 (H.B. 1442), § 1, eff. Sept. 1, 2017.

Art. 44.041. Conditions in Lieu of Bond

(a) If a defendant is confined in county jail pending appeal and is eligible for release on bond pending appeal but is financially unable to make bond, the court may release the defendant without bond pending the conclusion of the appeal only if the court determines that release under this article is reasonable given the circumstances of the defendant's offense and the sentence imposed.

(b) A court that releases a defendant under this article must require the defendant to participate in a program under Article 42.033, 42.034, 42.035, or 42.036 during the pendency of the appeal. A defendant required to participate in a program may receive credit toward completion of the defendant's sentence while participating in the program in the same manner and to the same extent provided by Article 42.033, 42.034, 42.035, or 42.036, as applicable.

Added by Acts 1989, 71st Leg., ch. 785, § 4.15, eff. Sept. 1, 1989. Amended by Acts 2009, 81st Leg., ch. 854, § 5, eff. June 19, 2009.

Arts. 44.05, 44.06.   Repealed by Texas Rules of Appellate Procedure effective September 1, 1986 (Acts 1985, 69th Leg., ch. 685, § 4)

Art. 44.07.   Right of appeal not abridged

The right of appeal, as otherwise provided by law, shall in no wise be abridged by any provision of this Chapter.

Act 1965, 59th Leg., vol. 2, p. 317, ch. 722.

Arts. 44.08, 44.09.   Repealed by Texas Rules of Appellate Procedure effective September 1, 1986 (Acts 1985, 69th Leg., ch. 685, § 4)

Art. 44.10.   Sheriff to report escape

When any such escape occurs, the sheriff who had the prisoner in custody shall immediately report the fact under oath to the district or county attorney of the county in which the conviction was had, who shall forthwith forward such report to the State prosecuting attorney. Such report shall be sufficient evidence of the fact of such escape to authorize the dismissal of the appeal.

Acts 1965, 59th Leg., vol. 2, p. 317, ch. 722.

Art. 44.11.   Repealed by Texas Rules of Appellate Procedure effective September 1, 1986 (Acts 1985, 69th Leg., ch. 685, § 4)

Art. 44.12.   Procedure as to bail pending appeal

The amount of any bail given in any felony or misdemeanor case to perfect an appeal from any court to the Court of Appeals shall be fixed by the court in which the judgment or order appealed from was rendered. The sufficiency of the security thereon shall be tested, and the same proceedings had in case of forfeiture, as in other cases regarding bail.

Acts 1965, 59th Leg., vol. 2, p. 317, ch. 722. Amended by Acts 1981, 67th Leg., p. 815, ch. 291, § 130, eff. Sept. 1, 1981.

Art. 44.13.   Repealed by Acts 1999, 76th Leg., ch. 1545, § 75(a), eff. Sept. 1, 1999

Art. 44.14.   Renumbered as Vernon's Ann.C.C.P. art. 45.0426 by Acts 1999, 76th Leg., ch. 1545, § 42, eff. Sept. 1, 1999

Art. 44.15.   Appellate court may allow new bond

When an appeal is taken from any court of this State, by filing a bond within the time prescribed by law in such cases, and the court to which appeal is taken determines that such bond is defective in form or substance, such appellate court may allow the appellant to amend such bond by filing a new bond, on such terms as the court may prescribe.

Acts 1965, 59th Leg., vol. 2, p. 317, ch. 722.

Art. 44.16.   Appeal bond given within what time

If the defendant is not in custody, a notice of appeal as provided in Article 44.13 shall have no effect whatever until the required appeal bond has been given and approved. The appeal bond shall be given within ten days after the sentence of the court has been rendered, except as provided in Article 27.14 of this code.

Acts 1965, 59th Leg., vol. 2, p. 317, ch. 722. Amended by Acts 1979, 66th Leg., p. 451, ch. 207, § 3, eff. Sept. 1, 1979.

Art. 44.17.   Appeal to county court, how conducted

In all appeals to a county court from justice courts and municipal courts other than municipal courts of record, the trial shall be de novo in the trial in the county court, the same as if the prosecution had been originally commenced in that court. An appeal to the county court from a municipal court of record may be based only on errors reflected in the record.

Acts 1965, 59th Leg., vol. 2, p. 317, ch. 722. Amended by Acts 1987, 70th Leg., ch. 641, § 3, eff. Sept. 1, 1987.

Art. 44.18.   Original papers sent up

In appeals from justice and corporation courts, all the original papers in the case, together with the appeal bond, if any, and together, with a certified transcript of all the proceedings had in the case before such court shall be delivered without delay to the clerk of the court to which the appeal was taken, who shall file the same and docket the case.

Acts 1965, 59th Leg., vol. 2, p. 317, ch. 722.

Art. 44.181.   Defect in complaint

(a) A court conducting a trial de novo based on an appeal from a justice or municipal court may dismiss the case because of a defect in the complaint only if the defendant objected to the defect before the trial began in the justice or municipal court.

(b) The attorney representing the state may move to amend a defective complaint before the trial de novo begins.

Added by Acts 1995, 74th Leg., ch. 478, § 2, eff. Sept. 1, 1995. Amended by Acts 1999, 76th Leg., ch. 1545, § 4, eff. Sept. 1, 1999.

Art. 44.19.   Witnesses not again summoned

In the cases mentioned in the preceding Article, the witnesses who have been summoned or attached to appear in the case before the court below, shall appear before the court to which the appeal is taken without further process. In case of their failure to do so, the same proceedings may be had as if they had been originally summoned or attached to appear before such court.

Acts 1965, 59th Leg., vol. 2, p. 317, ch. 722.

Art. 44.20.   Rules governing appeal bonds

The rules governing the taking and forfeiture of bail shall govern appeal bonds, and the forfeiture and collection of such appeal bonds shall be in the court to which such appeal is taken.

Acts 1965, 59th Leg., vol. 2, p. 317, ch. 722.

Arts. 44.21 to 44.24.   Repealed by Texas Rules of Appellate Procedure effective September 1, 1986 (Acts 1985, 69th Leg., ch. 685, § 4)

Art. 44.25.   Cases remanded

The courts of appeals or the Court of Criminal Appeals may reverse the judgment in a criminal action, as well upon the law as upon the facts.

Acts 1965, 59th Leg., vol. 2, p. 317, ch. 722. Amended by Acts 1981, 67th Leg., p. 817, ch. 291, § 134, eff. Sept. 1, 1981.

Art. 44.251.   Reformation of sentence in capital case

(a) The court of criminal appeals shall reform a sentence of death to a sentence of confinement in the Texas Department of Criminal Justice for life without parole if the court finds that there is legally insufficient evidence to support an affirmative answer to an issue submitted to the jury under Section 2(b), Article 37.071, or Section 2(b), Article 37.072.

(b) The court of criminal appeals shall reform a sentence of death to a sentence of confinement in the

Texas Department of Criminal Justice for life without parole if:

(1) the court finds reversible error that affects the punishment stage of the trial other than a finding of insufficient evidence under Subsection (a); and

(2) within 30 days after the date on which the opinion is handed down, the date the court disposes of a timely request for rehearing, or the date that the United States Supreme Court disposes of a timely filed petition for writ of certiorari, whichever date is later, the prosecuting attorney files a motion requesting that the sentence be reformed to confinement for life without parole.

(c) If the court of criminal appeals finds reversible error that affects the punishment stage of the trial only, as described by Subsection (b) of this article, and the prosecuting attorney does not file a motion for reformation of sentence in the period described by that subsection, the defendant shall receive a new sentencing trial in the manner required by Article 44.29(c) or (d), as applicable.

(d) The court of criminal appeals shall reform a sentence of death imposed under Section 12.42(c)(3), Penal Code, to a sentence of imprisonment in the Texas Department of Criminal Justice for life without parole if the United States Supreme Court:

(1) finds that the imposition of the death penalty under Section 12.42(c)(3), Penal Code, violates the United States Constitution; and

(2) issues an order that is not inconsistent with this article.

Added by Acts 1981, 67th Leg., p. 2673, ch. 725, § 2, eff. Aug. 31, 1981. Amended by Acts 1991, 72nd Leg., ch. 838, § 3, eff. Sept. 1, 1991; Acts 1993, 73rd Leg., ch. 781, § 3, eff. Aug. 30, 1993; Acts 2005, 79th Leg., ch. 787, § 10, eff. Sept. 1, 2005; Acts 2007, 80th Leg., ch. 593, § 3.18, eff. Sept. 1, 2007; Acts 2009, 81st Leg., ch. 87, § 25.036, eff. Sept. 1, 2009.

Art. 44.2511.   Reformation of Sentence in Capital Case for Offense Committed Before September 1, 1991

(a) This article applies to the reformation of a sentence of death in a capital case for an offense committed before September 1, 1991. For purposes of this subsection, an offense is committed before September 1, 1991, if every element of the offense occurred before that date.

(b) The court of criminal appeals shall reform a sentence of death to a sentence of confinement in the Texas Department of Criminal Justice for life if the court finds that there is legally insufficient evidence to support an affirmative answer to an issue submitted to the jury under Section 3(b), Article 37.0711.

(c) The court of criminal appeals shall reform a sentence of death to a sentence of confinement in the Texas Department of Criminal Justice for life if:

(1) the court finds reversible error that affects the punishment stage of the trial other than a finding of insufficient evidence under Subsection (b); and

(2) within 30 days after the date on which the opinion is handed down, the date the court disposes of a timely request for rehearing, or the date that the United States Supreme Court disposes of a timely filed petition for writ of certiorari, whichever date is later, the prosecuting attorney files a motion requesting that the sentence be reformed to confinement for life.

(d) If the court of criminal appeals finds reversible error that affects the punishment stage of the trial only, as described by Subsection (c), and the prosecuting attorney does not file a motion for reformation of sentence in the period described by that subsection, the defendant shall receive a new sentencing trial in the manner required by Article 44.29(c).

Added by Acts 2005, 79th Leg., ch. 787, § 11, eff. Sept. 1, 2005. Amended by Acts 2009, 81st Leg., ch. 87, § 25.037, eff. Sept. 1, 2009.

Arts. 44.26, 44.27. Repealed by Texas Rules of Appellate Procedure effective September 1, 1986 (Acts 1985, 69th Leg., ch. 685, § 4)

Art. 44.28. When misdemeanor is affirmed

In misdemeanor cases where there has been an affirmance, no proceedings need be had after filing the mandate, except to forfeit the bond of the defendant, or to issue a capias for the defendant, or an execution against his property, to enforce the judgment of the court, as if no appeal had been taken.

Acts 1965, 59th Leg., vol. 2, p. 317, ch. 722.

Art. 44.281. Disposition of Fines and Costs When Misdemeanor Affirmed

In misdemeanor cases affirmed on appeal from a municipal court, the fine imposed on appeal and the costs imposed on appeal shall be collected from the defendant, and the fine of the municipal court when collected shall be paid into the municipal treasury.

Acts 1965, 59th Leg., vol. 2, p. 317, ch. 722. Renumbered from Vernon's Ann.C.C.P. art. 45.11 and amended by Acts 1999, 76th Leg., ch. 1545, § 65, eff. Sept. 1, 1999.

Art. 44.2811. Records Relating to Certain Fine–Only Misdemeanors Committed by a Child

Text of article as amended by Acts 2013, 83rd Leg., ch. 1257 (H.B. 528), § 1. See, also, text of Art. 44.2811 as amended by Acts 2013, 83rd Leg., ch. 1319 (S.B. 394), § 1 and Acts 2013, 83rd Leg., ch. 1407 (S.B. 393), § 3.

All records and files and information stored by electronic means or otherwise, from which a record or file could be generated, relating to a criminal case for a fine-only misdemeanor, other than a traffic offense, that is committed by a child and that is appealed are confidential and may not be disclosed to the public except as provided under Article 45.0217(b).

Added by Acts 2011, 82nd Leg., ch. 731 (H.B. 961), § 1, eff. June 17, 2011. Amended by Acts 2013, 83rd Leg., ch. 1257 (H.B. 528), § 1, eff. Jan. 1, 2014.

Art. 44.2811. Records Relating to Children Convicted of or Receiving Deferred Disposition for Fine–Only Misdemeanors

Text of section as amended by Acts 2013, 83rd Leg., ch. 1319 (S.B. 394), § 1 and Acts 2013, 83rd Leg., ch. 1407 (S.B. 393), § 3. See, also, text of Art. 44.2811 as amended by Acts 2013, 83rd Leg., ch. 1257 (H.B. 528), § 1.

(a) This article applies only to a misdemeanor offense punishable by fine only, other than a traffic offense.

(b) All records and files and information stored by electronic means or otherwise, from which a record or file could be generated, relating to a child who is convicted of and has satisfied the judgment for or who has received a dismissal after deferral of disposition for an offense described by Subsection (a) are confidential and may not be disclosed to the public except as provided under Article 45.0217(b).

Added by Acts 2011, 82nd Leg., ch. 731 (H.B. 961), § 1, eff. June 17, 2011. Amended by Acts 2013, 83rd Leg., ch. 1319 (S.B. 394), § 1, eff. Sept. 1, 2013; Acts 2013, 83rd Leg., ch. 1407 (S.B. 393), § 3, eff. Sept. 1, 2013.

Art. 44.2812. Confidential records related to fine–only misdemeanor

(a) Except as provided by Subsection (b) and Article 45.0218(b), following the fifth anniversary of the date of a final conviction of, or of a dismissal after deferral of disposition for, a misdemeanor offense punishable by fine only, all records and files and information stored by electronic means or otherwise, from which a record or file could be generated, that are held or stored by or for an appellate court and relate to the person who was convicted of, or who received a dismissal after deferral of disposition for, the offense are confidential and may not be disclosed to the public.

(b) This article does not apply to:

(1) an opinion issued by an appellate court; or

(2) records, files, and information described by Subsection (a) that relate to an offense that is sexual in nature, as determined by the holder of the records, files, or information.

Added by Acts 2017, 85th Leg., ch. 811 (H.B. 681), § 1, eff. Sept. 1, 2017.

Section 3 of Acts 2017, 85th Leg., ch. 811 (H.B. 681) provides:

"The change in law made by this Act applies to the disclosure of information on or after the effective date [Sept. 1, 2017] of this Act regardless of whether the offense that is the subject of the information was committed before, on, or after the effective date of this Act."

Art. 44.29.   Effect of reversal

(a) Where the court of appeals or the Court of Criminal Appeals awards a new trial to the defendant on the basis of an error in the guilt or innocence stage of the trial or on the basis of errors in both the guilt or innocence stage of the trial and the punishment stage of the trial, the cause shall stand as it would have stood in case the new trial had been granted by the court below.

(b) If the court of appeals or the Court of Criminal Appeals awards a new trial to a defendant other than a defendant convicted of an offense under Section 19.03, Penal Code, only on the basis of an error or errors made in the punishment stage of the trial, the cause shall stand as it would have stood in case the new trial had been granted by the court below, except that the court shall commence the new trial as if a finding of guilt had been returned and proceed to the punishment stage of the trial under Subsection (b), Section 2, Article 37.07, of this code. If the defendant elects, the court shall empanel a jury for the sentencing stage of the trial in the same manner as a jury is empaneled by the court for other trials before the court. At the new trial, the court shall allow both the state and the defendant to introduce evidence to show the circumstances of the offense and other evidence as permitted by Section 3 of Article 37.07 of this code.

(c) If any court sets aside or invalidates the sentence of a defendant convicted of an offense under Section 19.03, Penal Code, and sentenced to death on the basis of any error affecting punishment only, the court shall not set the conviction aside but rather shall commence a new punishment hearing under Article 37.071 or Article 37.0711 of this code, as appropriate, as if a finding of guilt had been returned. The court shall empanel a jury for the sentencing stage of the trial in the same manner as a jury is to be empaneled by the court in other trials before the court for offenses under Section 19.03, Penal Code. At the new punishment hearing, the court shall permit both the state and the defendant to introduce evidence as permitted by Article 37.071 or Article 37.0711 of this code.

(d) If any court sets aside or invalidates the sentence of a defendant convicted of an offense punishable as a capital felony under Section 12.42(c)(3), Penal Code, and sentenced to death on the basis of any error affecting punishment only, the court shall not set the conviction aside but rather shall commence a new punishment hearing under Article 37.072, as if a finding of guilt had been returned. The court shall empanel a jury for the sentencing stage of the trial in the same manner as a jury is to be empaneled by the court in other trials before the court for the offense of which the defendant was convicted. At the new punishment hearing, the court shall permit both the state and the defendant to introduce evidence as permitted by Article 37.072.

Acts 1965, 59th Leg., vol. 2, p. 317, ch. 722. Amended by Acts 1981, 67th Leg., p. 817, ch. 291, § 137, eff. Sept. 1, 1981; Acts 1987, 70th Leg., ch. 179, § 1, eff. Aug. 31, 1987; Acts 1991, 72nd Leg., ch. 838, § 2, eff. Sept. 1, 1991; Acts 1993, 73rd Leg., ch. 781, § 4, eff. Aug. 30, 1993; Acts 2007, 80th Leg., ch. 593, § 3.19, eff. Sept. 1, 2007.

Arts. 44.30 to 44.32.   Repealed by Texas Rules of Appellate Procedure effective September 1, 1986 (Acts 1985, 69th Leg., ch. 685, § 4)

Art. 44.33.   Hearing in appellate court

(a) The Court of Criminal Appeals shall make rules of posttrial and appellate procedure as to the hearing of criminal actions not inconsistent with this Code. After the record is filed in the Court of Appeals or the Court of Criminal Appeals the parties may file such supplemental briefs as they may desire before the case is submitted to the court. Each party, upon filing any such supplemental brief, shall promptly cause true copy thereof to be delivered to the opposing party or to the latter's counsel. In every case at least two counsel for the defendant shall be heard in the Court of Appeals if such be desired by defendant. In every case heard by the Court of Criminal Appeals at least two counsel for the defendant shall be permitted oral argument if desired by the appellant.

(b) Appellant's failure to file his brief in the time prescribed shall not authorize a dismissal of the appeal by the Court of Appeals or the Court of Criminal Appeals, nor shall the Court of Appeals or the Court of Criminal Appeals, for such reason, refuse to consider appellant's case on appeal.

Acts 1965, 59th Leg., vol. 2, p. 317, ch. 722. Amended by Acts 1981, 67th Leg., p. 817, ch. 291, § 139, eff. Sept. 1, 1981.

Partial Repeal by Texas Rules of Appellate Procedure

By order of the Texas Court of Criminal Appeals dated December 18, 1985, effective September 1, 1986, adopting the Texas Rules of Appellate Procedure, pursuant to Acts 1985, 69th Leg., ch. 685, § 4, the court provided that this article was repealed except for the first sentence and subsec. (b). See, now, Rules App.Proc., rules 9.3 to 9.5, 38.1 et seq., 39.1 et seq.

Art. 44.34. Repealed by Texas Rules of Appellate Procedure effective September 1, 1986 (Acts 1985, 69th Leg., ch. 685, § 4)

Art. 44.35. Bail pending habeas corpus appeal

In any habeas corpus proceeding in any court or before any judge in this State where the defendant is remanded to the custody of an officer and an appeal is taken to an appellate court, the defendant shall be allowed bail by the court or judge so remanding the defendant, except in capital cases where the proof is evident. The fact that such defendant is released on bail shall not be grounds for a dismissal of the appeal except in capital cases where the proof is evident.

Acts 1965, 59th Leg., vol. 2, p. 317, ch. 722.

Arts. 44.36 to 44.38. Repealed by Texas Rules of Appellate Procedure effective September 1, 1986 (Acts 1985, 69th Leg., ch. 685, § 4)

Art. 44.39. Appellant detained by other than officer

If the appellant in a case of habeas corpus be detained by any person other than an officer, the sheriff receiving the mandate of the appellate court, shall immediately cause the person so held to be discharged; and the mandate shall be sufficient authority therefor.

Acts 1965, 59th Leg., vol. 2, p. 317, ch. 722. Amended by Acts 1981, 67th Leg., p. 818, ch. 291, § 144, eff. Sept. 1, 1981.

Art. 44.40. Repealed by Texas Rules of Appellate Procedure effective September 1, 1986 (Acts 1985, 69th Leg., ch. 685, § 4)

Art. 44.41. Who shall take bail bond

When, by the judgment of the appellate court upon cases of habeas corpus, the applicant is ordered to give bail, such judgment shall be certified to the officer holding him in custody; and if such officer be the sheriff, the bail bond may be executed before him; if any other officer, he shall take the person detained before some magistrate, who may receive a bail bond, and shall file the same in the proper court of the proper county; and such bond may be forfeited and enforced as provided by law.

Acts 1965, 59th Leg., vol. 2, p. 317, ch. 722. Amended by Acts 1981, 67th Leg., p. 819, ch. 291, § 146, eff. Sept. 1, 1981.

Art. 44.42. Appeal on forfeitures

An appeal may be taken by the defendant from every final judgment rendered upon a personal bond, bail bond or bond taken for the prevention or suppression of offenses, where such judgment is for twenty dollars or more, exclusive of costs, but not otherwise.

Acts 1965, 59th Leg., vol. 2, p. 317, ch. 722.

Art. 44.43. Writ of error

The defendant may also have any such judgment as is mentioned in the preceding Article, and which may have been rendered in courts other than the justice and corporation courts, reviewed upon writ of error.

Acts 1965, 59th Leg., vol. 2, p. 317, ch. 722.

Art. 44.44. Rules in forfeitures

In the cases provided for in the two preceding Articles, the proceeding shall be regulated by the same rules that govern civil actions where an appeal is taken or a writ of error sued out.

Acts 1965, 59th Leg., vol. 2, p. 317, ch. 722.

Art. 44.45. Review by Court of Criminal Appeals

(a) The Court of Criminal Appeals may review decisions of the court of appeals on its own motion. An order for review must be filed before the decision of the court of appeals becomes final as determined by Article 42.045.

(b) The Court of Criminal Appeals may review decisions of the court of appeals upon a petition for review.

(1) The state or a defendant in a case may petition the Court of Criminal Appeals for review of the decision of a court of appeals in that case.

(2) The petition shall be filed with the clerk of the court of appeals which rendered the decision within 30 days after the final ruling of the court of appeals.

(3) The petition for review shall be addressed to "The Court of Criminal Appeals of Texas," and shall state the name of the petitioning party and shall include a statement of the case and authorities and arguments in support of each ground for review.

(4) Upon filing a petition for review, the petitioning party shall cause a true copy to be delivered to the attorney representing the opposing party. The opposing party may file a reply to the petition with the Court of Criminal Appeals within 30 days after receipt of the petition from the petitioning party.

(5) Within 15 days after the filing of a petition for review, the clerk of the court of appeals shall note the filing on the record and forward the petition together with the original record and the opinion of the court of appeals to the Court of Criminal Appeals.

(6) The Court of Criminal Appeals shall either grant the petition and review the case or refuse the petition.

(7) Subsequent to granting the petition for review, the Court of Criminal Appeals may reconsider, set aside the order granting the petition, and refuse the petition as though the petition had never been granted.

(c) The Court of Criminal Appeals may promulgate rules pursuant to this article.

(d) Extensions of time for meeting the limits prescribed in Subdivisions (2) and (4) of Subsection (b) of this article may be granted by the Court of Criminal Appeals or a judge thereof for good cause shown on timely application to the Court of Criminal Appeals.

Added by Acts 1981, 67th Leg., p. 819, ch. 291, § 147, eff. Sept. 1, 1981; Acts 1983, 68th Leg., p. 1103, ch. 249, § 1, eff. Aug. 29, 1983. Amended by Acts 1987, 70th Leg., ch. 167, § 5.02(3), eff. Sept. 1, 1987.

Partial Repeal by Rules of Appellate Procedure

By order of the Texas Court of Criminal Appeals dated December 18, 1985, effective September 1, 1986, adopting the Texas Rules of Appellate Procedure, pursuant to Acts 1985, 69th Leg., ch. 685, § 4, the court provided that the second sentence of subsec. (a), subds. (1) to (7) of subsec. (b), and subsec. (d) only of this article are repealed. See, now, Rules App.Proc., rules 9.1 et seq., 25.2, 26.2, 26.3.

Art. 44.46. Reversal of Conviction on the Basis of Service on Jury by a Disqualified Juror

A conviction in a criminal case may be reversed on appeal on the ground that a juror in the case was absolutely disqualified from service under Article 35.19 of this code only if:

(1) the defendant raises the disqualification before the verdict is entered; or

(2) the disqualification was not discovered or brought to the attention of the trial court until after the verdict was entered and the defendant makes a showing of significant harm by the service of the disqualified juror.

Added by Acts 1993, 73rd Leg., ch. 372, § 1, eff. Sept. 1, 1993.

Art. 44.47. Repealed by Acts 2015, 84th Leg., ch. 74 (S.B. 888), § 4, eff. Sept. 1, 2015

Section 5 of Acts 2015, 84th Leg., ch. 74 (S.B. 888) provides:

"The change in law made by this Act applies only to an order of a juvenile court waiving jurisdiction and transferring a child to criminal court that is issued on or after the effective date [Sept. 1, 2015] of this Act. An order of a juvenile court waiving jurisdiction and transferring a child to criminal court that is issued before the effective date of this Act is governed by the law in effect on the date the order was issued, and the former law is continued in effect for that purpose."

JUSTICE AND MUNICIPAL COURTS

CHAPTER 45. JUSTICE AND MUNICIPAL COURTS

SUBCHAPTER A. GENERAL PROVISIONS

SUBCHAPTER B. PROCEDURES FOR JUSTICE AND MUNICIPAL COURTS

SUBCHAPTER A. GENERAL PROVISIONS

Art. 45.001. Objectives of Chapter

The purpose of this chapter is to establish procedures for processing cases that come within the criminal jurisdiction of the justice courts and municipal courts. This chapter is intended and shall be construed to achieve the following objectives:

(1) to provide fair notice to a person appearing in a criminal proceeding before a justice or municipal court and a meaningful opportunity for that person to be heard;

(2) to ensure appropriate dignity in court procedure without undue formalism;

(3) to promote adherence to rules with sufficient flexibility to serve the ends of justice; and

(4) to process cases without unnecessary expense or delay.

Added by Acts 1999, 76th Leg., ch. 1545, § 6, eff. Sept. 1, 1999.

Art. 45.002. Application of Chapter

Criminal proceedings in the justice and municipal courts shall be conducted in accordance with this chapter, including any other rules of procedure specifically made applicable to those proceedings by this chapter. If this chapter does not provide a rule of procedure governing any aspect of a case, the justice or judge shall apply the other general provisions of this code to the extent necessary to achieve the objectives of this chapter.

Added by Acts 1999, 76th Leg., ch. 1545, § 6, eff. Sept. 1, 1999.

Art. 45.003. Definition for Certain Prosecutions

For purposes of dismissing a charge under Section 502.407, Transportation Code, "day" does not include Saturday, Sunday, or a legal holiday.

Added by Acts 1999, 76th Leg., ch. 1545, § 6, eff. Sept. 1, 1999. Amended by Acts 2013, 83rd Leg., ch. 1291 (H.B. 2305), § 2, eff. March 1, 2015.

Art. 45.01. Repealed by Acts 1999, 76th Leg., ch. 1545, § 75(a), eff. Sept. 1, 1999

SUBCHAPTER B. PROCEDURES FOR JUSTICE AND MUNICIPAL COURTS

Art. 45.011. Rules of Evidence

The rules of evidence that govern the trials of criminal actions in the district court apply to a criminal proceeding in a justice or municipal court.

Acts 1965, 59th Leg., vol. 2, p. 317, ch. 722. Renumbered from Vernon's Ann.C.C.P. art. 45.38 and amended by Acts 1999, 76th Leg., ch. 1545, § 8, eff. Sept. 1, 1999.

Art. 45.012. Electronically Created Records

(a) Notwithstanding any other provision of law, a document that is issued or maintained by a justice or municipal court or a notice or a citation [1] issued by a law enforcement officer may be created by electronic means, including optical imaging, optical disk, digital imaging, or other electronic reproduction technique that does not permit changes, additions, or deletions to the originally created document.

(b) The court may use electronic means to:

(1) produce a document required by law to be written;

(2) record an instrument, paper, or notice that is permitted or required by law to be recorded or filed; or

(3) maintain a docket.

(c) The court shall maintain original documents as provided by law.

(d) An electronically recorded judgment has the same force and effect as a written signed judgment.

(e) A record created by electronic means is an original record or a certification of the original record.

(f) A printed copy of an optical image of the original record printed from an optical disk system is an accurate copy of the original record.

(g) A justice or municipal court shall have a court seal, the impression of which must be attached to all papers issued out of the court except subpoenas, and which must be used to authenticate the official acts of the clerk and of the recorder. A court seal may be created by electronic means, including optical imaging, optical disk, or other electronic reproduction technique that does not permit changes, additions, or deletions to an original document created by the same type of system.

(h) A statutory requirement that a document contain the signature of any person, including a judge, clerk of the court, or defendant, is satisfied if the document contains that signature as captured on an electronic device.

Added by Acts 1995, 74th Leg., ch. 735, § 2, eff. Sept. 1, 1995. Amended by Acts 1999, 76th Leg., ch. 701, § 2, eff. Aug. 30, 1999; Acts 1999, 76th Leg., ch. 1545, § 9, eff. Sept. 1, 1999; Acts 2001, 77th Leg., ch. 1420, § 21.001(12), eff. Sept. 1, 2001.

¹ Acts 1999, 76th Leg., ch. 701, § 2 reads "or citation".

Art. 45.013.   Filing With Clerk by Mail

(a) Notwithstanding any other law, for the purposes of this chapter a document is considered timely filed with the clerk of a court if:

(1) the document is deposited with the United States Postal Service in a first class postage prepaid envelope properly addressed to the clerk on or before the date the document is required to be filed with the clerk; and

(2) the clerk receives the document not later than the 10th day after the date the document is required to be filed with the clerk.

(b) A legible postmark affixed by the United States Postal Service is prima facie evidence of the date the document is deposited with the United States Postal Service.

(c) In this article, "day" does not include Saturday, Sunday, or a legal holiday.

Added by Acts 1999, 76th Leg., ch. 1545, § 10, eff. Sept. 1, 1999.

Art. 45.014.   Warrant of Arrest

(a) When a sworn complaint or affidavit based on probable cause has been filed before the justice or municipal court, the justice or judge may issue a warrant for the arrest of the accused and deliver the same to the proper officer to be executed.

(b) The warrant is sufficient if:

(1) it is issued in the name of "The State of Texas";

(2) it is directed to the proper peace officer or some other person specifically named in the warrant;

(3) it includes a command that the body of the accused be taken, and brought before the authority issuing the warrant, at the time and place stated in the warrant;

(4) it states the name of the person whose arrest is ordered, if known, or if not known, it describes the person as in the complaint;

(5) it states that the person is accused of some offense against the laws of this state, naming the offense; and

(6) it is signed by the justice or judge, naming the office of the justice or judge in the body of the warrant or in connection with the signature of the justice or judge.

(c) Chapter 15 applies to a warrant of arrest issued under this article, except as inconsistent or in conflict with this chapter.

(d) In a county with a population of more than two million that does not have a county attorney, a justice or judge may not issue a warrant under this section for an offense under Section 32.41, Penal Code, unless the district attorney has approved the complaint or affidavit on which the warrant is based.

(e) A justice or judge may not issue an arrest warrant for the defendant's failure to appear at the initial court setting, including failure to appear as required by a citation issued under Article 14.06(b), unless:

(1) the justice or judge provides by telephone or regular mail to the defendant notice that includes:

Text of (e)(1)(A), as added by Acts 2017, 85th Leg., ch. 977 (H.B. 351), § 9

(A) a date and time when the defendant must appear before the justice or judge;

Text of (e)(1)(A), as added by Acts 2017, 85th Leg., ch. 1127 (S.B. 1913), § 8

(A) a date and time, occurring within the 30–day period following the date that notice is provided, when the defendant must appear before the justice or judge;

(B) the name and address of the court with jurisdiction in the case;

(C) information regarding alternatives to the full payment of any fine or costs owed by the defendant, if the defendant is unable to pay that amount; and

(D) an explanation of the consequences if the defendant fails to appear before the justice or judge as required by this article; and

(2) the defendant fails to appear before the justice or judge as required by this article.

(f) A defendant who receives notice under Subsection (e) may request an alternative date or time to appear before the justice or judge if the defendant is unable to appear on the date and time included in the notice.

Text of (g), as added by Acts 2017, 85th Leg., ch. 977 (H.B. 351), § 9

(g) A justice or judge shall recall an arrest warrant for the defendant's failure to appear if, before the arrest warrant is executed:

(1) the defendant voluntarily appears to resolve the arrest warrant; and

(2) the arrest warrant is resolved in any manner authorized by this code.

Text of (g), as added by Acts 2017, 85th Leg., ch. 1127 (S.B. 1913), § 8

(g) A justice or judge shall recall an arrest warrant for the defendant's failure to appear if the defendant voluntarily appears and makes a good faith effort to resolve the arrest warrant before the warrant is executed.

Acts 1965, 59th Leg., vol. 2, p. 317, ch. 722. Renumbered from Vernon's Ann.C.C.P. art. 45.18 and amended by Acts 1999, 76th Leg., ch. 1545, § 11, eff. Sept. 1, 1999. Amended by Acts 2005, 79th Leg., ch. 644, § 1, eff. Sept. 1, 2005; Acts 2017, 85th Leg., ch. 977 (H.B. 351), § 9, eff. Sept. 1, 2017; Acts 2017, 85th Leg., ch. 1127 (S.B. 1913), § 8, eff. Sept. 1, 2017.

Section 33 of Acts 2017, 85th Leg., ch. 977 (H.B. 351) provides:

"The changes in law made by this Act to Articles 42.15, 43.09, 43.091, 45.014, 45.041, 45.046, 45.049, and 45.0491, Code of Criminal Procedure, and Articles 45.0492, Code of Criminal Procedure, as added by Chapter 227 (H.B. 350), Acts of the 82nd Legislature, Regular Session, 2011, and 45.0492, Code of Criminal Procedure, as added by Chapter 777 (H.B. 1964), Acts of the 82nd Legislature, Regular Session, 2011, apply to a sentencing proceeding that commences before, on, or after the effective date [Sept. 1, 2017] of this Act."

Section 29 of Acts 2017, 85th Leg., ch. 1127 (S.B. 1913) provides:

"The changes in law made by this Act to Articles 42.15, 43.09, 43.091, 45.014, 45.041, 45.046, 45.049, and 45.0491, Code of Criminal Procedure, and Articles 45.0492, Code of Criminal Procedure, as added by Chapter 227 (H.B. 350), Acts of the 82nd Legislature, Regular Session, 2011, and 45.0492, Code of Criminal Procedure, as added by Chapter 777 (H.B. 1964), Acts of the 82nd Legislature, Regular Session, 2011, apply to a sentencing proceeding that commences before, on, or after the effective date [Sept. 1, 2017] of this Act."

Art. 45.015. Defendant Placed in Jail

Whenever, by the provisions of this title, the peace officer is authorized to retain a defendant in custody, the peace officer may place the defendant in jail in accordance with this code or other law.

Acts 1965, 59th Leg., vol. 2, p. 317, ch. 722. Renumbered from Vernon's Ann. C.C.P. art. 45.43 and amended by Acts 1999, 76th Leg., ch. 1545, § 12, eff. Sept. 1, 1999.

Art. 45.016. Personal bond; bail bond

(a) The justice or judge may require the defendant to give a personal bond to secure the defendant's appearance in accordance with this code.

(b) The justice or judge may not, either instead of or in addition to the personal bond, require a defendant to give a bail bond unless:

(1) the defendant fails to appear in accordance with this code with respect to the applicable offense; and

(2) the justice or judge determines that:

(A) the defendant has sufficient resources or income to give a bail bond; and

(B) a bail bond is necessary to secure the defendant's appearance in accordance with this code.

Text of (c), as added by Acts 2017, 85th Leg., ch. 977 (H.B. 351), § 10

(c) If a defendant required to give a bail bond under Subsection (b) remains in custody, without giving the bond, for more than 48 hours after the issuance of the applicable order, the justice or judge shall reconsider the requirement for the defendant to give the bond.

Text of (c), as added by Acts 2017, 85th Leg., ch. 1127 (S.B. 1913), § 9

(c) If before the expiration of a 48–hour period following the issuance of the applicable order a defendant described by Subsections (b)(1) and (2) does not give a required bail bond, the justice or judge:

(1) shall reconsider the requirement for the defendant to give the bail bond and presume that the defendant does not have sufficient resources or income to give the bond; and

(2) may require the defendant to give a personal bond.

(d) If the defendant refuses to give a personal bond or, except as provided by Subsection (c), refuses or otherwise fails to give a bail bond, the defendant may be held in custody.

Acts 1965, 59th Leg., vol. 2, p. 317, ch. 722. Renumbered from Vernon's Ann.C.C.P. art. 45.41 and amended by Acts 1999, 76th Leg., ch. 1545, § 13, eff. Sept. 1, 1999. Amended by Acts 2017, 85th Leg., ch. 977 (H.B. 351), § 10, eff. Sept. 1, 2017; Acts 2017, 85th Leg., ch. 1127 (S.B. 1913), § 9, eff. Sept. 1, 2017.

Section 35 of Acts 2017, 85th Leg., ch. 977 (H.B. 351) provides:

"The changes in law made by this Act to Articles 45.016, 45.051, and 45.0511, Code of Criminal Procedure, apply only to a bond executed on or after the effective date [Sept. 1, 2017] of this Act. A bond executed before the effective date of this Act is governed by the law in effect when the bond was executed, and the former law is continued in effect for that purpose."

Section 31 of Acts 2017, 85th Leg., ch. 1127 (S.B. 1913) provides:

"The changes in law made by this Act to Articles 45.016, 45.051, and 45.0511, Code of Criminal Procedure, apply only to a bond executed on or after the effective date [Sept. 1, 2017] of this Act. A bond executed before the effective date of this Act is governed by the law in effect when the bond was executed, and the former law is continued in effect for that purpose."

Art. 45.017. Criminal Docket

(a) The justice or judge of each court, or, if directed by the justice or judge, the clerk of the court, shall keep a docket containing the following information:

(1) the style and file number of each criminal action;

(2) the nature of the offense charged;

(3) the plea offered by the defendant and the date the plea was entered;

(4) the date the warrant, if any, was issued and the return made thereon;

(5) the date the examination or trial was held, and if a trial was held, whether it was by a jury or by the justice or judge;

(6) the verdict of the jury, if any, and the date of the verdict;

(7) the judgment and sentence of the court, and the date each was given;

(8) the motion for new trial, if any, and the decision thereon; and

(9) whether an appeal was taken and the date of that action.

(b) The information in the docket may be processed and stored by the use of electronic data processing equipment, at the discretion of the justice of the peace or the municipal court judge.

Acts 1965, 59th Leg., vol. 2, p. 317, ch. 722. Amended by Acts 1989, 71st Leg., ch. 499, § 1, eff. Aug. 28, 1989. Renumbered from Vernon's Ann.C.C.P. art. 45.13 and amended by Acts 1999, 76th Leg., ch. 1545, § 14, eff. Sept. 1, 1999.

Art. 45.018. Complaint

(a) For purposes of this chapter, a complaint is a sworn allegation charging the accused with the commission of an offense.

(b) A defendant is entitled to notice of a complaint against the defendant not later than the day before the date of any proceeding in the prosecution of the defendant under the complaint. The defendant may waive the right to notice granted by this subsection.

Added by Acts 1999, 76th Leg., ch. 1545, § 15, eff. Sept. 1, 1999.

Art. 45.019. Requisites Of Complaint

(a) A complaint is sufficient, without regard to its form, if it substantially satisfies the following requisites:

(1) it must be in writing;

(2) it must commence "In the name and by the authority of the State of Texas";

(3) it must state the name of the accused, if known, or if unknown, must include a reasonably definite description of the accused;

(4) it must show that the accused has committed an offense against the law of this state, or state that the affiant has good reason to believe and does believe that the accused has committed an offense against the law of this state;

(5) it must state the date the offense was committed as definitely as the affiant is able to provide;

(6) it must bear the signature or mark of the affiant; and

(7) it must conclude with the words "Against the peace and dignity of the State" and, if the offense charged is an offense only under a municipal ordinance, it may also conclude with the words "Contrary to the said ordinance".

(b) A complaint filed in justice court must allege that the offense was committed in the county in which the complaint is made.

(c) A complaint filed in municipal court must allege that the offense was committed in the territorial limits of the municipality in which the complaint is made.

(d) A complaint may be sworn to before any officer authorized to administer oaths.

(e) A complaint in municipal court may be sworn to before:

(1) the municipal judge;

(2) the clerk of the court or a deputy clerk;

(3) the city secretary; or

(4) the city attorney or a deputy city attorney.

(f) If the defendant does not object to a defect, error, or irregularity of form or substance in a charging instrument before the date on which the trial on the merits commences, the defendant waives and forfeits the right to object to the defect, error, or irregularity. Nothing in this article prohibits a trial court from requiring that an objection to a charging instrument be made at an earlier time.

(g) In a county with a population of more than two million that does not have a county attorney, a complaint for an offense under Section 32.41, Penal Code, must be approved by the district attorney, regardless of whether a collection proceeding is initiated by the district attorney under Section 32.41(e), Penal Code.

Acts 1965, 59th Leg., vol. 2, p. 317, ch. 722. Renumbered from Vernon's Ann.C.C.P. art. 45.17 and amended by Acts 1999, 76th Leg., ch. 1545, § 16, eff. Sept. 1, 1999. Amended by Acts 2005, 79th Leg., ch. 644, § 2, eff. Sept. 1, 2005.

Art. 45.02.   Repealed by Acts 1999, 76th Leg., ch. 1545, § 75(a), eff. Sept. 1, 1999

Art. 45.020.   Appearance by Counsel

(a) The defendant has a right to appear by counsel as in all other cases.

(b) State's counsel may open and conclude the argument in the case.

Acts 1965, 59th Leg., vol. 2, p. 317, ch. 722. Renumbered from Vernon's Ann.C.C.P. art. 45.37 and amended by Acts 1999, 76th Leg., ch. 1545, § 17, eff. Sept. 1, 1999. Amended by Acts 2015, 84th Leg., ch. 528 (H.B. 1386), § 1, eff. Sept. 1, 2015.

Section 2 of Acts 2015, 84th Leg., ch. 528 (H.B. 1386) provides:

"The change in law made by this Act applies only to a criminal proceeding that commences on or after the effective date [Sept. 1, 2015] of this Act. A criminal proceeding that commences before the effective date of this Act is governed by the law in effect on the date the proceeding commences, and the former law is continued in effect for that purpose."

Art. 45.021.   Pleadings

All pleading of the defendant in justice or municipal court may be oral or in writing as the court may direct.

Acts 1965, 59th Leg., vol. 2, p. 317, ch. 722. Renumbered from Vernon's Ann.C.C.P. art. 45.33 and amended by Acts 1999, 76th Leg., ch. 1545, § 18, eff. Sept. 1, 1999.

Art. 45.0215.   Plea by Minor and Appearance of Parent

(a) This article applies to a defendant who has not had the disabilities of minority removed and has been:

(1) charged with an offense other than an offense under Section 43.261, Penal Code, if the defendant is younger than 17 years of age; or

(2) charged with an offense under Section 43.261, Penal Code, if the defendant is younger than 18 years of age.

(a–1) The judge or justice:

(1) must take the defendant's plea in open court; and

(2) shall issue a summons to compel the defendant's parent, guardian, or managing conservator to be present during:

(A) the taking of the defendant's plea; and

(B) all other proceedings relating to the case.

(b) If the court is unable to secure the appearance of the defendant's parent, guardian, or managing conservator by issuance of a summons, the court may, without the defendant's parent, guardian, or managing conservator present, take the defendant's plea and proceed against the defendant.

(c) If the defendant resides in a county other than the county in which the alleged offense occurred, the defendant may, with leave of the judge of the court of original jurisdiction, enter the plea, including a plea under Article 45.052, before a judge in the county in which the defendant resides.

(d) A justice or municipal court shall endorse on the summons issued to a parent an order to appear personally at a hearing with the child. The summons must include a warning that the failure of the parent to appear may result in arrest and is a Class C misdemeanor.

Added by Acts 1997, 75th Leg., ch. 193, § 1, eff. Sept. 1, 1997. Renumbered from Vernon's Ann.C.C.P. art. 45.331 and amended by Acts 1999, 76th Leg., ch. 1545, § 19, eff. Sept. 1, 1999. Amended by Acts 2005, 79th Leg., ch. 949, § 33, eff. Sept. 1, 2005; Acts 2011, 82nd Leg., ch. 1322 (S.B. 407), § 12, eff. Sept. 1, 2011.

Art. 45.0216.   Expunction of Certain Conviction Records

(a) In this article, "child" has the meaning assigned by Section 51.02, Family Code.

(b) A person may apply to the court in which the person was convicted to have the conviction expunged as provided by this article on or after the person's 17th birthday if:

(1) the person was convicted of not more than one offense described by Section 8.07(a)(4) or (5), Penal Code, while the person was a child; or

(2) the person was convicted only once of an offense under Section 43.261, Penal Code.

(c) The person must make a written request to have the records expunged. The request must be under oath.

(d) The request must contain the person's statement that the person was not convicted of any additional offense or found to have engaged in conduct indicating a need for supervision as described by Subsection (f)(1) or (2), as applicable.

(e) The judge shall inform the person and any parent in open court of the person's expunction rights and provide them with a copy of this article.

(f) The court shall order the conviction, together with all complaints, verdicts, sentences, and prosecutorial and law enforcement records, and any other documents relating to the offense, expunged from the person's record if the court finds that:

(1) for a person applying for the expunction of a conviction for an offense described by Section 8.07(a)(4) or (5), Penal Code, the person was not convicted of any other offense described by Section 8.07(a)(4) or (5), Penal Code, while the person was a child; and

(2) for a person applying for the expunction of a conviction for an offense described by Section 43.261, Penal Code, the person was not found to have engaged in conduct indicating a need for supervision described by Section 51.03(b)(6), Family Code, while the person was a child.

(f–1) After entry of an order under Subsection (f), the person is released from all disabilities resulting from the conviction and the conviction may not be shown or made known for any purpose.

(g) This article does not apply to any offense otherwise covered by:

(1) Chapter 106, Alcoholic Beverage Code; or

(2) Chapter 161, Health and Safety Code.

(h) Records of a person under 17 years of age relating to a complaint may be expunged under this article if:

(1) the complaint was dismissed under Article 45.051 or 45.052 or other law; or

(2) the person was acquitted of the offense.

(i) The justice or municipal court shall require a person who requests expungement under this article to pay a fee in the amount of $30 to defray the cost of notifying state agencies of orders of expungement under this article.

(j) The procedures for expunction provided under this article are separate and distinct from the expunction procedures under Chapter 55.

Added by Acts 2001, 77th Leg., ch. 1297, § 50, eff. Sept. 1, 2001. Amended by Acts 2005, 79th Leg., ch. 886, § 2, eff. Sept. 1, 2005; Acts 2011, 82nd Leg., ch. 1322 (S.B. 407), §§ 13, 14, eff. Sept. 1, 2011; Acts 2013, 83rd Leg., ch. 1299 (H.B. 2862), § 3, eff. Sept. 1, 2013; Acts 2015, 84th Leg., ch. 935 (H.B. 2398), § 2, eff. Sept. 1, 2015; Acts 2015, 84th Leg., ch. 1132 (S.B. 108), § 1, eff. Sept. 1, 2015; Acts 2017, 85th Leg., ch. 324 (S.B. 1488), § 5.002, eff. Sept. 1, 2017; Acts 2017, 85th Leg., ch. 685 (H.B. 29), § 13, eff. Sept. 1, 2017.

Sections 42 and 43 of Acts 2015, 84th Leg., ch. 935 (H.B. 2398) provide:

"Sec. 42. The changes in law made by this Act apply only to an offense committed or conduct that occurs on or after the effective date [Sept. 1, 2015] of this Act. An offense committed or conduct that occurs before the effective date of this Act is governed by the law in effect on the date the offense was committed or the conduct occurred, and the former law is continued in effect for that purpose. For purposes of this section, an offense is committed or conduct occurs before the effective date of this Act if any element of the offense or conduct occurs before that date.

"Sec. 43. To the extent of any conflict, this Act prevails over another Act of the 84th Legislature, Regular Session, 2015, relating to nonsubstantive additions to and corrections in enacted codes."

Section 7 of Acts 2015, 84th Leg., ch. 1132 (S.B. 108) provides:

"(a) Except as provided by Subsection (b) of this section, the changes in law made by this Act apply only to an offense committed on or after the effective date [Sept. 1, 2015] of this Act. An offense committed before the effective date of this Act is governed by the law in effect on the date the offense was committed, and the former law is continued in effect for that purpose. For purposes of this section, an offense was committed before the effective date of this Act if any element of the offense occurred before that date.

"(b) The change in law made by this Act to Article 45.0216(h), Code of Criminal Procedure, applies to arrest records and files created before, on, or after the effective date of this Act."

Section 45(a) of Acts 2017, 85th Leg., ch. 685 (H.B. 29) provides:

"(a) Except as provided by Subsection (b) of this section, the changes in law made by this Act apply only to an offense committed on or after the effective date [Sept. 1, 2017] of this Act. An offense committed before the effective date of this Act is governed by the law in effect on the date the offense was committed, and the former law is continued in effect for that purpose. For purposes of this subsection, an offense was committed before the effective date of this Act if any element of the offense occurred before that date."

Art. 45.0217. Confidential Records Related to Charges Against or the Conviction of a Child

Text of article as amended by Acts 2013, 83rd Leg., ch. 1257 (H.B. 528), §§ 2, 3. See, also, text of art. 45.0217 as amended by Acts 2013, 83rd Leg., ch. 1319 (S.B. 394), § 2 and Acts 2013, 83rd Leg., ch. 1407 (S.B. 393), § 4.

(a) Except as provided by Article 15.27 and Subsection (b), all records and files, including those held by law enforcement, and information stored by electronic means or otherwise, from which a record or file could be generated, relating to a child who is charged with, is convicted of, is found not guilty of, had a charge dismissed for, or is granted deferred disposition for a fine-only misdemeanor offense other than a traffic offense are confidential and may not be disclosed to the public.

(b) Information subject to Subsection (a) may be open to inspection only by:

(1) judges or court staff;

(2) a criminal justice agency for a criminal justice purpose, as those terms are defined by Section 411.082, Government Code;

(3) the Department of Public Safety;

(4) an attorney for a party to the proceeding;

(5) the child defendant; or

(6) the defendant's parent, guardian, or managing conservator.

Added by Acts 2011, 82nd Leg., ch. 731 (H.B. 961), § 2, eff. June 17, 2011. Amended by Acts 2013, 83rd Leg., ch. 1257 (H.B. 528), §§ 2, 3, eff. Jan. 1, 2014.

Art. 45.0217. Confidential Records Related to the Conviction of or Deferral of Disposition for a Child

Text of article as amended by Acts 2013, 83rd Leg., ch. 1319 (S.B. 394), § 2 and Acts 2013, 83rd Leg., ch. 1407 (S.B. 393), § 4. See, also, art. 45.0217 as amended by Acts 2013, 83rd Leg., ch. 1257 (H.B. 528), §§ 2, 3.

(a) This article applies only to a misdemeanor offense punishable by fine only, other than a traffic offense.

(a-1) Except as provided by Article 15.27 and Subsection (b), all records and files, including those held by law enforcement, and information stored by electronic means or otherwise, from which a record or file could be generated, relating to a child who is convicted of and has satisfied the judgment for or who has received a dismissal after deferral of disposition for an offense described by Subsection (a) are confidential and may not be disclosed to the public.

(b) Information subject to Subsection (a-1) may be open to inspection only by:

(1) judges or court staff;

(2) a criminal justice agency for a criminal justice purpose, as those terms are defined by Section 411.082, Government Code;

(3) the Department of Public Safety;

(4) an attorney for a party to the proceeding;

(5) the child defendant; or

(6) the defendant's parent, guardian, or managing conservator.

Added by Acts 2011, 82nd Leg., ch. 731 (H.B. 961), § 2, eff. June 17, 2011. Amended by Acts 2013, 83rd Leg., ch. 1319 (S.B. 394), § 2, eff. Sept. 1, 2013; Acts 2013, 83rd Leg., ch. 1407 (S.B. 393), § 4, eff. Sept. 1, 2013.

Art. 45.0218. Confidential records related to fine-only misdemeanor

(a) Except as provided by Subsections (b) and (c), following the fifth anniversary of the date of a final conviction of, or of a dismissal after deferral of disposition for, a misdemeanor offense punishable by fine only, all records and files and information stored by electronic means or otherwise, from which a record or file could be generated, that are held or stored by or for a municipal or justice court and relate to the person who was convicted of, or who received a dismissal after deferral of disposition for, the offense are confidential and may not be disclosed to the public.

(b) Records, files, and information subject to Subsection (a) may be open to inspection only:

(1) by judges or court staff;

(2) by a criminal justice agency for a criminal justice purpose, as those terms are defined by Section 411.082, Government Code;

(3) by the Department of Public Safety;

(4) by the attorney representing the state;

(5) by the defendant or the defendant's counsel;

(6) if the offense is a traffic offense, an insurance company or surety company authorized to write motor vehicle liability insurance in this state; or

(7) for the purpose of complying with a requirement under federal law or if federal law requires the disclosure as a condition of receiving federal highway funds.

(c) This article does not apply to records, files, and information described by Subsection (a) that relate to an offense that is sexual in nature, as determined by the holder of the records, files, or information.

Added by Acts 2017, 85th Leg., ch. 811 (H.B. 681), § 2, eff. Sept. 1, 2017.

Section 3 of Acts 2017, 85th Leg., ch. 811 (H.B. 681) provides:

"The change in law made by this Act applies to the disclosure of information on or after the effective date [Sept. 1, 2017] of this Act regardless of whether the offense that is the subject of the information was committed before, on, or after the effective date of this Act."

Art. 45.022. Plea of Guilty or Nolo Contendere

Proof as to the offense may be heard upon a plea of guilty or a plea of nolo contendere and the punishment assessed by the court.

Acts 1965, 59th Leg., vol. 2, p. 317, ch. 722. Renumbered from Vernon's Ann.C.C.P. art. 45.34 and amended by Acts 1999, 76th Leg., ch. 1545, § 20, eff. Sept. 1, 1999.

Art. 45.023. Defendant's Plea

(a) After the jury is impaneled, or after the defendant has waived trial by jury, the defendant may:

(1) plead guilty or not guilty;

(2) enter a plea of nolo contendere; or

(3) enter the special plea of double jeopardy as described by Article 27. 05.

(b) If a defendant is detained in jail before trial, the justice or judge may permit the defendant to enter any of the pleas described by Subsection (a).

(c) If a defendant who is detained in jail enters a plea of guilty or nolo contendere, the justice or judge may, after complying with Article 15.17 and advising the defendant of the defendant's right to trial by jury, as appropriate:

(1) accept the defendant's plea;

(2) assess a fine, determine costs, and accept payment of the fine and costs;

(3) give the defendant credit for time served;

(4) determine whether the defendant is indigent; or

(5) discharge the defendant.

(d) Notwithstanding Article 45.037, following a plea of guilty or nolo contendere entered under Subsection (b), a motion for new trial must be made not later than 10 days after the rendition of judgment and sentence, and not afterward. The justice or judge shall grant a motion for new trial made under this subsection.

Acts 1965, 59th Leg., vol. 2, p. 317, ch. 722. Renumbered from Vernon's Ann.C.C.P. art. 45.31 and amended by Acts 1999, 76th Leg., ch. 1545, § 21, eff. Sept. 1, 1999. Amended by Acts 2013, 83rd Leg., ch. 691 (H.B. 2679), § 1, eff. Sept. 1, 2013.

Art. 45.024. Defendant's Refusal to Plead

The justice or judge shall enter a plea of not guilty if the defendant refuses to plead.

Acts 1965, 59th Leg., vol. 2, p. 317, ch. 722. Renumbered from Vernon's Ann.C.C.P. art. 45.35 and amended by Acts 1999, 76th Leg., ch. 1545, § 22, eff. Sept. 1, 1999.

Art. 45.025. Defendant May Waive Jury

The accused may waive a trial by jury in writing. If the defendant waives a trial by jury, the justice or judge shall hear and determine the cause without a jury.

Acts 1965, 59th Leg., vol. 2, p. 317, ch. 722. Renumbered from Vernon's Ann.C.C.P. art. 45.24 and amended by Acts 1999, 76th Leg., ch. 1545, § 23, eff. Sept. 1, 1999.

Art. 45.026. Jury Trial; Failure to Appear

(a) A justice or municipal court may order a party who does not waive a jury trial in a justice or municipal court and who fails to appear for the trial to pay the costs incurred for impaneling the jury.

(b) The justice or municipal court may release a party from the obligation to pay costs under this section for good cause.

(c) An order issued by a justice or municipal court under this section may be enforced by contempt as prescribed by Section 21.002(c), Government Code.

Added by Acts 1995, 74th Leg., ch. 122, § 1, eff. Sept. 1, 1995. Renumbered from Vernon's Ann.C.C.P. art. 45.251 and amended by Acts 1999, 76th Leg., ch. 1545, § 24, eff. Sept. 1, 1999.

Art. 45.027. Jury Summoned

(a) If the accused does not waive a trial by jury, the justice or judge shall issue a writ commanding the proper officer to summon a venire from which six qualified persons shall be selected to serve as jurors in the case.

(b) The jurors when so summoned shall remain in attendance as jurors in all cases that may come up for hearing until discharged by the court.

(c) Any person so summoned who fails to attend may be fined an amount not to exceed $100 for contempt.

Acts 1965, 59th Leg., vol. 2, p. 317, ch. 722. Amended by Acts 1995, 74th Leg., ch. 802, § 1, eff. Sept. 1, 1995. Renumbered from Vernon's Ann.C.C.P. art. 45.25 and amended by Acts 1999, 76th Leg., ch. 1545, § 25, eff. Sept. 1, 1999.

Art. 45.028.　Other Jurors Summoned

If, from challenges or any other cause, a sufficient number of jurors are not in attendance, the justice or judge shall order the proper officer to summon a sufficient number of qualified persons to form the jury.

Acts 1965, 59th Leg., vol. 2, p. 317, ch. 722.　Renumbered from Vernon's Ann.C.C.P. art. 45.29 and amended by Acts 1999, 76th Leg., ch. 1545, § 26, eff. Sept. 1, 1999.

Art. 45.029.　Peremptory Challenges

In all jury trials in a justice or municipal court, the state and each defendant in the case is entitled to three peremptory challenges.

Acts 1965, 59th Leg., vol. 2, p. 317, ch. 722.　Renumbered from Vernon's Ann.C.C.P. art. 45.28 and amended by Acts 1999, 76th Leg., ch. 1545, § 27, eff. Sept. 1, 1999.

Art. 45.03.　Renumbered as Vernon's Ann.C.C.P. art. 45.201 by Acts 1999, 76th Leg., ch. 1545, § 59, eff. Sept. 1, 1999

Art. 45.030.　Formation Of Jury

The justice or judge shall form the jury and administer the appropriate oath in accordance with Chapter 35.

Acts 1965, 59th Leg., vol. 2, p. 317, ch. 722.　Renumbered from Vernon's Ann.C.C.P. art. 45.30 and amended by Acts 1999, 76th Leg., ch. 1545, § 28, eff. Sept. 1, 1999.

Art. 45.031.　Counsel for State Not Present

If the state is not represented by counsel when the case is called for trial, the justice or judge may:

(1) postpone the trial to a date certain;

(2) appoint an attorney pro tem as provided by this code to represent the state; or

(3) proceed to trial.

Acts 1965, 59th Leg., vol. 2, p. 317, ch. 722.　Renumbered from Vernon's Ann.C.C.P. art. 45.36 and amended by Acts 1999, 76th Leg., ch. 1545, § 29, eff. Sept. 1, 1999.

Art. 45.032.　Directed Verdict

If, upon the trial of a case in a justice or municipal court, the state fails to prove a prima facie case of the offense alleged in the complaint, the defendant is entitled to a directed verdict of "not guilty."

Added by Acts 1969, 61st Leg., p. 1655, ch. 520, § 2, eff. June 10, 1969.　Renumbered from Vernon's Ann.C.C.P. art. 45.031 and amended by Acts 1999, 76th Leg., ch. 1545, § 30, eff. Sept. 1, 1999.

Art. 45.033.　Jury Charge

The judge shall charge the jury.　The charge may be made orally or in writing, except that the charge shall be made in writing if required by law.

Added by Acts 1999, 76th Leg., ch. 1545, § 31, eff. Sept. 1, 1999.

Art. 45.034.　Jury Kept Together

The jury shall retire in charge of an officer when the cause is submitted to them, and be kept together until they agree to a verdict, are discharged, or the court recesses.

Acts 1965, 59th Leg., vol. 2, p. 317, ch. 722.　Renumbered from Vernon's Ann.C.C.P. art. 45.39 and amended by Acts 1999, 76th Leg., ch. 1545, § 32, eff. Sept. 1, 1999.

Art. 45.035.　Mistrial

A jury shall be discharged if it fails to agree to a verdict after being kept together a reasonable time. If a jury is discharged because it fails to agree to a verdict, the justice or judge may impanel another jury as soon as practicable to try such cause.

Acts 1965, 59th Leg., vol. 2, p. 317, ch. 722.　Amended by Acts 1995, 74th Leg., ch. 1005, § 1, eff. Sept. 1, 1995. Renumbered from Vernon's Ann.C.C.P. art. 45.40 and amended by Acts 1999, 76th Leg., ch. 1545, § 33, eff. Sept. 1, 1999.

Art. 45.036.　Verdict

(a) When the jury has agreed on a verdict, the jury shall bring the verdict into court.

(b) The justice or judge shall see that the verdict is in proper form and shall render the proper judgment and sentence on the verdict.

Acts 1965, 59th Leg., vol. 2, p. 317, ch. 722.　Renumbered from Vernon's Ann.C.C.P. art. 45.42 and amended by Acts 1999, 76th Leg., ch. 1545, § 34, eff. Sept. 1, 1999.

Art. 45.037.　Motion for New Trial

A motion for a new trial must be made within five days after the rendition of judgment and sentence, and not afterward.

Acts 1965, 59th Leg., vol. 2, p. 317, ch. 722.　Renumbered from Vernon's Ann.C.C.P. art. 45.45 and amended by Acts 1999, 76th Leg., ch. 1545, § 35, eff. Sept. 1, 1999.　Amended by Acts 2011, 82nd Leg., ch. 395 (S.B. 519), § 1, eff. Sept. 1, 2011.

Art. 45.038.　New Trial Granted

(a) Not later than the 10th day after the date that the judgment is entered, a justice or judge may, for good cause shown, grant the defendant a new trial, whenever the justice or judge considers that justice has not been done the defendant in the trial of the case.

(b) If a motion for a new trial is not granted before the 11th day after the date that the judgment is entered, the motion shall be considered denied.

Acts 1965, 59th Leg., vol. 2, p. 317, ch. 722. Renumbered from Vernon's Ann.C.C.P. art. 45.44 and amended by Acts 1999, 76th Leg., ch. 1545, § 36, eff. Sept. 1, 1999.

Art. 45.039.   Only One New Trial Granted

Not more than one new trial shall be granted the defendant in the same case. When a new trial has been granted, the justice or judge shall proceed, as soon as practicable, to try the case again.

Acts 1965, 59th Leg., vol. 2, p. 317, ch. 722. Renumbered from Vernon's Ann.C.C.P. art. 45.46 and amended by Acts 1999, 76th Leg., ch. 1545, § 37, eff. Sept. 1, 1999.

Art. 45.04.   Renumbered as Vernon's Ann.C.C.P. art. 45.202 by Acts 1999, 76th Leg., ch. 1545, § 60, eff. Sept. 1, 1999

Art. 45.040.   State Not Entitled to New Trial

In no case shall the state be entitled to a new trial.

Acts 1965, 59th Leg., vol. 2, p. 317, ch. 722. Renumbered from Vernon's Ann.C.C.P. art. 45.47 and amended by Acts 1999, 76th Leg., ch. 1545, § 38, eff. Sept. 1, 1999.

Art. 45.041.   Judgment

(a) The judgment and sentence, in case of conviction in a criminal action before a justice of the peace or municipal court judge, shall be that the defendant pay the amount of the fine and costs to the state.

Text of (a–1), as added by Acts 2017, 85th Leg., ch. 977 (H.B. 351), § 11

(a–1) Notwithstanding any other provision of this article, during or immediately after imposing a sentence in a case in which the defendant entered a plea in open court as provided by Article 27.14(a) or 27.16(a), the justice or judge shall inquire whether the defendant has sufficient resources or income to immediately pay all or part of the fine and costs. If the justice or judge determines that the defendant does not have sufficient resources or income to immediately pay all or part of the fine and costs, the justice or judge shall determine whether the fine and costs should be:

(1) required to be paid at some later date or in a specified portion at designated intervals;

(2) discharged by performing community service under, as applicable, Article 45.049, Article 45.0492, as added by Chapter 227 (H.B. 350), Acts of the 82nd Legislature, Regular Session, 2011, or Article 45.0492, as added by Chapter 777 (H.B. 1964), Acts of the 82nd Legislature, Regular Session, 2011;

(3) waived in full or in part under Article 45.0491; or

(4) satisfied through any combination of methods under Subdivisions (1)–(3).

Text of (a–1), as added by Acts 2017, 85th Leg., ch. 1127 (S.B. 1913), § 10

(a–1) Notwithstanding any other provision of this article, during or immediately after imposing a sentence in a case in which the defendant entered a plea in open court as provided by Article 27.14(a) or 27.16(a), the justice or judge shall inquire whether the defendant has sufficient resources or income to immediately pay all or part of the fine and costs. If the justice or judge determines that the defendant does not have sufficient resources or income to immediately pay all or part of the fine and costs, the justice or judge shall determine whether the fine and costs should be:

(1) subject to Subsection (b–2), required to be paid at some later date or in a specified portion at designated intervals;

(2) discharged by performing community service under, as applicable, Article 45.049, Article 45.0492, as added by Chapter 227 (H.B. 350), Acts of the 82nd Legislature, Regular Session, 2011, or Article 45.0492, as added by Chapter 777 (H.B. 1964), Acts of the 82nd Legislature, Regular Session, 2011;

(3) waived in full or in part under Article 45.0491; or

(4) satisfied through any combination of methods under Subdivisions (1)–(3).

(b) Subject to Subsections (b–2) and (b–3) and Article 45.0491, the justice or judge may direct the defendant:

(1) to pay:

(A) the entire fine and costs when sentence is pronounced;

(B) the entire fine and costs at some later date; or

(C) a specified portion of the fine and costs at designated intervals;

(2) if applicable, to make restitution to any victim of the offense; and

(3) to satisfy any other sanction authorized by law.

(b–1) Restitution made under Subsection (b)(2) may not exceed $5,000 for an offense under Section 32.41, Penal Code.

(b–2) When imposing a fine and costs, if the justice or judge determines that the defendant is unable to immediately pay the fine and costs, the justice or judge shall allow the defendant to pay the fine and costs in specified portions at designated intervals.

(b–3) A judge may allow a defendant who is a child, as defined by Article 45.058(h), to elect at the time of conviction, as defined by Section 133.101, Local Government Code, to discharge the fine and costs by:

(1) performing community service or receiving tutoring under Article 45.0492, as added by Chapter 227 (H.B. 350), Acts of the 82nd Legislature, Regular Session, 2011; or

(2) paying the fine and costs in a manner described by Subsection (b).

(b–4) The election under Subsection (b–3) must be made in writing, signed by the defendant, and, if present, signed by the defendant's parent, guardian, or managing conservator. The court shall maintain the written election as a record of the court and provide a copy to the defendant.

(b–5) The requirement under Article 45.0492(a), as added by Chapter 227 (H.B. 350), Acts of the 82nd Legislature, Regular Session, 2011, that an offense occur in a building or on the grounds of the primary or secondary school at which the defendant was enrolled at the time of the offense does not apply to the performance of community service or the receipt of tutoring to discharge a fine or costs under Subsection (b–3)(1).

(c) The justice or judge shall credit the defendant for time served in jail as provided by Article 42.03. The credit shall be applied to the amount of the fine and costs at the rate provided by Article 45.048.

(d) All judgments, sentences, and final orders of the justice or judge shall be rendered in open court.

Acts 1965, 59th Leg., vol. 2, p. 317, ch. 722. Amended by Acts 1971, 62nd Leg., p. 2990, ch. 987, § 5, eff. June 15, 1971. Renumbered from Vernon's Ann.C.C.P. art. 45.50 and amended by Acts 1999, 76th Leg., ch. 1545, § 39, eff. Sept. 1, 1999. Amended by Acts 2007, 80th Leg., ch. 1393, § 2, eff. Sept. 1, 2007; Acts 2011, 82nd Leg., ch. 464 (H.B. 27), § 3, eff. Sept. 1, 2011; Acts 2013, 83rd Leg., ch. 1320 (S.B. 395), § 3, eff. Sept. 1, 2013; Acts 2013, 83rd Leg., ch. 1407 (S.B. 393), § 5, eff. Sept. 1, 2013; Acts 2017, 85th Leg., ch. 977 (H.B. 351), § 11, eff. Sept. 1, 2017; Acts 2017, 85th Leg., ch. 1127 (S.B. 1913), § 10, eff. Sept. 1, 2017.

Section 33 of Acts 2017, 85th Leg., ch. 977 (H.B. 351) provides:

"The changes in law made by this Act to Articles 42.15, 43.09, 43.091, 45.014, 45.041, 45.046, 45.049, and 45.0491, Code of Criminal Procedure, and Articles 45.0492, Code of Criminal Procedure, as added by Chapter 227 (H.B. 350), Acts of the 82nd Legislature, Regular Session, 2011, and 45.0492, Code of Criminal Procedure, as added by Chapter 777 (H.B. 1964), Acts of the 82nd Legislature, Regular Session, 2011, apply to a sentencing proceeding that commences before, on, or after the effective date [Sept. 1, 2017] of this Act."

Section 29 of Acts 2017, 85th Leg., ch. 1127 (S.B. 1913) provides:

"The changes in law made by this Act to Articles 42.15, 43.09, 43.091, 45.014, 45.041, 45.046, 45.049, and 45.0491, Code of Criminal Procedure, and Articles 45.0492, Code of Criminal Procedure, as added by Chapter 227 (H.B. 350), Acts of the 82nd Legislature, Regular Session, 2011, and 45.0492, Code of Criminal Procedure, as added by Chapter 777 (H.B. 1964), Acts of the 82nd Legislature, Regular Session, 2011, apply to a sentencing proceeding that commences before, on, or after the effective date of this Act."

Art. 45.042. Appeal

(a) Appeals from a justice or municipal court, including appeals from final judgments in bond forfeiture proceedings, shall be heard by the county court except in cases where the county court has no jurisdiction, in which counties such appeals shall be heard by the proper court.

(b) Unless the appeal is taken from a municipal court of record and the appeal is based on error reflected in the record, the trial shall be de novo.

(c) In an appeal from the judgment and sentence of a justice or municipal court, if the defendant is in custody, the defendant is to be committed to jail unless the defendant gives bail.

Acts 1965, 59th Leg., vol. 2, p. 317, ch. 722. Amended by Acts 1987, 70th Leg., ch. 641, § 4, eff. Sept. 1, 1987. Renumbered from Vernon's Ann.C.C.P. art. 45.10 and amended by Acts 1999, 76th Leg., ch. 1545, § 40, eff. Sept. 1, 1999.

Art. 45.0425. Appeal Bond

(a) If the court from whose judgment and sentence the appeal is taken is in session, the court must approve the bail. The amount of an appeal bond may not be less than two times the amount of the fine and costs adjudged against the defendant, payable to the State of Texas. The appeal bond may not in any case be for an amount less than $50. If the appeal bond otherwise meets the requirements of this code, the court without requiring a court appearance by the defendant shall approve the appeal bond in the amount the court under Article 27.14(b) notified the defendant would be approved.

(b) An appeal bond shall recite that in the cause the defendant was convicted and has appealed and be conditioned that the defendant shall make the defendant's personal appearance before the court to which the appeal is taken instanter, if the court is in session, or, if the court is not in session, at its next regular term, stating the time and place of that session, and there remain from day to day and term to term, and answer in the cause in the court.

Added by Acts 1999, 76th Leg., ch. 1545, § 41, eff. Sept. 1, 1999. Amended by Acts 2017, 85th Leg., ch. 977 (H.B. 351), § 12, eff. Sept. 1, 2017; Acts 2017, 85th Leg., ch. 1127 (S.B. 1913), § 11, eff. Sept. 1, 2017.

Art. 45.0426. Filing Bond Perfects Appeal

(a) When the appeal bond has been filed with the justice or judge who tried the case not later than the 10th day after the date the judgment was entered, the appeal in such case shall be held to be perfected.

(b) If an appeal bond is not timely filed, the appellate court does not have jurisdiction over the case and shall remand the case to the justice or municipal court for execution of the sentence.

(c) An appeal may not be dismissed because the defendant failed to give notice of appeal in open court. An appeal by the defendant or the state may not be dismissed on account of any defect in the transcript.

Acts 1965, 59th Leg., vol. 2, p. 317, ch. 722. Amended by Acts 1995, 74th Leg., ch. 478, § 1, eff. Sept. 1, 1995. Renumbered from Vernon's Ann.C.C.P. art. 45.14 and amended by Acts 1999, 76th Leg., ch. 1545, § 42, eff. Sept. 1, 1999.

Art. 45.043. Effect of Appeal

When a defendant files the appeal bond required by law with the justice or municipal court, all further proceedings in the case in the justice or municipal court shall cease.

Acts 1965, 59th Leg., vol. 2, p. 317, ch. 722. Renumbered from Vernon's Ann.C.C.P. art. 45.48 and amended by Acts 1999, 76th Leg., ch. 1545, § 43, eff. Sept. 1, 1999.

Art. 45.044. Forfeiture of Cash Bond in Satisfaction of Fine

(a) A justice or judge may enter a judgment of conviction and forfeit a cash bond posted by the defendant in satisfaction of the defendant's fine and cost if the defendant:

(1) has entered a written and signed plea of nolo contendere and a waiver of jury trial; and

(2) fails to appear according to the terms of the defendant's release.

(b) A justice or judge who enters a judgment of conviction and forfeiture under Subsection (a) of this article shall immediately notify the defendant in writing, by regular mail addressed to the defendant at the defendant's last known address, that:

(1) a judgment of conviction and forfeiture of bond was entered against the defendant on a date certain and the forfeiture satisfies the defendant's fine and costs in the case; and

(2) the defendant has a right to a new trial in the case if the defendant applies for the new trial not later than the 10th day after the date of judgment and forfeiture.

(c) Notwithstanding Article 45.037 of this code, the defendant may file a motion for a new trial within the period provided by Subsection (b) of this article, and the court shall grant the motion if the motion is made within that period. On the new trial, the court shall permit the defendant to withdraw the previously entered plea of nolo contendere and waiver of jury trial.

Added by Acts 1993, 73rd Leg., ch. 109, § 1, eff. May 9, 1993. Renumbered from Vernon's Ann.C.C.P. art. 45.231 and amended by Acts 1999, 76th Leg., ch. 1545, § 44, eff. Sept. 1, 1999.

Art. 45.045. Capias Pro Fine

(a) If the defendant is not in custody when the judgment is rendered or if the defendant fails to satisfy the judgment according to its terms, the court may order a capias pro fine, as defined by Article 43.015, issued for the defendant's arrest. The capias pro fine shall state the amount of the judgment and sentence, and command the appropriate peace officer to bring the defendant before the court immediately or place the defendant in jail until the business day following the date of the defendant's arrest if the defendant cannot be brought before the court immediately.

Text of (a–1), as added by Acts 2015, 84th Leg., ch. 1171 (S.B. 873), § 2

(a–1) If the court that issued the capias pro fine is unavailable, the arresting officer may, in lieu of placing the defendant in jail, take the defendant to:

(1) a justice of the peace court or county criminal law magistrate court with jurisdiction over Class C misdemeanors that is located in the same county, if the court that issued the capias pro fine was a justice of the peace court; or

(2) a municipal court that is located in the same municipality, if the court that issued the capias pro fine was a municipal court.

Text of (a–1), as added by Acts 2015, 84th Leg., ch. 1182 (S.B. 1139), § 9.02

(a–1) If the court that issued the capias pro fine is unavailable, the arresting officer may take the defendant to one of the following locations in lieu of placing the defendant in jail:

(1) if the court that issued the capias pro fine was a justice of the peace, to a justice of the peace or county criminal law magistrate court with jurisdiction over Class C misdemeanors that is located within the same county; or

(2) if the court that issued the capias pro fine was a municipal court, to a municipal court judge that is located within the same city.

Text of (a–2), as added by Acts 2017, 85th Leg., ch. 977 (H.B. 351), § 13

(a–2) Before a court may issue a capias pro fine for the defendant's failure to satisfy the judgment according to its terms:

(1) the court must provide by regular mail to the defendant notice that includes:

(A) a statement that the defendant has failed to satisfy the judgment according to its terms; and

(B) a date and time when the court will hold a hearing on the defendant's failure to satisfy the judgment according to its terms; and

(2) either:

(A) the defendant fails to appear at the hearing; or

(B) based on evidence presented at the hearing, the court determines that the capias pro fine should be issued.

Text of (a–2), as added by Acts 2017, 85th Leg., ch. 1127 (S.B. 1913), § 12

(a–2) The court may not issue a capias pro fine for the defendant's failure to satisfy the judgment according to its terms unless the court holds a hearing on the defendant's ability to satisfy the judgment and:

(1) the defendant fails to appear at the hearing; or

(2) based on evidence presented at the hearing, the court determines that the capias pro fine should be issued.

(a–3) The court shall recall a capias pro fine if, before the capias pro fine is executed:

(1) the defendant voluntarily appears to resolve the amount owed; and

(2) the amount owed is resolved in any manner authorized by this chapter.

(b) A capias pro fine may not be issued for an individual convicted for an offense committed before the individual's 17th birthday unless:

(1) the individual is 17 years of age or older;

(2) the court finds that the issuance of the capias pro fine is justified after considering:

(A) the sophistication and maturity of the individual;

(B) the criminal record and history of the individual; and

(C) the reasonable likelihood of bringing about the discharge of the judgment through the use of procedures and services currently available to the court; and

(3) the court has proceeded under Article 45.050 to compel the individual to discharge the judgment.

(c) This article does not limit the authority of a court to order a child taken into custody under Article 45.058 or 45.059.

Acts 1965, 59th Leg., vol. 2, p. 317, ch. 722. Amended by Acts 1971, 62nd Leg., p. 2991, ch. 987, § 6, eff. June 15, 1971. Renumbered from Vernon's Ann.C.C.P. art. 45.51 and amended by Acts 1999, 76th Leg., ch. 1545, § 45, eff. Sept. 1, 1999. Amended by Acts 2003, 78th Leg., ch. 283, § 31, eff. Sept. 1, 2003; Acts 2007, 80th Leg., ch. 1263, § 16, eff. Sept. 1, 2007; Acts 2015, 84th Leg., ch. 1171 (S.B. 873), § 2, eff. Sept. 1, 2015; Acts 2015, 84th Leg., ch. 1182 (S.B. 1139), § 9.02, eff. Sept. 1, 2015; Acts 2017, 85th Leg., ch. 977 (H.B. 351), § 13, eff. Sept. 1, 2017; Acts 2017, 85th Leg., ch. 1127 (S.B. 1913), § 12, eff. Sept. 1, 2017.

Section 34 of Acts 2017, 85th Leg., ch. 977 (H.B. 351) provides:

"The change in law made by this Act to Articles 43.05 and 45.045, Code of Criminal Procedure, applies only to a capias pro fine issued on or after the effective date [Sept. 1, 2017] of this Act. A capias pro fine issued before the effective date of this Act is governed by the law in effect on the date the capias pro fine was issued, and the former law is continued in effect for that purpose."

Section 30 of Acts 2017, 85th Leg., ch. 1127 (S.B. 1913) provides:

"The change in law made by this Act to Articles 43.05 and 45.045, Code of Criminal Procedure, applies only to a capias pro fine issued on or after the effective date [Sept. 1, 2017] of this Act. A capias pro fine issued before the effective date of this Act is governed by the law in effect on the date the capias pro fine was issued, and the former law is continued in effect for that purpose."

Art. 45.046. Commitment

(a) When a judgment and sentence have been entered against a defendant and the defendant defaults in the discharge of the judgment, the judge may order the defendant confined in jail until discharged by law if the judge at a hearing makes a written determination that:

(1) the defendant is not indigent and has failed to make a good faith effort to discharge the fine or costs; or

(2) the defendant is indigent and:

(A) has failed to make a good faith effort to discharge the fine or costs under Article 45.049; and

(B) could have discharged the fine or costs under Article 45.049 without experiencing any undue hardship.

(b) A certified copy of the judgment, sentence, and order is sufficient to authorize such confinement.

(c) For purposes of a hearing described by Subsection (a), a defendant may be brought before the court in person or by means of an electronic broadcast system through which an image of the defendant is presented to the court. For purposes of this subsection, "electronic broadcast system" means a two-way electronic communication of image and sound between the defendant and the court and includes secure Internet videoconferencing.

Text of (d), as added by Acts 2015, 84th Leg., ch. 1171 (S.B. 873), § 3

(d) For purposes of a hearing described by Subsection (a), if the court that issued the capias pro fine is unavailable, the following judicial officers may conduct the hearing:

(1) a justice of the peace or county criminal law magistrate with jurisdiction over Class C misdemeanors who is located in the same county as the issuing court, if the issuing court was a justice of the peace court; or

(2) a municipal court judge who is located in the same municipality as the issuing court, if the issuing court was a municipal court.

Text of (d), as added by Acts 2015, 84th Leg., ch. 1182 (S.B. 1139), § 9.03

(d) For purposes of a hearing described by Subsection (a), if the court that issued the capias pro fine is unavailable, the following judicial officers may conduct the hearing:

(1) if the court that issued the capias pro fine was a justice of the peace, a justice of the peace or a county criminal law magistrate with jurisdiction over Class C misdemeanors that is located within the same county as the issuing court; or

(2) if the court that issued the capias pro fine was a municipal court, a municipal court judge that is located within the same city as the issuing municipal court.

Acts 1965, 59th Leg., vol. 2, p. 317, ch. 722. Amended by Acts 1971, 62nd Leg., p. 2991, ch. 987, § 7, eff. June 15, 1971. Renumbered from Vernon's Ann.C.C.P. art. 45.52 and amended by Acts 1999, 76th Leg., ch. 1545, § 46, eff. Sept. 1, 1999. Amended by Acts 2007, 80th Leg., ch. 1263, § 19, eff. Sept. 1, 2007; Acts 2009, 81st Leg., ch. 474, § 2, eff. Sept. 1, 2009; Acts 2015, 84th Leg., ch. 1171 (S.B. 873), § 3, eff. Sept. 1, 2015; Acts 2015, 84th Leg., ch. 1182 (S.B. 1139), § 9.03, eff. Sept. 1, 2015; Acts 2017, 85th Leg., ch. 977 (H.B. 351), § 14, eff. Sept. 1, 2017; Acts 2017, 85th Leg., ch. 1127 (S.B. 1913), § 13, eff. Sept. 1, 2017.

Section 33 of Acts 2017, 85th Leg., ch. 977 (H.B. 351) provides:

"The changes in law made by this Act to Articles 42.15, 43.09, 43.091, 45.014, 45.041, 45.046, 45.049, and 45.0491, Code of Criminal Procedure, and Articles 45.0492, Code of Criminal Procedure, as added by Chapter 227 (H.B. 350), Acts of the 82nd Legislature, Regular Session, 2011, and 45.0492, Code of Criminal Procedure, as added by Chapter 777 (H.B. 1964), Acts of the 82nd Legislature, Regular Session, 2011, apply to a sentencing proceeding that commences before, on, or after the effective date [Sept. 1, 2017] of this Act."

Section 29 of Acts 2017, 85th Leg., ch. 1127 (S.B. 1913) provides:

"The changes in law made by this Act to Articles 42.15, 43.09, 43.091, 45.014, 45.041, 45.046, 45.049, and 45.0491, Code of Criminal Procedure, and Articles 45.0492, Code of Criminal Procedure, as added by Chapter 227 (H.B. 350), Acts of the 82nd Legislature, Regular Session, 2011, and 45.0492, Code of Criminal Procedure, as added by Chapter 777 (H.B. 1964), Acts of the 82nd Legislature, Regular Session, 2011, apply to a sentencing proceeding that commences before, on, or after the effective date [Sept. 1, 2017] of this Act."

Art. 45.047. Civil Collection of Fines After Judgment

If after a judgment and sentence is entered the defendant defaults in payment of a fine, the justice or judge may order the fine and costs collected by execution against the defendant's property in the same manner as a judgment in a civil suit.

Added by Acts 1999, 76th Leg., ch. 1545, § 47, eff. Sept. 1, 1999.

Art. 45.048. Discharged from Jail

(a) A defendant placed in jail on account of failure to pay the fine and costs shall be discharged on habeas corpus by showing that the defendant:

(1) is too poor to pay the fine and costs; or

(2) has remained in jail a sufficient length of time to satisfy the fine and costs, at the rate of not less than $100 for each period served, as specified by the convicting court in the judgment in the case.

(b) A convicting court may specify a period that is not less than eight hours or more than 24 hours as the period for which a defendant who fails to pay the fine and costs in the case must remain in jail to satisfy $100 of the fine and costs.

Acts 1965, 59th Leg., vol. 2, p. 317, ch. 722. Amended by Acts 1981, 67th Leg., p. 2648, ch. 708, § 3, eff. Aug. 31, 1981. Renumbered from Vernon's Ann.C.C.P. art. 45.53 and amended by Acts 1999, 76th Leg., ch. 1545, § 48, eff. Sept. 1, 1999. Amended by Acts 2001, 77th Leg., ch. 872, § 1, eff. Sept. 1, 2001; Acts 2003, 78th Leg., ch. 209, § 65(a), eff. Jan. 1, 2004; Acts 2017, 85th Leg., ch. 977 (H.B. 351), § 15, eff. Sept. 1, 2017; Acts 2017, 85th Leg., ch. 1127 (S.B. 1913), § 14, eff. Sept. 1, 2017.

Section 36 of Acts 2017, 85th Leg., ch. 977 (H.B. 351) provides:

"The change in law made by this Act to Article 45.048, Code of Criminal Procedure, applies to a defendant who is placed in jail on or after the effective date [Sept. 1, 2017] of this Act for failure to pay the fine and costs imposed on conviction of an offense, regardless of whether the offense for which the defendant was convicted was committed before, on, or after the effective date of this Act."

Section 32 of Acts 2017, 85th Leg., ch. 1127 (S.B. 1913) provides:

"The change in law made by this Act to Article 45.048, Code of Criminal Procedure, applies to a defendant who is placed in jail on or after the effective date [Sept. 1, 2017] of this Act for failure to pay the fine and costs imposed on conviction of an offense, regardless of whether the offense for which the defendant was convicted was committed before, on, or after the effective date of this Act."

Art. 45.049. Community Service in Satisfaction of Fine or Costs

(a) A justice or judge may require a defendant who fails to pay a previously assessed fine or costs, or who is determined by the court to have insufficient resources or income to pay a fine or costs, to discharge all or part of the fine or costs by performing community service. A defendant may discharge an obligation to perform community service under this article by paying at any time the fine and costs assessed.

(b) In the justice's or judge's order requiring a defendant to perform community service under this article, the justice or judge must specify:

(1) the number of hours of community service the defendant is required to perform; and

(2) the date by which the defendant must submit to the court documentation verifying the defendant's completion of the community service.

Text of (c), as amended by Acts 2017, 85th Leg., ch. 977 (H.B. 351), § 16

(c) The justice or judge may order the defendant to perform community service under this article:

(1) by attending:

(A) a work and job skills training program;

(B) a preparatory class for the high school equivalency examination administered under Section 7.111, Education Code;

(C) an alcohol or drug abuse program;

(D) a rehabilitation program;

(E) a counseling program, including a self-improvement program;

(F) a mentoring program; or

(G) any similar activity; or

(2) for:

(A) a governmental entity;

(B) a nonprofit organization or another organization that provides services to the general public that enhance social welfare and the general well-being of the community, as determined by the justice or judge; or

(C) an educational institution.

Text of (c), as amended by Acts 2017, 85th Leg., ch. 1127 (S.B. 1913), § 15

(c) The justice or judge may order the defendant to perform community service under this article:

(1) by attending a work and job skills training program, a preparatory class for the high school equivalency examination administered under Section 7.111, Education Code, or similar activity; or

(2) for:

(A) a governmental entity;

(B) a nonprofit organization or another organization that provides services to the general public that enhance social welfare and the general well-being of the community, as determined by the justice or judge; or

(C) an educational institution.

(c-1) An entity that accepts a defendant under this article to perform community service must agree to supervise, either on-site or remotely, the defendant in the performance of the defendant's community service and report on the defendant's community service to the justice or judge who ordered the service.

(d) A justice or judge may not order a defendant to perform more than 16 hours per week of community service under this article unless the justice or judge determines that requiring the defendant to perform additional hours does not impose an undue hardship on the defendant or the defendant's dependents.

(e) A defendant is considered to have discharged not less than $100 of fines or costs for each eight hours of community service performed under this article.

(f) A sheriff, employee of a sheriff's department, county commissioner, county employee, county judge, justice of the peace, municipal court judge, or officer or employee of a political subdivision other than a county or an entity that accepts a defendant under this article to perform community service is not liable for damages arising from an act or failure to act in connection with community service performed by a defendant under this article if the act or failure to act:

(1) was performed pursuant to court order; and

(2) was not intentional, wilfully or wantonly negligent, or performed with conscious indifference or reckless disregard for the safety of others.

(g) This subsection applies only to a defendant who is charged with a traffic offense or an offense under Section 106.05, Alcoholic Beverage Code, and is a resident of this state. If under Article 45.051(b)(10), Code of Criminal Procedure, the judge requires the defendant to perform community service as a condition of the deferral, the defendant is entitled to elect whether to perform the required service in:

(1) the county in which the court is located; or

(2) the county in which the defendant resides, but only if the applicable entity agrees to:

(A) supervise, either on-site or remotely, the defendant in the performance of the defendant's community service; and

(B) report to the court on the defendant's community service.

(h) This subsection applies only to a defendant charged with an offense under Section 106.05, Alcoholic Beverage Code, who, under Subsection (g), elects to perform the required community service in the county in which the defendant resides. The community service must comply with Sections 106.071(d) and (e), Alcoholic Beverage Code, except that if the educational programs or services described by Section 106.071(e) are not available in the county of the defendant's residence, the court may order community service that it considers appropriate for rehabilitative purposes.

(i) A community supervision and corrections department or a court-related services office may provide the administrative and other services necessary for supervision of a defendant required to perform community service under this article.

Added by Acts 1993, 73rd Leg., ch. 298, § 1, eff. May 27, 1993. Renumbered from Vernon's Ann.C.C.P. art. 45.521 and amended by Acts 1999, 76th Leg., ch. 1545, § 49, eff. Sept. 1, 1999. Amended by Acts 2003, 78th Leg., ch. 209, § 66(a), eff. Jan. 1, 2004; Acts 2007, 80th Leg., ch. 1113, § 5, eff. Sept. 1, 2007; Acts 2007, 80th Leg., ch. 1263, § 17, eff. Sept. 1, 2007; Acts 2009, 81st Leg., ch. 87, 27.001(2), eff. Sept. 1, 2009; Acts 2017, 85th Leg., ch. 977 (H.B. 351), § 16, eff. Sept. 1, 2017; Acts 2017, 85th Leg., ch. 1127 (S.B. 1913), § 15, eff. Sept. 1, 2017.

Section 33 of Acts 2017, 85th Leg., ch. 977 (H.B. 351) provides:

"The changes in law made by this Act to Articles 42.15, 43.09, 43.091, 45.014, 45.041, 45.046, 45.049, and 45.0491, Code of Criminal Procedure, and Articles 45.0492, Code of Criminal Procedure, as added by Chapter 227 (H.B. 350), Acts of the 82nd Legislature, Regular Session, 2011, and 45.0492, Code of Criminal Procedure, as added by Chapter 777 (H.B. 1964), Acts of the 82nd Legislature, Regular Session, 2011, apply to a sentencing proceeding that commences before, on, or after the effective date [Sept. 1, 2017] of this Act."

Section 29 of Acts 2017, 85th Leg., ch. 1127 (S.B. 1913) provides:

"The changes in law made by this Act to Articles 42.15, 43.09, 43.091, 45.014, 45.041, 45.046, 45.049, and 45.0491, Code of Criminal Procedure, and Articles 45.0492, Code of Criminal Procedure, as added by Chapter 227 (H.B. 350), Acts of the 82nd Legislature, Regular Session, 2011, and 45.0492, Code of Criminal Procedure, as added by Chapter 777 (H.B. 1964), Acts of the 82nd Legislature, Regular Session, 2011, apply to a sentencing proceeding that commences before, on, or after the effective date [Sept. 1, 2017] of this Act."

Art. 45.0491. Waiver of payment of fines and costs for certain defendants and for children

(a) A municipal court, regardless of whether the court is a court of record, or a justice court may waive payment of all or part of a fine or costs imposed on a defendant if the court determines that:

(1) the defendant is indigent or does not have sufficient resources or income to pay all or part of the fine or costs or was, at the time the offense was committed, a child as defined by Article 45.058(h); and

(2) discharging the fine or costs under Article 45.049 or as otherwise authorized by this chapter would impose an undue hardship on the defendant.

(b) A defendant is presumed to be indigent or to not have sufficient resources or income to pay all or part of the fine or costs if the defendant:

(1) is in the conservatorship of the Department of Family and Protective Services, or was in the conservatorship of that department at the time of the offense; or

(2) is designated as a homeless child or youth or an unaccompanied youth, as those terms are defined by 42 U.S.C. Section 11434a, or was so designated at the time of the offense.

Added by Acts 2007, 80th Leg., ch. 1263, § 18, eff. Sept. 1, 2007. Amended by Acts 2013, 83rd Leg., ch. 1320 (S.B. 395), § 4, eff. Sept. 1, 2013; Acts 2013, 83rd Leg., ch. 1407 (S.B. 393), § 6, eff. Sept. 1, 2013; Acts 2017, 85th Leg., ch. 977 (H.B. 351), § 17, eff. Sept. 1, 2017; Acts 2017, 85th Leg., ch. 1127 (S.B. 1913), § 16, eff. Sept. 1, 2017.

Section 33 of Acts 2017, 85th Leg., ch. 977 (H.B. 351) provides:

"The changes in law made by this Act to Articles 42.15, 43.09, 43.091, 45.014, 45.041, 45.046, 45.049, and 45.0491, Code of Criminal Procedure, and Articles 45.0492, Code of Criminal Procedure, as added by Chapter 227 (H.B. 350), Acts of the 82nd Legislature,

Regular Session, 2011, and 45.0492, Code of Criminal Procedure, as added by Chapter 777 (H.B. 1964), Acts of the 82nd Legislature, Regular Session, 2011, apply to a sentencing proceeding that commences before, on, or after the effective date [Sept. 1, 2017] of this Act."

Section 29 of Acts 2017, 85th Leg., ch. 1127 (S.B. 1913) provides:

"The changes in law made by this Act to Articles 42.15, 43.09, 43.091, 45.014, 45.041, 45.046, 45.049, and 45.0491, Code of Criminal Procedure, and Articles 45.0492, Code of Criminal Procedure, as added by Chapter 227 (H.B. 350), Acts of the 82nd Legislature, Regular Session, 2011, and 45.0492, Code of Criminal Procedure, as added by Chapter 777 (H.B. 1964), Acts of the 82nd Legislature, Regular Session, 2011, apply to a sentencing proceeding that commences before, on, or after the effective date [Sept. 1, 2017] of this Act."

Art. 45.0492. Community service in satisfaction of fine or costs for certain juvenile defendants

Text of article as added by Acts 2011, 82nd Leg., ch. 227 (H.B. 350), § 1. See, also, art. 45.0492 as added by Acts 2011, 82nd Leg., ch. 777 (H.B. 1964), § 1.

(a) This article applies only to a defendant younger than 17 years of age who is assessed a fine or costs for a Class C misdemeanor occurring in a building or on the grounds of the primary or secondary school at which the defendant was enrolled at the time of the offense.

(b) A justice or judge may require a defendant described by Subsection (a) to discharge all or part of the fine or costs by performing community service. A defendant may discharge an obligation to perform community service under this article by paying at any time the fine and costs assessed.

(c) In the justice's or judge's order requiring a defendant to perform community service under this article, the justice or judge must specify:

(1) the number of hours of community service the defendant is required to perform; and

(2) the date by which the defendant must submit to the court documentation verifying the defendant's completion of the community service.

(d) The justice or judge may order the defendant to perform community service under this article:

(1) by attending:

(A) a work and job skills training program;

(B) a preparatory class for the high school equivalency examination administered under Section 7.111, Education Code;

(C) an alcohol or drug abuse program;

(D) a rehabilitation program;

(E) a counseling program, including a self-improvement program;

(F) a mentoring program;

(G) a tutoring program; or

(H) any similar activity; or

(2) for:

(A) a governmental entity;

(B) a nonprofit organization or another organization that provides services to the general public that enhance social welfare and the general well-being of the community, as determined by the justice or judge; or

(C) an educational institution.

(d-1) An entity that accepts a defendant under this article to perform community service must agree to supervise, either on-site or remotely, the defendant in the performance of the defendant's community service and report on the defendant's community service to the justice or judge who ordered the service.

(e) Repealed by Acts 2017, 85th Leg., ch. 977 (H.B. 351), § 31; Acts 2017, 85th Leg., ch. 1127 (S.B. 1913), § 27.

(f) A justice or judge may not order a defendant to perform more than 16 hours of community service per week under this article unless the justice or judge determines that requiring the defendant to perform additional hours does not impose an undue hardship on the defendant or the defendant's family. For purposes of this subsection, "family" has the meaning assigned by Section 71.003, Family Code.

(g) A defendant is considered to have discharged not less than $100 of fines or costs for each eight hours of community service performed under this article.

(h) A sheriff, employee of a sheriff's department, county commissioner, county employee, county judge, justice of the peace, municipal court judge, or officer or employee of a political subdivision other than a county or an entity that accepts a defendant under this article to perform community service is not liable for damages arising from an act or failure to act in connection with community service performed by a defendant under this article if the act or failure to act:

(1) was performed pursuant to court order; and

(2) was not intentional, grossly negligent, or performed with conscious indifference or reckless disregard for the safety of others.

(i) A local juvenile probation department or a court-related services office may provide the administrative and other services necessary for supervision of a defendant required to perform community service under this article.

Added by Acts 2011, 82nd Leg., ch. 227 (H.B. 350), § 1, eff. Sept. 1, 2011. Amended by Acts 2017, 85th Leg., ch. 977 (H.B. 351), §§ 18, 19, 31, eff. Sept. 1, 2017; Acts 2017, 85th Leg., ch. 1127 (S.B. 1913), §§ 17, 18, 27, eff. Sept. 1, 2017.

Section 33 of Acts 2017, 85th Leg., ch. 977 (H.B. 351) provides:

"The changes in law made by this Act to Articles 42.15, 43.09, 43.091, 45.014, 45.041, 45.046, 45.049, and 45.0491, Code of Criminal Procedure, and Articles 45.0492, Code of Criminal Procedure, as added by Chapter 227 (H.B. 350), Acts of the 82nd Legislature, Regular Session, 2011, and 45.0492, Code of Criminal Procedure, as added by Chapter 777 (H.B. 1964), Acts of the 82nd Legislature, Regular Session, 2011, apply to a sentencing proceeding that commences before, on, or after the effective date [Sept. 1, 2017] of this Act."

Art. 45.0492. Community Service in Satisfaction of Fine or Costs for Certain Juvenile Defendants

Text of article as added by Acts 2011, 82nd Leg., ch. 777 (H.B. 1964), § 1. See, also, art. 45.0492 as added by Acts 2011, 82nd Leg., ch. 227 (H.B. 350), § 1.

(a) This article applies only to a defendant younger than 17 years of age who is assessed a fine or costs for a Class C misdemeanor.

(b) A justice or judge may require a defendant described by Subsection (a) to discharge all or part of the fine or costs by performing community service. A defendant may discharge an obligation to perform community service under this article by paying at any time the fine and costs assessed.

(c) In the justice's or judge's order requiring a defendant to perform community service under this article, the justice or judge shall specify:

(1) the number of hours of community service the defendant is required to perform, not to exceed 200 hours; and

(2) the date by which the defendant must submit to the court documentation verifying the defendant's completion of the community service.

(d) The justice or judge may order the defendant to perform community service under this article:

(1) by attending:

(A) a work and job skills training program;

(B) a preparatory class for the high school equivalency examination administered under Section 7.111, Education Code;

(C) an alcohol or drug abuse program;

(D) a rehabilitation program;

(E) a counseling program, including a self-improvement program;

(F) a mentoring program; or

(G) any similar activity; or

(2) for:

(A) a governmental entity;

(B) a nonprofit organization or another organization that provides services to the general public that enhance social welfare and the general well-being of the community, as determined by the justice or judge; or

(C) an educational institution.

(d–1) An entity that accepts a defendant under this article to perform community service must agree to supervise, either on-site or remotely, the defendant in the performance of the defendant's community service and report on the defendant's community service to the justice or judge who ordered the service.

(e) A justice or judge may not order a defendant to perform more than 16 hours of community service per week under this article unless the justice or judge determines that requiring the defendant to perform additional hours does not impose an undue hardship on the defendant or the defendant's family. For purposes of this subsection, "family" has the meaning assigned by Section 71.003, Family Code.

(f) A sheriff, employee of a sheriff's department, county commissioner, county employee, county judge, justice of the peace, municipal court judge, or officer or employee of a political subdivision other than a county or an entity that accepts a defendant under this article to perform community service is not liable for damages arising from an act or failure to act in connection with community service performed by a defendant under this article if the act or failure to act:

(1) was performed pursuant to court order; and

(2) was not intentional, wilfully or wantonly negligent, or performed with conscious indifference or reckless disregard for the safety of others.

(g) A local juvenile probation department or a court-related services office may provide the administrative and other services necessary for supervision of a defendant required to perform community service under this article.

(h) A defendant is considered to have discharged not less than $100 of fines or costs for each eight hours of community service performed under this article.

Added by Acts 2011, 82nd Leg., ch. 777 (H.B. 1964), § 1, eff. Sept. 1, 2011. Amended by Acts 2017, 85th Leg., ch. 977 (H.B. 351), § 20, eff. Sept. 1, 2017; Acts 2017, 85th Leg., ch. 1127 (S.B. 1913), § 19, eff. Sept. 1, 2017.

Section 33 of Acts 2017, 85th Leg., ch. 977 (H.B. 351) provides:

"The changes in law made by this Act to Articles 42.15, 43.09, 43.091, 45.014, 45.041, 45.046, 45.049, and 45.0491, Code of Criminal Procedure, and Articles 45.0492, Code of Criminal Procedure, as added by Chapter 227 (H.B. 350), Acts of the 82nd Legislature, Regular Session, 2011, and 45.0492, Code of Criminal Procedure, as added by Chapter 777 (H.B. 1964), Acts of the 82nd Legislature, Regular Session, 2011, apply to a sentencing proceeding that commences before, on, or after the effective date [Sept. 1, 2017] of this Act."

Section 29 of Acts 2017, 85th Leg., ch. 1127 (S.B. 1913) provides:

"The changes in law made by this Act to Articles 42.15, 43.09, 43.091, 45.014, 45.041, 45.046, 45.049, and 45.0491, Code of Criminal Procedure, and Articles 45.0492, Code of Criminal Procedure, as added by Chapter 227 (H.B. 350), Acts of the 82nd Legislature, Regular Session, 2011, and 45.0492, Code of Criminal Procedure, as added by Chapter 777 (H.B. 1964), Acts of the 82nd Legislature, Regular Session, 2011, apply to a sentencing proceeding that commences before, on, or after the effective date of this Act."

Art. 45.05. Repealed by Acts 1999, 76th Leg., ch. 1545, § 75(a), eff. Sept. 1, 1999

Art. 45.050. Failure to Pay Fine; Failure to Appear; Contempt: Juveniles

(a) In this article, "child" has the meaning assigned by Article 45.058(h).

(b) A justice or municipal court may not order the confinement of a child for:

(1) the failure to pay all or any part of a fine or costs imposed for the conviction of an offense punishable by fine only;

(2) the failure to appear for an offense committed by the child; or

(3) contempt of another order of a justice or municipal court.

(c) If a child fails to obey an order of a justice or municipal court under circumstances that would constitute contempt of court, the justice or municipal court, after providing notice and an opportunity to be heard, may:

(1) refer the child to the appropriate juvenile court for delinquent conduct for contempt of the justice or municipal court order; or

(2) retain jurisdiction of the case, hold the child in contempt of the justice or municipal court, and order either or both of the following:

(A) that the contemnor pay a fine not to exceed $500; or

(B) that the Department of Public Safety suspend the contemnor's driver's license or permit or, if the contemnor does not have a license or permit, to deny the issuance of a license or permit to the contemnor until the contemnor fully complies with the orders of the court.

(d) A justice or municipal court may hold a person in contempt and impose a remedy authorized by Subsection (c)(2) if:

(1) the person was convicted for an offense committed before the person's 17th birthday;

(2) the person failed to obey the order while the person was 17 years of age or older; and

(3) the failure to obey occurred under circumstances that constitute contempt of court.

(e) A justice or municipal court may hold a person in contempt and impose a remedy authorized by Subsection (c)(2) if the person, while younger than 17 years of age, engaged in conduct in contempt of an order issued by the justice or municipal court, but contempt proceedings could not be held before the person's 17th birthday.

(f) A court that orders suspension or denial of a driver's license or permit under Subsection (c)(2)(B) shall notify the Department of Public Safety on receiving proof of compliance with the orders of the court.

(g) A justice or municipal court may not refer a child who violates a court order while 17 years of age or older to a juvenile court for delinquency proceedings for contempt of court.

Added by Acts 1995, 74th Leg., ch. 262, § 86, eff. Jan. 1, 1996. Amended by Acts 1999, 76th Leg., ch. 76, § 7, eff. Sept. 1, 1999. Renumbered from Vernon's Ann.C.C.P. art. 45.522 and amended by Acts 1999, 76th Leg., ch. 1545, § 49, eff. Sept. 1, 1999. Amended by Acts 2001, 77th Leg., ch. 1297, § 51, eff. Sept. 1, 2001; Acts 2001, 77th Leg., ch. 1514, § 8, eff. Sept. 1, 2001; Acts 2003, 78th Leg., ch. 283, § 32, eff. Sept. 1, 2003; Acts 2017, 85th Leg., ch. 1071 (H.B. 3272), §§ 1, 2, eff. Sept. 1, 2017.

Art. 45.051. Suspension of Sentence and Deferral of Final Disposition

(a) On a plea of guilty or nolo contendere by a defendant or on a finding of guilt in a misdemeanor case punishable by fine only and payment of all court costs, the judge may defer further proceedings without entering an adjudication of guilt and place the defendant on probation for a period not to exceed 180 days. In issuing the order of deferral, the judge may impose a special expense fee on the defendant in an amount not to exceed the amount of the fine that could be imposed on the defendant as punishment for the offense. The special expense fee may be collected at any time before the date on which the period of probation ends. The judge may elect not to impose the special expense fee for good cause shown by the defendant. If the judge orders the collection of a special expense fee, the judge shall require that the amount of the special expense fee be credited toward the payment of the amount of the fine imposed by the judge. An order of deferral under this subsection terminates any liability under a bond given for the charge.

(a–1) Notwithstanding any other provision of law, as an alternative to requiring a defendant charged with one or more offenses to make payment of all court costs as required by Subsection (a), the judge may:

(1) allow the defendant to enter into an agreement for payment of those costs in installments during the defendant's period of probation;

(2) require an eligible defendant to discharge all or part of those costs by performing community service or attending a tutoring program under Article 45.049 or 45.0492; or

(3) take any combination of actions authorized by Subdivision (1) or (2).

(b) During the deferral period, the judge may require the defendant to:

(1) post a bond in the amount of the fine assessed to secure payment of the fine;

(2) pay restitution to the victim of the offense in an amount not to exceed the fine assessed;

(3) submit to professional counseling;

(4) submit to diagnostic testing for alcohol or a controlled substance or drug;

(5) submit to a psychosocial assessment;

(6) participate in an alcohol or drug abuse treatment or education program, such as:

(A) a drug education program that is designed to educate persons on the dangers of drug abuse and is approved by the Department of State Health Services in accordance with Section 521.374, Transportation Code; or

(B) an alcohol awareness program described by Section 106.115, Alcoholic Beverage Code;

(7) pay the costs of any diagnostic testing, psychosocial assessment, or participation in a treatment or education program either directly or through the court as court costs;

(8) complete a driving safety course approved under Chapter 1001, Education Code, or another course as directed by the judge;

(9) present to the court satisfactory evidence that the defendant has complied with each requirement imposed by the judge under this article; and

(10) comply with any other reasonable condition.

(b–1) If the defendant is younger than 25 years of age and the offense committed by the defendant is a traffic offense classified as a moving violation:

(1) Subsection (b)(8) does not apply;

(2) during the deferral period, the judge:

(A) shall require the defendant to complete a driving safety course approved under Chapter 1001, Education Code; and

(B) may require the defendant to complete an additional driving safety course designed for drivers younger than 25 years of age and approved under Section 1001.111, Education Code; and

(3) if the defendant holds a provisional license, during the deferral period the judge shall require that the defendant be examined by the Department of Public Safety as required by Section 521.161(b)(2), Transportation Code; a defendant is not exempt from the examination regardless of whether the defendant was examined previously.

(b–2) A person examined as required by Subsection (b–1)(3) must pay a $10 examination fee.

(b–3) The fee collected under Subsection (b–2) must be deposited to the credit of a special account in the general revenue fund and may be used only by the Department of Public Safety for the administration of Chapter 521, Transportation Code.

(c) On determining that the defendant has complied with the requirements imposed by the judge under this article, the judge shall dismiss the complaint, and it shall be clearly noted in the docket that the complaint is dismissed and that there is not a final conviction.

(c–1) If the defendant fails to present within the deferral period satisfactory evidence of compliance with the requirements imposed by the judge under this article, the court shall:

(1) notify the defendant in writing, mailed to the address on file with the court or appearing on the notice to appear, of that failure; and

(2) require the defendant to appear at the time and place stated in the notice to show cause why the order of deferral should not be revoked.

(c-2) On the defendant's showing of good cause for failure to present satisfactory evidence of compliance with the requirements imposed by the judge under this article, the court may allow an additional period during which the defendant may present evidence of the defendant's compliance with the requirements.

(d) If on the date of a show cause hearing under Subsection (c-1) or, if applicable, by the conclusion of an additional period provided under Subsection (c-2) the defendant does not present satisfactory evidence that the defendant complied with the requirements imposed, the judge may impose the fine assessed or impose a lesser fine. The imposition of the fine or lesser fine constitutes a final conviction of the defendant. This subsection does not apply to a defendant required under Subsection (b-1) to complete a driving safety course approved under Chapter 1001, Education Code, or an examination under Section 521.161(b)(2), Transportation Code.

(d-1) If the defendant was required to complete a driving safety course or an examination under Subsection (b-1) and on the date of a show cause hearing under Subsection (c-1) or, if applicable, by the conclusion of an additional period provided under Subsection (c-2) the defendant does not present satisfactory evidence that the defendant completed that course or examination, the judge shall impose the fine assessed. The imposition of the fine constitutes a final conviction of the defendant.

(e) Records relating to a complaint dismissed as provided by this article may be expunged under Article 55.01. If a complaint is dismissed under this article, there is not a final conviction and the complaint may not be used against the person for any purpose.

(f) This article does not apply to:

(1) an offense to which Section 542.404, Transportation Code, applies; or

(2) a violation of a state law or local ordinance relating to motor vehicle control, other than a parking violation, committed by a person who:

(A) holds a commercial driver's license; or

(B) held a commercial driver's license when the offense was committed.

(g) If a judge requires a defendant under Subsection (b) to attend an alcohol awareness program or drug education program as described by Subdivision (6) of that subsection, unless the judge determines that the defendant is indigent and unable to pay the cost, the judge shall require the defendant to pay the cost of attending the program. The judge may allow the defendant to pay the cost of attending the program in installments during the deferral period.

Added by Acts 1981, 67th Leg., p. 894, ch. 318, § 1, eff. Sept. 1, 1981. Amended by Acts 1987, 70th Leg., ch. 226, § 1, eff. Sept. 1, 1987; Acts 1989, 71st Leg., ch. 399, § 1, eff. June 14, 1989; Acts 1991, 72nd Leg., ch. 775, § 19, eff. Sept. 1, 1991; Acts 1991, 72nd Leg., ch. 835, § 4, eff. Sept. 1, 1991; Acts 1993, 73rd Leg., ch. 900, § 5.07, eff. Sept. 1, 1993; Acts 1999, 76th Leg., ch. 532, § 1, eff. Sept. 1, 1999; Acts 1999, 76th Leg., ch. 1387, § 1, eff. Sept. 1, 1999. Renumbered from Vernon's Ann.C.C.P. art. 45.54 and amended by Acts 1999, 76th Leg., ch. 1545, § 50, eff. Sept. 1, 1999. Amended by Acts 2001, 77th Leg., ch. 1420, § 3.002, eff. Sept. 1, 2001; Acts 2003, 78th Leg., ch. 991, § 12, eff. Sept. 1, 2003; Acts 2003, 78th Leg., ch. 1182, § 1, eff. Sept. 1, 2003; Acts 2003, 78th Leg., 3rd C.S., ch. 8, §§ 4.01, 4.03, eff. Jan. 11, 2004; Acts 2005, 79th Leg., ch. 90, § 1, eff. Sept. 1, 2005; Acts 2005, 79th Leg., ch. 281, § 3.01(a), eff. June 14, 2005; Acts 2005, 79th Leg., ch. 357, § 6, eff. Sept. 1, 2005; Acts 2007, 80th Leg., ch. 508, § 1, eff. Sept. 1, 2007; Acts 2007, 80th Leg., ch. 714, § 1, eff. Sept. 1, 2007; Acts 2007, 80th Leg., ch. 921, § 3.001, eff. Sept. 1, 2007; Acts 2009, 81st Leg., ch. 1121, § 2, eff. Sept. 1, 2009; Acts 2011, 82nd Leg., ch. 227 (H.B. 350), § 2, eff. Sept. 1, 2011; Acts 2011, 82nd Leg., ch. 777 (H.B. 1964), § 2, eff. Sept. 1, 2011; Acts 2011, 82nd Leg., ch. 914 (S.B. 1330), § 1, eff. Jan. 1, 2012; Acts 2015, 84th Leg., ch. 1004 (H.B. 642), § 4, eff. Sept. 1, 2015; Acts 2017, 85th Leg., ch. 977 (H.B. 351), § 21, eff. Sept. 1, 2017; Acts 2017, 85th Leg., ch. 1127 (S.B. 1913), § 20, eff. Sept. 1, 2017.

Section 35 of Acts 2017, 85th Leg., ch. 977 (H.B. 351) provides:

"The changes in law made by this Act to Articles 45.016, 45.051, and 45.0511, Code of Criminal Procedure, apply only to a bond executed on or after the effective date [Sept. 1, 2017] of this Act. A bond executed before the effective date of this Act is governed by the law in effect when the bond was executed, and the former law is continued in effect for that purpose."

Section 31 of Acts 2017, 85th Leg., ch. 1127 (S.B. 1913) provides:

"The changes in law made by this Act to Articles 45.016, 45.051, and 45.0511, Code of Criminal Procedure, apply only to a bond executed on or after the effective date [Sept. 1, 2017] of this Act. A bond executed before the effective date of this Act is governed by the law in effect when the bond was executed, and the former law is continued in effect for that purpose."

Section 1 of Acts 2017, 85th Leg., ch. 1153 (S.B. 47) provides:

"Sec. 1. (a) The Office of Court Administration of the Texas Judicial System shall conduct a study on how records regarding misdemeanors punishable by fine only, other than traffic offenses, are held in different Texas counties.

"(b) The study must address, with respect to each county:

"(1) the public availability of conviction records for misdemeanors punishable by fine only;

"(2) the public availability of records relating to suspension of sentence and deferral of final disposition under Article 45.051, Code of Criminal Procedure, for misdemeanors punishable by fine only;

"(3) the public availability of records described by Subdivision (1) or (2) of this subsection that are related to a child younger than 18 years of age;

"(4) whether public access to and availability of records described by Subdivisions (1)–(3) of this subsection have been expanded or restricted by the county over time;

"(5) whether local agencies holding records described by Subdivisions (1)–(3) of this subsection destroy those records;

"(6) the reasons and criteria for any destruction of records described by Subdivisions (1)–(3) of this subsection; and

"(7) the retention schedule of each local agency holding records described by Subdivisions (1)–(3) of this subsection, if the agency routinely destroys those records.

"(c) Not later than January 1, 2019, the Office of Court Administration shall issue a report on the study required under this section to the lieutenant governor, the speaker of the house of representatives, and the appropriate standing committees of the house of representatives and the senate.

"(d) This section expires September 1, 2019."

Art. 45.0511. Driving Safety Course or Motorcycle Operator Course Dismissal Procedures

(a) Except as provided by Subsection (a–1), this article applies only to an alleged offense that:

(1) is within the jurisdiction of a justice court or a municipal court;

(2) involves the operation of a motor vehicle; and

(3) is defined by:

(A) Section 472.022, Transportation Code;

(B) Subtitle C, Title 7, Transportation Code; or

(C) Section 729.001(a)(3), Transportation Code.

(a–1) If the defendant is younger than 25 years of age, this article applies to any alleged offense that:

(1) is within the jurisdiction of a justice court or a municipal court;

(2) involves the operation of a motor vehicle; and

(3) is classified as a moving violation.

(b) The judge shall require the defendant to successfully complete a driving safety course approved by the Texas Department of Licensing and Regulation or a course under the motorcycle operator training and safety program approved by the designated state agency under Chapter 662, Transportation Code, if:

(1) the defendant elects driving safety course or motorcycle operator training course dismissal under this article;

(2) the defendant:

(A) has not completed an approved driving safety course or motorcycle operator training course, as appropriate, within the 12 months preceding the date of the offense; or

(B) does not have a valid Texas driver's license or permit, is a member, or the spouse or dependent child of a member, of the United States military forces serving on active duty, and has not completed a driving safety course or motorcycle operator training course, as appropriate, in another state within the 12 months preceding the date of the offense;

(3) the defendant enters a plea under Article 45.021 in person or in writing of no contest or guilty on or before the answer date on the notice to appear and:

(A) presents in person or by counsel to the court a request to take a course; or

(B) sends to the court by certified mail, return receipt requested, postmarked on or before the answer date on the notice to appear, a written request to take a course;

(4) the defendant:

(A) has a valid Texas driver's license or permit; or

(B) is a member, or the spouse or dependent child of a member, of the United States military forces serving on active duty;

(5) the defendant is charged with an offense to which this article applies, other than speeding at a speed of:

(A) 95 miles per hour or more; or

(B) 25 miles per hour or more over the posted speed limit; and

(6) the defendant provides evidence of financial responsibility as required by Chapter 601, Transportation Code.

(c) The court shall enter judgment on the defendant's plea of no contest or guilty at the time the plea is made, defer imposition of the judgment, and allow the defendant 90 days to successfully complete the approved driving safety course or motorcycle operator training course and present to the court:

(1) a uniform certificate of completion of the driving safety course or a verification of completion of the motorcycle operator training course;

(2) unless the judge proceeds under Subsection (c–1), the defendant's driving record as maintained by the Department of Public Safety, if any, showing that the defendant had not completed an approved driving safety course or motorcycle operator training course, as applicable, within the 12 months preceding the date of the offense;

(3) an affidavit stating that the defendant was not taking a driving safety course or motorcycle operator

training course, as applicable, under this article on the date the request to take the course was made and had not completed such a course that is not shown on the defendant's driving record within the 12 months preceding the date of the offense; and

(4) if the defendant does not have a valid Texas driver's license or permit and is a member, or the spouse or dependent child of a member, of the United States military forces serving on active duty, an affidavit stating that the defendant was not taking a driving safety course or motorcycle operator training course, as appropriate, in another state on the date the request to take the course was made and had not completed such a course within the 12 months preceding the date of the offense.

(c–1) In this subsection, "state electronic Internet portal" has the meaning assigned by Section 2054.003, Government Code. As an alternative to receiving the defendant's driving record under Subsection (c)(2), the judge, at the time the defendant requests a driving safety course or motorcycle operator training course dismissal under this article, may require the defendant to pay a fee in an amount equal to the sum of the amount of the fee established by Section 521.048, Transportation Code, and the state electronic Internet portal fee and, using the state electronic Internet portal, may request the Texas Department of Public Safety to provide the judge with a copy of the defendant's driving record that shows the information described by Section 521.047(b), Transportation Code. As soon as practicable and using the state electronic Internet portal, the Texas Department of Public Safety shall provide the judge with the requested copy of the defendant's driving record. The fee authorized by this subsection is in addition to any other fee required under this article. If the copy of the defendant's driving record provided to the judge under this subsection shows that the defendant has not completed an approved driving safety course or motorcycle operator training course, as appropriate, within the 12 months preceding the date of the offense, the judge shall allow the defendant to complete the appropriate course as provided by this article. The custodian of a municipal or county treasury who receives fees collected under this subsection shall keep a record of the fees and, without deduction or proration, forward the fees to the comptroller, with and in the manner required for other fees and costs received in connection with criminal cases. The comptroller shall credit fees received under this subsection to the Texas Department of Public Safety.

(d) Notwithstanding Subsections (b)(2) and (3), before the final disposition of the case, the court may grant a request to take a driving safety course or a motorcycle operator training course under this article.

(e) A request to take a driving safety course or motorcycle operator training course made at or before the time and at the place at which a defendant is required to appear in court is an appearance in compliance with the defendant's promise to appear.

(f) In addition to court costs and fees authorized or imposed by a law of this state and applicable to the offense, the court may:

(1) require a defendant requesting a course under Subsection (b) to pay an administrative fee set by the court to cover the cost of administering this article at an amount of not more than $10; or

(2) require a defendant requesting a course under Subsection (d) to pay a fee set by the court at an amount not to exceed the maximum amount of the fine for the offense committed by the defendant.

(g) A defendant who requests but does not take a course is not entitled to a refund of the fee.

(h) Fees collected by a municipal court shall be deposited in the municipal treasury. Fees collected by another court shall be deposited in the county treasury of the county in which the court is located.

(i) If a defendant requesting a course under this article fails to comply with Subsection (c), the court shall:

(1) notify the defendant in writing, mailed to the address on file with the court or appearing on the notice to appear, of that failure; and

(2) require the defendant to appear at the time and place stated in the notice to show cause why the evidence was not timely submitted to the court.

(j) If the defendant fails to appear at the time and place stated in the notice under Subsection (i), or appears at the time and place stated in the notice but does not show good cause for the defendant's failure to comply with Subsection (c), the court shall enter an adjudication of guilt and impose sentence.

(k) On a defendant's showing of good cause for failure to furnish evidence to the court, the court may allow an extension of time during which the defendant may present:

(1) a uniform certificate of course completion as evidence that the defendant successfully completed the driving safety course; or

(2) a verification of course completion as evidence that the defendant successfully completed the motorcycle operator training course.

(*l*) When a defendant complies with Subsection (c), the court shall:

(1) remove the judgment and dismiss the charge;

(2) report the fact that the defendant successfully completed a driving safety course or a motorcycle operator training course and the date of completion to the Texas Department of Public Safety for inclusion in the person's driving record; and

(3) state in that report whether the course was taken under this article to provide information necessary to determine eligibility to take a subsequent course under Subsection (b).

(m) The court may dismiss only one charge for each completion of a course.

(n) A charge that is dismissed under this article may not be part of a person's driving record or used for any purpose.

(*o*) An insurer delivering or issuing for delivery a motor vehicle insurance policy in this state may not cancel or increase the premium charged an insured under the policy because the insured completed a driving safety course or a motorcycle operator training course, or had a charge dismissed under this article.

(p) The court shall advise a defendant charged with a misdemeanor under Section 472.022, Transportation Code, Subtitle C, Title 7, Transportation Code,[1] or Section 729.001(a)(3), Transportation Code, committed while operating a motor vehicle of the defendant's right under this article to successfully complete a driving safety course or, if the offense was committed while operating a motorcycle, a motorcycle operator training course. The right to complete a course does not apply to a defendant charged with:

(1) a violation of Section 545.066, 550.022, or 550.023, Transportation Code;

(2) a serious traffic violation; or

(3) an offense to which Section 542.404, Transportation Code, applies.

(q) A notice to appear issued for an offense to which this article applies must inform a defendant charged with an offense under Section 472.022, Transportation Code, an offense under Subtitle C, Title 7, Transportation Code, or an offense under Section 729.001(a)(3), Transportation Code, committed while operating a motor vehicle of the defendant's right to complete a driving safety course or, if the offense was committed while operating a motorcycle, of the defendant's right to complete a motorcycle operator train-ing course. The notice required by this subsection must read substantially as follows:

"You may be able to require that this charge be dismissed by successfully completing a driving safety course or a motorcycle operator training course. You will lose that right if, on or before your appearance date, you do not provide the court with notice of your request to take the course."

(r) If the notice required by Subsection (q) is not provided to the defendant charged with the offense, the defendant may continue to exercise the defendant's right to take a driving safety course or a motorcycle operator training course until the notice required by Subsection (q) is provided to the defendant or there is a final disposition of the case.

(s) This article does not apply to an offense committed by a person who:

(1) holds a commercial driver's license; or

(2) held a commercial driver's license when the offense was committed.

(t) An order of deferral under Subsection (c) terminates any liability under a bond given for the charge.

(u) The requirement of Subsection (b)(2) does not apply to a defendant charged with an offense under Section 545.412, Transportation Code, if the judge requires the defendant to attend and present proof that the defendant has successfully completed a specialized driving safety course that includes four hours of instruction that encourages the use of child passenger safety seat systems, and any driving safety course taken by the defendant under this section within the 12 months preceding the date of the offense did not include that training. The person's driving record under Subsection (c)(2) and the affidavit of the defendant under Subsection (c)(3) is required to include only previous or concurrent courses that included that training.

Added by Acts 1999, 76th Leg., ch. 1545, § 51, eff. Sept. 1, 1999. Amended by Acts 2001, 77th Leg., ch. 1420, § 3.0021(a), eff. Sept. 1, 2001; Acts 2003, 78th Leg., ch. 1182, § 2, eff. Sept. 1, 2003; Acts 2003, 78th Leg., 3rd C.S., ch. 8, § 4.02, eff. Jan. 11, 2004; Acts 2005, 79th Leg., ch. 90, § 2, eff. Sept. 1, 2005; Acts 2005, 79th Leg., ch. 357, § 7, eff. Sept. 1, 2005; Acts 2005, 79th Leg., ch. 913, § 6, eff. Sept. 1, 2005; Acts 2005, 79th Leg., ch. 1194, § 1, eff. Sept. 1, 2005; Acts 2005, 79th Leg., ch. 1209, § 1, eff. Sept. 1, 2005; Acts 2007, 80th Leg., ch. 805, § 1, eff. Sept. 1, 2007; Acts 2007, 80th Leg., ch. 829, § 1, eff. Sept. 1, 2007; Acts 2011, 82nd Leg., ch. 973 (H.B. 1504), § 1, eff. June 17, 2011; Acts 2013, 83rd Leg., ch. 161 (S.B. 1093), § 3.009, eff. Sept. 1, 2013; Acts 2015, 84th Leg., ch. 1044 (H.B. 1786), § 54, eff. Sept. 1, 2015; Acts 2017, 85th Leg., ch. 977 (H.B. 351), § 22, eff. Sept. 1, 2017; Acts 2017, 85th Leg., ch. 1127 (S.B. 1913), § 21, eff. Sept. 1, 2017.

[1] V.T.C.A., Transportation Code § 541.001 et seq.

Sections 71 and 74 of Acts 2015, 84th Leg., ch. 1044 (H.B. 1786) provide:

"Sec. 71. The change in law made by this Act applies only to the imposition of an administrative penalty for a violation that occurs on or after the effective date [Sept. 1, 2015] of this Act. The imposition of an administrative penalty for a violation that occurs before the effective date of this Act is governed by the law in effect on the date the violation occurred, and that law is continued in effect for that purpose."

"Sec. 74. To the extent of any conflict, this Act prevails over another Act of the 84th Legislature, Regular Session, 2015, relating to nonsubstantive additions to and corrections in enacted codes."

Section 35 of Acts 2017, 85th Leg., ch. 977 (H.B. 351) provides:

"The changes in law made by this Act to Articles 45.016, 45.051, and 45.0511, Code of Criminal Procedure, apply only to a bond executed on or after the effective date [Sept. 1, 2017] of this Act. A bond executed before the effective date of this Act is governed by the law in effect when the bond was executed, and the former law is continued in effect for that purpose."

Section 31 of Acts 2017, 85th Leg., ch. 1127 (S.B. 1913) provides:

"The changes in law made by this Act to Articles 45.016, 45.051, and 45.0511, Code of Criminal Procedure, apply only to a bond executed on or after the effective date [Sept. 1, 2017] of this Act. A bond executed before the effective date of this Act is governed by the law in effect when the bond was executed, and the former law is continued in effect for that purpose."

Art. 45.052. Dismissal of Misdemeanor Charge on Completion of Teen Court Program

(a) A justice or municipal court may defer proceedings against a defendant who is under the age of 18 or enrolled full time in an accredited secondary school in a program leading toward a high school diploma for not more than 180 days if the defendant:

(1) is charged with an offense that the court has jurisdiction of under Article 4.11 or 4.14;

(2) pleads nolo contendere or guilty to the offense in open court with the defendant's parent, guardian, or managing conservator present;

(3) presents to the court an oral or written request to attend a teen court program or is recommended to attend the program by a school employee under Section 37.146, Education Code; and

(4) has not successfully completed a teen court program in the year preceding the date that the alleged offense occurred.

(b) The teen court program must be approved by the court.

(c) A defendant for whom proceedings are deferred under Subsection (a) shall complete the teen court program not later than the 90th day after the date the teen court hearing to determine punishment is held or the last day of the deferral period, whichever date is earlier. The justice or municipal court shall dismiss the charge at the time the defendant presents satisfactory evidence that the defendant has successfully completed the teen court program.

(d) A charge dismissed under this article may not be part of the defendant's criminal record or driving record or used for any purpose. However, if the charge was for a traffic offense, the court shall report to the Department of Public Safety that the defendant successfully completed the teen court program and the date of completion for inclusion in the defendant's driving record.

(e) The justice or municipal court may require a person who requests a teen court program to pay a fee not to exceed $10 that is set by the court to cover the costs of administering this article. Fees collected by a municipal court shall be deposited in the municipal treasury. Fees collected by a justice court shall be deposited in the county treasury of the county in which the court is located. A person who requests a teen court program and fails to complete the program is not entitled to a refund of the fee.

(f) A court may transfer a case in which proceedings have been deferred under this section to a court in another county if the court to which the case is transferred consents. A case may not be transferred unless it is within the jurisdiction of the court to which it is transferred.

(g) In addition to the fee authorized by Subsection (e) of this article, the court may require a child who requests a teen court program to pay a $10 fee to cover the cost to the teen court for performing its duties under this article. The court shall pay the fee to the teen court program, and the teen court program must account to the court for the receipt and disbursal of the fee. A child who pays a fee under this subsection is not entitled to a refund of the fee, regardless of whether the child successfully completes the teen court program.

(h) A justice or municipal court may exempt a defendant for whom proceedings are deferred under this article from the requirement to pay a court cost or fee that is imposed by another statute.

(i) Notwithstanding Subsection (e) or (g), a justice or municipal court that is located in the Texas–Louisiana border region, as defined by Section 2056.002, Government Code, may charge a fee of $20 under those subsections.

Added by Acts 1989, 71st Leg., ch. 1031, § 1, eff. Sept. 1, 1989. Amended by Acts 1995, 74th Leg., ch. 598, § 1, eff. Sept. 1, 1995; Acts 1995, 74th Leg., ch. 748, § 2, eff. Sept. 1, 1995; Acts 1997, 75th Leg., ch. 165, § 31.01(13), eff. Sept. 1, 1997; Acts 1999, 76th Leg., ch. 76, § 6, eff. Sept. 1, 1999. Renumbered from Vernon's Ann.C.C.P. art. 45.55 and amended by Acts 1999, 76th Leg., ch. 1545, § 52, eff. Sept. 1, 1999. Amended by Acts 2001, 77th Leg., ch. 216, § 1, eff. Sept. 1, 2001; Acts 2001, 77th Leg., ch. 216, § 1, eff. Sept. 1, 2001; Acts 2007, 80th Leg., ch. 910, § 1, eff. Sept. 1, 2007; Acts 2015, 84th Leg., ch. 1132 (S.B. 108), § 2, eff. Sept. 1, 2015.

Section 7(a) of Acts 2015, 84th Leg., ch. 1132 (S.B. 108) provides:

"(a) Except as provided by Subsection (b) of this section, the changes in law made by this Act apply only to an offense committed on or after the effective date [Sept. 1, 2015] of this Act. An offense committed before the effective date of this Act is governed by the law in effect on the date the offense was committed, and the former law is continued in effect for that purpose. For purposes of this section, an offense was committed before the effective date of this Act if any element of the offense occurred before that date."

Art. 45.053. Dismissal of Misdemeanor Charge on Commitment of Chemically Dependent Person

(a) On a plea of guilty or nolo contendere by a defendant or on a finding of guilt in a misdemeanor case punishable by a fine only, a justice or municipal court may defer further proceedings for 90 days without entering an adjudication of guilt if:

(1) the court finds that the offense resulted from or was related to the defendant's chemical dependency; and

(2) an application for court-ordered treatment of the defendant is filed in accordance with Chapter 462, Health and Safety Code.

(b) At the end of the deferral period, the justice or municipal court shall dismiss the charge if satisfactory evidence is presented that the defendant was committed for and completed court-ordered treatment in accordance with Chapter 462, Health and Safety Code, and it shall be clearly noted in the docket that the complaint is dismissed and that there is not a final conviction.

(c) If at the conclusion of the deferral period satisfactory evidence that the defendant was committed for and completed court-ordered treatment in accordance with Chapter 462, Health and Safety Code, is not presented, the justice or municipal court may impose the fine assessed or impose a lesser fine. The imposition of a fine constitutes a final conviction of the defendant.

(d) Records relating to a complaint dismissed under this article may be expunged under Article 55.01 of this code. If a complaint is dismissed under this article, there is not a final conviction and the complaint may not be used against the person for any purpose.

Added by Acts 1991, 72nd Leg., ch. 198, § 1, eff. Sept. 1, 1991. Renumbered from Vernon's Ann.C.C.P. art. 45.56 and amended by Acts 1999, 76th Leg., ch. 1545, § 53, eff. Sept. 1, 1999.

Art. 45.0531. Dismissal of Parent Contributing to Nonattendance Charge

Notwithstanding any other law, a county, justice, or municipal court, at the court's discretion, may dismiss a charge against a defendant alleging the defendant committed an offense under Section 25.093, Education Code, if the court finds that a dismissal would be in the interest of justice because:

(1) there is a low likelihood of recidivism by the defendant; or

(2) sufficient justification exists for the failure to attend school.

Added by Acts 2015, 84th Leg., ch. 935 (H.B. 2398), § 3, eff. Sept. 1, 2015.

Sections 42 and 43 of Acts 2015, 84th Leg., ch. 935 (H.B. 2398) provide:

"Sec. 42. The changes in law made by this Act apply only to an offense committed or conduct that occurs on or after the effective date [Sept. 1, 2015] of this Act. An offense committed or conduct that occurs before the effective date of this Act is governed by the law in effect on the date the offense was committed or the conduct occurred, and the former law is continued in effect for that purpose. For purposes of this section, an offense is committed or conduct occurs before the effective date of this Act if any element of the offense or conduct occurs before that date.

"Sec. 43. To the extent of any conflict, this Act prevails over another Act of the 84th Legislature, Regular Session, 2015, relating to nonsubstantive additions to and corrections in enacted codes."

Art. 45.054. Repealed by Acts 2015, 84th Leg., ch. 935 (H.B. 2398), § 41(1), eff. Sept. 1, 2015

Sections 42 and 43 of Acts 2015, 84th Leg., ch. 935 (H.B. 2398) provide:

"Sec. 42. The changes in law made by this Act apply only to an offense committed or conduct that occurs on or after the effective date [Sept. 1, 2015] of this Act. An offense committed or conduct that occurs before the effective date of this Act is governed by the law in effect on the date the offense was committed or the conduct occurred, and the former law is continued in effect for that purpose. For purposes of this section, an offense is committed or conduct occurs before the effective date of this Act if any element of the offense or conduct occurs before that date.

"Sec. 43. To the extent of any conflict, this Act prevails over another Act of the 84th Legislature, Regular Session, 2015, relating to nonsubstantive additions to and corrections in enacted codes."

Art. 45.0541. Expunction of Failure to Attend School Records

(a) In this article, "truancy offense" means an offense committed under the former Section 25.094, Education Code.

(b) An individual who has been convicted of a truancy offense or has had a complaint for a truancy offense dismissed is entitled to have the conviction or complaint and records relating to the conviction or complaint expunged.

(c) Regardless of whether the individual has filed a petition for expunction, the court in which the individual was convicted or a complaint for a truancy offense was filed shall order the conviction, complaints, verdicts, sentences, and other documents relating to the offense, including any documents in the possession of a school district or law enforcement agency, to be expunged from the individual's record. After entry of the order, the individual is released from all disabilities resulting from the conviction or complaint, and the conviction or complaint may not be shown or made known for any purpose.

Added by Acts 2015, 84th Leg., ch. 935 (H.B. 2398), § 3, eff. Sept. 1, 2015.

Sections 42 and 43 of Acts 2015, 84th Leg., ch. 935 (H.B. 2398) provide:

"Sec. 42. The changes in law made by this Act apply only to an offense committed or conduct that occurs on or after the effective date [Sept. 1, 2015] of this Act. An offense committed or conduct that occurs before the effective date of this Act is governed by the law in effect on the date the offense was committed or the conduct occurred, and the former law is continued in effect for that purpose. For purposes of this section, an offense is committed or conduct occurs before the effective date of this Act if any element of the offense or conduct occurs before that date.

"Sec. 43. To the extent of any conflict, this Act prevails over another Act of the 84th Legislature, Regular Session, 2015, relating to nonsubstantive additions to and corrections in enacted codes."

Art. 45.055.   Repealed by Acts 2015, 84th Leg., ch. 935 (H.B. 2398), § 41(1), eff. Sept. 1, 2015

Sections 42 and 43 of Acts 2015, 84th Leg., ch. 935 (H.B. 2398) provide:

"Sec. 42. The changes in law made by this Act apply only to an offense committed or conduct that occurs on or after the effective date [Sept. 1, 2015] of this Act. An offense committed or conduct that occurs before the effective date of this Act is governed by the law in effect on the date the offense was committed or the conduct occurred, and the former law is continued in effect for that purpose. For purposes of this section, an offense is committed or conduct occurs before the effective date of this Act if any element of the offense or conduct occurs before that date.

"Sec. 43. To the extent of any conflict, this Act prevails over another Act of the 84th Legislature, Regular Session, 2015, relating to nonsubstantive additions to and corrections in enacted codes."

Art. 45.056.   Juvenile Case Managers

(a) On approval of the commissioners court, city council, school district board of trustees, juvenile board, or other appropriate authority, a county court, justice court, municipal court, school district, juvenile probation department, or other appropriate governmental entity may:

(1) employ a case manager to provide services in cases involving juvenile offenders who are before a court consistent with the court's statutory powers or referred to a court by a school administrator or designee for misconduct that would otherwise be within the court's statutory powers prior to a case being filed, with the consent of the juvenile and the juvenile's parents or guardians;

(2) employ one or more juvenile case managers who:

(A) shall assist the court in administering the court's juvenile docket and in supervising the court's orders in juvenile cases; and

(B) may provide:

(i) prevention services to a child considered at risk of entering the juvenile justice system; and

(ii) intervention services to juveniles engaged in misconduct before cases are filed, excluding traffic offenses; or

(3) agree in accordance with Chapter 791, Government Code, with any appropriate governmental entity to jointly employ a case manager or to jointly contribute to the costs of a case manager employed by one governmental entity to provide services described by Subdivisions (1) and (2).

(b) A local entity may apply or more than one local entity may jointly apply to the criminal justice division of the governor's office for reimbursement of all or part of the costs of employing one or more juvenile case managers from funds appropriated to the governor's office or otherwise available for that purpose. To be eligible for reimbursement, the entity applying must present to the governor's office a comprehensive plan to reduce juvenile crimes in the entity's jurisdiction that addresses the role of the case manager in that effort.

Text of subsec. (c), as amended by Acts 2013, 83rd Leg., ch. 1213 (S.B. 1419), § 1

(c) An entity that jointly employs a case manager under Subsection (a)(3) employs a juvenile case manager for purposes of Chapter 102 of this code and Chapter 102, Government Code.

Text of subsec. (c), as amended by Acts 2013, 83rd Leg., ch. 1407 (S.B. 393), § 7

(c) A county or justice court on approval of the commissioners court or a municipality or municipal court on approval of the city council may employ one or more juvenile case managers who:

(1) shall assist the court in administering the court's juvenile docket and in supervising its court orders in juvenile cases; and

(2) may provide:

(A) prevention services to a child considered at-risk of entering the juvenile justice system; and

(B) intervention services to juveniles engaged in misconduct prior to cases being filed, excluding traffic offenses.

(d) Pursuant to Article 102.0174, the court or governing body may pay the salary and benefits of a juvenile case manager and the costs of training, travel, office supplies, and other necessary expenses relating to the position of the juvenile case manager from the juvenile case manager fund.

(e) A juvenile case manager employed under Subsection (c) shall give priority to cases brought under Sections 25.093 and 25.094, Education Code.

(f) The governing body of the employing governmental entity under Subsection (a) shall adopt reasonable rules for juvenile case managers that provide:

(1) a code of ethics, and for the enforcement of the code of ethics;

(2) appropriate educational preservice and in-service training standards for juvenile case managers; and

(3) training in:

(A) the role of the juvenile case manager;

(B) case planning and management;

(C) applicable procedural and substantive law;

(D) courtroom proceedings and presentation;

(E) services to at-risk youth under Subchapter D, Chapter 264, Family Code;

(F) local programs and services for juveniles and methods by which juveniles may access those programs and services; and

(G) detecting and preventing abuse, exploitation, and neglect of juveniles.

(g) The employing court or governmental entity under this article shall implement the rules adopted under Subsection (f).

(h) The commissioners court or governing body of the municipality that administers a juvenile case manager fund under Article 102.0174 shall require periodic review of juvenile case managers to ensure the implementation of the rules adopted under Subsection (f).

(i) The juvenile case manager shall timely report to the judge who signed the order or judgment and, on request, to the judge assigned to the case or the presiding judge any information or recommendations relevant to assisting the judge in making decisions that are in the best interest of the child.

(j) The judge who is assigned to the case shall consult with the juvenile case manager who is supervising the case regarding:

(1) the child's home environment;

(2) the child's developmental, psychological, and educational status;

(3) the child's previous interaction with the justice system; and

(4) any sanctions available to the court that would be in the best interest of the child.

(k) Subsections (i) and (j) do not apply to:

(1) a part-time judge; or

(2) a county judge of a county court that has one or more appointed full-time magistrates under Section 54.1172, Government Code.

Added by Acts 2001, 77th Leg., ch. 1514, § 9, eff. Sept. 1, 2001. Amended by Acts 2003, 78th Leg., ch. 283, § 33, eff. Sept. 1, 2003; Acts 2005, 79th Leg., ch. 949, § 34, eff. Sept. 1, 2005; Acts 2011, 82nd Leg., ch. 868 (S.B. 61), §§ 1, 2, eff. June 17, 2011; Acts 2011, 82nd Leg., ch. 1055 (S.B. 209), § 1, eff. Sept. 1, 2011; Acts 2011, 82nd Leg., ch. 1098 (S.B. 1489), § 16, eff. Sept. 1, 2011; Acts 2013, 83rd Leg., ch. 161 (S.B. 1093), §§ 22.001(8), 22.002(4), eff. Sept. 1, 2013; Acts 2013, 83rd Leg., ch. 1213 (S.B. 1419), § 1, eff. Sept. 1, 2013; Acts 2013, 83rd Leg., ch. 1407 (S.B. 393), § 7, eff. Sept. 1, 2013; Acts 2015, 84th Leg., ch. 935 (H.B. 2398), § 4, eff. Sept. 1, 2015.

Repeal of subsec. (e)

Without reference to the amendment of subsec. (e) by Acts 2011, 82nd Leg., ch. 1055 (S.B. 209), § 1, Acts 2011, 82nd Leg., ch. 1098 (S.B. 1489), § 16 repealed subsec. (e) effective Sept. 1, 2011.

Sections 42 and 43 of Acts 2015, 84th Leg., ch. 935 (H.B. 2398) provide:

"Sec. 42. The changes in law made by this Act apply only to an offense committed or conduct that occurs on or after the effective date [Sept. 1, 2015] of this Act. An offense committed or conduct that occurs before the effective date of this Act is governed by the law in effect on the date the offense was committed or the conduct occurred, and the former law is continued in effect for that purpose. For purposes of this section, an offense is committed or conduct occurs before the effective date of this Act if any element of the offense or conduct occurs before that date.

"Sec. 43. To the extent of any conflict, this Act prevails over another Act of the 84th Legislature, Regular Session, 2015, relating to nonsubstantive additions to and corrections in enacted codes."

Art. 45.057. Offenses Committed by Juveniles

(a) In this article:

(1) "Child" has the meaning assigned by Article 45.058(h).

(2) "Residence" means any place where the child lives or resides for a period of at least 30 days.

(3) "Parent" includes a person standing in parental relation, a managing conservator, or a custodian.

(b) On a finding by a justice or municipal court that a child committed an offense that the court has jurisdiction of under Article 4.11 or 4.14, the court has jurisdiction to enter an order:

(1) referring the child or the child's parent for services under Section 264.302, Family Code;

(2) requiring that the child attend a special program that the court determines to be in the best interest of the child and, if the program involves the expenditure of municipal or county funds, that is approved by the governing body of the municipality or county commissioners court, as applicable, including a rehabilitation, counseling, self-esteem and leadership, work and job skills training, job interviewing and work preparation, self-improvement, parenting, manners, violence avoidance, tutoring, sensitivity training, parental responsibility, community service, restitution, advocacy, or mentoring program; or

(3) requiring that the child's parent do any act or refrain from doing any act that the court determines will increase the likelihood that the child will comply with the orders of the court and that is reasonable and necessary for the welfare of the child, including:

(A) attend a parenting class or parental responsibility program; and

(B) attend the child's school classes or functions.

(c) The justice or municipal court may order the parent, managing conservator, or guardian of a child required to attend a program under Subsection (b) to pay an amount not greater than $100 to pay for the costs of the program.

(d) A justice or municipal court may require a child, parent, managing conservator, or guardian required to attend a program, class, or function under this article to submit proof of attendance to the court.

(e) A justice or municipal court shall endorse on the summons issued to a parent an order to appear personally at the hearing with the child. The summons must include a warning that the failure of the parent to appear may result in arrest and is a Class C misdemeanor.

(f) An order under this article involving a child is enforceable under Article 45.050.

(g) A person commits an offense if the person is a parent, managing conservator, or guardian who fails to attend a hearing under this article after receiving an order under Subsection (e). An offense under this subsection is a Class C misdemeanor.

(h) A child and parent required to appear before the court have an obligation to provide the court in writing with the current address and residence of the child. The obligation does not end when the child reaches age 17. On or before the seventh day after the date the child or parent changes residence, the child or parent shall notify the court of the current address in the manner directed by the court. A violation of this subsection may result in arrest and is a Class C misdemeanor. The obligation to provide notice terminates on discharge and satisfaction of the judgment or final disposition not requiring a finding of guilt.

(i) If an appellate court accepts an appeal for a trial de novo, the child and parent shall provide the notice under Subsection (h) to the appellate court.

(j) The child and parent are entitled to written notice of their obligation under Subsections (h) and (i), which may be satisfied by being given a copy of those subsections by:

(1) the court during their initial appearance before the court;

(2) a peace officer arresting and releasing a child under Article 45.058(a) on release; and

(3) a peace officer that issues a citation under Section 543.003, Transportation Code, or Article 14.06(b) of this code.

(k) It is an affirmative defense to prosecution under Subsection (h) that the child and parent were not informed of their obligation under this article.

(l) Any order under this article is enforceable by the justice or municipal court by contempt.

Added by Acts 2001, 77th Leg., ch. 1514, § 9, eff. Sept. 1, 2001. Amended by Acts 2003, 78th Leg., ch. 283, § 34, eff. Sept. 1, 2003. Amended by Acts 2011, 82nd Leg., ch. 777 (H.B. 1964), § 3, eff. Sept. 1, 2011.

Art. 45.058.   Children Taken Into Custody

(a) A child may be released to the child's parent, guardian, custodian, or other responsible adult as provided by Section 52.02(a)(1), Family Code, if the child is taken into custody for an offense that a justice or municipal court has jurisdiction of under Article 4.11 or 4.14.

(b) A child described by Subsection (a) must be taken only to a place previously designated by the head of the law enforcement agency with custody of the child as an appropriate place of nonsecure custody for children unless the child:

(1) is released under Section 52.02(a)(1), Family Code; or

(2) is taken before a justice or municipal court.

(c) A place of nonsecure custody for children must be an unlocked, multipurpose area. A lobby, office, or interrogation room is suitable if the area is not designated, set aside, or used as a secure detention area and is not part of a secure detention area. A place of nonsecure custody may be a juvenile processing office designated under Section 52.025, Family Code, if the area is not locked when it is used as a place of nonsecure custody.

(d) The following procedures shall be followed in a place of nonsecure custody for children:

(1) a child may not be secured physically to a cuffing rail, chair, desk, or other stationary object;

(2) the child may be held in the nonsecure facility only long enough to accomplish the purpose of identification, investigation, processing, release to parents, or the arranging of transportation to the appropriate juvenile court, juvenile detention facility, secure detention facility, justice court, or municipal court;

(3) residential use of the area is prohibited; and

(4) the child shall be under continuous visual supervision by a law enforcement officer or facility staff person during the time the child is in nonsecure custody.

(e) Notwithstanding any other provision of this article, a child may not, under any circumstances, be detained in a place of nonsecure custody for more than six hours.

(f) A child taken into custody for an offense that a justice or municipal court has jurisdiction of under Article 4.11 or 4.14 may be presented or detained in a detention facility designated by the juvenile court under Section 52.02(a)(3), Family Code, only if:

(1) the child's non-traffic case is transferred to the juvenile court by a justice or municipal court under Section 51.08(b), Family Code; or

(2) the child is referred to the juvenile court by a justice or municipal court for contempt of court under Article 45.050.

(g) Except as provided by Subsection (g–1) and Section 37.143(a), Education Code, a law enforcement officer may issue a field release citation as provided by Article 14.06 in place of taking a child into custody for a traffic offense or an offense punishable by fine only.

(g–1) A law enforcement officer may issue a field release citation as provided by Article 14.06 in place of taking a child into custody for conduct constituting a violation of Section 49.02, Penal Code, only if the officer releases the child to the child's parent, guardian, custodian, or other responsible adult.

(h) In this article, "child" means a person who is:

(1) at least 10 years of age and younger than 17 years of age; and

(2) charged with or convicted of an offense that a justice or municipal court has jurisdiction of under Article 4.11 or 4.14.

(i) If a law enforcement officer issues a citation or files a complaint in the manner provided by Article 45.018 for conduct by a child 12 years of age or older that is alleged to have occurred on school property or on a vehicle owned or operated by a county or independent school district, the officer shall submit to the court the offense report, a statement by a witness to the alleged conduct, and a statement by a victim of the alleged conduct, if any. An attorney representing the state may not proceed in a trial of an offense unless the law enforcement officer complied with the requirements of this subsection.

(j) Notwithstanding Subsection (g) or (g–1), a law enforcement officer may not issue a citation or file a complaint in the manner provided by Article 45.018 for conduct by a child younger than 12 years of age that is alleged to have occurred on school property or on a vehicle owned or operated by a county or independent school district.

Added by Acts 2001, 77th Leg., ch. 1514, § 9, eff. Sept. 1, 2001. Amended by Acts 2009, 81st Leg., ch. 311, § 2, eff. Sept. 1, 2009; Acts 2013, 83rd Leg., ch. 1409 (S.B. 1114), § 1, eff. Sept. 1, 2013; Acts 2015, 84th Leg., ch. 1132 (S.B. 108), § 3, eff. Sept. 1, 2015.

Section 7(a) of Acts 2015, 84th Leg., ch. 1132 (S.B. 108) provides:

"(a) Except as provided by Subsection (b) of this section, the changes in law made by this Act apply only to an offense committed on or after the effective date [Sept. 1, 2015] of this Act. An offense committed before the effective date of this Act is governed by the law in effect on the date the offense was committed, and the former law is continued in effect for that purpose. For purposes of this section, an offense was committed before the effective date of this Act if any element of the offense occurred before that date."

Art. 45.059.   Children Taken Into Custody for Violation of Juvenile Curfew or Order

(a) A peace officer taking into custody a person younger than 17 years of age for violation of a juvenile curfew ordinance of a municipality or order of the commissioners court of a county shall, without unnecessary delay:

(1) release the person to the person's parent, guardian, or custodian;

(2) take the person before a justice or municipal court to answer the charge; or

(3) take the person to a place designated as a juvenile curfew processing office by the head of the law enforcement agency having custody of the person.

(b) A juvenile curfew processing office must observe the following procedures:

(1) the office must be an unlocked, multipurpose area that is not designated, set aside, or used as a secure detention area or part of a secure detention area;

(2) the person may not be secured physically to a cuffing rail, chair, desk, or stationary object;

(3) the person may not be held longer than necessary to accomplish the purposes of identification, investigation, processing, release to a parent, guardian, or custodian, or arrangement of transportation to school or court;

(4) a juvenile curfew processing office may not be designated or intended for residential purposes;

(5) the person must be under continuous visual supervision by a peace officer or other person during the time the person is in the juvenile curfew processing office; and

(6) a person may not be held in a juvenile curfew processing office for more than six hours.

(c) A place designated under this article as a juvenile curfew processing office is not subject to the approval of the juvenile board having jurisdiction where the governmental entity is located.

Added by Acts 2001, 77th Leg., ch. 1514, § 9, eff. Sept. 1, 2001.

Art. 45.06.   Renumbered as Vernon's Ann.C.C.P. art. 45.203 by Acts 1999, 76th Leg., ch. 1545, § 61, eff. Sept. 1, 1999

Art. 45.060.   Unadjudicated Children, Now Adults; Notice on Reaching Age of Majority; Offense

(a) Except as provided by Articles 45.058 and 45.059, an individual may not be taken into secured custody for offenses alleged to have occurred before the individual's 17th birthday.

(b) On or after an individual's 17th birthday, if the court has used all available procedures under this chapter to secure the individual's appearance to answer allegations made before the individual's 17th birthday, the court may issue a notice of continuing obligation to appear by personal service or by mail to the last known address and residence of the individual. The notice must order the individual to appear at a designated time, place, and date to answer the allegations detailed in the notice.

(c) Failure to appear as ordered by the notice under Subsection (b) is a Class C misdemeanor independent of Section 38.10, Penal Code, and Section 543.003, Transportation Code.

(d) It is an affirmative defense to prosecution under Subsection (c) that the individual was not informed of the individual's obligation under Articles 45.057(h) and (i) or did not receive notice as required by Subsection (b).

(e) A notice of continuing obligation to appear issued under this article must contain the following statement provided in boldfaced type or capital letters:

"WARNING: COURT RECORDS REVEAL THAT BEFORE YOUR 17TH BIRTHDAY YOU WERE ACCUSED OF A CRIMINAL OFFENSE AND HAVE FAILED TO MAKE AN APPEARANCE OR ENTER A PLEA IN THIS MATTER. AS AN ADULT, YOU ARE NOTIFIED THAT YOU HAVE A CONTINUING OBLIGATION TO APPEAR IN THIS CASE. FAILURE TO APPEAR AS REQUIRED BY THIS NOTICE MAY BE AN ADDITIONAL CRIMINAL OFFENSE AND RESULT IN A WARRANT BEING ISSUED FOR YOUR ARREST."

Added by Acts 2003, 78th Leg., ch. 283, § 35, eff. Sept. 1, 2003.

Art. 45.061.   Proceedings Concerning Electronic Transmission of Certain Visual Material Depicting Minor

(a) In this article, "parent" means a natural or adoptive parent, managing or possessory conservator, or legal guardian. The term does not include a parent whose parental rights have been terminated.

(b) If a justice or municipal court finds that a defendant has committed an offense under Section 43.261, Penal Code, the court may enter an order requiring the defendant to attend and successfully complete an educational program described by Section 37.218, Education Code, or another equivalent educational program.

(c) A court that enters an order under Subsection (b) shall require the defendant or the defendant's parent to pay the cost of attending an educational program under Subsection (b) if the court determines that the defendant or the defendant's parent is financially able to make payment.

Added by Acts 2011, 82nd Leg., ch. 1322 (S.B. 407), § 15, eff. Sept. 1, 2011.

Arts. 45.07 to 45.09. Repealed by Acts 1999, 76th Leg., ch. 1545, § 75(a), eff. Sept. 1, 1999

Art. 45.10. Renumbered as Vernon's Ann.C.C.P. art. 45.042 by Acts 1999, 76th Leg., ch. 1545, § 40, eff. Sept. 1, 1999

SUBCHAPTER C.   PROCEDURES IN JUSTICE COURT

Art. 45.101.   Justice Court Prosecutions

(a) All prosecutions in a justice court shall be conducted by the county or district attorney or a deputy county or district attorney.

(b) Except as otherwise provided by law, appeals from justice court may be prosecuted by the district attorney or a deputy district attorney with the consent of the county attorney.

Added by Acts 1999, 76th Leg., ch. 1545, § 55, eff. Sept. 1, 1999.

Art. 45.102.   Offenses Committed in Another County

Whenever complaint is made before any justice of the peace that a felony has been committed in any other than a county in which the complaint is made, the justice shall issue a warrant for the arrest of the accused, directed as in other cases, commanding that the accused be arrested and taken before any magistrate of the county where such felony is alleged to have been committed, forthwith, for examination as in other cases.

Acts 1965, 59th Leg., vol. 2, p. 317, ch. 722. Renumbered from Vernon's Ann.C.C.P. art. 45.21 and amended by Acts 1999, 76th Leg., ch. 1545, § 56, eff. Sept. 1, 1999.

Art. 45.103.   Warrant Without Complaint

If a criminal offense that a justice of the peace has jurisdiction to try is committed within the view of the justice, the justice may issue a warrant for the arrest of the offender.

Acts 1965, 59th Leg., vol. 2, p. 317, ch. 722. Renumbered from Vernon's Ann.C.C.P. art. 45.15 and amended by Acts 1999, 76th Leg., ch. 1545, § 57, eff. Sept. 1, 1999.

Art. 45.11.   Renumbered as Vernon's Ann.C.C.P. art. 44.281 by Acts 1999, 76th Leg., ch. 1545, § 65, eff. Sept. 1, 1999

Art. 45.12.   Repealed by Acts 1999, 76th Leg., ch. 1545, § 75(a), eff. Sept. 1, 1999

Art. 45.13.   Renumbered as Vernon's Ann.C.C.P. art. 45.017 by Acts 1999, 76th Leg., ch. 1545, § 14, eff. Sept. 1, 1999

Art. 45.14.   Repealed by Acts 1989, 71st Leg., ch. 499, § 2, eff. Aug. 28, 1989

Art. 45.15.   Renumbered as Vernon's Ann.C.C.P. art. 45.103 by Acts 1999, 76th Leg., ch. 1545, § 57, eff. Sept. 1, 1999

Art. 45.16.   Repealed by Acts 1999, 76th Leg., ch. 1545, § 75(a), eff. Sept. 1, 1999

Art. 45.17.   Renumbered as Vernon's Ann.C.C.P. art. 45.019 by Acts 1999, 76th Leg., ch. 1545, § 16, eff. Sept. 1, 1999

Art. 45.18.   Renumbered as Vernon's Ann.C.C.P. art. 45.014 by Acts 1999, 76th Leg., ch. 1545, § 11, eff. Sept. 1, 1999

Art. 45.19.   Repealed by Acts 1999, 76th Leg., ch. 1545, § 75(a), eff. Sept. 1, 1999

Art. 45.20.   Repealed by Acts 1991, 72nd Leg., ch. 446, § 2, eff. June 11, 1991

SUBCHAPTER D.   PROCEDURES IN MUNICIPAL COURT

Art. 45.201.   Municipal Prosecutions

(a) All prosecutions in a municipal court shall be conducted by the city attorney of the municipality or by a deputy city attorney.

(b) The county attorney of the county in which the municipality is situated may, if the county attorney so desires, also represent the state in such prosecutions. In such cases, the county attorney is not entitled to receive any fees or other compensation for those services.

(c) With the consent of the county attorney, appeals from municipal court to a county court, county court at law, or any appellate court may be prosecuted by the city attorney or a deputy city attorney.

(d) It is the primary duty of a municipal prosecutor not to convict, but to see that justice is done.

Acts 1965, 59th Leg., vol. 2, p. 317, ch. 722. Amended by Acts 1987, 70th Leg., ch. 923, § 1, eff. Aug. 31, 1987. Renumbered from Vernon's Ann.C.C.P. art. 45.03 and amended by Acts 1999, 76th Leg., ch. 1545, § 59, eff. Sept. 1, 1999.

Art. 45.202. Service of Process

(a) All process issuing out of a municipal court may be served and shall be served when directed by the court, by a peace officer or marshal of the municipality within which it is situated, under the same rules as are provided by law for the service by sheriffs and constables of process issuing out of the justice court, so far as applicable.

(b) The peace officer or marshal may serve all process issuing out of a municipal court anywhere in the county in which the municipality is situated. If the municipality is situated in more than one county, the peace officer or marshal may serve the process throughout those counties.

Acts 1965, 59th Leg., vol. 2, p. 317, ch. 722. Amended by Acts 1967, 60th Leg., p. 1171, ch. 523, § 1, eff. Aug. 28, 1967. Renumbered from Vernon's Ann.C.C.P. art. 45.04 and amended by Acts 1999, 76th Leg., ch. 1545, § 60, eff. Sept. 1, 1999.

Art. 45.203. Collection Of Fines, Costs, and Special Expenses

(a) The governing body of each municipality shall by ordinance prescribe rules, not inconsistent with any law of this state, as may be proper to enforce the collection of fines imposed by a municipal court. In addition to any other method of enforcement, the municipality may enforce the collection of fines by:

(1) execution against the property of the defendant; or

(2) imprisonment of the defendant.

(b) The governing body of a municipality may adopt such rules and regulations, not inconsistent with any law of this state, concerning the practice and procedure in the municipal court as the governing body may consider proper.

(c) The governing body of each municipality may prescribe by ordinance the collection, after due notice, of a special expense, not to exceed $25 for the issuance and service of a warrant of arrest for an offense under Section 38.10, Penal Code, or Section 543.009, Transportation Code. Money collected from the special expense shall be paid into the municipal treasury for the use and benefit of the municipality.

(d) Costs may not be imposed or collected in criminal cases in municipal court by municipal ordinance.

Acts 1965, 59th Leg., vol. 2, p. 317, ch. 722. Amended by Acts 1983, 68th Leg., p. 2140, ch. 389, § 1, eff. Sept. 1, 1983; Acts 1987, 70th Leg., ch. 124, § 1, eff. Sept. 1, 1987; Acts 1995, 74th Leg., ch. 76, § 14.26, eff. Sept. 1, 1995. Renumbered from Vernon's Ann.C.C.P. art. 45.06 and amended by Acts 1999, 76th Leg., ch. 1545, § 61, eff. Sept. 1, 1999.

Art. 45.21. Renumbered as Vernon's Ann.C.C.P. art. 45.102 by Acts 1999, 76th Leg., ch. 1545, § 56, eff. Sept. 1, 1999

Arts. 45.22, 45.23. Repealed by Acts 1999, 76th Leg., ch. 1545, § 75(a), eff. Sept. 1, 1999

Art. 45.231. Renumbered as Vernon's Ann.C.C.P. art. 45.044 by Acts 1999, 76th Leg., ch. 1545, § 44, eff. Sept. 1, 1999

Art. 45.24. Renumbered as Vernon's Ann.C.C.P. art. 45.025 by Acts 1999, 76th Leg., ch. 1545, § 23, eff. Sept. 1, 1999

Art. 45.25. Renumbered as Vernon's Ann.C.C.P. art. 45.027 by Acts 1999, 76th Leg., ch. 1545, § 25, eff. Sept. 1, 1999

Art. 45.251. Renumbered as Vernon's Ann.C.C.P. art. 45.026 by Acts 1999, 76th Leg., ch. 1545, § 24, eff. Sept. 1, 1999

Arts. 45.26, 45.27. Repealed by Acts 1999, 76th Leg., ch. 1545, § 75(a), eff. Sept. 1, 1999

Art. 45.28. Renumbered as Vernon's Ann.C.C.P. art. 45.029 by Acts 1999, 76th Leg., ch. 1545, § 27, eff. Sept. 1, 1999

Art. 45.29. Renumbered as Vernon's Ann.C.C.P. art. 45.028 by Acts 1999, 76th Leg., ch. 1545, § 26, eff. Sept. 1, 1999

Art. 45.30. Renumbered as Vernon's Ann.C.C.P. art. 45.030 by Acts 1999, 76th Leg., ch. 1545, § 28, eff. Sept. 1, 1999

Art. 45.31. Renumbered as Vernon's Ann.C.C.P. art. 45.023 by Acts 1999, 76th Leg., ch. 1545, § 21, eff. Sept. 1, 1999

Art. 45.32. Repealed by Acts 1999, 76th Leg., ch. 1545, § 75(a), eff. Sept. 1, 1999

Art. 45.33. Renumbered as Vernon's Ann.C.C.P. art. 45.021 by Acts 1999, 76th Leg., ch. 1545, § 18, eff. Sept. 1, 1999

Art. 45.331. Renumbered as Vernon's Ann.C.C.P. art. 45.0215 by Acts 1999, 76th Leg., ch. 1545, § 19, eff. Sept. 1, 1999

Art. 45.34. Renumbered as Vernon's Ann.C.C.P. art. 45.022 by Acts 1999, 76th Leg., ch. 1545, § 20, eff. Sept. 1, 1999

Art. 45.35. Renumbered as Vernon's Ann.C.C.P. art. 45.024 by Acts 1999, 76th Leg., ch. 1545, § 22, eff. Sept. 1, 1999

Art. 45.36. Renumbered as Vernon's Ann.C.C.P. art. 45.031 by Acts 1999, 76th Leg., ch. 1545, § 29, eff. Sept. 1, 1999

Art. 45.37. Renumbered as Vernon's Ann.C.C.P. art. 45.020 by Acts 1999, 76th Leg., ch. 1545, § 17, eff. Sept. 1, 1999

Art. 45.38. Renumbered as Vernon's Ann.C.C.P. art. 45.011 by Acts 1999, 76th Leg., ch. 1545, § 8, eff. Sept. 1, 1999

Art. 45.39. Renumbered as Vernon's Ann.C.C.P. art. 45.034 by Acts 1999, 76th Leg., ch. 1545, § 32, eff. Sept. 1, 1999

Art. 45.40. Renumbered as Vernon's Ann.C.C.P. art. 45.035 by Acts 1999, 76th Leg., ch. 1545, § 33, eff. Sept. 1, 1999

Art. 45.41. Renumbered as Vernon's Ann.C.C.P. art. 45.016 by Acts 1999, 76th Leg., ch. 1545, § 13, eff. Sept. 1, 1999

Art. 45.42. Renumbered as Vernon's Ann.C.C.P. art. 45.036 by Acts 1999, 76th Leg., ch. 1545, § 34, eff. Sept. 1, 1999

Art. 45.43. Renumbered as Vernon's Ann.C.C.P. art. 45.015 by Acts 1999, 76th Leg., ch. 1545, § 12, eff. Sept. 1, 1999

Art. 45.44. Renumbered as Vernon's Ann.C.C.P. art. 45.038 by Acts 1999, 76th Leg., ch. 1545, § 36, eff. Sept. 1, 1999

Art. 45.45. Renumbered as Vernon's Ann.C.C.P. art. 45.037 by Acts 1999, 76th Leg., ch. 1545, § 35, eff. Sept. 1, 1999

Art. 45.46. Renumbered as Vernon's Ann.C.C.P. art. 45.039 by Acts 1999, 76th Leg., ch. 1545, § 37, eff. Sept. 1, 1999

Art. 45.47. Renumbered as Vernon's Ann.C.C.P. art. 45.040 by Acts 1999, 76th Leg., ch. 1545, § 38, eff. Sept. 1, 1999

Art. 45.48. Renumbered as Vernon's Ann.C.C.P. art. 45.043 by Acts 1999, 76th Leg., ch. 1545, § 43, eff. Sept. 1, 1999

Art. 45.49. Repealed by Acts 1999, 76th Leg., ch. 1545, § 75(a), eff. Sept. 1, 1999

Art. 45.50. Renumbered as Vernon's Ann.C.C.P. art. 45.041 by Acts 1999, 76th Leg., ch. 1545, § 39, eff. Sept. 1, 1999

Art. 45.51. Renumbered as Vernon's Ann.C.C.P. art. 45.045 by Acts 1999, 76th Leg., ch. 1545, § 45, eff. Sept. 1, 1999

Art. 45.52. Renumbered as Vernon's Ann.C.C.P. art. 45.046 by Acts 1999, 76th Leg., ch. 1545, § 46, eff. Sept. 1, 1999

Arts. 45.521, 45.522. Renumbered as Vernon's Ann. C.C.P. arts. 45.049, 45.050 by Acts 1999, 76th Leg., ch. 1545, § 49, eff. Sept. 1, 1999

Art. 45.53. Renumbered as Vernon's Ann.C.C.P. art. 45.048 by Acts 1999, 76th Leg., ch. 1545, § 48, eff. Sept. 1, 1999

Art. 45.54. Renumbered as Vernon's Ann.C.C.P. art. 45.051 by Acts 1999, 76th Leg., ch. 1545, § 50, eff. Sept. 1, 1999

Art. 45.541. Repealed by Acts 2001, 77th Leg., ch. 1420, § 3.0021(b), eff. Sept. 1, 2001

Art. 45.55. Renumbered as Vernon's Ann.C.C.P. art. 45.052 by Acts 1999, 76th Leg., ch. 1545, § 52, eff. Sept. 1, 1999

Art. 45.56. Renumbered as Vernon's Ann.C.C.P. art. 45.053 by Acts 1999, 76th Leg., ch. 1545, § 53, eff. Sept. 1, 1999

MISCELLANEOUS PROCEEDINGS

CHAPTER 46. INSANITY AS DEFENSE

Art. 46.01. Repealed by Acts 1999, 76th Leg., ch. 561, § 8, eff. September 1, 1999

Art. 46.02. Repealed by Acts 2003, 78th Leg., ch. 35, § 15, eff. Jan. 1, 2004

Art. 46.03. Repealed in part and renumbered in part by Acts 2005, 79th Leg., ch. 831, § 1, eff. Sept. 1, 2005; Acts 2011, 82nd Leg., ch. 787 (H.B. 2124), § 1, eff. June 17, 2011

Art. 46.04. Transportation to a Mental Health Facility or Residential Care Facility

Persons Accompanying Transport

Sec. 1. (a) A patient transported from a jail or detention facility to a mental health facility or a residential care facility shall be transported by a special officer for mental health assignment certified under Section 1701.404, Occupations Code, or by a sheriff or constable.

(b) The court ordering the transport shall require appropriate medical personnel to accompany the person transporting the patient, at the expense of the county from which the patient is transported, if there is reasonable cause to believe the patient will require medical assistance or will require the administration of medication during the transportation.

(c) A female patient must be accompanied by a female attendant.

Requirements for Transport

Sec. 2. The transportation of a patient from a jail or detention facility to a mental health facility or residential care facility must meet the following requirements:

(1) the patient must be transported directly to the facility within a reasonable amount of time and without undue delay;

(2) a vehicle used to transport the patient must be adequately heated in cold weather and adequately ventilated in warm weather;

(3) a special diet or other medical precautions recommended by the patient's physician must be followed;

(4) the person transporting the patient shall give the patient reasonable opportunities to get food and water and to use a bathroom; and

(5) the patient may not be transported with a state prisoner.

Added by Acts 1999, 76th Leg., ch. 1512, § 6, eff. Sept. 1, 1999. Amended by Acts 2001, 77th Leg., ch. 1420, § 14.736, eff. Sept. 1, 2001.

Art. 46.05. Competency to be Executed

(a) A person who is incompetent to be executed may not be executed.

(b) The trial court retains jurisdiction over motions filed by or for a defendant under this article.

(c) A motion filed under this article must identify the proceeding in which the defendant was convicted, give the date of the final judgment, set forth the fact that an execution date has been set if the date has been set, and clearly set forth alleged facts in support of the assertion that the defendant is presently incompetent to be executed. The defendant shall attach affidavits, records, or other evidence supporting the defendant's allegations or shall state why those items are not attached. The defendant shall identify any previous proceedings in which the defendant challenged the defendant's competency in relation to the conviction and sentence in question, including any challenge to the defendant's competency to be executed, competency to stand trial, or sanity at the time of the offense. The motion must be verified by the oath of some person on the defendant's behalf.

(d) On receipt of a motion filed under this article, the trial court shall determine whether the defendant has raised a substantial doubt of the defendant's competency to be executed on the basis of:

(1) the motion, any attached documents, and any responsive pleadings; and

(2) if applicable, the presumption of competency under Subsection (e).

(e) If a defendant is determined to have previously filed a motion under this article, and has previously been determined to be competent to be executed, the previous adjudication creates a presumption of competency and the defendant is not entitled to a hearing on the subsequent motion filed under this article, unless the defendant makes a prima facie showing of a substantial change in circumstances sufficient to raise a significant question as to the defendant's competency to be executed at the time of filing the subsequent motion under this article.

(f) If the trial court determines that the defendant has made a substantial showing of incompetency, the court shall order at least two mental health experts to examine the defendant using the standard described by Subsection (h) to determine whether the defendant is incompetent to be executed.

(g) If the trial court does not determine that the defendant has made a substantial showing of incompetency, the court shall deny the motion and may set an execution date as otherwise provided by law.

(h) A defendant is incompetent to be executed if the defendant does not understand:

(1) that he or she is to be executed and that the execution is imminent; and

(2) the reason he or she is being executed.

(i) Mental health experts who examine a defendant under this article shall provide within a time ordered by the trial court copies of their reports to the attorney representing the state, the attorney representing the defendant, and the court.

(j) By filing a motion under this article, the defendant waives any claim of privilege with respect to, and consents to the release of, all mental health and medical records relevant to whether the defendant is incompetent to be executed.

(k) The trial court shall determine whether, on the basis of reports provided under Subsection (i), the motion, any attached documents, any responsive pleadings, and any evidence introduced in the final competency hearing, the defendant has established by a preponderance of the evidence that the defendant is incompetent to be executed. If the court makes a finding that the defendant is not incompetent to be executed, the court may set an execution date as otherwise provided by law.

(*l*) Following the trial court's determination under Subsection (k) and on motion of a party, the clerk shall send immediately to the court of criminal appeals in accordance with Section 8(d), Article 11.071, the appropriate documents for that court's review and entry of a judgment of whether to adopt the trial court's order, findings, or recommendations issued under Subsection (g) or (k). The court of criminal appeals also shall determine whether any existing execution date should be withdrawn and a stay of execution issued while that court is conducting its review or, if a stay is not issued during the review, after entry of its judgment.

(l–1) Notwithstanding Subsection (*l*), the court of criminal appeals may not review any finding of the defendant's competency made by a trial court as a result of a motion filed under this article if the motion is filed on or after the 20th day before the defendant's scheduled execution date.

(m) If a stay of execution is issued by the court of criminal appeals, the trial court periodically shall order that the defendant be reexamined by mental health experts to determine whether the defendant is no longer incompetent to be executed.

(n) If the court of criminal appeals enters a judgment that a defendant is not incompetent to be executed, the court may withdraw any stay of execution issued under Subsection (*l*), and the trial court may set an execution date as otherwise provided by law.

Added by Acts 1999, 76th Leg., ch. 654, § 1, eff. Sept. 1, 1999. Renumbered from Vernon's Ann. C.C.P. art. 46.04 by Acts 2001, 77th Leg., ch. 1420, § 21.001(13), eff. Sept. 1, 2001. Amended by Acts 2007, 80th Leg., ch. 677, § 1, eff. Sept. 1, 2007.

This article has been declared unconstitutional. See Wood v. Quarterman, 572 F.Supp.2d 814 (W.D.Tex. 2008).

CHAPTER 46A. AIDS AND HIV TESTING IN COUNTY AND MUNICIPAL JAILS

Article
46A.01. Testing; segregation; disclosure.

Art. 46A.01. Testing; segregation; disclosure

(a) In this article "AIDS" and "HIV" have the meanings assigned those terms by Section 81.101, Health and Safety Code.

(b) A county or municipality may test an inmate confined in the county or municipal jail or in a contract facility authorized by Article 5115d, Revised Statutes, or Article 5115e, Revised Statutes, to determine the proper medical treatment of the inmate or the proper social management of the inmate or other inmates in the jail or facility.

(c) If the county or municipality determines that an inmate has a positive test result for AIDS or HIV, the county or municipality may segregate the inmate from other inmates in the jail or facility.

(d) This article does not provide a duty to test for AIDS or HIV, and a cause of action does not arise under this article from a failure to test for AIDS or HIV.

Added by Acts 1989, 71st Leg., ch. 1195, § 13, eff. Sept. 1, 1989. Amended by Acts 1991, 72nd Leg., ch. 14, § 284(10), eff. Sept. 1, 1991.

CHAPTER 46B. INCOMPETENCY TO STAND TRIAL

SUBCHAPTER A. GENERAL PROVISIONS

SUBCHAPTER A. GENERAL PROVISIONS

Art. 46B.001. Definitions

In this chapter:

(1) "Inpatient mental health facility" has the meaning assigned by Section 571.003, Health and Safety Code.

(2) "Intellectual disability" has the meaning assigned by Section 591.003, Health and Safety Code.

(3) "Local mental health authority" has the meaning assigned by Section 571.003, Health and Safety Code.

(4) "Local intellectual and developmental disability authority" has the meaning assigned by Section 531.002, Health and Safety Code.

(5) "Mental health facility" has the meaning assigned by Section 571.003, Health and Safety Code.

(6) "Mental illness" has the meaning assigned by Section 571.003, Health and Safety Code.

(7) "Residential care facility" has the meaning assigned by Section 591.003, Health and Safety Code.

(8) "Electronic broadcast system" means a two-way electronic communication of image and sound between the defendant and the court and includes secure Internet videoconferencing.

(9) "Competency restoration" means the treatment or education process for restoring a person's ability to consult with the person's attorney with a reasonable degree of rational understanding, including a rational and factual understanding of the court proceedings and charges against the person.

Added by Acts 2003, 78th Leg., ch. 35, § 1, eff. Jan. 1, 2004. Amended by Acts 2005, 79th Leg., ch. 324, § 1, eff. Sept. 1, 2005; Acts 2015, 84th Leg., ch. 1 (S.B. 219), § 6.006, eff. April 2, 2015; Acts 2017, 85th Leg., ch. 748 (S.B. 1326), § 5, eff. Sept. 1, 2017.

Section 37 of Acts 2017, 85th Leg., ch. 748 (S.B. 1326) provides:

"The changes in law made by this Act apply only to a defendant charged with an offense committed on or after the effective date [Sept. 1, 2017] of this Act. A defendant charged with an offense committed before the effective date of this Act is governed by the law in effect on the date the offense was committed, and the former law is continued in effect for that purpose. For purposes of this section, an offense was committed before the effective date of this Act if any element of the offense occurred before that date."

Art. 46B.002. Applicability

This chapter applies to a defendant charged with a felony or with a misdemeanor punishable by confinement.

Added by Acts 2003, 78th Leg., ch. 35, § 1, eff. Jan. 1, 2004.

Art. 46B.003. Incompetency; Presumptions

(a) A person is incompetent to stand trial if the person does not have:

(1) sufficient present ability to consult with the person's lawyer with a reasonable degree of rational understanding; or

(2) a rational as well as factual understanding of the proceedings against the person.

(b) A defendant is presumed competent to stand trial and shall be found competent to stand trial unless proved incompetent by a preponderance of the evidence.

Added by Acts 2003, 78th Leg., ch. 35, § 1, eff. Jan. 1, 2004.

Art. 46B.004. Raising Issue of Incompetency to Stand Trial

(a) Either party may suggest by motion, or the trial court may suggest on its own motion, that the defendant may be incompetent to stand trial. A motion suggesting that the defendant may be incompetent to stand trial may be supported by affidavits setting out the facts on which the suggestion is made.

(b) If evidence suggesting the defendant may be incompetent to stand trial comes to the attention of the court, the court on its own motion shall suggest that the defendant may be incompetent to stand trial.

(c) On suggestion that the defendant may be incompetent to stand trial, the court shall determine by informal inquiry whether there is some evidence from any source that would support a finding that the defendant may be incompetent to stand trial.

(c-1) A suggestion of incompetency is the threshold requirement for an informal inquiry under Subsection (c) and may consist solely of a representation from any credible source that the defendant may be incompetent. A further evidentiary showing is not required to initiate the inquiry, and the court is not required to have a bona fide doubt about the competency of the defendant. Evidence suggesting the need for an informal inquiry may be based on observations made in relation to one or more of the factors described by Article 46B.024 or on any other indication that the defendant is incompetent within the meaning of Article 46B.003.

(d) If the court determines there is evidence to support a finding of incompetency, the court, except as provided by Subsection (e) and Article 46B.005(d), shall stay all other proceedings in the case.

(e) At any time during the proceedings under this chapter after the issue of the defendant's incompetency to stand trial is first raised, the court on the motion of the attorney representing the state may dismiss all charges pending against the defendant, regardless of whether there is any evidence to support a finding of the defendant's incompetency under Subsection (d) or whether the court has made a finding of incompetency under this chapter. If the court dismisses the charges against the defendant, the court may not continue the proceedings under this chapter, except that, if there is evidence to support a finding of the defendant's incompetency under Subsection (d), the court may proceed under Subchapter F. If the court does not elect to proceed under Subchapter F, the court shall discharge the defendant.

Added by Acts 2003, 78th Leg., ch. 35, § 1, eff. Jan. 1, 2004. Amended by Acts 2005, 79th Leg., ch. 324, § 2, eff. Sept. 1, 2005; Acts 2005, 79th Leg., ch. 324, § 2, eff. Sept. 1, 2005; Acts 2011, 82nd Leg., ch. 822 (H.B. 2725), § 2, eff. Sept. 1, 2011.

Art. 46B.005.   Determining Incompetency to Stand Trial

(a) If after an informal inquiry the court determines that evidence exists to support a finding of incompetency, the court shall order an examination under Subchapter B to determine whether the defendant is incompetent to stand trial in a criminal case.

(b) Except as provided by Subsection (c), the court shall hold a trial under Subchapter C before determining whether the defendant is incompetent to stand trial on the merits.

(c) A trial under this chapter is not required if:

(1) neither party's counsel requests a trial on the issue of incompetency;

(2) neither party's counsel opposes a finding of incompetency; and

(3) the court does not, on its own motion, determine that a trial is necessary to determine incompetency.

(d) If the issue of the defendant's incompetency to stand trial is raised after the trial on the merits begins, the court may determine the issue at any time before the sentence is pronounced. If the determination is delayed until after the return of a verdict, the court shall make the determination as soon as reasonably possible after the return. If a verdict of not guilty is returned, the court may not determine the issue of incompetency.

Added by Acts 2003, 78th Leg., ch. 35, § 1, eff. Jan. 1, 2004. Amended by Acts 2005, 79th Leg., ch. 324, § 3, eff. Sept. 1, 2005.

Art. 46B.006.   Appointment of and Representation by Counsel

(a) A defendant is entitled to representation by counsel before any court-ordered competency evaluation and during any proceeding at which it is suggested that the defendant may be incompetent to stand trial.

(b) If the defendant is indigent and the court has not appointed counsel to represent the defendant, the court shall appoint counsel as necessary to comply with Subsection (a).

Added by Acts 2003, 78th Leg., ch. 35, § 1, eff. Jan. 1, 2004.

Art. 46B.007.   Admissibility of Statements and Certain Other Evidence

A statement made by a defendant during an examination or trial on the defendant's incompetency, the testimony of an expert based on that statement, and evidence obtained as a result of that statement may not be admitted in evidence against the defendant in any criminal proceeding, other than at:

(1) a trial on the defendant's incompetency; or

(2) any proceeding at which the defendant first introduces into evidence a statement, testimony, or evidence described by this article.

Added by Acts 2003, 78th Leg., ch. 35, § 1, eff. Jan. 1, 2004. Amended by Acts 2005, 79th Leg., ch. 324, § 3, eff. Sept. 1, 2005.

Art. 46B.008.   Rules of Evidence

Notwithstanding Rule 101, Texas Rules of Evidence, the Texas Rules of Evidence apply to a trial under Subchapter C or other proceeding under this chapter whether the proceeding is before a jury or before the court.

Added by Acts 2003, 78th Leg., ch. 35, § 1, eff. Jan. 1, 2004. Amended by Acts 2005, 79th Leg., ch. 324, § 3, eff. Sept. 1, 2005.

Art. 46B.009. Time Credits

A court sentencing a person convicted of a criminal offense shall credit to the term of the person's sentence each of the following periods for which the person may be confined in a mental health facility, residential care facility, or jail:

(1) any period of confinement that occurs pending a determination under Subchapter C as to the defendant's competency to stand trial; and

(2) any period of confinement that occurs between the date of any initial determination of the defendant's incompetency under that subchapter and the date the person is transported to jail following a final judicial determination that the person has been restored to competency.

Added by Acts 2003, 78th Leg., ch. 35, § 1, eff. Jan. 1, 2004. Amended by Acts 2005, 79th Leg., ch. 324, § 3, eff. Sept. 1, 2005; Acts 2007, 80th Leg., ch. 1307, § 2, eff. Sept. 1, 2007; Acts 2011, 82nd Leg., ch. 718 (H.B. 748), § 2, eff. Sept. 1, 2011; Acts 2011, 82nd Leg., ch. 822 (H.B. 2725), § 3, eff. Sept. 1, 2011.

Art. 46B.0095. Maximum period of commitment or program participation determined by maximum term for offense

(a) A defendant may not, under Subchapter D or E or any other provision of this chapter, be committed to a mental hospital or other inpatient or residential facility or to a jail-based competency restoration program, ordered to participate in an outpatient competency restoration or treatment program, or subjected to any combination of inpatient treatment, outpatient competency restoration or treatment program participation, or jail-based competency restoration under this chapter for a cumulative period that exceeds the maximum term provided by law for the offense for which the defendant was to be tried, except that if the defendant is charged with a misdemeanor and has been ordered only to participate in an outpatient competency restoration or treatment program under Subchapter D or E, the maximum period of restoration is two years.

(b) On expiration of the maximum restoration period under Subsection (a), the mental hospital, facility, or program provider identified in the most recent order of commitment or order of outpatient competency restoration or treatment program participation under this chapter shall assess the defendant to determine if civil proceedings under Subtitle C or D, Title 7, Health and Safety Code, are appropriate. The defendant may be confined for an additional period in a mental hospital or other facility or may be ordered to participate for an additional period in an outpatient treatment program, as appropriate, only pursuant to civil proceedings conducted under Subtitle C or D, Title 7, Health and Safety Code, by a court with probate jurisdiction.

(c) The cumulative period described by Subsection (a):

(1) begins on the date the initial order of commitment or initial order for outpatient competency restoration or treatment program participation is entered under this chapter; and

(2) in addition to any inpatient or outpatient competency restoration periods or program participation periods described by Subsection (a), includes any time that, following the entry of an order described by Subdivision (1), the defendant is confined in a correctional facility, as defined by Section 1.07, Penal Code, or is otherwise in the custody of the sheriff during or while awaiting, as applicable:

(A) the defendant's transfer to:

(i) a mental hospital or other inpatient or residential facility; or

(ii) a jail-based competency restoration program;

(B) the defendant's release on bail to participate in an outpatient competency restoration or treatment program; or

(C) a criminal trial following any temporary restoration of the defendant's competency to stand trial.

(d) The court shall credit to the cumulative period described by Subsection (a) any time that a defendant, following arrest for the offense for which the defendant was to be tried, is confined in a correctional facility, as defined by Section 1.07, Penal Code, before the initial order of commitment or initial order for outpatient competency restoration or treatment program participation is entered under this chapter.

(e) In addition to the time credit awarded under Subsection (d), the court may credit to the cumulative period described by Subsection (a) any good conduct time the defendant may have been granted under Article 42.032 in relation to the defendant's confinement as described by Subsection (d).

Added by Acts 2007, 80th Leg., ch. 1307, § 2, eff. Sept. 1, 2007. Amended by Acts 2011, 82nd Leg., ch. 718 (H.B. 748), § 3, eff. Sept. 1, 2011; Acts 2011, 82nd Leg., ch. 822 (H.B. 2725), § 4, eff. Sept. 1, 2011; Acts 2013, 83rd Leg., ch. 161 (S.B. 1093), § 3.010, eff. Sept. 1, 2013; Acts 2015, 84th Leg., ch. 627 (S.B. 1326), §§ 1, 3, eff. Sept. 1, 2015; Acts 2017, 85th Leg., ch. 748 (S.B. 1326), §§ 6, 7, eff. Sept. 1, 2017.

Section 4 of Acts 2015, 84th Leg., ch. 627 (S.B. 1326) provides:

"The change in law made by this Act applies only to a defendant with respect to whom any proceeding under Chapter 46B, Code of Criminal Procedure, is conducted on or after the effective date [Sept. 1, 2015] of this Act."

Section 37 of Acts 2017, 85th Leg., ch. 748 (S.B. 1326) provides:

"The changes in law made by this Act apply only to a defendant charged with an offense committed on or after the effective date [Sept. 1, 2017] of this Act. A defendant charged with an offense committed before the effective date of this Act is governed by the law in effect on the date the offense was committed, and the former law is continued in effect for that purpose. For purposes of this section, an offense was committed before the effective date of this Act if any element of the offense occurred before that date."

Art. 46B.010.   Mandatory dismissal of misdemeanor charges

If a court orders that a defendant charged with a misdemeanor punishable by confinement be committed to a mental hospital or other inpatient or residential facility or to a jail-based competency restoration program, that the defendant participate in an outpatient competency restoration or treatment program, or that the defendant be subjected to any combination of inpatient treatment, outpatient competency restoration or treatment program participation, or jail-based competency restoration under this chapter, and the defendant is not tried before the expiration of the maximum period of restoration described by Article 46B.0095:

(1) on the motion of the attorney representing the state, the court shall dismiss the charge; or

(2) on the motion of the attorney representing the defendant and notice to the attorney representing the state, the court:

(A) shall set the matter to be heard not later than the 10th day after the date of filing of the motion; and

(B) may dismiss the charge on a finding that the defendant was not tried before the expiration of the maximum period of restoration.

Added by Acts 2003, 78th Leg., ch. 35, § 1, eff. Jan. 1, 2004. Amended by Acts 2007, 80th Leg., ch. 1307, § 2, eff. Sept. 1, 2007; Acts 2011, 82nd Leg., ch. 718 (H.B. 748), § 4, eff. Sept. 1, 2011; Acts 2011, 82nd Leg., ch. 822 (H.B. 2725), § 5, eff. Sept. 1, 2011; Acts 2015, 84th Leg., ch. 627 (S.B. 1326), § 2, eff. Sept. 1, 2015; Acts 2017, 85th Leg., ch. 748 (S.B. 1326), § 8, eff. Sept. 1, 2017.

Section 4 of Acts 2015, 84th Leg., ch. 627 (S.B. 1326) provides:

"The change in law made by this Act applies only to a defendant with respect to whom any proceeding under Chapter 46B, Code of Criminal Procedure, is conducted on or after the effective date [Sept. 1, 2015] of this Act."

Section 37 of Acts 2017, 85th Leg., ch. 748 (S.B. 1326) provides:

"The changes in law made by this Act apply only to a defendant charged with an offense committed on or after the effective date [Sept. 1, 2017] of this Act. A defendant charged with an offense committed before the effective date of this Act is governed by the law

in effect on the date the offense was committed, and the former law is continued in effect for that purpose. For purposes of this section, an offense was committed before the effective date of this Act if any element of the offense occurred before that date."

Art. 46B.011.   Appeals

Neither the state nor the defendant is entitled to make an interlocutory appeal relating to a determination or ruling under Article 46B.005.

Added by Acts 2003, 78th Leg., ch. 35, § 1, eff. Jan. 1, 2004. Amended by Acts 2005, 79th Leg., ch. 324, § 3, eff. Sept. 1, 2005.

Art. 46B.012.   Compliance With Chapter

The failure of a person to comply with this chapter does not provide a defendant with a right to dismissal of charges.

Added by Acts 2003, 78th Leg., ch. 35, § 1, eff. Jan. 1, 2004.

Art. 46B.013.   Use of Electronic Broadcast System in Certain Proceedings Under This Chapter

(a) A hearing may be conducted using an electronic broadcast system as permitted by this chapter and in accordance with the other provisions of this code if:

(1) written consent to the use of an electronic broadcast system is filed with the court by:

(A) the defendant or the attorney representing the defendant; and

(B) the attorney representing the state;

(2) the electronic broadcast system provides for a simultaneous, compressed full motion video, and interactive communication of image and sound between the judge, the attorney representing the state, the attorney representing the defendant, and the defendant; and

(3) on request of the defendant or the attorney representing the defendant, the defendant and the attorney representing the defendant are able to communicate privately without being recorded or heard by the judge or the attorney representing the state.

(b) On the motion of the defendant, the attorney representing the defendant, or the attorney representing the state or on the court's own motion, the court may terminate an appearance made through an electronic broadcast system at any time during the appearance and require an appearance by the defendant in open court.

(c) A recording of the communication shall be made and preserved until any appellate proceedings have been concluded. The defendant may obtain a copy of the recording on payment of a reasonable amount to cover the costs of reproduction or, if the defendant is indigent, the court shall provide a copy to the defendant without charging a cost for the copy.

Added by Acts 2005, 79th Leg., ch. 324, § 4, eff. Sept. 1, 2005.

SUBCHAPTER B. EXAMINATION

Art. 46B.021. Appointment of Experts

(a) On a suggestion that the defendant may be incompetent to stand trial, the court may appoint one or more disinterested experts to:

(1) examine the defendant and report to the court on the competency or incompetency of the defendant; and

(2) testify as to the issue of competency or incompetency of the defendant at any trial or hearing involving that issue.

(b) On a determination that evidence exists to support a finding of incompetency to stand trial, the court shall appoint one or more experts to perform the duties described by Subsection (a).

(c) An expert involved in the treatment of the defendant may not be appointed to examine the defendant under this article.

(d) The movant or other party as directed by the court shall provide to experts appointed under this article information relevant to a determination of the defendant's competency, including copies of the indictment or information, any supporting documents used to establish probable cause in the case, and previous mental health evaluation and treatment records.

(e) The court may appoint as experts under this chapter qualified psychiatrists or psychologists employed by the local mental health authority or local intellectual and developmental disability authority. The local mental health authority or local intellectual and developmental disability authority is entitled to compensation and reimbursement as provided by Article 46B.027.

(f) If a defendant wishes to be examined by an expert of the defendant's own choice, the court on timely request shall provide the expert with reasonable opportunity to examine the defendant.

Added by Acts 2003, 78th Leg., ch. 35, § 1, eff. Jan. 1, 2004. Amended by Acts 2015, 84th Leg., ch. 1 (S.B. 219), § 6.007, eff. April 2, 2015.

Art. 46B.022. Experts: Qualifications

(a) To qualify for appointment under this subchapter as an expert, a psychiatrist or psychologist must:

(1) as appropriate, be a physician licensed in this state or be a psychologist licensed in this state who has a doctoral degree in psychology; and

(2) have the following certification or training:

(A) as appropriate, certification by:

(i) the American Board of Psychiatry and Neurology with added or special qualifications in forensic psychiatry; or

(ii) the American Board of Professional Psychology in forensic psychology; or

(B) training consisting of:

(i) at least 24 hours of specialized forensic training relating to incompetency or insanity evaluations; and

(ii) at least eight hours of continuing education relating to forensic evaluations, completed in the 12 months preceding the appointment.

(b) In addition to meeting qualifications required by Subsection (a), to be appointed as an expert a psychiatrist or psychologist must have completed six hours of required continuing education in courses in forensic psychiatry or psychology, as appropriate, in either of the reporting periods in the 24 months preceding the appointment.

(c) A court may appoint as an expert a psychiatrist or psychologist who does not meet the requirements of Subsections (a) and (b) only if exigent circumstances require the court to base the appointment on professional training or experience of the expert that directly provides the expert with a specialized expertise to examine the defendant that would not ordinarily be possessed by a psychiatrist or psychologist who meets the requirements of Subsections (a) and (b).

Added by Acts 2003, 78th Leg., ch. 35, § 1, eff. Jan. 1, 2004. Amended by Acts 2011, 82nd Leg., ch. 822 (H.B. 2725), § 6, eff. Sept. 1, 2011.

Art. 46B.023. Custody Status

During an examination under this subchapter, except as otherwise ordered by the court, the defendant shall be maintained under the same custody or status as the defendant was maintained under immediately before the examination began.

Added by Acts 2003, 78th Leg., ch. 35, § 1, eff. Jan. 1, 2004.

Art. 46B.024. Factors Considered in Examination

During an examination under this subchapter and in any report based on that examination, an expert shall consider, in addition to other issues determined relevant by the expert, the following:

(1) the capacity of the defendant during criminal proceedings to:

(A) rationally understand the charges against the defendant and the potential consequences of the pending criminal proceedings;

(B) disclose to counsel pertinent facts, events, and states of mind;

(C) engage in a reasoned choice of legal strategies and options;

(D) understand the adversarial nature of criminal proceedings;

(E) exhibit appropriate courtroom behavior; and

(F) testify;

(2) as supported by current indications and the defendant's personal history, whether the defendant:

(A) is a person with mental illness; or

(B) is a person with an intellectual disability;

(3) whether the identified condition has lasted or is expected to last continuously for at least one year;

(4) the degree of impairment resulting from the mental illness or intellectual disability, if existent, and the specific impact on the defendant's capacity to engage with counsel in a reasonable and rational manner; and

(5) if the defendant is taking psychoactive or other medication:

(A) whether the medication is necessary to maintain the defendant's competency; and

(B) the effect, if any, of the medication on the defendant's appearance, demeanor, or ability to participate in the proceedings.

Added by Acts 2003, 78th Leg., ch. 35, § 1, eff. Jan. 1, 2004. Amended by Acts 2011, 82nd Leg., ch. 822 (H.B. 2725), § 7, eff. Sept. 1, 2011; Acts 2015, 84th Leg., ch. 1 (S.B. 219), § 6.008, eff. April 2, 2015.

Art. 46B.025. Expert's Report

(a) An expert's report to the court must state an opinion on a defendant's competency or incompetency to stand trial or explain why the expert is unable to state such an opinion and must also:

(1) identify and address specific issues referred to the expert for evaluation;

(2) document that the expert explained to the defendant the purpose of the evaluation, the persons to whom a report on the evaluation is provided, and the limits on rules of confidentiality applying to the relationship between the expert and the defendant;

(3) in specific terms, describe procedures, techniques, and tests used in the examination, the purpose of each procedure, technique, or test, and the conclusions reached; and

(4) state the expert's clinical observations, findings, and opinions on each specific issue referred to the expert by the court, state the specific criteria supporting the expert's diagnosis, and state specifically any issues on which the expert could not provide an opinion.

(a–1) The expert's opinion on the defendant's competency or incompetency may not be based solely on the defendant's refusal to communicate during the examination.

(b) If in the opinion of an expert appointed under Article 46B.021 the defendant is incompetent to proceed, the expert shall state in the report:

(1) the symptoms, exact nature, severity, and expected duration of the deficits resulting from the defendant's mental illness or intellectual disability, if any, and the impact of the identified condition on the factors listed in Article 46B.024;

(2) an estimate of the period needed to restore the defendant's competency, including whether the defendant is likely to be restored to competency in the foreseeable future; and

(3) prospective treatment options, if any, appropriate for the defendant.

(c) An expert's report may not state the expert's opinion on the defendant's sanity at the time of the alleged offense, if in the opinion of the expert the defendant is incompetent to proceed.

(d) The court shall direct an expert to provide the expert's report to the court and the appropriate parties in the form approved by the Texas Correctional Office on Offenders with Medical or Mental Impairments under Section 614.0032(b), Health and Safety Code.

Added by Acts 2003, 78th Leg., ch. 35, § 1, eff. Jan. 1, 2004. Amended by Acts 2005, 79th Leg., ch. 1269, § 1, eff. June 18, 2005. Amended by Acts 2011, 82nd Leg., ch. 822 (H.B. 2725), § 8, eff. Sept. 1, 2011; Acts 2015, 84th Leg., ch. 1 (S.B. 219), § 6.009, eff. April 2, 2015.

Art. 46B.026. Report Deadline

(a) Except as provided by Subsection (b), an expert examining the defendant shall provide the report on the defendant's competency or incompetency to stand trial to the court, the attorney representing the state, and the attorney representing the defendant not later than the 30th day after the date on which the expert was ordered to examine the defendant and prepare the report.

(b) For good cause shown, the court may permit an expert to complete the examination and report and provide the report to the court and attorneys at a date later than the date required by Subsection (a).

(c) Repealed by Acts 2017, 85th Leg., ch. 748 (S.B. 1326), § 35(1).

(d) The court shall submit to the Office of Court Administration of the Texas Judicial System on a monthly basis the number of reports provided to the court under this article.

Added by Acts 2003, 78th Leg., ch. 35, § 1, eff. Jan. 1, 2004. Amended by Acts 2005, 79th Leg., ch. 1269, § 2, eff. June 18, 2005; Acts 2017, 85th Leg., ch. 748 (S.B. 1326), §§ 9, 35(1), eff. Sept. 1, 2017.

Section 37 of Acts 2017, 85th Leg., ch. 748 (S.B. 1326) provides:

"The changes in law made by this Act apply only to a defendant charged with an offense committed on or after the effective date [Sept. 1, 2017] of this Act. A defendant charged with an offense committed before the effective date of this Act is governed by the law in effect on the date the offense was committed, and the former law is continued in effect for that purpose. For purposes of this section, an offense was committed before the effective date of this Act if any element of the offense occurred before that date."

Art. 46B.027. Compensation of Experts; Reimbursement of Facilities

(a) For any appointment under this chapter, the county in which the indictment was returned or information was filed shall pay for services described by Articles 46B.021(a)(1) and (2). If those services are provided by an expert who is an employee of the local mental health authority or local intellectual and developmental disability authority, the county shall pay the authority for the services.

(b) The county in which the indictment was returned or information was filed shall reimburse a facility that accepts a defendant for examination under this chapter for expenses incurred that are reasonably necessary and incidental to the proper examination of the defendant.

Added by Acts 2003, 78th Leg., ch. 35, § 1, eff. Jan. 1, 2004. Amended by Acts 2015, 84th Leg., ch. 1 (S.B. 219), § 6.010, eff. April 2, 2015.

SUBCHAPTER C. INCOMPETENCY TRIAL

Acts 2005, 79th Leg., ch. 324, § 5, amended the subchapter heading.

Art. 46B.051. Trial Before Judge or Jury

(a) If a court holds a trial to determine whether the defendant is incompetent to stand trial, on the request of either party or the motion of the court, a jury shall make the determination.

(b) The court shall make the determination of incompetency if a jury determination is not required by Subsection (a).

(c) If a jury determination is required by Subsection (a), a jury that has not been selected to determine the guilt or innocence of the defendant must determine the issue of incompetency.

Added by Acts 2003, 78th Leg., ch. 35, § 1, eff. Jan. 1, 2004. Amended by Acts 2005, 79th Leg., ch. 324, § 6, eff. Sept. 1, 2005.

Art. 46B.052. Jury Verdict

(a) If a jury determination of the issue of incompetency to stand trial is required by Article 46B.051(a), the court shall require the jury to state in its verdict whether the defendant is incompetent to stand trial.

(b) The verdict must be concurred in by each juror.

Added by Acts 2003, 78th Leg., ch. 35, § 1, eff. Jan. 1, 2004.

Art. 46B.053. Procedure After Finding of Competency

If the court or jury determines that the defendant is competent to stand trial, the court shall continue the trial on the merits. If a jury determines that the defendant is competent and the trial on the merits is to be held before a jury, the court shall continue the trial with another jury selected for that purpose.

Added by Acts 2003, 78th Leg., ch. 35, § 1, eff. Jan. 1, 2004. Amended by Acts 2005, 79th Leg., ch. 324, § 7, eff. Sept. 1, 2005.

Art. 46B.054. Uncontested Incompetency

If the court finds that evidence exists to support a finding of incompetency to stand trial and the court and the counsel for each party agree that the defendant is incompetent to stand trial, the court shall proceed in the same manner as if a jury had been impaneled and had found the defendant incompetent to stand trial.

Added by Acts 2003, 78th Leg., ch. 35, § 1, eff. Jan. 1, 2004. Amended by Acts 2005, 79th Leg., ch. 324, § 7, eff. Sept. 1, 2005.

Art. 46B.055. Procedure After Finding of Incompetency

If the defendant is found incompetent to stand trial, the court shall proceed under Subchapter D.

Added by Acts 2003, 78th Leg., ch. 35, § 1, eff. Jan. 1, 2004.

SUBCHAPTER D. PROCEDURES AFTER DETERMINATION OF INCOMPETENCY

Acts 2005, 79th Leg., ch. 324, § 8, amended the subchapter heading.

Art. 46B.071. Options on Determination of Incompetency

(a) Except as provided by Subsection (b), on a determination that a defendant is incompetent to stand trial, the court shall:

(1) if the defendant is charged with an offense punishable as a Class B misdemeanor:

(A) release the defendant on bail under Article 46B.0711; or

(B) commit the defendant to:

(i) a jail-based competency restoration program under Article 46B.073(e); or

(ii) a mental health facility or residential care facility under Article 46B.073(f); or

(2) if the defendant is charged with an offense punishable as a Class A misdemeanor or any higher category of offense:

(A) release the defendant on bail under Article 46B.072; or

(B) commit the defendant to a facility or a jail-based competency restoration program under Article 46B.073(c) or (d).

(b) On a determination that a defendant is incompetent to stand trial and is unlikely to be restored to competency in the foreseeable future, the court shall:

(1) proceed under Subchapter E or F; or

(2) release the defendant on bail as permitted under Chapter 17.

Added by Acts 2003, 78th Leg., ch. 35, § 1, eff. Jan. 1, 2004. Amended by Acts 2011, 82nd Leg., ch. 822 (H.B. 2725), § 9, eff. Sept. 1, 2011; Acts 2017, 85th Leg., ch. 748 (S.B. 1326), § 10, eff. Sept. 1, 2017.

Section 37 of Acts 2017, 85th Leg., ch. 748 (S.B. 1326) provides:

"The changes in law made by this Act apply only to a defendant charged with an offense committed on or after the effective date [Sept. 1, 2017] of this Act. A defendant charged with an offense committed before the effective date of this Act is governed by the law in effect on the date the offense was committed, and the former law is continued in effect for that purpose. For purposes of this section, an offense was committed before the effective date of this Act if any element of the offense occurred before that date."

Art. 46B.0711. Release on bail for Class B misdemeanor

(a) This article applies only to a defendant who is subject to an initial restoration period based on Article 46B.071.

(b) Subject to conditions reasonably related to ensuring public safety and the effectiveness of the defendant's treatment, if the court determines that a defendant charged with an offense punishable as a Class B misdemeanor and found incompetent to stand trial is not a danger to others and may be safely treated on an outpatient basis with the specific objective of attaining competency to stand trial, and an appropriate outpatient competency restoration program is available for the defendant, the court shall:

(1) release the defendant on bail or continue the defendant's release on bail; and

(2) order the defendant to participate in an outpatient competency restoration program for a period not to exceed 60 days.

(c) Notwithstanding Subsection (b), the court may order a defendant to participate in an outpatient competency restoration program under this article only if:

(1) the court receives and approves a comprehensive plan that:

(A) provides for the treatment of the defendant for purposes of competency restoration; and

(B) identifies the person who will be responsible for providing that treatment to the defendant; and

(2) the court finds that the treatment proposed by the plan will be available to and will be provided to the defendant.

(d) An order issued under this article may require the defendant to participate in:

(1) as appropriate, an outpatient competency restoration program administered by a community center or an outpatient competency restoration program administered by any other entity that provides competency restoration services; and

(2) an appropriate prescribed regimen of medical, psychiatric, or psychological care or treatment.

Added by Acts 2017, 85th Leg., ch. 748 (S.B. 1326), § 11, eff. Sept. 1, 2017.

Section 37 of Acts 2017, 85th Leg., ch. 748 (S.B. 1326) provides:

"The changes in law made by this Act apply only to a defendant charged with an offense committed on or after the effective date [Sept. 1, 2017] of this Act. A defendant charged with an offense committed before the effective date of this Act is governed by the law in effect on the date the offense was committed, and the former law is continued in effect for that purpose. For purposes of this section, an offense was committed before the effective date of this Act if any element of the offense occurred before that date."

Art. 46B.072. Release on bail for felony or Class A misdemeanor

(a) This article applies only to a defendant who is subject to an initial restoration period based on Article 46B.071.

(a–1) Subject to conditions reasonably related to ensuring public safety and the effectiveness of the defendant's treatment, if the court determines that a defendant charged with an offense punishable as a felony or a Class A misdemeanor and found incompetent to stand trial is not a danger to others and may be safely treated on an outpatient basis with the specific objective of attaining competency to stand trial, and an appropriate outpatient competency restoration program is available for the defendant, the court:

(1) may release on bail a defendant found incompetent to stand trial with respect to an offense punishable as a felony or may continue the defendant's release on bail; and

(2) shall release on bail a defendant found incompetent to stand trial with respect to an offense punishable as a Class A misdemeanor or shall continue the defendant's release on bail.

(b) The court shall order a defendant released on bail under Subsection (a–1) to participate in an outpatient competency restoration program for a period not to exceed 120 days.

(c) Notwithstanding Subsection (a–1), the court may order a defendant to participate in an outpatient competency restoration program under this article only if:

(1) the court receives and approves a comprehensive plan that:

(A) provides for the treatment of the defendant for purposes of competency restoration; and

(B) identifies the person who will be responsible for providing that treatment to the defendant; and

(2) the court finds that the treatment proposed by the plan will be available to and will be provided to the defendant.

(d) An order issued under this article may require the defendant to participate in:

(1) as appropriate, an outpatient competency restoration program administered by a community center or an outpatient competency restoration program administered by any other entity that provides outpatient competency restoration services; and

(2) an appropriate prescribed regimen of medical, psychiatric, or psychological care or treatment, including care or treatment involving the administration of psychoactive medication, including those required under Article 46B.086.

Added by Acts 2003, 78th Leg., ch. 35, § 1, eff. Jan. 1, 2004. Amended by Acts 2007, 80th Leg., ch. 1307, § 3, eff. Sept. 1, 2007; Acts 2011, 82nd Leg., ch. 822 (H.B. 2725), § 10, eff. Sept. 1, 2011; Acts 2017, 85th Leg., ch. 748 (S.B. 1326), §§ 12, 13, eff. Sept. 1, 2017.

Section 37 of Acts 2017, 85th Leg., ch. 748 (S.B. 1326) provides:

"The changes in law made by this Act apply only to a defendant charged with an offense committed on or after the effective date [Sept. 1, 2017] of this Act. A defendant charged with an offense committed before the effective date of this Act is governed by the law in effect on the date the offense was committed, and the former law is continued in effect for that purpose. For purposes of this section, an offense was committed before the effective date of this Act if any element of the offense occurred before that date."

Art. 46B.073. Commitment for Restoration to Competency

(a) This article applies only to a defendant not released on bail who is subject to an initial restoration period based on Article 46B.071.

(b) For purposes of further examination and competency restoration services with the specific objective of the defendant attaining competency to stand trial, the court shall commit a defendant described by Subsection (a) to a mental health facility, residential care facility, or jail-based competency restoration program for the applicable period as follows:

(1) a period of not more than 60 days, if the defendant is charged with an offense punishable as a misdemeanor; or

(2) a period of not more than 120 days, if the defendant is charged with an offense punishable as a felony.

(c) If the defendant is charged with an offense listed in Article 17.032(a), other than an offense under Section 22.01(a)(1), Penal Code, or the indictment alleges an affirmative finding under Article 42A.054(c) or (d), the court shall enter an order committing the defendant for competency restoration services to the maximum security unit of any facility designated by the Department of State Health Services, to an agency of the United States operating a mental hospital, or to a Department of Veterans Affairs hospital.

(d) If the defendant is not charged with an offense described by Subsection (c) and the indictment does not allege an affirmative finding under Article 42A.054(c) or (d), the court shall enter an order committing the defendant to a mental health facility or residential care facility determined to be appropriate by the local mental health authority or local intellectual and developmental disability authority or to a jail-based competency restoration program. A defendant may be committed to a jail-based competency restoration program only if the program provider determines the defendant will begin to receive competency restoration services within 72 hours of arriving at the program.

(e) Except as provided by Subsection (f), a defendant charged with an offense punishable as a Class B misdemeanor may be committed under this subchapter only to a jail-based competency restoration program.

(f) A defendant charged with an offense punishable as a Class B misdemeanor may be committed to a mental health facility or residential care facility described by Subsection (d) only if a jail-based competency restoration program is not available or a licensed or qualified mental health professional determines that a jail-based competency restoration program is not appropriate.

Added by Acts 2003, 78th Leg., ch. 35, § 1, eff. Jan. 1, 2004. Amended by Acts 2005, 79th Leg., ch. 324, § 9, eff. Sept. 1, 2005; Acts 2007, 80th Leg., ch. 1307, § 4, eff. Sept. 1, 2007. Amended by Acts 2011, 82nd Leg., ch. 822 (H.B. 2725), § 11, eff. Sept. 1, 2011; Acts 2013, 83rd Leg., ch. 797 (S.B. 1475), § 1, eff. Sept. 1, 2013; Acts 2015, 84th Leg., ch. 1 (S.B. 219), § 6.011, eff. April 2, 2015; Acts 2015, 84th Leg., ch. 770 (H.B. 2299), § 2.20, eff. Jan. 1, 2017; Acts 2015, 84th Leg., ch. 946 (S.B. 277), § 1.15(b), eff. Sept. 1, 2015; Acts 2017, 85th Leg., ch. 748 (S.B. 1326), § 14, eff. Sept. 1, 2017.

Section 37 of Acts 2017, 85th Leg., ch. 748 (S.B. 1326) provides:

"The changes in law made by this Act apply only to a defendant charged with an offense committed on or after the effective date

[Sept. 1, 2017] of this Act. A defendant charged with an offense committed before the effective date of this Act is governed by the law in effect on the date the offense was committed, and the former law is continued in effect for that purpose. For purposes of this section, an offense was committed before the effective date of this Act if any element of the offense occurred before that date."

Art. 46B.074.   Competent Testimony Required

(a) A defendant may be committed to a jail-based competency restoration program, mental health facility, or residential care facility under this subchapter only on competent medical or psychiatric testimony provided by an expert qualified under Article 46B.022.

(b) The court may allow an expert to substitute the expert's report under Article 46B.025 for any testimony by the expert that may be required under this article.

Added by Acts 2003, 78th Leg., ch. 35, § 1, eff. Jan. 1, 2004. Amended by Acts 2005, 79th Leg., ch. 324, § 10, eff. Sept. 1, 2005; Acts 2017, 85th Leg., ch. 748 (S.B. 1326), § 15, eff. Sept. 1, 2017.

Section 37 of Acts 2017, 85th Leg., ch. 748 (S.B. 1326) provides:

"The changes in law made by this Act apply only to a defendant charged with an offense committed on or after the effective date [Sept. 1, 2017] of this Act. A defendant charged with an offense committed before the effective date of this Act is governed by the law in effect on the date the offense was committed, and the former law is continued in effect for that purpose. For purposes of this section, an offense was committed before the effective date of this Act if any element of the offense occurred before that date."

Art. 46B.075.   Transfer of defendant to facility or program

An order issued under Article 46B.0711, 46B.072, or 46B.073 must place the defendant in the custody of the sheriff or sheriff's deputy for transportation to the facility or program, as applicable, in which the defendant is to receive competency restoration services.

Added by Acts 2003, 78th Leg., ch. 35, § 1, eff. Jan. 1, 2004. Amended by Acts 2007, 80th Leg., ch. 1307, § 5, eff. Sept. 1, 2007; Acts 2017, 85th Leg., ch. 748 (S.B. 1326), § 16, eff. Sept. 1, 2017.

Section 37 of Acts 2017, 85th Leg., ch. 748 (S.B. 1326) provides:

"The changes in law made by this Act apply only to a defendant charged with an offense committed on or after the effective date [Sept. 1, 2017] of this Act. A defendant charged with an offense committed before the effective date of this Act is governed by the law in effect on the date the offense was committed, and the former law is continued in effect for that purpose. For purposes of this section, an offense was committed before the effective date of this Act if any element of the offense occurred before that date."

Art. 46B.0755.   Procedures on Credible Evidence of Immediate Restoration

(a) Notwithstanding any other provision of this subchapter, if the court receives credible evidence indicating that the defendant has been restored to competency at any time after the defendant's incompetency trial under Subchapter C but before the defendant is transported under Article 46B.075 to the facility or program, as applicable, the court may appoint disinterested experts to reexamine the defendant in accordance with Subchapter B. The court is not required to appoint the same expert or experts who performed the initial examination of the defendant under that subchapter.

(b) If after a reexamination of the defendant the applicable expert's report states an opinion that the defendant remains incompetent, the court's order under Article 46B.0711, 46B.072, or 46B.073 remains in effect, and the defendant shall be transported to the facility or program as required by Article 46B.075. If after a reexamination of the defendant the applicable expert's report states an opinion that the defendant has been restored to competency, the court shall withdraw its order under Article 46B.0711, 46B.072, or 46B.073 and proceed under Subsection (c) or (d).

(c) The court shall find the defendant competent to stand trial and proceed in the same manner as if the defendant had been found restored to competency at a hearing if:

(1) both parties agree that the defendant is competent to stand trial; and

(2) the court concurs.

(d) The court shall hold a hearing to determine whether the defendant has been restored to competency if any party fails to agree or if the court fails to concur that the defendant is competent to stand trial. If a court holds a hearing under this subsection, on the request of the counsel for either party or the motion of the court, a jury shall make the competency determination. For purposes of the hearing, incompetency is presumed, and the defendant's competency must be proved by a preponderance of the evidence. If after the hearing the defendant is again found to be incompetent to stand trial, the court shall issue a new order under Article 46B.0711, 46B.072, or 46B.073, as appropriate based on the defendant's current condition.

Added by Acts 2011, 82nd Leg., ch. 822 (H.B. 2725), § 12, eff. Sept. 1, 2011. Amended by Acts 2017, 85th Leg., ch. 748 (S.B. 1326), § 17, eff. Sept. 1, 2017.

Section 37 of Acts 2017, 85th Leg., ch. 748 (S.B. 1326) provides:

"The changes in law made by this Act apply only to a defendant charged with an offense committed on or after the effective date [Sept. 1, 2017] of this Act. A defendant charged with an offense committed before the effective date of this Act is governed by the law in effect on the date the offense was committed, and the former law is continued in effect for that purpose. For purposes of this section, an offense was committed before the effective date of this Act if any element of the offense occurred before that date."

Art. 46B.076.   Court's Order

(a) If the defendant is found incompetent to stand trial, not later than the date of the order of commitment or of release on bail, as applicable, the court shall send a copy of the order to the applicable facility or program. The court shall also provide to the facility or program copies of the following made available to the court during the incompetency trial:

(1) reports of each expert;

(2) psychiatric, psychological, or social work reports that relate to the mental condition of the defendant;

(3) documents provided by the attorney representing the state or the attorney representing the defendant that relate to the defendant's current or past mental condition;

(4) copies of the indictment or information and any supporting documents used to establish probable cause in the case;

(5) the defendant's criminal history record; and

(6) the addresses of the attorney representing the state and the attorney representing the defendant.

(b) The court shall order that the transcript of all medical testimony received by the jury or court be promptly prepared by the court reporter and forwarded to the applicable facility or program.

Added by Acts 2003, 78th Leg., ch. 35, § 1, eff. Jan. 1, 2004. Amended by Acts 2005, 79th Leg., ch. 324, § 11, eff. Sept. 1, 2005; Acts 2007, 80th Leg., ch. 1307, § 5, eff. Sept. 1, 2007; Acts 2015, 84th Leg., ch. 1 (S.B. 219), § 6.012, eff. April 2, 2015; Acts 2017, 85th Leg., ch. 748 (S.B. 1326), § 18, eff. Sept. 1, 2017.

Section 37 of Acts 2017, 85th Leg., ch. 748 (S.B. 1326) provides:

"The changes in law made by this Act apply only to a defendant charged with an offense committed on or after the effective date [Sept. 1, 2017] of this Act. A defendant charged with an offense committed before the effective date of this Act is governed by the law in effect on the date the offense was committed, and the former law is continued in effect for that purpose. For purposes of this section, an offense was committed before the effective date of this Act if any element of the offense occurred before that date."

Art. 46B.077.   Individual treatment program

(a) The facility or jail-based competency restoration program to which the defendant is committed or the outpatient competency restoration program to which the defendant is released on bail shall:

(1) develop an individual program of treatment;

(2) assess and evaluate whether the defendant is likely to be restored to competency in the foreseeable future; and

(3) report to the court and to the local mental health authority or to the local intellectual and developmental disability authority on the defendant's progress toward achieving competency.

(b) If the defendant is committed to an inpatient mental health facility, residential care facility, or jail-based competency restoration program, the facility or program shall report to the court at least once during the commitment period.

(c) If the defendant is released to an outpatient competency restoration program, the program shall report to the court:

(1) not later than the 14th day after the date on which the defendant's competency restoration services begin; and

(2) until the defendant is no longer released to the program, at least once during each 30–day period following the date of the report required by Subdivision (1).

Added by Acts 2003, 78th Leg., ch. 35, § 1, eff. Jan. 1, 2004. Amended by Acts 2007, 80th Leg., ch. 1307, § 6, eff. Sept. 1, 2007; Acts 2011, 82nd Leg., ch. 822 (H.B. 2725), § 13, eff. Sept. 1, 2011; Acts 2015, 84th Leg., ch. 1 (S.B. 219), § 6.013, eff. April 2, 2015; Acts 2017, 85th Leg., ch. 748 (S.B. 1326), § 19, eff. Sept. 1, 2017.

Section 37 of Acts 2017, 85th Leg., ch. 748 (S.B. 1326) provides:

"The changes in law made by this Act apply only to a defendant charged with an offense committed on or after the effective date [Sept. 1, 2017] of this Act. A defendant charged with an offense committed before the effective date of this Act is governed by the law in effect on the date the offense was committed, and the former law is continued in effect for that purpose. For purposes of this section, an offense was committed before the effective date of this Act if any element of the offense occurred before that date."

Art. 46B.078. Charges subsequently dismissed

If the charges pending against a defendant are dismissed, the court that issued the order under Article 46B.0711, 46B.072, or 46B.073 shall send a copy of the order of dismissal to the sheriff of the county in which the court is located and to the head of the facility, the provider of the jail-based competency restoration program, or the provider of the outpatient competency restoration program, as appropriate. On receipt of the copy of the order, the facility or program shall discharge the defendant into the care of the sheriff or sheriff's deputy for transportation in the manner described by Article 46B.082.

Added by Acts 2003, 78th Leg., ch. 35, § 1, eff. Jan. 1, 2004. Amended by Acts 2007, 80th Leg., ch. 1307, § 7, eff. Sept. 1, 2007; Acts 2017, 85th Leg., ch. 748 (S.B. 1326), § 20, eff. Sept. 1, 2017.

Section 37 of Acts 2017, 85th Leg., ch. 748 (S.B. 1326) provides:

"The changes in law made by this Act apply only to a defendant charged with an offense committed on or after the effective date [Sept. 1, 2017] of this Act. A defendant charged with an offense committed before the effective date of this Act is governed by the law in effect on the date the offense was committed, and the former law is continued in effect for that purpose. For purposes of this section, an offense was committed before the effective date of this Act if any element of the offense occurred before that date."

Art. 46B.079. Notice and report to court

(a) The head of the facility, the provider of the jail-based competency restoration program, or the provider of the outpatient competency restoration program, as appropriate, not later than the 15th day before the date on which the initial restoration period is to expire according to the terms of the order or under Article 46B.0095 or other applicable provisions of this chapter, shall notify the applicable court that the period is about to expire.

(b) The head of the facility or jail-based competency restoration program provider shall promptly notify the court when the head of the facility or program provider believes that:

(1) the defendant is clinically ready and can be safely transferred to a competency restoration program for education services but has not yet attained competency to stand trial;

(2) the defendant has attained competency to stand trial; or

(3) the defendant is not likely to attain competency in the foreseeable future.

(b–1) The outpatient competency restoration program provider shall promptly notify the court when the program provider believes that:

(1) the defendant has attained competency to stand trial; or

(2) the defendant is not likely to attain competency in the foreseeable future.

(c) When the head of the facility or program provider gives notice to the court under Subsection (a), (b), or (b–1), the head of the facility or program provider also shall file a final report with the court stating the reason for the proposed discharge or transfer under this chapter and including a list of the types and dosages of medications prescribed for the defendant while the defendant was receiving competency restoration services in the facility or through the program. The court shall provide to the attorney representing the defendant and the attorney representing the state copies of a report based on notice under this article, other than notice under Subsection (b)(1), to enable any objection to the findings of the report to be made in a timely manner as required under Article 46B.084(a–1).

(d) If the head of the facility or program provider notifies the court that the initial restoration period is about to expire, the notice may contain a request for an extension of the period for an additional period of 60 days and an explanation for the basis of the request. An explanation provided under this subsection must include a description of any evidence indicating a reduction in the severity of the defendant's symptoms or impairment.

Added by Acts 2003, 78th Leg., ch. 35, § 1, eff. Jan. 1, 2004. Amended by Acts 2005, 79th Leg., ch. 324, § 12, eff. Sept. 1, 2005; Acts 2007, 80th Leg., ch. 1307, § 7, eff. Sept. 1, 2007; Acts 2011, 82nd Leg., ch. 822 (H.B. 2725), § 14, eff. Sept. 1, 2011; Acts 2015, 84th Leg., ch. 994 (H.B. 211), § 1, eff. June 19, 2015; Acts 2017, 85th Leg., ch. 748 (S.B. 1326), § 21, eff. Sept. 1, 2017.

Section 3 of Acts 2015, 84th Leg., ch. 994 (H.B. 211) provides:

"The change in law made by this Act applies only to a proceeding under Chapter 46B, Code of Criminal Procedure, that commences on or after the effective date [June 21, 2015] of this Act, regardless of when the defendant may have committed the underlying offense for which the defendant became subject to the proceeding."

Section 37 of Acts 2017, 85th Leg., ch. 748 (S.B. 1326) provides:

"The changes in law made by this Act apply only to a defendant charged with an offense committed on or after the effective date [Sept. 1, 2017] of this Act. A defendant charged with an offense committed before the effective date of this Act is governed by the law in effect on the date the offense was committed, and the former law is continued in effect for that purpose. For purposes of this section, an offense was committed before the effective date of this Act if any element of the offense occurred before that date."

Art. 46B.080.   Extension of Order

(a) On a request of the head of a facility or a program provider that is made under Article 46B.079(d) and notwithstanding any other provision of this subchapter, the court may enter an order extending the initial restoration period for an additional period of 60 days.

(b) The court may enter an order under Subsection (a) only if the court determines that:

(1) the defendant has not attained competency; and

(2) an extension of the initial restoration period will likely enable the facility or program to restore the defendant to competency within the period of the extension.

(c) The court may grant only one 60–day extension under this article in connection with the specific offense with which the defendant is charged.

Added by Acts 2003, 78th Leg., ch. 35, § 1, eff. Jan. 1, 2004. Amended by Acts 2005, 79th Leg., ch. 324, § 12, eff. Sept. 1, 2005; Acts 2007, 80th Leg., ch. 1307, § 7, eff. Sept. 1, 2007; Acts 2011, 82nd Leg., ch. 822 (H.B. 2725), § 15, eff. Sept. 1, 2011; Acts 2017, 85th Leg., ch. 748 (S.B. 1326), § 22, eff. Sept. 1, 2017.

Section 37 of Acts 2017, 85th Leg., ch. 748 (S.B. 1326) provides:

"The changes in law made by this Act apply only to a defendant charged with an offense committed on or after the effective date [Sept. 1, 2017] of this Act. A defendant charged with an offense committed before the effective date of this Act is governed by the law in effect on the date the offense was committed, and the former law is continued in effect for that purpose. For purposes of this section, an offense was committed before the effective date of this Act if any element of the offense occurred before that date."

Art. 46B.0805.   Competency restoration education services

(a) On notification from the head of a facility or a jail-based competency restoration program provider under Article 46B.079(b)(1), the court shall order the defendant to receive competency restoration education services in a jail-based competency restoration program or an outpatient competency restoration program, as appropriate and if available.

(b) If a defendant for whom an order is entered under Subsection (a) was committed for competency restoration to a facility other than a jail-based competency restoration program, the court shall send a copy of that order to:

(1) the sheriff of the county in which the court is located;

(2) the head of the facility to which the defendant was committed for competency restoration; and

(3) the local mental health authority or local intellectual and developmental disability authority, as appropriate.

(c) As soon as practicable but not later than the 10th day after the date of receipt of a copy of an order under Subsection (b)(2), the applicable facility shall discharge the defendant into the care of the sheriff of the county in which the court is located or into the care of the sheriff's deputy. The sheriff or sheriff's deputy shall transport the defendant to the jail-based competency restoration program or outpatient competency restoration program, as appropriate.

(d) A jail-based competency restoration program or outpatient competency restoration program that receives a defendant under this article shall give to the court:

(1) notice regarding the defendant's entry into the program for purposes of receiving competency restoration education services; and

(2) subsequent notice as otherwise required under Article 46B.079.

Added by Acts 2017, 85th Leg., ch. 748 (S.B. 1326), § 23, eff. Sept. 1, 2017.

Section 37 of Acts 2017, 85th Leg., ch. 748 (S.B. 1326) provides:

"The changes in law made by this Act apply only to a defendant charged with an offense committed on or after the effective date [Sept. 1, 2017] of this Act. A defendant charged with an offense committed before the effective date of this Act is governed by the law in effect on the date the offense was committed, and the former law is continued in effect for that purpose. For purposes of this section, an offense was committed before the effective date of this Act if any element of the offense occurred before that date."

Art. 46B.081.   Return to court

Subject to Article 46B.082(b), a defendant committed or released on bail under this subchapter shall be returned to the applicable court as soon as practicable after notice to the court is provided under Article 46B.079(a), (b)(2), (b)(3), or (b–1), but not later than the date of expiration of the period for restoration specified by the court under Article 46B.0711, 46B.072, or 46B.073.

Added by Acts 2003, 78th Leg., ch. 35, § 1, eff. Jan. 1, 2004. Amended by Acts 2005, 79th Leg., ch. 324, § 13, eff. Sept. 1, 2005; Acts 2007, 80th Leg., ch. 1307, § 7, eff. Sept. 1, 2007; Acts 2017, 85th Leg., ch. 748 (S.B. 1326), § 24, eff. Sept. 1, 2017.

Section 37 of Acts 2017, 85th Leg., ch. 748 (S.B. 1326) provides:

"The changes in law made by this Act apply only to a defendant charged with an offense committed on or after the effective date [Sept. 1, 2017] of this Act. A defendant charged with an offense committed before the effective date of this Act is governed by the law in effect on the date the offense was committed, and the former law is continued in effect for that purpose. For purposes of this section, an offense was committed before the effective date of this Act if any element of the offense occurred before that date."

Art. 46B.082.   Transportation of defendant to court

(a) On notification from the court under Article 46B.078, the sheriff of the county in which the court is located or the sheriff's deputy shall transport the defendant to the court.

(b) If before the 15th day after the date on which the court received notification under Article 46B.079(a), (b)(2), (b)(3), or (b–1) a defendant committed to a facility or jail-based competency restoration program or ordered to participate in an outpatient competency restoration program has not been transported to the court that issued the order under Article 46B.0711, 46B.072, or 46B.073, as applicable, the head of the facility or provider of the jail-based competency restoration program to which the defendant is committed or the provider of the outpatient competency restoration program in which the defendant is participating shall cause the defendant to be promptly transported to the court and placed in the custody of the sheriff of the county in which the court is located. The county in which the court is located shall reimburse the Health and Human Services Commission or program provider, as appropriate, for the mileage and per diem expenses of the personnel required to trans-

port the defendant, calculated in accordance with rates provided in the General Appropriations Act for state employees.

Added by Acts 2003, 78th Leg., ch. 35, § 1, eff. Jan. 1, 2004. Amended by Acts 2007, 80th Leg., ch. 1307, § 7, eff. Sept. 1, 2007; Acts 2015, 84th Leg., ch. 1 (S.B. 219), § 6.014, eff. April 2, 2015; Acts 2017, 85th Leg., ch. 748 (S.B. 1326), § 25, eff. Sept. 1, 2017.

Section 37 of Acts 2017, 85th Leg., ch. 748 (S.B. 1326) provides:

"The changes in law made by this Act apply only to a defendant charged with an offense committed on or after the effective date [Sept. 1, 2017] of this Act. A defendant charged with an offense committed before the effective date of this Act is governed by the law in effect on the date the offense was committed, and the former law is continued in effect for that purpose. For purposes of this section, an offense was committed before the effective date of this Act if any element of the offense occurred before that date."

Art. 46B.0825.   Administration of medication while in custody of sheriff

(a) A sheriff or sheriff's deputy having custody of a defendant for transportation as required by Article 46B.0805 or 46B.082 or during proceedings described by Article 46B.084 shall, according to information available at the time and unless directed otherwise by a physician treating the defendant, ensure that the defendant is provided with the types and dosages of medication prescribed for the defendant.

(b) To the extent funds are appropriated for that purpose, a sheriff is entitled to reimbursement from the state for providing the medication required by Subsection (a).

(c) If the sheriff determines that funds are not available from the state to reimburse the sheriff as provided by Subsection (b), the sheriff is not required to comply with Subsection (a).

Added by Acts 2017, 85th Leg., ch. 748 (S.B. 1326), § 23, eff. Sept. 1, 2017.

Section 37 of Acts 2017, 85th Leg., ch. 748 (S.B. 1326) provides:

"The changes in law made by this Act apply only to a defendant charged with an offense committed on or after the effective date [Sept. 1, 2017] of this Act. A defendant charged with an offense committed before the effective date of this Act is governed by the law in effect on the date the offense was committed, and the former law is continued in effect for that purpose. For purposes of this section, an offense was committed before the effective date of this Act if any element of the offense occurred before that date."

Art. 46B.083.   Supporting commitment information provided by facility or program

(a) If the head of the facility, the jail-based competency restoration program provider, or the outpatient competency restoration program provider believes that the defendant is a person with mental illness and meets the criteria for court-ordered mental health services under Subtitle C¹, Title 7, Health and Safety Code, the head of the facility or the program provider shall have submitted to the court a certificate of medical examination for mental illness.

(b) If the head of the facility, the jail-based competency restoration program provider, or the outpatient competency restoration program provider believes that the defendant is a person with an intellectual disability, the head of the facility or the program provider shall have submitted to the court an affidavit stating the conclusions reached as a result of the examination.

Added by Acts 2003, 78th Leg., ch. 35, § 1, eff. Jan. 1, 2004. Amended by Acts 2005, 79th Leg., ch. 324, § 14, eff. Sept. 1, 2005; Acts 2007, 80th Leg., ch. 1307, § 7, eff. Sept. 1, 2007; Acts 2015, 84th Leg., ch. 1 (S.B. 219), § 6.015, eff. April 2, 2015; Acts 2017, 85th Leg., ch. 748 (S.B. 1326), § 26, eff. Sept. 1, 2017.

¹ V.T.C.A., Health & Safety Code § 571.001 et seq.

Section 37 of Acts 2017, 85th Leg., ch. 748 (S.B. 1326) provides:

"The changes in law made by this Act apply only to a defendant charged with an offense committed on or after the effective date [Sept. 1, 2017] of this Act. A defendant charged with an offense committed before the effective date of this Act is governed by the law in effect on the date the offense was committed, and the former law is continued in effect for that purpose. For purposes of this section, an offense was committed before the effective date of this Act if any element of the offense occurred before that date."

Art. 46B.084. Proceedings on Return of Defendant to Court

(a)(1) Not later than the next business day following the return of a defendant to the court, the court shall notify the attorney representing the state and the attorney for the defendant regarding the return. Within three business days of the date that notice is received under this subsection or, on a showing of good cause, a later date specified by the court, the attorney for the defendant shall meet and confer with the defendant to evaluate whether there is any suggestion that the defendant has not yet regained competency.

(2) Notwithstanding Subdivision (1), in a county with a population of less than one million or in a county with a population of four million or more, as soon as practicable following the date of the defendant's return to the court, the court shall provide the notice required by that subdivision to the attorney representing the state and the attorney for the defendant, and the attorney for the defendant shall meet and confer with the defendant as soon as practicable after the date of receipt of that notice.

(a–1) (1) Following the defendant's return to the court, the court shall make a determination with re-

gard to the defendant's competency to stand trial. The court may make the determination based only on the most recent report that is filed under Article 46B.079(c) and based on notice under that article, other than notice under Subsection (b)(1) of that article, and on other medical information or personal history information relating to the defendant. A party may object in writing or in open court to the findings of the most recent report not later than the 15th day after the date on which the court received the applicable notice under Article 46B.079. The court shall make the determination not later than the 20th day after the date on which the court received the applicable notice under Article 46B.079, or not later than the fifth day after the date of the defendant's return to court, whichever occurs first, regardless of whether a party objects to the report as described by this subsection and the issue is set for hearing under Subsection (b).

(2) Notwithstanding Subdivision (1), in a county with a population of less than one million or in a county with a population of four million or more, the court shall make the determination described by that subdivision not later than the 20th day after the date on which the court received notification under Article 46B.079, regardless of whether a party objects to the report as described by that subdivision and the issue is set for a hearing under Subsection (b).

(b) If a party objects under Subsection (a–1), the issue shall be set for a hearing. The hearing is before the court, except that on motion by the defendant, the defense counsel, the prosecuting attorney, or the court, the hearing shall be held before a jury.

(b–1) If the hearing is before the court, the hearing may be conducted by means of an electronic broadcast system as provided by Article 46B.013. Notwithstanding any other provision of this chapter, the defendant is not required to be returned to the court with respect to any hearing that is conducted under this article in the manner described by this subsection.

(c) Repealed by Acts 2007, 80th Leg., ch. 1307, § 21.

(d)(1) If the defendant is found competent to stand trial, on the court's own motion criminal proceedings in the case against the defendant shall be resumed not later than the 14th day after the date of the court's determination under this article that the defendant's competency has been restored.

(2) Notwithstanding Subdivision (1), in a county with a population of less than one million or in a

county with a population of four million or more, on the court's own motion criminal proceedings in the case against the defendant shall be resumed as soon as practicable after the date of the court's determination under this article that the defendant's competency has been restored.

(d–1) This article does not require the criminal case to be finally resolved within any specific period.

(e) If the defendant is found incompetent to stand trial and if all charges pending against the defendant are not dismissed, the court shall proceed under Subchapter E.

(f) If the defendant is found incompetent to stand trial and if all charges pending against the defendant are dismissed, the court shall proceed under Subchapter F.

Added by Acts 2003, 78th Leg., ch. 35, § 1, eff. Jan. 1, 2004. Amended by Acts 2005, 79th Leg., ch. 324, § 15, eff. Sept. 1, 2005; Acts 2007, 80th Leg., ch. 1307, §§ 8, 21, eff. Sept. 1, 2007; Acts 2011, 82nd Leg., ch. 822 (H.B. 2725), § 16, eff. Sept. 1, 2011; Acts 2015, 84th Leg., ch. 994 (H.B. 211), § 2, eff. June 19, 2015; Acts 2017, 85th Leg., ch. 748 (S.B. 1326), § 27, eff. Sept. 1, 2017.

Section 3 of Acts 2015, 84th Leg., ch. 994 (H.B. 211) provides:

"The change in law made by this Act applies only to a proceeding under Chapter 46B, Code of Criminal Procedure, that commences on or after the effective date [June 21, 2015] of this Act, regardless of when the defendant may have committed the underlying offense for which the defendant became subject to the proceeding."

Section 37 of Acts 2017, 85th Leg., ch. 748 (S.B. 1326) provides:

"The changes in law made by this Act apply only to a defendant charged with an offense committed on or after the effective date [Sept. 1, 2017] of this Act. A defendant charged with an offense committed before the effective date of this Act is governed by the law in effect on the date the offense was committed, and the former law is continued in effect for that purpose. For purposes of this section, an offense was committed before the effective date of this Act if any element of the offense occurred before that date."

Art. 46B.085. Subsequent Restoration Periods and Extensions of Those Periods Prohibited

(a) The court may order only one initial period of restoration and one extension under this subchapter in connection with the same offense.

(b) After an initial restoration period and an extension are ordered as described by Subsection (a), any subsequent court orders for treatment must be issued under Subchapter E or F.

Added by Acts 2003, 78th Leg., ch. 35, § 1, eff. Jan. 1, 2004. Amended by Acts 2005, 79th Leg., ch. 324, § 16, eff. Sept. 1, 2005; Acts 2007, 80th Leg., ch. 1307, § 9, eff. Sept. 1, 2007.

Art. 46B.086. Court–Ordered Medications

(a) This article applies only to a defendant:

(1) who is determined under this chapter to be incompetent to stand trial;

(2) who either:

(A) remains confined in a correctional facility, as defined by Section 1.07, Penal Code, for a period exceeding 72 hours while awaiting transfer to an inpatient mental health facility, a residential care facility, or an outpatient competency restoration program;

(B) is committed to an inpatient mental health facility, a residential care facility, or a jail-based competency restoration program for the purpose of competency restoration;

(C) is confined in a correctional facility while awaiting further criminal proceedings following competency restoration; or

(D) is subject to Article 46B.072, if the court has made the determinations required by Subsection (a–1) of that article;

(3) for whom a correctional facility or jail-based competency restoration program that employs or contracts with a licensed psychiatrist, an inpatient mental health facility, a residential care facility, or an outpatient competency restoration program provider has prepared a continuity of care plan that requires the defendant to take psychoactive medications; and

(4) who, after a hearing held under Section 574.106 or 592.156, Health and Safety Code, if applicable, has been found to not meet the criteria prescribed by Sections 574.106(a) and (a–1) or 592.156(a) and (b), Health and Safety Code, for court-ordered administration of psychoactive medications.

(b) If a defendant described by Subsection (a) refuses to take psychoactive medications as required by the defendant's continuity of care plan, the director of the facility or the program provider, as applicable, shall notify the court in which the criminal proceedings are pending of that fact not later than the end of the next business day following the refusal. The court shall promptly notify the attorney representing the state and the attorney representing the defendant of the defendant's refusal. The attorney representing the state may file a written motion to compel medication. The motion to compel medication must be filed not later than the 15th day after the date a judge issues an order stating that the defendant does not meet the criteria for court-ordered administration of psychoactive medications under Section 574.106 or 592.156, Health and Safety Code, except that, for a defendant in an outpatient competency restoration program, the motion may be filed at any time.

(c) The court, after notice and after a hearing held not later than the 10th day after the motion to compel medication is filed, may authorize the director of the facility or the program provider, as applicable, to have the medication administered to the defendant, by reasonable force if necessary. A hearing under this subsection may be conducted using an electronic broadcast system as provided by Article 46B.013.

(d) The court may issue an order under this article only if the order is supported by the testimony of two physicians, one of whom is the physician at or with the applicable facility or program who is prescribing the medication as a component of the defendant's continuity of care plan and another who is not otherwise involved in proceedings against the defendant. The court may require either or both physicians to examine the defendant and report on the examination to the court.

(e) The court may issue an order under this article if the court finds by clear and convincing evidence that:

(1) the prescribed medication is medically appropriate, is in the best medical interest of the defendant, and does not present side effects that cause harm to the defendant that is greater than the medical benefit to the defendant;

(2) the state has a clear and compelling interest in the defendant obtaining and maintaining competency to stand trial;

(3) no other less invasive means of obtaining and maintaining the defendant's competency exists; and

(4) the prescribed medication will not unduly prejudice the defendant's rights or use of defensive theories at trial.

(f) A statement made by a defendant to a physician during an examination under Subsection (d) may not be admitted against the defendant in any criminal proceeding, other than at:

(1) a hearing on the defendant's incompetency; or

(2) any proceeding at which the defendant first introduces into evidence the contents of the statement.

(g) For a defendant described by Subsection (a)(2)(A), an order issued under this article:

(1) authorizes the initiation of any appropriate mental health treatment for the defendant awaiting transfer; and

(2) does not constitute authorization to retain the defendant in a correctional facility for competency restoration treatment.

Added by Acts 2003, 78th Leg., ch. 35, § 1, eff. Jan. 1, 2004. Amended by Acts 2005, 79th Leg., ch. 717, § 8, eff. June 17, 2005; Acts 2007, 80th Leg., ch. 1307, § 9, eff. Sept. 1, 2007; Acts 2009, 81st Leg., ch. 624, § 4, eff. June 19, 2009; Acts 2011, 82nd Leg., ch. 822 (H.B. 2725), § 17, eff. Sept. 1, 2011; Acts 2013, 83rd Leg., ch. 504 (S.B. 34), § 4, eff. Sept. 1, 2013; Acts 2017, 85th Leg., ch. 748 (S.B. 1326), § 28, eff. Sept. 1, 2017.

Section 37 of Acts 2017, 85th Leg., ch. 748 (S.B. 1326) provides:

"The changes in law made by this Act apply only to a defendant charged with an offense committed on or after the effective date [Sept. 1, 2017] of this Act. A defendant charged with an offense committed before the effective date of this Act is governed by the law in effect on the date the offense was committed, and the former law is continued in effect for that purpose. For purposes of this section, an offense was committed before the effective date of this Act if any element of the offense occurred before that date."

Art. 46B.090. Jail–Based Restoration of Competency Pilot Program

(a) In this article, "department" means the Department of State Health Services.

(a–1) If the legislature appropriates to the department the funding necessary for the department to operate a jail-based restoration of competency pilot program as described by this article, the department shall develop and implement the pilot program in one or two counties in this state that choose to participate in the pilot program. In developing the pilot program, the department shall coordinate and allow for input from each participating county.

(b) The department shall contract with a provider of jail-based competency restoration services to provide services under the pilot program if the department develops a pilot program under this article.

(c) Not later than November 1, 2013, the commissioner of the department shall adopt rules as necessary to implement the pilot program. In adopting rules under this article, the commissioner shall specify the types of information the department must collect during the operation of the pilot program for use in evaluating the outcome of the pilot program.

(d) Repealed by Acts 2015, 84th Leg., ch. 946 (S.B. 277), § 1.15(d).

(e) Repealed by Acts 2015, 84th Leg., ch. 946 (S.B. 277), § 1.15(d).

(f) To contract with the department under Subsection (b), a provider of jail-based competency restoration services must demonstrate to the department that:

(1) the provider:

(A) has previously provided jail-based competency restoration services for one or more years; or

(B) is a local mental health authority that has previously provided competency restoration services;

(2) the provider's jail-based competency restoration program:

(A) uses a multidisciplinary treatment team to provide clinical treatment that is:

(i) directed toward the specific objective of restoring the defendant's competency to stand trial; and

(ii) similar to the clinical treatment provided as part of a competency restoration program at an inpatient mental health facility;

(B) employs or contracts for the services of at least one psychiatrist; and

(C) provides weekly treatment hours commensurate to the treatment hours provided as part of a competency restoration program at an inpatient mental health facility;

(3) the provider is certified by a nationwide nonprofit organization that accredits health care organizations and programs, such as the Joint Commission on Health Care Staffing Services, or the provider is a local mental health authority in good standing with the department; and

(4) the provider has a demonstrated history of successful jail-based competency restoration outcomes or, if the provider is a local mental health authority, a demonstrated history of successful competency restoration outcomes.

(g) A contract under Subsection (b) must require the designated provider to collect and submit to the department the information specified by rules adopted under Subsection (c).

(h) The designated provider shall enter into a contract with the participating county or counties. The contract must require the participating county or counties to:

(1) ensure the safety of defendants who participate in the jail-based restoration of competency pilot program;

(2) designate a separate space in the jail for the provider to conduct the pilot program;

(3) provide the same basic care to the participants as is provided to other inmates of a jail; and

(4) supply clinically appropriate psychoactive medications to the mental health service provider for purposes of administering court-ordered medication to the participants in accordance with Article 46B.086 of this code and Section 574.106, Health and Safety Code.

(i) The psychiatrist for the provider shall conduct at least two full psychiatric evaluations of the defendant during the period the defendant receives competency restoration services in the jail. The psychiatrist must conduct one evaluation not later than the 21st day and one evaluation not later than the 55th day after the date the defendant begins to participate in the pilot program. The psychiatrist shall submit to the court a report concerning each evaluation required under this subsection.

(j) If at any time during a defendant's participation in the jail-based restoration of competency pilot program the psychiatrist for the provider determines that the defendant has attained competency to stand trial:

(1) the psychiatrist for the provider shall promptly issue and send to the court a report demonstrating that fact; and

(2) the court shall consider that report as the report of an expert stating an opinion that the defendant has been restored to competency for purposes of Article 46B.0755(a) or (b).

(k) If at any time during a defendant's participation in the jail-based restoration of competency pilot program the psychiatrist for the provider determines that the defendant's competency to stand trial is unlikely to be restored in the foreseeable future:

(1) the psychiatrist for the provider shall promptly issue and send to the court a report demonstrating that fact; and

(2) the court shall:

(A) proceed under Subchapter E or F and order the transfer of the defendant, without unnecessary delay, to the first available facility that is appropriate for that defendant, as provided under Subchapter E or F, as applicable; or

(B) release the defendant on bail as permitted under Chapter 17.

(*l*) If the psychiatrist for the provider determines that a defendant ordered to participate in the pilot program has not been restored to competency by the end of the 60th day after the date the defendant began to receive services in the pilot program:

(1) for a defendant charged with a felony, the defendant shall be transferred, without unnecessary delay and for the remainder of the period prescribed by Article 46B.073(b), to the first available facility that is appropriate for that defendant as provided by Article 46B.073(c) or (d); and

(2) for a defendant charged with a misdemeanor, the court may:

(A) order a single extension under Article 46B.080 and the transfer of the defendant without unnecessary delay to the appropriate mental health facility or residential care facility as provided by Article 46B.073(d) for the remainder of the period under the extension;

(B) proceed under Subchapter E or F;

(C) release the defendant on bail as permitted under Chapter 17; or

(D) dismiss the charges in accordance with Article 46B.010.

(m) Unless otherwise provided by this article, the provisions of this chapter, including the maximum periods prescribed by Article 46B.0095, apply to a defendant receiving competency restoration services under the pilot program in the same manner as those provisions apply to any other defendant who is subject to proceedings under this chapter.

(n) If the department develops and implements a jail-based restoration of competency pilot program under this article, not later than December 1, 2018, the commissioner of the department shall submit a report concerning the pilot program to the presiding officers of the standing committees of the senate and house of representatives having primary jurisdiction over health and human services issues and over criminal justice issues. The report must include the information collected by the department during the pilot program and the commissioner's evaluation of the outcome of the program as of the date the report is submitted.

(*o*) Repealed by Acts 2017, 85th Leg., ch. 748 (S.B. 1326), § 35(2).

Added by Acts 2013, 83rd Leg., ch. 797 (S.B. 1475), § 2, eff. Sept. 1, 2013. Amended by Acts 2015, 84th Leg., ch. 1 (S.B. 219), § 6.016, eff. April 2, 2015; Acts 2015, 84th Leg., ch. 946 (S.B. 277), § 1.15(c), (d), eff. Sept. 1, 2015; Acts 2017, 85th Leg., ch. 748 (S.B. 1326), §§ 29, 35(2), eff. Sept. 1, 2017.

Section 37 of Acts 2017, 85th Leg., ch. 748 (S.B. 1326) provides:

"The changes in law made by this Act apply only to a defendant charged with an offense committed on or after the effective date [Sept. 1, 2017] of this Act. A defendant charged with an offense committed before the effective date of this Act is governed by the law in effect on the date the offense was committed, and the former law is continued in effect for that purpose. For purposes of this section, an offense was committed before the effective date of this Act if any element of the offense occurred before that date."

Art. 46B.091.   Jail–based competency restoration program implemented by county

(a) In this article:

(1) "Commission" means the Health and Human Services Commission.

(2) "Executive commissioner" means the executive commissioner of the Health and Human Services Commission.

(b) A county or counties jointly may develop and implement a jail-based competency restoration program.

(c) A county that implements a program under this article shall contract with a provider of jail-based competency restoration services that is a local mental health authority or local behavioral health authority that is in good standing with the commission, which may include an authority that is in good standing with the commission and subcontracts with a provider of jail-based competency restoration services.

(d) A jail-based competency restoration program must:

(1) provide jail-based competency restoration services through the use of a multidisciplinary treatment team that are:

(A) directed toward the specific objective of restoring the defendant's competency to stand trial; and

(B) similar to other competency restoration programs;

(2) employ or contract for the services of at least one psychiatrist;

(3) provide jail-based competency restoration services through licensed or qualified mental health professionals;

(4) provide weekly competency restoration hours commensurate to the hours provided as part of a competency restoration program at an inpatient mental health facility;

(5) operate in the jail in a designated space that is separate from the space used for the general population of the jail;

(6) ensure coordination of general health care;

(7) provide mental health treatment and substance use disorder treatment to defendants, as necessary, for competency restoration; and

(8) supply clinically appropriate psychoactive medications for purposes of administering court-ordered medication to defendants as applicable and in accordance with Article 46B.086 of this code or Section 574.106, Health and Safety Code.

(e) The executive commissioner shall adopt rules as necessary for a county to develop and implement a program under this article. The commission shall, as part of the rulemaking process, establish contract monitoring and oversight requirements for a local mental health authority or local behavioral health authority that contracts with a county to provide jail-based competency restoration services under this article. The contract monitoring and oversight requirements must be consistent with local mental health authority or local behavioral health authority performance contract monitoring and oversight requirements, as applicable.

(f) The commission may inspect on behalf of the state any aspect of a program implemented under this article.

(g) A psychiatrist or psychologist for the provider shall conduct at least two full psychiatric or psychological evaluations of the defendant during the period the defendant receives competency restoration services in the jail. The psychiatrist or psychologist must conduct one evaluation not later than the 21st day and one evaluation not later than the 55th day after the date the defendant is committed to the program. The psychiatrist or psychologist shall submit to the court a report concerning each evaluation required under this subsection.

(h) If at any time during a defendant's commitment to a program implemented under this article the psychiatrist or psychologist for the provider determines that the defendant has attained competency to stand trial:

(1) the psychiatrist or psychologist for the provider shall promptly issue and send to the court a report demonstrating that fact; and

(2) the court shall consider that report as the report of an expert stating an opinion that the defendant has been restored to competency for purposes of Article 46B.0755(a) or (b).

(i) If at any time during a defendant's commitment to a program implemented under this article the psychiatrist or psychologist for the provider determines that the defendant's competency to stand trial is unlikely to be restored in the foreseeable future:

(1) the psychiatrist or psychologist for the provider shall promptly issue and send to the court a report demonstrating that fact; and

(2) the court shall:

(A) proceed under Subchapter E or F and order the transfer of the defendant, without unnecessary delay, to the first available facility that is appropriate for that defendant, as provided under Subchapter E or F, as applicable; or

(B) release the defendant on bail as permitted under Chapter 17.

(j) If the psychiatrist or psychologist for the provider determines that a defendant committed to a program implemented under this article has not been restored to competency by the end of the 60th day after the date the defendant began to receive services in the program:

(1) for a defendant charged with a felony, the defendant shall be transferred, without unnecessary delay and for the remainder of the period prescribed by Article 46B.073(b), to the first available facility that is appropriate for that defendant as provided by Article 46B.073(c) or (d); and

(2) for a defendant charged with a misdemeanor, the court may:

(A) order a single extension under Article 46B.080 and, notwithstanding Articles 46B.073(e) and (f), the transfer of the defendant without unnecessary delay to the appropriate mental health facility or residential care facility as provided by Article 46B.073(d) for the remainder of the period under the extension;

(B) proceed under Subchapter E or F;

(C) release the defendant on bail as permitted under Chapter 17; or

(D) dismiss the charges in accordance with Article 46B.010.

(k) Unless otherwise provided by this article, the provisions of this chapter, including the maximum periods prescribed by Article 46B.0095, apply to a defendant receiving competency restoration services, including competency restoration education services, under a program implemented under this article in the same manner as those provisions apply to any other defendant who is subject to proceedings under this chapter.

(*l*) This article does not affect the responsibility of a county to ensure the safety of a defendant who is committed to the program and to provide the same adequate care to the defendant as is provided to other inmates of the jail in which the defendant is located.

Added by Acts 2017, 85th Leg., ch. 748 (S.B. 1326), § 30, eff. Sept. 1, 2017.

Section 37 of Acts 2017, 85th Leg., ch. 748 (S.B. 1326) provides:

"The changes in law made by this Act apply only to a defendant charged with an offense committed on or after the effective date [Sept. 1, 2017] of this Act. A defendant charged with an offense committed before the effective date of this Act is governed by the law in effect on the date the offense was committed, and the former law is continued in effect for that purpose. For purposes of this section, an offense was committed before the effective date of this Act if any element of the offense occurred before that date."

SUBCHAPTER E. CIVIL COMMITMENT: CHARGES PENDING

Acts 2005, 79th Leg., ch. 324, § 17, amended the subchapter heading.

Art. 46B.101. Applicability

This subchapter applies to a defendant against whom a court is required to proceed according to Article 46B.084(e) or according to the court's appropriate determination under Article 46B.071.

Added by Acts 2003, 78th Leg., ch. 35, § 1, eff. Jan. 1, 2004. Amended by Acts 2011, 82nd Leg., ch. 822 (H.B. 2725), § 18, eff. Sept. 1, 2011.

Art. 46B.102. Civil Commitment Hearing: Mental Illness

(a) If it appears to the court that the defendant may be a person with mental illness, the court shall hold a hearing to determine whether the defendant should be court-ordered to mental health services under Subtitle C, Title 7, Health and Safety Code.

(b) Proceedings for commitment of the defendant to court-ordered mental health services are governed by Subtitle C, Title 7,[1] Health and Safety Code, to the extent that Subtitle C applies and does not conflict with this chapter, except that the criminal court shall conduct the proceedings whether or not the criminal court is also the county court.

(c) If the court enters an order committing the defendant to a mental health facility, the defendant shall be:

(1) treated in conformity with Subtitle C, Title 7, Health and Safety Code, except as otherwise provided by this chapter; and

(2) released in conformity with Article 46B.107.

(d) In proceedings conducted under this subchapter for a defendant described by Subsection (a):

(1) an application for court-ordered temporary or extended mental health services may not be required;

(2) the provisions of Subtitle C, Title 7, Health and Safety Code, relating to notice of hearing do not apply; and

(3) appeals from the criminal court proceedings are to the court of appeals as in the proceedings for court-ordered inpatient mental health services under Subtitle C, Title 7, Health and Safety Code.

Added by Acts 2003, 78th Leg., ch. 35, § 1, eff. Jan. 1, 2004. Amended by Acts 2005, 79th Leg., ch. 324, § 18, eff. Sept. 1, 2005; Acts 2007, 80th Leg., ch. 1307, § 10, eff. Sept. 1, 2007.

[1] V.T.C.A., Health & Safety Code § 571.001 et seq.

Art. 46B.103. Civil Commitment Hearing: Intellectual Disability

(a) If it appears to the court that the defendant may be a person with an intellectual disability, the court shall hold a hearing to determine whether the defendant is a person with an intellectual disability.

(b) Proceedings for commitment of the defendant to a residential care facility are governed by Subtitle D, Title 7, Health and Safety Code, to the extent that Subtitle D applies and does not conflict with this chapter, except that the criminal court shall conduct the proceedings whether or not the criminal court is also a county court.

(c) If the court enters an order committing the defendant to a residential care facility, the defendant shall be:

(1) treated and released in accordance with Subtitle D, Title 7, Health and Safety Code, except as otherwise provided by this chapter; and

(2) released in conformity with Article 46B.107.

(d) In the proceedings conducted under this subchapter for a defendant described by Subsection (a):

(1) an application to have the defendant declared a person with an intellectual disability may not be required;

(2) the provisions of Subtitle D, Title 7, Health and Safety Code, relating to notice of hearing do not apply; and

(3) appeals from the criminal court proceedings are to the court of appeals as in the proceedings for

commitment to a residential care facility under Subtitle D, Title 7, Health and Safety Code.

Added by Acts 2003, 78th Leg., ch. 35, § 1, eff. Jan. 1, 2004. Amended by Acts 2005, 79th Leg., ch. 324, § 19, eff. Sept. 1, 2005; Acts 2007, 80th Leg., ch. 1307, § 11, eff. Sept. 1, 2007; Acts 2015, 84th Leg., ch. 1 (S.B. 219), §§ 6.017, 6.018, eff. April 2, 2015.

Art. 46B.104.   Civil Commitment Placement: Finding of Violence

A defendant committed to a facility as a result of proceedings initiated under this chapter shall be committed to the maximum security unit of any facility designated by the Department of State Health Services if:

(1) the defendant is charged with an offense listed in Article 17.032(a), other than an offense listed in Article 17.032(a)(6); or

(2) the indictment charging the offense alleges an affirmative finding under Article 42A.054(c) or (d).

Added by Acts 2003, 78th Leg., ch. 35, § 1, eff. Jan. 1, 2004. Amended by Acts 2005, 79th Leg., ch. 324, § 20, eff. Sept. 1, 2005; Acts 2007, 80th Leg., ch. 1307, § 12, eff. Sept. 1, 2007; Acts 2015, 84th Leg., ch. 1 (S.B. 219), § 6.019, eff. April 2, 2015; Acts 2015, 84th Leg., ch. 770 (H.B. 2299), § 2.21, eff. Jan. 1, 2017.

Art. 46B.105.   Transfer Following Civil Commitment Placement

(a) Unless a defendant is determined to be manifestly dangerous by a review board established under Subsection (b), not later than the 60th day after the date the defendant arrives at the maximum security unit, the defendant shall be transferred to:

(1) a unit of an inpatient mental health facility other than a maximum security unit;

(2) a residential care facility; or

(3) a program designated by a local mental health authority or a local intellectual and developmental disability authority.

(b) The commissioner of state health services shall appoint a review board of five members, including one psychiatrist licensed to practice medicine in this state and two persons who work directly with persons with mental illness or an intellectual disability, to determine whether the defendant is manifestly dangerous and, as a result of the danger the defendant presents, requires continued placement in a maximum security unit.

(c) The review board may not make a determination as to the defendant's need for treatment.

(d) A finding that the defendant is not manifestly dangerous is not a medical determination that the defendant no longer meets the criteria for involuntary civil commitment under Subtitle C[1] or D,[2] Title 7, Health and Safety Code.

(e) If the superintendent of the facility at which the maximum security unit is located disagrees with the determination, the matter shall be referred to the commissioner of state health services. The commissioner shall decide whether the defendant is manifestly dangerous.

Added by Acts 2003, 78th Leg., ch. 35, § 1, eff. Jan. 1, 2004. Amended by Acts 2005, 79th Leg., ch. 324, § 21, eff. Sept. 1, 2005; Acts 2015, 84th Leg., ch. 1 (S.B. 219), § 6.020, eff. April 2, 2015.

[1] V.T.C.A., Health & Safety Code § 571.001 et seq.

[2] V.T.C.A., Health & Safety § 591.001 et seq.

Art. 46B.106.   Civil Commitment Placement: No Finding of Violence

(a) A defendant committed to a facility as a result of the proceedings initiated under this chapter, other than a defendant described by Article 46B.104, shall be committed to:

(1) a facility designated by the Department of State Health Services or the Department of Aging and Disability Services, as appropriate; or

(2) an outpatient treatment program.

(b) A facility or outpatient treatment program may not refuse to accept a placement ordered under this article on the grounds that criminal charges against the defendant are pending.

Added by Acts 2003, 78th Leg., ch. 35, § 1, eff. Jan. 1, 2004. Amended by Acts 2005, 79th Leg., ch. 324, § 22, eff. Sept. 1, 2005; Acts 2007, 80th Leg., ch. 1307, § 13, eff. Sept. 1, 2007; Acts 2015, 84th Leg., ch. 1 (S.B. 219), § 6.021, eff. April 2, 2015.

Art. 46B.107.   Release of Defendant After Civil Commitment

(a) The release of a defendant committed under this chapter from the Department of State Health Services, the Department of Aging and Disability Services, an outpatient treatment program, or another facility is subject to disapproval by the committing court if the court or the attorney representing the state has notified the head of the facility or outpatient treatment provider, as applicable, to which the defendant has been committed that a criminal charge remains pending against the defendant.

(b) If the head of the facility or outpatient treatment provider to which a defendant has been committed under this chapter determines that the defendant should be released from the facility, the head of the facility or outpatient treatment provider shall notify the committing court and the sheriff of the county from which the defendant was committed in writing of the release not later than the 14th day before the date on which the facility or outpatient treatment provider intends to release the defendant.

(c) The head of the facility or outpatient treatment provider shall provide with the notice a written statement that states an opinion as to whether the defendant to be released has attained competency to stand trial.

(d) The court may, on motion of the attorney representing the state or on its own motion, hold a hearing to determine whether release is appropriate under the applicable criteria in Subtitle C[1] or D,[2] Title 7, Health and Safety Code. The court may conduct the hearing:

(1) at the facility; or

(2) by means of an electronic broadcast system as provided by Article 46B.013.

(e) If the court determines that release is not appropriate, the court shall enter an order directing the head of the facility or the outpatient treatment provider to not release the defendant.

(f) If an order is entered under Subsection (e), any subsequent proceeding to release the defendant is subject to this article.

Added by Acts 2003, 78th Leg., ch. 35, § 1, eff. Jan. 1, 2004. Amended by Acts 2005, 79th Leg., ch. 324, §§ 23, 24, eff. Sept. 1, 2005; Acts 2007, 80th Leg., ch. 1307, § 14, eff. Sept. 1, 2007; Acts 2015, 84th Leg., ch. 1 (S.B. 219), § 6.022, eff. April 2, 2015.

[1] V.T.C.A., Health & Safety Code § 571.001 et seq.
[2] V.T.C.A., Health & Safety § 591.001 et seq.

Art. 46B.108. Redetermination of Competency

(a) If criminal charges against a defendant found incompetent to stand trial have not been dismissed, the trial court at any time may determine whether the defendant has been restored to competency.

(b) An inquiry into restoration of competency under this subchapter may be made at the request of the head of the mental health facility, outpatient treatment provider, or residential care facility to which the defendant has been committed, the defendant, the attorney representing the defendant, or the attorney representing the state, or may be made on the court's own motion.

Added by Acts 2003, 78th Leg., ch. 35, § 1, eff. Jan. 1, 2004. Amended by Acts 2005, 79th Leg., ch. 324, § 25, eff. Sept. 1, 2005; Acts 2007, 80th Leg., ch. 1307, § 15, eff. Sept. 1, 2007.

Art. 46B.109. Request by Head of Facility or Outpatient Treatment Provider

(a) The head of a facility or outpatient treatment provider to which a defendant has been committed as a result of a finding of incompetency to stand trial may request the court to determine that the defendant has been restored to competency.

(b) The head of the facility or outpatient treatment provider shall provide with the request a written statement that in their opinion the defendant is competent to stand trial.

Added by Acts 2003, 78th Leg., ch. 35, § 1, eff. Jan. 1, 2004. Amended by Acts 2007, 80th Leg., ch. 1307, § 16, eff. Sept. 1, 2007.

Art. 46B.110. Motion by Defendant, Attorney Representing Defendant, or Attorney Representing State

(a) The defendant, the attorney representing the defendant, or the attorney representing the state may move that the court determine that the defendant has been restored to competency.

(b) A motion for a determination of competency may be accompanied by affidavits supporting the moving party's assertion that the defendant is competent.

Added by Acts 2003, 78th Leg., ch. 35, § 1, eff. Jan. 1, 2004. Amended by Acts 2005, 79th Leg., ch. 324, § 26, eff. Sept. 1, 2005.

Art. 46B.111. Appointment of Examiners

On the filing of a request or motion to determine that the defendant has been restored to competency or on the court's decision on its own motion to inquire into restoration of competency, the court may appoint disinterested experts to examine the defendant in accordance with Subchapter B.

Added by Acts 2003, 78th Leg., ch. 35, § 1, eff. Jan. 1, 2004.

Art. 46B.112. Determination of Restoration With Agreement

On the filing of a request or motion to determine that the defendant has been restored to competency or on the court's decision on its own motion to inquire into restoration of competency, the court shall find the defendant competent to stand trial and proceed in the same manner as if the defendant had been found restored to competency at a hearing if:

(1) both parties agree that the defendant is competent to stand trial; and

(2) the court concurs.

Added by Acts 2003, 78th Leg., ch. 35, § 1, eff. Jan. 1, 2004.

Art. 46B.113. Determination of Restoration Without Agreement

(a) The court shall hold a hearing on a request by the head of a facility or outpatient treatment provider to which a defendant has been committed as a result of a finding of incompetency to stand trial to determine whether the defendant has been restored to competency.

(b) The court may hold a hearing on a motion to determine whether the defendant has been restored to competency or on the court's decision on its own motion to inquire into restoration of competency, and shall hold a hearing if a motion and any supporting material establish good reason to believe the defendant may have been restored to competency.

(c) If a court holds a hearing under this article, on the request of the counsel for either party or the motion of the court, a jury shall make the competency determination. If the competency determination will be made by the court rather than a jury, the court may conduct the hearing:

(1) at the facility; or

(2) by means of an electronic broadcast system as provided by Article 46B.013.

(d) If the head of a facility or outpatient treatment provider to which the defendant was committed as a result of a finding of incompetency to stand trial has provided an opinion that the defendant has regained competency, competency is presumed at a hearing under this subchapter and continuing incompetency must be proved by a preponderance of the evidence.

(e) If the head of a facility or outpatient treatment provider has not provided an opinion described by Subsection (d), incompetency is presumed at a hearing under this subchapter and the defendant's competency must be proved by a preponderance of the evidence.

Added by Acts 2003, 78th Leg., ch. 35, § 1, eff. Jan. 1, 2004. Amended by Acts 2005, 79th Leg., ch. 324, § 27, eff. Sept. 1, 2005; Acts 2007, 80th Leg., ch. 1307, § 17, eff. Sept. 1, 2007.

Art. 46B.114. Transportation of Defendant to Court

If the hearing is not conducted at the facility to which the defendant has been committed under this chapter or conducted by means of an electronic broadcast system as described by this subchapter, an order setting a hearing to determine whether the defendant has been restored to competency shall direct that, as soon as practicable but not earlier than 72 hours before the date the hearing is scheduled, the defendant be placed in the custody of the sheriff of the county in which the committing court is located or the sheriff's designee for transportation to the court. The sheriff or the sheriff's designee may not take custody of the defendant under this article until 72 hours before the date the hearing is scheduled.

Added by Acts 2003, 78th Leg., ch. 35, § 1, eff. Jan. 1, 2004. Amended by Acts 2005, 79th Leg., ch. 324, § 28, eff. Sept. 1, 2005.

Art. 46B.115. Subsequent Redeterminations of Competency

(a) If the court has made a determination that a defendant has not been restored to competency under this subchapter, a subsequent request or motion for a redetermination of competency filed before the 91st day after the date of that determination must:

(1) explain why the person making the request or motion believes another inquiry into restoration is appropriate; and

(2) provide support for the belief.

(b) The court may hold a hearing on a request or motion under this article only if the court first finds reason to believe the defendant's condition has materially changed since the prior determination that the defendant was not restored to competency.

(c) If the competency determination will be made by the court, the court may conduct the hearing at the facility to which the defendant has been committed under this chapter or may conduct the hearing by means of an electronic broadcast system as provided by Article 46B.013.

Added by Acts 2003, 78th Leg., ch. 35, § 1, eff. Jan. 1, 2004. Amended by Acts 2005, 79th Leg., ch. 324, § 29, eff. Sept. 1, 2005.

Art. 46B.116. Disposition on Determination of Competency

If the defendant is found competent to stand trial, the proceedings on the criminal charge may proceed.

Added by Acts 2003, 78th Leg., ch. 35, § 1, eff. Jan. 1, 2004.

Art. 46B.117. Disposition on Determination of Incompetency

If a defendant under order of commitment to a facility or outpatient treatment program is found to not have been restored to competency to stand trial, the court shall remand the defendant pursuant to that order of commitment, and, if applicable, order the defendant placed in the custody of the sheriff or the sheriff's designee for transportation back to the facility or outpatient treatment program.

Added by Acts 2003, 78th Leg., ch. 35, § 1, eff. Jan. 1, 2004. Amended by Acts 2005, 79th Leg., ch. 324, § 30, eff. Sept. 1, 2005; Acts 2007, 80th Leg., ch. 1307, § 18, eff. Sept. 1, 2007.

SUBCHAPTER F. CIVIL COMMITMENT: CHARGES DISMISSED

Acts 2005, 79th Leg., ch. 324, § 31, amended the subchapter heading.

Art. 46B.151. Court Determination Related to Civil Commitment

(a) If a court is required by Article 46B.084(f) or by its appropriate determination under Article 46B.071 to proceed under this subchapter, or if the court is permitted by Article 46B.004(e) to proceed under this subchapter, the court shall determine whether there is evidence to support a finding that the defendant is either a person with mental illness or a person with an intellectual disability.

(b) If it appears to the court that there is evidence to support a finding of mental illness or an intellectual disability, the court shall enter an order transferring the defendant to the appropriate court for civil commitment proceedings and stating that all charges pending against the defendant in that court have been dismissed. The court may order the defendant:

(1) detained in jail or any other suitable place pending the prompt initiation and prosecution by the attorney for the state or other person designated by the court of appropriate civil proceedings to determine whether the defendant will be committed to a mental health facility or residential care facility; or

(2) placed in the care of a responsible person on satisfactory security being given for the defendant's proper care and protection.

(c) Notwithstanding Subsection (b), a defendant placed in a facility of the Department of State Health Services or the Department of Aging and Disability Services pending civil hearing under this article may be detained in that facility only with the consent of the head of the facility and pursuant to an order of protective custody issued under Subtitle C, Title 7, Health and Safety Code.

(d) If the court does not detain or place the defendant under Subsection (b), the court shall release the defendant.

Added by Acts 2003, 78th Leg., ch. 35, § 1, eff. Jan. 1, 2004. Amended by Acts 2005, 79th Leg., ch. 324, §§ 32, 33, eff. Sept. 1, 2005; Acts 2011, 82nd Leg., ch. 822 (H.B. 2725), § 19, eff. Sept. 1, 2011; Acts 2015, 84th Leg., ch. 1 (S.B. 219), § 6.023, eff. April 2, 2015.

SUBCHAPTER G. PROVISIONS APPLICABLE TO SUBCHAPTERS E AND F

Art. 46B.171. Transcripts and Other Records

(a) The court shall order that:

(1) a transcript of all medical testimony received in both the criminal proceedings and the civil commitment proceedings under Subchapter E or F be prepared as soon as possible by the court reporters; and

(2) copies of documents listed in Article 46B.076 accompany the defendant to the mental health facility, outpatient treatment program, or residential care facility.

(b) On the request of the defendant or the attorney representing the defendant, a mental health facility, an outpatient treatment program, or a residential care facility shall provide to the defendant or the attorney copies of the facility's records regarding the defendant.

Added by Acts 2003, 78th Leg., ch. 35, § 1, eff. Jan. 1, 2004. Amended by Acts 2005, 79th Leg., ch. 324, § 34, eff. Sept. 1, 2005; Acts 2007, 80th Leg., ch. 1307, § 19, eff. Sept. 1, 2007.

CHAPTER 46C. INSANITY DEFENSE

SUBCHAPTER A. GENERAL PROVISIONS

SUBCHAPTER A. GENERAL PROVISIONS

Art. 46C.001. Definitions

In this chapter:

(1) "Commissioner" means the commissioner of state health services.

(2) "Department" means the Department of State Health Services.

(3) "Mental illness" has the meaning assigned by Section 571.003, Health and Safety Code.

(4) "Mental retardation" has the meaning assigned by Section 591.003, Health and Safety Code.

(5) "Residential care facility" has the meaning assigned by Section 591.003, Health and Safety Code.

Added by Acts 2005, 79th Leg., ch. 831, § 2, eff. Sept. 1, 2005.

Art. 46C.002. Maximum Period of Commitment Determined by Maximum Term for Offense

(a) A person acquitted by reason of insanity may not be committed to a mental hospital or other inpatient or residential care facility or ordered to receive outpatient or community-based treatment and supervision under Subchapter F for a cumulative period that exceeds the maximum term provided by law for the offense for which the acquitted person was tried.

(b) On expiration of that maximum term, the acquitted person may be further confined in a mental hospital or other inpatient or residential care facility or ordered to receive outpatient or community-based treatment and supervision only under civil commitment proceedings.

Added by Acts 2005, 79th Leg., ch. 831, § 2, eff. Sept. 1, 2005.

Art. 46C.003. Victim Notification of Release

If the court issues an order that requires the release of an acquitted person on discharge or on a regimen of outpatient care, the clerk of the court issuing the order, using the information provided on any victim impact statement received by the court under Article 56.03 or other information made available to the court, shall notify the victim or the victim's guardian or close relative of the release. Notwithstanding Article 56.03(f), the clerk of the court may inspect a victim impact statement for the purpose of notification under this article. On request, a victim assistance coordinator may provide the clerk of the court with information or other assistance necessary for the clerk to comply with this article.

Added by Acts 1975, 64th Leg., p. 1100, ch. 415, § 2, eff. June 19, 1975. Amended by Acts 1977, 65th Leg., p. 1467, ch. 596, § 2, eff. Sept. 1, 1977; Acts 1983, 68th Leg., p. 2640, ch. 454, §§ 2, 3, eff. Aug. 29, 1983; Acts 1989, 71st Leg., ch. 393, §§ 7 to 9, eff. June 14, 1989; Acts 2001, 77th Leg., ch. 985, § 1, eff. Sept. 1, 2001; Acts 2003, 78th Leg., ch. 35, § 5, eff. Jan. 1, 2004; Acts 2005, 79th Leg., ch. 485, § 1, eff. Sept. 1, 2005; Acts 2005, 79th Leg., ch. 831, § 1, eff. Sept. 1, 2005. Redesignated from Vernon's Ann.C.C.P. art. 46.03, § 4(d)(8) and amended by Acts 2011, 82nd Leg., ch. 787 (H.B. 2124), § 1, eff. June 17, 2011. Amended by Acts 2013, 83rd Leg., ch. 1276 (H.B. 1435), § 1, eff. Sept. 1, 2013.

SUBCHAPTER B. RAISING THE INSANITY DEFENSE

Art. 46C.051. Notice of Intent to Raise Insanity Defense

(a) A defendant planning to offer evidence of the insanity defense must file with the court a notice of the defendant's intention to offer that evidence.

(b) The notice must:

(1) contain a certification that a copy of the notice has been served on the attorney representing the state; and

(2) be filed at least 20 days before the date the case is set for trial, except as described by Subsection (c).

(c) If before the 20–day period the court sets a pretrial hearing, the defendant shall give notice at the hearing.

Added by Acts 2005, 79th Leg., ch. 831, § 2, eff. Sept. 1, 2005.

Art. 46C.052. Effect of Failure to Give Notice

Unless notice is timely filed under Article 46C.051, evidence on the insanity defense is not admissible unless the court finds that good cause exists for failure to give notice.

Added by Acts 2005, 79th Leg., ch. 831, § 2, eff. Sept. 1, 2005.

SUBCHAPTER C. COURT–ORDERED EXAMINATION AND REPORT

Art. 46C.101. Appointment of Experts

(a) If notice of intention to raise the insanity defense is filed under Article 46C.051, the court may, on its own motion or motion by the defendant, the defendant's counsel, or the attorney representing the state, appoint one or more disinterested experts to:

(1) examine the defendant with regard to the insanity defense; and

(2) testify as to the issue of insanity at any trial or hearing involving that issue.

(b) The court shall advise an expert appointed under this article of the facts and circumstances of the offense with which the defendant is charged and the elements of the insanity defense.

Added by Acts 2005, 79th Leg., ch. 831, § 2, eff. Sept. 1, 2005.

Art. 46C.102. Experts: Qualifications

(a) The court may appoint qualified psychiatrists or psychologists as experts under this chapter. To qualify for appointment under this subchapter as an expert, a psychiatrist or psychologist must:

(1) as appropriate, be a physician licensed in this state or be a psychologist licensed in this state who has a doctoral degree in psychology; and

(2) have the following certification or experience or training:

(A) as appropriate, certification by:

(i) the American Board of Psychiatry and Neurology with added or special qualifications in forensic psychiatry; or

(ii) the American Board of Professional Psychology in forensic psychology; or

(B) experience or training consisting of:

(i) at least 24 hours of specialized forensic training relating to incompetency or insanity evaluations;

(ii) at least five years of experience in performing criminal forensic evaluations for courts; and

(iii) eight or more hours of continuing education relating to forensic evaluations, completed in the 12 months preceding the appointment and documented with the court.

(b) In addition to meeting qualifications required by Subsection (a), to be appointed as an expert a psychiatrist or psychologist must have completed six hours of required continuing education in courses in forensic psychiatry or psychology, as appropriate, in the 24 months preceding the appointment.

(c) A court may appoint as an expert a psychiatrist or psychologist who does not meet the requirements of Subsections (a) and (b) only if exigent circumstances require the court to base the appointment on professional training or experience of the expert that directly provides the expert with a specialized expertise to examine the defendant that would not ordinarily be possessed by a psychiatrist or psychologist who meets the requirements of Subsections (a) and (b).

Added by Acts 2005, 79th Leg., ch. 831, § 2, eff. Sept. 1, 2005.

Art. 46C.103.   Competency to Stand Trial: Concurrent Appointment

(a) An expert appointed under this subchapter to examine the defendant with regard to the insanity defense also may be appointed by the court to examine the defendant with regard to the defendant's competency to stand trial under Chapter 46B, if the expert files with the court separate written reports concerning the defendant's competency to stand trial and the insanity defense.

(b) Notwithstanding Subsection (a), an expert may not examine the defendant for purposes of determining the defendant's sanity and may not file a report regarding the defendant's sanity if in the opinion of the expert the defendant is incompetent to proceed.

Added by Acts 2005, 79th Leg., ch. 831, § 2, eff. Sept. 1, 2005.

Art. 46C.104.   Order Compelling Defendant to Submit to Examination

(a) For the purposes described by this chapter, the court may order any defendant to submit to examination, including a defendant who is free on bail. If the defendant fails or refuses to submit to examination, the court may order the defendant to custody for examination for a reasonable period not to exceed 21 days. Custody ordered by the court under this subsection may include custody at a facility operated by the department.

(b) If a defendant who has been ordered to a facility operated by the department for examination re-

mains in the facility for a period that exceeds 21 days, the head of that facility shall cause the defendant to be immediately transported to the committing court and placed in the custody of the sheriff of the county in which the committing court is located. That county shall reimburse the facility for the mileage and per diem expenses of the personnel required to transport the defendant, calculated in accordance with the state travel rules in effect at that time.

(c) The court may not order a defendant to a facility operated by the department for examination without the consent of the head of that facility.

Added by Acts 2005, 79th Leg., ch. 831, § 2, eff. Sept. 1, 2005.

Art. 46C.105.   Reports Submitted by Experts

(a) A written report of the examination shall be submitted to the court not later than the 30th day after the date of the order of examination. The court shall provide copies of the report to the defense counsel and the attorney representing the state.

(b) The report must include a description of the procedures used in the examination and the examiner's observations and findings pertaining to the insanity defense.

(c) The examiner shall submit a separate report stating the examiner's observations and findings concerning:

(1) whether the defendant is presently a person with a mental illness and requires court-ordered mental health services under Subtitle C,[1] Title 7, Health and Safety Code; or

(2) whether the defendant is presently a person with mental retardation.

Added by Acts 2005, 79th Leg., ch. 831, § 2, eff. Sept. 1, 2005.

[1] V.T.C.A., Health & Safety Code § 571.001 et seq.

Art. 46C.106.   Compensation of Experts

(a) The appointed experts shall be paid by the county in which the indictment was returned or information was filed.

(b) The county in which the indictment was returned or information was filed shall reimburse a facility operated by the department that accepts a defendant for examination under this subchapter for expenses incurred that are determined by the department to be reasonably necessary and incidental to the proper examination of the defendant.

Added by Acts 2005, 79th Leg., ch. 831, § 2, eff. Sept. 1, 2005.

Art. 46C.107. Examination by Expert of Defendant's Choice

. If a defendant wishes to be examined by an expert of the defendant's own choice, the court on timely request shall provide the examiner with reasonable opportunity to examine the defendant.

Added by Acts 2005, 79th Leg., ch. 831, § 2, eff. Sept. 1, 2005.

SUBCHAPTER D. DETERMINATION OF ISSUE OF DEFENDANT'S SANITY

Art. 46C.151. Determination of Sanity Issue by Jury

(a) In a case tried to a jury, the issue of the defendant's sanity shall be submitted to the jury only if the issue is supported by competent evidence. The jury shall determine the issue.

(b) If the issue of the defendant's sanity is submitted to the jury, the jury shall determine and specify in the verdict whether the defendant is guilty, not guilty, or not guilty by reason of insanity.

Added by Acts 2005, 79th Leg., ch. 831, § 2, eff. Sept. 1, 2005.

Art. 46C.152. Determination of Sanity Issue by Judge

(a) If a jury trial is waived and if the issue is supported by competent evidence, the judge as trier of fact shall determine the issue of the defendant's sanity.

(b) The parties may, with the consent of the judge, agree to have the judge determine the issue of the defendant's sanity on the basis of introduced or stipulated competent evidence, or both.

(c) If the judge determines the issue of the defendant's sanity, the judge shall enter a finding of guilty, not guilty, or not guilty by reason of insanity.

Added by Acts 2005, 79th Leg., ch. 831, § 2, eff. Sept. 1, 2005.

Art. 46C.153. General Provisions Relating to Determination of Sanity Issue by Judge or Jury

(a) The judge or jury shall determine that a defendant is not guilty by reason of insanity if:

(1) the prosecution has established beyond a reasonable doubt that the alleged conduct constituting the offense was committed; and

(2) the defense has established by a preponderance of the evidence that the defendant was insane at the time of the alleged conduct.

(b) The parties may, with the consent of the judge, agree to both:

(1) dismissal of the indictment or information on the ground that the defendant was insane; and

(2) entry of a judgment of dismissal due to the defendant's insanity.

(c) An entry of judgment under Subsection (b)(2) has the same effect as a judgment stating that the defendant has been found not guilty by reason of insanity.

Added by Acts 2005, 79th Leg., ch. 831, § 2, eff. Sept. 1, 2005.

Art. 46C.154. Informing Jury Regarding Consequences of Acquittal

The court, the attorney representing the state, or the attorney for the defendant may not inform a juror or a prospective juror of the consequences to the defendant if a verdict of not guilty by reason of insanity is returned.

Added by Acts 2005, 79th Leg., ch. 831, § 2, eff. Sept. 1, 2005.

Art. 46C.155. Finding of Not Guilty by Reason of Insanity Considered Acquittal

(a) Except as provided by Subsection (b), a defendant who is found not guilty by reason of insanity stands acquitted of the offense charged and may not be considered a person charged with an offense.

(b) A defendant who is found not guilty by reason of insanity is not considered to be acquitted for purposes of Chapter 55.

Added by Acts 2005, 79th Leg., ch. 831, § 2, eff. Sept. 1, 2005.

Art. 46C.156. Judgment

(a) In each case in which the insanity defense is raised, the judgment must reflect whether the defendant was found guilty, not guilty, or not guilty by reason of insanity.

(b) If the defendant was found not guilty by reason of insanity, the judgment must specify the offense of which the defendant was found not guilty.

(c) If the defendant was found not guilty by reason of insanity, the judgment must reflect the finding made under Article 46C.157.

Added by Acts 2005, 79th Leg., ch. 831, § 2, eff. Sept. 1, 2005.

Art. 46C.157. Determination Regarding Dangerous Conduct of Acquitted Person

If a defendant is found not guilty by reason of insanity, the court immediately shall determine whether the offense of which the person was acquitted involved conduct that:

(1) caused serious bodily injury to another person;

(2) placed another person in imminent danger of serious bodily injury; or

(3) consisted of a threat of serious bodily injury to another person through the use of a deadly weapon.

Added by Acts 2005, 79th Leg., ch. 831, § 2, eff. Sept. 1, 2005.

Art. 46C.158. Continuing Jurisdiction of Dangerous Acquitted Person

If the court finds that the offense of which the person was acquitted involved conduct that caused serious bodily injury to another person, placed another person in imminent danger of serious bodily injury, or consisted of a threat of serious bodily injury to another person through the use of a deadly weapon, the court retains jurisdiction over the acquitted person until either:

(1) the court discharges the person and terminates its jurisdiction under Article 46C.268; or

(2) the cumulative total period of institutionalization and outpatient or community-based treatment and supervision under the court's jurisdiction equals the maximum term provided by law for the offense of which the person was acquitted by reason of insanity and the court's jurisdiction is automatically terminated under Article 46C.269.

Added by Acts 2005, 79th Leg., ch. 831, § 2, eff. Sept. 1, 2005.

Art. 46C.159. Proceedings Regarding Nondangerous Acquitted Person

If the court finds that the offense of which the person was acquitted did not involve conduct that caused serious bodily injury to another person, placed another person in imminent danger of serious bodily injury, or consisted of a threat of serious bodily injury

to another person through the use of a deadly weapon, the court shall proceed under Subchapter E.

Added by Acts 2005, 79th Leg., ch. 831, § 2, eff. Sept. 1, 2005.

Art. 46C.160. Detention Pending Further Proceedings

(a) On a determination by the judge or jury that the defendant is not guilty by reason of insanity, pending further proceedings under this chapter, the court may order the defendant detained in jail or any other suitable place for a period not to exceed 14 days.

(b) The court may order a defendant detained in a facility of the department or a facility of the Department of Aging and Disability Services under this article only with the consent of the head of the facility.

Added by Acts 2005, 79th Leg., ch. 831, § 2, eff. Sept. 1, 2005.

SUBCHAPTER E. DISPOSITION FOLLOWING ACQUITTAL BY REASON OF INSANITY: NO FINDING OF DANGEROUS CONDUCT

Art. 46C.201. Disposition: Nondangerous Conduct

(a) If the court determines that the offense of which the person was acquitted did not involve conduct that caused serious bodily injury to another person, placed another person in imminent danger of serious bodily injury, or consisted of a threat of serious bodily injury to another person through the use of a deadly weapon, the court shall determine whether there is evidence to support a finding that the person is a person with a mental illness or with mental retardation.

(b) If the court determines that there is evidence to support a finding of mental illness or mental retardation, the court shall enter an order transferring the person to the appropriate court for civil commitment proceedings to determine whether the person should receive court-ordered mental health services under Subtitle C,[1] Title 7, Health and Safety Code, or be committed to a residential care facility to receive mental retardation services under Subtitle D,[2] Title 7, Health and Safety Code. The court may also order the person:

(1) detained in jail or any other suitable place pending the prompt initiation and prosecution of appropriate civil proceedings by the attorney representing the state or other person designated by the court; or

(2) placed in the care of a responsible person on satisfactory security being given for the acquitted person's proper care and protection.

Added by Acts 2005, 79th Leg., ch. 831, § 2, eff. Sept. 1, 2005.

[1] V.T.C.A., Health & Safety Code § 571.001 et seq.
[2] V.T.C.A., Health & Safety § 591.001 et seq.

Art. 46C.202. Detention or Release

(a) Notwithstanding Article 46C.201(b), a person placed in a department facility or a facility of the Department of Aging and Disability Services pending civil hearing as described by that subsection may be detained only with the consent of the head of the facility and under an Order of Protective Custody issued under Subtitle C or D, Title 7, Health and Safety Code.

(b) If the court does not detain or place the person under Article 46C.201(b), the court shall release the person.

Added by Acts 2005, 79th Leg., ch. 831, § 2, eff. Sept. 1, 2005.

SUBCHAPTER F. DISPOSITION FOLLOWING ACQUITTAL BY REASON OF INSANITY: FINDING OF DANGEROUS CONDUCT

Art. 46C.251. Commitment for Evaluation and Treatment; Report

(a) The court shall order the acquitted person to be committed for evaluation of the person's present mental condition and for treatment to the maximum security unit of any facility designated by the department. The period of commitment under this article may not exceed 30 days.

(b) The court shall order that:

(1) a transcript of all medical testimony received in the criminal proceeding be prepared as soon as possible by the court reporter and the transcript be forwarded to the facility to which the acquitted person is committed; and

(2) the following information be forwarded to the facility and, as applicable, to the department or the Department of Aging and Disability Services:

(A) the complete name, race, and gender of the person;

(B) any known identifying number of the person, including social security number, driver's license number, or state identification number;

(C) the person's date of birth; and

(D) the offense of which the person was found not guilty by reason of insanity and a statement of the facts and circumstances surrounding the alleged offense.

(c) The court shall order that a report be filed with the court under Article 46C.252.

(d) To determine the proper disposition of the acquitted person, the court shall hold a hearing on disposition not later than the 30th day after the date of acquittal.

Added by Acts 2005, 79th Leg., ch. 831, § 2, eff. Sept. 1, 2005.

Art. 46C.252. Report After Evaluation

(a) The report ordered under Article 46C.251 must be filed with the court as soon as practicable before the hearing on disposition but not later than the fourth day before that hearing.

(b) The report in general terms must describe and explain the procedure, techniques, and tests used in the examination of the person.

(c) The report must address:

(1) whether the acquitted person has a mental illness or mental retardation and, if so, whether the mental illness or mental retardation is severe;

(2) whether as a result of any severe mental illness or mental retardation the acquitted person is likely to cause serious harm to another;

(3) whether as a result of any impairment the acquitted person is subject to commitment under Subtitle C[1] or D,[2] Title 7, Health and Safety Code;

(4) prospective treatment and supervision options, if any, appropriate for the acquitted person; and

(5) whether any required treatment and supervision can be safely and effectively provided as outpatient or community-based treatment and supervision.

Added by Acts 2005, 79th Leg., ch. 831, § 2, eff. Sept. 1, 2005.

[1] V.T.C.A., Health & Safety Code § 571.001 et seq.
[2] V.T.C.A., Health & Safety § 591.001 et seq.

Art. 46C.253. Hearing on Disposition

(a) The hearing on disposition shall be conducted in the same manner as a hearing on an application for involuntary commitment under Subtitle C or D, Title 7, Health and Safety Code, except that the use of a jury is governed by Article 46C.255.

(b) At the hearing, the court shall address:

(1) whether the person acquitted by reason of insanity has a severe mental illness or mental retardation;

(2) whether as a result of any mental illness or mental retardation the person is likely to cause serious harm to another; and

(3) whether appropriate treatment and supervision for any mental illness or mental retardation rendering the person dangerous to another can be safely and effectively provided as outpatient or community-based treatment and supervision.

(c) The court shall order the acquitted person committed for inpatient treatment or residential care under Article 46C.256 if the grounds required for that order are established.

(d) The court shall order the acquitted person to receive outpatient or community-based treatment and supervision under Article 46C.257 if the grounds required for that order are established.

(e) The court shall order the acquitted person transferred to an appropriate court for proceedings under Subtitle C[1] or D,[2] Title 7, Health and Safety Code, if the state fails to establish the grounds required for an order under Article 46C.256 or 46C.257 but the evidence provides a reasonable basis for believing the acquitted person is a proper subject for those proceedings.

(f) The court shall order the acquitted person discharged and immediately released if the evidence fails to establish that disposition under Subsection (c), (d), or (e) is appropriate.

Added by Acts 2005, 79th Leg., ch. 831, § 2, eff. Sept. 1, 2005.

[1] V.T.C.A., Health & Safety Code § 571.001 et seq.
[2] V.T.C.A., Health & Safety § 591.001 et seq.

Art. 46C.254.　Effect of Stabilization on Treatment Regimen

If an acquitted person is stabilized on a treatment regimen, including medication and other treatment modalities, rendering the person no longer likely to cause serious harm to another, inpatient treatment or residential care may be found necessary to protect the safety of others only if:

(1) the person would become likely to cause serious harm to another if the person fails to follow the treatment regimen on an Order to Receive Outpatient or Community–Based Treatment and Supervision; and

(2) under an Order to Receive Outpatient or Community–Based Treatment and Supervision either:

(A) the person is likely to fail to comply with an available regimen of outpatient or community-based treatment, as determined by the person's insight into the need for medication, the number, severity, and controllability of side effects, the availability of support and treatment programs for the person from community members, and other appropriate considerations; or

(B) a regimen of outpatient or community-based treatment will not be available to the person.

Added by Acts 2005, 79th Leg., ch. 831, § 2, eff. Sept. 1, 2005.

Art. 46C.255.　Trial by Jury

(a) The following proceedings under this chapter must be before the court, and the underlying matter determined by the court, unless the acquitted person or the state requests a jury trial or the court on its own motion sets the matter for jury trial:

(1) a hearing under Article 46C.253;

(2) a proceeding for renewal of an order under Article 46C.261;

(3) a proceeding on a request for modification or revocation of an order under Article 46C.266; and

(4) a proceeding seeking discharge of an acquitted person under Article 46C.268.

(b) The following proceedings may not be held before a jury:

(1) a proceeding to determine outpatient or community-based treatment and supervision under Article 46C.262; or

(2) a proceeding to determine modification or revocation of outpatient or community-based treatment and supervision under Article 46C.267.

(c) If a hearing is held before a jury and the jury determines that the person has a mental illness or mental retardation and is likely to cause serious harm to another, the court shall determine whether inpatient treatment or residential care is necessary to protect the safety of others.

Added by Acts 2005, 79th Leg., ch. 831, § 2, eff. Sept. 1, 2005.

Art. 46C.256.　Order of Commitment to Inpatient Treatment or Residential Care

(a) The court shall order the acquitted person committed to a mental hospital or other appropriate facility for inpatient treatment or residential care if the state establishes by clear and convincing evidence that:

(1) the person has a severe mental illness or mental retardation;

(2) the person, as a result of that mental illness or mental retardation, is likely to cause serious bodily injury to another if the person is not provided with treatment and supervision; and

(3) inpatient treatment or residential care is necessary to protect the safety of others.

(b) In determining whether inpatient treatment or residential care has been proved necessary, the court shall consider whether the evidence shows both that:

(1) an adequate regimen of outpatient or community-based treatment will be available to the person; and

(2) the person will follow that regimen.

(c) The order of commitment to inpatient treatment or residential care expires on the 181st day following the date the order is issued but is subject to renewal as provided by Article 46C.261.

Added by Acts 2005, 79th Leg., ch. 831, § 2, eff. Sept. 1, 2005.

Art. 46C.257. Order to Receive Outpatient or Community–based Treatment and Supervision

(a) The court shall order the acquitted person to receive outpatient or community-based treatment and supervision if:

(1) the state establishes by clear and convincing evidence that the person:

(A) has a severe mental illness or mental retardation; and

(B) as a result of that mental illness or mental retardation is likely to cause serious bodily injury to another if the person is not provided with treatment and supervision; and

(2) the state fails to establish by clear and convincing evidence that inpatient treatment or residential care is necessary to protect the safety of others.

(b) The order of commitment to outpatient or community-based treatment and supervision expires on the first anniversary of the date the order is issued but is subject to renewal as provided by Article 46C.261.

Added by Acts 2005, 79th Leg., ch. 831, § 2, eff. Sept. 1, 2005.

Art. 46C.258. Responsibility of Inpatient or Residential Care Facility

(a) The head of the facility to which an acquitted person is committed has, during the commitment period, a continuing responsibility to determine:

(1) whether the acquitted person continues to have a severe mental illness or mental retardation and is likely to cause serious harm to another because of any severe mental illness or mental retardation; and

(2) if so, whether treatment and supervision cannot be safely and effectively provided as outpatient or community-based treatment and supervision.

(b) The head of the facility must notify the committing court and seek modification of the order of commitment if the head of the facility determines that an acquitted person no longer has a severe mental illness or mental retardation, is no longer likely to cause serious harm to another, or that treatment and supervision can be safely and effectively provided as outpatient or community-based treatment and supervision.

(c) Not later than the 60th day before the date of expiration of the order, the head of the facility shall transmit to the committing court a psychological evaluation of the acquitted person, a certificate of medical examination of the person, and any recommendation for further treatment of the person. The committing court shall make the documents available to the attorneys representing the state and the acquitted person.

Added by Acts 2005, 79th Leg., ch. 831, § 2, eff. Sept. 1, 2005.

Art. 46C.259. Status of Committed Person

If an acquitted person is committed under this subchapter, the person's status as a patient or resident is governed by Subtitle C or D, Title 7, Health and Safety Code, except that:

(1) transfer to a nonsecure unit is governed by Article 46C.260;

(2) modification of the order to direct outpatient or community-based treatment and supervision is governed by Article 46C.262; and

(3) discharge is governed by Article 46C.268.

Added by Acts 2005, 79th Leg., ch. 831, § 2, eff. Sept. 1, 2005.

Art. 46C.260. Transfer of Committed Person to Nonsecure Facility

(a) A person committed to a facility under this subchapter shall be committed to the maximum security unit of any facility designated by the department.

(b) A person committed under this subchapter shall be transferred to the maximum security unit immediately on the entry of the order of commitment.

(c) Unless the person is determined to be manifestly dangerous by a review board within the department, not later than the 60th day following the date of the person's arrival at the maximum security unit the person shall be transferred to a nonsecure unit of a facility designated by the department or the Department of Aging and Disability Services, as appropriate.

(d) The commissioner shall appoint a review board of five members, including one psychiatrist licensed to practice medicine in this state and two persons who work directly with persons with mental illnesses or with mental retardation, to determine whether the person is manifestly dangerous and, as a result of the danger the person presents, requires continued placement in a maximum security unit.

(e) If the head of the facility at which the maximum security unit is located disagrees with the determination, then the matter shall be referred to the commissioner. The commissioner shall decide whether the person is manifestly dangerous.

Added by Acts 2005, 79th Leg., ch. 831, § 2, eff. Sept. 1, 2005.

Art. 46C.261. Renewal of Orders for Inpatient Commitment or Outpatient or Community-based Treatment and Supervision

(a) A court that orders an acquitted person committed to inpatient treatment or orders outpatient or community-based treatment and supervision annually shall determine whether to renew the order.

(b) Not later than the 30th day before the date an order is scheduled to expire, the institution to which a person is committed, the person responsible for providing outpatient or community-based treatment and supervision, or the attorney representing the state may file a request that the order be renewed. The request must explain in detail the reasons why the person requests renewal under this article. A request to renew an order committing the person to inpatient treatment must also explain in detail why outpatient or community-based treatment and supervision is not appropriate.

(c) The request for renewal must be accompanied by a certificate of medical examination for mental illness signed by a physician who examined the person during the 30-day period preceding the date on which the request is filed.

(d) On the filing of a request for renewal under this article, the court shall:

(1) set the matter for a hearing; and

(2) appoint an attorney to represent the person.

(e) The court shall act on the request for renewal before the order expires.

(f) If a hearing is held, the person may be transferred from the facility to which the acquitted person was committed to a jail for purposes of participating in the hearing only if necessary but not earlier than 72 hours before the hearing begins. If the order is renewed, the person shall be transferred back to the facility immediately on renewal of the order.

(g) If no objection is made, the court may admit into evidence the certificate of medical examination for mental illness. Admitted certificates constitute competent medical or psychiatric testimony, and the court may make its findings solely from the certificate and the detailed request for renewal.

(h) A court shall renew the order only if the court finds that the party who requested the renewal has established by clear and convincing evidence that continued mandatory supervision and treatment are appropriate. A renewed order authorizes continued inpatient commitment or outpatient or community-based treatment and supervision for not more than one year.

(i) The court, on application for renewal of an order for inpatient or residential care services, may modify the order to provide for outpatient or community-based treatment and supervision if the court finds the acquitted person has established by a preponderance of the evidence that treatment and supervision can be safely and effectively provided as outpatient or community-based treatment and supervision.

Added by Acts 2005, 79th Leg., ch. 831, § 2, eff. Sept. 1, 2005.

Art. 46C.262. Court-ordered Outpatient or Community-based Treatment and Supervision After Inpatient Commitment

(a) An acquitted person, the head of the facility to which the acquitted person is committed, or the attorney representing the state may request that the court modify an order for inpatient treatment or residential care to order outpatient or community-based treatment and supervision.

(b) The court shall hold a hearing on a request made by the head of the facility to which the acquitted person is committed. A hearing under this subsection must be held not later than the 14th day after the date of the request.

(c) If a request is made by an acquitted person or the attorney representing the state, the court must act on the request not later than the 14th day after the date of the request. A hearing under this subsection is at the discretion of the court, except that the court shall hold a hearing if the request and any accompanying material provide a basis for believing modification of the order may be appropriate.

(d) If a request is made by an acquitted person not later than the 90th day after the date of a hearing on a previous request, the court is not required to act on the request except on the expiration of the order or on the expiration of the 90-day period following the date of the hearing on the previous request.

(e) The court shall rule on the request during or as soon as practicable after any hearing on the request but not later than the 14th day after the date of the request.

(f) The court shall modify the commitment order to direct outpatient or community-based treatment and supervision if at the hearing the acquitted person establishes by a preponderance of the evidence that treatment and supervision can be safely and effectively provided as outpatient or community-based treatment and supervision.

Added by Acts 2005, 79th Leg., ch. 831, § 2, eff. Sept. 1, 2005.

Art. 46C.263. Court–ordered Outpatient or Community–based Treatment and Supervision

(a) The court may order an acquitted person to participate in an outpatient or community-based regimen of treatment and supervision:

(1) as an initial matter under Article 46C.253;

(2) on renewal of an order of commitment under Article 46C.261; or

(3) after a period of inpatient treatment or residential care under Article 46C.262.

(b) An acquitted person may be ordered to participate in an outpatient or community-based regimen of treatment and supervision only if:

(1) the court receives and approves an outpatient or community-based treatment plan that comprehensively provides for the outpatient or community-based treatment and supervision; and

(2) the court finds that the outpatient or community-based treatment and supervision provided for by the plan will be available to and provided to the acquitted person.

(c) The order may require the person to participate in a prescribed regimen of medical, psychiatric, or psychological care or treatment, and the regimen may include treatment with psychoactive medication.

(d) The court may order that supervision of the acquitted person be provided by the appropriate community supervision and corrections department or the facility administrator of a community center that provides mental health or mental retardation services.

(e) The court may order the acquitted person to participate in a supervision program funded by the Texas Correctional Office on Offenders with Medical or Mental Impairments.

(f) An order under this article must identify the person responsible for administering an ordered regimen of outpatient or community-based treatment and supervision.

(g) In determining whether an acquitted person should be ordered to receive outpatient or community-based treatment and supervision rather than inpatient care or residential treatment, the court shall have as its primary concern the protection of society.

Added by Acts 2005, 79th Leg., ch. 831, § 2, eff. Sept. 1, 2005.

Art. 46C.264. Location of Court–ordered Outpatient or Community–based Treatment and Supervision

(a) The court may order the outpatient or community-based treatment and supervision to be provided in any appropriate county where the necessary resources are available.

(b) This article does not supersede any requirement under the other provisions of this subchapter to obtain the consent of a treatment and supervision provider to administer the court-ordered outpatient or community-based treatment and supervision.

Added by Acts 2005, 79th Leg., ch. 831, § 2, eff. Sept. 1, 2005.

Art. 46C.265.　Supervisory Responsibility for Outpatient or Community–based Treatment and Supervision

(a) The person responsible for administering a regimen of outpatient or community-based treatment and supervision shall:

(1) monitor the condition of the acquitted person; and

(2) determine whether the acquitted person is complying with the regimen of treatment and supervision.

(b) The person responsible for administering a regimen of outpatient or community-based treatment and supervision shall notify the court ordering that treatment and supervision and the attorney representing the state if the person:

(1) fails to comply with the regimen; and

(2) becomes likely to cause serious harm to another.

Added by Acts 2005, 79th Leg., ch. 831, § 2, eff. Sept. 1, 2005.

Art. 46C.266.　Modification or Revocation of Order for Outpatient or Community–based Treatment and Supervision

(a) The court, on its own motion or the motion of any interested person and after notice to the acquitted person and a hearing, may modify or revoke court-ordered outpatient or community-based treatment and supervision.

(b) At the hearing, the court without a jury shall determine whether the state has established clear and convincing evidence that:

(1) the acquitted person failed to comply with the regimen in a manner or under circumstances indicating the person will become likely to cause serious harm to another if the person is provided continued outpatient or community-based treatment and supervision; or

(2) the acquitted person has become likely to cause serious harm to another if provided continued outpatient or community-based treatment and supervision.

(c) On a determination under Subsection (b), the court may take any appropriate action, including:

(1) revoking court-ordered outpatient or community-based treatment and supervision and ordering the person committed for inpatient or residential care; or

(2) imposing additional or more stringent terms on continued outpatient or community-based treatment.

(d) An acquitted person who is the subject of a proceeding under this article is entitled to representation by counsel in the proceeding.

(e) The court shall set a date for a hearing under this article that is not later than the seventh day after the applicable motion was filed. The court may grant one or more continuances of the hearing on the motion of a party or of the court and for good cause shown.

Added by Acts 2005, 79th Leg., ch. 831, § 2, eff. Sept. 1, 2005.

Art. 46C.267.　Detention Pending Proceedings to Modify or Revoke Order for Outpatient or Community–based Treatment and Supervision

(a) The state or the head of the facility or other person responsible for administering a regimen of outpatient or community-based treatment and supervision may file a sworn application with the court for the detention of an acquitted person receiving court-ordered outpatient or community-based treatment and supervision. The application must state that the person meets the criteria of Article 46C.266 and provide a detailed explanation of that statement.

(b) If the court determines that the application establishes probable cause to believe the order for outpatient or community-based treatment and supervision should be revoked, the court shall issue an order to an on-duty peace officer authorizing the acquitted person to be taken into custody and brought before the court.

(c) An acquitted person taken into custody under an order of detention shall be brought before the court without unnecessary delay.

(d) When an acquitted person is brought before the court, the court shall determine whether there is probable cause to believe that the order for outpatient or community-based treatment and supervision should be revoked. On a finding that probable cause for revocation exists, the court shall order the person held in protective custody pending a determination of whether the order should be revoked.

(e) An acquitted person may be detained under an order for protective custody for a period not to exceed 72 hours, excluding Saturdays, Sundays, legal holidays, and the period prescribed by Section 574.025(b), Health and Safety Code, for an extreme emergency.

(f) This subchapter does not affect the power of a peace officer to take an acquitted person into custody under Section 573.001, Health and Safety Code.

Added by Acts 2005, 79th Leg., ch. 831, § 2, eff. Sept. 1, 2005.

Art. 46C.268. Advance Discharge of Acquitted Person and Termination of Jurisdiction

(a) An acquitted person, the head of the facility to which the acquitted person is committed, the person responsible for providing the outpatient or community-based treatment and supervision, or the state may request that the court discharge an acquitted person from inpatient commitment or outpatient or community-based treatment and supervision.

(b) Not later than the 14th day after the date of the request, the court shall hold a hearing on a request made by the head of the facility to which the acquitted person is committed or the person responsible for providing the outpatient or community-based treatment and supervision.

(c) If a request is made by an acquitted person, the court must act on the request not later than the 14th day after the date of the request. A hearing under this subsection is at the discretion of the court, except that the court shall hold a hearing if the request and any accompanying material indicate that modification of the order may be appropriate.

(d) If a request is made by an acquitted person not later than the 90th day after the date of a hearing on a previous request, the court is not required to act on the request except on the expiration of the order or on the expiration of the 90–day period following the date of the hearing on the previous request.

(e) The court shall rule on the request during or shortly after any hearing that is held and in any case not later than the 14th day after the date of the request.

(f) The court shall discharge the acquitted person from all court-ordered commitment and treatment and supervision and terminate the court's jurisdiction over the person if the court finds that the acquitted person has established by a preponderance of the evidence that:

(1) the acquitted person does not have a severe mental illness or mental retardation; or

(2) the acquitted person is not likely to cause serious harm to another because of any severe mental illness or mental retardation.

Added by Acts 2005, 79th Leg., ch. 831, § 2, eff. Sept. 1, 2005.

Art. 46C.269. Termination of Court's Jurisdiction

(a) The jurisdiction of the court over a person covered by this subchapter automatically terminates on the date when the cumulative total period of institutionalization and outpatient or community-based treatment and supervision imposed under this subchapter equals the maximum term of imprisonment provided by law for the offense of which the person was acquitted by reason of insanity.

(b) On the termination of the court's jurisdiction under this article, the person must be discharged from any inpatient treatment or residential care or outpatient or community-based treatment and supervision ordered under this subchapter.

(c) An inpatient or residential care facility to which a person has been committed under this subchapter or a person responsible for administering a regimen of outpatient or community-based treatment and supervision under this subchapter must notify the court not later than the 30th day before the court's jurisdiction over the person ends under this article.

(d) This subchapter does not affect whether a person may be ordered to receive care or treatment under Subtitle C or D, Title 7, Health and Safety Code.

Added by Acts 2005, 79th Leg., ch. 831, § 2, eff. Sept. 1, 2005.

Art. 46C.270. Appeals

(a) An acquitted person may appeal a judgment reflecting an acquittal by reason of insanity on the basis of the following:

(1) a finding that the acquitted person committed the offense; or

(2) a finding that the offense on which the prosecution was based involved conduct that:

(A) caused serious bodily injury to another person;

(B) placed another person in imminent danger of serious bodily injury; or

(C) consisted of a threat of serious bodily injury to another person through the use of a deadly weapon.

(b) Either the acquitted person or the state may appeal from:

(1) an Order of Commitment to Inpatient Treatment or Residential Care entered under Article 46C.256;

(2) an Order to Receive Outpatient or Community-Based Treatment and Supervision entered under Article 46C.257 or 46C.262;

(3) an order renewing or refusing to renew an Order for Inpatient Commitment or Outpatient or Community-Based Treatment and Supervision entered under Article 46C.261;

(4) an order modifying or revoking an Order for Outpatient or Community-Based Treatment and Supervision entered under Article 46C.266 or refusing a request to modify or revoke that order; or

(5) an order discharging an acquitted person under Article 46C.268 or denying a request for discharge of an acquitted person.

(c) An appeal under this subchapter may not be considered moot solely due to the expiration of an order on which the appeal is based.

Added by Acts 2005, 79th Leg., ch. 831, § 2, eff. Sept. 1, 2005.

CHAPTER 47. DISPOSITION OF STOLEN PROPERTY

Art. 47.01. Subject to Order of Court

(a) Except as provided by Subsection (b), an officer who comes into custody of property alleged to have been stolen shall hold it subject to the order of the proper court only if the ownership of the property is contested or disputed.

(b) An officer who comes into custody of property governed by Chapter 371, Finance Code, that is alleged to have been stolen shall hold the property subject to the order of the proper court regardless of whether the ownership of the property is contested or disputed.

Acts 1965, 59th Leg., vol. 2, p. 317, ch. 722. Amended by Acts 1993, 73rd Leg., ch. 860, § 1, eff. Aug. 30, 1993; Acts 1999, 76th Leg., ch. 62, § 3.07, eff. Sept. 1, 1999; Acts 2001, 77th Leg., ch. 752, § 1, eff. Sept. 1, 2001.

Art. 47.01a. Restoration when no trial is pending

(a) If a criminal action relating to allegedly stolen property is not pending, a district judge, county court judge, statutory county court judge, or justice of the peace having jurisdiction as a magistrate in the county in which the property is held or in which the property was alleged to have been stolen or a municipal judge having jurisdiction as a magistrate in the municipality in which the property is being held or in which the property was alleged to have been stolen may hold a hearing to determine the right to possession of the property, upon the petition of an interested person, a county, a city, or the state. Jurisdiction under this article is based solely on jurisdiction as a criminal magistrate under this code and not jurisdiction as a civil court. The court shall:

(1) order the property delivered to whoever has the superior right to possession, without conditions;

(2) on the filing of a written motion before trial by an attorney representing the state, order the property delivered to whoever has the superior right to possession, subject to the condition that the property be made available to the prosecuting authority should it be needed in future prosecutions; or

(3) order the property awarded to the custody of the peace officer, pending resolution of criminal investigations regarding the property.

(b) If it is shown in a hearing that probable cause exists to believe that the property was acquired by theft or by another manner that makes its acquisition an offense and that the identity of the actual owner of the property cannot be determined, the court shall order the peace officer to:

(1) deliver the property to a government agency for official purposes;

(2) deliver the property to a person authorized by Article 18.17 of this code to receive and dispose of the property; or

(3) destroy the property.

(c) At a hearing under Subsection (a) of this article, any interested person may present evidence showing that the property was not acquired by theft or another offense or that the person is entitled to possess the property. At the hearing, hearsay evidence is admissible.

(d) Venue for a hearing under this article is in any justice, county, statutory county, or district court in the county in which the property is seized or in which the property was alleged to have been stolen or in any municipal court in any municipality in which the property is seized or in which the property was alleged to have been stolen, except that the court may transfer venue to a court in another county on the motion of any interested party.

(e) The person who has the superior right to possession of the property, as determined in a hearing under Subsection (a), is responsible for any transportation necessary to deliver the property to the person as ordered under that subsection.

Added by Acts 1977, 65th Leg., p. 2034, ch. 813, § 1, eff. Aug. 29, 1977. Amended by Acts 1987, 70th Leg., ch. 548, § 1, eff. Aug. 31, 1987; Acts 1993, 73rd Leg., ch. 860, § 1, eff. Aug. 30, 1993; Acts 1995, 74th Leg., ch. 184, § 3, eff. May 23, 1995; Acts 2017, 85th Leg., ch. 565 (S.B. 631), § 1, eff. Sept. 1, 2017.

Art. 47.02. Restored on Trial

(a) On the trial of any criminal action for theft or any other offense involving the illegal acquisition of property, the court trying the case shall order the property to be restored to the person appearing by the proof to be the owner of the property.

(b) On written consent of the prosecuting attorney and following an order described by Subsection (a), any magistrate having jurisdiction in the county in which the property was alleged to have been stolen or, if the criminal action for theft or any other offense involving the illegal acquisition of property is pending in another county, the county in which the action is pending may hold a hearing to determine the right to possession of the property. If it is proved to the satisfaction of the magistrate that any person is a true owner of the property alleged to have been stolen, and the property is under the control of a peace officer, the magistrate may, by written order, direct the property to be restored to that person.

(c) The owner of the property is responsible for any transportation necessary to restore the property to the owner as ordered under this article.

Acts 1965, 59th Leg., vol. 2, p. 317, ch. 722. Amended by Acts 1997, 75th Leg., ch. 1415, § 1, eff. Sept. 1, 1997; Acts 2009, 81st Leg., ch. 613, § 2, eff. Sept. 1, 2009; Acts 2017, 85th Leg., ch. 565 (S.B. 631), § 2, eff. Sept. 1, 2017.

Art. 47.03. Schedule

When an officer seizes property alleged to have been stolen, he shall immediately file a schedule of the same, and its value, with the court having jurisdiction of the case, certifying that the property has been seized by him, and the reason therefor. The officer shall notify the court of the names and addresses of each party known to the officer who has a claim to possession of the seized property.

Acts 1965, 59th Leg., vol. 2, p. 317, ch. 722. Amended by Acts 1993, 73rd Leg., ch. 860, § 1, eff. Aug. 30, 1993.

Art. 47.04. Restored to owner

Upon an examining trial, if it is proven to the satisfaction of the court that any person is the true owner of property alleged to have been stolen, and which is in possession of a peace officer, the court may upon motion by the state, by written order direct the property to be restored to such owner subject to the conditions that such property shall be made available to the state or by order of any court having jurisdiction over the offense to be used for evidentiary purposes.

Acts 1965, 59th Leg., vol. 2, p. 317, ch. 722. Amended by Acts 1993, 73rd Leg., ch. 860, § 1, eff. Aug. 30, 1993.

Art. 47.05. Bond required

If the court has any doubt as to the ownership of the property, the court may require a bond of the claimant for its re-delivery in case it should thereafter be shown not to belong to such claimant; or the court may, in its discretion, direct the property to be retained by the sheriff until further orders as to its possession. Such bond shall be in a sum equal to the value of the property, with sufficient security, payable to and approved by the county judge of the county in which the property is in custody. Such bond shall be filed in the office of the county clerk of such county, and in case of a breach thereof may be sued upon in such county by any claimant of the property; or by the county treasurer of such county.

Acts 1965, 59th Leg., vol. 2, p. 317, ch. 722. Amended by Acts 1993, 73rd Leg., ch. 860, § 1, eff. Aug. 30, 1993.

Art. 47.06. Property sold

If the property is not claimed within 30 days from the conviction of the person accused of illegally acquiring it, the same procedure for its disposition as set out in Article 18.17 of this Code shall be followed.

Acts 1965, 59th Leg., vol. 2, p. 317, ch. 722. Amended by Acts 1987, 70th Leg., ch. 66, § 2, eff. May 6, 1987.

Art. 47.07. Owner may recover

The real owner of the property sold under the provisions of Article 47.06 may recover such property under the same terms as prescribed in Subsection (e) of Article 18.17 of this Code.

Acts 1965, 59th Leg., vol. 2, p. 317, ch. 722. Amended by Acts 1987, 70th Leg., ch. 66, § 2, eff. May 6, 1987.

Art. 47.08. Written instrument

If the property is a written instrument, it shall be deposited with the county clerk of the county where the proceedings are had, subject to the claim of any person who may establish his right thereto. The claimant of any such written instrument shall file his written sworn claim thereto with the county judge. If such judge be satisfied that such claimant is the real owner of the written instrument, the same shall be delivered to him. The county judge may, in his discretion, require a bond of such claimant, as in other cases of property claimed under any provision of this Chapter, and may also before such delivery require the written instrument to be recorded in the minutes of his court.

Acts 1965, 59th Leg., vol. 2, p. 317, ch. 722.

Art. 47.09. Claimant to pay charges

The claimant of the property, before he shall be entitled to have the same delivered to him, shall pay all reasonable charges for the safekeeping of the same while in the custody of the law, which charges shall be verified by the affidavit of the officer claiming the same, and determined by the court having jurisdiction thereof. If said charges are not paid, the property shall be sold as under execution; and the proceeds of sale, after the payment of said charges and costs of sale, paid to the owner of such property.

Acts 1965, 59th Leg., vol. 2, p. 317, ch. 722. Amended by Acts 1993, 73rd Leg., ch. 860, § 1, eff. Aug. 30, 1993.

Art. 47.10. Charges of officer

When property is sold, and the proceeds of sale are ready to be paid into the county treasury, the amount of expenses for keeping the same and the costs of sale shall be determined by the county judge. The account thereof shall be in writing and verified by the officer claiming the same, with the approval of the county judge thereto for the amount allowed and shall be filed in the office of the county treasurer at the time of paying into his hands the balance of the proceeds of such sale.

Acts 1965, 59th Leg., vol. 2, p. 317, ch. 722.

Art. 47.11. Scope of Chapter

Each provision of this Chapter relating to stolen property applies as well to property acquired in any manner which makes the acquisition a penal offense.

Acts 1965, 59th Leg., vol. 2, p. 317, ch. 722.

Art. 47.12. Appeal

(a) Appeals from a hearing in a district court, county court, or statutory county court under Article 47.01a of this code shall be heard by a court of appeals. The appeal is governed by the applicable rules of procedure for appeals of civil cases to a court of appeals.

(b) Appeals from a hearing in a municipal court or justice court under Article 47.01a of this code shall be heard by a county court or statutory county court. The appeal is governed by the applicable rules of procedure for appeals for civil cases in justice courts to a county court or statutory county court.

(c) Only an interested person who appears at a hearing under this article may appeal, and such person must give an oral notice of appeal at the conclusion of the hearing and must post an appeal bond by the end of the next business day, exclusive of Saturdays, Sundays, and legal holidays.

(d) The court may require an appeal bond, in an amount determined appropriate by the court, but not to exceed twice the value of the property. The bond shall be made payable to the party who was awarded possession at the hearing, with sufficient sureties approved by the court, and conditioned that appellant will prosecute his appeal to conclusion.

Added by Acts 1993, 73rd Leg., ch. 860, § 2, eff. Aug. 30, 1993.

CHAPTER 48. PARDON AND PAROLE

Article

Art. 48.01. Governor May Pardon

(a) In all criminal cases, except treason and impeachment, the Governor shall have power, after conviction or successful completion of a term of deferred adjudication community supervision, on the written signed recommendation and advice of the Board of

Pardons and Paroles, or a majority thereof, to grant reprieves and commutations of punishments and pardons; and upon the written recommendation and advice of a majority of the Board of Pardons and Paroles, he shall have the power to remit fines and forfeitures. The Governor shall have the power to grant one reprieve in any capital case for a period not to exceed 30 days; and he shall have power to revoke conditional pardons. With the advice and consent of the Legislature, the Governor may grant reprieves, commutations of punishment and pardons in cases of treason.

(b) The Board of Pardons and Paroles may recommend that the Governor grant a pardon to a person who:

(1) is placed on deferred adjudication community supervision under Subchapter C, Chapter 42A, and subsequently receives a discharge and dismissal under Article 42A.111; and

(2) on or after the 10th anniversary of the date of discharge and dismissal, submits a written request to the board for a recommendation under this subsection.

Acts 1965, 59th Leg., vol. 2, p. 317, ch. 722. Amended by Acts 1995, 74th Leg., ch. 321, § 2.019, eff. Sept. 1, 1995; Acts 2011, 82nd Leg., ch. 1053 (S.B. 144), § 1, eff. Jan. 1, 2012; Acts 2015, 84th Leg., ch. 770 (H.B. 2299), § 2.22, eff. Jan. 1, 2017.

Art. 48.02. Shall file reasons

When the Governor remits fines or forfeitures, or grants reprieves, commutation of punishment or pardons, he shall file in the office of Secretary of State his reasons therefor.

Acts 1965, 59th Leg., vol. 2, p. 317, ch. 722.

Art. 48.03. Governor's acts under seal

All remissions of fines and forfeitures, and all reprieves, commutations of punishment and pardons, shall be signed by the Governor, and certified by the Secretary of State, under the state seal, and shall be forthwith obeyed by any officer to whom the same may be presented.

Acts 1965, 59th Leg., vol. 2, p. 317, ch. 722. Amended by Acts 1993, 73rd Leg., ch. 300, § 26, eff. Aug. 30, 1993.

Art. 48.04. Power to remit fines and forfeitures

The Governor shall have the power to remit forfeitures of bail bonds.

Acts 1965, 59th Leg., vol. 2, p. 317, ch. 722.

Art. 48.05. Restoration of Civil Rights

(a)(1) An individual convicted of an offense described by Subdivision (2) of this subsection may, except as provided by Subsection (b) of this article, submit an application for restoration of any civil rights forfeited under the laws of this state as a result of the conviction.

(2) This article applies to:

(A) a federal offense, other than an offense involving:

(i) violence or the threat of violence;

(ii) drugs; or

(iii) firearms; and

(B) an offense under the laws of another country, other than an offense involving:

(i) violence or the threat of violence;

(ii) drugs; or

(iii) firearms, if the elements of the offense are substantially similar to elements of an offense under the laws of this state punishable as a felony.

(b) An individual may not apply for restoration of civil rights under this article unless:

(1) the individual has completed the sentence for the offense;

(2) the conviction occurred:

(A) three or more years before the date of application, if the offense is a federal offense; or

(B) two or more years before the date of application, if the offense is an offense under the laws of another country; and

(3) the individual has not been convicted at any other time of an offense under the laws of this state, another state, or the United States.

(c) An application for restoration of civil rights must contain:

(1) a completed application on a form adopted by the Board of Pardons and Paroles;

(2) three or more affidavits attesting to the good character of the applicant; and

(3) proof that the applicant has completed the sentence for the offense.

(d) The applicant must submit the application to:

(1) the sheriff of the county in which the applicant resides at the time of application or resided at the

time of conviction of the offense, if the individual resided in this state at that time; or

(2) the Board of Pardons and Paroles.

(e) If an application is submitted to a sheriff, the sheriff shall review the application and recommend to the Board of Pardons and Paroles whether the individual's civil rights should be restored. If the sheriff recommends restoration of the individual's civil rights, the board may either:

(1) concur in the recommendation and forward the recommendation to the governor; or

(2) independently review the application to determine whether to recommend to the governor the restoration of the individual's civil rights.

(f) If the sheriff does not recommend the restoration of the individual's civil rights, the individual may apply directly to the Board of Pardons and Paroles.

(g) If an application is submitted to the Board of Pardons and Paroles without first being submitted to a sheriff, the board shall review the application and recommend to the governor as to whether the individual's civil rights should be restored.

(h) The Board of Pardons and Paroles may require or obtain additional information as necessary to perform a review under Subsection (e)(2) or Subsection (g) of this article.

(i) On receipt from the Board of Pardons and Paroles of a recommendation to restore the civil rights of an individual, the governor may either grant or deny the restoration of civil rights to the individual. If the governor grants the restoration of civil rights to the individual, the governor shall issue a certificate of restoration of civil rights.

(j) If an application under this article is denied by the Board of Pardons and Paroles or the governor, the individual may not file another application under this article before the first anniversary of the date of the denial.

(k) A restoration of civil rights under this article is a form of pardon that restores all civil rights under the laws of this state that an individual forfeits as a result of the individual's conviction of an offense, except as specifically provided in the certificate of restoration.

Added by Acts 1993, 73rd Leg., ch. 900, § 7.01(a), eff. Sept. 1, 1993. Amended by Acts 2001, 77th Leg., ch. 150, § 1, eff. May 16, 2001.

Art. 48.06. Educational Materials Concerning Pardons for Certain Victims of Trafficking of Persons

(a) The Board of Pardons and Paroles shall develop educational materials specifically for persons convicted of or placed on deferred adjudication community supervision for an offense the person committed solely as a victim of trafficking of persons under Section 20A.02, Penal Code. The board shall include in the educational materials a detailed description of the process by which the person may submit a request to the board for a written signed recommendation advising the governor to grant the person a pardon.

(b) The Board of Pardons and Paroles shall post educational materials described by Subsection (a) on the board's Internet website.

Added by Acts 2013, 83rd Leg., ch. 1252 (H.B. 8), § 7, eff. Sept. 1, 2013.

CHAPTER 49. INQUESTS UPON DEAD BODIES

SUBCHAPTER A. DUTIES PERFORMED BY JUSTICES OF THE PEACE

SUBCHAPTER B. DUTIES PERFORMED BY MEDICAL EXAMINERS

SUBCHAPTER A. DUTIES PERFORMED BY JUSTICES OF THE PEACE

Art. 49.01. Definitions

In this article:

(1) "Autopsy" means a post mortem examination of the body of a person, including X-rays and an examination of the internal organs and structures after dissection, to determine the cause of death or the nature of any pathological changes that may have contributed to the death.

(2) "Inquest" means an investigation into the cause and circumstances of the death of a person, and a determination, made with or without a formal court hearing, as to whether the death was caused by an unlawful act or omission.

(3) "Inquest hearing" means a formal court hearing held to determine whether the death of a person was caused by an unlawful act or omission and, if the death was caused by an unlawful act or omission, to obtain evidence to form the basis of a criminal prosecution.

(4) "Institution" means any place where health care services are rendered, including a hospital, clinic, health facility, nursing home, extended-care facility, out-patient facility, foster-care facility, and retirement home.

(5) "Physician" means a practicing doctor of medicine or doctor of osteopathic medicine who is licensed by the Texas State Board of Medical Examiners under Subtitle B[1], Title 3, Occupations Code.

Amended by Acts 1987, 70th Leg., ch. 529, § 1, eff. Sept. 1, 1987; Acts 1989, 71st Leg., ch. 72, § 1, eff. May 9, 1989; Acts 2001, 77th Leg., ch. 1420, § 14.737, eff. Sept. 1, 2001.

[1] V.T.C.A., Occupations Code § 151.001 et seq.

Art. 49.02. Applicability

This subchapter applies to the inquest into a death occurring in a county that does not have a medical examiner's office or that is not part of a medical examiner's district.

Amended by Acts 1987, 70th Leg., ch. 529, § 1, eff. Sept. 1, 1987.

Art. 49.03. Powers and duties

The powers granted and duties imposed on a justice of the peace under this article are independent of the powers and duties of a law enforcement agency investigating a death.

Amended by Acts 1987, 70th Leg., ch. 529, § 1, eff. Sept. 1, 1987.

Art. 49.04. Deaths requiring an inquest

(a) A justice of the peace shall conduct an inquest into the death of a person who dies in the county served by the justice if:

(1) the person dies in prison under circumstances other than those described by Section 501.055(b), Government Code, or in jail;

(2) the person dies an unnatural death from a cause other than a legal execution;

(3) the body or a body part of a person is found, the cause or circumstances of death are unknown, and:

(A) the person is identified; or

(B) the person is unidentified;

(4) the circumstances of the death indicate that the death may have been caused by unlawful means;

(5) the person commits suicide or the circumstances of the death indicate that the death may have been caused by suicide;

(6) the person dies without having been attended by a physician;

(7) the person dies while attended by a physician who is unable to certify the cause of death and who requests the justice of the peace to conduct an inquest; or

(8) the person is a child younger than six years of age and an inquest is required by Chapter 264, Family Code.

(b) Except as provided by Subsection (c) of this section, a physician who attends the death of a person and who is unable to certify the cause of death shall report the death to the justice of the peace of the precinct where the death occurred and request that the justice conduct an inquest.

(c) If a person dies in a hospital or other institution and an attending physician is unable to certify the cause of death, the superintendent or general manager of the hospital or institution shall report the death to the justice of the peace of the precinct where the hospital or institution is located.

(d) A justice of the peace investigating a death described by Subsection (a)(3)(B) shall report the death to the missing children and missing persons information clearinghouse of the Department of Public Safety and the national crime information center not later than the 10th working day after the date the investigation began.

Amended by Acts 1987, 70th Leg., ch. 529, § 1, eff. Sept. 1, 1987; Acts 1995, 74th Leg., ch. 255, § 3, eff. Sept. 1, 1995; Acts 1995, 74th Leg., ch. 321, § 1.105, eff. Sept. 1, 1995; Acts 1995, 74th Leg., ch. 878, § 2, eff. Sept. 1, 1995; Acts 1997, 75th Leg., ch. 656, § 1, eff. Sept. 1, 1997; Acts 1999, 76th Leg., ch. 785, § 2, eff. Sept. 1, 1999; Acts 2003, 78th Leg., ch. 826, § 1, eff. Sept. 1, 2003; Acts 2003, 78th Leg., ch. 1295, § 1, eff. Sept. 1, 2003.

Art. 49.041.   Reopening an Inquest

A justice of the peace may reopen an inquest if, based on information provided by a credible person or facts within the knowledge of the justice of the peace, the justice of the peace determines that reopening the inquest may reveal a different cause or different circumstances of death.

Added by Acts 1997, 75th Leg., ch. 897, § 1, eff. Sept. 1, 1997.

Art. 49.05.   Time and place of inquest; removal of property and body from place of death

(a) A justice of the peace shall conduct an inquest immediately or as soon as practicable after the justice receives notification of the death.

(b) A justice of the peace may conduct an inquest:

(1) at the place where the death occurred;

(2) where the body was found; or

(3) at any other place determined to be reasonable by the justice.

(c) A justice of the peace may direct the removal of a body from the scene of death or move any part of the physical surroundings of a body only after a law enforcement agency is notified of the death and a peace officer has conducted an investigation or, if a law enforcement agency has not begun an investiga-

tion, a reasonable time has elapsed from the time the law enforcement agency was notified.

(d) A law enforcement agency that is notified of a death requiring an inquest under Article 49.04 of this code shall begin its investigation immediately or as soon as practicable after the law enforcement agency receives notification of the death.

(e) Except in emergency circumstances, a peace officer or other person conducting a death investigation for a law enforcement agency may not move the body or any part of the physical surroundings of the place of death without authorization from a justice of the peace.

(f) A person not authorized by law to move the body of a decedent or any part of the physical surroundings of the body commits an offense if the person tampers with a body that is subject to an inquest under Article 49.04 of this code or any part of the physical surroundings of the body. An offense under this section is punishable by a fine in an amount not to exceed $500.

Amended by Acts 1987, 70th Leg., ch. 529, § 1, eff. Sept. 1, 1987.

Art. 49.06.   Hindering an inquest

(a) A person commits an offense if the person intentionally or knowingly hinders the entrance of a justice of the peace to a premises where a death occurred or a body is found.

(b) An offense under this article is a Class B misdemeanor.

Amended by Acts 1987, 70th Leg., ch. 529, § 1, eff. Sept. 1, 1987.

Art. 49.07.   Notification of investigating official

(a) A physician or other person who has possession of a body or body part of a person whose death requires an inquest under Article 49.04 of this code shall immediately notify the justice of the peace who serves the precinct in which the body or body part was found.

(b) A peace officer who has been notified of the death of a person whose death requires an inquest under Article 49.04 of this code shall immediately notify the justice of the peace who serves the precinct in which the body or body part was found.

(c)(1) If the justice of the peace who serves the precinct in which the body or body part was found is not available to conduct an inquest, a person required to give notice under this article shall notify the nearest available justice of the peace serving the county in which the body or body part was found, and that justice of the peace shall conduct the inquest.

(2) If no justice of the peace serving the county in which the body or body part was found is available to conduct an inquest, a person required to give notice under this article shall notify the county judge, and the county judge shall initiate the inquest. The county judge may exercise any power and perform any duty otherwise granted to or imposed under this subchapter on the justice of the peace serving the county in which the body or body part was found, except that not later than the fifth day after the day on which the inquest is initiated, the county judge shall transfer all information obtained by the judge to the justice of the peace in whose precinct the body or body part was found for final disposition of the matter.

(3) If a justice of the peace or the county judge serving the county in which the body or body part was found is not available to conduct an inquest, a person required to give notice under this article may ask the justice of the peace of the precinct in which the body or body part was found or the county judge to request a justice of the peace of another county to which this subchapter applies to conduct the inquest. The justice of the peace that conducts the inquest shall, not later than the fifth day after the date the inquest is initiated, transfer all information related to the inquest to the justice of the peace of the precinct in which the body or body part was found for final disposition of the matter. All expenses related to the inquest must be paid as provided by this chapter.

(d) A person commits an offense if the person is required by this article to give notice and intentionally or knowingly fails to give the notice. An offense under this subsection is a Class C misdemeanor.

Amended by Acts 1987, 70th Leg., ch. 529, § 1, eff. Sept. 1, 1987; Acts 1997, 75th Leg., ch. 656, § 2, eff. Sept. 1, 1997; Acts 2001, 77th Leg., ch. 229, § 1, eff. May 22, 2001; Acts 2003, 78th Leg., ch. 826, § 2, eff. Sept. 1, 2003; Acts 2003, 78th Leg., ch. 1295, § 2, eff. Sept. 1, 2003; Acts 2017, 85th Leg., ch. 84 (H.B. 799), § 3, eff. Sept. 1, 2017.

Art. 49.08. Information leading to an inquest

A justice of the peace conducting an inquest may act on information the justice receives from any credible person or on facts within his knowledge.

Amended by Acts 1987, 70th Leg., ch. 529, § 1, eff. Sept. 1, 1987.

Art. 49.09. Body disinterred or cremated

(a) If a body or body part subject to investigation under Article 49.04 of this code is interred and an authorized person has not conducted an inquest required under this subchapter, a justice of the peace may direct the disinterment of the body or body part in order to conduct an inquest.

(b) A person may not cremate or direct the cremation of a body subject to investigation under Article 49.04 unless the body is identified and the person has received from the justice of the peace a certificate signed by the justice stating that:

(1) an autopsy was performed on the body under Article 49.10 of this code; or

(2) no autopsy was necessary.

(c) An owner or operator of a crematory shall retain a certificate received under Subsection (b) of this article for a period of 10 years from the date of cremation of the body named on the certificate.

(d) A person commits an offense if the person cremates or directs the cremation of a body without obtaining a certificate from a justice of the peace as required by Subsection (b) of this article. An offense under this section is a Class B misdemeanor.

(e) If the body of a deceased person is unidentified, a person may not cremate or direct the cremation of the body under this article. If the body is buried, the justice of the peace shall record and maintain for not less than 10 years all information pertaining to the body and the location of burial.

Amended by Acts 1987, 70th Leg., ch. 529, § 1, eff. Sept. 1, 1987; Acts 1997, 75th Leg., ch. 656, § 3, eff. Sept. 1, 1997; Acts 2003, 78th Leg., ch. 826, § 3, eff. Sept. 1, 2003; Acts 2003, 78th Leg., ch. 1295, § 3, eff. Sept. 1, 2003.

Art. 49.10. Autopsies and tests

(a) At his discretion, a justice of the peace may obtain the opinion of a county health officer or a physician concerning the necessity of obtaining an autopsy in order to determine or confirm the nature and cause of a death.

(b) The commissioners court of the county shall pay a reasonable fee for a consultation obtained by a justice of the peace under Subsection (a) of this article.

(c) Except as required by Section 264.514, Family Code, for each body that is the subject of an inquest by a justice of the peace, the justice, in the justice's discretion, shall:

(1) direct a physician to perform an autopsy; or

(2) certify that no autopsy is necessary.

(d) A justice of the peace may not order a person to perform an autopsy on the body of a deceased person whose death was caused by Asiatic cholera, bubonic plague, typhus fever, or smallpox. A justice of the peace may not order a person to perform an autopsy on the body of a deceased person whose death was caused by a communicable disease during a public health disaster.

(e) A justice of the peace shall order an autopsy performed on a body if:

(1) the justice determines that an autopsy is necessary to determine or confirm the nature and cause of death;

(2) the deceased was a child younger than six years of age and the death is determined under Section 264.514, Family Code, to be unexpected or the result of abuse or neglect; or

(3) directed to do so by the district attorney, criminal district attorney, or, if there is no district or criminal district attorney, the county attorney.

(f) A justice of the peace shall request a physician to perform the autopsy.

(g) The commissioners court shall pay a reasonable fee to a physician performing an autopsy on the order of a justice of the peace, if a fee is assessed.

(h) The commissioners court shall pay a reasonable fee for the transportation of a body to a place where an autopsy can be performed under this article if a justice of the peace orders the body to be transported to the place.

(i) If a justice of the peace determines that a complete autopsy is unnecessary to confirm or determine the cause of death, the justice may order a physician to take or remove from a body a sample of body fluids, tissues, or organs in order to determine the nature and cause of death. Except as provided by Subsection (j) of this article, a justice may not order any person other than a physician to take samples from the body of a deceased person.

(j) A justice of the peace may order a physician, qualified technician, paramedic, chemist, registered professional nurse, or licensed vocational nurse to take a specimen of blood from the body of a person who died as the result of a motor vehicle accident if the justice determines that circumstances indicate that the person may have been driving while intoxicated.

(k) A justice of the peace may order an investigative or laboratory test to determine the identity of a deceased person. After proper removal of a sample from a body, a justice may order any person specially trained in identification work to complete any tests necessary to determine the identity of the deceased person.

(l) A medical examination on an unidentified person shall include the following information to enable a timely and accurate identification of the person:

(1) all available fingerprints and palm prints;

(2) dental charts and radiographs (X-rays) of the person's teeth;

(3) frontal and lateral facial photographs with scale indicated;

(4) notation and photographs, with scale indicated, of a significant scar, mark, tattoo, or item of clothing or other personal effect found with or near the body;

(5) notation of antemortem medical conditions;

(6) notation of observations pertinent to the estimation of time of death; and

(7) precise documentation of the location of burial of the remains.

(m) A medical examination on an unidentified person may include the following information to enable a timely and accurate identification of the person:

(1) full body radiographs (X-rays); and

(2) hair specimens with roots.

(n) On discovering the body or body part of a deceased person in the circumstances described by Article 49.04(a)(3)(B), the justice of the peace may request the aid of a forensic anthropologist in the examination of the body or body part. The forensic anthropologist must hold a doctoral degree in anthropology with an emphasis in physical anthropology. The forensic anthropologist shall attempt to establish whether the body or body part is of a human or animal, whether evidence of childbirth, injury, or disease exists, and the sex, race, age, stature, and physical anomalies of the body or body part. The forensic anthropologist may also attempt to establish the cause, manner, and time of death.

(o) If a person is injured in one county and dies as a result of those injuries, with the death occurring in another county, the attorney representing the state in the prosecution of felonies in the county in which the injury occurred may request a justice of the peace in the county in which the death occurred to order an autopsy be performed on the body of the deceased person. If the justice of the peace orders that the autopsy be performed, the county in which the injury occurred shall reimburse the county in which the death occurred.

Amended by Acts 1987, 70th Leg., ch. 529, § 1, eff. Sept. 1, 1987; Acts 1995, 74th Leg., ch. 255, § 4, eff. Sept. 1, 1995; Acts 1995, 74th Leg., ch. 878, § 3, eff. Sept. 1, 1995; Acts 1997, 75th Leg., ch. 656, § 4, eff. Sept. 1, 1997; Acts 1997, 75th Leg., ch. 1022, § 102, eff. Sept. 1, 1997; Acts 1997, 75th Leg., ch. 1301, § 1, eff. Sept. 1, 1997; Acts 1999, 76th Leg., ch. 1071, § 1, eff. August 30, 1999; Acts 1999, 76th Leg., ch. 1132, § 1, eff. Sept. 1, 1999; Acts 2001, 77th Leg., ch. 237, § 1, eff. May 22, 2001; Acts 2001, 77th Leg., ch. 240, § 1, eff. Sept. 1, 2001; Acts 2003, 78th Leg., ch. 198, § 2.190, eff. Sept. 1, 2003; Acts 2003, 78th Leg., ch. 826, § 4, eff. Sept. 1, 2003; Acts 2003, 78th Leg., ch. 1295, § 4, eff. Sept. 1, 2003.

Art. 49.11. Chemical analysis

(a) A justice of the peace may obtain a chemical analysis of a sample taken from a body in order to determine whether death was caused, in whole or in part, by the ingestion, injection, or introduction into the body of a poison or other chemical substance. A justice may obtain a chemical analysis under this article from a chemist, toxicologist, pathologist, or other medical expert.

(b) A justice of the peace shall obtain a chemical analysis under Subsection (a) of this article if requested to do so by the physician who performed an autopsy on the body.

(c) The commissioners court shall pay a reasonable fee to a person who conducts a chemical analysis at the request of a justice of the peace.

Amended by Acts 1987, 70th Leg., ch. 529, § 1, eff. Sept. 1, 1987.

Art. 49.12. Liability of person performing autopsy or test

A person who performs an autopsy or makes a test on a body on the order of a justice of the peace in the good faith belief that the order is valid is not liable for damages if the order is invalid.

Amended by Acts 1987, 70th Leg., ch. 529, § 1, eff. Sept. 1, 1987.

Art. 49.13. Repealed by Acts 2011, 82nd Leg., ch. 950 (H.B. 1009), § 4, eff. Jan. 1, 2012

Art. 49.14. Inquest hearing

(a) A justice of the peace conducting an inquest may hold an inquest hearing if the justice determines that the circumstances warrant the hearing. The justice shall hold an inquest hearing if requested to do so by a district attorney or a criminal district attorney who serves the county in which the body was found.

(b) An inquest hearing may be held with or without a jury unless the district attorney or criminal district attorney requests that the hearing be held with a jury.

(c) A jury in an inquest hearing is composed of six persons. Jurors shall be summoned in the same manner as are jurors for county court. A juror who is properly summoned and fails to appear, other than a juror exempted by law, commits an offense. An offense under this subsection is punishable by a fine not to exceed $100.

(d) A justice of the peace may hold a public or a private inquest hearing. If a person has been arrested and charged with causing the death of the deceased, the defendant and the defendant's counsel are entitled to be present at the inquest hearing, examine witnesses, and introduce evidence.

(e) A justice of the peace may issue a subpoena to enforce the attendance of a witness at an inquest hearing and may issue an attachment for a person who is subpoenaed and fails to appear at the time and place cited on the subpoena.

(f) A justice of the peace may require bail of a witness to secure the appearance of the witness at an inquest hearing or before a grand jury, examining court, or other court investigating a death.

(g) The justice of the peace shall swear witnesses appearing at an inquest hearing. The justice and an attorney representing the state may examine witnesses at an inquest hearing. The justice shall direct that all sworn testimony be reduced to writing and the justice shall subscribe the transcription.

(h) Only the justice of the peace, a person charged in the death under investigation, the counsel for the person charged, and an attorney representing the state may question a witness at an inquest hearing.

(i) A justice of the peace may hold a person who disrupts the proceedings of an inquest hearing in contempt of court. A person who is found in contempt of court under this subsection may be fined in an amount not to exceed $100 and removed from court by a peace officer.

Amended by Acts 1987, 70th Leg., ch. 529, § 1, eff. Sept. 1, 1987.

Art. 49.15. Inquest record

(a) A justice of the peace or other person authorized under this subchapter to conduct an inquest shall make an inquest record for each inquest he conducts. The inquest record must include a report of the events, proceedings, findings, and conclusions of the inquest. The record must also include any autopsy prepared in the case and all other papers of the case. All papers of the inquest record must be marked with the case number and be clearly indexed and be maintained in the office of the justice of the peace and be made available to the appropriate officials upon request.

(b) As part of the inquest record, the justice of the peace shall make and keep complete and permanent records of all inquest hearings. The inquest hearing records must include:

(1) the name of the deceased person or, if the person is unidentified, a description of the body;

(2) the time, date, and place where the body was found;

(3) the time, date, and place where the inquest was held;

(4) the name of every witness who testified at the inquest;

(5) the name of every person who provided to the justice information pertinent to the inquest;

(6) the amount of bail set for each witness and person charged in the death;

(7) a transcript of the testimony given by each witness at the inquest hearing;

(8) the autopsy report, if an autopsy was performed; and

(9) the name of every person arrested as a suspect in the death who appeared at the inquest and the details of that person's arrest.

(c) The commissioners court shall pay a reasonable fee to a person who records or transcribes sworn testimony during an inquest hearing.

(d) The justice of the peace shall certify a copy of the inquest summary report and deliver the certified copy in a sealed envelope to the clerk of the district court. The clerk of the district court shall retain the summary report subject to an order by the district court.

Amended by Acts 1987, 70th Leg., ch. 529, § 1, eff. Sept. 1, 1987.

Art. 49.16. Orders and death certificates

The justice of the peace or other person who conducts an inquest under this subchapter shall sign the death certificate and all orders made as a necessary part of the inquest.

Amended by Acts 1987, 70th Leg., ch. 529, § 1, eff. Sept. 1, 1987.

Art. 49.17. Evidence

A justice of the peace shall preserve all tangible evidence that the justice accumulates in the course of an inquest that tends to show the real cause of death or identify the person who caused the death. The justice shall:

(1) deposit the evidence with the appropriate law enforcement agency to be stored in the agency's property room for safekeeping; or

(2) deliver the evidence to the district clerk for safekeeping subject to the order of the court.

Amended by Acts 1987, 70th Leg., ch. 529, § 1, eff. Sept. 1, 1987.

Art. 49.18. Death in custody

(a) If a person confined in a penal institution dies, the sheriff or other person in charge of the penal institution shall as soon as practicable inform the justice of the peace of the precinct where the penal institution is located of the death.

(b) If a person dies while in the custody of a peace officer or as a result of a peace officer's use of force or if a person incarcerated in a jail, correctional facility, or state juvenile facility dies, the director of the law enforcement agency of which the officer is a member or of the facility in which the person was incarcerated shall investigate the death and file a written report of the cause of death with the attorney general no later than the 30th day after the date on which the person in custody or the incarcerated person died. The director shall make a good faith effort to obtain all facts relevant to the death and include those facts in the report. The attorney general shall make the report, with the exception of any portion of the report that the attorney general determines is privileged, available to any interested person.

(c) Subsection (a) does not apply to a death that occurs in a facility operated by or under contract with the Texas Department of Criminal Justice. Subsection (b) does not apply to a death that occurs in a facility operated by or under contract with the Texas Department of Criminal Justice if the death occurs under circumstances described by Section 501.055(b)(2), Government Code.

(d) In this article:

(1) "Correctional facility" means a confinement facility or halfway house operated by or under contract with any division of the Texas Department of Criminal Justice.

(2) "In the custody of a peace officer" means:

(A) under arrest by a peace officer; or

(B) under the physical control or restraint of a peace officer.

(3) "State juvenile facility" means any facility or halfway house:

(A) operated by or under contract with the Texas Juvenile Justice Department; or

(B) described by Section 51.02(13) or (14), Family Code.

Amended by Acts 1987, 70th Leg., ch. 529, § 1, eff. Sept. 1, 1987; Acts 1995, 74th Leg., ch. 321, § 1.106, eff. Sept. 1, 1995; Acts 1997, 75th Leg., ch. 1422, § 1, eff. June 20, 1997; Acts 2003, 78th Leg., ch. 894, § 1, eff. Sept. 1, 2003; Acts 2015, 84th Leg., ch. 734 (H.B. 1549), § 5, eff. Sept. 1, 2015.

Section 150 of Acts 2015, 84th Leg., ch. 734 (H.B. 1549) provides:

"If any provision of this Act conflicts with a provision of another Act of the 84th Legislature, Regular Session, 2015, the provision of the other Act controls to the extent of the conflict, regardless of the date of enactment."

Art. 49.19. Warrant of arrest

(a) A justice of the peace who is conducting an inquest of a death under this subchapter may issue a warrant for the arrest of a person suspected of causing the death if:

(1) the justice has knowledge that the person caused the death of the deceased;

(2) the justice receives an affidavit stating that the person caused the death; or

(3) evidence is adduced at an inquest hearing that shows probable cause to believe the person caused the death.

(b) A peace officer who receives an arrest warrant issued by a justice of the peace shall:

(1) execute the warrant without delay; and

(2) detain the person arrested until the person's discharge is ordered by the justice of the peace or other proper authority.

(c) A person who is charged in a death and arrested under a warrant of a justice of the peace shall remain in the custody of the arresting peace officer and may not be removed from the peace officer's custody on the authority of a warrant from another magistrate. A person charged in a death who has not been arrested under a warrant of a justice of the peace may be arrested on the order of a magistrate other than the justice of the peace and examined by that magistrate while an inquest is pending.

Amended by Acts 1987, 70th Leg., ch. 529, § 1, eff. Sept. 1, 1987.

Art. 49.20. Requisites of warrant

A warrant of arrest issued under Article 49.19 of this code is sufficient if it:

(1) is issued in the name of "The State of Texas";

(2) specifies the name of the person whose arrest is ordered or, if the person's name is unknown, reasonably describes the person;

(3) recites in plain language the offense with which the person is charged; and

(4) is signed and dated by a justice of the peace.

Amended by Acts 1987, 70th Leg., ch. 529, § 1, eff. Sept. 1, 1987.

Art. 49.21. Commitment of homicide suspect

At the conclusion of an inquest, if a justice of the peace finds that a person who has been arrested in the case caused or contributed to the death of the deceased, the justice may:

(1) commit the person to jail; or

(2) require the person to execute a bail bond with security for the person's appearance before the proper court to answer for the offense.

Amended by Acts 1987, 70th Leg., ch. 529, § 1, eff. Sept. 1, 1987.

Art. 49.22. Sealing premises of deceased

(a) If a body or body part that is subject to an inquest under Article 49.04 of this code is found on premises that were under the sole control of the deceased, a justice of the peace or other person authorized under this subchapter to conduct an inquest may direct that the premises be locked and sealed to prohibit entrance by any person other than a peace officer conducting an investigation of the death.

(b) Rent, utility charges, taxes, and all other reasonable expenses accruing against the property of the deceased during the time the premises of the deceased are locked and sealed under this article may be charged against the estate of the deceased.

(c) A person other than a peace officer commits an offense if the person tampers with or removes a lock or seal placed on premises under this article.

(d) An offense under this article is a Class B misdemeanor.

Amended by Acts 1987, 70th Leg., ch. 529, § 1, eff. Sept. 1, 1987; Acts 1997, 75th Leg., ch. 656, § 5, eff. Sept. 1, 1997; Acts 2003, 78th Leg., ch. 826, § 5, eff. Sept. 1, 2003; Acts 2003, 78th Leg., ch. 1295, § 5, eff. Sept. 1, 2003.

Art. 49.23. Office of death investigator

(a) The commissioners court of a county may establish an office of death investigator and employ one or more death investigators to provide assistance to those persons in the county who conduct inquests. A death investigator employed under this article is entitled to receive compensation from the county in an amount set by the commissioners court. A death investigator serves at the will of the commissioners court and on terms and conditions set by the commissioners court.

(b) To be eligible for employment as a death investigator, a person must have experience or training in investigative procedures concerning the circumstances, manner, and cause of the death of a deceased person.

(c) At the request of and under the supervision of a justice of the peace or other person conducting an inquest, a death investigator may assist the person conducting the inquest to investigate the time, place, and manner of death and lock and seal the premises of the deceased. A death investigator who assists in an inquest under this subsection shall make a complete report of the death investigator's activities, findings, and conclusions to the justice of the peace or other person conducting the inquest not later than eight hours after the death investigator completes the investigation.

Amended by Acts 1987, 70th Leg., ch. 529, § 1, eff. Sept. 1, 1987.

Art. 49.24. Notification and Report of Death of Resident of Institution

(a) A superintendent or general manager of an institution who is required by Article 49.04 to report to a justice of the peace the death of an individual under the care, custody, or control of or residing in the institution shall:

(1) notify the office of the attorney general of the individual's death within 24 hours of the death; and

(2) prepare and submit to the office of the attorney general a report containing all facts relevant to the individual's death within 72 hours of the death.

(b) The superintendent or general manager of the institution shall make a good faith effort to obtain all facts relevant to an individual's death and to include those facts in the report submitted under Subsection (a)(2).

(c) The office of the attorney general may investigate each death reported to the office by an institution that receives payments through the medical assistance program under Chapter 32, Human Resources Code.

(d) Except as provided by Subsection (e), the office of the attorney general shall make a report submitted under Subsection (a)(2) available to any interested person who submits a written request for access to the report.

(e) The office of the attorney general may deny a person access to a report or a portion of a report filed under Subsection (a)(2) if the office determines that the report or a portion of the report is:

(1) privileged from discovery; or

(2) exempt from required public disclosure under Chapter 552, Government Code.

(f) This article does not relieve a superintendent or general manager of an institution of the duty of making any other notification or report of an individual's death as required by law.

(g) For the purposes of this article, the definition of "institution" excludes hospitals.

Added by Acts 2003, 78th Leg., ch. 894, § 2, eff. Sept. 1, 2003. Amended by Acts 2005, 79th Leg., ch. 392, § 1, eff. June 17, 2005.

SUBCHAPTER B. DUTIES PERFORMED BY MEDICAL EXAMINERS

Art. 49.25. Medical examiners

Office authorized

Sec. 1. Subject to the provisions of this Act, the Commissioners Court of any county having a population of more than one million and not having a reputable medical school as defined in Articles 4501 and 4503, Revised Civil Statutes of Texas, shall establish and maintain the office of medical examiner, and the Commissioners Court of any county may establish and provide for the maintenance of the office of medical examiner. Population shall be according to the last preceding federal census.

Multi-county District; Joint Office

Sec. 1-a. (a) The commissioners courts of two or more counties may enter into an agreement to create a medical examiners district and to jointly operate and maintain the office of medical examiner of the district. The district must include the entire area of all counties involved. The counties within the district must, when taken together, form a continuous area.

(b) There may be only one medical examiner in a medical examiners district, although he may employ, within the district, necessary staff personnel. When a county becomes a part of a medical examiners district, the effect is the same within the county as if the office of medical examiner had been established in that county alone. The district medical examiner has all the powers and duties within the district that a medical examiner who serves in a single county has within that county.

(c) The commissioners court of any county which has become a part of a medical examiners district may withdraw the county from the district, but twelve months' notice of withdrawal must be given to the commissioners courts of all other counties in the district.

Appointments and Qualifications

Sec. 2. (a) The commissioners court shall appoint the medical examiner, who serves at the pleasure of the commissioners court. A person appointed as the medical examiner must be:

(1) a physician licensed by the Texas Medical Board; or

(2) a person who:

(A) is licensed and in good standing as a physician in another state;

(B) has applied to the Texas Medical Board for a license to practice medicine in this state; and

(C) has been granted a provisional license under Section 155.101, Occupations Code.

(b) To the greatest extent possible, the medical examiner shall be appointed from persons having training and experience in pathology, toxicology, histology and other medico-legal sciences.

(c) The medical examiner shall devote the time and energy necessary to perform the duties conferred by this Article.

Assistants

Sec. 3. The medical examiner may, subject to the approval of the commissioners court, employ such deputy examiners, scientific experts, trained technicians, officers and employees as may be necessary to the proper performance of the duties imposed by this Article upon the medical examiner.

Salaries

Sec. 4. The commissioners court shall establish and pay the salaries and compensations of the medical examiner and his staff.

Offices

Sec. 5. The commissioners court shall provide the medical examiner and his staff with adequate office space and shall provide laboratory facilities or make arrangements for the use of existing laboratory facilities in the county, if so requested by the medical examiner.

Death investigations

Sec. 6. (a) Any medical examiner, or his duly authorized deputy, shall be authorized, and it shall be his duty, to hold inquests with or without a jury within his county, in the following cases:

1. When a person shall die within twenty-four hours after admission to a hospital or institution or in prison or in jail;

2. When any person is killed; or from any cause dies an unnatural death, except under sentence of the law; or dies in the absence of one or more good witnesses;

3. When the body or a body part of a person is found, the cause or circumstances of death are unknown, and:

(A) the person is identified; or

(B) the person is unidentified;

4. When the circumstances of the death of any person are such as to lead to suspicion that he came to his death by unlawful means;

5. When any person commits suicide, or the circumstances of his death are such as to lead to suspicion that he committed suicide;

6. When a person dies without having been attended by a duly licensed and practicing physician, and the local health officer or registrar required to report the cause of death under Section 193.005, Health and Safety Code, does not know the cause of death. When the local health officer or registrar of vital statistics whose duty it is to certify the cause of death does not know the cause of death, he shall so notify the medical examiner of the county in which the death occurred and request an inquest;

7.　When the person is a child who is younger than six years of age and the death is reported under Chapter 264, Family Code; and

8.　When a person dies who has been attended immediately preceding his death by a duly licensed and practicing physician or physicians, and such physician or physicians are not certain as to the cause of death and are unable to certify with certainty the cause of death as required by Section 193.004, Health and Safety Code.　In case of such uncertainty the attending physician or physicians, or the superintendent or general manager of the hospital or institution in which the deceased shall have died, shall so report to the medical examiner of the county in which the death occurred, and request an inquest.

(b) The inquests authorized and required by this Article shall be held by the medical examiner of the county in which the death occurred.

(c) In making such investigations and holding such inquests, the medical examiner or an authorized deputy may administer oaths and take affidavits.　In the absence of next of kin or legal representatives of the deceased, the medical examiner or authorized deputy shall take charge of the body and all property found with it.

Organ Transplant Donors; Notice; Inquests

Sec. 6a.　(a) When death occurs to an individual designated a prospective organ donor for transplantation by a licensed physician under circumstances requiring the medical examiner of the county in which death occurred, or the medical examiner's authorized deputy, to hold an inquest, the medical examiner, or a member of his staff will be so notified by the administrative head of the facility in which the transplantation is to be performed.

(b) When notified pursuant to Subsection (a) of this Section, the medical examiner or the medical examiner's deputy shall perform an inquest on the deceased prospective organ donor.

Reports of Death

Sec. 7.　(a) Any police officer, superintendent or general manager of an institution, physician, or private citizen who shall become aware of a death under any of the circumstances set out in Section 6(a) of this Article, shall immediately report such death to the office of the medical examiner or to the city or county police departments; any such report to a city or county police department shall be immediately transmitted to the office of the medical examiner.

(b) A person investigating a death described by Subdivision 3(B) of Section 6(a) shall report the death to the missing children and missing persons information clearinghouse of the Department of Public Safety and the national crime information center not later than the 10th working day after the date the investigation began.

(c) A superintendent or general manager of an institution who reports a death under Subsection (a) must comply with the notice and reporting requirements of Article 49.24.　The office of the attorney general has the same powers and duties provided the office under that article regarding the dissemination and investigation of the report.

Removal of Bodies

Sec. 8.　When any death under circumstances set out in Section 6 shall have occurred, the body shall not be disturbed or removed from the position in which it is found by any person without authorization from the medical examiner or authorized deputy, except for the purpose of preserving such body from loss or destruction or maintaining the flow of traffic on a highway, railroad or airport.

Autopsy

Sec. 9.　(a) If the cause of death shall be determined beyond a reasonable doubt as a result of the investigation, the medical examiner shall file a report thereof setting forth specifically the cause of death with the district attorney or criminal district attorney, or in a county in which there is no district attorney or criminal district attorney with the county attorney, of the county in which the death occurred.　If in the opinion of the medical examiner an autopsy is necessary, or if such is requested by the district attorney or criminal district attorney, or county attorney where there is no district attorney or criminal district attorney, the autopsy shall be immediately performed by the medical examiner or a duly authorized deputy.　In those cases where a complete autopsy is deemed unnecessary by the medical examiner to ascertain the cause of death, the medical examiner may perform a limited autopsy involving the taking of blood samples or any other samples of body fluids, tissues or organs, in order to ascertain the cause of death or whether a crime has been committed.　In the case of a body of a human being whose identity is unknown, the medical examiner may authorize such investigative and laboratory tests and processes as are required to determine its identity as well as the cause of death.　In performing an autopsy the medical examiner or authorized deputy may use the facilities of any city or county hospital within the county or such other facilities as are made available. Upon completion of the autopsy, the medical examiner shall file a report setting forth the findings in detail with the office of the district attorney or criminal district attorney of the county, or if there is no district attorney or criminal district attorney, with the county attorney of the county.

(b) A medical examination on an unidentified person shall include the following information to enable a timely and accurate identification of the person:

(1) all available fingerprints and palm prints;

(2) dental charts and radiographs (X-rays) of the person's teeth;

(3) frontal and lateral facial photographs with scale indicated;

(4) notation and photographs, with scale indicated, of a significant scar, mark, tattoo, or item of clothing or other personal effect found with or near the body;

(5) notation of antemortem medical conditions;

(6) notation of observations pertinent to the estimation of time of death; and

(7) precise documentation of the location of burial of the remains.

(c) A medical examination on an unidentified person may include the following information to enable a timely and accurate identification of the person:

(1) full body radiographs (X-rays); and

(2) hair specimens with roots.

Disinterments and Cremations

Sec. 10. When a body upon which an inquest ought to have been held has been interred, the medical examiner may cause it to be disinterred for the purpose of holding such inquest.

Before any body, upon which an inquest is authorized by the provisions of this Article, can be lawfully cremated, an autopsy shall be performed thereon as provided in this Article, or a certificate that no autopsy was necessary shall be furnished by the medical examiner. Before any dead body can be lawfully cremated, the owner or operator of the crematory shall demand and be furnished with a certificate, signed by the medical examiner of the county in which the death occurred showing that an autopsy was performed on said body or that no autopsy thereon was necessary. It shall be the duty of the medical examiner to determine whether or not, from all the circumstances surrounding the death, an autopsy is necessary prior to issuing a certificate under the provisions of this section. No autopsy shall be required by the medical examiner as a prerequisite to cremation in case death is caused by the pestilential diseases of Asiatic cholera, bubonic plague, typhus fever, or smallpox. All certificates furnished to the owner or operator of a crematory by any medical examiner, under the terms of this Article, shall be preserved by such owner or operator of such crematory for a period of two years from the date of the cremation of said body. A medical examiner is not required to perform an autopsy on the body of a deceased person whose death was caused by a communicable disease during a public health disaster.

Waiting Period Between Death and Cremation

Sec. 10a. The body of a deceased person shall not be cremated within 48 hours after the time of death as indicated on the regular death certificate, unless the death certificate indicates death was caused by the pestilential diseases of Asiatic cholera, bubonic plague, typhus fever, or smallpox, or unless the time requirement is waived in writing by the county medical examiner or, in counties not having a county medical examiner, a justice of the peace. In a public health disaster, the commissioner of public health may designate other communicable diseases for which cremation within 48 hours of the time of death is authorized.

Disposal of Unidentified Body

Sec. 10b. If the body of a deceased person is unidentified, a person may not cremate or direct the cremation of the body under this article. If the body is buried, the investigating agency responsible for the burial shall record and maintain for not less than 10 years all information pertaining to the body and the location of burial.

Records

Sec. 11. (a) The medical examiner shall keep full and complete records properly indexed, giving the name if known of every person whose death is investigated, the place where the body was found, the date, the cause and manner of death, and shall issue a death certificate. The full report and detailed findings of the autopsy, if any, shall be a part of the record. Copies of all records shall promptly be delivered to the proper district, county, or criminal district attorney in any case where further investigation is advisable. The records may not be withheld, subject to a discretionary exception under Chapter 552, Government Code, except that a photograph or x-ray of a body taken during an autopsy is excepted from required public disclosure in accordance with Chapter 552, Government Code, but is subject to disclosure:

(1) under a subpoena or authority of other law; or

(2) if the photograph or x-ray is of the body of a person who died while in the custody of law enforcement.

(b) Under the exception to public disclosure provided by Subsection (a), a governmental body as defined by Section 552.003, Government Code, may withhold a photograph or x-ray described by Subsection (a) without requesting a decision from the attorney general under Subchapter G, Chapter 552, Government Code. This subsection does not affect the required disclosure of a photograph or x-ray under Subsection (a)(1) or (2).

Transfer of Duties of Justice of Peace

Sec. 12. When the commissioners court of any county shall establish the office of medical examiner, all powers and duties of justices of the peace in such county relating to the investigation of deaths and inquests shall vest in the office of the medical examiner. Any subsequent General Law pertaining to the duties of justices of the peace in death investigations and inquests shall apply to the medical examiner in such counties as to the extent not inconsistent with this Article, and all laws or parts of laws otherwise in conflict herewith are hereby declared to be inapplicable to this Article.

Use of Forensic Anthropologist

Sec. 13. On discovering the body or body part of a deceased person in the circumstances described by Subdivision 3(B) of Section 6(a), the medical examiner may request the aid of a forensic anthropologist in the examination of the body or body part. The forensic anthropologist must hold a doctoral degree in anthropology with an emphasis in physical anthropology. The forensic anthropologist shall attempt to establish whether the body or body part is of a human or animal, whether evidence of childbirth, injury, or disease exists, and the sex, race, age, stature, and physical anomalies of the body or body part. The forensic anthropologist may also attempt to establish the cause, manner, and time of death.

Fees

Sec. 13A. (a) A medical examiner may charge reasonable fees for services provided by the office of medical examiner under this article, including crema-

tion approvals, court testimonies, consultations, and depositions.

(b) The commissioners court must approve the amount of the fee before the fee may be assessed. The fee may not exceed the amount necessary to provide the services described by Subsection (a).

(c) The fee may not be assessed against the county's district attorney or a county office.

Penalty

Sec. 14. (a) A person commits an offense if the person knowingly violates this article.

(b) An offense under this section is a Class B misdemeanor.

Acts 1965, 59th Leg., vol. 2, p. 317, ch. 722. Amended by Acts 1969, 61st Leg., p. 1033, ch. 336, § 1, eff. May 27, 1969; Acts 1969, 61st Leg., p. 1619, ch. 500, § 1, eff. June 10, 1969; Acts 1971, 62nd Leg., p. 1165, ch. 270, § 1, eff. Aug. 30, 1971; Acts 1975, 64th Leg., p. 1826, ch. 562, § 1, eff. Sept. 1, 1975; Acts 1989, 71st Leg., ch. 1205, § 1, eff. June 16, 1989; Acts 1991, 72nd Leg., ch. 14, §§ 284(66), (67), (69), eff. Sept. 1, 1991; Acts 1991, 72nd Leg., ch. 597, § 58, eff. Sept. 1, 1991; Acts 1995, 74th Leg., ch. 255, § 5, eff. Sept. 1, 1995; Acts 1995, 74th Leg., ch. 878, § 4, eff. Sept. 1, 1995; Acts 1997, 75th Leg., ch. 656, § 6, eff. Sept. 1, 1997; Acts 1999, 76th Leg., ch. 607, § 2, eff. Sept. 1, 1999; Acts 2003, 78th Leg., ch. 198, § 2.191, eff. Sept. 1, 2003; Acts 2003, 78th Leg., ch. 826, §§ 6, 7, eff. Sept. 1, 2003; Acts 2003, 78th Leg., ch. 894, § 3, eff. Sept. 1, 2003; Acts 2003, 78th Leg., ch. 1295, §§ 6, 7, eff. Sept. 1, 2003; Acts 2011, 82nd Leg., ch. 1341 (S.B. 1233), § 8, eff. June 17, 2011; Acts 2013, 83rd Leg., ch. 22 (S.B. 336), § 1, eff. Sept. 1, 2013; Acts 2013, 83rd Leg., ch. 25 (S.B. 457), § 1, eff. Sept. 1, 2013.

SUBCHAPTER C. INFORMED CONSENT FOR POSTMORTEM EXAMINATION OR AUTOPSY

Art. 49.31. Applicability

This subchapter does not apply to an autopsy that:

(1) is ordered by the Texas Department of Criminal Justice or an authorized official of the department in accordance with Section 501.055, Government Code; or

(2) a justice of the peace or medical examiner determines is required under this chapter or other law.

Added by Acts 2011, 82nd Leg., ch. 950 (H.B. 1009), § 2, eff. Sept. 1, 2011.

Art. 49.32. Consent to Postmortem Examination or Autopsy

(a) Except as provided by Subsection (b) of this article, a physician may not perform, or assist in the performance of, a postmortem examination or autopsy on the body of a deceased person unless the physician obtains the written informed consent of a person authorized to provide consent under Article 49.33 of this code. The consent must be provided on the form prescribed under Article 49.34 of this code.

(b) If, after due diligence, a physician is unable to identify or contact a person authorized to give consent under Article 49.33 of this code, the physician may, as authorized by a medical examiner, justice of the peace, or county judge, as appropriate, perform a postmortem examination or autopsy on the body of a deceased person not less than 24 hours and not more than 48 hours from the time of the decedent's death or the time the physician or other person took possession of the body.

Added by Acts 2011, 82nd Leg., ch. 950 (H.B. 1009), § 2, eff. Sept. 1, 2011.

Art. 49.33. Persons Authorized to Consent to Postmortem Examination or Autopsy

(a) Subject to Subsections (b) and (c) of this article, consent for a postmortem examination or autopsy may be given by any member of the following classes of persons who is reasonably available, in the order of priority listed:

(1) the spouse of the decedent;

(2) the person acting as guardian of the person of the decedent at the time of death or the executor or administrator of the decedent's estate;

(3) the adult children of the decedent;

(4) the parents of the decedent; and

(5) the adult siblings of the decedent.

(b) If there is more than one member of a class listed in Subsection (a)(2), (3), (4), or (5) of this article entitled to give consent to a postmortem examination or autopsy, consent may be given by a member of the class unless another member of the class files an objection with the physician, medical examiner, justice of the peace, or county judge. If an objection is filed, the consent may be given only by a majority of the members of the class who are reasonably available.

(c) A person may not give consent under this article if, at the time of the decedent's death, a person in a class granted higher priority under Subsection (a) of this article is reasonably available to give consent or

to file an objection to a postmortem examination or autopsy.

Added by Acts 2011, 82nd Leg., ch. 950 (H.B. 1009), § 2, eff. Sept. 1, 2011.

Art. 49.34. Postmortem Examination or Autopsy Consent Form

The commissioner of state health services, in consultation with the Texas Medical Board, shall prescribe a standard written consent form for a postmortem examination or autopsy. The form must:

(1) include the name of the hospital or other institution and the department that will perform the examination or autopsy;

(2) include a statement that the removal from the deceased person's body and retention by the physician of organs, fluids, prosthetic devices, or tissue may be required for purposes of comprehensive evaluation or accurate determination of a cause of death;

(3) provide the family of the deceased person with an opportunity to place restrictions or special limitations on the examination or autopsy;

(4) include a separate section regarding the disposition of organs, fluids, prosthetic devices, or tissue after the examination or autopsy, including a prioritized list of the persons authorized to control that disposition, as provided by Chapter 692A, Health and Safety Code;

(5) provide for documented and witnessed consent;

(6) allow authorization for the release of human remains to a funeral home or individual designated by the person giving consent for the postmortem examination or autopsy;

(7) include information regarding the rights described by Article 49.35 of this code;

(8) list the circumstances under which a medical examiner is required by law to conduct an investigation, inquest, or autopsy under Article 49.25 of this code;

(9) include a statement that the form is required by state law; and

(10) be written in plain language designed to be easily understood by the average person.

Added by Acts 2011, 82nd Leg., ch. 950 (H.B. 1009), § 2, eff. Sept. 1, 2011.

Art. 49.35. Right to Nonaffiliated Physician

(a) A person authorized to consent to a postmortem examination or autopsy under Article 49.33 of this code may request that a physician who is not affiliated with the hospital or other institution where the deceased person died:

(1) perform the postmortem examination or autopsy at another hospital or institution; or

(2) review the postmortem examination or autopsy conducted by a physician affiliated with the hospital or other institution where the deceased person died.

(b) A representative of the hospital or other institution shall inform the person of the person's right to request the performance or review of a postmortem examination or autopsy by a nonaffiliated physician under Subsection (a) before the person consents to the postmortem examination or autopsy.

(c) A person requesting a nonaffiliated physician to perform or review a postmortem examination or autopsy shall bear the additional costs incurred as a result of the nonaffiliated physician's performance or review of the examination or autopsy under Subsection (a) of this article.

Added by Acts 2011, 82nd Leg., ch. 950 (H.B. 1009), § 2, eff. Sept. 1, 2011.

SUBCHAPTER D. PARENTAL RIGHT TO VIEW DECEASED CHILD

Art. 49.51. Definitions

In this subchapter:

(1) "Child" means a person younger than 18 years of age.

(2) "Parent" has the meaning assigned by Section 160.102(11), Family Code.

Added by Acts 2017, 85th Leg., ch. 777 (S.B. 239), § 1, eff. Sept. 1, 2017.

Art. 49.52. Parental Right to View Deceased Child

(a) Except as provided by Subsection (b) or (c), a parent of a deceased child is entitled to view the child's body before a justice of the peace or the medical examiner, as applicable, for the county in which the death occurred assumes control over the body under Subchapter A or B, as applicable. If the child's death occurred at a hospital or other health care facility, the viewing may be conducted at the hospital or facility.

(b) A parent of a deceased child may not view the child's body after a justice of the peace or medical examiner described by Subsection (a) assumes control over the body under Subchapter A or B, as applicable,

unless the parent first obtains the consent of the justice of the peace or medical examiner or a person acting on behalf of the justice of the peace or medical examiner.

(c) A viewing of the body of a deceased child whose death is determined to be subject to an inquest under Article 49.04 or 49.25, as applicable, must be conducted in compliance with the following conditions:

(1) the viewing must be supervised by:

(A) if law enforcement has assumed control over the body at the time of the viewing, an appropriate peace officer or, with the officer's consent, a person described by Paragraph (B); or

(B) a physician, registered nurse, or licensed vocational nurse or the justice of the peace or the medical examiner or a person acting on behalf of the justice of the peace or medical examiner;

(2) a parent of the deceased child may not have contact with the child's body unless the parent first obtains the consent of the justice of the peace or medical examiner or a person acting on behalf of the justice of the peace or medical examiner; and

(3) a person may not remove a medical device from the child's body or otherwise alter the condition of the body for purposes of conducting the viewing unless the person first obtains the consent of the justice of the peace or medical examiner or a person acting on behalf of the justice of the peace or medical examiner.

(d) A person is not entitled to compensation for performing duties on behalf of a justice of the peace or medical examiner under this article unless the commissioners court of the applicable county approves the compensation.

Added by Acts 2017, 85th Leg., ch. 777 (S.B. 239), § 1, eff. Sept. 1, 2017.

CHAPTER 50.   FIRE INQUESTS

Article

Art. 50.01.   Investigations

When an affidavit is made by a credible person before any justice of the peace that there is ground to believe that any building has been unlawfully set or attempted to be set on fire, such justice shall cause the truth of such complaint to be investigated.

Acts 1965, 59th Leg., vol. 2, p. 317, ch. 722.

Art. 50.02. Proceedings

The proceedings in such case shall be governed by the laws relating to inquests upon dead bodies. The officer conducting such investigations shall have the same powers as are conferred upon justices of the peace in the preceding Articles of this Chapter.

Acts 1965, 59th Leg., vol. 2, p. 317, ch. 722.

Art. 50.03. Verdict in fire inquest

The jury after inspecting the place in question and after hearing the testimony, shall deliver to the justice holding such inquest its written signed verdict in which it shall find and certify how and in what manner such fire happened or was attempted, and all the circumstances attending the same, and who are guilty thereof, and in what manner. If such a jury is unable to so ascertain, it shall find and certify accordingly.

Acts 1965, 59th Leg., vol. 2, p. 317, ch. 722. Amended by Acts 1973, 63rd Leg., p. 968, ch. 399, § 2(A), eff. Jan. 1, 1974.

Art. 50.04. Witnesses bound over

If the jury finds that any building has been unlawfully set on fire or has been attempted so to be, the justice holding such inquest shall bind over the witnesses to appear and testify before the next grand jury of the county in which such offense was committed.

Acts 1965, 59th Leg., vol. 2, p. 317, ch. 722.

Art. 50.05. Warrant for accused

If the person charged with the offense, if any, be not in custody, the justice of the peace shall issue a warrant for his arrest, and when arrested, such person shall be dealt with as in other like cases.

Acts 1965, 59th Leg., vol. 2, p. 317, ch. 722.

Art. 50.06. Testimony written down

In all such investigations, the testimony of all witnesses examined before the jury shall be reduced to writing by or under the direction of the justice and signed by each witness. Such testimony together with the verdict and all bail bonds taken in the case shall be certified to and returned by the justice to the next district or criminal district court of his county.

Acts 1965, 59th Leg., vol. 2, p. 317, ch. 722.

Art. 50.07. Compensation

The pay of the officers and jury making such investigation shall be the same as that allowed for the holding of an inquest upon a dead body, so far as applicable, and shall be paid in like manner.

Acts 1965, 59th Leg., vol. 2, p. 317, ch. 722.

CHAPTER 51. FUGITIVES FROM JUSTICE

Article
51.01. Delivered up.
51.02. To aid in arrest.
51.03. Magistrate's warrant.
51.04. Complaint.
51.05. Bail or commitment.
51.06. Notice of arrest.
51.07. Discharge.
51.08. Second arrest.
51.09. Governor may demand fugitive.
51.10. Pay of agent; traveling expenses.
51.11. Reward.
51.12. Sheriff to report.
51.13. Uniform Criminal Extradition Act.
51.14. Interstate Agreement on Detainers.

Art. 51.01. Delivered up

A person in any other State of the United States charged with treason or any felony who shall flee from justice and be found in this State, shall on demand of the executive authority of the State from which he fled, be delivered up, to be removed to the State having jurisdiction of the crime.

Acts 1965, 59th Leg., vol. 2, p. 317, ch. 722.

Art. 51.02. To aid in arrest

All peace officers of the State shall give aid in the arrest and detention of a fugitive from any other State that he may be held subject to a requisition by the Governor of the State from which he fled.

Acts 1965, 59th Leg., vol. 2, p. 317, ch. 722.

Art. 51.03. Magistrate's warrant

When a complaint is made to a magistrate that any person within his jurisdiction is a fugitive from justice from another State, he shall issue a warrant of arrest directing a peace officer to apprehend and bring the accused before him.

Acts 1965, 59th Leg., vol. 2, p. 317, ch. 722.

Art. 51.04. Complaint

The complaint shall be sufficient if it recites:

1. The name of the person accused;

2. The State from which he has fled;

3. The offense committed by the accused;

4. That he has fled to this State from the State where the offense was committed; and

5. That the act alleged to have been committed by the accused is a violation of the penal law of the State from which he fled.

Acts 1965, 59th Leg., vol. 2, p. 317, ch. 722.

Art. 51.05.   Bail or commitment

When the accused is brought before the magistrate, he shall hear proof, and if satisfied that the accused is charged in another State with the offense named in the complaint, he shall require of him bail with sufficient security, in such amount as the magistrate deems reasonable, to appear before such magistrate at a specified time. In default of such bail, he may commit the defendant to jail to await a requisition from the Governor of the State from which he fled. A properly certified transcript of an indictment against the accused is sufficient to show that he is charged with the crime alleged. One arrested under the provisions of this title shall not be committed or held to bail for a longer time than ninety days.

Acts 1965, 59th Leg., vol. 2, p. 317, ch. 722.

Art. 51.06.   Notice of arrest

The magistrate who held or committed such fugitive shall immediately notify the Secretary of State and the district or county attorney of his county of such fact and the date thereof, stating the name of such fugitive, the State from which he fled, and the crime with which he is charged; and such officers so notified shall in turn notify the Governor of the proper State.

Acts 1965, 59th Leg., vol. 2, p. 317, ch. 722.

Art. 51.07.   Discharge

A fugitive not arrested under a warrant from the Governor of this State before the expiration of ninety days from the day of his commitment or the date of the bail shall be discharged.

Acts 1965, 59th Leg., vol. 2, p. 317, ch. 722.

Art. 51.08.   Second arrest

A person who has once been arrested under the provisions of this title and discharged under the provisions of the preceding Article or by habeas corpus shall not be again arrested upon a charge of the same offense, except by a warrant from the Governor of this State.

Acts 1965, 59th Leg., vol. 2, p. 317, ch. 722.

Art. 51.09.   Governor may demand fugitive

When the Governor deems it proper to demand a person who has committed an offense in this State and has fled to another State, he may commission any suitable person to take such requisition. The accused, if brought back to the State, shall be delivered up to the sheriff of the county in which it is alleged he has committed the offense.

Acts 1965, 59th Leg., vol. 2, p. 317, ch. 722.

Art. 51.10.   Pay of agent; traveling expenses

Sec. 1. The officer or person so commissioned shall receive as compensation the actual and necessary traveling expenses upon requisition of the Governor to be allowed by such Governor and to be paid out of the State Treasury upon a certificate of the Governor reciting the services rendered and the allowance therefor.

Sec. 2. The commissioners court of the county where an offense is committed may in its discretion, on the request of the sheriff and the recommendation of the district attorney, pay the actual and necessary traveling expenses of the officer or person so commissioned out of any fund or funds not otherwise pledged.

Acts 1965, 59th Leg., vol. 2, p. 317, ch. 722.

Art. 51.11.   Reward

The Governor may offer a reward for the apprehension of one accused of a felony in this State who is evading arrest, by causing such offer to be published in such manner as he deems most likely to effect the arrest. The reward shall be paid out of the State Treasury to the person who becomes entitled to it upon a certificate of the Governor reciting the facts which entitle such person to receive it.

Acts 1965, 59th Leg., vol. 2, p. 317, ch. 722.

Art. 51.12.   Sheriff to report

Each sheriff upon the close of any regular term of the district or criminal district court in his county, or within thirty days thereafter, shall make out and mail to the Director of the Department of Public Safety a certified list of all persons, who, after indictment for a felony, have fled from said county. Such lists shall contain the full name of each such fugitive, the offense with which he is charged, and a description giving his age, height, weight, color and occupation, the complexion of the skin and the color of eyes and hair, and any peculiarity in person, speech, manner or gait that may serve to identify such person so far as the sheriff may be able to give them. The Director of the Department of Public Safety shall prescribe and forward to all sheriffs the necessary blanks upon which are to be made the lists herein required.

Acts 1965, 59th Leg., vol. 2, p. 317, ch. 722.

Art. 51.13. Uniform Criminal Extradition Act
Definitions

Sec. 1. Where appearing in this Article, the term "Governor" includes any person performing the functions of Governor by authority of the laws of this State. The term "Executive Authority" includes the Governor, and any person performing the functions of Governor in a State other than this State, and the term "State", referring to a State other than this State, includes any other State organized or unorganized of the United States of America.

Fugitives from Justice; Duty of Governor

Sec. 2. Subject to the provisions of this Article, the provisions of the Constitution of the United States controlling, and any and all Acts of Congress enacted in pursuance thereof, it is the duty of the Governor of this State to have arrested and delivered up to the Executive Authority of any other State of the United States any person charged in that State with treason, felony, or other crime, who has fled from justice and is found in this State.

Form of Demand

Sec. 3. No demand for the extradition of a person charged with crime in another State shall be recognized by the Governor unless in writing, alleging, except in cases arising under Section 6, that the accused was present in the demanding State at the time of the commission of the alleged crime, and that thereafter he fled from the State, and accompanied by a copy of an indictment found or by information supported by affidavit in the State having jurisdiction of the crime, or by a copy of an affidavit before a magistrate there, together with a copy of any warrant which issued thereupon; or by a copy of a judgment of conviction or of a sentence imposed in execution thereof, together with a statement by the Executive Authority of the demanding State that the person claimed has escaped from confinement or has broken the terms of his bail, probation or parole. The indictment, information, or affidavit made before the magistrate must substantially charge the person demanded with having committed a crime under the law of that State; and the copy of indictment, information, affidavit, judgment of conviction or sentence must be authenticated by the Executive Authority making the

demand; provided, however, that all such copies of the aforesaid instruments shall be in duplicate, one complete set of such instruments to be delivered to the defendant or to his attorney.

Governor May Investigate Case

Sec. 4. When a demand shall be made upon the Governor of this State by the Executive Authority of another State for the surrender of a person so charged with crime, the Governor may call upon the Secretary of State, Attorney General or any prosecuting officer in this State to investigate or assist in investigating the demand, and to report to him the situation and circumstances of the person so demanded, and whether he ought to be surrendered.

Extradition of Persons Imprisoned or Awaiting Trial in Another State or Who have Left the Demanding State Under Compulsion

Sec. 5. When it is desired to have returned to this State a person charged in this State with a crime, and such person is imprisoned or is held under criminal proceedings then pending against him in another State, the Governor of this State may agree with the Executive Authority of such other State for the extradition of such person before the conclusion of such proceedings or his term of sentence in such other State, upon condition that such person be returned to such other State at the expense of this State as soon as the prosecution in this State is terminated.

The Governor of this State may also surrender on demand of the Executive Authority of any other State any person in this State who is charged in the manner provided in Section 23 of this Act with having violated the laws of the State whose Executive Authority is making the demand, even though such person left the demanding State involuntarily.

Extradition of Persons Not Present in Demanding State at Time of Commission of Crime

Sec. 6. The Governor of this State may also surrender, on demand of the Executive Authority of any other State, any person in this State charged in such other State in the manner provided in Section 3 with committing an act in this State, or in a third State, intentionally resulting in a crime in the State whose Executive Authority is making the demand, and the provisions of this Article not otherwise inconsistent, shall apply to such cases, even though the accused was not in that State at the time of the commission of the crime, and has not fled therefrom.

Issue of Governor's Warrant of Arrest; Its Recitals

Sec. 7. If the Governor decides that the demand should be complied with, he shall sign a warrant of arrest, which shall be sealed with the state seal and be directed to any peace officer or other person whom he may think fit to entrust with the execution thereof. The warrant must substantially recite the facts necessary to the validity of its issuance.

Manner and Place of Execution

Sec. 8. Such warrant shall authorize the peace officer or other person to whom directed to arrest the accused at any time and any place where he may be found within the State and to command the aid of all peace officers and other persons in the execution of the warrant, and to deliver the accused, subject to the provisions of this Article to the duly authorized agent of the demanding State.

Authority of Arresting Officer

Sec. 9. Every such peace officer or other person empowered to make the arrest, shall have the same authority, in arresting the accused, to command assistance therein, as peace officers have by law in the execution of any criminal process directed to them, with like penalties against those who refuse their assistance.

Rights of Accused Person; Application for Writ of Habeas Corpus.

Sec. 10. (a) No person arrested upon such warrant shall be delivered over to the agent whom the Executive Authority demanding him shall have appointed to receive him unless he shall first be taken forthwith before a judge of a court of record in this State, or before a justice of the peace serving a precinct that is located in a county bordering another state, who shall inform him of the demand made for his surrender and of the crime with which he is charged, and that he has the right to demand and procure legal counsel; and if the prisoner or his counsel shall state that he or they desire to test the legality of his arrest, the judge of the court of record shall fix a reasonable time to be allowed the prisoner in which to apply for a writ of habeas corpus, or the justice of the peace shall direct the prisoner to a court of record for purposes of obtaining such a writ. When the writ is applied for, notice thereof, and of the time and place of hearing thereon, shall be given to the prosecuting officer of the county in which the arrest is made and in which the accused is in custody, and to the said agent of the demanding State.

(b) Before a justice of the peace who is not an attorney may perform a duty or function permitted by Subsection (a), the justice must take, through the Texas Justice Court Training Center, a training course that focuses on extradition law. The center shall develop a course to satisfy the requirements of this subsection.

(c) Each justice of the peace who performs a duty or function permitted by Subsection (a) shall ensure that the applicable proceeding is transcribed or videotaped and that the record of the proceeding is retained in the records of the court for at least 270 days.

Penalty for Non-compliance With Preceding Section

Sec. 11. Any officer who shall deliver to the agent for extradition of the demanding State a person in his custody under the Governor's warrant, in wilful disobedience to Section 10 of this Act, shall be guilty of a misdemeanor and, on conviction, shall be fined not more than one thousand dollars or be imprisoned not more than six months, or both.

Confinement in Jail, When Necessary

Sec. 12. The officer or persons executing the Governor's warrant of arrest, or the agent of the demanding State to whom the prisoner may have been delivered may, when necessary, confine the prisoner in the jail of any county or city through which he may pass; and the keeper of such jail must receive and safely keep the prisoner until the officer or person having charge of him is ready to proceed on his route, such officer or person being chargeable with the expense of keeping.

The officer or agent of a demanding State to whom a prisoner may have been delivered following extradition proceedings in another State, or to whom a prisoner may have been delivered after waiving extradition in such other State, and who is passing through this State with such a prisoner for the purpose of immediately returning such prisoner to the demanding State may, when necessary, confine the prisoner in the jail of any county or city through which he may pass; and the keeper of such jail must receive and safely keep the prisoner until the officer or agent having charge of him is ready to proceed on his route, such officer or agent, however, being chargeable with the expense of keeping; provided, however, that such officer or agent shall produce and show to the keeper of such jail satisfactory written evidence of the fact that he is actually transporting such prisoner to the demanding State after a requisition by the Executive Authority of such demanding State. Such prisoner shall not be entitled to demand a new requisition while in this State.

Arrest Prior to Requisition

Sec. 13. Whenever any person within this State shall be charged on the oath of any credible person before any judge or magistrate of this State with the commission of any crime in any other State and except in cases arising under Section 6, with having fled from justice, or with having been convicted of a crime in that State and having escaped from confinement, or having broken the terms of his bail, probation or parole, or whenever complaint shall have been made before any judge or magistrate in this State setting forth on the affidavit of any credible person in another State that a crime has been committed in such other State and that the accused has been charged in such State with the commission of the crime, and except in cases arising under Section 6, has fled from justice, or with having been convicted of a crime in that State and having escaped from confinement, or having broken the terms of his bail, probation or parole and is believed to be in this State, the judge or magistrate shall issue a warrant directed to any peace officer commanding him to apprehend the person named therein, wherever he may be found in this State, and to bring him before the same or any other judge, magistrate or court who or which may be available in or convenient of access to the place where the arrest may be made, to answer the charge or complaint and affidavit, and a certified copy of the sworn charge or complaint and affidavit upon which the warrant is issued shall be attached to the warrant.

Arrest Without a Warrant

Sec. 14. The arrest of a person may be lawfully made also by any peace officer or private person, without a warrant upon reasonable information that the accused stands charged in the courts of a State with a crime punishable by death or imprisonment for a term exceeding one year, but when so arrested the accused must be taken before a judge or magistrate with all practicable speed and complaint must be made against him under oath setting forth the ground for the arrest as in the preceding section; and thereafter his answer shall be heard as if he had been arrested on a warrant.

Commitment to Await Requisition; Bail

Sec. 15. If from the examination before the judge or magistrate it appears that the person held is the person charged with having committed the crime alleged and except in cases arising under Section 6, that

he has fled from justice, the judge or magistrate must, by warrant reciting the accusation, commit him to the county jail for such time not exceeding thirty days and specified in the warrant, as will enable the arrest of the accused to be made under a warrant of the Governor on a requisition of the Executive Authority of the State having jurisdiction of the offense, unless the accused give bail as provided in the next section, or until he shall be legally discharged.

Bail; In What Cases; Conditions of Bond

Sec. 16. Unless the offense with which the prisoner is charged is shown to be an offense punishable by death or life imprisonment under the laws of the State in which it was committed, a judge or magistrate in this State may admit the person arrested to bail by bond, with sufficient sureties and in such sum as he deems proper, conditioned for his appearance before him at a time specified in such bond, and for his surrender, to be arrested upon the warrant of the Governor in this State.

Extension of Time of Commitment; Adjournment

Sec. 17. If the accused is not arrested under warrant of the Governor by the expiration of the time specified in the warrant or bond, a judge or magistrate may discharge him or may recommit him for a further period not to exceed sixty days, or a judge or magistrate may again take bail for his appearance and surrender, as provided in Section 16, but within a period not to exceed sixty days after the date of such new bond.

Forfeiture of Bail

Sec. 18. If the prisoner is admitted to bail and fails to appear and surrender himself according to the conditions of his bond, the judge, or magistrate by proper order, shall declare the bond forfeited and order his immediate arrest without warrant if he be within this State. Recovery may be had on such bond in the name of the State as in the case of other bonds given by the accused in criminal proceedings within this State.

Persons Under Criminal Prosecution in this State at the Time of Requisition

Sec. 19. If a criminal prosecution has been instituted against such person under the laws of this State and is still pending, the Governor, in his discretion, either may surrender him on demand of the Executive Authority of another State or hold him until he has been tried and discharged or convicted and punished in this State.

Guilt or Innocence of Accused, When Inquired Into

Sec. 20. The guilt or innocence of the accused as to the crime of which he is charged may not be inquired into by the Governor or in any proceeding after the demand for extradition accompanied by a charge of crime in legal form as above provided shall have been presented to the Governor, except as it may be involved in identifying the person held as the person charged with the crime.

Governor May Recall Warrant or Issue Alias

Sec. 21. The governor may recall his warrant of the arrest or may issue another warrant whenever he deems proper. Each warrant issued by the Governor shall expire and be of no force and effect when not executed within one year from the date thereof.

Fugitives from this State; Duty of Governor

Sec. 22. Whenever the Governor of this State shall demand a person charged with crime or with escaping from confinement or breaking the terms of his bail, probation or parole in this State, from the Executive Authority of any other State, or from the Chief Justice or an Associate Justice of the Supreme Court of the District of Columbia authorized to receive such demand under the laws of the United States, he shall issue a warrant under the state seal, to some agent, commanding him to receive the person so charged if delivered to him and convey him to the proper officer of the county in this State in which the offense was committed, or in which the prosecution for such offense is then pending.

Application for Issuance of Requisition; By Whom Made; Contents

Sec. 23. 1. When the return to this State of a person charged with crime in this State is required, the State's attorney shall present to the Governor his written motion for a requisition for the return of the person charged, in which motion shall be stated the name of the person so charged, the crime charged against him, the approximate time, place and circumstances of its commission, the State in which he is believed to be, including the location of the accused therein at the time the motion is made and certifying that, in the opinion of the said State's attorney the ends of justice require the arrest and return of the accused to this State for trial and that the proceeding is not instituted to enforce a private claim.

2. When the return to this State is required of a person who has been convicted of a crime in this State and has escaped from confinement, or broken the terms of his bail, probation or parole, the prosecuting attorney of the county in which the offense was committed, the parole board, or the warden of the institution or sheriff of the county, from which escape was made, shall present to the Governor a written application for a requisition for the return of such person, in which application shall be stated the name of the person, the crime of which he was convicted, the circumstances of his escape from confinement, or the circumstances of the breach of the terms of his bail, probation or parole, the State in which he is believed to be, including the location of the person therein at the time application is made.

3. The application shall be verified by affidavit, shall be executed in duplicate and shall be accompanied by two certified copies of the indictment returned, or information and affidavit filed, or of the complaint made to the judge or magistrate, stating the offense with which the accused is charged, or of the judgment of conviction or of the sentence. The prosecuting officer, parole board, warden or sheriff may also attach such further affidavits and other documents in duplicate as he shall deem proper to be submitted with such application. One copy of the application, with the action of the Governor indicated by endorsement thereon, and one of the certified copies of the indictment, complaint, information, and affidavits, or of the judgment of conviction or of the sentence shall be filed in the office of the Governor. The other copies of all papers shall be forwarded with the Governor's requisition.

Costs and Expenses

Sec. 24. In all cases of extradition, the commissioners court of the county where an offense is alleged to have been committed, or in which the prosecution is then pending may in its discretion, on request of the sheriff and the recommendation of the prosecuting attorney, pay the actual and necessary expenses of the officer or person commissioned to receive the person charged, out of any county fund or funds not otherwise pledged.

Immunity from Service of Process in Certain Civil Cases

Sec. 25. A person brought into this State by, or after waiver of, extradition based on a criminal charge shall not be subject to service of personal process in civil actions arising out of the same facts as the criminal proceeding to answer which he is being or has been returned, until he has been convicted in the criminal proceeding, or if acquitted, until he has had reasonable opportunity to return to the State from which he was extradited.

Written Waiver of Extradition Proceedings

Sec. 25a. (a) Any person arrested in this State charged with having committed any crime in another State or alleged to have escaped from confinement, or broken the terms of his bail, probation, or parole may waive the issuance and service of the warrant provided for in Sections 7 and 8 and all other procedure incidental to extradition proceedings, by executing or subscribing in the presence of a judge or any court of record within this State, or in the presence of a justice of the peace serving a precinct that is located in a county bordering another state, a writing which states that the arrested person consents to return to the demanding State; provided, however, that before such waiver shall be executed or subscribed by such person the judge or justice of the peace shall inform such person of his:

(1) right to the issuance and service of a warrant of extradition; and

(2) right to obtain a writ of habeas corpus as provided for in Section 10.

If and when such consent has been duly executed it shall forthwith be forwarded to the office of the Governor of this State and filed therein. The judge or justice of the peace shall direct the officer having such person in custody to deliver forthwith such person to the duly accredited agent or agents of the demanding State, and shall deliver or cause to be delivered to such agent or agents a copy of such consent; provided, however, that nothing in this section shall be deemed to limit the rights of the accused person to return voluntarily and without formality to the demanding State, nor shall this waiver procedure be deemed to be an exclusive procedure or to limit the powers, rights or duties of the officers of the demanding State or of this State.

(b) Before a justice of the peace who is not an attorney may perform a duty or function permitted by Subsection (a), the justice must take, through the Texas Justice Court Training Center, a training course that focuses on extradition law. The center shall develop a course to satisfy the requirements of this subsection.

(c) Each justice of the peace who performs a duty or function permitted by Subsection (a) shall ensure that the applicable proceeding is transcribed or videotaped and that the record of the proceeding is retained in the records of the court for at least 270 days.

Non-waiver by this State

Sec. 25b. Nothing in this Act contained shall be deemed to constitute a waiver by this State of its right, power or privilege to try such demanded person for crime committed within this State, or of its right, power or privilege to regain custody of such person by extradition proceedings or otherwise for the purpose of trial, sentence or punishment for any crime committed within this State, nor shall any proceedings had under this Article which result, or fail to result in, extradition to be deemed a waiver by this State of any of its rights, privileges or jurisdiction in any way whatsoever.

No Right of Asylum, No Immunity from Other Criminal Prosecutions While in this State

Sec. 26. After a person has been brought back to this State by, or after waiver of extradition proceedings, he may be tried in this State for other crimes which he may be charged with having committed here as well as that specified in the requisition for his extradition.

Interpretation

Sec. 27. The provisions of this Article shall be interpreted and construed as to effectuate its general purposes to make uniform the law of those States which enact it.

Acts 1965, 59th Leg., vol. 2, p. 317, ch. 722. Amended by Acts 1993, 73rd Leg., ch. 300, § 27, eff. Aug. 30, 1993; Acts 1997, 75th Leg., ch. 701, § 1, eff. Sept. 1, 1997; Acts 2013, 83rd Leg., ch. 1271 (H.B. 1125), §§ 1, 2, eff. June 14, 2013.

Art. 51.14. Interstate Agreement on Detainers

This article may be cited as the "Interstate Agreement on Detainers Act." This agreement on detainers is hereby enacted into law and entered into by this state with all other jurisdictions legally joined therein in the form substantially as follows:

The contracting states solemnly agree that:

ARTICLE I.

The party states find that charges outstanding against a prisoner, detainers based on untried indictments, informations, or complaints, and difficulties in securing speedy trial of persons already incarcerated in other jurisdictions, produce uncertainties which obstruct programs of prisoner treatment and rehabilitation. Accordingly, it is the policy of the party states and the purpose of this agreement to encourage the expeditious and orderly disposition of such charges and determination of the proper status of any and all detainers based on untried indictments, informations, or complaints. The party states also find that proceedings with reference to such charges and detainers, when emanating from another jurisdiction, cannot properly be had in the absence of cooperative procedures. It is the further purpose of this agreement to provide such cooperative procedures.

ARTICLE II.

As used is this agreement:

(a) "State" shall mean a state of the United States; the United States of America; a territory or possession of the United States; the District of Columbia; the Commonwealth of Puerto Rico.

(b) "Sending state" shall mean a state in which a prisoner is incarcerated at the time that he initiates a request for final disposition pursuant to Article III hereof or at the time that a request for custody or availability is initiated pursuant to Article IV hereof.

ARTICLE III.

(a) Whenever a person has entered upon a term of imprisonment in a penal or correctional institution of a party state, and whenever during the continuance of the term of imprisonment there is pending in any other party state any untried indictment, information, or complaint on the basis of which a detainer has been lodged against the prisoner, he shall be brought to trial within 180 days after he shall have caused to be delivered to the prosecuting officer and the appropriate court of the prosecuting officer's jurisdiction written notice of the place of his imprisonment and his request for a final disposition to be made of the indictment, information, or complaint; provided that for good cause shown in open court, the prisoner or his counsel being present, the court having jurisdiction of the matter may grant any necessary or reasonable continuance. The request of the prisoner shall be accompanied by a certificate of the appropriate official having custody of the prisoner, stating the term of commitment under which the prisoner is being held, the time already served, the time remaining to be served on the sentence, the amount of good time earned, the time of parole eligibility of the prisoner, and any decision of the state parole agency relating to the prisoner.

(b) The written notice and request for final disposition referred to in Paragraph (a) hereof shall be given or sent by the prisoner to the warden, commissioner of corrections, or other official having custody of him, who shall promptly forward it together with the certif-icate to the appropriate prosecuting official and court by registered or certified mail, return receipt requested.

(c) The warden, commissioner of corrections, or other official having custody of the prisoner shall promptly inform him of the source and contents of any detainer lodged against him and shall also inform him of his right to make a request for final disposition of the indictment, information, or complaint on which the detainer is based.

(d) Any request for final disposition made by a prisoner pursuant to Paragraph (a) hereof shall operate as a request for final disposition of all untried indictments, informations, or complaints on the basis of which detainers have been lodged against the prisoner from the state to whose prosecuting official the request for final disposition is specifically directed. The warden, commissioner of corrections, or other official having custody of the prisoner shall forthwith notify all appropriate prosecuting officers and courts in the several jurisdictions within the state to which the prisoner's request for final disposition is being sent of the proceeding being initiated by the prisoner. Any notification sent pursuant to this paragraph shall be accompanied by copies of the prisoner's written notice, request, and the certificate. If trial is not had on any indictment, information, or complaint contemplated hereby prior to the return of the prisoner to the original place of imprisonment, such indictment, information, or complaint shall not be of any further force or effect, and the court shall enter an order dismissing the same with prejudice.

(e) Any request for final disposition made by a prisoner pursuant to Paragraph (a) hereof shall also be deemed to be a waiver of extradition with respect to any charge or proceeding contemplated thereby or included therein by reason of Paragraph (d) hereof, and a waiver of extradition to the receiving state to serve any sentence there imposed upon him after completion of his term of imprisonment in the sending state. The request for final disposition shall also constitute a consent by the prisoner to the production of his body in any court where his presence may be required in order to effectuate the purposes of this agreement and a further consent voluntarily to be returned to the original place of imprisonment in accordance with the provisions of this agreement. Nothing in this paragraph shall prevent the imposition of a concurrent sentence if otherwise permitted by law.

(f) Escape from custody by the prisoner subsequent to his execution of the request for final disposition referred to in Paragraph (a) hereof shall void the request.

ARTICLE IV.

(a) The appropriate officer of the jurisdiction in which an untried indictment, information, or complaint is pending shall be entitled to have a prisoner against whom he has lodged a detainer and who is serving a term of imprisonment in any party state made available in accordance with Paragraph (a) of Article V hereof upon presentation of a written request for temporary custody or availability to the appropriate authorities of the state in which the prisoner is incarcerated; provided that the court having jurisdiction of such indictment, information, or complaint shall have duly approved, recorded, and transmitted the request; and provided further that there shall be a period of 30 days after receipt by the appropriate authorities before the request be honored, within which period the governor of the sending state may disapprove the request for temporary custody or availability, either upon his own motion or upon motion of the prisoner.

(b) Upon receipt of the officer's written request as provided in Paragraph (a) hereof, the appropriate authorities having the prisoner in custody shall furnish the officer with a certificate stating the term of commitment under which the prisoner is being held, the time already served, the time remaining to be served on the sentence, the amount of good time earned, the time of parole eligibility of the prisoner, and any decisions of the state parole agency relating to the prisoner. Said authorities simultaneously shall furnish all other officers and appropriate courts in the receiving state who have lodged detainers against the prisoner with similar certificates and with notices informing them of the request for custody or availability and of the reasons therefor.

(c) In respect of any proceeding made possible by this article, trial shall be commenced within 120 days of the arrival of the prisoner in the receiving state, but for good cause shown in open court, the prisoner or his counsel being present, the court having jurisdiction of the matter may grant any necessary or reasonable continuance.

(d) Nothing contained in this article shall be construed to deprive any prisoner of any right which he may have to contest the legality of his delivery as provided in Paragraph (a) hereof, but such delivery may not be opposed or denied on the ground that the executing authority of the sending state has not affirmatively consented to or ordered such delivery.

(e) If trial is not had on any indictment, information, or complaint contemplated hereby prior to the prisoner's being returned to the original place of imprisonment pursuant to Paragraph (e) of Article V hereof, such indictment, information, or complaint shall not be of any further force or effect, and the court shall enter an order dismissing the same with prejudice.

ARTICLE V.

(a) In response to a request made under Article III or Article IV hereof, the appropriate authority in a sending state shall offer to deliver temporary custody of such prisoner to the appropriate authority in the state where such indictment, information, or complaint is pending against such person in order that speedy and efficient prosecution may be had. If the request for final disposition is made by the prisoner, the offer of temporary custody shall accompany the written notice provided for in Article III of this agreement. In the case of a federal prisoner, the appropriate authority in the receiving state shall be entitled to temporary custody as provided by this agreement or to the prisoner's presence in federal custody at the place of trial, whichever custodial arrangement may be approved by the custodian.

(b) The officer or other representative of a state accepting an offer of temporary custody shall present the following upon demand:

(1) proper identification and evidence of his authority to act for the state into whose temporary custody this prisoner is to be given;

(2) a duly certified copy of the indictment, information, or complaint on the basis of which the detainer has been lodged and on the basis of which the request for temporary custody of the prisoner has been made.

(c) If the appropriate authority shall refuse or fail to accept temporary custody of said person, or in the event that an action on the indictment, information, or complaint on the basis of which the detainer has been lodged is not brought to trial within the period provided in Article III or Article IV hereof, the appropriate court of the jurisdiction where the indictment, information, or complaint has been pending shall enter an order dismissing the same with prejudice, and any detainer based thereon shall cease to be of any force or effect.

(d) The temporary custody referred to in this agreement shall be only for the purpose of permitting prosecution on the charge or charges contained in one or more untried indictments, informations, or complaints which form the basis of the detainer or detainers or for prosecution on any other charge or charges arising out of the same transaction. Except for his attendance at court and while being transported to or from any place at which his presence may be required, the prisoner shall be held in a suitable jail or other facility regularly used for persons awaiting prosecution.

(e) At the earliest practicable time consonant with the purposes of this agreement, the prisoner shall be returned to the sending state.

(f) During the continuance of temporary custody or while the prisoner is otherwise being made available for trial as required by this agreement, time being served on the sentence shall continue to run but good time shall be earned by the prisoner only if, and to the extent that, the law and practice of the jurisdiction which imposed the sentence may allow.

(g) For all purposes other than that for which temporary custody as provided in this agreement is exercised, the prisoner shall be deemed to remain in the custody of and subject to the jurisdiction of the sending state and any escape from temporary custody may be dealt with in the same manner as an escape from the original place of imprisonment or in any other manner permitted by law.

(h) From the time that a party state receives custody of a prisoner pursuant to this agreement until such prisoner is returned to the territory and custody of the sending state, the state in which the one or more untried indictments, informations, or complaints are pending or in which trial is being had shall be responsible for the prisoner and shall also pay all costs of transporting, caring for, keeping, and returning the prisoner. The provisions of this paragraph shall govern unless the states concerned shall have entered into a supplementary agreement providing for a different allocation of costs and responsibilities as between or among themselves. Nothing herein contained shall be construed to alter or affect any internal relationship among the departments, agencies, and officers of and in the government of a party state, or between a party state and its subdivisions, as to the payment of costs, or responsibilities therefor.

ARTICLE VI.

(a) In determining the duration and expiration dates of the time periods provided in Articles III and IV of this agreement, the running of said time periods shall be tolled whenever and for as long as the prisoner is unable to stand trial, as determined by the court having jurisdiction of the matter.

(b) No provision of this agreement, and no remedy made available by this agreement shall apply to any person who is adjudged to be mentally ill.

ARTICLE VII.

Each state party to this agreement shall designate an officer who, acting jointly with like officers of other party states, shall promulgate rules and regulations to carry out more effectively the terms and provisions of this agreement, and who shall provide, within and without the state, information necessary to the effective operation of this agreement.

ARTICLE VIII.

This agreement shall enter into full force and effect as to a party state when such state has enacted the same into law. A state party to this agreement may withdraw herefrom by enacting a statute repealing the same. However, the withdrawal of any state shall not affect the status of any proceedings already initiated by inmates or by state officers at the time such withdrawal takes effect, nor shall it affect their rights in respect thereof.

ARTICLE IX.

(a) This agreement shall be liberally construed so as to effectuate its purposes. The provisions of this agreement shall be severable and if any phrase, clause, sentence, or provision of this agreement is declared to be contrary to the constitution of any party state or of the United States or the applicability thereof to any government, agency, person, or circumstance is held invalid, the validity of the remainder of this agreement and the applicability thereof to any government, agency, person, or circumstance shall not be affected thereby. If this agreement shall be held contrary to the constitution of any state party hereto, the agreement shall remain in full force and effect as to the remaining states and in full force and effect as to the state affected as to all severable matters.

(b) As used in this article, "appropriate court" means a court of record with criminal jurisdiction.

(c) All courts, departments, agencies, officers, and employees of this state and its political subdivisions are hereby directed to enforce this article and to cooperate with one another and with other party states in enforcing the agreement and effectuating its purpose.

(d) Any prisoner escapes from lawful custody while in another state as a result of the application of this article shall be punished as though such escape had occurred within this state.

(e) The governor is empowered to designate the officer who will serve as central administrator of and information agent for the agreement on detainers pursuant to the provisions of Article VII hereof.

(f) Copies of this article, upon its enactment, shall be transmitted to the governor of each state, the Attorney General and the Secretary of State of the United States, and the council of state governments.

Added by Acts 1975, 64th Leg., p. 920, ch. 343, § 1, eff. June 19, 1975.

CHAPTER 52. COURT OF INQUIRY

Art. 52.01. Courts of Inquiry conducted by district judges

(a) When a judge of any district court of this state, acting in his capacity as magistrate, has probable cause to believe that an offense has been committed against the laws of this state, he may request that the presiding judge of the administrative judicial district appoint a district judge to commence a Court of Inquiry. The judge, who shall be appointed in accordance with Subsection (b), may summon and examine any witness in relation to the offense in accordance with the rules hereinafter provided, which procedure is defined as a "Court of Inquiry".

(b)(1) Before requesting the presiding judge to appoint a district judge to commence a Court of Inquiry, a judge must enter into the minutes of his court a sworn affidavit stating the substantial facts establishing probable cause that a specific offense has been committed against the laws of this state.

(2) After the affidavit has been entered into the minutes of his court and a copy filed with the district clerk, the judge shall request the presiding judge of the administrative judicial district in which the affidavit is filed to appoint a judge to commence the Court of Inquiry. The judge appointed to commence the Court of Inquiry shall issue a written order commencing the Court of Inquiry and stating its scope. The presiding judge shall not name the judge who requests the Court of Inquiry to preside over the Court of Inquiry.

(c) The district or county attorney of the district or county in which the Court of Inquiry is held shall assist the district judge in conducting the Court of Inquiry. The attorney shall examine witnesses and evidence admitted before the court to determine if an offense has been committed and shall render other assistance to the judge as is necessary in the proceeding.

(d) If the Court of Inquiry pertains to the activities of the district or county attorney or to the attorney's office, deputies, or employees, or if the attorney is otherwise disqualified in the proceeding, the judge shall appoint one attorney pro tem to assist in the proceeding. In any other circumstance, the judge may appoint an attorney pro tem to assist in the proceeding.

(e) If more than one Court of Inquiry is commenced which pertains to the activities of a state governmental entity or public servant thereof, then, upon motion of the state governmental entity or public servant, made to the presiding judge or judges of the administrative judicial region or regions where the Courts of Inquiry have been commenced, the presiding judge or judges shall transfer the Courts of Inquiry to the presiding administrative judge of Travis County. The presiding administrative judge of Travis County shall consolidate the Courts of Inquiry for further proceedings and shall assign a district judge to preside over the consolidated Courts of Inquiry.

Acts 1965, 59th Leg., vol. 2, p. 317, ch. 722: Amended by Acts 1967, 60th Leg., p. 1751, ch. 659, § 34, eff. Aug. 28, 1967; Acts 1987, 70th Leg., ch. 534, § 1, eff. Sept. 1, 1987. Acts 1995, 74th Leg., ch. 318, § 65, eff. Sept. 1, 1995.

Art. 52.02. Evidence; deposition; affidavits

At the hearing at a Court of Inquiry, evidence may be taken orally or by deposition, or, in the discretion of the judge, by affidavit. If affidavits are admitted, any witness against whom they may bear has the right to propound written interrogatories to the affiants or to file answering affidavits. The judge in hearing such evidence, at his discretion, may conclude not to sustain objections to all or to any portion of the evidence taken nor exclude same; but any of the witnesses or attorneys engaged in taking the testimony may have any objections they make recorded with the testimony and reserved for the action of any court in which such evidence is thereafter sought to be admitted, but such court is not confined to objections made at the taking of the testimony at the Court of Inquiry. Without restricting the foregoing, the judge may allow the introduction of any documentary or real evidence which he deems reliable, and the testimony adduced before any grand jury.

Acts 1965, 59th Leg., vol. 2, p. 317, ch. 722. Amended by Acts 1967, 60th Leg., p. 1751, ch. 659, § 35, eff. Aug. 28, 1967.

Art. 52.03. Subpoenas

The judge or his clerk has power to issue subpoenas which may be served within the same territorial limits as subpoenas issued in felony prosecutions or to summon witnesses before grand juries in this state.

Acts 1965, 59th Leg., vol. 2, p. 317, ch. 722. Amended by Acts 1967, 60th Leg., p. 1751, ch. 659, § 36, eff. Aug. 28, 1967.

Art. 52.04. Rights of witnesses

(a) All witnesses testifying in any Court of Inquiry have the same rights as to testifying as do defendants in felony prosecutions in this state. Before any witness is sworn to testify in any Court of Inquiry, he shall be instructed by the judge that he is entitled to counsel; that he cannot be forced to testify against himself; and that such testimony may be taken down and used against him in a later trial or trials ensuing from the instant Court of Inquiry. Any witness or his counsel has the right to fully cross-examine any of the witnesses whose testimony bears in any manner against him.

(b) If the Court of Inquiry pertains to the activities of a state governmental entity or its officers or employees, the officers and employees of that state governmental entity shall be indemnified for attorney's fees incurred as a result of exercising the employees' or officers' right to counsel under Subsection (a) if:

(1) the officer or employee is found not guilty after a trial or appeal or the complaint, information, or indictment is dismissed without a plea of guilty or nolo contendere being entered; and

(2) the judge commencing the Court of Inquiry, or the judge to whom the Court of Inquiry was transferred pursuant to Article 52.01(e), determines that the complaint, information, or indictment presented against the person was dismissed because:

(A) the presentment was made on mistake, false information, or other similar basis, indicating absence of probable cause to believe, at the time of dismissal, the person committed the offense; or

(B) the complaint, information, or indictment was void.

(c) The county in which the affidavit under Article 52.01 was filed shall be responsible for any attorney's fees awarded under Subsection (b).

Acts 1965, 59th Leg., vol. 2, p. 317, ch. 722. Amended by Acts 1967, 60th Leg., p. 1751, ch. 659, § 37, eff. Aug. 28, 1967; Acts 1995, 74th Leg., ch. 318, § 66, eff. Sept. 1, 1995.

Art. 52.05. Witness must testify

A person may be compelled to give testimony or produce evidence when legally called upon to do so at any Court of Inquiry; however, if any person refuses or declines to testify or produce evidence on the ground that it may incriminate him under laws of this state, then the judge may, in his discretion, compel such person to testify or produce evidence but the person shall not be prosecuted or subjected to any penalty or forfeiture for, or on account of, any transaction, matter or thing concerning which he may be compelled to testify or produce evidence at such Court of Inquiry.

Acts 1965, 59th Leg., vol. 2, p. 317, ch. 722. Amended by Acts 1967, 60th Leg., p. 1751, ch. 659, § 38, eff. Aug. 28, 1967.

Art. 52.06. Contempt

Contempt of court in a Court of Inquiry may be punished by a fine not exceeding One Hundred Dollars ($100.00) and any witness refusing to testify may be attached and imprisoned until he does testify.

Acts 1965, 59th Leg., vol. 2, p. 317, ch. 722.

Art. 52.07. Stenographic record; public hearing

All evidence taken at a Court of Inquiry shall be transcribed by the court reporter and all proceedings shall be open to the public.

Acts 1965, 59th Leg., vol. 2, p. 317, ch. 722.

Art. 52.08. Criminal prosecutions

If it appear from a Court of Inquiry or any testimony adduced therein, that an offense has been committed, the Judge shall issue a warrant for the arrest of the offender as if complaint had been made and filed.

Acts 1965, 59th Leg., vol. 2, p. 317, ch. 722.

Art. 52.09. Costs and attorney's fees

(a) All costs incurred in conducting a Court of Inquiry, including compensation of an attorney pro tem, shall be borne by the county in which said Court of Inquiry is conducted; provided, however, that where the Attorney General of Texas has submitted a request in writing to the judge for the holding of such Court of Inquiry, then and in that event the costs shall be borne by the State of Texas and shall be taxed to the attorney general and paid in the same manner and from the same funds as other court costs.

(b) Assistance by a county or district attorney to a Court of Inquiry is a duty of the attorney's office, and the attorney may not receive a fee for the service. A county is not liable for attorney's fees claimed for assistance in a Court of Inquiry by any attorney other than an attorney pro tem appointed under Article 52.01(d) of this code.

(c) An attorney pro tem appointed under Article 52.01(d) of this code is entitled to compensation in the same manner as an attorney pro tem appointed under Article 2.07 of this code. The district judge shall set the compensation of the attorney pro tem based on the sworn testimony of the attorney or other evidence that is given in open court.

Acts 1965, 59th Leg., vol. 2, p. 317, ch. 722. Amended by Acts 1967, 60th Leg., p. 1752, ch. 659, § 39, eff. Aug. 28, 1967; Acts 1987, 70th Leg., ch. 534, § 1, eff. Sept. 1, 1987.

CHAPTER 53. COSTS AND FEES [REPEALED]

Art. 53.01. Repealed by Acts 1987, 70th Leg., ch. 167, § 4.01(b), eff. Sept. 1, 1987

Art. 53.02. Repealed by Acts 1985, 69th Leg., ch. 269, § 5(1), eff. Sept. 1, 1985

Arts. 53.03 to 53.06. Repealed by Acts 1987, 70th Leg., ch. 167, § 4.01(b), eff. Sept. 1, 1987

Art. 53.07. Repealed by Acts 1985, 69th Leg., ch. 269, § 5(1), eff. Sept. 1, 1985

Art. 53.08. Repealed by Acts 1987, 70th Leg., ch. 167, § 4.01(b), eff. Sept. 1, 1987

Art. 53.09. Repealed by Acts 1987, 70th Leg., ch. 167, § 4.01(b), eff. Sept. 1, 1987

Art. 53.10. [Blank]

Art. 53.11. Renumbered from art. 53.08 by Acts 1987, 70th Leg., ch. 167, § 5.01(a)(10), eff. Sept. 1, 1987

CHAPTER 54. MISCELLANEOUS PROVISIONS

Article
54.01. Severability Clause.
54.02. Repealing Clause.
54.03. Emergency Clause.

Art. 54.01. Severability Clause

If any provision, section or clause of this Act or application thereof to any person or circumstances is held invalid, such invalidity shall not affect other provisions or applications hereof which can be given effect without the invalid provision, section or clause, and to this end the provisions of this Act are declared to be severable.

Acts 1965, 59th Leg., vol. 2, p. 317, ch. 722.

Art. 54.02. Repealing Clause

Sec. 1. (a) Except as otherwise provided in this Article 54.02, all laws relating to criminal procedure in this State that are not embraced, incorporated, or included in this Act and that have not been enacted during the Regular Session of the 59th Legislature are repealed.

(b) None of the following articles of the Code of Criminal Procedure of Texas, 1925, in force on the effective date of this Act, is repealed: 52; 52–1 through 52–161, both inclusive; 367D through 367K, both inclusive; 781B–1, 781B–2; 944 through 951, both inclusive; 1009 through 1035, both inclusive; 1037 through 1056, both inclusive; 1058 through 1064, both inclusive; and 1075 through 1082, both inclusive.

Sec. 2. (a) All laws and parts of laws relating to criminal procedure omitted from this Act have been intentionally omitted, and all additions to and changes in such procedure have been intentionally made. This Act shall be construed to be an independent Act of the Legislature, enacted under its caption, and the articles contained in this Act, as revised, rewritten, changed, combined, and codified, may not be construed as a continuation of former laws except as otherwise provided in this Act. The existing statutes of the Revised Civil Statutes of Texas, 1925, as amended, and of the Penal Code of Texas, 1925, as amended, which contain special or specific provisions of criminal procedure covering specific instances are not repealed by this Act.

(b) A person under recognizance or bond on the effective date of this Act continues under such recognizance or bond pending final disposition of any action pending against him.

Acts 1965, 59th Leg., vol. 2, p. 317, ch. 722.

Art. 54.03. Emergency Clause

The fact that the laws relating to criminal procedure in this State have not been completely revised and re-codified in more than a century past and the further fact that the administration of justice, in the field of criminal law, has undergone changes, through judicial construction and interpretation of constitutional provisions, which have been, in certain instances, modified or nullified, as the case may be, necessitates important changes requiring the revision or modernization of the laws relating to criminal procedure, and the further fact that it is desirous and desirable to strengthen, and to conform, various provisions in such laws to current interpretation and application, emphasizes the importance of this legislation and all of which, together with the crowded condition of the calendar in both Houses, create an emergency and an imperative public necessity that the Constitutional Rule requiring bills to be read on three several days be suspended, and said Rule is hereby suspended, and that this Act shall take effect and be in force and effect from and after 12 o'clock Meridian on the 1st day of January, Anno Domini, 1966, and it is so enacted.

Acts 1965, 59th Leg., vol. 2, p. 317, ch. 722.

CHAPTER 55. EXPUNCTION OF CRIMINAL RECORDS

Art. 55.01. Right to Expunction

(a) A person who has been placed under a custodial or noncustodial arrest for commission of either a felony or misdemeanor is entitled to have all records and files relating to the arrest expunged if:

(1) the person is tried for the offense for which the person was arrested and is:

(A) acquitted by the trial court, except as provided by Subsection (c); or

(B) convicted and subsequently:

(i) pardoned for a reason other than that described by Subparagraph (ii); or

(ii) pardoned or otherwise granted relief on the basis of actual innocence with respect to that offense, if the applicable pardon or court order clearly indicates on its face that the pardon or order was granted or rendered on the basis of the person's actual innocence; or

(2) the person has been released and the charge, if any, has not resulted in a final conviction and is no longer pending and there was no court-ordered community supervision under Chapter 42A for the offense, unless the offense is a Class C misdemeanor, provided that:

(A) regardless of whether any statute of limitations exists for the offense and whether any limitations period for the offense has expired, an indictment or information charging the person with the commission of a misdemeanor offense based on the person's arrest or charging the person with the commission of any felony offense arising out of the same transaction for which the person was arrested:

(i) has not been presented against the person at any time following the arrest, and:

(a) at least 180 days have elapsed from the date of arrest if the arrest for which the expunction was sought was for an offense punishable as a Class C misdemeanor and if there was no felony charge arising out of the same transaction for which the person was arrested;

(b) at least one year has elapsed from the date of arrest if the arrest for which the expunction was sought was for an offense punishable as a Class B or A misdemeanor and if there was no felony charge arising out of the same transaction for which the person was arrested;

(c) at least three years have elapsed from the date of arrest if the arrest for which the expunction was sought was for an offense punishable as a felony or if there was a felony charge arising out of the same transaction for which the person was arrested; or

(d) the attorney representing the state certifies that the applicable arrest records and files are not needed for use in any criminal investigation or prosecution, including an investigation or prosecution of another person; or

(ii) if presented at any time following the arrest, was dismissed or quashed, and the court finds that the indictment or information was dismissed or quashed because:

(a) the person completed a veterans treatment court program created under Chapter 124, Government Code, or former law, subject to Subsection (a–3);

(b) the person completed a pretrial intervention program authorized under Section 76.011, Government

Code, other than a veterans treatment court program created under Chapter 124, Government Code, or former law;

(c) the presentment had been made because of mistake, false information, or other similar reason indicating absence of probable cause at the time of the dismissal to believe the person committed the offense; or

(d) the indictment or information was void; or

(B) prosecution of the person for the offense for which the person was arrested is no longer possible because the limitations period has expired.

(a–1) Notwithstanding any other provision of this article, a person may not expunge records and files relating to an arrest that occurs pursuant to a warrant issued under Article 42A.751(b).

(a–2) Notwithstanding any other provision of this article, a person who intentionally or knowingly absconds from the jurisdiction after being released under Chapter 17 following an arrest is not eligible under Subsection (a)(2)(A)(i)(a), (b), or (c) or Subsection (a)(2)(B) for an expunction of the records and files relating to that arrest.

(a–3) A person is eligible under Subsection (a)(2)(A)(ii)(a) for an expunction of arrest records and files only if:

(1) the person has not previously received an expunction of arrest records and files under that subsubparagraph; and

(2) the person submits to the court an affidavit attesting to that fact.

(b) Except as provided by Subsection (c) and subject to Subsection (b–1), a district court, a justice court, or a municipal court of record may expunge all records and files relating to the arrest of a person under the procedure established under Article 55.02 if:

(1) the person is:

(A) tried for the offense for which the person was arrested;

(B) convicted of the offense; and

(C) acquitted by the court of criminal appeals or, if the period for granting a petition for discretionary review has expired, by a court of appeals; or

(2) an office of the attorney representing the state authorized by law to prosecute the offense for which the person was arrested recommends the expunction to the court before the person is tried for the offense, regardless of whether an indictment or information has been presented against the person in relation to the offense.

(b–1) A justice court or a municipal court of record may only expunge records and files under Subsection (b) that relate to the arrest of a person for an offense punishable by fine only.

(c) A court may not order the expunction of records and files relating to an arrest for an offense for which a person is subsequently acquitted, whether by the trial court, a court of appeals, or the court of criminal appeals, if the offense for which the person was acquitted arose out of a criminal episode, as defined by Section 3.01, Penal Code, and the person was convicted of or remains subject to prosecution for at least one other offense occurring during the criminal episode.

(d) A person is entitled to obtain the expunction of any information that identifies the person, including the person's name, address, date of birth, driver's license number, and social security number, contained in records and files relating to the person's arrest or the arrest of another person if:

(1) the expunction of identifying information is sought with respect to the arrest of the person asserting the entitlement and the person was arrested solely as a result of identifying information that was inaccurate due to a clerical error; or

(2) the expunction of identifying information is sought with respect to the arrest of a person other than the person asserting the entitlement and:

(A) the information identifying the person asserting the entitlement was falsely given by the arrested person as the arrested person's identifying information without the consent of the person asserting the entitlement; and

(B) the only reason why the identifying information of the person asserting the entitlement is contained in the applicable arrest records and files is because of the deception of the arrested person.

Added by Acts 1977, 65th Leg., p. 1880, ch. 747, § 1, eff. Aug. 29, 1977. Amended by Acts 1979, 66th Leg., p. 1333, ch. 604, § 1, eff. Aug. 27, 1979; Acts 1989, 71st Leg., ch. 803, § 1, eff. Sept. 1, 1989; Acts 1991, 72nd Leg., ch. 14, § 284(53), eff. Sept. 1, 1991; Acts 1993, 73rd Leg., ch. 900, § 7.02(a), eff. Sept. 1, 1993; Acts 1999, 76th Leg., ch. 1236, § 1, eff. Aug. 30, 1999; Acts 2001, 77th Leg., ch. 945, § 1, eff. June 14, 2001; Acts 2001, 77th Leg., ch. 1021, § 1, eff. Sept. 1, 2001; Acts 2003, 78th Leg., ch. 1236, § 1, eff. Sept. 1, 2003; Acts 2005, 79th Leg., ch. 1309, § 1, eff. Sept. 1, 2005; Acts 2009, 81st Leg., ch. 840, § 5, eff. June 19, 2009; Acts 2009, 81st Leg., ch. 1103, § 17(b), eff. Sept. 1, 2009; Acts 2011, 82nd Leg., ch. 690 (H.B. 351), § 1, eff. Sept. 1, 2011; Acts 2011, 82nd Leg., ch. 894 (S.B. 462), § 1, eff. Sept. 1, 2011; Acts 2015, 84th Leg., ch. 770 (H.B. 2299), § 2.23, eff. Jan. 1, 2017; Acts 2017, 85th Leg., ch. 693 (H.B. 322), § 1, eff. Sept. 1, 2017; Acts 2017, 85th Leg., ch. 1062 (H.B. 3147), § 1, eff. Sept. 1, 2017; Acts 2017, 85th Leg., ch. 1149 (H.B. 557), § 1, eff. Sept. 1, 2017.

Sections 6 and 7 of Acts 2017, 85th Leg., ch. 693 (H.B. 322) provide:

"Sec. 6.   (a) Except as provided by Subsection (b) of this section, this Act applies to the expunction of arrest records and files for a person who successfully completes a veterans treatment court program under Chapter 124, Government Code, or former law before, on, or after the effective date [Sept. 1, 2017] of this Act, regardless of when the underlying arrest occurred.

"(b) The change in law made by this Act to Article 102.006, Code of Criminal Procedure, applies to the fees charged or costs assessed for an expunction order entered on or after the effective date of this Act, regardless of whether the underlying arrest occurred before, on, or after the effective date of this Act.

"(c) For a person who is entitled to expunction under Article 55.01(a)(2)(A)(ii)(a), Code of Criminal Procedure, as amended by this Act, based on a successful completion of a veterans treatment court program under Chapter 124, Government Code, or former law before the effective date of this Act, notwithstanding the 30-day time limit provided for the court to enter an automatic order of expunction under Section 1a(a–1), Article 55.02, Code of Criminal Procedure, as added by this Act, the court may, with the consent of the attorney representing the state, enter an order of expunction for the person as soon as practicable after the court receives written notice from any party to the case about the person's entitlement to the expunction.

"Sec. 7.   The change in law made by this Act applies to a person whose conviction for an offense is set aside under Article 42A.701, Code of Criminal Procedure, on or after the effective date [Sept. 1, 2017] of this Act, regardless of when the person committed the offense for which the person was convicted."

Section 3 of Acts 2017, 85th Leg., ch. 1062 (H.B. 3147) provides:

"This Act applies to the expunction of arrest records and files for a person whose entitlement to expunction under Article 55.01(d), Code of Criminal Procedure, as amended by this Act, arises before, on, or after the effective date [Sept. 1, 2017] of this Act, regardless of when the underlying arrest occurred."

Section 10(a) of Acts 2017, 85th Leg., ch. 1149 (H.B. 557) provides:

"(a) Except as otherwise provided by this section, this Act applies to an expunction of records and files relating to any criminal offense that occurred before, on, or after the effective date [Sept. 1, 2017] of this Act."

Art. 55.011.   Right of Close Relative to Seek Expunction on Behalf of Deceased Person

(a) In this article, "close relative of a deceased person" means the grandparent, parent, spouse, or adult brother, sister, or child of a deceased person.

(b) A close relative of a deceased person who, if not deceased, would be entitled to expunction of records and files under Article 55.01 may file on behalf of the deceased person an ex parte petition for expunction under Section 2 or 2a, Article 55.02. If the court finds that the deceased person would be entitled to expunction of any record or file that is the subject of the petition, the court shall enter an order directing expunction.

Added by Acts 2009, 81st Leg., ch. 659, § 1, eff. June 19, 2009.

Art. 55.02.   Procedure for Expunction

Sec. 1.   At the request of the acquitted person and after notice to the state, or at the request of the attorney for the state with the consent of the acquitted person, the trial court presiding over the case in which the person was acquitted, if the trial court is a district court, a justice court, or a municipal court of record, or a district court in the county in which the trial court is located shall enter an order of expunction for a person entitled to expunction under Article 55.01(a)(1)(A) not later than the 30th day after the date of the acquittal. On acquittal, the trial court shall advise the acquitted person of the right to expunction. The party requesting the order of expunction shall provide to the court all of the information required in a petition for expunction under Section 2(b). The attorney for the acquitted person in the case in which the person was acquitted, if the person was represented by counsel, or the attorney for the state, if the person was not represented by counsel or if the attorney for the state requested the order of expunction, shall prepare the order for the court's signature.

Sec. 1a.   (a) The trial court presiding over a case in which a person is convicted and subsequently granted relief or pardoned on the basis of actual innocence of the offense of which the person was convicted, if the trial court is a district court, a justice court, or a municipal court of record, or a district court in the county in which the trial court is located shall enter an order of expunction for a person entitled to expunction under Article 55.01(a)(1)(B)(ii) not later than the 30th day after the date the court receives notice of the pardon or other grant of relief. The person shall provide to the court all of the information required in a petition for expunction under Section 2(b).

(a–1) A trial court dismissing a case following a person's successful completion of a veterans treatment court program created under Chapter 124, Government Code, or former law, if the trial court is a district court, or a district court in the county in which the trial court is located may, with the consent of the attorney representing the state, enter an order of expunction for a person entitled to expunction under Article 55.01(a)(2)(A)(ii)(a) not later than the 30th day after the date the court dismisses the case or receives the information regarding that dismissal, as applicable. Notwithstanding any other law, a court that enters an order for expunction under this subsection may not charge any fee or assess any cost for the expunction.

(b) The attorney for the state shall:

(1) prepare an expunction order under this section for the court's signature; and

(2) notify the Texas Department of Criminal Justice if the person is in the custody of the department.

(c) The court shall include in an expunction order under this section a listing of each official, agency, or other entity of this state or political subdivision of this state and each private entity that there is reason to believe has any record or file that is subject to the order. The court shall also provide in an expunction order under this section that:

(1) the Texas Department of Criminal Justice shall send to the court the documents delivered to the department under Section 8(a), Article 42.09; and

(2) the Department of Public Safety and the Texas Department of Criminal Justice shall delete or redact, as appropriate, from their public records all index references to the records and files that are subject to the expunction order.

(d) The court shall retain all documents sent to the court under Subsection (c)(1) until the statute of limitations has run for any civil case or proceeding relating to the wrongful imprisonment of the person subject to the expunction order.

Sec. 2. (a) A person who is entitled to expunction of records and files under Article 55.01(a)(1)(A), 55.01(a)(1)(B)(i), or 55.01(a)(2) or a person who is eligible for expunction of records and files under Article 55.01(b) may file an ex parte petition for expunction in a district court for the county in which:

(1) the petitioner was arrested; or

(2) the offense was alleged to have occurred.

(a–1) If the arrest for which expunction is sought is for an offense punishable by fine only, a person who is entitled to expunction of records and files under Article 55.01(a) or a person who is eligible for expunction of records and files under Article 55.01(b) may file an ex parte petition for expunction in a justice court or a municipal court of record in the county in which:

(1) the petitioner was arrested; or

(2) the offense was alleged to have occurred.

(b) A petition filed under Subsection (a) or (a–1) must be verified and must include the following or an explanation for why one or more of the following is not included:

(1) the petitioner's:

(A) full name;

(B) sex;

(C) race;

(D) date of birth;

(E) driver's license number;

(F) social security number; and

(G) address at the time of the arrest;

(2) the offense charged against the petitioner;

(3) the date the offense charged against the petitioner was alleged to have been committed;

(4) the date the petitioner was arrested;

(5) the name of the county where the petitioner was arrested and if the arrest occurred in a municipality, the name of the municipality;

(6) the name of the agency that arrested the petitioner;

(7) the case number and court of offense; and

(8) together with the applicable physical or e-mail addresses, a list of all:

(A) law enforcement agencies, jails or other detention facilities, magistrates, courts, prosecuting attorneys, correctional facilities, central state depositories of criminal records, and other officials or agencies or other entities of this state or of any political subdivision of this state;

(B) central federal depositories of criminal records that the petitioner has reason to believe have records or files that are subject to expunction; and

(C) private entities that compile and disseminate for compensation criminal history record information that the petitioner has reason to believe have information related to records or files that are subject to expunction.

(c) The court shall set a hearing on the matter no sooner than thirty days from the filing of the petition and shall give to each official or agency or other governmental entity named in the petition reasonable notice of the hearing by:

(1) certified mail, return receipt requested; or

(2) secure electronic mail, electronic transmission, or facsimile transmission.

(c–1) An entity described by Subsection (c) may be represented by the attorney responsible for providing the entity with legal representation in other matters.

(d) If the court finds that the petitioner, or a person for whom an ex parte petition is filed under Subsection (e), is entitled to expunction of any records and files that are the subject of the petition, it shall enter an order directing expunction.

(e) The director of the Department of Public Safety or the director's authorized representative may file on behalf of a person described by Subsection (a) of this section or by Section 2a an ex parte petition for expunction in a district court for the county in which:

(1) the person was arrested; or

(2) the offense was alleged to have occurred.

(f) An ex parte petition filed under Subsection (e) must be verified and must include the following or an explanation for why one or more of the following is not included:

(1) the person's:

(A) full name;

(B) sex;

(C) race;

(D) date of birth;

(E) driver's license number;

(F) social security number; and

(G) address at the time of the arrest;

(2) the offense charged against the person;

(3) the date the offense charged against the person was alleged to have been committed;

(4) the date the person was arrested;

(5) the name of the county where the person was arrested and if the arrest occurred in a municipality, the name of the municipality;

(6) the name of the agency that arrested the person;

(7) the case number and court of offense; and

(8) together with the applicable physical or e-mail addresses, a list of all:

(A) law enforcement agencies, jails or other detention facilities, magistrates, courts, prosecuting attorneys, correctional facilities, central state depositories of criminal records, and other officials or agencies or other entities of this state or of any political subdivision of this state;

(B) central federal depositories of criminal records that the person has reason to believe have records or files that are subject to expunction; and

(C) private entities that compile and disseminate for compensation criminal history record information that the person has reason to believe have information relating to records or files that are subject to expunction.

Sec. 2a. (a) A person who is entitled to expunction of information contained in records and files under Article 55.01(d) may file an application for expunction with the attorney representing the state in the prosecution of felonies in the county in which the person resides.

(b) The application must be verified, include authenticated fingerprint records of the applicant, and include the following or an explanation for why one or more of the following is not included:

(1) the applicant's full name, sex, race, date of birth, driver's license number, social security number, and address at the time of the applicable arrest;

(2) the following information regarding the arrest:

(A) the date of arrest;

(B) the offense charged against the person arrested;

(C) the name of the county or municipality in which the arrest occurred; and

(D) the name of the arresting agency; and

(3) a statement, as appropriate, that the applicant:

(A) was arrested solely as a result of identifying information that was inaccurate due to a clerical error; or

(B) is not the person arrested and for whom the arrest records and files were created and did not give the arrested person consent to falsely identify himself or herself as the applicant.

(c) After verifying the allegations in an application received under Subsection (a), the attorney representing the state shall:

(1) include on the application information regarding the arrest that was requested of the applicant but was unknown by the applicant;

(2) forward a copy of the application to the district court for the county;

(3) together with the applicable physical or e-mail addresses, attach to the copy a list of all:

(A) law enforcement agencies, jails or other detention facilities, magistrates, courts, prosecuting attorneys, correctional facilities, central state depositories of criminal records, and other officials or agencies or other entities of this state or of any political subdivision of this state;

(B) central federal depositories of criminal records that are reasonably likely to have records or files containing information that is subject to expunction; and

(C) private entities that compile and disseminate for compensation criminal history record information that are reasonably likely to have records or files containing information that is subject to expunction; and

(4) request the court to enter an order directing expunction based on an entitlement to expunction under Article 55.01(d).

(d) On receipt of a request under Subsection (c), the court shall, without holding a hearing on the matter, enter a final order directing expunction.

Sec. 3. (a) In an order of expunction issued under this article, the court shall require any state agency that sent information concerning the arrest to a central federal depository to request the depository to return all records and files subject to the order of expunction. The person who is the subject of the expunction order or an agency protesting the expunction may appeal the court's decision in the same manner as in other civil cases.

Text of 3(b) effective until January 1, 2019

(b) The order of expunction entered by the court shall have attached and incorporate by reference a copy of the judgment of acquittal and shall include:

(1) the following information on the person who is the subject of the expunction order:

(A) full name;

(B) sex;

(C) race;

(D) date of birth;

(E) driver's license number; and

(F) social security number;

(2) the offense charged against the person who is the subject of the expunction order;

(3) the date the person who is the subject of the expunction order was arrested;

(4) the case number and court of offense; and

(5) the tracking incident number (TRN) assigned to the individual incident of arrest under Article 60.07(b)(1) by the Department of Public Safety.

Text of 3(b) effective January 1, 2019

(b) The order of expunction entered by the court shall have attached and incorporate by reference a copy of the judgment of acquittal and shall include:

(1) the following information on the person who is the subject of the expunction order:

(A) full name;

(B) sex;

(C) race;

(D) date of birth;

(E) driver's license number; and

(F) social security number;

(2) the offense charged against the person who is the subject of the expunction order;

(3) the date the person who is the subject of the expunction order was arrested;

(4) the case number and court of offense; and

(5) the tracking incident number (TRN) assigned to the individual incident of arrest under Article 66.251(b)(1) by the Department of Public Safety.

(c) When the order of expunction is final, the clerk of the court shall send a certified copy of the order to the Crime Records Service of the Department of Public Safety and to each official or agency or other governmental entity of this state or of any political subdivision of this state named in the order. The certified copy of the order must be sent by secure electronic mail, electronic transmission, or facsimile transmission or otherwise by certified mail, return receipt requested. In sending the order to a governmental entity named in the order, the clerk may elect to substitute hand delivery for certified mail under this subsection, but the clerk must receive a receipt for that hand-delivered order.

(c–1) The Department of Public Safety shall notify any central federal depository of criminal records by any means, including secure electronic mail, electronic transmission, or facsimile transmission, of the order with an explanation of the effect of the order and a request that the depository, as appropriate, either:

(1) destroy or return to the court the records in possession of the depository that are subject to the order, including any information with respect to the order; or

(2) comply with Section 5(f) pertaining to information contained in records and files of a person entitled to expunction under Article 55.01(d).

(c–2) The Department of Public Safety shall also provide, by secure electronic mail, electronic transmission, or facsimile transmission, notice of the order to any private entity that is named in the order or that purchases criminal history record information from the department. The notice must include an explanation of the effect of the order and a request that the entity destroy any information in the possession of the entity that is subject to the order. The department may charge to a private entity that purchases criminal history record information from the department a fee in an amount sufficient to recover costs incurred by the department in providing notice under this subsection to the entity.

(d) Any returned receipts received by the clerk from notices of the hearing and copies of the order shall be maintained in the file on the proceedings under this chapter.

Sec. 4. (a) If the state establishes that the person who is the subject of an expunction order is still subject to conviction for an offense arising out of the transaction for which the person was arrested because the statute of limitations has not run and there is reasonable cause to believe that the state may proceed against the person for the offense, the court may provide in its expunction order that the law enforcement agency and the prosecuting attorney responsible for investigating the offense may retain any records and files that are necessary to the investigation.

(a–1) The court shall provide in its expunction order that the applicable law enforcement agency and prosecuting attorney may retain the arrest records and files of any person who becomes entitled to an expunction of those records and files based on the expiration of a period described by Article 55.01(a)(2)(A)(i)(a), (b), or (c), but without the certification of the prosecuting attorney as described by Article 55.01(a)(2)(A)(i)(d).

(a–2) In the case of a person who is the subject of an expunction order on the basis of an acquittal, the court may provide in the expunction order that the law enforcement agency and the prosecuting attorney retain records and files if:

(1) the records and files are necessary to conduct a subsequent investigation and prosecution of a person other than the person who is the subject of the expunction order; or

(2) the state establishes that the records and files are necessary for use in:

(A) another criminal case, including a prosecution, motion to adjudicate or revoke community supervision, parole revocation hearing, mandatory supervision revocation hearing, punishment hearing, or bond hearing; or

(B) a civil case, including a civil suit or suit for possession of or access to a child.

(b) Unless the person who is the subject of the expunction order is again arrested for or charged with an offense arising out of the transaction for which the person was arrested or unless the court provides for the retention of records and files under Subsection

(a–1) or (a–2), the provisions of Articles 55.03 and 55.04 apply to files and records retained under this section.

Sec. 5. (a) Except as provided by Subsections (f) and (g), on receipt of the order, each official or agency or other governmental entity named in the order shall:

(1) return all records and files that are subject to the expunction order to the court or in cases other than those described by Section 1a, if removal is impracticable, obliterate all portions of the record or file that identify the person who is the subject of the order and notify the court of its action; and

(2) delete from its public records all index references to the records and files that are subject to the expunction order.

(b) Except in the case of a person who is the subject of an expunction order on the basis of an acquittal or an expunction order based on an entitlement under Article 55.01(d), the court may give the person who is the subject of the order all records and files returned to it pursuant to its order.

(c) Except in the case of a person who is the subject of an expunction order based on an entitlement under Article 55.01(d) and except as provided by Subsection (g), if an order of expunction is issued under this article, the court records concerning expunction proceedings are not open for inspection by anyone except the person who is the subject of the order unless the order permits retention of a record under Section 4 of this article and the person is again arrested for or charged with an offense arising out of the transaction for which the person was arrested or unless the court provides for the retention of records and files under Section 4(a) of this article. The clerk of the court issuing the order shall obliterate all public references to the proceeding and maintain the files or other records in an area not open to inspection.

(d) Except in the case of a person who is the subject of an expunction order on the basis of an acquittal or an expunction order based on an entitlement under Article 55.01(d) and except as provided by Subsection (g), the clerk of the court shall destroy all the files or other records maintained under Subsection (c) not earlier than the 60th day after the date the order of expunction is issued or later than the first anniversary of that date unless the records or files were released under Subsection (b).

(d–1) Not later than the 30th day before the date on which the clerk destroys files or other records under Subsection (d), the clerk shall provide notice by mail, electronic mail, or facsimile transmission to the attorney representing the state in the expunction proceeding. If the attorney representing the state in the expunction proceeding objects to the destruction not later than the 20th day after receiving notice under this subsection, the clerk may not destroy the files or other records until the first anniversary of the date the order of expunction is issued or the first business day after that date.

(e) The clerk shall certify to the court the destruction of files or other records under Subsection (d) of this section.

(f) On receipt of an order granting expunction to a person entitled to expunction under Article 55.01(d), each official, agency, or other governmental entity named in the order:

(1) shall:

(A) obliterate all portions of the record or file that identify the petitioner; and

(B) substitute for all obliterated portions of the record or file any available information that identifies the person arrested; and

(2) may not return the record or file or delete index references to the record or file.

(g) Notwithstanding any other provision in this section, an official, agency, court, or other entity may retain receipts, invoices, vouchers, or similar records of financial transactions that arose from the expunction proceeding or prosecution of the underlying criminal cause in accordance with internal financial control procedures. An official, agency, court, or other entity that retains records under this subsection shall obliterate all portions of the record or the file that identify the person who is the subject of the expunction order.

Amended by Acts 1979, 66th Leg., p. 1333, ch. 604, § 1, eff. Aug. 27, 1979; Acts 1989, 71st Leg., ch. 803, §§ 2 to 4, eff. Sept. 1, 1989; Acts 1991, 72nd Leg., ch. 380, § 1, eff. Aug. 26, 1991; Acts 1999, 76th Leg., ch. 1236, § 2, eff. Aug. 30, 1999; Acts 2001, 77th Leg., ch. 945, § 2, 3, eff. June 14, 2001; Acts 2001, 77th Leg., ch. 1021, § 2, eff. Sept. 1, 2001; Acts 2003, 78th Leg., ch. 339, §§ 2 to 4, 7 eff. Sept. 1, 2003; Acts 2003, 78th Leg., ch. 404, §§ 1, 2, eff. Sept. 1, 2003; Acts 2003, 78th Leg., ch. 1126, § 1, eff. June 20, 2003; Acts 2003, 78th Leg., ch. 1236, § 2, eff. Sept. 1, 2003; Acts 2005, 79th Leg., ch. 728, § 4.006, eff. Sept. 1, 2005; Acts 2005, 79th Leg., ch. 177, §§ 1, 2, eff. Sept. 1, 2005; Acts 2005, 79th Leg., ch. 1309, § 2, eff. Sept. 1, 2005; Acts 2007, 80th Leg., ch. 120, § 1, eff. Sept. 1, 2007; Acts 2007, 80th Leg., ch. 1017, §§ 1 to 4, eff. Sept. 1, 2007; Acts 2011, 82nd Leg., ch. 91 (S.B. 1303), § 6.002, eff. Sept. 1, 2011; Acts 2011, 82nd Leg., ch. 278 (H.B. 1573), §§ 3, 4, eff. Sept. 1, 2011; Acts 2011, 82nd Leg., ch. 690 (H.B. 351), §§ 2 to 6, eff. Sept. 1, 2011; Acts 2011, 82nd Leg., ch. 894 (S.B. 462), § 2, eff. Sept. 1, 2011; Acts 2017, 85th Leg., ch. 693 (H.B. 322), § 2, eff. Sept. 1, 2017; Acts 2017, 85th Leg., ch. 1058 (H.B. 2931), § 4.04, eff. Jan. 1, 2019; Acts 2017, 85th Leg., ch. 1062 (H.B. 3147), § 2, eff. Sept. 1, 2017; Acts 2017, 85th Leg., ch. 1149 (H.B. 557), §§ 2 to 4, eff. Sept. 1, 2017.

Sections 6 and 7 of Acts 2017, 85th Leg., ch. 693 (H.B. 322) provide:

"Sec. 6. (a) Except as provided by Subsection (b) of this section, this Act applies to the expunction of arrest records and files for a person who successfully completes a veterans treatment court program under Chapter 124, Government Code, or former law before, on, or after the effective date [Sept. 1, 2017] of this Act, regardless of when the underlying arrest occurred.

"(b) The change in law made by this Act to Article 102.006, Code of Criminal Procedure, applies to the fees charged or costs assessed for an expunction order entered on or after the effective date of this Act, regardless of whether the underlying arrest occurred before, on, or after the effective date of this Act.

"(c) For a person who is entitled to expunction under Article 55.01(a)(2)(A)(ii)(a), Code of Criminal Procedure, as amended by this Act, based on a successful completion of a veterans treatment court program under Chapter 124, Government Code, or former law before the effective date of this Act, notwithstanding the 30–day time limit provided for the court to enter an automatic order of expunction under Section 1a(a–1), Article 55.02, Code of Criminal Procedure, as added by this Act, the court may, with the consent of the attorney representing the state, enter an order of expunction for the person as soon as practicable after the court receives written notice from any party to the case about the person's entitlement to the expunction.

"Sec. 7. The change in law made by this Act applies to a person whose conviction for an offense is set aside under Article 42A.701, Code of Criminal Procedure, on or after the effective date [Sept. 1, 2017] of this Act, regardless of when the person committed the offense for which the person was convicted."

Section 3 of Acts 2017, 85th Leg., ch. 1062 (H.B. 3147) provides:

"This Act applies to the expunction of arrest records and files for a person whose entitlement to expunction under Article 55.01(d), Code of Criminal Procedure, as amended by this Act, arises before, on, or after the effective date [Sept. 1, 2017] of this Act, regardless of when the underlying arrest occurred."

Section 10(a) and (b) of Acts 2017, 85th Leg., ch. 1149 (H.B. 557) provides:

"(a) Except as otherwise provided by this section, this Act applies to an expunction of records and files relating to any criminal offense that occurred before, on, or after the effective date [Sept. 1, 2017] of this Act.

"(b) Section 1, Article 55.02, Code of Criminal Procedure, as amended by this Act, applies only to the expunction of arrest records and files related to a criminal offense for which the trial of the offense begins on or after the effective date of this Act. The expunction of arrest records and files under Section 1, Article 55.02, Code of Criminal Procedure, related to a criminal offense for which the trial of the offense begins before the effective date of this Act is governed by the law in effect on the date the trial begins, and the former law is continued in effect for that purpose."

Art. 55.03. Effect of Expunction

When the order of expunction is final:

(1) the release, maintenance, dissemination, or use of the expunged records and files for any purpose is prohibited;

(2) except as provided in Subdivision (3) of this article, the person arrested may deny the occurrence of the arrest and the existence of the expunction order; and

(3) the person arrested or any other person, when questioned under oath in a criminal proceeding about an arrest for which the records have been expunged,

may state only that the matter in question has been expunged.

Added by Acts 1977, 65th Leg., p. 1880, ch. 747, § 1, eff. Aug. 29, 1977. Amended by Acts 1979, 66th Leg., p. 1333, ch. 604, § 1, eff. Aug. 27, 1979; Acts 1999, 76th Leg., ch. 1236, § 3, eff. Aug. 30, 1999; Acts 2001, 77th Leg., ch. 1021, § 3, eff. Sept. 1, 2001; Acts 2003, 78th Leg., ch. 1236, § 3, eff. Sept. 1, 2003; Acts 2005, 79th Leg., ch. 790, § 1, eff. June 17, 2005; Acts 2005, 79th Leg., ch. 919, § 1, eff. June 18, 2005.

Art. 55.04. Violation of Expunction Order

Sec. 1. A person who acquires knowledge of an arrest while an officer or employee of the state or of any agency or other entity of the state or any political subdivision of the state and who knows of an order expunging the records and files relating to that arrest commits an offense if he knowingly releases, disseminates, or otherwise uses the records or files.

Sec. 2. A person who knowingly fails to return or to obliterate identifying portions of a record or file ordered expunged under this chapter commits an offense.

Sec. 3. An offense under this article is a Class B misdemeanor.

Added by Acts 1977, 65th Leg., p. 1880, ch. 747, § 1, eff. Aug. 29, 1977. Amended by Acts 1979, 66th Leg., p. 1333, ch. 604, § 1, eff. Aug. 27, 1979.

Art. 55.05. Notice of Right to Expunction

On release or discharge of an arrested person, the person responsible for the release or discharge shall give him a written explanation of his rights under this chapter and a copy of the provisions of this chapter.

Added by Acts 1977, 65th Leg., p. 1880, ch. 747, § 1, eff. Aug. 29, 1977. Amended by Acts 1979, 66th Leg., p. 1333, ch. 604, § 1, eff. Aug. 27, 1979.

Art. 55.06. License Suspensions and Revocations

Records relating to the suspension or revocation of a driver's license, permit, or privilege to operate a motor vehicle may not be expunged under this chapter except as provided in Section 524.015, Transportation Code, or Section 724.048 of that code.

Added by Acts 1993, 73rd Leg., ch. 886, § 16, eff. Jan. 1, 1995. Amended by Acts 1999, 76th Leg., ch. 62, § 3.08, eff. Sept. 1, 1999; Acts 1999, 76th Leg., ch. 1236, § 4, eff. Aug. 30, 1999.

CHAPTER 56. RIGHTS OF CRIME VICTIMS

SUBCHAPTER A. CRIME VICTIMS' RIGHTS

SUBCHAPTER A. CRIME VICTIMS' RIGHTS

Art. 56.01. Definitions

In this chapter:

(1) "Close relative of a deceased victim" means a person who was the spouse of a deceased victim at the time of the victim's death or who is a parent or adult brother, sister, or child of the deceased victim.

(2) "Guardian of a victim" means a person who is the legal guardian of the victim, whether or not the legal relationship between the guardian and victim exists because of the age of the victim or the physical or mental incompetency of the victim.

(2–a) "Sexual assault" means an offense under Section 21.02, 21.11(a)(1), 22.011, or 22.021, Penal Code.

(3) "Victim" means a person who is the victim of the offense of sexual assault, kidnapping, aggravated robbery, trafficking of persons, or injury to a child, elderly individual, or disabled individual or who has suffered personal injury or death as a result of the criminal conduct of another.

Added by Acts 1985, 69th Leg., ch. 588, § 1, eff. Sept. 1, 1985. Amended by Acts 2005, 79th Leg., ch. 66, § 1, eff. Sept. 1, 2005; Acts 2005, 79th Leg., ch. 268, § 1.126, eff. Sept. 1, 2007; Acts 2007, 80th Leg., ch. 593, § 3.20, eff. Sept. 1, 2007; Acts 2009, 81st Leg., ch. 372, § 1, eff. June 19, 2009; Acts 2013, 83rd Leg., ch. 1345 (S.B. 1192), § 1, eff. Sept. 1, 2013.

Art. 56.02. Crime victims' rights

(a) A victim, guardian of a victim, or close relative of a deceased victim is entitled to the following rights within the criminal justice system:

(1) the right to receive from law enforcement agencies adequate protection from harm and threats of harm arising from cooperation with prosecution efforts;

(2) the right to have the magistrate take the safety of the victim or his family into consideration as an element in fixing the amount of bail for the accused;

(3) the right, if requested, to be informed:

(A) by the attorney representing the state of relevant court proceedings, including appellate proceedings, and to be informed if those proceedings have been canceled or rescheduled prior to the event; and

(B) by an appellate court of decisions of the court, after the decisions are entered but before the decisions are made public;

(4) the right to be informed, when requested, by a peace officer concerning the defendant's right to bail and the procedures in criminal investigations and by the district attorney's office concerning the general procedures in the criminal justice system, including general procedures in guilty plea negotiations and arrangements, restitution, and the appeals and parole process;

(5) the right to provide pertinent information to a probation department conducting a presentencing investigation concerning the impact of the offense on the victim and his family by testimony, written statement, or any other manner prior to any sentencing of the offender;

(6) the right to receive information regarding compensation to victims of crime as provided by Subchapter B,[1] including information related to the costs that may be compensated under that subchapter and the amount of compensation, eligibility for compensation, and procedures for application for compensation under that subchapter, the payment for a medical examination under Article 56.06 for a victim of a sexual assault, and when requested, to referral to available social service agencies that may offer additional assistance;

(7) the right to be informed, upon request, of parole procedures, to participate in the parole process, to be notified, if requested, of parole proceedings concerning a defendant in the victim's case, to provide to the Board of Pardons and Paroles[2] for inclusion in the defendant's file information to be considered by the board prior to the parole of any defendant convicted of any crime subject to this subchapter, and to be notified, if requested, of the defendant's release;

(8) the right to be provided with a waiting area, separate or secure from other witnesses, including the offender and relatives of the offender, before testifying in any proceeding concerning the offender; if a separate waiting area is not available, other safeguards should be taken to minimize the victim's contact with the offender and the offender's relatives and witnesses, before and during court proceedings;

(9) the right to prompt return of any property of the victim that is held by a law enforcement agency or the attorney for the state as evidence when the property is no longer required for that purpose;

(10) the right to have the attorney for the state notify the employer of the victim, if requested, of the necessity of the victim's cooperation and testimony in a proceeding that may necessitate the absence of the victim from work for good cause;

(11) the right to request victim-offender mediation coordinated by the victim services division of the Texas Department of Criminal Justice;

(12) the right to be informed of the uses of a victim impact statement and the statement's purpose in the criminal justice system, to complete the victim impact statement, and to have the victim impact statement considered:

(A) by the attorney representing the state and the judge before sentencing or before a plea bargain agreement is accepted; and

(B) by the Board of Pardons and Paroles before an inmate is released on parole;

(13) for a victim of an assault or sexual assault who is younger than 17 years of age or whose case involves family violence, as defined by Section 71.004, Family Code, the right to have the court consider the impact on the victim of a continuance requested by the defendant; if requested by the attorney representing the state or by counsel for the defendant, the court shall state on the record the reason for granting or denying the continuance; and

(14) if the offense is a capital felony, the right to:

(A) receive by mail from the court a written explanation of defense-initiated victim outreach if the court has authorized expenditures for a defense-initiated victim outreach specialist;

(B) not be contacted by the victim outreach specialist unless the victim, guardian, or relative has consented to the contact by providing a written notice to the court; and

(C) designate a victim service provider to receive all communications from a victim outreach specialist acting on behalf of any person.

(b) A victim, guardian of a victim, or close relative of a deceased victim is entitled to the right to be present at all public court proceedings related to the offense, subject to the approval of the judge in the case.

(c) The office of the attorney representing the state, and the sheriff, police, and other law enforcement agencies shall ensure to the extent practicable that a victim, guardian of a victim, or close relative of a deceased victim is afforded the rights granted by this article and Article 56.021 and, on request, an explanation of those rights.

(d) A judge, attorney for the state, peace officer, or law enforcement agency is not liable for a failure or inability to provide a right enumerated in this article or Article 56.021. The failure or inability of any person to provide a right or service enumerated in this article or Article 56.021 may not be used by a defendant in a criminal case as a ground for appeal, a ground to set aside the conviction or sentence, or a ground in a habeas corpus petition. A victim, guardian of a victim, or close relative of a deceased victim does not have standing to participate as a party in a criminal proceeding or to contest the disposition of any charge.

Added by Acts 1985, 69th Leg., ch. 588, § 1, eff. Sept. 1, 1985. Amended by Acts 1987, 70th Leg., ch. 433, § 1, eff. Aug. 31, 1987; Acts 1987, 70th Leg., ch. 929, § 1, eff. Sept. 1, 1987; Acts 1989, 71st Leg., ch. 996, § 1, eff. Sept. 1, 1989; Acts 1991, 72nd Leg., ch. 202, § 3, eff. Sept. 1, 1991; Acts 1993, 73rd Leg., ch. 811, § 3, eff. Sept. 1, 1993; Acts 1995, 74th Leg., ch. 76, § 5.95(108), eff. Sept. 1, 1995; Acts 2001, 77th Leg., ch. 1034, § 3, eff. Sept. 1, 2001. Acts 2005, 79th Leg., ch. 498, § 1, eff. Sept. 1, 2005; Acts 2007, 80th Leg., ch. 593, § 3.21, eff. Sept. 1, 2007; Acts 2009, 81st Leg., ch. 664, § 1, eff. Sept. 1, 2009; Acts 2009, 81st Leg., ch. 1140, § 1, eff. June 19, 2009; Acts 2013, 83rd Leg., ch. 651 (H.B. 899), § 1, eff. June 14, 2013; Acts 2013, 83rd Leg., ch. 1345 (S.B. 1192), § 2, eff. Sept. 1, 2013; Acts 2015, 84th Leg., ch. 1236 (S.B. 1296), §§ 4.002, 4.003, eff. Sept. 1, 2015.

[1] Vernon's Ann.C.C.P. art. 56.31 et seq.

[2] References to the Board of Pardons and Paroles shall mean either the Board of Pardons and Paroles or the pardon and paroles division of the Texas Department of Criminal Justice as provided by Acts 1989, 71st Leg., ch. 785, § 1.20(f)(2) as amended by Acts 1990, 71st Leg., 6th C.S., ch. 25, § 5.

Art. 56.021. Rights of Victim of Sexual Assault or Abuse, Stalking, or Trafficking

(a) In addition to the rights enumerated in Article 56.02, if the offense is a sexual assault, the victim, guardian of a victim, or close relative of a deceased victim is entitled to the following rights within the criminal justice system:

(1) if requested, the right to a disclosure of information regarding any evidence that was collected during the investigation of the offense, unless disclosing the information would interfere with the investigation or prosecution of the offense, in which event the victim, guardian, or relative shall be informed of the estimated date on which that information is expected to be disclosed;

(2) if requested, the right to a disclosure of information regarding the status of any analysis being performed of any evidence that was collected during the investigation of the offense;

(3) if requested, the right to be notified:

(A) at the time a request is submitted to a crime laboratory to process and analyze any evidence that was collected during the investigation of the offense;

(B) at the time of the submission of a request to compare any biological evidence collected during the investigation of the offense with DNA profiles maintained in a state or federal DNA database; and

(C) of the results of the comparison described by Paragraph (B), unless disclosing the results would interfere with the investigation or prosecution of the offense, in which event the victim, guardian, or relative shall be informed of the estimated date on which those results are expected to be disclosed;

(4) if requested, the right to counseling regarding acquired immune deficiency syndrome (AIDS) and human immunodeficiency virus (HIV) infection;

(5) for the victim of the offense, testing for acquired immune deficiency syndrome (AIDS), human immunodeficiency virus (HIV) infection, antibodies to HIV, or infection with any other probable causative agent of AIDS; and

(6) to the extent provided by Articles 56.06 and 56.065, for the victim of the offense, the right to a forensic medical examination if, within 96 hours of the offense, the offense is reported to a law enforcement agency or a forensic medical examination is otherwise conducted at a health care facility.

(b) A victim, guardian, or relative who requests to be notified under Subsection (a)(3) must provide a current address and phone number to the attorney representing the state and the law enforcement agency that is investigating the offense. The victim, guardian, or relative must inform the attorney repre-senting the state and the law enforcement agency of any change in the address or phone number.

(c) A victim, guardian, or relative may designate a person, including an entity that provides services to victims of sexual assault, to receive any notice requested under Subsection (a)(3).

(d) This subsection applies only to a victim of an offense under Section 20A.02, 20A.03, 21.02, 21.11, 22.011, 22.021, 42.072, or 43.05, Penal Code. In addition to the rights enumerated in Article 56.02 and, if applicable, Subsection (a) of this article, a victim described by this subsection or a parent or guardian of the victim is entitled to the following rights within the criminal justice system:

(1) the right to request that the attorney representing the state, subject to the Texas Disciplinary Rules of Professional Conduct, file an application for a protective order under Article 7A.01 on behalf of the victim;

(2) the right to be informed:

(A) that the victim or the victim's parent or guardian, as applicable, may file an application for a protective order under Article 7A.01;

(B) of the court in which the application for a protective order may be filed; and

(C) that, on request of the victim or of the victim's parent or guardian, as applicable, and subject to the Texas Disciplinary Rules of Professional Conduct, the attorney representing the state may file the application for a protective order;

(3) if the victim or the victim's parent or guardian, as applicable, is present when the defendant is convicted or placed on deferred adjudication community supervision, the right to be given by the court the information described by Subdivision (2) and, if the court has jurisdiction over applications for protective orders that are filed under Article 7A.01, the right to file an application for a protective order immediately following the defendant's conviction or placement on deferred adjudication community supervision; and

(4) if the victim or the victim's parent or guardian, as applicable, is not present when the defendant is convicted or placed on deferred adjudication community supervision, the right to be given by the attorney representing the state the information described by Subdivision (2).

Added by Acts 2013, 83rd Leg., ch. 1345 (S.B. 1192), § 3, eff. Sept. 1, 2013. Amended by Acts 2015, 84th Leg., ch. 1032 (H.B. 1447), §§ 2, 3, eff. Sept. 1, 2015; Acts 2015, 84th Leg., ch. 1153 (S.B. 630), §§ 2, 3, eff. Sept. 1, 2015; Acts 2017, 85th Leg., ch. 324 (S.B. 1488), § 5.003, eff. Sept. 1, 2017.

Section 4 of Acts 2015, 84th Leg., ch. 1032 (H.B. 1447) provides:

"The change in law made by this Act applies to a victim of criminally injurious conduct for which a judgment of conviction is entered or a grant of deferred adjudication is made on or after the effective date [Sept. 1, 2015] of this Act, regardless of whether the criminally injurious conduct occurred before, on, or after the effective date of this Act."

Section 4 of Acts 2015, 84th Leg., ch. 1153 (S.B. 630) provides:

"The change in law made by this Act applies to a victim of criminally injurious conduct for which a judgment of conviction is entered or a grant of deferred adjudication is made on or after the effective date [Sept. 1, 2015] of this Act, regardless of whether the criminally injurious conduct occurred before, on, or after the effective date of this Act."

Art. 56.03. Victim impact statement

(a) The Texas Crime Victim Clearinghouse, with the participation of the community justice assistance division of the Texas Department of Criminal Justice and the Board of Pardons and Paroles, shall develop a form to be used by law enforcement agencies, prosecutors, and other participants in the criminal justice system to record the impact of an offense on a victim of the offense, guardian of a victim, or a close relative of a deceased victim and to provide the agencies, prosecutors, and participants with information needed to contact the victim, guardian, or relative if needed at any stage of a prosecution of a person charged with the offense. The Texas Crime Victim Clearinghouse, with the participation of the community justice assistance division of the Texas Department of Criminal Justice and the Board of Pardons and Paroles,[1] shall also develop a victims' information booklet that provides a general explanation of the criminal justice system to victims of an offense, guardians of victims, and relatives of deceased victims.

(b) The victim impact statement must be in a form designed to inform a victim, guardian of a victim, or a close relative of a deceased victim with a clear statement of rights provided by Articles 56.02 and 56.021 and to collect the following information:

(1) the name of the victim of the offense or, if the victim has a legal guardian or is deceased, the name of a guardian or close relative of the victim;

(2) the address and telephone number of the victim, guardian, or relative through which the victim, guardian of a victim, or a close relative of a deceased victim, may be contacted;

(3) a statement of economic loss suffered by the victim, guardian, or relative as a result of the offense;

(4) a statement of any physical or psychological injury suffered by the victim, guardian, or relative as a result of the offense, as described by the victim, guardian, relative, or by a physician or counselor;

(5) a statement of any psychological services requested as a result of the offense;

(6) a statement of any change in the victim's, guardian's, or relative's personal welfare or familial relationship as a result of the offense;

(7) a statement as to whether or not the victim, guardian, or relative wishes to be notified in the future of any parole hearing for the defendant and an explanation as to the procedures by which the victim, guardian, or relative may obtain information concerning the release of the defendant from the Texas Department of Criminal Justice; and

(8) any other information, other than facts related to the commission of the offense, related to the impact of the offense on the victim, guardian, or relative.

(c) The victim assistance coordinator, designated in Article 56.04(a) of this code, shall send to a victim, guardian of a victim, or close relative of a deceased victim a victim impact statement, a victims' information booklet, and an application for compensation under Subchapter B, Chapter 56,[2] along with an offer to assist in completing those forms on request. The victim assistance coordinator, on request, shall explain the possible use and consideration of the victim impact statement at sentencing and future parole hearing of the offender.

(d) If a victim, guardian of a victim, or close relative of a deceased victim states on the victim impact statement that he wishes to be notified of parole proceedings, the victim, guardian, or relative is responsible for notifying the Board of Pardons and Paroles of any change of address.

(e) Prior to the imposition of a sentence by the court in a criminal case, the court shall, as applicable in the case, inquire as to whether a victim impact statement has been returned to the attorney representing the state and, if a victim impact statement has been returned to the attorney representing the state, consider the information provided in the statement. Before sentencing the defendant, the court shall permit the defendant or the defendant's counsel a reasonable time to read the statement, excluding the victim's name, address, and telephone number, comment on the statement, and, with the approval of the court, introduce testimony or other information alleging a factual inaccuracy in the statement. If the court sentences the defendant to a term of community supervision, the attorney representing the state shall forward any victim's impact statement received in the case to the community supervision and corrections department supervising the defendant.

(f) The court may not inspect a victim impact statement until after a finding of guilt or until deferred adjudication [3] is ordered and the contents of the statement may not be disclosed to any person unless:

(1) the defendant pleads guilty or nolo contendere or is convicted of the offense; or

(2) the defendant in writing authorizes the court to inspect the statement.

(g) A victim impact statement is subject to discovery under Article 39.14 of this code before the testimony of the victim is taken only if the court determines that the statement contains exculpatory material.

(h) Not later than December 1 of each odd-numbered year, the Texas Crime Victim Clearinghouse, with the participation of the community justice assistance division of the Texas Department of Criminal Justice and the Board of Pardons and Paroles, shall update the victim impact statement form and any other information provided by the commission to victims, guardians of victims, and relatives of deceased victims, if necessary, to reflect changes in law relating to criminal justice and the rights of victims and guardians and relatives of victims.

(i) In addition to the information described by Subsections (b)(1)–(8), the victim impact statement must be in a form designed to collect information on whether, if the victim is a child, there is an existing court order granting to the defendant possession of or access to the victim. If information collected under this subsection indicates the defendant is granted access or possession under court order and the defendant is subsequently confined by the Texas Department of Criminal Justice as a result of the commission of the offense, the victim services office of the department shall contact the court issuing the order before the defendant is released from the department on parole or mandatory supervision.

Added by Acts 1985, 69th Leg., ch. 588, § 1, eff. Sept. 1, 1985. Amended by Acts 1987, 70th Leg., ch. 433, § 2, eff. Aug. 31, 1987; Acts 1987, 70th Leg., ch. 929, §§ 2, 3, eff. Sept. 1, 1987; Acts 1989, 71st Leg., ch. 996, § 2, eff. Sept. 1, 1989; Acts 1995, 74th Leg., ch. 76, § 5.95(108), eff. Sept. 1, 1995; Acts 1997, 75th Leg., ch. 670, § 5, eff. Sept. 1, 1997; Acts 2001, 77th Leg., ch. 1034, § 4, eff. Sept. 1, 2001; Acts 2009, 81st Leg., ch. 87, § 25.038, eff. Sept. 1, 2009; Acts 2013, 83rd Leg., ch. 1154 (S.B. 213), § 25, eff. Sept. 1, 2013; Acts 2013, 83rd Leg., ch. 1345 (S.B. 1192), § 4, eff. Sept. 1, 2013.

[1] References to the Board of Pardons and Paroles shall mean either the Board of Pardons and Paroles or the pardon and paroles division

of the Texas Department of Criminal Justice as provided by Acts 1989, 71st Leg., ch. 785, § 1.20(f)(2) as amended by Acts 1990, 71st Leg., 6th C.S., ch. 25, § 5.

[2] Vernon's Ann.C.C.P. art. 56.31 et seq.

[3] A reference to "probation" or "deferred adjudication" means "community supervision", pursuant to Acts 1993, 73rd Leg., ch. 900, § 4.04(a).

Art. 56.04. Victim assistance coordinator; crime victim liaison

(a) The district attorney, criminal district attorney, or county attorney who prosecutes criminal cases shall designate a person to serve as victim assistance coordinator in that jurisdiction.

(b) The duty of the victim assistance coordinator is to ensure that a victim, guardian of a victim, or close relative of a deceased victim is afforded the rights granted victims, guardians, and relatives by Articles 56.02 and 56.021. The victim assistance coordinator shall work closely with appropriate law enforcement agencies, prosecuting attorneys, the Board of Pardons and Paroles, [1] and the judiciary in carrying out that duty.

(c) Each local law enforcement agency shall designate one person to serve as the agency's crime victim liaison. Each agency shall consult with the victim assistance coordinator in the office of the attorney representing the state to determine the most effective manner in which the crime victim liaison can perform the duties imposed on the crime victim liaison under this article.

(d) The duty of the crime victim liaison is to ensure that a victim, guardian of a victim, or close relative of a deceased victim is afforded the rights granted victims, guardians, or close relatives of deceased victims by Subdivisions (4), (6), and (9) of Article 56.02(a) of this code.

(d–1) The victim services division of the Texas Department of Criminal Justice, in consultation with the Board of Pardons and Paroles, law enforcement agencies, prosecutors' offices, and other participants in the criminal justice system, shall develop recommendations to ensure that completed victim impact statements are submitted to the Texas Department of Criminal Justice as provided by this chapter.

(e) On inquiry by the court, the attorney representing the state shall make available a copy of a victim impact statement for consideration by the court sentencing the defendant. If the court sentences the defendant to imprisonment in the Texas Department of Criminal Justice, the court shall attach the copy of the victim impact statement to the commitment papers.

(f) The commissioners court may approve a program in which the crime victim liaison or victim assistance coordinator may offer not more than 10 hours of post-investigation or posttrial psychological counseling for a person who serves as a grand juror, alternate grand juror, juror, or alternate juror in a grand jury investigation or criminal trial involving graphic evidence or testimony and who requests the post-investigation or posttrial psychological counseling not later than the 180th day after the date on which the grand jury or jury is dismissed. The crime victim liaison or victim assistance coordinator may provide the counseling using a provider that assists local criminal justice agencies in providing similar services to victims.

Added by Acts 1985, 69th Leg., ch. 588, § 1, eff. Sept. 1, 1985. Amended by Acts 1989, 71st Leg., ch. 996, § 3, eff. Sept. 1, 1989; Acts 1991, 72nd Leg., ch. 202, § 4, eff. Sept. 1, 1991; Acts 2007, 80th Leg., ch. 1378, § 6, eff. Sept. 1, 2007; Acts 2009, 81st Leg., ch. 87, § 25.039, eff. Sept. 1, 2009; Acts 2009, 81st Leg., ch. 93, § 1, eff. Sept. 1, 2009; Acts 2013, 83rd Leg., ch. 1154 (S.B. 213), § 26, eff. Sept. 1, 2013; Acts 2013, 83rd Leg., ch. 1345 (S.B. 1192), § 5, eff. Sept. 1, 2013; Acts 2017, 85th Leg., ch. 1160 (S.B. 1264), § 1, eff. Sept. 1, 2017.

[1] References to the Board of Pardons and Paroles shall mean the Board of Pardons and Paroles division of the Texas Department of Criminal Justice by Acts 1989, 71st Leg., ch. 785, § 1.20(f)(2).

Art. 56.045. Presence of Advocate or Representative During Forensic Medical Examination

(a) Before conducting a forensic medical examination of a person who consents to such an examination for the collection of evidence for an alleged sexual assault, the physician or other medical services personnel conducting the examination shall offer the person the opportunity to have an advocate from a sexual assault program as defined by Section 420.003, Government Code, who has completed a sexual assault training program described by Section 420.011(b), Government Code, present with the person during the examination, if the advocate is available at the time of the examination.

(b) The advocate may only provide the injured person with:

(1) counseling and other support services; and

(2) information regarding the rights of crime victims under Articles 56.02 and 56.021.

(c) Notwithstanding Subsection (a), the advocate and the sexual assault program providing the advocate may not delay or otherwise impede the screening or stabilization of an emergency medical condition.

(d) The sexual assault program providing the advocate shall pay all costs associated with providing the advocate.

(e) Any individual or entity, including a health care facility, that provides an advocate with access to a person consenting to an examination under Subsection (a) is not subject to civil or criminal liability for providing that access. In this subsection, "health care facility" includes a hospital licensed under Chapter 241, Health and Safety Code.

(f) If a person alleging to have sustained injuries as the victim of a sexual assault was confined in a penal institution, as defined by Section 1.07, Penal Code, at the time of the alleged assault, the penal institution shall provide, at the person's request, a representative to be present with the person at any forensic medical examination conducted for the purpose of collecting and preserving evidence related to the investigation or prosecution of the alleged assault. The representative may only provide the injured person with counseling and other support services and with information regarding the rights of crime victims under Articles 56.02 and 56.021 and may not delay or otherwise impede the screening or stabilization of an emergency medical condition. The representative must be approved by the penal institution and must be a:

(1) psychologist;

(2) sociologist;

(3) chaplain;

(4) social worker;

(5) case manager; or

(6) volunteer who has completed a sexual assault training program described by Section 420.011(b), Government Code.

Added by Acts 2001, 77th Leg., ch. 1019, § 1, eff. Sept. 1, 2001. Amended by Acts 2013, 83rd Leg., ch. 1345 (S.B. 1192), § 6, eff. Sept. 1, 2013.

Art. 56.05. Reports Required

(a) The Board of Pardons and Paroles, the community justice assistance division of the Texas Department of Criminal Justice, and the Texas Crime Victim Clearinghouse, designated as the planning body for the purposes of this article, shall develop a survey plan to maintain statistics on the numbers and types of persons to whom state and local agencies provide victim impact statements during each year.

(b) At intervals specified in the plan, the planning body may require any state or local agency to submit, in a form prescribed for the reporting of the information, statistical data on the numbers and types of persons to whom the agency provides victim impact statements and any other information required by the planning body. The form must be designed to protect the privacy of persons afforded rights under this chapter and to determine whether the selected agency or office is making a good faith effort to protect the rights of the persons served.

(c) The Texas Crime Victim Clearinghouse shall develop crime victim assistance standards and distribute those standards to law enforcement officers and attorneys representing the state to aid those officers and prosecutors in performing duties imposed by this chapter.

Added by Acts 1985, 69th Leg., ch. 588, § 1, eff. Sept. 1, 1985. Amended by Acts 1989, 71st Leg., ch. 996, § 4, eff. Sept. 1, 1989; Acts 2009, 81st Leg., ch. 87, § 25.040, eff. Sept. 1, 2009.

Art. 56.06. Forensic Medical Examination for Sexual Assault Victim Who Has Reported Assault; Costs

(a) If a sexual assault is reported to a law enforcement agency within 96 hours of the assault, the law enforcement agency, with the consent of the victim, a person authorized to act on behalf of the victim, or an employee of the Department of Family and Protective Services, shall request a forensic medical examination of the victim of the alleged assault for use in the investigation or prosecution of the offense. A law enforcement agency may decline to request a forensic medical examination under this subsection only if the person reporting the sexual assault has made one or more false reports of sexual assault to any law enforcement agency and if there is no other evidence to corroborate the current allegations of sexual assault.

(b) If a sexual assault is not reported within the period described by Subsection (a), on receiving the consent described by that subsection the law enforcement agency may request a forensic medical examination of a victim of an alleged sexual assault as considered appropriate by the agency.

(c) A law enforcement agency that requests a forensic medical examination of a victim of an alleged sexual assault for use in the investigation or prosecution of the offense shall pay all costs of the examina-

tion. On application to the attorney general, the law enforcement agency is entitled to be reimbursed for the reasonable costs of that examination if the examination was performed by a physician or by a sexual assault examiner or sexual assault nurse examiner, as defined by Section 420.003, Government Code.

(d) A law enforcement agency or prosecuting attorney's office may pay all costs related to the testimony of a licensed health care professional in a criminal proceeding regarding the results of the forensic medical examination or manner in which it was performed.

(e) This article does not require a law enforcement agency to pay any costs of treatment for injuries.

(f) The attorney general may make a payment to or on behalf of an individual for the reasonable costs incurred for medical care provided in accordance with Section 323.004, Health and Safety Code.

Added by Acts 1989, 71st Leg., ch. 2, § 5.05(a), eff. Aug. 28, 1989. Amended by Acts 1991, 72nd Leg., ch. 75, § 1, eff. Sept. 1, 1991; Acts 2001, 77th Leg., ch. 1507, § 1, eff. June 15, 2001; Acts 2005, 79th Leg., ch. 498, § 2, eff. Sept. 1, 2005; Acts 2009, 81st Leg., ch. 1140, § 2, eff. June 19, 2009; Acts 2015, 84th Leg., ch. 924 (H.B. 1446), §§ 1, 2, eff. Sept. 1, 2015.

Sections 8 and 9 of Acts 2015, 84th Leg., ch. 924 (H.B. 1446) provide:

"Sec. 8. The change in law made by this Act relating to reimbursement of certain medical costs applies only to payments made for medical care provided on or after the effective date [Sept. 1, 2015] of this Act. Payments made for medical care provided before the effective date of this Act are governed by the law in effect on the date the care was provided, and the former law is continued in effect for that purpose.

"Sec. 9. The change in law made by this Act relating to compensation for relocation and housing rental expenses applies only to a victim of a criminal offense committed or a violation that occurs on or after the effective date of this Act. The victim of a criminal offense committed or a violation that occurs before the effective date of this Act is governed by the law in effect on the date the offense was committed or the violation occurred, and the former law is continued in effect for that purpose. For purposes of this section, a criminal offense was committed or a violation occurred before the effective date of this Act if any element of the offense or violation occurred before that date."

Art. 56.065. Medical Examination for Sexual Assault Victim Who Has Not Reported Assault; Costs

(a) In this article:

(1) "Crime laboratory" has the meaning assigned by Article 38.35.

(2) "Department" means the Department of Public Safety.

(3) "Sexual assault examiner" and "sexual assault nurse examiner" have the meanings assigned by Section 420.003, Government Code.

(b) This article applies to the following health care facilities that provide diagnosis or treatment services to victims of sexual assault:

(1) a general or special hospital licensed under Chapter 241, Health and Safety Code;

(2) a general or special hospital owned by this state;

(3) an outpatient clinic; and

(4) a private physician's office.

(c) In accordance with Subchapter B, Chapter 420, Government Code, and except as provided by Subsection (e), a health care facility shall conduct a forensic medical examination of the victim of an alleged sexual assault if:

(1) the victim arrives at the facility within 96 hours after the assault occurred;

(2) the victim consents to the examination; and

(3) at the time of the examination the victim has not reported the assault to a law enforcement agency.

(d) The department shall pay the appropriate fees, as set by attorney general rule, for the forensic portion of the medical examination and for the evidence collection kit if a physician, sexual assault examiner, or sexual assault nurse examiner conducts the forensic portion of the examination within 96 hours after the alleged sexual assault occurred. The attorney general shall reimburse the department for fees paid under this subsection.

(e) If a health care facility does not provide diagnosis or treatment services to victims of sexual assault, the facility shall refer a victim seeking a forensic medical examination under Subsection (c) to a health care facility that provides services to those victims.

(f) The department, consistent with Chapter 420, Government Code, may develop procedures regarding the submission or collection of additional evidence of the alleged sexual assault other than through an examination as described by this article.

(g) The department, consistent with Chapter 420, Government Code, shall develop procedures for the transfer and preservation of evidence collected under this article to a crime laboratory or other suitable location designated by the public safety director of the department.The receiving entity shall preserve the evidence until the earlier of:

(1) the second anniversary of the date the evidence was collected; or

(2) the date on which written consent to release the evidence is obtained as provided by Section 420.0735, Government Code.

(h) The victim may not be required to:

(1) participate in the investigation or prosecution of an offense as a condition of receiving a forensic medical examination under this article; or

(2) pay for the forensic portion of the medical examination or for the evidence collection kit.

(i) The attorney general and the department each shall adopt rules as necessary to implement this article.

(j) A communication or record that contains identifying information regarding a person who receives a forensic medical examination under this article and that is created by, provided to, or in the control or possession of the department is confidential for purposes of Section 552.101, Government Code. In this subsection, "identifying information" includes:

(1) information revealing the identity, personal history, or background of the person; or

(2) information concerning the victimization of the person.

(k) The attorney general may make a payment to or on behalf of an individual for the reasonable costs incurred for medical care provided in accordance with Section 323.004, Health and Safety Code.

Added by Acts 2009, 81st Leg., ch. 1140, § 3, eff. June 19, 2009. Amended by Acts 2011, 82nd Leg., ch. 826 (H.B. 2966), § 1, eff. June 17, 2011; Acts 2011, 82nd Leg., ch. 1105 (S.B. 1636), § 12, eff. Sept. 1, 2011; Acts 2015, 84th Leg., ch. 924 (H.B. 1446), § 3, eff. Sept. 1, 2015.

Sections 8 and 9 of Acts 2015, 84th Leg., ch. 924 (H.B. 1446) provide:

"Sec. 8. The change in law made by this Act relating to reimbursement of certain medical costs applies only to payments made for medical care provided on or after the effective date [Sept. 1, 2015] of this Act. Payments made for medical care provided before the effective date of this Act are governed by the law in effect on the date the care was provided, and the former law is continued in effect for that purpose.

"Sec. 9. The change in law made by this Act relating to compensation for relocation and housing rental expenses applies only to a victim of a criminal offense committed or a violation that occurs on or after the effective date of this Act. The victim of a criminal offense committed or a violation that occurs before the effective date of this Act is governed by the law in effect on the date the offense was committed or the violation occurred, and the former law is continued in effect for that purpose. For purposes of this section, a criminal offense was committed or a violation occurred before the effective date of this Act if any element of the offense or violation occurred before that date."

Art. 56.07. Notification

(a) At the initial contact or at the earliest possible time after the initial contact between the victim of a reported crime and the law enforcement agency having the responsibility for investigating that crime, that agency shall provide the victim a written notice containing:

(1) information about the availability of emergency and medical services, if applicable;

(2) notice that the victim has the right to receive information regarding compensation to victims of crime as provided by Subchapter B, Chapter 56,[1] including information about:

(A) the costs that may be compensated under that Act and the amount of compensation, eligibility for compensation, and procedures for application for compensation under that Act;

(B) the payment for a medical examination for a victim of a sexual assault under Article 56.06 of this code; and

(C) referral to available social service agencies that may offer additional assistance;

(3) the name, address, and phone number of the law enforcement agency's victim assistance liaison;

(4) the address, phone number, and name of the crime victim assistance coordinator of the office of the attorney representing the state;

(5) the following statement:

"You may call the law enforcement agency's telephone number for the status of the case and information about victims' rights"; and

(6) the rights of crime victims under Articles 56.02 and 56.021.

(b) At the same time a law enforcement agency provides notice under Subsection (a), the agency shall provide, if the agency possesses the relevant information, a referral to a sexual assault program as defined by Section 420.003, Government Code, and a written description of the services provided by that program. A sexual assault program may provide a written description of its services to a law enforcement agency.

Added by Acts 1991, 72nd Leg., ch. 202, § 5, eff. Sept. 1, 1991. Amended by Acts 1995, 74th Leg., ch. 76, § 5.95(108), eff. Sept. 1, 1995; Acts 2003, 78th Leg., ch. 788, § 1, eff. June 20, 2003. Amended by Acts 2013, 83rd Leg., ch. 1345 (S.B. 1192), § 7, eff. Sept. 1, 2013.

[1] Vernon's Ann.C.C.P. art. 56.31 et seq.

Art. 56.08. Notification of rights by attorney representing the state

(a) Not later than the 10th day after the date that an indictment or information is returned against a defendant for an offense, the attorney representing the state shall give to each victim of the offense a written notice containing:

(1) a brief general statement of each procedural stage in the processing of a criminal case, including bail, plea bargaining, parole restitution, and appeal;

(2) notification of the rights and procedures under this chapter;

(3) suggested steps the victim may take if the victim is subjected to threats or intimidation;

(4) notification of the right to receive information regarding compensation to victims of crime as provided by Subchapter B,[1] including information about:

(A) the costs that may be compensated under Subchapter B, eligibility for compensation, and procedures for application for compensation under Subchapter B of this chapter;

(B) the payment for a medical examination for a victim of a sexual assault under Article 56.06; and

(C) referral to available social service agencies that may offer additional assistance;

(5) the name, address, and phone number of the local victim assistance coordinator;

(6) the case number and assigned court for the case;

(7) the right to file a victim impact statement with the office of the attorney representing the state and the Texas Department of Criminal Justice; and

(8) notification of the right of a victim, guardian of a victim, or close relative of a deceased victim, as defined by Section 508.117, Government Code, to appear in person before a member of the Board of Pardons and Paroles as provided by Section 508.153, Government Code.

(b) If requested by the victim, the attorney representing the state, as far as reasonably practical, shall give to the victim notice of any scheduled court proceedings, changes in that schedule, and the filing of a request for continuance of a trial setting.

(b–1) The attorney representing the state, as far as reasonably practical, shall give to the victim, guardian of a victim, or close relative of a deceased victim notice of the existence and terms of any plea bargain agreement to be presented to the court.

(c) A victim who receives a notice under Subsection (a) and who chooses to receive other notice under law about the same case must keep the following persons informed of the victim's current address and phone number:

(1) the attorney representing the state; and

(2) the Texas Department of Criminal Justice if after sentencing the defendant is confined in the department.

(d) An attorney representing the state who receives information concerning a victim's current address and phone number shall immediately provide that information to the community supervision and corrections department supervising the defendant, if the defendant is placed on community supervision.

(e) The brief general statement describing the plea bargaining stage in a criminal trial required by Subsection (a)(1) shall include a statement that:

(1) the victim impact statement provided by the victim, guardian of a victim, or close relative of a deceased victim will be considered by the attorney representing the state in entering into the plea bargain agreement; and

(2) the judge before accepting the plea bargain agreement is required under Article 26.13(e) to ask:

(A) whether a victim impact statement has been returned to the attorney;

(B) if a victim impact statement has been returned, for a copy of the statement; and

(C) whether the attorney representing the state has given the victim, guardian of a victim, or close relative of a deceased victim notice of the existence and terms of the plea bargain agreement.

Added by Acts 1991, 72nd Leg., ch. 202, § 5, eff. Sept. 1, 1991. Amended by Acts 1995, 74th Leg., ch. 76, § 5.95(108), eff. Sept. 1, 1995; Acts 1995, 74th Leg., ch. 252, § 2, eff. Sept. 1, 1995; Acts 1995, 74th Leg., ch. 253, § 2, eff. Sept. 1, 1995; Acts 1997, 75th Leg., ch. 165, § 12.04, eff. Sept. 1, 1997; Acts 2001, 77th Leg., ch. 1034, § 5, eff. Sept. 1, 2001; Acts 2009, 81st Leg., ch. 87, § 25.041, eff. Sept. 1, 2009; Acts 2011, 82nd Leg., ch. 1073 (S.B. 1010), § 2, eff. Sept. 1, 2011.

[1] Vernon's Ann.C.C.P. art. 56.31 et seq.

Art. 56.09. Victim's right to privacy

As far as reasonably practical, the address of the victim may not be a part of the court file except as necessary to identify the place of the crime. The phone number of the victim may not be a part of the court file.

Added by Acts 1991, 72nd Leg., ch. 202, § 5, eff. Sept. 1, 1991.

Art. 56.10. Victim's discovery attendance

Unless absolutely necessary, victims or witnesses who are not incarcerated may not be required to attend depositions in a correctional facility.

Added by Acts 1991, 72nd Leg., ch. 202, § 5, eff. Sept. 1, 1991.

Art. 56.11. Notification to Victim or Witness of Release or Escape of Defendant

(a) The Texas Department of Criminal Justice or the sheriff, whichever has custody of the defendant in the case of a felony, or the sheriff in the case of a misdemeanor, shall notify the victim of the offense or a witness who testified against the defendant at the trial for the offense, other than a witness who testified in the course and scope of the witness's official or professional duties, whenever a defendant convicted of an offense described by Subsection (c):

(1) completes the defendant's sentence and is released; or

(2) escapes from a correctional facility.

(a–1) The Texas Department of Criminal Justice, in the case of an inmate released on parole or to mandatory supervision following a term of imprisonment for an offense described by Subsection (c), or a community supervision and corrections department supervising a defendant, in the case of a defendant convicted of an offense described by Subsection (c) and subsequently released on community supervision, shall notify a victim or witness described by Subsection (a) whenever the inmate or defendant, if subject to electronic monitoring as a condition of release, ceases to be electronically monitored.

(b) If the Texas Department of Criminal Justice is required by Subsection (a) to give notice to a victim or witness, the department shall also give notice to local law enforcement officials in the county in which the victim or witness resides.

(c) This article applies to a defendant convicted of:

(1) an offense under Title 5, Penal Code, that is punishable as a felony;

(2) an offense described by Section 508.187(a), Government Code, other than an offense described by Subdivision (1); or

(3) an offense involving family violence, stalking, or violation of a protective order or magistrate's order.

(d) It is the responsibility of a victim or witness desiring notification of the defendant's release to provide the Texas Department of Criminal Justice, the sheriff, or the community supervision and corrections department supervising the defendant, as appropriate, with the e-mail address, mailing address, and telephone number of the victim, witness, or other person through whom the victim or witness may be contacted and to notify the appropriate department or the sheriff of any change of address or telephone number of the victim, witness, or other person. Information obtained and maintained by the Texas Department of Criminal Justice, a sheriff, or a community supervision and corrections department under this subsection is privileged and confidential.

(e) The Texas Department of Criminal Justice, the sheriff, or the community supervision and corrections department supervising the defendant, as appropriate:

(1) shall make a reasonable attempt to give any notice required by Subsection (a) or (a–1):

(A) not later than the 30th day before the date the defendant completes the sentence and is released or ceases to be electronically monitored as a condition of release; or

(B) immediately if the defendant escapes from the correctional facility; and

(2) may give any notice required by Subsection (a) or (a–1) by e-mail, if possible.

(f) An attempt by the Texas Department of Criminal Justice, the sheriff, or the community supervision and corrections department supervising the defendant to give notice to a victim or witness at the victim's or witness's last known mailing address or, if notice via e-mail is possible, last known e-mail address, as shown on the records of the appropriate department or agency, constitutes a reasonable attempt to give notice under this article.

(g) Not later than immediately following the conviction of a defendant described by Subsection (c), the attorney who represented the state in the prosecution of the case shall notify in writing a victim or witness described by Subsection (a) of the victim's or witness's right to receive notice under this article.

(h) In this article:

(1) "Correctional facility" has the meaning assigned by Section 1.07, Penal Code.

(2) "Family violence" has the meaning assigned by Section 71.004, Family Code.

Added by Acts 1993, 73rd Leg., ch. 10, § 6, eff. March 19, 1993. Amended by Acts 1995, 74th Leg., ch. 657, § 6, eff. June 14, 1995; Acts 1997, 75th Leg., ch. 1, § 8, eff. Jan. 28, 1997; Acts 1997, 75th Leg., ch. 670, § 6, eff. Sept. 1, 1997; Acts 2001, 77th Leg., ch. 978, § 3, eff. Sept. 1, 2001; Acts 2003, 78th Leg., ch. 1276, § 7.002(k), eff. Sept. 1, 2003; Acts 2007, 80th Leg., ch. 458, § 1, eff. Sept. 1, 2007; Acts 2009, 81st Leg., ch. 618, § 1, eff. Sept. 1, 2009.

Art. 56.12. Notification of Escape or Transfer

(a) The Texas Department of Criminal Justice shall immediately notify the victim of an offense, the victim's guardian, or the victim's close relative, if the victim is deceased, if the victim, victim's guardian, or victim's close relative has notified the department as provided by Subsection (b), whenever the defendant:

(1) escapes from a facility operated by the department for the imprisonment of individuals convicted of felonies other than state jail felonies; or

(2) is transferred from the custody of a facility operated by the department for the imprisonment of individuals convicted of felonies other than state jail felonies to the custody of a peace officer under a writ of attachment or a bench warrant.

(a–1) The Texas Department of Criminal Justice shall immediately notify a witness who testified against a defendant at the trial for the offense for which the defendant is incarcerated, the witness's guardian, or the witness's close relative, if the witness is deceased, if the witness, witness's guardian, or witness's close relative has notified the department as provided by Subsection (b), whenever the defendant:

(1) escapes from a facility operated by the department for the imprisonment of individuals convicted of felonies other than state jail felonies; or

(2) is transferred from the custody of a facility operated by the department for the imprisonment of individuals convicted of felonies other than state jail felonies to the custody of a peace officer under a writ of attachment or a bench warrant.

(b) It is the responsibility of the victim, witness, guardian, or close relative desiring notification of a defendant's escape or transfer from custody under a writ of attachment or bench warrant to notify the Texas Department of Criminal Justice of the desire for notification and any change of address.

(c) In providing notice under Subsection (a)(2) or (a–1)(2), the department shall include the name, address, and telephone number of the peace officer receiving the defendant into custody. On returning the defendant to the custody of the department, the victim services division of the department shall notify the victim, witness, guardian, or close relative, as applicable, of that fact.

(d) In this article, "witness's close relative" means a person who was the spouse of the deceased witness at the time of the witness's death or who is a parent or adult brother, sister, or child of the deceased witness.

Added by Acts 1995, 74th Leg., ch. 251, § 1, eff. May 29, 1995. Amended by Acts 2001, 77th Leg., ch. 1034, § 6, eff. Sept. 1, 2001; Acts 2007, 80th Leg., ch. 458, § 2, eff. Sept. 1, 2007; Acts 2009, 81st Leg., ch. 87, § 25.042, eff. Sept. 1, 2009.

Art. 56.13.   Victim-Offender Mediation

The victim services division of the Texas Department of Criminal Justice shall:

(1) train volunteers to act as mediators between victims, guardians of victims, and close relatives of deceased victims and offenders whose criminal conduct caused bodily injury or death to victims; and

(2) provide mediation services through referral of a trained volunteer, if requested by a victim, guardian of a victim, or close relative of a deceased victim.

Added by Acts 2001, 77th Leg., ch. 1034, § 7, eff. Sept. 1, 2001.

Art. 56.14.   Clearinghouse Annual Conference

(a) The Texas Crime Victim Clearinghouse may conduct an annual conference to provide to participants in the criminal justice system training containing information on crime victims' rights.

(b) The clearinghouse may charge fees to persons attending the conference described by Subsection (a).

Added by Acts 2001, 77th Leg., ch. 1034, § 7, eff. Sept. 1, 2001.

Art. 56.15.   Computerized Database; Defendant Release Information

The Texas Department of Criminal Justice shall:

(1) create and maintain a computerized database containing the release information and release date of a defendant described by Article 56.11(c); and

(2) allow a victim or witness entitled to notice under Article 56.11 or 56.12 to access via the Internet the computerized database maintained under Subdivision (1).

Added by Acts 2007, 80th Leg., ch. 458, § 3, eff. Sept. 1, 2007.

SUBCHAPTER B.   CRIME VICTIMS' COMPENSATION

Art. 56.31.   Short Title

This subchapter may be cited as the Crime Victims' Compensation Act.

Added by Acts 1993, 73rd Leg., ch. 268, § 6, eff. Sept. 1, 1993. Amended by Acts 1995, 74th Leg., ch. 76, § 5.84(a), eff. Sept. 1, 1995; Acts 1995, 74th Leg., ch. 779, § 1, eff. Sept. 1, 1995.

Art. 56.311.   Legislative Findings and Intent

The legislature recognizes that many innocent individuals suffer personal injury or death as a result of criminal acts. Crime victims and persons who intervene to prevent criminal acts often suffer disabilities, incur financial burdens, or become dependent on public assistance. The legislature finds that there is a need for the compensation of victims of crime and those who suffer personal injury or death in the prevention of crime or in the apprehension of criminals. It is the legislature's intent that the compensation of innocent victims of violent crime encourage greater public cooperation in the successful apprehension and prosecution of criminals.

Added by Acts 1995, 74th Leg., ch. 779, § 1, eff. Sept. 1, 1995.

Art. 56.32.   Definitions

(a) In this subchapter:

(1) "Child" means an individual younger than 18 years of age who:

(A) is not married; or

(B) has not had the disabilities of minority removed for general purposes under Chapter 31, Family Code.

(2) "Claimant" means, except as provided by Subsection (b), any of the following individuals who is entitled to file or has filed a claim for compensation under this subchapter:

(A) an authorized individual acting on behalf of a victim;

(B) an individual who legally assumes the obligation or who voluntarily pays medical or burial expenses of a victim incurred as a result of the criminally injurious conduct of another;

(C) a dependent of a victim who died as a result of criminally injurious conduct;

(D) an immediate family member or household member of a victim who:

(i) requires psychiatric care or counseling as a result of the criminally injurious conduct; or

(ii) as a result of the criminally injurious conduct, incurs with respect to a deceased victim expenses for traveling to and attending the victim's funeral or suffers wage loss from bereavement leave taken in connection with the death of that victim; or

(E) an authorized individual acting on behalf of an individual who is described by Subdivision (C) or (D) and who is a child.

(3) "Collateral source" means any of the following sources of benefits or advantages for pecuniary loss that a claimant or victim has received or that is readily available to the claimant or victim from:

(A) the offender under an order of restitution to the claimant or victim imposed by a court as a condition of community supervision;

(B) the United States, a federal agency, a state or any of its political subdivisions, or an instrumentality of two or more states, unless the law providing for the benefits or advantages makes them in excess of or secondary to benefits under this subchapter;

(C) social security, Medicare, or Medicaid;

(D) another state's or another country's crime victims' compensation program;

(E) workers' compensation;

(F) an employer's wage continuation program, not including vacation and sick leave benefits;

(G) proceeds of an insurance contract payable to or on behalf of the claimant or victim for loss that the claimant or victim sustained because of the criminally injurious conduct;

(H) a contract or self-funded program providing hospital and other health care services or benefits; or

(I) proceeds awarded to the claimant or victim as a result of third-party litigation.

(4) "Criminally injurious conduct" means conduct that:

(A) occurs or is attempted;

(B) poses a substantial threat of personal injury or death;

(C) is punishable by fine, imprisonment, or death, or would be punishable by fine, imprisonment, or death if the person engaging in the conduct possessed capacity to commit the conduct; and

(D) does not arise out of the ownership, maintenance, or use of a motor vehicle, aircraft, or water vehicle, unless the conduct is intended to cause personal injury or death or the conduct is in violation of Section 545.157 or 545.401, Transportation Code, and results in bodily injury or death, or is in violation of Section 550.021, Transportation Code, or one or more of the following sections of the Penal Code:

(i) Section 19.04 (manslaughter);

(ii) Section 19.05 (criminally negligent homicide);

(iii) Section 22.02 (aggravated assault);

(iv) Section 22.05 (deadly conduct);

(v) Section 49.04 (driving while intoxicated);

(vi) Section 49.05 (flying while intoxicated);

(vii) Section 49.06 (boating while intoxicated);

(viii) Section 49.07 (intoxication assault); or

(ix) Section 49.08 (intoxication manslaughter).

(5) "Dependent" means:

(A) a surviving spouse;

(B) a person who is a dependent, within the meaning of the Internal Revenue Code, of a victim; and

(C) a posthumous child of a deceased victim.

(6) "Household member" means an individual who resided in the same permanent household as the victim at the time that the criminally injurious conduct occurred and who is related by consanguinity or affinity to the victim.

(7) "Immediate family member" means an individual who is related to a victim within the second degree by affinity or consanguinity.

(8) "Intervenor" means an individual who goes to the aid of another and is killed or injured in the good faith effort to prevent criminally injurious conduct, to apprehend a person reasonably suspected of having engaged in criminally injurious conduct, or to aid a peace officer.

(9) "Pecuniary loss" means the amount of expense reasonably and necessarily incurred as a result of personal injury or death for:

(A) medical, hospital, nursing, or psychiatric care or counseling, or physical therapy;

(B) actual loss of past earnings and anticipated loss of future earnings and necessary travel expenses because of:

(i) a disability resulting from the personal injury;

(ii) the receipt of medically indicated services related to the disability resulting from the personal injury; or

(iii) participation in or attendance at investigative, prosecutorial, or judicial processes related to the criminally injurious conduct and participation in or attendance at any postconviction or postadjudication proceeding relating to criminally injurious conduct;

(C) care of a child or dependent, including specialized care for a child who is a victim;

(D) funeral and burial expenses, including, for an immediate family member or household member of the victim, the necessary expenses of traveling to and attending the funeral;

(E) loss of support to a dependent, consistent with Article 56.41(b)(5);

(F) reasonable and necessary costs of cleaning the crime scene;

(G) reasonable replacement costs for clothing, bedding, or property of the victim seized as evidence or rendered unusable as a result of the criminal investigation;

(H) reasonable and necessary costs for relocation and housing rental assistance payments as provided by Article 56.42(d);

(I) for an immediate family member or household member of a deceased victim, bereavement leave of not more than 10 work days; and

(J) reasonable and necessary costs of traveling to and from a place of execution for the purpose of witnessing the execution, including one night's lodging near the place at which the execution is conducted.

(10) "Personal injury" means physical or mental harm.

(11) "Victim" means, except as provided by Subsection (c):

(A) an individual who:

(i) suffers personal injury or death as a result of criminally injurious conduct or as a result of actions taken by the individual as an intervenor, if the conduct or actions occurred in this state; and

(ii) is a resident of this state, another state of the United States, the District of Columbia, the Commonwealth of Puerto Rico, or a possession or territory of the United States;

(B) an individual who:

(i) suffers personal injury or death as a result of criminally injurious conduct or as a result of actions taken by the individual as an intervenor, if the conduct or actions occurred in a state or country that does not have a crime victims' compensation program that meets the requirements of Section 1403(b), Crime Victims Compensation Act of 1984 (42 U.S.C. Section 10602(b));

(ii) is a resident of this state; and

(iii) would be entitled to compensation under this subchapter if the criminally injurious conduct or actions had occurred in this state; or

(C) an individual who:

(i) suffers personal injury or death as a result of criminally injurious conduct caused by an act of international terrorism as defined by 18 U.S.C. Section 2331 committed outside of the United States; and

(ii) is a resident of this state.

(12) "Family violence" has the meaning assigned by Section 71.004(1), Family Code.

(13) "Victim–related services or assistance" means compensation, services, or assistance provided directly to a victim or claimant for the purpose of supporting or assisting the recovery of the victim or claimant from the consequences of criminally injurious conduct.

(14) "Trafficking of persons" means any offense that results in a person engaging in forced labor or services, including sexual conduct, and that may be prosecuted under Section 20A.02, 20A.03, 43.03, 43.04, 43.05, 43.25, 43.251, or 43.26, Penal Code.

(b) In this subchapter "claimant" does not include a service provider.

Added by Acts 1993, 73rd Leg., ch. 268, § 6, eff. Sept. 1, 1993. Amended by Acts 1993, 73rd Leg., ch. 805, §§ 3, 4, eff. Aug. 30, 1993; Acts 1995, 74th Leg., ch. 76, §§ 5.84(a), 9.55, 14.27, eff. Sept. 1, 1995; Acts 1995, 74th Leg., ch. 779, § 1, eff. Sept. 1, 1995; Acts 1997, 75th Leg., ch. 1434, § 1, eff. Sept. 1, 1997; Acts 1999, 76th Leg., ch. 1470, § 1, eff. June 19, 1999; Acts 2001, 77th Leg., ch. 11, §§ 1, 2, eff. Sept. 1, 2001; Acts 2003, 78th Leg., ch. 1286, § 1, eff. Sept. 1, 2003; Acts 2003, 78th Leg., ch. 1303, § 2, eff. June 21, 2003; Acts 2005, 79th Leg., ch. 66, § 2, eff. Sept. 1, 2005; Acts 2005, 79th Leg., ch. 728, § 4.007, eff. Sept. 1, 2005; Acts 2007, 80th Leg., ch. 1374, § 1, eff. Sept. 1, 2007; Acts 2013, 83rd Leg., ch. 1252 (H.B. 8), § 8, eff. Sept. 1, 2013; Acts 2015, 84th Leg., ch. 332 (H.B. 10), § 2, eff. Sept. 1, 2015; Acts 2015, 84th Leg., ch. 924 (H.B. 1446), § 4, eff. Sept. 1, 2015; Acts 2017, 85th Leg., ch. 685 (H.B. 29), § 14, eff. Sept. 1, 2017.

Section 16 of Acts 2015, 84th Leg., ch. 332 (H.B. 10) provides:

"The changes in law made by this Act to Chapter 56, Code of Criminal Procedure, apply only to a criminal offense committed or a violation that occurs on or after the effective date [Sept. 1, 2015] of this Act. A criminal offense committed or a violation that occurs before the effective date of this Act is governed by the law in effect on the date the offense was committed or the violation occurred, and the former law is continued in effect for that purpose. For purposes of this section, a criminal offense was committed or a violation occurred before the effective date of this Act if any element of the offense or violation occurred before that date."

Sections 8 and 9 of Acts 2015, 84th Leg., ch. 924 (H.B. 1446) provide:

"Sec. 8. The change in law made by this Act relating to reimbursement of certain medical costs applies only to payments made for medical care provided on or after the effective date [Sept. 1, 2015] of this Act. Payments made for medical care provided before the effective date of this Act are governed by the law in effect on the date the care was provided, and the former law is continued in effect for that purpose.

"Sec. 9. The change in law made by this Act relating to compensation for relocation and housing rental expenses applies only to a victim of a criminal offense committed or a violation that occurs on or after the effective date of this Act. The victim of a criminal offense committed or a violation that occurs before the effective date of this Act is governed by the law in effect on the date the offense was committed or the violation occurred, and the former law is continued in effect for that purpose. For purposes of this section, a criminal offense was committed or a violation occurred before the effective date of this Act if any element of the offense or violation occurred before that date."

Section 45 of Acts 2017, 85th Leg., ch. 685 (H.B. 29) provides:

"(a) Except as provided by Subsection (b) of this section, the changes in law made by this Act apply only to an offense committed on or after the effective date [Sept. 1, 2017] of this Act. An offense committed before the effective date of this Act is governed by the law in effect on the date the offense was committed, and the former law is continued in effect for that purpose. For purposes of this subsection, an offense was committed before the effective date of this Act if any element of the offense occurred before that date.

"(b) The changes in law made by this Act in amending Chapter 62, Code of Criminal Procedure, apply only to a person who is required to register under Chapter 62, Code of Criminal Procedure, on the basis of a conviction or adjudication for or based on an offense committed on or after the effective date of this Act. A person who is required to register under Chapter 62, Code of Criminal Procedure, solely on the basis of a conviction or adjudication for or based on an offense committed before the effective date of this Act is governed by the law in effect on the date the offense was committed, and the former law is continued in effect for that purpose. For purposes of this subsection, an offense was committed before the effective date of this Act if any element of the offense occurred before that date."

Art. 56.33. Administration; Rules

(a) The attorney general shall adopt rules consistent with this subchapter governing its administration, including rules relating to the method of filing claims and the proof of entitlement to compensation and the review of health care services subject to compensation under this chapter. Subchapters A and B, Chapter 2001, Government Code, except Sections 2001.004(3) and 2001.005, apply to the attorney general.

(b) The attorney general may delegate a power, duty, or responsibility given to the attorney general under this subchapter to a person in the attorney general's office.

Added by Acts 1993, 73rd Leg., ch. 268, § 6, eff. Sept. 1, 1993. Amended by Acts 1995, 74th Leg., ch. 76, § 5.84(a), eff. Sept. 1, 1995; Acts 1995, 74th Leg., ch. 779, § 1, eff. Sept. 1, 1995.

Art. 56.34. Compensation

(a) The attorney general shall award compensation for pecuniary loss arising from criminally injurious conduct if the attorney general is satisfied by a preponderance of the evidence that the requirements of this subchapter are met.

(b) The attorney general, shall establish whether, as a direct result of criminally injurious conduct, a claimant or victim suffered personal injury or death that resulted in a pecuniary loss for which the claimant or victim is not compensated from a collateral source.

(c) The attorney general shall award compensation for health care services according to the medical fee guidelines prescribed by Subtitle A, Title 5, Labor Code.

(d) The attorney general, a claimant, or a victim is not liable for health care service charges in excess of the medical fee guidelines. A health care provider shall accept compensation from the attorney general as payment in full for the charges unless an investigation of the charges by the attorney general determines that there is a reasonable health care justification for the deviation from the guidelines.

(e) A claimant or victim is not liable for the balance of service charges left as a result of an adjustment of payment for the charges under Article 56.58.

(f) The compensation to victims of crime fund and the compensation to victims of crime auxiliary fund are the payers of last resort.

Added by Acts 1993, 73rd Leg., ch. 268, § 6, eff. Sept. 1, 1993. Amended by Acts 1995, 74th Leg., ch. 76, § 5.84(a), eff. Sept. 1, 1995; Acts 1995, 74th Leg., ch. 779, § 1, eff. Sept. 1, 1995; Acts 1997, 75th Leg., ch. 1434, § 1, eff. Sept. 1, 1997.

Art. 56.35. Types of Assistance

If the attorney general approves an application for compensation under Article 56.41, the attorney general shall determine what type of state assistance will best aid the claimant or victim. The attorney general may do one or more of the following:

(1) authorize cash payment or payments to or on behalf of a claimant or victim for pecuniary loss;

(2) refer a claimant or victim to a state agency for vocational or other rehabilitative services; or

(3) provide counseling services for a claimant or victim or contract with a private entity to provide counseling services.

Added by Acts 1993, 73rd Leg., ch. 268, § 6, eff. Sept. 1, 1993. Amended by Acts 1995, 74th Leg., ch. 76, § 5.84(a), eff. Sept. 1, 1995; Acts 1995, 74th Leg., ch. 779, § 1, eff. Sept. 1, 1995.

Art. 56.36. Application

(a) An applicant for compensation under this subchapter must apply in writing on a form prescribed by the attorney general.

(b) An application must be verified and must contain:

(1) the date on which the criminally injurious conduct occurred;

(2) a description of the nature and circumstances of the criminally injurious conduct;

(3) a complete financial statement, including:

(A) the cost of medical care or burial expenses and the loss of wages or support the claimant or victim has incurred or will incur; and

(B) the extent to which the claimant or victim has been indemnified for those expenses from a collateral source;

(4) if appropriate, a statement indicating the extent of a disability resulting from the injury incurred;

(5) an authorization permitting the attorney general to verify the contents of the application; and

(6) other information the attorney general requires.

Added by Acts 1993, 73rd Leg., ch. 268, § 6, eff. Sept. 1, 1993. Amended by Acts 1995, 74th Leg., ch. 76, § 5.84(a), eff. Sept. 1, 1995; Acts 1995, 74th Leg., ch. 779, § 1, eff. Sept. 1, 1995; Acts 1997, 75th Leg., ch. 1434, § 1, eff. Sept. 1, 1997.

Art. 56.37. Time for Filing

(a) Except as otherwise provided by this article, a claimant or victim must file an application not later than three years from the date of the criminally injurious conduct.

(b) The attorney general may extend the time for filing for good cause shown by the claimant or victim.

(c) If the victim is a child, the application must be filed within three years from the date the claimant or victim is made aware of the crime but not after the child is 21 years of age.

(d) If a claimant or victim presents medically documented evidence of a physical or mental incapacity that was incurred by the claimant or victim as a result of the criminally injurious conduct and that reasonably prevented the claimant or victim from filing the application within the limitations period under Subsection (a), the period of the incapacity is not included.

(e) For a claim that is based on criminally injurious conduct in violation of Chapter 19, Penal Code, the claimant must file an application not later than three years after the date the identity of the victim is established by a law enforcement agency.

Added by Acts 1993, 73rd Leg., ch. 268, § 6, eff. Sept. 1, 1993. Amended by Acts 1993, 73rd Leg., ch. 805, § 10, eff. Aug. 30, 1993; Acts 1995, 74th Leg., ch. 76, § 5.84(a), eff. Sept. 1, 1995; Acts 1995, 74th Leg., ch. 779, § 1, eff. Sept. 1, 1995; Acts 1997, 75th Leg., ch. 1434, § 1, eff. Sept. 1, 1997; Acts 2009, 81st Leg., ch. 496, § 1, eff. Sept. 1, 2009; Acts 2009, 81st Leg., ch. 716, § 1, eff. June 19, 2009.

Art. 56.38. Review; Verification

(a) The attorney general shall appoint a clerk to review each application for compensation under Article 56.36 to ensure the application is complete. If an application is not complete, the clerk shall return it to the claimant or victim and give a brief statement showing the additional information required. Not later than the 30th day after receiving a returned application, a claimant or victim may:

(1) supply the additional information; or

(2) appeal the action to the attorney general, who shall review the application to determine whether it is complete.

(b) The attorney general may investigate an application.

(c) Incident to the attorney general's review, verification, and hearing duties under this subchapter, the attorney general may:

(1) subpoena witnesses and administer oaths to determine whether and the extent to which a claimant or victim qualifies for an award; and

(2) order a claimant or victim to submit to a mental or physical examination by a physician or psychologist or order an autopsy of a deceased victim as provided by Article 56.39, if the mental, physical, or emotional condition of a claimant or victim is material to a claim.

(d) On request by the attorney general and not later than the 14th business day after the date of the request, a law enforcement agency shall release to the attorney general all reports, including witness statements and criminal history record information, for the purpose of allowing the attorney general to determine whether a claimant or victim qualifies for an award and the extent of the qualification.

Added by Acts 1993, 73rd Leg., ch. 268, § 6, eff. Sept. 1, 1993. Amended by Acts 1995, 74th Leg., ch. 76, § 5.84(a), eff. Sept. 1, 1995; Acts 1995, 74th Leg., ch. 779, § 1, eff. Sept. 1, 1995.

Art. 56.385.   Review of Health Care Services

(a) The attorney general may review the actual or proposed health care services for which a claimant or victim seeks compensation in an application filed under Article 56.36.

(b) The attorney general may not compensate a claimant or victim for health care services that the attorney general determines are not medically necessary.

(c) The attorney general, a claimant, or a victim is not liable for a charge that is not medically necessary.

Added by Acts 1995, 74th Leg., ch. 779, § 1, eff. Sept. 1, 1995.

Art. 56.39.   Mental or Physical Examination; Autopsy

(a) An order for a mental or physical examination or an autopsy as provided by Article 56.38(c)(2) may be made for good cause shown on notice to the individual to be examined and to all persons who have appeared.

(b) An order shall:

(1) specify the time, place, manner, conditions, and scope of the examination or autopsy;

(2) specify the person by whom the examination or autopsy is to be made; and

(3) require the person making the examination or autopsy to file with the attorney general a detailed written report of the examination or autopsy.

(c) A report shall set out the findings of the person making the examination or autopsy, including:

(1) the results of any tests made; and

(2) diagnoses, prognoses, and other conclusions and reports of earlier examinations of the same conditions.

(d) On request of the individual examined, the attorney general shall furnish the individual with a copy of the report. If the victim is deceased, the attorney general on request shall furnish the claimant with a copy of the report.

(e) A physician or psychologist making an examination or autopsy under this article shall be compensated from funds appropriated for the administration of this subchapter.

Added by Acts 1993, 73rd Leg., ch. 268, § 6, eff. Sept. 1, 1993. Amended by Acts 1995, 74th Leg., ch. 76, § 5.84(a), eff. Sept. 1, 1995; Acts 1995, 74th Leg., ch. 779, § 1, eff. Sept. 1, 1995; Acts 2013, 83rd Leg., ch. 161 (S.B. 1093), § 3.011, eff. Sept. 1, 2013; Acts 2013, 83rd Leg., ch. 1173 (S.B. 745), § 1, eff. Sept. 1, 2013.

Art. 56.40.   Hearings

(a) The attorney general shall determine whether a hearing on an application for compensation under this subchapter is necessary.

(b) If the attorney general determines that a hearing is not necessary, the attorney general may approve the application in accordance with the provisions of Article 56.41.

(c) If the attorney general determines that a hearing is necessary or if the claimant or victim requests a hearing, the attorney general shall consider the application at a hearing at a time and place of the attorney general's choosing. The attorney general shall notify all interested persons not less than 10 days before the date of the hearing.

(d) At the hearing the attorney general shall:

(1) review the application for assistance and the report prepared under Article 56.39 and any other evidence obtained as a result of the attorney general's investigation; and

(2) receive other evidence that the attorney general finds necessary or desirable to evaluate the application properly.

(e) The attorney general may appoint hearing officers to conduct hearings or prehearing conferences under this subchapter.

(f) A hearing or prehearing conference is open to the public unless in a particular case the hearing officer or attorney general determines that the hearing or prehearing conference or a part of it should be held in private because a criminal suspect has not been apprehended or because it is in the interest of the claimant or victim.

(g) The attorney general may suspend the proceedings pending disposition of a criminal prosecution that has been commenced or is imminent, but may make an emergency award under Article 56.50.

(h) Subchapters C through H, Chapter 2001, Government Code,[1] do not apply to the attorney general or the attorney general's orders and decisions.

Added by Acts 1993, 73rd Leg., ch. 268, § 6, eff. Sept. 1, 1993. Amended by Acts 1995, 74th Leg., ch. 76, § 5.84(a), eff. Sept. 1, 1995; Acts 1995, 74th Leg., ch. 779, § 1, eff. Sept. 1, 1995.

[1] V.T.C.A., Government Code §§ 2001.051 et seq. through 2001.201, 2001.202.

Art. 56.41.   Approval of Claim

(a) The attorney general shall approve an application for compensation under this subchapter if the attorney general finds by a preponderance of the evidence that grounds for compensation under this subchapter exist.

(b) The attorney general shall deny an application for compensation under this subchapter if:

(1) the criminally injurious conduct is not reported as provided by Article 56.46;

(2) the application is not made in the manner provided by Articles 56.36 and 56.37;

(3) the claimant or victim knowingly and willingly participated in the criminally injurious conduct;

(4) the claimant or victim is the offender or an accomplice of the offender;

(5) an award of compensation to the claimant or victim would benefit the offender or an accomplice of the offender;

(6) the claimant or victim was incarcerated in a penal institution, as defined by Section 1.07, Penal Code, at the time the offense was committed; or

(7) the claimant or victim knowingly or intentionally submits false or forged information to the attorney general.

(b–1) Subsection (b)(3) does not apply to a claimant or victim who seeks compensation for criminally injurious conduct that is:

(1) in violation of Section 20A.02(a)(7), Penal Code; or

(2) trafficking of persons, other than an offense described by Subdivision (1), if the criminally injurious conduct the claimant or victim participated in was the result of force, fraud, or coercion.

(c) Except as provided by rules adopted by the attorney general to prevent the unjust enrichment of an offender, the attorney general may not deny an award otherwise payable to a claimant or victim because the claimant or victim:

(1) is an immediate family member of the offender; or

(2) resides in the same household as the offender.

Added by Acts 1993, 73rd Leg., ch. 268, § 6, eff. Sept. 1, 1993. Amended by Acts 1995, 74th Leg., ch. 76, §§ 5.84(a), 14.28, eff. Sept. 1, 1995; Acts 1995, 74th Leg., ch. 779, § 1, eff. Sept. 1, 1995; Acts 1997, 75th Leg., ch. 1434, § 1, eff. Sept. 1, 1997; Acts 2015, 84th Leg., ch. 332 (H.B. 10), § 3, eff. Sept. 1, 2015.

Section 16 of Acts 2015, 84th Leg., ch. 332 (H.B. 10) provides:

"The changes in law made by this Act to Chapter 56, Code of Criminal Procedure, apply only to a criminal offense committed or a violation that occurs on or after the effective date [Sept. 1, 2015] of this Act. A criminal offense committed or a violation that occurs before the effective date of this Act is governed by the law in effect on the date the offense was committed or the violation occurred, and the former law is continued in effect for that purpose. For purposes of this section, a criminal offense was committed or a violation occurred before the effective date of this Act if any element of the offense or violation occurred before that date."

Art. 56.42.   Limits on Compensation

(a) Except as otherwise provided by this article, awards payable to a victim and all other claimants sustaining pecuniary loss because of injury or death of that victim may not exceed $50,000 in the aggregate.

(b) In addition to an award payable under Subsection (a), the attorney general may award an additional $75,000 for extraordinary pecuniary losses, if the personal injury to a victim is catastrophic and results in a total and permanent disability to the victim, for lost wages and reasonable and necessary costs of:

(1) making a home or automobile accessible;

(2) obtaining job training and vocational rehabilitation;

(3) training in the use of special appliances;

(4) receiving home health care;

(5) durable medical equipment;

(6) rehabilitation technology; and

(7) long-term medical expenses incurred as a result of medically indicated treatment for the personal injury.

(c) The attorney general may by rule establish limitations on any other pecuniary loss compensated for under this subchapter, including limitations on pecuniary loss incurred as a result of a claimant's travel to and attendance of a deceased victim's funeral.

(d) A victim who is a victim of stalking, family violence, or trafficking of persons, or a victim of sexual assault who is assaulted in the victim's place of residence, may receive a onetime-only assistance payment in an amount not to exceed:

(1) $2,000 to be used for relocation expenses, including expenses for rental deposit, utility connections, expenses relating to the moving of belongings, motor vehicle mileage expenses, and for out-of-state moves, transportation, lodging, and meals; and

(2) $1,800 to be used for housing rental expenses.

(e) An immediate family member or household member of a deceased victim may not receive more than $1,000 in lost wages as a result of bereavement leave taken by the family or household member.

Added by Acts 1993, 73rd Leg., ch. 268, § 6, eff. Sept. 1, 1993. Amended by Acts 1995, 74th Leg., ch. 76, § 5.84(a), eff. Sept. 1, 1995; Acts 1995, 74th Leg., ch. 779, § 1, eff. Sept. 1, 1995; Acts 1997, 75th Leg., ch. 1434, § 1, eff. Sept. 1, 1997; Acts 1999, 76th Leg., ch. 1470, § 2, eff. June 19, 1999; Acts 2001, 77th Leg., ch. 11, § 3, eff. Sept. 1, 2001; Acts 2001, 77th Leg., ch. 274, § 1, eff. Sept. 1, 2001; Acts 2003, 78th Leg., ch. 1286, § 2, eff. Sept. 1, 2003; Acts 2013, 83rd Leg., ch. 1252 (H.B. 8), § 9, eff. Sept. 1, 2013; Acts 2015, 84th Leg., ch. 924 (H.B. 1446), § 5, eff. Sept. 1, 2015.

Sections 8 and 9 of Acts 2015, 84th Leg., ch. 924 (H.B. 1446) provide:

"Sec. 8. The change in law made by this Act relating to reimbursement of certain medical costs applies only to payments made for medical care provided on or after the effective date [Sept. 1, 2015] of this Act. Payments made for medical care provided before the effective date of this Act are governed by the law in effect on the date the care was provided, and the former law is continued in effect for that purpose.

"Sec. 9. The change in law made by this Act relating to compensation for relocation and housing rental expenses applies only to a victim of a criminal offense committed or a violation that occurs on or after the effective date of this Act. The victim of a criminal offense committed or a violation that occurs before the effective date of this Act is governed by the law in effect on the date the offense was committed or the violation occurred, and the former law is continued in effect for that purpose. For purposes of this section, a criminal offense was committed or a violation occurred before the effective date of this Act if any element of the offense or violation occurred before that date."

Art. 56.43.   Attorney Fees

(a) As part of an order, the attorney general shall determine and award reasonable attorney's fees, commensurate with legal services rendered, to be paid by the state to the attorney representing the claimant or victim. Attorney fees shall not exceed 25 percent of the amount the attorney assisted the claimant or victim in obtaining. Where there is no dispute of the attorney general's determination of the amount of the award due to the claimant or victim and where no hearing is held, the attorney fee shall be the lesser of either 25 percent of the amount the attorney assisted the claimant or victim in obtaining or $300.

(b) Attorney fees may be denied on a finding that the claim or appeal is frivolous.

(c) An award of attorney fees is in addition to an award of compensation.

(d) An attorney may not contract for or receive an amount larger than that allowed under this article.

(e) Attorney fees may not be paid to an attorney of a claimant or victim unless an award is made to the claimant or victim.

Added by Acts 1993, 73rd Leg., ch. 268, § 6, eff. Sept. 1, 1993. Amended by Acts 1993, 73rd Leg., ch. 805, § 9, eff. Aug. 30, 1993; Acts 1995, 74th Leg., ch. 76, § 5.84(a), eff. Sept. 1, 1995; Acts 1995, 74th Leg., ch. 779, § 1, eff. Sept. 1, 1995.

Art. 56.44.   Payments

(a) The attorney general may provide for the payment of an award in a lump sum or in installments. The attorney general shall provide that the part of an award equal to the amount of pecuniary loss accrued to the date of the award be paid in a lump sum. Except as provided in Subsection (b), the attorney general shall pay the part of an award for allowable expense that accrues after the award is made in installments.

(b) At the request of the claimant or victim, the attorney general may provide that an award for future pecuniary loss be paid in a lump sum if the attorney general finds that:

(1) paying the award in a lump sum will promote the interests of the claimant or victim; or

(2) the present value of all future pecuniary loss does not exceed $1,000.

(c) The attorney general may not provide for an award for future pecuniary loss payable in installments for a period for which the attorney general cannot reasonably determine the future pecuniary loss.

(d) The attorney general may make payments only to an individual who is a claimant or a victim or to a provider on the individual's behalf.

Added by Acts 1993, 73rd Leg., ch. 268, § 6, eff. Sept. 1, 1993. Amended by Acts 1995, 74th Leg., ch. 76, § 5.84(a), eff. Sept. 1, 1995; Acts 1995, 74th Leg., ch. 779, § 1, eff. Sept. 1, 1995; Acts 1997, 75th Leg., ch. 1434, § 1, eff. Sept. 1, 1997.

Art. 56.45.   Denial or Reduction of Award

(a) The attorney general may deny or reduce an award otherwise payable:

(1) if the claimant or victim has not substantially cooperated with an appropriate law enforcement agency;

(2) if the claimant or victim bears a share of the responsibility for the act or omission giving rise to the claim because of the claimant's or victim's behavior;

(3) to the extent that pecuniary loss is recouped from a collateral source; or

(4) if the claimant or victim was engaging in an activity that at the time of the criminally injurious conduct was prohibited by law or a rule made under law.

(b) Subsection (a)(4) does not apply to a claimant or victim who seeks compensation for criminally injurious conduct that is:

(1) in violation of Section 20A.02(a)(7), Penal Code; or

(2) trafficking of persons, other than an offense described by Subdivision (1), if the activity the claimant or victim engaged in was the result of force, fraud, or coercion.

Added by Acts 1993, 73rd Leg., ch. 268, § 6, eff. Sept. 1, 1993. Amended by Acts 1995, 74th Leg., ch. 76, § 5.84(a), eff. Sept. 1, 1995; Acts 1995, 74th Leg., ch. 779, § 1, eff. Sept. 1, 1995; Acts 1997, 75th Leg., ch. 1434, § 1, eff. Sept. 1, 1997; Acts 2015, 84th Leg., ch. 332 (H.B. 10), § 4, eff. Sept. 1, 2015.

Section 16 of Acts 2015, 84th Leg., ch. 332 (H.B. 10) provides:

"The changes in law made by this Act to Chapter 56, Code of Criminal Procedure, apply only to a criminal offense committed or a violation that occurs on or after the effective date [Sept. 1, 2015] of this Act. A criminal offense committed or a violation that occurs before the effective date of this Act is governed by the law in effect on the date the offense was committed or the violation occurred, and the former law is continued in effect for that purpose. For purposes of this section, a criminal offense was committed or a violation occurred before the effective date of this Act if any element of the offense or violation occurred before that date."

Art. 56.46. Reporting of Crime

(a) Except as otherwise provided by this article, a claimant or victim may not file an application unless the victim reports the criminally injurious conduct to the appropriate state or local public safety or law enforcement agency within a reasonable period of time, but not so late as to interfere with or hamper the investigation and prosecution of the crime after the criminally injurious conduct is committed.

(b) The attorney general may extend the time for reporting the criminally injurious conduct if the attorney general determines that the extension is justified by extraordinary circumstances.

(c) Subsection (a) does not apply if the victim is a child.

Added by Acts 1993, 73rd Leg., ch. 268, § 6, eff. Sept. 1, 1993. Amended by Acts 1995, 74th Leg., ch. 76, § 5.84(a), eff. Sept. 1, 1995; Acts 1995, 74th Leg., ch. 779, § 1, eff. Sept. 1, 1995; Acts 1997, 75th Leg., ch. 1434, § 1, eff. Sept. 1, 1997.

Art. 56.47. Reconsideration

(a) The attorney general, on the attorney general's own motion or on request of a claimant or victim, may reconsider:

(1) a decision to make or deny an award; or

(2) the amount of an award.

(b) At least annually, the attorney general shall reconsider each award being paid in installments.

(c) An order on reconsideration may require a refund of an award if:

(1) the award was obtained by fraud or mistake; or

(2) newly discovered evidence shows the claimant or victim to be ineligible for the award under Article 56.41 or 56.45.

Added by Acts 1993, 73rd Leg., ch. 268, § 6, eff. Sept. 1, 1993. Amended by Acts 1993, 73rd Leg., ch. 805, § 6, eff. Aug. 30, 1993; Acts 1995, 74th Leg., ch. 76, § 5.84(a), 5.85(b), eff. Sept. 1, 1995; Acts 1995, 74th Leg., ch. 779, § 1, eff. Sept. 1, 1995; Acts 1997, 75th Leg., ch. 1434, § 1, eff. Sept. 1, 1997.

Art. 56.48. Judicial Review

(a) Not later than the 40th day after the attorney general renders a final decision, a claimant or victim may file with the attorney general a notice of dissatisfaction with the decision. Not later than the 40th day after the claimant or victim gives notice, the claimant or victim shall bring suit in the district court having jurisdiction in the county in which:

(1) the injury or death occurred;

(2) the victim resided at the time the injury or death occurred; or

(3) if the victim resided out of state at the time of the injury or death, in the county where the injury or death occurred or in a district court of Travis County.

(b) While judicial review of a decision by the attorney general is pending, the attorney general:

(1) shall suspend payments to the claimant or victim; and

(2) may not reconsider the award.

(c) The court shall determine the issues by trial de novo. The burden of proof is on the party who filed the notice of dissatisfaction.

(d) A court may award not more than 25 percent of the total recovery by the claimant or victim for attorney fees in the event of review.

(e) In computing a period under this article, if the last day is a legal holiday or Sunday, the last day is not counted, and the time is extended to include the next business day.

Added by Acts 1993, 73rd Leg., ch. 268, § 6, eff. Sept. 1, 1993. Amended by Acts 1995, 74th Leg., ch. 76, § 5.84(a), eff. Sept. 1, 1995; Acts 1995, 74th Leg., ch. 779, § 1, eff. Sept. 1, 1995; Acts 1997, 75th Leg., ch. 1434, § 1, eff. Sept. 1, 1997.

Art. 56.49. Exemption; Assignability

(a) An award is not subject to execution, attachment, garnishment, or other process, except that an award is not exempt from a claim of a creditor to the extent that the creditor provided products, services, or accommodations, the costs of which are included in the award.

(b) An assignment or agreement to assign a right to benefits for loss accruing in the future is unenforceable except:

(1) an assignment of a right to benefits for loss of earnings is enforceable to secure payment of alimony, maintenance, or child support; and

(2) an assignment of a right to benefits is enforceable to the extent that the benefits are for the cost of products, services, or accommodations:

(A) made necessary by the injury or death on which the claim is based; and

(B) provided or to be provided by the assignee.

Added by Acts 1993, 73rd Leg., ch. 268, § 6, eff. Sept. 1, 1993. Amended by Acts 1995, 74th Leg., ch. 76, § 5.84(a), eff. Sept. 1, 1995; Acts 1995, 74th Leg., ch. 779, § 1, eff. Sept. 1, 1995.

Art. 56.50. Emergency Award

(a) The attorney general may make an emergency award if, before acting on an application for compensation under this subchapter, it appears likely that:

(1) a final award will be made; and

(2) the claimant or victim will suffer undue hardship if immediate economic relief is not obtained.

(b) An emergency award may not exceed $1,500.

(c) The amount of an emergency award shall be:

(1) deducted from the final award; or

(2) repaid by and recoverable from the claimant or victim to the extent the emergency award exceeds the final award.

Added by Acts 1993, 73rd Leg., ch. 268, § 6, eff. Sept. 1, 1993. Amended by Acts 1995, 74th Leg., ch. 76, § 5.84(a), eff. Sept. 1, 1995; Acts 1995, 74th Leg., ch. 779, § 1, eff. Sept. 1, 1995.

Art. 56.51. Subrogation

If compensation is awarded under this subchapter, the state is subrogated to all the claimant's or victim's rights to receive or recover benefits for pecuniary loss to the extent compensation is awarded from a collateral source.

Added by Acts 1993, 73rd Leg., ch. 268, § 6, eff. Sept. 1, 1993. Amended by Acts 1995, 74th Leg., ch. 76, § 5.84(a), eff. Sept. 1, 1995; Acts 1995, 74th Leg., ch. 779, § 1, eff. Sept. 1, 1995.

Art. 56.52. Notice of Private Action

(a) Before a claimant or victim may bring an action to recover damages related to criminally injurious conduct for which compensation under this subchapter is claimed or awarded, the claimant or victim must give the attorney general written notice of the proposed action. After receiving the notice, the attorney general shall promptly:

(1) join in the action as a party plaintiff to recover benefits awarded;

(2) require the claimant or victim to bring the action in the claimant's or victim's name as a trustee on behalf of the state to recover benefits awarded; or

(3) reserve the attorney general's rights and do neither in the proposed action.

(b) If the claimant or victim brings the action as trustee and recovers compensation awarded by the attorney general, the claimant or victim may deduct from the benefits recovered on behalf of the state the reasonable expenses of the suit, including attorney fees, expended in pursuing the recovery for the state. The claimant or victim must justify this deduction in writing to the attorney general on a form provided by the attorney general.

(c) A claimant or victim shall not settle or resolve any such action without written authorization to do so from the attorney general. No third party or agents, insurers, or attorneys for third parties shall participate in the settlement or resolution of such an action if they actually know, or should know, that the claimant or victim has received moneys from the fund and is subject to the subrogation provisions of this article. Any attempt by such third party, or agents, insurers, or attorneys of third parties to settle an action is void and shall result in no release from liability to the fund for any rights subrogated pursuant to this article. All such agents, insurers, and attorneys are personally liable to the fund for any moneys paid to a claimant or victim in violation of this subsection, up to the full amount of the fund's right to reimbursement. A claimant, victim, third party, or any agents, attorneys, or insurers of third parties who knowingly or intentionally fail to comply with the requirements of this chapter commits a Class B misdemeanor.

(d) A person adjudged guilty of a Class B misdemeanor shall be punished by:

(1) a fine not to exceed $500;

(2) confinement in jail for a term not to exceed 180 days; or

(3) both such fine and imprisonment.

Added by Acts 1993, 73rd Leg., ch. 268, § 6, eff. Sept. 1, 1993. Amended by Acts 1993, 73rd Leg., ch. 805, § 11, eff. Aug. 30, 1993; Acts 1995, 74th Leg., ch. 76, § 5.84(a), eff. Sept. 1, 1995; Acts 1995, 74th Leg., ch. 779, § 1, eff. Sept. 1, 1995.

Art. 56.53. Annual Report

Annually, the attorney general shall report to the governor and the legislature on the attorney general's activities, including a statistical summary of claims and awards made and denied. The reporting period is the state fiscal year. The attorney general shall file the report not later than the 100th day after the end of the fiscal year.

Added by Acts 1993, 73rd Leg., ch. 268, § 6, eff. Sept. 1, 1993. Amended by Acts 1995, 74th Leg., ch. 76, § 5.84(a), eff. Sept. 1, 1995; Acts 1995, 74th Leg., ch. 779, § 1, eff. Sept. 1, 1995.

Art. 56.54. Funds

(a) The compensation to victims of crime fund is in the state treasury.

(b) Except as provided by Subsections (h), (i), (j), and (k) and Article 56.541, the compensation to victims of crime fund may be used only by the attorney general for the payment of compensation to claimants or victims under this subchapter. For purposes of this subsection, compensation to claimants or victims includes money allocated from the fund to the Crime Victims' Institute created by Section 96.65, Education Code, for the operation of the institute and for other expenses in administering this subchapter. The insti-

tute shall use money allocated from the fund only for the purposes of Sections 96.65, 96.651, and 96.652, Education Code.

(c) Repealed by Acts 2017, 85th Leg., ch. 351 (H.B. 1866), § 5(1).

(d) The attorney general may not make compensation payments in excess of the amount of money available in the compensation to victims of crime fund.

(e) General revenues may not be used for payments under this subchapter.

(f) The office of the attorney general is authorized to accept gifts, grants, and donations to be credited to the compensation to victims of crime fund and shall file annually with the governor and the presiding officer of each house of the legislature a complete and detailed written report accounting for all gifts, grants, and donations received and disbursed, used, or maintained by the office for the attorney general that are credited to the fund.

(g) Money in the compensation to victims of crime fund may be used only as provided by this subchapter and is not available for any other purpose. Section 403.095, Government Code, does not apply to the fund.

(h) An amount of money deposited to the credit of the compensation to victims of crime fund not to exceed one-quarter of the amount disbursed from that fund in the form of compensation payments during a fiscal year shall be carried forward into the next succeeding fiscal year and applied toward the amount listed in the next succeeding fiscal year's method of financing.

(i) If the sums available in the compensation to victims of crime fund are sufficient in a fiscal year to make all compensation payments, the attorney general may retain any portion of the fund that was deposited during the fiscal year that was in excess of compensation payments made during that fiscal year as an emergency reserve for the next fiscal year. Such emergency reserve may not exceed $10,000,000. The emergency reserve fund may be used only to make compensation awards in claims and for providing emergency relief and assistance, including crisis intervention, emergency housing, travel, food, or expenses and technical assistance expenses incurred in the implementation of this subsection in incidents resulting from an act of mass violence or from an act of international terrorism as defined by 18 U.S.C. Section 2331, occurring in the state or for Texas residents injured or killed in an act of terrorism outside of the United States.

(j) The legislature may appropriate money in the compensation to victims of crime fund to administer the associate judge program under Subchapter C, Chapter 201, Family Code.

(k) The attorney general may use the compensation to victims of crime fund to:

(1) reimburse a law enforcement agency for the reasonable costs of a forensic medical examination that are incurred by the agency under Article 56.06 or 56.065; and

(2) make a payment to or on behalf of an individual for the reasonable costs incurred for medical care provided under Article 56.06 or 56.065 in accordance with Section 323.004, Health and Safety Code.

(*l*) As appropriated by the legislature, the attorney general may use the compensation to victims of crime auxiliary fund to cover costs incurred by the attorney general in administering the address confidentiality program established under Subchapter C.

(m) Not later than September 15 of each year, the attorney general, after consulting with the comptroller, shall certify the amount of money remaining in the compensation to victims of crime auxiliary fund at the end of the preceding state fiscal year. If the amount remaining in the fund exceeds $5 million, as soon as practicable after the date of certification, the attorney general may transfer from that excess amount in the compensation to victims of crime auxiliary fund to the compensation to victims of crime fund an amount that is not more than 50 percent of the excess amount in the auxiliary fund, to be used only for the purpose of making compensation payments during the fiscal year in which the amount is transferred.

(m–1) Notwithstanding Subsection (m), the attorney general may not transfer money under that subsection during a fiscal year beginning September 1, 2017, or September 1, 2018. This subsection expires September 1, 2019.

Added by Acts 1993, 73rd Leg., ch. 268, § 6, eff. Sept. 1, 1993. Amended by Acts 1993, 73rd Leg., ch. 805, § 1, eff. Aug. 30, 1993; Acts 1995, 74th Leg., ch. 76, § 5.84(a), eff. Sept. 1, 1995; Acts 1995, 74th Leg., ch. 779, § 1, eff. Sept. 1, 1995; Acts 1997, 75th Leg., ch. 1042, § 2, eff. Sept. 1, 1997; Acts 1997, 75th Leg., ch. 1042, § 1, eff. June 19, 1997; Acts 1997, 75th Leg., ch. 1434, § 1, eff. Sept. 1, 1997; Acts 1999, 76th Leg., ch. 1302, § 13, eff. Sept. 1, 1999; Acts 2001, 77th Leg., ch. 1507, §§ 2, 3, eff. June 15, 2001; Acts 2003, 78th Leg., ch. 927, § 2, eff. Sept. 1, 2003; Acts 2007, 80th Leg., ch. 1295, § 2, eff. June 15, 2007; Acts 2009, 81st Leg., ch. 532, § 1, eff. Sept. 1, 2009; Acts 2015, 84th Leg., ch. 924 (H.B. 1446), § 6, eff. Sept. 1, 2015; Acts 2017, 85th Leg., ch. 351 (H.B. 1866), §§ 1, 5(1), eff. Sept. 1, 2017.

Sections 8 and 9 of Acts 2015, 84th Leg., ch. 924 (H.B. 1446) provide:

"Sec. 8. The change in law made by this Act relating to reimbursement of certain medical costs applies only to payments made for medical care provided on or after the effective date [Sept. 1, 2015] of this Act. Payments made for medical care provided before the effective date of this Act are governed by the law in effect on the date the care was provided, and the former law is continued in effect for that purpose.

"Sec. 9. The change in law made by this Act relating to compensation for relocation and housing rental expenses applies only to a victim of a criminal offense committed or a violation that occurs on or after the effective date of this Act. The victim of a criminal offense committed or a violation that occurs before the effective date of this Act is governed by the law in effect on the date the offense was committed or the violation occurred, and the former law is continued in effect for that purpose. For purposes of this section, a criminal offense was committed or a violation occurred before the effective date of this Act if any element of the offense or violation occurred before that date."

Art. 56.541. Appropriation of Excess Money for Other Crime Victim Assistance

(a) Not later than December 15 of each even-numbered year, the attorney general, after consulting with the comptroller, shall prepare forecasts and certify estimates of:

(1) the amount of money that the attorney general anticipates will be received from deposits made to the credit of the compensation to victims of crime fund during the next state fiscal biennium, other than deposits of:

(A) gifts, grants, and donations; and

(B) money received from the United States;

(2) the amount of money from the fund that the attorney general anticipates will be obligated during the next state fiscal biennium to comply with this chapter; and

(3) the amount of money in the fund that the attorney general anticipates will remain unexpended at the end of the current state fiscal year and that is available for appropriation in the next state fiscal biennium.

(b) At the time the attorney general certifies the estimates made under Subsection (a), the attorney general shall also certify for the next state fiscal biennium the amount of excess money in the compensation to victims of crime fund available for the purposes of Subsection (c), calculated by multiplying the amount estimated under Subsection (a)(2) by 105 percent, and subtracting that product from the sum of the amounts estimated under Subsections (a)(1) and (a)(3).

(c) For a state fiscal biennium, the legislature may appropriate from the compensation to victims of crime fund the amount of excess money in the fund certified for the biennium under Subsection (b) to state agencies that deliver or fund victim-related services or assistance.

(d) The attorney general and the comptroller shall cooperate in determining the proper allocation of the various sources of revenue deposited to the credit of the compensation to victims of crime fund for purposes of this article.

(e) The attorney general may use money appropriated from the compensation to victims of crime fund for grants or contracts supporting victim-related services or assistance, including support for private Texas nonprofit corporations that provide victim-related civil legal services directly to victims, immediate family members of victims, or claimants. A grant supporting victim-related services or assistance is governed by Chapter 783, Government Code.

(f) The attorney general shall adopt rules necessary to carry out this article.

Added by Acts 1997, 75th Leg., ch. 1042, § 3, eff. Sept. 1, 1997. Amended by Acts 1999, 76th Leg., ch. 1077, § 1, eff. Aug. 30, 1999; Acts 2005, 79th Leg., ch. 66, § 3, eff. Sept. 1, 2005; Acts 2009, 81st Leg., ch. 532, § 2, eff. Sept. 1, 2009.

Art. 56.542. Payments for Certain Disabled Peace Officers

(a) In this article, "peace officer":

(1) means an individual elected, appointed, or employed to serve as a peace officer for a governmental entity under Article 2.12 or other law; and

(2) includes a former peace officer who because of an injury suffered while performing duties as a peace officer is entitled to receive payments under this article.

(b) If a peace officer employed by the state or a local governmental entity in this state sustains an injury as a result of criminally injurious conduct on or after September 1, 1989, in the performance of the officer's duties as a peace officer and presents evidence satisfactory to the attorney general that the officer's condition is a total disability resulting in permanent incapacity for work and that the total disability has persisted for more than 12 months, the officer is entitled to an annual payment equal to the difference between:

(1) any amounts received by the officer on account of the injury or disability from other sources of income, including settlements related to the injury or disability, insurance benefits, federal disability benefits, workers' compensation benefits, and benefits from another governmental entity, if those amounts do not exceed the amount described by Subdivision (2); and

(2) an amount equal to the officer's average annual salary during the officer's final three years as a peace officer.

(c) The amount of the payment under Subsection (b) is subject to an annual cost-of-living adjustment computed by the attorney general. The attorney general shall compute the amount of the cost-of-living adjustment by multiplying the amount of the annual payment received by the peace officer under this section during the previous year times the percentage by which the Consumer Price Index for All Urban Consumers published by the Bureau of Labor Statistics of the United States Department of Labor, or its successor index, increased during the previous calendar year.

(d) The attorney general shall compute the amount of an initial payment based on an injury suffered after September 1, 1989, by:

(1) computing the amount to which the officer is entitled under Subsection (b); and

(2) adding to that amount the cumulative successive cost-of-living adjustments for the intervening years computed from the date of the injury.

(e) To receive a payment under this section, a peace officer must furnish to the attorney general:

(1) proof that the injury was sustained in the performance of the applicant's duties as a peace officer and is a total disability resulting in permanent incapacity for work; and

(2) other information or evidence the attorney general requires.

(f) The attorney general may approve the application without a hearing or may conduct a hearing under Article 56.40. The decision of the attorney general is subject to judicial review under Article 56.48.

(g) The attorney general may appoint a panel of physicians to periodically review each application for assistance under this article to ensure the validity of the application and the necessity of continued assistance to the peace officer.

(h) The attorney general shall notify the comptroller of the attorney general's determination that a claim under this section is valid and justifies payment. On receipt of the notice, the comptroller shall issue a warrant to or in behalf of the claimant in the proper amount from amounts in the compensation to victims of crime fund. A payment under this section to or in behalf of a peace officer is payable as soon as possible after the attorney general notifies the comptroller.

(*i*) The attorney general and the comptroller by rule shall adopt a memorandum of understanding to establish procedures under which annual payments continue to a peace officer until continued assistance is no longer necessary.

(j) Article 56.37 does not apply to the filing of an application under this article. Other provisions of this chapter apply to this article to the extent applicable and consistent with this article.

(k) The limits on compensation imposed by Article 56.42 do not apply to payments made under this article, but the total aggregate amount of all annual payments made to an individual peace officer under this section may not exceed $200,000.

(*l*) A peace officer who is entitled to an annual payment under Subsection (b) may elect to receive the payment in:

(1) a single payment paid each year; or

(2) equal monthly installments.

Added by Acts 2001, 77th Leg., ch. 1512, § 2, eff. Sept. 1, 2001. Amended by Acts 2005, 79th Leg., ch. 751, § 1, eff. June 17, 2005.

Arts. 56.55 to 56.57. Repealed by Acts 2003, 78th Leg., ch. 209, § 85(a)(1) to (3), eff. Jan. 1, 2004

Art. 56.58. Adjustment of Awards and Payments

(a) The attorney general shall establish a policy to adjust awards and payments so that the total amount of awards granted in each calendar year does not exceed the amount of money credited to the fund during that year.

(b) If the attorney general establishes a policy to adjust awards under Subsection (a), the attorney general, the claimant, or the victim is not liable for the amount of charges incurred in excess of the adjusted amount for the service on which the adjusted payment is determined.

(c) A service provider who accepts a payment that has been adjusted by a policy established under Subsection (a) agrees to accept the adjusted payment as payment in full for the service and is barred from legal action against the claimant or victim for collection.

Added by Acts 1993, 73rd Leg., ch. 268, § 6, eff. Sept. 1, 1993. Amended by Acts 1995, 74th Leg., ch. 76, § 5.84(a), eff. Sept. 1, 1995; Acts 1995, 74th Leg., ch. 779, § 1, eff. Sept. 1, 1995.

Art. 56.59. Repealed by Acts 2003, 78th Leg., ch. 209, § 85(a)(4), eff. Jan. 1, 2004

Art. 56.60. Public Notice

(a) A hospital licensed under the laws of this state shall display prominently in its emergency room posters giving notification of the existence and general provisions of this subchapter. The attorney general shall set standards for the location of the display and shall provide posters, application forms, and general information regarding this subchapter to each hospital and physician licensed to practice in this state.

(b) Each local law enforcement agency shall inform a claimant or victim of criminally injurious conduct of the provisions of this subchapter and make application forms available. The attorney general shall provide application forms and all other documents that local law enforcement agencies may require to comply with this article. The attorney general shall set standards to be followed by local law enforcement agencies for this purpose and may require them to file with the attorney general a description of the procedures adopted by each agency to comply.

Added by Acts 1993, 73rd Leg., ch. 268, § 6, eff. Sept. 1, 1993. Amended by Acts 1995, 74th Leg., ch. 76, § 5.84(a), eff. Sept. 1, 1995; Acts 1995, 74th Leg., ch. 779, § 1, eff. Sept. 1, 1995.

Art. 56.61. Compensation for Certain Criminally Injurious Conduct Prohibited; Exception

(a) Except as provided by Subsection (b), the attorney general may not award compensation for pecuniary loss arising from criminally injurious conduct that occurred before January 1, 1980.

(b) The attorney general may award compensation for pecuniary loss arising from criminally injurious conduct that occurred before January 1, 1980, if:

(1) the conduct was in violation of Chapter 19, Penal Code;

(2) the identity of the victim is established by a law enforcement agency on or after January 1, 2009; and

(3) the claimant files the application for compensation within the limitations period provided by Article 56.37(e).

Added by Acts 1993, 73rd Leg., ch. 268, § 6, eff. Sept. 1, 1993. Amended by Acts 1995, 74th Leg., ch. 76, § 5.84(a), eff. Sept. 1, 1995; Acts 1995, 74th Leg., ch. 779, § 1, eff. Sept. 1, 1995; Acts 2009, 81st Leg., ch. 496, § 2, eff. Sept. 1, 2009; Acts 2009, 81st Leg., ch. 716, § 2, eff. June 19, 2009; Acts 2013, 83rd Leg., ch. 1173 (S.B. 745), § 2, eff. Sept. 1, 2013.

Art. 56.62.   Public Letter of Reprimand

(a) The attorney general may issue a letter of reprimand against an individual if the attorney general finds that the person has filed or has caused to be filed under this subchapter an application for benefits or claim for pecuniary loss that contains a statement or representation that the person knows to be false.

(b) The attorney general must give the person notice of the proposed action before issuing the letter.

(c) A person may challenge the denial of compensation and the issuance of a letter of reprimand in a contested case hearing under Chapter 2001, Government Code (Administrative Procedure Act).

(d) A letter of reprimand issued under this article is public information.

Added by Acts 1995, 74th Leg., ch. 779, § 1, eff. Sept. 1, 1995.

Art. 56.63.   Civil Penalty

(a) A person is subject to a civil penalty of not less than $2,500 or more than $25,000 for each application for compensation that:

(1) is filed under this subchapter by the person or is filed under this subchapter as a result of conduct of the person; and

(2) contains a material statement or representation that the person knows to be false.

(b) The attorney general shall institute and conduct the suit to collect the civil penalty authorized by this article on behalf of the state.

(c) A civil penalty recovered under this article shall be deposited to the credit of the compensation to victims of crime fund.

(d) The civil penalty authorized by this article is in addition to any other civil, administrative, or criminal penalty provided by law.

(e) In addition to the civil penalty authorized by this article, the attorney general may recover expenses incurred by the attorney general in the investigation, institution, and prosecution of the suit, including investigative costs, witness fees, attorney's fees, and deposition expenses.

Added by Acts 1995, 74th Leg., ch. 779, § 1, eff. Sept. 1, 1995.

Art. 56.64.   Administrative Penalty

(a) A person who presents to the attorney general under this subchapter, or engages in conduct that results in the presentation to the attorney general

under this subchapter of, an application for compensation under this subchapter that contains a statement or representation the person knows to be false is liable to the attorney general for:

(1) the amount paid in reliance on the application and interest on that amount determined at the rate provided by law for legal judgments and accruing from the date on which the payment was made;

(2) payment of an administrative penalty not to exceed twice the amount paid because of the false application for benefits or claim for pecuniary loss; and

(3) payment of an administrative penalty of not more than $10,000 for each item or service for which payment was claimed.

(b) In determining the amount of the penalty to be assessed under Subsection (a)(3), the attorney general shall consider:

(1) the seriousness of the violation;

(2) whether the person has previously submitted a false application for benefits or a claim for pecuniary loss; and

(3) the amount necessary to deter the person from submitting future false applications for benefits or claims for pecuniary loss.

(c) If the attorney general determines that a violation has occurred, the attorney general may issue a report that states the facts on which the determination is made and the attorney general's recommendation on the imposition of a penalty, including a recommendation on the amount of the penalty.

(d) The attorney general shall give written notice of the report to the person. Notice under this subsection may be given by certified mail and must:

(1) include a brief summary of the alleged violation;

(2) include a statement of the amount of the recommended penalty; and

(3) inform the person of the right to a hearing on:

(A) the occurrence of the violation;

(B) the amount of the penalty; or

(C) both the occurrence of the violation and the amount of the penalty.

(e) Not later than the 20th day after the date the person receives the notice, the person, in writing, may:

(1) accept the attorney general's determination and recommended penalty; or

(2) request in writing a hearing on:

(A) the occurrence of the violation;

(B) the amount of the penalty; or

(C) both the occurrence of the violation and the amount of the penalty.

(f) If the person accepts the determination and recommended penalty of the attorney general, the attorney general by order shall approve the determination and impose the recommended penalty.

(g) If the person requests a hearing as provided by Subsection (e) or fails to respond to the notice in a timely manner, the attorney general shall set a contested case hearing under Chapter 2001, Government Code (Administrative Procedure Act), and notify the person of the hearing. The administrative law judge shall make findings of facts and conclusions of law and promptly issue to the attorney general a proposal for a decision regarding the occurrence of the violation and the amount of a proposed penalty. Based on the findings of fact, conclusions of law, and proposal for a decision, the attorney general by order may:

(1) find that a violation has occurred and impose a penalty; or

(2) find that a violation has not occurred.

(h) Notice of the attorney general's order given to the person under Chapter 2001, Government Code, must include a statement of the right of the person to judicial review of the order.

(i) Not later than the 30th day after the date that the attorney general's order is final under Section 2001.144, Government Code, the person shall:

(1) pay the amount of the penalty;

(2) pay the amount of the penalty and file a petition for judicial review contesting:

(A) the occurrence of the violation;

(B) the amount of the penalty; or

(C) the occurrence of the violation and the amount of the penalty; or

(3) without paying the amount of the penalty, file a petition for judicial review contesting:

(A) the occurrence of the violation;

(B) the amount of the penalty; or

(C) the occurrence of the violation and the amount of the penalty.

(j) Within the 30–day period, a person who acts under Subsection (i)(3) may:

(1) stay enforcement of the penalty by:

(A) paying the amount of the penalty to the court for placement in an escrow account; or

(B) giving to the court a supersedeas bond that is approved by the court for the amount of the penalty and that is effective until all judicial review of the attorney general's order is final; or

(2) request the court to stay enforcement of the penalty by:

(A) filing with the court a sworn affidavit of the person stating that the person is financially unable to pay the amount of the penalty or to give the supersedeas bond; and

(B) delivering a copy of the affidavit to the attorney general by certified mail.

(k) On receipt by the attorney general of a copy of an affidavit under Subsection (j)(2), the attorney general may file with the court, not later than the fifth day after the date the copy is received, a contest to the affidavit. The court shall hold a hearing on the facts alleged in the affidavit as soon as practicable and shall stay the enforcement of the penalty on finding that the alleged facts are true. A person who files an affidavit under Subsection (j)(2) has the burden of proving that the person is financially unable to pay the amount of the penalty or to give a supersedeas bond.

(*l*) If the person does not pay the amount of the penalty and the enforcement of the penalty is not stayed, the attorney general may file suit for collection of the amount of the penalty.

(m) Judicial review of the order of the attorney general:

(1) is instituted by filing a petition as provided by Section 2001.176, Government Code; and

(2) is governed by the substantial evidence rule.

(n) If the court upholds the finding that a violation occurred, the court may order the person to pay the full or reduced amount of the penalty. If the court does not uphold the finding, the court shall order that no penalty is owed.

(o) If the person paid the amount of the penalty and if that amount is reduced or is not upheld by the court, the court shall order that the appropriate amount plus accrued interest be remitted to the person. The rate of the interest is the rate charged on loans to depository institutions by the New York

Federal Reserve Bank, and the interest shall be paid for the period beginning on the date the penalty was paid and ending on the date the penalty is remitted. If the person gave a supersedeas bond and if the amount of the penalty is not upheld by the court, the court shall order the release of the bond. If the person gave a supersedeas bond and if the amount of the penalty is reduced, the court shall order the release of the bond after the person pays the amount.

(p) A penalty collected under this article shall be sent to the comptroller and deposited to the credit of the compensation to victims of crime fund.

(q) All proceedings under this article are subject to Chapter 2001, Government Code.

(r) In addition to the administrative penalty authorized by this article, the attorney general may recover all expenses incurred by the attorney general in the investigation, institution, and prosecution of the suit, including investigative costs, witness fees, attorney's fees, and deposition expenses.

Added by Acts 1995, 74th Leg., ch. 779, § 1, eff. Sept. 1, 1995.

Art. 56.65. Disclosure and use of information

(a) This article does not apply to information made confidential by law.

(b) An application for compensation under this subchapter and any information, document, summary, or other record provided to or received, maintained, or created by the attorney general under this subchapter is:

(1) except as provided by Section 552.132(c), Government Code, not subject to disclosure under Chapter 552 of that code; and

(2) except as provided by Subsection (c), not subject to disclosure, discovery, subpoena, or other means of legal compulsion for release.

(c) The attorney general may not release or disclose an application for compensation under this subchapter, or any information, document, summary, or other record provided to or received, maintained, or created by the attorney general under this subchapter, except:

(1) by court order for good cause shown, if the order includes a finding that the information is not available from any other source;

(2) with the consent of:

(A) the claimant or victim; or

(B) the person that provided the information to the attorney general;

(3) to an employee or other person under the direction of the attorney general;

(4) to another crime victims' compensation program that meets the requirements of 42 U.S.C. Section 10602(b);

(5) to a person authorized by the attorney general to receive the information in order to:

(A) conduct an audit as required by state or federal law;

(B) provide a review or examination under Article 56.38, 56.385, or 56.39 or under another provision of this subchapter for the purpose of determining the appropriateness of an award under this subchapter;

(C) prevent, deter, or punish fraud related to this subchapter; or

(D) assert subrogation or restitution rights;

(6) as the attorney general determines necessary to enforce this chapter, including presenting the application, information, document, summary, or record in court; or

(7) in response to a subpoena that is issued in a criminal proceeding and that requests an application for compensation under this subchapter, subject to Subsection (d).

(d) If responding to a subpoena described by Subsection (c)(7), the attorney general shall release only the victim's completed application form as described by Article 56.36(a) after redacting any confidential information described by Section 552.132(b), Government Code. The release of a victim's completed application form under this subsection does not affect the authority of the court to order the release or disclosure of additional information under this article.

Added by Acts 2017, 85th Leg., ch. 8 (S.B. 843), § 1, eff. Sept. 1, 2017.

Section 2 of Acts 2017, 85th Leg., ch. 8 (S.B. 843) provides:

"The change in law made by this Act applies only to a request for information that is received on or after the effective date [Sept. 1, 2017] of this Act. A request for information that was received before the effective date of this Act is governed by the law in effect on the date the request was received, and the former law is continued in effect for that purpose."

SUBCHAPTER C. ADDRESS CONFIDENTIALITY PROGRAM FOR VICTIMS OF FAMILY VIOLENCE, SEXUAL ASSAULT OR ABUSE, STALKING, OR TRAFFICKING OF PERSONS

Art. 56.81. Definitions

In this subchapter:

(1) "Applicant" means a person who applies to participate in the program.

(2) "Family violence" has the meaning assigned by Section 71.004, Family Code.

(3) "Family violence shelter center" has the meaning assigned by Section 51.002, Human Resources Code.

(3–a) "Household" has the meaning assigned by Section 71.005, Family Code.

(4) "Mail" means first class mail and any mail sent by a government agency. The term does not include a package, regardless of size or type of mailing.

(5) "Participant" means an applicant who is certified for participation in the program.

(6) "Program" means the address confidentiality program created under this subchapter.

(6–a) "Sexual abuse" means any conduct that constitutes an offense under Section 21.02, 21.11, or 25.02, Penal Code.

(6–b) "Sexual assault" means any conduct that constitutes an offense under Section 22.011 or 22.021, Penal Code.

(6–c) "Stalking" means any conduct that constitutes an offense under Section 42.072, Penal Code.

(7) "Trafficking of persons" means any conduct that constitutes an offense under Section 20A.02, 20A.03, 43.03, 43.04, 43.05, 43.25, 43.251, or 43.26, Penal Code, and that results in a person:

(A) engaging in forced labor or services; or

(B) otherwise becoming a victim of the offense.

Added by Acts 2007, 80th Leg., ch. 1295, § 1, eff. June 15, 2007. Amended by Acts 2013, 83rd Leg., ch. 1252 (H.B. 8), § 10, eff. Sept. 1, 2013; Acts 2017, 85th Leg., ch. 41 (S.B. 256), § 2, eff. May 19, 2017.

Art. 56.82. Address Confidentiality Program

(a) The attorney general shall establish an address confidentiality program, as provided by this subchapter, to assist a victim of family violence, sexual assault or abuse, stalking, or trafficking of persons in maintaining a confidential address.

(b) The attorney general shall:

(1) designate a substitute post office box address that a participant may use in place of the participant's true residential, business, or school address;

(2) act as agent to receive service of process and mail on behalf of the participant; and

(3) forward to the participant mail received by the office of the attorney general on behalf of the participant.

(c) A summons, writ, notice, demand, or process may be served on the attorney general on behalf of the participant by delivery of two copies of the document to the office of the attorney general. The attorney general shall retain a copy of the summons, writ, notice, demand, or process and forward the original to the participant not later than the third day after the date of service on the attorney general.

(d) The attorney general shall make and retain a copy of the envelope in which certified mail is received on behalf of the participant.

Added by Acts 2007, 80th Leg., ch. 1295, § 1, eff. June 15, 2007. Amended by Acts 2013, 83rd Leg., ch. 1252 (H.B. 8), § 11, eff. Sept. 1, 2013; Acts 2017, 85th Leg., ch. 41 (S.B. 256), § 3, eff. May 19, 2017.

Art. 56.83. Eligibility to Participate in Program

(a) To be eligible to participate in the program, an applicant must:

(1) either:

(A) meet with a victim's assistance counselor from a state or local agency or other entity, whether for-profit or nonprofit, that is identified by the attorney general as an entity that provides shelter or civil legal services or counseling to victims of family violence, sexual assault or abuse, stalking, or trafficking of persons;

(B) be protected under, or be filing an application on behalf of a victim who is the applicant's child or another person in the applicant's household and who is protected under:

(i) a temporary injunction issued under Subchapter F, Chapter 6, Family Code;

(ii) a temporary ex parte order issued under Chapter 83, Family Code;

(iii) an order issued under Chapter 7A or Article 6.09 of this code or Chapter 85, Family Code; or

(iv) a magistrate's order for emergency protection issued under Article 17.292; or

(C) possess documentation of family violence, as identified by the rules adopted under this section, or of sexual assault or abuse or stalking, as described by Section 92.0161, Property Code;

(2) file an application for participation with the attorney general or a state or local agency or other

entity identified by the attorney general under Subdivision (1);

(3) file an affirmation that the applicant has discussed safety planning with a victim's assistance counselor described by Subdivision (1)(A);

(4) designate the attorney general as agent to receive service of process and mail on behalf of the applicant; and

(5) live at a residential address, or relocate to a residential address, that is unknown to the person who committed or is alleged to have committed the family violence, sexual assault or abuse, stalking, or trafficking of persons.

(b) An application under Subsection (a)(2) must contain:

(1) a signed, sworn statement by the applicant stating that the applicant fears for the safety of the applicant, the applicant's child, or another person in the applicant's household because of a threat of immediate or future harm caused by the person who committed or is alleged to have committed the family violence, sexual assault or abuse, stalking, or trafficking of persons;

(2) the applicant's true residential address and, if applicable, the applicant's business and school addresses; and

(3) a statement by the applicant of whether there is an existing court order or a pending court case for child support or child custody or visitation that involves the applicant, the applicant's child, or another person in the applicant's household and, if so, the name and address of:

(A) the legal counsel of record; and

(B) each parent involved in the court order or pending case.

(c) An application under Subsection (a)(2) must be completed by the applicant in person at the state or local agency or other entity with which the application is filed. An applicant who knowingly or intentionally makes a false statement in an application under Subsection (a)(2) is subject to prosecution under Chapter 37, Penal Code.

(d) A state or local agency or other entity with which an application is filed under Subsection (a)(2) shall forward the application to the office of the attorney general.

(e) The attorney general by rule may establish additional eligibility requirements for participation in the program that are consistent with the purpose of the program as stated in Article 56.82(a).

(e–1) The attorney general may establish procedures for requiring an applicant, in appropriate circumstances, to submit with the application under Subsection (a)(2) independent documentary evidence of family violence, sexual assault or abuse, stalking, or trafficking of persons in the form of:

(1) an active or recently issued order described by Subsection (a)(1)(B);

(2) an incident report or other record maintained by a law enforcement agency or official;

(3) a statement of a physician or other health care provider regarding the medical condition of the applicant, applicant's child, or other person in the applicant's household as a result of the family violence, sexual assault or abuse, stalking, or trafficking of persons;

(4) a statement of a mental health professional, a member of the clergy, an attorney or other legal advocate, a trained staff member of a family violence center, or another professional who has assisted the applicant, applicant's child, or other person in the applicant's household in addressing the effects of the family violence, sexual assault or abuse, stalking, or trafficking of persons; or

(5) any other independent documentary evidence necessary to show the applicant's eligibility to participate in the program.

(f) Any assistance or counseling provided by the attorney general or an employee or agent of the attorney general to an applicant does not constitute legal advice.

Added by Acts 2007, 80th Leg., ch. 1295, § 1, eff. June 15, 2007. Amended by Acts 2013, 83rd Leg., ch. 1252 (H.B. 8), § 12, eff. Sept. 1, 2013; Acts 2017, 85th Leg., ch. 41 (S.B. 256), § 4, eff. May 19, 2017.

Art. 56.84. Certification; Expiration

(a) The attorney general shall certify for participation in the program an applicant who satisfies the eligibility requirements under Article 56.83.

(b) A certification under this article expires on the third anniversary of the date of certification.

Added by Acts 2007, 80th Leg., ch. 1295, § 1, eff. June 15, 2007.

Art. 56.85. Renewal

To renew a certification under Article 56.84, a participant must satisfy the eligibility requirements under

Article 56.83 as if the participant were originally applying for participation in the program.

Added by Acts 2007, 80th Leg., ch. 1295, § 1, eff. June 15, 2007.

Art. 56.86. Ineligibility and Cancellation

(a) An applicant is ineligible for, and a participant may be excluded from, participation in the program if the applicant or participant knowingly makes a false statement on an application filed under Article 56.83(a)(2).

(b) A participant may be excluded from participation in the program if:

(1) mail forwarded to the participant by the attorney general is returned undeliverable on at least four occasions;

(2) the participant changes the participant's true residential address as provided in the application filed under Article 56.83(a)(2) and does not notify the attorney general of the change at least 10 days before the date of the change; or

(3) the participant changes the participant's name.

Added by Acts 2007, 80th Leg., ch. 1295, § 1, eff. June 15, 2007.

Art. 56.87. Withdrawal

A participant may withdraw from the program by notifying the attorney general in writing of the withdrawal.

Added by Acts 2007, 80th Leg., ch. 1295, § 1, eff. June 15, 2007.

Art. 56.88. Confidentiality; Destruction of Information

(a) Information relating to a participant:

(1) is confidential, except as provided by Article 56.90; and

(2) may not be disclosed under Chapter 552, Government Code.

(b) Except as provided by Article 56.82(d), the attorney general may not make a copy of any mail received by the office of the attorney general on behalf of the participant.

(c) The attorney general shall destroy all information relating to a participant on the third anniversary of the date participation in the program ends.

Added by Acts 2007, 80th Leg., ch. 1295, § 1, eff. June 15, 2007.

Art. 56.89. Acceptance of Substitute Address; Exemptions

(a) Except as provided by Subsection (b), a state or local agency must accept the substitute post office box address designated by the attorney general if the substitute address is presented to the agency by a participant in place of the participant's true residential, business, or school address.

(b) The attorney general by rule may permit an agency to require a participant to provide the participant's true residential, business, or school address, if necessary for the agency to perform a duty or function that is imposed by law or administrative requirement.

Added by Acts 2007, 80th Leg., ch. 1295, § 1, eff. June 15, 2007.

Art. 56.90. Exceptions

(a) The attorney general:

(1) shall disclose a participant's true residential, business, or school address if:

(A) requested by:

(i) a law enforcement agency for the purpose of conducting an investigation;

(ii) the Department of Family and Protective Services for the purpose of conducting a child protective services investigation under Chapter 261, Family Code; or

(iii) the Department of State Health Services or a local health authority for the purpose of making a notification described by Article 21.31 of this code, Section 54.033, Family Code, or Section 81.051, Health and Safety Code; or

(B) required by court order; and

(2) may disclose a participant's true residential, business, or school address if:

(A) the participant consents to the disclosure; and

(B) the disclosure is necessary to administer the program.

(b) A person to whom a participant's true residential, business, or school address is disclosed under this section shall maintain the requested information in a manner that protects the confidentiality of the participant's true residential, business, or school address.

Added by Acts 2007, 80th Leg., ch. 1295, § 1, eff. June 15, 2007. Amended by Acts 2017, 85th Leg., ch. 41 (S.B. 256), § 5, eff. May 19, 2017.

Art. 56.91.   Liability

(a) The attorney general or an agent or employee of the attorney general is immune from liability for any act or omission by the agent or employee in administering the program if the agent or employee was acting in good faith and in the course and scope of assigned responsibilities and duties.

(b) An agent or employee of the attorney general who does not act in good faith and in the course and scope of assigned responsibilities and duties in disclosing a participant's true residential, business, or school address is subject to prosecution under Chapter 39, Penal Code.

Added by Acts 2007, 80th Leg., ch. 1295, § 1, eff. June 15, 2007.

Art. 56.92.   Program Information and Application Materials

The attorney general shall make program information and application materials available online.

Added by Acts 2007, 80th Leg., ch. 1295, § 1, eff. June 15, 2007.

Art. 56.93.   Rules

The attorney general shall adopt rules to administer the program.

Added by Acts 2007, 80th Leg., ch. 1295, § 1, eff. June 15, 2007.

CHAPTER 57. CONFIDENTIALITY OF IDENTIFYING INFORMATION OF SEX OFFENSE VICTIMS

Article

Art. 57.01.   Definitions

In this chapter:

(1) "Name" means the legal name of a person.

(2) "Pseudonym" means a set of initials or a fictitious name chosen by a victim to designate the victim in all public files and records concerning the offense, including police summary reports, press releases, and records of judicial proceedings.

(3) "Public servant" has the meaning assigned by Subsection (a), Section 1.07, Penal Code.

(4) "Victim" means a person who was the subject of:

(A) an offense the commission of which leads to a reportable conviction or adjudication under Chapter 62; or

(B) an offense that is part of the same criminal episode, as defined by Section 3.01, Penal Code, as an offense described by Paragraph (A).

Added by Acts 1987, 70th Leg., ch. 571, § 1, eff. Sept. 1, 1987. Amended by Acts 1997, 75th Leg., ch. 680, § 1, eff. Sept. 1, 1997; Acts 2003, 78th Leg., ch. 451, § 1, eff. Sept. 1, 2003; Acts 2003, 78th Leg., ch. 1276, § 5.0025, eff. Sept. 1, 2003.

Art. 57.02.   Confidentiality of files and records

(a) The Sexual Assault Prevention and Crisis Services Program of the office of the attorney general shall develop and distribute to all law enforcement agencies of the state a pseudonym form to record the name, address, telephone number, and pseudonym of a victim.

(b) A victim may choose a pseudonym to be used instead of the victim's name to designate the victim in all public files and records concerning the offense, including police summary reports, press releases, and records of judicial proceedings. A victim who elects to use a pseudonym as provided by this article must complete a pseudonym form developed under this article and return the form to the law enforcement agency investigating the offense.

(c) A victim who completes and returns a pseudonym form to the law enforcement agency investigating the offense may not be required to disclose the victim's name, address, and telephone number in connection with the investigation or prosecution of the offense.

(d) A completed and returned pseudonym form is confidential and may not be disclosed to any person other than a defendant in the case or the defendant's attorney, except on an order of a court of competent jurisdiction. The court finding required by Subsection (g) of this article is not required to disclose the confidential pseudonym form to the defendant in the case or to the defendant's attorney.

(e) If a victim completes and returns a pseudonym form to a law enforcement agency under this article, the law enforcement agency receiving the form shall:

(1) remove the victim's name and substitute the pseudonym for the name on all reports, files, and records in the agency's possession;

(2) notify the attorney for the state of the pseudonym and that the victim has elected to be designated by the pseudonym; and

(3) maintain the form in a manner that protects the confidentiality of the information contained on the form.

(f) An attorney for the state who receives notice that a victim has elected to be designated by a pseudonym shall ensure that the victim is designated by the pseudonym in all legal proceedings concerning the offense.

(g) A court of competent jurisdiction may order the disclosure of a victim's name, address, and telephone number only if the court finds that the information is essential in the trial of the defendant for the offense or the identity of the victim is in issue.

(h) Except as required or permitted by other law or by court order, a public servant or other person who has access to or obtains the name, address, telephone number, or other identifying information of a victim younger than 17 years of age may not release or disclose the identifying information to any person who is not assisting in the investigation, prosecution, or defense of the case. This subsection does not apply to the release or disclosure of a victim's identifying information by:

(1) the victim; or

(2) the victim's parent, conservator, or guardian, unless the parent, conservator, or guardian is a defendant in the case.

Text of subsec. (i) as added by Acts 2007, 80th Leg., ch. 619, § 1

(i) This article does not prohibit the inspector general of the Texas Department of Criminal Justice from disclosing a victim's identifying information to an employee of the department if the victim is an inmate or state jail defendant confined in a facility operated by or under contract with the department.

Text of subsec. (i) as added by Acts 2007, 80th Leg., ch. 1217, § 1

(i) This article does not prohibit the inspector general of the Texas Department of Criminal Justice from disclosing a victim's identifying information to the department's ombudsperson if the victim is an inmate or state jail defendant confined in a facility operated by or under contract with the department.

Added by Acts 1987, 70th Leg., ch. 571, § 1, eff. Sept. 1, 1987. Amended by Acts 2001, 77th Leg., ch. 1337, § 3, eff. Sept. 1, 2001; Acts 2005, 79th Leg., ch. 93, § 1, eff. Sept. 1, 2005; Acts 2007, 80th Leg., ch. 619, § 1, eff. Sept. 1, 2007; Acts 2007, 80th Leg., ch. 1217, § 1, eff. June 15, 2007.

Art. 57.03. Offense

(a) A public servant with access to the name, address, or telephone number of a victim 17 years of age or older who has chosen a pseudonym under this chapter commits an offense if the public servant knowingly discloses the name, address, or telephone number of the victim to any person who is not assisting in the investigation or prosecution of the offense or to any person other than the defendant, the defendant's attorney, or the person specified in the order of a court of competent jurisdiction.

(b) Unless the disclosure is required or permitted by other law, a public servant or other person commits an offense if the person:

(1) has access to or obtains the name, address, or telephone number of a victim younger than 17 years of age; and

(2) knowingly discloses the name, address, or telephone number of the victim to any person who is not assisting in the investigation or prosecution of the offense or to any person other than the defendant, the defendant's attorney, or a person specified in an order of a court of competent jurisdiction.

(c) It is an affirmative defense to prosecution under Subsection (b) that the actor is:

(1) the victim; or

(2) the victim's parent, conservator, or guardian, unless the actor is a defendant in the case.

(c-1) It is an exception to the application of this article that:

(1) the person who discloses the name, address, or telephone number of a victim is the inspector general of the Texas Department of Criminal Justice;

(2) the victim is an inmate or state jail defendant confined in a facility operated by or under contract with the Texas Department of Criminal Justice; and

Text of subsec. (c–1)(3) as added by Acts 2007, 80th Leg., ch. 619, § 2

(3) the person to whom the disclosure is made is an employee of the department.

Text of subsec. (c–1)(3) as added by Acts 2007, 80th Leg., ch. 1217, § 2

(3) the person to whom the disclosure is made is the department's ombudsperson.

(d) An offense under this article is a Class C misdemeanor.

Added by Acts 1987, 70th Leg., ch. 571, § 1, eff. Sept. 1, 1987. Amended by Acts 2001, 77th Leg., ch. 1337, § 4, eff. Sept. 1, 2001; Acts 2007, 80th Leg., ch. 619, § 2, eff. Sept. 1, 2007; Acts 2007, 80th Leg., ch. 1217, § 2, eff. June 15, 2007.

CHAPTER 57A. CONFIDENTIALITY OF IDENTIFYING INFORMATION OF VICTIMS OF STALKING

Article
57A.01. Definitions.
57A.02. Confidentiality of Files and Records.
57A.03. Offense.
57A.04. Effect on Other Law.

Art. 57A.01. Definitions

In this chapter:

(1) "Name" means the legal name of a person.

(2) "Pseudonym" means a set of initials or a fictitious name chosen by a victim to designate the victim in all public files and records concerning the offense, including police summary reports, press releases, and records of judicial proceedings.

(3) "Public servant" has the meaning assigned by Section 1.07(a), Penal Code.

(4) "Victim" means a person who is the subject of:

(A) an offense that allegedly constitutes stalking under Section 42.072, Penal Code; or

(B) an offense that is part of the same criminal episode, as defined by Section 3.01, Penal Code, as an offense under Section 42.072, Penal Code.

Added by Acts 2015, 84th Leg., ch. 394 (H.B. 1293), § 1, eff. Sept. 1, 2015.

Art. 57A.02. Confidentiality of Files and Records

(a) The office of the attorney general shall develop and distribute to all law enforcement agencies of the state a pseudonym form to record the name, address, telephone number, and pseudonym of a victim.

(b) A victim may choose a pseudonym to be used instead of the victim's name to designate the victim in all public files and records concerning the offense, including police summary reports, press releases, and records of judicial proceedings. A victim who elects to use a pseudonym as provided by this article must complete a pseudonym form developed under this article and return the form to the law enforcement agency investigating the offense.

(c) A victim who completes and returns a pseudonym form to the law enforcement agency investigating the offense may not be required to disclose the victim's name, address, and telephone number in connection with the investigation or prosecution of the offense.

(d) A completed and returned pseudonym form is confidential and may not be disclosed to any person other than the victim identified by the pseudonym form, a defendant in the case, or the defendant's attorney, except on an order of a court of competent jurisdiction. The court finding required by Subsection (g) is not required to disclose the confidential pseudonym form to the victim identified by the pseudonym form, the defendant in the case, or the defendant's attorney.

(e) If a victim completes and returns a pseudonym form to a law enforcement agency under this article, the law enforcement agency receiving the form shall:

(1) remove the victim's name and substitute the pseudonym for the name on all reports, files, and records in the agency's possession;

(2) notify the attorney for the state of the pseudonym and that the victim has elected to be designated by the pseudonym;

(3) provide to the victim a copy of the completed pseudonym form showing that the form was returned to the law enforcement agency; and

(4) maintain the form in a manner that protects the confidentiality of the information contained on the form.

(f) An attorney for the state who receives notice that a victim has elected to be designated by a pseudonym shall ensure that the victim is designated by the pseudonym in all legal proceedings concerning the offense.

(g) A court of competent jurisdiction may order the disclosure of a victim's name, address, and telephone number only if the court finds that:

(1) the information is essential in the trial of the defendant for the offense;

(2) the identity of the victim is in issue; or

(3) the disclosure is in the best interest of the victim.

(h) Except as required or permitted by other law or by court order, a public servant or other person who has access to or obtains the name, address, telephone number, or other identifying information of a victim younger than 17 years of age may not release or disclose the identifying information to any person who is not assisting in the investigation, prosecution, or defense of the case. This subsection does not apply to the release or disclosure of a victim's identifying information by:

(1) the victim; or

(2) the victim's parent, conservator, or guardian, unless the victim's parent, conservator, or guardian allegedly committed the offense described by Article 57A.01(4).

Added by Acts 2015, 84th Leg., ch. 394 (H.B. 1293), § 1, eff. Sept. 1, 2015.

Art. 57A.03. Offense

(a) A public servant with access to the name, address, or telephone number of a victim 17 years of age or older who has chosen a pseudonym under this chapter commits an offense if the public servant knowingly discloses the name, address, or telephone number of the victim to any person who is not assisting in the investigation or prosecution of the offense or to any person other than the defendant, the defendant's attorney, or the person specified in the order of a court of competent jurisdiction.

(b) Unless the disclosure is required or permitted by other law, a public servant or other person commits an offense if the person:

(1) has access to or obtains the name, address, or telephone number of a victim younger than 17 years of age; and

(2) knowingly discloses the name, address, or telephone number of the victim to any person who is not assisting in the investigation or prosecution of the offense or to any person other than the defendant, the defendant's attorney, or a person specified in an order of a court of competent jurisdiction.

(c) It is an affirmative defense to prosecution under Subsection (b) that the actor is:

(1) the victim; or

(2) the victim's parent, conservator, or guardian, unless the victim's parent, conservator, or guardian allegedly committed the offense described by Article 57A.01(4).

(d) An offense under this article is a Class C misdemeanor.

Added by Acts 2015, 84th Leg., ch. 394 (H.B. 1293), § 1, eff. Sept. 1, 2015.

Art. 57A.04. Effect on Other Law

This chapter does not affect:

(1) a victim's responsibility to provide documentation of stalking under Section 92.0161, Property Code; or

(2) a person's power or duty to disclose the documented information as provided by Subsection (j) of that section.

Added by Acts 2015, 84th Leg., ch. 394 (H.B. 1293), § 1, eff. Sept. 1, 2015.

CHAPTER 57B. CONFIDENTIALITY OF IDENTIFYING INFORMATION OF FAMILY VIOLENCE VICTIMS

Art. 57B.01. Definitions

In this chapter:

(1) "Name" means the legal name of a person.

(2) "Pseudonym" means a set of initials or a fictitious name chosen by a victim to designate the victim in all public files and records concerning the offense, including police summary reports, press releases, and records of judicial proceedings.

(3) "Public servant" has the meaning assigned by Subsection (a), Section 1.07, Penal Code.

(4) "Victim" means a person who is the subject of:

(A) an offense that allegedly constitutes family violence, as defined by Section 71.004, Family Code; or

(B) an offense that is part of the same criminal episode, as defined by Section 3.01, Penal Code, as an offense described by Paragraph (A).

Added by Acts 2007, 80th Leg., ch. 1295, § 3, eff. June 15, 2007.

Art. 57B.02. Confidentiality of Files and Records

(a) The office of the attorney general shall develop and distribute to all law enforcement agencies of the state a pseudonym form to record the name, address, telephone number, and pseudonym of a victim.

(b) A victim may choose a pseudonym to be used instead of the victim's name to designate the victim in all public files and records concerning the offense, including police summary reports, press releases, and records of judicial proceedings. A victim who elects to use a pseudonym as provided by this article must complete a pseudonym form developed under this article and return the form to the law enforcement agency investigating the offense.

(c) A victim who completes and returns a pseudonym form to the law enforcement agency investigating the offense may not be required to disclose the victim's name, address, and telephone number in connection with the investigation or prosecution of the offense.

(d) A completed and returned pseudonym form is confidential and may not be disclosed to any person other than a defendant in the case or the defendant's attorney, except on an order of a court of competent jurisdiction. The court finding required by Subsection (g) is not required to disclose the confidential pseudonym form to the defendant in the case or to the defendant's attorney.

(e) If a victim completes and returns a pseudonym form to a law enforcement agency under this article, the law enforcement agency receiving the form shall:

(1) remove the victim's name and substitute the pseudonym for the name on all reports, files, and records in the agency's possession;

(2) notify the attorney for the state of the pseudonym and that the victim has elected to be designated by the pseudonym; and

(3) maintain the form in a manner that protects the confidentiality of the information contained on the form.

(f) An attorney for the state who receives notice that a victim has elected to be designated by a pseudonym shall ensure that the victim is designated by the pseudonym in all legal proceedings concerning the offense.

(g) A court of competent jurisdiction may order the disclosure of a victim's name, address, and telephone number only if the court finds that the information is essential in the trial of the defendant for the offense or the identity of the victim is in issue.

(h) Except as required or permitted by other law or by court order, a public servant or other person who has access to or obtains the name, address, telephone number, or other identifying information of a victim younger than 17 years of age may not release or disclose the identifying information to any person who is not assisting in the investigation, prosecution, or

defense of the case. This subsection does not apply to the release or disclosure of a victim's identifying information by:

(1) the victim; or

(2) the victim's parent, conservator, or guardian, unless the victim's parent, conservator, or guardian allegedly committed the offense described by Article 57B.01(4).

Added by Acts 2007, 80th Leg., ch. 1295, § 3, eff. June 15, 2007.

Art. 57B.03. Offense

(a) A public servant with access to the name, address, or telephone number of a victim 17 years of age or older who has chosen a pseudonym under this chapter commits an offense if the public servant knowingly discloses the name, address, or telephone number of the victim to any person who is not assisting in the investigation or prosecution of the offense or to any person other than the defendant, the defendant's attorney, or the person specified in the order of a court of competent jurisdiction.

(b) Unless the disclosure is required or permitted by other law, a public servant or other person commits an offense if the person:

(1) has access to or obtains the name, address, or telephone number of a victim younger than 17 years of age; and

(2) knowingly discloses the name, address, or telephone number of the victim to any person who is not assisting in the investigation or prosecution of the offense or to any person other than the defendant, the defendant's attorney, or a person specified in an order of a court of competent jurisdiction.

(c) It is an affirmative defense to prosecution under Subsection (b) that the actor is:

(1) the victim; or

(2) the victim's parent, conservator, or guardian, unless the victim's parent, conservator, or guardian allegedly committed the offense described by Article 57B.01(4).

(d) An offense under this article is a Class C misdemeanor.

Added by Acts 2007, 80th Leg., ch. 1295, § 3, eff. June 15, 2007.

Art. 57B.04. Applicability of Chapter to Department of Family and Protective Services

Nothing in this chapter requires the Department of Family and Protective Services to use a pseudonym in a department report, file, or record relating to the abuse, neglect, or exploitation of a child or adult who may also be the subject of an offense described by Article 57B.01(4). To the extent permitted by law, the Department of Family and Protective Services and a department employee, as necessary in performing department duties, may disclose the name of a victim who elects to use a pseudonym under this chapter.

Added by Acts 2007, 80th Leg., ch. 1295, § 3, eff. June 15, 2007.

Art. 57B.05. Applicability of Chapter to Political Subdivisions

Nothing in this chapter requires a political subdivision to use a pseudonym in a report, file, or record that is not:

(1) intended for distribution to the public; or

(2) the subject of an open records request under Chapter 552, Government Code.

Added by Acts 2007, 80th Leg., ch. 1295, § 3, eff. June 15, 2007.

CHAPTER 57C. SEALING OF COURT RECORDS CONTAINING MEDICAL INFORMATION FOR CERTAIN CHILD VICTIMS

Article
57C.01. Definitions.
57C.02. Sealing of Records.

Art. 57C.01. Definitions

In this chapter:

(1) "Child" means a person who is younger than 18 years of age.

(2) "Medical records" means any information used or generated by health care providers, including records relating to emergency room treatment, rehabilitation therapy, or counseling.

Added by Acts 2009, 81st Leg., ch. 1010, § 1, eff. June 19, 2009.

Art. 57C.02. Sealing of Records

(a) Except as provided by Subsection (c), on a motion filed by a person described by Subsection (b), the court shall seal the medical records of a child who is a victim of an offense described by Section 1, Article 38.071.

(b) A motion under this article may be filed on the court's own motion or by:

(1) the attorney representing the state;

(2) the defendant; or

(3) the parent or guardian of the victim or, if the victim is no longer a child, the victim.

(c) The court is not required to seal the records described by this article on a finding of good cause after a hearing held under Subsection (d).

(d) The court shall grant the motion without a hearing unless the motion is contested not later than the seventh day after the date the motion is filed.

(e) Medical records sealed under this chapter are not open for inspection by any person except:

(1) on further order of the court after:

(A) notice to a parent or guardian of the victim whose information is sealed or, if the victim is no longer a child, notice to the victim; and

(B) a finding of good cause;

(2) in connection with a criminal or civil proceeding as otherwise provided by law; or

(3) on request of a parent or legal guardian of the victim whose information is being sealed or, if the victim is no longer a child, on request of the victim.

(f) A clerk of court is not liable for any failure to seal medical records after a motion under this chapter is granted, except on a showing of bad faith.

Added by Acts 2009, 81st Leg., ch. 1010, § 1, eff. June 19, 2009.

CHAPTER 57D. CONFIDENTIALITY OF IDENTIFYING INFORMATION OF VICTIMS OF TRAFFICKING OF PERSONS

Article
57D.01. Definitions.
57D.02. Confidentiality of Files and Records.
57D.03. Offense.

Art. 57D.01. Definitions

In this chapter:

(1) "Name" means the legal name of a person.

(2) "Pseudonym" means a set of initials or a fictitious name chosen by a victim to designate the victim in all public files and records concerning the offense,

including police summary reports, press releases, and records of judicial proceedings.

(3) "Public servant" has the meaning assigned by Section 1.07(a), Penal Code.

(4) "Victim" means a person who is the subject of:

(A) an offense under Section 20A.02, Penal Code; or

(B) an offense that is part of the same criminal episode, as defined by Section 3.01, Penal Code, as an offense under Section 20A.02, Penal Code.

Added by Acts 2011, 82nd Leg., ch. 1008 (H.B. 2329), § 2, eff. Sept. 1, 2011.

Art. 57D.02.　Confidentiality of Files and Records

(a) The office of the attorney general shall develop and distribute to all law enforcement agencies of the state a pseudonym form to record the name, address, telephone number, and pseudonym of a victim.

(b) A victim may choose a pseudonym to be used instead of the victim's name to designate the victim in all public files and records concerning the offense, including police summary reports, press releases, and records of judicial proceedings. A victim who elects to use a pseudonym as provided by this article must complete a pseudonym form developed under this article and return the form to the law enforcement agency investigating the offense.

(c) A victim who completes and returns a pseudonym form to the law enforcement agency investigating the offense may not be required to disclose the victim's name, address, and telephone number in connection with the investigation or prosecution of the offense.

(d) A completed and returned pseudonym form is confidential and may not be disclosed to any person other than a defendant in the case or the defendant's attorney, except on an order of a court of competent jurisdiction. The court finding required by Subsection (g) is not required to disclose the confidential pseudonym form to the defendant in the case or to the defendant's attorney.

(e) If a victim completes and returns a pseudonym form to a law enforcement agency under this article, the law enforcement agency receiving the form shall:

(1) remove the victim's name and substitute the pseudonym for the name on all reports, files, and records in the agency's possession;

(2) notify the attorney for the state of the pseudonym and that the victim has elected to be designated by the pseudonym; and

(3) maintain the form in a manner that protects the confidentiality of the information contained on the form.

(f) An attorney for the state who receives notice that a victim has elected to be designated by a pseudonym shall ensure that the victim is designated by the pseudonym in all legal proceedings concerning the offense.

(g) A court of competent jurisdiction may order the disclosure of a victim's name, address, and telephone number only if the court finds that the information is essential in the trial of the defendant for the offense or the identity of the victim is in issue.

(h) Except as required or permitted by other law or by court order, a public servant or other person who has access to or obtains the name, address, telephone number, or other identifying information of a victim younger than 18 years of age may not release or disclose the identifying information to any person who is not assisting in the investigation, prosecution, or defense of the case. This subsection does not apply to the release or disclosure of a victim's identifying information by:

(1) the victim; or

(2) the victim's parent, conservator, or guardian, unless the victim's parent, conservator, or guardian allegedly committed the offense described by Article 57D.01(4).

Added by Acts 2011, 82nd Leg., ch. 1008 (H.B. 2329), § 2, eff. Sept. 1, 2011.

Art. 57D.03.　Offense

(a) A public servant with access to the name, address, or telephone number of a victim 18 years of age or older who has chosen a pseudonym under this chapter commits an offense if the public servant knowingly discloses the name, address, or telephone number of the victim to any person who is not assisting in the investigation or prosecution of the offense or to any person other than the defendant, the defendant's attorney, or the person specified in the order of a court of competent jurisdiction.

(b) Unless the disclosure is required or permitted by other law, a public servant or other person commits an offense if the person:

(1) has access to or obtains the name, address, or telephone number of a victim younger than 18 years of age; and

(2) knowingly discloses the name, address, or telephone number of the victim to any person who is not assisting in the investigation or prosecution of the offense or to any person other than the defendant, the defendant's attorney, or a person specified in an order of a court of competent jurisdiction.

(c) It is an affirmative defense to prosecution under Subsection (b) that the actor is:

(1) the victim; or

(2) the victim's parent, conservator, or guardian, unless the victim's parent, conservator, or guardian allegedly committed the offense described by Article 57D.01(4).

(d) An offense under this article is a Class C misdemeanor.

Added by Acts 2011, 82nd Leg., ch. 1008 (H.B. 2329), § 2, eff. Sept. 1, 2011.

CHAPTER 58. SEALING FILES AND RECORDS OF CHILDREN [REPEALED]

Art. 58.01. Repealed by Acts 2001, 77th Leg., ch. 1297, § 71(3), eff. Sept. 1, 2001

CHAPTER 59. FORFEITURE OF CONTRABAND

Art. 59.01. Definitions

In this chapter:

(1) "Attorney representing the state" means the prosecutor with felony jurisdiction in the county in which a forfeiture proceeding is held under this chapter or, in a proceeding for forfeiture of contraband as defined under Subdivision (2)(B)(v) of this article, the city attorney of a municipality if the property is seized in that municipality by a peace officer employed by that municipality and the governing body of the municipality has approved procedures for the city attorney acting in a forfeiture proceeding. In a proceeding for forfeiture of contraband as defined under Subdivision (2)(B)(vi) of this article, the term includes the attorney general.

(2) "Contraband" means property of any nature, including real, personal, tangible, or intangible, that is:

(A) used in the commission of:

(i) any first or second degree felony under the Penal Code;

(ii) any felony under Section 15.031(b), 20.05, 20.06, 21.11, 38.04, or Chapter 43, 20A, 29, 30, 31, 32, 33, 33A, or 35, Penal Code;

(iii) any felony under The Securities Act (Article 581–1 et seq., Vernon's Texas Civil Statutes); or

(iv) any offense under Chapter 49, Penal Code, that is punishable as a felony of the third degree or state jail felony, if the defendant has been previously convicted three times of an offense under that chapter;

(B) used or intended to be used in the commission of:

(i) any felony under Chapter 481, Health and Safety Code (Texas Controlled Substances Act);

(ii) any felony under Chapter 483, Health and Safety Code;

(iii) a felony under Chapter 151, Finance Code;

(iv) any felony under Chapter 34, Penal Code;

(v) a Class A misdemeanor under Subchapter B, Chapter 365, Health and Safety Code,[1] if the defendant has been previously convicted twice of an offense under that subchapter;

(vi) any felony under Chapter 32, Human Resources Code, or Chapter 31, 32, 35A, or 37, Penal Code, that involves the state Medicaid program;

(vii) a Class B misdemeanor under Chapter 522, Business & Commerce Code;

(viii) a Class A misdemeanor under Section 306.051, Business & Commerce Code;

(ix) any offense under Section 42.10, Penal Code;

(x) any offense under Section 46.06(a)(1) or 46.14, Penal Code;

(xi) any offense under Chapter 71, Penal Code;

(xii) any offense under Section 20.05 or 20.06, Penal Code; or

(xiii) an offense under Section 326.002, Business & Commerce Code;

(C) the proceeds gained from the commission of a felony listed in Paragraph (A) or (B) of this subdivision, a misdemeanor listed in Paragraph (B)(vii), (ix), (x), or (xi) of this subdivision, or a crime of violence;

(D) acquired with proceeds gained from the commission of a felony listed in Paragraph (A) or (B) of this subdivision, a misdemeanor listed in Paragraph (B)(vii), (ix), (x), or (xi) of this subdivision, or a crime of violence;

(E) used to facilitate or intended to be used to facilitate the commission of a felony under Section 15.031 or 43.25, Penal Code; or

(F) used to facilitate or intended to be used to facilitate the commission of a felony under Section 20A.02 or Chapter 43, Penal Code.

(3) "Crime of violence" means:

(A) any criminal offense defined in the Penal Code or in a federal criminal law that results in a personal injury to a victim; or

(B) an act that is not an offense under the Penal Code involving the operation of a motor vehicle, aircraft, or water vehicle that results in injury or death sustained in an accident caused by a driver in violation of Section 550.021, Transportation Code.

(4) "Interest holder" means the bona fide holder of a perfected lien or a perfected security interest in property.

(5) "Law enforcement agency" means an agency of the state or an agency of a political subdivision of the state authorized by law to employ peace officers.

(6) "Owner" means a person who claims an equitable or legal ownership interest in property.

(7) "Proceeds" includes income a person accused or convicted of a crime or the person's representative or assignee receives from:

(A) a movie, book, magazine article, tape recording, phonographic record, radio or television presentation, telephone service, electronic media format, including an Internet website, or live entertainment in which the crime was reenacted; or

(B) the sale of tangible property the value of which is increased by the notoriety gained from the convic-

tion of an offense by the person accused or convicted of the crime.

(8) "Seizure" means the restraint of property by a peace officer under Article 59.03(a) or (b) of this code, whether the officer restrains the property by physical force or by a display of the officer's authority, and includes the collection of property or the act of taking possession of property.

(9) "Depository account" means the obligation of a regulated financial institution to pay the account owner under a written agreement, including a checking account, savings account, money market account, time deposit, NOW account, or certificate of deposit.

(10) "Primary state or federal financial institution regulator" means the state or federal regulatory agency that chartered and comprehensively regulates a regulated financial institution.

(11) "Regulated financial institution" means a depository institution chartered by a state or federal government, the deposits of which are insured by the Federal Deposit Insurance Corporation or the National Credit Union Administration.

Added by Acts 1989, 71st Leg., 1st C.S., ch. 12, § 1, eff. Oct. 18, 1989. Amended by Acts 1991, 72nd Leg., ch. 102, § 2, eff. Sept. 1, 1991; Acts 1993, 73rd Leg., ch. 761, § 5, eff. Sept. 1, 1993; Acts 1993, 73rd Leg., ch. 780, § 1, eff. Sept. 1, 1993; Acts 1993, 73rd Leg., ch. 828, § 1, eff. Sept. 1, 1993; Acts 1995, 74th Leg., ch. 76, §§ 5.91, 5.95(112), eff. Sept. 1, 1995; Acts 1995, 74th Leg., ch. 621, § 3, eff. Sept. 1, 1995; Acts 1995, 74th Leg., ch. 708, § 2, eff. Sept. 1, 1995; Acts 1997, 75th Leg., ch. 306, § 6, eff. Sept. 1, 1997; Acts 1999, 76th Leg., ch. 62, §§ 3.09, 7.48, eff. Sept. 1, 1999; Acts 2001, 77th Leg., ch. 124, § 1, eff. Sept. 1, 2001; Acts 2001, 77th Leg., ch. 438, § 1, eff. Sept. 1, 2001; Acts 2001, 77th Leg., ch. 467, § 1, eff. Sept. 1, 2001; Acts 2003, 78th Leg., ch. 198, § 2.141, eff. Sept. 1, 2003; Acts 2003, 78th Leg., ch. 257, § 17, eff. Sept. 1, 2003; Acts 2003, 78th Leg., ch. 428, § 1, eff. Sept. 1, 2003; Acts 2003, 78th Leg., ch. 649, § 3, eff. Sept. 1, 2003; Acts 2003, 78th Leg., ch. 1005, § 7, eff. Sept. 1, 2003; Acts 2005, 79th Leg., ch. 617, § 1, eff. Sept. 1, 2005; Acts 2005, 79th Leg., ch. 728, § 4.008, eff. Sept. 1, 2005; Acts 2005, 79th Leg., ch. 944, §§ 1, 2, eff. Sept. 1, 2005; Acts 2005, 79th Leg., ch. 1026, §§ 3, 4, eff. Sept. 1, 2005; Acts 2007, 80th Leg., ch. 127, § 6, eff. Sept. 1, 2007; Acts 2007, 80th Leg., ch. 822, § 2, eff. Sept. 1, 2007; Acts 2007, 80th Leg., ch. 885, § 2.14, eff. April 1, 2009; Acts 2009, 81st Leg., ch. 87, § 6.006, eff. Sept. 1, 2009; Acts 2009, 81st Leg., ch. 153, § 3, eff. Sept. 1, 2009; Acts 2009, 81st Leg., ch. 1130, § 11, eff. Sept. 1, 2009; Acts 2009, 81st Leg., ch. 1357, § 3, eff. Sept. 1, 2009; Acts 2011, 82nd Leg., ch. 91 (S.B. 1303), § 6.003, eff. Sept. 1, 2011; Acts 2011, 82nd Leg., ch. 223 (H.B. 260), § 5, eff. Sept. 1, 2011; Acts 2011, 82nd Leg., ch. 515 (H.B. 2014), § 2.04, eff. Sept. 1, 2011; Acts 2013, 83rd Leg., ch. 427 (S.B. 529), § 2, eff. Sept. 1, 2013; Acts 2013, 83rd Leg., ch. 1357 (S.B. 1451), § 1, eff. Sept. 1, 2013; Acts 2015, 84th Leg., ch. 333 (H.B. 11), § 3, eff. Sept. 1, 2015; Acts 2015, 84th Leg., ch. 1236 (S.B. 1296), § 4.004, eff. Sept. 1, 2015.

[1] V.T.C.A., Health & Safety Code § 365.011 et seq.

Art. 59.011.   Election of Forfeiture Proceeding

If property described by Article 59.01(2)(B)(ix), (x), or (xi) is subject to forfeiture under this chapter and Article 18.18, the attorney representing the state may proceed under either this chapter or that article.

Added by Acts 2009, 81st Leg., ch. 153, § 4, eff. Sept. 1, 2009; Acts 2009, 81st Leg., ch. 1130, § 12, eff. Sept. 1, 2009; Acts 2009, 81st Leg., ch. 1357, § 4, eff. Sept. 1, 2009. Amended by Acts 2011, 82nd Leg., ch. 91 (S.B. 1303), § 6.004, eff. Sept. 1, 2011; Acts 2013, 83rd Leg., ch. 1357 (S.B. 1451), § 2, eff. Sept. 1, 2013.

Art. 59.02.   Forfeiture of contraband

(a) Property that is contraband is subject to seizure and forfeiture under this chapter.

(b) Any property that is contraband other than property held as evidence in a criminal investigation or a pending criminal case, money, a negotiable instrument, or a security that is seized under this chapter may be replevied by the owner or interest holder of the property, on execution of a good and valid bond with sufficient surety in a sum equal to the appraised value of the property replevied.   The bond may be approved as to form and substance by the court after the court gives notice of the bond to the authority holding the seized property.   The bond must be conditioned:

(1) on return of the property to the custody of the state on the day of hearing of the forfeiture proceedings; and

(2) that the interest holder or owner of the property will abide by the decision that may be made in the cause.

(c) An owner or interest holder's interest in property may not be forfeited under this chapter if the owner or interest holder proves by a preponderance of the evidence that the owner or interest holder acquired and perfected the interest:

(1) before or during the act or omission giving rise to forfeiture or, if the property is real property, he acquired an ownership interest, security interest, or lien interest before a lis pendens notice was filed under Article 59.04(g) of this code and did not know or should not reasonably have known of the act or omission giving rise to the forfeiture or that it was likely to occur at or before the time of acquiring and perfecting the interest or, if the property is real property, at or before the time of acquiring the ownership interest, security interest, or lien interest; or

(2) after the act or omission giving rise to the forfeiture, but before the seizure of the property, and only if the owner or interest holder:

(A) was, at the time that the interest in the property was acquired, an owner or interest holder for value; and

(B) was without reasonable cause to believe that the property was contraband and did not purposefully avoid learning that the property was contraband.

(d) Notwithstanding any other law, if property is seized from the possession of an owner or interest holder who asserts an ownership interest, security interest, or lien interest in the property under applicable law, the owner or interest holder's rights remain in effect during the pendency of proceedings under this chapter as if possession of the property had remained with the owner or interest holder.

(e) On motion by any party or on the motion of the court, after notice in the manner provided by Article 59.04 of this code to all known owners and interest holders of property subject to forfeiture under this chapter, and after a hearing on the matter, the court may make appropriate orders to preserve and maintain the value of the property until a final disposition of the property is made under this chapter, including the sale of the property if that is the only method by which the value of the property may be preserved until final disposition.

(f) Any property that is contraband and has been seized by the Texas Department of Criminal Justice shall be forfeited to the department under the same rules and conditions as for other forfeitures.

(g) An individual, firm, corporation, or other entity insured under a policy of title insurance may not assert a claim or cause of action on or because of the policy if the claim or cause of action is based on forfeiture under this chapter and, at or before the time of acquiring the ownership of real property, security interest in real property, or lien interest against real property, the insured knew or reasonably should have known of the act or omission giving rise to the forfeiture or that the act or omission was likely to occur.

(h)(1) An owner or interest holder's interest in property may not be forfeited under this chapter if at the forfeiture hearing the owner or interest holder proves by a preponderance of the evidence that the owner or interest holder was not a party to the offense giving rise to the forfeiture and that the contraband:

(A) was stolen from the owner or interest holder before being used in the commission of the offense giving rise to the forfeiture;

(B) was purchased with:

(i) money stolen from the owner or interest holder; or

(ii) proceeds from the sale of property stolen from the owner or interest holder; or

(C) was used or intended to be used without the effective consent of the owner or interest holder in the commission of the offense giving rise to the forfeiture.

(2) An attorney representing the state who has a reasonable belief that property subject to forfeiture is described by Subdivision (1) and who has a reasonable belief as to the identity of the rightful owner or interest holder of the property shall notify the owner or interest holder as provided by Article 59.04.

(3) An attorney representing the state is not liable in an action for damages resulting from an act or omission in the performance of the duties imposed by Subdivision (2).

(4) The exclusive remedy for failure by the attorney representing the state to provide the notice required under Subdivision (2) is submission of that failure as a ground for new trial in a motion for new trial or bill of review.

(i) The forfeiture provisions of this chapter apply to contraband as defined by Article 59.01(2)(B)(v) of this code only in a municipality with a population of 250,000 or more.

Added by Acts 1989, 71st Leg., 1st C.S., ch. 12, § 1, eff. Oct. 18, 1989. Amended by Acts 1993, 73rd Leg., ch. 828, § 2, eff. Sept. 1, 1993; Acts 2001, 77th Leg., ch. 438, § 2, eff. Sept. 1, 2001; Acts 2001, 77th Leg., ch. 929, § 1, eff. Sept. 1, 2001; Acts 2001, 77th Leg. ch. 438, § 2 renumbered as subsec. (i) by Acts 2003, 78th Leg., ch. 1275, § 2(9), eff. Sept. 1, 2003; Acts 2009, 81st Leg., ch. 87, § 25.043, eff. Sept. 1, 2009.

Art. 59.021. Forfeiture of Substitute Property

(a) In this article, "substitute property" means property:

(1) that is not contraband; and

(2) that is owned by a person who is or was the owner of, or has or had an interest in, contraband with an aggregate value of $200,000 or more.

(b) Substitute property may be seized under authority of a search warrant issued under Subsection (c) if property that is contraband:

(1) can no longer be located after the exercise of reasonable diligence;

(2) has been transferred, conveyed, sold to, or deposited with a person other than the owner or interest holder;

(3) is not within the jurisdiction of the court;

(4) has substantially diminished in value;

(5) has been commingled with other property and cannot be readily distinguished or separated; or

(6) is proceeds described by Article 59.01(2)(C) and was used to acquire other property that is not within the jurisdiction of the court.

(c) A district court may issue a search warrant authorizing a peace officer to seize substitute property if the officer submits an affidavit that states:

(1) probable cause for the commission of an offense giving rise to forfeiture of contraband;

(2) a description of the contraband involved and the estimated current fair market value of the substitute property to be seized;

(3) the reasons the contraband is unavailable for forfeiture;

(4) probable cause to believe that the owner of the substitute property owned or had an interest in contraband with an aggregate value of $200,000 or more in connection with the commission of an underlying offense giving rise to the forfeiture; and

(5) that due diligence has been exercised in identifying the minimum amount of substitute property necessary to approximate the estimated highest fair market value of the contraband during the period in which the owner of the substitute property owned, or had an interest in, the contraband.

(d) After seizure of the substitute property, the disposition shall proceed as other cases in this chapter except that the attorney representing the state must prove by a preponderance of the evidence:

(1) that the contraband described by Subsection (b) was subject to seizure and forfeiture under this chapter;

(2) the highest fair market value of that contraband during the period in which the owner of the substitute property owned, or had an interest in, the contraband;

(3) the fair market value of the substitute property at the time it was seized; and

(4) that the owner of the substitute property owned or had an interest in contraband with an aggregate

value of $200,000 or more in connection with the commission of an underlying offense giving rise to the forfeiture.

(e) For purposes of determining the aggregate value of contraband under Subsection (c) or (d), the owner or interest holder is not required to have simultaneously owned or had an interest in all of the property constituting contraband.

(f) If the fair market value of the substitute property seized exceeds the highest fair market value of the contraband described by Subsection (b) during the period in which the owner of the substitute property owned, or had an interest in, the contraband, the court shall make appropriate orders to ensure that property equal in value to the excess is returned to the person or persons from whom the substitute property was seized.

Added by Acts 2013, 83rd Leg., ch. 1357 (S.B. 1451), § 3, eff. Sept. 1, 2013.

Art. 59.022. Property Removed From This State

(a) This article applies to contraband, other than real property, that is determined to be located outside of this state.

(b) A peace officer who identifies contraband described by Subsection (a) shall provide the attorney representing the state a sworn statement that identifies the contraband and the reasons the contraband is subject to seizure. On receiving the sworn statement, the attorney representing the state may file, in the name of the state, a notice of intended forfeiture in a district court in:

(1) the county in which the contraband, or proceeds used to acquire the contraband, was known to be situated before its removal out of this state;

(2) the county in which any owner or possessor of the contraband was prosecuted for an underlying offense for which the property is subject to forfeiture;

(3) the county in which venue existed for prosecution of an underlying offense for which the property is subject to forfeiture; or

(4) Travis County.

(c) The attorney representing the state shall request that citation be served on any person who owns or is in possession or control of the contraband to which this article applies and, on service in accordance with the Texas Rules of Civil Procedure, may move to have the court order that the contraband be:

(1) returned or brought to the jurisdiction of the court; or

(2) delivered to an agent of this state for transportation to the jurisdiction of the court.

(d) The attorney representing the state is entitled to all reasonable discovery in accordance with the Texas Rules of Civil Procedure to assist in identifying and locating contraband described by Subsection (a).

(e) If the court orders the return of contraband under this article, the contraband, after return, is subject to seizure and forfeiture as otherwise provided by this chapter.

(f) If it is found that any person after being served with a citation under Subsection (c) has transported, concealed, disposed of, or otherwise acted to prevent the seizure and forfeiture of contraband described by Subsection (a), the court may:

(1) order the payment to the attorney representing the state of costs incurred in investigating and identifying the location of the contraband, including discovery costs, reasonable attorney's fees, expert fees, other professional fees incurred by the attorney, and travel expenses;

(2) enter a judgment for civil contempt and impose:

(A) a fine of not more than $10,000 or less than $1,000;

(B) confinement in jail for a term of not more than 30 days or less than 10 days; or

(C) both fine and confinement;

(3) enter a judgment of forfeiture of the person's interest in the contraband;

(4) enter a judgment in the amount of the fair market value of the contraband;

(5) impose a civil penalty of not more than $25,000 or less than $1,000 for each item of contraband, or each separate fund, of which the person transported, concealed, disposed, or otherwise acted to prevent the seizure and forfeiture; or

(6) order any combination of Subdivisions (1) through (5).

Added by Acts 2013, 83rd Leg., ch. 1357 (S.B. 1451), § 3, eff. Sept. 1, 2013.

Art. 59.023. Suit for Proceeds

(a) A peace officer who identifies proceeds that are gained from the commission of an offense listed in Article 59.01(2)(A) or (B) shall provide the attorney representing the state with an affidavit that identifies the amount of the proceeds and that states probable cause that the proceeds are contraband subject to forfeiture. On receiving the affidavit, the attorney representing the state may file for a judgment in the amount of the proceeds in a district court in:

(1) the county in which the proceeds were gained;

(2) the county in which any owner or possessor of the property was prosecuted for an underlying offense for which the property is subject to forfeiture;

(3) the county in which venue existed for prosecution of an underlying offense for which the property is subject to forfeiture;

(4) the county in which the proceeds were seized; or

(5) Travis County.

(b) If the court determines that, based on an examination of the affidavit described by Subsection (a), probable cause exists for the suit to proceed, the court shall order that citation be served on all defendants named in the suit in accordance with the Texas Rules of Civil Procedure.

(c) Each person who is shown to have been a party to an underlying offense for which the proceeds are subject to forfeiture is jointly and severally liable in a suit under this article, regardless of whether the person has been charged for the offense.

Added by Acts 2013, 83rd Leg., ch. 1357 (S.B. 1451), § 3, eff. Sept. 1, 2013.

Art. 59.024. Multiple Recovery Prohibited

The attorney representing the state may proceed under Article 59.02, 59.021, 59.022, or 59.023, or any combination of those articles. If property or proceeds are awarded or forfeited to the state under this chapter for an underlying offense, a court may not award or forfeit additional property or proceeds that would exceed the highest fair market value of the contraband subject to forfeiture for that offense. For purposes of this article, the highest fair market value may be calculated at any time during the period in which the applicable person owned, possessed, or had an interest in the contraband.

Added by Acts 2013, 83rd Leg., ch. 1357 (S.B. 1451), § 3, eff. Sept. 1, 2013.

Art. 59.03. Seizure of contraband

(a) Property subject to forfeiture under this chapter, other than property described by Article 59.12, may be seized by any peace officer under authority of a search warrant.

(b) Seizure of property subject to forfeiture may be made without warrant if:

(1) the owner, operator, or agent in charge of the property knowingly consents;

(2) the seizure is incident to a search to which the owner, operator, or agent in charge of the property knowingly consents;

(3) the property subject to seizure has been the subject of a prior judgment in favor of the state in a forfeiture proceeding under this chapter; or

(4) the seizure was incident to a lawful arrest, lawful search, or lawful search incident to arrest.

(c) A peace officer who seizes property under this chapter has custody of the property, subject only to replevy under Article 59.02 of this code or an order of a court. A peace officer who has custody of property shall provide the attorney representing the state with a sworn statement that contains a schedule of the property seized, an acknowledgment that the officer has seized the property, and a list of the officer's reasons for the seizure. Not later than 72 hours after the seizure, the peace officer shall:

(1) place the property under seal;

(2) remove the property to a place ordered by the court; or

(3) require a law enforcement agency of the state or a political subdivision to take custody of the property and move it to a proper location.

(d) A person in the possession of property at the time a peace officer seizes the property under this chapter may at the time of seizure assert the person's interest in or right to the property. A peace officer, including the peace officer who seizes the property, may not request, require, or in any manner induce any person, including a person who asserts an interest in or right to the property, to execute a document purporting to waive the person's interest in or rights to property seized under this chapter.

(e) At any time before notice is filed under Article 59.04(b), an attorney representing the state may not request, require, or in any manner induce any person, including a person who asserts an interest in or right to property seized under this chapter, to execute a document purporting to waive the person's interest in or rights to the property.

Added by Acts 1989, 71st Leg., 1st C.S., ch. 12, § 1, eff. Oct. 18, 1989. Amended by Acts 2001, 77th Leg., ch. 438, § 3, eff. Sept. 1, 2001; Acts 2001, 77th Leg., ch. 929, § 2, eff. Sept. 1, 2001; Acts 2011, 82nd Leg., ch. 1321 (S.B. 316), § 1, eff. Sept. 1, 2011.

Art. 59.04. Notification of forfeiture proceeding

(a) If a peace officer seizes property under this chapter, the attorney representing the state shall commence proceedings under this section not later than the 30th day after the date of the seizure.

(b) A forfeiture proceeding commences under this chapter when the attorney representing the state files a notice of the seizure and intended forfeiture in the name of the state with the clerk of the district court in the county in which the seizure is made. The attorney representing the state must attach to the notice the peace officer's sworn statement under Article 59.03 of this code or, if the property has been seized under Article 59.12(b), the statement of the terms and amount of the depository account or inventory of assets provided by the regulated financial institution to the peace officer executing the warrant in the manner described by Article 59.12(b). Except as provided by Subsection (c) of this article, the attorney representing the state shall cause certified copies of the notice to be served on the following persons in the same manner as provided for the service of process by citation in civil cases:

(1) the owner of the property; and

(2) any interest holder in the property.

(c) If the property is a motor vehicle, and if there is reasonable cause to believe that the vehicle has been registered under the laws of this state, the attorney representing the state shall ask the Texas Department of Motor Vehicles to identify from its records the record owner of the vehicle and any interest holder. If the addresses of the owner and interest holder are not otherwise known, the attorney representing the state shall request citation be served on such persons at the address listed with the Texas Department of Motor Vehicles. If the citation issued to such address is returned unserved, the attorney representing the state shall cause a copy of the notice of the seizure and intended forfeiture to be posted at the courthouse door, to remain there for a period of not less than 30 days. If the owner or interest holder does not answer or appear after the notice has been so posted, the court shall enter a judgment by default as to the owner or interest holder, provided that the attorney representing the state files a written motion supported by affidavit setting forth the attempted service. An owner or interest holder whose interest is forfeited in this manner shall not be liable for court costs. If the person in possession of the vehicle at the time of the seizure is not the owner or the interest holder of the vehicle, notification shall be provided to the possessor in the same manner specified for notification to an owner or interest holder.

(d) If the property is a motor vehicle and is not registered in this state, the attorney representing the state shall attempt to ascertain the name and address of the person in whose name the vehicle is licensed in another state. If the vehicle is licensed in a state that has a certificate of title law, the attorney representing the state shall request the appropriate agency of that state to identify the record owner of the vehicle and any interest holder.

(e) If a financing statement is required by law to be filed to perfect a security interest affecting the property, and if there is reasonable cause to believe that a financing statement has been filed, the attorney representing the state who commences the proceedings shall ask the appropriate official designated by Chapter 9, Business & Commerce Code, to identify the record owner of the property and the person who is an interest holder.

(f) If the property is an aircraft or a part of an aircraft, and if there is reasonable cause to believe that a perfected security instrument affects the property, the attorney representing the state shall request an administrator of the Federal Aviation Administration to identify from the records of that agency the record owner of the property and the holder of the perfected security instrument. The attorney representing the state shall also notify the Department of Public Safety in writing of the fact that an aircraft has been seized and shall provide the department with a description of the aircraft.

(g) If the property is real property, the attorney representing the state, not later than the third day after the date proceedings are commenced, shall file a lis pendens notice describing the property with the county clerk of each county in which the property is located.

(h) For all other property subject to forfeiture, if there is reasonable cause to believe that a perfected security instrument affects the property, the attorney representing the state shall make a good faith inquiry to identify the holder of the perfected security instrument.

(i) Except as provided by Section (c) of this article, the attorney representing the state who commences the proceedings shall cause the owner and any interest holder to be named as a party and to be served with citation as provided by the Texas Rules of Civil Procedure.

(j) A person who was in possession of the property at the time it was seized shall be made a party to the proceeding.

(k) If no person was in possession of the property at the time it was seized, and if the owner of the property is unknown, the attorney representing the state shall file with the clerk of the court in which the proceedings are pending an affidavit stating that no person was in possession of the property at the time it was seized and that the owner of the property is unknown. The clerk of the court shall issue a citation for service by publication addressed to "The Unknown Owner of _____," filling in the blank space with a reasonably detailed description of the property subject to forfeiture. The citation must contain the other requisites prescribed by and be served as provided by Rules 114, 115, and 116, Texas Rules of Civil Procedure.

(*l*) Proceedings commenced under this chapter may not proceed to hearing unless the judge who is to conduct the hearing is satisfied that this article has been complied with and that the attorney representing the state will introduce into evidence at the hearing any answer received from an inquiry required by Subsections (c)–(h) of this article.

Added by Acts 1989, 71st Leg., 1st C.S., ch. 12, § 1, eff. Oct. 18, 1989. Amended by Acts 1991, 72nd Leg., ch. 14, § 282, eff. Sept. 1, 1991; Acts 1995, ch. 165, § 22(25), eff. Sept. 1, 1995; Acts 1995, 74th Leg., ch. 533, § 1, eff. Sept. 1, 1995; Acts 2001, 77th Leg., ch. 438, § 4, eff. Sept. 1, 2001; Acts 2009, 81st Leg., ch. 933, § 3B.02, eff. Sept. 1, 2009.

Art. 59.05. Forfeiture hearing

(a) All parties must comply with the rules of pleading as required in civil suits.

(b) All cases under this chapter shall proceed to trial in the same manner as in other civil cases. The state has the burden of proving by a preponderance of the evidence that property is subject to forfeiture.

(c) It is an affirmative defense to forfeiture under this chapter of property belonging to the spouse of a person whose acts gave rise to the seizure of community property that, because of an act of family violence, as defined by Section 71.004, Family Code, the spouse was unable to prevent the act giving rise to the seizure.

(d) A final conviction for an underlying offense is not a requirement for forfeiture under this chapter. An owner or interest holder may present evidence of a dismissal or acquittal of an underlying offense in a forfeiture proceeding, and evidence of an acquittal raises a presumption that the property or interest that is the subject of the hearing is nonforfeitable. This presumption can be rebutted by evidence that the owner or interest holder knew or should have known that the property was contraband.

(e) It is the intention of the legislature that asset forfeiture is remedial in nature and not a form of punishment. If the court finds that all or any part of the property is subject to forfeiture, the judge shall forfeit the property to the state, with the attorney representing the state as the agent for the state, except that if the court finds that the nonforfeitable interest of an interest holder in the property is valued in an amount greater than or substantially equal to the present value of the property, the court shall order the property released to the interest holder. If the court finds that the nonforfeitable interest of an interest holder is valued in an amount substantially less than the present value of the property and that the property is subject to forfeiture, the court shall order the property forfeited to the state with the attorney representing the state acting as the agent of the state, and making necessary orders to protect the nonforfeitable interest of the interest holder. On final judgment of forfeiture, the attorney representing the state shall dispose of the property in the manner required by Article 59.06 of this code.

(f) On forfeiture to the state of an amount greater than $2,500, the clerk of the court in which the forfeiture proceeding was held is entitled to court costs in that proceeding as in other civil proceedings unless the forfeiture violates federal requirements for multijurisdictional task force cases authorized under Chapter 362, Local Government Code. The procedure for collecting the costs is the procedure established under Subsections (a) and (c), Article 59.06.

(g) If property is seized at a federal checkpoint, the notice of seizure and intended forfeiture may be filed in and the proceeding may be held in:

(1) the county in which the seizure occurred; or

(2) with the consent of the owner, operator, or agent in charge of the property, a county that is adjacent to the county in which the seizure occurred, if both counties are in the same judicial district.

Added by Acts 1989, 71st Leg., 1st C.S., ch. 12, § 1, eff. Oct. 18, 1989. Amended by Acts 1993, 73rd Leg., ch. 780, § 2, eff. Sept. 1, 1993; Acts 1995, 74th Leg., ch. 533, § 2, eff. Sept. 1, 1995; Acts 1999, 76th Leg., ch. 582, § 1, eff. Sept. 1, 1999; Acts 2003, 78th Leg., ch. 1153, § 1, eff. Sept. 1, 2003; Acts 2003, 78th Leg., ch. 1276, § 7.002(*l*), eff. Sept. 1, 2003.

Art. 59.06. Disposition of Forfeited Property

(a) Except as provided by Subsection (k), all forfeited property shall be administered by the attorney representing the state, acting as the agent of the state, in accordance with accepted accounting practices and with the provisions of any local agreement entered into between the attorney representing the state and law enforcement agencies. If a local agreement has not been executed, the property shall be sold on the 75th day after the date of the final judgment of forfeiture at public auction under the direction of the county sheriff, after notice of public auction as provided by law for other sheriff's sales. The proceeds of the sale shall be distributed as follows:

(1) to any interest holder to the extent of the interest holder's nonforfeitable interest;

(2) after any distributions under Subdivision (1), if the Title IV–D agency has filed a child support lien in the forfeiture proceeding, to the Title IV–D agency in an amount not to exceed the amount of child support arrearages identified in the lien; and

(3) the balance, if any, after the deduction of court costs to which a district court clerk is entitled under Article 59.05(f) and, after that deduction, the deduction of storage and disposal costs, to be deposited not later than the 30th day after the date of the sale in the state treasury to the credit of the general revenue fund.

(b) If a local agreement exists between the attorney representing the state and law enforcement agencies, the attorney representing the state may transfer the property to law enforcement agencies to maintain, repair, use, and operate the property for official purposes if the property is free of any interest of an interest holder. The agency receiving the forfeited property may purchase the interest of an interest holder so that the property can be released for use by the agency. The agency receiving the forfeited property may maintain, repair, use, and operate the property with money appropriated for current operations. If the property is a motor vehicle subject to registration under the motor vehicle registration laws of this state, the agency receiving the forfeited vehicle is considered to be the purchaser and the certificate of title shall issue to the agency. A law enforcement agency to which property is transferred under this subsection at any time may transfer or loan the property to any other municipal or county agency, a groundwater conservation district governed by Chapter 36, Water Code, or a school district for the use of that agency or district. A municipal or county agen-cy, a groundwater conservation district, or a school district to which a law enforcement agency loans a motor vehicle under this subsection shall maintain any automobile insurance coverage for the vehicle that is required by law.

(b–1) If a loan is made by a sheriff's office or by a municipal police department, the commissioners court of the county in which the sheriff has jurisdiction or the governing body of the municipality in which the department has jurisdiction, as applicable, may revoke the loan at any time by notifying the receiving agency or district, by mail, that the receiving agency or district must return the loaned vehicle to the loaning agency before the seventh day after the date the receiving agency or district receives the notice.

(b–2) An agency that loans property under this article shall:

(1) keep a record of the loan, including the name of the agency or district to which the vehicle was loaned, the fair market value of the vehicle, and where the receiving agency or district will use the vehicle; and

(2) update the record when the information relating to the vehicle changes.

(c) If a local agreement exists between the attorney representing the state and law enforcement agencies, all money, securities, negotiable instruments, stocks or bonds, or things of value, or proceeds from the sale of those items, shall be deposited, after the deduction of court costs to which a district court clerk is entitled under Article 59.05(f), according to the terms of the agreement into one or more of the following funds:

(1) a special fund in the county treasury for the benefit of the office of the attorney representing the state, to be used by the attorney solely for the official purposes of his office;

(2) a special fund in the municipal treasury if distributed to a municipal law enforcement agency, to be used solely for law enforcement purposes;

(3) a special fund in the county treasury if distributed to a county law enforcement agency, to be used solely for law enforcement purposes; or

(4) a special fund in the state law enforcement agency if distributed to a state law enforcement agency, to be used solely for law enforcement purposes.

(c–1) Notwithstanding Subsection (a), the attorney representing the state and special rangers of the Texas and Southwestern Cattle Raisers Association who meet the requirements of Article 2.125 may enter into a local agreement that allows the attorney representing the state to transfer proceeds from the sale of forfeited property described by Subsection (c), after the deduction of court costs as described by that subsection, to a special fund established for the special rangers. Proceeds transferred under this subsection must be used by the special rangers solely for law enforcement purposes. Any expenditures of the proceeds are subject to the audit provisions established under this article.

(c–2) Any postjudgment interest from money, securities, negotiable instruments, stocks or bonds, or things of value, or proceeds from the sale of those items, that are deposited in an interest-bearing bank account under Subsection (c) shall be used for the same purpose as the principal.

(c–3) Notwithstanding Subsection (a), with respect to forfeited property seized in connection with a violation of Chapter 481, Health and Safety Code (Texas Controlled Substances Act), by a peace officer employed by the Department of Public Safety, in a proceeding under Article 59.05 in which a default judgment is rendered in favor of the state, the attorney representing the state shall enter into a local agreement with the department that allows the attorney representing the state either to:

(1) transfer forfeited property to the department to maintain, repair, use, and operate for official purposes in the manner provided by Subsection (b); or

(2) allocate proceeds from the sale of forfeited property described by Subsection (c), after the deduction of court costs as described by that subsection, in the following proportions:

(A) 40 percent to a special fund in the department to be used solely for law enforcement purposes;

(B) 30 percent to a special fund in the county treasury for the benefit of the office of the attorney representing the state, to be used by the attorney solely for the official purposes of the attorney's office; and

(C) 30 percent to the general revenue fund.

(c–4) Notwithstanding Subsections (a) and (c–3), with respect to forfeited property seized in connection with a violation of Chapter 481, Health and Safety Code (Texas Controlled Substances Act), by the Department of Public Safety concurrently with any other law enforcement agency, in a proceeding under Article 59.05 in which a default judgment is rendered in favor of the state, the attorney representing the state may allocate property or proceeds in accordance with a memorandum of understanding between the law en-

forcement agencies and the attorney representing the state.

(d) Proceeds awarded under this chapter to a law enforcement agency or to the attorney representing the state may be spent by the agency or the attorney after a budget for the expenditure of the proceeds has been submitted to the commissioners court or governing body of the municipality. The budget must be detailed and clearly list and define the categories of expenditures, but may not list details that would endanger the security of an investigation or prosecution. Expenditures are subject to the audit and enforcement provisions established under this chapter. A commissioners court or governing body of a municipality may not use the existence of an award to offset or decrease total salaries, expenses, and allowances that the agency or the attorney receives from the commissioners court or governing body at or after the time the proceeds are awarded.

(d–1) The head of a law enforcement agency or an attorney representing the state may not use proceeds or property received under this chapter to:

(1) contribute to a political campaign;

(2) make a donation to any entity, except as provided by Subsection (d–2);

(3) pay expenses related to the training or education of any member of the judiciary;

(4) pay any travel expenses related to attendance at training or education seminars if the expenses violate generally applicable restrictions established by the commissioners court or governing body of the municipality, as applicable;

(5) purchase alcoholic beverages;

(6) make any expenditure not approved by the commissioners court or governing body of the municipality, as applicable, if the head of a law enforcement agency or attorney representing the state holds an elective office and:

(A) the deadline for filing an application for a place on the ballot as a candidate for reelection to that office in the general primary election has passed and the person did not file an application for a place on that ballot; or

(B) during the person's current term of office, the person was a candidate in a primary, general, or runoff election for reelection to that office and was not the prevailing candidate in that election; or

(7) increase a salary, expense, or allowance for an employee of the law enforcement agency or attorney

representing the state who is budgeted by the commissioners court or governing body of the municipality unless the commissioners court or governing body first approves the increase.

(d–2) The head of a law enforcement agency or an attorney representing the state may use as an official purpose of the agency or attorney proceeds or property received under this chapter to make a donation to an entity that assists in:

(1) the detection, investigation, or prosecution of:

(A) criminal offenses; or

(B) instances of abuse, as defined by Section 261.001, Family Code;

(2) the provision of:

(A) mental health, drug, or rehabilitation services; or

(B) services for victims or witnesses of criminal offenses or instances of abuse described by Subdivision (1); or

(3) the provision of training or education related to duties or services described by Subdivision (1) or (2).

(d–3) Except as otherwise provided by this article, an expenditure of proceeds or property received under this chapter is considered to be for a law enforcement purpose if the expenditure is made for an activity of a law enforcement agency that relates to the criminal and civil enforcement of the laws of this state, including an expenditure made for:

(1) equipment, including vehicles, computers, firearms, protective body armor, furniture, software, uniforms, and maintenance equipment;

(2) supplies, including office supplies, mobile phone and data account fees for employees, and Internet services;

(3) investigative and training-related travel expenses, including payment for hotel rooms, airfare, meals, rental of and fuel for a motor vehicle, and parking;

(4) conferences and training expenses, including fees and materials;

(5) investigative costs, including payments to informants and lab expenses;

(6) crime prevention and treatment programs;

(7) facility costs, including building purchase, lease payments, remodeling and renovating, maintenance, and utilities;

(8) witness-related costs, including travel and security; and

(9) audit costs and fees, including audit preparation and professional fees.

(d–4) Except as otherwise provided by this article, an expenditure of proceeds or property received under this chapter is considered to be for an official purpose of an attorney's office if the expenditure is made for an activity of an attorney or office of an attorney representing the state that relates to the preservation, enforcement, or administration of the laws of this state, including an expenditure made for:

(1) equipment, including vehicles, computers, visual aid equipment for litigation, firearms, body armor, furniture, software, and uniforms;

(2) supplies, including office supplies, legal library supplies and access fees, mobile phone and data account fees for employees, and Internet services;

(3) prosecution and training-related travel expenses, including payment for hotel rooms, airfare, meals, rental of and fuel for a motor vehicle, and parking;

(4) conferences and training expenses, including fees and materials;

(5) investigative costs, including payments to informants and lab expenses;

(6) crime prevention and treatment programs;

(7) facility costs, including building purchase, lease payments, remodeling and renovating, maintenance, and utilities;

(8) legal fees, including court costs, witness fees, and related costs, including travel and security, audit costs, and professional fees; and

(9) state bar and legal association dues.

(e) On the sale of contraband under this article, the appropriate state agency shall issue a certificate of title to the recipient if a certificate of title is required for the property by other law.

(f) A final judgment of forfeiture under this chapter perfects the title of the state to the property as of the date that the contraband was seized or the date the forfeiture action was filed, whichever occurred first, except that if the property forfeited is real property, the title is perfected as of the date a notice of lis pendens is filed on the property.

(g)(1) All law enforcement agencies and attorneys representing the state who receive proceeds or property under this chapter shall account for the seizure, forfeiture, receipt, and specific expenditure of all the proceeds and property in an audit, which is to be performed annually by the commissioners court or governing body of a municipality, as appropriate. The annual period of the audit for a law enforcement agency is the fiscal year of the appropriate county or municipality and the annual period for an attorney representing the state is the state fiscal year. The audit must be completed on a form provided by the attorney general and must include a detailed report and explanation of all expenditures, including salaries and overtime pay, officer training, investigative equipment and supplies, and other items. Certified copies of the audit shall be delivered by the law enforcement agency or attorney representing the state to the attorney general not later than the 60th day after the date on which the annual period that is the subject of the audit ends.

(2) If a copy of the audit is not delivered to the attorney general within the period required by Subdivision (1), within five days after the end of the period the attorney general shall notify the law enforcement agency or the attorney representing the state of that fact. On a showing of good cause, the attorney general may grant an extension permitting the agency or attorney to deliver a copy of the audit after the period required by Subdivision (1) and before the 76th day after the date on which the annual period that is the subject of the audit ends. If the law enforcement agency or the attorney representing the state fails to establish good cause for not delivering the copy of the audit within the period required by Subdivision (1) or fails to deliver a copy of an audit within the extension period, the attorney general shall notify the comptroller of that fact.

(3) On notice under Subdivision (2), the comptroller shall perform the audit otherwise required by Subdivision (1). At the conclusion of the audit, the comptroller shall forward a copy of the audit to the attorney general. The law enforcement agency or attorney representing the state is liable to the comptroller for the costs of the comptroller in performing the audit.

(h) As a specific exception to the requirement of Subdivisions (1)–(3) of Subsection (c) of this article that the funds described by those subdivisions be used only for the official purposes of the attorney representing the state or for law enforcement purposes, on agreement between the attorney representing the state or the head of a law enforcement agency and the governing body of a political subdivision, the attorney representing the state or the head of the law enforcement agency shall comply with the request of the governing body to deposit not more than a total of 10 percent of the gross amount credited to the attorney's or agency's fund into the treasury of the political subdivision. The governing body of the political subdivision shall, by ordinance, order, or resolution, use funds received under this subsection for:

(1) nonprofit programs for the prevention of drug abuse;

(2) nonprofit chemical dependency treatment facilities licensed under Chapter 464, Health and Safety Code;

(3) nonprofit drug and alcohol rehabilitation or prevention programs administered or staffed by professionals designated as qualified and credentialed by the Texas Commission on Alcohol and Drug Abuse; or

(4) financial assistance as described by Subsection (o).

(i) The governing body of a political subdivision may not use funds received under this subchapter for programs or facilities listed under Subsections (h)(1)–(3) if an officer of or member of the Board of Directors of the entity providing the program or facility is related to a member of the governing body, the attorney representing the state, or the head of the law enforcement agency within the third degree by consanguinity or the second degree by affinity.

(j) As a specific exception to Subdivision (4) of Subsection (c) of this article, the director of a state law enforcement agency may use not more than 10 percent of the amount credited to the special fund of the agency under that subdivision for the prevention of drug abuse and the treatment of persons with drug-related problems.

(k)(1) The attorney for the state shall transfer all forfeited property that is income from, or acquired with the income from, a movie, book, magazine article, tape recording, phonographic record, radio or television presentation, telephone service, electronic media format, including an Internet website, or live entertainment in which a crime is reenacted to the attorney general.

(2) The attorney for the state shall transfer to the attorney general all income from the sale of tangible property the value of which is increased by the notoriety gained from the conviction of an offense by the person accused or convicted of the crime, minus the deduction authorized by this subdivision. The attorney for the state shall determine the fair market value

of property that is substantially similar to the property that was sold but that has not been increased in value by notoriety and deduct that amount from the proceeds of the sale. After transferring income to the attorney general, the attorney for the state shall transfer the remainder of the proceeds of the sale to the owner of the property. The attorney for the state, the attorney general, or a person who may be entitled to claim money from the escrow account described by Subdivision (3) in satisfaction of a claim may at any time bring an action to enjoin the waste of income described by this subdivision.

(3) The attorney general shall deposit the money or proceeds from the sale of the property into an escrow account. The money in the account is available to satisfy a judgment against the person who committed the crime in favor of a victim of the crime if the judgment is for damages incurred by the victim caused by the commission of the crime. The attorney general shall transfer the money in the account that has not been ordered paid to a victim in satisfaction of a judgment to the compensation to victims of crime fund on the fifth anniversary of the date the account was established. In this subsection, "victim" has the meaning assigned by Article 56.32.

(*l*) A law enforcement agency that, or an attorney representing the state who, does not receive proceeds or property under this chapter during an annual period as described by Subsection (g) shall, not later than the 30th day after the date on which the annual period ends, report to the attorney general that the agency or attorney, as appropriate, did not receive proceeds or property under this chapter during the annual period.

(m) As a specific exception to Subdivisions (1)–(3) of Subsection (c), a law enforcement agency or attorney representing the state may use proceeds received under this chapter to contract with a person or entity to prepare an audit as required by Subsection (g).

(n) As a specific exception to Subsection (c)(2) or (3), a local law enforcement agency may transfer not more than a total of 10 percent of the gross amount credited to the agency's fund to a separate special fund in the treasury of the political subdivision. The agency shall administer the separate special fund, and expenditures from the fund are at the sole discretion of the agency and may be used only for financial assistance as described by Subsection (o).

(o) The governing body of a political subdivision or a local law enforcement agency may provide financial assistance under Subsection (h)(4) or (n) only to a person who is a Texas resident, who plans to enroll or is enrolled at an institution of higher education in an undergraduate degree or certificate program in a field related to law enforcement, and who plans to return to that locality to work for the political subdivision or the agency in a field related to law enforcement. To ensure the promotion of a law enforcement purpose of the political subdivision or the agency, the governing body of the political subdivision or the agency shall impose other reasonable criteria related to the provision of this financial assistance, including a requirement that a recipient of the financial assistance work for a certain period of time for the political subdivision or the agency in a field related to law enforcement and including a requirement that the recipient sign an agreement to perform that work for that period of time. In this subsection, "institution of higher education" has the meaning assigned by Section 61.003, Education Code.

(p) Notwithstanding Subsection (a), and to the extent necessary to protect the commission's ability to recover amounts wrongfully obtained by the owner of the property and associated damages and penalties to which the commission may otherwise be entitled by law, the attorney representing the state shall transfer to the Health and Human Services Commission all forfeited property defined as contraband under Article 59.01(2)(B)(vi). If the forfeited property consists of property other than money or negotiable instruments, the attorney representing the state may, if approved by the commission, sell the property and deliver to the commission the proceeds from the sale, minus costs attributable to the sale. The sale must be conducted in a manner that is reasonably expected to result in receiving the fair market value for the property.

(q)(1) Notwithstanding any other provision of this article, a multicounty drug task force, or a county or municipality participating in the task force, that is not established in accordance with Section 362.004, Local Government Code, or that fails to comply with the policies and procedures established by the Department of Public Safety under that section, and that participates in the seizure of contraband shall forward to the comptroller all proceeds received by the task force from the forfeiture of the contraband. The comptroller shall deposit the proceeds in the state treasury to the credit of the general revenue fund.

(2) The attorney general shall ensure the enforcement of Subdivision (1) by filing any necessary legal proceedings in the county in which the contraband is forfeited or in Travis County.

(r) As a specific exception to Subsection (c)(2), (3), or (4), a law enforcement agency may transfer not more than 10 percent of the gross amount credited to the agency's fund to a separate special fund established in the treasury of the political subdivision or maintained by the state law enforcement agency, as applicable. The law enforcement agency shall administer the separate special fund. Interest received from the investment of money in the fund shall be credited to the fund. The agency may use money in the fund only to provide scholarships to children of peace officers who were employed by the agency or by another law enforcement agency with which the agency has overlapping geographic jurisdiction and who were killed in the line of duty. Scholarships under this subsection may be used only to pay the costs of attendance at an institution of higher education or private or independent institution of higher education, including tuition and fees and costs for housing, books, supplies, transportation, and other related personal expenses. In this subsection, "institution of higher education" and "private or independent institution of higher education" have the meanings assigned by Section 61.003, Education Code.

(s) Not later than April 30 of each year, the attorney general shall develop a report based on information submitted by law enforcement agencies and attorneys representing the state under Subsection (g) detailing the total amount of funds forfeited, or credited after the sale of forfeited property, in this state in the preceding calendar year. The attorney general shall maintain in a prominent location on the attorney general's publicly accessible Internet website a link to the most recent annual report developed under this subsection.

Added by Acts 1989, 71st Leg., 1st C.S., ch. 12, § 1, eff. Oct. 18, 1989. Amended by Acts 1991, 72nd Leg., ch. 312, §§ 1, 2, eff. Sept. 1, 1991; Acts 1993, 73rd Leg., ch. 780, §§ 3, 4, eff. Sept. 1, 1993; Acts 1993, 73rd Leg., ch. 814, § 1, eff. Aug. 30, 1993; Acts 1995, 74th Leg., ch. 76, § 5.95(112), eff. Sept. 1, 1995; Acts 1997, 75th Leg., ch. 975, § 1, eff. Sept. 1, 1997; Acts 1999, 76th Leg., ch. 481, § 1, 2, eff. Sept. 1, 1999; Acts 1999, 76th Leg., ch. 582, § 2, eff. Sept. 1, 1999; Acts 1999, 76th Leg., ch. 707, § 1, eff. Sept. 1, 1999; Acts 2001, 77th Leg., ch. 124, § 2, eff. Sept. 1, 2001; Acts 2001, 77th Leg., ch. 929, § 3, eff. Sept. 1, 2001; Acts 2003, 78th Leg., ch. 198, § 2.142, eff. Sept. 1, 2003; Acts 2003, 78th Leg., ch. 257, § 18, eff. Sept. 1, 2003; Acts 2003, 78th Leg., ch. 428, § 2, eff. Sept. 1, 2003; Acts 2005, 79th Leg., ch. 556, § 4, eff. Sept. 1, 2005; Acts 2007, 80th Leg., ch. 120, § 2, eff. Sept. 1, 2007; Acts 2007, 80th Leg., ch. 446, § 1, eff. Sept. 1, 2007; Acts 2009, 81st Leg., ch. 187, § 1, eff. May 27, 2009; Acts 2009, 81st Leg., ch. 941, § 1, eff. Sept. 1, 2009; Acts 2011, 82nd Leg., ch. 508 (H.B. 1674), § 23, eff. Sept. 1, 2011; Acts 2011, 82nd Leg., ch. 1321 (S.B. 316), § 2, eff. Sept. 1, 2011; Acts 2013, 83rd Leg., ch. 157 (S.B. 878), § 1, eff. Sept. 1, 2013; Acts 2013, 83rd Leg., ch. 1357 (S.B. 1451), § 4, eff. Sept. 1, 2013; Acts 2015, 84th Leg., ch. 920 (H.B. 530), § 1, eff. Sept. 1, 2015.

Art. 59.061.   Audits and Investigations

(a) The state auditor may at any time perform an audit or conduct an investigation, in accordance with this article and Chapter 321, Government Code, related to the seizure, forfeiture, receipt, and specific expenditure of proceeds and property received under this chapter.

(b) The state auditor is entitled at any time to access any book, account, voucher, confidential or nonconfidential report, or other record of information, including electronic data, maintained under Article 59.06, except that if the release of the applicable information is restricted under state or federal law, the state auditor may access the information only with the approval of a court or federal administrative agency, as appropriate.

(c) If the results of an audit or investigation under this article indicate that a law enforcement agency or attorney representing the state has knowingly violated or is knowingly violating a provision of this chapter relating to the disposition of proceeds or property received under this chapter, the state auditor shall promptly notify the attorney general for the purpose of initiating appropriate enforcement proceedings under Article 59.062.

(d) The law enforcement agency or attorney representing the state shall reimburse the state auditor for costs incurred by the state auditor in performing an audit under this article.

Added by Acts 2011, 82nd Leg., ch. 1321 (S.B. 316), § 3, eff. Sept. 1, 2011.

Art. 59.062.   Enforcement

(a) In the name of the state, the attorney general may institute in a district court in Travis County or in a county served by the law enforcement agency or attorney representing the state, as applicable, a suit for injunctive relief, to recover a civil penalty, or for both injunctive relief and a civil penalty if the results of an audit or investigation under Article 59.061 indicate that the law enforcement agency or attorney representing the state has knowingly violated or is knowingly violating a provision of this chapter relating to the disposition of proceeds or property received under this chapter.

(b) On application for injunctive relief and a finding that the law enforcement agency or attorney representing the state is knowingly violating a provision of this chapter relating to the disposition of proceeds or property received under this chapter, the district court shall grant the injunctive relief the facts may warrant, without requirement for bond.

(c) A law enforcement agency or attorney representing the state who knowingly commits a violation described by Subsection (a) is liable to the state for a civil penalty in an amount not to exceed $100,000 as determined by the district court to be appropriate for the nature and seriousness of the violation. In determining an appropriate penalty for the violation, the court shall consider:

(1) any previous violations committed by the agency or attorney;

(2) the seriousness of the violation, including the nature, circumstances, extent, and gravity of the violation;

(3) the demonstrated good faith of the agency or attorney; and

(4) the amount necessary to deter future violations.

(d) If the attorney general brings a suit under this article and an injunction is granted or a civil penalty is imposed, the attorney general may recover reasonable expenses, court costs, investigative costs, and attorney's fees.

(e) Notwithstanding any other provision of this article, a law enforcement agency or attorney representing the state ordered to pay a civil penalty, expense, cost, or fee under this article shall make the payment out of money available in any fund established by the agency or attorney, as applicable, for the purpose of administering proceeds or property received under this chapter. If sufficient money is not available to make payment in full at the time the court enters an order requiring payment, the agency or attorney shall continue to make payments out of money available in any fund described by this subsection until the payment is made in full.

(f) A civil penalty collected under this article shall be deposited to the credit of the drug court account in the general revenue fund to help fund specialty court programs established under Chapter 122, 123, 124, 125, or 129, Government Code, or former law.

(g) A law enforcement agency or attorney representing the state is immune from liability under this article if the agency or attorney reasonably relied on:

(1) the advice, consent, or approval of an entity that conducts an audit of the agency or attorney under this chapter; or

(2) a written opinion of the attorney general relating to:

(A) the statute or other provision of law the agency or attorney is alleged to have knowingly violated; or

(B) a fact situation that is substantially similar to the fact situation in which the agency or attorney is involved.

Added by Acts 2011, 82nd Leg., ch. 1321 (S.B. 316), § 3, eff. Sept. 1, 2011. Amended by Acts 2013, 83rd Leg., ch. 747 (S.B. 462), § 2.02, eff. Sept. 1, 2013; Acts 2017, 85th Leg., ch. 369 (H.B. 3391), § 2, eff. Sept. 1, 2017.

Art. 59.07.   Immunity

This chapter does not impose any additional liability on any authorized state, county, or municipal officer engaged in the lawful performance of the officer's duties.

Added by Acts 1989, 71st Leg., 1st C.S., ch. 12, § 1, eff. Oct. 18, 1989.

Art. 59.08.   Deposit of money pending disposition

(a) If money that is contraband is seized, the attorney representing the state may deposit the money in an interest-bearing bank account in the jurisdiction of the attorney representing the state until a final judgment is rendered concerning the contraband.

(b) If a final judgment is rendered concerning contraband, money that has been placed in an interest-bearing bank account under Subsection (a) of this article shall be distributed in the same manner as proceeds are distributed under Article 59.06 of this code, with any interest being distributed in the same manner and used for the same purpose as the principal.

Added by Acts 1989, 71st Leg., 1st C.S., ch. 12, § 1, eff. Oct. 18, 1989.

Art. 59.09.   Right to attorney not to be abridged

This chapter is not intended to abridge an accused person's right to counsel in a criminal case.

Added by Acts 1989, 71st Leg., 1st C.S., ch. 12, § 1, eff. Oct. 18, 1989.

Art. 59.10.   Election of laws

If property is subject to forfeiture under this chapter and under any other law of this state, the attorney representing the state may bring forfeiture proceedings under either law.

Added by Acts 1989, 71st Leg., 1st C.S., ch. 12, § 1, eff. Oct. 18, 1989.

Art. 59.11. Report of Seized and Forfeited Aircraft

Not later than the 10th day after the last day of each quarter of the fiscal year, the Department of Public Safety shall report to the Texas Department of Transportation:

(1) a description of each aircraft that the Department of Public Safety has received by forfeiture under this chapter during the preceding quarter and the purposes for which the Department of Public Safety intends to use the aircraft; and

(2) a description of each aircraft the Department of Public Safety knows to have been seized under this chapter during the preceding quarter and the purposes for which the Department of Public Safety would use the aircraft if it were forfeited to the Department of Public Safety.

Added by Acts 1991, 72nd Leg., ch. 14, § 283, eff. Sept. 1, 1991. Amended by Acts 2013, 83rd Leg., ch. 1312 (S.B. 59), § 4, eff. Sept. 1, 2013.

Art. 59.12. Seizure of Accounts and Assets at Regulated Financial Institution

(a) This article applies to property consisting of a depository account or assets in a regulated financial institution.

(b) A regulated financial institution, at the time a seizure warrant issued under Chapter 18 is served on the institution, may either:

(1) pay an account or tender assets held as security for an obligation owed to the institution at the time of the service of the seizure warrant; or

(2) transfer the depository account or assets to a segregated interest-bearing account in the name of the attorney representing the state as trustee, to remain in the account until the time has expired for an appeal from a decision of the court relating to the forfeiture of accounts or assets under Article 59.05.

(c) Immediately on service of the seizure warrant, the regulated financial institution shall take action as necessary to segregate the account or assets and shall provide evidence, certified by an officer of the institution, of the terms and amount of the account or a detailed inventory of the assets to the peace officer serving the warrant. Except as otherwise provided by this article, a transaction involving an account or assets, other than the deposit or reinvestment of interest, dividends, or other normally recurring payments on the account or assets that do not involve distribution of proceeds to the owner, is not authorized unless approved by the court that issued the seizure warrant or, if a forfeiture action has been instituted, the court in which that action is pending.

(d) Any accrual to the value of the account or assets during the pendency of the forfeiture proceedings is subject to the procedures for the disbursement of interest under Article 59.08.

(e) If the regulated financial institution fails to release the depository account or assets to a peace officer pursuant to a seizure warrant or transfer the account or assets as required by Subsection (b), and as a result cannot comply with the court's forfeiture order, the court:

(1) shall order the regulated financial institution and its culpable officers, agents, or employees to pay actual damages, attorney's fees, and court costs incurred as a result of the institution's failure to comply; and

(2) may find the regulated financial institution and its culpable officers, agents, or employees in contempt.

(f) A regulated financial institution that complies with this article is not liable in damages because of the compliance.

(g) This article does not:

(1) impair the right of the state to obtain possession of physical evidence or to seize a depository account or other assets for purposes other than forfeiture under this chapter; or

(2) waive criminal or civil remedies available under other law.

Added by Acts 2001, 77th Leg., ch. 438, § 5, eff. Sept. 1, 2001.

Art. 59.13. Disclosure of Information Relating to Accounts and Assets at Regulated Financial Institution

(a) The attorney representing the state may disclose information to the primary state or federal financial institution regulator, including grand jury information or otherwise confidential information, relating to any action contemplated or brought under this chapter that involves property consisting of a depository account in a regulated financial institution or assets held by a regulated financial institution as security for an obligation owed to a regulated financial institution. An attorney representing the state who discloses information as permitted by this subsection is not subject to contempt under Article 20.02 for that disclosure.

(b) A primary state or federal financial institution regulator shall keep confidential any information provided by the attorney representing the state under Subsection (a). The sharing of information under Subsection (a) by a representative of the state is not considered a waiver by the state of any privilege or claim of confidentiality.

(c) A regulator described by Subsection (b) commits an offense if the regulator knowingly discloses information in violation of this article. An offense under this subsection is punishable by confinement in jail for a period not to exceed 30 days, a fine not to exceed $500, or both such confinement and fine.

Added by Acts 2001, 77th Leg., ch. 438, § 5, eff. Sept. 1, 2001.

Art. 59.14. Notice to Primary State and Federal Financial Institution Regulators

(a) Before taking any action under this chapter that implicates a potentially culpable officer or director of a regulated financial institution, the attorney representing the state shall notify the banking commissioner, who shall notify the appropriate state or federal financial institution regulator.

(b) A state or federal financial institution regulator shall keep confidential any information provided by the attorney representing the state under Subsection (a).

(c) A regulator described by Subsection (b) commits an offense if the regulator knowingly discloses information in violation of this article. An offense under this subsection is punishable by confinement in jail for a period not to exceed 30 days, a fine not to exceed $500, or both such confinement and fine.

(d) The provision of notice under Subsection (a) is not considered a waiver by the state of any privilege or claim of confidentiality.

Added by Acts 2001, 77th Leg., ch. 438, § 5, eff. Sept. 1, 2001.

CHAPTER 60. CRIMINAL HISTORY RECORD SYSTEM

Art. 60.01. Definitions

In this chapter:

(1) "Administration of criminal justice" means the performance of any of the following activities: detection, apprehension, detention, pretrial release, post-trial release, prosecution, adjudication, correctional supervision, or rehabilitation of an offender. The term includes criminal identification activities and the collection, storage, and dissemination of criminal history record information.

(2) "Appeal" means the review of a decision of a lower court by a superior court other than by collateral attack.

(3) "Computerized criminal history system" means the data base containing arrest, disposition, and other criminal history maintained by the Department of Public Safety.

(4) "Corrections tracking system" means the data base maintained by the Texas Department of Criminal Justice on all offenders under its supervision.

(5) "Council" means the Criminal Justice Policy Council.

(6) "Criminal justice agency" means a federal or state agency that is engaged in the administration of criminal justice under a statute or executive order and allocates a substantial part of its annual budget to the administration of criminal justice.

(7) "Criminal justice information system" means the computerized criminal history system and the corrections tracking system.

(8) "Disposition" means an action that results in the termination, transfer to another jurisdiction, or inde-

terminate suspension of the prosecution of a criminal charge.

(9) "Incident number" means a unique number assigned to a specific person during a specific arrest.

(10) "Offender" means any person who is assigned an incident number.

(11) "Offense code" means a numeric code for each offense category.

(12) "Rejected case" means:

(A) a charge that, after the arrest of the offender, the prosecutor declines to include in an information or present to a grand jury; or

(B) an information or indictment that, after the arrest of the offender, the prosecutor refuses to prosecute.

(13) "Release" means the termination of jurisdiction over an individual by the criminal justice system.

(14) "State identification number" means a unique number assigned by the Department of Public Safety to each person whose name appears in the criminal justice information system.

(15) "Uniform incident fingerprint card" means a multiple part form containing a unique incident number with space for information relating to the charge or charges for which a person is being arrested, the person's fingerprints, and other information relevant to the arrest.

(16) "Electronic means" means the transmission of data between word processors, data processors, or similar automated information equipment over dedicated cables, commercial lines, or other similar methods of transmission.

Added by Acts 1989, 71st Leg., ch. 785, § 6.01, eff. Sept. 1, 1989. Amended by Acts 1990, 71st Leg., 6th C.S., ch. 25, § 28, eff. June 18, 1990; Acts 1993, 73rd Leg., ch. 790, § 37, eff. Sept. 1, 1993; Acts 1993, 73rd Leg., ch. 1025, § 1, eff. Sept. 1, 1993.

Repeal

This article is repealed by Acts 2017, 85th Leg., ch. 1058 (H.B. 2931), § 5.01(3), effective Jan. 1, 2019.

Art. 60.02. Information systems

(a) The Texas Department of Criminal Justice is responsible for recording data and establishing and maintaining a data base for a corrections tracking system.

(b) The Department of Public Safety is responsible for recording data and maintaining a data base for a computerized criminal history system that serves as the record creation point for criminal history information maintained by the state.

(c) The criminal justice information system shall be established and maintained to supply the state with a system:

(1) that provides law enforcement officers with an accurate criminal history record depository;

(2) that provides criminal justice agencies with an accurate criminal history record depository for operational decision making;

(3) from which accurate criminal justice system modeling can be conducted;

(4) that improves the quality of data used to conduct impact analyses of proposed legislative changes in the criminal justice system; and

(5) that improves the ability of interested parties to analyze the functioning of the criminal justice system.

(d) The data bases must contain the information required by this chapter.

(e) The Department of Public Safety shall designate the offense codes and has the sole responsibility for designating the state identification number for each person whose name appears in the criminal justice information system.

(f) The Department of Public Safety and the Texas Department of Criminal Justice shall implement a system to link the computerized criminal history system and the corrections tracking system. Data received by the Texas Department of Criminal Justice that is required by the Department of Public Safety for the preparation of a criminal history record shall be made available to the computerized criminal history system not later than the seventh day after the date on which the Texas Department of Criminal Justice receives the request for the data from the Department of Public Safety.

(g) The Department of Public Safety is responsible for the operation of the computerized criminal history system and shall develop the necessary interfaces in the system to accommodate inquiries from a statewide automated fingerprint identification system, if such a system is implemented by the department.

(h) Whenever possible, the reporting of information relating to dispositions and subsequent offender processing data shall be conducted electronically.

(i) The Department of Public Safety and the Texas Department of Criminal Justice, with advice from the council and the Department of Information Resources, shall develop biennial plans to improve the reporting and accuracy of the criminal justice information system and to develop and maintain monitoring systems capable of identifying missing information.

(j) At least once during each five-year period the council shall coordinate an examination of the records and operations of the criminal justice information system to ensure the accuracy and completeness of information in the system and to ensure the promptness of information reporting. The state auditor, or other appropriate entity selected by the council, shall conduct the examination with the cooperation of the council, the Department of Public Safety, and the Texas Department of Criminal Justice. The Department of Public Safety, the council, and the Texas Department of Criminal Justice may examine the records of the agencies required to report information to the Department of Public Safety or the Texas Department of Criminal Justice. The examining entity shall submit to the legislature and the council a report that summarizes the findings of each examination and contains recommendations for improving the system. Not later than the first anniversary after the date the examining entity submits its report, the Department of Public Safety shall report to the Legislative Budget Board, the governor, and the council on the department's progress in implementing the examining entity's recommendations, including for each recommendation not implemented the reason for not implementing the recommendation. The Department of Public Safety shall submit a similar report each year following the submission of the first report until each of the examining entity's recommendations is implemented.

(k) The council, the Department of Public Safety, the criminal justice division of the governor's office, and the Department of Information Resources cooperatively shall develop and adopt a grant program, to be implemented by the criminal justice division at a time and in a manner determined by the division, to aid local law enforcement agencies, prosecutors, and court personnel in obtaining equipment and training necessary to operate a telecommunications network capable of:

(1) making inquiries to and receiving responses from the statewide automated fingerprint identification system and from the computerized criminal history system; and

(2) transmitting information to those systems.

(m) [1] Notwithstanding Subsection (j), work performed under this section by the state auditor is subject to approval by the legislative audit committee for inclusion in the audit plan under Section 321.013(c), Government Code.

Added by Acts 1989, 71st Leg., ch. 785, § 6.01, eff. Sept. 1, 1989. Amended by Acts 1990, 71st Leg., 6th C.S., ch. 25, § 28, eff. June 18, 1990; Acts 1991, 72nd Leg., ch. 362, § 1, eff. Aug. 26, 1991; Acts 2001, 77th Leg., ch. 474, § 1, eff. Sept. 1, 2001; Acts 2003, 78th Leg., ch. 785, § 72, eff. Sept. 1, 2003; Acts 2013, 83rd Leg., ch. 1312 (S.B. 59), § 5, eff. Sept. 1, 2013.

[1] So in original.

Repeal

This article is repealed by Acts 2017, 85th Leg., ch. 1058 (H.B. 2931), § 5.01(3), effective Jan. 1, 2019.

Art. 60.03. Interagency cooperation; confidentiality

(a) Criminal justice agencies, the Legislative Budget Board, and the council are entitled to access to the data bases of the Department of Public Safety, the Texas Juvenile Justice Department, and the Texas Department of Criminal Justice in accordance with applicable state or federal law or regulations. The access granted by this subsection does not grant an agency, the Legislative Budget Board, or the council the right to add, delete, or alter data maintained by another agency.

(b) The council or the Legislative Budget Board may submit to the Department of Public Safety, the Texas Juvenile Justice Department, and the Texas Department of Criminal Justice an annual request for a data file containing data elements from the departments' systems. The Department of Public Safety, the Texas Juvenile Justice Department, and the Texas Department of Criminal Justice shall provide the council and the Legislative Budget Board with that data file for the period requested, in accordance with state and federal law and regulations. If the council submits data file requests other than the annual data file request, the director of the agency maintaining the requested records must approve the request. The Legislative Budget Board may submit data file requests other than the annual data file request without the approval of the director of the agency maintaining the requested records.

(c) Neither a criminal justice agency, the council, nor the Legislative Budget Board may disclose to the public information in an individual's criminal history record if the record is protected by state or federal law or regulation.

Added by Acts 1989, 71st Leg., ch. 785, § 6.01, eff. Sept. 1, 1989. Amended by Acts 1990, 71st Leg., 6th C.S., ch. 25, § 28, eff. June 18, 1990; Acts 2005, 79th Leg., ch. 741, § 1, eff. June 17, 2005; Acts 2015, 84th Leg., ch. 734 (H.B. 1549), § 6, eff. Sept. 1, 2015.

Repeal

This article is repealed by Acts 2017, 85th Leg., ch. 1058 (H.B. 2931), § 5.01(3), effective Jan. 1, 2019.

Section 150 of Acts 2015, 84th Leg., ch. 734 (H.B. 1549) provides:

"If any provision of this Act conflicts with a provision of another Act of the 84th Legislature, Regular Session, 2015, the provision of the other Act controls to the extent of the conflict, regardless of the date of enactment."

Art. 60.04.   Compatibility of data

(a) Data supplied to the criminal justice information system must be compatible with the system and must contain both incident numbers and state identification numbers.

(b) A discrete submission of information under any article of this chapter must contain, in conjunction with information required, the defendant's name and state identification number.

Added by Acts 1989, 71st Leg., ch. 785, § 6.01, eff. Sept. 1, 1989. Amended by Acts 1990, 71st Leg., 6th C.S., ch. 25, § 28, eff. June 18, 1990.

Repeal

This article is repealed by Acts 2017, 85th Leg., ch. 1058 (H.B. 2931), § 5.01(3), effective Jan. 1, 2019.

Art. 60.05.   Types of information collected

The criminal justice information system must contain but is not limited to the following types of information for each arrest for a felony or a misdemeanor not punishable by fine only:

(1) information relating to offenders;

(2) information relating to arrests;

(3) information relating to prosecutions;

(4) information relating to the disposition of cases by courts;

(5) information relating to sentencing; and

(6) information relating to the handling of offenders received by a correctional agency, facility, or other institution.

Added by Acts 1989, 71st Leg., ch. 785, § 6.01, eff. Sept. 1, 1989. Amended by Acts 1990, 71st Leg., 6th C.S., ch. 25, § 28, eff. June 18, 1990.

Repeal

This article is repealed by Acts 2017, 85th Leg., ch. 1058 (H.B. 2931), § 5.01(3), effective Jan. 1, 2019.

Art. 60.051.   Information in computerized criminal history system

(a) Information in the computerized criminal history system relating to an offender must include:

(1) the offender's name, including other names by which the offender is known;

(2) the offender's date of birth;

(3) the offender's physical description, including sex, weight, height, race, ethnicity, eye color, hair color, scars, marks, and tattoos; and

(4) the offender's state identification number.

(b) Information in the computerized criminal history system relating to an arrest must include:

(1) the name of the offender;

(2) the offender's state identification number;

(3) the arresting agency;

(4) the arrest charge by offense code and incident number;

(5) whether the arrest charge is a misdemeanor or felony;

(6) the date of the arrest;

(7) the exact disposition of the case by a law enforcement agency following the arrest; and

(8) the date of disposition of the case by the law enforcement agency.

(c) Information in the computerized criminal history system relating to a prosecution must include:

(1) each charged offense by offense code and incident number;

(2) the level of the offense charged or the degree of the offense charged for each offense in Subdivision (1) of this subsection; and

(3) for a rejected case, the date of rejection, offense code, and incident number, and whether the rejection is a result of a successful pretrial diversion program.

(d) Information in the computerized criminal history system relating to the disposition of a case that was not rejected must include:

(1) the final pleading to each charged offense and the level of the offense;

(2) a listing of each charged offense disposed of by the court and:

(A) the date of disposition;

(B) the offense code for the disposed charge and incident number; and

(C) the type of disposition; and

(3) for a conviction that is appealed the final court decision and the final disposition of the offender on appeal.

(e) Information in the computerized criminal history system relating to sentencing must include for each sentence:

(1) the sentencing date;

(2) the sentence for each offense by offense code and incident number;

(3) if the offender was sentenced to confinement:

(A) the agency that receives custody of the offender;

(B) the length of sentence for each offense; and

(C) if multiple sentences were ordered, whether they were ordered to be served consecutively or concurrently;

(4) if the offender was sentenced to a fine, the amount of the fine;

(5) if a sentence to confinement or fine was ordered but was deferred, probated, suspended, or otherwise not imposed:

(A) the length of sentence or the amount of the fine that was deferred, probated, suspended, or otherwise not imposed; and

(B) the offender's name, offense code, and incident number; and

(6) if a sentence other than fine or confinement was ordered, a description of the sentence ordered.

(f) The department shall maintain in the computerized criminal history system any information the department maintains in the central database under Article 62.005.

(g) In addition to the information described by Subsections (a)–(f), information in the computerized criminal history system must include the age of the victim of the offense if the defendant was arrested for or charged with an offense under:

(1) Section 21.02 (Continuous sexual abuse of young child or children), Penal Code;

(2) Section 21.11 (Indecency with a child), Penal Code;

(3) Section 22.011 (Sexual assault) or 22.021 (Aggravated sexual assault), Penal Code;

(4) Section 43.25 (Sexual performance by a child), Penal Code;

(5) Section 20.04(a)(4) (Aggravated kidnapping), Penal Code, if the defendant committed the offense with intent to violate or abuse the victim sexually;

(6) Section 30.02 (Burglary), Penal Code, if the offense is punishable under Subsection (d) of that section and the defendant committed the offense with intent to commit an offense described by Subdivision (2), (3), or (5);

(7) Section 20A.02 (Trafficking of persons), Penal Code, if the defendant:

(A) trafficked a person with the intent or knowledge that the person would engage in sexual conduct, as defined by Section 43.25, Penal Code; or

(B) benefited from participating in a venture that involved a trafficked person engaging in sexual conduct, as defined by Section 43.25, Penal Code; or

(8) Section 43.05(a)(2) (Compelling prostitution), Penal Code.

Added by Acts 1989, 71st Leg., ch. 785, § 6.01, eff. Sept. 1, 1989. Renumbered from art. 60.05(b) to (f) and amended by Acts 1990, 71st Leg., 6th C.S., ch. 25, § 28, eff. June 18, 1990. Amended by Acts 1993, 73rd Leg., ch. 1025, § 9, eff. Sept. 1, 1993; Acts 1995, 74th Leg., ch. 258, § 14, eff. Sept. 1, 1995; Acts 1997, 75th Leg., ch. 668, § 8, eff. Sept. 1, 1997; Acts 2005, 79th Leg., ch. 1008, § 2.03, eff. Sept. 1, 2005; Acts 2007, 80th Leg., ch. 593, § 1.08, eff. Sept. 1, 2007; Acts 2011, 82nd Leg., ch. 515 (H.B. 2014), § 2.05, eff. Sept. 1, 2011.

Repeal

This article is repealed by Acts 2017, 85th Leg., ch. 1058 (H.B. 2931), § 5.01(3), effective Jan. 1, 2019.

Art. 60.052. Information in corrections tracking system

(a) Information in the corrections tracking system relating to a sentence to be served under the jurisdiction of the Texas Department of Criminal Justice must include:

(1) the offender's name;

(2) the offender's state identification number;

(3) the sentencing date;

(4) the sentence for each offense by offense code and incident number;

(5) if the offender was sentenced to imprisonment:

(A) the unit of imprisonment;

(B) the length of sentence for each offense; and

(C) if multiple sentences were ordered, whether they were ordered to be served consecutively or concurrently; and

(6) if a sentence other than a fine or imprisonment was ordered, a description of the sentence ordered.

(b) Sentencing information in the corrections tracking system must also include the following information about each deferred adjudication,[1] probation, or other alternative to imprisonment ordered:

(1) each conviction for which sentence was ordered but was deferred, probated, suspended, or otherwise not imposed, by offense code and incident number; and

(2) if a sentence or portion of a sentence of imprisonment was deferred, probated, suspended, or otherwise not imposed:

(A) the offense, the sentence, and the amount of the sentence deferred, probated, suspended, or otherwise not imposed;

(B) a statement of whether a return to confinement or other imprisonment was a condition of probation or an alternative sentence;

(C) the community supervision and corrections department exercising jurisdiction over the offender;

(D) the date the offender was received by a community supervision and corrections department;

(E) any program in which an offender is placed or has previously been placed and the level of supervision the offender is placed on while under the jurisdiction of a community supervision and corrections department;

(F) the date a program described by Paragraph (E) of this subdivision begins, the date the program ends, and whether the program was completed successfully;

(G) the date a level of supervision described by Paragraph (E) of this subdivision begins and the date the level of supervision ends;

(H) if the offender's probation is revoked:

(i) the reason for the revocation and the date of revocation by offense code and incident number; and

(ii) other current sentences of probation or other alternatives to confinement that have not been revoked, by offense code and incident number; and

(I) the date of the offender's release from the community supervision and corrections department.

(c) Information in the corrections tracking system relating to the handling of offenders must include the following information about each imprisonment, confinement, or execution of an offender:

(1) the date of the imprisonment or confinement;

(2) if the offender was sentenced to death:

(A) the date of execution; and

(B) if the death sentence was commuted, the sentence to which the sentence of death was commuted and the date of commutation;

(3) the date the offender was released from imprisonment or confinement and whether the release was a discharge or a release on parole or mandatory supervision;

(4) if the offender is released on parole or mandatory supervision:

(A) the offense for which the offender was convicted by offense code and incident number;

(B) the date the offender was received by an office of the parole division;

(C) the county in which the offender resides while under supervision;

(D) any program in which an offender is placed or has previously been placed and the level of supervision the offender is placed on while under the jurisdiction of the parole division;

(E) the date a program described by Paragraph (D) begins, the date the program ends, and whether the program was completed successfully;

(F) the date a level of supervision described by Paragraph (D) begins and the date the level of supervision ends;

(G) if the offender's release status is revoked, the reason for the revocation and the date of revocation;

(H) the expiration date of the sentence; and

(I) the date of the offender's release from the parole division or the date on which the offender is granted clemency; and

(5) if the offender is released under Article 42A.202(b), the date of the offender's release.

Renumbered from art. 60.05(g) to (i) and amended by Acts 1990, 71st Leg., 6th C.S., ch. 25, § 28, eff. June 18, 1990. Amended by Acts 2009, 81st Leg., ch. 87, § 25.044, eff. Sept. 1, 2009; Acts 2015, 84th Leg., ch. 770 (H.B. 2299), § 2.24, eff. Jan. 1, 2017.

1 A reference to "probation" or "deferred adjudication" means "community supervision", pursuant to Acts 1993, 73rd Leg., ch. 900, § 4.04(a).

Repeal

This article is repealed by Acts 2017, 85th Leg., ch. 1058 (H.B. 2931), § 5.01(3), effective Jan. 1, 2019.

Art. 60.06. Duties of agencies

(a) Each criminal justice agency shall:

(1) compile and maintain records needed for reporting data required by the Texas Department of Criminal Justice and the Department of Public Safety;

(2) transmit to the Texas Department of Criminal Justice and the Department of Public Safety, when and in the manner the Texas Department of Criminal Justice and the Department of Public Safety direct, all data required by the Texas Department of Criminal Justice and the Department of Public Safety;

(3) give the Department of Public Safety and the Texas Department of Criminal Justice or their accredited agents access to the agency for the purpose of inspection to determine the completeness and accuracy of data reported;

(4) cooperate with the Department of Public Safety and the Texas Department of Criminal Justice so that the Department of Public Safety and the Texas Department of Criminal Justice may properly and efficiently perform their duties under this chapter; and

(5) cooperate with the Department of Public Safety and the Texas Department of Criminal Justice to identify and eliminate redundant reporting of information to the criminal justice information system.

(b) Information on an individual that consists of an identifiable description and notation of an arrest, detention, indictment, information, or other formal criminal charge and a disposition of the charge, including sentencing, correctional supervision, and release that is collected and compiled by the Department of Public Safety and the Texas Department of Criminal Justice from criminal justice agencies and maintained in a central location is not subject to public disclosure except as authorized by federal or state law or regulation.

(c) Subsection (b) of this section does not apply to a document maintained by a criminal justice agency that is the source of information collected by the Department of Public Safety or the Texas Department of Criminal Justice. Each criminal justice agency shall retain documents described by this subsection.

(d) An optical disk or other technology may be used instead of microfilm as a medium to store information if allowed by the applicable state laws or regulations relating to the archiving of state agency information.

(e) An official of an agency may not intentionally conceal or destroy any record with intent to violate this section.

(f) The duties imposed on a criminal justice agency under this article are also imposed on district court and county court clerks.

Added by Acts 1989, 71st Leg., ch. 785, § 6.01, eff. Sept. 1, 1989. Amended by Acts 1990, 71st Leg., 6th C.S., ch. 25, § 28, eff. June 18, 1990; Acts 1995, 74th Leg., ch. 750, § 1, eff. Aug. 28, 1995.

Repeal

This article is repealed by Acts 2017, 85th Leg., ch. 1058 (H.B. 2931), § 5.01(3), effective Jan. 1, 2019.

Art. 60.061. Information on persons licensed by certain agencies

(a) The Texas State Board of Medical Examiners, the Texas State Board of Podiatric Medical Examiners, the State Board of Dental Examiners, the Texas State Board of Pharmacy, the Texas State Board of Examiners of Psychologists, and the State Board of Veterinary Medical Examiners shall provide to the Department of Public Safety through electronic means, magnetic tape, or disk, as specified by the department, a list including the name, date of birth, and any other personal descriptive information required by the department for each person licensed by the respective agency. Each agency shall update this information and submit to the Department of Public Safety the updated information quarterly.

(b) The Department of Public Safety shall perform at least quarterly a computer match of the licensing list against the convictions maintained in the computerized criminal history system. The Department of Public Safety shall report to the appropriate licensing agency for verification and administrative action, as considered appropriate by the licensing agency, the name of any person found to have a record of conviction, except a defendant whose prosecution is deferred during a period of community supervision without an adjudication or plea of guilt. The Department of Public Safety may charge the licensing agency a fee not to exceed the actual direct cost incurred by the department in performing a computer match and reporting to the agency.

(c) The transmission of information by electronic means under Subsection (a) of this article does not affect whether the information is subject to disclosure under Chapter 552, Government Code.

Added by Acts 1993, 73rd Leg., ch. 790, § 38, eff. Sept. 1, 1993; Acts 1993, 73rd Leg., ch. 1025, § 2, eff. Sept. 1, 1993. Amended by Acts 1995, 74th Leg., ch. 76, § 3.21, 5.95(88), eff. Sept. 1, 1995; Acts 1995, 74th Leg., ch. 965, § 78, eff. Sept. 1, 1995; Acts 1999, 76th Leg., ch. 1189, § 43, eff. Sept. 1, 1999; Acts 2005, 79th Leg., ch. 143, § 23, eff. Sept. 1, 2005.

Repeal

This article is repealed by Acts 2017, 85th Leg., ch. 1058 (H.B. 2931), § 5.01(3), effective Jan. 1, 2019.

Art. 60.07.   Uniform incident fingerprint card

(a) The Department of Public Safety, in consultation with the council, shall design, print, and distribute to each law enforcement agency in the state a uniform incident fingerprint card.

(b) The incident card must:

(1) be serially numbered with an incident number in such a manner that the individual incident of arrest may be readily ascertained; and

(2) be a multiple part form that can be transmitted with the offender through the criminal justice process and that allows each agency to report required data to the Department of Public Safety or the Texas Department of Criminal Justice.

(c) Subject to available telecommunications capacity, the Department of Public Safety shall develop the capability to receive by electronic means from a law enforcement agency the information on the uniform incident fingerprint card. The information must be in a form that is compatible to the form required of data supplied to the criminal justice information system.

Added by Acts 1989, 71st Leg., ch. 785, § 6.01, eff. Sept. 1, 1989. Amended by Acts 1990, 71st Leg., 6th C.S., ch. 25, § 28, eff. June 18, 1990; Acts 1993, 73rd Leg., ch. 790, § 39, eff. Sept. 1, 1993; Acts 1993, 73rd Leg., ch. 1025, § 3, eff. Sept. 1, 1993.

Repeal

This article is repealed by Acts 2017, 85th Leg., ch. 1058 (H.B. 2931), § 5.01(3), effective Jan. 1, 2019.

Art. 60.08.   Reporting

(a) The Department of Public Safety and the Texas Department of Criminal Justice shall, by rule, develop reporting procedures that:

(1) ensure that the offender processing data is reported from the time an offender is arrested until the time an offender is released; and

(2) provide measures and policies designed to identify and eliminate redundant reporting of information to the criminal justice information system.

(b) The arresting agency shall prepare a uniform incident fingerprint card and initiate the reporting process for each offender charged with a felony or a misdemeanor not punishable by fine only.

(c) The clerk of the court exercising jurisdiction over a case shall report the disposition of the case to the Department of Public Safety.

(d) Except as otherwise required by applicable state laws or regulations, information or data required by this chapter to be reported to the Texas Department of Criminal Justice or the Department of Public Safety shall be reported promptly but not later than the 30th day after the date on which the information or data is received by the agency responsible for reporting it except in the case of an arrest. An offender's arrest shall be reported to the Department of Public Safety not later than the seventh day after the date of the arrest.

(e) A court that orders the release of an offender under Article 42A.202(b) at a time when the offender is under a bench warrant and not physically imprisoned in the Texas Department of Criminal Justice shall report the release to the department not later than the seventh day after the date of the release.

Added by Acts 1989, 71st Leg., ch. 785, § 6.01, eff. Sept. 1, 1989. Amended by Acts 1990, 71st Leg., 6th C.S., ch. 25, § 28, eff. June 18, 1990; Acts 1995, 74th Leg., ch. 750, § 2, eff. Aug. 28, 1995; Acts 2009, 81st Leg., ch. 87, § 25.045, eff. Sept. 1, 2009; Acts 2015, 84th Leg., ch. 770 (H.B. 2299), § 2.25, eff. Jan. 1, 2017.

Repeal

This article is repealed by Acts 2017, 85th Leg., ch. 1058 (H.B. 2931), § 5.01(3), effective Jan. 1, 2019.

Art. 60.09.   Local data advisory boards

(a) The commissioners court of each county may create local data advisory boards to, among other duties:

(1) analyze the structure of local automated and manual data systems to identify redundant data entry and data storage;

(2) develop recommendations for the commissioners to improve the local data systems;

(3) develop recommendations, when appropriate, for the effective electronic transfer of required data from local agencies to state agencies; and

(4) perform any related duties to be determined by the commissioners court.

(b) Local officials responsible for collecting, storing, reporting, and using data may be appointed to the local data advisory board.

(c) The council and the Department of Public Safety shall, to the extent that resources allow, provide technical assistance and advice on the request of the local data advisory board.

Added by Acts 1989, 71st Leg., ch. 785, § 6.01, eff. Sept. 1, 1989. Amended by Acts 1990, 71st Leg., 6th C.S., ch. 25, § 28, eff. June 18, 1990.

Repeal

This article is repealed by Acts 2017, 85th Leg., ch. 1058 (H.B. 2931), § 5.01(3), effective Jan. 1, 2019.

Art. 60.10.   Expired

Art. 60.11.   Repealed by Acts 2005, 79th Leg., ch. 1218, § 6(1), (2), eff. Sept. 1, 2005

Art. 60.12.   Fingerprint and arrest information in computerized system

(a) The Department of Public Safety shall, when a jurisdiction transmits fingerprints and arrest information by a remote terminal accessing the statewide automated fingerprint identification system, use that transmission either to create a permanent record in the criminal justice information system or to create a temporary arrest record in the criminal justice information system to be maintained by the department until the department receives and processes the physical copy of the arrest information.

(b) The Department of Public Safety shall make available to a criminal justice agency making a background criminal inquiry any information contained in a temporary arrest record maintained by the department, including a statement that a physical copy of the arrest information was not available at the time the information was entered in the system.

Added by Acts 1991, 72nd Leg., 2nd C.S., ch. 10, § 7.05, eff. Dec. 1, 1991. Amended by Acts 1993, 73rd Leg., ch. 790, § 40, eff. Sept. 1, 1993; Acts 1993, 73rd Leg., ch. 1025, § 4, eff. Sept. 1, 1993.

Repeal

This article is repealed by Acts 2017, 85th Leg., ch. 1058 (H.B. 2931), § 5.01(3), effective Jan. 1, 2019.

Art. 60.13.   Repealed by Acts 2005, 79th Leg., ch. 1218, § 6(3), eff. Sept. 1, 2005

Art. 60.14.   Allocation of grant program money for criminal justice programs

An agency of the state, before allocating money to a county from any federal or state grant program for the enhancement of criminal justice programs, shall certify that the county has taken or will take, using all or part of the allocated funds, all action necessary to provide the Texas Department of Criminal Justice and the Department of Public Safety any criminal history records maintained by the county in the manner specified for purposes of those departments.

Added by Acts 1991, 72nd Leg., 2nd C.S., ch. 10, § 7.05, eff. Dec. 1, 1991.

Repeal

This article is repealed by Acts 2017, 85th Leg., ch. 1058 (H.B. 2931), § 5.01(3), effective Jan. 1, 2019.

Arts. 60.15 to 60.17.   Repealed by Acts 2005, 79th Leg., ch. 1218, § 6(4) to (6), eff. Sept. 1, 2005

Art. 60.18.   Information on Subsequent Arrest of Certain Individuals

The Texas Department of Criminal Justice and the Department of Public Safety shall develop the capability to send by electronic means information about the subsequent arrest of a person under supervision to, as applicable:

(1) the community supervision and corrections department serving the court of original jurisdiction; or

(2) the district parole office supervising the person.

Added by Acts 1993, 73rd Leg., ch. 790, § 41, eff. Sept. 1, 1993; Acts 1993, 73rd Leg., ch. 1025, § 5, eff. Sept. 1, 1993. Amended by Acts 2005, 79th Leg., ch. 1218, § 2, eff. Sept. 1, 2005.

Repeal

This article is repealed by Acts 2017, 85th Leg., ch. 1058 (H.B. 2931), § 5.01(3), effective Jan. 1, 2019.

Art. 60.19. Information Related to Misused Identity

(a) On receipt of information from a local law enforcement agency under Article 2.28, the department shall:

(1) provide the notice described by Subdivision (1) of that article to the person whose identity was misused, if the local law enforcement agency was unable to notify the person under that subdivision;

(2) take action to ensure that the information maintained in the computerized criminal history system reflects the use of the person's identity as a stolen alias; and

(3) notify the Texas Department of Criminal Justice that the person's identifying information may have been falsely used by an inmate in the custody of the department.

(b) On receipt of a declaration under Section 411.0421, Government Code, or on receipt of information similar to that contained in a declaration, the department shall separate information maintained in the computerized criminal history system regarding an individual whose identity has been misused from information maintained in that system regarding the person who misused the identity.

Added by Acts 1999, 76th Leg., ch. 1334, § 2, eff. Sept. 1, 1999.   Amended by Acts 2003, 78th Leg., ch. 339, § 5, eff. Sept. 1, 2003.

Repeal

This article is repealed by Acts 2017, 85th Leg., ch. 1058 (H.B. 2931), § 5.01(3), effective Jan. 1, 2019.

Art. 60.20. Information Related to Non-Fingerprint Supported Actions

On receipt of a report of prosecution or court disposition information from a jurisdiction for which corresponding arrest data does not exist in the computerized criminal history system, the Department of Public Safety shall enter the report into a non-fingerprint supported file that is separate from the computerized criminal history system. The department shall grant access to records in the non-fingerprint supported file that include the subject's name or other identifier in the same manner as the department is required to grant access to criminal history record information under Subchapter F[1], Chapter 411, Government Code. On receipt of a report of arrest information that corresponds to a record in the non-fingerprint supported file, the department shall transfer the record from the non-fingerprint supported file to the computerized criminal history system.

Added by Acts 2001, 77th Leg., ch. 474, § 2, eff. Sept. 1, 2001.

[1] V.T.C.A., Government Code § 411.081 et seq.

Repeal

This article is repealed by Acts 2017, 85th Leg., ch. 1058 (H.B. 2931), § 5.01(3), effective Jan. 1, 2019.

Art. 60.21. Monitoring Tracking; Information Submission

(a) The Department of Information Resources shall monitor the development of the corrections tracking system by the Texas Department of Criminal Justice to ensure implementation of the system not later than June 1, 2005.

(b) The Department of Public Safety shall:

(1) monitor the submission of arrest and disposition information by local jurisdictions;

(2) annually submit to the Legislative Budget Board, the governor, the lieutenant governor, the state auditor, and the standing committees in the senate and house of representatives that have primary jurisdiction over criminal justice and the Department of Public Safety a report regarding the level of reporting by local jurisdictions;

(3) identify local jurisdictions that do not report arrest or disposition information or that partially report information; and

(4) for use in determining the status of outstanding dispositions, publish monthly on the Department of Public Safety's Internet website or on another electronic publication a report listing each arrest by local jurisdiction for which there is no corresponding final court disposition.

(c) The report described by Subsection (b)(2) must contain a disposition completeness percentage for each county in this state. For purposes of this subsection, "disposition completeness percentage" means the percentage of arrest charges a county reports to the Department of Public Safety to be entered in the computerized criminal history system under this chapter that were brought against a person in the county for which a disposition has been subsequently reported and entered into the computerized criminal history system.

Added by Acts 2001, 77th Leg., ch. 474, § 2, eff. Sept. 1, 2001. Amended by Acts 2005, 79th Leg., ch. 1218, § 3, eff. Sept. 1, 2005; Acts 2009, 81st Leg., ch. 1146, § 21.002, eff. Sept. 1, 2009.

Repeal

This article is repealed by Acts 2017, 85th Leg., ch. 1058 (H.B. 2931), § 5.01(3), effective Jan. 1, 2019.

CHAPTER 61. COMPILATION OF INFORMATION PERTAINING TO CRIMINAL COMBINATIONS AND CRIMINAL STREET GANGS

Art. 61.01. Definitions

In this chapter:

(1) "Combination" and "criminal street gang" have the meanings assigned by Section 71.01, Penal Code.

(2) "Child" has the meaning assigned by Section 51.02, Family Code.

(3) "Criminal information" means facts, material, photograph, or data reasonably related to the investigation or prosecution of criminal activity.

(4) "Criminal activity" means conduct that is subject to prosecution.

(5) "Criminal justice agency" has the meaning assigned by Article 60.01 and also means a municipal or county agency, or school district law enforcement agency, that is engaged in the administration of criminal justice under a statute or executive order.

(6) "Administration of criminal justice" has the meaning assigned by Article 60.01.

(7) "Department" means the Department of Public Safety of the State of Texas.

(8) "Intelligence database" means a collection or compilation of data organized for search and retrieval to evaluate, analyze, disseminate, or use intelligence information relating to a criminal combination or a criminal street gang for the purpose of investigating or prosecuting criminal offenses.

(9) "Law enforcement agency" does not include the Texas Department of Criminal Justice, the Texas Juvenile Justice Department, or a local juvenile probation department.

(10) "Juvenile justice agency" has the meaning assigned by Section 58.101, Family Code.

Added by Acts 1995, 74th Leg., ch. 671, § 1, eff. Aug. 28, 1995. Amended by Acts 1999, 76th Leg., ch. 1154, § 2, eff. Sept. 1, 1999; Acts 2011, 82nd Leg., ch. 380 (S.B. 315), § 1, eff. June 17, 2011; Acts 2015, 84th Leg., ch. 734 (H.B. 1549), § 7, eff. Sept. 1, 2015.

Repeal

This article is repealed by Acts 2017, 85th Leg., ch. 1058 (H.B. 2931), § 5.01(4), effective Jan. 1, 2019.

Section 150 of Acts 2015, 84th Leg., ch. 734 (H.B. 1549) provides:

"If any provision of this Act conflicts with a provision of another Act of the 84th Legislature, Regular Session, 2015, the provision of the other Act controls to the extent of the conflict, regardless of the date of enactment."

Art. 61.02. Criminal Combination and Criminal Street Gang Intelligence Database; Submission Criteria

(a) Subject to Subsection (b), a criminal justice agency or a juvenile justice agency shall compile criminal information into an intelligence database for the purpose of investigating or prosecuting the criminal activities of criminal combinations or criminal street gangs.

(b) A law enforcement agency in a municipality with a population of 50,000 or more or in a county with a population of 100,000 or more shall compile and maintain in a local or regional intelligence database criminal information relating to a criminal street gang as provided by Subsection (a). The information must be compiled and maintained in accordance with the criminal intelligence systems operating policies established under 28 C.F.R. Section 23.1 et seq. and the submission criteria established under Subsection (c).

(b–1) Information described by this article may be compiled on paper, by computer, or in any other useful manner by a criminal justice agency, juvenile justice agency, or law enforcement agency.

(c) Criminal information collected under this chapter relating to a criminal street gang must:

(1) be relevant to the identification of an organization that is reasonably suspected of involvement in criminal activity; and

(2) consist of:

(A) a judgment under any law that includes, as a finding or as an element of a criminal offense, participation in a criminal street gang;

(B) a self-admission by the individual of criminal street gang membership that is made during a judicial proceeding; or

(C) except as provided by Subsection (d), any two of the following:

(i) a self-admission by the individual of criminal street gang membership that is not made during a judicial proceeding, including the use of the Internet or other electronic format or medium to post photographs or other documentation identifying the individual as a member of a criminal street gang;

(ii) an identification of the individual as a criminal street gang member by a reliable informant or other individual;

(iii) a corroborated identification of the individual as a criminal street gang member by an informant or other individual of unknown reliability;

(iv) evidence that the individual frequents a documented area of a criminal street gang and associates with known criminal street gang members;

(v) evidence that the individual uses, in more than an incidental manner, criminal street gang dress, hand signals, tattoos, or symbols, including expressions of letters, numbers, words, or marks, regardless of how or the means by which the symbols are displayed, that are associated with a criminal street gang that operates in an area frequented by the individual and described by Subparagraph (iv);

(vi) evidence that the individual has been arrested or taken into custody with known criminal street gang members for an offense or conduct consistent with criminal street gang activity;

(vii) evidence that the individual has visited a known criminal street gang member, other than a family member of the individual, while the gang member is confined in or committed to a penal institution; or

(viii) evidence of the individual's use of technology, including the Internet, to recruit new criminal street gang members.

(d) Evidence described by Subsections (c)(2)(C)(iv) and (vii) is not sufficient to create the eligibility of a person's information to be included in an intelligence database described by this chapter unless the evidence is combined with information described by another subparagraph of Subsection (c)(2)(C).

(e) In this article:

(1) "Family member" means a person related to another person within the third degree by consanguinity or affinity, as described by Subchapter B, Chapter 573, Government Code, except that the term does not include a person who is considered to be related to another person by affinity only as described by Section 573.024(b), Government Code.

(2) "Penal institution" means a confinement facility operated by or under a contract with any division of the Texas Department of Criminal Justice, a confinement facility operated by or under contract with the Texas Juvenile Justice Department, or a juvenile secure pre-adjudication or post-adjudication facility operated by or under a local juvenile probation department, or a county jail.

Added by Acts 1995, 74th Leg., ch. 671, § 1, eff. Aug. 28, 1995. Amended by Acts 1999, 76th Leg., ch. 1154, § 3, eff. Sept. 1, 1999; Acts 2007, 80th Leg., ch. 258, § 18.05, eff. Sept. 1, 2007; Acts 2009, 81st Leg., ch. 736, § 1, eff. Sept. 1, 2009; Acts 2009, 81st Leg., ch. 1130, § 36, eff. Sept. 1, 2009; Acts 2011, 82nd Leg., ch. 380 (S.B. 315), § 2, eff. June 17, 2011; Acts 2015, 84th Leg., ch. 734 (H.B. 1549), § 8, eff. Sept. 1, 2015.

Repeal

This article is repealed by Acts 2017, 85th Leg., ch. 1058 (H.B. 2931), § 5.01(4), effective Jan. 1, 2019.

Section 150 of Acts 2015, 84th Leg., ch. 734 (H.B. 1549) provides: "If any provision of this Act conflicts with a provision of another Act of the 84th Legislature, Regular Session, 2015, the provision of the other Act controls to the extent of the conflict, regardless of the date of enactment."

Art. 61.03.   Release of information

(a) A criminal justice agency may release on request information maintained under this chapter to:

(1) another criminal justice agency;

(2) a court; or

(3) a defendant in a criminal proceeding who is entitled to the discovery of the information under Chapter 39.

(b) A criminal justice agency or court may use information received under this article only for the administration of criminal justice. A defendant may use information received under this article only for a defense in a criminal proceeding.

(c) A local law enforcement agency described by Article 61.02(b) shall send to the department information compiled and maintained under this chapter.

(d) The department shall establish an intelligence database and shall maintain information received from an agency under Subsection (c) in the database in accordance with the policies established under 28 C.F.R. Section 23.1 et seq. and the submission criteria under Article 61.02(c).

(e) The department shall designate a code to distinguish criminal information contained in the intelligence database relating to a child from criminal information contained in the database relating to an adult offender.

Added by Acts 1995, 74th Leg., ch. 671, § 1, eff. Aug. 28, 1995. Amended by Acts 1997, 75th Leg., ch. 898, § 1, eff. Sept. 1, 1997; Acts 1999, 76th Leg., ch. 1154, § 4, eff. Sept. 1, 1999; Acts 2009, 81st Leg., ch. 736, § 2, eff. Sept. 1, 2009.

Repeal

This article is repealed by Acts 2017, 85th Leg., ch. 1058 (H.B. 2931), § 5.01(4), effective Jan. 1, 2019.

Art. 61.04. Criminal information relating to child

(a) Notwithstanding Chapter 58, Family Code, criminal information relating to a child associated with a combination or a criminal street gang may be compiled and released under this chapter regardless of the age of the child.

(b) A criminal justice agency or a juvenile justice agency may release information maintained under this chapter to an attorney representing a child who is a party to a proceeding under Title 3,[1] Family Code, if the juvenile court determines the information:

(1) is material to the proceeding; and

(2) is not privileged under law.

(c) An attorney may use information received under this article only for a child's defense in a proceeding under Title 3, Family Code.

(d) The governing body of a county or municipality served by a law enforcement agency described by Article 61.02(b) may adopt a policy to notify the parent or guardian of a child of the agency's observa-tions relating to the child's association with a criminal street gang.

Added by Acts 1995, 74th Leg., ch. 671, § 1, eff. Aug. 28, 1995. Amended by Acts 1997, 75th Leg., ch. 165, § 7.05, eff. Sept. 1, 1997; Acts 1997, 75th Leg., ch. 898, § 2, eff. Sept. 1, 1997; Acts 1999, 76th Leg., ch. 1154, § 5, eff. Sept. 1, 1999; Acts 2009, 81st Leg., ch. 736, § 3, eff. Sept. 1, 2009; Acts 2011, 82nd Leg., ch. 380 (S.B. 315), § 3, eff. June 17, 2011.

[1] V.T.C.A., Family Code § 51.01 et seq.

Repeal

This article is repealed by Acts 2017, 85th Leg., ch. 1058 (H.B. 2931), § 5.01(4), effective Jan. 1, 2019.

Art. 61.05. Unauthorized use or release of criminal information

(a) A person commits an offense if the person knowingly:

(1) uses criminal information obtained under this chapter for an unauthorized purpose; or

(2) releases the information to a person who is not entitled to the information.

(b) An offense under this article is a Class A misdemeanor.

Added by Acts 1995, 74th Leg., ch. 671, § 1, eff. Aug. 28, 1995.

Repeal

This article is repealed by Acts 2017, 85th Leg., ch. 1058 (H.B. 2931), § 5.01(4), effective Jan. 1, 2019.

Art. 61.06. Removal of Records Relating to an Individual Other Than a Child

(a) This article does not apply to information collected under this chapter by the Texas Department of Criminal Justice or the Texas Juvenile Justice Department.

(b) Subject to Subsection (c), information collected under this chapter relating to a criminal street gang must be removed from an intelligence database established under Article 61.02 and the intelligence database maintained by the department under Article 61.03 after five years if:

(1) the information relates to the investigation or prosecution of criminal activity engaged in by an individual other than a child; and

(2) the individual who is the subject of the information has not been arrested for criminal activity reported to the department under Chapter 60.

(c) In determining whether information is required to be removed from an intelligence database under Subsection (b), the five-year period does not include any period during which the individual who is the subject of the information is:

(1) confined in a correctional facility operated by or under contract with the Texas Department of Criminal Justice;

(2) committed to a secure correctional facility operated by or under contract with the Texas Juvenile Justice Department, as defined by Section 51.02, Family Code; or

(3) confined in a county jail or confined in or committed to a facility operated by a juvenile board in lieu of being confined in a correctional facility operated by or under contract with the Texas Department of Criminal Justice or being committed to a secure correctional facility operated by or under contract with the Texas Juvenile Justice Department.

Added by Acts 1995, 74th Leg., ch. 671, § 1, eff. Aug. 28, 1995. Amended by Acts 1997, 75th Leg., ch. 898, § 3, eff. Sept. 1, 1997; Acts 1999, 76th Leg., ch. 1154, § 6, eff. Sept. 1, 1999; Acts 2007, 80th Leg., ch. 258, § 18.06, eff. Sept. 1, 2007; Acts 2007, 80th Leg., ch. 263, § 2, eff. June 8, 2007; Acts 2007, 80th Leg., ch. 1308, § 10, eff. June 15, 2007; Acts 2009, 81st Leg., ch. 87, § 6.007, eff. Sept. 1, 2009; Acts 2009, 81st Leg., ch. 1130, §§ 37, 38, eff. Sept. 1, 2009; Acts 2015, 84th Leg., ch. 734 (H.B. 1549), § 9, eff. Sept. 1, 2015.

Repeal

This article is repealed by Acts 2017, 85th Leg., ch. 1058 (H.B. 2931), § 5.01(4), effective Jan. 1, 2019.

Section 150 of Acts 2015, 84th Leg., ch. 734 (H.B. 1549) provides:

"If any provision of this Act conflicts with a provision of another Act of the 84th Legislature, Regular Session, 2015, the provision of the other Act controls to the extent of the conflict, regardless of the date of enactment."

Art. 61.07. Removal of Records Relating to a Child

(a) This article does not apply to information collected under this chapter by the Texas Department of Criminal Justice or the Texas Juvenile Justice Department.

(b) Subject to Subsection (c), information collected under this chapter relating to a criminal street gang must be removed from an intelligence database established under Article 61.02 and the intelligence database maintained by the department under Article 61.03 after two years if:

(1) the information relates to the investigation or prosecution of criminal activity engaged in by a child; and

(2) the child who is the subject of the information has not been:

(A) arrested for criminal activity reported to the department under Chapter 60; or

(B) taken into custody for delinquent conduct reported to the department under Chapter 58, Family Code.

(c) In determining whether information is required to be removed from an intelligence database under Subsection (b), the two-year period does not include any period during which the child who is the subject of the information is:

(1) committed to the Texas Juvenile Justice Department for conduct that violates a penal law of the grade of felony; or

(2) confined in the Texas Department of Criminal Justice.

Added by Acts 1999, 76th Leg., ch. 1154, § 7, eff. Sept. 1, 1999. Amended by Acts 2009, 81st Leg., ch. 87, § 25.046, eff. Sept. 1, 2009; Acts 2015, 84th Leg., ch. 734 (H.B. 1549), § 10, eff. Sept. 1, 2015.

Repeal

This article is repealed by Acts 2017, 85th Leg., ch. 1058 (H.B. 2931), § 5.01(4), effective Jan. 1, 2019.

Section 150 of Acts 2015, 84th Leg., ch. 734 (H.B. 1549) provides:

"If any provision of this Act conflicts with a provision of another Act of the 84th Legislature, Regular Session, 2015, the provision of the other Act controls to the extent of the conflict, regardless of the date of enactment."

Art. 61.075. Right to Request Existence of Criminal Information

(a) A person or the parent or guardian of a child may request a law enforcement agency to determine whether the agency has collected or is maintaining, under criteria established under Article 61.02(c), criminal information relating solely to the person or child. The law enforcement agency shall respond to the request not later than the 10th business day after the date the agency receives the request.

(b) Before responding to a request under Subsection (a), a law enforcement agency may require reasonable written verification of the identity of the person making the request and the relationship between the parent or guardian and the child, if applicable, including written verification of an address, date of birth, driver's license number, state identification card number, or social security number.

Added by Acts 2007, 80th Leg., ch. 258, § 18.07, eff. Sept. 1, 2007.

Repeal

This article is repealed by Acts 2017, 85th Leg., ch. 1058 (H.B. 2931), § 5.01(4), effective Jan. 1, 2019.

Art. 61.08. Right to Request Review of Criminal Information

(a) On receipt of a written request of a person or the parent or guardian of a child that includes a showing by the person or the parent or guardian that a law enforcement agency may have collected criminal information under this chapter relating to the person or child that is inaccurate or that does not comply with the submission criteria under Article 61.02(c), the head of the agency or the designee of the agency head shall review criminal information collected by the agency under this chapter relating to the person or child to determine if:

(1) reasonable suspicion exists to believe that the information is accurate; and

(2) the information complies with the submission criteria established under Article 61.02(c).

(b) If, after conducting a review of criminal information under Subsection (a), the agency head or designee determines that:

(1) reasonable suspicion does not exist to believe that the information is accurate or the information does not comply with the submission criteria, the agency shall:

(A) destroy all records containing the information; and

(B) notify the department and the person who requested the review of the agency's determination and the destruction of the records; or

(2) reasonable suspicion does exist to believe that the information is accurate and the information complies with the submission criteria, the agency shall notify the person who requested the review of the agency's determination and that the person is entitled to seek judicial review of the agency's determination under Article 61.09.

(c) On receipt of notice under Subsection (b), the department shall immediately destroy all records containing the information that is the subject of the notice

in the intelligence database maintained by the department under Article 61.03.

(d) A person who is committed to the Texas Juvenile Justice Department or confined in the Texas Department of Criminal Justice does not while committed or confined have the right to request review of criminal information under this article.

Added by Acts 1999, 76th Leg., ch. 1154, § 7, eff. Sept. 1, 1999. Amended by Acts 2009, 81st Leg., ch. 87, § 25.047, eff. Sept. 1, 2009; Acts 2015, 84th Leg., ch. 734 (H.B. 1549), § 11, eff. Sept. 1, 2015.

Repeal

This article is repealed by Acts 2017, 85th Leg., ch. 1058 (H.B. 2931), § 5.01(4), effective Jan. 1, 2019.

Section 150 of Acts 2015, 84th Leg., ch. 734 (H.B. 1549) provides:

"If any provision of this Act conflicts with a provision of another Act of the 84th Legislature, Regular Session, 2015, the provision of the other Act controls to the extent of the conflict, regardless of the date of enactment."

Art. 61.09. Judicial Review

(a) A person who is entitled to seek judicial review of a determination made under Article 61.08(b)(2) may file a petition for review in district court in the county in which the person resides.

(b) On the filing of a petition for review under Subsection (a), the district court shall conduct an in camera review of the criminal information that is the subject of the determination to determine if:

(1) reasonable suspicion exists to believe that the information is accurate; and

(2) the information complies with the submission criteria under Article 61.02(c).

(c) If, after conducting an in camera review of criminal information under Subsection (b), the court finds that reasonable suspicion does not exist to believe that the information is accurate or that the information does not comply with the submission criteria, the court shall:

(1) order the law enforcement agency that collected the information to destroy all records containing the information; and

(2) notify the department of the court's determination and the destruction of the records.

(d) A petitioner may appeal a final judgment of a district court conducting an in camera review under this article.

(e) Information that is the subject of an in camera review under this article is confidential and may not be disclosed.

Added by Acts 1999, 76th Leg., ch. 1154, § 7, eff. Sept. 1, 1999.

Repeal

This article is repealed by Acts 2017, 85th Leg., ch. 1058 (H.B. 2931), § 5.01(4), effective Jan. 1, 2019.

Art. 61.10.   Texas Violent Gang Task Force

(a) In this article, "task force" means the Texas Violent Gang Task Force.

(b) The purpose of the task force is to form a strategic partnership among local, state, and federal criminal justice, juvenile justice, and correctional agencies to better enable those agencies to take a proactive stance towards tracking gang activity and the growth and spread of gangs statewide.

(c) The task force shall focus its efforts on:

(1) developing, through regional task force meetings, a statewide networking system that will provide timely access to gang information;

(2) establishing communication between different criminal justice, juvenile justice, and correctional agencies, combining independent agency resources, and joining agencies together in a cooperative effort to focus on gang membership, gang activity, and gang migration trends; and

(3) forming a working group of criminal justice, juvenile justice, and correctional representatives from throughout the state to discuss specific cases and investigations involving gangs and other related gang activities.

(d) The task force may take any other actions as necessary to accomplish the purposes of this article.

(e) The Department of Public Safety shall support the task force to assist in coordinating statewide antigang initiatives.

(f) The task force shall consist of:

(1) a representative of the Department of Public Safety designated by the director of that agency;

(2) two representatives of the Texas Department of Criminal Justice, including a representative of the parole division, designated by the executive director of that agency;

(3) a representative of the office of the inspector general of the Texas Department of Criminal Justice designated by the inspector general;

(4) two representatives of the Texas Juvenile Justice Department designated by the executive director of that agency;

(5) a representative of the office of the attorney general designated by the attorney general;

(6) six representatives who are local law enforcement officers or local community supervision personnel, including juvenile probation personnel, designated by the governor;

(7) two representatives who are local prosecutors designated by the governor; and

(8) a representative of the Texas Alcoholic Beverage Commission designated by the executive director of that agency.

(g) If practicable, the task force shall consult with representatives from one or more United States Attorneys' Offices in this state and with representatives from the following federal agencies who are available and assigned to a duty station in this state:

(1) the Federal Bureau of Investigation;

(2) the Federal Bureau of Prisons;

(3) the United States Drug Enforcement Administration;

(4) United States Immigration and Customs Enforcement;

(5) United States Customs and Border Protection;

(6) the Bureau of Alcohol, Tobacco, Firearms and Explosives;

(7) the United States Marshals Service; and

(8) the United States Probation and Pretrial Services System.

Added by Acts 1999, 76th Leg., ch. 492, § 1, eff. June 18, 1999. Renumbered from Vernon's Ann. C.C.P. art. 61.07 by Acts 2001, 77th Leg., ch. 1420, § 21.001(14), eff. Sept. 1, 2001. Amended by Acts 2011, 82nd Leg., ch. 380 (S.B. 315), § 4, eff. June 17, 2011; Acts 2015, 84th Leg., ch. 734 (H.B. 1549), § 12, eff. Sept. 1, 2015; Acts 2015, 84th Leg., ch. 1232 (S.B. 2019), § 1, eff. June 19, 2015.

Repeal

This article is repealed by Acts 2017, 85th Leg., ch. 1058 (H.B. 2931), § 5.01(4), effective Jan. 1, 2019.

Section 150 of Acts 2015, 84th Leg., ch. 734 (H.B. 1549) provides:

"If any provision of this Act conflicts with a provision of another Act of the 84th Legislature, Regular Session, 2015, the provision of the other Act controls to the extent of the conflict, regardless of the date of enactment."

Art. 61.11. Gang Resource System

(a) The office of the attorney general shall establish an electronic gang resource system to provide criminal justice agencies and juvenile justice agencies with information about criminal street gangs in the state. The system may include the following information with regard to any gang:

(1) gang name;

(2) gang identifiers, such as colors used, tattoos, and clothing preferences;

(3) criminal activities;

(4) migration trends;

(5) recruitment activities; and

(6) a local law enforcement contact.

(b) Upon request by the office of the attorney general, criminal justice agencies and juvenile justice agencies shall make a reasonable attempt to provide gang information to the office of the attorney general for the purpose of maintaining an updated, comprehensive gang resource system.

(c) The office of the attorney general shall cooperate with criminal justice agencies and juvenile justice agencies in collecting and maintaining the accuracy of the information included in the gang resource system.

(d) Information relating to the identity of a specific offender or alleged offender may not be maintained in the gang resource system.

(e) Information in the gang resource system may be used in investigating gang-related crimes but may be included in affidavits or subpoenas or used in connection with any other legal or judicial proceeding only if the information from the system is corroborated by information not provided or maintained in the system.

(f) Access to the gang resource system shall be limited to criminal justice agency personnel and juvenile justice agency personnel.

(g) Information in the gang resource system shall be accessible by:

(1) municipality or county; and

(2) gang name.

(h) The office of the attorney general may coordinate with the Texas Department of Criminal Justice to include information in the gang resource system regarding groups which have been identified by the Security Threat Group Management Office of the Texas Department of Criminal Justice.

Added by Acts 1999, 76th Leg., ch. 491, § 1, eff. Aug. 30, 1999. Renumbered from Vernon's Ann. C.C.P. art. 61.08 by Acts 2001, 77th Leg., ch. 1420, § 21.001(15), eff. Sept. 1, 2001.

Repeal

This article is repealed by Acts 2017, 85th Leg., ch. 1058 (H.B. 2931), § 5.01(4), effective Jan. 1, 2019.

Art. 61.12. Database User Training

(a) The department shall enter into a memorandum of understanding with the United States Department of Justice or other appropriate federal department or agency to provide any person in this state who enters information into or retrieves information from an intelligence database described by this chapter with training regarding the operating principles described by 28 C.F.R. Part 23, as those principles relate to an intelligence database established or maintained under this chapter.

(b) A person in this state who enters information into or retrieves information from an intelligence database described by this chapter shall complete continuing education training on the material described by Subsection (a) at least once for each continuous two-year period the person has primary responsibility for performing a function described by this subsection.

(c) The department shall adopt the rules necessary to implement this article.

Added by Acts 2009, 81st Leg., ch. 736, § 4, eff. Sept. 1, 2009.

Repeal

This article is repealed by Acts 2017, 85th Leg., ch. 1058 (H.B. 2931), § 5.01(4), effective Jan. 1, 2019.

CHAPTER 62. SEX OFFENDER REGISTRATION PROGRAM

SUBCHAPTER A. GENERAL PROVISIONS

CODE OF CRIMINAL PROCEDURE

SUBCHAPTER A. GENERAL PROVISIONS

Art. 62.001. Definitions

In this chapter:

(1) "Department" means the Department of Public Safety.

(2) "Local law enforcement authority" means, as applicable, the office of the chief of police of a municipality, the office of the sheriff of a county in this state, or a centralized registration authority.

(3) "Penal institution" means a confinement facility operated by or under a contract with any division of the Texas Department of Criminal Justice, a confinement facility operated by or under contract with the Texas Juvenile Justice Department, or a juvenile secure pre-adjudication or post-adjudication facility operated by or under a local juvenile probation department, or a county jail.

(4) "Released" means discharged, paroled, placed in a nonsecure community program for juvenile offenders, or placed on juvenile probation, community supervision, or mandatory supervision.

(5) "Reportable conviction or adjudication" means a conviction or adjudication, including an adjudication of delinquent conduct or a deferred adjudication, that, regardless of the pendency of an appeal, is a conviction for or an adjudication for or based on:

(A) a violation of Section 21.02 (Continuous sexual abuse of young child or children), 21.09 (Bestiality), 21.11 (Indecency with a child), 22.011 (Sexual assault), 22.021 (Aggravated sexual assault), or 25.02 (Prohibited sexual conduct), Penal Code;

(B) a violation of Section 43.05 (Compelling prostitution), 43.25 (Sexual performance by a child), or 43.26 (Possession or promotion of child pornography), Penal Code;

(B–1) a violation of Section 43.02 (Prostitution), Penal Code, if the offense is punishable under Subsection (c–1)(3) of that section;

(C) a violation of Section 20.04(a)(4) (Aggravated kidnapping), Penal Code, if the actor committed the offense or engaged in the conduct with intent to violate or abuse the victim sexually;

(D) a violation of Section 30.02 (Burglary), Penal Code, if the offense or conduct is punishable under Subsection (d) of that section and the actor committed the offense or engaged in the conduct with intent to commit a felony listed in Paragraph (A) or (C);

(E) a violation of Section 20.02 (Unlawful restraint), 20.03 (Kidnapping), or 20.04 (Aggravated kidnapping), Penal Code, if, as applicable:

(i) the judgment in the case contains an affirmative finding under Article 42.015; or

(ii) the order in the hearing or the papers in the case contain an affirmative finding that the victim or intended victim was younger than 17 years of age;

(F) the second violation of Section 21.08 (Indecent exposure), Penal Code, but not if the second violation results in a deferred adjudication;

(G) an attempt, conspiracy, or solicitation, as defined by Chapter 15, Penal Code, to commit an offense or engage in conduct listed in Paragraph (A), (B), (C), (D), (E), (K), or (L);

(H) a violation of the laws of another state, federal law, the laws of a foreign country, or the Uniform Code of Military Justice for or based on the violation of an offense containing elements that are substantially similar to the elements of an offense listed under Paragraph (A), (B), (B–1), (C), (D), (E), (G), (J), (K), or (L), but not if the violation results in a deferred adjudication;

(I) the second violation of the laws of another state, federal law, the laws of a foreign country, or the Uniform Code of Military Justice for or based on the violation of an offense containing elements that are substantially similar to the elements of the offense of indecent exposure, but not if the second violation results in a deferred adjudication;

(J) a violation of Section 33.021 (Online solicitation of a minor), Penal Code;

(K) a violation of Section 20A.02(a)(3), (4), (7), or (8) (Trafficking of persons), Penal Code; or

(L) a violation of Section 20A.03 (Continuous trafficking of persons), Penal Code, if the offense is based partly or wholly on conduct that constitutes an offense under Section 20A.02(a)(3), (4), (7), or (8) of that code.

(6) "Sexually violent offense" means any of the following offenses committed by a person 17 years of age or older:

(A) an offense under Section 21.02 (Continuous sexual abuse of young child or children), 21.11(a)(1) (Indecency with a child), 22.011 (Sexual assault), or 22.021 (Aggravated sexual assault), Penal Code;

(B) an offense under Section 43.25 (Sexual performance by a child), Penal Code;

(C) an offense under Section 20.04(a)(4) (Aggravated kidnapping), Penal Code, if the defendant committed the offense with intent to violate or abuse the victim sexually;

(D) an offense under Section 30.02 (Burglary), Penal Code, if the offense is punishable under Subsection (d) of that section and the defendant committed the offense with intent to commit a felony listed in Paragraph (A) or (C) of Subdivision (5); or

(E) an offense under the laws of another state, federal law, the laws of a foreign country, or the Uniform Code of Military Justice if the offense contains elements that are substantially similar to the elements of an offense listed under Paragraph (A), (B), (C), or (D).

(7) "Residence" includes a residence established in this state by a person described by Article 62.152(e).

(8) "Public or private institution of higher education" includes a college, university, community college, or technical or trade institute.

(9) "Authority for campus security" means the authority with primary law enforcement jurisdiction over property under the control of a public or private institution of higher education, other than a local law enforcement authority.

(10) "Extrajurisdictional registrant" means a person who:

(A) is required to register as a sex offender under:

(i) the laws of another state with which the department has entered into a reciprocal registration agreement;

(ii) federal law or the Uniform Code of Military Justice; or

(iii) the laws of a foreign country; and

(B) is not otherwise required to register under this chapter because:

(i) the person does not have a reportable conviction for an offense under the laws of the other state, federal law, the laws of the foreign country, or the Uniform Code of Military Justice containing elements that are substantially similar to the elements of an offense requiring registration under this chapter; or

(ii) the person does not have a reportable adjudication of delinquent conduct based on a violation of an offense under the laws of the other state, federal law, or the laws of the foreign country containing elements that are substantially similar to the elements of an offense requiring registration under this chapter.

(11) "Centralized registration authority" means a mandatory countywide registration location designated under Article 62.0045.

(12) "Online identifier" means electronic mail address information or a name used by a person when sending or receiving an instant message, social networking communication, or similar Internet communication or when participating in an Internet chat. The term includes an assumed name, nickname, pseudonym, moniker, or user name established by a person for use in connection with an electronic mail address, chat or instant chat room platform, commercial social networking site, or online picture-sharing service.

Added by Acts 1991, 72nd Leg., ch. 572, § 1, eff. Sept. 1, 1991. Amended by Acts 1993, 73rd Leg., ch. 866, § 1, eff. Aug. 30, 1993; Acts 1995, 74th Leg., ch. 76, § 14.62, eff. Sept. 1, 1995; Acts 1995, 74th Leg., ch. 258, § 1, eff. Sept. 1, 1995. Redesignated from Vernon's Ann.Civ.St. art. 6252–13c.1, § 1 and amended by Acts 1997, 75th Leg., ch. 668, § 1, eff. Sept. 1, 1997. Amended by Acts 1999, 76th Leg., ch. 1193, § 4, eff. Sept. 1, 1999; Acts 1999, 76th Leg., ch. 1415, §§ 7, 8, eff. Sept. 1, 1999; Acts 2003, 78th Leg., ch. 347, § 1, eff. Sept. 1, 2003; Acts 2003, 78th Leg., ch. 1005, § 8, eff. Sept. 1, 2003; Acts 2003, 78th Leg., ch. 1275, § 3(4), eff. Sept. 1, 2003; Acts 2005, 79th Leg., ch. 1273, § 2, eff. June 18, 2005. Redesignated from Vernon's Ann.C.C.P. art. 62.01 and amended by Acts 2005, 79th Leg., ch. 1008, § 1.01, eff. Sept. 1, 2005. Amended by Acts 2007, 80th Leg., ch. 593, §§ 3.22(a), 3.22(b), 3.23, eff. Sept. 1, 2007; Acts 2007, 80th Leg., ch. 921, § 3.002(a), eff. Sept. 1, 2007; Acts 2009, 81st Leg., ch. 566, § 1, eff. June 19, 2009; Acts 2009, 81st Leg., ch. 755, § 2, eff. Sept. 1, 2009; Acts 2011, 82nd Leg., ch. 1 (S.B. 24), § 2.10, eff. Sept. 1, 2011; Acts 2011, 82nd Leg., ch. 91 (S.B. 1303), § 27.001(4), eff. Sept. 1, 2011; Acts 2011, 82nd Leg., ch. 233 (H.B. 530), § 1, eff. June 17, 2011; Acts 2015, 84th Leg., ch. 332 (H.B. 10), § 5, eff. Sept. 1, 2015; Acts 2015, 84th Leg., ch. 734 (H.B. 1549), § 13, eff. Sept. 1, 2015; Acts 2017, 85th Leg., ch. 685 (H.B. 29), § 15, eff. Sept. 1, 2017; Acts 2017, 85th Leg., ch. 739 (S.B. 1232), § 5, eff. Sept. 1, 2017.

Section 17 of Acts 2015, 84th Leg., ch. 332 (H.B. 10) provides:

"The changes in law made by this Act to Article 62.001(5), Code of Criminal Procedure, and Sections 20A.03 and 43.02, Penal Code, apply only to an offense committed on or after the effective date [Sept. 1, 2015] of this Act. An offense committed before the effective date of this Act is governed by the law in effect on the date the offense was committed, and the former law is continued in effect for that purpose. For purposes of this section, an offense was committed before the effective date of this Act if any element of the offense occurred before that date."

Section 150 of Acts 2015, 84th Leg., ch. 734 (H.B. 1549) provides:

"If any provision of this Act conflicts with a provision of another Act of the 84th Legislature, Regular Session, 2015, the provision of the other Act controls to the extent of the conflict, regardless of the date of enactment."

Section 45 of Acts 2017, 85th Leg., ch. 685 (H.B. 29) provides:

"(a) Except as provided by Subsection (b) of this section, the changes in law made by this Act apply only to an offense committed on or after the effective date [Sept. 1, 2017] of this Act. An offense committed before the effective date of this Act is governed by the law in effect on the date the offense was committed, and the former law is continued in effect for that purpose. For purposes of this subsection, an offense was committed before the effective date of this Act if any element of the offense occurred before that date.

"(b) The changes in law made by this Act in amending Chapter 62, Code of Criminal Procedure, apply only to a person who is required to register under Chapter 62, Code of Criminal Procedure, on the basis of a conviction or adjudication for or based on an offense committed on or after the effective date of this Act. A person who is required to register under Chapter 62, Code of Criminal Procedure, solely on the basis of a conviction or adjudication for or based on an offense committed before the effective date of this Act is governed by the law in effect on the date the offense was committed, and the former law is continued in effect for that purpose. For purposes of this subsection, an offense was committed before the effective date of this Act if any element of the offense occurred before that date."

Section 9 of Acts 2017, 85th Leg., ch. 739 (S.B. 1232) provides:

"The change in law made by this Act applies only to an offense committed on or after the effective date [Sept. 1, 2017] of this Act. An offense committed before the effective date of this Act is governed by the law in effect on the date the offense was committed, and the former law is continued in effect for that purpose. For purposes of this section, an offense was committed before the effective date of this Act if any element of the offense occurred before that date."

Art. 62.0015. Renumbered as Vernon's Ann.C.C.P. art. 63.0015 by Acts 2009, 81st Leg., ch. 87, § 27.001(3), eff. Sept. 1, 2009

Art. 62.002. Applicability of Chapter

(a) This chapter applies only to a reportable conviction or adjudication occurring on or after September 1, 1970.

(b) Except as provided by Subsection (c), the duties imposed on a person required to register under this chapter on the basis of a reportable conviction or adjudication, and the corresponding duties and powers of other entities in relation to the person required to register on the basis of that conviction or adjudication, are not affected by:

(1) an appeal of the conviction or adjudication; or

(2) a pardon of the conviction or adjudication.

(c) If a conviction or adjudication that is the basis of a duty to register under this chapter is set aside on appeal by a court or if the person required to register under this chapter on the basis of a conviction or adjudication receives a pardon on the basis of subsequent proof of innocence, the duties imposed on the person by this chapter and the corresponding duties and powers of other entities in relation to the person are terminated.

Added by Acts 2005, 79th Leg., ch. 1008, § 1.01, eff. Sept. 1, 2005.

Art. 62.003. Determination Regarding Substantially Similar Elements of Offense

(a) For the purposes of this chapter, the department is responsible for determining whether an offense under the laws of another state, federal law, the laws of a foreign country, or the Uniform Code of Military Justice contains elements that are substantially similar to the elements of an offense under the laws of this state.

(b) The department annually shall provide or make available to each prosecuting attorney's office in this state:

(1) the criteria used in making a determination under Subsection (a); and

(2) any existing record or compilation of offenses under the laws of another state, federal law, the laws of a foreign country, and the Uniform Code of Military Justice that the department has already determined to contain elements that are substantially similar to the elements of offenses under the laws of this state.

(c) An appeal of a determination made under this article shall be brought in a district court in Travis County.

Added by Acts 2001, 77th Leg., ch. 211, § 2, eff. Sept. 1, 2001. Amended by Acts 2003, 78th Leg., ch. 1005, § 9, eff. Sept. 1, 2003. Redesignated from Vernon's Ann.C.C.P. art. 62.0101 and amended by Acts 2005, 79th Leg., ch. 1008, § 1.01, eff. Sept. 1, 2005.

Art. 62.004. Determination Regarding Primary Registration Authority

(a) Except as provided by Subsection (a–1), for each person subject to registration under this chapter, the department shall determine which local law enforcement authority serves as the person's primary registration authority based on the municipality or county in which the person resides or, as provided by Article 62.152, the municipality or county in which the person works or attends school.

(a–1) Notwithstanding any other provision of this chapter, if a person resides or, as described by Article 62.152, works or attends school in a county with a centralized registration authority, the centralized registration authority serves as the person's primary registration authority under this chapter, regardless of whether the person resides, works, or attends school, as applicable, in any municipality located in that county.

(b) The department shall notify each person subject to registration under this chapter of the person's primary registration authority in a timely manner.

Added by Acts 2003, 78th Leg., ch. 347, § 2, eff. Sept. 1, 2003. Redesignated from Vernon's Ann.C.C.P. art. 62.0102 and amended by Acts 2005, 79th Leg., ch. 1008, § 1.01, eff. Sept. 1, 2005; Acts 2009, 81st Leg., ch. 566, § 2, eff. June 19, 2009.

Art. 62.0045. Centralized Registration Authority

(a) The commissioners court of a county may designate the office of the sheriff of the county or may, through interlocal agreement, designate the office of a chief of police of a municipality in that county to serve as a mandatory countywide registration location for persons subject to this chapter.

(b) Notwithstanding any other provision of this chapter, a person subject to this chapter is required to perform the registration and verification requirements of Articles 62.051 and 62.058 and the change of address requirements of Article 62.055 only with respect to the centralized registration authority for the county, regardless of whether the person resides in any municipality located in that county. If the person resides in a municipality, and the local law enforcement authority in the municipality does not serve as the person's centralized registration authority, the centralized registration authority, not later than the third day after the date the person registers or verifies registration or changes address with that authority, shall provide to the local law enforcement authority in that municipality notice of the person's registration, verification of registration, or change of address, as applicable, with the centralized registration authority.

(c) This section does not affect a person's duty to register with secondary sex offender registries under this chapter, such as those described by Articles 62.059 and 62.153.

Added by Acts 2009, 81st Leg., ch. 566, § 3, eff. June 19, 2009. Amended by Acts 2013, 83rd Leg., ch. 1036 (H.B. 2825), § 1, eff. June 14, 2013.

Art. 62.005. Central Database; Public Information

(a) The department shall maintain a computerized central database containing the information required for registration under this chapter. The department may include in the computerized central database the numeric risk level assigned to a person under this chapter.

(b) The information contained in the database, including the numeric risk level assigned to a person under this chapter, is public information, with the exception of any information:

(1) regarding the person's social security number or driver's license number, or any home, work, or cellular telephone number of the person;

(2) that is described by Article 62.051(c)(7) or required by the department under Article 62.051(c)(9),

including any information regarding an employer's name, address, or telephone number; or

(3) that would identify the victim of the offense for which the person is subject to registration.

(c) Notwithstanding Chapter 730, Transportation Code, the department shall maintain in the database, and shall post on any department website related to the database, any photograph of the person that is available through the process for obtaining or renewing a personal identification certificate or driver's license under Section 521.103 or 521.272, Transportation Code. The department shall update the photograph in the database and on the website annually or as the photograph otherwise becomes available through the renewal process for the certificate or license.

(d) A local law enforcement authority shall release public information described under Subsection (b) to any person who requests the information from the authority. The authority may charge the person a fee not to exceed the amount reasonably necessary to cover the administrative costs associated with the authority's release of information to the person under this subsection.

(e) The department shall provide a licensing authority with notice of any person required to register under this chapter who holds or seeks a license that is issued by the authority. The department shall provide the notice required by this subsection as the applicable licensing information becomes available through the person's registration or verification of registration.

(f) On the written request of a licensing authority that identifies an individual and states that the individual is an applicant for or a holder of a license issued by the authority, the department shall release any information described by Subsection (a) to the licensing authority.

(g) For the purposes of Subsections (e) and (f):

(1) "License" means a license, certificate, registration, permit, or other authorization that:

(A) is issued by a licensing authority; and

(B) a person must obtain to practice or engage in a particular business, occupation, or profession.

(2) "Licensing authority" means a department, commission, board, office, or other agency of the state or a political subdivision of the state that issues a license.

(h) Not later than the third day after the date on which the applicable information becomes available through the person's registration or verification of registration or under Article 62.058, the department shall send notice of any person required to register under this chapter who is or will be employed, carrying on a vocation, or a student at a public or private institution of higher education in this state to:

(1) for an institution in this state:

(A) the authority for campus security for that institution; or

(B) if an authority for campus security for that institution does not exist, the local law enforcement authority of:

(i) the municipality in which the institution is located; or

(ii) the county in which the institution is located, if the institution is not located in a municipality; or

(2) for an institution in another state, any existing authority for campus security at that institution.

(i) On the written request of an institution of higher education described by Subsection (h) that identifies an individual and states that the individual has applied to work or study at the institution, the department shall release any information described by Subsection (a) to the institution.

(j) The department, for law enforcement purposes, shall release all relevant information described by Subsection (a), including information that is not public information under Subsection (b), to a peace officer, an employee of a local law enforcement authority, or the attorney general on the request of the applicable person or entity.

Added by Acts 2005, 79th Leg., ch. 1008, § 1.01, eff. Sept. 1, 2005. Amended by Acts 2009, 81st Leg., ch. 755, § 3, eff. Sept. 1, 2009; Acts 2013, 83rd Leg., ch. 521 (S.B. 369), § 1, eff. Sept. 1, 2013; Acts 2017, 85th Leg., ch. 685 (H.B. 29), § 16, eff. Sept. 1, 2017.

Section 45 of Acts 2017, 85th Leg., ch. 685 (H.B. 29) provides:

"(a) Except as provided by Subsection (b) of this section, the changes in law made by this Act apply only to an offense committed on or after the effective date [Sept. 1, 2017] of this Act. An offense committed before the effective date of this Act is governed by the law in effect on the date the offense was committed, and the former law is continued in effect for that purpose. For purposes of this subsection, an offense was committed before the effective date of this Act if any element of the offense occurred before that date.

"(b) The changes in law made by this Act in amending Chapter 62, Code of Criminal Procedure, apply only to a person who is required to register under Chapter 62, Code of Criminal Procedure, on the basis of a conviction or adjudication for or based on an offense committed on or after the effective date of this Act. A person who is required to register under Chapter 62, Code of Criminal Procedure, solely on the basis of a conviction or adjudication for or based on an offense committed before the effective date of this Act is governed by the law in effect on the date the offense was committed, and the former law is continued in effect for that purpose. For purposes of this subsection, an offense was committed before the effective date of this Act if any element of the offense occurred before that date."

Art. 62.006. Information Provided to Peace Officer on Request

The department shall establish a procedure by which a peace officer or employee of a law enforcement agency who provides the department with a driver's license number, personal identification certificate number, or license plate number is automatically provided information as to whether the person to whom the driver's license or personal identification certificate is issued is required to register under this chapter or whether the license plate number is entered in the computerized central database under Article 62.005 as assigned to a vehicle owned or driven by a person required to register under this chapter.

Added by Acts 2005, 79th Leg., ch. 1008, § 1.01, eff. Sept. 1, 2005.

Art. 62.0061. Request for Online Identifiers by Social Networking Sites.

(a) On request by a commercial social networking site, the department may provide to the commercial social networking site:

(1) all public information that is contained in the database maintained under Article 62.005; and

(2) notwithstanding Article 62.005(b)(2), any online identifier established or used by a person who uses the site, is seeking to use the site, or is precluded from using the site.

(b) The department by rule shall establish a procedure through which a commercial social networking site may request information under Subsection (a), including rules regarding the eligibility of commercial social networking sites to request information under Subsection (a). The department shall consult with the attorney general, other appropriate state agencies, and other appropriate entities in adopting rules under this subsection.

(c) A commercial social networking site or the site's agent:

(1) may use information received under Subsection (a) only to:

(A) prescreen persons seeking to use the site; or

(B) preclude persons registered under this chapter from using the site; and

(2) may not use any information received under Subsection (a) that the networking site obtained solely under Subsection (a) in any manner not described by Subdivision (1).

(d) A commercial social networking site that uses information received under Subsection (a) in any manner not described by Subsection (c)(1) or that violates a rule adopted by the department under Subsection (b) is subject to a civil penalty of $1,000 for each misuse of information or rule violation. A commercial social networking site that is assessed a civil penalty under this article shall pay, in addition to the civil penalty, all court costs, investigative costs, and attorney's fees associated with the assessment of the penalty. A civil penalty assessed under this subsection shall be deposited to the compensation to victims of crime fund established under Subchapter B, Chapter 56.

(e) This article does not create a private cause of action against a commercial social networking site, including a cause of action that is based on the site:

(1) identifying, removing, disabling, blocking, or otherwise affecting the user of a commercial social networking site, based on a good faith belief that the person is required to register as a sex offender under this chapter or federal law; or

(2) failing to identify, remove, disable, block, or otherwise affect the user of a commercial social networking site who is required to register as a sex offender under this chapter or federal law.

(f) In this article, "commercial social networking site":

(1) means an Internet website that:

(A) allows users, through the creation of Internet web pages or profiles or other similar means, to provide personal information to the public or other users of the Internet website;

(B) offers a mechanism for communication with other users of the Internet website; and

(C) has the primary purpose of facilitating online social interactions; and

(2) does not include an Internet service provider, unless the Internet service provider separately operates and directly derives revenue from an Internet website described by Subdivision (1).

Added by Acts 2009, 81st Leg., ch. 755, § 4, eff. Sept. 1, 2009.

Art. 62.007. Risk Assessment Review Committee; Sex Offender Screening Tool

(a) The Texas Department of Criminal Justice shall establish a risk assessment review committee composed of at least seven members, each of whom serves on the review committee in addition to the member's other employment-related duties. The review committee, to the extent feasible, must include at least:

(1) one member having experience in law enforcement;

(2) one member having experience working with juvenile sex offenders;

(3) one member having experience as a sex offender treatment provider;

(4) one member having experience working with victims of sex offenses;

(5) the executive director of the Council on Sex Offender Treatment; and

(6) one sex offender treatment provider registered under Chapter 110, Occupations Code, and selected by the executive director of the Council on Sex Offender Treatment to serve on the review committee.

(b) The risk assessment review committee functions in an oversight capacity. The committee shall:

(1) develop or select, from among existing tools or from any tool recommended by the Council on Sex Offender Treatment, a sex offender screening tool to be used in determining the level of risk of a person subject to registration under this chapter;

(2) ensure that staff is trained on the use of the screening tool;

(3) monitor the use of the screening tool in the state; and

(4) analyze other screening tools as they become available and revise or replace the existing screening tool if warranted.

(c) The sex offender screening tool must use an objective point system under which a person is assigned a designated number of points for each of various factors. In developing or selecting the sex offender screening tool, the risk assessment review committee shall use or shall select a screening tool that may be adapted to use the following general guidelines:

(1) level one (low): a designated range of points on the sex offender screening tool indicating that the

person poses a low danger to the community and will not likely engage in criminal sexual conduct;

(2) level two (moderate): a designated range of points on the sex offender screening tool indicating that the person poses a moderate danger to the community and might continue to engage in criminal sexual conduct; and

(3) level three (high): a designated range of points on the sex offender screening tool indicating that the person poses a serious danger to the community and will continue to engage in criminal sexual conduct.

(d) The risk assessment review committee, the Texas Department of Criminal Justice, the Texas Juvenile Justice Department, or a court may override a risk level only if the entity:

(1) believes that the risk level assessed is not an accurate prediction of the risk the offender poses to the community; and

(2) documents the reason for the override in the offender's case file.

(e) Records and files, including records that have been sealed under Chapter 58, Family Code, relating to a person for whom a court, the Texas Department of Criminal Justice, or the Texas Juvenile Justice Department is required under this article to determine a level of risk shall be released to the court, the Texas Department of Criminal Justice, or the Texas Juvenile Justice Department, as appropriate, for the purpose of determining the person's risk level.

(f) Chapter 551, Government Code, does not apply to a meeting of the risk assessment review committee.

(g) The numeric risk level assigned to a person using the sex offender screening tool described by this article is not confidential and is subject to disclosure under Chapter 552, Government Code.

Added by Acts 2005, 79th Leg., ch. 1008, § 1.01, eff. Sept. 1, 2005. Amended by Acts 2015, 84th Leg., ch. 734 (H.B. 1549), § 14, eff. Sept. 1, 2015; Acts 2017, 85th Leg., ch. 746 (S.B. 1304), § 1, eff. Sept. 1, 2017.

Section 150 of Acts 2015, 84th Leg., ch. 734 (H.B. 1549) provides:

"If any provision of this Act conflicts with a provision of another Act of the 84th Legislature, Regular Session, 2015, the provision of the other Act controls to the extent of the conflict, regardless of the date of enactment."

Section 22 of Acts 2017, 85th Leg., ch. 746 (S.B. 1304) provides:

"The changes in law made by this Act apply to records created before, on, or after the effective date [Sept. 1, 2017] of this Act."

Art. 62.008. General Immunity

The following persons are immune from liability for good faith conduct under this chapter:

(1) an employee or officer of the Texas Department of Criminal Justice, the Texas Juvenile Justice Department, the Department of Public Safety, the Board of Pardons and Paroles, or a local law enforcement authority;

(2) an employee or officer of a community supervision and corrections department or a juvenile probation department;

(3) a member of the judiciary; and

(4) a member of the risk assessment review committee established under Article 62.007.

Added by Acts 2005, 79th Leg., ch. 1008, § 1.01, eff. Sept. 1, 2005. Amended by Acts 2015, 84th Leg., ch. 734 (H.B. 1549), § 15, eff. Sept. 1, 2015.

Section 150 of Acts 2015, 84th Leg., ch. 734 (H.B. 1549) provides:

"If any provision of this Act conflicts with a provision of another Act of the 84th Legislature, Regular Session, 2015, the provision of the other Act controls to the extent of the conflict, regardless of the date of enactment."

Art. 62.009. Immunity for Release of Public Information

(a) The department, a penal institution, a local law enforcement authority, or an authority for campus security may release to the public information regarding a person required to register under this chapter only if the information is public information under this chapter.

(b) An individual, agency, entity, or authority is not liable under Chapter 101, Civil Practice and Remedies Code, or any other law for damages arising from conduct authorized by Subsection (a).

(c) For purposes of determining liability, the release or withholding of information by an appointed or elected officer of an agency, entity, or authority is a discretionary act.

(d) A private primary or secondary school, public or private institution of higher education, or administrator of a private primary or secondary school or public or private institution of higher education may release to the public information regarding a person required to register under this chapter only if the information is public information under this chapter and is released to the administrator under Article 62.005, 62.053, 62.054, 62.055, or 62.153. A private primary or secondary school, public or private institution of higher education, or administrator of a private primary or secondary school or public or private institution of higher education is not liable under any law for damages arising from conduct authorized by this subsection.

Added by Acts 2005, 79th Leg., ch. 1008, § 1.01, eff. Sept. 1, 2005.

Art. 62.010. Rulemaking Authority

The Texas Department of Criminal Justice, the Texas Juvenile Justice Department, and the department may adopt any rule necessary to implement this chapter.

Added by Acts 2005, 79th Leg., ch. 1008, § 1.01, eff. Sept. 1, 2005. Amended by Acts 2015, 84th Leg., ch. 734 (H.B. 1549), § 16, eff. Sept. 1, 2015.

Section 150 of Acts 2015, 84th Leg., ch. 734 (H.B. 1549) provides:

"If any provision of this Act conflicts with a provision of another Act of the 84th Legislature, Regular Session, 2015, the provision of the other Act controls to the extent of the conflict, regardless of the date of enactment."

Art. 62.01. Redesignated as Vernon's Ann.C.C.P. art. 62.001 and amended by Acts 2005, 79th Leg., ch. 1008, § 1.01, eff. Sept. 1, 2005

Arts. 62.0101, 62.0102. Redesignated as Vernon's Ann.C.C.P. arts. 62.003, 62.004 and amended by Acts 2005, 79th Leg., ch. 1008, § 1.01, eff. Sept. 1, 2005

Arts. 62.0105, 62.011. Deleted by Acts 2005, 79th Leg., ch. 1008, § 1.01, eff. Sept. 1, 2005

Arts. 62.012 to 62.018. Renumbered as Vernon's Ann.C.C.P. arts. 63.012 to 63.018 by Acts 1999, 76th Leg., ch. 62, § 19.01(8)(A), eff. Sept. 1, 1999

Arts. 62.019, 62.020. Renumbered as Vernon's Ann. C.C.P. Arts. 63.019, 63.020 by Acts 1999, 76th Leg., ch. 62, § 19.01(8)(B), eff. Sept. 1, 1999

Arts. 62.02, 62.021. Redesignated as Vernon's Ann. C.C.P. arts. 62.051, 62.052 and amended by Acts 2005, 79th Leg., ch. 1008, § 1.01, eff. Sept. 1, 2005

Art. 62.022. Renumbered as Vernon's Ann.C.C.P. Art. 63.022 by Acts 1999, 76th Leg., ch. 62, § 19.01(8)(B), eff. Sept. 1, 1999

Arts. 62.023, 62.024. Repealed by Acts 1999, 76th Leg., ch. 1081, § 8, eff. Sept. 1, 1999

Art. 62.03. Redesignated as Vernon's Ann.C.C.P. art. 62.053 and amended by Acts 2005, 79th Leg., ch. 1008, § 1.01, eff. Sept. 1, 2005

Art. 62.031. Deleted by Acts 2005, 79th Leg., ch. 1008, § 1.01, eff. Sept. 1, 2005

Art. 62.032. Redesignated as Vernon's Ann.C.C.P. art. 62.054 and amended by Acts 2005, 79th Leg., ch. 1008, § 1.01, eff. Sept. 1, 2005

Art. 62.035. Deleted by Acts 2005, 79th Leg., ch. 1008, § 1.01, eff. Sept. 1, 2005

Art. 62.04. Redesignated as Vernon's Ann.C.C.P. art. 62.055 and amended by Acts 2005, 79th Leg., ch. 1008, § 1.01, eff. Sept. 1, 2005

Art. 62.041. Deleted by Acts 2005, 79th Leg., ch. 1008, § 1.01, eff. Sept. 1, 2005

Art. 62.045. Redesignated as Vernon's Ann.C.C.P. art. 62.056 and amended by Acts 2005, 79th Leg., ch. 1008, § 1.01, eff. Sept. 1, 2005

Art. 62.0451. Deleted by Acts 2005, 79th Leg., ch. 1008, § 1.01, eff. Sept. 1, 2005

Art. 62.05. Redesignated as Vernon's Ann.C.C.P. art. 62.057 and amended by Acts 2005, 79th Leg., ch. 1008, § 1.01, eff. Sept. 1, 2005

SUBCHAPTER B. REGISTRATION AND VERIFICATION REQUIREMENTS; RELATED NOTICE

Art. 62.051. Registration: General

(a) A person who has a reportable conviction or adjudication or who is required to register as a condition of parole, release to mandatory supervision, or community supervision shall register or, if the person is a person for whom registration is completed under this chapter, verify registration as provided by Subsection (f), with the local law enforcement authority in any municipality where the person resides or intends to reside for more than seven days. If the person does not reside or intend to reside in a municipality, the person shall register or verify registration in any county where the person resides or intends to reside for more than seven days. The person shall satisfy the requirements of this subsection not later than the later of:

(1) the seventh day after the person's arrival in the municipality or county; or

(2) the first date the local law enforcement authority of the municipality or county by policy allows the person to register or verify registration, as applicable.

(b) The department shall provide the Texas Department of Criminal Justice, the Texas Juvenile Justice Department, and each local law enforcement authority, authority for campus security, county jail, and court with a form for registering persons required by this chapter to register.

(c) The registration form shall require:

(1) the person's full name, date of birth, sex, race, height, weight, eye color, hair color, social security number, driver's license number, and shoe size;

(1-a) the address at which the person resides or intends to reside or, if the person does not reside or intend to reside at a physical address, a detailed description of each geographical location at which the person resides or intends to reside;

(1-b) each alias used by the person and any home, work, or cellular telephone number of the person;

(2) a recent color photograph or, if possible, an electronic digital image of the person and a complete set of the person's fingerprints;

(3) the type of offense the person was convicted of, the age of the victim, the date of conviction, and the punishment received;

(4) an indication as to whether the person is discharged, paroled, or released on juvenile probation, community supervision, or mandatory supervision;

(5) an indication of each license, as defined by Article 62.005(g), that is held or sought by the person;

(6) an indication as to whether the person is or will be employed, carrying on a vocation, or a student at a particular public or private institution of higher education in this state or another state, and the name and address of that institution;

(7) the identification of any online identifier established or used by the person;

(8) the vehicle registration information, including the make, model, vehicle identification number, color, and license plate number, of any vehicle owned by the person, if the person has a reportable conviction or adjudication for an offense under:

(A) Section 20A.02(a)(3), (4), (7), or (8), Penal Code; or

(B) Section 20A.03, Penal Code, if based partly or wholly on conduct that constitutes an offense under Section 20A.02(a)(3), (4), (7), or (8) of that code; and

(9) any other information required by the department.

(d) The registration form must contain a statement and description of any registration duties the person has or may have under this chapter.

(e) Not later than the third day after a person's registering, the local law enforcement authority with whom the person registered shall send a copy of the registration form to the department and, if the person resides on the campus of a public or private institution of higher education, to any authority for campus security for that institution.

(f) Not later than the seventh day after the date on which the person is released, a person for whom registration is completed under this chapter shall report to the applicable local law enforcement authority to verify the information in the registration form received by the authority under this chapter. The authority shall require the person to produce proof of the person's identity and residence before the authority gives the registration form to the person for verification. If the information in the registration form is complete and accurate, the person shall verify registration by signing the form. If the information is not complete or not accurate, the person shall make any necessary additions or corrections before signing the form.

(g) A person who is required to register or verify registration under this chapter shall ensure that the person's registration form is complete and accurate with respect to each item of information required by the form in accordance with Subsection (c).

(h) If a person subject to registration under this chapter does not move to an intended residence by the end of the seventh day after the date on which the person is released or the date on which the person leaves a previous residence, the person shall:

(1) report to the juvenile probation officer, community supervision and corrections department officer, or parole officer supervising the person by not later than the seventh day after the date on which the person is released or the date on which the person leaves a previous residence, as applicable, and provide the officer with the address of the person's temporary residence; and

(2) continue to report to the person's supervising officer not less than weekly during any period of time in which the person has not moved to an intended residence and provide the officer with the address of the person's temporary residence.

(i) If the other state has a registration requirement for sex offenders, a person who has a reportable conviction or adjudication, who resides in this state, and who is employed, carries on a vocation, or is a student in another state shall, not later than the 10th day after the date on which the person begins to work or attend school in the other state, register with the law enforcement authority that is identified by the department as the authority designated by that state to receive registration information. If the person is employed, carries on a vocation, or is a student at a public or private institution of higher education in the other state and if an authority for campus security exists at the institution, the person shall also register with that authority not later than the 10th day after the date on which the person begins to work or attend school.

(j) If a person subject to registration under this chapter is released from a penal institution without being released to parole or placed on any other form of supervision and the person does not move to the address indicated on the registration form as the person's intended residence or does not indicate an address on the registration form, the person shall, not later than the seventh day after the date on which the person is released:

(1) report in person to the local law enforcement authority for the municipality or county, as applicable, in which the person is residing and provide that authority with the address at which the person is residing or, if the person's residence does not have a physical address, a detailed description of the geographical location of the person's residence; and

(2) until the person indicates the person's current address as the person's intended residence on the registration form or otherwise complies with the requirements of Article 62.055, as appropriate, continue to report, in the manner required by Subdivision (1), to that authority not less than once in each succeeding 30–day period and provide that authority with the address at which the person is residing or, if applicable, a detailed description of the geographical location of the person's residence.

(k) A person required to register under this chapter may not refuse or otherwise fail to provide any information required for the accurate completion of the registration form.

Added by Acts 1991, 72nd Leg., ch. 572, § 1, eff. Sept. 1, 1991. Amended by Acts 1995, 74th Leg., ch. 258, § 2, eff. Sept. 1, 1995; Acts 1995, 74th Leg., ch. 676, § 1, eff. Sept. 1, 1995. Redesignated from Vernon's Ann.Civ.St. art. 6252–13c.1, § 2 and amended by Acts 1997, 75th Leg., ch. 668, § 1, eff. Sept. 1, 1997. Amended by Acts 1999, 76th Leg., ch. 444, § 1, eff. Sept. 1, 1999; Acts 1999, 76th Leg., ch. 1193, § 5, eff. Sept. 1, 1999; Acts 1999, 76th Leg., ch. 1415, § 10, eff. Sept. 1, 1999; Acts 2001, 77th Leg., ch. 932, § 1, eff. Sept. 1, 2001; Acts 2003, 78th Leg., ch. 347, § 4, eff. Sept. 1, 2003; Acts 2003, 78th Leg., ch. 1276, § 5.003(b), eff. Sept. 1, 2003. Redesignated from Vernon's Ann.C.C.P. art. 62.02 and amended by Acts 2005, 79th Leg., ch. 1008, § 1.01, eff. Sept. 1, 2005; Acts 2009, 81st Leg., ch. 661, § 2, eff. Sept. 1, 2009; Acts 2009, 81st Leg., ch. 755, § 5, eff. Sept. 1, 2009. Amended by Acts 2011, 82nd Leg., ch. 91 (S.B. 1303), § 6.005, eff. Sept. 1, 2011; Acts 2015, 84th Leg., ch. 734 (H.B. 1549), § 17, eff. Sept. 1, 2015; Acts 2017, 85th Leg., ch. 685 (H.B. 29), § 17, eff. Sept. 1, 2017.

Section 150 of Acts 2015, 84th Leg., ch. 734 (H.B. 1549) provides:

"If any provision of this Act conflicts with a provision of another Act of the 84th Legislature, Regular Session, 2015, the provision of the other Act controls to the extent of the conflict, regardless of the date of enactment."

Section 45 of Acts 2017, 85th Leg., ch. 685 (H.B. 29) provides:

"(a) Except as provided by Subsection (b) of this section, the changes in law made by this Act apply only to an offense committed on or after the effective date [Sept. 1, 2017] of this Act. An offense committed before the effective date of this Act is governed by the law in effect on the date the offense was committed, and the former law is continued in effect for that purpose. For purposes of this subsection, an offense was committed before the effective date of this Act if any element of the offense occurred before that date.

"(b) The changes in law made by this Act in amending Chapter 62, Code of Criminal Procedure, apply only to a person who is required to register under Chapter 62, Code of Criminal Procedure, on the basis of a conviction or adjudication for or based on an offense committed on or after the effective date of this Act. A person who is required to register under Chapter 62, Code of Criminal Procedure, solely on the basis of a conviction or adjudication for or based on an offense committed before the effective date of this Act is governed by the law in effect on the date the offense was committed, and the former law is continued in effect for that purpose. For purposes of this subsection, an offense was committed before the effective date of this Act if any element of the offense occurred before that date."

Art. 62.052. Registration: Extrajurisdictional Registrants

(a) An extrajurisdictional registrant is required to comply with the annual verification requirements of Article 62.058 in the same manner as [1] a person who is required to verify registration on the basis of a reportable conviction or adjudication.

(b) The duty to register for an extrajurisdictional registrant expires on the date the person's duty to register would expire under the laws of the other state or foreign country had the person remained in that state or foreign country, under federal law, or under the Uniform Code of Military Justice, as applicable.

(c) The department may negotiate and enter into a reciprocal registration agreement with any other state to prevent residents of this state and residents of the other state from frustrating the public purpose of the registration of sex offenders by moving from one state to the other.

Added by Acts 1999, 76th Leg., ch. 444, § 2, eff. Sept. 1, 1999; Acts 1999, 76th Leg., ch. 1415, § 11, eff. Sept. 1, 1999. Amended by Acts 2001, 77th Leg., ch. 211, § 3, eff. Sept. 1, 2001; Acts 2003, 78th Leg., ch. 1005, § 10, eff. Sept. 1, 2003. Redesignated from Vernon's Ann.C.C.P. art. 62.021 and amended by Acts 2005, 79th Leg., ch. 1008, § 1.01, eff. Sept. 1, 2005.

[1] Acts 1999, 76th Leg., ch. 444, § 2 here reads "manner as is".

Art. 62.053. Prerelease Notification

(a) Before a person who will be subject to registration under this chapter is due to be released from a penal institution, the Texas Department of Criminal Justice or the Texas Juvenile Justice Department shall determine the person's level of risk to the community using the sex offender screening tool developed or selected under Article 62.007 and assign to the person a numeric risk level of one, two, or three. Before releasing the person, an official of the penal institution shall:

(1) inform the person that:

(A) not later than the later of the seventh day after the date on which the person is released or after the date on which the person moves from a previous residence to a new residence in this state or not later than the first date the applicable local law enforcement authority by policy allows the person to register or verify registration, the person must register or verify registration with the local law enforcement authority in the municipality or county in which the person intends to reside;

(B) not later than the seventh day after the date on which the person is released or the date on which the person moves from a previous residence to a new residence in this state, the person must, if the person has not moved to an intended residence, report to the applicable entity or entities as required by Article 62.051(h) or (j) or 62.055(e);

(C) not later than the seventh day before the date on which the person moves to a new residence in this state or another state, the person must report in person to the local law enforcement authority designated as the person's primary registration authority by the department and to the juvenile probation officer, community supervision and corrections department officer, or parole officer supervising the person;

(D) not later than the 10th day after the date on which the person arrives in another state in which the person intends to reside, the person must register with the law enforcement agency that is identified by the department as the agency designated by that state to receive registration information, if the other state has a registration requirement for sex offenders;

(E) not later than the 30th day after the date on which the person is released, the person must apply to the department in person for the issuance of an original or renewal driver's license or personal identification certificate and a failure to apply to the department as required by this paragraph results in the automatic revocation of any driver's license or personal identification certificate issued by the department to the person;

(F) the person must notify appropriate entities of any change in status as described by Article 62.057;

(G) certain types of employment are prohibited under Article 62.063 for a person with a reportable conviction or adjudication for a sexually violent offense involving a victim younger than 14 years of age and occurring on or after September 1, 2013; and

Text of (a)(1)(H), as added by Acts 2017, 85th Leg., ch. 329 (H.B. 355), § 2

(H) certain locations of residence are prohibited under Article 62.064 for a person with a reportable conviction or adjudication for an offense occurring on or after September 1, 2017, except as otherwise provided by that article;

Text of (a)(1)(H), as added by Acts 2017, 85th Leg., ch. 924 (S.B. 1553), § 1

(H) if the person enters the premises of a school as described by Article 62.064 and is subject to the requirements of that article, the person must immediately notify the administrative office of the school of the person's presence and the person's registration status under this chapter;

(2) require the person to sign a written statement that the person was informed of the person's duties as described by Subdivision (1) or Subsection (g) or, if the person refuses to sign the statement, certify that the person was so informed;

(3) obtain the address or, if applicable, a detailed description of each geographical location where the person expects to reside on the person's release and other registration information, including a photograph and complete set of fingerprints; and

(4) complete the registration form for the person.

(b) On the seventh day before the date on which a person who will be subject to registration under this chapter is due to be released from a penal institution, or on receipt of notice by a penal institution that a person who will be subject to registration under this chapter is due to be released in less than seven days, an official of the penal institution shall send the person's completed registration form and numeric risk level to the department and to:

(1) the applicable local law enforcement authority in the municipality or county in which the person expects to reside, if the person expects to reside in this state; or

(2) the law enforcement agency that is identified by the department as the agency designated by another state to receive registration information, if the person expects to reside in that other state and that other state has a registration requirement for sex offenders.

(c) If a person who is subject to registration under this chapter receives an order deferring adjudication, placing the person on community supervision or juvenile probation, or imposing only a fine, the court pronouncing the order or sentence shall make a determination of the person's numeric risk level using the sex offender screening tool developed or selected under Article 62.007, assign to the person a numeric risk level of one, two, or three, and ensure that the prerelease notification and registration requirements specified in this article are conducted on the day of entering the order or sentencing. If a community supervision and corrections department representative is available in court at the time a court pronounces a sentence of deferred adjudication or community supervision, the representative shall immediately obtain the person's numeric risk level from the court and conduct the prerelease notification and registration requirements specified in this article. In any other case in which the court pronounces a sentence under this subsection, the court shall designate another appropriate individual to obtain the person's numeric risk level from the court and conduct the prerelease notification and registration requirements specified in this article.

(d) If a person who has a reportable conviction described by Article 62.001(5)(H) or (I) is placed under the supervision of the parole division of the Texas Department of Criminal Justice or a community supervision and corrections department under Section 510.017, Government Code, the division or community supervision and corrections department shall conduct the prerelease notification and registration require- ments specified in this article on the date the person is placed under the supervision of the division or community supervision and corrections department. If a person who has a reportable adjudication of delinquent conduct described by Article 62.001(5)(H) or (I) is, as permitted by Section 60.002, Family Code, placed under the supervision of the Texas Youth Commission, a public or private vendor operating under contract with the Texas Youth Commission, a local juvenile probation department, or a juvenile secure pre-adjudication or post-adjudication facility, the commission, vendor, probation department, or facility shall conduct the prerelease notification and registration requirements specified in this article on the date the person is placed under the supervision of the commission, vendor, probation department, or facility.

(e) Not later than the eighth day after receiving a registration form under Subsection (b), (c), or (d), the local law enforcement authority shall verify the age of the victim, the basis on which the person is subject to registration under this chapter, and the person's numeric risk level. The local law enforcement authority shall immediately provide notice to the superintendent of the public school district and to the administrator of any private primary or secondary school located in the public school district in which the person subject to registration intends to reside by mail to the office of the superintendent or administrator, as appropriate, in accordance with Article 62.054. On receipt of a notice under this subsection, the superintendent shall release the information contained in the notice to appropriate school district personnel, including peace officers and security personnel, principals, nurses, and counselors.

(f) The local law enforcement authority shall include in the notice to the superintendent of the public school district and to the administrator of any private primary or secondary school located in the public school district any information the authority determines is necessary to protect the public, except:

(1) the person's social security number or driver's license number, or any home, work, or cellular telephone number of the person; and

(2) any information that would identify the victim of the offense for which the person is subject to registration.

(g) Before a person who will be subject to registration under this chapter is due to be released from a penal institution in this state, an official of the penal institution shall inform the person that:

(1) if the person intends to reside in another state and to work or attend school in this state, the person must, not later than the later of the seventh day after the date on which the person begins to work or attend school or the first date the applicable local law enforcement authority by policy allows the person to register or verify registration, register or verify registration with the local law enforcement authority in the municipality or county in which the person intends to work or attend school;

(2) if the person intends to reside in this state and to work or attend school in another state and if the other state has a registration requirement for sex offenders, the person must:

(A) not later than the 10th day after the date on which the person begins to work or attend school in the other state, register with the law enforcement authority that is identified by the department as the authority designated by that state to receive registration information; and

(B) if the person intends to be employed, carry on a vocation, or be a student at a public or private institution of higher education in the other state and if an authority for campus security exists at the institution, register with that authority not later than the 10th day after the date on which the person begins to work or attend school; and

(3) regardless of the state in which the person intends to reside, if the person intends to be employed, carry on a vocation, or be a student at a public or private institution of higher education in this state, the person must:

(A) not later than the later of the seventh day after the date on which the person begins to work or attend school or the first date the applicable authority by policy allows the person to register, register with:

(i) the authority for campus security for that institution; or

(ii) except as provided by Article 62.153(e), if an authority for campus security for that institution does not exist, the local law enforcement authority of:

(a) the municipality in which the institution is located; or

(b) the county in which the institution is located, if the institution is not located in a municipality; and

(B) not later than the seventh day after the date the person stops working or attending school, notify the appropriate authority for campus security or local law enforcement authority of the termination of the person's status as a worker or student.

Added by Acts 1991, 72nd Leg., ch. 572, § 1, eff. Sept. 1, 1991. Amended by Acts 1993, 73rd Leg., ch. 866, § 2, eff. Aug. 30, 1993; Acts 1995, 74th Leg., ch. 258, § 3, eff. Sept. 1, 1995; Acts 1997, 75th Leg., ch. 667, § 5, eff. Sept. 1, 1997; Acts 1997, 75th Leg., ch. 1430, § 8, eff. Sept. 1, 1997. Redesignated from Vernon's Ann.Civ.St. art. 6252–13c.1, § 3 and amended by Acts 1997, 75th Leg., ch. 668, § 1, eff. Sept. 1, 1997. Amended by Acts 1999, 76th Leg., ch. 444, § 3, eff. Sept. 1, 1999; Acts 1999, 76th Leg., ch. 1193, §§ 6, 7, eff. Sept. 1, 1999; Acts 1999, 76th Leg., ch. 1401, § 2, eff. Sept. 1, 2000; Acts 1999, 76th Leg., ch. 1415, § 12, eff. Sept. 1, 1999; Acts 1999, 76th Leg., ch. 1557, § 1, eff. Aug. 30, 1999; Acts 2001, 77th Leg., ch. 177, § 1, eff. Sept. 1, 2001; Acts 2001, 77th Leg., ch. 211, § 4, eff. Sept. 1, 2001; Acts 2001, 77th Leg., ch. 1420, § 3.003, eff. Sept. 1, 2001; Acts 2003, 78th Leg., ch. 347, § 5, eff. Sept. 1, 2003. Redesignated from Vernon's Ann.C.C.P. art. 62.03 and amended by Acts 2005, 79th Leg., ch. 1008, § 1.01, eff. Sept. 1, 2005. Amended by Acts 2009, 81st Leg., ch. 87, § 25.048, eff. Sept. 1, 2009; Acts 2009, 81st Leg., ch. 661, § 3, eff. Sept. 1, 2009; Acts 2009, 81st Leg., ch. 755, § 6, eff. Sept. 1, 2009; Acts 2013, 83rd Leg., ch. 663 (H.B. 1302), § 4, eff. Sept. 1, 2013; Acts 2017, 85th Leg., ch. 329 (H.B. 355), § 2, eff. Sept. 1, 2017; Acts 2017, 85th Leg., ch. 924 (S.B. 1553), § 1, eff. Sept. 1, 2017.

Section 4 of Acts 2017, 85th Leg., ch. 329 (H.B. 355) provides:

"(a) The change in law made by this Act in adding Article 62.064, Code of Criminal Procedure, applies only to a person who is required to register under Chapter 62, Code of Criminal Procedure, on the basis of a conviction or adjudication for an offense committed on or after the effective date [Sept. 1, 2017] of this Act. An offense committed before the effective date of this Act is governed by the law in effect on the date the offense was committed, and the former law is continued in effect for that purpose.

"(b) A person who is required to register under Chapter 62, Code of Criminal Procedure, solely on the basis of a conviction or adjudication that occurs before the effective date [Sept. 1, 2017] of this Act is governed by the law in effect when the conviction or adjudication occurred, and the former law is continued in effect for that purpose."

Section 6 of Acts 2017, 85th Leg., ch. 924 (S.B. 1553) provides:

"Articles 62.053 and 62.058, Code of Criminal Procedure, as amended by this Act, and Article 62.064, Code of Criminal Procedure, as added by this Act, apply to a person subject to registration under Chapter 62, Code of Criminal Procedure, for an offense committed or conduct that occurs before, on, or after September 1, 2017."

Art. 62.054. Circumstances Requiring Notice to Superintendent or School Administrator

(a) A local law enforcement authority shall provide notice to the superintendent and each administrator under Article 62.053(e) or 62.055(f) only if:

(1) the victim was at the time of the offense a child younger than 17 years of age or a student enrolled in a public or private secondary school;

(2) the person subject to registration is a student enrolled in a public or private secondary school; or

(3) the basis on which the person is subject to registration is a conviction, a deferred adjudication, or

an adjudication of delinquent conduct for an offense under Section 43.25 or 43.26, Penal Code, or an offense under the laws of another state, federal law, or the Uniform Code of Military Justice that contains elements substantially similar to the elements of an offense under either of those sections.

(b) A local law enforcement authority may not provide notice to the superintendent or any administrator under Article 62.053(e) or 62.055(f) if the basis on which the person is subject to registration is a conviction, a deferred adjudication, or an adjudication of delinquent conduct for an offense under Section 25.02, Penal Code, or an offense under the laws of another state, federal law, or the Uniform Code of Military Justice that contains elements substantially similar to the elements of an offense under that section.

Added by Acts 2003, 78th Leg., ch. 347, § 6, eff. Sept. 1, 2003. Redesignated from Vernon's Ann.C.C.P. art. 62.032 and amended by Acts 2005, 79th Leg., ch. 1008, § 1.01, eff. Sept. 1, 2005.

Art. 62.055. Change of Address; Lack of Address

(a) If a person required to register under this chapter intends to change address, regardless of whether the person intends to move to another state, the person shall, not later than the seventh day before the intended change, report in person to the local law enforcement authority designated as the person's primary registration authority by the department and to the juvenile probation officer, community supervision and corrections department officer, or parole officer supervising the person and provide the authority and the officer with the person's anticipated move date and new address. If a person required to register changes address, the person shall, not later than the later of the seventh day after changing the address or the first date the applicable local law enforcement authority by policy allows the person to report, report in person to the local law enforcement authority in the municipality or county in which the person's new residence is located and provide the authority with proof of identity and proof of residence.

(b) Not later than the third day after receipt of notice under Subsection (a), the person's juvenile probation officer, community supervision and corrections department officer, or parole officer shall forward the information provided under Subsection (a) to the local law enforcement authority designated as the person's primary registration authority by the department and, if the person intends to move to another municipality or county in this state, to the applicable local law enforcement authority in that municipality or county.

(c) If the person moves to another state that has a registration requirement for sex offenders, the person shall, not later than the 10th day after the date on which the person arrives in the other state, register with the law enforcement agency that is identified by the department as the agency designated by that state to receive registration information.

(d) Not later than the third day after receipt of information under Subsection (a) or (b), whichever is earlier, the local law enforcement authority shall forward this information to the department and, if the person intends to move to another municipality or county in this state, to the applicable local law enforcement authority in that municipality or county.

(e) If a person who reports to a local law enforcement authority under Subsection (a) does not move on or before the anticipated move date or does not move to the new address provided to the authority, the person shall:

(1) not later than the seventh day after the anticipated move date, and not less than weekly after that seventh day, report to the local law enforcement authority designated as the person's primary registration authority by the department and provide an explanation to the authority regarding any changes in the anticipated move date and intended residence; and

(2) report to the juvenile probation officer, community supervision and corrections department officer, or parole officer supervising the person not less than weekly during any period in which the person has not moved to an intended residence.

(f) If the person moves to another municipality or county in this state, the department shall inform the applicable local law enforcement authority in the new area of the person's residence not later than the third day after the date on which the department receives information under Subsection (a). Not later than the eighth day after the date on which the local law enforcement authority is informed under Subsection (a) or under this subsection, the authority shall verify the age of the victim, the basis on which the person is subject to registration under this chapter, and the person's numeric risk level. The local law enforcement authority shall immediately provide notice to the superintendent of the public school district and to the administrator of any private primary or secondary school located in the public school district in which the person subject to registration intends to reside by mail to the office of the superintendent or administrator, as appropriate, in accordance with Article 62.054. On receipt of a notice under this subsection, the superintendent shall release the information contained in the notice to appropriate school district personnel, including peace officers and security personnel, principals, nurses, and counselors.

(g) The local law enforcement authority shall include in the notice to the superintendent of the public school district and the administrator of any private primary or secondary school located in the public school district any information the authority determines is necessary to protect the public, except:

(1) the person's social security number or driver's license number, or any home, work, or cellular telephone number of the person; and

(2) any information that would identify the victim of the offense for which the person is subject to registration.

(h) If the person moves to another state, the department shall, immediately on receiving information under Subsection (d):

(1) inform the agency that is designated by the other state to receive registration information, if that state has a registration requirement for sex offenders; and

(2) send to the Federal Bureau of Investigation a copy of the person's registration form, including the record of conviction and a complete set of fingerprints.

(i) If a person required to register under this chapter resides for more than seven days at a location or locations to which a physical address has not been assigned by a governmental entity, the person, not less than once in each 30–day period, shall confirm the person's location or locations by:

(1) reporting to the local law enforcement authority in the municipality where the person resides or, if the person does not reside in a municipality, the local law enforcement authority in the county in which the person resides; and

(2) providing a detailed description of the applicable location or locations.

Added by Acts 1991, 72nd Leg., ch. 572, § 1, eff. Sept. 1, 1991. Amended by Acts 1995, 74th Leg., ch. 258, § 4, eff. Sept. 1, 1995; Acts 1997, 75th Leg., ch. 667, § 6, eff. Sept. 1, 1997; Acts 1997, 75th Leg., ch. 1430, § 9, eff. Sept. 1, 1997. Redesignated from Vernon's Ann.Civ.St. art. 6252–13c.1, § 4 and amended by Acts 1997, 75th Leg., ch. 668, § 1, eff. Sept. 1, 1997. Amended by Acts 1999, 76th Leg., ch. 444, § 4, eff. Sept. 1, 1999; Acts 1999, 76th Leg., ch. 1415, § 13, eff. Sept. 1, 1999; Acts 1999, 76th Leg., ch. 1557, § 3, eff. Aug. 30, 1999; Acts 2001, 77th Leg., ch. 177, § 3, eff. Sept. 1, 2001; Acts 2001, 77th Leg., ch. 211, § 5, eff. Sept. 1, 2001; Acts 2001, 77th Leg., ch. 1420, § 3.004, eff. Sept. 1, 2001; Acts 2003, 78th Leg., ch. 347, § 7, eff. Sept. 1, 2003. Redesignated from Vernon's Ann.C.C.P. art. 62.04 and amended by Acts 2005, 79th Leg., ch. 1008, § 1.01, eff. Sept. 1, 2005. Amended by Acts 2009, 81st Leg., ch. 661, §§ 4, 5, eff. Sept. 1, 2009; Acts 2009, 81st Leg., ch. 755, § 7, eff. Sept. 1, 2009.

Art. 62.0551.   Change in Online Identifiers

(a) If a person required to register under this chapter changes any online identifier included on the person's registration form or establishes any new online identifier not already included on the person's registration form, the person, not later than the later of the seventh day after the change or establishment or the first date the applicable authority by policy allows the person to report, shall report the change or establishment to the person's primary registration authority in the manner prescribed by the authority.

(b) A primary registration authority that receives information under this article shall forward information in the same manner as information received by the authority under Article 62.055.

Added by Acts 2009, 81st Leg., ch. 755, § 8, eff. Sept. 1, 2009.

Art. 62.056.   Additional Public Notice for Certain Offenders

(a) On receipt of notice under this chapter that a person subject to registration is due to be released from a penal institution, has been placed on community supervision or juvenile probation, or intends to move to a new residence in this state, the department shall verify the person's numeric risk level assigned under this chapter. If the person is assigned a numeric risk level of three, the department shall, not later than the seventh day after the date on which the person is released or the 10th day after the date on which the person moves, provide written notice mailed or delivered to at least each address, other than a post office box, within a one-mile radius, in an area that has not been subdivided, or a three-block area, in an area that has been subdivided, of the place where the person intends to reside. In providing written notice under this subsection, the department shall use employees of the department whose duties in providing the notice are in addition to the employees' regular duties.

(b) The department shall provide the notice in English and Spanish and shall include in the notice any information that is public information under this chapter. The department may not include any information that is not public information under this chapter.

(c) The department shall establish procedures for a person with respect to whom notice is provided under Subsection (a), other than a person subject to registration on the basis of an adjudication of delinquent conduct, to pay to the department all costs incurred by the department in providing the notice. The person shall pay those costs in accordance with the procedures established under this subsection.

(d) On receipt of notice under this chapter that a person subject to registration under this chapter is required to register or verify registration with a local law enforcement authority and has been assigned a numeric risk level of three, the local law enforcement authority may provide notice to the public in any manner determined appropriate by the local law enforcement authority, including publishing notice in a newspaper or other periodical or circular in circulation in the area where the person intends to reside, holding a neighborhood meeting, posting notices in the area where the person intends to reside, distributing printed notices to area residents, or establishing a specialized local website. The local law enforcement authority may include in the notice only information that is public information under this chapter.

(e) An owner, builder, seller, or lessor of a single-family residential real property or any improvement to residential real property or that person's broker, salesperson, or other agent or representative in a residential real estate transaction does not have a duty to make a disclosure to a prospective buyer or lessee about registrants under this chapter. To the extent of any conflict between this subsection and another law imposing a duty to disclose information about registered sex offenders, this subsection controls.

Added by Acts 1999, 76th Leg., ch. 1557, § 4, eff. Aug. 30, 1999. Amended by Acts 2001, 77th Leg., ch. 177, § 4, eff. Sept. 1, 2001; Acts 2001, 77th Leg., ch. 211, §§ 6, 7, eff. Sept. 1, 2001. Redesignated from Vernon's Ann.C.C.P. art. 62.045 and amended by Acts 2005, 79th Leg., ch. 1008, § 1.01, eff. Sept. 1, 2005.

Art. 62.057. Status Report by Supervising Officer or Local Law Enforcement Authority

(a) If the juvenile probation officer, community supervision and corrections department officer, or parole officer supervising a person subject to registration under this chapter receives information to the effect that the person's status has changed in any manner that affects proper supervision of the person, including a change in the person's name, online identifiers, physical health, job or educational status, including higher educational status, incarceration, or terms of release, the supervising officer shall promptly notify the appropriate local law enforcement authority or authorities of that change. If the person required to register intends to change address, the supervising officer shall notify the local law enforcement authorities designated by Article 62.055(b). Not later than the seventh day after the date the supervising officer receives the relevant information, the supervising officer shall notify the local law enforcement authority of any change in the person's job or educational status in which the person:

(1) becomes employed, begins to carry on a vocation, or becomes a student at a particular public or private institution of higher education; or

(2) terminates the person's status in that capacity.

(b) Not later than the later of the seventh day after the date of the change or the first date the applicable authority by policy allows the person to report, a person subject to registration under this chapter shall report to the local law enforcement authority designated as the person's primary registration authority by the department any change in the person's name, online identifiers, physical health, or job or educational status, including higher educational status.

(c) For purposes of Subsection (b):

(1) a person's job status changes if the person leaves employment for any reason, remains employed by an employer but changes the location at which the person works, or begins employment with a new employer;

(2) a person's health status changes if the person is hospitalized as a result of an illness;

(3) a change in a person's educational status includes the person's transfer from one educational facility to another; and

(4) regarding a change of name, notice of the proposed name provided to a local law enforcement authority as described by Sections 45.004 and 45.103, Family Code, is sufficient, except that the person shall promptly notify the authority of any denial of the person's petition for a change of name.

(d) Not later than the seventh day after the date the local law enforcement authority receives the relevant information, the local law enforcement authority shall notify the department of any change in the person's job or educational status in which the person:

(1) becomes employed, begins to carry on a vocation, or becomes a student at a particular public or private institution of higher education; or

(2) terminates the person's status in that capacity.

Added by Acts 1997, 75th Leg., ch. 668, § 1, eff. Sept. 1, 1997. Amended by Acts 1999, 76th Leg., ch. 444, § 6, eff. Sept. 1, 1999; Acts 1999, 76th Leg., ch. 1415, § 14, eff. Sept. 1, 1999; Acts 2001, 77th Leg., ch. 19, § 1, eff. Sept. 1, 2001; Acts 2003, 78th Leg., ch. 347, § 8, eff. Sept. 1, 2003; Acts 2003, 78th Leg., ch. 1300, § 4, eff. Sept. 1, 2003. Redesignated from Vernon's Ann.C.C.P. art. 62.05 and amended by Acts 2005, 79th Leg., ch. 1008, § 1.01, eff. Sept. 1, 2005. Amended by Acts 2009, 81st Leg., ch. 755, § 9, eff. Sept. 1, 2009.

Art. 62.058. Law Enforcement Verification of Registration Information

(a) A person subject to registration under this chapter who has for a sexually violent offense been convicted two or more times, received an order of deferred adjudication two or more times, or been convicted and received an order of deferred adjudication shall report to the local law enforcement authority designated as the person's primary registration authority by the department not less than once in each 90–day period following the date the person first registered under this chapter to verify the information in the registration form maintained by the authority for that person. A person subject to registration under this chapter who is not subject to the 90–day reporting requirement described by this subsection shall report to the local law enforcement authority designated as the person's primary registration authority by the department once each year not earlier than the 30th day before and not later than the 30th day after the anniversary of the person's date of birth to verify the information in the registration form maintained by the authority for that person. For purposes of this subsection, a person complies with a requirement that the person register within a 90–day period following a date if the person registers at any time on or after the 83rd day following that date but before the 98th day after that date.

(b) A local law enforcement authority designated as a person's primary registration authority by the department may direct the person to report to the authority to verify the information in the registration form maintained by the authority for that person. The authority may direct the person to report under this subsection once in each 90–day period following the date the person first registered under this chapter, if the person is required to report not less than once in each 90–day period under Subsection (a) or once in each year not earlier than the 30th day before and not later than the 30th day after the anniversary of the person's date of birth, if the person is required to report once each year under Subsection (a). A local law enforcement authority may not direct a person to report to the authority under this subsection if the person is required to report under Subsection (a) and is in compliance with the reporting requirements of that subsection.

(c) A local law enforcement authority with whom a person reports under this article shall require the person to produce proof of the person's identity and residence before the authority gives the registration form to the person for verification. If the information in the registration form is complete and accurate, the person shall verify registration by signing the form. If the information is not complete or not accurate, the person shall make any necessary additions or corrections before signing the form.

(d) A local law enforcement authority designated as a person's primary registration authority by the department may at any time mail a nonforwardable verification form to the last reported address of the person. Not later than the 21st day after receipt of a verification form under this subsection, the person shall:

(1) indicate on the form whether the person still resides at the last reported address and, if not, provide on the form the person's new address;

(2) complete any other information required by the form;

(3) sign the form; and

(4) return the form to the authority.

(e) For purposes of this article, a person receives multiple convictions or orders of deferred adjudication regardless of whether:

(1) the judgments or orders are entered on different dates; or

(2) the offenses for which the person was convicted or placed on deferred adjudication arose out of different criminal transactions.

(f) A local law enforcement authority that provides to a person subject to the prohibitions described by Article 62.063 a registration form for verification as required by this chapter shall include with the form a statement summarizing the types of employment that are prohibited for that person.

Text of (g), as added by Acts 2017, 85th Leg., ch. 329 (H.B. 355), § 3

(g) A local law enforcement authority that provides to a person a registration form for verification as required by this chapter shall include with the form a statement describing the prohibition under Article 62.064.

Text of (g), as added by Acts 2017, 85th Leg., ch. 924 (S.B. 1553), § 2

(g) A local law enforcement authority who provides a person with a registration form for verification as required by this chapter shall include with the form a statement and, if applicable, a description of the person's duty to provide notice under Article 62.064.

Added by Acts 1997, 75th Leg., ch. 668, § 1, eff. Sept. 1, 1997. Amended by Acts 1999, 76th Leg., ch. 444, § 7, eff. Sept. 1, 1999; Acts 1999, 76th Leg., ch. 1415, § 15, eff. Sept. 1, 1999; Acts 2001, 77th Leg., ch. 211, § 9, eff. Sept. 1, 2001; Acts 2003, 78th Leg., ch. 347, § 9, eff. Sept. 1, 2003. Redesignated from Vernon's Ann.C.C.P. art. 62.06 by Acts 2005, 79th Leg., ch. 1008, § 1.01, eff. Sept. 1, 2005. Amended by Acts 2013, 83rd Leg., ch. 663 (H.B. 1302), § 5, eff. Sept. 1, 2013; Acts 2017, 85th Leg., ch. 329 (H.B. 355), § 3, eff. Sept. 1, 2017; Acts 2017, 85th Leg., ch. 924 (S.B. 1553), § 2, eff. Sept. 1, 2017.

Section 4 of Acts 2017, 85th Leg., ch. 329 (H.B. 355) provides:

"(a) The change in law made by this Act in adding Article 62.064, Code of Criminal Procedure, applies only to a person who is required to register under Chapter 62, Code of Criminal Procedure, on the basis of a conviction or adjudication for an offense committed on or after the effective date [Sept. 1, 2017] of this Act. An offense committed before the effective date of this Act is governed by the law in effect on the date the offense was committed, and the former law is continued in effect for that purpose.

"(b) A person who is required to register under Chapter 62, Code of Criminal Procedure, solely on the basis of a conviction or adjudication that occurs before the effective date [Sept. 1, 2017] of this Act is governed by the law in effect when the conviction or adjudication occurred, and the former law is continued in effect for that purpose."

Section 6 of Acts 2017, 85th Leg., ch. 924 (S.B. 1553) provides:

"Articles 62.053 and 62.058, Code of Criminal Procedure, as amended by this Act, and Article 62.064, Code of Criminal Procedure, as added by this Act, apply to a person subject to registration under Chapter 62, Code of Criminal Procedure, for an offense committed or conduct that occurs before, on, or after September 1, 2017."

Art. 62.059. Registration of Persons Regularly Visiting Location

(a) A person subject to this chapter who on at least three occasions during any month spends more than 48 consecutive hours in a municipality or county in this state, other than the municipality or county in which the person is registered under this chapter, before the last day of that month shall report that fact to:

(1) the local law enforcement authority of the municipality in which the person is a visitor; or

(2) if the person is a visitor in a location that is not a municipality, the local law enforcement authority of the county in which the person is a visitor.

(b) A person described by Subsection (a) shall provide the local law enforcement authority with:

(1) all information the person is required to provide under Article 62.051(c);

(2) the address of any location in the municipality or county, as appropriate, at which the person was lodged during the month; and

(3) a statement as to whether the person intends to return to the municipality or county during the succeeding month.

(c) This article does not impose on a local law enforcement authority requirements of public notification or notification to schools relating to a person about whom the authority is not otherwise required by this chapter to make notifications.

Added by Acts 1999, 76th Leg., ch. 444, § 8, eff. Sept. 1, 1999; Acts 1999, 76th Leg., ch. 1415, § 16, eff. Sept. 1, 1999. Redesignated from Vernon's Ann.C.C.P. art. 62.062 and amended by Acts 2005, 79th Leg., ch. 1008, § 1.01, eff. Sept. 1, 2005.

Art. 62.060. Requirements Relating to Driver's License or Personal Identification Certificate

(a) A person subject to registration under this chapter shall apply to the department in person for the issuance of, as applicable, an original or renewal driver's license under Section 521.272, Transportation Code, an original or renewal personal identification certificate under Section 521.103, Transportation Code, or an original or renewal commercial driver's license or commercial learner's permit under Section 522.033, Transportation Code, not later than the 30th day after the date:

(1) the person is released from a penal institution or is released by a court on community supervision or juvenile probation; or

(2) the department sends written notice to the person of the requirements of this article.

(b) The person shall annually renew in person each driver's license or personal identification certificate issued by the department to the person, including each renewal, duplicate, or corrected license or certificate, until the person's duty to register under this chapter expires.

Added by Acts 1999, 76th Leg., ch. 1401, § 3, eff. Sept. 1, 2000. Amended by Acts 2001, 77th Leg., ch. 546, § 1, eff. Sept. 1, 2001. Redesignated from Vernon's Ann.C.C.P. art. 62.065 and amended by Acts 2005, 79th Leg., ch. 1008, § 1.01, eff. Sept. 1, 2005. Amended by Acts 2015, 84th Leg., ch. 752 (H.B. 1888), § 42, eff. Jan. 1, 2016.

Art. 62.06. Redesignated as Vernon's Ann.C.C.P. art. 62.058 and amended by Acts

2005, 79th Leg., ch. 1008, § 1.01, eff. Sept. 1, 2005

Art. 62.061. DNA Specimen

A person required to register under this chapter shall comply with a request for a DNA specimen made by a law enforcement agency under Section 411.1473, Government Code.

Amended by Acts 2005, 79th Leg., ch. 1008, § 1.01, eff. Sept. 1, 2005.

Art. 62.062. Limitation on Newspaper Publication

(a) Except as provided by Subsection (b), a local law enforcement authority may not publish notice in a newspaper or other periodical or circular concerning a person's registration under this chapter if the only basis on which the person is subject to registration is one or more adjudications of delinquent conduct.

(b) This article does not apply to a publication of notice under Article 62.056.

Amended by Acts 2005, 79th Leg., ch. 1008, § 1.01, eff. Sept. 1, 2005.

Art. 62.063. Prohibited Employment

(a) In this article:

(1) "Amusement ride" has the meaning assigned by Section 2151.002, Occupations Code.

(2) "Bus" has the meaning assigned by Section 541.201, Transportation Code.

(b) A person subject to registration under this chapter because of a reportable conviction or adjudication for which an affirmative finding is entered under Article 42.015(b) or 42A.105(a), as appropriate, may not, for compensation:

(1) operate or offer to operate a bus;

(2) provide or offer to provide a passenger taxicab or limousine transportation service;

(3) provide or offer to provide any type of service in the residence of another person unless the provision of service will be supervised; or

(4) operate or offer to operate any amusement ride.

Added by Acts 2013, 83rd Leg., ch. 663 (H.B. 1302), § 6, eff. Sept. 1, 2013. Amended by Acts 2015, 84th Leg., ch. 770 (H.B. 2299), § 2.26, eff. Jan. 1, 2017.

Art. 62.064. Prohibited location of residence

Text of article as added by Acts 2017, 85th Leg., ch. 329 (H.B. 355), § 1. See, also, Art. 62.064 as added by Acts 2017, 85th Leg., ch. 924 (S.B. 1553), § 3.

A person subject to registration under this chapter may not reside on the campus of a public or private institution of higher education unless:

(1) the person is assigned a numeric risk level of one based on an assessment conducted using the sex offender screening tool developed or selected under Article 62.007; and

(2) the institution approves the person to reside on the institution's campus.

Added by Acts 2017, 85th Leg., ch. 329 (H.B. 355), § 1, eff. Sept. 1, 2017.

Section 4 of Acts 2017, 85th Leg., ch. 329 (H.B. 355) provides:

"(a) The change in law made by this Act in adding Article 62.064, Code of Criminal Procedure, applies only to a person who is required to register under Chapter 62, Code of Criminal Procedure, on the basis of a conviction or adjudication for an offense committed on or after the effective date [Sept. 1, 2017] of this Act. An offense committed before the effective date of this Act is governed by the law in effect on the date the offense was committed, and the former law is continued in effect for that purpose.

"(b) A person who is required to register under Chapter 62, Code of Criminal Procedure, solely on the basis of a conviction or adjudication that occurs before the effective date [Sept. 1, 2017] of this Act is governed by the law in effect when the conviction or adjudication occurred, and the former law is continued in effect for that purpose."

Art. 62.064. Entry onto school premises; notice required

Text of article as added by Acts 2017, 85th Leg., ch. 924 (S.B. 1553), § 3. See, also, Art. 62.064 as added by Acts 2017, 85th Leg., ch. 329 (H.B. 355), § 1.

(a) In this article:

(1) "Premises" means a building or portion of a building and the grounds on which the building is located, including any public or private driveway, street, sidewalk or walkway, parking lot, or parking garage on the grounds.

(2) "School" has the meaning assigned by Section 481.134, Health and Safety Code.

(b) A person subject to registration under this chapter who enters the premises of any school in this state during the standard operating hours of the school shall immediately notify the administrative office of the school of the person's presence on the premises of the school and the person's registration status under this chapter. The office may provide a chaperon to accompany the person while the person is on the premises of the school.

(c) The requirements of this article:

(1) are in addition to any requirement associated with the imposition of a child safety zone on the person under Section 508.187, Government Code, or Article 42A.453 of this code; and

(2) do not apply to:

(A) a student enrolled at the school;

(B) a student from another school participating at an event at the school; or

(C) a person who has entered into a written agreement with the school that exempts the person from those requirements.

Added by Acts 2017, 85th Leg., ch. 924 (S.B. 1553), § 3, eff. Sept. 1, 2017.

Section 6 of Acts 2017, 85th Leg., ch. 924 (S.B. 1553) provides:

"Articles 62.053 and 62.058, Code of Criminal Procedure, as amended by this Act, and Article 62.064, Code of Criminal Procedure, as added by this Act, apply to a person subject to registration under Chapter 62, Code of Criminal Procedure, for an offense committed or conduct that occurs before, on, or after September 1, 2017."

Art. 62.065.   **Redesignated as Vernon's Ann.C.C.P. art. 62.060 and amended by Acts 2005, 79th Leg., ch. 1008, § 1.01, eff. Sept. 1, 2005**

Arts. 62.07 to 62.091.   **Deleted by Acts 2005, 79th Leg., ch. 1008, § 1.01, eff. Sept. 1, 2005**

Art. 62.10.   **Redesignated as Vernon's Ann.C.C.P. art. 62.102 and amended by Acts 2005, 79th Leg., ch. 1008, § 1.01, eff. Sept. 1, 2005**

SUBCHAPTER C. EXPIRATION OF DUTY TO REGISTER; GENERAL PENALTIES FOR NONCOMPLIANCE

Art. 62.101. Expiration of Duty to Register

(a) Except as provided by Subsection (b) and Subchapter I, the duty to register for a person ends when the person dies if the person has a reportable conviction or adjudication, other than an adjudication of delinquent conduct, for:

(1) a sexually violent offense;

(2) an offense under Section 20A.02(a)(3), (4), (7), or (8), 25.02, 43.05(a)(2), or 43.26, Penal Code;

(3) an offense under Section 20A.03, Penal Code, if based partly or wholly on conduct that constitutes an offense under Section 20A.02(a)(3), (4), (7), or (8) of that code;

(4) an offense under Section 21.11(a)(2), Penal Code, if before or after the person is convicted or adjudicated for the offense under Section 21.11(a)(2), Penal Code, the person receives or has received another reportable conviction or adjudication, other than an adjudication of delinquent conduct, for an offense or conduct that requires registration under this chapter;

(5) an offense under Section 20.02, 20.03, or 20.04, Penal Code, if:

(A) the judgment in the case contains an affirmative finding under Article 42.015 or, for a deferred adjudication, the papers in the case contain an affirmative finding that the victim or intended victim was younger than 17 years of age; and

(B) before or after the person is convicted or adjudicated for the offense under Section 20.02, 20.03, or 20.04, Penal Code, the person receives or has received another reportable conviction or adjudication, other than an adjudication of delinquent conduct, for an offense or conduct that requires registration under this chapter; or

(6) an offense under Section 43.23, Penal Code, that is punishable under Subsection (h) of that section.

(b) Except as provided by Subchapter I, the duty to register for a person otherwise subject to Subsection (a) ends on the 10th anniversary of the date on which the person is released from a penal institution or discharges community supervision or the court dismisses the criminal proceedings against the person and discharges the person, whichever date is later, if the person's duty to register is based on a conviction or an order of deferred adjudication in a cause that was transferred to a district court or criminal district court under Section 54.02, Family Code.

(c) Except as provided by Subchapter I, the duty to register for a person with a reportable conviction or adjudication for an offense other than an offense described by Subsection (a) ends:

(1) if the person's duty to register is based on an adjudication of delinquent conduct, on the 10th anniversary of the date on which the disposition is made or the person completes the terms of the disposition, whichever date is later; or

(2) if the person's duty to register is based on a conviction or on an order of deferred adjudication, on the 10th anniversary of the date on which the court dismisses the criminal proceedings against the person and discharges the person, the person is released from

a penal institution, or the person discharges community supervision, whichever date is later.

Added by Acts 2005, 79th Leg., ch. 1008, § 1.01, eff. Sept. 1, 2005. Amended by Acts 2011, 82nd Leg., ch. 1 (S.B. 24), § 2.11, eff. Sept. 1, 2011; Acts 2017, 85th Leg., ch. 685 (H.B. 29), § 18, eff. Sept. 1, 2017.

Section 45 of Acts 2017, 85th Leg., ch. 685 (H.B. 29) provides:

"(a) Except as provided by Subsection (b) of this section, the changes in law made by this Act apply only to an offense committed on or after the effective date [Sept. 1, 2017] of this Act. An offense committed before the effective date of this Act is governed by the law in effect on the date the offense was committed, and the former law is continued in effect for that purpose. For purposes of this subsection, an offense was committed before the effective date of this Act if any element of the offense occurred before that date.

"(b) The changes in law made by this Act in amending Chapter 62, Code of Criminal Procedure, apply only to a person who is required to register under Chapter 62, Code of Criminal Procedure, on the basis of a conviction or adjudication for or based on an offense committed on or after the effective date of this Act. A person who is required to register under Chapter 62, Code of Criminal Procedure, solely on the basis of a conviction or adjudication for or based on an offense committed before the effective date of this Act is governed by the law in effect on the date the offense was committed, and the former law is continued in effect for that purpose. For purposes of this subsection, an offense was committed before the effective date of this Act if any element of the offense occurred before that date."

Art. 62.102. Failure to Comply With Registration Requirements

(a) A person commits an offense if the person is required to register and fails to comply with any requirement of this chapter.

(b) An offense under this article is:

(1) a state jail felony if the actor is a person whose duty to register expires under Article 62.101(b) or (c);

(2) a felony of the third degree if the actor is a person whose duty to register expires under Article 62.101(a) and who is required to verify registration once each year under Article 62.058; and

(3) a felony of the second degree if the actor is a person whose duty to register expires under Article 62.101(a) and who is required to verify registration once each 90–day period under Article 62.058.

(c) If it is shown at the trial of a person for an offense or an attempt to commit an offense under this article that the person has previously been convicted of an offense or an attempt to commit an offense under this article, the punishment for the offense or the attempt to commit the offense is increased to the punishment for the next highest degree of felony.

(d) If it is shown at the trial of a person for an offense under this article or an attempt to commit an offense under this article that the person fraudulently used identifying information in violation of Section 32.51, Penal Code, during the commission or attempt-ed commission of the offense, the punishment for the offense or the attempt to commit the offense is increased to the punishment for the next highest degree of felony.

Added by Acts 1991, 72nd Leg., ch. 572, § 1, eff. Sept. 1, 1991. Redesignated from Vernon's Ann.Civ.St. art. 6252–13c.1, § 7 and amended by Acts 1997, 75th Leg., ch. 668, § 1, eff. Sept. 1, 1997. Amended by Acts 1999, 76th Leg., ch. 444, § 9, eff. Sept. 1, 1999; Acts 1999, 76th Leg., ch. 1415, § 18, eff. Sept. 1, 1999. Redesignated from Vernon's Ann.C.C.P. art. 62.10 and amended by Acts 2005, 79th Leg., ch. 1008, § 1.01, eff. Sept. 1, 2005. Amended by Acts 2013, 83rd Leg., ch. 362 (H.B. 2637), § 1, eff. Sept. 1, 2013.

Arts. 62.11 to 62.13. Deleted by Acts 2005, 79th Leg., ch. 1008, § 1.01, eff. Sept. 1, 2005

Art. 62.14. Redesignated as Vernon's Ann.C.C.P. art. 62.251 and amended by Acts 2005, 79th Leg., ch. 1008, § 1.01, eff. Sept. 1, 2005

SUBCHAPTER D. PROVISIONS APPLICABLE TO CERTAIN WORKERS AND STUDENTS

Art. 62.151. Definitions

For purposes of this subchapter, a person:

(1) is employed or carries on a vocation if the person works or volunteers on a full-time or part-time basis for a consecutive period exceeding 14 days or for an aggregate period exceeding 30 days in a calendar year;

(2) works regardless of whether the person works for compensation or for governmental or educational benefit; and

(3) is a student if the person enrolls on a full-time or part-time basis in any educational facility, including:

(A) a public or private primary or secondary school, including a high school or alternative learning center; or

(B) a public or private institution of higher education.

Added by Acts 2005, 79th Leg., ch. 1008, § 1.01, eff. Sept. 1, 2005.

Art. 62.152. Registration of Certain Workers or Students

(a) A person is subject to this subchapter and, except as otherwise provided by this article, to the other subchapters of this chapter if the person:

(1) has a reportable conviction or adjudication;

(2) resides in another state; and

(3) is employed, carries on a vocation, or is a student in this state.

(b) A person described by Subsection (a) is subject to the registration and verification requirements of Articles 62.051 and 62.058 and to the change of address requirements of Article 62.055, except that the registration and verification and the reporting of a change of address are based on the municipality or county in which the person works or attends school. The person is subject to the school notification requirements of Articles 62.053–62.055, except that notice provided to the superintendent and any administrator is based on the public school district in which the person works or attends school.

(c) A person described by Subsection (a) is not subject to Article 62.101.

(d) The duty to register for a person described by Subsection (a) ends when the person no longer works or studies in this state, provides notice of that fact to the local law enforcement authority in the municipality or county in which the person works or attends school, and receives notice of verification of that fact from the authority. The authority must verify that the person no longer works or studies in this state and must provide to the person notice of that verification within a reasonable time.

(e) Notwithstanding Subsection (a), this article does not apply to a person who has a reportable conviction or adjudication, who resides in another state, and who is employed, carries on a vocation, or is a student in this state if the person establishes another residence in this state to work or attend school in this state. However, that person remains subject to the other articles of this chapter based on that person's residence in this state.

Added by Acts 2005, 79th Leg., ch. 1008, § 1.01, eff. Sept. 1, 2005.

Art. 62.153. Registration of Workers or Students at Institutions of Higher Education

(a) Not later than the later of the seventh day after the date on which the person begins to work or attend school or the first date the applicable authority by policy allows the person to register, a person required to register under Article 62.152 or any other provision of this chapter who is employed, carries on a vocation, or is a student at a public or private institution of higher education in this state shall report that fact to:

(1) the authority for campus security for that institution; or

(2) if an authority for campus security for that institution does not exist, the local law enforcement authority of:

(A) the municipality in which the institution is located; or

(B) the county in which the institution is located, if the institution is not located in a municipality.

(b) A person described by Subsection (a) shall provide the authority for campus security or the local law enforcement authority with all information the person is required to provide under Article 62.051(c).

(c) A person described by Subsection (a) shall notify the authority for campus security or the local law enforcement authority not later than the seventh day after the date of termination of the person's status as a worker or student at the institution.

(d) The authority for campus security or the local law enforcement authority shall promptly forward to the administrative office of the institution any information received from the person under this article and any information received from the department under Article 62.005.

(e) Subsection (a)(2) does not require a person to register with a local law enforcement authority if the person is otherwise required by this chapter to register with that authority.

(f) This article does not impose the requirements of public notification or notification to public or private primary or secondary schools on:

(1) an authority for campus security; or

(2) a local law enforcement authority, if those requirements relate to a person about whom the authority is not otherwise required by this chapter to make notifications.

(g) Notwithstanding Article 62.059, the requirements of this article supersede those of Article 62.059 for a person required to register under both this article and Article 62.059.

Added by Acts 2005, 79th Leg., ch. 1008, § 1.01, eff. Sept. 1, 2005.

SUBCHAPTER E. PROVISIONS APPLICABLE TO PERSONS SUBJECT TO CIVIL COMMITMENT

Art. 62.201. Additional Public Notice for Individuals Subject to Civil Commitment

(a) On receipt of notice under this chapter that a person subject to registration who is civilly committed as a sexually violent predator is due to be released from a penal institution or intends to move to a new residence in this state, the department shall, not later than the seventh day after the date on which the person is released or the seventh day after the date on which the person moves, provide written notice mailed or delivered to at least each address, other than a post office box, within a one-mile radius, in an area that has not been subdivided, or a three-block area, in an area that has been subdivided, of the place where the person intends to reside.

(b) The department shall provide the notice in English and Spanish and shall include in the notice any information that is public information under this chapter. The department may not include any information that is not public information under this chapter.

(c) The department shall establish procedures for a person with respect to whom notice is provided under this article to pay to the department all costs incurred by the department in providing the notice. The person shall pay those costs in accordance with the procedures established under this subsection.

(d) The department's duty to provide notice under this article in regard to a particular person ends on the date on which a court releases the person from all requirements of the civil commitment process.

Added by Acts 2005, 79th Leg., ch. 1008, § 1.01, eff. Sept. 1, 2005.

Art. 62.202. Verification of Individuals Subject to Commitment

(a) Notwithstanding Article 62.058, if an individual subject to registration under this chapter is civilly committed as a sexually violent predator, the person shall report to the local law enforcement authority designated as the person's primary registration authority by the department to verify the information in the registration form maintained by the authority for that person as follows:

(1) if the person resides at a civil commitment center, not less than once each year; or

(2) if the person does not reside at a civil commitment center, not less than once in each 30–day period following:

(A) the date the person first registered under this chapter; or

(B) if applicable, the date the person moved from the center.

(a–1) For purposes of Subsection (a)(2), a person complies with a requirement that the person register within a 30–day period following a date if the person registers at any time on or after the 27th day following that date but before the 33rd day after that date.

(b) On the date a court releases a person described by Subsection (a) from all requirements of the civil commitment process:

(1) the person's duty to verify registration as a sex offender is no longer imposed by this article; and

(2) the person is required to verify registration as provided by Article 62.058.

Added by Acts 2005, 79th Leg., ch. 1008, § 1.01, eff. Sept. 1, 2005. Amended by Acts 2017, 85th Leg., ch. 34 (S.B. 1576), § 5, eff. Sept. 1, 2017.

Section 42 of Acts 2017, 85th Leg., ch. 34 (S.B. 1576) provides:

"Chapter 62, Code of Criminal Procedure, as amended by this Act, applies to any person who, on or after the effective date [Sept. 1, 2017] of this Act, is required to register under that chapter, regardless of whether the offense or conduct for which the person is required to register occurs before, on, or after the effective date of this Act."

Art. 62.2021. Requirements Relating to Driver's License or Personal Identification Certificate: Individuals Residing at Civil Commitment Center

(a) Notwithstanding Article 62.060(b), a person subject to registration who is civilly committed as a sexually violent predator and resides at a civil commitment center shall renew the person's department-issued driver's license or personal identification certificate as prescribed by Section 521.103, 521.272, or 522.033, Transportation Code, as applicable.

(b) On the date that a person described by Subsection (a) no longer resides at a civil commitment center, the person is required to renew a driver's license or personal identification certificate only as provided by Article 62.060(b).

Added by Acts 2017, 85th Leg., ch. 34 (S.B. 1576), § 6, eff. Sept. 1, 2017.

Section 42 of Acts 2017, 85th Leg., ch. 34 (S.B. 1576) provides:

"Chapter 62, Code of Criminal Procedure, as amended by this Act, applies to any person who, on or after the effective date [Sept. 1, 2017] of this Act, is required to register under that chapter, regardless of whether the offense or conduct for which the person is required to register occurs before, on, or after the effective date of this Act."

Art. 62.203. Failure to Comply: Individuals Subject to Commitment

(a) A person commits an offense if the person, after commitment as a sexually violent predator but before the person is released from all requirements of the civil commitment process, fails to comply with any requirement of this chapter.

(b) An offense under this article is a felony of the second degree.

Added by Acts 1999, 76th Leg., ch. 444, § 5(c). Redesignated from Vernon's Ann.C.C.P. art. 62.101 and amended by Acts 2005, 79th Leg., ch. 1008, § 1.01, eff. Sept. 1, 2005.

SUBCHAPTER F. REMOVAL OF REGISTRATION INFORMATION

Art. 62.251. Removing Registration Information When Duty to Register Expires

(a) When a person is no longer required to register as a sex offender under this chapter, the department shall remove all information about the person from the sex offender registry.

(b) The duty to remove information under Subsection (a) arises if:

(1) the department has received notice from a local law enforcement authority under Subsection (c) or (d) that the person is no longer required to register or will no longer be required to renew registration and the department verifies the correctness of that information;

(2) the court having jurisdiction over the case for which registration is required requests removal and the department determines that the duty to register has expired; or

(3) the person or the person's representative requests removal and the department determines that the duty to register has expired.

(c) When a person required to register under this chapter appears before a local law enforcement authority to renew or modify registration information, the authority shall determine whether the duty to register has expired. If the authority determines that the duty to register has expired, the authority shall remove all information about the person from the sex offender registry and notify the department that the person's duty to register has expired.

(d) When a person required to register under this chapter appears before a local law enforcement authority to renew registration information, the authority shall determine whether the renewal is the final annual renewal of registration required by law. If the authority determines that the person's duty to register will expire before the next annual renewal is scheduled, the authority shall automatically remove all information about the person from the sex offender registry on expiration of the duty to register and notify the department that the information about the person has been removed from the registry.

(e) When the department has removed information under Subsection (a), the department shall notify all local law enforcement authorities that have provided registration information to the department about the person of the removal. A local law enforcement authority that receives notice from the department under this subsection shall remove all registration information about the person from its registry.

(f) When the department has removed information under Subsection (a), the department shall notify all public and private agencies or organizations to which it has provided registration information about the person of the removal. On receiving notice, the public or private agency or organization shall remove all registration information about the person from any registry the agency or organization maintains that is accessible to the public with or without charge.

Added by Acts 2003, 78th Leg., ch. 283, § 37, eff. Sept. 1, 2003. Redesignated from Vernon's Ann.C.C.P. art. 62.14 and amended by Acts 2005, 79th Leg., ch. 1008, § 1.01, eff. Sept. 1, 2005.

SUBCHAPTER G. EXEMPTION FROM REGISTRATION FOR CERTAIN YOUNG ADULT SEX OFFENDERS

Art. 62.301. Exemption From Registration for Certain Young Adult Sex Offenders

(a) If eligible under Subsection (b) or (c), a person required to register under this chapter may petition the court having jurisdiction over the case for an order exempting the person from registration under this chapter at any time on or after the date of the person's sentencing or the date the person is placed on deferred adjudication community supervision, as applicable.

(b) A person is eligible to petition the court as described by Subsection (a) if:

(1) the person is required to register only as a result of a single reportable conviction or adjudication, other than an adjudication of delinquent conduct; and

(2) the court has entered in the appropriate judgment or has filed with the appropriate papers a statement of an affirmative finding described by Article 42.017 or 42A.105(c).

(c) A defendant who before September 1, 2011, is convicted of or placed on deferred adjudication community supervision for an offense under Section 21.11 or 22.011, Penal Code, is eligible to petition the court as described by Subsection (a). The court may consider the petition only if the petition states and the court finds that the defendant would have been entitled to the entry of an affirmative finding under Article 42.017 or 42A.105(c), as appropriate, had the conviction or placement on deferred adjudication community supervision occurred after September 1, 2011.

(c–1) At a hearing on the petition described by Subsection (a), the court may consider:

(1) testimony from the victim or intended victim, or a member of the victim's or intended victim's family, concerning the requested exemption;

(2) the relationship between the victim or intended victim and the petitioner at the time of the hearing; and

(3) any other evidence that the court determines is relevant and admissible.

(d) After a hearing on the petition described by Subsection (a), the court may issue an order exempting the person from registration under this chapter if it appears by a preponderance of the evidence that:

(1) the exemption does not threaten public safety;

(2) the person's conduct did not occur without the consent of the victim or intended victim as described by Section 22.011(b), Penal Code;

(3) the exemption is in the best interest of the victim or intended victim; and

(4) the exemption is in the best interest of justice.

(e) An order exempting the person from registration under this chapter does not expire, but the court shall withdraw the order if after the order is issued the person receives a reportable conviction or adjudication under this chapter.

Added by Acts 2005, 79th Leg., ch. 1008, § 1.01, eff. Sept. 1, 2005. Amended by Acts 2011, 82nd Leg., ch. 134 (S.B. 198), § 3, eff. Sept. 1, 2011; Acts 2015, 84th Leg., ch. 770 (H.B. 2299), § 2.27, eff. Jan. 1, 2017.

SUBCHAPTER H. EXEMPTIONS FROM REGISTRATION FOR CERTAIN JUVENILES

Art. 62.351. Motion and Hearing Generally

(a) During or after disposition of a case under Section 54.04, Family Code, for adjudication of an offense for which registration is required under this chapter, the juvenile court on motion of the respondent shall conduct a hearing to determine whether the interests of the public require registration under this chapter. The motion may be filed and the hearing held regardless of whether the respondent is under 18 years of age. Notice of the motion and hearing shall be provided to the prosecuting attorney.

(b) The hearing is without a jury and the burden of persuasion is on the respondent to show by a preponderance of evidence that the criteria of Article 62.352(a) have been met. The court at the hearing may make its determination based on:

(1) the receipt of exhibits;

(2) the testimony of witnesses;

(3) representations of counsel for the parties; or

(4) the contents of a social history report prepared by the juvenile probation department that may include the results of testing and examination of the respondent by a psychologist, psychiatrist, or counselor.

(c) All written matter considered by the court shall be disclosed to all parties as provided by Section 54.04(b), Family Code.

(d) If a respondent, as part of a plea agreement, promises not to file a motion seeking an order exempting the respondent from registration under this chapter, the court may not recognize a motion filed by a respondent under this article.

Added by Acts 2005, 79th Leg., ch. 1008, § 1.01, eff. Sept. 1, 2005.

Art. 62.352. Order Generally

(a) The court shall enter an order exempting a respondent from registration under this chapter if the court determines:

(1) that the protection of the public would not be increased by registration of the respondent under this chapter; or

(2) that any potential increase in protection of the public resulting from registration of the respondent is clearly outweighed by the anticipated substantial harm to the respondent and the respondent's family that would result from registration under this chapter.

(b) After a hearing under Article 62.351 or under a plea agreement described by Article 62.355(b), the juvenile court may enter an order:

(1) deferring decision on requiring registration under this chapter until the respondent has completed

treatment for the respondent's sexual offense as a condition of probation or while committed to the Texas Juvenile Justice Department; or

(2) requiring the respondent to register as a sex offender but providing that the registration information is not public information and is restricted to use by law enforcement and criminal justice agencies, the Council on Sex Offender Treatment, and public or private institutions of higher education.

(c) If the court enters an order described by Subsection (b)(1), the court retains discretion and jurisdiction to require, or exempt the respondent from, registration under this chapter at any time during the treatment or on the successful or unsuccessful completion of treatment, except that during the period of deferral, registration may not be required. Following successful completion of treatment, the respondent is exempted from registration under this chapter unless a hearing under this subchapter is held on motion of the prosecuting attorney, regardless of whether the respondent is 18 years of age or older, and the court determines the interests of the public require registration. Not later than the 10th day after the date of the respondent's successful completion of treatment, the treatment provider shall notify the juvenile court and prosecuting attorney of the completion.

(d) Information that is the subject of an order described by Subsection (b)(2) may not be posted on the Internet or released to the public.

Added by Acts 2005, 79th Leg., ch. 1008, § 1.01, eff. Sept. 1, 2005. Amended by Acts 2013, 83rd Leg., ch. 1299 (H.B. 2862), § 4, eff. Sept. 1, 2013.

Art. 62.353. Motion, Hearing, and Order Concerning Person Already Registered

(a) A person who has registered as a sex offender for an adjudication of delinquent conduct, regardless of when the delinquent conduct or the adjudication for the conduct occurred, may file a motion in the adjudicating juvenile court for a hearing seeking:

(1) exemption from registration under this chapter as provided by Article 62.351; or

(2) an order under Article 62.352(b)(2) that the registration become nonpublic.

(b) The person may file a motion under Subsection (a) in the original juvenile case regardless of whether the person, at the time of filing the motion, is 18 years of age or older. Notice of the motion shall be provided to the prosecuting attorney. A hearing on the

motion shall be provided as in other cases under this subchapter.

(c) Only one subsequent motion may be filed under Subsection (a) if a previous motion under this article has been filed concerning the case.

(d) To the extent feasible, the motion under Subsection (a) shall identify those public and private agencies and organizations, including public or private institutions of higher education, that possess sex offender registration information about the case.

(e) The juvenile court, after a hearing, may:

(1) deny a motion filed under Subsection (a);

(2) grant a motion described by Subsection (a)(1); or

(3) grant a motion described by Subsection (a)(2).

(f) If the court grants a motion filed under Subsection (a), the clerk of the court shall by certified mail, return receipt requested, send a copy of the order to the department, to each local law enforcement authority that the person has proved to the juvenile court has registration information about the person, and to each public or private agency or organization that the person has proved to the juvenile court has information about the person that is currently available to the public with or without payment of a fee. The clerk of the court shall by certified mail, return receipt requested, send a copy of the order to any other agency or organization designated by the person. The person shall identify the agency or organization and its address and pay a fee of $20 to the court for each agency or organization the person designates.

(g) In addition to disseminating the order under Subsection (f), at the request of the person, the clerk of the court shall by certified mail, return receipt requested, send a copy of the order to each public or private agency or organization that at any time following the initial dissemination of the order under Subsection (f) gains possession of sex offender registration information pertaining to that person, if the agency or organization did not otherwise receive a copy of the order under Subsection (f).

(h) An order under Subsection (f) must require the recipient to conform its records to the court's order either by deleting the sex offender registration information or changing its status to nonpublic, as applicable. A public or private institution of higher education may not be required to delete the sex offender registration information under this subsection.

(i) A private agency or organization that possesses sex offender registration information the agency or organization obtained from a state, county, or local governmental entity is required to conform the agency's or organization's records to the court's order on or before the 30th day after the date of the entry of the order. Unless the agency or organization is a public or private institution of higher education, failure to comply in that period automatically bars the agency or organization from obtaining sex offender registration information from any state, county, or local governmental entity in this state in the future.

Added by Acts 2005, 79th Leg., ch. 1008, § 1.01, eff. Sept. 1, 2005.

Art. 62.354. Motion, Hearing, and Order Concerning Person Required to Register Because of Out–of–State Adjudication

(a) A person required to register as a sex offender in this state because of an out-of-state adjudication of delinquent conduct may file in the juvenile court of the person's county of residence a petition under Article 62.351 for an order exempting the person from registration under this chapter.

(b) If the person is already registered as a sex offender in this state because of an out-of-state adjudication of delinquent conduct, the person may file in the juvenile court of the person's county of residence a petition under Article 62.353 for an order removing the person from sex offender registries in this state.

(c) On receipt of a petition under this article, the juvenile court shall conduct a hearing and make rulings as in other cases under this subchapter.

(d) An order entered under this article requiring removal of registration information applies only to registration information derived from registration in this state.

Added by Acts 2005, 79th Leg., ch. 1008, § 1.01, eff. Sept. 1, 2005.

Art. 62.355. Waiver of Hearing

(a) The prosecuting attorney may waive the state's right to a hearing under this subchapter and agree that registration under this chapter is not required. A waiver under this subsection must state whether the waiver is entered under a plea agreement.

(b) If the waiver is entered under a plea agreement, the court, without a hearing, shall:

(1) enter an order exempting the respondent from registration under this chapter; or

(2) under Section 54.03(j), Family Code, inform the respondent that the court believes a hearing under this article is required and give the respondent the opportunity to:

(A) withdraw the respondent's plea of guilty, nolo contendere, or true; or

(B) affirm the respondent's plea and participate in the hearing.

(c) If the waiver is entered other than under a plea agreement, the court, without a hearing, shall enter an order exempting the respondent from registration under this chapter.

Added by Acts 2005, 79th Leg., ch. 1008, § 1.01, eff. Sept. 1, 2005.

Art. 62.356. Effect of Certain Orders

(a) A person who has an adjudication of delinquent conduct that would otherwise be reportable under Article 62.001(5) does not have a reportable adjudication of delinquent conduct for purposes of this chapter if the juvenile court enters an order under this subchapter exempting the person from the registration requirements of this chapter.

(b) If the juvenile court enters an order exempting a person from registration under this chapter, the respondent may not be required to register in this or any other state for the offense for which registration was exempted.

Added by Acts 2005, 79th Leg., ch. 1008, § 1.01, eff. Sept. 1, 2005.

Art. 62.357. Appeal of Certain Orders

(a) Notwithstanding Section 56.01, Family Code, on entry by a juvenile court of an order under Article 62.352(a) exempting a respondent from registration under this chapter, the prosecuting attorney may appeal that order by giving notice of appeal within the time required under Rule 26.2(b), Texas Rules of Appellate Procedure. The appeal is civil and the standard of review in the appellate court is whether the juvenile court committed procedural error or abused its discretion in exempting the respondent from registration under this chapter. The appeal is limited to review of the order exempting the respondent from registration under this chapter and may not include any other issues in the case.

(b) A respondent may under Section 56.01, Family Code, appeal a juvenile court's order under Article

62.352(a) requiring registration in the same manner as the appeal of any other legal issue in the case. The standard of review in the appellate court is whether the juvenile court committed procedural error or abused its discretion in requiring registration.

Added by Acts 2005, 79th Leg., ch. 1008, § 1.01, eff. Sept. 1, 2005.

SUBCHAPTER I. EARLY TERMINATION OF CERTAIN PERSONS' OBLIGATION TO REGISTER

Art. 62.401. Definition

In this subchapter, "council" means the Council on Sex Offender Treatment.

Added by Acts 2005, 79th Leg., ch. 1008, § 1.01, eff. Sept. 1, 2005.

Art. 62.402. Determination of Minimum Required Registration Period

(a) The department by rule shall determine the minimum required registration period under federal law for each reportable conviction or adjudication under this chapter.

(b) After determining the minimum required registration period for each reportable conviction or adjudication under Subsection (a), the department shall compile and publish a list of reportable convictions or adjudications for which a person must register under this chapter for a period that exceeds the minimum required registration period under federal law.

(c) To the extent possible, the department shall periodically verify with the United States Department of Justice's Office of Sex Offender Sentencing, Monitoring, Apprehending, Registering, and Tracking or another appropriate federal agency or office the accuracy of the list of reportable convictions or adjudications described by Subsection (b).

Added by Acts 2005, 79th Leg., ch. 1008, § 1.01, eff. Sept. 1, 2005. Amended by Acts 2011, 82nd Leg., ch. 134 (S.B. 198), § 4, eff. Sept. 1, 2011.

Art. 62.403. Individual Risk Assessment

(a) The council by rule shall establish, develop, or adopt an individual risk assessment tool or a group of individual risk assessment tools that:

(1) evaluates the criminal history of a person required to register under this chapter; and

(2) seeks to predict:

(A) the likelihood that the person will engage in criminal activity that may result in the person receiving a second or subsequent reportable adjudication or conviction; and

(B) the continuing danger, if any, that the person poses to the community.

(b) On the written request of a person with a single reportable adjudication or conviction that appears on the list published under Article 62.402(b), the council shall:

(1) evaluate the person using the individual risk assessment tool or group of individual risk assessment tools established, developed, or adopted under Subsection (a); and

(2) provide to the person a written report detailing the outcome of an evaluation conducted under Subdivision (1).

(c) An individual risk assessment provided to a person under this subchapter is confidential and is not subject to disclosure under Chapter 552, Government Code.

Added by Acts 2005, 79th Leg., ch. 1008, § 1.01, eff. Sept. 1, 2005.

Art. 62.404. Motion for Early Termination

(a) A person required to register under this chapter who has requested and received an individual risk assessment under Article 62.403 may file with the trial court that sentenced the person for the reportable conviction or adjudication a motion for early termination of the person's obligation to register under this chapter.

(b) A motion filed under this article must be accompanied by:

(1) a written explanation of how the reportable conviction or adjudication giving rise to the movant's registration under this chapter qualifies as a reportable conviction or adjudication that appears on the list published under Article 62.402(b); and

(2) a certified copy of a written report detailing the outcome of an individual risk assessment evaluation conducted under Article 62.403(b)(1).

Added by Acts 2005, 79th Leg., ch. 1008, § 1.01, eff. Sept. 1, 2005.

Art. 62.405. Hearing on Petition

(a) After reviewing a motion filed with the court under Article 62.404, the court may:

(1) deny without a hearing the movant's request for early termination; or

(2) hold a hearing on the motion to determine whether to grant or deny the motion.

(b) The court may not grant a motion filed under Article 62.404 if:

(1) the motion is not accompanied by the documents required under Article 62.404(b); or

(2) the court determines that the reportable conviction or adjudication for which the movant is required to register under this chapter is not a reportable conviction or adjudication for which the movant is required to register for a period that exceeds the minimum required registration period under federal law.

Added by Acts 2005, 79th Leg., ch. 1008, § 1.01, eff. Sept. 1, 2005.

Art. 62.406. Costs of Individual Risk Assessment and of Court

A person required to register under this chapter who files a motion for early termination of the person's registration obligation under this chapter is responsible for and shall remit to the council and to the court, as applicable, all costs associated with and incurred by the council in providing the individual risk assessment or by the court in holding a hearing under this subchapter.

Added by Acts 2005, 79th Leg., ch. 1008, § 1.01, eff. Sept. 1, 2005.

Art. 62.407. Effect of Order Granting Early Termination

(a) If, after notice to the person and to the prosecuting attorney and a hearing, the court grants a motion filed under Article 62.404 for the early termination of a person's obligation to register under this chapter, notwithstanding Article 62.101, the person's obligation to register under this chapter ends on the later of:

(1) the date the court enters the order of early termination; or

(2) the date the person has paid each cost described by Section 62.406.

(b) If the court grants a motion filed under Article 62.404 for the early termination of a person's obligation to register under this chapter, all conditions of the person's parole, release to mandatory supervision, or community supervision shall be modified in accordance with the court's order.

Added by Acts 2005, 79th Leg., ch. 1008, § 1.01, eff. Sept. 1, 2005.

Art. 62.408. Nonapplicability

This subchapter does not apply to a person without a reportable conviction or adjudication who is required to register as a condition of parole, release to mandatory supervision, or community supervision.

Added by Acts 2005, 79th Leg., ch. 1008, § 1.01, eff. Sept. 1, 2005.

CHAPTER 63. MISSING CHILDREN AND MISSING PERSONS

SUBCHAPTER A. GENERAL PROVISIONS

Chapter 63, Missing Children and Missing Persons, was renumbered from Chapter 62 by Acts 1999, 76th Leg., ch. 62, § 19.01(8)(A).

SUBCHAPTER A. GENERAL PROVISIONS

Art. 63.001. Definitions

In this chapter:

(1) "Abduct" has the meaning assigned by Section 20.01, Penal Code.

(1–a) "Child" means a person under 18 years of age.

(2) "Missing person" means a person 18 years old or older whose disappearance is possibly not voluntary.

(3) "Missing child" means a child whose whereabouts are unknown to the child's legal custodian, the circumstances of whose absence indicate that:

(A) the child did not voluntarily leave the care and control of the custodian, and the taking of the child was not authorized by law;

(B) the child voluntarily left the care and control of the custodian without the custodian's consent and without intent to return;

(C) the child was taken or retained in violation of the terms of a court order for possession of or access to the child; or

(D) the child was taken or retained without the permission of the custodian and with the effect of depriving the custodian of possession of or access to the child unless the taking or retention of the child was prompted by the commission or attempted commission of family violence, as defined by Section 71.004, Family Code, against the child or the actor.

(4) "Missing child" or "missing person" also includes a person of any age who is missing and:

(A) is under proven physical or mental disability or is senile, and because of one or more of these conditions is subject to immediate danger or is a danger to others;

(B) is in the company of another person or is in a situation the circumstances of which indicate that the missing child's or missing person's safety is in doubt; or

(C) is unemancipated as defined by the law of this state.

(5) "Missing child or missing person report" means information that is:

(A) given to a law enforcement agency on a form used for sending information to the national crime information center; and

(B) about a child or missing person whose whereabouts are unknown to the reporter and who is alleged in the form by the reporter to be missing.

(6) "Legal custodian of a child" means a parent of a child if no managing conservator or guardian of the person of the child has been appointed, the managing conservator of a child or a guardian of a child if a managing conservator or guardian has been appointed for the child, a possessory conservator of a child if the child is absent from the possessory conservator of the child at a time when the possessory conservator is entitled to possession of the child and the child is not believed to be with the managing conservator, or any other person who has assumed temporary care and control of a child if at the time of disappearance the child was not living with his parent, guardian, managing conservator, or possessory conservator.

(7) "Clearinghouse" means the missing children and missing persons information clearinghouse.

(8) "Law enforcement agency" means a police department of a city in this state, a sheriff of a county in this state, or the Department of Public Safety.

(9) "Possible match" occurs if the similarities between an unidentified body and a missing child or person would lead one to believe they are the same person.

(10) "City or state agency" means an employment commission, the Texas Department of Human Services, the Texas Department of Transportation, and

any other agency that is funded or supported by the state or a city government.

(11) "Birth certificate agency" means a municipal or county official that records and maintains birth certificates and the bureau of vital statistics.

(12) "Bureau of vital statistics" means the bureau of vital statistics of the Texas Department of Health.

(13) "School" means a public primary school or private primary school that charges a fee for tuition and has more than 25 students enrolled and attending courses at a single location.

Added by Acts 1985, 69th Leg., ch. 132, § 1, eff. May 22, 1985. Amended by Acts 1987, 70th Leg., ch. 657, § 1, eff. June 18, 1987; Acts 1987, 70th Leg., ch. 1052, § 7.03, eff. Sept. 1, 1987. Renumbered from V.T.C.A., Human Resources Code § 74.001 by Acts 1987, 70th Leg., ch. 167, § 5.01(a)(26), eff. Sept. 1, 1987. Amended by Acts 1995, 74th Leg., ch. 165, § 22(43), eff. Sept. 1, 1995; Acts 1995, 74th Leg., ch. 178, § 1, eff. Sept. 1, 1995; Acts 1997, 75th Leg., ch. 51, § 1, eff. May 7,1997; Acts 1997, 75th Leg., ch. 1084, § 1, eff. Sept. 1, 1997. Renumbered from V.T.C.A., Human Resources Code § 79.001 and amended by Acts 1997, 75th Leg., ch. 1427, § 1, eff. Sept. 1, 1997. Amended by Acts 1999, 76th Leg., ch. 62, § 3.10, eff. Sept. 1, 1999. Renumbered from Vernon's Ann.C.C.P. art. 62.001 and amended by Acts 1999, 76th Leg., ch. 62, § 19.01(8)(A), eff. Sept. 1, 1999. Amended by Acts 2011, 82nd Leg., ch. 840 (H.B. 3439), § 1, eff. Sept. 1, 2011; Acts 2011, 82nd Leg., ch. 1100 (S.B. 1551), § 2, eff. Sept. 1, 2011; Acts 2011, 82nd Leg., ch. 1019 (H.B. 2662), § 1, eff. Sept. 1, 2011; Acts 2013, 83rd Leg., ch. 571 (S.B. 742), § 1, eff. Sept. 1, 2013.

Art. 63.0015. Presumption Regarding Parentage

For purposes of this chapter, a person named as a child's mother or father in the child's birth certificate is presumed to be the child's parent.

Added by Acts 1999, 76th Leg., ch. 685, § 2, eff. Sept. 1, 1999. Renumbered from Vernon's Ann.C.C.P. art. 62.0015 by Acts 2009, 81st Leg., ch. 87, § 27.001(3), eff. Sept. 1, 2009.

Art. 63.0016. Attempted Child Abduction by Relative

For purposes of this chapter, "attempted child abduction" does not include an attempted abduction in which the actor was a relative, as defined by Section 20.01, Penal Code, of the person intended to be abducted.

Added by Acts 2013, 83rd Leg., ch. 571 (S.B. 742), § 2, eff. Sept. 1, 2013.

Art. 63.002. Missing Children and Missing Persons Information Clearinghouse

(a) The missing children and missing persons information clearinghouse is established within the Department of Public Safety.

(b) The clearinghouse is under the administrative direction of the director of the department.

(c) The clearinghouse shall be used by all law enforcement agencies of the state.

Added by Acts 1985, 69th Leg., ch. 132, § 1, eff. May 22, 1985. Renumbered from V.T.C.A., Human Resources Code § 74.002 by Acts 1987, 70th Leg., ch. 167, § 5.01(a)(26), eff. Sept. 1, 1987. Renumbered from V.T.C.A., Human Resources Code § 79.002 by Acts 1997, 75th Leg., ch. 1427, § 1, eff. Sept. 1, 1997. Renumbered from Vernon's Ann.C.C.P. art. 62.002 by Acts 1999, 76th Leg., ch. 62, § 19.01(8)(A), eff. Sept. 1, 1999.

Art. 63.003. Function of Clearinghouse

(a) The clearinghouse is a central repository of information on missing children, missing persons, and attempted child abductions.

(b) The clearinghouse shall:

(1) establish a system of intrastate communication of information relating to missing children and missing persons;

(2) provide a centralized file for the exchange of information on missing children, missing persons, and unidentified dead bodies within the state;

(3) communicate with the national crime information center for the exchange of information on missing children and missing persons suspected of interstate travel;

(4) collect, process, maintain, and disseminate accurate and complete information on missing children and missing persons;

(5) provide a statewide toll-free telephone line for the reporting of missing children and missing persons and for receiving information on missing children and missing persons;

(6) provide and disseminate to legal custodians, law enforcement agencies, and the Texas Education Agency information that explains how to prevent child abduction and what to do if a child becomes missing; and

(7) receive and maintain information on attempted child abductions in this state.

Added by Acts 1985, 69th Leg., ch. 132, § 1, eff. May 22, 1985. Renumbered from V.T.C.A., Human Resources Code § 74.003 by Acts 1987, 70th Leg., ch. 167, § 5.01(a)(26), eff. Sept. 1, 1987. Amended by Acts 1997, 75th Leg., ch. 165, § 6.59, eff. Sept. 1, 1997. Renumbered from V.T.C.A., Human Resources Code § 79.003 and amended by Acts 1997, 75th Leg., ch. 1427, § 1, eff. Sept. 1, 1997. Renumbered from Vernon's Ann.C.C.P. art. 62.003 by Acts 1999, 76th Leg., ch. 62, § 19.01(8)(A), eff. Sept. 1, 1999. Amended by Acts 2013, 83rd Leg., ch. 571 (S.B. 742), § 3, eff. Sept. 1, 2013.

Art. 63.004. Report Forms

(a) The Department of Public Safety shall distribute missing children and missing person report forms.

(b) A missing child or missing person report may be made to a law enforcement officer authorized by that department to receive reports in person or by telephone or other indirect method of communication and the officer may enter the information on the form for the reporting person. A report form may also be completed by the reporting person and delivered to a law enforcement officer.

Added by Acts 1985, 69th Leg., ch. 132, § 1, eff. May 22, 1985. Renumbered from V.T.C.A., Human Resources Code § 74.004 by Acts 1987, 70th Leg., ch. 167, § 5.01(a)(26), eff. Sept. 1, 1987. Renumbered from V.T.C.A., Human Resources Code § 79.004 by Acts 1997, 75th Leg., ch. 1427, § 1, eff. Sept. 1, 1997. Renumbered from Vernon's Ann.C.C.P. art. 62.004 by Acts 1999, 76th Leg., ch. 62, § 19.01(8)(A), eff. Sept. 1, 1999.

Art. 63.0041. Reporting of Attempted Child Abduction

(a) A local law enforcement agency, on receiving a report of an attempted child abduction, shall as soon as practicable, but not later than eight hours after receiving the report, provide any relevant information regarding the attempted child abduction to the clearinghouse. Information not immediately available shall be obtained by the agency and entered into the clearinghouse as a supplement to the original entry as soon as possible.

(b) A law enforcement officer or local law enforcement agency reporting an attempted child abduction to the clearinghouse shall make the report by use of the Texas Law Enforcement Telecommunications System or a successor system of telecommunication used by law enforcement agencies and operated by the Department of Public Safety.

Added by Acts 2013, 83rd Leg., ch. 571 (S.B. 742), § 4, eff. Sept. 1, 2013. Amended by Acts 2017, 85th Leg., ch. 1016 (H.B. 1503), § 1, eff. Sept. 1, 2017.

Art. 63.005. Distribution of Information

(a) The clearinghouse shall print and distribute posters, flyers, and other forms of information containing descriptions of missing children.

(b) The clearinghouse shall also provide to the Texas Education Agency information about missing children who may be located in the school systems.

(c) The clearinghouse may also receive information about missing children from the Public Education Information Management System of the Texas Education Agency and from school districts.

Added by Acts 1985, 69th Leg., ch. 132, § 1, eff. May 22, 1985. Renumbered from V.T.C.A., Human Resources Code § 74.005 by Acts 1987, 70th Leg., ch. 167, § 5.01(a)(26), eff. Sept. 1, 1987. Amended by Acts 1989, 71st Leg., ch. 190, § 2, eff. Aug. 28, 1989; Acts 1997, 75th Leg., ch. 165, § 6.60, eff. Sept. 1, 1997. Renumbered from V.T.C.A., Human Resources Code § 79.005 and amended by Acts 1997, 75th Leg., ch. 1427, § 1, eff. Sept. 1, 1997. Renumbered from Vernon's Ann.C.C.P. art. 62.005 by Acts 1999, 76th Leg., ch. 62, § 19.01(8)(A), eff. Sept. 1, 1999.

Art. 63.006. Release of Dental Records

(a) At the time a report is made for a missing child, the person to whom the report is given shall give or mail to the reporter a dental record release form. The officer receiving the report shall endorse the form with the notation that a missing child report has been made in compliance with this chapter. When the form is properly completed by the reporter, and contains the endorsement, the form is sufficient to permit any dentist or physician in this state to release dental records relating to the child reported missing.

(b) At any time a report is made for a missing person the law enforcement officer taking the report shall complete a dental release form that states that the person is missing and that there is reason to believe that the person has not voluntarily relocated or removed himself from communications with others and that authorizes the bearer of the release to obtain dental information records from any dentist or physician in this state.

(c) Any person who obtains dental records through the use of the form authorized by this article shall send the records to the clearinghouse.

(d) The judge of any court of record of this state may for good cause shown authorize the release of dental records of a missing child or missing person.

(e) A dentist or physician who releases dental records to a person presenting a proper release executed or ordered under this article is immune from civil liability or criminal prosecution for the release of those records.

Added by Acts 1985, 69th Leg., ch. 132, § 1, eff. May 22, 1985. Renumbered from V.T.C.A., Human Resources Code § 74.006 by Acts 1987, 70th Leg., ch. 167, § 5.01(a)(26), eff. Sept. 1, 1987. Renumbered from V.T.C.A., Human Resources Code § 79.006 and amended by Acts 1997, 75th Leg., ch. 1427, § 1, eff. Sept. 1, 1997. Amended by Acts 1999, 76th Leg., ch. 685, § 3, eff. Sept. 1, 1999. Renumbered from Vernon's Ann.C.C.P. art. 62.006 by Acts 1999, 76th Leg., ch. 62, § 19.01(8)(A), eff. Sept. 1, 1999.

Art. 63.007. Release of Medical Records

(a) At the time a report is made for a missing child or adult, the law enforcement officer taking the report shall give a medical record release form to the parent, spouse, adult child, or legal guardian who is making the report. The officer receiving the report shall endorse the form with the notation that a missing child or missing adult report has been made in compliance with this chapter. When the form is properly completed by the parent, spouse, adult child, or legal guardian, and contains the endorsement, the form is sufficient to permit any physician, health care facility, or other licensed health care provider in this state to release to the law enforcement officer presenting the release dental records, blood type, height, weight, X rays, and information regarding scars, allergies, or any unusual illnesses suffered by the person who is reported missing. Except as provided by Subsection (d), a medical record of a missing child may be released only if the medical record release form is signed by a parent or legal guardian.

(b) At any time a report is made for an adult missing person, the law enforcement officer taking the report shall complete a medical release form that states that the person is missing and that there is reason to believe that the person has not voluntarily relocated or removed himself or herself from communications with others. A release under this subsection is not valid unless it is signed by the adult missing person's:

(1) spouse;

(2) adult child who is reasonably available;

(3) parent; or

(4) legal guardian.

(c) A law enforcement officer who obtains medical records under this article shall send a copy of the records to the clearinghouse. A law enforcement officer who obtains records under this article, a law enforcement agency using the records, and the clearinghouse are prohibited from disclosing the information contained in or obtained through the medical records unless permitted by law. Information contained in or obtained through medical records may be used only for purposes directly related to locating the missing person.

(d) The judge of any court of record of this state may for good cause shown authorize the release of pertinent medical records of a missing child or missing adult.

(e) A physician, health care facility, or other licensed health care provider releasing a medical record to a person presenting a proper release executed or ordered under this article is immune from civil liability or criminal prosecution for the release of the record.

Added by Acts 1995, 74th Leg., ch. 438, § 1, eff. Aug. 28, 1995. Renumbered from V.T.C.A., Human Resources Code § 79.0065 and amended by Acts 1997, 75th Leg., ch. 1427, § 1, eff. Sept. 1, 1997. Renumbered from Vernon's Ann. C.C.P. art. 62.007 by Acts 1999, 76th Leg., ch. 62, § 19.01(8)(A), eff. Sept. 1, 1999.

Art. 63.008. Missing Children Program

(a) The Texas Education Agency shall develop and administer a program for the location of missing children who may be enrolled within the Texas school system, including nonpublic schools, and for the reporting of children who may be missing or who may be unlawfully removed from schools.

(b) The program shall include the use of information received from the missing children and missing persons information clearinghouse and shall be coordinated with the operations of that information clearinghouse.

(c) The State Board of Education may adopt rules for the operation of the program and shall require the participation of all school districts and accredited private schools in this state.

Added by Acts 1985, 69th Leg., ch. 132, § 1, eff. May 22, 1985. Renumbered from V.T.C.A., Human Resources Code § 74.007 by Acts 1987, 70th Leg., ch. 167, § 5.01(a)(26), eff. Sept. 1, 1987. Amended by Acts 1997, 75th Leg., ch. 165, § 6.61, eff. Sept. 1, 1997. Renumbered from V.T.C.A., Human Resources Code § 79.007 and amended by Acts 1997, 75th Leg., ch. 1427, § 1, eff. Sept. 1, 1997. Renumbered from Vernon's Ann.C.C.P. art. 62.008 by Acts 1999, 76th Leg., ch. 62, § 19.01(8)(A), eff. Sept. 1, 1999.

Art. 63.009. Law Enforcement Requirements

(a) Local law enforcement agencies, on receiving a report of a missing child or a missing person, shall:

(1) if the subject of the report is a child and the child is at a high risk of harm or is otherwise in danger or if the subject of the report is a person who is known by the agency to have or is reported to have chronic dementia, including Alzheimer's dementia, whether caused by illness, brain defect, or brain injury, immediately start an investigation in order to determine the present location of the child or person;

(2) if the subject of the report is a child or person other than a child or person described by Subdivision

(1), start an investigation with due diligence in order to determine the present location of the child or person;

(3) immediately, but not later than two hours after receiving the report, enter the name of the child or person into the clearinghouse, the national crime information center missing person file if the child or person meets the center's criteria, and the Alzheimer's Association Safe Return crisis number, if applicable, with all available identifying features such as dental records, fingerprints, other physical characteristics, and a description of the clothing worn when last seen, and all available information describing any person reasonably believed to have taken or retained the missing child or missing person; and

(4) inform the person who filed the report of the missing child or missing person that the information will be entered into the clearinghouse, the national crime information center missing person file, and the Alzheimer's Association Safe Return crisis number, if applicable.

(a-1) A local law enforcement agency, on receiving a report of a child missing under the circumstances described by Article 63.001(3)(D) for a period of not less than 48 hours, shall immediately make a reasonable effort to locate the child and determine the well-being of the child. On determining the location of the child, if the agency has reason to believe that the child is a victim of abuse or neglect as defined by Section 261.001, Family Code, the agency:

(1) shall notify the Department of Family and Protective Services; and

(2) may take possession of the child under Subchapter B, Chapter 262, Family Code.

(a-2) The Department of Family and Protective Services, on receiving notice under Subsection (a-1), may initiate an investigation into the allegation of abuse or neglect under Section 261.301, Family Code, and take possession of the child under Chapter 262, Family Code.

(a-3) Repealed by Acts 2017, 85th Leg., ch. 1016 (H.B. 1503), § 2.

(b) Information not immediately available shall be obtained by the agency and entered into the clearinghouse and the national crime information center file as a supplement to the original entry as soon as possible.

(c) All Texas law enforcement agencies are required to enter information about all unidentified bodies into the clearinghouse and the national crime information center unidentified person file. A law enforcement agency shall, not later than the 10th working day after the date the death is reported to the agency, enter all available identifying features of the unidentified body (fingerprints, dental records, any unusual physical characteristics, and a description of the clothing found on the body) into the clearinghouse and the national crime information center file. If an information entry into the national crime information center file results in an automatic entry of the information into the clearinghouse, the law enforcement agency is not required to make a direct entry of that information into the clearinghouse.

(d) If a local law enforcement agency investigating a report of a missing child or missing person obtains a warrant for the arrest of a person for taking or retaining the missing child or missing person, the local law enforcement agency shall immediately enter the name and other descriptive information of the person into the national crime information center wanted person file if the person meets the center's criteria. The local law enforcement agency shall also enter all available identifying features, including dental records, fingerprints, and other physical characteristics of the missing child or missing person. The information shall be cross-referenced with the information in the national crime information center missing person file.

(e) A local law enforcement agency that has access to the national crime information center database shall cooperate with other law enforcement agencies in entering or retrieving information from the national crime information center database.

(f) Immediately after the return of a missing child or missing person or the identification of an unidentified body, the local law enforcement agency having jurisdiction of the investigation shall cancel the entry in the national crime information center database.

(g) On determining the location of a child under Subsection (a)(1) or (2), other than a child who is subject to the continuing jurisdiction of a district court, an officer shall take possession of the child and shall deliver or arrange for the delivery of the child to a person entitled to possession of the child. If the person entitled to possession of the child is not immediately available, the law enforcement officer shall deliver the child to the Department of Protective and Regulatory Services.

Added by Acts 1985, 69th Leg., ch. 132, § 1, eff. May 22, 1985. Amended by Acts 1987, 70th Leg., ch. 657, § 2, eff. June 18, 1987. Renumbered from V.T.C.A., Human Resources Code § 74.008 by Acts 1987, 70th Leg., ch. 167, § 5.01(a)(26), eff. Sept. 1, 1987. Amended by Acts 1989, 71st Leg., ch. 190, § 3, eff. Aug. 28, 1989; Acts 1997, 75th Leg., ch. 51, § 2, eff. May 7, 1997; Acts 1997, 75th Leg., ch. 771, § 1, eff. Sept. 1, 1997. Renumbered from V.T.C.A., Human Resources Code § 79.008 and amended by Acts 1997, 75th Leg., ch. 1427, § 1, eff. Sept. 1, 1997. Amended by Acts 1999, 76th Leg., ch. 62, §§ 3.11, 3.12, eff. Sept. 1, 1999; Acts 1999, 76th Leg., ch. 200, §§ 1, 2, eff. Sept. 1, 1999; Acts 1999, 76th Leg., ch. 685, § 4, 5, eff. Sept. 1, 1999. Renumbered from Vernon's Ann.C.C.P. art. 62.009 and amended by Acts 1999, 76th Leg., ch. 62, § 19.01(8)(A), eff. Sept. 1, 1999. Amended by Acts 2001, 77th Leg., ch. 1420, § 3.005, eff. Sept. 1, 2001; Acts 2011, 82nd Leg., ch. 1130 (H.B. 943), § 2, eff. Sept. 1, 2011; Acts 2013, 83rd Leg., ch. 571 (S.B. 742), § 5, eff. Sept. 1, 2013; Acts 2013, 83rd Leg., ch. 906 (H.B. 1206), § 1, eff. Sept. 1, 2013; Acts 2015, 84th Leg., ch. 745 (H.B. 1793), § 1, eff. Sept. 1, 2015; Acts 2015, 84th Leg., ch. 1236 (S.B. 1296), § 21.001(6), eff. Sept. 1, 2015; Acts 2017, 85th Leg., ch. 1016 (H.B. 1503), § 2, eff. Sept. 1, 2017.

Section 5 of Acts 2015, 84th Leg., ch. 745 (H.B. 1793) provides:

"Articles 63.009(a) and 63.0091, Code of Criminal Procedure, as amended by this Act, and Article 63.0092, Code of Criminal Procedure, as added by this Act, apply only to a missing child report that is received by a law enforcement agency on or after the effective date of this Act. A report that is received before the effective date of this Act is governed by the law in effect on the date the report was received, and the former law is continued in effect for that purpose."

Art. 63.0091. Law Enforcement Requirements Regarding Reports of Certain Missing Children

(a) The public safety director of the Department of Public Safety shall adopt rules regarding the procedures for a local law enforcement agency on receiving a report of a missing child who:

(1) had been reported missing on four or more occasions in the 24–month period preceding the date of the current report;

(2) is in foster care or in the conservatorship of the Department of Family and Protective Services and had been reported missing on two or more occasions in the 24–month period preceding the date of the current report; or

(3) is under 14 years of age and otherwise determined by the local law enforcement agency or the Department of Public Safety to be at a high risk of human trafficking, sexual assault, exploitation, abuse, or neglectful supervision.

(b) The rules adopted under this article must require that in entering information regarding the report into the national crime information center missing person file as required by Article 63.009(a)(3) for a missing child described by Subsection (a), the local law enforcement agency shall indicate, in the manner specified in the rules, that the child is at a high risk of harm and include relevant information regarding any prior occasions on which the child was reported missing.

(c) If, at the time the initial entry into the national crime information center missing person file is made, the local law enforcement agency has not determined that the requirements of this article apply to the report of the missing child, the information required by Subsection (b) must be added to the entry promptly after the agency investigating the report or the Department of Public Safety determines that the missing child is described by Subsection (a).

Added by Acts 2013, 83rd Leg., ch. 571 (S.B. 742), § 6, eff. Sept. 1, 2013. Amended by Acts 2015, 84th Leg., ch. 745 (H.B. 1793), § 2, eff. Sept. 1, 2015.

Section 5 of Acts 2015, 84th Leg., ch. 745 (H.B. 1793) provides:

"Articles 63.009(a) and 63.0091, Code of Criminal Procedure, as amended by this Act, and Article 63.0092, Code of Criminal Procedure, as added by this Act, apply only to a missing child report that is received by a law enforcement agency on or after the effective date of this Act. A report that is received before the effective date of this Act is governed by the law in effect on the date the report was received, and the former law is continued in effect for that purpose."

Art. 63.0092. Option to Designate Missing Child as High Risk

(a) This article applies to a report of a missing child who is at least 14 years of age and who a local law enforcement agency or the Department of Public Safety determines is at a high risk of human trafficking, sexual assault, exploitation, abuse, or neglectful supervision.

(b) In entering information regarding a report described by Subsection (a) into the national crime information center missing person file as required by Article 63.009(a)(3), the local law enforcement agency may indicate that the child is at a high risk of harm and may include any other relevant information.

Added by Acts 2015, 84th Leg., ch. 745 (H.B. 1793), § 3, eff. Sept. 1, 2015.

Section 5 of Acts 2015, 84th Leg., ch. 745 (H.B. 1793) provides:

"Articles 63.009(a) and 63.0091, Code of Criminal Procedure, as amended by this Act, and Article 63.0092, Code of Criminal Procedure, as added by this Act, apply only to a missing child report that is received by a law enforcement agency on or after the effective date of this Act. A report that is received before the effective date of this Act is governed by the law in effect on the date the report was received, and the former law is continued in effect for that purpose."

Art. 63.010. Attorney General to Require Compliance

The attorney general shall require each law enforcement agency to comply with this chapter and may seek writs of mandamus or other appropriate remedies to enforce this chapter.

Added by Acts 1985, 69th Leg., ch. 132, § 1, eff. May 22, 1985. Renumbered from V.T.C.A., Human Resources Code § 74.009 by Acts 1987, 70th Leg., ch. 167, § 5.01(a)(26), eff. Sept. 1, 1987. Renumbered from V.T.C.A., Human Resources Code § 79.009 by Acts 1997, 75th Leg., ch. 1427, § 1, eff. Sept. 1, 1997. Renumbered from Vernon's Ann.C.C.P. art. 62.010 by Acts 1999, 76th Leg., ch. 62, § 19.01(8)(A), eff. Sept. 1, 1999.

Art. 63.011. Missing Children Investigations

On the written request made to a law enforcement agency by a parent, foster parent, managing or possessory conservator, guardian of the person or the estate, or other court-appointed custodian of a child whose whereabouts are unknown, the law enforcement agency shall request from the missing children and missing persons information clearinghouse information concerning the child that may aid the person making the request in the identification or location of the child.

Added by Acts 1985, 69th Leg., ch. 132, § 1, eff. May 22, 1985. Renumbered from V.T.C.A., Human Resources Code § 74.010 by Acts 1987, 70th Leg., ch. 167, § 5.01(a)(26), eff. Sept. 1, 1987. Renumbered from V.T.C.A., Human Resources Code § 79.010 by Acts 1997, 75th Leg., ch. 1427, § 1, eff. Sept. 1, 1997. Renumbered from Vernon's Ann.C.C.P. art. 62.011 by Acts 1999, 76th Leg., ch. 62, § 19.01(8)(A), eff. Sept. 1, 1999.

Art. 63.012. Report of Inquiry

A law enforcement agency to which a request has been made under Article 63.011 of this code shall report to the parent on the results of its inquiry within 14 days after the day that the written request is filed with the law enforcement agency.

Added by Acts 1985, 69th Leg., ch. 132, § 1, eff. May 22, 1985. Renumbered from V.T.C.A., Human Resources Code § 74.011 and amended by Acts 1987, 70th Leg., ch. 167, § 5.01(a)(26), (27), eff. Sept. 1, 1987. Renumbered from V.T.C.A., Human Resources Code § 79.011 and amended by Acts 1997, 75th Leg., ch. 1427, § 1, eff. Sept. 1, 1997. Renumbered from Vernon's Ann.C.C.P. art. 62.012 and amended by Acts 1999, 76th Leg., ch. 62, § 19.01(8)(A), eff. Sept. 1, 1999. Amended by Acts 1999, 76th Leg., ch. 62, § 19.02(1), eff. Sept. 1, 1999.

Art. 63.013. Information to Clearinghouse

Each law enforcement agency shall provide to the missing children and missing persons information clearinghouse:

(1) any information that would assist in the location or identification of any missing child who has been reported to the agency as missing; and

(2) any information regarding an attempted child abduction that has been reported to the agency or that the agency has received from any person or another agency.

Added by Act 1985, 69th Leg., ch. 132, § 1, eff. May 22, 1985. Renumbered from V.T.C.A., Human Resources Code § 74.012 by Acts 1987, 70th Leg., ch. 167, § 5.01(a)(26), eff. Sept. 1, 1987. Renumbered from V.T.C.A., Human Resources Code § 79.012 by Acts 1997, 75th Leg., ch. 1427, § 1, eff. Sept. 1, 1997. Renumbered from Vernon's Ann.C.C.P. art. 62.013 by Acts 1999, 76th Leg., ch. 62, § 19.01(8)(A), eff. Sept. 1, 1999. Amended by Acts 2013, 83rd Leg., ch. 571 (S.B. 742), § 7, eff. Sept. 1, 2013.

Art. 63.014. Cross-Checking and Matching

(a) The clearinghouse shall cross-check and attempt to match unidentified bodies with missing children or missing persons. When the clearinghouse discovers a possible match between an unidentified body and a missing child or missing person, the Department of Public Safety shall notify the appropriate law enforcement agencies.

(b) Those law enforcement agencies that receive notice of a possible match shall make arrangements for positive identification and complete and close out the investigation with notification to the clearinghouse.

Added by Acts 1985, 69th Leg., ch. 132, § 1, eff. May 22, 1985. Renumbered from V.T.C.A., Human Resources Code § 74.013 by Acts 1987, 70th Leg., ch. 167, § 5.01(a)(26), eff. Sept. 1, 1987. Renumbered from V.T.C.A., Human Resources Code § 79.013 by Acts 1997, 75th Leg., ch. 1427, § 1, eff. Sept. 1, 1997. Renumbered from Vernon's Ann.C.C.P. art. 62.014 by Acts 1999, 76th Leg., ch. 62, § 19.01(8)(A), eff. Sept. 1, 1999.

Art. 63.015. Availability of Information Through Other Agencies

(a) On the request of any law enforcement agency, a city or state agency shall furnish the law enforcement agency with any information about a missing child or missing person that will assist in completing the investigation.

(b) The information given under Subsection (a) of this article is confidential and may not be released to any other person outside of the law enforcement agency.

Added by Acts 1985, 69th Leg., ch. 132, § 1, eff. May 22, 1985. Renumbered from V.T.C.A., Human Resources Code § 74.014 by Acts 1987, 70th Leg., ch. 167, § 5.01(a)(26), eff. Sept. 1, 1987. Renumbered from V.T.C.A., Human Resources Code § 79.014 and amended by Acts 1997, 75th Leg., ch. 1427, § 1, eff. Sept. 1, 1997. Renumbered from Vernon's Ann.C.C.P. art. 62.015 by Acts 1999, 76th Leg., ch. 62, § 19.01(8)(A), eff. Sept. 1, 1999.

Art. 63.016. Donations

The Department of Public Safety may accept money donated from any source to assist in financing the activities and purposes of the missing children and missing persons information clearinghouse.

Added by Acts 1987, 70th Leg., ch. 894, § 1, eff. June 19, 1987. Renumbered from V.T.C.A., Human Resources Code § 79.015 by Acts 1997, 75th Leg., ch. 1427, § 1, eff. Sept. 1, 1997. Renumbered from Vernon's Ann.C.C.P. art. 62.016 by Acts 1999, 76th Leg., ch. 62, § 19.01(8)(A), eff. Sept. 1, 1999.

Art. 63.017. Confidentiality of Certain Records

Clearinghouse records that relate to the investigation by a law enforcement agency of a missing child, a missing person, or an unidentified body and records or notations that the clearinghouse maintains for internal use in matters relating to missing children, missing persons, or unidentified bodies are confidential.

Added by Acts 1989, 71st Leg., ch. 190, § 1, eff. Aug. 28, 1989. Renumbered from V.T.C.A., Human Resources Code § 79.016 by Acts 1997, 75th Leg., ch. 1427, § 1, eff. Sept. 1, 1997. Renumbered from Vernon's Ann.C.C.P. art. 62.017 by Acts 1999, 76th Leg., ch. 62, § 19.01(8)(A), eff. Sept. 1, 1999

Art. 63.018. Death Certificates

A physician who performs a postmortem examination on the body of an unidentified person shall complete and file a death certificate in accordance with Chapter 193, Health and Safety Code. The physician shall note on the certificate the name of the law enforcement agency that submitted the body for examination and shall send a copy of the certificate to the clearinghouse not later than the 10th working day after the date the physician files the certificate.

Added by Acts 1997, 75th Leg., ch. 1427, § 1, eff. Sept. 1, 1997. Renumbered from Vernon's Ann.C.C.P. art. 62.018 by Acts 1999, 76th Leg., ch. 62, § 19.01(8)(A), eff. Sept. 1, 1999.

Art. 63.019. School Records System

(a) On enrollment of a child under 11 years of age in a school for the first time at the school, the school shall:

(1) request from the person enrolling the child the name of each previous school attended by the child;

(2) request from each school identified in Subdivision (1), the school records for the child and, if the person enrolling the child provides copies of previous school records, request verification from the school of the child's name, address, birth date, and grades and dates attended; and

(3) notify the person enrolling the student that not later than the 30th day after enrollment, or the 90th day if the child was not born in the United States, the person must provide:

(A) a certified copy of the child's birth certificate; or

(B) other reliable proof of the child's identity and age and a signed statement explaining the person's inability to produce a copy of the child's birth certificate.

(b) If a person enrolls a child under 11 years of age in school and does not provide the valid prior school information or documentation required by this section, the school shall notify the appropriate law enforcement agency before the 31st day after the person fails to comply with this section. On receipt of notification, the law enforcement agency shall immediately check the clearinghouse to determine if the child has been reported missing. If the child has been reported missing, the law enforcement agency shall immediately notify other appropriate law enforcement agencies that the missing child has been located.

Added by Acts 1997, 75th Leg., ch. 1084, § 2, eff. Sept. 1, 1997. Renumbered from V.T.C.A., Human Resources Code § 79.017 by Acts 1999, 76th Leg., ch. 62, § 19.01(8)(B), eff. Sept. 1, 1999.

Art. 63.020. Duty of Schools and Other Entities to Flag Missing Children's Records

(a) When a report that a child under 11 years of age is missing is received by a law enforcement agency, the agency shall immediately notify each school and day care facility that the child attended or in which the child was enrolled as well as the bureau of vital statistics, if the child was born in the state, that the child is missing.

(b) On receipt of notice that a child under 11 years of age is missing, the bureau of vital statistics shall notify the appropriate municipal or county birth certificate agency that the child is missing.

(c) A school, day care facility, or birth certificate agency that receives notice concerning a child under this section shall flag the child's records that are maintained by the school, facility, or agency.

(d) The law enforcement agency shall notify the clearinghouse that the notification required under this section has been made. The clearinghouse shall provide the notice required under this section if the clearinghouse determines that the notification has not been made by the law enforcement agency.

(e) If a missing child under 11 years of age, who was the subject of a missing child report made in this state, was born in or attended a school or licensed day care facility in another state, the law enforcement agency shall notify law enforcement or the missing and exploited children clearinghouse in each appropriate state regarding the missing child and request the law enforcement agency or clearinghouse to contact the state birth certificate agency and each school or licensed day care facility the missing child attended to flag the missing child's records.

Added by Acts 1997, 75th Leg., ch. 1084, § 2, eff. Sept. 1, 1997. Renumbered from V.T.C.A., Human Resources Code § 79.018 by Acts 1999, 76th Leg., ch. 62, § 19.01(8)(B), eff. Sept. 1, 1999.

Art. 63.021. System for Flagging Records

(a) On receipt of notification by a law enforcement agency or the clearinghouse regarding a missing child under 11 years of age, the school, day care facility, or birth certificate agency shall maintain the child's records in its possession so that on receipt of a request regarding the child, the school, day care facility, or agency will be able to notify law enforcement or the clearinghouse that a request for a flagged record has been made.

(b) When a request concerning a flagged record is made in person, the school, day care facility, or agency may not advise the requesting party that the request concerns a missing child and shall:

(1) require the person requesting the flagged record to complete a form stating the person's name, address, telephone number, and relationship to the child for whom a request is made and the name, address, and birth date of the child;

(2) obtain a copy of the requesting party's driver's license or other photographic identification, if possible;

(3) if the request is for a birth certificate, inform the requesting party that a copy of a certificate will be sent by mail; and

(4) immediately notify the appropriate law enforcement agency that a request has been made concerning a flagged record and include a physical description of the requesting party, the identity and address of the requesting party, and a copy of the requesting party's driver's license or other photographic identification.

(c) After providing the notification required under Subsection (a)(4), the school, day care facility, or agency shall mail a copy of the requested record to the requesting party on or after the 21st day after the date of the request.

(d) When a request concerning a flagged record is made in writing, the school, day care facility, or agency may not advise the party that the request concerns a missing child and shall immediately notify the appropriate law enforcement agency that a request has been made concerning a flagged record and provide to the law enforcement agency a copy of the written request. After providing the notification under this subsection, the school, day care facility, or agency shall mail a copy of the requested record to the requesting party on or after the 21st day after the date of the request.

Added by Acts 1997, 75th Leg., ch. 1084, § 2, eff. Sept. 1, 1997. Renumbered from V.T.C.A., Human Resources Code § 79.019 by Acts 1999, 76th Leg., ch. 62, § 19.01(8)(B), eff. Sept. 1, 1999.

Art. 63.022. Removal of Flag From Records

(a) On the return of a missing child under 11 years of age, the law enforcement agency shall notify each school or day care facility that has maintained flagged records for the child and the bureau of vital statistics that the child is no longer missing. The law enforcement agency shall notify the clearinghouse that notification under this section has been made. The bureau of vital statistics shall notify the appropriate municipal or county birth certificate agency. The clearinghouse shall notify the school, day care facility, or bureau of vital statistics that the missing child is no longer missing if the clearinghouse determines that the notification was not provided by the law enforcement agency.

(b) On notification by the law enforcement agency or the clearinghouse that a missing child has been recovered, the school, day care facility, or birth certificate agency that maintained flagged records shall remove the flag from the records.

(c) A school, day care facility, or birth certificate agency that has reason to believe a missing child has been recovered may request confirmation that the missing child has been recovered from the appropriate law enforcement agency or the clearinghouse. If a response is not received after the 45th day after the date of the request for confirmation, the school, day care facility, or birth certificate agency may remove the flag from the record and shall inform the law enforcement agency or the clearinghouse that the flag has been removed.

Added by Acts 1997, 75th Leg., ch. 1084, § 2, eff. Sept. 1, 1997. Renumbered from V.T.C.A., Human Resources Code § 79.020 by Acts 1999, 76th Leg., ch. 62, § 19.01(8)(B), eff. Sept. 1, 1999.

SUBCHAPTER B. UNIVERSITY OF NORTH TEXAS HEALTH SCIENCE CENTER AT FORT WORTH MISSING PERSONS DNA DATABASE

Art. 63.051. Definitions

In this subchapter:

(1) "Board" means the board of regents of the University of North Texas System.

(2) "Center" means the University of North Texas Health Science Center at Fort Worth.

(3) "DNA" means deoxyribonucleic acid.

(4) "DNA database" means the database containing forensic DNA analysis results, including any known name of the person who is the subject of the forensic DNA analysis, that is maintained by the center.

(5) "High–risk missing person" means:

(A) a person missing as a result of an abduction by a stranger;

(B) a person missing under suspicious or unknown circumstances; or

(C) a person who has been missing more than 30 days, or less than 30 days at the discretion of the investigating agency, if there is reason to believe that the person is in danger or deceased.

(6) "Law enforcement agency" means the law enforcement agency primarily responsible for investigating a report of a high-risk missing person.

Added by Acts 2001, 77th Leg., ch. 1496, § 1, eff. Sept. 1, 2001. Renumbered from V.T.C.A., Education Code § 105.111 by Acts 2003, 78th Leg., ch. 1275, § 2(48), eff. Sept. 1, 2003. Redesignated from V.T.C.A., Education Code § 105.451 and amended by Acts 2005, 79th Leg., ch. 319, § 2, eff. June 17, 2005.

Art. 63.0515. Criminal Justice Agency

For purposes of this subchapter, the center is a criminal justice agency that performs forensic DNA analyses on evidence, including evidence related to a case involving unidentified human remains or a high-risk missing person. The center shall comply with 42 U.S.C. Section 14132.

Added by Acts 2011, 82nd Leg., ch. 320 (H.B. 2385), § 1, eff. June 17, 2011.

Art. 63.052. Establishment of DNA Database for Missing or Unidentified Persons

(a) The board shall develop at the University of North Texas Health Science Center at Fort Worth a DNA database for any case based on the report of unidentified human remains or a report of a high-risk missing person.

(b) The database may be used to identify unidentified human remains and high-risk missing persons.

(c) Repealed by Acts 2011, 82nd Leg., ch. 320 (H.B. 2385), § 3.

Added by Acts 2001, 77th Leg., ch. 1496, § 1, eff. Sept. 1, 2001. Renumbered from V.T.C.A., Education Code § 105.112 by Acts 2003, 78th Leg., ch. 1275, § 2(48), eff. Sept. 1, 2003. Redesignated from V.T.C.A., Education Code § 105.452 and amended by Acts 2005, 79th Leg., ch. 319, § 2, eff. June 17, 2005. Amended by Acts 2011, 82nd Leg., ch. 320 (H.B. 2385), §§ 2, 3, eff. June 17, 2011.

Art. 63.053. Information Stored in Database

(a) The database required in Article 63.052 may contain only DNA genetic markers that are commonly recognized as appropriate for human identification. Except to the extent that those markers are appropriate for human identification, the database may not contain DNA genetic markers that predict biological function. The center shall select the DNA genetic markers for inclusion in the DNA database based on existing technology for forensic DNA analysis.

(b) The results of the forensic DNA analysis must be compatible with the CODIS DNA database established by the Federal Bureau of Investigation and the center must make the results available for inclusion in that database.

Added by Acts 2001, 77th Leg., ch. 1496, § 1, eff. Sept. 1, 2001. Renumbered from V.T.C.A., Education Code § 105.113 and amended by Acts 2003, 78th Leg., ch. 1275, §§ 2(48), 3(18), eff. Sept. 1, 2003. Redesignated from V.T.C.A., Education Code § 105.453 and amended by Acts 2005, 79th Leg., ch. 319, § 2, eff. June 17, 2005.

Art. 63.054. Comparison of Samples

The center shall compare DNA samples taken from unidentified human remains with DNA samples taken from personal articles belonging to high-risk missing persons or from parents of high-risk missing persons or other appropriate persons.

Added by Acts 2001, 77th Leg., ch. 1496, § 1, eff. Sept. 1, 2001. Renumbered from V.T.C.A., Education Code § 105.114 by Acts 2003, 78th Leg., ch. 1275, § 2(48), eff. Sept. 1, 2003. Redesignated from V.T.C.A., Education Code § 105.454 and amended by Acts 2005, 79th Leg., ch. 319, § 2, eff. June 17, 2005.

Art. 63.055. Standards Collection; Storage

In consultation with the center, the board by rule shall develop standards and guidelines for the collection of DNA samples submitted to the center and the center's storage of DNA samples.

Added by Acts 2001, 77th Leg., ch. 1496, § 1, eff. Sept. 1, 2001. Renumbered from V.T.C.A., Education Code § 105.115 by Acts 2003, 78th Leg., ch. 1275, § 2(48), eff. Sept. 1, 2003. Redesignated from V.T.C.A., Education Code § 105.455 and amended by Acts 2005, 79th Leg., ch. 319, § 2, eff. June 17, 2005.

Art. 63.056. Collection of Samples From Unidentified Human Remains

(a) A physician acting on the request of a justice of the peace under Subchapter A, Chapter 49, a county coroner, a county medical examiner, or other law enforcement entity, as appropriate, shall collect samples from unidentified human remains. The justice of the peace, coroner, medical examiner, or other law enforcement entity shall submit those samples to the center for forensic DNA analysis and inclusion of the results in the DNA database.

(b) After the center has performed the forensic DNA analysis, the center shall return the remaining sample to the entity that submitted the sample under Subsection (a).

Added by Acts 2001, 77th Leg., ch. 1496, § 1, eff. Sept. 1, 2001. Renumbered from V.T.C.A., Education Code § 105.116 by Acts 2003, 78th Leg., ch. 1275, § 2(48), eff. Sept. 1, 2003. Redesignated from V.T.C.A., Education Code § 105.456 and amended by Acts 2005, 79th Leg., ch. 319, § 2, eff. June 17, 2005.

Art. 63.057. Duty of Law Enforcement Agency to Notify Appropriate Persons Regarding Provision of Voluntary Sample

Not later than the 30th day after the date a report of a high-risk missing person is filed, the law enforcement agency shall inform a parent or any other person considered appropriate by the agency that the person may provide:

(1) a DNA sample for forensic DNA analysis; or

(2) for purposes of DNA sampling, a personal article belonging to the high-risk missing person.

Added by Acts 2001, 77th Leg., ch. 1496, § 1, eff. Sept. 1, 2001. Renumbered from V.T.C.A., Education Code § 105.117 by Acts 2003, 78th Leg., ch. 1275, § 2(48), eff. Sept. 1, 2003. Redesignated from V.T.C.A., Education Code § 105.457 and amended by Acts 2005, 79th Leg., ch. 319, § 2, eff. June 17, 2005.

Art. 63.058. Release Form

(a) The center shall develop a standard release form that authorizes a parent or other appropriate person to voluntarily provide under Article 63.057 a DNA sample or a personal article for purposes of DNA sampling. The release must explain that the DNA sample is to be used only to identify the high-risk missing person.

(b) A law enforcement agency may not use any form of incentive or coercion to compel the parent or other appropriate person to provide a sample or article under this subchapter.

Added by Acts 2001, 77th Leg., ch. 1496, § 1, eff. Sept. 1, 2001. Renumbered from V.T.C.A., Education Code § 105.118 and amended by Acts 2003, 78th Leg., ch. 1275, §§ 2(48), 3(19), eff. Sept. 1, 2003. Redesignated from V.T.C.A., Education Code § 105.458 and amended by Acts 2005, 79th Leg., ch. 319, § 2, eff. June 17, 2005.

Art. 63.059. Protocol for Obtaining Samples Relating to High-risk Missing Persons

(a) The law enforcement agency shall take DNA samples from parents or other appropriate persons under Article 63.057 in any manner prescribed by the center.

(b) The center shall develop a model kit to be used by a law enforcement agency to take DNA samples from parents or other appropriate persons.

Added by Acts 2001, 77th Leg., ch. 1496, § 1, eff. Sept. 1, 2001. Renumbered from V.T.C.A., Education Code § 105.119 and amended by Acts 2003, 78th Leg., ch. 1275, §§ 2(48), 3(20), eff. Sept. 1, 2003. Redesignated from V.T.C.A., Education Code § 105.459 and amended by Acts 2005, 79th Leg., ch. 319, § 2, eff. June 17, 2005.

Art. 63.060. Submission of Sample to Center

(a) Before submitting to the center a DNA sample obtained under Article 63.057, the law enforcement agency shall reverify the status of a high-risk missing person.

(b) As soon as practicable after a DNA sample is obtained, the law enforcement agency shall submit the DNA sample, a copy of the missing person's report, and any supplemental information to the center.

Added by Acts 2001, 77th Leg., ch. 1496, § 1, eff. Sept. 1, 2001. Renumbered from V.T.C.A., Education Code § 105.120 and amended by Acts 2003, 78th Leg., ch. 1275, §§ 2(48), 3(21), eff. Sept. 1, 2003. Redesignated from V.T.C.A., Education Code § 105.460 and amended by Acts 2005, 79th Leg., ch. 319, § 2, eff. June 17, 2005.

Art. 63.061. Destruction of Samples

All DNA samples extracted from a living person shall be destroyed after a positive identification is made and a report is issued.

Added by Acts 2001, 77th Leg., ch. 1496, § 1, eff. Sept. 1, 2001. Renumbered from V.T.C.A., Education Code § 105.121 by Acts 2003, 78th Leg., ch. 1275, § 2(48), eff. Sept. 1, 2003. Redesignated from V.T.C.A., Education Code § 105.461 and amended by Acts 2005, 79th Leg., ch. 319, § 2, eff. June 17, 2005.

Art. 63.062. Confidentiality

(a) Except as provided by Subsection (b), the results of a forensic DNA analysis performed by the center are confidential.

(b) The center may disclose the results of a forensic DNA analysis only to:

(1) personnel of the center;

(2) law enforcement agencies;

(3) justices of the peace, coroners, medical examiners, or other law enforcement entities submitting a sample to the center under Article 63.056;

(4) attorneys representing the state; and

(5) a parent or other appropriate person voluntarily providing a DNA sample or an article under Article 63.057.

Added by Acts 2001, 77th Leg., ch. 1496, § 1, eff. Sept. 1, 2001. Renumbered from V.T.C.A., Education Code § 105.122 and amended by Acts 2003, 78th Leg., ch. 1275, §§ 2(48), 3(22), eff. Sept. 1, 2003. Redesignated from V.T.C.A., Education Code § 105.462 and amended by Acts 2005, 79th Leg., ch. 319, § 2, eff. June 17, 2005.

Art. 63.063. Criminal Penalty

(a) A person who collects, processes, or stores a DNA sample from a living person for forensic DNA analysis under this subchapter commits an offense if the person intentionally violates Article 63.061 or 63.062.

(b) An offense under this section is a Class B misdemeanor.

Added by Acts 2001, 77th Leg., ch. 1496, § 1, eff. Sept. 1, 2001. Renumbered from V.T.C.A., Education Code § 105.123 and amended by Acts 2003, 78th Leg., ch. 1275, §§ 2(48), 3(23), eff. Sept. 1, 2003. Redesignated from V.T.C.A., Education Code § 105.463 and amended by Acts 2005, 79th Leg., ch. 319, § 2, eff. June 17, 2005.

Art. 63.064. Civil Penalty

A person who collects, processes, or stores a DNA sample from a living person for forensic DNA analysis under this subchapter and who intentionally violates Article 63.061 or 63.062 is liable in civil damages to the donor of the DNA in the amount of $5,000 for each violation, plus reasonable attorney's fees and court costs.

Added by Acts 2001, 77th Leg., ch. 1496, § 1, eff. Sept. 1, 2001. Renumbered from V.T.C.A., Education Code § 105.124 and amended by Acts 2003, 78th Leg., ch. 1275, §§ 2(48), 3(24), eff. Sept. 1, 2003. Redesignated from V.T.C.A., Education Code § 105.464 and amended by Acts 2005, 79th Leg., ch. 319, § 2, eff. June 17, 2005.

Art. 63.065. Missing Persons DNA Database Fund

(a) The missing persons DNA database fund is a separate account in the general revenue fund.

(b) Notwithstanding Article 56.54(g), the legislature may appropriate money in the compensation to victims of crime fund and the compensation to victims of crime auxiliary fund to fund the University of North Texas Health Science Center at Fort Worth missing persons DNA database. Legislative appropriations under this subsection shall be deposited to the credit of the account created under Subsection (a).

(c) Money in the account may be used only for purposes of developing and maintaining the DNA database as described by this section.

(d) The center may use money in the account only to:

(1) establish and maintain center infrastructure;

(2) pay the costs of DNA sample storage, forensic DNA analysis, and labor costs for cases of high-risk missing persons and unidentified human remains;

(3) reimburse counties for the purposes of pathology and exhumation as considered necessary by the center;

(4) publicize the DNA database for the purpose of contacting parents and other appropriate persons so that they may provide a DNA sample or a personal article for DNA sampling;

(5) educate law enforcement officers about the DNA database and DNA sampling; and

(6) provide outreach programs related to the purposes of this chapter.

(e) Section 403.095(b), Government Code, does not apply to the account established under Subsection (a).

Added by Acts 2001, 77th Leg., ch. 1496, § 1, eff. Sept. 1, 2001. Renumbered from V.T.C.A., Education Code § 105.125 by Acts 2003, 78th Leg., ch. 1275, § 2(48), eff. Sept. 1, 2003. Redesignated from V.T.C.A., Education Code § 105.465 and amended by Acts 2005, 79th Leg., ch. 319, § 2, eff. June 17, 2005.

Art. 63.066. Backlog of Unidentified Human Remains: Advisory Committee and Outsourcing

(a) The center shall create an advisory committee, consisting of medical examiners, law enforcement officials, and other interested persons as determined appropriate by the center, to impose priorities regarding the identification of the backlog of high-risk missing person cases and unidentified human remains.

(b) The center shall use any available federal funding to assist in reducing the backlog of high-risk missing person cases and unidentified human remains.

(c) The reduction of the backlog may be outsourced to other appropriate laboratories at the center's discretion.

Added by Acts 2001, 77th Leg., ch. 1496, § 1, eff. Sept. 1, 2001. Renumbered from V.T.C.A., Education Code § 105.126 by Acts 2003, 78th Leg., ch. 1275, § 2(48), eff. Sept. 1, 2003. Redesignated from V.T.C.A., Education Code § 105.466 and amended by Acts 2005, 79th Leg., ch. 319, § 2, eff. June 17, 2005.

Art. 63.067.   Expired

CHAPTER 64.   MOTION FOR FORENSIC DNA TESTING

Art. 64.01.   Motion

(a) In this section, "biological material":

(1) means an item that is in possession of the state and that contains blood, semen, hair, saliva, skin tissue or cells, fingernail scrapings, bone, bodily fluids, or other identifiable biological evidence that may be suitable for forensic DNA testing; and

(2) includes the contents of a sexual assault evidence collection kit.

(a–1) A convicted person may submit to the convicting court a motion for forensic DNA testing of evidence that has a reasonable likelihood of containing biological material. The motion must be accompanied by an affidavit, sworn to by the convicted person, containing statements of fact in support of the motion.

(b) The motion may request forensic DNA testing only of evidence described by Subsection (a–1) that was secured in relation to the offense that is the basis of the challenged conviction and was in the possession of the state during the trial of the offense, but:

(1) was not previously subjected to DNA testing; or

(2) although previously subjected to DNA testing:

(A) can be subjected to testing with newer testing techniques that provide a reasonable likelihood of

results that are more accurate and probative than the results of the previous test; or

(B) was tested:

(i) at a laboratory that ceased conducting DNA testing after an audit by the Texas Forensic Science Commission revealed the laboratory engaged in faulty testing practices; and

(ii) during the period identified in the audit as involving faulty testing practices.

(c) A convicted person is entitled to counsel during a proceeding under this chapter. The convicting court shall appoint counsel for the convicted person if the person informs the court that the person wishes to submit a motion under this chapter, the court finds reasonable grounds for a motion to be filed, and the court determines that the person is indigent. Counsel must be appointed under this subsection not later than the 45th day after the date the court finds reasonable grounds or the date the court determines that the person is indigent, whichever is later. Compensation of counsel is provided in the same manner as is required by:

(1) Article 11.071 for the representation of a petitioner convicted of a capital felony; and

(2) Chapter 26 for the representation in a habeas corpus hearing of an indigent defendant convicted of a felony other than a capital felony.

Added by Acts 2001, 77th Leg., ch. 2, § 2, eff. April 5, 2001. Amended by Acts 2003, 78th Leg., ch. 13, § 1, eff. Sept. 1, 2003; Acts 2007, 80th Leg., ch. 1006, § 2, eff. Sept. 1, 2007; Acts 2011, 82nd Leg., ch. 278 (H.B. 1573), § 5, eff. Sept. 1, 2011; Acts 2011, 82nd Leg., ch. 366 (S.B. 122), § 1, eff. Sept. 1, 2011; Acts 2015, 84th Leg., ch. 70 (S.B. 487), § 1, eff. Sept. 1, 2015; Acts 2017, 85th Leg., ch. 903 (H.B. 3872), § 2, eff. June 15, 2017.

Section 3 of Acts 2015, 84th Leg., ch. 70 (S.B. 487) provides:

"The change in law made by this Act applies to a motion for forensic DNA testing filed on or after the effective date [Sept. 1, 2015] of this Act. A motion for forensic DNA testing filed before the effective date of this Act is governed by the law in effect on the date the motion was filed, and the former law is continued in effect for that purpose."

Art. 64.011.   Guardians and Other Representatives

(a) In this chapter, "guardian of a convicted person" means a person who is the legal guardian of the convicted person, whether the legal relationship between the guardian and convicted person exists because of the age of the convicted person or because of the physical or mental incompetency of the convicted person.

(b) A guardian of a convicted person may submit motions for the convicted person under this chapter and is entitled to counsel otherwise provided to a convicted person under this chapter.

Added by Acts 2003, 78th Leg., ch. 13, § 2, eff. Sept. 1, 2003.

Art. 64.02. Notice to State; Response

(a) On receipt of the motion, the convicting court shall:

(1) provide the attorney representing the state with a copy of the motion; and

(2) require the attorney representing the state to take one of the following actions in response to the motion not later than the 60th day after the date the motion is served on the attorney representing the state:

(A) deliver the evidence to the court, along with a description of the condition of the evidence; or

(B) explain in writing to the court why the state cannot deliver the evidence to the court.

(b) The convicting court may proceed under Article 64.03 after the response period described by Subsection (a)(2) has expired, regardless of whether the attorney representing the state submitted a response under that subsection.

Added by Acts 2001, 77th Leg., ch. 2, § 2, eff. April 5, 2001. Amended by Acts 2007, 80th Leg., ch. 1006, § 3, eff. Sept. 1, 2007.

Art. 64.03. Requirements; Testing

(a) A convicting court may order forensic DNA testing under this chapter only if:

(1) the court finds that:

(A) the evidence:

(i) still exists and is in a condition making DNA testing possible; and

(ii) has been subjected to a chain of custody sufficient to establish that it has not been substituted, tampered with, replaced, or altered in any material respect;

(B) there is a reasonable likelihood that the evidence contains biological material suitable for DNA testing; and

(C) identity was or is an issue in the case; and

(2) the convicted person establishes by a preponderance of the evidence that:

(A) the person would not have been convicted if exculpatory results had been obtained through DNA testing; and

(B) the request for the proposed DNA testing is not made to unreasonably delay the execution of sentence or administration of justice.

(b) A convicted person who pleaded guilty or nolo contendere or, whether before or after conviction, made a confession or similar admission in the case may submit a motion under this chapter, and the convicting court is prohibited from finding that identity was not an issue in the case solely on the basis of that plea, confession, or admission, as applicable.

(b–1) Notwithstanding Subsection (c), a convicting court shall order that the requested DNA testing be done with respect to evidence described by Article 64.01(b)(2)(B) if the court finds in the affirmative the issues listed in Subsection (a)(1), regardless of whether the convicted person meets the requirements of Subsection (a)(2). The court may order the test to be conducted by any laboratory that the court may order to conduct a test under Subsection (c).

(c) If the convicting court finds in the affirmative the issues listed in Subsection (a)(1) and the convicted person meets the requirements of Subsection (a)(2), the court shall order that the requested forensic DNA testing be conducted. The court may order the test to be conducted by:

(1) the Department of Public Safety;

(2) a laboratory operating under a contract with the department; or

(3) on the request of the convicted person, another laboratory if that laboratory is accredited under Article 38.01.

(d) If the convicting court orders that the forensic DNA testing be conducted by a laboratory other than a Department of Public Safety laboratory or a laboratory under contract with the department, the State of Texas is not liable for the cost of testing under this subsection unless good cause for payment of that cost has been shown. A political subdivision of the state is not liable for the cost of testing under this subsection, regardless of whether good cause for payment of that cost has been shown. If the court orders that the testing be conducted by a laboratory described by this subsection, the court shall include in the order requirements that:

(1) the DNA testing be conducted in a timely and efficient manner under reasonable conditions designed

to protect the integrity of the evidence and the testing process;

(2) the DNA testing employ a scientific method sufficiently reliable and relevant to be admissible under Rule 702, Texas Rules of Evidence; and

(3) on completion of the DNA testing, the results of the testing and all data related to the testing required for an evaluation of the test results be immediately filed with the court and copies of the results and data be served on the convicted person and the attorney representing the state.

(e) The convicting court, not later than the 30th day after the conclusion of a proceeding under this chapter, shall forward the results to the Department of Public Safety.

Added by Acts 2001, 77th Leg., ch. 2, § 2, eff. April 5, 2001. Amended by Acts 2003, 78th Leg., ch. 13, § 3, eff. Sept. 1, 2003; Acts 2007, 80th Leg., ch. 1006, § 4, eff. Sept. 1, 2007; Acts 2015, 84th Leg., ch. 70 (S.B. 487), § 2, eff. Sept. 1, 2015; Acts 2015, 84th Leg., ch. 1276 (S.B. 1287), § 11, eff. Sept. 1, 2015; Acts 2017, 85th Leg., ch. 903 (H.B. 3872), § 3, eff. June 15, 2017.

Section 3 of Acts 2015, 84th Leg., ch. 70 (S.B. 487) provides:

"The change in law made by this Act applies to a motion for forensic DNA testing filed on or after the effective date [Sept. 1, 2015] of this Act. A motion for forensic DNA testing filed before the effective date of this Act is governed by the law in effect on the date the motion was filed, and the former law is continued in effect for that purpose."

Art. 64.035. Unidentified DNA Profiles

If an analyzed sample meets the applicable requirements of state or federal submission policies, on completion of the testing under Article 64.03, the convicting court shall order any unidentified DNA profile to be compared with the DNA profiles in:

(1) the DNA database established by the Federal Bureau of Investigation; and

(2) the DNA database maintained by the Department of Public Safety under Subchapter G, Chapter 411, Government Code.

Added by Acts 2011, 82nd Leg., ch. 278 (H.B. 1573), § 6, eff. Sept. 1, 2011; Acts 2011, 82nd Leg., ch. 366 (S.B. 122), § 2, eff. Sept. 1, 2011.

Art. 64.04. Finding

After examining the results of testing under Article 64.03 and any comparison of a DNA profile under Article 64.035, the convicting court shall hold a hearing and make a finding as to whether, had the results been available during the trial of the offense, it is reasonably probable that the person would not have been convicted.

Added by Acts 2001, 77th Leg., ch. 2, § 2, eff. April 5, 2001. Amended by Acts 2003, 78th Leg., ch. 13, § 4, eff. Sept. 1, 2003; Acts 2011, 82nd Leg., ch. 278 (H.B. 1573), § 7, eff. Sept. 1, 2011; Acts 2011, 82nd Leg., ch. 366 (S.B. 122), § 3, eff. Sept. 1, 2011.

Art. 64.05. Appeals

An appeal under this chapter is to a court of appeals in the same manner as an appeal of any other criminal matter, except that if the convicted person was convicted in a capital case and was sentenced to death, the appeal is a direct appeal to the court of criminal appeals.

Added by Acts 2001, 77th Leg., ch. 2, § 2, eff. April 5, 2001. Amended by Acts 2003, 78th Leg., ch. 13, § 5, eff. Sept. 1, 2003.

CHAPTER 66. CRIMINAL HISTORY RECORD SYSTEM

SUBCHAPTER A. GENERAL PROVISIONS

Art. 66.001. Definitions

Text of article effective Jan. 1, 2019

In this chapter:

(1) "Administration of criminal justice" means the detection, apprehension, detention, pretrial release, post-trial release, prosecution, adjudication, correctional supervision, or rehabilitation of an offender. The term includes criminal identification activities and the collection, storage, and dissemination of criminal history record information.

(2) "Computerized criminal history system" means the database containing arrest, disposition, and other criminal history maintained by the Department of Public Safety.

(3) "Corrections tracking system" means the database maintained by the Texas Department of Criminal Justice on all offenders under the department's supervision.

(4) "Council" means the Criminal Justice Policy Council.

(5) "Criminal justice agency" means a federal or state agency that is engaged in the administration of criminal justice under a statute or executive order and allocates a substantial part of the agency's annual budget to the administration of criminal justice.

(6) "Criminal justice information system" means the computerized criminal history system and the corrections tracking system.

(7) "Disposition" means an action that results in the termination, transfer to another jurisdiction, or indeterminate suspension of the prosecution of a criminal charge.

(8) "Electronic means" means the transmission of data between word processors, data processors, or similar automated information equipment over dedicated cables, commercial lines, or other similar methods of transmission.

(9) "Incident number" means the unique number assigned to a specific person during a specific arrest.

(10) "Offender" means any person who is assigned an incident number.

(11) "Offense code" means the numeric code for each offense category.

(12) "Release" means the termination of jurisdiction over an individual by the criminal justice system.

(13) "State identification number" means the unique number assigned by the Department of Public Safety to each person whose name appears in the criminal justice information system. (Code Crim. Proc., Arts. 60.01(1), (3), (4), (5), (6), (7), (8), (9), (10), (11), (13), (14), (16).)

Added by Acts 2017, 85th Leg., ch. 1058 (H.B. 2931), § 1.03, eff. Jan. 1, 2019.

SUBCHAPTER B. CRIMINAL JUSTICE INFORMATION SYSTEM

Art. 66.051. Purpose and Functions

Text of article effective Jan. 1, 2019

The criminal justice information system shall be maintained to supply the state with a system:

(1) that provides an accurate criminal history record depository to:

(A) law enforcement officers; and

(B) criminal justice agencies for operational decision making;

(2) from which accurate criminal justice system modeling can be conducted; and

(3) that improves:

(A) the quality of data used to conduct impact analyses of proposed legislative changes in the criminal justice system; and

(B) the ability of interested parties to analyze the functioning of the criminal justice system. (Code Crim. Proc., Art. 60.02(c).)

Added by Acts 2017, 85th Leg., ch. 1058 (H.B. 2931), § 1.03, eff. Jan. 1, 2019.

Art. 66.052. Implementation and Operation of Criminal Justice Information System

Text of article effective Jan. 1, 2019

(a) The Department of Public Safety shall designate offense codes and has the sole responsibility for designating the state identification number for each person whose name appears in the criminal justice information system.

(b) The Department of Public Safety and the Texas Department of Criminal Justice shall implement a system to link the computerized criminal history system and the corrections tracking system. (Code Crim. Proc., Arts. 60.02(e), (f) (part).)

Added by Acts 2017, 85th Leg., ch. 1058 (H.B. 2931), § 1.03, eff. Jan. 1, 2019.

Art. 66.053. Information Collected

Text of article effective Jan. 1, 2019

For each arrest for a felony or misdemeanor other than a misdemeanor punishable by fine only, the criminal justice information system must include information relating to:

(1) offenders;

(2) arrests;

(3) prosecutions;

(4) the disposition of cases by courts;

(5) sentencing; and

(6) the handling of offenders received by a correctional agency, facility, or other institution. (Code Crim. Proc., Art. 60.05.)

Added by Acts 2017, 85th Leg., ch. 1058 (H.B. 2931), § 1.03, eff. Jan. 1, 2019.

Art. 66.054. Fingerprint and Arrest Information in Criminal Justice Information System

Text of article effective Jan. 1, 2019

(a) When a jurisdiction transmits fingerprints and arrest information by a remote terminal accessing the statewide automated fingerprint identification system, the Department of Public Safety shall use that transmission to create:

(1) a permanent record in the criminal justice information system; or

(2) a temporary arrest record in the criminal justice information system to be maintained by the department until the department receives and processes the physical copy of the arrest information.

(b) The Department of Public Safety shall make available to a criminal justice agency making a background criminal inquiry any information contained in a temporary arrest record maintained by the department, including a statement that a physical copy of the arrest information was not available at the time the information was entered in the criminal justice information system. (Code Crim. Proc., Art. 60.12.)

Added by Acts 2017, 85th Leg., ch. 1058 (H.B. 2931), § 1.03, eff. Jan. 1, 2019.

SUBCHAPTER C. COMPUTERIZED CRIMINAL HISTORY SYSTEM

Art. 66.101. Computerized Criminal History System Database

Text of article effective Jan. 1, 2019

(a) The Department of Public Safety shall record data and maintain the computerized criminal history system that serves as the record creation point for criminal history information maintained by the state.

(b) The computerized criminal history system must contain the information required by this chapter.

(c) The Department of Public Safety shall operate the computerized criminal history system and develop the necessary interfaces in the system to accommodate inquiries from the statewide automated fingerprint identification system implemented by the department. (Code Crim. Proc., Arts. 60.02(b), (d), (g).)

Added by Acts 2017, 85th Leg., ch. 1058 (H.B. 2931), § 1.03, eff. Jan. 1, 2019.

Art. 66.102. Information Contained in Computerized Criminal History System

Text of article effective Jan. 1, 2019

(a) In this article:

(1) "Appeal" means the review of a decision of a lower court by a superior court other than by collateral attack.

(2) "Rejected case" means:

(A) a charge that, after the arrest of the offender, the prosecutor declines to include in an information or present to a grand jury; or

(B) an information or indictment that, after the arrest of the offender, the prosecutor refuses to prosecute.

(b) Information in the computerized criminal history system relating to an offender must include the offender's:

(1) name, including other names by which the offender is known;

(2) date of birth;

(3) physical description, including sex, weight, height, race, ethnicity, eye color, hair color, scars, marks, and tattoos; and

(4) state identification number.

(c) Information in the computerized criminal history system relating to an arrest must include:

(1) the offender's name;

(2) the offender's state identification number;

(3) the arresting law enforcement agency;

(4) the arrest charge, by offense code and incident number;

(5) whether the arrest charge is a misdemeanor or felony;

(6) the date of the arrest;

(7) the exact disposition of the case by a law enforcement agency following the arrest; and

(8) the date of disposition of the case by the law enforcement agency.

(d) Information in the computerized criminal history system relating to a prosecution must include:

(1) each charged offense, by offense code and incident number;

(2) the level of the offense charged or the degree of the offense charged for each offense in Subdivision (1); and

(3) for a rejected case:

(A) the date of rejection;

(B) the offense code;

(C) the incident number; and

(D) whether the rejection is a result of a successful pretrial diversion program.

(e) Information in the computerized criminal history system relating to the disposition of a case other than a rejected case must include:

(1) the final pleading to each charged offense and the level of the offense;

(2) a listing of each charged offense disposed of by the court and:

(A) the date of disposition;

(B) the offense code for the disposed charge and incident number; and

(C) the type of disposition; and

(3) for a conviction that is appealed, the final court decision and the final disposition of the offender's case on appeal.

(f) Information in the computerized criminal history system relating to sentencing must include for each sentence:

(1) the sentencing date;

(2) the sentence for each offense, by offense code and incident number;

(3) if the offender was sentenced to confinement:

(A) the agency that receives custody of the offender;

(B) the length of the sentence for each offense; and

(C) if multiple sentences were ordered, whether the sentences were ordered to be served consecutively or concurrently;

(4) if the offender was sentenced to pay a fine, the amount of the fine;

(5) if a sentence to pay a fine or to confinement was ordered but was deferred, probated, suspended, or otherwise not imposed:

(A) the length of the sentence or the amount of the fine that was deferred, probated, suspended, or otherwise not imposed; and

(B) the offender's name, offense code, and incident number; and

(6) if a sentence other than a fine or confinement was ordered, a description of the sentence ordered.

(g) The Department of Public Safety shall maintain in the computerized criminal history system any information the department maintains in the central database under Article 62.005.

(h) In addition to the information described by this article, information in the computerized criminal history system must include the age of the victim of the offense if the offender was arrested for or charged with an offense under the following provisions of the Penal Code:

(1) Section 20.04(a)(4) (Aggravated Kidnapping), if the offender committed the offense with the intent to violate or abuse the victim sexually;

(2) Section 20A.02 (Trafficking of Persons), if the offender:

(A) trafficked a person with the intent or knowledge that the person would engage in sexual conduct, as defined by Section 43.25, Penal Code; or

(B) benefited from participating in a venture that involved a trafficked person engaging in sexual conduct, as defined by Section 43.25, Penal Code;

(3) Section 21.02 (Continuous Sexual Abuse of Young Child or Children);

(4) Section 21.11 (Indecency with a Child);

(5) Section 22.011 (Sexual Assault) or 22.021 (Aggravated Sexual Assault);

(6) Section 30.02 (Burglary), if the offense is punishable under Subsection (d) of that section and the offender committed the offense with the intent to commit an offense described by Subdivision (1), (4), or (5);

(7) Section 43.05(a)(2) (Compelling Prostitution); or

(8) Section 43.25 (Sexual Performance by a Child). (Code Crim. Proc., Arts. 60.01(2), (12), 60.051.)

Added by Acts 2017, 85th Leg., ch. 1058 (H.B. 2931), § 1.03, eff. Jan. 1, 2019.

Art. 66.103.   Duties of Texas Department of Criminal Justice Regarding Criminal Justice Information System

Text of article effective Jan. 1, 2019

Data received by the Texas Department of Criminal Justice that is required by the Department of Public Safety for the preparation of a criminal history record shall be made available to the computerized criminal history system not later than the seventh day after the date on which the Texas Department of Criminal Justice receives the request for the data from the Department of Public Safety. (Code Crim. Proc., Art. 60.02(f) (part).)

Added by Acts 2017, 85th Leg., ch. 1058 (H.B. 2931), § 1.03, eff. Jan. 1, 2019.

Art. 66.104.   Duties of Licensing Agencies to Provide Information Regarding License Holders

Text of article effective Jan. 1, 2019

(a) The Texas Medical Board, the Texas State Board of Podiatric Medical Examiners, the State Board of Dental Examiners, the Texas State Board of Pharmacy, the Texas State Board of Examiners of Psychologists, and the State Board of Veterinary Medical Examiners shall provide to the Department of Public Safety through electronic means, magnetic tape, or disk, as specified by the department, a list of each person licensed by the respective agency, including the person's name and date of birth and any other personal descriptive information required by the department. Each agency shall update the information and submit the updated information quarterly to the department.

(b) The Department of Public Safety shall:

(1) perform at least quarterly a computer match of the licensing list against the convictions maintained in the computerized criminal history system; and

(2) report to the appropriate licensing agency for verification and administrative action, as considered appropriate by the licensing agency, the name of any person found to have a record of conviction, other than a defendant whose prosecution is deferred during a period of community supervision without an adjudication of guilt or a plea of guilty.

(c) The Department of Public Safety may charge a licensing agency a fee not to exceed the actual direct cost incurred by the department in performing a computer match and reporting to the agency under Subsection (b).

(d) The transmission of information by electronic means under Subsection (a) does not affect whether the information is subject to disclosure under Chapter 552, Government Code. (Code Crim. Proc., Art. 60.061.)

Added by Acts 2017, 85th Leg., ch. 1058 (H.B. 2931), § 1.03, eff. Jan. 1, 2019.

Art. 66.105.   Information Related to Misused Identity

Text of article effective Jan. 1, 2019

(a) On receipt of information from a local law enforcement agency under Article 2.28, the Department of Public Safety shall:

(1) provide the notice described by Article 2.28(1) to the person whose identity was misused, if the local law enforcement agency was unable to notify the person under that subdivision;

(2) take action to ensure that the information maintained in the computerized criminal history system reflects the use of the person's identity as a stolen alias; and

(3) notify the Texas Department of Criminal Justice that the person's identifying information may have been falsely used by an inmate in the custody of the Texas Department of Criminal Justice.

(b) On receipt of a declaration under Section 411.0421, Government Code, or on receipt of information similar to that contained in a declaration filed under that section, the Department of Public Safety shall separate information maintained in the computerized criminal history system regarding an individual whose identity has been misused from information maintained in that system regarding the person who misused the identity. (Code Crim. Proc., Art. 60.19.)

Added by Acts 2017, 85th Leg., ch. 1058 (H.B. 2931), § 1.03, eff. Jan. 1, 2019.

Art. 66.106. Information Related to Non–Fingerprint Supported Actions

Text of article effective Jan. 1, 2019

(a) On receipt of a report of prosecution or court disposition information from a jurisdiction for which corresponding arrest data does not exist in the computerized criminal history system, the Department of Public Safety shall enter the report into a non-fingerprint supported file that is separate from the computerized criminal history system.

(b) The Department of Public Safety shall grant access to records in a non-fingerprint supported file created under Subsection (a) that include the subject's name or other identifier in the same manner as the department is required to grant access to criminal history record information under Subchapter F, Chapter 411, Government Code.

(c) On receipt of a report of arrest information that corresponds to a record in a non-fingerprint supported file created under Subsection (a), the Department of Public Safety shall transfer the record from the non-fingerprint supported file to the computerized criminal history system. (Code Crim. Proc., Art. 60.20.)

Added by Acts 2017, 85th Leg., ch. 1058 (H.B. 2931), § 1.03, eff. Jan. 1, 2019.

SUBCHAPTER D. CORRECTIONS TRACKING SYSTEM

Art. 66.151. Corrections Tracking System Database

Text of article effective Jan. 1, 2019

(a) The Texas Department of Criminal Justice shall record data and establish and maintain the corrections tracking system.

(b) The corrections tracking system must contain the information required by this chapter. (Code Crim. Proc., Arts. 60.02(a), (d).)

Added by Acts 2017, 85th Leg., ch. 1058 (H.B. 2931), § 1.03, eff. Jan. 1, 2019.

Art. 66.152. Information Contained in Corrections Tracking System

Text of article effective Jan. 1, 2019

(a) Information in the corrections tracking system relating to a sentence to be served under the jurisdiction of the Texas Department of Criminal Justice must include:

(1) the offender's name;

(2) the offender's state identification number;

(3) the sentencing date;

(4) the sentence for each offense, by offense code and incident number;

(5) if the offender was sentenced to imprisonment:

(A) the unit of imprisonment;

(B) the length of the sentence for each offense; and

(C) if multiple sentences were ordered, whether the sentences were ordered to be served consecutively or concurrently; and

(6) if a sentence other than a fine or imprisonment was ordered, a description of the sentence ordered.

(b) Sentencing information in the corrections tracking system must also include the following information about each community supervision, including deferred adjudication community supervision, or other alternative to imprisonment ordered:

(1) each conviction for which a sentence was ordered but was deferred, probated, suspended, or otherwise not imposed, by offense code and incident number; and

(2) if a sentence or portion of a sentence of imprisonment was deferred, probated, suspended, or otherwise not imposed:

(A) the offense, the sentence, and the amount of the sentence deferred, probated, suspended, or otherwise not imposed;

(B) a statement of whether any return to imprisonment or confinement was a condition of community supervision or an alternative sentence;

(C) the community supervision and corrections department exercising jurisdiction over the offender;

(D) the date the offender was received by a community supervision and corrections department;

(E) any program in which the offender is placed or has previously been placed and the level of supervision on which the offender is placed while under the jurisdiction of a community supervision and corrections department;

(F) the date a program described by Paragraph (E) begins, the date the program ends, and whether the program was completed successfully;

(G) the date a level of supervision described by Paragraph (E) begins and the date the level of supervision ends;

(H) if the offender's community supervision is revoked:

(i) the reason for the revocation and the date of revocation, by offense code and incident number; and

(ii) other current sentences of community supervision or other alternatives to confinement that have not been revoked, by offense code and incident number; and

(I) the date of the offender's release from the community supervision and corrections department.

(c) Information in the corrections tracking system relating to the handling of offenders must include the following information about each imprisonment, confinement, or execution of an offender:

(1) the date of the imprisonment or confinement;

(2) if the offender was sentenced to death:

(A) the date of execution; and

(B) if the death sentence was commuted, the sentence to which the sentence of death was commuted and the date of commutation;

(3) the date the offender was released from imprisonment or confinement and whether the release was a discharge or a release on parole or to mandatory supervision;

(4) if the offender is released on parole or to mandatory supervision:

(A) the offense for which the offender was convicted, by offense code and incident number;

(B) the date the offender was received by an office of the parole division of the Texas Department of Criminal Justice;

(C) the county in which the offender resides while under supervision;

(D) any program in which the offender is placed or has previously been placed and the level of supervision on which the offender is placed while under the jurisdiction of the parole division;

(E) the date a program described by Paragraph (D) begins, the date the program ends, and whether the program was completed successfully;

(F) the date a level of supervision described by Paragraph (D) begins and the date the level of supervision ends;

(G) if the offender's release status is revoked, the reason for the revocation and the date of revocation;

(H) the expiration date of the sentence; and

(I) the date on which the offender is:

(i) released from the parole division; or

(ii) granted clemency; and

(5) if the offender is released under Article 42A.202(b), the date of the offender's release. (Code Crim. Proc., Art. 60.052.)

Added by Acts 2017, 85th Leg., ch. 1058 (H.B. 2931), § 1.03, eff. Jan. 1, 2019.

SUBCHAPTER E. ACCESS TO INFORMATION IN CRIMINAL JUSTICE INFORMATION SYSTEM

Art. 66.201. Access to Databases by Criminal Justice Agencies and Other Entities

Text of article effective Jan. 1, 2019

(a) Criminal justice agencies, the Legislative Budget Board, and the council are entitled to access the databases of the Department of Public Safety, the Texas Juvenile Justice Department, and the Texas Department of Criminal Justice in accordance with applicable state or federal law or regulations.

(b) The access granted by this article does not entitle a criminal justice agency, the Legislative Budget Board, or the council to add, delete, or alter data maintained by another agency. (Code Crim. Proc., Art. 60.03(a).)

Added by Acts 2017, 85th Leg., ch. 1058 (H.B. 2931), § 1.03, eff. Jan. 1, 2019.

Art. 66.202. Request for Data File from Databases

Text of article effective Jan. 1, 2019

(a) The council or the Legislative Budget Board may submit to the Department of Public Safety, the Texas Juvenile Justice Department, and the Texas Department of Criminal Justice an annual request for a data file containing data elements from the departments' systems.

(b) The Department of Public Safety, the Texas Juvenile Justice Department, and the Texas Department of Criminal Justice shall provide the council and the Legislative Budget Board with the data file for the period requested, in accordance with state and federal law and regulations.

(c) If the council submits a data file request other than the annual data file request, the director of the agency maintaining the requested records must approve the request.

(d) The Legislative Budget Board may submit a data file request other than the annual data file request without the approval of the director of the agency maintaining the requested records. (Code Crim. Proc., Art. 60.03(b).)

Added by Acts 2017, 85th Leg., ch. 1058 (H.B. 2931), § 1.03, eff. Jan. 1, 2019.

Art. 66.203. Public Disclosure of Data Prohibited

Text of article effective Jan. 1, 2019

A criminal justice agency, the council, and the Legislative Budget Board may not disclose to the public information in an individual's criminal history record if the record is protected by state or federal law or regulation. (Code Crim. Proc., Art. 60.03(c).)

Added by Acts 2017, 85th Leg., ch. 1058 (H.B. 2931), § 1.03, eff. Jan. 1, 2019.

SUBCHAPTER F. DATA COLLECTION AND SUBMISSION

Art. 66.251. Uniform Incident Fingerprint Card

Text of article effective Jan. 1, 2019

(a) The Department of Public Safety, in consultation with the council, shall design, print, and distribute a uniform incident fingerprint card to each law enforcement agency in this state.

(b) The uniform incident fingerprint card must be:

(1) serially numbered with an incident number in such a manner that the individual incident of arrest may be readily ascertained; and

(2) a multiple-part form that:

(A) has space for information relating to each charge for which a person is arrested, the person's fingerprints, and other information relevant to the arrest;

(B) can be transmitted with the offender through the criminal justice process; and

(C) allows each law enforcement agency to report required data to the Department of Public Safety or the Texas Department of Criminal Justice.

(c) Subject to available telecommunications capacity, the Department of Public Safety shall develop the capability to receive the information on the uniform incident fingerprint card by electronic means from a law enforcement agency. The information must be in a form that is compatible with the form required for data supplied to the criminal justice information system. (Code Crim. Proc., Arts. 60.01(15), 60.07.)

Added by Acts 2017, 85th Leg., ch. 1058 (H.B. 2931), § 1.03, eff. Jan. 1, 2019.

Art. 66.252. Reporting of Information by Local Entities

Text of article effective Jan. 1, 2019

(a) The Department of Public Safety and the Texas Department of Criminal Justice by rule shall develop reporting procedures that:

(1) ensure that the offender processing data is reported from the time an offender is arrested until the time an offender is released; and

(2) provide measures and policies designed to identify and eliminate redundant reporting of information to the criminal justice information system.

(b) The arresting law enforcement agency shall prepare a uniform incident fingerprint card described by Article 66.251 and initiate the reporting process for each offender charged with a felony or a misdemeanor other than a misdemeanor punishable by fine only.

(c) The clerk of the court exercising jurisdiction over a case shall report the disposition of the case to the Department of Public Safety.

(d) Except as provided by Subsection (e) or as otherwise required by applicable state law or rule, information or data required by this chapter to be reported to the Department of Public Safety or the Texas Department of Criminal Justice shall be reported promptly but not later than the 30th day after the date on which the information or data is received by the agency responsible for reporting it.

(e) An offender's arrest shall be reported to the Department of Public Safety not later than the seventh day after the date of the arrest.

(f) A court that orders the release of an offender under Article 42A.202(b) when the offender is under a bench warrant and not physically imprisoned in the Texas Department of Criminal Justice shall report the release to the department not later than the seventh day after the date of the release. (Code Crim. Proc., Art. 60.08.)

Added by Acts 2017, 85th Leg., ch. 1058 (H.B. 2931), § 1.03, eff. Jan. 1, 2019.

Art. 66.253. Compatibility of Data

Text of article effective Jan. 1, 2019

(a) Data supplied to the criminal justice information system must:

(1) be compatible with the system; and

(2) contain both incident numbers and state identification numbers.

(b) A discrete submission of information under this chapter must contain, in conjunction with the required information, the person's name and state identification number. (Code Crim. Proc., Art. 60.04.)

Added by Acts 2017, 85th Leg., ch. 1058 (H.B. 2931), § 1.03, eff. Jan. 1, 2019.

Art. 66.254. Electronic Reporting of Information

Text of article effective Jan. 1, 2019

Whenever possible, information relating to dispositions and subsequent offender processing data shall be reported electronically. (Code Crim. Proc., Art. 60.02(h).)

Added by Acts 2017, 85th Leg., ch. 1058 (H.B. 2931), § 1.03, eff. Jan. 1, 2019.

Art. 66.255. Information on Subsequent Arrests

Text of article effective Jan. 1, 2019

The Department of Public Safety and the Texas Department of Criminal Justice shall develop the ca-pability to send by electronic means information about the subsequent arrest of a person under supervision to:

(1) the community supervision and corrections department serving the court of original jurisdiction; or

(2) the district parole office supervising the person. (Code Crim. Proc., Art. 60.18.)

Added by Acts 2017, 85th Leg., ch. 1058 (H.B. 2931), § 1.03, eff. Jan. 1, 2019.

SUBCHAPTER G. DUTIES OF CRIMINAL JUSTICE AGENCIES AND CERTAIN COURT CLERKS

Art. 66.301. Duties of Criminal Justice Agencies

Text of article effective Jan. 1, 2019

(a) Each criminal justice agency shall:

(1) compile and maintain records needed for reporting data required by the Department of Public Safety and the Texas Department of Criminal Justice;

(2) transmit to the Department of Public Safety and the Texas Department of Criminal Justice, when and in the manner each department directs, all data required by the appropriate department;

(3) give the Department of Public Safety and the Texas Department of Criminal Justice, or the departments' accredited agents, access to the agency for the purpose of inspection to determine the completeness and accuracy of data reported;

(4) cooperate with the Department of Public Safety and the Texas Department of Criminal Justice so that each department may properly and efficiently perform the department's duties under this chapter; and

(5) cooperate with the Department of Public Safety and the Texas Department of Criminal Justice to identify and eliminate redundant reporting of information to the criminal justice information system.

(b) An optical disk or other technology may be used instead of microfilm as a medium to store information if allowed by the applicable state laws or rules relating to the archiving of state agency information. (Code Crim. Proc., Arts. 60.06(a), (d).)

Added by Acts 2017, 85th Leg., ch. 1058 (H.B. 2931), § 1.03, eff. Jan. 1, 2019.

Art. 66.302. Public Disclosure Not Authorized

Text of article effective Jan. 1, 2019

(a) An individual's identifiable description or a notation of an individual's arrest, detention, indictment, information, or other formal criminal charge and of any disposition of the charge, including sentencing, correctional supervision, and release, that is collected and compiled by the Department of Public Safety or the Texas Department of Criminal Justice from criminal justice agencies and maintained in a central location is not subject to public disclosure except as authorized by federal or state law or regulation.

(b) Subsection (a) does not apply to a document maintained by a criminal justice agency that is the source of information collected by the Department of Public Safety or the Texas Department of Criminal Justice. Each criminal justice agency shall retain the documents described by this subsection. (Code Crim. Proc., Arts. 60.06(b), (c).)

Added by Acts 2017, 85th Leg., ch. 1058 (H.B. 2931), § 1.03, eff. Jan. 1, 2019.

Art. 66.303. Prohibited Acts

Text of article effective Jan. 1, 2019

An agency official may not intentionally conceal or destroy any record with the intent to violate this subchapter. (Code Crim. Proc., Art. 60.06(e).)

Added by Acts 2017, 85th Leg., ch. 1058 (H.B. 2931), § 1.03, eff. Jan. 1, 2019.

Art. 66.304. Applicability to District Court and County Court Clerks

Text of article effective Jan. 1, 2019

The duties imposed on a criminal justice agency under this subchapter are also imposed on district court and county court clerks. (Code Crim. Proc., Art. 60.06(f).)

Added by Acts 2017, 85th Leg., ch. 1058 (H.B. 2931), § 1.03, eff. Jan. 1, 2019.

SUBCHAPTER H. OVERSIGHT AND REPORTING

Art. 66.351. Biennial Plans

Text of article effective Jan. 1, 2019

The Department of Public Safety and the Texas Department of Criminal Justice, with advice from the council and the Department of Information Resources, shall develop biennial plans to:

(1) improve the reporting and accuracy of the criminal justice information system; and

(2) develop and maintain monitoring systems capable of identifying missing information. (Code Crim. Proc., Art. 60.02(i).)

Added by Acts 2017, 85th Leg., ch. 1058 (H.B. 2931), § 1.03, eff. Jan. 1, 2019.

Art. 66.352. Examination of Records and Operations

Text of article effective Jan. 1, 2019

(a) At least once during each five-year period, the council shall coordinate an examination of the records and operations of the criminal justice information system to ensure:

(1) the accuracy and completeness of information in the system; and

(2) the promptness of information reporting.

(b) The state auditor or other appropriate entity selected by the council shall conduct the examination under Subsection (a) with the cooperation of the council, the Department of Public Safety, and the Texas Department of Criminal Justice.

(c) The council, the Department of Public Safety, and the Texas Department of Criminal Justice may examine the records of the agencies required to report information to the Department of Public Safety or the Texas Department of Criminal Justice.

(d) The examining entity under Subsection (b) shall submit to the legislature and the council a report that summarizes the findings of each examination and contains recommendations for improving the criminal justice information system.

(e) Not later than the first anniversary of the date the examining entity under Subsection (b) submits a report under Subsection (d), the Department of Public Safety shall report to the Legislative Budget Board, the governor, and the council the department's progress in implementing the examining entity's recommendations, including the reason for not implementing any recommendation.

(f) Each year following the submission of the report described by Subsection (e), the Department of Public Safety shall submit a similar report until each of the examining entity's recommendations is implemented.

(g) Notwithstanding any other provision of this article, work performed under this article by the state auditor is subject to approval by the legislative audit committee for inclusion in the audit plan under Section 321.013(c), Government Code. (Code Crim. Proc., Arts. 60.02(j), (m).)

Added by Acts 2017, 85th Leg., ch. 1058 (H.B. 2931), § 1.03, eff. Jan. 1, 2019.

Art. 66.353. Monitoring and Reporting Duties of Department of Public Safety

Text of article effective Jan. 1, 2019

(a) The Department of Public Safety shall:

(1) monitor the submission of arrest and disposition information by local jurisdictions;

(2) annually submit to the Legislative Budget Board, the governor, the lieutenant governor, the state auditor, and the standing committees in the senate and house of representatives with primary jurisdiction over criminal justice and the department a report regarding the level of reporting by local jurisdictions;

(3) identify local jurisdictions that do not report arrest or disposition information or that partially report information; and

(4) for use in determining the status of outstanding dispositions, publish monthly on the department's Internet website or in another electronic publication a report listing by local jurisdiction each arrest for which there is no corresponding final court disposition.

(b) The report described by Subsection (a)(2) must contain a disposition completeness percentage for each county in this state. For purposes of this subsection, "disposition completeness percentage" means the percentage of arrest charges a county reports to the Department of Public Safety, to be entered in the computerized criminal history system under this chapter, that were brought against a person in the county and for which a disposition has been subsequently reported and entered in the computerized criminal history system. (Code Crim. Proc., Arts. 60.21(b), (c).)

Added by Acts 2017, 85th Leg., ch. 1058 (H.B. 2931), § 1.03, eff. Jan. 1, 2019.

Art. 66.354. Local Data Advisory Boards

Text of article effective Jan. 1, 2019

(a) The commissioners court of each county may create a local data advisory board to:

(1) analyze the structure of local automated and manual data systems to identify redundant data entry and data storage;

(2) develop recommendations for the commissioners to improve the local data systems;

(3) develop recommendations, when appropriate, for the effective electronic transfer of required data from local agencies to state agencies; and

(4) perform any related duties to be determined by the commissioners court.

(b) Local officials responsible for collecting, storing, reporting, and using data may be appointed to a local data advisory board.

(c) The council and the Department of Public Safety shall, to the extent that resources allow, provide technical assistance and advice on the request of a local data advisory board. (Code Crim. Proc., Art. 60.09.)

Added by Acts 2017, 85th Leg., ch. 1058 (H.B. 2931), § 1.03, eff. Jan. 1, 2019.

SUBCHAPTER I. GRANTS

Art. 66.401. Grants for Criminal Justice Programs

Text of article effective Jan. 1, 2019

The council, the Department of Public Safety, the criminal justice division of the governor's office, and the Department of Information Resources cooperatively shall develop and adopt a grant program, to be implemented by the criminal justice division at a time and in a manner determined by the division, to aid local law enforcement agencies, prosecutors, and court personnel in obtaining equipment and training necessary to operate a telecommunications network capable of:

(1) making inquiries to and receiving responses from the statewide automated fingerprint identification system and from the computerized criminal history system; and

(2) transmitting information to those systems. (Code Crim. Proc., Art. 60.02(k).)

Added by Acts 2017, 85th Leg., ch. 1058 (H.B. 2931), § 1.03, eff. Jan. 1, 2019.

Art. 66.402. Certification Required

Text of article effective Jan. 1, 2019

Before allocating money to a county from any federal or state grant program for the enhancement of criminal justice programs, an agency of the state must certify that, using all or part of the allocated money, the county has taken or will take all action necessary to provide the Department of Public Safety and the

Texas Department of Criminal Justice any criminal history records maintained by the county in the manner specified for purposes of those departments. (Code Crim. Proc., Art. 60.14.)

Added by Acts 2017, 85th Leg., ch. 1058 (H.B. 2931), § 1.03, eff. Jan. 1, 2019.

CHAPTER 67. COMPILATION OF INFORMATION PERTAINING TO COMBINATIONS AND CRIMINAL STREET GANGS

SUBCHAPTER A. GENERAL PROVISIONS

Art. 67.001. Definitions

Text of article effective Jan. 1, 2019

In this chapter:

(1) "Administration of criminal justice" has the meaning assigned by Article 66.001.

(2) "Child" has the meaning assigned by Section 51.02, Family Code.

(3) "Combination" has the meaning assigned by Section 71.01, Penal Code.

(4) "Criminal activity" means conduct that is subject to prosecution.

(5) "Criminal information" means facts, material, photographs, or data reasonably related to the investigation or prosecution of criminal activity.

(6) "Criminal justice agency" means:

(A) an entity defined as a criminal justice agency under Article 66.001; or

(B) a municipal or county agency, or school district law enforcement agency, that is engaged in the administration of criminal justice under a statute or executive order.

(7) "Criminal street gang" has the meaning assigned by Section 71.01, Penal Code.

(8) "Department" means the Department of Public Safety of the State of Texas.

(9) "Intelligence database" means a collection or compilation of data organized for search and retrieval to evaluate, analyze, disseminate, or use intelligence information relating to a combination or criminal street gang for the purpose of investigating or prosecuting a criminal offense.

(10) "Juvenile justice agency" has the meaning assigned by Section 58.101, Family Code.

(11) "Law enforcement agency" does not include the Texas Department of Criminal Justice, the Texas Juvenile Justice Department, or a local juvenile probation department. (Code Crim. Proc., Art. 61.01.)

Added by Acts 2017, 85th Leg., ch. 1058 (H.B. 2931), § 1.04, eff. Jan. 1, 2019.

SUBCHAPTER B. INTELLIGENCE DATABASES

Art. 67.051. Intelligence Databases Required

Text of article effective Jan. 1, 2019

(a) Subject to Subsection (b), a criminal justice agency or juvenile justice agency shall compile criminal information into an intelligence database for the purpose of investigating or prosecuting the criminal activities of combinations or criminal street gangs.

(b) A law enforcement agency in a municipality with a population of 50,000 or more or in a county with a population of 100,000 or more shall compile and maintain in a local or regional intelligence database criminal information relating to a criminal street gang as provided by Subsection (a). The agency must compile and maintain the information in accordance with the criminal intelligence systems operating policies established under 28 C.F.R. Section 23.1 et seq. and the submission criteria established under Article 67.054(b).

(c) Information described by this article may be compiled on paper, by computer, or in any other useful manner by a criminal justice agency, juvenile justice agency, or law enforcement agency.

(d) A local law enforcement agency described by Subsection (b) shall send to the department information the agency compiles and maintains under this chapter. (Code Crim. Proc., Arts. 61.02(a), (b), (b–1), 61.03(c).)

Added by Acts 2017, 85th Leg., ch. 1058 (H.B. 2931), § 1.04, eff. Jan. 1, 2019.

Art. 67.052. Department Intelligence Database

Text of article effective Jan. 1, 2019

(a) The department shall establish an intelligence database and shall maintain information received from an agency under Article 67.051(d) in the database in accordance with the criminal intelligence systems operating policies established under 28 C.F.R. Section 23.1 et seq. and the submission criteria under Article 67.054(b).

(b) The department shall designate a code to distinguish criminal information relating to a child and contained in the department's intelligence database from criminal information relating to an adult offender and contained in the database. (Code Crim. Proc., Arts. 61.02(b) (part), 61.03(d), (e).)

Added by Acts 2017, 85th Leg., ch. 1058 (H.B. 2931), § 1.04, eff. Jan. 1, 2019.

Art. 67.053. Intelligence Database User Training; Rules

Text of article effective Jan. 1, 2019

(a) The department shall enter into a memorandum of understanding with the United States Department of Justice or other appropriate federal department or agency to provide any person in this state who enters information into or retrieves information from an intelligence database described by this chapter with training regarding the operating principles described by 28 C.F.R. Part 23, as those principles relate to an intelligence database established or maintained under this chapter.

(b) A person in this state who enters information into or retrieves information from an intelligence database described by this chapter shall complete continuing education training on the material described by Subsection (a) at least once for each continuous two-year period the person has primary responsibility for performing a function described by this subsection.

(c) The department shall adopt rules necessary to implement this article. (Code Crim. Proc., Art. 61.12.)

Added by Acts 2017, 85th Leg., ch. 1058 (H.B. 2931), § 1.04, eff. Jan. 1, 2019.

Art. 67.054. Submission Criteria

Text of article effective Jan. 1, 2019

(a) In this article:

(1) "Family member" means a person related to another person within the third degree by consanguinity or affinity, as described by Subchapter B, Chapter 573, Government Code, except that the term does not include a person who is considered to be related to another person by affinity only as described by Section 573.024(b), Government Code.

(2) "Penal institution" means:

(A) a confinement facility operated by or under contract with any division of the Texas Department of Criminal Justice;

(B) a confinement facility operated by or under contract with the Texas Juvenile Justice Department;

(C) a juvenile secure pre-adjudication or post-adjudication facility operated by or under a local juvenile probation department; or

(D) a county jail.

(b) Criminal information collected under this chapter relating to a criminal street gang must:

(1) be relevant to the identification of an organization that is reasonably suspected of involvement in criminal activity; and

(2) consist of:

(A) a judgment under any law that includes, as a finding or as an element of a criminal offense, participation in a criminal street gang;

(B) a self-admission by an individual of criminal street gang membership that is made during a judicial proceeding; or

(C) except as provided by Subsection (c), any two of the following:

(i) a self-admission by the individual of criminal street gang membership that is not made during a judicial proceeding, including the use of the Internet or other electronic format or medium to post photographs or other documentation identifying the individual as a member of a criminal street gang;

(ii) an identification of the individual as a criminal street gang member by a reliable informant or other individual;

(iii) a corroborated identification of the individual as a criminal street gang member by an informant or other individual of unknown reliability;

(iv) evidence that the individual frequents a documented area of a criminal street gang and associates with known criminal street gang members;

(v) evidence that the individual uses, in more than an incidental manner, criminal street gang dress, hand signals, tattoos, or symbols, including expressions of letters, numbers, words, or marks, regardless of how or the means by which the symbols are displayed, that are associated with a criminal street gang that operates in an area frequented by the individual and described by Subparagraph (iv);

(vi) evidence that the individual has been arrested or taken into custody with known criminal street gang members for an offense or conduct consistent with criminal street gang activity;

(vii) evidence that the individual has visited a known criminal street gang member, other than a family member of the individual, while the gang member is confined in or committed to a penal institution; or

(viii) evidence of the individual's use of technology, including the Internet, to recruit new criminal street gang members.

(c) Evidence described by Subsections (b)(2)(C)(iv) and (vii) is not sufficient to create the eligibility of a person's information to be included in an intelligence database described by this chapter unless the evidence is combined with information described by an-

other subparagraph of Subsection (b)(2)(C). (Code Crim. Proc., Arts. 61.02(c), (d), (e).)

Added by Acts 2017, 85th Leg., ch. 1058 (H.B. 2931), § 1.04, eff. Jan. 1, 2019.

SUBCHAPTER C. RELEASE AND USE OF INFORMATION

Art. 67.101. Release and Use of Information

Text of article effective Jan. 1, 2019

(a) On request, a criminal justice agency may release information maintained under this chapter to:

(1) another criminal justice agency;

(2) a court; or

(3) a defendant in a criminal proceeding who is entitled to the discovery of the information under Chapter 39.

(b) A criminal justice agency or court may use information received under this article or Article 67.051(d) or 67.052 only for the administration of criminal justice.

(c) A defendant may use information received under this article or Article 67.051(d) or 67.052 only for a defense in a criminal proceeding. (Code Crim. Proc., Arts. 61.03(a), (b).)

Added by Acts 2017, 85th Leg., ch. 1058 (H.B. 2931), § 1.04, eff. Jan. 1, 2019.

Art. 67.102. Criminal Information Relating to Child

Text of article effective Jan. 1, 2019

(a) Notwithstanding Chapter 58, Family Code, criminal information relating to a child associated with a combination or criminal street gang may be compiled and released under this chapter regardless of the age of the child.

(b) A criminal justice agency or juvenile justice agency may release information maintained under this chapter to an attorney representing a child who is a party to a proceeding under Title 3, Family Code, if the juvenile court determines the information:

(1) is material to the proceeding; and

(2) is not privileged under law.

(c) An attorney may use information received under this article only for a child's defense in a proceeding under Title 3, Family Code.

(d) The governing body of a county or municipality served by a law enforcement agency described by Article 67.051(b) may adopt a policy to notify the parent or guardian of a child of the agency's observations relating to the child's association with a criminal street gang. (Code Crim. Proc., Art. 61.04.)

Added by Acts 2017, 85th Leg., ch. 1058 (H.B. 2931), § 1.04, eff. Jan. 1, 2019.

Art. 67.103. Unauthorized Release or Use of Criminal Information; Penalty

Text of article effective Jan. 1, 2019

(a) A person commits an offense if the person knowingly:

(1) uses criminal information obtained under this chapter for an unauthorized purpose; or

(2) releases the information to a person who is not entitled to the information.

(b) An offense under this article is a Class A misdemeanor. (Code Crim. Proc., Art. 61.05.)

Added by Acts 2017, 85th Leg., ch. 1058 (H.B. 2931), § 1.04, eff. Jan. 1, 2019.

SUBCHAPTER D. REMOVAL OF INFORMATION

Art. 67.151. Removal of Information Relating to Individual Other than Child

Text of article effective Jan. 1, 2019

(a) This article does not apply to information collected under this chapter by the Texas Department of Criminal Justice or the Texas Juvenile Justice Department.

(b) Subject to Subsection (c), information collected under this chapter relating to a criminal street gang must be removed after five years from an intelligence database established under Article 67.051 and the intelligence database maintained by the department under Article 67.052 if:

(1) the information relates to the investigation or prosecution of criminal activity engaged in by an individual other than a child; and

(2) the individual who is the subject of the information has not been arrested for criminal activity reported to the department under Chapter 66.

(c) The five-year period described by Subsection (b) does not include any period during which the individual who is the subject of the information is:

(1) confined in a correctional facility operated by or under contract with the Texas Department of Criminal Justice;

(2) committed to a secure correctional facility, as defined by Section 51.02, Family Code, operated by or under contract with the Texas Juvenile Justice Department; or

(3) confined in a county jail or confined in or committed to a facility operated by a juvenile board in lieu of being confined in a correctional facility described by Subdivision (1) or committed to a secure correctional facility described by Subdivision (2). (Code Crim. Proc., Art. 61.06.)

Added by Acts 2017, 85th Leg., ch. 1058 (H.B. 2931), § 1.04, eff. Jan. 1, 2019.

Art. 67.152. Removal of Information Relating to Child

Text of article effective Jan. 1, 2019

(a) This article does not apply to information collected under this chapter by the Texas Department of Criminal Justice or the Texas Juvenile Justice Department.

(b) Subject to Subsection (c), information collected under this chapter relating to a criminal street gang must be removed after two years from an intelligence database established under Article 67.051 and the intelligence database maintained by the department under Article 67.052 if:

(1) the information relates to the investigation or prosecution of criminal activity engaged in by a child; and

(2) the child who is the subject of the information has not been:

(A) arrested for criminal activity reported to the department under Chapter 66; or

(B) taken into custody for delinquent conduct reported to the department under Chapter 58, Family Code.

(c) The two-year period described by Subsection (b) does not include any period during which the child who is the subject of the information is:

(1) committed to the Texas Juvenile Justice Department for conduct that violates a penal law of the grade of felony; or

(2) confined in the Texas Department of Criminal Justice. (Code Crim. Proc., Art. 61.07.)

Added by Acts 2017, 85th Leg., ch. 1058 (H.B. 2931), § 1.04, eff. Jan. 1, 2019.

SUBCHAPTER E. RIGHTS OF SUBJECT OF CRIMINAL INFORMATION

Art. 67.201. Right to Request Existence of Criminal Information

Text of article effective Jan. 1, 2019

(a) A person or the parent or guardian of a child may request that a law enforcement agency determine whether the agency has collected or is maintaining, under submission criteria established under Article 67.054(b), criminal information relating solely to the person or child. The law enforcement agency shall respond to the request not later than the 10th business day after the date the agency receives the request.

(b) Before responding to a request under Subsection (a), a law enforcement agency may require reasonable written verification of the identity of the person making the request and the relationship between the parent or guardian and the child, if applicable, including written verification of an address, date of birth, driver's license number, state identification card number, or social security number. (Code Crim. Proc., Art. 61.075.)

Added by Acts 2017, 85th Leg., ch. 1058 (H.B. 2931), § 1.04, eff. Jan. 1, 2019.

Art. 67.202. Right to Request Review of Criminal Information

Text of article effective Jan. 1, 2019

(a) On receipt of a written request of a person or the parent or guardian of a child that includes a showing by the person or the parent or guardian that a law enforcement agency may have collected criminal information under this chapter relating to the person or child that is inaccurate or does not comply with the submission criteria under Article 67.054(b), the head of the agency or the designee of the agency head shall review criminal information collected by the agency under this chapter relating to the person or child to determine if:

(1) reasonable suspicion exists to believe that the information is accurate; and

(2) the information complies with the submission criteria established under Article 67.054(b).

(b) If, after conducting a review of criminal information under Subsection (a), the agency head or designee determines that reasonable suspicion does not exist to believe that the information is accurate, or determines that the information does not comply with the submission criteria, the agency shall:

(1) destroy all records containing the information; and

(2) notify the department and the person who requested the review of the agency's determination and the destruction of the records.

(c) If, after conducting a review of criminal information under Subsection (a), the agency head or designee determines that reasonable suspicion exists to believe that the information is accurate, and determines that the information complies with the submission criteria, the agency shall notify the person who requested the review:

(1) of the agency's determination; and

(2) that the person is entitled to seek judicial review of the agency's determination under Article 67.203.

(d) On receipt of notice under Subsection (b)(2), the department immediately shall destroy all records containing the information that is the subject of the notice in the intelligence database maintained by the department under Article 67.052.

(e) A person who is committed to the Texas Juvenile Justice Department or confined in the Texas Department of Criminal Justice does not, while committed or confined, have the right to request review of criminal information under this article. (Code Crim. Proc., Art. 61.08.)

Added by Acts 2017, 85th Leg., ch. 1058 (H.B. 2931), § 1.04, eff. Jan. 1, 2019.

Art. 67.203. Judicial Review

Text of article effective Jan. 1, 2019

(a) A person who is entitled to seek judicial review of a determination made under Article 67.202(c) may file a petition for review in district court in the county in which the person resides.

(b) On the filing of a petition for review under Subsection (a), the district court shall conduct an in camera review of the criminal information that is the subject of the determination to determine if:

(1) reasonable suspicion exists to believe that the information is accurate; and

(2) the information complies with the submission criteria under Article 67.054(b).

(c) If, after conducting an in camera review of criminal information under Subsection (b), the court finds that reasonable suspicion does not exist to believe that the information is accurate, or finds that the information does not comply with the submission criteria, the court shall:

(1) order the law enforcement agency that collected the information to destroy all records containing the information; and

(2) notify the department of the court's determination and the destruction of the records.

(d) A petitioner may appeal a final judgment of a district court conducting an in camera review under this article.

(e) Information that is the subject of an in camera review under this article is confidential and may not be disclosed. (Code Crim. Proc., Art. 61.09.)

Added by Acts 2017, 85th Leg., ch. 1058 (H.B. 2931), § 1.04, eff. Jan. 1, 2019.

SUBCHAPTER F. GANG RESOURCE SYSTEM

Art. 67.251. Establishment of Gang Resource System

Text of article effective Jan. 1, 2019

The office of the attorney general shall establish an electronic gang resource system to provide criminal justice agencies and juvenile justice agencies with information about criminal street gangs in this state. (Code Crim. Proc., Art. 61.11(a) (part).)

Added by Acts 2017, 85th Leg., ch. 1058 (H.B. 2931), § 1.04, eff. Jan. 1, 2019.

Art. 67.252. Information Included in Gang Resource System

Text of article effective Jan. 1, 2019

(a) The gang resource system established under Article 67.251 may include the following information with regard to any gang:

(1) gang name;

(2) gang identifiers, such as colors used, tattoos, and clothing preferences;

(3) criminal activities;

(4) migration trends;

(5) recruitment activities; and

(6) a local law enforcement contact.

(b) Information in the gang resource system shall be accessible according to:

(1) municipality or county; and

(2) gang name.

(c) The office of the attorney general may coordinate with the Texas Department of Criminal Justice to include information in the gang resource system regarding groups that have been identified by the Security Threat Group Management Office of the Texas Department of Criminal Justice. (Code Crim. Proc., Arts. 61.11(a) (part), (g), (h).)

Added by Acts 2017, 85th Leg., ch. 1058 (H.B. 2931), § 1.04, eff. Jan. 1, 2019.

Art. 67.253. Inclusion of Certain Information Prohibited

Text of article effective Jan. 1, 2019

Information relating to the identity of a specific offender or alleged offender may not be maintained in the gang resource system. (Code Crim. Proc., Art. 61.11(d).)

Added by Acts 2017, 85th Leg., ch. 1058 (H.B. 2931), § 1.04, eff. Jan. 1, 2019.

Art. 67.254. Collection of Information

Text of article effective Jan. 1, 2019

(a) On request by the office of the attorney general, a criminal justice agency or juvenile justice agency shall make a reasonable attempt to provide gang information to the office of the attorney general for the purpose of maintaining an updated, comprehensive gang resource system.

(b) The office of the attorney general shall cooperate with criminal justice agencies and juvenile justice agencies in collecting and maintaining the accuracy of the information included in the gang resource system. (Code Crim. Proc., Arts. 61.11(b), (c).)

Added by Acts 2017, 85th Leg., ch. 1058 (H.B. 2931), § 1.04, eff. Jan. 1, 2019.

Art. 67.255. Use of Information

Text of article effective Jan. 1, 2019

Information in the gang resource system may be used in investigating gang-related crimes. Information from the system may be included in an affidavit or subpoena or used in connection with any other legal or judicial proceeding only if the information is corroborated by information not provided by or maintained in the system. (Code Crim. Proc., Art. 61.11(e).)

Added by Acts 2017, 85th Leg., ch. 1058 (H.B. 2931), § 1.04, eff. Jan. 1, 2019.

Art. 67.256. Access to Information

Text of article effective Jan. 1, 2019

Access to the gang resource system shall be limited to criminal justice agency personnel and juvenile justice agency personnel. (Code Crim. Proc., Art. 61.11(f).)

Added by Acts 2017, 85th Leg., ch. 1058 (H.B. 2931), § 1.04, eff. Jan. 1, 2019.

SUBCHAPTER G. TEXAS VIOLENT GANG TASK FORCE

Art. 67.301. Definition

Text of article effective Jan. 1, 2019

In this subchapter, "task force" means the Texas Violent Gang Task Force. (Code Crim. Proc., Art. 61.10(a).)

Added by Acts 2017, 85th Leg., ch. 1058 (H.B. 2931), § 1.04, eff. Jan. 1, 2019.

Art. 67.302. Purpose

Text of article effective Jan. 1, 2019

The purpose of the task force is to form a strategic partnership among local, state, and federal criminal justice, juvenile justice, and correctional agencies to better enable those agencies to take a proactive stance toward tracking gang activity and the growth and spread of gangs statewide. (Code Crim. Proc., Art. 61.10(b).)

Added by Acts 2017, 85th Leg., ch. 1058 (H.B. 2931), § 1.04, eff. Jan. 1, 2019.

Art. 67.303. Task Force Members

Text of article effective Jan. 1, 2019

The task force shall consist of:

(1) a representative of the department designated by the director of the department;

(2) two representatives of the Texas Department of Criminal Justice, including a representative of the parole division, designated by the executive director of that agency;

(3) a representative of the office of the inspector general of the Texas Department of Criminal Justice designated by the inspector general;

(4) two representatives of the Texas Juvenile Justice Department designated by the executive director of that agency;

(5) a representative of the office of the attorney general designated by the attorney general;

(6) six representatives who are local law enforcement officers or local community supervision personnel, including juvenile probation personnel, designated by the governor;

(7) two representatives who are local prosecutors designated by the governor; and

(8) a representative of the Texas Alcoholic Beverage Commission designated by the executive director of that agency. (Code Crim. Proc., Art. 61.10(f).)

Added by Acts 2017, 85th Leg., ch. 1058 (H.B. 2931), § 1.04, eff. Jan. 1, 2019.

Art. 67.304. Duties of Task Force

Text of article effective Jan. 1, 2019

(a) The task force shall focus its efforts on:

(1) developing, through regional task force meetings, a statewide networking system that will provide timely access to gang information;

(2) establishing communication between different criminal justice, juvenile justice, and correctional agencies, combining independent agency resources, and joining agencies together in a cooperative effort to focus on gang membership, gang activity, and gang migration trends; and

(3) forming a working group of criminal justice, juvenile justice, and correctional representatives from throughout this state to discuss specific cases and investigations involving gangs and other related gang activities.

(b) The task force may take any other actions necessary to accomplish the purposes of this subchapter.

(c) If practicable, the task force shall consult with representatives from one or more United States attorneys' offices in this state and with representatives from the following federal agencies who are available and assigned to a duty station in this state:

(1) the Federal Bureau of Investigation;

(2) the Federal Bureau of Prisons;

(3) the United States Drug Enforcement Administration;

(4) United States Immigration and Customs Enforcement;

(5) United States Customs and Border Protection;

(6) the Bureau of Alcohol, Tobacco, Firearms and Explosives;

(7) the United States Marshals Service; and

(8) the United States Probation and Pretrial Services System. (Code Crim. Proc., Arts. 61.10(c), (d), (g).)

Added by Acts 2017, 85th Leg., ch. 1058 (H.B. 2931), § 1.04, eff. Jan. 1, 2019.

Art. 67.305. Duties of Department Regarding Task Force

Text of article effective Jan. 1, 2019

The department shall support the task force to assist in coordinating statewide antigang initiatives. (Code Crim. Proc., Art. 61.10(e).)

Added by Acts 2017, 85th Leg., ch. 1058 (H.B. 2931), § 1.04, eff. Jan. 1, 2019.

TITLE 2

DISPOSITION TABLE

Showing where former provisions of Part 2 of the Code of Criminal Procedure are now covered in Title 2 of the Code of Criminal Procedure.

CHAPTER 101. GENERAL PROVISIONS

Art. 101.001. Purpose of title

(a) This title is enacted as a part of the state's continuing statutory revision program, begun by the Texas Legislative Council in 1963 as directed by the legislature in Chapter 448, Acts of the 58th Legislature, Regular Session, 1963 (Article 5429b–1, Vernon's Texas Civil Statutes). The program contemplates a topic-by-topic revision of the state's general and permanent statute law without substantive change.

(b) Consistent with the objectives of the statutory revision program, the purpose of this title is to make the law encompassed by this title more accessible and understandable by:

(1) rearranging the statutes into a more logical order;

(2) employing a format and numbering system designed to facilitate citation of the law and to accommodate future expansion of the law;

(3) eliminating repealed, duplicative, unconstitutional, expired, executed, and other ineffective provisions; and

(4) restating the law in modern American English to the greatest extent possible.

Added by Acts 1985, 69th Leg., ch. 269, § 1, eff. Sept. 1, 1985.

Art. 101.002. Construction of title

The Code Construction Act (Article 5429b–2, Vernon's Texas Civil Statutes[1]) applies to the construction of each provision in this title, except as otherwise expressly provided by this title.

Added by Acts 1985, 69th Leg., ch. 269, § 1, eff. Sept. 1, 1985.

[1] Repealed; see, now, V.T.C.A. Government Code, § 311.001 et seq.

Art. 101.003. Internal references

In this title:

(1) a reference to a chapter or article without further identification is a reference to a chapter or article of this title; and

(2) a reference to a subchapter, article, subsection, subdivision, paragraph, or other numbered or lettered unit without further identification is a reference to a unit of the next larger unit of this title in which the reference appears.

Added by Acts 1985, 69th Leg., ch. 269, § 1, eff. Sept. 1, 1985.

Arts. 1001 to 1008. Repealed by Acts 1985, 69th Leg., ch. 269, § 5(2), eff. Sept. 1, 1985

CHAPTER 102. COSTS PAID BY DEFENDANTS

SUBCHAPTER A. GENERAL COSTS

SUBCHAPTER B. CRIMINAL JUSTICE PLANNING FUND

SUBCHAPTER C. COURT COSTS AND FEES

SUBCHAPTER D. COMPREHENSIVE REHABILITATION FUND

A former Chapter 102, which related to taxation of costs and consisted of articles 1009 to 1017, was repealed by Acts 1985, 69th Leg., ch. 269, § 5(2), eff. Sept. 1, 1985.

SUBCHAPTER A. GENERAL COSTS

Art. 102.001. Fees for Services of Peace Officers

(a) Repealed by Acts 1989, 71st Leg., ch. 826, § 2, eff. Sept. 1, 1989.

(b) In addition to fees provided by Subsection (a), a defendant required to pay fees under this article shall also pay 15 cents per mile for mileage required of an officer to perform a service listed in this subsection and to return from performing that service. If the service provided is the execution of a writ and the writ is directed to two or more persons or the officer executes more than one writ in a case, the defendant is required to pay only mileage actually and necessarily traveled. In calculating mileage, the officer must use the railroad or the most practical route by private conveyance. This subsection applies to:

(1) conveying a prisoner after conviction to the county jail;

(2) conveying a prisoner arrested on a warrant or capias issued in another county to the court or jail of the county in which the warrant or capias was issued; and

(3) traveling to execute criminal process, to summon or attach a witness, and to execute process not otherwise described by this article.

(c) to (e) Repealed by Acts 1989, 71st Leg., ch. 826, § 2, eff. Sept. 1, 1989.

(f) An officer who receives fees imposed under Subsection (a)(1) of this section in a municipal court shall keep separate records of the funds collected and shall deposit the funds in the municipal treasury. The officer collecting the fees under Subsection (a)(1) or (a)(2) of this article in a justice, county, or district court shall keep separate records of the funds collected and shall deposit the funds in the county treasury.

(g) Relettered from (e) by Acts 1989, 71st Leg., ch. 2, § 16.01(12), eff. Aug. 28, 1989, and repealed by Acts 1989, 71st Leg., ch. 826, § 2, eff. Sept. 1, 1989.

(h) The custodian of a municipal or county treasury who receives fees under Subsection (a)(1) of this article for services performed by peace officers employed by the state shall remit all fees to the comptroller of public accounts in the manner directed by the comptroller. The custodian of a county treasury who receives fees under Subsection (a)(2) of this article for services performed by peace officers employed by the state may retain $2 of the fee for the county and shall forward the remainder to the comptroller in the manner directed by the comptroller. All custodians of municipal and county treasuries who receive fees under Subsection (a)(1) or (a)(2) of this article shall keep records of the amount of funds collected that are on deposit with them and, not later than the last day of the month following each calendar quarter, shall remit to the comptroller funds collected under Subsection (a)(1) or (a)(2) of this article during the preceding quarter in a manner directed by the comptroller. The municipality or county may retain all interest earned on those funds. The comptroller shall credit funds received under this subsection to the General Revenue Fund.

Added by Acts 1985, 69th Leg., ch. 269, § 1, eff. Sept. 1, 1985. Amended by Acts 1987, 70th Leg., ch. 167, § 4.01(a), eff. Sept. 1, 1987; Acts 1987, 70th Leg., ch. 821, § 1, eff. Sept. 1, 1987; Acts 1989, 71st Leg., ch. 2, § 16.01(12), eff. Aug. 28, 1989; Acts 1989, 71st Leg., ch. 347, § 1, eff. Oct. 1, 1989.

Repeal

Without reference to amendment of subsecs. (b), (f), and (h) by Acts 1989, 71st Leg., ch. 347, § 1, this article was repealed by Acts 1989, 71st Leg., ch. 826, § 2, effective September 1, 1989.

Art. 102.002. Witness Fees

(a) Repealed by Acts 1999, 76th Leg., ch. 580, § 11(a), eff. Sept. 1, 1999.

(b) The justices of the peace and municipal courts shall maintain a record of and the clerks of district and county courts and county courts at law shall keep a book and record in the book:

(1) the number and style of each criminal action before the court;

(2) the name of each witness subpoenaed, attached, or recognized to testify in the action; and

(3) whether the witness was a witness for the state or for the defendant.

(c) Except as otherwise provided by this subsection, a defendant is liable on conviction for the fees provided by this article for witnesses in the defendant's case. If a defendant convicted of a misdemeanor does not pay the defendant's fines and costs, the county or municipality, as appropriate, is liable for the fees provided by this article for witnesses in the defendant's case.

(d) If a person is subpoenaed as a witness in a criminal case and fails to appear, the person is liable for the costs of an attachment, unless he shows good cause to the court why he did not appear.

Added by Acts 1985, 69th Leg., ch. 269, § 1, eff. Sept. 1, 1985. Amended by Acts 1999, 76th Leg., ch. 580, § 11(a), eff. Sept. 1, 1999; Acts 1999, 76th Leg., ch. 1545, § 63, eff. Sept. 1, 1999.

Repeal of subsecs. (b) and (c)

Without reference to the amendment of subsecs. (b) and (c) by Acts 1999, 76th Leg., ch. 1545, § 63, Acts 1999, 76th Leg., ch. 580, § 11(a), repealed subsecs. (b) and (c) eff. Sept. 1, 1999.

Art. 102.003. Repealed by Acts 1995, 74th Leg., ch. 122, § 4, eff. Sept. 1, 1995

Art. 102.004. Jury Fee

(a) A defendant convicted by a jury in a trial before a justice or municipal court shall pay a jury fee of $3. A defendant in a justice or municipal court who requests a trial by jury and who withdraws the request not earlier than 24 hours before the time of trial shall pay a jury fee of $3, if the defendant is convicted of the offense or final disposition of the defendant's case is deferred. A defendant convicted by a jury in a county court, a county court at law, or a district court shall pay a jury fee of $40.

(b) If two or more defendants are tried jointly in a justice or municipal court, only one jury fee of $3 may be imposed under this article. If the defendants sever and are tried separately, each defendant convicted shall pay a jury fee.

(c) In this article, "conviction" has the meaning assigned by Section 133.101, Local Government Code.

Added by Acts 1985, 69th Leg., ch. 269, § 1, eff. Sept. 1, 1985. Amended by Acts 1989, 71st Leg., ch. 1080, § 3, eff. Sept. 1, 1989; Acts 1995, 74th Leg., ch. 122, § 2, eff. Sept. 1, 1995; Acts 1999, 76th Leg., ch. 1545, § 64, eff. Sept. 1, 1999; Acts 2003, 78th Leg., ch. 209, § 67(a), eff. Jan. 1, 2004; Acts 2015, 84th Leg., ch. 654 (H.B. 2182), § 2, eff. Sept. 1, 2015.

Section 7 of Acts 2015, 84th Leg., ch. 654 (H.B. 2182) provides:

"The changes in law made by this Act apply only to a fee that becomes payable on or after the effective date [Sept. 1, 2015] of this Act. A fee that becomes payable before that date is governed by the law in effect when the fee became payable, and the former law is continued in effect for that purpose."

Art. 102.0045. Fee for Jury Reimbursement to Counties

(a) A person convicted of any offense, other than an offense relating to a pedestrian or the parking of a motor vehicle, shall pay as a court cost, in addition to all other costs, a fee of $4 to be used to reimburse counties for the cost of juror services as provided by Section 61.0015, Government Code.

(b) The clerk of the court shall remit the fees collected under this article to the comptroller in the manner provided by Subchapter B,[1] Chapter 133, Local Government Code. The comptroller shall deposit the fees in the jury service fund.

(c) The jury service fund is created in the state treasury. If, at any time, the unexpended balance of the jury service fund exceeds $10 million, the comptroller shall transfer the amount in excess of $10 million to the fair defense account.

(d) Fees deposited in the jury service fund under this article are exempt from the application of Section 403.095, Government Code.

Added by Acts 2005, 79th Leg., ch. 1360, § 5, eff. Sept. 1, 2005. Amended by Acts 2011, 82nd Leg., ch. 91 (S.B. 1303), § 6.006, eff. Sept. 1, 2011.

[1] V.T.C.A., Local Government Code § 133.051 et seq.

Art. 102.005. Fees to Clerks

(a) A defendant convicted of an offense in a county court, a county court at law, or a district court shall pay for the services of the clerk of the court a fee of $40.

(b) In this article, a person is considered convicted if:

(1) a sentence is imposed on the person;

(2) the person receives community supervision, including deferred adjudication; or

(3) the court defers final disposition of the person's case.

(c) Except as provided by Subsection (d), the fee imposed under Subsection (a) is for all clerical duties performed by the clerk, including:

(1) filing a complaint or information;

(2) docketing the case;

(3) taxing costs against the defendant;

(4) issuing original writs and subpoenas;

(5) swearing in and impaneling a jury;

(6) receiving and recording the verdict;

(7) filing each paper entered in the case; and

(8) swearing in witnesses in the case.

(d) The fee imposed by law for issuing a certified or noncertified copy is in addition to the fee imposed by Subsection (a). The clerk may issue a copy only if a person requests the copy and pays the appropriate fee as required by Sections 118.011, 118.014, 118.0145, 118.052, 118.060, and 118.0605, Local Government Code, and Sections 51.318 and 51.319, Government Code.

(e) Repealed by Acts 1999, 76th Leg., ch. 580, § 11(b), eff. Sept. 1, 1999.

(f) A defendant convicted of an offense in a county court, a county court at law, or a district court shall pay a fee of $25 for records management and preservation services performed by the county as required by Chapter 203, Local Government Code. The fee shall be collected and distributed by the clerk of the court to the county treasurer, or to an official who discharges the duties commonly delegated to the county treasurer, for deposit as follows:

(1) $22.50 to the county records management and preservation fund for records management and preservation, including automation, in various county offices; and

(2) $2.50 to the records management and preservation fund of the clerk of the court for records management and preservation services performed by the clerk of the court.

(g) A fee deposited in accordance with Subsection (f) may be used only to provide funds for specific records management and preservation, including for automation purposes, on approval by the commissioners court of a budget as provided by Chapter 111, Local Government Code.

(h) An expenditure from a records management and preservation fund must comply with Subchapter C,[1] Chapter 262, Local Government Code.

Added by Acts 1985, 69th Leg., ch. 269, § 1, eff. Sept. 1, 1985. Amended by Acts 1989, 71st Leg., ch. 1080, § 4, eff. Sept. 1, 1989; Acts 1993, 73rd Leg., ch. 675, § 6, eff. Sept. 1, 1993; Acts 1995, 74th Leg., ch. 764, § 1, eff. Aug. 28, 1995; Acts 1999, 76th Leg., ch. 580, § 11(b), eff. Sept. 1, 1999; Acts 1999, 76th Leg., ch. 1031, § 1, eff. Sept. 1, 1999; Acts 2005, 79th Leg., ch. 804, § 2, eff. June 17, 2005.

[1] V.T.C.A., Local Government Code § 262.021 et seq.

Art. 102.006. Fees in Expunction Proceedings

(a) In addition to any other fees required by other law and except as provided by Subsection (b), a petitioner seeking expunction of a criminal record in a district court shall pay the following fees:

(1) the fee charged for filing an ex parte petition in a civil action in district court;

(2) $1 plus postage for each certified mailing of notice of the hearing date; and

(3) $2 plus postage for each certified mailing of certified copies of an order of expunction.

(a-1) In addition to any other fees required by other law and except as provided by Subsection (b), a petitioner seeking expunction of a criminal record in a justice court or a municipal court of record under Chapter 55 shall pay a fee of $100 for filing an ex parte petition for expunction to defray the cost of notifying state agencies of orders of expunction under that chapter.

Text of (b), as amended by Acts 2017, 85th Leg., ch. 693 (H.B. 322), § 3

(b) The fees under Subsection (a) shall be waived if the petitioner:

(1) seeks expunction of a criminal record that relates to an arrest for an offense of which the person was acquitted, other than an acquittal for an offense described by Article 55.01(c), and the petition for

expunction is filed not later than the 30th day after the date of the acquittal; or

(2) is entitled to expunction under Article 55.01(a)(2)(A)(ii)(a) after successful completion of a veterans treatment court program created under Chapter 124, Government Code, or former law.

Text of (b), as amended by Acts 2017, 85th Leg., ch. 1149 (H.B. 557), § 5

(b) The fees under Subsection (a) or the fee under Subsection (a-1), as applicable, shall be waived if:

(1) the petitioner seeks expunction of a criminal record that relates to an arrest for an offense of which the person was acquitted, other than an acquittal for an offense described by Article 55.01(c); and

(2) the petition for expunction is filed not later than the 30th day after the date of the acquittal.

(c) A court that grants a petition for expunction of a criminal record may order that any fee, or portion of a fee, required to be paid under Subsection (a) be returned to the petitioner.

Added by Acts 1985, 69th Leg., ch. 269, § 1, eff. Sept. 1, 1985. Amended by Acts 2005, 79th Leg., ch. 886, § 4, eff. Sept. 1, 2005; Acts 2009, 81st Leg., ch. 140, § 1, eff. Sept. 1, 2009; Acts 2017, 85th Leg., ch. 693 (H.B. 322), § 3, eff. Sept. 1, 2017; Acts 2017, 85th Leg., ch. 1149 (H.B. 557), § 5, eff. Sept. 1, 2017.

Sections 6 and 7 of Acts 2017, 85th Leg., ch. 693 (H.B. 322) provide:

"Sec. 6. (a) Except as provided by Subsection (b) of this section, this Act applies to the expunction of arrest records and files for a person who successfully completes a veterans treatment court program under Chapter 124, Government Code, or former law before, on, or after the effective date [Sept. 1, 2017] of this Act, regardless of when the underlying arrest occurred.

"(b) The change in law made by this Act to Article 102.006, Code of Criminal Procedure, applies to the fees charged or costs assessed for an expunction order entered on or after the effective date of this Act, regardless of whether the underlying arrest occurred before, on, or after the effective date of this Act.

"(c) For a person who is entitled to expunction under Article 55.01(a)(2)(A)(ii)(a), Code of Criminal Procedure, as amended by this Act, based on a successful completion of a veterans treatment court program under Chapter 124, Government Code, or former law before the effective date of this Act, notwithstanding the 30-day time limit provided for the court to enter an automatic order of expunction under Section 1a(a-1), Article 55.02, Code of Criminal Procedure, as added by this Act, the court may, with the consent of the attorney representing the state, enter an order of expunction for the person as soon as practicable after the court receives written notice from any party to the case about the person's entitlement to the expunction.

"Sec. 7. The change in law made by this Act applies to a person whose conviction for an offense is set aside under Article 42A.701, Code of Criminal Procedure, on or after the effective date [Sept. 1, 2017] of this Act, regardless of when the person committed the offense for which the person was convicted."

Section 10(a) and (c) of Acts 2017, 85th Leg., ch. 1149 (H.B. 557) provides:

"(a) Except as otherwise provided by this section, this Act applies to an expunction of records and files relating to any criminal offense that occurred before, on, or after the effective date [Sept. 1, 2017] of this Act."

"(c) Article 102.006(c), Code of Criminal Procedure, as added by this Act, applies only to a petition for expunction filed on or after the effective date of this Act. A petition for expunction filed before the effective date of this Act is governed by the law in effect on the date the petition was filed, and the former law is continued in effect for that purpose."

Art. 102.007. Fee for Collecting and Processing Check or Similar Sight Order

(a) A county attorney, district attorney, or criminal district attorney may collect a fee if the attorney's office collects and processes a check or similar sight order, as defined by Section 1.07, Penal Code, if the check or similar sight order:

(1) has been issued or passed in a manner that makes the issuance or passing an offense under:

(A) Section 31.03, Penal Code;

(B) Section 31.04, Penal Code; or

(C) Section 32.41, Penal Code; or

(2) has been forged, as defined by Section 32.21, Penal Code.

(b) The county attorney, district attorney, or criminal district attorney may collect the fee from any person who is a party to the offense described in Subsection (a).

(c) The amount of the fee may not exceed:

(1) $10 if the face amount of the check or sight order does not exceed $10;

(2) $15 if the face amount of the check or sight order is greater than $10 but does not exceed $100;

(3) $30 if the face amount of the check or sight order is greater than $100 but does not exceed $300;

(4) $50 if the face amount of the check or sight order is greater than $300 but does not exceed $500; and

(5) $75 if the face amount of the check or sight order is greater than $500.

(d) If the person from whom the fee is collected was a party to the offense of forgery, as defined by Section 32.21, Penal Code, committed by altering the face amount of the check or sight order, the face amount as altered governs for the purposes of determining the amount of the fee.

(e) In addition to the collection fee specified in Subsection (c), the county attorney, district attorney, or criminal district attorney may collect the fee authorized by Section 3.506, Business & Commerce Code, for the benefit of the holder of a check or similar sight order or the holder's assignee, agent, representative, or any other person retained by the holder to seek collection of the check or order.

(f) Fees collected under Subsection (c) of this article shall be deposited in the county treasury in a special fund to be administered by the county attorney, district attorney, or criminal district attorney. Expenditures from this fund shall be at the sole discretion of the attorney and may be used only to defray the salaries and expenses of the prosecutor's office, but in no event may the county attorney, district attorney, or criminal district attorney supplement his or her own salary from this fund.

(g) In addition to the collection fee specified in Subsections (b) and (c), the issuer of a check or similar sight order that has been issued or passed as described by Subsection (a)(1) is liable for a fee in an amount equal to the costs of delivering notification by registered or certified mail with return receipt requested. The fee under this subsection must be collected in all cases described by Subsection (a)(1), and on receipt of proof of the actual costs expended, the fee shall be remitted to the holder of the check or similar sight order.

Added by Acts 1985, 69th Leg., ch. 269, § 1, eff. Sept. 1, 1985. Amended by Acts 1991, 72nd Leg., ch. 396, § 2, eff. Sept. 1, 1991; Acts 1997, 75th Leg., ch. 256, § 1, eff. Sept. 1, 1997; Acts 1999, 76th Leg., ch. 49, § 1, eff. Sept. 1, 1999; Acts 2001, 77th Leg., ch. 1420, § 2.001(b), eff. Sept. 1, 2001; Acts 2007, 80th Leg., ch. 976, § 3, eff. Sept. 1, 2007; Acts 2013, 83rd Leg., ch. 128 (S.B. 821), §§ 7, 8, eff. Sept. 1, 2013.

Art. 102.0071. Justice court dishonored check or similar sight order

On conviction in justice court of an offense under Section 32.41, Penal Code, or an offense under Section 31.03, 31.04, or 32.21, Penal Code, in which it is shown that the defendant committed the offense by issuing, passing, or forging a check or similar sight order, as defined by Section 1.07, Penal Code, that was subsequently dishonored, the court may collect from the defendant and pay to the holder of the check or order the fee permitted by Section 3.506, Business & Commerce Code.

Added by Acts 1991, 72nd Leg., ch. 396, § 2, eff. Sept. 1, 1991. Amended by Acts 2001, 77th Leg., ch. 1420, § 2.001(c), eff. Sept. 1, 2001; Acts 2013, 83rd Leg., ch. 128 (S.B. 821), § 9, eff. Sept. 1, 2013; Acts 2017, 85th Leg., ch. 977 (H.B. 351), § 23, eff. Sept. 1, 2017.

Section 37 of Acts 2017, 85th Leg., ch. 977 (H.B. 351) provides:

"The change in law made by this Act in amending Article 102.0071, Code of Criminal Procedure, and Section 32.21, Penal Code, applies only to an offense committed on or after the effective date [Sept. 1, 2017] of this Act. An offense committed before the effective date of this Act is governed by the law in effect when the offense was committed, and the former law is continued in effect for that purpose. For purposes of this section, an offense was committed before the effective date of this Act if any element of the offense occurred before that date."

Art. 102.008. Fees for Services of Prosecutors

(a) Except as provided by Subsection (b), a defendant convicted of a misdemeanor or a gambling offense shall pay a fee of $25 for the trying of the case by the district or county attorney. If the court appoints an attorney to represent the state in the absence of the district or county attorney, the appointed attorney is entitled to the fee otherwise due.

(b) No fee for the trying of a case may be charged against a defendant prosecuted in a justice court for violation of a penal statute or of the Uniform Act Regulating Traffic on Highways.

(c) If two or more defendants are tried jointly, only one fee may be charged under this article. If the defendants sever and are tried separately, each defendant shall pay the fee.

(d) A defendant is liable for fees imposed by Subsection (a) if the defendant is convicted of an offense and:

(1) the defendant does not appeal the conviction; or

(2) the conviction is affirmed on appeal.

Added by Acts 1985, 69th Leg., ch. 269, § 1, eff. Sept. 1, 1985. Amended by Acts 1989, 71st Leg., ch. 1080, § 5, eff. Sept. 1, 1989.

Art. 102.009. Repealed by Acts 2015, 84th Leg., ch. 1141 (S.B. 287), § 4(1), eff. June 19, 2015

Art. 102.010. [Blank]

Art. 102.011. Fees for Services of Peace Officers

(a) A defendant convicted of a felony or a misdemeanor shall pay the following fees for services performed in the case by a peace officer:

(1) $5 for issuing a written notice to appear in court following the defendant's violation of a traffic law, municipal ordinance, or penal law of this state, or for making an arrest without a warrant;

(2) $50 for executing or processing an issued arrest warrant, capias, or capias pro fine with the fee imposed for the services of:

(A) the law enforcement agency that executed the arrest warrant or capias, if the agency requests of the court, not later than the 15th day after the date of the execution of the arrest warrant or capias, the imposition of the fee on conviction; or

(B) the law enforcement agency that processed the arrest warrant or capias, if:

(i) the arrest warrant or capias was not executed; or

(ii) the executing law enforcement agency failed to request the fee within the period required by Paragraph (A) of this subdivision;

(3) $5 for summoning a witness;

(4) $35 for serving a writ not otherwise listed in this article;

(5) $10 for taking and approving a bond and, if necessary, returning the bond to the courthouse;

(6) $5 for commitment or release;

(7) $5 for summoning a jury, if a jury is summoned; and

(8) $8 for each day's attendance of a prisoner in a habeas corpus case if the prisoner has been remanded to custody or held to bail.

(b) In addition to fees provided by Subsection (a) of this article, a defendant required to pay fees under this article shall also pay 29 cents per mile for mileage required of an officer to perform a service listed in this subsection and to return from performing that service. If the service provided is the execution of a writ and the writ is directed to two or more persons or the officer executes more than one writ in a case, the defendant is required to pay only mileage actually and necessarily traveled. In calculating mileage, the officer must use the railroad or the most practical route by private conveyance. The defendant shall also pay all necessary and reasonable expenses for meals and lodging incurred by the officer in the performance of services under this subsection, to the extent such expenses meet the requirements of Section 611.001, Government Code. This subsection applies to:

(1) conveying a prisoner after conviction to the county jail;

(2) conveying a prisoner arrested on a warrant or capias issued in another county to the court or jail of the county; and

(3) traveling to execute criminal process, to summon or attach a witness, and to execute process not otherwise described by this article.

(c) If an officer attaches a witness on the order of a court outside the county, the defendant shall pay $10 per day or part of a day spent by the officer conveying the witness and actual necessary expenses for travel by the most practical public conveyance. In order to receive expenses under this subsection, the officer must make a sworn statement of the expenses and the judge issuing the attachment must approve the statement.

(d) A defendant shall pay for the services of a sheriff or constable who serves process and attends an examining trial in a felony or a misdemeanor case the same fees allowed for those services in the trial of a felony or a misdemeanor, not to exceed $5.

(e) A fee under Subsection (a)(1) or (a)(2) of this article shall be assessed on conviction, regardless of whether the defendant was also arrested at the same time for another offense, and shall be assessed for each arrest made of a defendant arising out of the offense for which the defendant has been convicted.

(f) to (h) Repealed by Acts 2003, 78th Leg., ch. 209, § 85(a)(5).

(i) In addition to fees provided by Subsections (a) through (g) of this article, a defendant required to pay fees under this article shall also pay the costs of overtime paid to a peace officer for time spent testifying in the trial of the case or for traveling to or from testifying in the trial of the case.

(j) In this article, "conviction" has the meaning assigned by Section 133.101, Local Government Code.

Added by Acts 1987, 70th Leg., ch. 821, § 2, eff. Sept. 1, 1987. Amended by Acts 1989, 71st Leg., ch. 826, § 1, eff. Sept. 1, 1989; Acts 1991, 72nd Leg., ch. 575, § 1, eff. Sept. 1, 1991; Acts 1993, 73rd Leg., ch. 988, § 2.04(a), eff. Sept. 1, 1993; Acts 1995, 74th Leg., ch. 267, § 1, eff. Sept. 1, 1995; Acts 1995, 74th Leg., ch. 560, § 1, eff. Sept. 1, 1995; Acts 1999, 76th Leg., ch. 44, § 1, eff. Sept. 1, 1999; Acts 2003, 78th Leg., ch. 209, §§ 68(a), 85(a)(5), eff. Jan. 1, 2004; Acts 2007, 80th Leg., ch. 1263, §§ 20, 21 eff. Sept. 1, 2007; Acts 2009, 81st Leg., ch. 87, § 6.008, eff. Sept. 1, 2009.

Art. 102.012. Fees for Pretrial Intervention Programs

(a) A court that authorizes a defendant to participate in a pretrial intervention program established under Section 76.011, Government Code, may order the defendant to pay to the court a supervision fee in an amount not more than $60 per month as a condition of participating in the program.

(b) In addition to or in lieu of the supervision fee authorized by Subsection (a), the court may order the defendant to pay or reimburse a community supervision and corrections department for any other expense that is:

(1) incurred as a result of the defendant's participation in the pretrial intervention program, other than an expense described by Article 102.0121; or

(2) necessary to the defendant's successful completion of the program.

Added by Acts 1990, 71st Leg., 6th C.S., ch. 25, § 20, eff. June 18, 1990. Amended by Acts 1995, 74th Leg., ch. 76, § 7.16, eff. Sept. 1, 1995; Acts 2005, 79th Leg., ch. 91, § 2, eff. Sept. 1, 2005; Acts 2007, 80th Leg., ch. 1226, § 1, eff. Sept. 1, 2007.

Art. 102.0121. Fees for Certain Expenses Related to Pretrial Intervention Programs

(a) A district attorney, criminal district attorney, or county attorney may collect a fee in an amount not to exceed $500 to be used to reimburse a county for expenses, including expenses of the district attorney's, criminal district attorney's, or county attorney's office, related to a defendant's participation in a pretrial intervention program offered in that county.

(b) The district attorney, criminal district attorney, or county attorney may collect the fee from any defendant who participates in a pretrial intervention program administered in any part by the attorney's office.

(c) Fees collected under this article shall be deposited in the county treasury in a special fund to be used solely to administer the pretrial intervention program. An expenditure from the fund may be made only in accordance with a budget approved by the commissioners court.

Added by Acts 2007, 80th Leg., ch. 1226, § 2, eff. Sept. 1, 2007.

Art. 102.013. Court Costs; Crime Stoppers Assistance Account

(a) The legislature shall appropriate funds from the crime stoppers assistance account to the Criminal Justice Division of the Governor's Office. The Criminal Justice Division may use 10 percent of the funds for the operation of the free statewide telephone service or other appropriate systems for the reporting of crime under Section 414.012, Government Code, and shall distribute the remainder of the funds only to crime stoppers organizations. The Criminal Justice Division may adopt a budget and rules to implement the distribution of these funds.

(b) All funds distributed by the Criminal Justice Division under Subsection (a) of this article are subject to audit by the state auditor. All funds collected or distributed are subject to audit by the Governor's Division of Planning Coordination.

(c) In this article, "crime stoppers organization" has the meaning assigned by Section 414.001, Government Code.

Added by Acts 1990, 71st Leg., 6th C.S., ch. 28, § 1, eff. Sept. 6, 1990. Renumbered from art. 102.012 by Acts 1991, 72nd Leg., ch. 16, § 19.01(7), eff. Aug. 26, 1991. Amended by Acts 1991, 72nd Leg., ch. 727, § 2, eff. Sept. 1, 1991; Acts 1993, 73rd Leg., ch. 807, § 2, eff. Aug. 30, 1993; Acts 1997, 75th Leg., ch. 700, § 13, eff. Sept. 1, 1997; Acts 1997, 75th Leg., ch. 1100, § 1, eff. Sept. 1, 1997; Acts 2017, 85th Leg., ch. 707 (H.B. 3690), § 3, eff. Sept. 1, 2017.

Art. 102.014. Court Costs for Child Safety Fund in Municipalities

(a) The governing body of a municipality with a population greater than 850,000 according to the most recent federal decennial census that has adopted an ordinance, regulation, or order regulating the stopping, standing, or parking of vehicles as allowed by Section 542.202, Transportation Code, or Chapter 682, Transportation Code, shall by order assess a court cost on each parking violation not less than $2 and not to exceed $5. The court costs under this subsection shall be collected in the same manner that other fines in the case are collected.

(b) The governing body of a municipality with a population less than 850,000 according to the most recent federal decennial census that has adopted an ordinance, regulation, or order regulating the stopping, standing, or parking of vehicles as allowed by Section 542.202, Transportation Code, or Chapter 682, Transportation Code, may by order assess a court cost on each parking violation not to exceed $5. The additional court cost under this subsection shall be collected in the same manner that other fines in the case are collected.

(c) A person convicted of an offense under Subtitle C, Title 7, Transportation Code,[1] when the offense occurs within a school crossing zone as defined by Section 541.302 of that code, shall pay as court costs $25 in addition to other taxable court costs. A person convicted of an offense under Section 545.066, Transportation Code, shall pay as court costs $25 in addition to other taxable court costs. The additional court costs under this subsection shall be collected in the same manner that other fines and taxable court costs

in the case are collected and shall be assessed only in a municipality.

(d) A person convicted of an offense under Section 25.093, Education Code, shall pay as taxable court costs $20 in addition to other taxable court costs. The additional court costs under this subsection shall be collected in the same manner that other fines and taxable court costs in the case are collected.

(e) In this article, a person is considered to have been convicted in a case if the person would be considered to have been convicted under Section 133.101, Local Government Code.

(f) In a municipality with a population greater than 850,000 according to the most recent federal decennial census, the officer collecting the costs in a municipal court case shall deposit money collected under this article in the municipal child safety trust fund established as required by Chapter 106, Local Government Code.

(g) In a municipality with a population less than 850,000 according to the most recent federal decennial census, the money collected under this article in a municipal court case must be used for a school crossing guard program if the municipality operates one. If the municipality does not operate a school crossing guard program or if the money received from court costs from municipal court cases exceeds the amount necessary to fund the school crossing guard program, the municipality may:

(1) deposit the additional money in an interest-bearing account;

(2) expend the additional money for programs designed to enhance child safety, health, or nutrition, including child abuse prevention and intervention and drug and alcohol abuse prevention; or

(3) expend the additional money for programs designed to enhance public safety and security.

(h) Money collected under this article in a justice, county, or district court shall be used to fund school crossing guard programs in the county where they are collected. If the county does not operate a school crossing guard program, the county may:

(1) remit fee revenues to school districts in its jurisdiction for the purpose of providing school crossing guard services;

(2) fund programs the county is authorized by law to provide which are designed to enhance child safety, health, or nutrition, including child abuse prevention

and intervention and drug and alcohol abuse prevention;

(3) provide funding to the sheriff's department for school-related activities;

(4) provide funding to the county juvenile probation department; or

(5) deposit the money in the general fund of the county.

(i) Each collecting officer shall keep separate records of money collected under this article.

Added by Acts 1991, 72nd Leg., ch. 830, § 2, eff. July 1, 1991. Amended by Acts 1995, 74th Leg., ch. 76, § 10.03, eff. Sept. 1, 1995; Acts 1997, 75th Leg., ch. 50, § 1, eff. Sept. 1, 1997; Acts 1997, 75th Leg., ch. 165, § 6.05, eff. Sept. 1, 1997; Acts 1997, 75th Leg., ch. 1384, § 1, eff. Sept. 1, 1997; Acts 2001, 77th Leg., ch. 983, § 1, eff. Sept. 1, 2001; Acts 2001, 77th Leg., ch. 1514, § 10, eff. Sept. 1, 2001; Acts 2003, 78th Leg., ch. 209, § 69(a), eff. Jan. 1, 2004; Acts 2009, 81st Leg., ch. 162, § 1, eff. May 26, 2009; Acts 2015, 84th Leg., ch. 935 (H.B. 2398), § 5, eff. Sept. 1, 2015.

[1] V.T.C.A., Transportation Code § 541.001 et seq.

Sections 42 and 43 of Acts 2015, 84th Leg., ch. 935 (H.B. 2398) provide:

"Sec. 42. The changes in law made by this Act apply only to an offense committed or conduct that occurs on or after the effective date [Sept. 1, 2015] of this Act. An offense committed or conduct that occurs before the effective date of this Act is governed by the law in effect on the date the offense was committed or the conduct occurred, and the former law is continued in effect for that purpose. For purposes of this section, an offense is committed or conduct occurs before the effective date of this Act if any element of the offense or conduct occurs before that date.

"Sec. 43. To the extent of any conflict, this Act prevails over another Act of the 84th Legislature, Regular Session, 2015, relating to nonsubstantive additions to and corrections in enacted codes."

Art. 102.015. Court Costs: Truancy Prevention and Diversion Fund

(a) The truancy prevention and diversion fund is a dedicated account in the general revenue fund.

(b) A person convicted in municipal or justice court of an offense, other than an offense relating to a pedestrian or the parking of a motor vehicle, shall pay as a court cost $2 in addition to other court costs.

(c) For purposes of this article, a person is considered to have been convicted if:

(1) a sentence is imposed; or

(2) the defendant receives deferred disposition in the case.

(d) Court costs under this article are collected in the same manner as other fines or costs. An officer collecting the costs shall keep separate records of the funds collected as costs under this article and shall

deposit the funds in the county treasury or municipal treasury, as applicable.

(e) The custodian of a county treasury or municipal treasury, as applicable, shall:

(1) keep records of the amount of funds on deposit collected under this article; and

(2) send to the comptroller before the last day of the first month following each calendar quarter the funds collected under this article during the preceding quarter, except that the custodian may retain 50 percent of funds collected under this article for the purpose of operating or establishing a juvenile case manager program, if the county or municipality has established or is attempting to establish a juvenile case manager program.

(f) If no funds due as costs under this article are deposited in a county treasury or municipal treasury in a calendar quarter, the custodian of the treasury shall file the report required for the quarter in the regular manner and must state that no funds were collected.

(g) The comptroller shall deposit the funds received under this article to the credit of a dedicated account in the general revenue fund to be known as the truancy prevention and diversion fund. The legislature may appropriate money from the account only to the criminal justice division of the governor's office for distribution to local governmental entities for truancy prevention and intervention services.

(h) A local governmental entity may request funds from the criminal justice division of the governor's office for providing truancy prevention and intervention services. The division may award the requested funds based on the availability of appropriated funds and subject to the application procedure and eligibility requirements specified by division rule.

(i) Funds collected under this article are subject to audit by the comptroller.

Added by Acts 2013, 83rd Leg., ch. 1213 (S.B. 1419), § 2, eff. Sept. 1, 2013.

Art. 102.016. Costs for Breath Alcohol Testing Program

(a) The custodians of municipal and county treasuries may deposit funds collected under this article in interest-bearing accounts and retain for the municipality or county interest earned on the funds. The custodians shall keep records of funds received and disbursed under this article and shall provide a yearly report of all funds received and disbursed under this article to the comptroller, the Department of Public Safety, and to each agency in the county served by the court that participates in or maintains a certified breath alcohol testing program. The comptroller shall approve the form of the report.

(b) The custodian of a municipal or county treasury in a county that maintains a certified breath alcohol testing program but does not use the services of a certified technical supervisor employed by the department may, to defray the costs of maintaining and supporting a certified breath alcohol testing program, retain $22.50 of each court cost collected under Section 133.102, Local Government Code, on conviction of an offense under Chapter 49, Penal Code, other than an offense that is a Class C misdemeanor.

(c) The legislature may appropriate money deposited to the credit of the breath alcohol testing account in the general revenue fund under this subsection to the Department of Public Safety for use by the department in the implementation, administration, and maintenance of the statewide certified breath alcohol testing program.

(d) The Department of Public Safety shall maintain a list of counties that do not use the services of a certified technical supervisor employed by the department.

Added by Acts 1991, 72nd Leg., 1st C.S., ch. 5, § 5.03(a), eff. Sept. 1, 1991. Amended by Acts 1993, 73rd Leg., ch. 900, § 3.03, eff. Sept. 1, 1994; Acts 1997, 75th Leg., ch. 1100, § 2, eff. Sept. 1, 1997; Acts 2009, 81st Leg., ch. 1204, § 1, eff. Sept. 1, 2009.

Art. 102.0169. Court Costs; County and District Court Technology Fund

(a) A defendant convicted of a criminal offense in a county court, statutory county court, or district court shall pay a $4 county and district court technology fee as a cost of court.

(b) In this article, a person is considered convicted if:

(1) a sentence is imposed on the person;

(2) the person receives community supervision, including deferred adjudication; or

(3) the court defers final disposition of the person's case.

(c) The clerks of the courts described by Subsection (a) shall collect the costs and pay them to the county treasurer or to any other official who discharges the duties commonly delegated to the county treasurer, as

appropriate, for deposit in a fund to be known as the county and district court technology fund.

(d) A fund designated by this article may be used only to finance:

(1) the cost of continuing education and training for county court, statutory county court, or district court judges and clerks regarding technological enhancements for those courts; and

(2) the purchase and maintenance of technological enhancements for a county court, statutory county court, or district court, including:

(A) computer systems;

(B) computer networks;

(C) computer hardware;

(D) computer software;

(E) imaging systems;

(F) electronic kiosks; and

(G) docket management systems.

(e) The county and district court technology fund shall be administered by or under the direction of the commissioners court of the county.

Added by Acts 2009, 81st Leg., ch. 1183, § 1, eff. Sept. 1, 2009.

Art. 102.017. Court Costs; Courthouse Security Fund; Municipal Court Building Security Fund; Justice Court Building Security Fund

(a) A defendant convicted of a felony offense in a district court shall pay a $5 security fee as a cost of court.

(b) A defendant convicted of a misdemeanor offense in a county court, county court at law, or district court shall pay a $3 security fee as a cost of court. A defendant convicted of a misdemeanor offense in a justice court shall pay a $4 security fee as a cost of court. The governing body of a municipality by ordinance may create a municipal court building security fund and may require a defendant convicted of a misdemeanor offense in a municipal court to pay a $3 security fee as a cost of court.

(c) In this article, a person is considered convicted if:

(1) a sentence is imposed on the person;

(2) the person receives community supervision, including deferred adjudication; or

(3) the court defers final disposition of the person's case.

(d) Except as provided by Subsection (d–2), the clerks of the respective courts shall collect the costs and pay them to the county or municipal treasurer, as appropriate, or to any other official who discharges the duties commonly delegated to the county or municipal treasurer, as appropriate, for deposit in a fund to be known as the courthouse security fund or a fund to be known as the municipal court building security fund, as appropriate. Money deposited in a courthouse security fund may be used only for security personnel, services, and items related to buildings that house the operations of district, county, or justice courts, and money deposited in a municipal court building security fund may be used only for security personnel, services, and items related to buildings that house the operations of municipal courts. For purposes of this subsection, operations of a district, county, or justice court include the activities of associate judges, masters, magistrates, referees, hearing officers, criminal law magistrate court judges, and masters in chancery appointed under:

(1) Section 61.311, Alcoholic Beverage Code;

(2) Section 51.04(g) or Chapter 201, Family Code;

(3) Section 574.0085, Health and Safety Code;

(4) Section 33.71, Tax Code;

(5) Chapter 54A, Government Code; or

(6) Rule 171, Texas Rules of Civil Procedure.

(d–1) For purposes of this article, the term "security personnel, services, and items" includes:

(1) the purchase or repair of X-ray machines and conveying systems;

(2) handheld metal detectors;

(3) walkthrough metal detectors;

(4) identification cards and systems;

(5) electronic locking and surveillance equipment;

(6) video teleconferencing systems;

(7) bailiffs, deputy sheriffs, deputy constables, or contract security personnel during times when they are providing appropriate security services;

(8) signage;

(9) confiscated weapon inventory and tracking systems;

(10) locks, chains, alarms, or similar security devices;

(11) the purchase or repair of bullet-proof glass;

(12) continuing education on security issues for court personnel and security personnel; and

(13) warrant officers and related equipment.

(d–2)(1) This subsection applies only to a justice court located in a county in which one or more justice courts are located in a building that is not the county courthouse.

(2) The county treasurer shall deposit one-fourth of the cost of court collected under Subsection (b) in a justice court described by Subdivision (1) into a fund to be known as the justice court building security fund. A fund designated by this subsection may be used only for the purpose of providing security personnel, services, and items for a justice court located in a building that is not the county courthouse.

(e) The courthouse security fund and the justice court building security fund shall be administered by or under the direction of the commissioners court. The municipal court building fund shall be administered by or under the direction of the governing body of the municipality.

(f) The sheriff, constable, or other law enforcement agency or entity that provides security for a court shall provide to the Office of Court Administration of the Texas Judicial System a written report regarding any security incident involving court security that occurs in or around a building housing a court for which the sheriff, constable, agency, or entity provides security not later than the third business day after the date the incident occurred. A copy of the report must be provided to the presiding judge of the court in which the incident occurred. The report is confidential and exempt from disclosure under Chapter 552, Government Code.

Added by Acts 1993, 73rd Leg., ch. 818, § 1, eff. Sept. 1, 1993. Amended by Acts 1995, 74th Leg., ch. 764, § 2, eff. Aug. 28, 1995; Acts 1997, 75th Leg., ch. 12, § 1, eff. Sept. 1, 1997; Acts 1999, 76th Leg., ch. 110, § 1, eff. May 17, 1999; Acts 2005, 79th Leg., ch. 83, § 2, eff. Sept. 1, 2005; Acts 2005, 79th Leg., ch. 1087, §§ 1, 2, eff. Sept. 1, 2005; Acts 2007, 80th Leg., ch. 221, § 1, eff. Sept. 1, 2007; Acts 2011, 82nd Leg., ch. 664 (S.B. 1521), § 1, eff. June 17, 2011; Acts 2011, 82nd Leg., ch. 1031 (H.B. 2847), § 7, eff. Sept. 1, 2011; Acts 2011, 82nd Leg., 1st C.S., ch. 3 (H.B. 79), § 6.07, eff. Jan. 1, 2012; Acts 2013, 83rd Leg., ch. 161 (S.B. 1093), § 3.012, eff. Sept. 1, 2013; Acts 2017, 85th Leg., ch. 190 (S.B. 42), § 2, eff. Sept. 1, 2017.

Art. 102.0171. Court Costs: Juvenile Delinquency Prevention Funds

(a) A defendant convicted of an offense under Section 28.08, Penal Code, in a county court, county court at law, or district court shall pay a $50 juvenile delinquency prevention and graffiti eradication fee as a cost of court.

(b) In this article, a person is considered convicted if:

(1) a sentence is imposed on the person;

(2) the person receives community supervision, including deferred adjudication; or

(3) the court defers final disposition of the person's case.

(c) The clerks of the respective courts shall collect the costs and pay them to the county treasurer or to any other official who discharges the duties commonly delegated to the county treasurer for deposit in a fund to be known as the county juvenile delinquency prevention fund. A fund designated by this subsection may be used only to:

(1) repair damage caused by the commission of offenses under Section 28.08, Penal Code;

(2) provide educational and intervention programs and materials, including printed educational materials for distribution to primary and secondary school students, designed to prevent individuals from committing offenses under Section 28.08, Penal Code;

(3) provide to the public rewards for identifying and aiding in the apprehension and prosecution of offenders who commit offenses under Section 28.08, Penal Code;

(4) provide funding for teen recognition and teen recreation programs;

(5) provide funding for local teen court programs;

(6) provide funding for the local juvenile probation department; and

(7) provide educational and intervention programs designed to prevent juveniles from engaging in delinquent conduct.

(d) The county juvenile delinquency prevention fund shall be administered by or under the direction of the commissioners court.

Added by Acts 1997, 75th Leg., ch. 593, § 2, eff. Sept. 1, 1997. Amended by Acts 2003, 78th Leg., ch. 601, §§ 1, 2, eff. Sept. 1, 2003; Acts 2007, 80th Leg., ch. 1053, § 3, eff. Sept. 1, 2007.

Art. 102.0172. Court Costs; Municipal Court Technology Fund

(a) The governing body of a municipality by ordinance may create a municipal court technology fund and may require a defendant convicted of a misdemeanor offense in a municipal court or municipal court of record to pay a technology fee not to exceed $4 as a cost of court.

(b) In this article, a person is considered convicted if:

(1) a sentence is imposed on the person;

(2) the person is placed on community supervision, including deferred adjudication community supervision; or

(3) the court defers final disposition of the person's case.

(c) The municipal court clerk shall collect the costs and pay the funds to the municipal treasurer, or to any other official who discharges the duties commonly delegated to the municipal treasurer, for deposit in a fund to be known as the municipal court technology fund.

(d) A fund designated by this article may be used only to finance the purchase of or to maintain technological enhancements for a municipal court or municipal court of record, including:

(1) computer systems;

(2) computer networks;

(3) computer hardware;

(4) computer software;

(5) imaging systems;

(6) electronic kiosks;

(7) electronic ticket writers; and

(8) docket management systems.

(e) The municipal court technology fund shall be administered by or under the direction of the governing body of the municipality.

(f) Repealed by Acts 2003, 78th Leg., ch. 502, § 2, eff. Sept. 1, 2003.

Added by Acts 1999, 76th Leg., ch. 285, § 1, eff. Sept. 1, 1999. Amended by Acts 2003, 78th Leg., ch. 502, §§ 1, 2, eff. Sept. 1, 2003.

Art. 102.0173. Court Costs; Justice Court Technology Fund

(a) The commissioners court of a county by order shall create a justice court technology fund. A defendant convicted of a misdemeanor offense in justice court shall pay a $4 justice court technology fee as a cost of court for deposit in the fund.

(b) In this article, a person is considered convicted if:

(1) a sentence is imposed on the person; or

(2) the court defers final disposition of the person's case.

(c) The justice court clerk shall collect the costs and pay the funds to the county treasurer, or to any other official who discharges the duties commonly delegated to the county treasurer, for deposit in a fund to be known as the justice court technology fund.

(d) A fund designated by this article may be used only to finance:

(1) the cost of continuing education and training for justice court judges and clerks regarding technological enhancements for justice courts; and

(2) the purchase and maintenance of technological enhancements for a justice court, including:

(A) computer systems;

(B) computer networks;

(C) computer hardware;

(D) computer software;

(E) imaging systems;

(F) electronic kiosks;

(G) electronic ticket writers; and

(H) docket management systems.

(e) The justice court technology fund shall be administered by or under the direction of the commissioners court of the county.

(f) A justice court may, subject to the approval of the commissioners court, use a fund designated by this article to assist a constable's office or other county department with a technological enhancement, or cost related to the enhancement, described by Subsection (d)(1) or (2) if the enhancement directly relates to the operation or efficiency of the justice court. This subsection applies only to a county that:

(1) has a population of 125,000 or more;

(2) is not adjacent to a county of two million or more;

(3) contains a portion of the Guadalupe River; and

(4) contains a portion of Interstate Highway 10.

Added by Acts 2001, 77th Leg., ch. 977, § 1, eff. Sept. 1, 2001. Amended by Acts 2005, 79th Leg., ch. 240, §§ 1, 3, eff. Sept. 1, 2005; Acts 2013, 83rd Leg., ch. 304 (H.B. 1448), § 1, eff. Sept. 1, 2013.

Art. 102.0174. Court Costs; Juvenile Case Manager Fund

(a) In this article, "fund" means a juvenile case manager fund.

(b) The governing body of a municipality by ordinance may create a juvenile case manager fund and may require a defendant convicted of a fine-only misdemeanor offense in a municipal court to pay a juvenile case manager fee not to exceed $5 as a cost of court if the municipality employs a juvenile case manager. A municipality that does not employ a juvenile case manager may not collect a fee under this subsection.

(c) The commissioners court of a county by order may create a juvenile case manager fund and may require a defendant convicted of a fine-only misdemeanor offense in a justice court, county court, or county court at law to pay a juvenile case manager fee not to exceed $5 as a cost of court if the court employs a juvenile case manager. A justice court, county court, or county court at law that does not employ a juvenile case manager may not collect a fee under this subsection.

(d) The ordinance or order must authorize the judge or justice to waive the fee required by Subsection (b) or (c) in a case of financial hardship.

(e) In this article, a defendant is considered convicted if:

(1) a sentence is imposed on the defendant;

(2) the defendant receives deferred disposition, including deferred proceedings under Article 45.052 or 45.053; or

(3) the defendant receives deferred adjudication in county court.

(f) The clerks of the respective courts shall collect the costs and pay them to the county or municipal treasurer, as applicable, or to any other official who discharges the duties commonly delegated to the county or municipal treasurer for deposit in the fund.

(g) A fund created under this section may be used to finance the salary, benefits, training, travel expenses, office supplies, and other necessary expenses relating to the position of a juvenile case manager employed under Article 45.056. If there is money in the fund after those costs are paid, on approval by the employing court, a juvenile case manager may direct the remaining money to be used to implement programs directly related to the duties of the juvenile case manager, including juvenile alcohol and substance abuse programs, educational and leadership programs, and any other projects designed to prevent or reduce the number of juvenile referrals to the court. The fund may not be used to supplement the income of an employee whose primary role is not that of a juvenile case manager.

(h) A fund must be administered by or under the direction of the commissioners court or under the direction of the governing body of the municipality.

Added by Acts 2005, 79th Leg., ch. 949, § 35, eff. Sept. 1, 2005. Amended by Acts 2011, 82nd Leg., ch. 868 (S.B. 61), § 3, eff. June 17, 2011; Acts 2011, 82nd Leg., ch. 1098 (S.B. 1489), § 8, eff. Sept. 1, 2011; Acts 2015, 84th Leg., ch. 801 (H.B. 2945), § 1, eff. June 17, 2015.

Art. 102.0178. Costs Attendant to Certain Intoxication and Drug Convictions

(a) In addition to other costs on conviction imposed by this chapter, a person shall pay $60 as a court cost on conviction of an offense punishable as a Class B misdemeanor or any higher category of offense under:

(1) Chapter 49, Penal Code; or

(2) Chapter 481, Health and Safety Code.

(b) For purposes of this article, a person is considered to have been convicted if:

(1) a sentence is imposed; or

(2) the defendant receives community supervision or deferred adjudication.

(c) Court costs under this article are collected in the same manner as other fines or costs. An officer collecting the costs shall keep separate records of the funds collected as costs under this article and shall deposit the funds in the county treasury, as appropriate.

(d) The custodian of a county treasury shall:

(1) keep records of the amount of funds on deposit collected under this article; and

(2) except as provided by Subsection (e), send to the comptroller before the last day of the first month following each calendar quarter the funds collected under this article during the preceding quarter.

(e) A county is entitled to:

(1) if the custodian of the county treasury complies with Subsection (d), retain 10 percent of the funds collected under this article by an officer of the county during the calendar quarter as a service fee; and

(2) if the county has established a drug court program or establishes a drug court program before the expiration of the calendar quarter, retain in addition to the 10 percent authorized by Subdivision (1) another 50 percent of the funds collected under this article by an officer of the county during the calendar quarter to be used exclusively for the development and maintenance of drug court programs operated within the county.

(f) If no funds due as costs under this article are deposited in a county treasury in a calendar quarter, the custodian of the treasury shall file the report required for the quarter in the regular manner and must state that no funds were collected.

(g) The comptroller shall deposit the funds received under this article to the credit of the drug court account in the general revenue fund to help fund drug court programs established under Chapter 122, 123, 124, 125, or 129, Government Code, or former law. The legislature shall appropriate money from the account solely to the criminal justice division of the governor's office for distribution to drug court programs that apply for the money.

(h) Funds collected under this article are subject to audit by the comptroller.

Added by Acts 2007, 80th Leg., ch. 625, § 8, eff. June 15, 2007. Amended by Acts 2009, 81st Leg., ch. 902, § 1, eff. Sept. 1, 2009; Acts 2013, 83rd Leg., ch. 747 (S.B. 462), § 2.03, eff. Sept. 1, 2013; Acts 2017, 85th Leg., ch. 369 (H.B. 3391), § 3, eff. Sept. 1, 2017.

Art. 102.018. Costs Attendant to Intoxication Convictions

(a) Except as provided by Subsection (d) of this article, on conviction of an offense relating to the driving or operating of a motor vehicle under Section 49.04, Penal Code, the court shall impose a cost of $15 on a defendant if, subsequent to the arrest of the defendant, a law enforcement agency visually recorded the defendant with an electronic device. Costs imposed under this subsection are in addition to other court costs and are due whether or not the defendant is granted probation in the case. The court shall collect the costs in the same manner as other costs are collected in the case.

(b) Except as provided by Subsection (d), on conviction of an offense relating to the driving or operating of a motor vehicle punishable under Section 49.04(b), Penal Code, the court shall impose as a cost of court on the defendant an amount that is equal to the cost of an evaluation of the defendant performed under Article 42A.402(a). Costs imposed under this subsection are in addition to other court costs and are due whether or not the defendant is granted community supervision in the case, except that if the court determines that the defendant is indigent and unable to pay the cost, the court may waive the imposition of the cost.

(c)(1) Except as provided by Subsection (d) of this article, if a person commits an offense under Chapter 49, Penal Code, and as a direct result of the offense the person causes an incident resulting in an accident response by a public agency, the person is liable on conviction for the offense for the reasonable expense to the agency of the accident response. In this article, a person is considered to have been convicted in a case if:

(A) sentence is imposed;

(B) the defendant receives probation or deferred adjudication; or

(C) the court defers final disposition of the case.

(2) The liability authorized by this subsection may be established by civil suit; however, if a determination is made during a criminal trial that a person committed an offense under Chapter 49, Penal Code, and as a direct result of the offense the person caused an incident resulting in an accident response by a public agency, the court may include the obligation for the liability as part of the judgment. A judgment that includes such an obligation is enforceable as any other judgment.

(3) The liability is a debt of the person to the public agency, and the public agency may collect the debt in the same manner as the public agency collects an express or implied contractual obligation to the agency.

(4) A person's liability under this subsection for the reasonable expense of an accident response may not exceed $1,000 for a particular incident. For the purposes of this subdivision, a reasonable expense for an accident response includes only those costs to the public agency arising directly from an accident response to a particular incident, such as the cost of providing police, fire-fighting, rescue, ambulance, and emergency medical services at the scene of the incident and the salaries of the personnel of the public agency responding to the incident.

(5) A bill for the expense of an accident response sent to a person by a public agency under this subsection must contain an itemized accounting of the components of the total charge. A bill that complies with this subdivision is prima facie evidence of the reasonableness of the costs incurred in the accident response to which the bill applies.

(6) A policy of motor vehicle insurance delivered, issued for delivery, or renewed in this state may not cover payment of expenses charged to a person under this subsection.

(7) In this subsection, "public agency" means the state, a county, a municipality district, or a public authority located in whole or in part in this state that provides police, fire-fighting, rescue, ambulance, or emergency medical services.

(d) Subsections (a), (b), and (c) of this article do not apply to an offense under Section 49.02 or 49.03, Penal Code.

Added by Acts 1993, 73rd Leg., ch. 900, § 1.07, eff. Sept. 1, 1994. Renumbered from art. 102.017 by Acts 1995, 74th Leg., ch. 76, § 17.01(4), eff. Sept. 1, 1995. Amended by Acts 2015, 84th Leg., ch. 770 (H.B. 2299), § 2.28, eff. Jan. 1, 2017.

Art. 102.0185. Additional Costs Attendant to Intoxication Convictions: Emergency Medical Services, Trauma Facilities, and Trauma Care Systems

(a) In addition to the costs on conviction imposed by Articles 102.016 and 102.018, a person convicted of an offense under Chapter 49, Penal Code, except for Sections 49.02 and 49.031, shall pay $100 on conviction of the offense.

(b) Costs imposed under this article are imposed without regard to whether the defendant is placed on community supervision after being convicted of the offense or receives deferred disposition or deferred adjudication for the offense.

(c) Costs imposed under this article are collected in the manner provided by Subchapter B, Chapter 133, Local Government Code.

(d) The officer collecting the costs under this article shall keep separate records of the money collected and shall pay the money to the custodian of the municipal or county treasury.

(e) The custodian of the municipal or county treasury shall:

(1) keep records of the amount of money collected under this article that is deposited with the treasury under this article; and

(2) not later than the last day of the first month following each calendar quarter:

(A) pay the money collected under this article during the preceding calendar quarter to the comptroller; or

(B) if, in the calendar quarter, the custodian of the municipal or county treasury did not receive any money attributable to costs paid under this article, file a report with the comptroller stating that fact.

(f) The comptroller shall deposit the funds received under this article to the credit of the account established under Section 773.006, Health and Safety Code.

Added by Acts 2003, 78th Leg., ch. 1213, § 4, eff. Sept. 1, 2003. Amended by Acts 2011, 82nd Leg., ch. 91 (S.B. 1303), § 6.007, eff. Sept. 1, 2011.

Art. 102.0186. Additional Costs Attendant to Certain Child Sexual Assault and Related Convictions

(a) A person convicted of an offense under Section 21.02, 21.11, 22.011(a)(2), 22.021(a)(1)(B), 43.25, 43.251, or 43.26, Penal Code, shall pay $100 on conviction of the offense.

(b) Costs imposed under this article are imposed without regard to whether the defendant is placed on community supervision after being convicted of the offense or receives deferred adjudication for the offense.

(c) The clerks of the respective courts shall collect the costs and pay them to the county treasurer or to any other official who discharges the duties commonly delegated to the county treasurer for deposit in a fund to be known as the county child abuse prevention fund. A fund designated by this subsection may be used only to fund child abuse prevention programs in the county where the court is located.

(d) The county child abuse prevention fund shall be administered by or under the direction of the commissioners court.

Added by Acts 2005, 79th Leg., ch. 268, § 1.127(a), eff. Sept. 1, 2005. Amended by Acts 2007, 80th Leg., ch. 593, § 3.24, eff. Sept. 1, 2007.

Art. 102.019. Repealed by Acts 2003, 78th Leg., ch. 209, § 85(a)(6), eff. Jan. 1, 2004

Art. 102.020. Costs Related to DNA Testing

(a) A person shall pay as a cost of court:

(1) $250 on conviction of an offense listed in Section 411.1471(a)(1), Government Code;

(2) $50 on conviction of an offense described by Section 411.1471(a)(3), Government Code; or

(3) $34 on placement of the person on community supervision, including deferred adjudication community supervision, if the person is required to submit a DNA sample under Article 42A.352.

(b) The court shall assess and make a reasonable effort to collect the cost due under this article whether or not any other court cost is assessed or collected.

(c) For purposes of this article, a person is considered to have been convicted if:

(1) a sentence is imposed; or

(2) the defendant receives community supervision or deferred adjudication.

(d) Court costs under this article are collected in the same manner as other fines or costs. An officer collecting the costs shall keep separate records of the funds collected as costs under this article and shall deposit the funds in the county treasury.

(e) The custodian of a county treasury shall:

(1) keep records of the amount of funds on deposit collected under this article; and

(2) send to the comptroller before the last day of the first month following each calendar quarter the funds collected under this article during the preceding quarter.

(f) A county may retain 10 percent of the funds collected under this article by an officer of the county as a collection fee if the custodian of the county treasury complies with Subsection (e).

(g) If no funds due as costs under this article are deposited in a county treasury in a calendar quarter, the custodian of the treasury shall file the report required for the quarter in the regular manner and must state that no funds were collected.

(h) Except as provided by Subsection (h–1), the comptroller shall deposit 35 percent of the funds received under this article in the state treasury to the credit of the state highway fund and 65 percent of the funds received under this article to the credit of the criminal justice planning account in the general revenue fund.

(h–1) The clerk of the court shall transfer to the comptroller any funds received under Subsection (a)(2) or (3). The comptroller shall credit the funds to the Department of Public Safety to help defray the cost of collecting or analyzing DNA samples provided by defendants who are required to pay a court cost under this article.

(i) Funds collected under this article are subject to audit by the comptroller.

(j) The court may waive the imposition of a court cost under this article if the court determines that the defendant is indigent and unable to pay the cost.

Added by Acts 2001, 77th Leg., ch. 1490, § 6, eff. Sept. 1, 2001. Amended by Acts 2009, 81st Leg., ch. 1209, §§ 1, 2, eff. Sept. 1, 2009; Acts 2015, 84th Leg., ch. 221 (H.B. 941), § 1, eff. Sept. 1, 2015; Acts 2015, 84th Leg., ch. 770 (H.B. 2299), § 2.29, eff. Jan. 1, 2017.

For validity of this section, see Peraza v. State, Tex.App.–Hous. (1 Dist.), 2014, 457 S.W.3d 134.

Section 6 of Acts 2015, 84th Leg., ch. 221 (H.B. 941) provides:

"The change in law made by this Act in amending Article 102.020, Code of Criminal Procedure, and Section 411.1471, Government Code, applies only to an offense committed on or after the effective date [Sept. 1, 2015] of this Act. An offense committed before the effective date of this Act is governed by the law in effect at the time the offense was committed, and the former law is continued in effect for that purpose. For purposes of this section, an offense was committed before the effective date of this Act if any element of the offense occurred before that date."

Art. 102.022. Costs on Conviction to Fund Statewide Repository for Data Related to Civil Justice

(a) In this article, "moving violation" means an offense that:

(1) involves the operation of a motor vehicle; and

(2) is classified as a moving violation by the Department of Public Safety under Section 708.052, Transportation Code.

(b) A defendant convicted of a moving violation in a justice court, county court, county court at law, or municipal court shall pay a fee of 10 cents as a cost of court.

(c) In this article, a person is considered convicted if:

(1) a sentence is imposed on the person;

(2) the person receives community supervision, including deferred adjudication; or

(3) the court defers final disposition of the person's case.

(d) The clerks of the respective courts shall collect the costs described by this article. The clerk shall keep separate records of the funds collected as costs under this article and shall deposit the funds in the county or municipal treasury, as appropriate.

(e) The custodian of a county or municipal treasury shall:

(1) keep records of the amount of funds on deposit collected under this article; and

(2) send to the comptroller before the last day of the first month following each calendar quarter the funds collected under this article during the preceding quarter.

(f) A county or municipality may retain 10 percent of the funds collected under this article by an officer of the county or municipality as a collection fee if the custodian of the county or municipal treasury complies with Subsection (e).

(g) If no funds due as costs under this article are deposited in a county or municipal treasury in a calendar quarter, the custodian of the treasury shall file the report required for the quarter in the regular manner and must state that no funds were collected.

(h) The comptroller shall deposit the funds received under this article to the credit of the Civil Justice Data Repository fund in the general revenue fund, to be used only by the Texas Commission on Law Enforcement to implement duties under Section 1701.162, Occupations Code.

(i) Funds collected under this article are subject to audit by the comptroller.

Added by Acts 2009, 81st Leg., ch. 1172, § 30, eff. Sept. 1, 2009. Amended by Acts 2013, 83rd Leg., ch. 93 (S.B. 686), § 2.10, eff. May 18, 2013.

SUBCHAPTER B. CRIMINAL JUSTICE PLANNING FUND

Arts. 102.051 to 102.055. Repealed by Acts 1997, 75th Leg., ch. 1100, § 6(3), eff. Sept. 1, 1997

Art. 102.056. Distribution of Funds

(a) The legislature shall determine and appropriate the necessary amount from the criminal justice planning fund to the criminal justice division of the governor's office for expenditure for state and local criminal justice projects and for costs of administering the funds for the projects. The criminal justice division shall allocate not less than 20 percent of these funds to juvenile justice programs. The distribution of the funds to local units of government shall be in an amount equal at least to the same percentage as local expenditures for criminal justice activities are to total state and local expenditures for criminal justice activities for the preceding state fiscal year. Funds shall be allocated among combinations of local units of government taking into consideration the population of the combination of local units of government as compared to the population of the state and the incidence of crime in the jurisdiction of the combination of local units of government as compared to the incidence of crime in the state. All funds collected are subject to audit by the comptroller of public accounts. All funds expended are subject to audit by the State Auditor. All funds collected or expended are subject to audit by the governor's division of planning coordination.

(b) The legislature may appropriate any unobligated balance of the criminal justice planning fund for any court-related purpose.

(c) Notwithstanding any other provision of this article, the criminal justice division shall allocate to a local unit of government or combination of local units of government located in an impacted region occurring as the result of the establishment of a significant new naval military facility an amount that exceeds by 10 percent the amount it would otherwise receive under this article.

(d) In this article, "significant new naval military facility" and "impacted region" have the meanings assigned by Section 4, Article 1, National Defense Impacted Region Assistance Act of 1985.

(e) The legislature shall determine and appropriate the necessary amount from the criminal justice planning account to the criminal justice division of the governor's office for reimbursement in the form of grants to the Department of Public Safety of the State of Texas and other law enforcement agencies for expenses incurred in performing duties imposed on those agencies under Section 411.1471 or Subchapter B–1, Chapter 420, Government Code, as applicable. On the first day after the end of a calendar quarter, a law enforcement agency incurring expenses described by this subsection in the previous calendar quarter shall send a certified statement of the costs incurred to the criminal justice division. The criminal justice division through a grant shall reimburse the law enforcement agency for the costs not later than the 30th day after the date the certified statement is received. If the criminal justice division does not reimburse the law enforcement agency before the 90th day after the date the certified statement is received, the agency is not required to perform duties imposed under Section 411.1471 or Subchapter B–1, Chapter 420, Government Code, as applicable, until the agency has been compensated for all costs for which the agency has submitted a certified statement under this subsection.

Added by Acts 1985, 69th Leg., ch. 269, § 1, eff. Sept. 1, 1985. Amended by Acts 1986, 69th Leg., 2nd C.S., ch. 11, § 8, eff. Sept. 22, 1986; Acts 1991, 72nd Leg., ch. 16, § 4.07(a), eff. Aug. 26, 1991; Acts 2001, 77th Leg., ch. 1490, § 7, eff. Sept. 1, 2001. Amended by Acts 2011, 82nd Leg., ch. 91 (S.B. 1303), § 6.008, eff. Sept. 1, 2011; Acts 2011, 82nd Leg., ch. 1105 (S.B. 1636), § 13, eff. Sept. 1, 2011.

SUBCHAPTER C. COURT COSTS AND FEES

Art. 102.071. Collection, Allocation, and Administration

The comptroller of public accounts may require state court costs and fees in criminal cases to be reported in lump-sum amounts. The comptroller shall allocate the amounts received to the appropriate fund, with each fund receiving the same amount of money the fund would have received if the costs and fees had been reported individually.

Added by Acts 1989, 71st Leg., ch. 347, § 4, eff. Oct. 1, 1989.

Art. 102.072. Administrative Fee

An officer listed in Article 103.003 or a community supervision and corrections department may assess an administrative fee for each transaction made by the officer or department relating to the collection of fines, fees, restitution, or other costs imposed by a court. The fee may not exceed $2 for each transaction. This article does not apply to a transaction relating to the collection of child support.

Added by Acts 1995, 74th Leg., ch. 217, § 2, eff. May 23, 1995. Amended by Acts 1999, 76th Leg., ch. 1345, § 1, eff. Sept. 1, 1999.

Art. 102.073. Assessment of Court Costs and Fees in a Single Criminal Action

(a) In a single criminal action in which a defendant is convicted of two or more offenses or of multiple counts of the same offense, the court may assess each court cost or fee only once against the defendant.

(b) In a criminal action described by Subsection (a), each court cost or fee the amount of which is determined according to the category of offense must be assessed using the highest category of offense that is possible based on the defendant's convictions.

(c) This article does not apply to a single criminal action alleging only the commission of two or more offenses punishable by fine only.

Added by Acts 2015, 84th Leg., ch. 1160 (S.B. 740), § 1, eff. Sept. 1, 2015.

Section 2 of Acts 2015, 84th Leg., ch. 1160 (S.B. 740) provides:

"The change in law made by this Act applies to a court cost or fee imposed on or after the effective date [Sept. 1, 2015] of this Act, regardless of whether the offense for which the cost or fee was imposed was committed before, on, or after that date."

Art. 102.075. Repealed by Acts 2003, 78th Leg., ch. 209, § 85(a)(7), eff. Jan. 1, 2004

SUBCHAPTER D. COMPREHENSIVE REHABILITATION FUND

Arts. 102.081 to 102.085. Repealed by Acts 1997, 75th Leg., ch. 1100, § 6(4), eff. Sept. 1, 1997

Arts. 1009 to 1017. Repealed by Acts 1985, 69th Leg., ch. 269, § 5(2), eff. Sept. 1, 1985

CHAPTER 103. PAYMENT, COLLECTION, AND RECORDKEEPING

A former Chapter 103, relating to costs paid by state, and consisting of articles 1018 to 1036, was repealed by Acts 1985, 69th Leg., ch. 269, § 5(2), eff. Sept. 1, 1989, 71st Leg., ch. 2, § 5.06, eff. Aug. 28, 1989.

Art. 103.001. Costs Payable

(a) In a justice or municipal court, a cost is not payable by the person charged with the cost until a written bill is:

(1) produced or ready to be produced, containing the items of cost; and

(2) signed by the officer who charged the cost or the officer who is entitled to receive payment for the cost.

(b) In a court other than a justice or municipal court, a cost is not payable by the person charged with the cost until a written bill containing the items of cost is:

(1) produced;

(2) signed by the officer who charged the cost or the officer who is entitled to receive payment for the cost; and

(3) provided to the person charged with the cost.

Added by Acts 1985, 69th Leg., ch. 269, § 1, eff. Sept. 1, 1985. Amended by Acts 2015, 84th Leg., ch. 1141 (S.B. 287), § 1, eff. June 19, 2015.

Section 5 of Acts 2015, 84th Leg., ch. 1141 (S.B. 287) provides:

"Article 103.001, Code of Criminal Procedure, as amended by this Act, applies only to a cost incurred on or after the effective date [June 21, 2015] of this Act. A cost incurred before the effective date of this Act is governed by the law in effect on the date the cost was incurred, and the former law is continued in effect for that purpose."

Art. 103.002. Certain Costs Barred

An officer may not impose a cost for a service not performed or for a service for which a cost is not expressly provided by law.

Added by Acts 1985, 69th Leg., ch. 269, § 1, eff. Sept. 1, 1985.

Art. 103.0025. Alternative Payment Procedure for Certain Past Due Fines and Costs

(a) This article applies to a defendant's past due payment on a judgment for a fine and related court costs if a capias pro fine has been issued in the case.

(b) Notwithstanding any other provision of law, the court may adopt an alternative procedure for collecting a past due payment described by Subsection (a). Under the procedure, a peace officer who executes a capias pro fine or who is authorized to arrest a defendant on other grounds and knows that the defendant owes a past due payment described by Subsection (a):

(1) shall inform the defendant of:

(A) the possibility of making an immediate payment of the fine and related court costs by use of a credit or debit card; and

(B) the defendant's available alternatives to making an immediate payment; and

(2) may accept, on behalf of the court, the defendant's immediate payment of the fine and related

court costs by use of a credit or debit card, after which the peace officer may release the defendant as appropriate based on the officer's authority for the arrest.

(c) A peace officer accepting a payment under Subsection (b)(2) may also accept payment for fees for the issuance and execution of the capias pro fine.

Added by Acts 2015, 84th Leg., ch. 450 (H.B. 121), § 2, eff. June 15, 2015.

Art. 103.003. Collection

(a) District and county attorneys, clerks of district and county courts, sheriffs, constables, and justices of the peace may collect money payable under this title.

(b) A community supervision and corrections department and a county treasurer may collect money payable under this title with the written approval of the clerk of the court or fee officer, and may collect money payable as otherwise provided by law.

(b–1) The commissioners court of a county that has implemented a collection improvement program under Article 103.0033 may collect money payable under this title or under other law.

(c) This article does not limit the authority of a commissioners court to contract with a private vendor or private attorney for the provision of collection services under Article 103.0031.

Added by Acts 1985, 69th Leg., ch. 269, § 1, eff. Sept. 1, 1985. Amended by Acts 1995, 74th Leg., ch. 217, § 3, eff. May 23, 1995; Acts 2001, 77th Leg., ch. 1279, § 1, eff. June 15, 2001; Acts 2005, 79th Leg., ch. 1064, § 1, eff. June 18, 2005. Amended by Acts 2011, 82nd Leg., ch. 270 (H.B. 1426), § 1, eff. June 17, 2011; Acts 2011, 82nd Leg., ch. 606 (S.B. 373), § 1, eff. Sept. 1, 2011.

Art. 103.0031. Collection Contracts

(a) The commissioners court of a county or the governing body of a municipality may enter into a contract with a private attorney or a public or private vendor for the provision of collection services for one or more of the following items:

(1) debts and accounts receivable such as unpaid fines, fees, court costs, forfeited bonds, and restitution ordered paid by:

(A) a court serving the county or a court serving the municipality, as applicable; or

(B) a hearing officer serving the municipality under Chapter 682, Transportation Code;

(2) amounts in cases in which the accused has failed to appear:

(A) as promised under Subchapter A[1], Chapter 543, Transportation Code, or other law;

(B) in compliance with a lawful written notice to appear issued under Article 14.06(b) or other law;

(C) in compliance with a lawful summons issued under Article 15.03(b) or other law;

(D) in compliance with a lawful order of a court serving the county or municipality; or

(E) as specified in a citation, summons, or other notice authorized by Section 682.002, Transportation Code, that charges the accused with a parking or stopping offense; and

(3) false alarm penalties or fees imposed by a county under Chapter 118 or 233, Local Government Code, or by a municipality under a municipal ordinance.

(b) A commissioners court or governing body of a municipality that enters into a contract with a private attorney or private vendor under this article may authorize the addition of a collection fee in the amount of 30 percent on each item described in Subsection (a) that is more than 60 days past due and has been referred to the attorney or vendor for collection. The collection fee does not apply to a case that has been dismissed by a court of competent jurisdiction or to any amount that has been satisfied through time-served credit or community service. The collection fee may be applied to any balance remaining after a partial credit for time served or community service if the balance is more than 60 days past due. Unless the contract provides otherwise, the court shall calculate the amount of any collection fee due to the governmental entity or to the private attorney or private vendor performing the collection services and shall receive all fees, including the collection fee. With respect to cases described by Subsection (a)(2), the amount to which the 30 percent collection fee applies is:

(1) the amount to be paid that is communicated to the accused as acceptable to the court under its standard policy for resolution of the case, if the accused voluntarily agrees to pay that amount; or

(2) the amount ordered paid by the court after plea or trial.

(c) The governing body of a municipality with a population of more than 1.9 million may authorize the addition of collection fees under Subsection (b) for a collection program performed by employees of the governing body.

(d) A defendant is not liable for the collection fees authorized under Subsection (b) if the court of original jurisdiction has determined the defendant is indigent, or has insufficient resources or income, or is otherwise unable to pay all or part of the underlying fine or costs.

(e) If a county or municipality has entered into a contract under Subsection (a) and a person pays an amount that is less than the aggregate total to be collected under Subsections (a) and (b), the allocation to the comptroller, the county or municipality, and the private attorney or vendor shall be reduced proportionately.

(f) An item subject to collection services under Subsection (a) and to the additional collection fee authorized by Subsection (b) is considered more than 60 days past due under Subsection (b) if it remains unpaid on the 61st day after the following appropriate date:

(1) with respect to an item described by Subsection (a)(1), the date on which the debt, fine, fee, forfeited bond, or court cost must be paid in full as determined by the court or hearing officer;

(2) with respect to an item described by Subsection (a)(2), the date by which the accused promised to appear or was notified, summoned, or ordered to appear; or

(3) with respect to an item described by Subsection (a)(3), the date on which a penalty or fee is due under a rule or order adopted under Chapter 233, Local Government Code, or an ordinance, policy, procedure, or rule of a municipality.

(g) A county or municipality that enters into a contract under Subsection (a) may not use the additional 30 percent collection fee authorized by Subsection (b) for any purpose other than compensating the private attorney or private vendor who earns the fee.

(h) This section does not apply to the collection of commercial bail bonds.

(i) The commissioners court of a county or the governing body of a municipality may enter into a contract as described in this article to collect a debt incurred as a result of the commission of a criminal or civil offense committed before the effective date of this subsection. The collection fee does not apply to a debt collected pursuant to a contract entered into under this subsection.

(j) A communication to the accused person regarding the amount of payment that is acceptable to the court under the court's standard policy for resolution of a case must include:

(1) a notice of the person's right to enter a plea or go to trial on any offense charged; and

(2) a statement that, if the person is unable to pay the full amount of payment that is acceptable to the court, the person should contact the court regarding the alternatives to full payment that are available to resolve the case.

Added by Acts 1993, 73rd Leg., ch. 809, § 3, eff. Aug. 30, 1993. Amended by Acts 2001, 77th Leg., ch. 1279, § 2, eff. June 15, 2001; Acts 2003, 78th Leg., ch. 346, § 1, eff. June 18, 2003; Acts 2005, 79th Leg., ch. 1296, § 4, eff. June 18, 2005; Acts 2017, 85th Leg., ch. 977 (H.B. 351), § 24, eff. Sept. 1, 2017; Acts 2017, 85th Leg., ch. 1127 (S.B. 1913), § 22, eff. Sept. 1, 2017.

[1] V.T.C.A., Transportation Code § 543.201 et seq.

Art. 103.0032.　Collection Improvement Plans

Not later than January 1 of each even-numbered year, the Office of Court Administration of the Texas Judicial System may award grants to counties and municipalities to prepare a collection plan. The grants shall reimburse the county or municipality for the cost of preparing the plan. The plan shall provide methods to improve the collection of court costs, fees, and fines imposed in criminal cases. The Office of Court Administration of the Texas Judicial System may require that the county or municipality reimburse the state from the additional collections as a condition of the grant.

Added by Acts 2001, 77th Leg., ch. 1469, § 1, eff. Sept. 1, 2001.

Art. 103.0033.　Collection Improvement Program

(a) In this article:

(1) "Eligible case" means a criminal case in which the judgment has been entered by a trial court. The term does not include a criminal case in which a defendant has been placed on deferred disposition or has elected to take a driving safety course.

(2) "Office" means the Office of Court Administration of the Texas Judicial System.

(3) "Program" means the program to improve the collection of court costs, fees, and fines imposed in criminal cases, as developed and implemented under this article.

(b) This article applies only to a county or municipality with a population of 100,000 or greater.

(c) Unless granted a waiver under Subsection (h)(2) or (h–1), each county and municipality shall develop and implement a program that complies with the prioritized implementation schedule under Subsection (h)(1). A county program must include district, county, and justice courts.

(d) The program must consist of:

(1) a component that conforms with a model developed by the office and designed to improve in-house collections for eligible cases through the application of best practices; and

(2) a component designed to improve the collection of balances for eligible cases more than 60 days past due, which may be implemented by entering into a contract with a private attorney or public or private vendor in accordance with Article 103.0031.

(e) Not later than June 1 of each year, the office shall identify those counties and municipalities that:

(1) have not implemented a program; and

(2) are able to implement a program before April 1 of the following year.

(f) The office shall develop a methodology for determining the collection rate of counties and municipalities described by Subsection (e) before implementation of a program. The office shall determine the rate for each county and municipality not later than the first anniversary of the county's or municipality's adoption of a program.

(g) The office shall:

(1) make available on the office's Internet website requirements for a program; and

(2) assist counties and municipalities in implementing a program by providing training and consultation, except that the office may not provide employees for implementation of a program.

(h) The office may:

(1) use case dispositions, population, revenue data, or other appropriate measures to develop a prioritized implementation schedule for programs; and

(2) determine whether it is not cost-effective to implement a program in a county or municipality and grant a waiver to the county or municipality.

(h–1) The office shall grant a waiver to a county that:

(1) contains within its borders a correctional facility operated by or under contract with the Texas Department of Criminal Justice; and

(2) has a population of 50,000 or more only because the inmate population of all correctional facilities described by Subdivision (1) is included in that population.

(i) Each county and municipality shall at least annually submit to the office a written report that includes updated information regarding the program, as determined by the office. The report must be in a form approved by the office.

(j) The office shall periodically audit counties and municipalities to verify information reported under Subsection (i) and confirm that the county or municipality is conforming with requirements relating to the program.

Added by Acts 2005, 79th Leg., ch. 899, § 10.01, eff. Aug. 29, 2005. Amended by Acts 2011, 82nd Leg., ch. 1171 (H.B. 2949), § 1, eff. Sept. 1, 2011; Acts 2011, 82nd Leg., 1st C.S., ch. 4 (S.B. 1), § 41.01, eff. Sept. 28, 2011; Acts 2013, 83rd Leg., ch. 24 (S.B. 387), § 1, eff. May 10, 2013; Acts 2017, 85th Leg., ch. 364 (H.B. 3167), § 1, eff. June 1, 2017.

Art. 103.004. Disposition of Collected Money

(a) Except as provided by Subsection (c), an officer who collects recognizances, bail bonds, fines, forfeitures, judgments, jury fees, and other obligations recovered in the name of the state under any provision of this title shall deposit the money in the county treasury not later than the next regular business day after the date that the money is collected. If it is not possible for the officer to deposit the money in the county treasury by that date, the officer shall deposit the money in the county treasury as soon as possible, but not later than the fifth regular business day after the date that the money is collected.

(b) Repealed by Acts 2011, 82nd Leg., ch. 606 (S.B. 373), § 31(a).

(c) The commissioners court of a county with a population of less than 50,000 may authorize an officer who is required to deposit money under Subsection (a) to deposit the money in the county treasury not later than the 15th day after the date that the money is collected.

(d) The custodian of the county treasury shall deposit money received from fees imposed under Article 102.012 in the special fund of the county treasury for the community supervision and corrections department serving the county.

Added by Acts 1985, 69th Leg., ch. 269, § 1, eff. Sept. 1, 1985. Amended by Acts 1990, 71st Leg., 6th C.S., ch. 25, § 21, eff. June 18, 1990; Acts 1999, 76th Leg., ch. 1462, § 1, eff. Sept. 1, 1999; Acts 2011, 82nd Leg., ch. 606 (S.B. 373), §§ 2, 31(a), eff. Sept. 1, 2011.

Art. 103.005. Report Required

(a) An officer listed in Article 103.003 who collects money other than taxes for a county shall report to the commissioners court of the county for which the money was collected during each term of the court.

(b) An officer listed in Article 103.003 who collects money other than taxes for the state shall report to the district court having jurisdiction in the county the officer serves on the first day of each term of the court.

(c) The report must state for the reporting period:

(1) the amount of money collected by the officer;

(2) when and from whom the money was collected;

(3) the process by which the money was collected; and

(4) the disposition of the money.

(d) The report must be in writing and under the oath of the officer.

(e) If an officer has not collected money since the last report required to be filed with the court or the commissioners court, the officer shall report that fact to the court or commissioners court.

Added by Acts 1985, 69th Leg., ch. 269, § 1, eff. Sept. 1, 1985.

Art. 103.006. Transfer of Bill of Costs

If a criminal action or proceeding is transferred from one court to another or is appealed, an officer of the court shall certify and sign a bill of costs stating the costs that have accrued and send the bill of costs to the court to which the action or proceeding is transferred or appealed.

Added by Acts 1985, 69th Leg., ch. 269, § 1, eff. Sept. 1, 1985.

Art. 103.007. Additional Costs After Payment

After a defendant has paid costs, no more costs may be charged against the defendant unless the court rules on a motion presented to the court that additional costs are due.

Added by Acts 1985, 69th Leg., ch. 269, § 1, eff. Sept. 1, 1985.

Art. 103.008. Correction of Costs

(a) On the filing of a motion by a defendant not later than one year after the date of the final disposition of a case in which costs were imposed, the court in which the case is pending or was last pending shall correct any error in the costs.

(b) The defendant must notify each person affected by the correction of costs in the same manner as notice of a similar motion is given in a civil action.

Added by Acts 1985, 69th Leg., ch. 269, § 1, eff. Sept. 1, 1985.

Art. 103.0081. Uncollectible Fees

(a) Any officer authorized by this chapter to collect a fee or item of cost may request the trial court in which a criminal action or proceeding was held to make a finding that a fee or item of cost imposed in the action or proceeding is uncollectible if the officer believes:

(1) the defendant is deceased;

(2) the defendant is serving a sentence for imprisonment for life or life without parole; or

(3) the fee has been unpaid for at least 15 years.

(b) On a finding by a court that any condition described by Subsections (a)(1)–(3) is true, the court may order the officer to designate the fee or item of cost as uncollectible in the fee record. The officer shall attach a copy of the court's order to the fee record.

(c) This article applies only to a county with a population of more than 780,000 but less than 790,000.

Added by Acts 2017, 85th Leg., ch. 446 (S.B. 413), § 1, eff. Sept. 1, 2017.

Art. 103.009. Fee Records

(a) Each clerk of a court, county judge, justice of the peace, sheriff, constable, and marshal shall keep a fee record. The record must contain:

(1) a statement of each fee or item of cost charged for a service rendered in a criminal action or proceeding;

(2) the number and style of the action or proceeding; and

(3) the name of the officer or person who is entitled to receive the fee.

(b) Any person may inspect a fee record described by Subsection (a).

(c) A statement of an item of cost in a fee record is prima facie evidence of the correctness of the statement.

(d) The county shall provide to officers required to keep a fee record by this article equipment and supplies necessary to keep the record.

Added by Acts 1985, 69th Leg., ch. 269, § 1, eff. Sept. 1, 1985. Amended by Acts 1993, 73rd Leg., ch. 988, § 2.05, eff. Sept. 1, 1993.

Art. 103.010. Receipt Book

(a) Each county shall provide a receipt book to each officer collecting fines and fees in criminal cases for the county. The book must contain duplicate official receipts. Each receipt must bear a distinct number and a facsimile of the official seal of the county.

(b) An officer who collects fines or fees in a criminal case shall give the person paying the money a receipt from the receipt book. The receipt must show:

(1) the amount of money paid;

(2) the date the money was paid;

(3) the style and number of the case in which the costs were accrued;

(4) the item of costs;

(5) the name of the person paying the money; and

(6) the official signature of the officer receiving the money.

(c) Instead of a receipt book, each officer collecting fines or fees in criminal cases for the county may maintain the information listed in Subsections (b)(1)–(5) in a computer database. The officer shall provide a receipt to each person paying a fine or fee.

Added by Acts 1985, 69th Leg., ch. 269, § 1, eff. Sept. 1, 1985. Amended by Acts 1999, 76th Leg., ch. 412, § 1, eff. June 18, 1999.

Art. 103.011. Audit

An officer shall deliver the receipt book or a copy of any receipt records contained in a computer database to the county auditor at the end of each month's business or at the end of each month shall allow the county auditor electronic access to receipt records contained in the computer database. The county auditor shall examine the receipt book or computer records and determine whether the money collected has been properly disposed of. If each receipt in a receipt book has been used, the county auditor shall keep the book. If any receipt in the book has not been used, the auditor shall return the book to the officer. The county auditor may keep a copy of computer generated receipt records delivered to the county auditor.

Any person may inspect a receipt book or a computer generated receipt record kept by the county auditor.

Added by Acts 1985, 69th Leg., ch. 269, § 1, eff. Sept. 1, 1985. Amended by Acts 1999, 76th Leg., ch. 412, § 2, eff. June 18, 1999.

Art. 103.012. Penalty

(a) An officer commits an offense if the officer violates a provision of Article 103.010 or Article 103.011.

(b) An offense under this article is a Class C misdemeanor.

(c) An officer who violates a provision of Article 103.010 or Article 103.011 or whose deputy violates a provision of those articles may be removed from office on the petition of the county or district attorney.

Added by Acts 1985, 69th Leg., ch. 269, § 1, eff. Sept. 1, 1985.

Art. 103.013. Repealed by Acts 2003, 78th Leg., ch. 1276, § 5.004, eff. Sept. 1, 2003

Arts. 1018 to 1035. Repealed by Acts 1985, 69th Leg., ch. 269, § 5(2), eff. Sept. 1, 1985

Art. 1036. Repealed by Acts 1985, 69th Leg., ch. 269, § 5(2), eff. Sept. 1, 1985; Acts 1989, 71st Leg., ch. 2, § 5.06(b), eff. Aug. 28, 1989

CHAPTER 104.   CERTAIN EXPENSES PAID BY STATE OR COUNTY

Art. 104.001. Jury Pay and Expenses for Jurors

(a) The sheriff of a county shall, with the approval of the commissioners court, provide food and lodging for jurors impaneled in a felony case tried in the county. A juror may pay his own expenses and draw his script.

(b) A juror in a felony case is entitled to receive as jury pay the amount authorized by Article 2122, Revised Statutes.

(c) The county treasurer shall pay a juror the amount due the juror for expenses under this article after receiving a certificate from a clerk of a court or justice of the peace stating the amount due the juror.

(d) A draft or certificate issued under this article may be transferred by delivery and, without further action of any authority except registration by the county treasurer, may be used at par to pay county taxes owed by the holder of the draft or certificate.

(e) If a defendant is indicted in one county and tried in another county after a change of venue, the county in which the defendant was indicted is liable for jury pay and expenses paid to jurors by the county trying the case.

(f) At each regular meeting of the commissioners court of a county, the court shall determine whether, since the last regular meeting of the court, a defendant described by Subsection (e) has been tried in the county. The commissioners court shall prepare an account against another county liable for jury pay and expenses under this article. The account must show the number of days the jury was impaneled in the case and the jury pay and expenses incurred by the county in the case.

(g) The county judge of the county in which the defendant was tried shall certify the correctness of the account and send the account to the county judge of the county in which the defendant was indicted. The county in which the defendant was indicted shall pay the account in the same manner required for payment of the expenses of transferred prisoners under Article 104.002.

Added by Acts 1985, 69th Leg., ch. 269, § 1, eff. Sept. 1, 1985.

Art. 104.002. Expenses for Prisoners

(a) Except as otherwise provided by this article, a county is liable for all expenses incurred in the safekeeping of prisoners confined in the county jail or kept under guard by the county. If a prisoner is transferred to a county from another county on a change of venue, for safekeeping, or for a habeas corpus hearing, the county transferring the prisoner is liable for the expenses described by this article.

(b) If a county incurs expenses for the safekeeping of a prisoner from another county, the sheriff shall submit to the county judge an account of expenses incurred by the county for the prisoner. The county judge shall approve the amount he determines is a correct statement of the expenses and sign and date the account.

(c) The county judge shall submit to the commissioners court of the county for which the prisoner was kept, at a regular term of the court, his signed statement of the account described by Subsection (b). If the commissioners court determines that the account is in accordance with the law, it shall order the county treasurer to issue to the sheriff of the county submitting the statement a draft in an amount approved by the court.

(d) A person who is or was a prisoner in a county jail and received medical, dental, or health related services from a county or a hospital district shall be required to pay for such services when they are rendered. If such prisoner is an eligible county resident as defined in Section 61.002, Health and Safety Code, the county or hospital district providing the services has a right of subrogation to the prisoner's right of recovery from any source, limited to the cost of services provided. A prisoner, unless the prisoner fully pays for the cost of services received, shall remain obligated to reimburse the county or hospital district for any medical, dental, or health services provided, and the county or hospital district may apply for reimbursement in the manner provided by Chapter 61, Health and Safety Code. A county or hospital district shall have authority to recover the amount expended in a civil action.

Added by Acts 1985, 69th Leg., ch. 269, § 1, eff. Sept. 1, 1985. Amended by Acts 1987, 70th Leg., ch. 1010, § 1, eff. June 19, 1987; Acts 1991, 72nd Leg., ch. 14, § 284(19), eff. Sept. 1, 1991; Acts 1991, 72nd Leg., ch. 434, § 1, eff. Aug. 26, 1991; Acts 1995, 74th Leg., ch. 76, § 3.22, eff. Sept. 1, 1995.

Art. 104.003. State Payment of Certain Prosecution Costs

(a) In a prosecution of a criminal offense or delinquent conduct committed on property owned or operated by or under contract with the Texas Department of Criminal Justice or the Texas Juvenile Justice Department, or committed by or against a person in the custody of the Texas Department of Criminal Justice or the Texas Juvenile Justice Department while the person is performing a duty away from Texas Department of Criminal Justice or Texas Juvenile Justice Department property, the state shall reimburse the county for expenses incurred by the county, in an amount that the court determines to be reasonable, for payment of:

(1) salaries and expenses of foreign language interpreters and interpreters for deaf persons whose services are necessary to the prosecution;

(2) consultation fees of experts whose assistance is directly related to the prosecution;

(3) travel expenses for witnesses;

(4) expenses for the food, lodging, and compensation of jurors;

(5) compensation of witnesses;

(6) the cost of preparation of a statement of facts and a transcript of the trial for purposes of appeal;

(7) if the death of a person is an element of the offense, expenses of an inquest relating to the death;

(8) food, lodging, and travel expenses incurred by the prosecutor's staff during travel essential to the prosecution of the offense;

(9) court reporter's fees; and

(10) the cost of special security officers.

(b) If there is a change of venue, the court may, in its discretion, determine that a special prosecutor should be hired for the prosecution of an offense described in Section (a), and the state shall reimburse the county for the salary and expenses of the special prosecutor if the court determines that the hiring of the special prosecutor was reasonable and necessary for effective prosecution. The amount of reimbursement may not exceed an amount that the court determines to be reasonable.

(c) The court shall certify the amount of reimbursement for expenses under Sections (a) and (b) on presentation by the county of an itemized and verified receipt for those expenses.

(d) The state shall reimburse the county for expenses incurred by the county for the investigation of an offense described in Section (a), whether or not the investigation results in the prosecution of an offense, and shall reimburse the county for reasonable operational expenses of the special prison prosecution unit, including educational activities for the staff and general expenses relating to its investigative and prosecutorial duties.

(e) The court shall certify the amount of reimbursement for expenses under Sections (a) and (b) to the comptroller. The comptroller shall issue a warrant in that amount to the commissioners court of the county or, if the comptroller determines that the amount certified by the court is unreasonable, in an amount that the comptroller determines to be reasonable.

(f) The commissioners court of the county shall certify the amount of reimbursement for expenses under Section (d) to the comptroller. The comptroller shall issue a warrant in that amount to the commissioners court or, if the comptroller determines that the amount certified by the commissioners court is unreasonable, in an amount that the comptroller determines to be reasonable.

(g) Notwithstanding any other provision of this article, the expenses submitted by the county for reimbursement may not exceed the amount the county would pay for the same activity or service, if that activity or service was not reimbursed by the state. The county judge shall certify compliance with this section on request by the comptroller.

Added by Acts 1989, 71st Leg., ch. 2, § 5.06(a), eff. Aug. 28, 1989. Amended by Acts 1989, 71st Leg., ch. 461, § 1, eff. June 14, 1989; Acts 1991, 72nd Leg., ch. 14, § 284(60), eff. Sept. 1, 1991; Acts 2007, 80th Leg., ch. 263, § 3, eff. June 8, 2007; Acts 2015, 84th Leg., ch. 734 (H.B. 1549), § 18, eff. Sept. 1, 2015.

Section 150 of Acts 2015, 84th Leg., ch. 734 (H.B. 1549) provides:

"If any provision of this Act conflicts with a provision of another Act of the 84th Legislature, Regular Session, 2015, the provision of the other Act controls to the extent of the conflict, regardless of the date of enactment."

Art. 104.004. Extraordinary Costs of Prosecution

(a) The criminal justice division of the governor's office may distribute money appropriated by the legislature for the purposes of this article to a county for the reimbursement of expenses incurred by the county during the fiscal year during which application is made or the fiscal year preceding the year during which application is made for the investigation or prosecution of an offense under Section 19.03, Penal Code, or an offense under the Penal Code alleged by the attorney representing the state to have been committed for a purpose or reason described by Article 42.014.

(b) For each fiscal year, the division shall distribute at least 50 percent of the money distributed under this article during that year to counties with a population of less than 50,000, except that if the total distributions applied for by those counties is less than 50 percent of the money distributed during that year, the division is only required to distribute to those counties the amount of money for which applications have been made.

(c) The division may adopt a budget and rules for the distribution of money under this article.

(d) All money distributed to a county under this article and its expenditure by the county are subject to audit by the state auditor.

Added by Acts 1999, 76th Leg., ch. 664, § 1, eff. Sept. 1, 1999. Amended by Acts 2001, 77th Leg., ch. 85, § 2.01, eff. Sept. 1, 2001.

Arts. 1037 to 1055. Repealed by Acts 1985, 69th Leg., ch. 269, § 5(2), eff. Sept. 1, 1985

Art. 1056. Repealed by Acts 1975, 64th Leg., p. 1353, ch. 510, § 2, eff. Sept. 1, 1975

Art. 1057. Repealed by Acts 1945, 49th Leg., p. 372, ch. 239, § 4, eff. May 24, 1945

Arts. 1058 to 1060. Repealed by Acts 1985, 69th Leg., ch. 269, § 5(2), eff. Sept. 1, 1985

CHAPTER 105. COSTS TO BE PAID BY DEFENDANT [REPEALED]

1. IN DISTRICT AND COUNTY COURTS

Arts. 1061 to 1065. Repealed by Acts 1985, 69th Leg., ch. 269, § 5(2), eff. Sept. 1, 1985

2. JURY AND JURY FEES

Arts. 1075 to 1077. Repealed by Acts 1985, 69th Leg., ch. 269, § 5(2), eff. Sept. 1, 1985

3. WITNESS FEES

Arts. 1078 to 1082. Repealed by Acts 1985, 69th Leg., ch. 269, § 5(2), eff. Sept. 1, 1985

4. CRIMINAL JUSTICE PLANNING FUND

Art. 1083. Repealed by Acts 1985, 69th Leg., ch. 269, § 5(2), eff. Sept. 1, 1985; Acts 1991, 72nd Leg., ch. 16, § 4.07(b), eff. Aug. 26, 1991

GOVERNMENT CODE

TITLE 4. EXECUTIVE BRANCH

SUBTITLE G. CORRECTIONS

CHAPTER 508. PAROLE AND MANDATORY SUPERVISION

DISPOSITION TABLE

Showing where provisions of former Vernon's Ann.C.C.P. art. 42.18 may be found in Chapter 508 of the Government Code.

SUBCHAPTER A. GENERAL PROVISIONS

§ 508.001. Definitions

In this chapter:

(1) "Board" means the Board of Pardons and Paroles.

(2) "Community supervision and corrections department" means a department established under Chapter 76.

(3) "Director" means the director of the pardons and paroles division.

(4) "Division" means the pardons and paroles division.

(5) "Mandatory supervision" means the release of an eligible inmate sentenced to the institutional division so that the inmate may serve the remainder of the inmate's sentence not on parole but under the supervision of the pardons and paroles division.

(6) "Parole" means the discretionary and conditional release of an eligible inmate sentenced to the institutional division so that the inmate may serve the remainder of the inmate's sentence under the supervision of the pardons and paroles division.

(7) "Parole officer" means a person appointed by the director and assigned the duties of assessment of risks and needs, investigation, case management, and supervision of releasees to ensure that releasees are complying with the conditions of parole or mandatory supervision.

(8) "Parole commissioner" means a person employed by the board to perform the duties described by Section 508.0441.

(9) "Releasee" means a person released on parole or to mandatory supervision.

(10) "Presiding officer" means the presiding officer of the Board of Pardons and Paroles.

Added by Acts 1997, 75th Leg., ch. 165, § 12.01, eff. Sept. 1, 1997. Amended by Acts 1999, 76th Leg., ch. 62, § 10.01, eff. Sept. 1, 1999; Acts 2003, 78th Leg., 3rd C.S., ch. 3, § 11.02, eff. Jan. 11, 2004.

§ 508.002. Clemency, Commutation Distinguished

Neither parole nor mandatory supervision is a commutation of sentence or any other form of clemency.

Added by Acts 1997, 75th Leg., ch. 165, § 12.01, eff. Sept. 1, 1997.

§ 508.003. Inapplicable to Juveniles and Certain Inmates

(a) This chapter does not apply to an emergency absence under escort granted to an inmate by the institutional division under Section 501.006.

(b) Except as provided by Subsection (c), this chapter does not apply to release on parole from an institution for juveniles.

(c) The provisions of this chapter not in conflict with Section 508.156 apply to parole of a person from the Texas Juvenile Justice Department or from a post-adjudication secure correctional facility operated by or under contract with a juvenile board or local juvenile probation department under that section.

Added by Acts 1997, 75th Leg., ch. 165, § 12.01, eff. Sept. 1, 1997. Amended by Acts 2015, 84th Leg., ch. 734 (H.B. 1549), § 100, eff. Sept. 1, 2015; Acts 2015, 84th Leg., ch. 854 (S.B. 1149), § 6, eff. Sept. 1, 2015.

Section 150 of Acts 2015, 84th Leg., ch. 734 (H.B. 1549) provides:

"If any provision of this Act conflicts with a provision of another Act of the 84th Legislature, Regular Session, 2015, the provision of the other Act controls to the extent of the conflict, regardless of the date of enactment."

SUBCHAPTER B. BOARD OF PARDONS AND PAROLES

§ 508.031. Composition of Board

(a) The board consists of seven members appointed by the governor with the advice and consent of the senate.

(b) Appointments to the board must be made without regard to the race, color, disability, sex, religion, age, or national origin of the appointed members.

Added by Acts 1997, 75th Leg., ch. 165, § 12.01, eff. Sept. 1, 1997. Amended by Acts 1999, 76th Leg., ch. 554, § 1, eff. Sept. 1, 1999; Acts 2003, 78th Leg., 3rd C.S., ch. 3, § 11.03, eff. Jan. 11, 2004.

§ 508.032. Requirements for Membership

(a) Board members must be representative of the general public.

(b) A member must have resided in this state for the two years before appointment.

(c)(1) A person who is a former employee of the department may not serve on the board before the second anniversary of the date the person terminated employment with the department.

(2) A person who is employed by the department on August 1, 2003, may not serve on the board before August 1, 2005.

(d) At any time not more than three members of the board may be former employees of the department.

(e) For purposes of Subsections (c) and (d), previous service as a board member is not considered to be employment with the department.

Added by Acts 1997, 75th Leg., ch. 165, § 12.01, eff. Sept. 1, 1997. Amended by Acts 2003, 78th Leg., 3rd C.S., ch. 3, § 11.04, eff. Jan. 11, 2004.

§ 508.033. Disqualifications

(a) A person is not eligible for appointment as a member of the board or for employment as a parole commissioner if the person or the person's spouse:

(1) is employed by or participates in the management of a business entity or other organization receiving funds from the department or the board;

(2) owns or controls, directly or indirectly, more than a 10–percent interest in a business entity or other organization:

(A) regulated by the department; or

(B) receiving funds from the department or the board; or

(3) uses or receives a substantial amount of tangible goods, services, or funds from the department or the board, other than compensation or reimbursement authorized by law for board membership, attendance, or expenses.

(b) In determining eligibility under Subsection (a)(3), the compensation or reimbursement that a board member's spouse or parole commissioner's spouse receives as an employee of the board or the department may not be considered. This subsection does not affect any restriction on employment or board membership imposed by any other law.

(c) A person may not serve as a parole commissioner, may not be a member of the board, and may not be an employee of the division or the board employed in a "bona fide executive, administrative, or professional capacity," as that phrase is used for purposes of establishing an exemption to the overtime provisions of the federal Fair Labor Standards Act of 1938 (29 U.S.C. Section 201 et seq.) and its subsequent amendments, if:

(1) the person is an officer, employee, or paid consultant of a Texas trade association in the field of criminal justice; or

(2) the person's spouse is an officer, manager, or paid consultant of a Texas trade association in the field of criminal justice.

(d) A person who is required to register as a lobbyist under Chapter 305 because of the person's activities for compensation in or on behalf of a profession related to the operation of the board may not:

(1) serve as a member of the board or as a parole commissioner; or

(2) act as the general counsel to the board or division.

(e) In this section, "Texas trade association" means a cooperative and voluntarily joined association of business or professional competitors in this state designed to assist its members and its industry or profession in:

(1) dealing with mutual business or professional problems; and

(2) promoting their common interests.

(f) A person who is a current or former employee of the department may not serve as a parole commissioner before the second anniversary of the date the person's employment with the department ceases, and a member of the board may not serve as a parole commissioner before the second anniversary of the date the person's membership on the board ceases.

Added by Acts 1997, 75th Leg., ch. 165, § 12.01, eff. Sept. 1, 1997. Amended by Acts 1999, 76th Leg., ch. 62, § 10.04, eff. Sept. 1, 1999; Acts 1999, 76th Leg., ch. 554, § 2, eff. Sept. 1, 1999; Acts 2007, 80th Leg., ch. 1308, § 33, eff. June 15, 2007.

§ 508.034. Grounds for Removal

(a) It is a ground for removal from the board that a member:

(1) does not have at the time of taking office the qualification required by Section 508.032(b) for appointment to the board;

(2) is ineligible for membership under Section 508.033;

(3) is unable to discharge the member's duties for a substantial part of the term for which the member is appointed because of illness or disability; or

(4) is absent from more than half of the regularly scheduled board or panel meetings that the member is eligible to attend during each calendar year.

(b) The board administrator or the board administrator's designee shall provide to members of the board and to employees, as often as necessary, information regarding their qualification for office or employment under this chapter and their responsibilities under applicable laws relating to standards of conduct for state officers or employees.

(c) The validity of an action of the board or panel is not affected by the fact that the action is taken when a ground for removal of a board member exists.

(d) If the general counsel to the board has knowledge that a potential ground for removal exists, the general counsel shall notify the presiding officer of the board of the potential ground. The presiding officer shall notify the governor and the attorney general that a potential ground for removal exists. If the potential ground for removal involves the presiding officer, the general counsel to the board shall notify the governor and the attorney general that a potential ground for removal exists.

(e) It is a ground for removal from the board that a member fails to comply with policies or rules adopted by the board.

Added by Acts 1997, 75th Leg., ch. 165, § 12.01, eff. Sept. 1, 1997. Amended by Acts 1999, 76th Leg., ch. 62, § 10.05, eff. Sept. 1, 1999; Acts 1999, 76th Leg., ch. 554, § 3, eff. Sept. 1, 1999; Acts 2001, 77th Leg., ch. 856, § 1, eff. Sept. 1, 2001; Acts 2003, 78th Leg., 3rd C.S., ch. 3, § 11.05, eff. Jan. 11, 2004.

§ 508.035. Presiding Officer

(a) The governor shall designate one member to serve as presiding officer of the board.

(b) The presiding officer serves in that capacity at the pleasure of the governor.

(c) The presiding officer reports directly to the governor and serves as the administrative head of the board.

(d) The presiding officer may:

(1) delegate responsibilities and authority to other members of the board, parole commissioners, or to employees of the board;

(2) appoint advisory committees from the membership of the board or from parole commissioners to further the efficient administration of board business; and

(3) establish policies and procedures to further the efficient administration of the business of the board.

Added by Acts 1997, 75th Leg., ch. 165, § 12.01, eff. Sept. 1, 1997. Amended by Acts 2001, 77th Leg., ch. 856, § 2, eff. Sept. 1, 2001; Acts 2003, 78th Leg., 3rd C.S., ch. 3, § 11.06, eff. Jan. 11, 2004.

§ 508.036. General Administrative Duties

(a) The presiding officer shall:

(1) develop and implement policies that clearly separate the policy-making responsibilities of the board and the management responsibilities of the board administrator, parole commissioners, and the staff of the board;

(2) establish caseloads and required work hours for members of the board and parole commissioners;

(3) update parole guidelines, assign precedential value to previous decisions of the board relating to

the granting of parole and the revocation of parole or mandatory supervision, and develop policies to ensure that members of the board and parole commissioners use guidelines and previous decisions of the board and parole commissioners in making decisions under this chapter;

(4) require members of the board and parole commissioners to file activity reports that provide information on release decisions made by members of the board and parole commissioners, the workload and hours worked of the members of the board and parole commissioners, and the use of parole guidelines by members of the board and parole commissioners; and

(5) report at least annually to the governor and the legislature on the activities of the board and parole commissioners, parole release decisions, and the use of parole guidelines by the board and parole commissioners.

(b) The board shall:

(1) adopt rules relating to the decision-making processes used by the board and parole panels;

(2) prepare information of public interest describing the functions of the board and make the information available to the public and appropriate state agencies;

(3) comply with federal and state laws related to program and facility accessibility; and

(4) develop and implement policies that provide the public with a reasonable opportunity to appear before the board and to speak on any issue under the jurisdiction of the board, with the exception of an individual parole determination or clemency recommendation.

(c) The board administrator shall prepare and maintain a written plan that describes how a person who does not speak English can be provided reasonable access to the board's programs and services.

(d) The board, in performing its duties, is subject to the open meetings law, Chapter 551, and the administrative procedure law, Chapter 2001. This subsection does not affect the provisions of Section 2001.223 exempting hearings and interviews conducted by the board or the division from Section 2001.038 and Subchapters C–H, Chapter 2001.[1]

(e) The board, in accordance with the rules and procedures of the Legislative Budget Board, shall prepare, approve, and submit a legislative appropriations request that is separate from the legislative appropriations request for the department and is used to develop the board's budget structure. The board shall maintain the board's legislative appropriations request and budget structure separately from those of the department.

Added by Acts 1997, 75th Leg., ch. 165, § 12.01, eff. Sept. 1, 1997. Amended by Acts 1999, 76th Leg., ch. 62, § 10.06, eff. Sept. 1, 1999; Acts 2001, 77th Leg., ch. 856, § 3, eff. Sept. 1, 2001; Acts 2003, 78th Leg., ch. 1170, § 31.01, eff. Sept. 1, 2003; Acts 2003, 78th Leg., 3rd C.S., ch. 3, § 11.07, eff. Jan. 11, 2004; Acts 2007, 80th Leg., ch. 1308, §§ 34, 35, eff. June 15, 2007; Acts 2011, 82nd Leg., ch. 1083 (S.B. 1179), § 9, eff. June 17, 2011.

[1] V.T.C.A., Government Code § 2001.051 et seq.

§ 508.0361. Repealed by Acts 2003, 78th Leg., 3rd C.S., ch. 3, § 11.22(a), eff. Jan. 11, 2004

§ 508.0362. Training Required

(a)(1) A person who is appointed to and qualifies for office as a member of the board may not vote, deliberate, or be counted as a member in attendance at a meeting of the board until the person completes at least one course of a training program that complies with this section.

(2) A parole commissioner employed by the board may not vote or deliberate on a matter described by Section 508.0441 until the person completes at least one course of a training program that complies with this section.

(b) A training program must provide information to the person regarding:

(1) the enabling legislation that created the board;

(2) the programs operated by the board;

(3) the role and functions of the board and parole commissioners;

(4) the rules of the board;

(5) the current budget for the board;

(6) the results of the most recent formal audit of the board;

(7) the requirements of the:

(A) open meetings law, Chapter 551;

(B) open records law, Chapter 552; and

(C) administrative procedure law, Chapter 2001;

(8) the requirements of the conflict of interest laws and other laws relating to public officials; and

(9) any applicable ethics policies adopted by the board or the Texas Ethics Commission.

(c) A person appointed to the board is entitled to reimbursement, as provided by the General Appropriations Act, for the travel expenses incurred in attending the training program regardless of whether the attendance at the program occurs before or after the person qualifies for office.

Added by Acts 1999, 76th Leg., ch. 62, § 10.08, eff. Sept. 1, 1999. Amended by Acts 1999, 76th Leg., ch. 554, § 4, eff. Sept. 1, 1999; Acts 2003, 78th Leg., 3rd C.S., ch. 3, § 11.08, eff. Jan. 11, 2004.

§ 508.037. Terms; Removal

(a) A board member holds office for a term of six years.

(b) The terms of one-third of the members expire February 1 of each odd-numbered year.

(c) The governor may remove a board member, other than a member appointed by another governor, at any time and for any reason.

Added by Acts 1997, 75th Leg., ch. 165, § 12.01, eff. Sept. 1, 1997.

§ 508.038. Vacancies

If a vacancy occurs, the governor shall appoint in the same manner as other appointments are made a person to serve the remainder of the unexpired term.

Added by Acts 1997, 75th Leg., ch. 165, § 12.01, eff. Sept. 1, 1997.

§ 508.039. Compensation

A board member is paid the salary the legislature determines in the General Appropriations Act.

Added by Acts 1997, 75th Leg., ch. 165, § 12.01, eff. Sept. 1, 1997.

§ 508.040. Personnel

(a) The presiding officer is responsible for the employment and supervision of:

(1) parole commissioners;

(2) a general counsel to the board;

(3) a board administrator to manage the day-to-day activities of the board;

(4) hearing officers;

(5) personnel to assist in clemency and hearing matters; and

(6) secretarial or clerical personnel.

(b) The board administrator or the board administrator's designee shall prepare and maintain a written policy statement that implements a program of equal employment opportunity under which all personnel decisions of the board are made without regard to race, color, disability, sex, religion, age, or national origin. The policy statement must include:

(1) personnel policies, including policies relating to recruitment, evaluation, selection, training, and promotion of personnel, that show the intent of the board to avoid the unlawful employment practices described by Chapter 21, Labor Code; and

(2) an analysis of the extent to which the composition of the board's personnel is in accordance with state and federal law and a description of reasonable methods to achieve compliance with state and federal law.

(c) The policy statement must be updated annually, be reviewed by the Commission on Human Rights for compliance with Subsection (b)(1), and be filed with the governor's office.

(d) The board administrator or the board administrator's designee shall develop an intra-agency career ladder program that addresses opportunities for mobility and advancement for employees within the board. The program shall require intra-agency posting of all positions concurrently with any public posting.

(e) The board administrator or the board administrator's designee shall develop a system of annual performance evaluations that are based on documented employee performance. All merit pay for board employees must be based on the system established under this subsection.

Added by Acts 1997, 75th Leg., ch. 165, § 12.01, eff. Sept. 1, 1997. Amended by Acts 1999, 76th Leg., ch. 62, § 10.09, eff. Sept. 1, 1999; Acts 1999, 76th Leg., ch. 554, § 5, eff. Sept. 1, 1999; Acts 2003, 78th Leg., 3rd C.S., ch. 3, § 11.09, eff. Jan. 11, 2004.

§ 508.041. Designee Training; Handbook

(a) The board shall develop and implement:

(1) a training program that each newly hired employee of the board designated to conduct hearings under Section 508.281 must complete before conducting a hearing without the assistance of a board member or experienced parole commissioner or designee; and

(2) a training program to provide an annual update to designees of the board on issues and procedures relating to the revocation process.

(b) The board shall prepare and biennially update a procedural manual to be used by designees of the board. The board shall include in the manual:

(1) descriptions of decisions in previous hearings determined by the board to have value as precedents for decisions in subsequent hearings;

(2) laws and court decisions relevant to decision making in hearings; and

(3) case studies useful in decision making in hearings.

(c) The board shall prepare and update as necessary a handbook to be made available to participants in hearings under Section 508.281, such as defense attorneys, persons released on parole or mandatory supervision, and witnesses. The handbook must describe in plain language the procedures used in a hearing under Section 508.281.

Added by Acts 1997, 75th Leg., ch. 165, § 12.01, eff. Sept. 1, 1997. Amended by Acts 1999, 76th Leg., ch. 62, § 10.10, eff. Sept. 1, 1999; Acts 2003, 78th Leg., 3rd C.S., ch. 3, § 11.10, eff. Jan. 11, 2004.

§ 508.042. Training Program for Members and Parole Commissioners

(a) The board shall develop for board members and parole commissioners a comprehensive training and education program on the criminal justice system, with special emphasis on the parole process.

(b)(1) A new member may not participate in a vote of the board or a panel, deliberate, or be counted as a member in attendance at a meeting of the board until the member completes the program.

(2) A new parole commissioner may not participate in a vote of a panel until the commissioner completes the program. This subdivision does not apply to a new parole commissioner who as a board member completed the program.

Added by Acts 1997, 75th Leg., ch. 165, § 12.01, eff. Sept. 1, 1997. Amended by Acts 1999, 76th Leg., ch. 62, § 10.11, eff. Sept. 1, 1999; Acts 1999, 76th Leg., ch. 554, § 6, eff. Sept. 1, 1999; Acts 2003, 78th Leg., 3rd C.S., ch. 3, § 11.11, eff. Jan. 11, 2004.

§ 508.043. Gifts and Grants

The board may apply for and accept gifts or grants from any public or private source for use in any lawful purpose of the board.

Added by Acts 1997, 75th Leg., ch. 165, § 12.01, eff. Sept. 1, 1997.

§ 508.044. Powers and Duties of Board

A board member shall give full time to the duties of the member's office, including duties imposed on the board by the Texas Constitution and other law.

Added by Acts 1997, 75th Leg., ch. 165, § 12.01, eff. Sept. 1, 1997. Amended by Acts 1999, 76th Leg., ch. 62, §§ 10.12 to 10.14, eff. Sept. 1, 1999; Acts 2001, 77th Leg., ch. 856, § 4, eff. Sept. 1, 2001; Acts 2003, 78th Leg., 3rd C.S., ch. 3, § 11.12, eff. Jan. 11, 2004.

§ 508.0441. Release and Revocation Duties

(a) Board members and parole commissioners shall determine:

(1) which inmates are to be released on parole or mandatory supervision;

(2) conditions of parole or mandatory supervision, including special conditions;

(3) the modification and withdrawal of conditions of parole or mandatory supervision;

(4) which releasees may be released from supervision and reporting; and

(5) the continuation, modification, and revocation of parole or mandatory supervision.

(b) The board shall develop and implement a policy that clearly defines circumstances under which a board member or parole commissioner should disqualify himself or herself from voting on:

(1) a parole decision; or

(2) a decision to revoke parole or mandatory supervision.

(c) The board may adopt reasonable rules as proper or necessary relating to:

(1) the eligibility of an inmate for release on parole or release to mandatory supervision;

(2) the conduct of a parole or mandatory supervision hearing; or

(3) conditions to be imposed on a releasee.

(d) The presiding officer may provide a written plan for the administrative review of actions taken by a parole panel by a review panel.

(e) Board members and parole commissioners shall, at the direction of the presiding officer, file activity reports on duties performed under this chapter.

Added by Acts 1997, 75th Leg., ch. 165, § 12.01, eff. Sept. 1, 1997. Amended by Acts 1999, 76th Leg., ch. 62, §§ 10.12 to 10.14, eff. Sept. 1, 1999; Acts 2001, 77th Leg., ch. 856, § 4, eff. Sept. 1, 2001. Redesignated from V.T.C.A., Government Code § 508.044(b) to (f) and amended by Acts 2003, 78th Leg., 3rd C.S., ch. 3, § 11.12, eff. Jan. 11, 2004.

§ 508.045. Parole Panels

(a) Except as provided by Section 508.046, board members and parole commissioners shall act in panels composed of three in matters of:

(1) release on parole;

(2) release to mandatory supervision; and

(3) revocation of parole or mandatory supervision.

(b) The presiding officer shall designate the composition of each panel and shall designate panels composed of at least one board member and any combination of board members and parole commissioners.

(c) A parole panel may:

(1) grant, deny, or revoke parole;

(2) revoke mandatory supervision; and

(3) conduct parole revocation hearings and mandatory supervision revocation hearings.

Added by Acts 1997, 75th Leg., ch. 165, § 12.01, eff. Sept. 1, 1997. Amended by Acts 2003, 78th Leg., 3rd C.S., ch. 3, § 11.13, eff. Jan. 11, 2004.

§ 508.046. Extraordinary Vote Required

To release on parole an inmate who was convicted of an offense under Section 20A.03, 21.02, 21.11(a)(1), or 22.021, Penal Code, or who is required under Section 508.145(c) to serve 35 calendar years before becoming eligible for release on parole, all members of the board must vote on the release on parole of the inmate, and at least two-thirds of the members must vote in favor of the release on parole. A member of the board may not vote on the release unless the member first receives a copy of a written report from the department on the probability that the inmate would commit an offense after being released on parole.

Added by Acts 1997, 75th Leg., ch. 165, § 12.01, eff. Sept. 1, 1997. Amended by Acts 2005, 79th Leg., ch. 787, § 3, eff. Sept. 1, 2005; Acts 2007, 80th Leg., ch. 593, § 3.38, eff. Sept. 1, 2007; Acts 2011, 82nd Leg., ch. 122 (H.B. 3000), § 9, eff. Sept. 1, 2011.

§ 508.047. Meetings

(a) The members of the board shall meet at least once in each quarter of the calendar year at a site determined by the presiding officer.

(b) The members of the board are not required to meet as a body to perform the members' duties in clemency matters.

(c) A majority of each parole panel constitutes a quorum for the transaction of the panel's business. A panel's decision must be by majority vote.

(d) The members of a parole panel are not required to meet as a body to perform the members' duties, except to conduct a hearing under Section 508.281.

Added by Acts 1997, 75th Leg., ch. 165, § 12.01, eff. Sept. 1, 1997. Amended by Acts 1999, 76th Leg., ch. 62, § 10.15, eff. Sept. 1, 1999; Acts 2003, 78th Leg., 3rd C.S., ch. 3, § 11.14, eff. Jan. 11, 2004.

§ 508.048. Subpoenas

(a) A parole panel may issue a subpoena requiring the attendance of a witness or the production of any record, book, paper, or document the panel considers necessary for investigation of the case of a person before the panel.

(b) A member of the board may sign a subpoena and administer an oath.

(c) A peace officer, parole officer, or community supervision and corrections department officer may serve the subpoena in the same manner as similar process in a court of record having original jurisdiction of criminal actions is served.

(d) A person who testifies falsely, fails to appear when subpoenaed, or fails or refuses to produce material under the subpoena is subject to the same orders and penalties to which a person taking those actions before a court is subject.

(e) On application of the board, a court of record having original jurisdiction of criminal actions may compel the attendance of a witness, the production of material, or the giving of testimony before the board, by an attachment for contempt or in the same manner as the court may otherwise compel the production of evidence.

Added by Acts 1997, 75th Leg., ch. 165, § 12.01, eff. Sept. 1, 1997.

§ 508.0481. Victim's Right to Representation

(a) If a victim, close relative of a deceased victim, or guardian of a victim is required by a subpoena issued under Section 508.048 to appear at a hearing, the victim, relative, or guardian is entitled to representation by counsel at the hearing.

(b) This section does not require the state to provide representation by counsel to a victim, close relative of a deceased victim, or guardian of a victim.

(c) In this section, "victim," "close relative of a deceased victim," and "guardian of a victim" have the meanings assigned by Section 508.117.

Added by Acts 2001, 77th Leg., ch. 1034, § 10, eff. Sept. 1, 2001.

§ 508.049. Mission Statement

(a) The board, after consultation with the governor and the Texas Board of Criminal Justice, shall adopt a mission statement that reflects the responsibilities for the operation of the parole process that are assigned to the board, the division, the department, or the Texas Board of Criminal Justice.

(b) The board shall include in the mission statement a description of specific locations at which the board intends to conduct business related to the operation of the parole process.

Added by Acts 1997, 75th Leg., ch. 165, § 12.01, eff. Sept. 1, 1997. Amended by Acts 1999, 76th Leg., ch. 62, § 10.16, eff. Sept. 1, 1999; Acts 2003, 78th Leg., 3rd C.S., ch. 3, § 11.15, eff. Jan. 11, 2004.

§ 508.050. Report to Governor

(a) On request of the governor, the board shall investigate a person being considered by the governor for:

(1) pardon;

(2) commutation of sentence;

(3) reprieve;

(4) remission of fine; or

(5) forfeiture.

(b) The board shall report to the governor on its investigation and make recommendations about the person to the governor.

Added by Acts 1997, 75th Leg., ch. 165, § 12.01, eff. Sept. 1, 1997.

§ 508.051. Sunset Provision

The Board of Pardons and Paroles is subject to review under Chapter 325 (Texas Sunset Act), but is not abolished under that chapter. The board shall be reviewed during the period in which the Texas Department of Criminal Justice is reviewed.

Added by Acts 1997, 75th Leg., ch. 165, § 12.01, eff. Sept. 1, 1997. Amended by Acts 1999, 76th Leg., ch. 62, § 10.17, eff. Sept. 1, 1999.

§ 508.052. Computers; Office Space; Other Equipment

(a) The department by interagency contract may provide to the board necessary computer equipment and computer access to all computerized records and physical access to all printed records in the custody of the department that are related to the duties and functions of the board.

(b) The department by interagency contract may provide to the board necessary and appropriate:

(1) office space at locations designated by the presiding officer of the board; and

(2) utilities and communications equipment.

Added by Acts 1997, 75th Leg., ch. 165, § 12.01, eff. Sept. 1, 1997.

§ 508.053. Use of Technology

The board shall implement a policy requiring the board to use appropriate technological solutions to improve the board's ability to perform its functions. The policy must ensure that the public is able to interact with the board on the Internet.

Added by Acts 2007, 80th Leg., ch. 1308, § 36, eff. June 15, 2007.

§ 508.054. Records of Complaints

(a) The board shall maintain a system to promptly and efficiently act on complaints filed with the board. The board shall maintain information about parties to the complaint, the subject matter of the complaint, a summary of the results of the review or investigation of the complaint, and its disposition.

(b) The board shall make information available describing its procedures for complaint investigation and resolution.

(c) The board shall periodically notify the complaint parties of the status of the complaint until final disposition.

(d) This section does not apply to a complaint about an individual parole determination or clemency recommendation.

Added by Acts 2007, 80th Leg., ch. 1308, § 36, eff. June 15, 2007.

§ 508.055. Negotiated Rulemaking and Alternative Dispute Resolution

(a) The board shall develop and implement a policy to encourage the use of:

(1) negotiated rulemaking procedures under Chapter 2008 for the adoption of board rules; and

(2) appropriate alternative dispute resolution procedures under Chapter 2009 to assist in the resolution of internal disputes under the board's jurisdiction.

(b) The board's procedures relating to alternative dispute resolution must conform, to the extent possible, to any model guidelines issued by the State Office of Administrative Hearings for the use of alternative dispute resolution by state agencies.

(c) The board shall designate a trained person to:

(1) coordinate the implementation of the policy adopted under Subsection (a);

(2) serve as a resource for any training needed to implement the procedures for negotiated rulemaking or alternative dispute resolution; and

(3) collect data concerning the effectiveness of those procedures, as implemented by the board.

Added by Acts 2007, 80th Leg., ch. 1308, § 36, eff. June 15, 2007.

SUBCHAPTER C. REPRESENTATION OF INMATES

§ 508.081. Definitions

In this subchapter:

(1) "Compensation" has the meaning assigned by Section 305.002.

(2) "Inmate" includes:

(A) an administrative releasee;

(B) an inmate imprisoned in the institutional division; and

(C) a person confined in a transfer facility or county jail awaiting:

(i) transfer to the institutional division; or

(ii) a revocation hearing.

(3) "Represent" means to directly or indirectly contact in person or by telephone, facsimile transmission, or correspondence a member or employee of the board or an employee of the department on behalf of an inmate.

Added by Acts 1997, 75th Leg., ch. 165, § 12.01, eff. Sept. 1, 1997.

§ 508.082. Rules

The board shall adopt rules relating to:

(1) the submission and presentation of information and arguments to the board, a parole panel, and the department for and in behalf of an inmate; and

(2) the time, place, and manner of contact between a person representing an inmate and:

(A) a member of the board or a parole commissioner;

(B) an employee of the board; or

(C) an employee of the department.

Added by Acts 1997, 75th Leg., ch. 165, § 12.01, eff. Sept. 1, 1997. Amended by Acts 1999, 76th Leg., ch. 62, § 10.18, eff. Sept. 1, 1999; Acts 2003, 78th Leg., 3rd C.S., ch. 3, § 11.16, eff. Jan. 11, 2004.

§ 508.083. Eligibility to Represent Inmates

(a) A person who represents an inmate for compensation must:

(1) be an attorney licensed in this state; and

(2) register with the division.

(b) A person serving as a member or employee of the board or the Texas Board of Criminal Justice may not, before the second anniversary of the date the person ceases to be a board member or employee:

(1) represent any person in a matter before the board or a parole panel; or

(2) receive compensation for services rendered on behalf of any person regarding a matter pending before the board or a parole panel.

(c) A person, other than a person subject to Subsection (b), who is employed by the department may not, before the second anniversary of the date the person terminates service with the department:

(1) represent an inmate in a matter before the board or a parole panel; or

(2) receive compensation for services rendered on behalf of any person regarding a matter pending before the board or a parole panel.

(d) Repealed by Acts 2003, 78th Leg., ch. 1007, § 2.

Added by Acts 1997, 75th Leg., ch. 165, § 12.01, eff. Sept. 1, 1997. Amended by Acts 2003, 78th Leg., ch. 1007, §§ 1, 2, eff. Sept. 1, 2003.

§ 508.084. Fee Affidavit

(a) A person required to register under Section 508.083, before the person first contacts a member of the board, an employee of the board, or an employee of the department on behalf of an inmate, shall file a fee affidavit with the department in a form prescribed by the department for each inmate the person represents for compensation.

(b) The fee affidavit must be written and verified and contain a statement of:

(1) the registrant's full name and address;

(2) the registrant's normal business, business phone number, and business address;

(3) the full name of any former member or employee of the board or the Texas Board of Criminal Justice or any former employee of the department with whom the registrant:

(A) is associated;

(B) has a relationship as an employer or employee; or

(C) maintains a contractual relationship to provide services;

(4) the full name and institutional identification number of the inmate the registrant represents;

(5) the amount of compensation the registrant has received or expects to receive in exchange for the representation; and

(6) the name of the person providing the compensation.

(c) If a registrant receives compensation in excess of the amount reported on the fee affidavit, the registrant shall file with the department, not later than the fifth day after the date the registrant receives compensation in excess of the reported amount, a supplemental fee affidavit in a form prescribed by the department indicating the total amount of compensation received for representing the inmate.

(d) For each fee affidavit and supplemental fee affidavit received, the department shall:

(1) keep a copy of the affidavit in a central location; and

(2) not later than the third day after the date the affidavit is filed, place a copy of the affidavit in the inmate's file that is reviewed by a parole panel or the board.

Added by Acts 1997, 75th Leg., ch. 165, § 12.01, eff. Sept. 1, 1997.

§ 508.085.　Representation Summary Form

(a) A person required to register under Section 508.083 shall, for each calendar year in which the person represents an inmate, file a representation summary form with the division on a form prescribed by the division.

(b) The form must be filed not later than January 31 of the year succeeding the year for which the report is filed and must include a statement of:

(1) the registrant's full name and address;

(2) the registrant's normal business, business phone number, and business address;

(3) the full name of any former member or employee of the board or the Texas Board of Criminal Justice or any former employee of the department with whom the registrant:

(A) is associated;

(B) has a relationship as an employer or employee; or

(C) maintains a contractual relationship to provide services;

(4) the full name and institutional identification number of each inmate the registrant represented in the previous calendar year; and

(5) the amount of compensation the registrant has received for representing each inmate in the previous calendar year.

(c) A person who files a form under this section and for whom the information required for the form has changed shall, not later than the 10th day after the date the information changes, file a supplemental statement with the division indicating the change.

Added by Acts 1997, 75th Leg., ch. 165, § 12.01, eff. Sept. 1, 1997.

§ 508.086.　Criminal Penalties

(a) A former member or employee of the board or the Texas Board of Criminal Justice or a former employee of the department commits an offense if the former member or employee violates Section 508.083(b), (c), or (d).

(b) A person who represents an inmate for compensation commits an offense if the person is not an attorney licensed in this state.

(c) A person who is required to file an affidavit under Section 508.084(a) or (c) or a form or statement under Section 508.085 commits an offense if the person fails to file the affidavit, form, or statement.

(d) An offense under Subsection (a) is a Class A misdemeanor. An offense under Subsection (b) or (c) is a Class C misdemeanor.

Added by Acts 1997, 75th Leg., ch. 165, § 12.01, eff. Sept. 1, 1997.

SUBCHAPTER D.　PARDONS AND PAROLES DIVISION

§ 508.111.　Director

(a) The executive director shall hire the director of the division.

(b) The director is responsible for the administration of the division.

Added by Acts 1997, 75th Leg., ch. 165, § 12.01, eff. Sept. 1, 1997.

§ 508.112.　Duty of Division

The division is responsible for the investigation and supervision of all releasees.

Added by Acts 1997, 75th Leg., ch. 165, § 12.01, eff. Sept. 1, 1997.

§ 508.113. Parole Officers, Supervisors: Qualifications

(a) This subsection and Subsection (b) apply only to a person employed as a parole officer or supervisor on or before September 1, 1990. A person may not be employed as a parole officer or supervisor, or be responsible for investigating or supervising a releasee, unless the person has:

(1) four years of successfully completed education in an accredited college or university;

(2) two years of full-time paid employment in responsible correctional work with adults or juveniles or in a related field; and

(3) any other qualifications that may be specified by the director.

(b) Additional experience in a category described by Subsection (a)(2) may be substituted year for year for the required college education, with a maximum substitution of two years.

(c) The director shall establish qualifications for parole officers and supervisors that are the same as qualifications for community supervision and corrections department officers imposed by Section 76.005. A person may not begin employment as a parole officer or supervisor after September 1, 1990, unless the person meets the qualifications established by the director.

(d) A person who is serving as a peace officer or as a prosecuting attorney may not act as a parole officer or be responsible for supervising a releasee.

Added by Acts 1997, 75th Leg., ch. 165, § 12.01, eff. Sept. 1, 1997.

§ 508.1131. Salary Career Ladder for Parole Officers

(a) The executive director shall adopt a salary career ladder for parole officers. The salary career ladder must base a parole officer's salary on the officer's classification and years of service with the department.

(b) For purposes of the salary schedule, the department shall classify all parole officer positions as Parole Officer I, Parole Officer II, Parole Officer III, Parole Officer IV, or Parole Officer V.

(c) Under the salary career ladder adopted under Subsection (a), a parole officer to whom the schedule applies and who received an overall evaluation of at least satisfactory in the officer's most recent annual evaluation is entitled to an annual salary increase, during each of the officer's first 10 years of service in

a designated parole officer classification as described by Subsection (b), equal to one-tenth of the difference between:

(1) the officer's current annual salary; and

(2) the minimum annual salary of a parole officer in the next highest classification.

Added by Acts 2007, 80th Leg., ch. 1308, § 37, eff. June 15, 2007.

§ 508.114. Parole Officers, Supervisors: Additional Duties

(a) The judge of a court having original jurisdiction of criminal actions may, with the approval of the director, designate a parole officer or supervisor as a community supervision and corrections department officer. The director must give prior written approval for the payment of a proportional part of the salary paid to the parole officer or supervisor in compensation for service as a community supervision and corrections department officer. The director shall periodically report to the governor and the legislature the proportional salary payments.

(b) A parole officer or supervisor, on request of the governor or on order of the director, shall be responsible for supervising an inmate placed on conditional pardon or granted an emergency absence under escort.

Added by Acts 1997, 75th Leg., ch. 165, § 12.01, eff. Sept. 1, 1997.

§ 508.1141. Specialized Training; Gang Members

The department shall develop and provide specialized training for parole officers supervising releasees previously identified by the department as being members of prison gangs, criminal street gangs, or security threat groups.

Added by Acts 1999, 76th Leg., ch. 490, § 1, eff. Sept. 1, 1999.

§ 508.1142. Parole Officer Maximum Caseloads

(a) The department shall adopt a policy that establishes guidelines for a maximum caseload for each parole officer of:

(1) 60 active releasees, if the releasees are not in a specialized program described by Subdivisions (2)–(6);

(2) 35 active releasees, if the releasees are in the special needs offender program;

(3) 35 active releasees, if the releasees are in the therapeutic community substance abuse aftercare treatment program;

(4) 24 active releasees, if the releasees are in the sex offender program;

(5) 20 active releasees, if the releasees are electronically monitored; and

(6) 11 active releasees, if the releasees are in the super-intensive supervision program.

(b) If the department is unable to meet the maximum caseload guidelines, the department shall submit a report to the Legislative Budget Board, at the end of each fiscal year in which the department fails to meet the guidelines, stating the amount of money needed by the department to meet the guidelines.

Added by Acts 2007, 80th Leg., ch. 1421, § 1, eff. June 15, 2007.

§ 508.115. Notification of Release of Inmate

(a) Not later than the 11th day before the date a parole panel orders the release on parole of an inmate or not later than the 11th day after the date the board recommends that the governor grant executive clemency, the division shall notify the sheriffs, each chief of police, the prosecuting attorneys, and the district judges in the county in which the inmate was convicted and the county to which the inmate is released that a parole panel is considering release on parole or the governor is considering clemency.

(b) In a case in which there was a change of venue, the division shall notify the sheriff, the prosecuting attorney, and the district judge in the county in which the prosecution was originated if, not later than the 30th day after the date the inmate was sentenced, those officials request in writing that the division give the officials notice under this section of a release of the inmate.

(c) Not later than the 10th day after the date a parole panel orders the transfer of an inmate to a halfway house under this chapter, the division shall give notice in accordance with Subsection (d) to:

(1) the sheriff of the county in which the inmate was convicted;

(2) the sheriff of the county in which the halfway house is located and each chief of police in the county; and

(3) the attorney who represents the state in the prosecution of felonies in the county in which the halfway house is located.

(d) The notice must state:

(1) the inmate's name;

(2) the county in which the inmate was convicted; and

(3) the offense for which the inmate was convicted.

(e) The notice must be provided by e-mail or other electronic communication.

Added by Acts 1997, 75th Leg., ch. 165, § 12.01, eff. Sept. 1, 1997. Amended by Acts 1999, 76th Leg., ch. 62, § 10.19, eff. Sept. 1, 1999; Acts 2001, 77th Leg., ch. 856, § 5, eff. Sept. 1, 2001; Acts 2011, 82nd Leg., ch. 1123 (H.B. 200), § 5, eff. Sept. 1, 2011.

§ 508.116. Parole Information Program

(a) The division shall develop and implement a comprehensive program to inform inmates, the inmates' families, and other interested parties about the parole process.

(b) The division shall update the program annually.

Added by Acts 1997, 75th Leg., ch. 165, § 12.01, eff. Sept. 1, 1997.

§ 508.117. Victim Notification

(a) Before a parole panel considers for release on parole an inmate who is serving a sentence for an offense in which a person was a victim, the division, using the name and address provided on the victim impact statement, shall make a reasonable effort to notify:

(1) the victim;

(2) if the victim has a guardian, the guardian; or

(3) if the victim is deceased, a close relative of the deceased victim.

(b) A victim, guardian of a victim, or close relative of a deceased victim who would have been entitled to notification of parole consideration by the division but failed to provide a victim impact statement containing the person's name and address may file with the division a written request for notification. After receiving the written request, the division shall grant to the person all privileges, including notification under this section, to which the person would have been entitled had the person submitted a completed victim impact statement.

(c) If the notice is sent to a guardian or close relative of a deceased victim, the notice must contain a request by the division that the guardian or relative inform other persons having an interest in the matter that the inmate is being considered for release on parole.

(d) The failure of the division to comply with notice requirements of this section is not a ground for revocation of parole.

(e) Before an inmate is released from the institutional division on parole or to mandatory supervision, the pardons and paroles division shall give notice of the release to a person entitled to notification of parole consideration for the inmate under Subsection (a) or (b).

(f) Except as necessary to comply with this section, the board or the department may not disclose to any person the name or address of a person entitled to notice under this section unless:

(1) the person approves the disclosure; or

(2) a court determines that there is good cause for disclosure and orders the board or the department to disclose the information.

(g) In this section:

(1) "Close relative of a deceased victim" means a person who was:

(A) the spouse of the victim at the time of the victim's death;

(B) a parent of the deceased victim;

(C) an adult brother, sister, or child of the deceased victim; or

(D) the nearest relative of the deceased victim by consanguinity, if the persons described by Paragraphs (A) through (C) are deceased or are incapacitated due to physical or mental illness or infirmity.

(2) "Guardian of a victim" means a person who is the legal guardian of a victim, whether or not the legal relationship between the guardian and the victim exists because of the age of the victim or the physical or mental incompetency of the victim.

(2–a) "Sexual assault" includes an offense under Section 21.02, Penal Code.

(3) "Victim" means a person who:

(A) is a victim of sexual assault, kidnapping, aggravated robbery, or felony stalking; or

(B) has suffered bodily injury or death as the result of the criminal conduct of another.

Added by Acts 1997, 75th Leg., ch. 165, § 12.01, eff. Sept. 1, 1997. Amended by Acts 2007, 80th Leg., ch. 593, § 3.39, eff. Sept. 1, 2007; Acts 2007, 80th Leg., ch. 826, § 1, eff. June 15, 2007; Acts 2007, 80th Leg., ch. 1308, § 38, eff. June 15, 2007.

§ 508.118. Halfway Houses

(a) The division, in conjunction with the institutional division, shall use halfway houses to divert from housing in regular units of the institutional division suitable low-risk inmates and other inmates who would benefit from a smoother transition from incarceration to supervised release.

(b) Before transferring an inmate to a halfway house, the division shall send to the director of the halfway house all information relating to the inmate that the division determines will aid the halfway house in helping the inmate make a transition from the institutional division to supervised release.

(c) The division is responsible for supervising an inmate:

(1) for whom a presumptive parole date has been established; and

(2) who is transferred into a preparole residence in a halfway house under Subchapter A, Chapter 499.[1]

Added by Acts 1997, 75th Leg., ch. 165, § 12.01, eff. Sept. 1, 1997.

[1] V.T.C.A., Government Code § 499.001 et seq.

§ 508.119. Community Residential Facilities

(a) The purpose of a community residential facility is to provide housing, supervision, counseling, personal, social, and work adjustment training, and other programs to:

(1) releasees who are required by a parole panel as a condition of release on parole or to mandatory supervision to serve a period in a community residential facility; and

(2) releasees whose parole or mandatory supervision has been continued or modified under Section 508.283 and on whom sanctions have been imposed under that section.

(b) The division may establish and operate, or contract for the operation of, community residential facilities.

(c) The division may contract with a public or private vendor for the financing, construction, operation, or management of a community residential facility using a lease-purchase or installment sale contract to provide or supplement housing, board, or supervision for releasees placed in a community residential facility. A releasee housed or supervised in a facility operated by a vendor under a contract is subject to the same laws as if the housing or supervision were provided directly by the division.

(d) Unless the division or a vendor proposing to operate a community residential facility provides notice of a following proposed action and a hearing on the issues in the same manner as required under Section 509.010, the division may not:

(1) establish or contract for a community residential facility;

(2) change the use of a community residential facility;

(3) significantly increase the capacity of a community residential facility; or

(4) increase the capacity of a community residential facility to more than 500 residents, regardless of whether the increase is significant.

(e) Subsection (d) applies to any residential facility that the division establishes or contracts for under:

(1) this chapter;

(2) Subchapter C, Chapter 497;[1] or

(3) Subchapter A, Chapter 499.

(f) The Texas Board of Criminal Justice shall adopt rules necessary for the management of a community residential facility.

(g) The division may charge to a releasee housed in a community residential facility a reasonable fee for the cost of housing, board, and the part of the administrative costs of the facility that is properly allocable to the releasee. The fee may not exceed the actual costs to the division for services to that releasee. The division may not deny placement in a community residential facility to a releasee because the releasee is unable to pay the fee.

(h) A parole panel or a designated agent of the division may grant a limited release to a releasee placed in a community residential facility to maintain or seek employment or participation in an education or training course or to seek housing after release from the facility.

(i) The notice required by Subsection (d) must clearly state that the proposed action concerns a facility in which persons who have been released from prison on parole or to mandatory supervision are to be housed.

Added by Acts 1997, 75th Leg., ch. 165, § 12.01, eff. Sept. 1, 1997. Amended by Acts 1999, 76th Leg., ch. 62, § 10.20, eff. Sept. 1, 1999.

[1] V.T.C.A., Government Code § 497.051 et seq.

SUBCHAPTER E. PAROLE AND MANDATORY SUPERVISION; RELEASE PROCEDURES

§ 508.141. Authority to Consider and Order Release on Parole

(a) A parole panel may consider for release and release on parole an inmate who:

(1) has been sentenced to a term of imprisonment in the institutional division;

(2) is confined in a penal or correctional institution, including a jail in this state, a federal correctional institution, or a jail or a correctional institution in another state; and

(3) is eligible for release on parole.

(b) A parole is issued only on the order of a parole panel.

(c) Before releasing an inmate on parole, a parole panel may have the inmate appear before the panel and interview the inmate.

(d) A parole panel may release an inmate on parole during the parole month established for the inmate if the panel determines that the inmate's release will not increase the likelihood of harm to the public.

(e) A parole panel may release an inmate on parole only when:

(1) arrangements have been made for the inmate's employment or for the inmate's maintenance and care, which may include the issuance of payment for the cost of temporary post-release housing under Section 508.157; and

(2) the parole panel believes that the inmate is able and willing to fulfill the obligations of a law-abiding citizen.

(f) A parole panel may order a parole only for the best interest of society and not as an award of clemency.

(g) The board shall adopt a policy establishing the date on which the board may reconsider for release an inmate who has previously been denied release. The policy must require the board to reconsider for release:

(1) an inmate serving a sentence for an offense listed in Section 508.149(a) or for an offense punishable as a felony of the second or third degree under Section 22.04, Penal Code, during a month designated under Subsection (g–1) by the parole panel that denied release; and

(2) an inmate other than an inmate described by Subdivision (1) as soon as practicable after the first anniversary of the date of the denial.

(g–1) The month designated under Subsection (g)(1) by the parole panel that denied release must begin after the first anniversary of the date of the denial and end before the fifth anniversary of the date of the denial, unless the inmate is serving a sentence for an offense under Section 22.021, Penal Code, or a life sentence for a capital felony, in which event the designated month must begin after the first anniversary of the date of the denial and end before the 10th anniversary of the date of the denial.

Added by Acts 1997, 75th Leg., ch. 165, § 12.01, eff. Sept. 1, 1997. Amended by Acts 2003, 78th Leg., ch. 349, § 1, eff. June 18, 2003; Acts 2003, 78th Leg., 3rd C.S., ch. 3, § 11.17, eff. Jan. 11, 2004; Acts 2009, 81st Leg., ch. 944, § 2, eff. June 19, 2009; Acts 2013, 83rd Leg., ch. 1256 (H.B. 431), § 2, eff. June 14, 2013; Acts 2015, 84th Leg., ch. 358 (H.B. 1914), § 1, eff. Sept. 1, 2015.

Section 2 of Acts 2015, 84th Leg., ch. 358 (H.B. 1914) provides:

"The Board of Pardons and Paroles shall adopt a policy consistent with Section 508.141(g–1), Government Code, as amended by this Act, as soon as practicable after the effective date of this Act."

§ 508.1411. Notification of Parole Panel Decision

(a) For each decision of a parole panel granting or denying the release of an inmate on parole, or denying the release of an inmate on mandatory supervision, the parole panel shall:

(1) produce a written statement, in clear and understandable language, that explains:

(A) the decision; and

(B) the reasons for the decision only to the extent those reasons relate specifically to the inmate;

(2) provide a copy of the statement to the inmate; and

(3) place a copy of the statement in the inmate's file.

(b) In a written statement produced under Subsection (a), the parole panel may withhold information that:

(1) is confidential and not subject to public disclosure under Chapter 552; or

(2) the parole panel considers to possibly jeopardize the health or safety of any individual.

(c) The board shall keep a copy of each statement produced under Subsection (a) in a central location.

Added by Acts 2013, 83rd Leg., ch. 1154 (S.B. 213), § 14, eff. Sept. 1, 2013.

§ 508.142. Period of Parole

(a) The institutional division shall provide the board with sentence time credit information for each inmate who is eligible for release on parole.

(b) Good conduct time credit is computed for an inmate as if the inmate were confined in the institutional division during the entire time the inmate was actually confined.

(c) The period of parole is computed by subtracting from the term for which the inmate was sentenced the calendar time served on the sentence.

Added by Acts 1997, 75th Leg., ch. 165, § 12.01, eff. Sept. 1, 1997.

§ 508.143. Legal Custody of Releasee

(a) A releasee while on parole is in the legal custody of the division.

(b) A releasee while on mandatory supervision is in the legal custody of the state.

Added by Acts 1997, 75th Leg., ch. 165, § 12.01, eff. Sept. 1, 1997.

§ 508.144. Parole Guidelines and Range of Recommended Parole Approval Rates

(a) The board shall:

(1) develop according to an acceptable research method the parole guidelines that are the basic criteria on which a parole decision is made;

(2) base the guidelines on the seriousness of the offense and the likelihood of a favorable parole outcome;

(3) ensure that the guidelines require consideration of an inmate's progress in any programs in which the inmate participated during the inmate's term of confinement;

(4) establish and maintain a range of recommended parole approval rates for each category or score within the guidelines; and

(5) implement the guidelines.

(b) The board shall meet annually to review and discuss the parole guidelines and range of recommended parole approval rates. The board may consult outside experts to assist with the review. The board shall prioritize the use of outside experts, technical assistance, and training in taking any action under Subsection (c). The board must consider:

(1) how the parole guidelines and range of recommended parole approval rates serve the needs of parole decision-making; and

(2) the extent to which the parole guidelines and range of recommended parole approval rates reflect parole panel decisions and predict successful parole outcomes.

(c) Based on the board's review under Subsection (b), the board may:

(1) update the guidelines by:

(A) including new risk factors; or

(B) changing the values of offense severity or risk factor scores; or

(2) modify the range of recommended parole approval rates under the guidelines, if parole approval rates differ significantly from the range of recommended parole approval rates.

(d) The board is not required to hold an open meeting to review the parole guidelines and range of recommended parole approval rates as required by Subsection (b), but any modifications or updates to the guidelines or range of recommended parole approval rates made by the board under Subsection (c) must occur in an open meeting.

Added by Acts 1997, 75th Leg., ch. 165, § 12.01, eff. Sept. 1, 1997. Amended by Acts 2003, 78th Leg., 3rd C.S., ch. 3, § 11.18, eff. Jan. 11, 2004; Acts 2007, 80th Leg., ch. 1308, § 39, eff. June 15, 2007; Acts 2013, 83rd Leg., ch. 1154 (S.B. 213), § 15, eff. Sept. 1, 2013.

§ 508.144. Annual Report on Guidelines Required

(a) The board annually shall submit a report to the Criminal Justice Legislative Oversight Committee, the lieutenant governor, the speaker of the house of representatives, and the presiding officers of the standing committees in the senate and house of representatives primarily responsible for criminal justice regarding the board's application of the parole guidelines adopted under Section 508.144.

(b) The report must include:

(1) a brief explanation of the parole guidelines, including how the board:

(A) defines the risk factors and offense severity levels; and

(B) determines the range of recommended parole approval rates for each guideline score;

(2) a comparison of the range of recommended parole approval rates under the parole guidelines to the actual approval rates for individual parole panel members, regional offices, and the state as a whole; and

(3) a description of instances in which the actual parole approval rates do not meet the range of recommended parole approval rates under the parole guidelines, an explanation of the variations, and a list of actions that the board has taken or will take to meet the guidelines.

Added by Acts 2007, 80th Leg., ch. 1308, § 40, eff. June 15, 2007. Amended by Acts 2013, 83rd Leg., ch. 1154 (S.B. 213), § 16, eff. Sept. 1, 2013.

§ 508.145. Eligibility for Release on Parole; Computation of Parole Eligibility Date

(a) An inmate under sentence of death, serving a sentence of life imprisonment without parole, serving a sentence for an offense under Section 21.02, Penal Code, or serving a sentence for an offense under Section 22.021, Penal Code, that is punishable under Subsection (f) of that section is not eligible for release on parole.

(b) An inmate serving a life sentence under Section 12.31(a)(1), Penal Code, for a capital felony is not eligible for release on parole until the actual calendar time the inmate has served, without consideration of good conduct time, equals 40 calendar years.

(c) An inmate serving a sentence under Section 12.42(c)(2), Penal Code, is not eligible for release on parole until the actual calendar time the inmate has served, without consideration of good conduct time, equals 35 calendar years.

(d)(1) This subsection applies only to an inmate who is serving a sentence for:

(A) an offense described by Article 42A.054(a), Code of Criminal Procedure, other than an offense under Section 19.03, Penal Code;

(B) an offense for which the judgment contains an affirmative finding under Article 42A.054(c) or (d), Code of Criminal Procedure;

(C) an offense under Section 20A.03, Penal Code; or

(D) an offense under Section 71.02 or 71.023, Penal Code.

(2) An inmate described by Subdivision (1) is not eligible for release on parole until the inmate's actual calendar time served, without consideration of good conduct time, equals one-half of the sentence or 30 calendar years, whichever is less, but in no event is the inmate eligible for release on parole in less than two calendar years.

(3) Notwithstanding Subdivision (2), an inmate who is serving a sentence for an offense under Section 22.021, Penal Code, is not eligible for release on parole if the inmate is serving a sentence for an offense for which punishment was enhanced under Section 12.42(c)(4), Penal Code.

(d–1) Notwithstanding Subsection (d), for every 12 months that elapse between the date an arrest warrant is issued for the inmate following an indictment for the offense and the date the inmate is arrested for the offense, the earliest date on which an inmate is eligible for parole is delayed by three years from the date otherwise provided by Subsection (d), if the inmate is serving a sentence for an offense under Section 19.02, 22.011, or 22.021, Penal Code.

(e) An inmate serving a sentence for which the punishment is increased under Section 481.134, Health and Safety Code, is not eligible for release on parole until the inmate's actual calendar time served, without consideration of good conduct time, equals five years or the term to which the inmate was sentenced, whichever is less.

(f) Except as provided by Section 508.146, any other inmate is eligible for release on parole when the inmate's actual calendar time served plus good conduct time equals one-fourth of the sentence imposed or 15 years, whichever is less.

Added by Acts 1997, 75th Leg., ch. 165, § 12.01, eff. Sept. 1, 1997. Amended by Acts 1999, 76th Leg., ch. 62, § 10.21, eff. Sept. 1, 1999; Acts 2005, 79th Leg., ch. 787, §§ 4, 12, eff. Sept. 1, 2005; Acts 2007, 80th Leg., ch. 405, § 2, eff. Sept. 1, 2007; Acts 2007, 80th Leg., ch. 593, § 1.10, eff. Sept. 1, 2007; Acts 2009, 81st Leg., ch. 87, § 11.008, eff. Sept. 1, 2009; Acts 2009, 81st Leg., ch. 146, § 2, eff. Sept. 1, 2009; Acts 2009, 81st Leg., ch. 765, § 2, eff. Sept. 1, 2009; Acts 2009, 81st Leg., ch. 1400, § 3, eff. Sept. 1, 2009; Acts 2011, 82nd Leg., ch. 122 (H.B. 3000), § 10, eff. Sept. 1, 2011; Acts 2011, 82nd Leg., ch. 1119 (H.B. 3), § 2, eff. Sept. 1, 2011; Acts 2013, 83rd Leg., ch. 126 (S.B. 727), § 2, eff. Sept. 1, 2013; Acts 2013, 83rd Leg., ch. 1252 (H.B. 8), § 13, eff. Sept. 1, 2013; Acts 2013, 83rd Leg., ch. 1325 (S.B. 549), § 2, eff. Sept. 1, 2013; Acts 2015, 84th Leg., ch. 770 (H.B. 2299), § 2.51, eff. Jan. 1, 2017.

§ 508.146. Medically Recommended Intensive Supervision

(a) An inmate other than an inmate who is serving a sentence of death or life without parole may be released on medically recommended intensive supervision on a date designated by a parole panel described by Subsection (e), except that an inmate with an instant offense that is an offense described in Article 42A.054, Code of Criminal Procedure, or an inmate who has a reportable conviction or adjudication under Chapter 62, Code of Criminal Procedure, may only be considered if a medical condition of terminal illness or long-term care has been diagnosed by a physician, if:

(1) the Texas Correctional Office on Offenders with Medical or Mental Impairments, in cooperation with the Correctional Managed Health Care Committee, identifies the inmate as being:

(A) a person who is elderly or terminally ill, a person with mental illness, an intellectual disability, or a physical disability, or a person who has a condition requiring long-term care, if the inmate is

an inmate with an instant offense that is described in Article 42A.054, Code of Criminal Procedure; or

(B) in a persistent vegetative state or being a person with an organic brain syndrome with significant to total mobility impairment, if the inmate is an inmate who has a reportable conviction or adjudication under Chapter 62, Code of Criminal Procedure;

(2) the parole panel determines that, based on the inmate's condition and a medical evaluation, the inmate does not constitute a threat to public safety; and

(3) the Texas Correctional Office on Offenders with Medical or Mental Impairments, in cooperation with the pardons and paroles division, has prepared for the inmate a medically recommended intensive supervision plan that requires the inmate to submit to electronic monitoring, places the inmate on super-intensive supervision, or otherwise ensures appropriate supervision of the inmate.

(b) An inmate may be released on medically recommended intensive supervision only if the inmate's medically recommended intensive supervision plan under Subsection (a)(3) is approved by the Texas Correctional Office on Offenders with Medical or Mental Impairments.

(c) The parole panel shall require as a condition of release under Subsection (a) that the releasee remain under the care of a physician and in a medically suitable placement. At least once each calendar quarter, the Texas Correctional Office on Offenders with Medical or Mental Impairments shall report to the parole panel on the releasee's medical and placement status. On the basis of the report, the parole panel may modify conditions of release and impose any condition on the releasee that a panel could impose on a releasee released under Section 508.145, including a condition that the releasee reside in a halfway house or community residential facility.

(d) The Texas Correctional Office on Offenders with Medical or Mental Impairments and the Texas Department of Human Services shall jointly request proposals from public or private vendors to provide under contract services for inmates released on medically recommended intensive supervision. A request for proposals under this subsection may require that the services be provided in a medical care facility located in an urban area. For the purposes of this subsection, "urban area" means the area in this state within a metropolitan statistical area, according to the standards of the United States Bureau of the Census.

(e) Only parole panels composed of the presiding officer of the board and two members appointed to the panel by the presiding officer may make determinations regarding the release of inmates on medically recommended intensive supervision under Subsection (a) or of inmates released pending deportation. If the Texas Council on Offenders with Mental Impairments identifies an inmate as a candidate for release under the guidelines established by Subsection (a)(1), the council shall present to a parole panel described by this subsection relevant information concerning the inmate and the inmate's potential for release under this section.

(f) An inmate who is not a citizen of the United States, as defined by federal law, who is not under a sentence of death or life without parole, and who does not have a reportable conviction or adjudication under Chapter 62, Code of Criminal Procedure, or an instant offense described in Article 42A.054, Code of Criminal Procedure, may be released to immigration authorities pending deportation on a date designated by a parole panel described by Subsection (e) if the parole panel determines that on release the inmate would be deported to another country and that the inmate does not constitute a threat to public safety in the other country or this country and is unlikely to reenter this country illegally.

Added by Acts 1997, 75th Leg., ch. 165, § 12.01, eff. Sept. 1, 1997. Amended by Acts 2001, 77th Leg., ch. 1435, § 1, eff. Sept. 1, 2001; Acts 2003, 78th Leg., ch. 252, § 1, eff. Sept. 1, 2003; Acts 2003, 78th Leg., ch. 856, § 21, eff. Sept. 1, 2003; Acts 2005, 79th Leg., ch. 787, § 5, eff. Sept. 1, 2005; Acts 2007, 80th Leg., ch. 1247, § 1, eff. Sept. 1, 2007; Acts 2015, 84th Leg., ch. 770 (H.B. 2299), § 2.52, eff. Jan. 1, 2017.

§ 508.147. Release to Mandatory Supervision

(a) Except as provided by Section 508.149, a parole panel shall order the release of an inmate who is not on parole to mandatory supervision when the actual calendar time the inmate has served plus any accrued good conduct time equals the term to which the inmate was sentenced.

(b) An inmate released to mandatory supervision is considered to be released on parole.

(c) To the extent practicable, arrangements for the inmate's proper employment, maintenance, and care must be made before the inmate's release to mandatory supervision.

Added by Acts 1997, 75th Leg., ch. 165, § 12.01, eff. Sept. 1, 1997.

§ 508.148. Period of Mandatory Supervision

(a) The period of mandatory supervision is computed by subtracting from the term for which the inmate was sentenced the calendar time served on the sentence.

(b) The time served on mandatory supervision is computed as calendar time.

Added by Acts 1997, 75th Leg., ch. 165, § 12.01, eff. Sept. 1, 1997.

§ 508.149. Inmates Ineligible for Mandatory Supervision

(a) An inmate may not be released to mandatory supervision if the inmate is serving a sentence for or has been previously convicted of:

(1) an offense for which the judgment contains an affirmative finding under Article 42A.054(c) or (d), Code of Criminal Procedure;

(2) a first degree felony or a second degree felony under Section 19.02, Penal Code;

(3) a capital felony under Section 19.03, Penal Code;

(4) a first degree felony or a second degree felony under Section 20.04, Penal Code;

(5) an offense under Section 21.11, Penal Code;

(6) a felony under Section 22.011, Penal Code;

(7) a first degree felony or a second degree felony under Section 22.02, Penal Code;

(8) a first degree felony under Section 22.021, Penal Code;

(9) a first degree felony under Section 22.04, Penal Code;

(10) a first degree felony under Section 28.02, Penal Code;

(11) a second degree felony under Section 29.02, Penal Code;

(12) a first degree felony under Section 29.03, Penal Code;

(13) a first degree felony under Section 30.02, Penal Code;

(14) a felony for which the punishment is increased under Section 481.134 or Section 481.140, Health and Safety Code;

(15) an offense under Section 43.25, Penal Code;

(16) an offense under Section 21.02, Penal Code;

(17) a first degree felony under Section 15.03, Penal Code;

(18) an offense under Section 43.05, Penal Code;

(19) an offense under Section 20A.02, Penal Code;

(20) an offense under Section 20A.03, Penal Code; or

(21) a first degree felony under Section 71.02 or 71.023, Penal Code.

(b) An inmate may not be released to mandatory supervision if a parole panel determines that:

(1) the inmate's accrued good conduct time is not an accurate reflection of the inmate's potential for rehabilitation; and

(2) the inmate's release would endanger the public.

(c) A parole panel that makes a determination under Subsection (b) shall specify in writing the reasons for the determination.

(d) A determination under Subsection (b) is not subject to administrative or judicial review, except that the parole panel making the determination shall reconsider the inmate for release to mandatory supervision at least twice during the two years after the date of the determination.

Added by Acts 1997, 75th Leg., ch. 165, § 12.01, eff. Sept. 1, 1997. Amended by Acts 1999, 76th Leg., ch. 62, § 10.22, eff. Sept. 1, 1999; Acts 2001, 77th Leg., ch. 786, § 3, eff. June 14, 2001; Acts 2007, 80th Leg., ch. 593, § 1.11, eff. Sept. 1, 2007; Acts 2009, 81st Leg., ch. 146, § 3, eff. Sept. 1, 2009; Acts 2011, 82nd Leg., ch. 1 (S.B. 24), § 5.02, eff. Sept. 1, 2011; Acts 2011, 82nd Leg., ch. 122 (H.B. 3000), § 11, eff. Sept. 1, 2011; Acts 2013, 83rd Leg., ch. 161 (S.B. 1093), § 9.011, eff. Sept. 1, 2013; Acts 2013, 83rd Leg., ch. 1325 (S.B. 549), § 3, eff. Sept. 1, 2013; Acts 2015, 84th Leg., ch. 770 (H.B. 2299), § 2.53, eff. Jan. 1, 2017.

§ 508.150. Consecutive Felony Sentences

(a) If an inmate is sentenced to consecutive felony sentences under Article 42.08, Code of Criminal Procedure, a parole panel shall designate during each sentence the date, if any, the inmate would have been eligible for release on parole if the inmate had been sentenced to serve a single sentence.

(b) For the purposes of Article 42.08, Code of Criminal Procedure, the judgment and sentence of an inmate sentenced for a felony, other than the last sentence in a series of consecutive sentences, cease to operate:

(1) when the actual calendar time served by the inmate equals the sentence imposed by the court; or

(2) on the date a parole panel designates as the date the inmate would have been eligible for release on parole if the inmate had been sentenced to serve a single sentence.

(c) A parole panel may not:

(1) consider consecutive sentences as a single sentence for purposes of parole; or

(2) release on parole an inmate sentenced to serve consecutive felony sentences before the date the inmate becomes eligible for release on parole from the last sentence imposed on the inmate.

(d) A parole panel may not use calendar time served and good conduct time accrued by an inmate that are used by the panel in determining when a judgment and sentence cease to operate:

(1) for the same purpose in determining that date in a subsequent sentence in the same series of consecutive sentences; or

(2) for determining the date an inmate becomes eligible for release on parole from the last sentence in a series of consecutive sentences.

Added by Acts 1997, 75th Leg., ch. 165, § 12.01, eff. Sept. 1, 1997.

§ 508.151. Presumptive Parole Date

(a) For the purpose of diverting inmates to halfway houses under Section 508.118, a parole panel, after reviewing all available pertinent information, may designate a presumptive parole date for an inmate who:

(1) has never been convicted of an offense listed under Article 42A.054(a), Code of Criminal Procedure, or an offense under Section 20A.03 or 21.02, Penal Code; and

(2) has never had a conviction with a judgment that contains an affirmative finding under Article 42A.054(c) or (d), Code of Criminal Procedure.

(b) The presumptive parole date may not be a date that is earlier than the inmate's initial parole eligibility date computed under Section 508.145.

(c) A parole panel may rescind or postpone a previously established presumptive parole date on the basis of a report from an agent of the division responsible for supervision or an agent of the institutional division acting in the case.

(d) If an inmate transferred to preparole status has satisfactorily served the inmate's sentence in the halfway house to which the inmate is assigned from the date of transfer to the presumptive parole date, without rescission or postponement of the date, the parole panel shall order the inmate's release on parole and issue an appropriate certificate of release. The releasee is subject to the provisions of this chapter governing release on parole.

Added by Acts 1997, 75th Leg., ch. 165, § 12.01, eff. Sept. 1, 1997. Amended by Acts 2007, 80th Leg., ch. 593, § 3.40, eff. Sept. 1, 2007; Acts 2011, 82nd Leg., ch. 122 (H.B. 3000), § 12, eff. Sept. 1, 2011; Acts 2015, 84th Leg., ch. 770 (H.B. 2299), § 2.54, eff. Jan. 1, 2017.

§ 508.152. Individual Treatment Plan

(a) Not later than the 120th day after the date an inmate is admitted to the institutional division, the department shall obtain all pertinent information relating to the inmate, including:

(1) the court judgment;

(2) any sentencing report;

(3) the circumstances of the inmate's offense;

(4) the inmate's previous social history and criminal record;

(5) the inmate's physical and mental health record;

(6) a record of the inmate's conduct, employment history, and attitude in the institutional division; and

(7) any written comments or information provided by local trial officials or victims of the offense.

(b) The department shall:

(1) establish for the inmate an individual treatment plan; and

(2) submit the plan to the board at the time of the board's consideration of the inmate's case for release.

(b–1) The department shall include in an inmate's individual treatment plan:

(1) a record of the inmate's institutional progress that includes the inmate's participation in any program, including an intensive volunteer program as defined by the department;

(2) the results of any assessment of the inmate, including any assessment made using the risk and needs assessment instrument adopted under Section 501.0921 and any vocational, educational, or substance abuse assessment;

(3) the dates on which the inmate must participate in any subsequent assessment; and

(4) all of the treatment and programming needs of the inmate, prioritized based on the inmate's assessed needs.

(b–2) At least once in every 12–month period, the department shall review each inmate's individual treatment plan to assess the inmate's institutional progress and revise or update the plan as necessary. The department shall make reasonable efforts to provide an inmate the opportunity to complete any classes or programs included in the inmate's individual treatment plan, other than classes or programs that are to be completed immediately before the inmate's release on parole, in a timely manner so that the inmate's release on parole is not delayed due to any uncompleted classes or programs.

(c) The board shall conduct an initial review of an eligible inmate not later than the 180th day after the date of the inmate's admission to the institutional division. The board shall identify any classes or programs that the board intends to require the inmate to complete before releasing the inmate on parole. The department shall provide the inmate with a list of those classes or programs.

(d) Before the inmate is approved for release on parole, the inmate must agree to participate in the programs and activities described by the individual treatment plan.

(e) The institutional division shall:

(1) work closely with the board to monitor the progress of the inmate in the institutional division; and

(2) report the progress to the board before the inmate's release.

(f) An attorney representing the state in the prosecution of an inmate serving a sentence for an offense described by Section 508.187(a) shall provide written comments to the department on the circumstances related to the commission of the offense and other information determined by the attorney to be relevant to any subsequent parole decisions regarding the inmate.

Added by Acts 1997, 75th Leg., ch. 165, § 12.01, eff. Sept. 1, 1997. Amended by Acts 2001, 77th Leg., ch. 978, § 1, eff. Sept. 1, 2001; Acts 2013, 83rd Leg., ch. 1154 (S.B. 213), §§ 17, 18, eff. Sept. 1, 2013; Acts 2017, 85th Leg., ch. 505 (H.B. 2888), § 1, eff. Sept. 1, 2017.

§ 508.153. Statements of Victim

(a) A parole panel considering for release on parole or mandatory supervision an inmate who is serving a sentence for an offense in which a person was a victim shall allow:

(1) the victim, a guardian of the victim, a close relative of the deceased victim, or a representative of the victim, the victim's guardian, or the victim's

close relative to provide a written statement to the panel; and

(2) the victim, guardian of the victim, or close relative of the deceased victim to appear in person before the board members to present a statement of the person's views about:

(A) the offense;

(B) the inmate; and

(C) the effect of the offense on the victim.

(b) If more than one person is entitled to appear in person before the board members or parole commissioners, only the person chosen by all persons entitled to appear as the persons' sole representative may appear.

(c) The panel shall consider the statements and the information provided in a victim impact statement in determining whether to recommend an inmate for release on parole.

(d) This section does not limit the number of persons who may provide written statements for or against the release of the inmate on parole.

(e) In this section, "close relative of a deceased victim," "guardian of a victim," and "victim" have the meanings assigned by Section 508.117.

Added by Acts 1997, 75th Leg., ch. 165, § 12.01, eff. Sept. 1, 1997. Amended by Acts 2001, 77th Leg., ch. 856, § 6, eff. Sept. 1, 2001; Acts 2003, 78th Leg., 3rd C.S., ch. 3, § 11.19, eff. Jan. 11, 2004.

§ 508.1531. Contact with Victim

A parole panel considering the release of an inmate on parole or to mandatory supervision may consider whether the inmate violated a policy adopted by the department under Section 498.0042(a) or a court order entered under Article 42.24, Code of Criminal Procedure.

Added by Acts 2011, 82nd Leg., ch. 491 (H.B. 1028), § 4, eff. Sept. 1, 2011.

§ 508.154. Contract on Release

(a) An inmate to be released on parole shall be furnished a contract stating in clear and intelligible language the conditions and rules of parole.

(b) Acceptance, signing, and execution of the contract by the inmate to be paroled is a precondition to release on parole.

(c) An inmate released to mandatory supervision shall be furnished a written statement stating in clear and intelligible language the conditions and rules of mandatory supervision.

(d) A releasee while on parole or mandatory supervision must be amenable to the conditions of supervision ordered by a parole panel.

Added by Acts 1997, 75th Leg., ch. 165, § 12.01, eff. Sept. 1, 1997.

§ 508.155. Completion of Parole Period

(a) To complete a parole period, a releasee must serve the entire period of parole.

(b) The time on parole is computed as calendar time.

(c) The division may allow a releasee to serve the remainder of the releasee's sentence without supervision and without being required to report if a parole supervisor at the regional level has approved the releasee's early release from supervision under Section 508.1555.

(d) The division may require a person released from supervision and reporting under Subsection (c) to resubmit to supervision and resume reporting at any time and for any reason.

Added by Acts 1997, 75th Leg., ch. 165, § 12.01, eff. Sept. 1, 1997. Amended by Acts 2007, 80th Leg., ch. 1308, § 41, eff. June 15, 2007.

§ 508.1555. Procedure for the Early Release From Supervision of Certain Releasees

(a) A parole officer annually shall identify the releasees under the parole officer's supervision who are eligible for early release from supervision under Section 508.155(c). A releasee is eligible for early release if:

(1) the releasee has been under supervision for at least one-half of the time that remained on the releasee's sentence when the releasee was released from imprisonment;

(2) during the preceding two-year period, the releasee has not committed any violation of the rules or conditions of release;

(3) during the period of supervision the releasee's parole or release to mandatory supervision has not been revoked; and

(4) the division determines:

(A) that the releasee has made a good faith effort to comply with any restitution order imposed on the releasee by a court; and

(B) that allowing the releasee to serve the remainder of the releasee's sentence without supervision and reporting is in the best interest of society.

(b) After identifying any releasees who are eligible for early release under Subsection (a), the parole officer shall review the eligible releasees, including any releasees the parole officer has previously declined to recommend for early release, to determine if a recommendation for early release from supervision is appropriate. In conducting the review and determining recommendations, the parole officer shall consider whether the releasee:

(1) has a low risk of recidivism as determined by an assessment developed by the department; and

(2) has made a good faith effort to comply with the conditions of release.

(c) A parole officer shall forward to the parole supervisor at the regional level any recommendations for early release the parole officer makes under Subsection (b). If the parole supervisor approves the recommendation, the division shall allow a releasee to serve the remainder of the releasee's sentence without supervision and without being required to report as authorized by Section 508.155.

Added by Acts 2007, 80th Leg., ch. 1308, § 42, eff. June 15, 2007.

§ 508.156.　Determinate Sentence Parole

(a) Before the release of a person who is transferred under Section 152.0016(g), 152.00161(e), 245.051(c), or 245.151(e), Human Resources Code, to the department for release on parole, a parole panel shall review the person's records and may interview the person or any other person the panel considers necessary to determine the conditions of parole. The panel may impose any reasonable condition of parole on the person that the panel may impose on an adult inmate under this chapter.

(b) The panel shall furnish the person with a written statement clearly describing the conditions and rules of parole. The person must accept and sign the statement as a precondition to release on parole.

(c) While on parole, the person remains in the legal custody of the state and shall comply with the conditions of parole ordered by a panel under this section.

(d) The period of parole for a person released on parole under this section is the term for which the person was sentenced less calendar time served at the Texas Juvenile Justice Department or in the custody of a juvenile board or local juvenile probation department following a commitment under Section 54.04011(c)(2), Family Code, and in a juvenile detention facility in connection with the conduct for which the person was adjudicated.

(e) If a parole panel revokes the person's parole, the panel may require the person to serve the remaining portion of the person's sentence in the institutional division. The remaining portion of the person's sentence is computed without credit for the time from the date of the person's release to the date of revocation. The panel may not recommit the person to the Texas Juvenile Justice Department or to the custody of a juvenile board or local juvenile probation department.

(f) For purposes of this chapter, a person released from the Texas Juvenile Justice Department or the custody of a juvenile board or local juvenile probation department on parole under this section is considered to have been convicted of the offense for which the person has been adjudicated.

Added by Acts 1997, 75th Leg., ch. 165, § 12.01, eff. Sept. 1, 1997. Amended by Acts 2007, 80th Leg., ch. 263, § 19, eff. June 8, 2007; Acts 2011, 82nd Leg., ch. 85 (S.B. 653), § 3.014, eff. Sept. 1, 2011; Acts 2015, 84th Leg., ch. 734 (H.B. 1549), § 101, eff. Sept. 1, 2015; Acts 2015, 84th Leg., ch. 854 (S.B. 1149), § 7, eff. Sept. 1, 2015.

Section 150 of Acts 2015, 84th Leg., ch. 734 (H.B. 1549) provides:

"If any provision of this Act conflicts with a provision of another Act of the 84th Legislature, Regular Session, 2015, the provision of the other Act controls to the extent of the conflict, regardless of the date of enactment."

Section 13 of Acts 2015, 84th Leg., ch. 854 (S.B. 1149) provides:

"The change in law made by this Act applies to a person committed to or serving a sentence in a post-adjudication secure correctional facility on or after the effective date [Sept. 1, 2015] of this Act, regardless of whether the underlying conduct giving rise to the commitment and sentence occurred before, on, or after that date."

§ 508.157.　Temporary Housing on Release

(a) This section applies only to inmates who are eligible for release on parole or to mandatory supervision and to releasees.

(a–1) In this section, "residential correctional facility" means a facility operated by or under contract with the department to provide housing, supervision, and programmatic support to individuals released on parole or to mandatory supervision. The term includes a halfway house described by Section 508.118 or a community residential facility described by Section 508.119. The term does not include a transitional treatment center, a substance abuse felony punishment facility, or any other facility operated by or under contract with the department the primary purpose of which is to provide substance abuse treatment or aftercare.

(b) If the department does not operate or contract for the operation of a residential correctional facility in the county of legal residence of an inmate or releasee, the department may issue, for an inmate described by Subsection (a) or for a releasee, payment for the cost of temporary post-release housing that:

(1) meets any conditions or requirements imposed by a parole panel;

(2) is located in the county of legal residence of the inmate or releasee; and

(3) except as provided by Subsection (e–1), is in a structure that existed on June 1, 2009, as a multifamily residence or as a motel to which Section 156.001, Tax Code, applies.

(c) The amount of payment issued under Subsection (b) may not exceed an amount that is equal to the cost the department would incur, for the period for which the payment is issued, to:

(1) incarcerate the inmate or releasee in a facility operated by or under contract with the department; or

(2) house the inmate or releasee in a residential correctional facility.

(d) The department shall issue payment under Subsection (b) out of funds appropriated by the legislature to the department for use in administering the parole system with respect to the housing of inmates on their release.

(e) The executive director of the Texas Department of Criminal Justice shall adopt rules as necessary to implement this section.

(e–1) The department may issue payment for post-release housing under Subsection (b) for a structure not described by Subsection (b)(3) if, before issuing payment, the department or the owner of the structure provides, in the same manner as required for a community corrections facility under Section 509.010, notice of the proposed use of the structure under this section and a hearing on the issue of whether the use is appropriate.

(f) Expired.

(g) Expired.

Added by Acts 2009, 81st Leg., ch. 944, § 1, eff. June 19, 2009. Amended by Acts 2011, 82nd Leg., ch. 286 (H.B. 1770), § 1, eff. June 17, 2011.

SUBCHAPTER F. MANDATORY CONDITIONS OF PAROLE OR MANDATORY SUPERVISION

§ 508.181. Residence During Release

(a) Except as provided by Subsections (b) and (c), a parole panel shall require as a condition of parole or mandatory supervision that the releasee reside in the county in which:

(1) the releasee resided at the time of committing the offense for which the releasee was sentenced to the institutional division; or

(2) the releasee committed the offense for which the releasee was sentenced to the institutional division, if the releasee was not a resident of this state at the time of committing the offense.

(b) A parole panel may require a releasee to reside in a county other than the county required under Subsection (a) to:

(1) protect the life or safety of:

(A) a victim of the releasee's offense;

(B) the releasee;

(C) a witness in the case; or

(D) any other person; or

(2) increase the likelihood of the releasee's successful completion of parole or mandatory supervision, because of:

(A) written expressions of significant public concern in the county in which the releasee would otherwise be required to reside;

(B) the presence of family members or friends in the other county who have expressed a willingness to assist the releasee in successfully completing the conditions of the releasee's parole or mandatory supervision;

(C) the verified existence of a job offer in the other county; or

(D) the availability of a treatment program, educational program, or other social service program in the other county that is not available in the county in which the releasee is otherwise required to reside under Subsection (a).

(c) At any time after a releasee is released on parole or to mandatory supervision, a parole panel may modify the conditions of parole or mandatory supervision to require the releasee to reside in a county other than the county required by the original conditions. In making a decision under this subsection, a parole panel must consider the factors listed under Subsection (b).

(d) If a parole panel initially requires the releasee to reside in a county other than the county required under Subsection (a), the parole panel shall subsequently require the releasee to reside in the county described under Subsection (a) if the requirement that the releasee reside in the other county was based on:

(1) the verified existence of a job offer under Subsection (b)(2)(C) and the releasee is no longer employed or actively seeking employment; or

(2) the availability of a treatment program, educational program, or other social service program under Subsection (b)(2)(D) and the releasee:

(A) no longer regularly participates in the program as required by a condition of parole or mandatory supervision; or

(B) has successfully completed the program but has violated another condition of the releasee's parole or mandatory supervision.

(e) If a parole panel requires the releasee to reside in a county other than the county required under Subsection (a), the panel shall:

(1) state in writing the reason for the panel's decision; and

(2) place the statement in the releasee's permanent record.

(f) This section does not apply to a decision by a parole panel to require a releasee to serve the period of parole or mandatory supervision in another state.

(g) The division shall, on the first working day of each month, notify the sheriff of any county in which the total number of sex offenders under the supervision and control of the division residing in the county exceeds 10 percent of the total number of sex offenders in the state under the supervision and control of the division. The notice must be provided by e-mail or other electronic communication. If the total number of sex offenders under the supervision and control of the division residing in a county exceeds 22 percent of the total number of sex offenders in the state under the supervision and control of the division, a parole panel may require a sex offender to reside in that county only as required by Subsection (a) or for the reason stated in Subsection (b)(2)(B). In this subsection, "sex offender" means a person who is released on parole or to mandatory supervision after serving a sentence for an offense described by Section 508.187(a).

(h) If a parole panel requires a releasee to reside in a county other than the county required under Subsection (a), the division shall include the reason for residency exemption in the required notification to the sheriff of the county in which the defendant is to reside, the chief of police of the municipality in which the halfway house is located, and the attorney who represents the state in the prosecution of felonies in that county.

Added by Acts 1997, 75th Leg., ch. 165, § 12.01, eff. Sept. 1, 1997. Amended by Acts 1999, 76th Leg., ch. 62, §§ 10.23, 10.24, eff. Sept. 1, 1999; Acts 2011, 82nd Leg., ch. 1123 (H.B. 200), § 6, eff. Sept. 1, 2011.

§ 508.182. Parole Supervision Fee; Administrative Fee

(a) A parole panel shall require as a condition of parole or mandatory supervision that a releasee pay to the division for each month during which the releasee is under parole supervision:

(1) a parole supervision fee of $10; and

(2) an administrative fee of $8.

(b) A fee under this section applies to an inmate released in another state who is required as a condition of the inmate's release to report to a parole officer or supervisor in this state for parole supervision.

(c) On the request of the releasee, a parole panel may allow the releasee to defer one or more payments under this section. The releasee remains responsible for payment of the fee and shall pay the amount of the deferred payment not later than the second anniversary of the date the payment becomes due.

(d) The Texas Board of Criminal Justice shall adopt rules relating to the method of payment required of the releasee.

(e) The division shall remit fees collected under this section to the comptroller. The comptroller shall deposit the fees collected under:

(1) Subsection (a)(1) in the general revenue fund; and

(2) Subsection (a)(2) in the compensation to victims of crime fund.

(f) In a parole or mandatory supervision revocation hearing under Section 508.281 at which it is alleged only that the releasee failed to make a payment under this section, it is an affirmative defense to revocation that the releasee is unable to pay the amount as ordered by a parole panel. The releasee must prove the affirmative defense by a preponderance of the evidence.

Added by Acts 1997, 75th Leg., ch. 165, § 12.01, eff. Sept. 1, 1997.

§ 508.183. Educational Skill Level

(a) A parole panel shall require as a condition of release on parole or release to mandatory supervision that an inmate demonstrate to the parole panel whether the inmate has an educational skill level that is equal to or greater than the average skill level of students who have completed the sixth grade in a public school in this state.

(b) If the parole panel determines that the inmate has not attained that skill level, the parole panel shall require as a condition of parole or mandatory supervision that the inmate as a releasee attain that level of educational skill, unless the parole panel determines that the inmate lacks the intellectual capacity or the learning ability to ever achieve that level of skill.

Added by Acts 1997, 75th Leg., ch. 165, § 12.01, eff. Sept. 1, 1997.

§ 508.184. Controlled Substance Testing

(a) A parole panel shall require as a condition of parole or mandatory supervision that a releasee submit to testing for controlled substances on evidence that:

(1) a controlled substance is present in the releasee's body;

(2) the releasee has used a controlled substance; or

(3) the use of a controlled substance is related to the offense for which the releasee was convicted.

(b) The Texas Board of Criminal Justice by rule shall adopt procedures for the administration of a test required under this section.

Added by Acts 1997, 75th Leg., ch. 165, § 12.01, eff. Sept. 1, 1997.

§ 508.185. Substance Abuse Treatment

(a) A parole panel shall require as a condition of release on parole or release to mandatory supervision that an inmate who immediately before release is a participant in the program established under Section 501.0931 participate as a releasee in a drug or alcohol abuse continuum of care treatment program.

(b) The Texas Commission on Alcohol and Drug Abuse shall develop the continuum of care treatment program.

Added by Acts 1997, 75th Leg., ch. 165, § 12.01, eff. Sept. 1, 1997.

§ 508.186. Sex Offender Registration

A parole panel shall require as a condition of parole or mandatory supervision that a releasee required to register as a sex offender under Chapter 62, Code of Criminal Procedure:

(1) register under that chapter; and

(2) submit a blood sample or other specimen to the Department of Public Safety under Subchapter G, Chapter 411,[1] for the purpose of creating a DNA record of the releasee, unless the releasee has already submitted the required specimen under other state law.

Added by Acts 1997, 75th Leg., ch. 165, § 12.01, eff. Sept. 1, 1997. Amended by Acts 1999, 76th Leg., ch. 62, § 10.25, eff. Sept. 1, 1999; Acts 2001, 77th Leg., ch. 211, § 16, eff. Sept. 1, 2001; Acts 2003, 78th Leg., ch. 1300, § 9, eff. Sept. 1, 2003; Acts 2005, 79th Leg., ch. 1008, § 1.06, eff. Sept. 1, 2005.

[1] V.T.C.A., Government Code § 411.141 et seq.

§ 508.1861. Prohibitions on Internet Access for Certain Sex Offenders

(a) This section applies only to a person who, on release, will be required to register as a sex offender under Chapter 62, Code of Criminal Procedure, by court order or otherwise, and:

(1) is serving a sentence for an offense under Section 21.11, 22.011(a)(2), 22.021(a)(1)(B), 33.021, or 43.25, Penal Code;

(2) used the Internet or any other type of electronic device used for Internet access to commit the offense or engage in the conduct for which the person is required to register under Chapter 62, Code of Criminal Procedure; or

(3) is assigned a numeric risk level of two or three based on an assessment conducted under Article 62.007, Code of Criminal Procedure.

(b) If the parole panel releases on parole or to mandatory supervision a person described by Subsection (a), the parole panel as a condition of parole or mandatory supervision shall:

(1) prohibit the releasee from using the Internet to:

(A) access material that is obscene as defined by Section 43.21, Penal Code;

(B) access a commercial social networking site, as defined by Article 62.0061(f), Code of Criminal Procedure;

(C) communicate with any individual concerning sexual relations with an individual who is younger than 17 years of age; or

(D) communicate with another individual the releasee knows is younger than 17 years of age; and

(2) to ensure the releasee's compliance with Subdivision (1), require the releasee to submit to regu-

lar inspection or monitoring of each electronic device used by the releasee to access the Internet.

(c) The parole panel may modify at any time the condition described by Subsection (b)(1)(D) if:

(1) the condition interferes with the releasee's ability to attend school or become or remain employed and consequently constitutes an undue hardship for the releasee; or

(2) the releasee is the parent or guardian of an individual who is younger than 17 years of age and the releasee is not otherwise prohibited from communicating with that individual.

Added by Acts 2009, 81st Leg., ch. 755, § 10, eff. Sept. 1, 2009. Amended by Acts 2015, 84th Leg., ch. 684 (H.B. 372), § 2, eff. Sept. 1, 2015.

§ 508.1862. Sex Offender Treatment

A parole panel shall require as a condition of release on parole or to mandatory supervision that a releasee participate in a sex offender treatment program developed by the department if:

(1) the releasee:

(A) was serving a sentence for an offense under Chapter 21, Penal Code; or

(B) is required to register as a sex offender under Chapter 62, Code of Criminal Procedure; and

(2) immediately before release, the releasee is participating in a sex offender treatment program established under Section 499.054.

Added by Acts 2015, 84th Leg., ch. 1114 (H.B. 3387), § 1, eff. Sept. 1, 2015.

Section 3 of Acts 2015, 84th Leg., ch. 1114 (H.B. 3387) provides:

"Sections 508.1862 and 508.228, Government Code, as added by this Act, apply only to a decision of a parole panel made on or after the effective date of this Act. A decision of a parole panel made before the effective date of this Act is governed by the law in effect on the date the decision was made, and the former law is continued in effect for that purpose."

§ 508.187. Child Safety Zone

(a) This section applies only to a releasee serving a sentence for an offense under:

(1) Section 43.25 or 43.26, Penal Code;

(2) Section 21.02, 21.11, 22.011, 22.021, or 25.02, Penal Code;

(3) Section 20.04(a)(4), Penal Code, if the releasee committed the offense with the intent to violate or abuse the victim sexually;

(4) Section 30.02, Penal Code, punishable under Subsection (d) of that section, if the releasee committed the offense with the intent to commit a felony listed in Subdivision (2) or (3);

(5) Section 43.05(a)(2), Penal Code; or

(6) Section 20A.02, Penal Code, if the defendant:

(A) trafficked the victim with the intent or knowledge that the victim would engage in sexual conduct, as defined by Section 43.25, Penal Code; or

(B) benefited from participating in a venture that involved a trafficked victim engaging in sexual conduct, as defined by Section 43.25, Penal Code.

(b) A parole panel shall establish a child safety zone applicable to a releasee if the panel determines that a child as defined by Section 22.011(c), Penal Code, was the victim of the offense, by requiring as a condition of parole or mandatory supervision that the releasee:

(1) not:

(A) supervise or participate in any program that includes as participants or recipients persons who are 17 years of age or younger and that regularly provides athletic, civic, or cultural activities; or

(B) go in, on, or within a distance specified by the panel of premises where children commonly gather, including a school, day-care facility, playground, public or private youth center, public swimming pool, or video arcade facility; and

(2) attend for a period of time determined necessary by the panel psychological counseling sessions for sex offenders with an individual or organization that provides sex offender treatment or counseling as specified by the parole officer supervising the releasee after release.

(b–1) Notwithstanding Subsection (b)(1)(B), a requirement that a releasee not go in, on, or within a distance specified by a parole panel of certain premises does not apply to a releasee while the releasee is in or going immediately to or from:

(1) a parole office;

(2) premises at which the releasee is participating in a program or activity required as a condition of release;

(3) a residential facility in which the releasee is required to reside as a condition of release;

(4) a private residence in which the releasee is required to reside as a condition of release; or

(5) any other premises, facility, or location that is:

(A) designed to rehabilitate or reform the releasee; or

(B) authorized by the division as a premises, facility, or location where it is reasonable and necessary for the releasee to be present and at which the releasee has legitimate business, including a church, synagogue, or other established place of religious worship, a workplace, a health care facility, or a location of a funeral.

(c) A parole officer who under Subsection (b)(2) specifies a sex offender treatment provider to provide counseling to a releasee shall:

(1) contact the provider before the releasee is released;

(2) establish the date, time, and place of the first session between the releasee and the provider; and

(3) request the provider to immediately notify the officer if the releasee fails to attend the first session or any subsequent scheduled session.

(d) At any time after the imposition of a condition under Subsection (b)(1), the releasee may request the parole panel to modify the child safety zone applicable to the releasee because the zone as created by the panel:

(1) interferes with the releasee's ability to attend school or hold a job and consequently constitutes an undue hardship for the releasee; or

(2) is broader than necessary to protect the public, given the nature and circumstances of the offense.

(e) A parole officer supervising a releasee may permit the releasee to enter on an event-by-event basis into the child safety zone that the releasee is otherwise prohibited from entering if:

(1) the releasee has served at least two years of the period of supervision imposed on release;

(2) the releasee enters the zone as part of a program to reunite with the releasee's family;

(3) the releasee presents to the parole officer a written proposal specifying:

(A) where the releasee intends to go within the zone;

(B) why and with whom the releasee is going; and

(C) how the releasee intends to cope with any stressful situations that occur;

(4) the sex offender treatment provider treating the releasee agrees with the officer that the releasee should be allowed to attend the event; and

(5) the officer and the treatment provider agree on a chaperon to accompany the releasee, and the chaperon agrees to perform that duty.

(f) In this section, "playground," "premises," "school," "video arcade facility," and "youth center" have the meanings assigned by Section 481.134, Health and Safety Code.

Added by Acts 1997, 75th Leg., ch. 165, § 12.01, eff. Sept. 1, 1997. Amended by Acts 2001, 77th Leg., ch. 978, § 2, eff. Sept. 1, 2001; Acts 2007, 80th Leg., ch. 593, § 3.41, eff. Sept. 1, 2007; Acts 2011, 82nd Leg., ch. 515 (H.B. 2014), § 3.03, eff. Sept. 1, 2011; Acts 2017, 85th Leg., ch. 997 (H.B. 1111), § 1, eff. Sept. 1, 2017.

Section 4 of Acts 2017, 85th Leg., ch. 997 (H.B. 1111) provides:

"Sections 508.187 and 508.225, Government Code, as amended by this Act, apply to a person on parole or mandatory supervision on or after the effective date [Sept. 1, 2017] of this Act, regardless of whether the person was released on parole or to mandatory supervision before, on, or after that date."

§ 508.188. Community Service for Certain Releasees

A parole panel shall require as a condition of parole or mandatory supervision that a releasee for whom the court has made an affirmative finding under Article 42.014, Code of Criminal Procedure, perform not less than 300 hours of community service at a project designated by the parole panel that primarily serves the person or group that was the target of the releasee.

Added by Acts 1997, 75th Leg., ch. 165, § 12.01, eff. Sept. 1, 1997.

§ 508.189. Parole Fee for Certain Releasees

(a) A parole panel shall require as a condition of parole or mandatory supervision that a releasee convicted of an offense under Section 21.02, 21.08, 21.11, 22.011, 22.021, 25.02, 43.25, or 43.26, Penal Code, pay to the division a parole supervision fee of $5 each month during the period of parole supervision.

(b) The division shall send fees collected under this section to the comptroller. The comptroller shall deposit the fees in the general revenue fund to the credit of the sexual assault program fund established under Section 44.0061, Health and Safety Code.

Added by Acts 1997, 75th Leg., ch. 165, § 12.01, eff. Sept. 1, 1997. Amended by Acts 2007, 80th Leg., ch. 593, § 3.42, eff. Sept. 1, 2007.

§ 508.190. Avoiding Victim of Stalking Offense

(a) A parole panel shall require as a condition of parole or mandatory supervision that a releasee serving a sentence for an offense under Section 42.072, Penal Code, not:

(1) communicate directly or indirectly with the victim;

(2) go to or near the residence, place of employment, or business of the victim; or

(3) go to or near a school, day-care facility, or similar facility where a dependent child of the victim is in attendance.

(b) If a parole panel requires the prohibition contained in Subsection (a)(2) or (3) as a condition of parole or mandatory supervision, the parole panel shall specifically describe the prohibited locations and the minimum distances, if any, that the releasee must maintain from the locations.

Added by Acts 1999, 76th Leg., ch. 62, § 10.26, eff. Sept. 1, 1999.

§ 508.191.   No Contact With Victim

(a) If a parole panel releases a defendant on parole or to mandatory supervision, the panel shall require as a condition of parole or mandatory supervision that the defendant not intentionally or knowingly communicate directly or indirectly with a victim of the offense or intentionally or knowingly go near a residence, school, place of employment, or business of a victim. At any time after the defendant is released on parole or to mandatory supervision, a victim of the offense may petition the panel for a modification of the conditions of the defendant's parole or mandatory supervision allowing the defendant contact with the victim subject to reasonable restrictions.

(b) Notwithstanding Subsection (a), a defendant may participate in victim-offender mediation authorized by Section 508.324 on the request of the victim or a guardian of the victim or a close relative of a deceased victim.

(c) In this section, "victim" has the meaning assigned by Article 56.01(3), Code of Criminal Procedure.

Added by Acts 1999, 76th Leg., ch. 62, § 10.27, eff. Sept. 1, 1999.

§ 508.192.   Reentry Into the United States Prohibited

(a) In this section, "illegal criminal alien" has the meaning assigned by Section 493.015.

(b) A parole panel shall require as a condition of parole or mandatory supervision that an illegal criminal alien released to the custody of United States Immigration and Customs Enforcement:

(1) regardless of whether a final order of deportation is issued with reference to the illegal criminal alien, leave the United States as soon as possible after release; and

(2) not unlawfully return to or unlawfully reenter the United States in violation of the Immigration Reform and Control Act of 1986 (8 U.S.C. Section 1101 et seq.).

Added by Acts 2011, 82nd Leg., ch. 1025 (H.B. 2734), § 1, eff. Sept. 1, 2011.

SUBCHAPTER G.   DISCRETIONARY CONDITIONS OF PAROLE OR MANDATORY SUPERVISION

§ 508.221.   Conditions Permitted Generally

A parole panel may impose as a condition of parole or mandatory supervision any condition that a court may impose on a defendant placed on community supervision under Chapter 42A, Code of Criminal Procedure, including the condition that a releasee submit to testing for controlled substances or submit to electronic monitoring if the parole panel determines that without testing for controlled substances or participation in an electronic monitoring program the inmate would not be released on parole.

Added by Acts 1997, 75th Leg., ch. 165, § 12.01, eff. Sept. 1, 1997. Amended by Acts 2015, 84th Leg., ch. 770 (H.B. 2299), § 2.55, eff. Jan. 1, 2017.

§ 508.222.   Payment of Certain Damages

A parole panel may require as a condition of parole or mandatory supervision that a releasee make payments in satisfaction of damages for which the releasee is liable under Section 500.002.

Added by Acts 1997, 75th Leg., ch. 165, § 12.01, eff. Sept. 1, 1997.

§ 508.223.   Psychological Counseling

A parole panel may require as a condition of parole or mandatory supervision that a releasee serving a sentence for an offense under Section 42.072, Penal Code, attend psychological counseling sessions of a type and for a duration as specified by the parole panel, if the parole panel determines in consultation with a local mental health services provider that appropriate mental health services are available through the Texas Department of Mental Health and Mental Retardation in accordance with Section 534.053,

Health and Safety Code, or through another mental health services provider.

Added by Acts 1997, 75th Leg., ch. 165, § 12.01, eff. Sept. 1, 1997. Amended by Acts 1999, 76th Leg., ch. 62, § 10.28, eff. Sept. 1, 1999.

§ 508.224. Substance Abuse Counseling

A parole panel may require as a condition of parole or mandatory supervision that the releasee attend counseling sessions for substance abusers or participate in substance abuse treatment services in a program or facility approved or licensed by the Texas Commission on Alcohol and Drug Abuse if:

(1) the releasee was sentenced for an offense involving a controlled substance; or

(2) the panel determines that the releasee's substance abuse was related to the commission of the offense.

Added by Acts 1997, 75th Leg., ch. 165, § 12.01, eff. Sept. 1, 1997.

§ 508.225. Child Safety Zone

(a) If the nature of the offense for which an inmate is serving a sentence warrants the establishment of a child safety zone, a parole panel may establish a child safety zone applicable to an inmate serving a sentence for an offense listed in Article 42A.054(a), Code of Criminal Procedure, or for which the judgment contains an affirmative finding under Article 42A.054(c) or (d), Code of Criminal Procedure, by requiring as a condition of parole or release to mandatory supervision that the inmate not:

(1) supervise or participate in any program that includes as participants or recipients persons who are 17 years of age or younger and that regularly provides athletic, civic, or cultural activities; or

(2) go in or on, or within a distance specified by the panel of, a premises where children commonly gather, including a school, day-care facility, playground, public or private youth center, public swimming pool, or video arcade facility.

(a–1) Notwithstanding Subsection (a)(2), a requirement that an inmate not go in, on, or within a distance specified by a parole panel of certain premises does not apply to an inmate while the inmate is in or going immediately to or from:

(1) a parole office;

(2) premises at which the inmate is participating in a program or activity required as a condition of release;

(3) a residential facility in which the inmate is required to reside as a condition of release;

(4) a private residence in which the inmate is required to reside as a condition of release; or

(5) any other premises, facility, or location that is:

(A) designed to rehabilitate or reform the inmate; or

(B) authorized by the division as a premises, facility, or location where it is reasonable and necessary for the inmate to be present and at which the inmate has legitimate business, including a church, synagogue, or other established place of religious worship, a workplace, a health care facility, or a location of a funeral.

(b) At any time after the imposition of a condition under Subsection (a), the inmate may request the parole panel to modify the child safety zone applicable to the inmate because the zone as created by the panel:

(1) interferes with the ability of the inmate to attend school or hold a job and consequently constitutes an undue hardship for the inmate; or

(2) is broader than is necessary to protect the public, given the nature and circumstances of the offense.

(c) This section does not apply to an inmate described by Section 508.187.

(d) In this section, "playground," "premises," "school," "video arcade facility," and "youth center" have the meanings assigned by Section 481.134, Health and Safety Code.

Added by Acts 1999, 76th Leg., ch. 56, § 2, eff. Sept. 1, 1999. Amended by Acts 2015, 84th Leg., ch. 770 (H.B. 2299), § 2.56, eff. Jan. 1, 2017; Acts 2017, 85th Leg., ch. 997 (H.B. 1111), § 2, eff. Sept. 1, 2017.

Section 4 of Acts 2017, 85th Leg., ch. 997 (H.B. 1111) provides:

"Sections 508.187 and 508.225, Government Code, as amended by this Act, apply to a person on parole or mandatory supervision on or after the effective date [Sept. 1, 2017] of this Act, regardless of whether the person was released on parole or to mandatory supervision before, on, or after that date."

§ 508.226. Orchiectomy as Condition Prohibited

A parole panel may not require an inmate to undergo an orchiectomy as a condition of release on parole or to mandatory supervision.

Added by Acts 1999, 76th Leg., ch. 62, § 10.29, eff. Sept. 1, 1999. Renumbered from § 508.225 by Acts 2001, 77th Leg., ch. 1420, § 21.001(45), eff. Sept. 1, 2001.

§ 508.227. Electronic Monitoring of Certain Members of Criminal Street Gang

Text of (a) effective until January 1, 2019

(a) This section applies only to a releasee who:

(1) is identified as a member of a criminal street gang in an intelligence database established under Chapter 61, Code of Criminal Procedure; and

(2) has three or more times been convicted of, or received a grant of deferred adjudication community supervision or another functionally equivalent form of community supervision or probation for, a felony offense under the laws of this state, another state, or the United States.

Text of (a) effective January 1, 2019

(a) This section applies only to a releasee who:

(1) is identified as a member of a criminal street gang in an intelligence database established under Chapter 67, Code of Criminal Procedure; and

(2) has three or more times been convicted of, or received a grant of deferred adjudication community supervision or another functionally equivalent form of community supervision or probation for, a felony offense under the laws of this state, another state, or the United States.

(b) A parole panel may require as a condition of release on parole or to mandatory supervision that a releasee described by Subsection (a) submit to tracking under an electronic monitoring service or other appropriate technological service designed to track a person's location.

Added by Acts 2009, 81st Leg., ch. 1130, § 20, eff. Sept. 1, 2009. Amended by Acts 2017, 85th Leg., ch. 1058 (H.B. 2931), § 4.12, eff. Jan. 1, 2019.

§ 508.228. Sex Offender Treatment

A parole panel may require as a condition of release on parole or to mandatory supervision that a releasee participate in a sex offender treatment program as specified by the parole panel if:

(1) the releasee:

(A) was serving a sentence for an offense under Chapter 21, Penal Code; or

(B) is required to register as a sex offender under Chapter 62, Code of Criminal Procedure; or

(2) a designated agent of the board after conducting a hearing that allows the releasee to contest the evidence, on evidence that a sex offense occurred during the commission of the offense for which the releasee was serving a sentence, makes an affirmative finding that, regardless of the offense for which the releasee was serving a sentence, the releasee constitutes a threat to society because of the releasee's lack of sexual control.

Added by Acts 2015, 84th Leg., ch. 1114 (H.B. 3387), § 2, eff. Sept. 1, 2015.

Section 3 of Acts 2015, 84th Leg., ch. 1114 (H.B. 3387) provides:

"Sections 508.1862 and 508.228, Government Code, as added by this Act, apply only to a decision of a parole panel made on or after the effective date of this Act. A decision of a parole panel made before the effective date of this Act is governed by the law in effect on the date the decision was made, and the former law is continued in effect for that purpose."

SUBCHAPTER H. WARRANTS

§ 508.251. Issuance of Warrant or Summons

(a) In a case of parole or mandatory supervision, the director or a designated agent of the director or, in another case, the board on order by the governor, may issue a warrant as provided by Section 508.252 for the return of:

(1) a releasee;

(2) an inmate released although not eligible for release;

(3) a resident released to a preparole or work program;

(4) an inmate released on emergency reprieve or on emergency absence under escort; or

(5) a person released on a conditional pardon.

(b) A warrant issued under Subsection (a) must require the return of the person to the institution from which the person was paroled or released.

(c) Instead of the issuance of a warrant under this section, the division:

(1) may issue to the person a summons requiring the person to appear for a hearing under Section 508.281 if the person:

(A) is not a releasee who is:

(i) on intensive supervision or superintensive supervision;

(ii) an absconder; or

(iii) determined by the division to be a threat to public safety; or

(B) is charged only with committing a new offense that is alleged to have been committed after the first anniversary of the date the person was released on parole or to mandatory supervision if:

(i) the new offense is a Class C misdemeanor under the Penal Code, other than an offense committed against a child younger than 17 years of age or an offense involving family violence, as defined by Section 71.004, Family Code;

(ii) the person has maintained steady employment for at least one year;

(iii) the person has maintained a stable residence for at least one year; and

(iv) the person has not previously been charged with an offense after the person was released on parole or to mandatory supervision; and

(2) shall issue to the person a summons requiring the person to appear for a hearing under Section 508.281 if the person:

(A) is charged only with committing an administrative violation of release that is alleged to have been committed after the first anniversary of the date the person was released on parole or to mandatory supervision;

(B) is not serving a sentence for, and has not been previously convicted of, an offense listed in or described by Article 62.001(5), Code of Criminal Procedure; and

(C) is not a releasee with respect to whom a summons may not be issued under Subdivision (1).

(c–1) A summons issued under Subsection (c) must state the time, date, place, and purpose of the hearing.

(d) A designated agent of the director acts independently from a parole officer and must receive specialized training as determined by the director.

Added by Acts 1997, 75th Leg., ch. 165, § 12.01, eff. Sept. 1, 1997. Amended by Acts 2003, 78th Leg., ch. 264, § 1, eff. Sept. 1, 2003; Acts 2011, 82nd Leg., ch. 546 (H.B. 2735), § 1, eff. Sept. 1, 2011; Acts 2015, 84th Leg., ch. 693 (H.B. 710), § 1, eff. Sept. 1, 2015.

Section 3 of Acts 2015, 84th Leg., ch. 693 (H.B. 710) provides:

"The change in law made by this Act in amending Section 508.251(c), Government Code, applies only to a person who on or after the effective date [Sept. 1, 2015] of this Act is charged with a violation of the terms of the person's release on parole or to mandatory supervision. A person who before the effective date of this Act was charged with a violation of the terms of the person's release is governed by the law in effect when the violation was charged, and the former law is continued in effect for that purpose."

§ 508.252. Grounds for Issuance of Warrant or Summons

A warrant or summons may be issued under Section 508.251 if:

(1) there is reason to believe that the person has been released although not eligible for release;

(2) the person has been arrested for an offense;

(3) there is a document that is self-authenticating as provided by Rule 902, Texas Rules of Evidence,

stating that the person violated a rule or condition of release; or

(4) there is reliable evidence that the person has exhibited behavior during the person's release that indicates to a reasonable person that the person poses a danger to society that warrants the person's immediate return to custody.

Added by Acts 1997, 75th Leg., ch. 165, § 12.01, eff. Sept. 1, 1997. Amended by Acts 1999, 76th Leg., ch. 62, § 10.30, eff. Sept. 1, 1999; Acts 2003, 78th Leg., ch. 264, § 2, eff. Sept. 1, 2003.

§ 508.253. Effect on Sentence After Issuance of Warrant

If it appears a releasee has violated a condition or provision of the releasee's parole or mandatory supervision, the date of the issuance of the warrant to the date of the releasee's arrest is not counted as a part of the time served under the releasee's sentence.

Added by Acts 1997, 75th Leg., ch. 165, § 12.01, eff. Sept. 1, 1997.

§ 508.254. Detention Under Warrant

(a) A person who is the subject of a warrant may be held in custody pending a determination of all facts surrounding the alleged offense, violation of a rule or condition of release, or dangerous behavior.

(b) A warrant authorizes any officer named by the warrant to take custody of the person and detain the person until a parole panel orders the return of the person to the institution from which the person was released.

(c) Except as provided by Subsection (d), pending a hearing on a charge of parole violation, ineligible release, or violation of a condition of mandatory supervision, a person returned to custody shall remain confined.

(d) A magistrate of the county in which the person is held in custody may release the person on bond pending the hearing if:

(1) the person is arrested or held in custody only on a charge that the person committed an administrative violation of release;

(2) the division, in accordance with Subsection (e), included notice on the warrant for the person's arrest that the person is eligible for release on bond; and

(3) the magistrate determines that the person is not a threat to public safety.

(e) The division shall include a notice on the warrant for the person's arrest indicating that the person is eligible for release on bond under Subsection (d) if the division determines that the person:

(1) has not been previously convicted of:

(A) an offense under Chapter 29, Penal Code;

(B) an offense under Title 5, Penal Code, punishable as a felony; or

(C) an offense involving family violence, as defined by Section 71.004, Family Code;

(2) is not on intensive supervision or super-intensive supervision;

(3) is not an absconder; and

(4) is not a threat to public safety.

(f) The provisions of Chapters 17 and 22, Code of Criminal Procedure, apply to a person released under Subsection (d) in the same manner as those provisions apply to a person released pending an appearance before a court or magistrate, except that the release under that subsection is conditioned on the person's appearance at a hearing under this subchapter.

Added by Acts 1997, 75th Leg., ch. 165, § 12.01, eff. Sept. 1, 1997. Amended by Acts 2015, 84th Leg., ch. 472 (S.B. 790), § 1, eff. Sept. 1, 2015.

Section 3 of Acts 2015, 84th Leg., ch. 472 (S.B. 790) provides:

"The change in law made by this Act in amending Section 508.254, Government Code, applies only to a person who on or after the effective date [Sept. 1, 2015] of this Act is charged with a violation of the person's release on parole or mandatory supervision. A person who before the effective date of this Act was charged with a violation of release is governed by the law in effect when the violation was charged, and the former law is continued in effect for that purpose."

§ 508.255. Status as Fugitive From Justice

(a) After the issuance of a warrant, a person for whose return a warrant was issued is a fugitive from justice.

(b) The law relating to the right of the state to extradite a person and return a fugitive from justice and Article 42.11, Code of Criminal Procedure, relating to the waiver of all legal requirements to obtain extradition of a fugitive from justice from another state to this state, are not impaired by this chapter and remain in full force and effect.

Added by Acts 1997, 75th Leg., ch. 165, § 12.01, eff. Sept. 1, 1997.

§ 508.256. Withdrawal of Warrant

At any time before setting a revocation hearing date under Section 508.282, the division may withdraw a warrant and continue supervision of a releasee.

Added by Acts 1997, 75th Leg., ch. 165, § 12.01, eff. Sept. 1, 1997.

SUBCHAPTER I. HEARINGS AND SANCTIONS

§ 508.281. Hearing

(a) A releasee, a person released although ineligible for release, or a person granted a conditional pardon is entitled to a hearing before a parole panel or a designated agent of the board under the rules adopted by the board and within a period that permits a parole panel, a designee of the board, or the department to dispose of the charges within the periods established by Sections 508.282(a) and (b) if the releasee or person:

(1) is accused of a violation of the releasee's parole or mandatory supervision or the person's conditional pardon, on information and complaint by a peace officer or parole officer; or

(2) is arrested after an ineligible release.

(b) If a parole panel or designated agent of the board determines that a releasee or person granted a conditional pardon has been convicted of a felony offense committed while an administrative releasee and has been sentenced to a term of confinement in a penal institution, the determination is considered to be a sufficient hearing to revoke the parole or mandatory supervision or recommend to the governor revocation of a conditional pardon without further hearing, except that the parole panel or designated agent shall conduct a hearing to consider mitigating circumstances if requested by the releasee or person granted a conditional pardon.

Text of (c), as amended by Acts 2015, 84th Leg., ch. 472 (S.B. 790), § 2

(c) If a designated agent of the board determines that a releasee who appears in compliance with a summons has violated a condition of release, the agent shall notify the board. After the board or a parole panel makes a final determination regarding the violation, the division may issue a warrant requiring the releasee to be held in a county jail pending the return of the releasee to the institution from which the releasee was released.

Text of (c), as amended by Acts 2015, 84th Leg., ch. 693 (H.B. 710), § 2

(c) If a hearing before a designated agent of the board is held under this section for a releasee who appears in compliance with a summons, the sheriff of the county in which the releasee is required to appear shall provide the designated agent with a place at the county jail to hold the hearing. After the board or a parole panel makes a final determination that a releasee has violated a condition of release, a warrant may be issued requiring the releasee to be held in the county jail pending:

(1) transfer to an intermediate sanction facility; or

(2) the return of the releasee to the institution from which the releasee was released.

(d) If a parole panel or designated agent of the board determines that a releasee has violated a condition of release required under Section 508.192 and confirms the violation with a peace officer or other law enforcement officer of this state who is authorized under federal law to verify a person's immigration status or, in accordance with 8 U.S.C. Section 1373(c), with a federal law enforcement officer, the determination is considered to be a sufficient hearing to revoke the parole or mandatory supervision without further hearing or determination, except that the parole panel or designated agent shall conduct a hearing to consider mitigating circumstances, if requested by the releasee.

(e) A parole panel or designated agent of the board may not revoke the parole or mandatory supervision of a releasee if the parole panel or designated agent finds that the only evidence supporting the alleged violation of a condition of release is the uncorroborated results of a polygraph examination.

(f) Any hearing required to be conducted by a parole panel under this chapter may be conducted by a designated agent of the board. The designated agent may make recommendations to a parole panel that has responsibility for making a final determination.

Added by Acts 1997, 75th Leg., ch. 165, § 12.01, eff. Sept. 1, 1997. Amended by Acts 1999, 76th Leg., ch. 62, § 10.31, eff. Sept. 1, 1999; Acts 2003, 78th Leg., ch. 264, § 3, eff. Sept. 1, 2003; Acts 2003, 78th Leg., 3rd C.S., ch. 3, § 11.20, eff. Jan. 11, 2004; Acts 2011, 82nd Leg., ch. 1025 (H.B. 2734), § 2, eff. Sept. 1, 2011; Acts 2013, 83rd Leg., ch. 1154 (S.B. 213), § 19, eff. Sept. 1, 2013; Acts 2013, 83rd Leg., ch. 1160 (S.B. 358), § 3, eff. June 14, 2013; Acts 2015, 84th Leg., ch. 472 (S.B. 790), § 2, eff. Sept. 1, 2015; Acts 2015, 84th Leg., ch. 693 (H.B. 710), § 2, eff. Sept. 1, 2015; Acts 2015, 84th Leg., ch. 1236 (S.B. 1296), § 21.001(25), eff. Sept. 1, 2015.

Section 4 of Acts 2015, 84th Leg., ch. 472 (S.B. 790) provides:

"The change in law made by this Act in amending Section 508.281(c), Government Code, applies only to a determination made by a designated agent of the Board of Pardons and Paroles on or after the effective date [Sept. 1, 2015] of this Act. A determination made before the effective date of this Act is governed by the law in effect on the date the determination was made, and the former law is continued in effect for that purpose."

Section 4 of Acts 2015, 84th Leg., ch. 693 (H.B. 710) provides:

"The change in law made by this Act in amending Section 508.281(c), Government Code, applies only to a hearing held on or after the effective date [Sept. 1, 2015] of this Act. A hearing held before the effective date of this Act is governed by the law in effect on the date the hearing was held, and the former law is continued in effect for that purpose."

§ 508.2811. Preliminary Hearing

A parole panel or a designee of the board shall provide within a reasonable time to an inmate or person described by Section 508.281(a) a preliminary hearing to determine whether probable cause or reasonable grounds exist to believe that the inmate or person has committed an act that would constitute a violation of a condition of release, unless the inmate or person:

(1) waives the preliminary hearing; or

(2) after release:

(A) has been charged only with an administrative violation of a condition of release; or

(B) has been adjudicated guilty of or has pleaded guilty or nolo contendere to an offense committed after release, other than an offense punishable by fine only involving the operation of a motor vehicle, regardless of whether the court has deferred disposition of the case, imposed a sentence in the case, or placed the inmate or person on community supervision.

Added by Acts 1999, 76th Leg., ch. 62, § 10.32, eff. Sept. 1, 1999.

§ 508.282. Deadlines

(a) Except as provided by Subsection (b), a parole panel, a designee of the board, or the department shall dispose of the charges against an inmate or person described by Section 508.281(a):

(1) before the 41st day after the date on which:

(A) a warrant issued as provided by Section 508.251 is executed, if the inmate or person is arrested only on a charge that the inmate or person has committed an administrative violation of a condition of release, and the inmate or person is not charged before the 41st day with the commission of an offense described by Section 508.2811(2)(B); or

(B) the sheriff having custody of an inmate or person alleged to have committed an offense after release notifies the department that:

(i) the inmate or person has discharged the sentence for the offense; or

(ii) the prosecution of the alleged offense has been dismissed by the attorney representing the state in the manner provided by Article 32.02, Code of Criminal Procedure; or

(2) within a reasonable time after the date on which the inmate or person is returned to the custody of the department, if:

(A) immediately before the return the inmate or person was in custody in another state or in a federal correctional system; or

(B) the inmate or person is transferred to the custody of the department under Section 508.284.

(b) A parole panel, a designee of the board, or the department is not required to dispose of the charges against an inmate or person within the period required by Subsection (a) if:

(1) the inmate or person is in custody in another state or a federal correctional institution;

(2) the parole panel or a designee of the board is not provided a place by the sheriff to hold the hearing, in which event the department, parole panel, or designee is not required to dispose of the charges against the inmate or person until the 30th day after the date on which the sheriff provides a place to hold the hearing; or

(3) the inmate or person is granted a continuance by a parole panel or a designee of the board in the inmate's or person's hearing under Section 508.281(a), but in no event may a parole panel, a designee of the board, or the department dispose of the charges against the person later than the 15th day after the date on which the parole panel, designee, or department would otherwise be required to dispose of the charges under this section, unless the inmate or person is released from custody and a summons is issued under Section 508.251 requiring the inmate or person to appear for a hearing under Section 508.281.

(c) In Subsections (a), (b), and (f), charges against an inmate or person are disposed of when:

(1) the inmate's or person's conditional pardon, parole, or release to mandatory supervision is:

(A) revoked; or

(B) continued or modified and the inmate or person is released from the county jail;

(2) the warrant for the inmate or person issued under Section 508.251 is withdrawn; or

(3) the inmate or person is transferred to a facility described by Section 508.284 for further proceedings.

(d) A sheriff, not later than the 10th day before the date on which the sheriff intends to release from

custody an inmate or person described by Section 508.281(a) or transfer the inmate or person to the custody of an entity other than the department, shall notify the department of the intended release or transfer.

(e) If a warrant for an inmate or person issued under Section 508.251 is withdrawn, a summons may be issued requiring the inmate or person to appear for a hearing under Section 508.281.

(f) A parole panel, a designee of the board, or the department shall dispose of the charges against a releasee for whom a warrant is issued under Section 508.281(c) not later than the 31st day after the date on which the warrant is issued.

Added by Acts 1997, 75th Leg., ch. 165, § 12.01, eff. Sept. 1, 1997. Amended by Acts 1999, 76th Leg., ch. 62, § 10.33, eff. Sept. 1, 1999; Acts 2003, 78th Leg., ch. 264, § 4, eff. Sept. 1, 2003; Acts 2003, 78th Leg., ch. 1194, § 1, eff. Sept. 1, 2003.

§ 508.283. Sanctions

(a) After a parole panel or designated agent of the board has held a hearing under Section 508.281, in any manner warranted by the evidence:

(1) the board may recommend to the governor to continue, revoke, or modify the conditional pardon; and

(2) a parole panel may continue, revoke, or modify the parole or mandatory supervision.

(b) If the parole, mandatory supervision, or conditional pardon of a person described by Section 508.149(a) is revoked, the person may be required to serve the remaining portion of the sentence on which the person was released. The remaining portion is computed without credit for the time from the date of the person's release to the date of revocation.

(c) If the parole, mandatory supervision, or conditional pardon of a person other than a person described by Section 508.149(a) is revoked, the person may be required to serve the remaining portion of the sentence on which the person was released. For a person who on the date of issuance of a warrant or summons initiating the revocation process is subject to a sentence the remaining portion of which is greater than the amount of time from the date of the person's release to the date of issuance of the warrant or summons, the remaining portion is to be served without credit for the time from the date of the person's release to the date of revocation. For a person who on the date of issuance of the warrant or summons is subject to a sentence the remaining portion of which is less than the amount of time from the date of the person's release to the date of issuance of the warrant or summons, the remaining portion is to be served without credit for an amount of time equal to the remaining portion of the sentence on the date of issuance of the warrant or citation.

(d) If a warrant is issued charging a violation of a release condition or a summons is issued for a hearing under Section 508.281, the sentence time credit may be suspended until a determination is made in the case. The suspended time credit may be reinstated if the parole, mandatory supervision, or conditional pardon is continued.

(e) If a person's parole or mandatory supervision is modified after it is established that the person violated conditions of release, the board may require the releasee to remain under custodial supervision in a county jail for a period of not less than 60 days or more than 180 days. A sheriff is required to accept an inmate sanctioned under this subsection only if the commissioners court of the county in which the sheriff serves and the Texas Department of Criminal Justice have entered into a contract providing for the housing of persons sanctioned under this subsection.

Added by Acts 1997, 75th Leg., ch. 165, § 12.01, eff. Sept. 1, 1997. Amended by Acts 1999, 76th Leg., ch. 62, § 10.34, eff. Sept. 1, 1999; Acts 2001, 77th Leg., ch. 856, § 7, eff. Sept. 1, 2001; Acts 2001, 77th Leg., ch. 1197, § 1, eff. Sept. 1, 2001; Acts 2003, 78th Leg., ch. 1275, § 2(62), eff. Sept. 1, 2003.

§ 508.284. Transfer Pending Revocation Hearing

The department, as provided by Section 508.282(c), may authorize a facility that is otherwise required to detain and house an inmate or person to transfer the inmate or person to a correctional facility operated by the department or under contract with the department if:

(1) the department determines that adequate space is available in the facility to which the inmate or person is to be transferred; and

(2) the facility to which the inmate or person is to be transferred is located not more than 150 miles from the facility from which the inmate or person is to be transferred.

Added by Acts 1999, 76th Leg., ch. 62, § 10.35, eff. Sept. 1, 1999.

SUBCHAPTER J. MISCELLANEOUS

§ 508.311. Duty to Provide Information

On request of a member of the board or employee of the board or department, a public official of the state, including a judge, district attorney, county attorney, or police officer, who has information relating to an inmate eligible for parole shall send to the department in writing the information in the official's possession or under the official's control.

Added by Acts 1997, 75th Leg., ch. 165, § 12.01, eff. Sept. 1, 1997.

§ 508.312. Information on Recidivism of Releasees

The Texas Board of Criminal Justice shall collect information on recidivism of releasees under the supervision of the division and shall use the information to evaluate operations.

Added by Acts 1997, 75th Leg., ch. 165, § 12.01, eff. Sept. 1, 1997.

§ 508.313. Confidential Information

(a) All information obtained and maintained, including a victim protest letter or other correspondence, a victim impact statement, a list of inmates eligible for release on parole, and an arrest record of an inmate, is confidential and privileged if the information relates to:

(1) an inmate of the institutional division subject to release on parole, release to mandatory supervision, or executive clemency;

(2) a releasee; or

(3) a person directly identified in any proposed plan of release for an inmate.

(b) Statistical and general information relating to the parole and mandatory supervision system, including the names of releasees and data recorded relating to parole and mandatory supervision services, is not confidential or privileged and must be made available for public inspection at any reasonable time.

(c) The department, on request or in the normal course of official business, shall provide information that is confidential and privileged under Subsection (a) to:

(1) the governor;

(2) a member of the board or a parole commissioner;

(3) the Criminal Justice Policy Council in performing duties of the council under Section 413.017; or

(4) an eligible entity requesting information for a law enforcement, prosecutorial, correctional, clemency, or treatment purpose.

(d) In this section, "eligible entity" means:

(1) a government agency, including the office of a prosecuting attorney;

(2) an organization with which the department contracts or an organization to which the department provides a grant; or

(3) an organization to which inmates are referred for services by the department.

(e) This section does not apply to information relating to a sex offender that is authorized for release under Chapter 62, Code of Criminal Procedure.

(f) This section does not apply to information that is subject to required public disclosure under Section 552.029.

Added by Acts 1997, 75th Leg., ch. 165, § 12.01, eff. Sept. 1, 1997. Amended by Acts 1999, 76th Leg., ch. 62, § 10.36, eff. Sept. 1, 1999; Acts 1999, 76th Leg., ch. 783, § 3, eff. Aug. 30, 1999; Acts 2001, 77th Leg., ch. 856, § 8, eff. Sept. 1, 2001; Acts 2003, 78th Leg., ch. 6, § 3, eff. April 10, 2003; Acts 2003, 78th Leg., 3rd C.S., ch. 3, § 11.21, eff. Jan. 11, 2004.

§ 508.314.　Access to Inmates

The department shall:

(1) grant to a member or employee of the board access at all reasonable times to any inmate;

(2) provide for the member or employee or a representative of the member or employee facilities for communicating with or observing an inmate; and

(3) furnish to the member or employee:

(A) any report the member or employee requires relating to the conduct or character of an inmate; or

(B) other facts a parole panel considers pertinent in determining whether an inmate will be released on parole.

Added by Acts 1997, 75th Leg., ch. 165, § 12.01, eff. Sept. 1, 1997.

§ 508.315.　Electronic Monitoring Programs

(a) To establish and maintain an electronic monitoring program under this chapter, the department may:

(1) fund an electronic monitoring program in a parole office;

(2) develop standards for the operation of an electronic monitoring program in a parole office; and

(3) fund the purchase, lease, or maintenance of electronic monitoring equipment.

(b) In determining whether electronic monitoring equipment should be leased or purchased, the depart- ment shall consider the rate at which technological change makes electronic monitoring equipment obsolete.

Added by Acts 1997, 75th Leg., ch. 165, § 12.01, eff. Sept. 1, 1997.

§ 508.316.　Special Programs

(a) The department may contract for services for releasees if funds are appropriated to the department for the services, including services for releasees who have a history of:

(1) mental impairment or mental retardation;

(2) substance abuse; or

(3) sexual offenses.

(b) The department shall seek funding for a contract under this section as a priority item.

Added by Acts 1997, 75th Leg., ch. 165, § 12.01, eff. Sept. 1, 1997.

§ 508.317.　Intensive Supervision Program; Super-Intensive Supervision Program

(a) The department shall establish a program to provide intensive supervision to inmates released under Subchapter B, Chapter 499,[1] and other inmates determined by a parole panel or the department to require intensive supervision.

(b) The Texas Board of Criminal Justice shall adopt rules that establish standards for determining which inmates require intensive supervision.

(c) The program must provide the level of supervision the department provides that is higher than any level of supervision other than the level of supervision described by Subsection (d).

(d) The department shall establish a program to provide super-intensive supervision to inmates released on parole or mandatory supervision and determined by parole panels to require super-intensive supervision. The program must provide the highest level of supervision provided by the department.

Added by Acts 1997, 75th Leg., ch. 165, § 12.01, eff. Sept. 1, 1997. Amended by Acts 1999, 76th Leg., ch. 62, § 10.37, eff. Sept. 1, 1999.

[1] V.T.C.A., Government Code § 499.021 et seq.

§ 508.318.　Continuing Education Program

(a) The Texas Board of Criminal Justice and the Texas Education Agency shall adopt a memorandum of understanding that establishes the respective responsibilities of the board and the agency in implementing a continuing education program to increase the literacy of releasees.

(b) The Texas Board of Criminal Justice and the agency shall coordinate the development of the memorandum of understanding and each by rule shall adopt the memorandum.

Added by Acts 1997, 75th Leg., ch. 165, § 12.01, eff. Sept. 1, 1997.

§ 508.319. Program to Assess and Enhance Educational and Vocational Skills

(a) The department, with the assistance of public school districts, community and public junior colleges, public and private institutions of higher education, and other appropriate public and private entities, may establish a developmental program based on information obtained under Section 508.183 for an inmate to be released to the supervision of the division.

(b) The developmental program may provide the inmate with the educational and vocational training necessary to:

(1) meet the average skill level required under Section 508.183; and

(2) acquire employment while in the custody of the division to lessen the likelihood that the inmate will return to the institutional division.

(c) To decrease state expense for a program established under this section, the Texas Workforce Commission shall provide to the department and the other entities described by Subsection (a) information relating to obtaining financial assistance under applicable programs of public or private entities.

(d) The department may establish a developmental program similar to the program described by Subsection (a) for inmates released from the institutional division who will not be supervised by the department.

Added by Acts 1997, 75th Leg., ch. 165, § 12.01, eff. Sept. 1, 1997.

§ 508.320. Contracts for Lease of Federal Facilities

(a) The department may contract with the federal government for the lease of a military base or other federal facility that is not being used by the federal government.

(b) The department may use a facility leased under this section to house releasees in the custody of the division.

(c) The department may not enter into a contract under this section unless funds have been appropriated specifically to make payments on a contract under this section.

(d) The department shall attempt to enter into contracts that will provide the department with facilities located in various parts of the state.

Added by Acts 1997, 75th Leg., ch. 165, § 12.01, eff. Sept. 1, 1997.

§ 508.321. Reporting, Management, and Collection Services

The department, with the approval of the Texas Board of Criminal Justice, may contract with a public or private vendor to provide telephone reporting, automated caseload management, or collection services for:

(1) fines, fees, restitution, or other costs ordered to be paid by a court; or

(2) fees collected by the division.

Added by Acts 1997, 75th Leg., ch. 165, § 12.01, eff. Sept. 1, 1997.

§ 508.322. Releasee Restitution Fund

(a) The releasee restitution fund is a fund outside the treasury and consists of restitution payments made by releasees. Money in the fund may be used only to pay restitution as required by a condition of parole or mandatory supervision to victims of criminal offenses.

(b) The comptroller is the trustee of the releasee restitution fund as provided by Section 404.073.

(c) When a parole panel orders the payment of restitution from a releasee as provided by Article 42.037(h), Code of Criminal Procedure, the department shall:

(1) collect the payment for disbursement to the victim;

(2) deposit the payment in the releasee restitution fund; and

(3) transmit the payment to the victim as soon as practicable.

(d) If a victim who is entitled to restitution cannot be located, immediately after receiving a final payment in satisfaction of an order of restitution for the victim, the department shall attempt to notify the victim of that fact by certified mail, mailed to the last known address of the victim. If a victim then makes a claim for payment, the department promptly shall remit the payment to the victim.

(e) If a victim who is entitled to restitution does not make a claim for payment before the fifth anniversary of the date the department receives the initial restitution payment or if, after the victim makes a claim for payment, the department is unable to locate the victim for a period of five years after the date the department last made a payment to the victim, any unclaimed restitution payments being held by the department for payment to the victim are presumed abandoned. The department shall report and deliver to the comptroller all unclaimed restitution payments presumed abandoned under this section in the manner provided by Chapter 77, Property Code.

(f) If on March 1 a department is not holding unclaimed restitution payments that are presumed abandoned under this section, the department shall file a property report under Section 77.051, Property Code, that certifies that the department is not holding any unclaimed restitution payments that are presumed abandoned under this section.

Added by Acts 1997, 75th Leg., ch. 165, § 12.01, eff. Sept. 1, 1997. Amended by Acts 2001, 77th Leg., ch. 856, § 9, eff. Sept. 1, 2001; Acts 2017, 85th Leg., ch. 351 (H.B. 1866), § 3, eff. Sept. 1, 2017.

§ 508.323.　Audit

The financial transactions of the division and the board are subject to audit by the state auditor in accordance with Chapter 321.

Added by Acts 1997, 75th Leg., ch. 165, § 12.01, eff. Sept. 1, 1997.

§ 508.324.　Victim-Offender Mediation

If the pardons and paroles division receives notice from the victim services office of the department that a victim of the defendant, or the victim's guardian or close relative, wishes to participate in victim-offender mediation with a person released on parole or to mandatory supervision, the division shall cooperate and assist the person if the person chooses to participate in the mediation program provided by the office. The pardons and paroles division may not require the defendant to participate and may not reward the person for participation by modifying conditions of release or the person's level of supervision or by granting any other benefit to the person.

Added by Acts 1999, 76th Leg., ch. 62, § 10.38, eff. Sept. 1, 1999.

TEXAS RULES OF EVIDENCE

Effective March 1, 1998

Including Amendments Received Through September 1, 2017

Rule
903. Subscribing Witness's Testimony.

ARTICLE X. CONTENTS OF WRITINGS RECORDINGS, AND PHOTOGRAPHS

ARTICLE I. GENERAL PROVISIONS

Rule 101. Title, Scope, and Applicability of the Rules; Definitions

(a) Title. These rules may be cited as the Texas Rules of Evidence.

(b) Scope. These rules apply to proceedings in Texas courts except as otherwise provided in subdivisions (d)–(f).

(c) Rules on Privilege. The rules on privilege apply to all stages of a case or proceeding.

(d) Exception for Constitutional or Statutory Provisions or Other Rules. Despite these rules, a court must admit or exclude evidence if required to do so by the United States or Texas Constitution, a federal or Texas statute, or a rule prescribed by the United States or Texas Supreme Court or the Texas Court of Criminal Appeals. If possible, a court should resolve by reasonable construction any inconsistency between these rules and applicable constitutional or statutory provisions or other rules.

(e) Exceptions. These rules—except for those on privilege—do not apply to:

(1) the court's determination, under Rule 104(a), on a preliminary question of fact governing admissibility;

(2) grand jury proceedings; and

(3) the following miscellaneous proceedings:

(A) an application for habeas corpus in extradition, rendition, or interstate detainer proceedings;

(B) an inquiry by the court under Code of Criminal Procedure article 46B.004 to determine whether evidence exists that would support a finding that the defendant may be incompetent to stand trial;

(C) bail proceedings other than hearings to deny, revoke, or increase bail;

(D) hearings on justification for pretrial detention not involving bail;

(E) proceedings to issue a search or arrest warrant; and

(F) direct contempt determination proceedings.

(f) Exception for Justice Court Cases. These rules do not apply to justice court cases except as authorized by Texas Rule of Civil Procedure 500.3.

(g) Exception for Military Justice Hearings. The Texas Code of Military Justice, Tex. Gov't Code §§ 432.001–432.195, governs the admissibility of evidence in hearings held under that Code.

(h) Definitions. In these rules:

(1) "civil case" means a civil action or proceeding;

(2) "criminal case" means a criminal action or proceeding, including an examining trial;

(3) "public office" includes a public agency;

(4) "record" includes a memorandum, report, or data compilation;

(5) a "rule prescribed by the United States or Texas Supreme Court or the Texas Court of Criminal Appeals" means a rule adopted by any of those courts under statutory authority;

(6) "unsworn declaration" means an unsworn declaration made in accordance with Tex. Civ. Prac. & Rem. Code § 132.001; and

(7) a reference to any kind of written material or any other medium includes electronically stored information.

Eff. March 1, 1998. Amended by orders of Supreme Court March 10, 2015 and Court of Criminal Appeals March 12, 2015, eff. April 1, 2015.

Notes and Comments

Comment to 1998 change: "Criminal proceedings" rather than "criminal cases" is used since that was the terminology used in the prior Rules of Criminal Evidence. In subpart (b), the reference to "trials before magistrates" comes from prior Criminal Rule 1101(a). In the prior Criminal Rules, both Rule 101 and Rule 1101 dealt with the same thing—the applicability of the rules. Thus, Rules 101(c) and (d) have been written to incorporate the provisions of former Criminal Rule 1101 and that rule is omitted.

Rule 102. Purpose

These rules should be construed so as to administer every proceeding fairly, eliminate unjustifiable expense and delay, and promote the development of evidence law, to the end of ascertaining the truth and securing a just determination.

Eff. March 1, 1998. Amended by orders of Supreme Court March 10, 2015 and Court of Criminal Appeals March 12, 2015, eff. April 1, 2015.

Rule 103. Rulings on Evidence

(a) Preserving a Claim of Error. A party may claim error in a ruling to admit or exclude evidence only if the error affects a substantial right of the party and:

(1) if the ruling admits evidence, a party, on the record:

(A) timely objects or moves to strike; and

(B) states the specific ground, unless it was apparent from the context; or

(2) if the ruling excludes evidence, a party informs the court of its substance by an offer of proof, unless the substance was apparent from the context.

(b) Not Needing to Renew an Objection. When the court hears a party's objections outside the presence of the jury and rules that evidence is admissible, a party need not renew an objection to preserve a claim of error for appeal.

(c) Court's Statement About the Ruling; Directing an Offer of Proof. The court must allow a party to make an offer of proof outside the jury's presence as soon as practicable—and before the court reads its charge to the jury. The court may make any statement about the character or form of the evidence, the objection made, and the ruling. At a party's request, the court must direct that an offer of proof be made in question-and-answer form. Or the court may do so on its own.

(d) Preventing the Jury from Hearing Inadmissible Evidence. To the extent practicable, the court must conduct a jury trial so that inadmissible evidence is not suggested to the jury by any means.

(e) Taking Notice of Fundamental Error in Criminal Cases. In criminal cases, a court may take notice of a fundamental error affecting a substantial right, even if the claim of error was not properly preserved.

Eff. March 1, 1998. Amended by orders of Supreme Court March 10, 2015 and Court of Criminal Appeals March 12, 2015, eff. April 1, 2015.

Notes and Comments

Comment to 1998 change: The exception to the requirement of an offer of proof for matters that were apparent from the context within which ques-

tions were asked, found in paragraph (a)(2), is now applicable to civil as well as criminal cases.

Rule 104. Preliminary Questions

(a) In General. The court must decide any preliminary question about whether a witness is qualified, a privilege exists, or evidence is admissible. In so deciding, the court is not bound by evidence rules, except those on privilege.

(b) Relevance That Depends on a Fact. When the relevance of evidence depends on whether a fact exists, proof must be introduced sufficient to support a finding that the fact does exist. The court may admit the proposed evidence on the condition that the proof be introduced later.

(c) Conducting a Hearing So That the Jury Cannot Hear It. The court must conduct any hearing on a preliminary question so that the jury cannot hear it if:

(1) the hearing involves the admissibility of a confession in a criminal case;

(2) a defendant in a criminal case is a witness and so requests; or

(3) justice so requires.

(d) Cross–Examining a Defendant in a Criminal Case. By testifying outside the jury's hearing on a preliminary question, a defendant in a criminal case does not become subject to cross-examination on other issues in the case.

(e) Evidence Relevant to Weight and Credibility. This rule does not limit a party's right to introduce before the jury evidence that is relevant to the weight or credibility of other evidence.

Eff. March 1, 1998. Amended by orders of Supreme Court March 10, 2015 and Court of Criminal Appeals March 12, 2015, eff. April 1, 2015.

Rule 105. Evidence That Is Not Admissible Against Other Parties or for Other Purposes

(a) Limiting Admitted Evidence. If the court admits evidence that is admissible against a party or for a purpose—but not against another party or for another purpose—the court, on request, must restrict the evidence to its proper scope and instruct the jury accordingly.

(b) Preserving a Claim of Error.

(1) *Court Admits the Evidence Without Restriction.* A party may claim error in a ruling to admit evidence that is admissible against a party or

for a purpose—but not against another party or for another purpose—only if the party requests the court to restrict the evidence to its proper scope and instruct the jury accordingly.

(2) Court Excludes the Evidence. A party may claim error in a ruling to exclude evidence that is admissible against a party or for a purpose—but not against another party or for another purpose—only if the party limits its offer to the party against whom or the purpose for which the evidence is admissible.

Eff. March 1, 1998. Amended by orders of Supreme Court March 10, 2015 and Court of Criminal Appeals March 12, 2015, eff. April 1, 2015.

Rule 106. Remainder of or Related Writings or Recorded Statements

If a party introduces all or part of a writing or recorded statement, an adverse party may introduce, at that time, any other part—or any other writing or recorded statement—that in fairness ought to be considered at the same time. "Writing or recorded statement" includes depositions.

Eff. March 1, 1998. Amended by orders of Supreme Court March 10, 2015 and Court of Criminal Appeals March 12, 2015, eff. April 1, 2015.

Rule 107. Rule of Optional Completeness

If a party introduces part of an act, declaration, conversation, writing, or recorded statement, an adverse party may inquire into any other part on the same subject. An adverse party may also introduce any other act, declaration, conversation, writing, or recorded statement that is necessary to explain or allow the trier of fact to fully understand the part offered by the opponent. "Writing or recorded statement" includes a deposition.

Eff. March 1, 1998. Amended by orders of Supreme Court March 10, 2015 and Court of Criminal Appeals March 12, 2015,, eff. April 1, 2015.

Notes and Comments

Comment to 1998 change: This rule is the former Criminal Rule 107 except that the example regarding "when a letter is read" has been relocated in the rule so as to more accurately indicate the provision it explains. While this rule appeared only in the prior criminal rules, it is made applicable to civil cases because it accurately reflects the common law rule of optional completeness in civil cases.

ARTICLE II. JUDICIAL NOTICE

Rule 201. Judicial Notice of Adjudicative Facts

(a) Scope. This rule governs judicial notice of an adjudicative fact only, not a legislative fact.

(b) Kinds of Facts That May Be Judicially Noticed. The court may judicially notice a fact that is not subject to reasonable dispute because it:

    (1) is generally known within the trial court's territorial jurisdiction; or

    (2) can be accurately and readily determined from sources whose accuracy cannot reasonably be questioned.

(c) Taking Notice. The court:

    (1) may take judicial notice on its own; or

    (2) must take judicial notice if a party requests it and the court is supplied with the necessary information.

(d) Timing. The court may take judicial notice at any stage of the proceeding.

(e) Opportunity to Be Heard. On timely request, a party is entitled to be heard on the propriety of taking judicial notice and the nature of the fact to be noticed. If the court takes judicial notice before notifying a party, the party, on request, is still entitled to be heard.

(f) Instructing the Jury. In a civil case, the court must instruct the jury to accept the noticed fact as conclusive. In a criminal case, the court must instruct the jury that it may or may not accept the noticed fact as conclusive.

Eff. March 1, 1998. Amended by orders of Supreme Court March 10, 2015 and Court of Criminal Appeals March 12, 2015, eff. April 1, 2015.

Rule 202. Judicial Notice of Other States' Law

(a) Scope. This rule governs judicial notice of another state's, territory's, or federal jurisdiction's:

- Constitution;
- public statutes;
- rules;
- regulations;
- ordinances;
- court decisions; and
- common law.

(b) Taking Notice. The court:

    (1) may take judicial notice on its own; or

(2) must take judicial notice if a party requests it and the court is supplied with the necessary information.

(c) Notice and Opportunity to Be Heard.

(1) *Notice.* The court may require a party requesting judicial notice to notify all other parties of the request so they may respond to it.

(2) *Opportunity to Be Heard.* On timely request, a party is entitled to be heard on the propriety of taking judicial notice and the nature of the matter to be noticed. If the court takes judicial notice before a party has been notified, the party, on request, is still entitled to be heard.

(d) Timing. The court may take judicial notice at any stage of the proceeding.

(e) Determination and Review. The court—not the jury—must determine the law of another state, territory, or federal jurisdiction. The court's determination must be treated as a ruling on a question of law.

Eff. March 1, 1998. Amended by orders of Supreme Court March 10, 2015 and Court of Criminal Appeals March 12, 2015, eff. April 1, 2015.

Rule 203. Determining Foreign Law

(a) Raising a Foreign Law Issue. A party who intends to raise an issue about a foreign country's law must:

(1) give reasonable notice by a pleading or other writing; and

(2) at least 30 days before trial, supply all parties a copy of any written materials or sources the party intends to use to prove the foreign law.

(b) Translations. If the materials or sources were originally written in a language other than English, the party intending to rely on them must, at least 30 days before trial, supply all parties both a copy of the foreign language text and an English translation.

(c) Materials the Court May Consider; Notice. In determining foreign law, the court may consider any material or source, whether or not admissible. If the court considers any material or source not submitted by a party, it must give all parties notice and a reasonable opportunity to comment and submit additional materials.

(d) Determination and Review. The court—not the jury—must determine foreign law. The court's

determination must be treated as a ruling on a question of law.

Eff. March 1, 1998. Amended by orders of Supreme Court March 10, 2015 and Court of Criminal Appeals March 12, 2015, eff. April 1, 2015.

Rule 204. Judicial Notice of Texas Municipal and County Ordinances, Texas Register Contents, and Published Agency Rules

(a) Scope. This rule governs judicial notice of Texas municipal and county ordinances, the contents of the Texas Register, and agency rules published in the Texas Administrative Code.

(b) Taking Notice. The court:

(1) may take judicial notice on its own; or

(2) must take judicial notice if a party requests it and the court is supplied with the necessary information.

(c) Notice and Opportunity to Be Heard.

(1) *Notice.* The court may require a party requesting judicial notice to notify all other parties of the request so they may respond to it.

(2) *Opportunity to Be Heard.* On timely request, a party is entitled to be heard on the propriety of taking judicial notice and the nature of the matter to be noticed. If the court takes judicial notice before a party has been notified, the party, on request, is still entitled to be heard.

(d) Determination and Review. The court—not the jury—must determine municipal and county ordinances, the contents of the Texas Register, and published agency rules. The court's determination must be treated as a ruling on a question of law.

Eff. March 1, 1998. Amended by orders of Supreme Court March 10, 2015 and Court of Criminal Appeals March 12, 2015, eff. April 1, 2015.

ARTICLE III. PRESUMPTIONS

[No rules adopted at this time.]

ARTICLE IV. RELEVANCE AND ITS LIMITS

Rule 401. Test for Relevant Evidence

Evidence is relevant if:

(a) it has any tendency to make a fact more or less probable than it would be without the evidence; and

(b) the fact is of consequence in determining the action.

Eff. March 1, 1998. Amended by orders of Supreme Court March 10, 2015 and Court of Criminal Appeals March 12, 2015, eff. April 1, 2015.

Rule 402. General Admissibility of Relevant Evidence

Relevant evidence is admissible unless any of the following provides otherwise:

- the United States or Texas Constitution;
- a statute;
- these rules; or
- other rules prescribed under statutory authority.

Irrelevant evidence is not admissible.

Eff. March 1, 1998. Amended by orders of Supreme Court March 10, 2015 and Court of Criminal Appeals March 12, 2015, eff. April 1, 2015.

Rule 403. Excluding Relevant Evidence for Prejudice, Confusion, or Other Reasons

The court may exclude relevant evidence if its probative value is substantially outweighed by a danger of one or more of the following: unfair prejudice, confusing the issues, misleading the jury, undue delay, or needlessly presenting cumulative evidence.

Eff. March 1, 1998. Amended by orders of Supreme Court March 10, 2015 and Court of Criminal Appeals March 12, 2015, eff. April 1, 2015.

Rule 404. Character Evidence; Crimes or Other Acts

(a) Character Evidence.

(1) *Prohibited Uses.* Evidence of a person's character or character trait is not admissible to prove that on a particular occasion the person acted in accordance with the character or trait.

(2) *Exceptions for an Accused.*

(A) In a criminal case, a defendant may offer evidence of the defendant's pertinent trait, and if the evidence is admitted, the prosecutor may offer evidence to rebut it.

(B) In a civil case, a party accused of conduct involving moral turpitude may offer evidence of the party's pertinent trait, and if the evidence is admitted, the accusing party may offer evidence to rebut it.

(3) *Exceptions for a Victim.*

(A) In a criminal case, subject to the limitations in Rule 412, a defendant may offer evidence of a victim's pertinent trait, and if the evidence is admitted, the prosecutor may offer evidence to rebut it.

(B) In a homicide case, the prosecutor may offer evidence of the victim's trait of peacefulness to rebut evidence that the victim was the first aggressor.

(C) In a civil case, a party accused of assaultive conduct may offer evidence of the victim's trait of violence to prove self-defense, and if the evidence is admitted, the accusing party may offer evidence of the victim's trait of peacefulness.

(4) *Exceptions for a Witness.* Evidence of a witness's character may be admitted under Rules 607, 608, and 609.

(5) *Definition of "Victim."* In this rule, "victim" includes an alleged victim.

(b) Crimes, Wrongs, or Other Acts.

(1) *Prohibited Uses.* Evidence of a crime, wrong, or other act is not admissible to prove a person's character in order to show that on a particular occasion the person acted in accordance with the character.

(2) *Permitted Uses; Notice in Criminal Case.* This evidence may be admissible for another purpose, such as proving motive, opportunity, intent, preparation, plan, knowledge, identity, absence of mistake, or lack of accident. On timely request by a defendant in a criminal case, the prosecutor must provide reasonable notice before trial that the prosecution intends to introduce such evidence—other than that arising in the same transaction—in its case-in-chief.

Eff. March 1, 1998. Amended by orders of Supreme Court March 10, 2015 and Court of Criminal Appeals March 12, 2015, eff. April 1, 2015.

Rule 405. Methods of Proving Character

(a) By Reputation or Opinion.

(1) *In General.* When evidence of a person's character or character trait is admissible, it may be proved by testimony about the person's reputation or by testimony in the form of an opinion. On cross-examination of the character witness, inquiry may be made into relevant specific instances of the person's conduct.

(2) *Accused's Character in a Criminal Case.* In the guilt stage of a criminal case, a witness may testify to the defendant's character or character trait only if, before the day of the offense, the witness was familiar with the defendant's reputation or the facts or information that form the basis of the witness's opinion.

(b) By Specific Instances of Conduct. When a person's character or character trait is an essential element of a charge, claim, or defense, the character or trait may also be proved by relevant specific instances of the person's conduct.

Eff. March 1, 1998. Amended by orders of Supreme Court March 10, 2015 and Court of Criminal Appeals March 12, 2015, eff. April 1, 2015.

Rule 406. Habit; Routine Practice

Evidence of a person's habit or an organization's routine practice may be admitted to prove that on a particular occasion the person or organization acted in accordance with the habit or routine practice. The court may admit this evidence regardless of whether it is corroborated or whether there was an eyewitness.

Eff. March 1, 1998. Amended by orders of Supreme Court March 10, 2015 and Court of Criminal Appeals March 12, 2015, eff. April 1, 2015.

Rule 407. Subsequent Remedial Measures; Notification of Defect

(a) Subsequent Remedial Measures. When measures are taken that would have made an earlier injury or harm less likely to occur, evidence of the subsequent measures is not admissible to prove:

- negligence;
- culpable conduct;
- a defect in a product or its design; or
- a need for a warning or instruction.

But the court may admit this evidence for another purpose, such as impeachment or—if disputed—proving ownership, control, or the feasibility of precautionary measures.

(b) Notification of Defect. A manufacturer's written notification to a purchaser of a defect in one of its products is admissible against the manufacturer to prove the defect.

Eff. March 1, 1998; amended by Supreme Court Aug. 29, 2003, eff. July 1, 2003. Amended by orders of Supreme Court March 10, 2015 and Court of Criminal Appeals March 12, 2015, eff. April 1, 2015.

Rule 408. Compromise Offers and Negotiations

(a) Prohibited Uses. Evidence of the following is not admissible either to prove or disprove the validity or amount of a disputed claim:

(1) furnishing, promising, or offering—or accepting, promising to accept, or offering to accept—a valuable consideration in compromising or attempting to compromise the claim; and

(2) conduct or statements made during compromise negotiations about the claim.

(b) Permissible Uses. The court may admit this evidence for another purpose, such as proving a party's or witness's bias, prejudice, or interest, negating a contention of undue delay, or proving an effort to obstruct a criminal investigation or prosecution.

Eff. March 1, 1998. Amended by orders of Supreme Court March 10, 2015 and Court of Criminal Appeals March 12, 2015, eff. April 1, 2015.

Rule 409. Offers to Pay Medical and Similar Expenses

Evidence of furnishing, promising to pay, or offering to pay medical, hospital, or similar expenses resulting from an injury is not admissible to prove liability for the injury.

Eff. March 1, 1998. Amended by orders of Supreme Court March 10, 2015 and Court of Criminal Appeals March 12, 2015, eff. April 1, 2015.

Rule 410. Pleas, Plea Discussions, and Related Statements

(a) Prohibited Uses in Civil Cases. In a civil case, evidence of the following is not admissible against the defendant who made the plea or was a participant in the plea discussions:

(1) a guilty plea that was later withdrawn;

(2) a nolo contendere plea;

(3) a statement made during a proceeding on either of those pleas under Federal Rule of Criminal Procedure 11 or a comparable state procedure; or

(4) a statement made during plea discussions with an attorney for the prosecuting authority if the discussions did not result in a guilty plea or they resulted in a later-withdrawn guilty plea.

(b) Prohibited Uses in Criminal Cases. In a criminal case, evidence of the following is not admissible against the defendant who made the plea or was a participant in the plea discussions:

(1) a guilty plea that was later withdrawn;

(2) a nolo contendere plea that was later withdrawn;

(3) a statement made during a proceeding on either of those pleas under Federal Rule of Criminal Procedure 11 or a comparable state procedure; or

(4) a statement made during plea discussions with an attorney for the prosecuting authority if the discussions did not result in a guilty or nolo contendere plea or they resulted in a later-withdrawn guilty or nolo contendere plea.

(c) Exception. In a civil case, the court may admit a statement described in paragraph (a)(3) or (4) and in a criminal case, the court may admit a statement described in paragraph (b)(3) or (4), when another statement made during the same plea or plea discussions has been introduced and in fairness the statements ought to be considered together.

Eff. March 1, 1998. Amended by orders of Supreme Court March 10, 2015 and Court of Criminal Appeals March 12, 2015, eff. April 1, 2015.

Rule 411. Liability Insurance

Evidence that a person was or was not insured against liability is not admissible to prove whether the person acted negligently or otherwise wrongfully. But the court may admit this evidence for another purpose, such as proving a witness's bias or prejudice or, if disputed, proving agency, ownership, or control.

Eff. March 1, 1998. Amended by orders of Supreme Court March 10, 2015 and Court of Criminal Appeals March 12, 2015, eff. April 1, 2015.

Rule 412. Evidence of Previous Sexual Conduct in Criminal Cases

(a) In General. The following evidence is not admissible in a prosecution for sexual assault, aggravated sexual assault, or attempt to commit sexual assault or aggravated sexual assault:

(1) reputation or opinion evidence of a victim's past sexual behavior; or

(2) specific instances of a victim's past sexual behavior.

(b) Exceptions for Specific Instances. Evidence of specific instances of a victim's past sexual behavior is admissible if:

(1) the court admits the evidence in accordance with subdivisions (c) and (d);

(2) the evidence:

(A) is necessary to rebut or explain scientific or medical evidence offered by the prosecutor;

(B) concerns past sexual behavior with the defendant and is offered by the defendant to prove consent;

(C) relates to the victim's motive or bias;

(D) is admissible under Rule 609; or

(E) is constitutionally required to be admitted; and

(3) the probative value of the evidence outweighs the danger of unfair prejudice.

(c) Procedure for Offering Evidence. Before offering any evidence of the victim's past sexual behavior, the defendant must inform the court outside the jury's presence. The court must then conduct an in camera hearing, recorded by a court reporter, and determine whether the proposed evidence is admissible. The defendant may not refer to any evidence ruled inadmissible without first requesting and gaining the court's approval outside the jury's presence.

(d) Record Sealed. The court must preserve the record of the in camera hearing, under seal, as part of the record.

(e) Definition of "Victim." In this rule, "victim" includes an alleged victim.

Eff. March 1, 1998. Amended by Court of Criminal Appeals Dec. 13, 2006, eff. Jan. 1, 2007. Amended by orders of Supreme Court March 10, 2015 and Court of Criminal Appeals March 12, 2015, eff. April 1, 2015.

ARTICLE V. PRIVILEGES

Rule 501. Privileges in General

Unless a Constitution, a statute, or these or other rules prescribed under statutory authority provide otherwise, no person has a privilege to:

(a) refuse to be a witness;

(b) refuse to disclose any matter;

(c) refuse to produce any object or writing; or

(d) prevent another from being a witness, disclosing any matter, or producing any object or writing.

Eff. March 1, 1998. Amended by orders of Supreme Court March 10, 2015 and Court of Criminal Appeals March 12, 2015, eff. April 1, 2015.

Rule 502. Required Reports Privileged By Statute

(a) In General. If a law requiring a return or report to be made so provides:

(1) a person, corporation, association, or other organization or entity—whether public or private—that makes the required return or report has a privilege to refuse to disclose it and to prevent any other person from disclosing it; and

(2) a public officer or agency to whom the return or report must be made has a privilege to refuse to disclose it.

(b) Exceptions. This privilege does not apply in an action involving perjury, false statements, fraud in the return or report, or other failure to comply with the law in question.

Eff. March 1, 1998. Amended by orders of Supreme Court March 10, 2015 and Court of Criminal Appeals March 12, 2015, eff. April 1, 2015.

Rule 503. Lawyer–Client Privilege

(a) Definitions. In this rule:

(1) A "client" is a person, public officer, or corporation, association, or other organization or entity— whether public or private—that:

(A) is rendered professional legal services by a lawyer; or

(B) consults a lawyer with a view to obtaining professional legal services from the lawyer.

(2) A "client's representative" is:

(A) a person who has authority to obtain professional legal services for the client or to act for the client on the legal advice rendered; or

(B) any other person who, to facilitate the rendition of professional legal services to the client, makes or receives a confidential communication while acting in the scope of employment for the client.

(3) A "lawyer" is a person authorized, or who the client reasonably believes is authorized, to practice law in any state or nation.

(4) A "lawyer's representative" is:

(A) one employed by the lawyer to assist in the rendition of professional legal services; or

(B) an accountant who is reasonably necessary for the lawyer's rendition of professional legal services.

(5) A communication is "confidential" if not intended to be disclosed to third persons other than those:

(A) to whom disclosure is made to further the rendition of professional legal services to the client; or

(B) reasonably necessary to transmit the communication.

(b) Rules of Privilege.

(1) *General Rule.* A client has a privilege to refuse to disclose and to prevent any other person from disclosing confidential communications made to facilitate the rendition of professional legal services to the client:

(A) between the client or the client's representative and the client's lawyer or the lawyer's representative;

(B) between the client's lawyer and the lawyer's representative;

(C) by the client, the client's representative, the client's lawyer, or the lawyer's representative to a lawyer representing another party in a pending action or that lawyer's representative, if the communications concern a matter of common interest in the pending action;

(D) between the client's representatives or between the client and the client's representative; or

(E) among lawyers and their representatives representing the same client.

(2) *Special Rule in a Criminal Case.* In a criminal case, a client has a privilege to prevent a lawyer or lawyer's representative from disclosing any other fact that came to the knowledge of the lawyer or the lawyer's representative by reason of the attorney-client relationship.

(c) Who May Claim. The privilege may be claimed by:

(1) the client;

(2) the client's guardian or conservator;

(3) a deceased client's personal representative; or

(4) the successor, trustee, or similar representative of a corporation, association, or other organization or entity—whether or not in existence.

The person who was the client's lawyer or the lawyer's representative when the communication was made may claim the privilege on the client's behalf—and is presumed to have authority to do so.

(d) Exceptions. This privilege does not apply:

(1) *Furtherance of Crime or Fraud.* If the lawyer's services were sought or obtained to enable or aid anyone to commit or plan to commit what the client knew or reasonably should have known to be a crime or fraud.

(2) *Claimants Through Same Deceased Client.* If the communication is relevant to an issue between parties claiming through the same deceased client.

(3) *Breach of Duty By a Lawyer or Client.* If the communication is relevant to an issue of breach of duty by a lawyer to the client or by a client to the lawyer.

(4) *Document Attested By a Lawyer.* If the communication is relevant to an issue concerning an attested document to which the lawyer is an attesting witness.

(5) *Joint Clients.* If the communication:

(A) is offered in an action between clients who retained or consulted a lawyer in common;

(B) was made by any of the clients to the lawyer; and

(C) is relevant to a matter of common interest between the clients.

Eff. March 1, 1998. Amended by orders of Supreme Court March 10, 2015 and Court of Criminal Appeals March 12, 2015, eff. April 1, 2015.

Notes and Comments

Comment to 1998 change: The addition of subsection (a)(2)(B) adopts a subject matter test for the privilege of an entity, in place of the control group test previously used. See *National Tank Co. v. Brotherton*, 851 S.W.2d 193, 197-198 (Tex. 1993).

Rule 504. Spousal Privileges

(a) Confidential Communication Privilege.

(1) *Definition.* A communication is "confidential" if a person makes it privately to the person's spouse and does not intend its disclosure to any other person.

(2) *General Rule.* A person has a privilege to refuse to disclose and to prevent any other person from disclosing a confidential communication made to the person's spouse while they were married. This privilege survives termination of the marriage.

(3) *Who May Claim.* The privilege may be claimed by:

(A) the communicating spouse;

(B) the guardian of a communicating spouse who is incompetent; or

(C) the personal representative of a communicating spouse who is deceased.

The other spouse may claim the privilege on the communicating spouse's behalf—and is presumed to have authority to do so.

(4) *Exceptions.* This privilege does not apply:

(A) *Furtherance of Crime or Fraud.* If the communication is made—wholly or partially—to enable or aid anyone to commit or plan to commit a crime or fraud.

(B) *Proceeding Between Spouse and Other Spouse or Claimant Through Deceased Spouse.* In a civil proceeding:

(i) brought by or on behalf of one spouse against the other; or

(ii) between a surviving spouse and a person claiming through the deceased spouse.

(C) *Crime Against Family, Spouse, Household Member, or Minor Child.* In a:

(i) proceeding in which a party is accused of conduct that, if proved, is a crime against the person of the other spouse, any member of the household of either spouse, or any minor child; or

(ii) criminal proceeding involving a charge of bigamy under Section 25.01 of the Penal Code.

(D) *Commitment or Similar Proceeding.* In a proceeding to commit either spouse or otherwise to place the spouse or the spouse's property under another's control because of a mental or physical condition.

(E) *Proceeding to Establish Competence.* In a proceeding brought by or on behalf of either spouse to establish competence.

(b) Privilege Not to Testify in a Criminal Case.

(1) *General Rule.* In a criminal case, an accused's spouse has a privilege not to be called to testify for the state. But this rule neither prohibits a spouse from testifying voluntarily for the state nor gives a spouse a privilege to refuse to be called to testify for the accused.

(2) *Failure to Call Spouse.* If other evidence indicates that the accused's spouse could testify to relevant matters, an accused's failure to call the spouse to testify is a proper subject of comment by counsel.

(3) *Who May Claim.* The privilege not to testify may be claimed by the accused's spouse or the spouse's guardian or representative, but not by the accused.

(4) *Exceptions.* This privilege does not apply:

(A) *Certain Criminal Proceedings.* In a criminal proceeding in which a spouse is charged with:

(i) a crime against the other spouse, any member of the household of either spouse, or any minor child; or

(ii) bigamy under Section 25.01 of the Penal Code.

(B) *Matters That Occurred Before the Marriage.* If the spouse is called to testify about matters that occurred before the marriage.

Eff. March 1, 1998. Amended by Court of Criminal Appeals Dec. 13, 2006, eff. January 1, 2007. Amended by orders of Supreme Court March 10, 2015 and Court of Criminal Appeals March 12, 2015, eff. April 1, 2015.

Notes and Comments

Comment to 1998 change: The rule eliminates the spousal testimonial privilege for prosecutions in which the testifying spouse is the alleged victim of a crime by the accused. This is intended to be consistent with Code of Criminal Procedure article 38.10, effective September 1, 1995.

Rule 505. Privilege For Communications to a Clergy Member

(a) Definitions. In this rule:

(1) A "clergy member" is a minister, priest, rabbi, accredited Christian Science Practitioner, or other similar functionary of a religious organization or someone whom a communicant reasonably believes is a clergy member.

(2) A "communicant" is a person who consults a clergy member in the clergy member's professional capacity as a spiritual adviser.

(3) A communication is "confidential" if made privately and not intended for further disclosure except to other persons present to further the purpose of the communication.

(b) General Rule. A communicant has a privilege to refuse to disclose and to prevent any other person from disclosing a confidential communication by the communicant to a clergy member in the clergy member's professional capacity as spiritual adviser.

(c) Who May Claim. The privilege may be claimed by:

(1) the communicant;

(2) the communicant's guardian or conservator; or

(3) a deceased communicant's personal representative.

The clergy member to whom the communication was made may claim the privilege on the communicant's behalf—and is presumed to have authority to do so.

Eff. March 1, 1998. Amended by orders of Supreme Court March 10, 2015 and Court of Criminal Appeals March 12, 2015, eff. April 1, 2015.

Rule 506. Political Vote Privilege

A person has a privilege to refuse to disclose the person's vote at a political election conducted by secret ballot unless the vote was cast illegally.

Eff. March 1, 1998. Amended by orders of Supreme Court March 10, 2015 and Court of Criminal Appeals March 12, 2015, eff. April 1, 2015.

Rule 507. Trade Secrets Privilege

(a) General Rule. A person has a privilege to refuse to disclose and to prevent other persons from disclosing a trade secret owned by the person, unless the court finds that nondisclosure will tend to conceal fraud or otherwise work injustice.

(b) Who May Claim. The privilege may be claimed by the person who owns the trade secret or the person's agent or employee.

(c) Protective Measure. If a court orders a person to disclose a trade secret, it must take any protective measure required by the interests of the privilege holder and the parties and to further justice.

Eff. March 1, 1998. Amended by orders of Supreme Court March 10, 2015 and Court of Criminal Appeals March 12, 2015, eff. April 1, 2015.

Rule 508. Informer's Identity Privilege

(a) General Rule. The United States, a state, or a subdivision of either has a privilege to refuse to disclose a person's identity if:

(1) the person has furnished information to a law enforcement officer or a member of a legislative committee or its staff conducting an investigation of a possible violation of law; and

(2) the information relates to or assists in the investigation.

(b) Who May Claim. The privilege may be claimed by an appropriate representative of the public entity to which the informer furnished the information. The court in a criminal case must reject the privilege claim if the state objects.

(c) Exceptions.

(1) *Voluntary Disclosure; Informer a Witness.* This privilege does not apply if:

(A) the informer's identity or the informer's interest in the communication's subject matter has been disclosed—by a privilege holder or the informer's own action—to a person who would have cause to resent the communication; or

(B) the informer appears as a witness for the public entity.

(2) *Testimony About the Merits.*

(A) *Criminal Case.* In a criminal case, this privilege does not apply if the court finds a reasonable probability exists that the informer can give testimony necessary to a fair determination of guilt or innocence. If the court so finds and the public entity elects not to disclose the informer's identity:

(i) on the defendant's motion, the court must dismiss the charges to which the testimony would relate; or

(ii) on its own motion, the court may dismiss the charges to which the testimony would relate.

(B) *Certain Civil Cases.* In a civil case in which the public entity is a party, this privilege does not apply if the court finds a reasonable probability exists that the informer can give testimony necessary to a fair determination of a material issue on the merits. If the court so finds and the public entity elects not to disclose the informer's identity, the court may make any order that justice requires.

(C) *Procedures.*

(i) If it appears that an informer may be able to give the testimony required to invoke this exception and the public entity claims the privilege, the court must give the public entity an opportunity to show in camera facts relevant to determining whether this exception is met. The showing should ordinarily be made by affidavits, but the court may take testimony if it finds the matter cannot be satisfactorily resolved by affidavits.

(ii) No counsel or party may attend the in camera showing.

(iii) The court must seal and preserve for appeal evidence submitted under this subparagraph (2)(C). The evidence must not otherwise be revealed without the public entity's consent.

(3) *Legality of Obtaining Evidence.*

(A) *Court May Order Disclosure.* The court may order the public entity to disclose an informer's identity if:

(i) information from an informer is relied on to establish the legality of the means by which evidence was obtained; and

(ii) the court is not satisfied that the information was received from an informer reasonably believed to be reliable or credible.

(B) *Procedures.*

(i) On the public entity's request, the court must order the disclosure be made in camera.

(ii) No counsel or party may attend the in camera disclosure.

(iii) If the informer's identity is disclosed in camera, the court must seal and preserve for appeal the record of the in camera proceeding. The record of the in camera proceeding must not otherwise be revealed without the public entity's consent.

Eff. March 1, 1998. Amended by orders of Supreme Court March 10, 2015 and Court of Criminal Appeals March 12, 2015, eff. April 1, 2015.

Rule 509. Physician–Patient Privilege

(a) Definitions. In this rule:

(1) A "patient" is a person who consults or is seen by a physician for medical care.

(2) A "physician" is a person licensed, or who the patient reasonably believes is licensed, to practice medicine in any state or nation.

(3) A communication is "confidential" if not intended to be disclosed to third persons other than those:

(A) present to further the patient's interest in the consultation, examination, or interview;

(B) reasonably necessary to transmit the communication; or

(C) participating in the diagnosis and treatment under the physician's direction, including members of the patient's family.

(b) Limited Privilege in a Criminal Case. There is no physician-patient privilege in a criminal case. But a confidential communication is not admissible in a criminal case if made:

(1) to a person involved in the treatment of or examination for alcohol or drug abuse; and

(2) by a person being treated voluntarily or being examined for admission to treatment for alcohol or drug abuse.

(c) General Rule in a Civil Case. In a civil case, a patient has a privilege to refuse to disclose and to prevent any other person from disclosing:

(1) a confidential communication between a physician and the patient that relates to or was made in connection with any professional services the physician rendered the patient; and

(2) a record of the patient's identity, diagnosis, evaluation, or treatment created or maintained by a physician.

(d) Who May Claim in a Civil Case. The privilege may be claimed by:

(1) the patient; or

(2) the patient's representative on the patient's behalf.

The physician may claim the privilege on the patient's behalf—and is presumed to have authority to do so.

(e) Exceptions in a Civil Case. This privilege does not apply:

(1) *Proceeding Against Physician.* If the communication or record is relevant to a claim or defense in:

(A) a proceeding the patient brings against a physician; or

(B) a license revocation proceeding in which the patient is a complaining witness.

(2) *Consent.* If the patient or a person authorized to act on the patient's behalf consents in writing to the release of any privileged information, as provided in subdivision (f).

(3) *Action to Collect.* In an action to collect a claim for medical services rendered to the patient.

(4) *Party Relies on Patient's Condition.* If any party relies on the patient's physical, mental, or emotional condition as a part of the party's claim or defense and the communication or record is relevant to that condition.

(5) *Disciplinary Investigation or Proceeding.* In a disciplinary investigation of or proceeding against a physician under the Medical Practice Act, Tex. Occ. Code § 164.001 et seq., or a registered nurse under Tex. Occ. Code § 301.451 et seq. But the board conducting the investigation or proceeding must protect the identity of any patient whose medical records are examined unless:

(A) the patient's records would be subject to disclosure under paragraph (e)(1); or

(B) the patient has consented in writing to the release of medical records, as provided in subdivision (f).

(6) *Involuntary Civil Commitment or Similar Proceeding.* In a proceeding for involuntary civil commitment or court-ordered treatment, or a probable cause hearing under Tex. Health & Safety Code:

(A) chapter 462 (Treatment of Persons With Chemical Dependencies);

(B) title 7, subtitle C (Texas Mental Health Code); or

(C) title 7, subtitle D (Persons With an Intellectual Disability Act).

(7) *Abuse or Neglect of "Institution" Resident.* In a proceeding regarding the abuse or neglect, or the cause of any abuse or neglect, of a resident of an "institution" as defined in Tex. Health & Safety Code § 242.002.

(f) Consent For Release of Privileged Information.

(1) Consent for the release of privileged information must be in writing and signed by:

(A) the patient;

(B) a parent or legal guardian if the patient is a minor;

(C) a legal guardian if the patient has been adjudicated incompetent to manage personal affairs;

(D) an attorney appointed for the patient under Tex. Health & Safety Code title 7, subtitles C and D;

(E) an attorney ad litem appointed for the patient under Tex. Estates Code title 3, subtitle C;

(F) an attorney ad litem or guardian ad litem appointed for a minor under Tex. Fam. Code chapter 107, subchapter B; or

(G) a personal representative if the patient is deceased.

(2) The consent must specify:

(A) the information or medical records covered by the release;

(B) the reasons or purposes for the release; and

(C) the person to whom the information is to be released.

(3) The patient, or other person authorized to consent, may withdraw consent to the release of any information. But a withdrawal of consent does not affect any information disclosed before the patient or authorized person gave written notice of the withdrawal.

(4) Any person who receives information privileged under this rule may disclose the information only to the extent consistent with the purposes specified in the consent.

Eff. March 1, 1998. Amended by orders of Supreme Court March 10, 2015 and Court of Criminal Appeals March 12, 2015, eff. April 1, 2015. Amended by order of Supreme Court June 14, 2016, eff. June 14, 2016.

Notes and Comments

Comment to 1998 change: This comment is intended to inform the construction and application of this rule. Prior Criminal Rules of Evidence 509 and 510 are now in subparagraph (b) of this Rule. This rule governs disclosures of patient-physician communications only in judicial or administrative proceedings. Whether a physician may or must disclose such communications in other circumstances is governed by TEX.REV.CIV.STAT.ANN. art. 4495b, § 5.08. Former subparagraph (d)(6) of the Civil Evidence Rules, regarding disclosures in a suit affecting the parent-child relationship, is omitted, not because there should be no exception to the privilege in suits affecting the parent-child relationship, but because the exception in such suits is properly considered under subparagraph (e)(4) of the new rule (formerly subparagraph (d)(4)), as construed in *R.K. v. Ramirez*, 887 S.W.2d 836 (Tex. 1994). In determining the proper application of an exception in such suits, the trial court must ensure that the precise need for the information is not outweighed by legitimate privacy interests protected by the privilege. Subparagraph (e) of the new rule does not except from the privilege information relating to a nonparty patient who is or may be a consulting or testifying expert in the suit.

Rule 510. Mental Health Information Privilege in Civil Cases

(a) Definitions. In this rule:

(1) A "professional" is a person:

(A) authorized to practice medicine in any state or nation;

(B) licensed or certified by the State of Texas in the diagnosis, evaluation, or treatment of any mental or emotional disorder;

(C) involved in the treatment or examination of drug abusers; or

(D) who the patient reasonably believes to be a professional under this rule.

(2) A "patient" is a person who:

(A) consults or is interviewed by a professional for diagnosis, evaluation, or treatment of any mental or emotional condition or disorder, including alcoholism and drug addiction; or

(B) is being treated voluntarily or being examined for admission to voluntary treatment for drug abuse.

(3) A "patient's representative" is:

(A) any person who has the patient's written consent;

(B) the parent of a minor patient;

(C) the guardian of a patient who has been adjudicated incompetent to manage personal affairs; or

(D) the personal representative of a deceased patient.

(4) A communication is "confidential" if not intended to be disclosed to third persons other than those:

(A) present to further the patient's interest in the diagnosis, examination, evaluation, or treatment;

(B) reasonably necessary to transmit the communication; or

(C) participating in the diagnosis, examination, evaluation, or treatment under the professional's direction, including members of the patient's family.

(b) General Rule; Disclosure.

(1) In a civil case, a patient has a privilege to refuse to disclose and to prevent any other person from disclosing:

(A) a confidential communication between the patient and a professional; and

(B) a record of the patient's identity, diagnosis, evaluation, or treatment that is created or maintained by a professional.

(2) In a civil case, any person—other than a patient's representative acting on the patient's behalf—who receives information privileged under this rule may disclose the information only to the extent consistent with the purposes for which it was obtained.

(c) Who May Claim. The privilege may be claimed by:

(1) the patient; or

(2) the patient's representative on the patient's behalf.

The professional may claim the privilege on the patient's behalf—and is presumed to have authority to do so.

(d) Exceptions. This privilege does not apply:

(1) *Proceeding Against Professional.* If the communication or record is relevant to a claim or defense in:

(A) a proceeding the patient brings against a professional; or

(B) a license revocation proceeding in which the patient is a complaining witness.

(2) *Written Waiver.* If the patient or a person authorized to act on the patient's behalf waives the privilege in writing.

(3) *Action to Collect.* In an action to collect a claim for mental or emotional health services rendered to the patient.

(4) *Communication Made in Court–Ordered Examination.* To a communication the patient made to a professional during a court-ordered examination relating to the patient's mental or emotional condition or disorder if:

(A) the patient made the communication after being informed that it would not be privileged;

(B) the communication is offered to prove an issue involving the patient's mental or emotional health; and

(C) the court imposes appropriate safeguards against unauthorized disclosure.

(5) *Party Relies on Patient's Condition.* If any party relies on the patient's physical, mental, or emotional condition as a part of the party's claim or defense and the communication or record is relevant to that condition.

(6) *Abuse or Neglect of "Institution" Resident.* In a proceeding regarding the abuse or neglect, or the cause of any abuse or neglect, of a resident of an "institution" as defined in Tex. Health & Safety Code § 242.002.

Eff. March 1, 1998. Amended by orders of Supreme Court March 10, 2015 and Court of Criminal Appeals March 12, 2015, eff. April 1, 2015. Amended by Supreme Court order of June 14, 2016, eff. June 14, 2016.

Notes and Comments

Comment to 1998 change: This comment is intended to inform the construction and application of this rule. This rule governs disclosures of patient-professional communications only in judicial or administrative proceedings. Whether a professional may or must disclose such communications in other circumstances is governed by TEX.HEALTH & SAFETY CODE §§ 611.001-611.008. Former subparagraph (d)(6) of the Civil Evidence Rules, regarding disclosures in a suit affecting the parent-child relationship, is omitted, not because there should be no exception to the privilege in suits affecting the parent-child relationship, but because the exception in such suits is properly considered under subparagraph (d)(5), as construed in *R.K. v. Ramirez*, 887 S.W.2d 836 (Tex. 1994). In determining the proper application of an exception in such suits, the trial court must ensure that the precise need for the information is not outweighed by legitimate privacy interests protected by the privilege. Subparagraph (d) does not except from the privilege information relating to a nonparty patient who is or may be a consulting or testifying expert in the suit.

Rule 511.   Waiver by Voluntary Disclosure

(a) General Rule.

A person upon whom these rules confer a privilege against disclosure waives the privilege if:

(1) the person or a predecessor of the person while holder of the privilege voluntarily discloses or consents to disclosure of any significant part of the privileged matter unless such disclosure itself is privileged; or

(2) the person or a representative of the person calls a person to whom privileged communications have been made to testify as to the person's character or character trait insofar as such communications are relevant to such character or character trait.

(b) Lawyer–Client Privilege and Work Product; Limitations on Waiver.

Notwithstanding paragraph (a), the following provisions apply, in the circumstances set out, to disclosure of a communication or information covered by the lawyer-client privilege or work-product protection.

(1) *Disclosure Made in a Federal or State Proceeding or to a Federal or State Office or Agency; Scope of a Waiver.* When the disclosure is made in a federal proceeding or state proceeding of any state or to a federal office or agency or state office or agency of any state and waives the lawyer-client privilege or work-product protection, the waiver extends to an undisclosed communication or information only if:

(A) the waiver is intentional;

(B) the disclosed and undisclosed communications or information concern the same subject matter; and

(C) they ought in fairness to be considered together.

(2) *Inadvertent Disclosure in State Civil Proceedings.* When made in a Texas state proceeding, an inadvertent disclosure does not operate as a waiver if the holder followed the procedures of Rule of Civil Procedure 193.3(d).

(3) *Controlling Effect of a Court Order.* A disclosure made in litigation pending before a federal court or a state court of any state that has entered an order that the privilege or protection is not waived by disclosure connected with the litigation pending before that court is also not a waiver in a Texas state proceeding.

(4) *Controlling Effect of a Party Agreement.* An agreement on the effect of disclosure in a state proceeding of any state is binding only on the parties to the agreement, unless it is incorporated into a court order.

Eff. March 1, 1998. Amended by orders of Supreme Court March 10, 2015 and Court of Criminal Appeals March 12, 2015, eff. April 1, 2015.

Rule 512. Privileged Matter Disclosed Under Compulsion or Without Opportunity to Claim Privilege

A privilege claim is not defeated by a disclosure that was:

(a) compelled erroneously; or

(b) made without opportunity to claim the privilege.

Eff. March 1, 1998. Amended by orders of Supreme Court March 10, 2015 and Court of Criminal Appeals March 12, 2015, eff. April 1, 2015.

Rule 513. Comment On or Inference From a Privilege Claim; Instruction

(a) Comment or Inference Not Permitted. Except as permitted in Rule 504(b)(2), neither the court nor counsel may comment on a privilege claim—whether made in the present proceeding or previously—and the factfinder may not draw an inference from the claim.

(b) Claiming Privilege Without the Jury's Knowledge. To the extent practicable, the court must conduct a jury trial so that the making of a privilege claim is not suggested to the jury by any means.

(c) Claim of Privilege Against Self–Incrimination in a Civil Case. Subdivisions (a) and (b) do not apply to a party's claim, in the present civil case, of the privilege against self-incrimination.

(d) Jury Instruction. When this rule forbids a jury from drawing an inference from a privilege claim, the court must, on request of a party against whom the jury might draw the inference, instruct the jury accordingly.

Eff. March 1, 1998. Amended by orders of Supreme Court March 10, 2015 and Court of Criminal Appeals March 12, 2015, eff. April 1, 2015.

Notes and Comments

Comment to 1998 change. Subdivision (d) regarding a party's entitlement to a jury instruction about a claim of privilege is made applicable to civil cases.

ARTICLE VI. WITNESSES

Rule 601. Competency to Testify in General; "Dead Man's Rule"

(a) In General. Every person is competent to be a witness unless these rules provide otherwise. The following witnesses are incompetent:

(1) *Insane Persons.* A person who is now insane or was insane at the time of the events about which the person is called to testify.

(2) *Persons Lacking Sufficient Intellect.* A child—or any other person—whom the court examines and finds lacks sufficient intellect to testify concerning the matters in issue.

(b) The "Dead Man's Rule."

(1) *Applicability.* The "Dead Man's Rule" applies only in a civil case:

(A) by or against a party in the party's capacity as an executor, administrator, or guardian; or

(B) by or against a decedent's heirs or legal representatives and based in whole or in part on the decedent's oral statement.

(2) *General Rule.* In cases described in subparagraph (b)(1)(A), a party may not testify against another party about an oral statement by the testator, intestate, or ward. In cases described in subparagraph (b)(1)(B), a party may not testify against another party about an oral statement by the decedent.

(3) *Exceptions.* A party may testify against another party about an oral statement by the testator, intestate, ward, or decedent if:

(A) the party's testimony about the statement is corroborated; or

(B) the opposing party calls the party to testify at the trial about the statement.

(4) *Instructions.* If a court excludes evidence under paragraph (b)(2), the court must instruct the jury that the law prohibits a party from testifying about an oral statement by the testator, intestate, ward, or decedent unless the oral statement is corroborated or the opposing party calls the party to testify at the trial about the statement.

Eff. March 1, 1998. Amended by orders of Supreme Court March 10, 2015 and Court of Criminal Appeals March 12, 2015, eff. April 1, 2015.

Rule 602. Need for Personal Knowledge

A witness may testify to a matter only if evidence is introduced sufficient to support a finding that the witness has personal knowledge of the matter. Evidence to prove personal knowledge may consist of the witness's own testimony. This rule does not apply to a witness's expert testimony under Rule 703.

Eff. March 1, 1998. Amended by orders of Supreme Court March 10, 2015 and Court of Criminal Appeals March 12, 2015, eff. April 1, 2015.

Rule 603. Oath or Affirmation to Testify Truthfully

Before testifying, a witness must give an oath or affirmation to testify truthfully. It must be in a form designed to impress that duty on the witness's conscience.

Eff. March 1, 1998. Amended by orders of Supreme Court March 10, 2015 and Court of Criminal Appeals March 12, 2015, eff. April 1, 2015.

Rule 604. Interpreter

An interpreter must be qualified and must give an oath or affirmation to make a true translation.

Eff. March 1, 1998. Amended by orders of Supreme Court March 10, 2015 and Court of Criminal Appeals March 12, 2015, eff. April 1, 2015.

Rule 605. Judge's Competency as a Witness

The presiding judge may not testify as a witness at the trial. A party need not object to preserve the issue.

Eff. March 1, 1998. Amended by orders of Supreme Court March 10, 2015 and Court of Criminal Appeals March 12, 2015, eff. April 1, 2015.

Rule 606. Juror's Competency as a Witness

(a) At the Trial. A juror may not testify as a witness before the other jurors at the trial. If a juror is called to testify, the court must give a party an opportunity to object outside the jury's presence.

(b) During an Inquiry into the Validity of a Verdict or Indictment.

(1) *Prohibited Testimony or Other Evidence.* During an inquiry into the validity of a verdict or indictment, a juror may not testify about any statement made or incident that occurred during the jury's deliberations; the effect of anything on that juror's or another juror's vote; or any juror's mental processes concerning the verdict or indictment. The court may not receive a juror's affidavit or evidence of a juror's statement on these matters.

(2) *Exceptions.* A juror may testify:

(A) about whether an outside influence was improperly brought to bear on any juror; or

(B) to rebut a claim that the juror was not qualified to serve.

Eff. March 1, 1998. Amended by orders of Supreme Court March 10, 2015 and Court of Criminal Appeals March 12, 2015, eff. April 1, 2015.

Rule 607. Who May Impeach a Witness

Any party, including the party that called the witness, may attack the witness's credibility.

Eff. March 1, 1998. Amended by orders of Supreme Court March 10, 2015 and Court of Criminal Appeals March 12, 2015, eff. April 1, 2015.

Rule 608. A Witness's Character for Truthfulness or Untruthfulness

(a) Reputation or Opinion Evidence. A witness's credibility may be attacked or supported by testimony about the witness's reputation for having a character for truthfulness or untruthfulness, or by testimony in the form of an opinion about that character. But evidence of truthful character is admissible only after the witness's character for truthfulness has been attacked.

(b) Specific Instances of Conduct. Except for a criminal conviction under Rule 609, a party may not inquire into or offer extrinsic evidence to prove specific instances of the witness's conduct in order to attack or support the witness's character for truthfulness.

Eff. March 1, 1998. Amended by orders of Supreme Court March 10, 2015 and Court of Criminal Appeals March 12, 2015, eff. April 1, 2015.

Rule 609. Impeachment by Evidence of a Criminal Conviction

(a) In General. Evidence of a criminal conviction offered to attack a witness's character for truthfulness must be admitted if:

(1) the crime was a felony or involved moral turpitude, regardless of punishment;

(2) the probative value of the evidence outweighs its prejudicial effect to a party; and

(3) it is elicited from the witness or established by public record.

(b) Limit on Using the Evidence After 10 Years. This subdivision (b) applies if more than 10 years have passed since the witness's conviction or release from confinement for it, whichever is later. Evidence of the conviction is admissible only if its probative value, supported by specific facts and circumstances, substantially outweighs its prejudicial effect.

(c) Effect of a Pardon, Annulment, or Certificate of Rehabilitation. Evidence of a conviction is not admissible if:

(1) the conviction has been the subject of a pardon, annulment, certificate of rehabilitation, or other equivalent procedure based on a finding that the person has been rehabilitated, and the person has not been convicted of a later crime that was classified as a felony or involved moral turpitude, regardless of punishment;

(2) probation has been satisfactorily completed for the conviction, and the person has not been convicted of a later crime that was classified as a felony or involved moral turpitude, regardless of punishment; or

(3) the conviction has been the subject of a pardon, annulment, or other equivalent procedure based on a finding of innocence.

(d) Juvenile Adjudications. Evidence of a juvenile adjudication is admissible under this rule only if:

(1) the witness is a party in a proceeding conducted under title 3 of the Texas Family Code; or

(2) the United States or Texas Constitution requires that it be admitted.

(e) Pendency of an Appeal. A conviction for which an appeal is pending is not admissible under this rule.

(f) Notice. Evidence of a witness's conviction is not admissible under this rule if, after receiving from the adverse party a timely written request specifying the witness, the proponent of the conviction fails to provide sufficient written notice of intent to use the conviction. Notice is sufficient if it provides a fair opportunity to contest the use of such evidence.

Eff. March 1, 1998. Amended by orders of Supreme Court March 10, 2015 and Court of Criminal Appeals March 12, 2015, eff. April 1, 2015.

Rule 610. Religious Beliefs or Opinions

Evidence of a witness's religious beliefs or opinions is not admissible to attack or support the witness's credibility.

Eff. March 1, 1998. Amended by orders of Supreme Court March 10, 2015 and Court of Criminal Appeals March 12, 2015, eff. April 1, 2015.

Notes and Comments

Comment to 1998 change: This is prior Rule of Criminal Evidence 615.

Rule 611. Mode and Order of Examining Witnesses and Presenting Evidence

(a) Control by the Court; Purposes. The court should exercise reasonable control over the mode and order of examining witnesses and presenting evidence so as to:

(1) make those procedures effective for determining the truth;

(2) avoid wasting time; and

(3) protect witnesses from harassment or undue embarrassment.

(b) Scope of Cross–Examination. A witness may be cross-examined on any relevant matter, including credibility.

(c) Leading Questions. Leading questions should not be used on direct examination except as necessary to develop the witness's testimony. Ordinarily, the court should allow leading questions:

(1) on cross-examination; and

(2) when a party calls a hostile witness, an adverse party, or a witness identified with an adverse party.

Eff. March 1, 1998. Amended by orders of Supreme Court March 10, 2015 and Court of Criminal Appeals March 12, 2015, eff. April 1, 2015.

Rule 612. Writing Used to Refresh a Witness's Memory

(a) Scope. This rule gives an adverse party certain options when a witness uses a writing to refresh memory:

(1) while testifying;

(2) before testifying, in civil cases, if the court decides that justice requires the party to have those options; or

(3) before testifying, in criminal cases.

(b) Adverse Party's Options; Deleting Unrelated Matter. An adverse party is entitled to have the writing produced at the hearing, to inspect it, to cross-examine the witness about it, and to introduce in evidence any portion that relates to the witness's testimony. If the producing party claims that the writing includes unrelated matter, the court must examine the writing in camera, delete any unrelated portion, and order that the rest be delivered to the adverse party. Any portion deleted over objection must be preserved for the record.

(c) Failure to Produce or Deliver the Writing. If a writing is not produced or is not delivered as ordered, the court may issue any appropriate order. But if the prosecution does not comply in a criminal case, the court must strike the witness's testimony or—if justice so requires—declare a mistrial.

Eff. March 1, 1998. Amended by orders of Supreme Court March 10, 2015 and Court of Criminal Appeals March 12, 2015, eff. April 1, 2015.

Rule 613. Witness's Prior Statement and Bias or Interest

(a) Witness's Prior Inconsistent Statement.

(1) *Foundation Requirement.* When examining a witness about the witness's prior inconsistent statement—whether oral or written—a party must first tell the witness:

(A) the contents of the statement;

(B) the time and place of the statement; and

(C) the person to whom the witness made the statement.

(2) *Need Not Show Written Statement.* If the witness's prior inconsistent statement is written, a party need not show it to the witness before inquiring about it, but must, upon request, show it to opposing counsel.

(3) *Opportunity to Explain or Deny.* A witness must be given the opportunity to explain or deny the prior inconsistent statement.

(4) *Extrinsic Evidence.* Extrinsic evidence of a witness's prior inconsistent statement is not admissible unless the witness is first examined about the statement and fails to unequivocally admit making the statement.

(5) *Opposing Party's Statement.* This subdivision (a) does not apply to an opposing party's statement under Rule 801(e)(2).

(b) Witness's Bias or Interest.

(1) *Foundation Requirement.* When examining a witness about the witness's bias or interest, a party must first tell the witness the circumstances or statements that tend to show the witness's bias or interest. If examining a witness about a statement—whether oral or written—to prove the witness's bias or interest, a party must tell the witness:

(A) the contents of the statement;

(B) the time and place of the statement; and

(C) the person to whom the statement was made.

(2) *Need Not Show Written Statement.* If a party uses a written statement to prove the witness's bias or interest, a party need not show the

statement to the witness before inquiring about it, but must, upon request, show it to opposing counsel.

(3) *Opportunity to Explain or Deny.* A witness must be given the opportunity to explain or deny the circumstances or statements that tend to show the witness's bias or interest. And the witness's proponent may present evidence to rebut the charge of bias or interest.

(4) *Extrinsic Evidence.* Extrinsic evidence of a witness's bias or interest is not admissible unless the witness is first examined about the bias or interest and fails to unequivocally admit it.

(c) Witness's Prior Consistent Statement. Unless Rule 801(e)(1)(B) provides otherwise, a witness's prior consistent statement is not admissible if offered solely to enhance the witness's credibility.

Eff. March 1, 1998. Amended by orders of Supreme Court March 10, 2015 and Court of Criminal Appeals March 12, 2015, eff. April 1, 2015.

Rule 614. Excluding Witnesses

At a party's request, the court must order witnesses excluded so that they cannot hear other witnesses' testimony. Or the court may do so on its own. But this rule does not authorize excluding:

(a) a party who is a natural person and, in civil cases, that person's spouse;

(b) after being designated as the party's representative by its attorney:

(1) in a civil case, an officer or employee of a party that is not a natural person; or

(2) in a criminal case, a defendant that is not a natural person;

(c) a person whose presence a party shows to be essential to presenting the party's claim or defense; or

(d) the victim in a criminal case, unless the court determines that the victim's testimony would be materially affected by hearing other testimony at the trial.

Eff. March 1, 1998. Amended by orders of Supreme Court March 10, 2015 and Court of Criminal Appeals March 12, 2015, eff. April 1, 2015.

Rule 615. Producing a Witness's Statement in Criminal Cases

(a) Motion to Produce. After a witness other than the defendant testifies on direct examination, the court, on motion of a party who did not call the witness, must order an attorney for the state or the defendant and the defendant's attorney to produce, for the examination and use of the moving party, any statement of the witness that:

(1) is in their possession;

(2) relates to the subject matter of the witness's testimony; and

(3) has not previously been produced.

(b) Producing the Entire Statement. If the entire statement relates to the subject matter of the witness's testimony, the court must order that the statement be delivered to the moving party.

(c) Producing a Redacted Statement. If the party who called the witness claims that the statement contains information that does not relate to the subject matter of the witness's testimony, the court must inspect the statement in camera. After excising any unrelated portions, the court must order delivery of the redacted statement to the moving party. If a party objects to an excision, the court must preserve the entire statement with the excised portion indicated, under seal, as part of the record.

(d) Recess to Examine a Statement. If the court orders production of a witness's statement, the court, on request, must recess the proceedings to allow the moving party time to examine the statement and prepare for its use.

(e) Sanction for Failure to Produce or Deliver a Statement. If the party who called the witness disobeys an order to produce or deliver a statement, the court must strike the witness's testimony from the record. If an attorney for the state disobeys the order, the court must declare a mistrial if justice so requires.

(f) "Statement" Defined. As used in this rule, a witness's "statement" means:

(1) a written statement that the witness makes and signs, or otherwise adopts or approves;

(2) a substantially verbatim, contemporaneously recorded recital of the witness's oral statement that is contained in any recording or any transcription of a recording; or

(3) the witness's statement to a grand jury, however taken or recorded, or a transcription of such a statement.

Eff. March 1, 1998. Amended by orders of Supreme Court March 10, 2015, and Court of Criminal Appeals March 12, 2015, eff. April 1, 2015. Amended by orders of Supreme Court February 16, 2016, and Court of Criminal Appeals Dec. 7, 2015, and February 29, 2016, eff. Jan. 1, 2016.

Notes and Comments

Comment to 1998 change: This is prior Rule of Criminal Evidence 614.

ARTICLE VII. OPINIONS AND EXPERT TESTIMONY

Rule 701. Opinion Testimony by Lay Witnesses

If a witness is not testifying as an expert, testimony in the form of an opinion is limited to one that is:

(a) rationally based on the witness's perception; and

(b) helpful to clearly understanding the witness's testimony or to determining a fact in issue.

Eff. March 1, 1998. Amended by orders of Supreme Court March 10, 2015 and Court of Criminal Appeals March 12, 2015, eff. April 1, 2015.

Rule 702. Testimony by Expert Witnesses

A witness who is qualified as an expert by knowledge, skill, experience, training, or education may testify in the form of an opinion or otherwise if the expert's scientific, technical, or other specialized knowledge will help the trier of fact to understand the evidence or to determine a fact in issue.

Eff. March 1, 1998. Amended by orders of Supreme Court March 10, 2015 and Court of Criminal Appeals March 12, 2015, eff. April 1, 2015.

Rule 703. Bases of an Expert's Opinion Testimony

An expert may base an opinion on facts or data in the case that the expert has been made aware of, reviewed, or personally observed. If experts in the particular field would reasonably rely on those kinds of facts or data in forming an opinion on the subject, they need not be admissible for the opinion to be admitted.

Eff. March 1, 1998. Amended by orders of Supreme Court March 10, 2015 and Court of Criminal Appeals March 12, 2015, eff. April 1, 2015.

Notes and Comments

Comment to 1998 change: The former Civil Rule referred to facts or data "perceived by or reviewed by" the expert. The former Criminal Rule referred to facts or data "perceived by or made known to" the expert. The terminology is now conformed, but no change in meaning is intended.

Rule 704. Opinion on an Ultimate Issue

An opinion is not objectionable just because it embraces an ultimate issue.

Eff. March 1, 1998. Amended by orders of Supreme Court March 10, 2015 and Court of Criminal Appeals March 12, 2015, eff. April 1, 2015.

Rule 705. Disclosing the Underlying Facts or Data and Examining an Expert About Them

(a) Stating an Opinion Without Disclosing the Underlying Facts or Data. Unless the court orders otherwise, an expert may state an opinion—and give the reasons for it—without first testifying to the underlying facts or data. But the expert may be required to disclose those facts or data on cross-examination.

(b) Voir Dire Examination of an Expert About the Underlying Facts or Data. Before an expert states an opinion or discloses the underlying facts or data, an adverse party in a civil case may—or in a criminal case must—be permitted to examine the expert about the underlying facts or data. This examination must take place outside the jury's hearing.

(c) Admissibility of Opinion. An expert's opinion is inadmissible if the underlying facts or data do not provide a sufficient basis for the opinion.

(d) When Otherwise Inadmissible Underlying Facts or Data May Be Disclosed; Instructing the Jury. If the underlying facts or data would otherwise be inadmissible, the proponent of the opinion may not disclose them to the jury if their probative value in helping the jury evaluate the opinion is outweighed by their prejudicial effect. If the court allows the proponent to disclose those facts or data the court must, upon timely request, restrict the evidence to its proper scope and instruct the jury accordingly.

Eff. March 1, 1998. Amended by orders of Supreme Court March 10, 2015 and Court of Criminal Appeals March 12, 2015, eff. April 1, 2015.

Notes and Comments

Comment to 1998 change: Paragraphs (b), (c), and (d) are based on the former Criminal Rule and are made applicable to civil cases. This rule does not preclude a party in any case from conducting a *voir dire* examination into the qualifications of an expert.

Rule 706. Audit in Civil Cases

Notwithstanding any other evidence rule, the court must admit an auditor's verified report prepared under Rule of Civil Procedure 172 and offered by a party. If a party files exceptions to the report, a party may offer evidence supporting the exceptions to contradict the report.

Eff. March 1, 1998. Amended by orders of Supreme Court March 10, 2015 and Court of Criminal Appeals March 12, 2015, eff. April 1, 2015.

ARTICLE VIII. HEARSAY

Rule 801. Definitions That Apply to This Article; Exclusions from Hearsay

(a) Statement. "Statement" means a person's oral or written verbal expression, or nonverbal conduct that a person intended as a substitute for verbal expression.

(b) Declarant. "Declarant" means the person who made the statement.

(c) Matter Asserted. "Matter asserted" means:

(1) any matter a declarant explicitly asserts; and

(2) any matter implied by a statement, if the probative value of the statement as offered flows from the declarant's belief about the matter.

(d) Hearsay. "Hearsay" means a statement that:

(1) the declarant does not make while testifying at the current trial or hearing; and

(2) a party offers in evidence to prove the truth of the matter asserted in the statement.

(e) Statements That Are Not Hearsay. A statement that meets the following conditions is not hearsay:

(1) *A Declarant–Witness's Prior Statement.* The declarant testifies and is subject to cross-examination about a prior statement, and the statement:

(A) is inconsistent with the declarant's testimony and:

(i) when offered in a civil case, was given under penalty of perjury at a trial, hearing, or other proceeding or in a deposition; or

(ii) when offered in a criminal case, was given under penalty of perjury at a trial, hearing, or other proceeding—except a grand jury proceeding—or in a deposition;

(B) is consistent with the declarant's testimony and is offered to rebut an express or implied charge that the declarant recently fabricated it or acted from a recent improper influence or motive in so testifying; or

(C) identifies a person as someone the declarant perceived earlier.

(2) *An Opposing Party's Statement.* The statement is offered against an opposing party and:

(A) was made by the party in an individual or representative capacity;

(B) is one the party manifested that it adopted or believed to be true;

(C) was made by a person whom the party authorized to make a statement on the subject;

(D) was made by the party's agent or employee on a matter within the scope of that relationship and while it existed; or

(E) was made by the party's coconspirator during and in furtherance of the conspiracy.

(3) *A Deponent's Statement.* In a civil case, the statement was made in a deposition taken in the same proceeding. "Same proceeding" is defined in Rule of Civil Procedure 203.6(b). The deponent's unavailability as a witness is not a requirement for admissibility.

Adopted eff. March 1, 1998. Amended eff. Jan. 1, 1999. Amended by orders of Supreme Court March 10, 2015 and Court of Criminal Appeals March 12, 2015, eff. April 1, 2015.

Rule 802. The Rule Against Hearsay

Hearsay is not admissible unless any of the following provides otherwise:

- a statute;
- these rules; or
- other rules prescribed under statutory authority.

Inadmissible hearsay admitted without objection may not be denied probative value merely because it is hearsay.

Eff. March 1, 1998. Amended by orders of Supreme Court March 10, 2015 and Court of Criminal Appeals March 12, 2015, eff. April 1, 2015.

Rule 803. Exceptions to the Rule Against Hearsay—Regardless of Whether the Declarant Is Available as a Witness

The following are not excluded by the rule against hearsay, regardless of whether the declarant is available as a witness:

(1) *Present Sense Impression.* A statement describing or explaining an event or condition, made while or immediately after the declarant perceived it.

(2) *Excited Utterance.* A statement relating to a startling event or condition, made while the declarant was under the stress of excitement that it caused.

(3) *Then–Existing Mental, Emotional, or Physical Condition.* A statement of the declarant's then-existing state of mind (such as motive, intent, or plan) or emotional, sensory, or physical condition (such as mental feeling, pain, or bodily health), but not including a statement of memory or belief to prove the fact remembered or believed unless it relates to the validity or terms of the declarant's will.

(4) *Statement Made for Medical Diagnosis or Treatment.* A statement that:

(A) is made for—and is reasonably pertinent to—medical diagnosis or treatment; and

(B) describes medical history; past or present symptoms or sensations; their inception; or their general cause.

(5) *Recorded Recollection.* A record that:

(A) is on a matter the witness once knew about but now cannot recall well enough to testify fully and accurately;

(B) was made or adopted by the witness when the matter was fresh in the witness's memory; and

(C) accurately reflects the witness's knowledge, unless the circumstances of the record's preparation cast doubt on its trustworthiness.

If admitted, the record may be read into evidence but may be received as an exhibit only if offered by an adverse party.

(6) *Records of a Regularly Conducted Activity.* A record of an act, event, condition, opinion, or diagnosis if:

(A) the record was made at or near the time by—or from information transmitted by—someone with knowledge;

(B) the record was kept in the course of a regularly conducted business activity;

(C) making the record was a regular practice of that activity;

(D) all these conditions are shown by the testimony of the custodian or another qualified witness, or by an affidavit or unsworn declaration that complies with Rule 902(10); and

(E) the opponent fails to demonstrate that the source of information or the method or circumstances of preparation indicate a lack of trustworthiness. "Business" as used in this paragraph includes every kind of regular organized activity whether conducted for profit or not.

(7) *Absence of a Record of a Regularly Conducted Activity.* Evidence that a matter is not included in a record described in paragraph (6) if:

(A) the evidence is admitted to prove that the matter did not occur or exist;

(B) a record was regularly kept for a matter of that kind; and

(C) the opponent fails to show that the possible source of the information or other circumstances indicate a lack of trustworthiness.

(8) *Public Records.* A record or statement of a public office if:

(A) it sets out:

(i) the office's activities;

(ii) a matter observed while under a legal duty to report, but not including, in a criminal case, a matter observed by law-enforcement personnel; or

(iii) in a civil case or against the government in a criminal case, factual findings from a legally authorized investigation; and

(B) the opponent fails to demonstrate that the source of information or other circumstances indicate a lack of trustworthiness.

(9) *Public Records of Vital Statistics.* A record of a birth, death, or marriage, if reported to a public office in accordance with a legal duty.

(10) *Absence of a Public Record.* Testimony—or a certification under Rule 902—that a diligent search failed to disclose a public record or statement if the testimony or certification is admitted to prove that:

(A) the record or statement does not exist; or

(B) a matter did not occur or exist, if a public office regularly kept a record or statement for a matter of that kind.

(11) *Records of Religious Organizations Concerning Personal or Family History.* A statement of birth, legitimacy, ancestry, marriage, divorce, death, relationship by blood or marriage, or similar facts of personal or family history, contained in a regularly kept record of a religious organization.

(12) *Certificates of Marriage, Baptism, and Similar Ceremonies.* A statement of fact contained in a certificate:

(A) made by a person who is authorized by a religious organization or by law to perform the act certified;

(B) attesting that the person performed a marriage or similar ceremony or administered a sacrament; and

(C) purporting to have been issued at the time of the act or within a reasonable time after it.

(13) *Family Records.* A statement of fact about personal or family history contained in a family record, such as a Bible, genealogy, chart, engraving on a ring, inscription on a portrait, or engraving on an urn or burial marker.

(14) *Records of Documents That Affect an Interest in Property.* The record of a document that purports to establish or affect an interest in property if:

(A) the record is admitted to prove the content of the original recorded document, along with its signing and its delivery by each person who purports to have signed it;

(B) the record is kept in a public office; and

(C) a statute authorizes recording documents of that kind in that office.

(15) *Statements in Documents That Affect an Interest in Property.* A statement contained in a document that purports to establish or affect an interest in property if the matter stated was relevant to the document's purpose—unless later dealings with the property are inconsistent with the truth of the statement or the purport of the document.

(16) *Statements in Ancient Documents.* A statement in a document that is at least 20 years old and whose authenticity is established.

(17) *Market Reports and Similar Commercial Publications.* Market quotations, lists, directories, or other compilations that are generally relied on by the public or by persons in particular occupations.

(18) *Statements in Learned Treatises, Periodicals, or Pamphlets.* A statement contained in a treatise, periodical, or pamphlet if:

(A) the statement is called to the attention of an expert witness on cross-examination or relied on by the expert on direct examination; and

(B) the publication is established as a reliable authority by the expert's admission or testimony, by another expert's testimony, or by judicial notice.

If admitted, the statement may be read into evidence but not received as an exhibit.

(19) *Reputation Concerning Personal or Family History.* A reputation among a person's family by blood, adoption, or marriage—or among a person's associates or in the community—concerning the person's birth, adoption, legitimacy, ancestry, marriage, divorce, death, relationship by blood, adoption, or marriage, or similar facts of personal or family history.

(20) *Reputation Concerning Boundaries or General History.* A reputation in a community—arising before the controversy—concerning boundaries of land in the community or customs that affect the land, or concerning general historical events important to that community, state, or nation.

(21) *Reputation Concerning Character.* A reputation among a person's associates or in the community concerning the person's character.

(22) *Judgment of a Previous Conviction.* Evidence of a final judgment of conviction if:

(A) it is offered in a civil case and:

(i) the judgment was entered after a trial or guilty plea, but not a nolo contendere plea;

(ii) the conviction was for a felony;

(iii) the evidence is admitted to prove any fact essential to the judgment; and

(iv) an appeal of the conviction is not pending; or

(B) it is offered in a criminal case and:

(i) the judgment was entered after a trial or a guilty or nolo contendere plea;

(ii) the conviction was for a criminal offense;

(iii) the evidence is admitted to prove any fact essential to the judgment;

(iv) when offered by the prosecutor for a purpose other than impeachment, the judgment was against the defendant; and

(v) an appeal of the conviction is not pending.

(23) *Judgments Involving Personal, Family, or General History or a Boundary.* A judgment that is admitted to prove a matter of personal, family, or general history, or boundaries, if the matter:

(A) was essential to the judgment; and

(B) could be proved by evidence of reputation.

(24) *Statement Against Interest.* A statement that:

(A) a reasonable person in the declarant's position would have made only if the person believed it to be true because, when made, it was so contrary to the declarant's proprietary or pecuniary interest or had so great a tendency to invalidate the declarant's claim against someone else or to expose the declarant to civil or criminal liability or to make the

declarant an object of hatred, ridicule, or disgrace; and

(B) is supported by corroborating circumstances that clearly indicate its trustworthiness, if it is offered in a criminal case as one that tends to expose the declarant to criminal liability.

Eff. March 1, 1998. Amended by orders of Supreme Court March 10, 2015 and Court of Criminal Appeals March 12, 2015, eff. April 1, 2015.

Rule 804. Exceptions to the Rule Against Hearsay—When the Declarant Is Unavailable as a Witness

(a) Criteria for Being Unavailable. A declarant is considered to be unavailable as a witness if the declarant:

(1) is exempted from testifying about the subject matter of the declarant's statement because the court rules that a privilege applies;

(2) refuses to testify about the subject matter despite a court order to do so;

(3) testifies to not remembering the subject matter;

(4) cannot be present or testify at the trial or hearing because of death or a then-existing infirmity, physical illness, or mental illness; or

(5) is absent from the trial or hearing and the statement's proponent has not been able, by process or other reasonable means, to procure the declarant's attendance or testimony.

But this subdivision (a) does not apply if the statement's proponent procured or wrongfully caused the declarant's unavailability as a witness in order to prevent the declarant from attending or testifying.

(b) The Exceptions. The following are not excluded by the rule against hearsay if the declarant is unavailable as a witness:

(1) *Former Testimony.* Testimony that:

(A) when offered in a civil case:

(i) was given as a witness at a trial or hearing of the current or a different proceeding or in a deposition in a different proceeding; and

(ii) is now offered against a party and the party—or a person with similar interest—had an opportunity and similar motive to develop the testimony by direct, cross-, or redirect examination.

(B) when offered in a criminal case:

(i) was given as a witness at a trial or hearing of the current or a different proceeding; and

(ii) is now offered against a party who had an opportunity and similar motive to develop it by direct, cross-, or redirect examination; or

(iii) was taken in a deposition under—and is now offered in accordance with—chapter 39 of the Code of Criminal Procedure.

(2) *Statement Under the Belief of Imminent Death.* A statement that the declarant, while believing the declarant's death to be imminent, made about its cause or circumstances.

(3) *Statement of Personal or Family History.* A statement about:

(A) the declarant's own birth, adoption, legitimacy, ancestry, marriage, divorce, relationship by blood, adoption or marriage, or similar facts of personal or family history, even though the declarant had no way of acquiring personal knowledge about that fact; or

(B) another person concerning any of these facts, as well as death, if the declarant was related to the person by blood, adoption, or marriage or was so intimately associated with the person's family that the declarant's information is likely to be accurate.

Eff. March 1, 1998. Amended by orders of Supreme Court March 10, 2015 and Court of Criminal Appeals March 12, 2015, eff. April 1, 2015.

Rule 805. Hearsay Within Hearsay

Hearsay within hearsay is not excluded by the rule against hearsay if each part of the combined statements conforms with an exception to the rule.

Eff. March 1, 1998. Amended by orders of Supreme Court March 10, 2015 and Court of Criminal Appeals March 12, 2015, eff. April 1, 2015.

Rule 806. Attacking and Supporting the Declarant's Credibility

When a hearsay statement—or a statement described in Rule 801(e)(2)(C), (D), or (E), or, in a civil case, a statement described in Rule 801(e)(3)—has been admitted in evidence, the declarant's credibility may be attacked, and then supported, by any evidence that would be admissible for those purposes if the declarant had testified as a witness. The court may admit evidence of the declarant's statement or conduct, offered to impeach the declarant, regardless of when it occurred or whether the declarant had an opportunity to explain or deny it. If the party against whom the statement was admitted calls the declarant

as a witness, the party may examine the declarant on the statement as if on cross-examination.

Eff. March 1, 1998. Amended by orders of Supreme Court March 10, 2015 and Court of Criminal Appeals March 12, 2015, eff. April 1, 2015.

ARTICLE IX. AUTHENTICATION AND IDENTIFICATION

Rule 901. Authenticating or Identifying Evidence

(a) In General. To satisfy the requirement of authenticating or identifying an item of evidence, the proponent must produce evidence sufficient to support a finding that the item is what the proponent claims it is.

(b) Examples. The following are examples only— not a complete list—of evidence that satisfies the requirement:

(1) *Testimony of a Witness with Knowledge.* Testimony that an item is what it is claimed to be.

(2) *Nonexpert Opinion About Handwriting.* A nonexpert's opinion that handwriting is genuine, based on a familiarity with it that was not acquired for the current litigation.

(3) *Comparison by an Expert Witness or the Trier of Fact.* A comparison by an expert witness or the trier of fact with a specimen that the court has found is genuine.

(4) *Distinctive Characteristics and the Like.* The appearance, contents, substance, internal patterns, or other distinctive characteristics of the item, taken together with all the circumstances.

(5) *Opinion About a Voice.* An opinion identifying a person's voice—whether heard firsthand or through mechanical or electronic transmission or recording—based on hearing the voice at any time under circumstances that connect it with the alleged speaker.

(6) *Evidence About a Telephone Conversation.* For a telephone conversation, evidence that a call was made to the number assigned at the time to:

(A) a particular person, if circumstances, including self-identification, show that the person answering was the one called; or

(B) a particular business, if the call was made to a business and the call related to business reasonably transacted over the telephone.

(7) *Evidence About Public Records.* Evidence that:

(A) a document was recorded or filed in a public office as authorized by law; or

(B) a purported public record or statement is from the office where items of this kind are kept.

(8) *Evidence About Ancient Documents or Data Compilations.* For a document or data compilation, evidence that it:

(A) is in a condition that creates no suspicion about its authenticity;

(B) was in a place where, if authentic, it would likely be; and

(C) is at least 20 years old when offered.

(9) *Evidence About a Process or System.* Evidence describing a process or system and showing that it produces an accurate result.

(10) *Methods Provided by a Statute or Rule.* Any method of authentication or identification allowed by a statute or other rule prescribed under statutory authority.

Eff. March 1, 1998. Amended by orders of Supreme Court March 10, 2015 and Court of Criminal Appeals March 12, 2015, eff. April 1, 2015.

Rule 902.   Evidence That Is Self–Authenticating

The following items of evidence are self-authenticating; they require no extrinsic evidence of authenticity in order to be admitted:

(1) *Domestic Public Documents That Are Sealed and Signed.* A document that bears:

(A) a seal purporting to be that of the United States; any state, district, commonwealth, territory, or insular possession of the United States; the former Panama Canal Zone; the Trust Territory of the Pacific Islands; a political subdivision of any of these entities; or a department, agency, or officer of any entity named above; and

(B) a signature purporting to be an execution or attestation.

(2) *Domestic Public Documents That Are Not Sealed But Are Signed and Certified.* A document that bears no seal if:

(A) it bears the signature of an officer or employee of an entity named in Rule 902(1)(A); and

(B) another public officer who has a seal and official duties within that same entity certifies under seal—or its equivalent—that the signer has the official capacity and that the signature is genuine.

(3) *Foreign Public Documents.* A document that purports to be signed or attested by a person who is authorized by a foreign country's law to do so.

(A) *In General.* The document must be accompanied by a final certification that certifies the genuineness of the signature and official position of the signer or attester—or of any foreign official whose certificate of genuineness relates to the signature or attestation or is in a chain of certificates of genuineness relating to the signature or attestation. The certification may be made by a secretary of a United States embassy or legation; by a consul general, vice consul, or consular agent of the United States; or by a diplomatic or consular official of the foreign country assigned or accredited to the United States.

(B) *If Parties Have Reasonable Opportunity to Investigate.* If all parties have been given a reasonable opportunity to investigate the document's authenticity and accuracy, the court may, for good cause, either:

(i) order that it be treated as presumptively authentic without final certification; or

(ii) allow it to be evidenced by an attested summary with or without final certification.

(C) *If a Treaty Abolishes or Displaces the Final Certification Requirement.* If the United States and the foreign country in which the official record is located are parties to a treaty or convention that abolishes or displaces the final certification requirement, the record and attestation must be certified under the terms of the treaty or convention.

(4) *Certified Copies of Public Records.* A copy of an official record—or a copy of a document that was recorded or filed in a public office as authorized by law—if the copy is certified as correct by:

(A) the custodian or another person authorized to make the certification; or

(B) a certificate that complies with Rule 902(1), (2), or (3), a statute, or a rule prescribed under statutory authority.

(5) *Official Publications.* A book, pamphlet, or other publication purporting to be issued by a public authority.

(6) *Newspapers and Periodicals.* Printed material purporting to be a newspaper or periodical.

(7) *Trade Inscriptions and the Like.* An inscription, sign, tag, or label purporting to have been affixed in the course of business and indicating origin, ownership, or control.

(8) *Acknowledged Documents.* A document accompanied by a certificate of acknowledgment that is lawfully executed by a notary public or another officer who is authorized to take acknowledgments.

(9) Commercial Paper and Related Documents. Commercial paper, a signature on it, and related documents, to the extent allowed by general commercial law.

(10) Business Records Accompanied by Affidavit. The original or a copy of a record that meets the requirements of Rule 803(6) or (7), if the record is accompanied by an affidavit that complies with subparagraph (B) of this rule and any other requirements of law, and the record and affidavit are served in accordance with subparagraph (A). For good cause shown, the court may order that a business record be treated as presumptively authentic even if the proponent fails to comply with subparagraph (A).

(A) Service Requirement. The proponent of a record must serve the record and the accompanying affidavit on each other party to the case at least 14 days before trial. The record and affidavit may be served by any method permitted by Rule of Civil Procedure 21a.

(B) Form of Affidavit. An affidavit is sufficient if it includes the following language, but this form is not exclusive. The proponent may use an unsworn declaration made under penalty of perjury in place of an affidavit.

1. I am the custodian of records [*or* I am an employee or owner] of _____ and am familiar with the manner in which its records are created and maintained by virtue of my duties and responsibilities.

2. Attached are ___ pages of records. These are the original records or exact duplicates of the original records.

3. The records were made at or near the time of each act, event, condition, opinion, or diagnosis set forth. [*or* It is the regular practice of _____ to make this type of record at or near the time of each act, event, condition, opinion, or diagnosis set forth in the record.]

4. The records were made by, or from information transmitted by, persons with knowledge of the matters set forth. [*or* It is the regular practice of _____ for this type of record to be made by, or from information transmitted by, persons with knowledge of the matters set forth in them.]

5. The records were kept in the course of regularly conducted business activity. [*or* It is the regular practice of _____ to keep this type of

record in the course of regularly conducted business activity.]

6. It is the regular practice of the business activity to make the records.

(11) Presumptions Under a Statute or Rule. A signature, document, or anything else that a statute or rule prescribed under statutory authority declares to be presumptively or prima facie genuine or authentic.

Eff. March 1, 1998. Amended by orders of Feb. 12, 2013, and March 26, 2013, eff. March 1, 2013. Amended by orders of Supreme Court and Court of Criminal Appeals April 14, 2014, and August 19, 2014, eff. Sept. 1, 2014. Amended by order of orders of Supreme Court March 10, 2015 and Court of Criminal Appeals March 12, 2015, eff. April 1, 2015.

Rule 903. Subscribing Witness's Testimony

A subscribing witness's testimony is necessary to authenticate a writing only if required by the law of the jurisdiction that governs its validity.

Eff. March 1, 1998. Amended by orders of Supreme Court March 10, 2015 and Court of Criminal Appeals March 12, 2015, eff. April 1, 2015.

ARTICLE X. CONTENTS OF WRITINGS, RECORDINGS, AND PHOTOGRAPHS

Rule 1001. Definitions That Apply to This Article

In this article:

(a) A "writing" consists of letters, words, numbers, or their equivalent set down in any form.

(b) A "recording" consists of letters, words, numbers, or their equivalent recorded in any manner.

(c) A "photograph" means a photographic image or its equivalent stored in any form.

(d) An "original" of a writing or recording means the writing or recording itself or any counterpart intended to have the same effect by the person who executed or issued it. For electronically stored information, "original" means any printout—or other output readable by sight—if it accurately reflects the information. An "original" of a photograph includes the negative or a print from it.

(e) A "duplicate" means a counterpart produced by a mechanical, photographic, chemical, electronic, or other equivalent process or technique that accurately reproduces the original.

Eff. March 1, 1998. Amended by orders of Supreme Court March 10, 2015 and Court of Criminal Appeals March 12, 2015, eff. April 1, 2015.

Rule 1002. Requirement of the Original

An original writing, recording, or photograph is required in order to prove its content unless these rules or other law provides otherwise.

Eff. March 1, 1998. Amended by orders of Supreme Court March 10, 2015 and Court of Criminal Appeals March 12, 2015, eff. April 1, 2015.

Rule 1003. Admissibility of Duplicates

A duplicate is admissible to the same extent as the original unless a question is raised about the original's authenticity or the circumstances make it unfair to admit the duplicate.

Eff. March 1, 1998. Amended by orders of Supreme Court March 10, 2015 and Court of Criminal Appeals March 12, 2015, eff. April 1, 2015.

Rule 1004. Admissibility of Other Evidence of Content

An original is not required and other evidence of the content of a writing, recording, or photograph is admissible if:

(a) all the originals are lost or destroyed, unless the proponent lost or destroyed them in bad faith;

(b) an original cannot be obtained by any available judicial process;

(c) an original is not located in Texas;

(d) the party against whom the original would be offered had control of the original; was at that time put on notice, by pleadings or otherwise, that the original would be a subject of proof at the trial or hearing; and fails to produce it at the trial or hearing; or

(e) the writing, recording, or photograph is not closely related to a controlling issue.

Eff. March 1, 1998. Amended by orders of Supreme Court March 10, 2015 and Court of Criminal Appeals March 12, 2015, eff. April 1, 2015.

Rule 1005. Copies of Public Records to Prove Content

The proponent may use a copy to prove the content of an official record—or of a document that was recorded or filed in a public office as authorized by law—if these conditions are met: the record or document is otherwise admissible; and the copy is certified as correct in accordance with Rule 902(4) or is testified to be correct by a witness who has compared it with the original. If no such copy can be obtained by reasonable diligence, then the proponent may use other evidence to prove the content.

Eff. March 1, 1998. Amended by orders of Supreme Court March 10, 2015 and Court of Criminal Appeals March 12, 2015, eff. April 1, 2015.

Rule 1006. Summaries to Prove Content

The proponent may use a summary, chart, or calculation to prove the content of voluminous writings, recordings, or photographs that cannot be conveniently examined in court. The proponent must make the originals or duplicates available for examination or copying, or both, by other parties at a reasonable time and place. And the court may order the proponent to produce them in court.

Eff. March 1, 1998. Amended by orders of Supreme Court March 10, 2015 and Court of Criminal Appeals March 12, 2015, eff. April 1, 2015.

Rule 1007. Testimony or Statement of a Party to Prove Content

The proponent may prove the content of a writing, recording, or photograph by the testimony, deposition, or written statement of the party against whom the evidence is offered. The proponent need not account for the original.

Eff. March 1, 1998. Amended by orders of Supreme Court March 10, 2015 and Court of Criminal Appeals March 12, 2015, eff. April 1, 2015.

Rule 1008. Functions of the Court and Jury

Ordinarily, the court determines whether the proponent has fulfilled the factual conditions for admitting other evidence of the content of a writing, recording, or photograph under Rule 1004 or 1005. But in a jury trial, the jury determines—in accordance with Rule 104(b)—any issue about whether:

(a) an asserted writing, recording, or photograph ever existed;

(b) another one produced at the trial or hearing is the original; or

(c) other evidence of content accurately reflects the content.

Eff. March 1, 1998. Amended by orders of Supreme Court March 10, 2015 and Court of Criminal Appeals March 12, 2015, eff. April 1, 2015.

Rule 1009. Translating a Foreign Language Document

(a) **Submitting a Translation.** A translation of a foreign language document is admissible if, at least 45 days before trial, the proponent serves on all parties:

(1) the translation and the underlying foreign language document; and

(2) a qualified translator's affidavit or unsworn declaration that sets forth the translator's qualifications and certifies that the translation is accurate.

(b) Objection. When objecting to a translation's accuracy, a party should specifically indicate its inaccuracies and offer an accurate translation. A party must serve the objection on all parties at least 15 days before trial.

(c) Effect of Failing to Object or Submit a Conflicting Translation. If the underlying foreign language document is otherwise admissible, the court must admit—and may not allow a party to attack the accuracy of—a translation submitted under subdivision (a) unless the party has:

(1) submitted a conflicting translation under subdivision (a); or

(2) objected to the translation under subdivision (b).

(d) Effect of Objecting or Submitting a Conflicting Translation. If conflicting translations are submitted under subdivision (a) or an objection is made under subdivision (b), the court must determine whether there is a genuine issue about the accuracy of a material part of the translation. If so, the trier of fact must resolve the issue.

(e) Qualified Translator May Testify. Except for subdivision (c), this rule does not preclude a party from offering the testimony of a qualified translator to translate a foreign language document.

(f) Time Limits. On a party's motion and for good cause, the court may alter this rule's time limits.

(g) Court–Appointed Translator. If necessary, the court may appoint a qualified translator. The reasonable value of the translator's services must be taxed as court costs.

Eff. March 1, 1998. Amended by orders of Supreme Court March 10, 2015 and Court of Criminal Appeals March 12, 2015, eff. April 1, 2015.

Notes and Comments

Comment to 1998 change: This is a new rule.

TEXAS RULES OF APPELLATE PROCEDURE

As Amended by the Supreme Court and Court of Criminal Appeals of Texas

Effective September 1, 1997

Including Amendments Received Through September 1, 2017

746

APPENDIXES TO THE TEXAS RULES OF APPELLATE PROCEDURE

APPENDIX A.
APPENDIX B.
APPENDIX C.
APPENDIX D.
APPENDIX E.
APPENDIX F.
APPENDIX G [Renumbered as Appendix F by Order of Dec. 11, 2013, eff. Jan. 1, 2014]
APPENDIX H [Repealed by Order of Dec. 11, 2013, eff. Jan. 1, 2014]

SECTION ONE. GENERAL PROVISIONS

Rule 1. Scope of Rules; Local Rules of Courts of Appeals

Notes and Comments

Comment to 1997 change: Subdivision 1.1 is simplified without substantive change. Subdivision 1.2 is amended to make clear that any person is entitled to a copy of local rules. Paragraph 1.2(c), restricting dismissal of a case for noncompliance with a local rule, is added.

1.1. Scope

These rules govern procedure in appellate courts and before appellate judges and post-trial procedure in trial courts in criminal cases.

Eff. Sept. 1, 1997.

1.2. Local Rules

(a) *Promulgation.* A court of appeals may promulgate rules governing its practice that are not inconsistent with these rules. Local rules governing civil cases must first be approved by the Supreme Court. Local rules governing criminal cases must first be approved by the Court of Criminal Appeals.

(b) *Copies.* The clerk must provide a copy of the court's local rules to anyone who requests it.

(c) *Party's Noncompliance.* A court must not dismiss an appeal for noncompliance with a local rule without giving the noncomplying party notice and a reasonable opportunity to cure the noncompliance.

Eff. Sept. 1, 1997.

Rule 2. Suspension of Rules

On a party's motion or on its own initiative an appellate court may—to expedite a decision or for other good cause—suspend a rule's operation in a particular case and order a different procedure; but a court must not construe this rule to suspend any provision in the Code of Criminal Procedure or to alter the time for perfecting an appeal in a civil case.

Eff. Sept. 1, 1997.

Rule 3. Definitions; Uniform Terminology

Notes and Comments

Comment to 1997 change: The definition of *court below* and the reference to "suing out a writ of error to the court of appeals," are deleted as those terms are no longer used in these rules. Other changes are made.

3.1. Definitions

(a) *Appellant* means a party taking an appeal to an appellate court.

(b) *Appellate court* means the courts of appeals, the Court of Criminal Appeals, and the Supreme Court.

(c) *Appellee* means a party adverse to an appellant.

(d) *Applicant* means a person seeking relief by a habeas corpus in a criminal case.

(e) *Petitioner* means a party petitioning the Supreme Court or the Court of Criminal Appeals for review.

(f) *Relator* means a person seeking relief in an original proceeding in an appellate court other than by habeas corpus in a criminal case.

(g) *Reporter* or *court reporter* means the court reporter or court recorder.

(h) *Respondent* means:

(1) a party adverse to a petitioner in the Supreme Court or the Court of Criminal Appeals; or

(2) a party against whom relief is sought in an original proceeding in an appellate court.

Eff. Sept. 1, 1997.

3.2. Uniform Terminology in Criminal Cases

In documents filed in criminal appeals, the parties are the *State* and the *appellant.* But if the State has appealed under Article 44.01 of the Code of Criminal Procedure, the defendant is the *appellee.* Otherwise, papers should use real names for parties, and such labels as *appellee, petitioner, respondent,* and *movant* should be avoided unless necessary for clarity. In habeas corpus proceedings, the person for whose relief the writ is requested is the *applicant;* Code of Criminal Procedure article 11.13.

Eff. Sept. 1, 1997.

Rule 4. Time and Notice Provisions

Notes and Comments

Comment to 1997 change: This is former Rule 5. Paragraph 4.1(b) is added. Former paragraph (b)(1) is omitted because it is covered by other provisions of the rules. Former paragraphs (b)(2) and (b)(3) are omitted because they are duplicative of provisions in the Rules of Civil Procedure, which prescribes the applicable procedure. The phrase "modified, corrected or reformed in any respect" in paragraph 4.3(a) is changed to "modified in any respect," but no change in substance is intended. Former subdivision (e) regarding notice of judgment by the court of appeals is moved to Rule 12.6. Subdivision 4.5 is revised and now makes clear that the court must grant the motion for additional time if the court finds that the party did not receive the notice or acquire actual knowledge in time. Other changes are made throughout the rule.

4.1. Computing Time

(a) *In General.* The day of an act, event, or default after which a designated period begins to run is not included when computing a period prescribed or allowed by these rules, by court order, or by statute. The last day of the period is included, but if that day is a Saturday, Sunday, or legal holiday, the period extends to the end of the next day that is not a Saturday, Sunday, or legal holiday.

(b) *Clerk's Office Closed or Inaccessible.* If the act to be done is filing a document, and if the clerk's office where the document is to be filed is closed or inaccessible during regular hours on the last day for filing the document, the period for filing the document extends to the end of the next day when the clerk's office is open and accessible. The closing or inaccessibility of the clerk's office may be proved by a certificate of the clerk or counsel, by a party's affidavit, or by other satisfactory proof, and may be controverted in the same manner.

Eff. Sept. 1, 1997.

4.2. No Notice of Trial Court's Judgment in Civil Case

(a) *Additional Time to File Documents.*

(1) In general. If a party affected by a judgment or other appealable order has not—within 20 days after the judgment or order was signed—either received the notice required by Texas Rule of Civil Procedure 306a.3 or acquired actual knowledge of the signing, then a period that, under these rules, runs from the signing will begin for that party on the earlier of the date when the party receives notice or acquires actual knowledge of the signing.

But in no event may the period begin more than 90 days after the judgment or order was signed.

(2) Exception for restricted appeal. Subparagraph (1) does not extend the time for perfecting a restricted appeal.

(b) *Procedure to Gain Additional Time.* The procedure to gain additional time is governed by Texas Rule of Civil Procedure 306a.5.

(c) *The Court's Order.* After hearing the motion, the trial court must sign a written order that finds the date when the party or the party's attorney first either received notice or acquired actual knowledge that the judgment or order was signed.

Eff. Sept. 1, 1997.

4.3. Periods Affected by Modified Judgment in Civil Case

(a) *During Plenary-Power Period.* If a judgment is modified in any respect while the trial court retains plenary power, a period that, under these rules, runs from the date when the judgment is signed will run from the date when the modified judgment is signed.

(b) *After Plenary Power Expires.* If the trial court corrects or reforms the judgment under Texas Rule of Civil Procedure 316 after expiration of the trial court's plenary power, all periods provided in these rules that run from the date the judgment is signed run from the date the corrected judgment is signed for complaints that would not apply to the original judgment.

Eff. Sept. 1, 1997.

4.4. Periods Affected When Process Served by Publication

If process was served by publication and if a motion for new trial was filed under Texas Rule of Civil Procedure 329 more than 30 days after the judgment was signed, a period that, under these rules, runs from the date when the judgment is signed will be computed as if the judgment were signed on the date when the motion for new trial was filed.

Eff. Sept. 1, 1997.

4.5. No Notice of Judgment or Order of Appellate Court; Effect on Time to File Certain Documents

(a) *Additional Time to File Documents.* A party may move for additional time to file a motion for rehearing or en banc reconsideration in the court of appeals, a petition for review, or a petition for discretionary review, if the party did not—until after the time expired for filing the document—either receive

APPENDIXES TO THE TEXAS RULES OF APPELLATE PROCEDURE

SECTION ONE. GENERAL PROVISIONS

Rule 1. Scope of Rules; Local Rules of Courts of Appeals

Notes and Comments

Comment to 1997 change: Subdivision 1.1 is simplified without substantive change. Subdivision 1.2 is amended to make clear that any person is entitled to a copy of local rules. Paragraph 1.2(c), restricting dismissal of a case for noncompliance with a local rule, is added.

1.1. Scope

These rules govern procedure in appellate courts and before appellate judges and post-trial procedure in trial courts in criminal cases.

Eff. Sept. 1, 1997.

1.2. Local Rules

(a) *Promulgation.* A court of appeals may promulgate rules governing its practice that are not inconsistent with these rules. Local rules governing civil cases must first be approved by the Supreme Court. Local rules governing criminal cases must first be approved by the Court of Criminal Appeals.

(b) *Copies.* The clerk must provide a copy of the court's local rules to anyone who requests it.

(c) *Party's Noncompliance.* A court must not dismiss an appeal for noncompliance with a local rule without giving the noncomplying party notice and a reasonable opportunity to cure the noncompliance.

Eff. Sept. 1, 1997.

Rule 2. Suspension of Rules

On a party's motion or on its own initiative an appellate court may—to expedite a decision or for other good cause—suspend a rule's operation in a particular case and order a different procedure; but a court must not construe this rule to suspend any provision in the Code of Criminal Procedure or to alter the time for perfecting an appeal in a civil case.

Eff. Sept. 1, 1997.

Rule 3. Definitions; Uniform Terminology

Notes and Comments

Comment to 1997 change: The definition of *court below* and the reference to "suing out a writ of error to the court of appeals," are deleted as those terms are no longer used in these rules. Other changes are made.

3.1. Definitions

(a) *Appellant* means a party taking an appeal to an appellate court.

(b) *Appellate court* means the courts of appeals, the Court of Criminal Appeals, and the Supreme Court.

(c) *Appellee* means a party adverse to an appellant.

(d) *Applicant* means a person seeking relief by a habeas corpus in a criminal case.

(e) *Petitioner* means a party petitioning the Supreme Court or the Court of Criminal Appeals for review.

(f) *Relator* means a person seeking relief in an original proceeding in an appellate court other than by habeas corpus in a criminal case.

(g) *Reporter* or *court reporter* means the court reporter or court recorder.

(h) *Respondent* means:

(1) a party adverse to a petitioner in the Supreme Court or the Court of Criminal Appeals; or

(2) a party against whom relief is sought in an original proceeding in an appellate court.

Eff. Sept. 1, 1997.

3.2. Uniform Terminology in Criminal Cases

In documents filed in criminal appeals, the parties are the *State* and the *appellant.* But if the State has appealed under Article 44.01 of the Code of Criminal Procedure, the defendant is the *appellee.* Otherwise, papers should use real names for parties, and such labels as *appellee, petitioner, respondent,* and *movant* should be avoided unless necessary for clarity. In habeas corpus proceedings, the person for whose relief the writ is requested is the *applicant;* Code of Criminal Procedure article 11.13.

Eff. Sept. 1, 1997.

Rule 4. Time and Notice Provisions

Notes and Comments

Comment to 1997 change: This is former Rule 5. Paragraph 4.1(b) is added. Former paragraph (b)(1) is omitted because it is covered by other provisions of the rules. Former paragraphs (b)(2) and (b)(3) are omitted because they are duplicative of provisions in the Rules of Civil Procedure, which prescribes the applicable procedure. The phrase "modified, corrected or reformed in any respect" in paragraph 4.3(a) is changed to "modified in any respect," but no change in substance is intended. Former subdivision (e) regarding notice of judgment by the court of appeals is moved to Rule 12.6. Subdivision 4.5 is revised and now makes clear that the court must grant the motion for additional time if the court finds that the party did not receive the notice or acquire actual knowledge in time. Other changes are made throughout the rule.

4.1. Computing Time

(a) *In General.* The day of an act, event, or default after which a designated period begins to run is not included when computing a period prescribed or allowed by these rules, by court order, or by statute. The last day of the period is included, but if that day is a Saturday, Sunday, or legal holiday, the period extends to the end of the next day that is not a Saturday, Sunday, or legal holiday.

(b) *Clerk's Office Closed or Inaccessible.* If the act to be done is filing a document, and if the clerk's office where the document is to be filed is closed or inaccessible during regular hours on the last day for filing the document, the period for filing the document extends to the end of the next day when the clerk's office is open and accessible. The closing or inaccessibility of the clerk's office may be proved by a certificate of the clerk or counsel, by a party's affidavit, or by other satisfactory proof, and may be controverted in the same manner.

Eff. Sept. 1, 1997.

4.2. No Notice of Trial Court's Judgment in Civil Case

(a) *Additional Time to File Documents.*

(1) In general. If a party affected by a judgment or other appealable order has not—within 20 days after the judgment or order was signed—either received the notice required by Texas Rule of Civil Procedure 306a.3 or acquired actual knowledge of the signing, then a period that, under these rules, runs from the signing will begin for that party on the earlier of the date when the party receives notice or acquires actual knowledge of the signing.

But in no event may the period begin more than 90 days after the judgment or order was signed.

(2) Exception for restricted appeal. Subparagraph (1) does not extend the time for perfecting a restricted appeal.

(b) *Procedure to Gain Additional Time.* The procedure to gain additional time is governed by Texas Rule of Civil Procedure 306a.5.

(c) *The Court's Order.* After hearing the motion, the trial court must sign a written order that finds the date when the party or the party's attorney first either received notice or acquired actual knowledge that the judgment or order was signed.

Eff. Sept. 1, 1997.

4.3. Periods Affected by Modified Judgment in Civil Case

(a) *During Plenary-Power Period.* If a judgment is modified in any respect while the trial court retains plenary power, a period that, under these rules, runs from the date when the judgment is signed will run from the date when the modified judgment is signed.

(b) *After Plenary Power Expires.* If the trial court corrects or reforms the judgment under Texas Rule of Civil Procedure 316 after expiration of the trial court's plenary power, all periods provided in these rules that run from the date the judgment is signed run from the date the corrected judgment is signed for complaints that would not apply to the original judgment.

Eff. Sept. 1, 1997.

4.4. Periods Affected When Process Served by Publication

If process was served by publication and if a motion for new trial was filed under Texas Rule of Civil Procedure 329 more than 30 days after the judgment was signed, a period that, under these rules, runs from the date when the judgment is signed will be computed as if the judgment were signed on the date when the motion for new trial was filed.

Eff. Sept. 1, 1997.

4.5. No Notice of Judgment or Order of Appellate Court; Effect on Time to File Certain Documents

(a) *Additional Time to File Documents.* A party may move for additional time to file a motion for rehearing or en banc reconsideration in the court of appeals, a petition for review, or a petition for discretionary review, if the party did not—until after the time expired for filing the document—either receive motion to withdraw need not comply with (a) but must state only the substitute attorney's name, mailing address, telephone number, fax number, if any, and State Bar of Texas identification number. The withdrawing attorney must comply with (b) but not (c).

Eff. Sept. 1, 1997.

6.6. Agreements of Parties or Counsel

To be enforceable, an agreement of parties or their counsel concerning an appellate court proceeding must be in writing and signed by the parties or their counsel. Such an agreement is subject to any appellate court order necessary to ensure that the case is properly presented.

Eff. Sept. 1, 1997.

Rule 7. Substituting Parties

Notes and Comments

Comment to 1997 change: This is former Rule 9. Former subdivision (a) regarding death of a party in a civil case is now subparagraph 7.1(a)(1). Former subdivision (b) regarding death of a party in a criminal case is now subparagraph 7.1(a)(2). Former subdivision (c) regarding separation of office by public officers is now subdivision 7.2. Former paragraph (c)(3) regarding a successor's liability for costs is omitted as unnecessary. Former subdivision (d) regarding substitution for other causes is now paragraph 7.1(b). Subdivision 7.2 is revised to make it applicable to all cases in which a public officer is a party, and to make substitution automatic if appropriate.

7.1. Parties Who Are Not Public Officers

(a) *Death of a Party.*

(1) Civil Cases. If a party to a civil case dies after the trial court renders judgment but before the case has been finally disposed of on appeal, the appeal may be perfected, and the appellate court will proceed to adjudicate the appeal as if all parties were alive. The appellate court's judgment will have the same force and effect as if rendered when all parties were living. The decedent party's name may be used on all papers.

(2) Criminal Cases. If the appellant in a criminal case dies after an appeal is perfected but before the appellate court issues the mandate, the appeal will be permanently abated.

(b) *Substitution for Other Reasons.* If substitution of a party in the appellate court is necessary for a reason other than death, the appellate court may order substitution on any party's motion at any time.

Eff. Sept. 1, 1997.

7.2. Public Officers

(a) *Automatic Substitution of Officer.* When a public officer is a party in an official capacity to an appeal or original proceeding, and if that person ceases to hold office before the appeal or original proceeding is finally disposed of, the public officer's successor is automatically substituted as a party if appropriate. Proceedings following substitution are to be in the name of the substituted party, but any misnomer that does not affect the substantial rights of the parties may be disregarded. Substitution may be ordered at any time, but failure to order substitution of the successor does not affect the substitution.

(b) *Abatement.* If the case is an original proceeding under Rule 52, the court must abate the proceeding to allow the successor to reconsider the original party's decision. In all other cases, the suit will not abate, and the successor will be bound by the appellate court's judgment or order as if the successor were the original party.

Eff. Sept. 1, 1997.

Rule 8. Bankruptcy in Civil Cases

Notes and Comments

Comment to 1997 change: This is a new rule.

8.1 Notice of Bankruptcy

Any party may file a notice that a party is in bankruptcy. The notice must contain:

(a) the bankrupt party's name;

(b) the court in which the bankruptcy proceeding is pending;

(c) the bankruptcy proceeding's style and case number; and

(d) the date when the bankruptcy petition was filed.

Eff. Sept. 1, 1997. Amended by Supreme Court March 10, 2008, and Aug. 20, 2008, eff. Sept. 1, 2008. Approved by Court of Criminal Appeals Sept. 30, 2008, eff. Sept. 30, 2008.

8.2. Effect of Bankruptcy

A bankruptcy suspends the appeal and all periods in these rules from the date when the bankruptcy petition is filed until the appellate court reinstates or severs the appeal in accordance with federal law. A period that began to run and had not expired at the time the proceeding was suspended begins anew when the proceeding is reinstated or severed under 8.3. A document filed by a party while the proceeding is suspended will be deemed filed on the same day, but after, the court reinstates or severs the appeal and will not be considered ineffective because it was filed while the proceeding was suspended.

Eff. Sept. 1, 1997.

8.3. Motion to Reinstate or Sever Appeal Suspended by Bankruptcy

(a) *Motion to Reinstate.* If a case has been suspended by a bankruptcy filing, a party may move that the appellate court reinstate the appeal if permitted by federal law or the bankruptcy court. If the bankruptcy court has lifted or terminated the stay, a certified copy of the order must be attached to the motion.

(b) *Motion to Sever.* A party may move to sever the appeal with respect to the bankrupt party and to reinstate the appeal with respect to the other parties. The motion must show that the case is severable and must comply with applicable federal law regarding severance of a bankrupt party. The court may proceed under this paragraph on its own initiative.

Eff. Sept. 1, 1997.

Rule 9. Documents Generally

Notes and Comments

Comment to 1997 change: This is former Rule 4. Subdivision 9.4, prescribing the form of documents filed in the appellate courts, is changed and the form to be used is stated in significantly more detail. Former subdivisions (f) and (g), regarding service of documents, are merged into subdivision 9.5. Former Rule 6 is included as subdivision 9.6, but no substantive change is made. Other changes are made throughout the rule. Electronic filing is authorized by §§ 51.801–.807 of the Government Code.

9.1. Signing

(a) *Represented Parties.* If a party is represented by counsel, a document filed on that party's behalf must be signed by at least one of the party's attorneys. For each attorney whose name appears on a document as representing that party, the document must contain that attorney's State Bar of Texas identification number, mailing address, telephone number, and fax number, if any, and email address.

(b) *Unrepresented Parties.* A party not represented by counsel must sign any document that the party files and give the party's mailing address, telephone number, fax number, if any, and email address.

(c) *Electronic Signatures.* A document that is electronically served, filed, or issued by a court or clerk is considered signed if the document includes:

(1) a "/s/" and name typed in the space where the signature would otherwise appear, unless the document is notarized or sworn; or

(2) an electronic image or scanned image of the signature.

Eff. Sept. 1, 1997. Amended by Supreme Court Dec. 11, 2013, eff. Jan. 1, 2014. Approved by Court of Criminal Appeals Dec. 11, 2013, eff. Jan. 1, 2014.

9.2. Filing

(a) *With Whom.* A document is filed in an appellate court by delivering it to:

(1) the clerk of the court in which the document is to be filed; or

(2) a justice or judge of that court who is willing to accept delivery. A justice or judge who accepts delivery must note on the document the date and time of delivery, which will be considered the time of filing, and must promptly send it to the clerk.

(b) *Filing by Mail.*

(1) Timely Filing. A document received within ten days after the filing deadline is considered timely filed if:

(A) it was sent to the proper clerk by United States Postal Service or a commercial delivery service;

(B) it was placed in an envelope or wrapper properly addressed and stamped; and

(C) it was deposited in the mail or delivered to a commercial delivery service on or before the last day for filing.

(2) Proof of Mailing. Though it may consider other proof, the appellate court will accept the following as conclusive proof of the date of mailing:

(A) a legible postmark affixed by the United States Postal Service;

(B) a receipt for registered or certified mail if the receipt is endorsed by the United States Postal Service;

(C) a certificate of mailing by the United States Postal Service; or

(D) a receipt endorsed by the commercial delivery service.

(c) *Electronic Filing.*

(1) Requirement. Attorneys in civil cases must electronically file documents. Attorneys in criminal cases must electronically file documents except for good cause shown in a motion filed in the appellate court. Unrepresented parties in civil and criminal

cases may electronically file documents, but it is not required.

(2) Mechanism. Electronic filing must be done through the electronic filing manager established by the Office of Court Administration and an electronic filing service provider certified by the Office of Court Administration.

(3) Exceptions. Documents filed under seal, subject to a pending motion to seal, or to which access is otherwise restricted by law or court order must not be electronically filed. For good cause, an appellate court may permit a party to file other documents in paper form in a particular case.

(4) Timely Filing. Unless a document must be filed by a certain time of day, a document is considered timely filed if it is electronically filed at any time before midnight (in the court's time zone) on the filing deadline. An electronically filed document is deemed filed when transmitted to the filing party's electronic filing service provider, except:

(A) if a document is transmitted on a Saturday, Sunday, or legal holiday, it is deemed filed on the next day that is not a Saturday, Sunday, or legal holiday; and

(B) if a document requires a motion and an order allowing its filing, the document is deemed filed on the date the motion is granted.

(5) Technical Failure. If a document is untimely due to a technical failure or a system outage, the filing party may seek appropriate relief from the court.

(6) Confirmation of Filing. The electronic filing manager will send a filing confirmation notice to the filing party.

(7) Electronic Notices From the Court. The clerk may send notices, orders, or other communications about the case to the party electronically. A court seal may be electronic.

Eff. Sept. 1, 1997. Amended by Supreme Court Feb. 28, 2011, eff. June 30, 2011. Approved by Court of Criminal Appeals Feb. 28, 2011, eff. June 30, 2011. Amended by Supreme Court June 27, 2011, eff. June 30, 2011. Amended by Supreme Court Dec. 11, 2013, eff. Jan. 1, 2014. Approved by Court of Criminal Appeals Dec. 11, 2013, eff. Jan. 1, 2014.

9.3. Number of Copies

(a) *Courts of Appeals.*

(1) Document Filed in Paper Form. If a document is not electronically filed, a party must file the original and one unbound copy of the document unless otherwise required by local rule. The un-

bound copy of an appendix must contain a separate page before each document and must not include tabs that extend beyond the edge of the page.

(2) Electronically Filed Document. Unless required by local rule, a party need not file a paper copy of an electronically filed document.

(b) *Supreme Court and Court of Criminal Appeals.*

(1) Document Filed in Paper Form. If a document is not electronically filed, a party must file the original and 11 copies of any document addressed to either the Supreme Court or the Court of Criminal Appeals, except that in the Supreme Court only an original and one copy must be filed of any motion, response to the motion, and reply in support of the motion, and in the Court of Criminal Appeals, only the original must be filed of a motion for extension of time or a response to the motion, or a pleading under Code of Criminal Procedure article 11.07.

(2) Electronically Filed Document. Paper copies of each document that is electronically filed with the Supreme Court or the Court of Criminal Appeals must be mailed or hand-delivered to the Supreme Court or the Court of Criminal Appeals, as appropriate, within three business days after the document is electronically filed. The number of paper copies required shall be determined, respectively, by order of the Supreme Court or the Court of Criminal Appeals.

(c) *Exception for Record.* Only the original record need be filed in any proceeding.

Eff. Sept. 1, 1997. Amended by Supreme Court March 10, 2008, and Aug. 20, 2008, eff. Sept. 1, 2008. Approved by Court of Criminal Appeals Sept. 30, 2008, eff. Sept. 30, 2008. Amended by Supreme Court Feb. 28, 2011, eff. June 30, 2011. Approved by Court of Criminal Appeals Feb. 28, 2011, eff. June 30, 2011. Amended by Supreme Court June 27, 2011, eff. June 30, 2011. Amended by Supreme Court Dec. 11, 2013, eff. Jan. 1, 2014. Approved by Court of Criminal Appeals Dec. 11, 2013, eff. Jan. 1, 2014.

9.4. Form

Except for the record, a document filed with an appellate court, including a paper copy of an electronically filed document, must—unless the court accepts another form in the interest of justice — be in the following form:

(a) *Printing.* A document may be produced by standard typographic printing or by any duplicating process that produces a distinct black image. Printing must be on one side of the paper.

(b) *Paper Type and Size.* The paper on which a document is produced must be 8 1/2 by 11 inches, white or nearly white, and opaque.

(c) *Margins.* Documents must have at least one-inch margins on both sides and at the top and bottom.

(d) *Spacing.* Text must be double-spaced, but footnotes, block quotations, short lists, and issues or points of error may be single-spaced.

(e) *Typeface.* A document produced on a computer must be printed in a conventional typeface no smaller than 14–point except for footnotes, which must be no smaller than 12–point. A typewritten document must be printed in standard 10–character–per–inch (cpi) monospaced typeface.

(f) *Binding and Covering.* A paper document must be bound so as to ensure that it will not lose its cover or fall apart in regular use. A paper document should be stapled once in the top left-hand corner or be bound so that it will lie flat when open. A paper petition or brief should have durable front and back covers which must not be plastic or be red, black, or dark blue.

(g) *Contents of Cover.* A document's front cover, if any, must contain the case style, the case number, the title of the document being filed, the name of the party filing the document, and the name, mailing address, telephone number, fax number, if any, email address, and State Bar of Texas identification number of the lead counsel for the filing party. If a party requests oral argument in the court of appeals, the request must appear on the front cover of that party's first brief.

(h) *Appendix and Original Proceeding Record.* A paper appendix may be bound either with the document to which it is related or separately. If separately bound, the appendix must comply with paragraph (f). A paper record in an original proceeding or a paper appendix must be tabbed and indexed. An electronically filed record in an original proceeding or an electronically filed appendix that includes more than one item must contain bookmarks to assist in locating each item.

(i) Length.

(1) Contents Included and Excluded. In calculating the length of a document, every word and every part of the document, including headings, footnotes, and quotations, must be counted except the following: caption, identity of parties and counsel, statement regarding oral argument, table of contents, index of authorities, statement of the case, state-

ment of issues presented, statement of jurisdiction, statement of procedural history, signature, proof of service, certification, certificate of compliance, and appendix.

(2) Maximum Length. The documents listed below must not exceed the following limits:

(A) A brief and response in a direct appeal to the Court of Criminal Appeals in a case in which the death penalty has been assessed: 37,500 words if computer-generated, and 125 pages if not.

(B) A brief and response in an appellate court (other than a brief under subparagraph (A)) and a petition and response in an original proceeding in the court of appeals: 15,000 words if computer-generated, and 50 pages if not. In a civil case in the court of appeals, the aggregate of all briefs filed by a party must not exceed 27,000 words if computer-generated, and 90 pages if not.

(C) A reply brief in an appellate court and a reply to a response to a petition in an original proceeding in the court of appeals: 7,500 words if computer-generated, and 25 pages if not.

(D) A petition and response in an original proceeding in the Supreme Court and the Court of Criminal Appeals, except for petitions and responses in an original proceeding in a case in which the death penalty has been assessed, a petition for review and response in the Supreme Court, a petition for discretionary review in the Court of Criminal Appeals, and a motion for rehearing and response in an appellate court: 4,500 words if computer-generated, and 15 pages if not.

(E) A reply to a response to a petition for review in the Supreme Court, a reply to a response to a petition in an original proceeding in the Supreme Court and the Court of Criminal Appeals, except a reply to a response in an original proceeding in a case in which the death penalty has been assessed, and a reply to a petition for discretionary review in the Court of Criminal Appeals: 2,400 words if computer-generated, and 8 pages if not.

(F) A petition and response in an original proceeding in the Court of Criminal Appeals in a case in which the death penalty has been assessed: 9,000 words if computer-generated, and 30 pages if not.

(G) A reply to a response to a petition in an original proceeding in the Court of Criminal Appeals in a case in which the death penalty has been assessed: 4,800 words if computer-generated, and 16 pages if not.

(3) Certificate of Compliance. A computer-generated document that is subject to a word limit under this rule must include a certificate by counsel or an unrepresented party stating the number of words in the document. The person certifying may rely on the word count of the computer program used to prepare the document.

(4) Extensions. A court may, on motion, permit a document that exceeds the prescribed limit.

(j) *Electronically Filed Documents.* An electronically filed document must:

(1) be in text-searchable portable document format (PDF);

(2) be directly converted to PDF rather than scanned, if possible;

(3) not be locked;

(4) be combined with any appendix into one computer file, unless that file would exceed the size limit prescribed by the electronic filing manager; and

(5) otherwise comply with the Technology Standards set by the Judicial Committee on Information Technology and approved by the Supreme Court.

(k) *Nonconforming Documents.* If a document fails to conform with these rules, the court may strike the document or identify the error and permit the party to resubmit the document in a conforming format by a specified deadline.

Eff. Sept. 1, 1997. Amended by Supreme Court Nov. 13, 2012, eff. Dec. 1, 2012; March 4, 2013, eff. immediately. Amended by Supreme Court Dec. 11, 2013, eff. Jan. 1, 2014. Approved by Court of Criminal Appeals Dec. 11, 2013, eff. Jan. 1, 2014. Amended by Court of Criminal Appeals Jan. 23, 2017, and Supreme Court Jan. 25, 2017, eff. Feb. 1, 2017.

9.5. Service

(a) *Service of All Documents Required.* At or before the time of a document's filing, the filing party must serve a copy on all parties to the proceeding. Service on a party represented by counsel must be made on that party's lead counsel. Except in original proceedings, a party need not serve a copy of the record.

(b) *Manner of Service.*

(1) Documents Filed Electronically. A document filed electronically under Rule 9.2 must be served electronically through the electronic filing manager if the email address of the party or attorney to be served is on file with the electronic filing manager. If the email address of the party or attorney to be served is not on file with the electronic filing man-

ager, the document may be served on that party or attorney under subparagraph (2).

(2) Documents Not Filed Electronically. A document that is not filed electronically may be served in person, by mail, by commercial delivery service, by fax, or by email. Personal service includes delivery to any responsible person at the office of the lead counsel for the party served.

(c) *When Complete.*

(1) Service by mail is complete on mailing.

(2) Service by commercial delivery service is complete when the document is placed in the control of the delivery service.

(3) Service by fax is complete on receipt.

(4) Electronic service is complete on transmission of the document to the serving party's electronic filing service provider. The electronic filing manager will send confirmation of service to the serving party.

(d) *Proof of Service.* A document presented for filing must contain a proof of service in the form of either an acknowledgment of service by the person served or a certificate of service. Proof of service may appear on or be affixed to the filed document. The clerk may permit a document to be filed without proof of service, but will require the proof to be filed promptly.

(e) *Certificate Requirements.* A certificate of service must be signed by the person who made the service and must state:

(1) the date and manner of service;

(2) the name and address of each person served; and

(3) if the person served is a party's attorney, the name of the party represented by that attorney.

Eff. Sept. 1, 1997. Amended by Supreme Court Dec. 23, 2002, eff. Jan. 1, 2003. Amended by Supreme Court Dec. 11, 2013, eff. Jan. 1, 2014. Approved by Court of Criminal Appeals Dec. 11, 2013, eff. Jan. 1, 2014.

Notes and Comments

Comment to 2002 change: The change clarifies that the filing party must serve a copy of the document filed on all other parties, not only in an appeal or review, but in original proceedings as well. The rule applies only to filing *parties.* Thus, when the clerk or court reporter is responsible for filing the record, as in cases on appeal, a copy need not be served on the parties. The rule for original civil proceedings, in which a party is responsible for filing the record, is stated in subdivision 52.7.

9.6. Communications With the Court

Parties and counsel may communicate with the appellate court about a case only through the clerk.

Eff. Sept. 1, 1997. Amended by order of Jan. 1, 2014, eff. Jan. 1, 2014.

9.7. Adoption by Reference

Any party may join in or adopt by reference all or any part of a brief, petition, response, motion, or other document filed in an appellate court by another party in the same case.

Added by Supreme Court Dec. 23, 2002, eff. Jan. 1, 2003. Amended by order of Jan. 1, 2014, eff. Jan. 1, 2014.

Notes and Comments

Comment to 2002 change: Subdivision 9.7 is added to provide express authorization for the practice of adopting by reference all or part of another party's filing.

9.8. Protection of Minor's Identity in Parental–Rights Termination Cases and Juvenile Court Cases

(a) *Alias Defined.* For purposes of this rule, an alias means one or more of a person's initials or a fictitious name, used to refer to the person.

(b) *Parental–Rights Termination Cases.* In an appeal or an original proceeding in an appellate court, arising out of a case in which the termination of parental rights was at issue:

(1) except for a docketing statement, in all papers submitted to the court, including all appendix items submitted with a brief, petition, or motion:

(A) a minor must be identified only by an alias unless the court orders otherwise;

(B) the court may order that a minor's parent or other family member be identified only by an alias if necessary to protect a minor's identity, and

(C) all documents must be redacted accordingly;

(2) the court must, in its opinion, use an alias to refer to a minor, and if necessary to protect the minor's identity, to the minor's parent or other family member.

(c) *Juvenile Court Cases.* In an appeal or an original proceeding in an appellate court, arising out of a case under Title 3 of the Family Code:

(1) except for a docketing statement, in all papers submitted to the court, including all appendix items submitted with a brief, petition, or motion:

(A) a minor must be identified only by an alias;

(B) a minor's parent or other family member must be identified only by an alias; and

(C) all documents must be redacted accordingly;

(2) the court must, in its opinion, use an alias to refer to a minor and to the minor's parent or other family member.

(d) *No Alteration of Appellate Record.* Nothing in this rule permits alteration of the original appellate record except as specifically authorized by court order.

Added by Supreme Court March 10, 2008, eff. Sept. 1, 2008. Amended by Supreme Court Aug. 20, 2008, eff. Sept. 1, 2008. Approved by Court of Criminal Appeals Sept. 30, 2008, eff. Sept. 30, 2008. Amended by order of Jan. 1, 2014, eff. Jan. 1, 2014.

9.9. Privacy Protection for Documents Filed in Civil Cases

(a) *Sensitive Data Defined.* Sensitive data consists of:

(1) a driver's license number, passport number, social security number, tax identification number or similar government-issued personal identification number;

(2) a bank account number, credit card number, or other financial account number; and

(3) a birth date, home address, and the name of any person who was a minor when the underlying suit was filed.

(b) *Filing of Documents Containing Sensitive Data Prohibited.* Unless the inclusion of sensitive data is specifically required by a statute, court rule, or administrative regulation, an electronic or paper document containing sensitive data may not be filed with a court unless the sensitive data is redacted, except for the record in an appeal under Section Two.

(c) *Redaction of Sensitive Data; Retention Requirement.* Sensitive data must be redacted by using the letter "X" in place of each omitted digit or character or by removing the sensitive data in a manner indicating that the data has been redacted. The filing party must retain an unredacted version of the filed document during the pendency of the appeal and any related proceedings filed within six months of the date the judgment is signed.

(d) *Notice to Clerk.* If a document must contain sensitive data, the filing party must notify the clerk by:

(1) designating the document as containing sensitive data when the document is electronically filed; or

(2) if the document is not electronically filed, by including, on the upper left-hand side of the first page, the phrase: "NOTICE: THIS DOCUMENT CONTAINS SENSITIVE DATA."

(e) *Restriction on Remote Access.* Documents that contain unredacted sensitive data in violation of this rule must not be posted on the Internet.

Adopted by Supreme Court Dec. 11, 2013, eff. Jan. 1, 2014. Approved by Court of Criminal Appeals Dec. 11, 2013, eff. Jan. 1, 2014.

9.10. Privacy Protection for Documents Filed in Criminal Cases

(a) *Sensitive Data Defined.* Sensitive data consists of:

(1) a driver's license number, passport number, social security number, tax identification number or similar government-issued personal identification number;

(2) bank account number, credit card number, and other financial account number;

(3) a birth date, a home address, and the name of any person who was a minor at the time the offense was committed.

(b) *Redacted Filings.* Unless a court orders otherwise, an electronic or paper filing with the court, including the contents of any appendices, must not contain sensitive data.

(c) *Exemptions from the Redaction Requirement.* The redaction requirement does not apply to the following:

(1) A court filing that is related to a criminal matter or investigation and that is prepared before the filing of a criminal charge or is not filed as part of any docketed criminal case;

(2) An arrest or search warrant;

(3) A charging document and an affidavit filed in support of any charging document;

(4) A defendant's date of birth;

(5) A defendant's address; and

(6) Any government issued number intended to identify the defendant associated with a criminal filing, except for the defendant's social security number or driver's license number.

(d) *Redaction procedures.* Sensitive data must be redacted by using the letter "X" in place of each omitted digit or character or by removing the sensitive data in a manner indicating that the data has been redacted. The filer must retain an unredacted version of the filed document during the pendency of the appeal and any related proceedings filed within three years of the date the judgment is signed. If a district court clerk or appellate court clerk discovers unredacted sensitive data in the record, the clerk shall notify the parties and seek a ruling from the court.

(e) *Certification.* The filing of a document constitutes a certification by the filer that the document complies with paragraphs (a) and (b) of this rule.

(f) *Reference List.* If a filer believes any information described in paragraph (a) of this rule is essential to a document or that the document would be confusing without the information, the filer may submit the information to the court in a reference list that is in paper form and under seal. The reference list must specify an appropriate identifier that corresponds uniquely to each item listed. Any reference in the document to a listed identifier will be construed to refer to the corresponding item of information. If the filer provides a reference list pursuant to this rule, the front page of the document containing the redacted information must indicate that the reference list has been, or will be, provided. On its own initiative, the court may order a sealed reference list in any case.

(g) *Sealed materials.* Materials that are required by statute to be sealed, redacted, or kept confidential, such as the items set out in Articles 35.29 (Personal Information About Jurors), 38.45 (Evidence Depicting or Describing Abuse of or Sexual Conduct by Child or Minor), and 42.12, § 9(j), must be treated in accordance with the pertinent statutes and shall not be publicly available on the internet. A court may also order that a document be filed under seal in paper form or electronic form, without redaction. The court may later unseal the document or order the filer to provide a redacted version of the document for the public record. If a court orders material sealed, whether it be sensitive data or other materials, the court's sealing order must be affixed to the outside of the sealed container if the sealed material is filed in paper form, or be the first document that appears if filed in electronic form. Sealed portions of the clerk's and reporter's records should be clearly marked and separated from unsealed portions and tendered as separate records, whether in paper form or electronic form. Sealed material shall not be available either on the internet or in other form without court order.

(h) *Waiver of Protection of Identifiers.* A person waives the protection of this rule as to a person's own information by filing it without redaction and not under seal.

Adopted by Supreme Court Dec. 11, 2013, eff. Jan. 1, 2014. Approved by Court of Criminal Appeals Dec. 11, 2013, eff. Jan. 1, 2014. Amended by Court of Criminal Appeals Oct. 5, 2015, eff. Nov. 1, 2015.

Rule 10. Motions in the Appellate Courts

Notes and Comments

Comment to 1997 change: This is former Rule 19. Under subdivision 10.1, a response may be filed at any time before the court rules on the motion. The provision of former subdivision (b) regarding docketing motions is incorporated in Rule 12.2. The provision of former subdivision (b) for noting attorneys' names on the docket is incorporated in Rule 6.2. Former subdivision (c), requiring the clerk to send notices of the filing of motions is deleted as unnecessary because the parties must serve all motions under Rule 9.5. Subdivision 10.2 is amended to eliminate the requirement of an oath where the facts are within the personal knowledge of the attorney. Subdivision 10.5 is new and incorporates the provisions of other rules concerning motions, as follows: 10.5(a) from former Rule 71; 10.5(b) from former Rules 73, 130(d), and 160; and 10.5(c) from former Rule 70. Other changes are made.

10.1. Contents of Motions; Response

(a) *Motion.* Unless these rules prescribe another form, a party must apply by motion for an order or other relief. The motion must:

(1) contain or be accompanied by any matter specifically required by a rule governing such a motion;

(2) state with particularity the grounds on which it is based;

(3) set forth the order or relief sought;

(4) be served and filed with any brief, affidavit, or other paper filed in support of the motion; and

(5) in civil cases, except for motions for rehearing and en banc reconsideration, contain or be accompanied by a certificate stating that the filing party conferred, or made a reasonable attempt to confer, with all other parties about the merits of the motion and whether those parties oppose the motion.

(b) *Response.* A party may file a response to a motion at any time before the court rules on the motion or by any deadline set by the court. The court may determine a motion before a response is filed.

Eff. Sept. 1, 1997. Amended by Supreme Court March 10, 2008, and Aug. 20, 2008, eff. Sept. 1, 2008. Approved by Court of Criminal Appeals Sept. 30, 2008, eff. Sept. 30, 2008.

10.2. Evidence on Motions

A motion need not be verified unless it depends on the following types of facts, in which case the motion must be supported by affidavit or other satisfactory evidence. The types of facts requiring proof are those that are:

(a) not in the record;

(b) not within the court's knowledge in its official capacity; and

(c) not within the personal knowledge of the attorney signing the motion.

Eff. Sept. 1, 1997. Amended by Supreme Court March 10, 2008, and Aug. 20, 2008, eff. Sept. 1, 2008. Approved by Court of Criminal Appeals Sept. 30, 2008, eff. Sept. 30, 2008.

10.3. Determining Motions

(a) *Time for Determination.* A court should not hear or determine a motion until 10 days after the motion was filed, unless:

(1) the motion is to extend time to file a brief, a petition for review, or a petition for discretionary review;

(2) the motion states that the parties have conferred and that no party opposes the motion; or

(3) the motion is an emergency.

(b) *Reconsideration.* If a motion is determined prematurely, any party adversely affected may request the court to reconsider its order.

Eff. Sept. 1, 1997.

10.4. Power of Panel or Single Justice or Judge to Entertain Motions

(a) *Single Justice.* In addition to the authority expressly conferred by these rules or by law, a single justice or judge of an appellate court may grant or deny a request for relief that these rules allow to be sought by motion. But in a civil case, a single justice should not do the following:

(1) act on a petition for an extraordinary writ; or

(2) dismiss or otherwise determine an appeal or a motion for rehearing.

(b) *Panel.* An appellate court may provide, by order or rule, that a panel or the full court must act on any motion or class of motions.

Eff. Sept. 1, 1997.

10.5. Particular Motions

(a) *Motions Relating to Informalities in the Record.* A motion relating to informalities in the manner of bringing a case into court must be filed within 30 days after the record is filed in the court of appeals. The objection, if waivable, will otherwise be deemed waived.

(b) *Motions to Extend Time.*

(1) Contents of Motion in General. All motions to extend time, except a motion to extend time for filing a notice of appeal, must state:

(A) the deadline for filing the item in question;

(B) the length of the extension sought;

(C) the facts relied on to reasonably explain the need for an extension; and

(D) the number of previous extensions granted regarding the item in question.

(2) Contents of Motion to Extend Time to File Notice of Appeal. A motion to extend the time for filing a notice of appeal must:

(A) comply with (1)(A) and (C);

(B) identify the trial court;

(C) state the date of the trial court's judgment or appealable order; and

(D) state the case number and style of the case in the trial court.

(3) Contents of Motion to Extend Time to File Petition for Review or Petition for Discretionary Review. A motion to extend time to file a petition for review or petition for discretionary review must also specify:

(A) the court of appeals;

(B) the date of the court of appeals' judgment;

(C) the case number and style of the case in the court of appeals; and

(D) the date every motion for rehearing or en banc reconsideration was filed, and either the date and nature of the court of appeals' ruling on the motion, or that it remains pending.

(c) *Motions to Postpone Argument.* Unless all parties agree, or unless sufficient cause is apparent to the court, a motion to postpone argument of a case must be supported by sufficient cause.

Eff. Sept. 1, 1997. Amended by Supreme Court Aug. 20, 2008, eff. Sept. 1, 2008. Approved by Court of Criminal Appeals Sept. 30, 2008, eff. Sept. 30, 2008.

Rule 11. Amicus Curiae Briefs

An appellate clerk may receive, but not file, an amicus curiae brief. But the court for good cause may refuse to consider the brief and order that it be returned. An amicus curiae brief must:

(a) comply with the briefing rules for parties;

(b) identify the person or entity on whose behalf the brief is tendered;

(c) disclose the source of any fee paid or to be paid for preparing the brief; and

(d) certify that copies have been served on all parties.

Eff. Sept. 1, 1997. Amended by Supreme Court Dec. 23, 2002, eff. Jan. 1, 2003.

Notes and Comments

Comment to 1997 change: This is former Rule 20. The rule is rewritten and now requires disclosure of the identity of the person or entity on whose behalf the brief is filed, and the source of any fee paid.

Comment to 2002 change: The change expressly recognizes that a court may refuse to consider an amicus curiae brief for good cause.

Rule 12. Duties of Appellate Clerk

Notes and Comments

Comment to 1997 change: This is former Rule 18. Former subdivision (b), regarding the preparation of the record, is moved to the order concerning the preparation of the appellate record. Former Rule 14, which is revised and simplified, is relocated here as subdivision 12.5. Subdivision 12.6, requiring the clerk to send a notice of any order or judgment of an appellate court, is added. Other changes are made.

12.1. Docketing the Case

On receiving a copy of the notice of appeal, the petition for review, the petition for discretionary review, the petition in an original proceeding, or a certified question, the appellate clerk must:

(a) endorse on the document the date of receipt;

(b) collect any filing fee;

(c) docket the case;

(d) notify all parties of the receipt of the document; and

(e) if the document filed is a petition for review filed in the Supreme Court, notify the court of appeals clerk of the filing of the petition.

12.2. Docket Numbers

The clerk must put the case's docket number on each item received in connection with the case and must put the docket number on the envelope in which the record is stored.

(a) *Numbering System.* Each case filed in a court of appeals must be assigned a docket number consisting of the following four parts, separated by hyphens:

(1) the number of the court of appeals district;

(2) the last two digits of the year in which the case is filed;

(3) the number assigned to the case; and

(4) the designation "CV" for a civil case or "CR" for a criminal case.

(b) *Numbering Order.* Each case must be docketed in the order of its filing.

(c) *Multiple Notices of Appeal.* All notices of appeal filed in the same case must be given the same docket number.

(d) *Appeals Not Yet Filed.* A motion relating to an appeal that has been perfected but not yet filed must be docketed and assigned a docket number that will also be assigned to the appeal when it is filed.

Eff. Sept. 1, 1997.

12.3. Custody of Papers

The clerk must safeguard the record and every other item filed in a case. If the record or any part of it or any other item is missing, the court will make an order for the replacement of the record or item that is just under the circumstances.

Eff. Sept. 1, 1997.

12.4. Withdrawing Papers

The clerk may permit the record or other filed item to be taken from the clerk's office at any time, on the following conditions:

(a) the clerk must have a receipt for the record or item;

(b) the clerk should make reasonable conditions to ensure that the withdrawn record or item is preserved and returned;

(c) the clerk may demand the return of the record or item at any time;

(d) after the case is submitted to the court and before the court's decision, the record cannot be withdrawn;

(e) after the court's decision, the losing party must be given priority in withdrawing the record;

(f) the clerk may not allow original documents filed under Rule 34.5(f) or original exhibits filed under Rule 34.6(g) to be taken from the clerk's office;

(g) if the court allows an original document or exhibit to be taken by a party and it is not returned, the court may accept the opposing party's statement concerning the document's or exhibit's nature and contents;

(h) withdrawn material must not be removed from the court's jurisdiction; and

(i) the court may, on the motion of any party or its own initiative, modify any of these conditions.

12.5. Clerk's Duty to Account

The clerk of an appellate court who receives money due another court must promptly pay the money to the court to whom it is due. This rule is enforceable by the Supreme Court.

Eff. Sept. 1, 1997.

12.6. Notices of Court's Judgments and Orders

In any proceeding, the clerk of an appellate court must promptly send a notice of any judgment, mandate, or other court order to all parties to the proceeding.

Eff. Sept. 1, 1997. Amended by Supreme Court Dec. 23, 2002, eff. Jan. 1, 2003.

Notes and Comments

Comment to 2002 change: Subdivision 12.6 is amended to require the clerk to notify the parties of all of the court's rulings, including the mandate.

Rule 13. Court Reporters and Court Recorders

Notes and Comments

Comment to 1997 change: Former Rules 11 and 12 are merged. Former Rules 11(a), (c) and (d) now appear as subdivisions 13.1, 13.5 and 13.6. Former Rule 11(b) is omitted as unnecessary. The provisions of former Rule 12(a) are moved to Rule 35.3. Former Rules 12(b) and (c) now appear as subdivisions 13.3 and 13.4. The rule is made to apply to court recorders as well as court reporters. Paragraph 13.1(a) merges paragraphs (a)(1) and (2) of former Rule 11, and now requires the reporter to make a record of voir dire and closing argument unless excused by agreement of the parties. Paragraph 13.1(b) is new, but codifies current practice. Subdivision 13.2 is new and specifies rules for electronic recording of proceedings. A provision requiring a deputy court reporter to file with the trial court clerk a document identifying the proceedings in which the reporter worked is included in paragraph 13.5. Other changes are made.

13.1. Duties of Court Reporters and Recorders

The official court reporter or court recorder must:

(a) unless excused by agreement of the parties, attend court sessions and make a full record of the proceedings;

(b) take all exhibits offered in evidence during a proceeding and ensure that they are marked;

(c) file all exhibits with the trial court clerk after a proceeding ends;

(d) perform the duties prescribed by Rules 34.6 and 35; and

(e) perform other acts relating to the reporter's or recorder's official duties, as the trial court directs.

Eff. Sept. 1, 1997. Amended by Supreme Court Dec. 23, 2002, eff. Jan. 1, 2003.

Notes and Comments

Comment to 2002 change: Subdivision 13.1(a) is amended merely for clarification.

13.2. Additional Duties of Court Recorder

The official court recorder must also:

(a) ensure that the recording system functions properly throughout the proceeding and that a complete, clear, and transcribable recording is made;

(b) make a detailed, legible log of all proceedings being recorded, showing:

(1) the number and style of the case before the court;

(2) the name of each person speaking;

(3) the event being recorded such as the voir dire, the opening statement, direct and cross-examinations, and bench conferences;

(4) each exhibit offered, admitted, or excluded;

(5) the time of day of each event; and

(6) the index number on the recording device showing where each event is recorded;

(c) after a proceeding ends, file with the clerk the original log;

(d) have the original recording stored to ensure that it is preserved and is accessible; and

(e) ensure that no one gains access to the original recording without the court's written order.

Eff. Sept. 1, 1997.

13.3. Priorities of Reporters

The trial court must help ensure that the court reporter's work is timely accomplished by setting work priorities. The reporter's duties relating to proceedings before the court take preference over other work.

Eff. Sept. 1, 1997.

13.4. Report of Reporters

To aid the trial court in setting priorities under 13.3, each court reporter must give the trial court a monthly written report showing the amount and nature of the business pending in the reporter's office. A copy of this report must be filed with the appellate clerk of each district in which the court sits.

Eff. Sept. 1, 1997.

13.5. Appointing Deputy Reporter

When the official court reporter is unable to perform the duties in 13.1 or 13.2 because of illness, press of official work, or unavoidable absence or disability, the trial court may designate a deputy reporter. If the court appoints a deputy reporter, that person must file with the trial court clerk a document stating:

(a) the date the deputy worked;

(b) the court in which the deputy worked; and

(c) the number and style of the case on which the deputy worked.

Eff. Sept. 1, 1997.

13.6. Filing of Notes in a Criminal Case

When a defendant is convicted and sentenced, or is granted deferred adjudication for a felony other than a state jail felony, and does not appeal, the court reporter must—within 20 days after the time to perfect the appeal has expired—file the untranscribed notes or the original recording of the proceeding with the trial court clerk. The trial court clerk need not retain the notes beyond 15 years of their filing date.

Eff. Sept. 1, 1997.

Rule 14. Recording and Broadcasting Court Proceedings

Notes and Comments

Comment to 1997 change: This is former Rule 21. The rule is rewritten and now allows recording and broadcasting of court proceedings at the discretion of the court and subject to the stated guidelines.

14.1. Recording and Broadcasting Permitted

An appellate court may permit courtroom proceedings to be broadcast, televised, recorded, or photographed in accordance with this rule.

Eff. Sept. 1, 1997.

14.2. Procedure

(a) *Request to Cover Court Proceeding.*

(1) A person wishing to broadcast, televise, record, or photograph a court proceeding must file with the court clerk a request to cover the proceeding. The request must state:

(A) the case style and number;

(B) the date and time when the proceeding is to begin;

(C) the name of the requesting person or organization;

(D) the type of coverage requested (for example, televising or photographing); and

(E) the type and extent of equipment to be used.

(2) A request to cover argument of a case must be filed no later than five days before the date the case is set for argument and must be served on all parties to the case. A request to cover any other proceeding must be filed no later than two days before the date when the proceeding is to begin.

(b) *Response.* Any party may file a response to the request. If the request is to cover argument, the response must be filed no later than two days before the date set for argument. If a party objects to coverage of the argument, the response should state the injury that will allegedly result from coverage.

(c) *Court May Shorten Time.* The court may, in the interest of justice, shorten the time for filing a document under this rule if no party or interested person would be unduly prejudiced.

(d) *Decision of Court.* In deciding whether to allow coverage, the court may consider information known *ex parte* to the court. The court may allow, deny, limit, or terminate coverage for any reason the court considers necessary or appropriate, such as protecting the parties' rights or the dignity of the court and ensuring the orderly conduct of the proceedings.

Eff. Sept. 1, 1997.

14.3. Equipment and Personnel

The court may, among other things:

(a) require that a person seeking to cover a proceeding demonstrate or display the equipment that will be used;

(b) prohibit equipment that produces distracting sound or light;

(c) prohibit signal lights or devices showing when equipment is operating, or require their concealment;

(d) prohibit moving lights, flash attachments, or sudden lighting changes;

(e) require the use of the courtroom's existing video, audio, and lighting systems, if any;

(f) specify the placement of personnel and equipment;

(g) determine the number of cameras to be allowed in the courtroom; and

(h) require pooling of equipment if more than one person wishes to cover a proceeding.

Eff. Sept. 1, 1997.

14.4. Enforcement

The court may sanction a violation of this rule by measures that include barring a person or organization from access to future coverage of proceedings in that court for a defined period.

Eff. Sept. 1, 1997.

Rule 15. Issuance of Writ or Process by Appellate Court

Notes and Comments

Comment to 1997 change: This is former Rule 17. Nonsubstantive changes are made.

15.1. In General

(a) *Signature Under Seal.* A writ or process issuing from an appellate court must bear the court's seal and be signed by the clerk.

(b) *To Whom Directed; by Whom Served.* Unless a rule or statute provides otherwise, the writ or process must be directed to the person or court to be served. The writ or process may be served by the sheriff, constable, or other peace officer whose jurisdiction includes the county in which the person or court to be served may be found.

(c) *Return; Lack of Execution; Simultaneous Writs.* The writ or process must be returned to the issuing court according to the writ's direction. If the writ or process is not executed, the clerk may issue another writ or process if requested by the party who requested the former writ or process. At a party's request, the clerk may issue two or more writs simultaneously.

Eff. Sept. 1, 1997.

15.2. Appearance Without Service; Actual Knowledge

A party who appears in person or by attorney in an appellate court proceeding—or who has actual knowledge of the court's opinion, judgment, or order related to a writ or process—is bound by the opinion, judgment, or order to the same extent as if personally served under 15.1.

Eff. Sept. 1, 1997.

Rule 16. Disqualification or Recusal of Appellate Judges

Notes and Comments

Comment to 1997 change: Former Rules 15 and 15a are merged. Former Rule 15a appears as subdivision 16.2. For grounds for disqualification, reference is made to the Constitution and statutes rather than the Rules of Civil Procedure. The procedure for disqualification is not specified. The nature of prior participation in a proceeding that requires recusal is clarified. Former subdivision (b) of Rule 15, requiring service of the motion, is omitted as unnecessary. The remaining subdivisions of former Rule 15 are contained in subdivision 16.3. Other changes are made.

16.1. Grounds for Disqualification

The grounds for disqualification of an appellate court justice or judge are determined by the Constitution and laws of Texas.

Eff. Sept. 1, 1997.

16.2. Grounds for Recusal

The grounds for recusal of an appellate court justice or judge are the same as those provided in the Rules of Civil Procedure. In addition, a justice or judge must recuse in a proceeding if it presents a material issue which the justice or judge participated in deciding while serving on another court in which the proceeding was pending.

Eff. Sept. 1, 1997.

16.3. Procedure for Recusal

(a) *Motion.* A party may file a motion to recuse a justice or judge before whom the case is pending. The motion must be filed promptly after the party has reason to believe that the justice or judge should not participate in deciding the case.

(b) *Decision.* Before any further proceeding in the case, the challenged justice or judge must either remove himself or herself from all participation in the case or certify the matter to the entire court, which will decide the motion by a majority of the remaining judges sitting en banc. The challenged justice or judge must not sit with the remainder of the court to consider the motion as to him or her.

(c) *Appeal.* An order of recusal is not reviewable, but the denial of a recusal motion is reviewable.

Eff. Sept. 1, 1997.

Rule 17. Court of Appeals Unable to Take Immediate Action

Notes and Comments

Comment to 1997 change: This is former Rule 16. The rule is rewritten and simplified.

17.1. Inability to Act

A court of appeals is unable to take immediate action if it cannot—within the time when action must be taken—assemble a panel because members of the court are ill, absent, or unavailable. A justice who is disqualified or recused is unavailable. A court of appeals' inability to act immediately may be established by certificate of the clerk, a member of the court, or a party's counsel, or by affidavit of a party.

Eff. Sept. 1, 1997.

17.2. Nearest Available Court of Appeals

If a court of appeals is unable to take immediate action, the nearest court of appeals that is able to take immediate action may do so with the same effect as the other court. The nearest court of appeals is the one whose courthouse is nearest—measured by a straight line—the courthouse of the trial court.

Eff. Sept. 1, 1997.

17.3. Further Proceedings

After acting or refusing to act, the nearest court of appeals must promptly send a copy of its order, and the original or a copy of any document presented to it, to the other court, which will conduct any further proceedings in the matter.

Eff. Sept. 1, 1997.

Rule 18. Mandate

Notes and Comments

Comment to 1997 change: This is a new rule that combines the provisions of former Rules 43(g), 86, 186, 231, and 232.

18.1. Issuance

The clerk of the appellate court that rendered the judgment must issue a mandate in accordance with the judgment and send it to the clerk of the court to which it is directed and to all parties to the proceeding when one of the following periods expires:

(a) *In the Court of Appeals.*

(1) Ten days after the time has expired for filing a motion to extend time to file a petition for review or a petition for discretionary review if:

(A) no timely petition for review or petition for discretionary review has been filed;

(B) no timely filed motion to extend time to file a petition for review or petition for discretionary review is pending; and

(C) in a criminal case, the Court of Criminal Appeals has not granted review on its own initiative.

(2) Ten days after the time has expired for filing a motion to extend time to file a motion for rehearing of a denial, refusal, or dismissal of a petition for review, or a refusal or dismissal of a petition for discretionary review, if no timely filed motion for rehearing or motion to extend time is pending.

(b) *In the Supreme Court and the Court of Criminal Appeals.* Ten days after the time has expired for filing a motion to extend time to file a motion for rehearing if no timely filed motion for rehearing or motion to extend time is pending.

(c) *Agreement to Issue.* The mandate may be issued earlier if the parties so agree, or for good cause on the motion of a party.

Eff. Sept. 1, 1997. Amended by Supreme Court Dec. 23, 2002, eff. Jan. 1, 2003.

Notes and Comments

Comment to 2002 change: Subdivision 18.1 is amended consistent with the change in subdivision 12.6.

18.2. Stay of Mandate

A party may move to stay issuance of the mandate pending the United States Supreme Court's disposition of a petition for writ of certiorari. The motion must state the grounds for the petition and the circumstances requiring the stay. The appellate court authorized to issue the mandate may grant a stay if it finds that the grounds are substantial and that the petitioner or others would incur serious hardship from the mandate's issuance if the United States Supreme Court were later to reverse the judgment. In a criminal case, the stay will last for no more than 90 days, to permit the timely filing of a petition for writ of certiorari. After that period and others mentioned in this rule expire, the mandate will issue.

Eff. Sept. 1, 1997.

18.3. Trial Court Case Number

The mandate must state the trial court case number.

Eff. Sept. 1, 1997.

18.4. Filing of Mandate

The clerk receiving the mandate will file it with the case's other papers and note it on the docket.

Eff. Sept. 1, 1997.

18.5. Costs

The mandate will be issued without waiting for costs to be paid. If the Supreme Court declines to grant review, Supreme Court costs must be included in the court of appeals' mandate.

Eff. Sept. 1, 1997.

18.6. Mandate in Accelerated Appeals

The appellate court's judgment on an appeal from an interlocutory order takes effect when the mandate is issued. The court may issue the mandate with its judgment or delay the mandate until the appeal is finally disposed of. If the mandate is issued, any further proceeding in the trial court must conform to the mandate.

Eff. Sept. 1, 1997.

18.7. Recall of Mandate

If an appellate court vacates or modifies its judgment or order after issuing its mandate, the appellate clerk must promptly notify the clerk of the court to which the mandate was directed and all parties. The mandate will have no effect and a new mandate may be issued.

Eff. Sept. 1, 1997.

Rule 19. Plenary Power of the Courts of Appeals and Expiration of Term

Notes and Comments

Comment to 1997 change: This is a new rule except the provisions of former Rule 234 are incorporated in subdivision 19.4.

19.1. Plenary Power of Courts of Appeals

A court of appeals' plenary power over its judgment expires:

(a) 60 days after judgment if no timely filed motion for rehearing or en banc reconsideration, or timely filed motion to extend time to file such a motion, is then pending; or

(b) 30 days after the court overrules all timely filed motions for rehearing or en banc reconsideration, and all timely filed motions to extend time to file such a motion.

Eff. Sept. 1, 1997. Amended by Supreme Court Dec. 23, 2002, eff. Jan. 1, 2003; March 10, 2008, and Aug. 20, 2008, eff. Sept. 1, 2008. Approved by Court of Criminal Appeals Sept. 30, 2008, eff. Sept. 30, 2008.

Notes and Comments

Comment to 2002 change: Subdivision 19.1 amended to clarify that a motion for en banc reconsideration extends the court of appeals' plenary power in the same manner as a motion for rehearing addressed to the panel of justices who rendered the judgment or under consideration.

19.2. Plenary Power Continues After Petition Filed

In a civil case, the court of appeals retains plenary power to vacate or modify its judgment during the periods prescribed in 19.1 even if a party has filed a petition for review in the Supreme Court.

Eff. Sept. 1, 1997.

19.3. Proceedings After Plenary Power Expires

After its plenary power expires, the court cannot vacate or modify its judgment. But the court may:

(a) correct a clerical error in its judgment or opinion;

(b) issue and recall its mandate as these rules provide;

(c) enforce or suspend enforcement of its judgment as these rules or applicable law provide;

(d) order or modify the amount and type of security required to suspend a judgment, and decide the sufficiency of the sureties, under Rule 24[1]; and

(e) order its opinion published in accordance with Rule 47.[2]

Eff. Sept. 1, 1997.

[1] Vernon's Ann.Rules App.Proc., rule 24.1 et seq.
[2] Vernon's Ann.Rules App.Proc., rule 47.1 et seq.

19.4. Expiration of Term

The expiration of the appellate court's term does not affect the court's plenary power or its jurisdiction over a case that is pending when the court's term expires.

Eff. Sept. 1, 1997.

Rule 20. When Party Is Indigent

Notes and Comments

Comment to 1997 change: The rule is new and combines the provisions of former Rules 13(k), 40(a)(3), and 53(j). The procedure for proceeding in civil cases in an appellate court without advance payment of costs, in both appeals and original proceedings, is stated. The information that must be given in the affidavit is prescribed. An extension of time to file the affidavit is now available. The indigent party is no longer required to serve the court reporter, but must file the affidavit with the appropriate clerk who is to notify the court reporter. A contest need not be under oath. Provision is made for later ability to pay the costs. Nonsubstantive changes are made to the rule for criminal cases.

See also Civil Practice and Remedies Code § 13.003.

20.1. Civil Cases

(a) *Costs Defined.* In this rule, "costs" mean filing fees charged by the appellate court. Fees charged for preparation of the appellate record are governed by Texas Rule of Civil Procedure 145.

(b) *When a Statement Was Filed in the Trial Court.*

(1) *General Rule; Status in Trial Court Carries Forward.* A party who filed a Statement of Inability to Afford Payment of Court Costs in the trial court is not required to pay costs in the appellate court unless the trial court overruled the party's claim of indigence in an order that complies with Texas Rule of Civil Procedure 145. A party is not required to pay costs in the appellate court if the trial court ordered the party to pay partial costs or to pay costs in installments.

(2) *Establishing the Right to Proceed Under the General Rule.* To establish the right to proceed without payment of costs under (1), a party must communicate to the appellate court clerk in writing that the party is presumed indigent under this rule. In an appeal under Section Two of these rules, the applicability of the presumption should be stated in the notice of appeal and in the docketing statement.

(3) *Exception; Material Change in Circumstances.* An appellate court may permit a party who is not entitled to proceed under (1) to proceed without payment of costs if the party establishes that the party's financial circumstances have materially changed since the date of the trial court's order under Texas Rule of Civil Procedure 145.

(A) *Requirements.* The party must file a motion in the appellate court alleging that the party's financial circumstances have materially changed since the date of the trial court's order and a current Statement of Inability to Afford Payment of Court Costs that complies with Texas Rule of Civil Procedure 145. The Statement that was filed in the trial court does not meet the requirements of this rule.

(B) *Action by Appellate Court.* The appellate court may decide the motion based on the record or refer the motion to the trial court with instructions to hear evidence and issue findings of fact. If a motion is referred to the trial court, the appellate court must review the trial court's findings and the record of the hearing before ruling on the motion.

(c) *When No Statement Was Filed in the Trial Court.* An appellate court may permit a party who did not file a Statement of Inability to Afford Payment of Court Costs in the trial court to proceed without payment of costs. The court may require the party to file a Statement in the appellate court. If the court denies the party's request to proceed without payment of costs, it must do so in a written order.

Eff. Sept. 1, 1997. Amended by Supreme Court March 10, 2008, and Aug. 20, 2008, eff. Sept. 1, 2008. Approved by the Court of Criminal Appeals Sept. 30, 2008, eff. Sept. 30, 2008. Amended by Supreme Court Aug. 31, 2011, eff. Sept. 1, 2011; Feb. 13, 2012, eff. March 1, 2012; Aug. 31, 2016, eff. Sept. 1, 2016.

20.2. Criminal Cases

Within the time for perfecting the appeal, an appellant who is unable to pay for the appellate record may, by motion and affidavit, ask the trial court to have the appellate record furnished without charge. If after hearing the motion the court finds that the appellant cannot pay or give security for the appellate record, the court must order the reporter to transcribe the proceedings. When the court certifies that the appellate record has been furnished to the appellant, the reporter must be paid from the general funds of the county in which the offense was committed, in the amount set by the trial court.

Eff. Sept. 1, 1997.

SECTION TWO. APPEALS FROM TRIAL COURT JUDGMENTS AND ORDERS

Rule 21. New Trials in Criminal Cases

Notes and Comments

Comment to 1997 change: Former Rules 30, 31, and 32 are merged. Paragraph (b)(6) of former Rule 30 is deleted because the rule-making authori-

ty of the Court of Criminal Appeals was withdrawn. *See* Code of Criminal Procedure article 40.001. Other nonsubstantive changes are made.

21.1. Definitions

(a) *New trial* means the rehearing of a criminal action after the trial court has, on the defendant's motion, set aside a finding or verdict of guilt.

(b) *New trial on punishment* means a new hearing of the punishment stage of a criminal action after the trial court has, on the defendant's motion, set aside an assessment of punishment without setting aside a finding or verdict of guilt.

Eff. Sept. 1, 1997. Amended by Court of Criminal Appeals Dec. 13, 2006, eff. Jan. 1, 2007.

21.2. When Motion for New Trial Required

A motion for new trial is a prerequisite to presenting a point of error on appeal only when necessary to adduce facts not in the record.

Eff. Sept. 1, 1997.

21.3. Grounds

The defendant must be granted a new trial, or a new trial on punishment, for any of the following reasons:

(a) except in a misdemeanor case in which the maximum possible punishment is a fine, when the defendant has been unlawfully tried in absentia or has been denied counsel;

(b) when the court has misdirected the jury about the law or has committed some other material error likely to injure the defendant's rights;

(c) when the verdict has been decided by lot or in any manner other than a fair expression of the jurors' opinion;

(d) when a juror has been bribed to convict or has been guilty of any other corrupt conduct;

(e) when a material defense witness has been kept from court by force, threats, or fraud, or when evidence tending to establish the defendant's innocence has been intentionally destroyed or withheld, thus preventing its production at trial;

(f) when, after retiring to deliberate, the jury has received other evidence; when a juror has talked with anyone about the case; or when a juror became so intoxicated that his or her vote was probably influenced as a result;

(g) when the jury has engaged in such misconduct that the defendant did not receive a fair and impartial trial; or

(h) when the verdict is contrary to the law and the evidence.

Eff. Sept. 1, 1997. Amended by Court of Criminal Appeals Dec. 13, 2006, eff. Jan. 1, 2007.

21.4. Time to File and Amend Motion

(a) *To File.* The defendant may file a motion for new trial before, but no later than 30 days after, the date when the trial court imposes or suspends sentence in open court.

(b) *To Amend.* Within 30 days after the date when the trial court imposes or suspends sentence in open court but before the court overrules any preceding motion for new trial, a defendant may, without leave of court, file one or more amended motions for new trial.

Eff. Sept. 1, 1997.

21.5. State May Controvert; Effect

The State may oppose in writing any reason the defendant sets forth in the motion for new trial. The State's having opposed a motion for new trial does not affect a defendant's responsibilities under 21.6.

Eff. Sept. 1, 1997.

21.6. Time to Present

The defendant must present the motion for new trial to the trial court within 10 days of filing it, unless the trial court in its discretion permits it to be presented and heard within 75 days from the date when the court imposes or suspends sentence in open court.

Eff. Sept. 1, 1997.

21.7. Types of Evidence Allowed at Hearing

The court may receive evidence by affidavit or otherwise.

Eff. Sept. 1, 1997.

21.8. Court's Ruling

(a) *Time to Rule.* The court must rule on a motion for new trial within 75 days after imposing or suspending sentence in open court.

(b) *Ruling.* In ruling on a motion for new trial, the court may make oral or written findings of fact. The granting of a motion for new trial must be accomplished by written order. A docket entry does not constitute a written order.

(c) *Failure to Rule.* A motion not timely ruled on by written order will be deemed denied when the period prescribed in (a) expires.

Eff. Sept. 1, 1997. Amended by Court of Criminal Appeals Dec. 13, 2006, eff. Jan. 1, 2007.

21.9. Granting a New Trial

(a) A court must grant a new trial when it has found a meritorious ground for new trial, but a court must grant only a new trial on punishment when it has found a ground that affected only the assessment of punishment.

(b) Granting a new trial restores the case to its position before the former trial, including, at any party's option, arraignment or pretrial proceedings initiated by that party.

(c) Granting a new trial on punishment restores the case to its position after the defendant was found guilty. Unless the defendant, State, and trial court all agree to a change, punishment in a new trial shall be assessed in accordance with the defendant's original election under article 37.07, § 2(b) of the Code of Criminal Procedure.

(d) A finding or verdict of guilt in the former trial must not be regarded as a presumption of guilt, nor may it be alluded to in the presence of the jury that hears the case on retrial of guilt. A finding of fact or an assessment of punishment in the former trial may not be alluded to in the presence of the jury that hears the case on retrial of punishment.

Eff. Sept. 1, 1997. Amended by Court of Criminal Appeals Dec. 13, 2006, eff. Jan. 1, 2007.

Rule 22. Arrest of Judgment in Criminal Cases

Notes and Comments

Comment to 1997 change: Former Rules 33, 34, and 35 are merged without substantive change.

22.1. Definition

Motion in arrest of judgment means a defendant's oral or written suggestion that, for reasons stated in the motion, the judgment rendered against the defendant was contrary to law. Such a motion is made in the trial court.

Eff. Sept. 1, 1997.

22.2. Grounds

The motion may be based on any of the following grounds:

(a) that the indictment or information is subject to an exception on substantive grounds;

(b) that in relation to the indictment or information a verdict is substantively defective; or

(c) that the judgment is invalid for some other reason.

Eff. Sept. 1, 1997.

22.3. Time to File Motion

A defendant may file a motion in arrest of judgment before, but no later than 30 days after, the date when the trial court imposes or suspends sentence in open court.

Eff. Sept. 1, 1997.

22.4. Court's Ruling

(a) *Time to Rule; Form of Ruling.* The court must rule on a motion in arrest of judgment within 75 days after imposing or suspending sentence in open court. The ruling may be oral or in writing.

(b) *Failure to Rule.* A motion not timely ruled on will be deemed denied when the period prescribed in (a) expires.

Eff. Sept. 1, 1997.

22.5. Effect of Denying

For purposes of the defendant's giving notice of appeal, an order denying a motion in arrest of judgment will be considered an order denying a motion for new trial.

Eff. Sept. 1, 1997.

22.6. Effect of Granting

(a) *Defendant Restored.* If judgment is arrested, the defendant is restored to the position that he or she had before the indictment or information was presented.

(b) *Defendant Discharged or Remanded.* If the judgment is arrested, the defendant will be discharged. But the trial court may remand the defendant to custody or fix bail if the court determines, from the evidence adduced at trial, that the defendant may be convicted on a proper indictment or information, or on a proper verdict in relation to the indictment or information.

Eff. Sept. 1, 1997.

Rule 23. Nunc Pro Tunc Proceedings in Criminal Cases

Notes and Comments

Comment to 1997 change: This is former Rule 36. The rule is amended without substantive change.

23.1. Judgment and Sentence

Unless the trial court has granted a new trial or arrested the judgment, or unless the defendant has appealed, a failure to render judgment and pronounce sentence may be corrected at any time by the court's doing so.

Eff. Sept. 1, 1997.

23.2. Credit on Sentence

When sentence is pronounced, the trial court must give the defendant credit on that sentence for:

(a) all time the defendant has been confined since the time when judgment and sentence should have been entered and pronounced; and

(b) all time between the defendant's arrest and confinement to the time when judgment and sentence should have been entered and pronounced.

Eff. Sept. 1, 1997.

Rule 24. Suspension of Enforcement of Judgment Pending Appeal in Civil Cases

Notes and Comments

Comment to 1997 change: Former Rules 47, 48, and 49 are merged. The rule is substantially revised. Paragraph 24.1(a) now provides for superseding the judgment by agreement. Paragraph 24.1(c) is taken from former Rule 48 and provides for a deposit in lieu of the bond, including specific provisions for the release of the deposit. Paragraph 24.1(d) provides the conditions for the surety to honor the bond and for the deposit to be paid to the judgment creditor. In subdivision 24.2, the provisions for determining the amount of the bond or deposit are simplified. All provisions regarding superseding a judgment for an interest in property are merged into subparagraph 24.2(a)(2). The procedure for allowing security in a lesser amount is moved to paragraph 24.2(b) and is made applicable to all judgments. Subdivision 24.4 is taken from former Rule 49. The procedure for appellate review is more precisely stated.

24.1. Suspension of Enforcement

(a) *Methods.* Unless the law or these rules provide otherwise, a judgment debtor may supersede the judgment by:

(1) filing with the trial court clerk a written agreement with the judgment creditor for suspending enforcement of the judgment;

(2) filing with the trial court clerk a good and sufficient bond;

(3) making a deposit with the trial court clerk in lieu of a bond; or

(4) providing alternate security ordered by the court.

(b) *Bonds.*

(1) A bond must be:

(A) in the amount required by 24.2;

(B) payable to the judgment creditor;

(C) signed by the judgment debtor or the debtor's agent;

(D) signed by a sufficient surety or sureties as obligors; and

(E) conditioned as required by (d).

(2) To be effective a bond must be approved by the trial court clerk. On motion of any party, the trial court will review the bond.

(c) *Deposit in Lieu of Bond.*

(1) Types of Deposits. Instead of filing a surety bond, a party may deposit with the trial court clerk:

(A) cash;

(B) a cashier's check payable to the clerk, drawn on any federally insured and federally or state-chartered bank or savings-and-loan association; or

(C) with leave of court, a negotiable obligation of the federal government or of any federally insured and federally or state-chartered bank or savings-and-loan association.

(2) Amount of Deposit. The deposit must be in the amount required by 24.2.

(3) Clerk's Duties; Interest. The clerk must promptly deposit any cash or a cashier's check in accordance with law. The clerk must hold the deposit until the conditions of liability in (d) are extinguished. The clerk must then release any remaining funds in the deposit to the judgment debtor.

(d) *Conditions of Liability.* The surety or sureties on a bond, any deposit in lieu of a bond, or any alternate security ordered by the court is subject to liability for all damages and costs that may be awarded against the debtor—up to the amount of the bond, deposit, or security—if:

(1) the debtor does not perfect an appeal or the debtor's appeal is dismissed, and the debtor does not perform the trial court's judgment;

(2) the debtor does not perform an adverse judgment final on appeal; or

(3) the judgment is for the recovery of an interest in real or personal property, and the debtor does not pay the creditor the value of the property interest's rent or revenue during the pendency of the appeal.

(e) *Orders of Trial Court.* The trial court may make any order necessary to adequately protect the judgment creditor against loss or damage that the appeal might cause.

(f) *Effect of Supersedeas.* Enforcement of a judgment must be suspended if the judgment is superseded. Enforcement begun before the judgment is superseded must cease when the judgment is superseded. If execution has been issued, the clerk will promptly issue a writ of supersedeas.

Eff. Sept. 1, 1997.

24.2. Amount of Bond, Deposit or Security

(a) *Type of Judgment.*

(1) For Recovery of Money. When the judgment is for money, the amount of the bond, deposit, or security must equal the sum of compensatory damages awarded in the judgment, interest for the estimated duration of the appeal, and costs awarded in the judgment. But the amount must not exceed the lesser of:

(A) 50 percent of the judgment debtor's current net worth; or

(B) 25 million dollars.

(2) For Recovery of Property. When the judgment is for the recovery of an interest in real or personal property, the trial court will determine the type of security that the judgment debtor must post. The amount of that security must be at least:

(A) the value of the property interest's rent or revenue, if the property interest is real; or

(B) the value of the property interest on the date when the court rendered judgment, if the property interest is personal.

(3) Other Judgment. When the judgment is for something other than money or an interest in property, the trial court must set the amount and type of security that the judgment debtor must post. The security must adequately protect the judgment creditor against loss or damage that the appeal might cause. But the trial court may decline to permit the judgment to be superseded if the judgment creditor posts security ordered by the trial court in an amount and type that will secure the judgment debtor against any loss or damage caused

by the relief granted the judgment creditor if an appellate court determines, on final disposition, that that relief was improper.

(4) *Conservatorship or Custody.* When the judgment involves the conservatorship or custody of a minor or other person under legal disability, enforcement of the judgment will not be suspended, with or without security, unless ordered by the trial court. But upon a proper showing, the appellate court may suspend enforcement of the judgment with or without security.

(5) *For a Governmental Entity.* When a judgment in favor of a governmental entity in its governmental capacity is one in which the entity has no pecuniary interest, the trial court must determine whether to suspend enforcement, with or without security, taking into account the harm that is likely to result to the judgment debtor if enforcement is not suspended, and the harm that is likely to result to others if enforcement is suspended. The appellate court may review the trial court's determination and suspend enforcement of the judgment, with or without security, or refuse to suspend the judgment. If security is required, recovery is limited to the governmental entity's actual damages resulting from suspension of the judgment.

(b) *Lesser Amount.* The trial court must lower the amount of security required by (a) to an amount that will not cause the judgment debtor substantial economic harm if, after notice to all parties and a hearing, the court finds that posting a bond, deposit, or security in the amount required by (a) is likely to cause the judgment debtor substantial economic harm.

(c) *Determination of Net Worth.*

(1) Judgment Debtor's Affidavit Required; Contents; Prima Facie Evidence. A judgment debtor who provides a bond, deposit, or security under (a)(1)(A) in an amount based on the debtor's net worth must simultaneously file with the trial court clerk an affidavit that states the debtor's net worth and states complete, detailed information concerning the debtor's assets and liabilities from which net worth can be ascertained. An affidavit that meets these requirements is prima facie evidence of the debtor's net worth for the purpose of establishing the amount of the bond, deposit, or security required to suspend enforcement of the judgment. A trial court clerk must receive and file a net-worth affidavit tendered for filing by a judgment debtor.

(2) Contest; Discovery. A judgment creditor may file a contest to the debtor's claimed net worth.

The contest need not be sworn. The creditor may conduct reasonable discovery concerning the judgment debtor's net worth.

(3) Hearing; Burden of Proof; Findings; Additional Security. The trial court must hear a judgment creditor's contest of the judgment debtor's claimed net worth promptly after any discovery has been completed. The judgment debtor has the burden of proving net worth. The trial court must issue an order that states the debtor's net worth and states with particularity the factual basis for that determination. If the trial court orders additional or other security to supersede the judgment, the enforcement of the judgment will be suspended for twenty days after the trial court's order. If the judgment debtor does not comply with the order within that period, the judgment may be enforced against the judgment debtor.

(d) *Injunction.* The trial court may enjoin the judgment debtor from dissipating or transferring assets to avoid satisfaction of the judgment, but the trial court may not make any order that interferes with the judgment debtor's use, transfer, conveyance, or dissipation of assets in the normal course of business.

Eff. Sept. 1, 1997. Amended by Supreme Court Aug. 29, 2003 and Sept. 10, 2003, eff. Sept. 1, 2003; March 10, 2008, and Aug. 20, 2008, eff. Sept. 1, 2008. Approved by Court of Criminal Appeals Sept. 30, 2008, eff. Sept. 30, 2008.

24.3. Continuing Trial Court Jurisdiction; Duties of Judgment Debtor

(a) *Continuing Jurisdiction.* Even after the trial court's plenary power expires, the trial court has continuing jurisdiction to do the following:

(1) order the amount and type of security and decide the sufficiency of sureties; and

(2) if circumstances change, modify the amount or type of security required to continue the suspension of a judgment's execution.

(b) *Duties of Judgment Debtor.* If, after jurisdiction attaches in an appellate court, the trial court orders or modifies the security or decides the sufficiency of sureties, the judgment debtor must notify the appellate court of the trial court's action.

Eff. Sept. 1, 1997.

24.4. Appellate Review

(a) *Motions; Review.* A party may seek review of the trial court's ruling by motion filed in the court of appeals with jurisdiction or potential jurisdiction over the appeal from the judgment in the case. A party may seek review of the court of appeals' ruling on the motion by petition for writ of mandamus in the Supreme Court. The appellate court may review:

(1) the sufficiency or excessiveness of the amount of security, but when the judgment is for money, the appellate court must not modify the amount of security to exceed the limits imposed by Rule 24.2(a)(1);

(2) the sureties on any bond;

(3) the type of security;

(4) the determination whether to permit suspension of enforcement; and

(5) the trial court's exercise of discretion under Rule 24.3(a).

(b) *Grounds of Review.* Review may be based both on conditions as they existed at the time the trial court signed an order, and on changes in those conditions afterward.

(c) *Temporary Orders.* The appellate court may issue any temporary orders necessary to preserve the parties' rights.

(d) *Action by Appellate Court.* The motion must be heard at the earliest practicable time. The appellate court may require that the amount of a bond, deposit, or other security be increased or decreased, and that another bond, deposit, or security be provided and approved by the trial court clerk. The appellate court may require other changes in the trial court order. The appellate court may remand to the trial court for entry of findings of fact or for the taking of evidence.

(e) *Effect of Ruling.* If the appellate court orders additional or other security to supersede the judgment, enforcement will be suspended for 20 days after the appellate court's order. If the judgment debtor does not comply with the order within that period, the judgment may be enforced. When any additional bond, deposit, or security has been filed, the trial court clerk must notify the appellate court. The posting of additional security will not release the previously posted security or affect any alternative security arrangements that the judgment debtor previously made unless specifically ordered by the appellate court.

Eff. Sept. 1, 1997. Amended by Supreme Court Aug. 29, 2003, eff. Sept. 1, 2003; March 10, 2008, and Aug. 20, 2008, eff. Sept. 1, 2008. Approved by Court of Criminal Appeals Sept. 30, 2008, eff. Sept. 30, 2008.

Rule 25. Perfecting Appeal

Notes and Comments

Comment on 1997 change: This is former Rule 40. In civil cases, the requirement of an appeal bond is repealed. Appeal is perfected by filing a notice of appeal. A notice must be filed by any party seeking to alter the trial court's judgment. The restricted appeal—formerly the appeal by writ of error—is perfected by filing a notice of appeal in the trial court as in other appeals. The contents of the notice of appeal is prescribed. The notice of limitation of appeal is repealed. In criminal cases, the rule is amended to apply to notices by the State, and to refer to additional statutory requirements for the State's notice. In felony cases in which the defendant waived trial by jury, pleaded guilty or nolo contendere, and received a punishment that did not exceed what the defendant agreed to in a plea bargain, the rule is amended to make clear that regardless of when the alleged error occurred, an appeal must be based on a jurisdictional defect or a written motion ruled on before trial, or be with the permission of the trial court.

25.1. Civil Cases

(a) *Notice of Appeal.* An appeal is perfected when a written notice of appeal is filed with the trial court clerk. If a notice of appeal is mistakenly filed with the appellate court, the notice is deemed to have been filed the same day with the trial court clerk, and the appellate clerk must immediately send the trial court clerk a copy of the notice.

(b) *Jurisdiction of Appellate Court.* The filing of a notice of appeal by any party invokes the appellate court's jurisdiction over all parties to the trial court's judgment or order appealed from. Any party's failure to take any other step required by these rules, including the failure of another party to perfect an appeal under (c), does not deprive the appellate court of jurisdiction but is ground only for the appellate court to act appropriately, including dismissing the appeal.

(c) *Who Must File Notice.* A party who seeks to alter the trial court's judgment or other appealable order must file a notice of appeal. Parties whose interests are aligned may file a joint notice of appeal. The appellate court may not grant a party who does not file a notice of appeal more favorable relief than did the trial court except for just cause.

(d) *Contents of Notice.* The notice of appeal must:

(1) identify the trial court and state the case's trial court number and style;

(2) state the date of the judgment or order appealed from;

(3) state that the party desires to appeal;

(4) state the court to which the appeal is taken unless the appeal is to either the First or Fourteenth Court of Appeals, in which case the notice must state that the appeal is to either of those courts;

(5) state the name of each party filing the notice;

(6) in an accelerated appeal, state that the appeal is accelerated and state whether it is a parental termination or child protection case, as defined in Rule 28.4;

(7) in a restricted appeal:

(A) state that the appellant is a party affected by the trial court's judgment but did not participate—either in person or through counsel—in the hearing that resulted in the judgment complained of;

(B) state that the appellant did not timely file either a postjudgment motion, request for findings of fact and conclusions of law, or notice of appeal; and

(C) be verified by the appellant if the appellant does not have counsel.

(8) state, if applicable, that the appellant is presumed indigent and may proceed without paying costs under Rule 20.1.

(e) *Service of Notice.* The notice of appeal must be served on all parties to the trial court's final judgment or, in an interlocutory appeal, on all parties to the trial court proceeding.

(f) *Clerk's Duties.* The trial court clerk must immediately send a copy of the notice of appeal to the appellate court clerk and to the court reporter or court reporters responsible for preparing the reporter's record.

(g) *Amending the Notice.* An amended notice of appeal correcting a defect or omission in an earlier filed notice may be filed in the appellate court at any time before the appellant's brief is filed. The amended notice is subject to being struck for cause on the motion of any party affected by the amended notice. After the appellant's brief is filed, the notice may be amended only on leave of the appellate court and on such terms as the court may prescribe.

(h) *Enforcement of Judgment Not Suspended by Appeal.* The filing of a notice of appeal does not suspend enforcement of the judgment. Enforcement of the judgment may proceed unless:

(1) the judgment is superseded in accordance with Rule 24[1], or

(2) the appellant is entitled to supersede the judgment without security by filing a notice of appeal.

Eff. Sept. 1, 1997. Amended by Supreme Court Aug. 31, 2011, eff. Sept. 1, 2011; Feb. 13, 2012, eff. March 1, 2012; Aug. 31, 2016, eff. Sept. 1, 2016.

[1] Vernon's Ann.Rules App.Proc., rule 24.1 et seq.

25.2. Criminal Cases

(a) *Rights to Appeal.*

(1) Of the State. The State is entitled to appeal a court's order in a criminal case as provided by Code of Criminal Procedure article 44.01.

(2) Of the Defendant. A defendant in a criminal case has the right of appeal under Code of Criminal Procedure article 44.02 and these rules. The trial court shall enter a certification of the defendant's right of appeal each time it enters a judgment of guilt or other appealable order. In a plea bargain case—that is, a case in which a defendant's plea was guilty or nolo contendere and the punishment did not exceed the punishment recommended by the prosecutor and agreed to by the defendant—a defendant may appeal only:

(A) those matters that were raised by written motion filed and ruled on before trial, or

(B) after getting the trial court's permission to appeal.

(b) *Perfection of Appeal.* In a criminal case, appeal is perfected by timely filing a sufficient notice of appeal. In a death-penalty case it is unnecessary to file a notice of appeal, but, in every death-penalty case, the clerk of the trial court shall file a notice of conviction with the Court of Criminal Appeals within thirty days after the defendant is sentenced to death.

(c) *Form and Sufficiency of Notice.*

(1) Notice must be given in writing and filed with the trial court clerk. If the notice of appeal is received in the court of appeals, the clerk of that court shall immediately record on the notice the date that it was received and send the notice to the trial court clerk.

(2) Notice is sufficient if it shows the party's desire to appeal from the judgment or other appealable order, and, if the State is the appellant, the notice complies with Code of Criminal Procedure article 44.01.

(d) *Certification of Defendant's Rights of Appeal.* If the defendant is the appellant, the record must include the trial court's certification of the defendant's right of appeal under Rule 25.2(a)(2). The certification shall include a notice that the defendant has been informed of his rights concerning an appeal, as well as any right to file a *pro se* petition for discretionary review. This notification shall be signed by the defendant, with a copy given to him. The certification should be part of the record when notice is filed, but may be added by timely amendment or supplementation under this rule or Rule 34.5(c)(1) or Rule 37.1 or by order of the appellate court under Rule 34.5(c)(2). The appeal must be dismissed if a certification that shows the defendant has the right of appeal has not been made part of the record under these rules.

(e) *Clerk's Duties.* The trial court clerk must note on the copies of the notice of appeal and the trial court's certification of the defendant's right of appeal the case number and the date when each was filed. The clerk must then immediately send one copy of each to the clerk of the appropriate court of appeals and, if the defendant is the appellant, one copy of each to the State's attorney.

(f) *Amending the Notice or Certification.* An amended notice of appeal or trial court's certification of the defendant's right of appeal correcting a defect or omission in an earlier filed notice or certification, including a defect in the notification of the defendant's appellate rights, may be filed in the appellate court in accordance with Rule 37.1, or at any time before the appealing party's brief is filed if the court of appeals has not used Rule 37.1. The amended notice or certification is subject to being struck for cause on the motion of any party affected by the amended notice or certification. After the appealing party's brief is filed, the notice or certification may be amended only on leave of the appellate court and on such terms as the court may prescribe.

(g) *Effect of Appeal.* Once the record has been filed in the appellate court, all further proceedings in the trial court—except as provided otherwise by law or by these rules—will be suspended until the trial court receives the appellate-court mandate.

(h) *Advice of Right of Appeal.* When a court enters a judgment or other appealable order and the defendant has a right of appeal, the court (orally or in writing) shall advise the defendant of his right of appeal and of the requirements for timely filing a sufficient notice of appeal.

Eff. Sept. 1, 1997. Amended by Supreme Court Dec. 23, 2002, eff. Jan. 1, 2003; Aug. 20, 2008, eff. Sept. 1, 2008; Court of Criminal Appeals Dec. 13, 2006, eff. Jan. 1, 2007; May 2, 2007 and Aug. 20, 2007, eff. Sept. 1, 2007; June 30, 2008, eff. Sept. 1, 2008; Sept. 30, 2008, eff. Sept. 30, 2008.

Notes and Comments

Comment to 2002 change: Rule 25.2, for criminal cases, is amended. Subdivision 25.2(a) states the parties' rights of appeal that are established by Code of Criminal Procedure article 44.01 and by article 44.02, the proviso of which was repealed when rulemaking power was given to the Court of Criminal Appeals. Subdivision 25.2(b) is given the requirement that a notice of appeal be in "sufficient" form, which codifies the decisional law. The requirement in former subdivision 25.2(b)(3) that a plea-bargaining appellant's notice of appeal specify the right of appeal is replaced by a requirement in subdivision 25.2(d) that the trial court certify the defendant's right of appeal in every case in which a judgment or other appealable order is entered. The certificate should be signed at the time the judgment or other appealable order is pronounced. The form of certification of the defendant's right of appeal is provided in an appendix to these rules. If the record does not include the trial court's certification that the defendant has the right of appeal, the appeal must be dismissed. If a sufficient notice of appeal or certification is not filed after the appellate court deals with the defect (see Rules 34.5(c) and 37.1), preparation of an appellate record and representation by an appointed attorney may cease.

Rule 26. Time to Perfect Appeal

Notes and Comments

Comment to 1997 change: This is former Rule 41. All times for perfecting appeal in civil cases—including the time for perfecting a restricted appeal—are stated. An extension of time is available for all appeals. The provisions of former Rule 41(c) regarding prematurely filed documents are moved to Rule 27. Nonsubstantive changes are made in the rule for criminal cases.

26.1. Civil Cases

The notice of appeal must be filed within 30 days after the judgment is signed, except as follows:

(a) the notice of appeal must be filed within 90 days after the judgment is signed if any party timely files:

    (1) a motion for new trial;

    (2) a motion to modify the judgment;

    (3) a motion to reinstate under Texas Rule of Civil Procedure 165a; or

    (4) a request for findings of fact and conclusions of law if findings and conclusions either are required by the Rules of Civil Procedure or, if not required, could properly be considered by the appellate court;

(b) in an accelerated appeal, the notice of appeal must be filed within 20 days after the judgment or order is signed;

(c) in a restricted appeal, the notice of appeal must be filed within six months after the judgment or order is signed; and

(d) if any party timely files a notice of appeal, another party may file a notice of appeal within the applicable period stated above or 14 days after the first filed notice of appeal, whichever is later.

Eff. Sept. 1, 1997.

26.2. Criminal Cases

(a) *By the Defendant.* The notice of appeal must be filed:

(1) within 30 days after the day sentence is imposed or suspended in open court, or after the day the trial court enters an appealable order; or

(2) within 90 days after the day sentence is imposed or suspended in open court if the defendant timely files a motion for new trial.

(b) *By the State.* The notice of appeal must be filed within 20 days after the day the trial court enters the order, ruling, or sentence to be appealed.

Eff. Sept. 1, 1997. Amended by Court of Criminal Appeals March 4, 2008, and June 30, 2008, eff. Sept. 1, 2008 Sept. 30, 2008, eff. Sept. 30, 2008. Amended by Supreme Court March 10, 2008, and Aug. 20, 2008, eff. Sept. 1, 2008.

26.3. Extension of Time

The appellate court may extend the time to file the notice of appeal if, within 15 days after the deadline for filing the notice of appeal, the party:

(a) files in the trial court the notice of appeal; and

(b) files in the appellate court a motion complying with Rule 10.5(b).

Eff. Sept. 1, 1997.

Rule 27. Premature Filings

Notes and Comments

Comment to 1997 change: This rule is new and combines the provisions of former Rules 41(c) and 58.

27.1. Prematurely Filed Notice of Appeal

(a) *Civil Cases.* In a civil case, a prematurely filed notice of appeal is effective and deemed filed on the day of, but after, the event that begins the period for perfecting the appeal.

(b) *Criminal Cases.* In a criminal case, a prematurely filed notice of appeal is effective and deemed filed on the same day, but after, sentence is imposed or suspended in open court, or the appealable order is

signed by the trial court. But a notice of appeal is not effective if filed before the trial court makes a finding of guilt or receives a jury verdict.

Eff. Sept. 1, 1997.

27.2. Other Premature Actions

The appellate court may treat actions taken before an appealable order is signed as relating to an appeal of that order and give them effect as if they had been taken after the order was signed. The appellate court may allow an appealed order that is not final to be modified so as to be made final and may allow the modified order and all proceedings relating to it to be included in a supplemental record.

Eff. Sept. 1, 1997.

27.3. If Appealed Order Modified or Vacated

After an order or judgment in a civil case has been appealed, if the trial court modifies the order or judgment, or if the trial court vacates the order or judgment and replaces it with another appealable order or judgment, the appellate court must treat the appeal as from the subsequent order or judgment and may treat actions relating to the appeal of the first order or judgment as relating to the appeal of the subsequent order or judgment. The subsequent order or judgment and actions relating to it may be included in the original or supplemental record. Any party may nonetheless appeal from the subsequent order or judgment.

Eff. Sept. 1, 1997.

Rule 28. Accelerated, Agreed, and Permissive Appeals in Civil Cases

Notes and Comments

Comment to 1997 change: This is former Rule 42. A motion for new trial is now permitted in an appeal from an interlocutory order, but it does not extend the time to perfect appeal. The deadlines for filing items in an accelerated appeal are moved to other rules. *See* Rules 26.1, 35.1 and 38.6. Former Rule 42(b), regarding discretionary acceleration, is omitted as unnecessary. *See* Rule 40.1. The provision in former Rule 42(c) allowing the court to shorten the time to file briefs is omitted as unnecessary. *See* Rule 38.6.

28.1. Accelerated Appeal

(a) *Types of Accelerated Appeals.* Appeals from interlocutory orders (when allowed by statute), appeals in quo warranto proceedings, appeals required by statute to be accelerated or expedited, and appeals required by law to be filed or perfected within less than 30 days after the date of the order or judgment being appealed are accelerated appeals.

(b) *Perfection of Accelerated Appeal.* Unless otherwise provided by statute, an accelerated appeal is perfected by filing a notice of appeal in compliance with Rule 25.1 within the time allowed by Rule 26.1(b) or as extended by Rule 26.3. Filing a motion for new trial, any other post-trial motion, or a request for findings of fact will not extend the time to perfect an accelerated appeal.

(c) *Appeals of Interlocutory Orders.* The trial court need not file findings of fact and conclusions of law but may do so within 30 days after the order is signed.

(d) *Quo Warranto Appeals.* The trial court may grant a motion for new trial timely filed under Texas Rule of Civil Procedure 329b(a)–(b) until 50 days after the trial court's final judgment is signed. If not determined by signed written order within that period, the motion will be deemed overruled by operation of law on expiration of that period.

(e) *Record and Briefs.* In lieu of the clerk's record, the appellate court may hear an accelerated appeal on the original papers forwarded by the trial court or on sworn and uncontroverted copies of those papers. The appellate court may allow the case to be submitted without briefs. The deadlines and procedures for filing the record and briefs in an accelerated appeal are provided in Rules 35.1 and 38.6.

Eff. Sept. 1, 1997. Amended by Supreme Court March 10, 2008, Aug. 20, 2008, and Aug. 25, 2008, eff. Sept. 1, 2008. Approved by Court of Criminal Appeals Sept. 30, 2008, eff. Sept. 30, 2008. Amended by Supreme Court Sept. 9, 2011, eff. Sept. 9, 2011.

28.2. Agreed Interlocutory Appeals in Civil Cases

(a) *Perfecting Appeal.* An agreed appeal of an interlocutory order permitted by statute must be perfected as provided in Rule 25.1. The notice of appeal must be filed no later than the 20th day after the date the trial court signs a written order granting permission to appeal, unless the court of appeals extends the time for filing pursuant to Rule 26.3.

(b) *Other Requirements.* In addition to perfecting appeal, the appellant must file with the clerk of the appellate court a docketing statement as provided in Rule 32.1 and pay to the clerk of the appellate court all required fees authorized to be collected by the clerk.

(c) *Contents of Notice.* The notice of accelerated appeal must contain, in addition to the items required by Rule 25.1(d), the following:

(1) a list of the names of all parties to the trial court proceeding and the names, addresses, and telefax numbers of all trial and appellate counsel;

(2) a copy of the trial court's order granting permission to appeal;

(3) a copy of the trial court order appealed from;

(4) a statement that all parties to the trial court proceeding agreed to the trial court's order granting permission to appeal;

(5) a statement that all parties to the trial court proceeding agreed that the order granting permission to appeal involves a controlling question of law as to which there is a substantial ground for difference of opinion;

(6) a brief statement of the issues or points presented; and

(7) a concise explanation of how an immediate appeal may materially advance the ultimate termination of the litigation.

(d) *Determination of Jurisdiction.* If the court of appeals determines that a notice of appeal filed under this rule does not demonstrate the court's jurisdiction, it may order the appellant to file an amended notice of appeal. On a party's motion or its own initiative, the court of appeals may also order the appellant or any other party to file briefing addressing whether the appeal meets the statutory requirements, and may direct the parties to file supporting evidence. If, after providing an opportunity to file an amended notice of appeal or briefing addressing potential jurisdictional defects, the court of appeals concludes that a jurisdictional defect exists, it may dismiss the appeal for want of jurisdiction at any stage of the appeal.

(e) *Record; Briefs.* The rules governing the filing of the appellate record and briefs in accelerated appeals apply. A party may address in its brief any issues related to the court of appeals' jurisdiction, including whether the appeal meets the statutory requirements.

(f) *No Automatic Stay of Proceedings in Trial Court.* An agreed appeal of an interlocutory order permitted by statute does not stay proceedings in the trial court except as agreed by the parties and ordered by the trial court or the court of appeals.

Eff. Sept. 1, 1997. Amended by Supreme Court March 10, 2008, and Aug. 20, 2008, eff. Sept. 1, 2008. Approved by Court of Criminal Appeals Sept. 30, 2008, eff. Sept. 30, 2008.

28.3. Permissive Appeals in Civil Cases

(a) *Petition Required.* When a trial court has permitted an appeal from an interlocutory order that would not otherwise be appealable, a party seeking to appeal must petition the court of appeals for permission to appeal.

(b) *Where Filed.* The petition must be filed with the clerk of the court of appeals having appellate jurisdiction over the action in which the order to be appealed is issued. The First and Fourteenth Courts of Appeals must determine in which of those two courts a petition will be filed.

(c) *When Filed.* The petition must be filed within 15 days after the order to be appealed is signed. If the order is amended by the trial court, either on its own or in response to a party's motion, to include the court's permission to appeal, the time to petition the court of appeals runs from the date the amended order is signed.

(d) *Extension of Time to File Petition.* The court of appeals may extend the time to file the petition if the party:

(1) files the petition within 15 days after the deadline, and

(2) files a motion complying with Rule 10.5(b).

(e) *Contents.* The petition must:

(1) contain the information required by Rule 25.1(d) to be included in a notice of appeal:

(2) attach a copy of the order from which appeal is sought:

(3) contain a table of contents, index of authorities, issues presented, and a statement of facts; and

(4) argue clearly and concisely why the order to be appealed involves a controlling question of law as to which there is a substantial ground for difference of opinion and how an immediate appeal from the order may materially advance the ultimate termination of the litigation.

(f) *Response; Reply; Cross–Petition; Time for Filing.* If any party timely files a petition, any other party may file a response or a cross-petition within 10 days. A party may file a response to a cross-petition within 10 days of the date the cross-petition is filed. A petitioner or cross-petitioner may reply to any matter in a response within 7 days of the date the response is filed. The court of appeals may extend the time to file a response, reply, and cross-petition.

(g) *Length of Petition, Cross–Petition, Response, and Reply.* A petition, cross-petition, response, and reply must comply with the length limitations in Rule 9.4(i)(2)(D)–(E).

(h) *Service.* A petition, cross-petition, response, and reply must be served on all parties to the trial court proceeding.

(i) *Docketing Statement.* Upon filing the petition, the petitioner must file the docketing statement required by Rule 32.1.

(j) *Time for Determination.* Unless the court of appeals orders otherwise, a petition, and any cross-petition, response, and reply, will be determined without oral argument, no earlier than 10 days after the petition is filed.

(k) *When Petition Granted.* If the petition is granted, a notice of appeal is deemed to have been filed under Rule 26.1(b) on that date, and the appeal is governed by the rules for accelerated appeals. A separate notice of appeal need not be filed. A copy of the order granting the petition must be filed with the trial court clerk.

Adopted by Supreme Court Sept. 9, 2011, eff. Sept. 9, 2011. Amended by order of March 4, 2013, eff. immediately.

28.4. Accelerated Appeals in Parental Termination and Child Protection Cases

(a) *Application and Definitions.*

(1) Appeals in parental termination and child protection cases are governed by the rules of appellate procedure for accelerated appeals, except as otherwise provided in Rule 28.4.

(2) In Rule 28.4:

(A) a "parental termination case" means a suit in which termination of the parent-child relationship is at issue.

(B) a "child protection case" means a suit affecting the parent-child relationship filed by a governmental entity for managing conservatorship.

(b) *Appellate Record.*

(1) Responsibility for Preparation of Reporter's Record. In addition to the responsibility imposed on the trial court in Rule 35.3(c). when the reporter's responsibility to prepare, certify and timely file the reporter's record arises under Rule 35.3(b) the trial court must direct the official or deputy reporter to immediately commence the preparation of the reporter's record. The trial court must arrange for a substitute reporter, if necessary.

(2) Extension of Time. The appellate court may grant an extension of time to file a record under

Rule 35.3(c); however, the extension or extensions granted must not exceed 30 days cumulatively, absent extraordinary circumstances.

(3) Restriction on Preparation Inapplicable. Section 13.003 of the Civil Practice & Remedies Code does not apply to an appeal from a parental termination or child protection case.

(c) *Remand for New Trial.* If the judgment of the appellate court reverses and remands a parental termination or child protection case for a new trial, the judgment must instruct the trial court to commence the new trial no later than 180 days after the mandate is issued by the appellate court.

Adopted by order of Supreme Court Feb. 13, 2012, eff. March 1, 2012.

Rule 29. Orders Pending Interlocutory Appeal in Civil Cases

Notes and Comments

Comment to 1997 change: This is former Rule 43. The provision in the former rule that an appeal from an order certifying a class suspends the order is repealed. The provision in the former rule that an order denying interlocutory relief cannot be suspended is omitted as unnecessary because the rule provides for superseding only orders granting relief. No substantive change is intended. The provision in former Rule 43(d) prohibiting the trial court from making an order granting substantially the same relief as the order appealed is repealed as being too broad. The provisions of former Rule 43(g) regarding the mandate are moved to Rule 18.6 and 18.7. The provision of former Rule 43(h) regarding rehearings is moved to Rule 49.4.

29.1. Effect of Appeal

Perfecting an appeal from an order granting interlocutory relief does not suspend the order appealed from unless:

(a) the order is superseded in accordance with 29.2; or

(b) the appellant is entitled to supersede the order without security by filing a notice of appeal.

Eff. Sept. 1, 1997.

29.2. Security

The trial court may permit an order granting interlocutory relief to be superseded pending an appeal from the order, in which event the appellant may supersede the order in accordance with Rule 24.[1] If the trial court refuses to permit the appellant to supersede the order, the appellant may move the appellate court to review that decision for abuse of discretion.

Eff. Sept. 1, 1997.

[1] Vernon's Ann.Rules App.Proc., rule 24.1 et seq.

29.3. Temporary Orders of Appellate Court

When an appeal from an interlocutory order is perfected, the appellate court may make any temporary orders necessary to preserve the parties' rights until disposition of the appeal and may require appropriate security. But the appellate court must not suspend the trial court's order if the appellant's rights would be adequately protected by supersedeas or another order made under Rule 24.[1]

Eff. Sept. 1, 1997.

[1] Vernon's Ann.Rules App.Proc., rule 24.1 et seq.

29.4. Enforcement of Temporary Orders

While an appeal from an interlocutory order is pending, only the appellate court in which the appeal is pending may enforce the order. But the appellate court may refer any enforcement proceeding to the trial court with instructions to:

(a) hear evidence and grant appropriate relief; or

(b) make findings and recommendations and report them to the appellate court.

Eff. Sept. 1, 1997.

29.5. Further Proceedings in Trial Court

While an appeal from an interlocutory order is pending, the trial court retains jurisdiction of the case and unless prohibited by statute may make further orders, including one dissolving the order complained of on appeal. If permitted by law, the trial court may proceed with a trial on the merits. But the court must not make an order that:

(a) is inconsistent with any appellate court temporary order; or

(b) interferes with or impairs the jurisdiction of the appellate court or effectiveness of any relief sought or that may be granted on appeal.

Eff. Sept. 1, 1997. Amended by Supreme Court Dec. 23, 2002, eff. Jan. 1, 2003; March 10, 2008, and Aug. 20, 2008, eff. Sept. 1, 2008. Approved by Court of Criminal Appeals Sept. 30, 2008, eff. Sept. 30, 2008.

Notes and Comments

Comment to 2002 change: Rule 29.5 is amended to acknowledge that a trial court may be prohibited by law from proceeding to trial during the pendency of an interlocutory appeal, as for example by section

51.014(b) of the Texas Civil Practice and Remedies Code.

29.6. Review of Further Orders

(a) *Motion to Review Further Orders.* While an appeal from an interlocutory order is pending, on a party's motion or on the appellate court's own initiative, the appellate court may review the following:

(1) a further appealable interlocutory order concerning the same subject matter; and

(2) any interlocutory order that interferes with or impairs the effectiveness of the relief sought or that may be granted on appeal.

(b) *Record.* The party filing the motion may rely on the original record or may file a supplemental record with the motion.

Eff. Sept. 1, 1997.

Rule 30. Restricted Appeal to Court of Appeals in Civil Cases

A party who did not participate—either in person or through counsel—in the hearing that resulted in the judgment complained of and who did not timely file a postjudgment motion or request for findings of fact and conclusions of law, or a notice of appeal within the time permitted by Rule 26.1(a), may file a notice of appeal within the time permitted by Rule 26.1(c). Restricted appeals replace writ of error appeals to the court of appeals. Statutes pertaining to writ of error appeals to the court of appeals apply equally to restricted appeals.

Eff. Sept. 1, 1997.

Notes and Comments

Comment to 1997 change: This is former Rule 45. The appeal by writ of error procedure is repealed. A procedure for an appeal filed within 6 months— called a restricted appeal—is substituted. This rule sets out who may take a restricted appeal. Rules 25.1 and 26.1 set out the method of perfection and the time for perfecting the appeal.

Rule 31. Appeals in Habeas Corpus, Bail, and Extradition Proceedings in Criminal Cases

Notes and Comments

Comment to 1997 change: This is former Rule 44. Since the purpose of the appeal is to do substantial justice, it is extended to both parties in recognition that both parties now have the right to appeal. Other nonsubstantive changes are made.

31.1. Filing the Record; Submission

When written notice of appeal from a judgment or order in a habeas corpus or bail proceeding is filed, the trial court clerk must prepare and certify the clerk's record and, if the appellant requests, the court reporter must prepare and certify a reporter's record. The clerk must send the clerk's record and the court reporter must send the reporter's record to the appellate court within 15 days after the notice of appeal is filed. On reasonable explanation, the appellate court may shorten or extend the time to file the record. When the appellate court receives the record, the court will—if it desires briefs—set the time for filing briefs, and will set the appeal for submission.

Eff. Sept. 1, 1997.

31.2. Hearing

An appeal in a habeas corpus or bail proceeding will be heard at the earliest practicable time. The applicant need not personally appear, and the appeal will be heard and determined upon the law and the facts shown by the record. The appellate court will not review any incidental question that might have arisen on the hearing of the application before the trial court. The sole purpose of the appeal is to do substantial justice to the parties.

Eff. Sept. 1, 1997.

31.3. Orders on Appeal

The appellate court will render whatever judgment and make whatever orders the law and the nature of the case require. The court may make an appropriate order relating to costs, whether allowing costs and fixing the amount, or allowing no costs.

Eff. Sept. 1, 1997.

31.4. Stay of Mandate

(a) *When Motion for Stay Required.* Despite Rule 18 [1] or any other of these rules, in the following circumstances a party who in good faith intends to seek discretionary review must—within 15 days after the court of appeals renders judgment—file with the court of appeals clerk a motion for stay of mandate, to which is appended the party's petition for discretionary review showing reasons why the Court of Criminal Appeals should review the appellate court judgment:

(1) when a court of appeals affirms the judgment of the trial court in an extradition matter and thereby sanctions a defendant's extradition; or

(2) when a court of appeals reverses the trial court's judgment in a bail matter—including bail

pending appeal under Code of Criminal Procedure article 44.04(g)—and thereby grants or reduces the amount of bail.

(b) *Determination of the Motion.* The clerk must promptly submit the motion and appendix to the court of appeals, or to one or more judges as the court deems appropriate, for immediate consideration and determination.

(1) If the motion for stay is granted, the clerk will immediately forward the petition for discretionary review to the clerk of the Court of Criminal Appeals.

(2) If the motion is denied, the clerk will issue a mandate in accordance with the court of appeals' judgment.

(c) *Denial of Stay.* If the motion for stay is denied under 31.4(b)(2), the losing party may then present the motion and appendix to the clerk of the Court of Criminal Appeals, who will promptly submit them to the Court, or to one or more judges as the Court deems appropriate, for immediate consideration and determination. The Court of Criminal Appeals may deny the motion or stay or recall the mandate. If the mandate is stayed or recalled, the clerk of the Court of Criminal Appeals will file the petition for discretionary review and process the case in accordance with Rule 68.7.

Eff. Sept. 1, 1997. Amended by Supreme Court Oct. 17, 2011, eff. Oct. 17, 2011.

¹ Vernon's Ann.Rules App.Proc., rule 18.1 et seq.

31.5. Judgment Conclusive

The court of appeals' judgment is final and conclusive if the Court of Criminal Appeals does not grant discretionary review. If the Court of Criminal Appeals grants discretionary review, that court's judgment is final and conclusive. In either case, no further application in the same case can be made for the writ unless the law provides otherwise.

Eff. Sept. 1, 1997.

31.6. Defendant Detained by Other Than Officer

If the defendant is held by a person other than an officer, the sheriff receiving the appellate court mandate so ordering must immediately cause the defendant to be discharged, for which discharge the mandate is sufficient authority.

Eff. Sept. 1, 1997.

31.7. Judgment to Be Certified

The appellate court clerk will certify the court's judgment to the officer holding the defendant in custody or, if the defendant is held by a person other than an officer, to the appropriate sheriff.

Eff. Sept. 1, 1997.

Rule 32. Docketing Statement

Notes and Comments

Comment to 1997 change: The rule is new.

32.1. Civil Cases

Promptly upon filing the notice of appeal in a civil case, the appellant must file in the appellate court a docketing statement that includes the following information:

(a)(1) if the appellant filing the statement has counsel, the name of that appellant and the name, address, telephone number, fax number, if any, and State Bar of Texas identification number of the appellant's lead counsel; or

(2) if the appellant filing the statement is not represented by an attorney, that party's name, address, telephone number, and fax number, if any;

(b) the date the notice of appeal was filed in the court and, if mailed to the trial court clerk, the date of mailing;

(c) the trial court's name and county, the name of the judge who tried the case, and the date the judgment or order appealed from was signed;

(d) the date of filing of any motion for new trial, motion to modify the judgment, request for findings of fact, motion to reinstate, or other filing that affects the time for perfecting the appeal;

(e) the names of all other parties to the trial court's judgment or the order appealed from, and:

(1) if represented by counsel, their lead counsel's names, addresses, telephone numbers, and fax numbers, if any; or

(2) if not represented by counsel, the name, address, and telephone number of the party, or a statement that the appellant diligently inquired but could not discover that information;

(f) the general nature of the case—for example, personal injury, breach of contract, or temporary injunction;

(g) whether the appeal's submission should be given priority, whether the appeal is an accelerated one under Rule 28 ¹ or another rule or statute, and whether it is a parental termination or child protection case, as defined in Rule 28.4;

(h) whether the appellant has requested or will request a reporter's record, and whether the trial was electronically recorded;

(i) the name of the court reporter;

(j) whether the appellant intends to seek temporary or ancillary relief while the appeal is pending;

(k) if the appellant filed a Statement of Inability to Afford Payment of Court Costs in the trial court:

(1) the date that the Statement was filed;

(2) the date of filing of any motion challenging the Statement;

(3) the date of any hearing on the appellant's ability to afford costs; and

(4) if the trial court signed an order under Texas Rule of Civil Procedure 145, the court's findings regarding the appellant's ability to afford costs and the date that the order was signed;

(*l*) whether the appellant has filed or will file a supersedeas bond; and

(m) any other information the appellate court requires.

Eff. Sept. 1, 1997. Amended by order of Supreme Court Feb. 13, 2012, eff. March 1, 2012; Aug. 31, 2016, eff. Sept. 1, 2016.

[1] Vernon's Ann.Rules App.Proc., rule 28.1 et seq.

32.2. Criminal Cases

Upon perfecting the appeal in a criminal case, the appellant must file in the appellate court a docketing statement that includes the following information:

(a)(1) if the appellant has counsel, the name of the appellant and the name, address, telephone number, fax number, if any, and State Bar of Texas identification number of the appellant's counsel, and whether the counsel is appointed or retained; or

(2) if the appellant is not represented by an attorney, that party's name, address, telephone number, and fax number, if any;

(b) the date the notice of appeal was filed in the trial court and, if mailed to the trial court clerk, the date of mailing;

(c) the trial court's name and county, and the name of the judge who tried the case;

(d) the date the trial court imposed or suspended sentence in open court, or the date the judgment or order appealed from was signed;

(e) the date of filing any motion for new trial, motion in arrest of judgment, or any other filing that affects the time for perfecting the appeal;

(f) the offense charged and the date of the offense;

(g) the defendant's plea;

(h) whether the trial was jury or nonjury;

(i) the punishment assessed;

(j) whether the appeal is from a pretrial order;

(k) whether the appeal involves the validity of a statute, ordinance, or rule;

(*l*) whether a reporter's record has been or will be requested, and whether the trial was electronically recorded;

(m) the name of the court reporter;

(n)(1) the dates of filing of any motion and affidavit of indigence;

(2) the date of any hearing;

(3) the date of any order; and

(4) whether the motion was granted or denied; and

(*o*) any other information the appellate court requires.

Eff. Sept. 1, 1997.

32.3. Supplemental Statements

Any party may file a statement supplementing or correcting the docketing statement.

Eff. Sept. 1, 1997.

32.4. Purpose of Statement

The docketing statement is for administrative purposes and does not affect the appellate court's jurisdiction.

Eff. Sept. 1, 1997.

Rule 33. Preservation of Appellate Complaints

Notes and Comments

Comment to 1997 change: This is former Rule 52. Subdivision 33.1 is rewritten. Former Rule 52(b), regarding offers of proof, is omitted as unnecessary. *See* TEX.R.CIV.EVID. 103; TEX.R.CRIM.EVID. 103. Subdivision 33.2 is also rewritten and the procedure is more definitely stated. Former Rule 52(d), regarding motions for new trial, is omitted as unnecessary. *See* TEX.R.CIV.P. 324(a) & (b).

Rule 33.1. Preservation; How Shown

(a) *In General.* As a prerequisite to presenting a complaint for appellate review, the record must show that:

(1) the complaint was made to the trial court by a timely request, objection, or motion that:

(A) stated the grounds for the ruling that the complaining party sought from the trial court with sufficient specificity to make the trial court aware of the complaint, unless the specific grounds were apparent from the context; and

(B) complied with the requirements of the Texas Rules of Evidence or the Texas Rules of Civil or Appellate Procedure; and

(2) the trial court:

(A) ruled on the request, objection, or motion, either expressly or implicitly; or

(B) refused to rule on the request, objection, or motion, and the complaining party objected to the refusal.

(b) *Ruling by Operation of Law.* In a civil case, the overruling by operation of law of a motion for new trial or a motion to modify the judgment preserves for appellate review a complaint properly made in the motion, unless taking evidence was necessary to properly present the complaint in the trial court.

(c) *Formal Exception and Separate Order Not Required.* Neither a formal exception to a trial court ruling or order nor a signed, separate order is required to preserve a complaint for appeal.

(d) *Sufficiency of Evidence Complaints in Civil Nonjury Cases.* In a civil nonjury case, a complaint regarding the legal or factual insufficiency of the evidence—including a complaint that the damages found by the court are excessive or inadequate, as distinguished from a complaint that the trial court erred in refusing to amend a fact finding or to make an additional finding of fact—may be made for the first time on appeal in the complaining party's brief.

Eff. Sept. 1, 1997. Amended by Supreme Court Dec. 23, 2002, eff. Jan. 1, 2003. Amended by Supreme Court order of June 30, 2017, and Court of Criminal Appeals order of June 26, 2017, eff. July 1, 2017.

Notes and Comments

> **Comment to 2017 change:** The 2017 amendment is intended only to clarify, and not to change, existing law.

33.2. Formal Bills of Exception

To complain on appeal about a matter that would not otherwise appear in the record, a party must file a formal bill of exception.

(a) *Form.* No particular form of words is required in a bill of exception. But the objection to the court's ruling or action, and the ruling complained of, must be stated with sufficient specificity to make the trial court aware of the complaint.

(b) *Evidence.* When the appellate record contains the evidence needed to explain a bill of exception, the bill itself need not repeat the evidence, and a party may attach and incorporate a transcription of the evidence certified by the court reporter.

(c) *Procedure.*

(1) The complaining party must first present a formal bill of exception to the trial court.

(2) If the parties agree on the contents of the bill of exception, the judge must sign the bill and file it with the trial court clerk. If the parties do not agree on the contents of the bill, the trial judge must—after notice and hearing—do one of the following things:

(A) sign the bill of exception and file it with the trial court clerk if the judge finds that it is correct;

(B) suggest to the complaining party those corrections to the bill that the judge believes are necessary to make it accurately reflect the proceedings in the trial court, and if the party agrees to the corrections, have the corrections made, sign the bill, and file it with the trial court clerk; or

(C) if the complaining party will not agree to the corrections suggested by the judge, return the bill to the complaining party with the judge's refusal written on it, and prepare, sign, and file with the trial court clerk such bill as will, in the judge's opinion, accurately reflect the proceedings in the trial court.

(3) If the complaining party is dissatisfied with the bill of exception filed by the judge under (2)(C), the party may file with the trial court clerk the bill that was rejected by the judge. That party must also file the affidavits of at least three people who observed the matter to which the bill of exception is addressed. The affidavits must attest to the correctness of the bill as presented by the party. The matters contained in that bill of exception may be controverted and maintained by additional affidavits filed by any party within ten days after the filing of

that bill. The truth of the bill of exception will be determined by the appellate court.

(d) *Conflict.* If a formal bill of exception conflicts with the reporter's record, the bill controls.

(e) *Time to File.*

(1) Civil Cases. In a civil case, a formal bill of exception must be filed no later than 30 days after the filing party's notice of appeal is filed.

(2) Criminal Cases. In a criminal case, a formal bill of exception must be filed:

(A) no later than 60 days after the trial court pronounces or suspends sentence in open court; or

(B) if a motion for new trial has been timely filed, no later than 90 days after the trial court pronounces or suspends sentence in open court.

(3) Extension of Time. The appellate court may extend the time to file a formal bill of exception if, within 15 days after the deadline for filing the bill, the party files in the appellate court a motion complying with Rule 10.5(b).

(f) *Inclusion in Clerk's Record.* When filed, a formal bill of exception should be included in the appellate record.

Eff. Sept. 1, 1997.

Rule 34. Appellate Record

Notes and Comments

Comment to 1997 change: Former Rules 50, 51 and 53 are merged. *Clerk's record* is substituted for *transcript*, and *reporter's record* is substituted for *statement of facts* throughout the rules. In subdivision 34.2, the requisites of an agreed record are more clearly stated. Former Rule 50(d), regarding the burden to file a complete record, is repealed. Subdivision 34.4 is from former Rules 51(c) and 53(h). Former Rule 50(f), regarding a violation of the rules, is repealed. Subparagraph 34.5(b)(3) allows the appellate court to tax costs against a party for requiring unnecessary items to be included in the clerk's record. Paragraph 34.5(c) is new and provides for supplementation of the clerk's record. The provisions of paragraph 34.5(d) are from former Rule 55(b). The provisions of paragraph 34.5(e) are from former Rule 50(e). Paragraph 34.5(h) specifically allows the clerk to consult with the parties to determine the contents of the clerk's record. Paragraph 34.6(a), defining the reporter's record, is new. Former Rules 53(b) (Other Requests), (d) (Partial Statement), and (e) (Unnecessary Portions) are merged into paragraph 34.6(c). Paragraph 34.6(d) is new. Paragraph 34.6(e) is from former Rule 55. Paragraph 34.6(f) is from former Rule 50(d). The provisions of former Rules 53(f) (Certification by Court Reporter) and (h) (Form) are moved to the Order of the Supreme Court and the Court of Criminal Appeals on the preparation of the record. Former Rule 53(i) (Narrative Statement) is repealed. The provisions of former Rule 53(j) (Free Statement of Facts) are moved to Rule 20. Former Rule 53(k) (Duty of Appellant to File) is repealed; it is now the duty of the court reporter to file the reporter's record. Paragraph 34.6(g) is from former Rule 51(d). Former Rule 53(g) is now paragraph 34.6(i). Former Rule 53(*l*) is now paragraph 34.6(h). The need for two duplicate records in a death penalty case was created by the habeas corpus provision in Code of Criminal Procedure article 11.071.

34.1. Contents

The appellate record consists of the clerk's record and, if necessary to the appeal, the reporter's record. Even if more than one notice of appeal is filed, there should be only one appellate record in a case.

Eff. Sept. 1, 1997.

34.2. Agreed Record

By written stipulation filed with the trial court clerk, the parties may agree on the contents of the appellate record. An agreed record will be presumed to contain all evidence and filings relevant to the appeal. To request matter to be included in the agreed record, the parties must comply with the procedures in Rules 34.5 and 34.6.

Eff. Sept. 1, 1997.

34.3. Agreed Statement of the Case

In lieu of a reporter's record, the parties may agree on a brief statement of the case. The statement must be filed with the trial court clerk and included in the appellate record.

Eff. Sept. 1, 1997.

34.4. Form

The Supreme Court and Court of Criminal Appeals will prescribe the form of the appellate record.

Eff. Sept. 1, 1997.

34.5. Clerk's Record

(a) *Contents.* Unless the parties designate the filings in the appellate record by agreement under Rule 34.2, the record must include copies of the following:

(1) in civil cases, all pleadings on which the trial was held;

(2) in criminal cases, the indictment or information, any special plea or defense motion that was presented to the court and overruled, any written waiver, any written stipulation, and, in cases in

which a plea of guilty or nolo contendere has been entered, any documents executed for the plea;

(3) the court's docket sheet;

(4) the court's charge and the jury's verdict, or the court's findings of fact and conclusions of law;

(5) the court's judgment or other order that is being appealed;

(6) any request for findings of fact and conclusions of law, any post-judgment motion, and the court's order on the motion;

(7) the notice of appeal;

(8) any formal bill of exception;

(9) any request for a reporter's record, including any statement of points or issues under Rule 34.6(c);

(10) any request for preparation of the clerk's record;

(11) in civil cases, a certified bill of costs including the cost of preparing the clerk's record, showing credits for payments made;

(12) in criminal cases the trial court's certification of the defendant's right of appeal under Rule 25.2; and

(13) subject to (b), any filing that a party designates to have included in the record.

(b) *Request for Additional Items.*

(1) Time for Request. At any time before the clerk's record is prepared, any party may file with the trial court clerk a written designation specifying items to be included in the record.

(2) Request Must Be Specific. A party requesting that an item be included in the clerk's record must specifically describe the item so that the clerk can readily identify it. The clerk will disregard a general designation, such as one for "all papers filed in the case."

(3) Requesting Unnecessary Items. In a civil case, if a party requests that more items than necessary be included in the clerk's record or any supplement, the appellate court may—regardless of the appeal's outcome—require that party to pay the costs for the preparation of the unnecessary portion.

(4) Failure to Timely Request. An appellate court must not refuse to file the clerk's record or a supplemental clerk's record because of a failure to timely request items to be included in the clerk's record.

(c) *Supplementation.*

(1) If a relevant item has been omitted from the clerk's record, the trial court, the appellate court, or any party may by letter direct the trial court clerk to prepare, certify, and file in the appellate court a supplement containing the omitted item.

(2) If the appellate court in a criminal case orders the trial court to prepare and file findings of fact and conclusions of law as required by law, or certification of the defendant's right of appeal as required by these rules, the trial court clerk must prepare, certify, and file in the appellate court a supplemental clerk's record containing those findings and conclusions.

(3) Any supplemental clerk's record will be part of the appellate record.

(d) *Defects or Inaccuracies.* If the clerk's record is defective or inaccurate, the appellate clerk must inform the trial court clerk of the defect or inaccuracy and instruct the clerk to make the correction.

(e) *Clerk's Record Lost or Destroyed.* If a filing designated for inclusion in the clerk's record has been lost or destroyed, the parties may, by written stipulation, deliver a copy of that item to the trial court clerk for inclusion in the clerk's record or a supplement. If the parties cannot agree, the trial court must—on any party's motion or at the appellate court's request—determine what constitutes an accurate copy of the missing item and order it to be included in the clerk's record or a supplement.

(f) *Original Documents.* If the trial court determines that original documents filed with the trial court clerk should be inspected by the appellate court or sent to that court in lieu of copies, the trial court must make an order for the safekeeping, transportation, and return of those original documents. The order must list the original documents and briefly describe them. All the documents must be arranged in their listed sequence and bound firmly together. On any party's motion or its own initiative, the appellate court may direct the trial court clerk to send it any original document.

(g) *Additional Copies of Clerk's Record in Criminal Cases.* In a criminal case, the clerk's record must be made in duplicate, and in a case in which the death penalty was assessed, in triplicate. The trial court clerk must retain the copy or copies for the parties to use with the court's permission.

(h) *Clerk May Consult With Parties.* The clerk may consult with the parties concerning the contents of the clerk's record.

Eff. Sept. 1, 1997. Amended by Supreme Court Dec. 23, 2002, eff. Jan. 1, 2003.

Notes and Comments

Comment to 2002 change: Rule 34.5(a) is amended to require that the record in a criminal case include the certification of defendant's right of appeal; see Rule 25.2(d). Rule 34.5(c) is amended to make clear that an appellate court may order the trial court to make such a certification for inclusion in a supplemental clerk's record.

34.6. Reporter's Record

(a) *Contents.*

(1) Stenographic Recording. If the proceedings were stenographically recorded, the reporter's record consists of the court reporter's transcription of so much of the proceedings, and any of the exhibits, that the parties to the appeal designate.

(2) Electronic Recording. If the proceedings were electronically recorded, the reporter's record consists of certified copies of all tapes or other audio-storage devices on which the proceedings were recorded, any of the exhibits that the parties to the appeal designate, and certified copies of the logs prepared by the court recorder under Rule 13.2.

(b) *Request for Preparation.*

(1) Request to Court Reporter. At or before the time for perfecting the appeal, the appellant must request in writing that the official reporter prepare the reporter's record. The request must designate the exhibits to be included. A request to the court reporter—but not the court recorder—must also designate the portions of the proceedings to be included.

(2) Filing. The appellant must file a copy of the request with the trial court clerk.

(3) Failure to Timely Request. An appellate court must not refuse to file a reporter's record or a supplemental reporter's record because of a failure to timely request it.

(c) *Partial Reporter's Record.*

(1) Effect on Appellate Points or Issues. If the appellant requests a partial reporter's record, the appellant must include in the request a statement of the points or issues to be presented on appeal and will then be limited to those points or issues.

(2) Other Parties May Designate Additions. Any other party may designate additional exhibits and portions of the testimony to be included in the reporter's record.

(3) Costs; Requesting Unnecessary Matter. Additions requested by another party must be included in the reporter's record at the appellant's cost. But if the trial court finds that all or part of the designated additions are unnecessary to the appeal, the trial court may order the other party to pay the costs for the preparation of the unnecessary additions. This paragraph does not affect the appellate court's power to tax costs differently.

(4) Presumptions. The appellate court must presume that the partial reporter's record designated by the parties constitutes the entire record for purposes of reviewing the stated points or issues. This presumption applies even if the statement includes a point or issue complaining of the legal or factual insufficiency of the evidence to support a specific factual finding identified in that point or issue.

(5) Criminal Cases. In a criminal case, if the statement contains a point complaining that the evidence is insufficient to support a finding of guilt, the record must include all the evidence admitted at the trial on the issue of guilt or innocence and punishment.

(d) *Supplementation.* If anything relevant is omitted from the reporter's record, the trial court, the appellate court, or any party may by letter direct the official court reporter to prepare, certify, and file in the appellate court a supplemental reporter's record containing the omitted items. Any supplemental reporter's record is part of the appellate record.

(e) *Inaccuracies in the Reporter's Record.*

(1) Correction of Inaccuracies by Agreement. The parties may agree to correct an inaccuracy in the reporter's record, including an exhibit, without the court reporter's recertification.

(2) Correction of Inaccuracies by Trial Court. If the parties cannot agree on whether or how to correct the reporter's record so that the text accurately discloses what occurred in the trial court and the exhibits are accurate, the trial court must—after notice and hearing—settle the dispute. If the court finds any inaccuracy, it must order the court reporter to conform the reporter's record (including text and any exhibits) to what occurred in the trial court, and to file certified corrections in the appellate court.

(3) Correction After Filing in Appellate Court. If the dispute arises after the reporter's record has been filed in the appellate court, that court may submit the dispute to the trial court for resolution. The trial court must then proceed as under subparagraph (e)(2).

(f) *Reporter's Record Lost or Destroyed.* An appellant is entitled to a new trial under the following circumstances:

(1) if the appellant has timely requested a reporter's record;

(2) if, without the appellant's fault, a significant exhibit or a significant portion of the court reporter's notes and records has been lost or destroyed or—if the proceedings were electronically recorded—a significant portion of the recording has been lost or destroyed or is inaudible;

(3) if the lost, destroyed, or inaudible portion of the reporter's record, or the lost or destroyed exhibit, is necessary to the appeal's resolution; and

(4) if the lost, destroyed or inaudible portion of the reporter's record cannot be replaced by agreement of the parties, or the lost or destroyed exhibit cannot be replaced either by agreement of the parties or with a copy determined by the trial court to accurately duplicate with reasonable certainty the original exhibit.

(g) *Original Exhibits.*

(1) Reporter May Use in Preparing Reporter's Record. At the court reporter's request, the trial court clerk must give all original exhibits to the reporter for use in preparing the reporter's record. Unless ordered to include original exhibits in the reporter's record, the court reporter must return the original exhibits to the clerk after copying them for inclusion in the reporter's record. If someone other than the trial court clerk possesses an original exhibit, either the trial court or the appellate court may order that person to deliver the exhibit to the trial court clerk.

(2) Use of Original Exhibits by Appellate Court. If the trial court determines that original exhibits should be inspected by the appellate court or sent to that court in lieu of copies, the trial court must make an order for the safekeeping, transportation, and return of those exhibits. The order must list the exhibits and briefly describe them. To the extent practicable, all the exhibits must be arranged in their listed order and bound firmly together before being sent to the appellate clerk. On any party's motion or its own initiative, the appellate court may direct the trial court clerk to send it any original exhibit.

(h) *Additional Copies of Reporter's Record in Criminal Cases.* In a criminal case in which a party requests a reporter's record, the court reporter must prepare a duplicate of the reporter's record and file it with the trial court clerk. In a case where the death penalty was assessed, the court reporter must prepare two duplicates of the reporter's record.

(i) *Supreme Court and Court of Criminal Appeals May Set Fee.* From time to time, the Supreme Court and the Court of Criminal Appeals may set the fee that the court reporters may charge for preparing the reporter's record.

Eff. Sept. 1, 1997. Amended by Supreme Court Dec. 23, 2002, eff. Jan. 1, 2003.

Notes and Comments

Comment to 2002 change: Subparagraphs 34.6(e) and (f) are amended to clarify the application to exhibits. The language is subparagraphs (e)(2) referring to the text of the record is simplified without substantive change. Subparagraph (e)(3) incorporates the procedures specified in (e)(2). The language in subparagraph (f) is clarified to require agreement only as to the portion of the text at issue, and to provide that the trial court may determine that a copy of an exhibit should be used even if the parties cannot agree.

Rule 35. Time to File Record; Responsibility for Filing Record

Notes and Comments

Comment to 1997 change: This is former Rule 54. In subdivision 35.1, the time to file the record in civil cases is based on the date the judgment is signed except in accelerated and restricted appeals, in which the time to file the record is based on the date the notice of appeal is filed. Subdivision 35.3 is new and makes it the responsibility of the trial court clerk and court reporter to file the record. Former Rule 54(c), providing for an extension of time to file the record, is repealed as unnecessary. The trial court clerk and court reporter should make arrangements with the court of appeals if additional time is required to file the record, as suggested in Rule 37.3.

35.1. Civil Cases

The appellate record must be filed in the appellate court within 60 days after the judgment is signed, except as follows:

(a) if Rule 26.1(a) applies, within 120 days after the judgment is signed;

(b) if Rule 26.1(b) applies, within 10 days after the notice of appeal is filed; or

(c) if Rule 26.1(c) applies, within 30 days after the notice of appeal is filed.

Eff. Sept. 1, 1997.

35.2. Criminal Cases

The appellate record must be filed in the appellate court:

(a) if a motion for new trial is not filed, within 60 days after the date the sentence is imposed or suspended in open court or the order appealed from is signed;

(b) if a timely motion for new trial is filed and denied, within 120 days after the date the sentence is imposed or suspended in open court; or

(c) if a motion for new trial is granted, within 60 days after the order granting the motion is signed.

Eff. Sept. 1, 1997.

35.3. Responsibility for Filing Record

(a) *Clerk's Record.* The trial court clerk is responsible for preparing, certifying, and timely filing the clerk's record if:

(1) a notice of appeal has been filed, and in criminal proceedings, the trial court has certified the defendant's right of appeal, as required by Rule 25.2(d); and

(2) the party responsible for paying for the preparation of the clerk's record has paid the clerk's fee, has made satisfactory arrangements with the clerk to pay the fee, or is entitled to appeal without paying the fee.

(b) *Reporter's Record.* The official or deputy reporter is responsible for preparing, certifying, and timely filing the reporter's record if:

(1) a notice of appeal has been filed;

(2) the appellant has requested that the reporter's record be prepared; and

(3) the party responsible for paying for the preparation of the reporter's record has paid the reporter's fee, or has made satisfactory arrangements with the reporter to pay the fee, or is entitled to appeal without paying the fee.

(c) *Courts to Ensure Record Timely Filed.* The trial and appellate courts are jointly responsible for ensuring that the appellate record is timely filed. The appellate court may extend the deadline to file the record if requested by the clerk or reporter. Each extension must not exceed 30 days in an ordinary or restricted appeal, or 10 days in an accelerated appeal. The appellate court must allow the record to be filed late when the delay is not the appellant's fault, and may do so when the delay is the appellant's fault.

The appellate court may enter any order necessary to ensure the timely filing of the appellate record.

Eff. Sept. 1, 1997. Amended by Court of Criminal Appeals Dec. 13, 2006, eff. Jan. 1, 2007. Amended by order of Supreme Court Feb. 13, 2012, eff. March 1, 2012.

Rule 36. Agency Record in Administrative Appeals

Notes and Comments

Comment to 1997 change: The rule is new.

36.1. Scope

This rule applies only to cases involving judicial review of state agency decisions in contested cases under the Administrative Procedure Act.

Eff. Sept. 1, 1997.

36.2. Inclusion in Appellate Record

The record of an agency proceeding filed in the trial court may be included in either the clerk's record or the reporter's record.

Eff. Sept. 1, 1997.

36.3. Correcting the Record.

(a) *Correction by Agreement.* At any stage of the proceeding, the parties may agree to correct an agency record filed under Section 2001.175(b) of the Government Code to ensure that the agency record accurately reflects the contested case proceedings before the agency. The court reporter need not recertify the agency record.

(b) *Correction by Trial Court.* If the parties cannot agree to a correction to the agency record, the appellate court must—on any party's motion or its own incentive—send the question to the trial court. After notice and hearing, the trial court must determine what constitutes an accurate copy of the agency record and order the agency to send an accurate copy to the clerk of the court in which the case is pending.

Eff. Sept. 1, 1997.

Rule 37. Duties of the Appellate Clerk on Receiving the Notice of Appeal and Record

Notes and Comments

Comment to 1997 change: Former Rules 56 and 57(a) are merged. Subdivisions 37.2 and 37.3 are new.

37.1. On Receiving the Notice of Appeal

If the appellate clerk determines that the notice of appeal or certification of defendant's right of appeal in a criminal case is defective, the clerk must notify the parties of the defect so that it can be remedied, if possible. If a proper notice of appeal or certification of a criminal defendant's right of appeal is not filed in the trial court within 30 days of the date of the clerk's notice, the clerk must refer the matter to the appellate court, which will make an appropriate order under this rule or Rule 34.5(c)(2).

Eff. Sept. 1, 1997. Amended by Supreme Court Dec. 23, 2002, eff. Jan. 1, 2003.

37.2. On Receiving the Record

On receiving the clerk's record or the reporter's record, the appellate clerk must determine whether each complies with the Supreme Court's and Court of Criminal Appeals' order on preparation of the record. If so, the clerk must endorse on each the date of receipt, file it, and notify the parties of the filing and the date. If not, the clerk must endorse on the clerk's record or reporter's record — whichever is defective — the date of receipt and return it to the official responsible for filing it. The appellate court clerk must specify the defects and instruct the official to correct the defects and return the record to the appellate court by a specified date. In a criminal case, the record must not be posted on the Internet.

Eff. Sept. 1, 1997. Amended by Court of Criminal Appeals Dec. 11, 2013, eff. Jan. 1, 2014.

37.3. If No Record Filed

(a) *Notice of Late Record.*

(1) Civil Cases. If the clerk's record or reporter's record has not been timely filed, the appellate clerk must send notice to the official responsible for filing it, stating that the record is late and requesting that the record be filed within 30 days if an ordinary or restricted appeal, or 10 days if an accelerated appeal. The appellate clerk must send a copy of this notice to the parties and the trial court. If the clerk does not receive the record within the stated period, the clerk must refer the matter to the appellate court. The court must make whatever order is appropriate to avoid further delay and to preserve the parties' rights.

(2) Criminal Cases. If the clerk's record or reporter's record has not been timely filed, the appellate court clerk must refer the matter to the appellate court. The court must make whatever order is appropriate to avoid further delay and to preserve the parties' rights.

(b) *If No Clerk's Record Filed Due to Appellant's Fault.* If the trial court clerk failed to file the clerk's

record because the appellant failed to pay or make arrangements to pay the clerk's fee for preparing the clerk's record, the appellate court may—on a party's motion or its own initiative—dismiss the appeal for want of prosecution unless the appellant was entitled to proceed without payment of costs. The court must give the appellant a reasonable opportunity to cure before dismissal.

(c) *If No Reporter's Record Filed Due to Appellant's Fault.* Under the following circumstances, and if the clerk's record has been filed, the appellate court may—after first giving the appellant notice and a reasonable opportunity to cure—consider and decide those issues or points that do not require a reporter's record for a decision. The court may do this if no reporter's record has been filed because:

(1) the appellant failed to request a reporter's record; or

(2)(A) appellant failed to pay or make arrangements to pay the reporter's fee to prepare the reporter's record; and

(B) the appellant is not entitled to proceed without payment of costs.

Eff. Sept. 1, 1997.

Rule 38. Requisites of Briefs

Notes and Comments

Comment to 1997 change: This is former Rule 74. The rule is substantially rewritten. Paragraph 38.1(e) now specifically allows a party to either present issues or points of error. Paragraphs 38.1(f) and (g) are new and require a brief to include a statement of facts and summary of the argument. Paragraph 38.2(b) is new and gives specific requirements for cross-points. *See also* TEX.R.CIV.P. 324(c). Subdivision 38.3 is new and provides for a reply brief. Subdivision 38.4 imposes a total brief limit of 90 pages on each party. Thus, if more than one party has filed a notice of appeal, there will be multiple appellant's, appellee's, and reply briefs, but each party is limited to a total of 90 pages. Subdivision 38.5 is new and provides for an appendix in cases recorded electronically in the trial court. Paragraph 38.6(b) now provides that the appellee has 30—rather than 25—days to file a brief. The provisions of former Rules 74(i) (Number of Copies), (j) (Briefs Typewritten or Printed), and (q) (Service of Briefs) are omitted as unnecessary. *See* Rule 9.

38.1. Appellant's Brief

The appellant's brief must, under appropriate headings and in the order here indicated, contain the following:

(a) *Identity of Parties and Counsel.* The brief must give a complete list of all parties to the trial court's judgment or order appealed from, and the names and addresses of all trial and appellate counsel, except as otherwise provided in Rule 9.8.

(b) *Table of Contents.* The brief must have a table of contents with references to the pages of the brief. The table of contents must indicate the subject matter of each issue or point, or group of issues or points.

(c) *Index of Authorities.* The brief must have an index of authorities arranged alphabetically and indicating the pages of the brief where the authorities are cited.

(d) *Statement of the Case.* The brief must state concisely the nature of the case (e.g., whether it is a suit for damages, on a note, or involving a murder prosecution), the course of proceedings, and the trial court's disposition of the case. The statement should be supported by record references, should seldom exceed one-half page, and should not discuss the facts.

(e) *Any Statement Regarding Oral Argument.* The brief may include a statement explaining why oral argument should or should not be permitted. Any such statement must not exceed one page and should address how the court's decisional process would, or would not, be aided by oral argument. As required by Rule 39.7, any party requesting oral argument must note that request on the front cover of the party's brief.

(f) *Issues Presented.* The brief must state concisely all issues or points presented for review. The statement of an issue or point will be treated as covering every subsidiary question that is fairly included.

(g) *Statement of Facts.* The brief must state concisely and without argument the facts pertinent to the issues or points presented. In a civil case, the court will accept as true the facts stated unless another party contradicts them. The statement must be supported by record references.

(h) *Summary of the Argument.* The brief must contain a succinct, clear, and accurate statement of the arguments made in the body of the brief. This summary must not merely repeat the issues or points presented for review.

(i) *Argument.* The brief must contain a clear and concise argument for the contentions made, with appropriate citations to authorities and to the record.

(j) *Prayer.* The brief must contain a short conclusion that clearly states the nature of the relief sought.

(k) *Appendix in Civil Cases.*

(1) Necessary Contents. Unless voluminous or impracticable, the appendix must contain a copy of:

(A) the trial court's judgment or other appealable order from which relief is sought;

(B) the jury charge and verdict, if any, or the trial court's findings of fact and conclusions of law, if any; and

(C) the text of any rule, regulation, ordinance, statute, constitutional provision, or other law (excluding case law) on which the argument is based, and the text of any contract or other document that is central to the argument.

(2) Optional Contents. The appendix may contain any other item pertinent to the issues or points presented for review, including copies or excerpts of relevant court opinions, laws, documents on which the suit was based, pleadings, excerpts from the reporter's record, and similar material. Items should not be included in the appendix to attempt to avoid the page limits for the brief.

Eff. Sept. 1, 1997. Amended by Supreme Court March 10, 2008, and Aug. 20, 2008, eff. Sept. 1, 2008. Approved by Court of Criminal Appeals Sept. 30, 2008, eff. Sept. 30, 2008.

38.2. Appellee's Brief

(a) *Form of Brief.*

(1) An appellee's brief must conform to the requirements of Rule 38.1, except that:

(A) the list of parties and counsel is not required unless necessary to supplement or correct the appellant's list;

(B) the appellee's brief need not include a statement of the case, a statement of the issues presented, or a statement of facts, unless the appellee is dissatisfied with that portion of the appellant's brief; and

(C) the appendix to the appellee's brief need not contain any item already contained in an appendix filed by the appellant.

(2) When practicable, the appellee's brief should respond to the appellant's issues or points in the order the appellant presented those issues or points.

(b) *Cross-Points.*

(1) Judgment Notwithstanding the Verdict. When the trial court renders judgment notwithstanding the verdict on one or more questions, the appellee must bring forward by cross-point any

issue or point that would have vitiated the verdict or that would have prevented an affirmance of the judgment if the trial court had rendered judgment on the verdict. Failure to bring forward by cross-point an issue or point that would vitiate the verdict or prevent an affirmance of the judgment waives that complaint. Included in this requirement is a point that:

(A) the verdict or one or more jury findings have insufficient evidentiary support or are against the overwhelming preponderance of the evidence as a matter of fact; or

(B) the verdict should be set aside because of improper argument of counsel.

(2) When Evidentiary Hearing Needed. The appellate court must remand a case to the trial court to take evidence if:

(A) the appellate court has sustained a point raised by the appellant; and

(B) the appellee raised a cross-point that requires the taking of additional evidence.

Eff. Sept. 1, 1997. Amended by Supreme Court Dec. 23, 2002, eff. Jan. 1, 2003.

38.3. Reply Brief

The appellant may file a reply brief addressing any matter in the appellee's brief. However, the appellate court may consider and decide the case before a reply brief is filed.

Eff. Sept. 1, 1997.

38.4. Repealed by Order of Nov. 13, 2012, eff. Dec. 1, 2012

38.5. Appendix for Cases Recorded Electronically

In cases where the proceedings were electronically recorded, the following rules apply:

(a) *Appendix.*

(1) In General. At or before the time a party's brief is due, the party must file one copy of an appendix containing a transcription of all portions of the recording that the party considers relevant to the appellate issues or points. Unless another party objects, the transcription will be presumed accurate.

(2) Repetition Not Required. A party's appendix need not repeat evidence included in any previously filed appendix.

(3) Form. The form of the appendix and transcription must conform to any specifications of the Supreme Court and Court of Criminal Appeals con-cerning the form of the reporter's record except that it need not have the reporter's certificate.

(4) Notice. At the time the appendix is filed, the party must give written notice of the filing to all parties to the trial court's judgment or order. The notice must specify, by referring to the index numbers in the court recorder's logs, those parts of the recording that are included in the appendix. The filing party need not serve a copy of the appendix but must make a copy available to all parties for inspection and copying.

(b) *Presumptions.* The same presumptions that apply to a partial reporter's record under Rule 34.6(c)(4) apply to the parties' appendixes. The appellate court need not review any part of the electronic recording.

(c) *Supplemental Appendix.* The appellate court may direct or allow a party to file a supplemental appendix containing a transcription of additional portions of the recording.

(d) *Inability to Pay.* A party who cannot pay the cost of an appendix must file the affidavit provided for by Rule 20.[1] The party must also state in the affidavit or a supplemental affidavit that the party has neither the access to the equipment necessary nor the skill necessary to prepare the appendix. If a contest to the affidavit is not sustained by written order, the court recorder must transcribe or have transcribed those portions of the recording that the party designates and must file the transcription as that party's appendix, along with all exhibits.

(e) *Inaccuracies.*

(1) Correction by Agreement. The parties may agree to correct an inaccuracy in the transcription of the recording.

(2) Correction by Appellate or Trial Court. If the parties dispute whether an electronic recording or transcription accurately discloses what occurred in the trial court but cannot agree on corrections, the appellate court may:

(A) settle the dispute by reviewing the recording; or

(B) submit the dispute to the trial court, which must—after notice and hearing—settle the dispute and ensure that the recording or transcription is made to conform to what occurred in the trial court.

(f) *Costs.* The actual expense of preparing the appendixes or the amount prescribed for official reporters, whichever is less, is taxed as costs. The appellate court may disallow the cost of any portion of the appendixes that it considers surplusage or that does not conform to any specifications prescribed by the Supreme Court or Court of Criminal Appeals.

Eff. Sept. 1, 1997.

[1] Vernon's Ann.Rules App.Proc., rule 20.1 et seq.

38.6. Time to File Briefs

(a) *Appellant's Filing Date.* Except in a habeas corpus or bail appeal, which is governed by Rule 31,[1] an appellant must file a brief within 30 days—20 days in an accelerated appeal—after the later of:

(1) the date the clerk's record was filed; or

(2) the date the reporter's record was filed.

(b) *Appellee's Filing Date.* The appellee's brief must be filed within 30 days—20 days in an accelerated appeal—after the date the appellant's brief was filed. In a civil case, if the appellant has not filed a brief as provided in this rule, an appellee may file a brief within 30 days—20 days in an accelerated appeal—after the date the appellant's brief was due.

(c) *Filing Date for Reply Brief.* A reply brief, if any, must be filed within 20 days after the date the appellee's brief was filed.

(d) *Modifications of Filing Time.* On motion complying with Rule 10.5(b), the appellate court may extend the time for filing a brief and may postpone submission of the case. A motion to extend the time to file a brief may be filed before or after the date the brief is due. The court may also, in the interests of justice, shorten the time for filing briefs and for submission of the case.

Eff. Sept. 1, 1997. Amended by Supreme Court Dec. 23, 2002, eff. Jan. 1, 2003.

[1] Vernon's Ann.Rules App.Proc., rule 31.1 et seq.

Notes and Comments

Comment to 2002 change: Rule 38.6(d) is amended to clarify that an appellate court may postpone the filing of any brief, not just the appellant's brief.

38.7. Amendment or Supplementation

A brief may be amended or supplemented whenever justice requires, on whatever reasonable terms the court may prescribe.

Eff. Sept. 1, 1997.

38.8. Failure of Appellant to File Brief

(a) *Civil Cases.* If an appellant fails to timely file a brief, the appellate court may:

(1) dismiss the appeal for want of prosecution, unless the appellant reasonably explains the failure and the appellee is not significantly injured by the appellant's failure to timely file a brief;

(2) decline to dismiss the appeal and give further direction to the case as it considers proper; or

(3) if an appellee's brief is filed, the court may regard that brief as correctly presenting the case and may affirm the trial court's judgment upon that brief without examining the record.

(b) *Criminal Cases.*

(1) Effect. An appellant's failure to timely file a brief does not authorize either dismissal of the appeal or, except as provided in (4), consideration of the appeal without briefs.

(2) Notice. If the appellant's brief is not timely filed, the appellate clerk must notify counsel for the parties and the trial court of that fact. If the appellate court does not receive a satisfactory response within ten days, the court must order the trial court to immediately conduct a hearing to determine whether the appellant desires to prosecute his appeal, whether the appellant is indigent, or, if not indigent, whether retained counsel has abandoned the appeal, and to make appropriate findings and recommendations.

(3) Hearing. In accordance with (2), the trial court must conduct any necessary hearings, make appropriate findings and recommendations, and have a record of the proceedings prepared, which record—including any order and findings—must be sent to the appellate court.

(4) Appellate Court Action. Based on the trial court's record, the appellate court may act appropriately to ensure that the appellant's rights are protected, including initiating contempt proceedings against appellant's counsel. If the trial court has found that the appellant no longer desires to prosecute the appeal, or that the appellant is not indigent but has not made the necessary arrangements for filing a brief, the appellate court may consider the appeal without briefs, as justice may require.

Eff. Sept. 1, 1997.

38.9. Briefing Rules to Be Construed Liberally

Because briefs are meant to acquaint the court with the issues in a case and to present argument that will enable the court to decide the case, substantial compliance with this rule is sufficient, subject to the following.

(a) *Formal Defects.* If the court determines that this rule has been flagrantly violated, it may require a brief to be amended, supplemented, or redrawn. If another brief that does not comply with this rule is filed, the court may strike the brief, prohibit the party from filing another, and proceed as if the party had failed to file a brief.

(b) *Substantive Defects.* If the court determines, either before or after submission, that the case has not been properly presented in the briefs, or that the law and authorities have not been properly cited in the briefs, the court may postpone submission, require additional briefing, and make any other order necessary for a satisfactory submission of the case.

Eff. Sept. 1, 1997.

Rule 39. Oral Argument; Decision Without Argument

Notes and Comments

Comment to 1997 change: This is former Rule 75. Technical and nonsubstantive changes are made.

39.1. Right to Oral Argument

A party who has filed a brief and who has timely requested oral argument may argue the case to the court unless the court, after examining the briefs, decides that oral argument is unnecessary for any of the following reasons:

(a) the appeal is frivolous;

(b) the dispositive issue or issues have been authoritatively decided;

(c) the facts and legal arguments are adequately presented in the briefs and record; or

(d) the decisional process would not be significantly aided by oral argument.

Eff. Sept. 1, 1997. Amended by Supreme Court March 10, 2008, and Aug. 20, 2008, eff. Sept. 1, 2008. Approved by Court of Criminal Appeals Sept. 30, 2008, eff. Sept. 30, 2008.

39.2. Purpose of Argument

Oral argument should emphasize and clarify the written arguments in the briefs. Counsel should not merely read from prepared text. Counsel should assume that all members of the court have read the briefs before oral argument and counsel should be prepared to respond to questions. A party should not refer to or comment on matters not involved in or pertaining to what is in the record.

Eff. Sept. 1, 1997.

39.3. Time Allowed

The court will set the time that will be allowed for argument. Counsel must complete argument in the time allotted and may continue after the expiration of the allotted time only with permission of the court. Counsel is not required to use all the allotted time. The appellant must be allowed to conclude the argument.

Eff. Sept. 1, 1997.

39.4. Number of Counsel

Generally, only one counsel should argue for each side. Except on leave of court, no more than two counsel on each side may argue. Only one counsel may argue in rebuttal.

Eff. Sept. 1, 1997.

39.5. Argument by Amicus

With leave of court obtained before the argument and with a party's consent, an amicus curiae may share allotted time with that party. Otherwise, counsel for amicus may not argue.

Eff. Sept. 1, 1997.

39.6. When Only One Party Files a Brief

If counsel for only one party has filed a brief, the court may allow that party to argue.

Eff. Sept. 1, 1997.

39.7. Request and Waiver

A party desiring oral argument must note that request on the front cover of the party's brief. A party's failure to request oral argument waives the party's right to argue. But even if a party has waived oral argument, the court may direct the party to appear and argue.

Eff. Sept. 1, 1997.

39.8. Clerk's Notice.

The clerk must send to the parties—at least 21 days before the date the case is set for argument or submission without argument—a notice telling the parties:

(a) whether the court will allow oral argument or will submit the case without argument;

(b) the date of argument or submission without argument;

(c) if argument is allowed, the time allotted for argument; and

(d) the names of the members of the panel to which the case will be argued or submitted, subject to change by the court.

A party's failure to receive the notice does not prevent a case's argument or submission on the scheduled date.

Eff. Sept. 1, 1997. Amended by Supreme Court March 10, 2008, and Aug. 20, 2008, eff. Sept. 1, 2008. Approved by Court of Criminal Appeals Sept. 30, 2008, eff. Sept. 30, 2008.

39.9. [Deleted]

Rule 40. Order of Decision

Notes and Comments

Comment on 1997 change: The provisions of former Rules 76, 77 and 78 are merged. Civil cases involving the Railroad Commission, the State, and "cases submitted on oral argument for all parties" are no longer given preference unless given preference by law.

40.1. Civil Cases

The court of appeals may determine the order in which civil cases will be decided. But the following types of cases have precedence over all others:

(a) a case given precedence by law;

(b) an accelerated appeal; and

(c) a case that the court determines should be given precedence in the interest of justice.

Eff. Sept. 1, 1997.

40.2. Criminal Cases

In cases not otherwise given precedence by law, the court of appeals must hear and determine a criminal appeal at the earliest possible time, having due regard for the parties' rights and for the proper administration of justice.

Eff. Sept. 1, 1997.

Rule 41. Panel and En Banc Decision

Notes and Comments

Comment to 1997 change: This is former Rule 79. The rule is reorganized. Paragraphs 41.1(b) and (c) are amended to make clear that a three judge panel must hear the case. Therefore, only if a member of a panel is lost after argument do the provisions for appointment of another justice to break a deadlock come into play. Paragraph 41.2(a) is amended to define an en banc court.

41.1. Decision by Panel

(a) *Constitution of Panel.* Unless a court of appeals with more than three justices votes to decide a case en banc, a case must be assigned for decision to a panel of the court consisting of three justices, although not every member of the panel must be present for argument. If the case is decided without argument, three justices must participate in the decision. A majority of the panel, which constitutes a quorum, must agree on the judgment. Except as otherwise provided in these rules, a panel's opinion constitutes the court's opinion, and the court must render a judgment in accordance with the panel opinion.

(b) *When Panel Cannot Agree on Judgment.* After argument, if for any reason a member of the panel cannot participate in deciding a case, the case may be decided by the two remaining justices. If they cannot agree on a judgment, the chief justice of the court of appeals must:

(1) designate another justice of the court to sit on the panel to consider the case;

(2) request the Chief Justice of the Supreme Court to temporarily assign an eligible justice or judge to sit on the panel to consider the case; or

(3) convene the court en banc to consider the case.

The reconstituted panel or the en banc court may order the case reargued.

(c) *When Court Cannot Agree on Judgment.* After argument, if for any reason a member of a court consisting of only three justices cannot participate in deciding a case, the case may be decided by the two remaining justices. If they cannot agree on a judgment, that fact must be certified to the Chief Justice of the Supreme Court. The Chief Justice may then temporarily assign an eligible justice or judge to sit with the court of appeals to consider the case. The reconstituted court may order the case reargued.

Eff. Sept. 1, 1997. Amended by Supreme Court March 10, 2008, and Aug. 20, 2008, eff. Sept. 1, 2008. Approved by Court of Criminal Appeals Sept. 30, 2008, eff. Sept. 30, 2008.

41.2. Decision by En Banc Court

(a) *Constitution of En Banc Court.* An en banc court consists of all members of the court who are not disqualified or recused and—if the case was originally argued before or decided by a panel—any members of the panel who are not members of the court but remain eligible for assignment to the court. A majority of the en banc court constitutes a quorum. A majority of the en banc court must agree on a judgment.

(b) *When En Banc Court Cannot Agree on Judgment.* If a majority of an en banc court cannot agree on a judgment, that fact must be certified to the Chief Justice of the Supreme Court. The Chief Justice may then temporarily assign an eligible justice or judge to sit with the court of appeals to consider the case. The reconstituted court may order the case reargued.

(c) *En Banc Consideration Disfavored.* En banc consideration of a case is not favored and should not be ordered unless necessary to secure or maintain uniformity of the court's decisions or unless extraordinary circumstances require en banc consideration. A vote to determine whether a case will be heard or reheard en banc need not be taken unless a justice of the court requests a vote. If a vote is requested and a majority of the court's members vote to hear or rehear the case en banc, the en banc court will hear or rehear the case. Otherwise, a panel of the court will consider the case.

Eff. Sept. 1, 1997. Amended by Supreme Court March 10, 2008, and Aug. 20, 2008, eff. Sept. 1, 2008. Approved by Court of Criminal Appeals Sept. 30, 2008, eff. Sept. 30, 2008.

41.3. Precedent in Transferred Cases.

In cases transferred by the Supreme Court from one court of appeals to another, the court of appeals to which the case is transferred must decide the case in accordance with the precedent of the transferor court under principles of stare decisis if the transferee court's decision otherwise would have been inconsistent with the precedent of the transferor court. The court's opinion may state whether the outcome would have been different had the transferee court not been required to decide the case in accordance with the transferor court's precedent.

Added by Supreme Court March 10, 2008, and Aug. 20, 2008, eff. Sept. 1, 2008. Approved by Court of Criminal Appeals Sept. 30, 2008, eff. Sept. 30, 2008.

Rule 42. Dismissal

Notes and Comments

Comment to 1997 change: Former Rules 59 and 60 are merged. Paragraph 42.1(c), allowing a court of appeals to withdraw its opinion, is new. Provision is made in paragraph 42.3(c) for dismissal of an appeal for failure to comply with a notice from the clerk. Other changes are made.

42.1. Voluntary Dismissal in Civil Cases

(a) *On Motion or By Agreement.* The appellate court may dispose of an appeal as follows:

(1) On Motion of Appellant. In accordance with a motion of appellant, the court may dismiss the

appeal or affirm the appealed judgment or order unless disposition would prevent a party from seeking relief to which it would otherwise be entitled.

(2) By Agreement. In accordance with an agreement signed by the parties or their attorneys and filed with the clerk, the court may:

(A) render judgment effectuating the parties' agreements;

(B) set aside the trial court's judgment without regard to the merits and remand the case to the trial court for rendition of judgment in accordance with the agreements; or

(C) abate the appeal and permit proceedings in the trial court to effectuate the agreement.

(b) *Partial Disposition.* A severable portion of the proceeding may be disposed of under (a) if it will not prejudice the remaining parties.

(c) *Effect on Court's Opinion.* In dismissing a proceeding, the appellate court will determine whether to withdraw any opinion it has already issued. An agreement or motion for dismissal cannot be conditioned on withdrawal of the opinion.

(d) *Costs.* Absent agreement of the parties, the court will tax costs against the appellant.

Eff. Sept. 1, 1997. Amended by Supreme Court Dec. 23, 2002, eff. Jan. 1, 2003.

Notes and Comments

Comment to 2002 change: Rule 42.1 is amended to clarify the procedures for implementing settlements on appeal and to expressly give courts flexibility in effectuating settlements. The rule is also clarified to expressly permit the dismissal of appeal without dismissal of the action itself. The rules does not permit an appellate court to order a new trial merely on the agreement of the parties absent reversible error, or to vacate a trial court's judgment absent reversible error or a settlement.

42.2. Voluntary Dismissal in Criminal Cases

(a) At any time before the appellate court's decision, the appellate court may dismiss the appeal upon the appellant's motion. The appellant and his or her attorney must sign the written motion to dismiss and file it in duplicate with the appellate clerk, who must immediately send the duplicate copy to the trial court clerk.

(b) After the court of appeals hands down its opinion, it may not grant an appellant's motion to dismiss the appeal unless the other parties consent. If the other parties consent and the court of appeals grants the appellant's motion to dismiss the appeal, the appellate opinion must be withdrawn and the appeal dismissed. The appellate clerk must send notice of the dismissal to the trial court clerk.

Eff. Sept. 1, 1997. Amended by Court of Criminal Appeals Aug. 10, 2000 and Oct. 16, 2000, eff. Jan. 1, 2001; Supreme Court Sept. 12, 2000, eff. Jan. 1, 2001; Court of Criminal Appeals Dec. 13, 2006, eff. Jan. 1, 2007.

Notes and Comments

Comment to 2000 change: In the first sentence of Rule 42.2(a) "appellant" is replaced by "party that appealed," to make it clear that the rule applies to the State when it is the appealing party. See State v. Miles, 994 S.W.2d 410 (Tex.App.—Waco 1999). The requirement that the appellant's attorney must sign the withdrawal is deleted, and the last sentence is added, to remove any implication that the attorney may veto the appellant's decision to withdraw the notice of appeal. The word "personally" is added to emphasize that the appellant must participate in the withdrawal of his or her appeal. The provisions of Rule 9.1(a) do not restrict the appellant's ability to withdraw the notice of appeal.

42.3. Involuntary Dismissal in Civil Cases

Under the following circumstances, on any party's motion—or on its own initiative after giving ten days' notice to all parties—the appellate court may dismiss the appeal or affirm the appealed judgment or order. Dismissal or affirmance may occur if the appeal is subject to dismissal:

(a) for want of jurisdiction;

(b) for want of prosecution; or

(c) because the appellant has failed to comply with a requirement of these rules, a court order, or a notice from the clerk requiring a response or other action within a specified time.

Eff. Sept. 1, 1997.

42.4. Involuntary Dismissal in Criminal Cases

The appellate court must dismiss an appeal on the State's motion, supported by affidavit, showing that the appellant has escaped from custody pending the appeal and that to the affiant's knowledge, the appellant has not, within ten days after escaping, voluntarily returned to lawful custody within the state.

(a) *Timely Return to Custody; Reinstatement.* The appeal may not be dismissed—or, if dismissed, must be reinstated—if an affidavit of an officer or other credible person is filed showing that the appellant, within ten days after escaping, voluntarily returned to lawful custody within the state.

(b) *Life Sentence.* The appellate court may overrule the motion to dismiss—or, if the motion was granted, may reinstate the appeal—if:

(1) the appellant received a life sentence; and

(2) the appellant is recaptured or voluntarily surrenders within 30 days after escaping.

Eff. Sept. 1, 1997.

Rule 43. Judgment of the Court of Appeals

Notes and Comments

Comment to 1997 changes: Former Rules 80(a)–(c) and 82 are merged. Paragraph 43.2(e) allows the court of appeals to vacate the trial court's judgment and dismiss the case; paragraph 43.2(f) allows the court of appeals to dismiss the appeal. Both provisions are new but codify current practice. Paragraph 43.3(a) is moved here from former Rule 81(c). Paragraph 43.3(b), allowing a remand in the interest of justice, is new. Subdivisions 43.4 and 43.5 are from former Rule 82.

43.1. Time

The court of appeals should render its judgment promptly after submission of a case.

Eff. Sept. 1, 1997.

43.2. Types of Judgment

The court of appeals may:

(a) affirm the trial court's judgment in whole or in part;

(b) modify the trial court's judgment and affirm it as modified;

(c) reverse the trial court's judgment in whole or in part and render the judgment that the trial court should have rendered;

(d) reverse the trial court's judgment and remand the case for further proceedings;

(e) vacate the trial court's judgment and dismiss the case; or

(f) dismiss the appeal.

Eff. Sept. 1, 1997.

43.3. Rendition Appropriate Unless Remand Necessary

When reversing a trial court's judgment, the court must render the judgment that the trial court should have rendered, except when:

(a) a remand is necessary for further proceedings; or

(b) the interests of justice require a remand for another trial.

Eff. Sept. 1, 1997.

43.4. Judgment for Costs in Civil Cases

The court of appeals' judgment should award to the prevailing party costs incurred by that party related to the appeal, including filing fees in the court of appeals and costs for preparation of the record. The court of appeals may tax costs otherwise as required by law or for good cause. But the judgment must not require the payment of costs by a party who was entitled to proceed without payment of costs under Rule 20.1, and a provision in the judgment purporting to do so is void.

Eff. Sept. 1, 1997. Amended by order of Aug. 31, 2016, eff. Sept. 1, 2016.

43.5. Judgment Against Sureties in Civil Cases

When a court of appeals affirms the trial court judgment, or modifies that judgment and renders judgment against the appellant, the court of appeals must render judgment against the sureties on the appellant's supersedeas bond, if any, for the performance of the judgment and for any costs taxed against the appellant.

Eff. Sept. 1, 1997.

43.6. Other Orders

The court of appeals may make any other appropriate order that the law and the nature of the case require.

Eff. Sept. 1, 1997.

Rule 44. Reversible Error

Notes and Comments

Comment to 1997 change: Former Rules 80(d), 81 and 83 are merged. The reversible error standard in subdivision 44.1 is amended to omit the reference to an action "reasonably calculated to cause" an improper judgment, but no substantive change is intended. Paragraph 44.2(a) is amended to limit its standard of review to constitutional errors that are subject to harmless error review. Paragraph 44.2(b) is new and is taken from Federal Rule of Criminal Procedure 52(a) without substantive change. Paragraph 44.2(c) is former Rule 80(d) without substantive change. Subdivision 44.3 is amended to delete the reference to defects of "substance" and to delete the provisions regarding the late filing of the record.

44.1. Reversible Error in Civil Cases

(a) *Standard for Reversible Error.* No judgment may be reversed on appeal on the ground that the trial court made an error of law unless the court of appeals concludes that the error complained of:

(1) probably caused the rendition of an improper judgment; or

(2) probably prevented the appellant from properly presenting the case to the court of appeals.

(b) *Error Affecting Only Part of Case.* If the error affects part of, but not all, the matter in controversy and that part is separable without unfairness to the parties, the judgment must be reversed and a new trial ordered only as to the part affected by the error. The court may not order a separate trial solely on unliquidated damages if liability is contested.

Eff. Sept. 1, 1997.

44.2. Reversible Error in Criminal Cases

(a) *Constitutional Error.* If the appellate record in a criminal case reveals constitutional error that is subject to harmless error review, the court of appeals must reverse a judgment of conviction or punishment unless the court determines beyond a reasonable doubt that the error did not contribute to the conviction or punishment.

(b) *Other Errors.* Any other error, defect, irregularity, or variance that does not affect substantial rights must be disregarded.

(c) *Presumptions.* Unless the following matters were disputed in the trial court, or unless the record affirmatively shows the contrary, the court of appeals must presume:

(1) that venue was proved in the trial court;

(2) that the jury was properly impaneled and sworn;

(3) that the defendant was arraigned;

(4) that the defendant pleaded to the indictment or other charging instrument; and

(5) that the court's charge was certified by the trial court and filed by the clerk before it was read to the jury.

Eff. Sept. 1, 1997.

44.3. Defects in Procedure

A court of appeals must not affirm or reverse a judgment or dismiss an appeal for formal defects or irregularities in appellate procedure without allowing a reasonable time to correct or amend the defects or irregularities.

Eff. Sept. 1, 1997.

44.4. Remediable Error of the Trial Court

(a) *Generally.* A court of appeals must not affirm or reverse a judgment or dismiss an appeal if:

(1) the trial court's erroneous action or failure or refusal to act prevents the proper presentation of a case to the court of appeals; and

(2) the trial court can correct its action or failure to act.

(b) *Court of Appeals Direction if Error Remediable.* If the circumstances described in (a) exist, the court of appeals must direct the trial court to correct the error. The court of appeals will then proceed as if the erroneous action or failure to act had not occurred.

Eff. Sept. 1, 1997.

Rule 45. Damages for Frivolous Appeals in Civil Cases

If the court of appeals determines that an appeal is frivolous, it may—on motion of any party or on its own initiative, after notice and a reasonable opportunity for response—award each prevailing party just damages. In determining whether to award damages, the court must not consider any matter that does not appear in the record, briefs, or other papers filed in the court of appeals.

Eff. Sept. 1, 1997.

Notes and Comments

Comment to 1997 change: This is former Rule 84. The limit on the amount of the sanction that may be imposed is repealed. A requirement of notice and opportunity to respond is added.

Rule 46. Remittitur in Civil Cases

Notes and Comments

Comment to 1997 change: This is former Rule 85. The rule is revised without substantive change.

46.1. Remittitur After Appeal Perfected

If the trial court suggests a remittitur but the case is appealed before the remittitur is filed, the party who would make the remittitur may do so in the court of appeals in the same manner as in the trial court. The court of appeals must then render the judgment

that the trial court should have rendered if the remittitur had been made in the trial court.

Eff. Sept. 1, 1997.

46.2. Appeal on Remittitur

If a party makes the remittitur at the trial judge's suggestion and the party benefitting from the remittitur appeals, the remitting party is not barred from contending in the court of appeals that all or part of the remittitur should not have been required, but the remitting party must perfect an appeal to raise that point. If the court of appeals sustains the remitting party's contention that remittitur should not have been required, the court must render the judgment that the trial court should have rendered.

Eff. Sept. 1, 1997.

46.3. Suggestion of Remittitur by Court of Appeals

The court of appeals may suggest a remittitur. If the remittitur is timely filed, the court must reform and affirm the trial court's judgment in accordance with the remittitur. If the remittitur is not timely filed, the court must reverse the trial court's judgment.

Eff. Sept. 1, 1997.

46.4. Refusal to Remit Must Not Be Mentioned in Later Trial

If the court of appeals suggests a remittitur, but no remittitur is filed, evidence of the court's determination regarding remittitur is inadmissible in a later trial of the case.

Eff. Sept. 1, 1997.

46.5. Voluntary Remittitur

If a court of appeals reverses the trial court's judgment because of a legal error that affects only part of the damages awarded by the judgment, the affected party may—within 15 days after the court of appeals' judgment—voluntarily remit the amount that the affected party believes will cure the reversible error. A party may include in a motion for rehearing—without waiving any complaint that the court of appeals erred—a conditional request that the court accept the remittitur and affirm the trial court's judgment as reduced. If the court of appeals determines that the voluntary remittitur is not sufficient to cure the reversible error, but that remittitur is appropriate, the court must suggest a remittitur in accordance with Rule 46.3. If the remittitur is timely filed and the court of appeals determines that the voluntary remittitur cures the reversible error, then the court must accept the remittitur and reform and affirm the trial court judgment in accordance with the remittitur.

Eff. Sept. 1, 1997. Amended by Supreme Court Dec. 23, 2002, eff. Jan. 1, 2003.

Notes and Comments

Comment to 2002 change: Subdivision 46.5 is amended to clarify the procedure for offering a voluntary remittitur. The offer many be made in a motion for rehearing without waiving any complaint that the court of appeals erred, thereby extending the deadlines for further appeal.

Rule 47. Opinions, Publication, and Citation

Notes and Comments

Comment to 1997 change: This is former Rule 90. Subdivision 47.1 makes clear that a memorandum opinion should not be any longer than necessary. Subdivision 47.5 is amended to make clear that only justices who participated in the decision may file an opinion in the case. Judges who are not on a panel may file an opinion only in respect to a hearing or rehearing en banc. Former Rule 90(h), regarding publication of opinions after the Supreme Court grants review, is repealed.

Comment to 2002 change: The rule is substantively changed to discontinue the use of the "do not publish" designation in civil cases, to require that all opinions of the court of appeals be made available to public reporting services, and to remove prospectively any prohibition against the citation of opinions as authority in civil cases. The rule favors the use "memorandum opinions" designated as such except in certain types of cases but does not change other requirements, such as those in *Pool v. Ford Motor Co.*, 715 S.W.2d 629, 635–636 (Tex. 1986). An opinion previously designated "do not publish" has not precedential value but may be cited. The citation must include the notation, "(not designated for publication)." Of course, whenever an opinion not readily available is cited, copies should be furnished to the court and opposing counsel.

47.1. Written Opinions

The court of appeals must hand down a written opinion that is as brief as practicable but that addresses every issue raised and necessary to final disposition of the appeal.

Eff. Sept. 1, 1997. Amended by Supreme Court Dec. 23, 2002, eff. Jan. 1, 2003.

47.2. Designation and Signing of Opinions; Participating Justices

(a) *Civil and Criminal Cases.* Each opinion of the court must be designated either an "Opinion" or a "Memorandum Opinion." A majority of the justices who participate in considering the case must deter-mine whether the opinion will be signed by a justice or will be per curiam and whether it will be designated an opinion or memorandum opinion. The names of the participating justices must be noted on all written opinions or orders of the court or a panel of the court.

(b) *Criminal Cases.* In addition, each opinion and memorandum opinion in a criminal case must bear the notation "publish" or "do not publish" as determined—before the opinion is handed down—by a majority of the justices who participate in considering the case. Any party may move the appellate court to change the notation, but the court of appeals must not change the notation after the Court of Criminal Appeals has acted on any party's petition for discretionary review or other request for relief. The Court of Criminal Appeals may, at any time, order that a "do not publish" notation be changed to "publish."

(c) *Civil Cases.* Opinions and memorandum opinions in civil cases issued on or after January 1, 2003 shall not be designated "do not publish."

Eff. Sept. 1, 1997. Amended by Supreme Court Dec. 23, 2002, eff. Jan. 1, 2003; March 10, 2008, and Aug. 20, 2008, eff. Sept. 1, 2008. Approved by Court of Criminal Appeals Sept. 30, 2008, eff. Sept. 30, 2008.

47.3. Distribution of Opinions

All opinions of the courts of appeals are open to the public and must be made available to public reporting services, print or electronic.

Eff. Sept. 1, 1997. Amended by Supreme Court Dec. 23, 2002, eff. Jan. 1, 2003.

47.4. Memorandum Opinions

If the issues are settled, the court should write a brief memorandum opinion no longer than necessary to advise the parties of the court's decision and the basic reasons for it. An opinion may not be designated a memorandum opinion if the author of a concurrence or dissent opposes that designation. An opinion must be designated a memorandum opinion unless it does any of the following:

(a) establishes a new rule of law, alters or modifies an existing rule, or applies an existing rule to a novel fact situation likely to recur in future cases;

(b) involves issues of constitutional law or other legal issues important to the jurisprudence of Texas;

(c) criticizes existing law; or

(d) resolves an apparent conflict of authority.

Eff. Sept. 1, 1997. Amended by Supreme Court Dec. 23, 2002, eff. Jan. 1, 2003.

47.5. Concurring and Dissenting Opinions

Only a justice who participated in the decision of a case may file or join in an opinion concurring in or dissenting from the judgment of the court of appeals. Any justice on the court may file an opinion in connection with a denial of a hearing or rehearing en banc.

Eff. Sept. 1, 1997. Amended by Supreme Court Dec. 23, 2002, eff. Jan. 1, 2003.

47.6. Change in Designation by En Banc Court

A court en banc may change a panel's designation of an opinion.

Eff. Sept. 1, 1997. Amended by Supreme Court Dec. 23, 2002, eff. Jan. 1, 2003.

47.7. Citation of Unpublished Opinions

(a) *Criminal Cases.* Opinions and memorandum opinions not designated for publication by the court of appeals under these or prior rules have no precedential value but may be cited with the notation, "(not designated for publication)."

(b) *Civil Cases.* Opinions and memorandum opinions designated "do not publish" under these rules by the courts of appeals prior to January 1, 2003 have no precedential value but may be cited with the notation, "(not designated for publication)." If an opinion or memorandum opinion issued on or after that date is erroneously designated "do not publish," the erroneous designation will not affect the precedential value of the decision.

Eff. Sept. 1, 1997. Amended by Supreme Court Dec. 23, 2002, eff. Jan. 1, 2003; March 10, 2008, and Aug. 20, 2008, eff. Sept. 1, 2008. Approved by Court of Criminal Appeals Sept. 30, 2008, eff. Sept. 30, 2008.

Rule 48. Copy of Opinion and Judgment to Interested Parties and Other Courts

Notes and Comments

Comment to 1997 change: This is former Rule 91 with changes.

48.1. Recipients of Opinion and Judgment in All Cases

On the date when an appellate court's opinion is handed down, the appellate clerk must send or deliver copies of the opinion and judgment to the following persons:

(a) the trial judge;

(b) the trial court clerk;

(c) the regional administrative judge; and

(d) all parties to the appeal.

Eff. Sept. 1, 1997. Amended by Supreme Court Dec. 11, 2013, eff. Jan. 1, 2014. Approved by Court of Criminal Appeals Dec. 11, 2013, eff. Jan. 1, 2014.

48.2. Additional Recipients in Criminal Cases

In criminal cases, copies of the opinion and judgment will also be mailed or delivered to the State Prosecuting Attorney.

Eff. Sept. 1, 1997.

48.3. Filing Opinion and Judgment

The trial court clerk must file a copy of the opinion and judgment among the papers of the case in that court.

Eff. Sept. 1, 1997.

48.4. Opinion Sent to Criminal Defendant

In criminal cases, the attorney representing the defendant on appeal shall, within five days after the opinion is handed down, send his client a copy of the opinion and judgment, along with notification of the defendant's right to file a *pro se* petition for discretionary review under Rule 68. This notification shall be sent certified mail, return receipt requested, to the defendant at his last known address. The attorney shall also send the court of appeals a letter certifying his compliance with this rule and attaching a copy of the return receipt within the time for filing a motion for rehearing. The court of appeals shall file this letter in its record of the appeal.

Adopted by Court of Criminal Appeals May 2, 2007 and Aug. 20, 2007, eff. Sept. 1, 2007.

Rule 49. Motion for Rehearing and En Banc Reconsideration

Notes and Comments

Comment to 1997 change: This is former Rule 100. Subdivision 49.4 is moved here from former Rule 43(h). Subdivisions 49.9 and 49.10 are added.

49.1. Motion for Rehearing

A motion for rehearing may be filed within 15 days after the court of appeals' judgment or order is rendered. The motion must clearly state the points relied on for the rehearing.

Eff. Sept. 1, 1997.

49.2. Response

No response to a motion for rehearing need be filed unless the court so requests. A motion will not be granted unless a response has been filed or requested by the court.

Eff. Sept. 1, 1997.

49.3. Decision on Motion

A motion for rehearing may be granted by a majority of the justices who participated in the decision of the case. Otherwise, it must be denied. If rehearing is granted, the court or panel may dispose of the case with or without rebriefing and oral argument.

Eff. Sept. 1, 1997.

49.4. Accelerated Appeals

In an accelerated appeal, the appellate court may deny the right to file a motion for rehearing or shorten the time to file such a motion.

Eff. Sept. 1, 1997.

49.5 Further Motion for Rehearing.

After a motion for rehearing is decided, a further motion for rehearing may be filed within 15 days of the court's action if the court:

(a) modifies its judgment;

(b) vacates its judgment and renders a new judgment; or

(c) issues a different opinion.

Eff. Sept. 1, 1997. Amended by Supreme Court March 10, 2008, and Aug. 20, 2008, eff. Sept. 1, 2008. Approved by Court of Criminal Appeals Sept. 30, 2008, eff. Sept. 30, 2008.

49.6. Amendments

A motion for rehearing or en banc reconsideration may be amended as a matter of right anytime before the 15–day period allowed for filing the motion expires, and with leave of the court, anytime before the court of appeals decides the motion.

Eff. Sept. 1, 1997 Amended by Supreme Court March 10, 2008, and Aug. 20, 2008 eff. Sept. 1, 2008. Approved by Court of Criminal Appeals Sept. 30, 2008, eff. Sept. 30, 2008.

49.7. En Banc Reconsideration

A party may file a motion for en banc reconsideration as a separate motion, with or without filing a motion for rehearing. The motion must be filed within 15 days after the court of appeals' judgment or order, or when permitted, within 15 days after the court of appeals' denial of the party's last timely filed motion for rehearing or en banc reconsideration. While the court has plenary power, a majority of the en banc court may, with or without a motion, order en banc reconsideration of a panel's decision. If a major-

ity orders reconsideration, the panel's judgment or order does not become final, and the case will be resubmitted to the court for en banc review and disposition.

Eff. Sept. 1, 1997. Amended by Supreme Court March 10, 2008, Aug. 20, 2008, and Aug. 25, 2008, eff. Sept. 1, 2008. Approved by Court of Criminal Appeals Sept. 30, 2008, eff. Sept. 30, 2008.

49.8. Extension of Time

A court of appeals may extend the time for filing a motion for rehearing or en banc reconsideration if a party files a motion complying with Rule 10.5(b) no later than 15 days after the last date for filing the motion.

Eff. Sept. 1, 1997. Amended by Supreme Court March 10, 2008, and Aug. 20, 2008, eff. Sept. 1, 2008. Approved by Court of Criminal Appeals Sept. 30, 2008, eff. Sept. 30, 2008.

49.9. Not Required for Review

A motion for rehearing is not a prerequisite to filing a petition for review in the Supreme Court or a petition for discretionary review in the Court of Criminal Appeals nor is it required to preserve error.

Eff. Sept. 1, 1997.

49.10.   Repealed by Order of Nov. 13, 2012, eff. Dec. 1, 2012

49.11. Relationship to Petition for Review

A party may not file a motion for rehearing or en banc reconsideration in the court of appeals after that party has filed a petition for review in the Supreme Court unless the court of appeals modifies its opinion or judgment after the petition for review is filed. The filing of a petition for review does not preclude another party from filing a motion for rehearing or en banc reconsideration or preclude the court of appeals from ruling on the motion. If a motion for rehearing or en banc reconsideration is timely filed after a petition for review is filed, the petitioner must immediately notify the Supreme Court clerk of the filing of the motion, and must notify the clerk when the last timely filed motion is overruled by the court of appeals.

Eff. Sept. 1, 1997. Amended by Supreme Court March 10, 2008, and Aug. 20, 2008, eff. Sept. 1, 2008. Approved by Court of Criminal Appeals Sept. 30, 2008, eff. Sept. 30, 2008.

49.12. Certificate of Conference Not Required

A certificate of conference is not required for a motion for rehearing or en banc reconsideration of a panel's decision.

Added by Supreme Court March 10, 2008, and Aug. 20, 2008, eff. Sept. 1, 2008. Approved by Court of Criminal Appeals Sept. 30, 2008, eff. Sept. 30, 2008.

Rule 50. Abolished by Order of July 12, 2011, eff. Sept. 1, 2011

Rule 51. Enforcement of Judgments After Mandate

Notes and Comments

Comment to 1997 change: Former Rules 87 and 88 are merged. The reference to costs in tax suits is deleted.

51.1. Civil Cases

(a) *Statement of Costs.* The appellate clerk must prepare, and send to the trial court clerk with the mandate, a statement of costs showing:

(1) the preparation costs for the appellate record, and any court of appeals filing fees, with a notation of those items that have been paid and those that are owing; and

(2) the party or parties against whom costs have been adjudged.

(b) *Enforcement of Judgment.* When the trial court clerk receives the mandate, the appellate court's judgment must be enforced. Appellate court costs must be included with the trial court costs in any process to enforce the judgment. If all or part of the costs are collected, the trial court clerk must immediately remit to the appellate court clerk any amount due to that clerk. The trial court need not make any further order in the case, and the appellate court's judgment may be enforced as in other cases, when the appellate judgment:

(1) affirms the trial court's judgment;

(2) modifies the trial court's judgment and, as so modified, affirms that judgment; or

(3) renders the judgment the trial court should have rendered.

Eff. Sept. 1, 1997.

51.2. Criminal Cases

When the trial court clerk receives the mandate, the appellate court's judgment must be enforced as follows:

(a) *Clerk's Duties.* The trial court clerk must:

(1) send an acknowledgment to the appellate clerk of the mandate's receipt; and

(2) immediately file the mandate.

(b) *Judgment of Affirmance; Defendant Not in Custody.*

(1) Capias to Be Issued. If the judgment contains a sentence of confinement or imprisonment that has not been suspended, the trial court must promptly issue a capias for the defendant's arrest so that the court's sentence can be executed.

(2) Contents of Capias. The capias may issue to any county of this state and must be executed and returned as in felony cases, except that no bail may be taken. The capias must:

(A) recite the fact of conviction;

(B) set forth the offense and the court's judgment and sentence;

(C) state that the judgment was appealed from and affirmed, and that the mandate has been filed; and

(D) command the sheriff to arrest and take the defendant into his custody, and to place and keep the defendant in custody until delivered to the proper authorities as directed by the sentence.

(3) Sheriff's Duties. The sheriff must promptly execute the capias as directed. The sheriff must notify the trial court clerk and the appellate clerk when the mandate has been carried out and executed.

(c) *Judgment of Reversal.*

(1) When New Trial Ordered. When the appellate court reverses the trial court's judgment and grants the defendant a new trial, the procedure is governed by Code of Criminal Procedure article 44.29. If the defendant is in custody and entitled to bail, the defendant must be released upon giving bail.

(2) When Case Dismissed. When the appellate court reverses the trial court's judgment and orders the case to be dismissed, the defendant—if in custody—must be discharged.

(d) *Judgment of Acquittal.* When the appellate court reverses a judgment and orders the defendant's acquittal, the defendant—if in custody—must be discharged, and no further order or judgment of the trial court is necessary.

Eff. Sept. 1, 1997.

SECTION THREE. ORIGINAL PROCEEDINGS IN THE SUPREME COURT AND THE COURTS OF APPEALS

Rule 52. Original Proceedings

Notes and Comments

Comment to 1997 change: Former Rules 120, 121, and 122 are merged into this rule. The requirement of a motion for leave in original proceedings is repealed. The form of the petition and response, contents of the appendix and record, page limits, and relief that may be granted are specifically stated. Specific provision is now made for a motion for rehearing. A provision for sanctions is added.

52.1. Commencement

An original appellate proceeding seeking extraordinary relief—such as a writ of habeas corpus, mandamus, prohibition, injunction, or quo warranto—is commenced by filing a petition with the clerk of the appropriate appellate court. The petition must be captioned "*In re* [name of relator]."

Eff. Sept. 1, 1997.

52.2. Designation of Parties

The party seeking the relief is the relator. In original proceedings other than habeas corpus, the person against whom relief is sought—whether a judge, court, tribunal, officer, or other person—is the respondent. A person whose interest would be directly affected by the relief sought is a real party in interest and a party to the case.

Eff. Sept. 1, 1997.

52.3. Form and Contents of Petition.

The petition must, under appropriate headings and in the order here indicated, contain the following:

(a) *Identity of Parties and Counsel.* The petition must give a complete list of all parties, and the names, and addresses of all counsel.

(b) *Table of Contents.* The petition must include a table of contents with references to the pages of the petition. The table of contents must indicate the subject matter of each issue or point, or group of issues or points.

(c) *Index of Authorities.* The petition must include an index of authorities arranged alphabetically and indicating the pages of the petition where the authorities are cited.

(d) *Statement of the Case.* The petition must contain a statement of the case that should seldom exceed one page and should not discuss the facts. The statement must contain the following:

(1) a concise description of the nature of any underlying proceeding (e.g., a suit for damages, a contempt proceeding for failure to pay child support, or the certification of a candidate for inclusion on an election ballot);

(2) if the respondent is a judge, the name of the judge, the designation of the court in which the

judge was sitting, and the county in which the court is located; and if the respondent is an official other than a judge, the designation and location of the office held by the respondent;

(3) a concise description of the respondent's action from which the relator seeks relief;

(4) if the relator seeks a writ of habeas corpus, a statement describing how and where the relator is being deprived of liberty;

(5) if the petition is filed in the Supreme Court after a petition requesting the same relief was filed in the court of appeals:

(A) the date the petition was filed in the court of appeals;

(B) the district of the court of appeals and the names of the justices who participated in the decision;

(C) the author of any opinion for the court of appeals and the author of any separate opinion;

(D) the citation of the court's opinion;

(E) the disposition of the case by the court of appeals, and the date of the court of appeals' order.

(e) *Statement of Jurisdiction.* The petition must state, without argument, the basis of the court's jurisdiction. If the Supreme Court and the court of appeals have concurrent jurisdiction, the petition must be presented first to the court of appeals unless there is a compelling reason not to do so. If the petition is filed in the Supreme Court without first being presented to the court of appeals, the petition must state the compelling reason why the petition was not first presented to the court of appeals.

(f) *Issues Presented.* The petition must state concisely all issues or points presented for relief. The statement of an issue or point will be treated as covering every subsidiary question that is fairly included.

(g) *Statement of Facts.* The petition must state concisely and without argument the facts pertinent to the issues or points presented. Every statement of fact in the petition must be supported by citation to competent evidence included in the appendix or record.

(h) *Argument.* The petition must contain a clear and concise argument for the contentions made, with appropriate citations to authorities and to the appendix or record.

(i) *Prayer.* The petition must contain a short conclusion that clearly states the nature of the relief sought.

(j) *Certification.* The person filing the petition must certify that he or she has reviewed the petition and concluded that every factual statement in the petition is supported by competent evidence included in the appendix or record.

(k) *Appendix.*

(1) Necessary Contents. The appendix must contain:

(A) a certified or sworn copy of any order complained of, or any other document showing the matter complained of;

(B) any order or opinion of the court of appeals, if the petition is filed in the Supreme Court;

(C) unless voluminous or impracticable, the text of any rule, regulation, ordinance, statute, constitutional provision, or other law (excluding case law) on which the argument is based; and

(D) if a writ of habeas corpus is sought, proof that the relator is being restrained.

(2) Optional Contents. The appendix may contain any other item pertinent to the issues or points presented for review, including copies or excerpts of relevant court opinions, statutes, constitutional provisions, documents on which the suit was based, pleadings, and similar material. Items should not be included in the appendix to attempt to avoid the page limits for the petition. The appendix should not contain any evidence or other item that is not necessary for a decision.

Eff. Sept. 1, 1997. Amended by Supreme Court March 10, 2008, and Aug. 20, 2008, eff. Sept. 1, 2008. Approved by Court of Criminal Appeals Sept. 30, 2008, eff. Sept. 30, 2008.

52.4. Response

Any party may file a response to the petition, but it is not mandatory. The court must not grant relief—other than temporary relief—before a response has been filed or requested by the court. The response must conform to the requirements of 52.3, except that:

(a) the list of parties and counsel is not required unless necessary to supplement or correct the list contained in the petition;

(b) the response need not include a statement of the case, a statement of the issues presented, or a statement of the facts unless the responding party is dissatisfied with that portion of the petition;

(c) a statement of jurisdiction should be omitted unless the petition fails to assert valid grounds for jurisdiction, in which case the reasons why the court lacks jurisdiction must be concisely stated;

(d) the argument must be confined to the issues or points presented in the petition; and

(e) the appendix to the response need not contain any item already contained in an appendix filed by the relator.

Eff. Sept. 1, 1997.

52.5. Relator's Reply to Response

The relator may file a reply addressing any matter in the response. However, the court may consider and decide the case before a reply brief is filed.

Eff. Sept. 1, 1997.

52.6. Repealed by Order of Nov. 13, 2012, eff. Dec. 1, 2012

52.7. Record

(a) *Filing by Relator Required.* Relator must file with the petition:

(1) a certified or sworn copy of every document that is material to the relator's claim for relief and that was filed in any underlying proceeding; and

(2) a properly authenticated transcript of any relevant testimony from any underlying proceeding, including any exhibits offered in evidence, or a statement that no testimony was adduced in connection with the matter complained.

(b) *Supplementation Permitted.* After the record is filed, relator or any other party to the proceeding may file additional materials for inclusion in the record.

(c) *Service of Record on All Parties.* Relator and any party who files materials for inclusion in the record must—at the same time—serve each party.

(1) those materials not previously served on that party as part of the record in another original appellate proceeding in the same or another court; and

(2) an index listing the materials filed and describing them in sufficient detail to identify them.

Eff. Sept. 1, 1997. Amended by Supreme Court Dec. 23, 2002, eff. Jan. 1, 2003.

Notes and Comments

Comment to 2002 change: Subdivision 52.7(c) added to specify how record materials in original proceedings are to be served. Ordinarily, a party must serve records materials and an index of those materials on all other parties. But when materials have already been served in related original proceedings, they need not be served again. Examples are when original proceedings, raising the same issues are brought in both the court of appeals and the Supreme Court, or when separate original proceedings are filed arising out of the same underlying lawsuit. The purpose of this procedure is to ensure that all parties have record materials readily available without requiring unnecessary duplication.

52.8. Action on Petition

(a) *Relief Denied.* If the court determines from the petition and any response and reply that the relator is not entitled to the relief sought, the court must deny the petition. If the relator in a habeas corpus proceeding has been released on bond, the court must remand the relator to custody and issue an order of commitment. If the relator is not returned to custody, the court may declare the bond to be forfeited and render judgment against the surety.

(b) *Interim Action.* If the court is of the tentative opinion that relator is entitled to the relief sought or that a serious question concerning the relief requires further consideration:

   (1) the court must request a response if one has not been filed;

   (2) the Supreme Court may request full briefing under Rule 55;

   (3) in a habeas corpus proceeding, the court may order that relator be discharged on execution and filing of a bond in an amount set by the court; and

   (4) the court may set the case for oral argument.

(c) *Relief Granted.* If the court determines that relator is entitled to relief, it must make an appropriate order. The court may grant relief without hearing oral argument.

(d) *Opinion.* When denying relief, the court may hand down an opinion but is not required to do so. When granting relief, the court must hand down an opinion as in any other case. Rule 47 is applicable to an order or opinion by a court of appeals except that the court of appeals may not order an unpublished opinion published after the Supreme Court or Court of Criminal Appeals has acted on any party's petition for extraordinary relief addressing the same issues.

Eff. Sept. 1, 1997.

52.9. Motion for Rehearing

Any party may file a motion for rehearing within 15 days after the final order is rendered. The motion must clearly state the points relied on for the rehearing. No response to a motion for rehearing need be filed unless the court so requests. The court will not grant a motion for rehearing unless a response has been filed or requested.

Eff. Sept. 1, 1997. Amended by order of March 4, 2013, eff. immediately.

52.10. Temporary Relief

(a) *Motion for Temporary Relief; Certificate of Compliance.* The relator may file a motion to stay any underlying proceedings or for any other temporary relief pending the court's action on the petition. The relator must notify or make a diligent effort to notify all parties by expedited means (such as by telephone or fax) that a motion for temporary relief has been or will be filed and must certify to the court that the relator has complied with this paragraph before temporary relief will be granted.

(b) *Grant of Temporary Relief.* The court—on motion of any party or on its own initiative—may without notice grant any just relief pending the court's action on the petition. As a condition of granting temporary relief, the court may require a bond to protect the parties who will be affected by the relief. Unless vacated or modified, an order granting temporary relief is effective until the case is finally decided.

(c) *Motion to Reconsider.* Any party may move the court at any time to reconsider a grant of temporary relief.

Eff. Sept. 1, 1997.

52.11. Groundless Petition or Misleading Statement or Record

On motion of any party or on its own initiative, the court may—after notice and a reasonable opportunity to respond—impose just sanctions on a party or attorney who is not acting in good faith as indicated by any of the following:

(a) filing a petition that is clearly groundless;

(b) bringing the petition solely for delay of an underlying proceeding;

(c) grossly misstating or omitting an obviously important and material fact in the petition or response; or

(d) filing an appendix or record that is clearly misleading because of the omission of obviously important and material evidence or documents.

Eff. Sept. 1, 1997.

SECTION FOUR. PROCEEDINGS IN THE SUPREME COURT

Rule 53. Petition for Review

Notes and Comments

Comment to 1997 change: Former Rules 130 and 131 are merged. The 50–page application for writ of error is replaced by a 15–page petition for review, which is filed in the Supreme Court and should concentrate on the reasons the Court should exercise jurisdiction to hear the case. The contents of the petition and response, the length of the documents, the time for filing are all specifically stated.

53.1. Method of Review

The Supreme Court may review a court of appeals' final judgment on a petition for review addressed to "The Supreme Court of Texas." A party who seeks to alter the court of appeals' judgment must file a petition for review. The petition for review procedure replaces the writ of error procedure. Statutes pertaining to the writ of error in the Supreme Court apply equally to the petition for review.

Eff. Sept. 1, 1997.

53.2. Contents of Petition

The petition for review must, under appropriate headings and in the order here indicated, contain the following items:

(a) *Identity of Parties and Counsel.* The petition must give a complete list of all parties to the trial court's final judgment, and the names and addresses of all trial and appellate counsel.

(b) *Table of Contents.* The petition must have a table of contents with references to the pages of the petition. The table of contents must indicate the subject matter of each issue or point, or group of issues or points.

(c) *Index of Authorities.* The petition must have an index of authorities arranged alphabetically and indicating the pages of the petition where the authorities are cited.

(d) *Statement of the Case.* The petition must contain a statement of the case that should seldom exceed one page and should not discuss the facts. The statement must contain the following:

(1) a concise description of the nature of the case (e.g., whether it is a suit for damages, on a note, or in trespass to try title);

(2) the name of the judge who signed the order or judgment appealed from;

(3) the designation of the trial court and the county in which it is located;

(4) the disposition of the case by the trial court;

(5) the parties in the court of appeals;

(6) the district of the court of appeals;

(7) the names of the justices who participated in the decision in the court of appeals, the author of the opinion for the court, and the author of any separate opinion;

(8) the citation for the court of appeals' opinion; and

(9) the disposition of the case by the court of appeals, including the disposition of any motions for rehearing or en banc reconsideration, and whether any motions for rehearing or en banc reconsideration are pending in the court of appeals at the time the petition for review is filed.

(e) *Statement of Jurisdiction.* The petition must state, without argument, the basis of the Court's jurisdiction.

(f) *Issues Presented.* The petition must state concisely all issues or points presented for review. The statement of an issue or point will be treated as covering every subsidiary question that is fairly included. If the matter complained of originated in the trial court, it should have been preserved for appellate review in the trial court and assigned as error in the court of appeals.

(g) *Statement of Facts.* The petition must affirm that the court of appeals correctly stated the nature of the case, except in any particulars pointed out. The petition must state concisely and without argument the facts and procedural background pertinent to the issues or points presented. The statement must be supported by record references.

(h) *Summary of the Argument.* The petition must contain a succinct, clear, and accurate statement of the arguments made in the body of the petition. This summary must not merely repeat the issues or points presented for review.

(i) *Argument.* The petition must contain a clear and concise argument for the contentions made, with appropriate citations to authorities and to the record. The argument need not address every issue or point included in the statement of issues or points. Any issue or point not addressed may be addressed in the brief on the merits if one is requested by the Court. The argument should state the reasons why the Supreme Court should exercise jurisdiction to hear the case with specific reference to the factors listed in

Rule 56.1(a). The petition need not quote at length from a matter included in the appendix; a reference to the appendix is sufficient. The Court will consider the court of appeals' opinion along with the petition, so statements in that opinion need not be repeated.

(j) *Prayer.* The petition must contain a short conclusion that clearly states the nature of the relief sought.

(k) *Appendix.*

(1) Necessary Contents. Unless voluminous or impracticable, the appendix must contain a copy of:

(A) the judgment or other appealable order of the trial court from which relief in the court of appeals was sought;

(B) the jury charge and verdict, if any, or the trial court's findings of fact and conclusions of law, if any;

(C) the opinion and judgment of the court of appeals; and

(D) the text of any rule, regulation, ordinance, statute, constitutional provision, or other law on which the argument is based (excluding case law), and the text of any contract or other document that is central to the argument.

(2) Optional Contents. The appendix may contain any other item pertinent to the issues or points presented for review, including copies or excerpts of relevant court opinions, statutes, constitutional provisions, documents on which the suit was based, pleadings, and similar material. Items should not be included in the appendix to attempt to avoid the page limits for the petition.

Eff. Sept. 1, 1997. Amended by Supreme Court March 10, 2008, and Aug. 20, 2008, eff. Sept. 1, 2008. Approved by Court of Criminal Appeals Sept. 30, 2008, eff. Sept. 30, 2008.

53.3. Response to Petition for Review

Any other party to the appeal may file a response to the petition for review, but it is not mandatory. If no response is timely filed, or if a party files a waiver of response, the Court will consider the petition without a response. A petition will not be granted before a response has been filed or requested by the Court. The response must conform to the requirements of 53.2, except that:

(a) the list of parties and counsel is not required unless necessary to supplement or correct the list contained in the petition;

(b) a statement of the case and a statement of the facts need not be made unless the respondent is dissatisfied with that portion of the petition;

(c) a statement of the issues presented need not be made unless:

(1) the respondent is dissatisfied with the statement made in the petition;

(2) the respondent is asserting independent grounds for affirmance of the court of appeals' judgment; or

(3) the respondent is asserting grounds that establish the respondent's right to a judgment that is less favorable to the respondent than the judgment rendered by the court of appeals but more favorable to the respondent than the judgment that might be awarded to the petitioner (e.g., a remand for a new trial rather than a rendition of judgment in favor of the petitioner);

(d) a statement of jurisdiction should be omitted unless the petition fails to assert valid grounds for jurisdiction, in which case the reasons why the Supreme Court lacks jurisdiction must be concisely stated;

(e) the respondent's argument must be confined to the issues or points presented in the petition or asserted by the respondent in the respondent's statement of issues; and

(f) the appendix to the response need not contain any item already contained in an appendix filed by the petitioner.

Eff. Sept. 1, 1997.

53.4. Points Not Considered in Court of Appeals

To obtain a remand to the court of appeals for consideration of issues or points briefed in that court but not decided by that court, or to request that the Supreme Court consider such issues or points, a party may raise those issues or points in the petition, the response, the reply, any brief, or a motion for rehearing.

Eff. Sept. 1, 1997.

53.5. Petitioner's Reply to Response

The petitioner may file a reply addressing any matter in the response. However, the Court may consider and decide the case before a reply brief is filed.

Eff. Sept. 1, 1997.

53.6. Repealed by Order of Nov. 13, 2012, eff. Dec. 1, 2012

53.7. Time and Place of Filing

(a) *Petition.* Unless the Supreme Court orders an earlier filing deadline, the petition must be filed with the Supreme Court clerk within 45 days after the following:

(1) the date the court of appeals rendered judgment, if no motion for rehearing or en banc reconsideration is timely filed; or

(2) the date of the court of appeals' last ruling on all timely filed motions for rehearing or en banc reconsideration.

(b) *Premature Filing.* A petition filed before the last ruling on all timely filed motions for rehearing and en banc reconsideration is treated as having been filed on the date of, but after, the last ruling on any such motion. If a party files a petition for review while a motion for rehearing or en banc reconsideration is pending in the court of appeals, the party must include that information in its petition for review.

(c) *Petitions Filed by Other Parties.* If a party files a petition for review within the time specified in 53.7(a)—or within the time specified by the Supreme Court in an order granting an extension of time to file a petition—any other party required to file a petition may do so within 45 days after the last timely motion for rehearing is overruled or within 30 days after any preceding petition is filed, whichever date is later.

(d) *Response.* Any response must be filed with the Supreme Court clerk within 30 days after the petition is filed.

(e) *Reply.* Any reply must be filed with the Supreme Court clerk within 15 days after the response is filed.

(f) *Extension of Time.* The Supreme Court may extend the time to file a petition for review if a party files a motion complying with Rule 10.5(b) no later than 15 days after the last day for filing the petition. The Supreme Court may extend the time to file a response or reply if a party files a motion complying with Rule 10.5(b) either before or after the response or reply is due.

(g) *Petition Filed in Court of Appeals.* If a petition is mistakenly filed in the court of appeals, the petition is deemed to have been filed the same day with the Supreme Court clerk, and the court of appeals clerk must immediately send the petition to the Supreme Court clerk.

Eff. Sept. 1, 1997. Amended by Supreme Court March 10, 2008, and Aug. 20, 2008, eff. Sept. 1, 2008. Approved by Court of Criminal Appeals Sept. 30, 2008, eff. Sept. 30, 2008.

53.8. Amendment

On motion showing good cause, the Court may allow the petition, response, or reply to be amended on such reasonable terms as the Court may prescribe.

Eff. Sept. 1, 1997.

53.9. Court May Require Revision

If a petition, response, or reply does not conform with these rules, the Supreme Court may require the document to be revised or may return the document to the party who filed it and consider the case without allowing the document to be revised.

Eff. Sept. 1, 1997.

Rule 54. Filing the Record

Notes and Comments

Comment to 1997 change: This is former Rule 132. Subdivision 54.1 is new and provides for the Supreme Court to request the filing of the record. Other changes are made.

54.1. Request for Record

With or without granting the petition for review, the Supreme Court may request that the record from the court of appeals be filed with the clerk of the Supreme Court.

Eff. Sept. 1, 1997.

54.2. Duty of Court of Appeals Clerk

(a) *Request for Record.* The court of appeals clerk must not send the record to the Supreme Court unless it is requested. Upon receiving the Supreme Court clerk's request for the record, the court of appeals clerk must promptly send to the Supreme Court clerk all of the following:

(1) the original record;

(2) any motion filed in the court of appeals;

(3) copies of all orders of the court of appeals; and

(4) copies of all opinions and the judgment of the court of appeals.

(b) *Nondocumentary Exhibits.* The clerk should not send any nondocumentary exhibits unless the Supreme Court specifically requests.

Eff. Sept. 1, 1997.

54.3. Expenses

The petitioner must pay to the court of appeals clerk a sum sufficient to pay the cost of mailing or shipping the record to and from the Supreme Court clerk.

Eff. Sept. 1, 1997.

54.4. Duty of Supreme Court Clerk

Upon receiving the record, the Supreme Court clerk must file it and enter the filing on the docket. The clerk may refuse the record if the charges for mailing or shipping have not been paid.

Eff. Sept. 1, 1997.

Rule 55. Briefs on the Merits

Notes and Comments

Comment to 1997 change: The rule is new and provides for a 50 page brief on the merits if requested by the Supreme Court.

55.1. Request by Court

A brief on the merits must not be filed unless requested by the Court. With or without granting the petition for review, the Court may request the parties to file briefs on the merits. In appropriate cases, the Court may realign parties and direct that parties file consolidated briefs.

Eff. Sept. 1, 1997. Amended by Supreme Court Dec. 23, 2002, eff. Jan. 1, 2003.

Notes and Comments

Comment to 2002 change: Subdivision 55.1 is clarified to provide that the Court may realign parties require consolidated briefing for a clearer and more efficient presentation of the case.

55.2. Petitioner's Brief on the Merits

The petitioner's brief on the merits must be confined to the issues or points stated in the petition for review and must, under appropriate headings and in the order here indicated, contain the following items:

(a) *Identity of Parties and Counsel.* The brief must give a complete list of all parties to the trial court's final judgment, and the names and addresses of all trial and appellate counsel.

(b) *Table of Contents.* The brief must have a table of contents with references to the pages of the brief. The table of contents must indicate the subject matter of each issue or point, or group of issues or points.

(c) *Index of Authorities.* The brief must have an index of authorities arranged alphabetically and indicating the pages of the brief where the authorities are cited.

(d) *Statement of the Case.* The brief must contain a statement of the case that should seldom exceed one page and should not discuss the facts. The statement must contain the following:

(1) a concise description of the nature of the case (e.g., whether it is a suit for damages, on a note, or in trespass to try title);

(2) the name of the judge who signed the order or judgment appealed from;

(3) the designation of the trial court and the county in which it is located;

(4) the disposition of the case by the trial court;

(5) the parties in the court of appeals;

(6) the district of the court of appeals;

(7) the names of the justices who participated in the decision in the court of appeals, the author of the opinion for the court, and the author of any separate opinion;

(8) the citation for the court of appeals' opinion, if available, or a statement that the opinion was unpublished; and

(9) the disposition of the case by the court of appeals;

(e) *Statement of Jurisdiction.* The brief must state, without argument, the basis of the Court's jurisdiction.

(f) *Issues Presented.* The brief must state concisely all issues or points presented for review. The statement of an issue or point will be treated as covering every subsidiary question that is fairly included. The phrasing of the issues or points need not be identical to the statement of issues or points in the petition for review, but the brief may not raise additional issues or points or change the substance of the issues or points presented in the petition.

(g) *Statement of Facts.* The brief must affirm that the court of appeals correctly stated the nature of the case, except in any particulars pointed out. The brief must state concisely and without argument the facts and procedural background pertinent to the issues or points presented. The statement must be supported by record references.

(h) *Summary of the Argument.* The brief must contain a succinct, clear, and accurate statement of the arguments made in the body of the brief. This summary must not merely repeat the issues or points presented for review.

(i) *Argument.* The brief must contain a clear and concise argument for the contentions made, with appropriate citations to authorities and to the record.

(j) *Prayer.* The brief must contain a short conclusion that clearly states the nature of the relief sought.

Eff. Sept. 1, 1997. Amended by Supreme Court Dec. 23, 2002, eff. Jan. 1, 2003.

55.3. Respondent's Brief

If the petitioner files a brief on the merits, any other party to the appeal may file a brief in response, which must conform to 55.2, except that:

(a) the list of parties and counsel is not required unless necessary to supplement or correct the list contained in the petitioner's brief;

(b) a statement of the case and a statement of the facts need not be made unless the respondent is dissatisfied with that portion of the petitioner's brief; and

(c) a statement of the issues presented need not be made unless:

(1) the respondent is dissatisfied with the statement made in the petitioner's brief;

(2) the respondent is asserting independent grounds for affirmance of the court of appeals' judgment; or

(3) the respondent is asserting grounds that establish the respondent's right to a judgment that is less favorable to the respondent than the judgment rendered by the court of appeals but more favorable to the respondent than the judgment that might be awarded to the petitioner (e.g., a remand for a new trial rather than a rendition of judgment in favor of the petitioner);

(d) a statement of jurisdiction should be omitted unless the petition fails to assert valid grounds for jurisdiction; and

(e) the respondent's argument must be confined to the issues or points presented in the petitioner's brief or asserted by the respondent in the respondent's statement of issues.

Eff. Sept. 1, 1997.

55.4. Petitioner's Brief in Reply

The petitioner may file a reply brief addressing any matter in the brief in response. However, the Court may consider and decide the case before a reply brief is filed.

Eff. Sept. 1, 1997.

55.5. Reliance on Prior Brief

As a brief on the merits or a brief in response, a party may file the brief that the party filed in the court of appeals.

Eff. Sept. 1, 1997.

55.6. Repealed by Order of Nov. 13, 2012, eff. Dec. 1, 2012

55.7. Time and Place of Filing; Extension of Time

Briefs must be filed with the Supreme Court clerk in accordance with the schedule stated in the clerk's notice that the Court has requested briefs on the merits. If no schedule is stated in the notice, petitioner must file a brief on the merits within 30 days after the date of the notice, respondent must file a brief in response within 20 days after receiving petitioner's brief, and petitioner must file any reply brief within 15 days after receiving respondent's brief. On motion complying with Rule 10.5(b) either before or after the brief is due, the Supreme Court may extend the time to file a brief.

Eff. Sept. 1, 1997.

55.8. Amendment

On motion showing good cause, the Court may allow a party to amend a brief on such reasonable terms as the Court may prescribe.

Eff. Sept. 1, 1997.

55.9. Court May Require Revision

If a brief does not conform with these rules, the Supreme Court may require the brief to be revised or may return it to the party who filed it and consider the case without further briefing by that party.

Eff. Sept. 1, 1997.

Rule 56.   Orders on Petition for Review

Notes and Comments

Comment to 1997 change: The rule is from former Rule 133. Subdivision 56.3 regarding settled cases is added.

56.1. Orders on Petition for Review

(a) *Considerations in Granting Review.* Whether to grant review is a matter of judicial discretion. Among the factors the Supreme Court considers in deciding whether to grant a petition for review are the following:

(1) whether the justices of the court of appeals disagree on an important point of law;

(2) whether there is a conflict between the courts of appeals on an important point of law;

(3) whether a case involves the construction or validity of a statute;

(4) whether a case involves constitutional issues;

(5) whether the court of appeals appears to have committed an error of law of such importance to the state's jurisprudence that it should be corrected; and

(6) whether the court of appeals has decided an important question of state law that should be, but has not been, resolved by the Supreme Court.

(b) *Petition Denied or Dismissed.* When the petition has been on file in the Supreme Court for 30 days, the Court may deny or dismiss the petition—whether or not a response has been filed—with one of the following notations:

(1) "Denied." If the Supreme Court is not satisfied that the opinion of the court of appeals has correctly declared the law in all respects, but determines that the petition presents no error that requires reversal or that is of such importance to the jurisprudence of the state as to require correction, the Court will deny the petition with the notation "Denied."

(2) "Dismissed w.o.j." If the Supreme Court lacks jurisdiction, the Court will dismiss the petition with the notation "Dismissed for Want of Jurisdiction."

(c) *Petition Refused.* If the Supreme Court determines—after a response has been filed or requested—that the court of appeals' judgment is correct and that the legal principles announced in the opinion are likewise correct, the Court will refuse the petition with the notation "Refused." The court of appeals' opinion in the case has the same precedential value as an opinion of the Supreme Court.

(d) *Improvident Grant.* If the Court has granted review but later decides that review should not have been granted, the Court may, without opinion, set aside the order granting review and dismiss the petition or deny or refuse review as though review had never been granted.

Eff. Sept. 1, 1997.

56.2. Moot Cases

If a case is moot, the Supreme Court may, after notice to the parties, grant the petition and, without hearing argument, dismiss the case or the appealable portion of it without addressing the merits of the appeal.

Eff. Sept. 1, 1997.

56.3. Settled Cases

If a case is settled by agreement of the parties and all parties so move, the Supreme Court may grant the petition if it has not already been granted and, without hearing argument or considering the merits, render a judgment to effectuate the agreement. The Supreme Court's action may include setting aside the judgment of the court of appeals or the trial court without regard to the merits and remanding the case to the trial court for rendition of a judgment in accordance with the agreement. The Supreme Court may abate the case until the lower court's proceedings to effectuate the agreement are complete. A severable portion of the proceeding may be disposed of if it will not prejudice the remaining parties. In any event, the Supreme Court's order does not vacate the court of appeals' opinion unless the order specifically provides otherwise. An agreement or motion cannot be conditioned on vacating the court of appeals' opinion.

Eff. Sept. 1, 1997. Amended by Supreme Court Dec. 23, 2002, eff. Jan. 1, 2003.

Notes and Comments

Comment to 2002 change: Subdivision 56.3 is clarified to provide for partial settlements.

56.4. Notice to Parties

When the Supreme Court grants, denies, refuses, or dismisses a petition for review, the Supreme Court clerk must send a written notice of the disposition to the court of appeals, the trial court, and all parties to the appeal.

Eff. Sept. 1, 1997.

56.5. Return of Documents to Court of Appeals

When the Supreme Court denies, refuses, or dismisses a petition for review, the clerk will retain the petition, together with the record and accompanying papers, for 30 days after the order is rendered. If no motion for rehearing has been filed by the end of that period or when any motion for rehearing of the order has been overruled, the clerk must send a certified copy of its order to the court of appeals and return the record and all papers (except for documents filed in the Supreme Court) to the court of appeals clerk.

Eff. Sept. 1, 1997.

Rule 57. Direct Appeals to the Supreme Court

Notes and Comments

Comment to 1997 change: This is former Rule 140. The rule is amended without substantive change except subdivision 57.5 is amended to make clear that no party to the direct appeal may pursue the appeal in the court of appeals while the direct appeal is pending, but allowing 10 days to perfect a subsequent appeal.

57.1. Application

This rule governs direct appeals to the Supreme Court that are authorized by the Constitution and by statute. Except when inconsistent with a statute or this rule, the rules governing appeals to courts of appeals also apply to direct appeals to the Supreme Court.

Eff. Sept. 1, 1997.

57.2. Jurisdiction

The Supreme Court may not take jurisdiction over a direct appeal from the decision of any court other than a district court or county court, or over any question of fact. The Supreme Court may decline to exercise jurisdiction over a direct appeal of an interlocutory order if the record is not adequately developed, or if its decision would be advisory, or if the case is not of such importance to the jurisprudence of the state that a direct appeal should be allowed.

Eff. Sept. 1, 1997.

57.3. Statement of Jurisdiction

Appellant must file with the record a statement fully but plainly setting out the basis asserted for exercise of the Supreme Court's jurisdiction. Appellee may file a response to appellant's statement of jurisdiction within ten days after the statement is filed.

Eff. Sept. 1, 1997.

57.4. Preliminary Ruling on Jurisdiction

If the Supreme Court notes probable jurisdiction over a direct appeal, the parties must file briefs under Rule 38[1] as in any other case. If the Supreme Court does not note probable jurisdiction over a direct appeal, the appeal will be dismissed.

Eff. Sept. 1, 1997.

[1] Vernon's Ann.Rules App.Proc., rule 38.1 et seq.

57.5. Direct Appeal Exclusive While Pending

If a direct appeal to the Supreme Court is filed, the parties to the appeal must not, while that appeal is pending, pursue an appeal to the court of appeals. But if the direct appeal is dismissed, any party may pursue any other appeal available at the time when the direct appeal was filed. The other appeal must be perfected within ten days after dismissal of the direct appeal.

Eff. Sept. 1, 1997.

Rule 58. Certification of Questions of Law by United States Courts

Notes and Comments

Comment to 1997 change: This is former Rule 114. The rule is substantially revised, but no substantive change in procedure is intended.

58.1. Certification

The Supreme Court of Texas may answer questions of law certified to it by any federal appellate court if the certifying court is presented with determinative questions of Texas law having no controlling Supreme Court precedent. The Supreme Court may decline to answer the questions certified to it.

Eff. Sept. 1, 1997.

58.2. Contents of the Certification Order

An order from the certifying court must set forth:

(a) the questions of law to be answered; and

(b) a stipulated statement of all facts relevant to the questions certified, showing fully the nature of the controversy in which the questions arose.

Eff. Sept. 1, 1997.

58.3. Transmission of Certification Order

The clerk of the certifying court must send to the clerk of the Supreme Court of Texas the following:

(a) the certification order under the certifying court's official seal;

(b) a list of the names of all parties to the pending case, giving the address and telephone number, if known, of any party not represented by counsel; and

(c) a list of the names, addresses, and telephone numbers of counsel for each party.

Eff. Sept. 1, 1997.

58.4. Transmission of Record

The certifying court should not send the Supreme Court of Texas the record in the pending case with the certification order. The Supreme Court may later require the original or copies of all or part of the record before the certifying court to be filed with the Supreme Court clerk.

Eff. Sept. 1, 1997.

58.5. Fees and Costs

Unless the certifying court orders otherwise in its certification order, the parties must bear equally the fees under Rule 5.

Eff. Sept. 1, 1997.

58.6. Notice

If the Supreme Court agrees to answer the questions certified to it, the Court will notify all parties and the certifying court. The Supreme Court clerk must also send a notice to the Attorney General of Texas if:

(a) the constitutionality of a Texas statute is the subject of a certified question that the Supreme Court has agreed to answer; and

(b) the State of Texas or an officer, agency, or employee of the state is not a party to the proceeding in the certifying court.

Eff. Sept. 1, 1997.

58.7. Briefs and Oral Argument

(a) *Briefs.* The appealing party in the certifying court must file a brief with the Supreme Court clerk within 30 days after the date of the notice. Opposing parties must file an answering brief within 20 days after receiving the opening brief. Briefs must comply with Rule 55[1] to the extent its provisions apply. On motion complying with Rule 10.5(b), either before or after the brief is due, the Supreme Court may extend the time to file a brief.

(b) *Oral Argument.* Oral argument may be granted either on a party's request or on the Court's own initiative. Argument is governed by Rule 59.[2]

Eff. Sept. 1, 1997.

[1] Vernon's Ann.Rules App.Proc., rule 55.1 et seq.
[2] Vernon's Ann.Rules App.Proc., rule 59.1 et seq.

58.8. Intervention by the State

If the constitutionality of a Texas statute is the subject of a certified question that the Supreme Court has agreed to answer the State of Texas may intervene at any reasonable time for briefing and oral argument (if argument is allowed), on the question of constitutionality.

Eff. Sept. 1, 1997.

58.9. Opinion on Certified Questions

If the Supreme Court has agreed to answer a certified question, it will hand down an opinion as in any other case.

Eff. Sept. 1, 1997.

58.10. Answering Certified Questions

After all motions for rehearing have been overruled, the Supreme Court clerk must send to the certifying court the written opinion on the certified questions. The opinion must be under the Supreme Court's seal.

Eff. Sept. 1, 1997.

Rule 59. Submission and Argument

Notes and Comments

Comment to 1997 change: Former Rules 170, 171, and 172 are merged. Subdivisions 59.2 and 59.3 are new. Other changes are made.

59.1. Submission Without Argument

If at least six members of the Court so vote, a petition may be granted and an opinion handed down without oral argument.

Eff. Sept. 1, 1997.

59.2. Submission With Argument

If the Supreme Court decides that oral argument would aid the Court, the Court will set the case for argument. The clerk will notify all parties of the submission date.

Eff. Sept. 1, 1997.

59.3. Purpose of Argument

Oral argument should emphasize and clarify the written arguments in the briefs. Counsel should not merely read from a prepared text. Counsel should assume that all Justices have read the briefs before oral argument and should be prepared to respond to the Justices' questions.

Eff. Sept. 1, 1997.

59.4. Time for Argument

Each side is allowed only as much time as the Court orders. Counsel is not required to use all the allotted time. On motion filed before the day of argument, the Court may extend the time for argument. The Court may also align the parties for purposes of presenting argument.

Eff. Sept. 1, 1997.

59.5. Number of Counsel

Generally, only one counsel should argue for each side. Except on leave of court, no more than two counsel on each side may argue. Only one counsel may argue in rebuttal.

59.6. Argument by Amicus Curiae

With leave of court obtained before the argument and with a party's consent, an amicus may share allotted time with that party. Otherwise, counsel for amicus curiae may not argue.

Eff. Sept. 1, 1997.

Rule 60. Judgments in the Supreme Court

Notes and Comments

Comment to 1997 change: Former Rules 180 and 182(a) are merged. Subdivision 60.1 is from former Rule 181. Paragraphs 60.2(b), (e), and (f) are new but codify current practice. Subdivision 60.6 is new. Other changes are made.

60.1. Announcement of Judgments

The Court's judgments will be announced by the clerk.

Eff. Sept. 1, 1997.

60.2. Types of Judgment

The Supreme Court may:

(a) affirm the lower court's judgment in whole or in part;

(b) modify the lower court's judgment and affirm it as modified;

(c) reverse the lower court's judgment in whole or in part and render the judgment that the lower court should have rendered;

(d) reverse the lower court's judgment and remand the case for further proceedings;

(e) vacate the judgments of the lower courts and dismiss the case; or

(f) vacate the lower court's judgment and remand the case for further proceedings in light of changes in the law.

Eff. Sept. 1, 1997.

60.3. Remand in the Interest of Justice

When reversing the court of appeals' judgment, the Supreme Court may, in the interest of justice, remand the case to the trial court even if a rendition of judgment is otherwise appropriate.

Eff. Sept. 1, 1997.

60.4. Judgment for Costs

The Supreme Court's judgment will award to the prevailing party the costs incurred by that party in the Supreme Court. If appropriate, the judgment may also award the prevailing party the costs—including preparation costs for the record—incurred by that party in the court of appeals and in the trial court. But the Court may tax costs otherwise as required by law or for good cause.

Eff. Sept. 1, 1997.

60.5. Judgment Against Sureties

When affirming, modifying, or rendering a judgment against the party who was the appellant in the court of appeals, the Supreme Court must render judgment against the sureties on that party's supersedeas bond, if any, for the performance of the judgment. If the Supreme Court taxes costs against the party who was the appellant in the court of appeals, the Court must render judgment for those costs against the sureties on that party's supersedeas bond, if any.

60.6. Other Orders

The Supreme Court may make any other appropriate order required by the law and the nature of the case.

Eff. Sept. 1, 1997.

Rule 61. Reversible Error

Notes and Comments

Comment to 1997 change: Former Rules 184 and 185 are merged. The reversible error standard is amended to omit the reference to an action "reasonably calculated to cause" an improper judgment, but no substantive change is intended. Subdivision 61.3 is amended to delete the reference to defects of "substance."

61.1. Standard for Reversible Error

No judgment may be reversed on appeal on the ground that the trial court made an error of law unless the Supreme Court concludes that the error complained of:

(a) probably caused the rendition of an improper judgment; or

(b) probably prevented the petitioner from properly presenting the case to the appellate courts.

Eff. Sept. 1, 1997.

61.2. Error Affecting Only Part of the Case

If the error affects a part, but not all, of the matter in controversy, and that part is separable without unfairness to the parties, the judgment must be reversed and a new trial ordered only as to the part affected by the error. The Court may not order a separate trial solely on unliquidated damages if liability is contested.

Eff. Sept. 1, 1997.

61.3. Defects in Procedure

The Supreme Court will not affirm or reverse a judgment or dismiss a petition for review for formal defects or irregularities in appellate procedure without allowing a reasonable time to correct or amend the defects or irregularities.

Eff. Sept. 1, 1997.

61.4. Remediable Error of the Trial Court or Court of Appeals

(a) *Generally.* The Supreme Court will not affirm or reverse a judgment or dismiss a petition for review if:

(1) the trial court's or court of appeals' erroneous action or failure or refusal to act prevents the proper presentation of a case to the Supreme Court; and

(2) the trial court or court of appeals can correct its action or failure to act.

(b) *Supreme Court Direction if Error Remediable.* If the circumstances described in (a) exist, the Supreme Court will direct the trial court or court of appeals to correct the error. The Supreme Court will then proceed as if the error had not occurred.

Eff. Sept. 1, 1997.

Rule 62.   Damages for Frivolous Appeals

If the Supreme Court determines that a direct appeal or a petition for review is frivolous, it may—on motion of any party or on its own initiative, after notice and a reasonable opportunity for response—award to each prevailing party just damages. In determining whether to award damages, the Court must not consider any matter that does not appear in the record, briefs, or other papers filed in the court of appeals or the Supreme Court.

Eff. Sept. 1, 1997.

Notes and Comments

Comment to 1997 change: This is former Rule 182(b). The rule is changed from allowing a sanction when an appeal "filed for delay and without sufficient cause" to allowing a sanction when the appeal is "frivolous." A requirement for notice and an opportunity to respond is included.

Rule 63.   Opinions; Copy of Opinion and Judgment to Interested Parties and Other Courts

The Supreme Court will hand down a written opinion in all cases in which it renders a judgment. The clerk will send a copy of the opinion and judgment to the court of appeals clerk, the trial court clerk, the regional administrative judge, and all parties to the appeal.

Eff. Sept. 1, 1997.

Notes and Comments

Comment to 1997 change: This is former Rule 181 with changes.

Rule 64.   Motion for Rehearing

Notes and Comments

Comment to 1997 change: This is former Rule 190. The service and notice provisions of former subdivisions (b) and (c) are deleted. *See* Rule 9.5. Other changes are made.

64.1.   Time for Filing

A motion for rehearing may be filed with the Supreme Court clerk within 15 days from the date when the Court renders judgment or makes an order disposing of a petition for review. In exceptional cases, if justice requires, the Court may shorten the time within which the motion may be filed or even deny the right to file it altogether.

Eff. Sept. 1, 1997.

64.2.   Contents

The motion must specify the points relied on for the rehearing.

Eff. Sept. 1, 1997.

64.3.   Response and Decision

No response to a motion for rehearing need be filed unless the Court so requests. A motion will not be granted unless a response has been filed or requested by the Court. But in exceptional cases, if justice so requires, the Court may deny the right to file a response and act on a motion any time after it is filed.

Eff. Sept. 1, 1997.

64.4. Second Motion

The Court will not consider a second motion for rehearing unless the Court modifies its judgment, vacates its judgment and renders a new judgment, or issues a different opinion.

Eff. Sept. 1, 1997. Amended by Supreme Court Aug. 20, 2008, eff. Sept. 1, 2008. Approved by Court of Criminal Appeals Sept. 30, 2008, eff. Sept. 30, 2008.

64.5. Extensions of Time

The Court may extend the time to file a motion for rehearing in the Supreme Court, if a motion complying with Rule 10.5(b) is filed with the Court no later than 15 days after the last date for filing a motion for rehearing.

Eff. Sept. 1, 1997.

64.6. Repealed by Order of Nov. 13, 2012, eff. Dec. 1, 2012

Rule 65. Enforcement of Judgment after Mandate

Notes and Comments

Comment to 1997 change: Subdivision 65.1 is new. Subdivision 65.2 is from former Rule 183.

65.1. Statement of Costs

The Supreme Court clerk will prepare, and send to the clerk to whom the mandate is directed, a statement of costs showing:

(a) the costs that were incurred in the Supreme Court, with a notation of those items that have been paid and those that are owing; and

(b) the party or parties against whom costs have been adjudged.

Eff. Sept. 1, 1997.

65.2. Enforcement of Judgment

If the Supreme Court renders judgment, the trial court need not make any further order. Upon receiving the Supreme Court's mandate, the trial court clerk must proceed to enforce the judgment of the Supreme Court's as in any other case. Appellate court costs must be included with the trial court costs in any process to enforce the judgment. If all or part of the costs are collected, the trial court clerk must immediately remit to the appellate court clerk any amount due to that clerk.

Eff. Sept. 1, 1997.

SECTION FIVE. PROCEEDINGS IN THE COURT OF CRIMINAL APPEALS

Rule 66. Discretionary Review in General

Notes and Comments

Comment to 1997 change: This is former Rule 200. The former rule's reference to motions for rehearing now appears in Rule 49.9. The rule is otherwise amended without substantive change.

66.1. With or Without Petition

The Court of Criminal Appeals may review a court of appeals' decision in a criminal case on its own initiative under Rule 67[1] or on the petition of a party under Rule 68.[2]

Eff. Sept. 1, 1997.

[1] Vernon's Ann.Rules App.Proc., rule 67.1 et seq.
[2] Vernon's Ann.Rules App.Proc., rule 68.1 et seq.

66.2. Not a Matter of Right

Discretionary review by the Court of Criminal Appeals is not a matter of right, but of the Court's discretion.

Eff. Sept. 1, 1997.

66.3. Reasons for Granting Review

While neither controlling nor fully measuring the Court of Criminal Appeals' discretion, the following will be considered by the Court in deciding whether to grant discretionary review:

(a) whether a court of appeals' decision conflicts with another court of appeals' decision on the same issue;

(b) whether a court of appeals has decided an important question of state or federal law that has not been, but should be, settled by the Court of Criminal Appeals;

(c) whether a court of appeals has decided an important question of state or federal law in a way that conflicts with the applicable decisions of the Court of Criminal Appeals or the Supreme Court of the United States;

(d) whether a court of appeals has declared a statute, rule, regulation, or ordinance unconstitutional, or appears to have misconstrued a statute, rule, regulation, or ordinance;

(e) whether the justices of a court of appeals have disagreed on a material question of law necessary to the court's decision; and

(f) whether a court of appeals has so far departed from the accepted and usual course of judicial proceedings, or so far sanctioned such a departure by a lower court, as to call for an exercise of the Court of Criminal Appeals' power of supervision.

Eff. Sept. 1, 1997.

66.4. Documents to Aid Decision

(a) *Acquiring Documents.* The Court of Criminal Appeals—or any judge of the Court—may order the court of appeals clerk to promptly send the following items to the Court in order to aid it in deciding whether to grant discretionary review:

(1) the appellate record;

(2) a copy of the opinions of the court of appeals;

(3) a copy of the motions filed in the court of appeals; and

(4) certified copies of any judgment or order of the court of appeals.

(b) *Return of Documents.* If discretionary review is not granted, the clerk of the Court of Criminal Appeals will return the appellate record to the court of appeals clerk.

Eff. Sept. 1, 1997.

Rule 67. Discretionary Review Without Petition

Notes and Comments

Comment to 1997 change: This is former Rule 201. The rule is amended without substantive change.

67.1. Four Judges Vote

By a vote of at least four judges, the Court of Criminal Appeals may grant review of a court of appeals' decision in a criminal case at any time before the mandate of the court of appeals issues. An order granting review will be filed with the clerk of the Court of Criminal Appeals, who must send a copy to the court of appeals clerk.

Eff. Sept. 1, 1997. Amended by Court of Criminal Appeals Aug. 10, 2000 and Oct. 16, 2000, eff. Jan. 1, 2001; Supreme Court Sept. 12, 2000, eff. Jan. 1, 2001.

Notes and Comments

Comment to 2000 change: Language which was in the catchline of former Rule 201 has been deleted from Rule 67.1, to restore the substance of the rule, and to remove any implication that the court may not grant review on its own motion when a petition for discretionary review has been filed.

67.2. Order Staying Mandate

To provide enough time for the Court of Criminal Appeals to decide whether to grant discretionary review under 67.1, the Court—or any judge of the Court—may file with the clerk of the court of appeals an order staying the court of appeals' mandate. The order must be signed by a judge of the Court of Criminal Appeals. The clerk of the Court of Criminal Appeals must immediately send a copy of the order to the court of appeals clerk.

Eff. Sept. 1, 1997.

67.3. Time to Issue Mandate Extended

Unless otherwise limited in the order itself, an order staying the court of appeals' mandate under 67.2 will extend for an additional 45 days the time before issuance of the court of appeals' mandate. An order granting review prevents the issuance of the court of appeals' mandate pending the further order of the Court of Criminal Appeals. If four judges do not agree to grant review within that time the court of appeals clerk must issue the mandate.

Eff. Sept. 1, 1997.

Rule 68. Discretionary Review With Petition

Notes and Comments

Comment to 1997 change: This is former Rule 202. Subdivisions (k) and (*l*) of the former rule have been relocated to Rule 69. The new rule limits the length of a petition and reply. The time for amendment of a petition or reply is increased to conform with the amendment in Rule 50. The rule is otherwise amended without substantive change.

68.1. Generally

On petition by any party, the Court of Criminal Appeals may review a court of appeals' decision in a criminal case.

Eff. Sept. 1, 1997.

68.2. Time to File Petition

(a) *First Petition.* The petition must be filed within 30 days after either the day the court of appeals' judgment was rendered or the day the last timely motion for rehearing or timely motion for en banc reconsideration was overruled by the court of appeals.

(b) *Subsequent Petition.* Even if the time specified in (a) has expired, a party who otherwise may file a petition may do so within 10 days after the timely filing of another party's petition.

(c) *Extension of Time.* The Court of Criminal Appeals may extend the time to file a petition for discretionary review if a party files a motion complying with Rule 10.5(b) no later than 15 days after the last day for filing the petition. The Court of Criminal Appeals may extend the time to file a response or reply if a party files a motion complying with Rule 10.5(b) either before or after the response or reply is due.

Eff. Sept. 1, 1997. Amended by Court of Criminal Appeals July 12, 2011, eff. Sept. 1, 2011.

68.3. Where to File Petition

(a) The petition and all copies of the petition must be filed with the clerk of the Court of Criminal Appeals.

(b) *Petition filed in Court of Appeals.* If a petition is mistakenly filed in the court of appeals, the petition is deemed to have been filed the same day with the clerk of the Court of Criminal Appeals, and the court of appeals clerk must immediately send the petition to the clerk of the Court of Criminal Appeals.

Eff. Sept. 1, 1997. Amended by Court of Criminal Appeals July 12, 2011, eff. Sept. 1, 2011.

68.4. Contents of Petition

A petition for discretionary review must be as brief as possible. It must be addressed to the "Court of Criminal Appeals of Texas" and must state the name of the party or parties applying for review. The petition must contain the following items:

(a) *Identity of Judge, Parties, and Counsel.* The petition must list the trial court judge, all parties to the judgment or order appealed from, and the names and addresses of all trial and appellate counsel.

(b) *Table of Contents.* The petition must include a table of contents with references to the pages of the petition. The table of contents must indicate the subject matter of each ground or question presented for review.

(c) *Index of Authorities.* The petition must include an index of authorities arranged alphabetically and indicating the pages of the petition where the authorities are cited.

(d) *Statement Regarding Oral Argument.* The petition must include a short statement of why oral argument would be helpful, or a statement that oral argument is waived. If a reply or cross-petition is filed, it likewise must include a statement of why oral argument should or should not be heard.

(e) *Statement of the Case.* The petition must state briefly the nature of the case. This statement should

seldom exceed half a page. The details of the case should be reserved and stated with the pertinent grounds or questions.

(f) *Statement of Procedural History.* The petition must state:

(1) the date any opinion of the court of appeals was handed down, or the date of any order of the court of appeals disposing of the case without an opinion;

(2) the date any motion for rehearing was filed (or a statement that none was filed); and

(3) the date the motion for rehearing was overruled or otherwise disposed of.

(g) *Grounds for Review.* The petition must state briefly, without argument, the grounds on which the petition is based. The grounds must be separately numbered. If the petitioner has access to the record, the petitioner must (after each ground) refer to the page of the record where the matter complained of is found. Instead of listing grounds for review, the petition may contain the questions presented for review, expressed in the terms and circumstances of the case but without unnecessary detail. The statement of questions should be short and concise, not argumentative or repetitious.

(h) *Argument.* The petition must contain a direct and concise argument, with supporting authorities, amplifying the reasons for granting review. See Rule 66.3. The court of appeals' opinions will be considered with the petition, and statements in those opinions need not be repeated if counsel accepts them as correct.

(i) *Prayer for Relief.* The petition must state clearly the nature of the relief sought.

(j) *Appendix.* The petition must contain a copy of any opinion of the court of appeals.

Eff. Sept. 1, 1997. Amended by Supreme Court order of Dec. 23, 2002, eff. Jan. 1, 2003; Court of Criminal Appeals order of Dec. 11, 2013, eff. Jan. 1, 2014.

68.5. Repealed by Order of Nov. 13, 2012, eff. Dec. 1, 2012

68.6. Nonconforming Petition

The Court may strike, order redrawn, or summarily refuse a petition for discretionary review that is unnecessarily lengthy or that does not conform to these rules.

Eff. Sept. 1, 1997.

68.7. Court of Appeals Clerk's Duties

Within 15 days of receiving notice of the filing of a petition for discretionary review from the clerk of the Court of Criminal Appeals, the clerk of the court of appeals must send to the clerk of the Court of Criminal Appeals the record, any motions filed in the case, and copies of any judgments, opinions, and orders of the court of appeals. The clerk need not forward any nondocumentary exhibits unless ordered to do so by the Court of Criminal Appeals.

Eff. Sept. 1, 1997. Amended by Court of Criminal Appeals March 4, 2008, and June 30, 2008, eff. Sept. 1, 2008; Sept. 30, 2008, eff. Sept. 30, 2008; Supreme Court March 10, 2008, and Aug. 20, 2008, eff. Sept. 1, 2008. Amended by Court of Criminal Appeals July 12, 2011, eff. September 1, 2011.

68.8. Court of Criminal Appeals Clerk's Duties

Upon receipt of the record from the court of appeals, the clerk of the Court of Criminal Appeals will file the record and enter the filing on the docket.

Eff. Sept. 1, 1997. Amended by Court of Criminal Appeals July 12, 2011, eff. Sept. 1, 2011.

68.9. Reply

The opposing party has 15 days after the timely filing of the petition in the Court of Criminal Appeals to file a reply petition with the clerk of the Court of Criminal Appeals.

Added eff. Sept. 1, 2011.

68.10. Amendment

Upon motion the petition or a reply may be amended or supplemented at any time justice requires.

Eff. Sept. 1, 1997. Amended by Court of Criminal Appeals July 12, 2011, eff. Sept. 1, 2011.

68.11. Service on State Prosecuting Attorney

In addition to the service required by Rule 9.5, service of the petition, the reply, and any amendment or supplementation of a petition or reply must be made on the State Prosecuting Attorney.

Eff. Sept. 1, 1997. Amended by Court of Criminal Appeals July 12, 2011, eff. September 1, 2011.

Rule 69. Action of Court on Petition for Discretionary Review and After Granting Review

Notes and Comments

Comment to 1997 change: This is former subdivisions (k) and (*l*) of Rule 202. Internal procedures of the Court are deleted. Provisions are added in 69.4(a) and (b) for the clerk to send notice of the granting, refusal, or dismissal of a petition for dis-

cretionary review. Other nonsubstantive changes are made.

69.1. Granting or Refusal

If four judges do not vote to grant a petition for discretionary review, the Court will enter a docket notation that the petition is *refused*. If four judges vote to grant a petition, the Court will enter a docket notation that discretionary review is *granted*.

Eff. Sept. 1, 1997.

69.2. Setting Case for Submission

If discretionary review is granted, either on the petition of a party or by the Court on its own initiative, the case will be set for submission.

Eff. Sept. 1, 1997.

69.3. Improvident Grant of Review

If, after granting discretionary review, five judges are of the opinion that discretionary review should not have been granted, the case will be dismissed.

Eff. Sept. 1, 1997.

69.4. Clerk's Duties

(a) *On Refusal or Dismissal.* When the Court refuses or dismisses a petition, the clerk will send to the parties and the State Prosecuting Attorney a notice informing them that the petition was refused or dismissed. The clerk will retain the petition and all other items filed in the case for at least 15 days from the date of the refusal or dismissal. At the end of that time, if no motion for rehearing has been timely filed, or upon the overruling or dismissal of such a motion, the clerk will send to the court of appeals clerk a certified copy of the order refusing or dismissing the petition (as well as any order overruling a motion for rehearing). The clerk of the Court of Criminal Appeals will return the appellate record to the court of appeals clerk but will retain the petition, and other documents filed in the Court of Criminal Appeals.

(b) *On Granting Review.* If the Court grants discretionary review, the clerk will send to the parties and the State Prosecuting Attorney a notice informing them that discretionary review was granted.

Eff. Sept. 1, 1997.

Rule 70. Brief on the Merits

Notes and Comments

Comment to 1997 change: This is former Rule 203. The rule is amended without substantive change.

70.1. Initial Brief

If review is granted, the petitioner—or, if there was no petition, the party who lost in the court of appeals—must file a brief within 30 days after review is granted.

Eff. Sept. 1, 1997.

70.2. Respondent's Brief

The opposing party must file a brief within 30 days after the petitioner's brief is filed.

Eff. Sept. 1, 1997. Amended by Court of Criminal Appeals Dec. 11, 2013, eff. Jan. 1, 2014.

70.3. Brief Contents and Form

Briefs must comply with the requirements of Rules 9 and 38, except that they need not contain the appendix (Rule 38.1(k)). Copies must be served as required by Rule 68.11.

Eff. Sept. 1, 1997. Amended by Supreme Court March 10, 2008, and Aug. 20, 2008, eff. Sept. 1, 2008. Approved by Court of Criminal Appeals Sept. 30, 2008, eff. Sept. 30, 2008. Amended by Supreme Court Nov. 13, 2012, eff. Dec. 1, 2012.

70.4. Other Briefs

The Court of Criminal Appeals may direct that a party file a brief, or an additional brief, in a particular case. Additionally, upon motion by a party the Court may permit the filing of additional briefs.

Eff. Sept. 1, 1997. Amended by Court of Criminal Appeals Dec. 11, 2013, eff. Jan. 1, 2014.

Rule 71. Direct Appeals

Notes and Comments

Comment to 1997 change: This is former Rule 210. The rule is extended to all direct appeals. A page limit is added for death penalty cases. Other nonsubstantive changes are made.

71.1. Direct Appeal

Cases in which the death penalty has been assessed under Code of Criminal Procedure article 37.071, and cases in which bail has been denied in non-capital cases under Article I, Section 11a of the Constitution, are appealed directly to the Court of Criminal Appeals.

Eff. Sept. 1, 1997.

71.2. Record

The appellate record should be prepared and filed in accordance with Rules 31, 32, 34, 35 and 37,[1] except that the record must be filed in the Court of Criminal Appeals. After disposition of the appeal, the Court may discard copies of juror information cards or other portions of the clerk's record that are not relevant to an issue on appeal.

Eff. Sept. 1, 1997. Amended by Supreme Court Dec. 23, 2002, eff. Jan. 1, 2003.

[1] Vernon's Ann.Rules App.Proc., rules 31.1 et seq., 32.1 et seq., 34.1 et seq., 35.1 et seq., 37.1 et seq.

71.3. Briefs

Briefs in a direct appeal should be prepared and filed in accordance with Rules 9 and 38, except that the brief need not contain an appendix (Rule 38.1(k)). All briefs must be filed in the Court of Criminal Appeals. The brief must include a short statement of why oral argument would be helpful, or a statement that oral argument is waived.

Eff. Sept. 1, 1997. Amended by Supreme Court March 10, 2008, and Aug. 20, 2008, eff. Sept. 1, 2008. Approved by Court of Criminal Appeals Sept. 30, 2008, eff. Sept. 30, 2008. Amended by Supreme Court Nov. 13, 2012, eff. Dec. 1, 2012.

Notes and Comments

Comment to 2002 change: A requirement that briefs include a statement regarding oral argument is added.

71.4. Additional Briefs

Upon motion by a party the Court may permit the filing of additional briefs other than those provided for in Rule 38.

Adopted by Court of Criminal Appeals Dec. 11, 2013, eff. Jan. 1, 2014.

Rule 72. Extraordinary Matters

Notes and Comments

Comment to 1997 change: This is former Rule 211. The rule is amended to include all the Court's jurisdiction of extraordinary matters. Internal procedures of the Court are deleted. Other nonsubstantive changes are made.

72.1. Leave to File

A motion for leave to file must accompany an original petition for writ of habeas corpus, mandamus, procedendo, prohibition, certiorari, or other extraordinary writ, or any other motion not otherwise provided for in these rules.

Eff. Sept. 1, 1997.

72.2. Disposition

If five judges tentatively believe that the case should be filed and set for submission, the motion for leave will be granted and the case will then be handled and disposed of in accordance with Rule 52.8. If the motion for leave is denied, no motions for rehearing or reconsideration will be entertained. But the Court may, on its own initiative, reconsider a denial of a motion for leave.

Eff. Sept. 1, 1997. Amended by Court of Criminal Appeals Jan. 23, 2017, and Supreme Court Jan. 25, 2017, eff. Feb. 1, 2017.

Rule 73. Postconviction Applications for Writs of Habeas Corpus

Notes and Comments

Comment to 2000 change: Rules 73.1 and 73.2 are added, and a form is added in an appendix.

The Court of Criminal Appeals order dated October 16, 2000, provides in part:

"2. These changes take effect January 1, 2001. Unless this order provides otherwise, they shall govern all proceedings in motions for new trial, appeals, petitions for discretionary review, and petitions or applications for extraordinary writs thereafter brought and in all such proceedings then pending, except to the extent that in the opinion of the court their application in a particular proceeding then pending would not be feasible or would work injustice, in which case the former procedure may be followed.

"3. The notes and comments appended to these changes are incomplete, are included only for the convenience of the bench and bar, and are not a part of the rules."

Comment to 1997 change: This is former Rule 4 of the Appendix for Criminal Cases. The rule is amended without substantive change.

73.1. Form for Application Filed Under Article 11.07 of the Code of Criminal Procedure

(a) *Prescribed Form.* An application filed under Article 11.07 must be on the form prescribed by the Court of Criminal Appeals.

(b) *Availability of Form.* The district clerk of the county of conviction shall make the form available to applicants on request, without charge.

(c) *Contents.* The applicant or petitioner must provide all information required by the form. The form must include all grounds for relief and set forth in summary fashion the facts supporting each ground. Any ground not raised on the form will not be considered. Legal citations and arguments may be made in a separate memorandum. The form must be computer-generated, typewritten, or legibly handwritten.

(d) *Length.* Each ground for relief and supporting facts raised on the form shall not exceed the two pages provided for each ground in the form. The applicant or petitioner may file a separate memorandum. This memorandum shall comply with these rules and shall not exceed 15,000 words if computer-generated or 50 pages if not. If the total number of pages, including those in the original and any additional memoranda, exceed the word or page limits, an application may be dismissed unless the convicting court for good cause shown grants leave to exceed the prescribed limits. The prescribed limits do not include appendices, exhibits, cover page, table of contents, table of authorities, and certificate of compliance.

(e) *Typeface.* A computer-generated memorandum must be printed in a conventional typeface no smaller than 14–point except for footnotes, which must be no smaller than 12–point. A typewritten document must be printed in standard 10–character–per–inch (cpi) monospaced typeface.

(f) *Certificate of compliance.* A computer-generated memorandum, including any additional memoranda, must include a certificate by the applicant or petitioner stating the number of words in the document. The person certifying may rely on the word count of the computer program used to prepare the document.

(g) *Verification.* The application must be verified by either:

(1) oath made before a notary public or other officer authorized to administer oaths; or

(2) if the person making the application is an inmate in the Institutional Division of the Department of Criminal Justice or in a county jail, an unsworn declaration in substantially the form required in Civil Practices and Remedies Code chapter 132.

Adopted by Court of Criminal Appeals Aug. 10, 2000 and Oct. 16, 2000, eff. Jan. 1, 2001; adopted by Supreme Court Sept. 12, 2000, eff. Jan. 1, 2001. Amended by Court of Criminal Appeals Dec. 11, 2013, eff. Jan. 1, 2014.

73.2. Non–Compliant Applications

The Court of Criminal Appeals may dismiss an application that does not comply with these rules.

Adopted by Court of Criminal Appeals Aug. 10, 2000 and Oct. 16, 2000, eff. Jan. 1, 2001; adopted by Supreme Court Sept. 12, 2000, eff. Jan. 1, 2001. Amended by Court of Criminal Appeals Dec. 11, 2013, eff. Jan. 1, 2014.

73.3. State's Response

Any response by the State must comply with length, typeface, and certificate of compliance requirements set out in rule 73.1 (d),(e) and (f).

Adopted by Court of Criminal Appeals Dec. 11, 2013, eff. Jan. 1, 2014.

73.4. Filing and Transmission of Habeas Record

(a) The district clerk of the county of conviction shall accept and file all Code of Criminal Procedure article 11.07 applications.

(b) In addition to the duties set out in Article 11.07, the clerk shall do the following:

(1) If the convicting court enters an order designating issues, the clerk shall immediately transmit to the Court of Criminal Appeals a copy of that order and proof of the date the district attorney received the habeas application.

(2) When any pleadings, objections, motions, affidavits, exhibits, proposed or entered findings of fact and conclusions of law, or other orders are filed or made a part of the record, the district clerk shall immediately send a copy to all parties in the case. A party has ten days from the date he receives the trial court's findings of facts and conclusions of law to file objections, but the trial court may, nevertheless, order the district clerk to transmit the record to the Court of Criminal Appeals before the expiration of the ten days.

(3) When a district clerk transmits the record in a postconviction application for a writ of habeas corpus under Code of Criminal Procedure articles 11.07 or 11.071, the district clerk must prepare and transmit a summary sheet that includes the following information:

(A) the convicting court's name and county, and the name of the judge who tried the case;

(B) the applicant's name, the offense, the plea, the cause number, the sentence, and the date of sentence, as shown in the judgment of conviction;

(C) the cause number of any appeal from the conviction and the citation to any published report;

(D) whether a hearing was held on the application, whether findings of fact were made, any recommendation of the convicting court, and the name of the judge who presided over the application;

(E) the name of counsel if applicant is represented.

The Court of Criminal Appeals may by order adopt a form of summary sheet that the district clerks must use.

(4) The district clerk shall also include in the record transmitted to the Court of Criminal Appeals, among any other pertinent papers or supplements, the indictment or information, any plea papers, the court's docket sheet, the court's charge and the jury's verdict, any proposed findings of fact and conclusions of law, the court's findings of fact and conclusions of law, any objections to the court's findings of fact and conclusions of law filed by either party, and the transcript of any hearings held.

(5) On the 181st day from the date of receipt of the application by the State of a postconviction application for writ of habeas corpus under Article 11.07, the district clerk shall forward the writ record to this Court unless the district court has received an extension of time from the Court of Criminal Appeals pursuant to Rule 73.5.

Former Rule 73.1 adopted eff. Sept. 1, 1997. Renumbered as Rule 73.3 by Court of Criminal Appeals Nov. 8, 2000, eff. Jan. 1, 2001. Renumbered as Rule 73.4 and amended by Court of Criminal Appeals Dec. 11, 2013, eff. Jan. 1, 2014. Amended by orders of Supreme Court February 16, 2016, and Court of Criminal Appeals Dec. 7, 2015, and February 29, 2016, eff. Jan. 1, 2016.

73.5. Time Frame for Resolution of Claims Raised in Application

Within 180 days from the date of receipt of the application by the State, the convicting court shall resolve any issues that the court has timely designated for resolution. Any motion for extension of time must be filed in the Court of Criminal Appeals before the expiration of the 180–day period.

Adopted by Court of Criminal Appeals Dec. 11, 2013, eff. Jan. 1, 2014.

73.6. Action on Application

The Court may deny relief based upon its own review of the application or may issue such other instructions or orders as may be appropriate.

Former Rule 73.2 adopted eff. Sept. 1, 1997. Renumbered as Rule 73.4 by Court of Criminal Appeals Nov. 8, 2000, eff. Jan. 1, 2001. Renumbered as Rule 73.6 by Court of Criminal Appeals Dec. 11, 2013, eff. Jan. 1, 2014.

73.7. New Evidence After Application Forwarded to Court of Criminal Appeals

If an Article 11.07 or 11.071 application has been forwarded to this Court, and a party wishes this Court to consider evidence not filed in the trial court, then the party must comply with the following procedures or the evidence will not be considered.

(a) If the Court of Criminal Appeals has received an Article 11.07 or 11.071 application from the district clerk of the county of conviction and has filed and set the application for submission, a party has two options:

(1) The party may file the evidence directly in the Court of Criminal Appeals with a motion for the

Court of Criminal Appeals to consider the evidence. In this motion, the party should describe the evidence, explain its evidentiary value, and state why compelling and extraordinary circumstances exist for the Court of Criminal Appeals to consider the evidence directly. The moving party must immediately serve copies of the motion and the evidence the party seeks to file on the other party or parties in the case. If the Court of Criminal Appeals grants this motion, the Court will consider the evidence in its review of the application. The Court of Criminal Appeals will grant such a motion only if the Court concludes the circumstances are truly exceptional.

(2) The party may file in the Court of Criminal Appeals a motion to supplement the record in the trial court. In this motion, the party should describe the evidence the party intends to file, explain its evidentiary value, and state why the evidence could not have been filed in the trial court before the Court of Criminal Appeals filed and set the application for submission. The moving party must immediately serve copies of the motion and the evidence the party seeks to file on the other party or parties in the case. If the Court of Criminal Appeals grants the motion, the party may file the evidence with the district clerk of the county of conviction, and should attach a copy of the motion to supplement and the Court of Criminal Appeals' order granting said motion. The district clerk shall immediately send a copy of the filed materials to the trial judge assigned to the habeas case and to the other party or parties in the case, and otherwise comply with the procedures set out in Rule 73.4(b) of these rules.

(b) If the Court of Criminal Appeals has received an Article 11.07 or 11.071 application from the district clerk of the county of conviction, but the Court has not yet filed and set the application for submission, the party must file in the Court of Criminal Appeals a motion to stay the proceedings pending the filing of the evidence in the trial court. In this motion, the party should describe the evidence the party intends to file and explain its evidentiary value. The moving party must immediately serve copies of the motion and the evidence the party seeks to file on the other party or parties in the case. If the Court of Criminal Appeals grants the motion, the Court will specify a designated time frame for the party to file the evidence with the district clerk of the county of conviction. The party should attach a copy of the motion to stay proceedings and the Court of Criminal Appeals'

order granting said motion to the evidentiary filing. The district clerk of the county of conviction shall immediately send a copy of the filed materials to the trial judge assigned to the habeas case and to the other party or parties in the case, and otherwise comply with the procedures set out in Rule 73.4(b) of these rules.

Adopted by Court of Criminal Appeals Jan. 23, 2017 and Supreme Court Jan. 25, 2017, eff. Feb. 1, 2017.

Rule 74. Review of Certified State Criminal-Law Questions

Notes and Comments

Comment to 1997 change: This is former Rule 214. The rule is amended without substantive change.

74.1. Certification

The Court of Criminal Appeals may answer questions of Texas criminal law certified to it by any federal appellate court if the certifying court is presented with determinative questions of Texas criminal law having no controlling Court of Criminal Appeals precedent. The Court may decline to answer the questions certified to it.

Eff. Sept. 1, 1997.

74.2. Contents of the Certification Order

An order from the certifying court must set forth:

(a) the questions of law to be answered; and

(b) a stipulated statement of all facts relevant to the questions certified, showing fully the nature of the controversy in which the questions arose.

Eff. Sept. 1, 1997.

74.3. Transmission of Certification Order

The clerk of the certifying court must send to the clerk of the Court of Criminal Appeals the following:

(a) the certification order under the certifying court's official seal;

(b) a list of the names of each party to the pending case, giving the address and telephone number, if known, of any party not represented by counsel; and

(c) a list of the names and addresses of counsel for each party.

Eff. Sept. 1, 1997.

74.4. Transmission of Record

The certifying court should not send to the Court of Criminal Appeals the record in the pending case with the certification order. The Court of Criminal Appeals may later require the original or copies of all or part of the record before the certifying court to be filed with the Court of Criminal Appeals clerk.

Eff. Sept. 1, 1997.

74.5. Notice

If the Court of Criminal Appeals agrees to answer the questions certified to it, the Court will notify all parties and the certifying court. The Court of Criminal Appeals clerk must also send a notice to the Attorney General of Texas if:

(a) the constitutionality of a Texas statute is the subject of a certified question that the Court of Criminal Appeals has agreed to answer; and

(b) the State of Texas or an officer, agency, or employee of the State is not a party to the proceeding in the certifying court.

Eff. Sept. 1, 1997.

74.6. Briefs and Oral Argument

(a) *Briefs.* The appealing party in the certifying court must file a brief with the clerk of the Court of Criminal Appeals within 30 days after the date of the notice. Opposing parties must file an answering brief within 15 days of receiving the opening brief. Briefs must comply with Rule 38[1] to the extent that its provisions apply.

(b) *Oral Argument.* Oral argument may be granted either on a party's request or on the Court's own initiative. Argument is governed by Rule 39.[2]

Eff. Sept. 1, 1997.

[1] Vernon's Ann.Rules App.Proc., rule 38.1 et seq.
[2] Vernon's Ann.Rules App.Proc., rule 39.1 et seq.

74.7. Intervention by the State

If the constitutionality of a Texas statute is the subject of a certified question that the Court of Criminal Appeals has agreed to answer, the State of Texas may intervene at any reasonable time for briefing and oral argument (if argument is allowed) on the question of constitutionality.

Eff. Sept. 1, 1997.

74.8. Opinion on Certified Question

If the Court of Criminal Appeals has agreed to answer a certified question, it will hand down an opinion as in any other case.

Eff. Sept. 1, 1997.

74.9. Motion for Rehearing

Any party may file a motion for rehearing within 15 days after the opinion is handed down. The motion must clearly state the points relied on for the rehearing. No reply to a motion for rehearing need be filed unless the Court so requests. The Court will not grant a motion for rehearing unless a response has been filed or requested.

Eff. Sept. 1, 1997.

74.10. Answering Certified Questions

After all motions for rehearing have been overruled, the clerk of the Court of Criminal Appeals must send to the certifying court the written opinion on the certified questions. The opinion must be under the Court of Criminal Appeals' seal.

Eff. Sept. 1, 1997.

Rule 75. Notification; Oral Argument

Notes and Comments

Comment to 1997 change: This is former Rule 220. The rule is amended without substantive change.

75.1. Notification of Argument or Submission

Oral argument will be permitted only in cases designated by the Court of Criminal Appeals. If the Court permits argument in a case, the clerk will notify the parties of the date set for argument. If a case will be submitted without argument, the clerk will notify the parties of the date of submission. The clerk must use all reasonable diligence to notify counsel of settings, but counsel's failure to receive notice will not necessarily prevent argument or submission of the case on the day it is set.

Eff. Sept. 1, 1997.

75.2. Request for Argument

If a case is not designated for oral argument but counsel desires oral argument, counsel may—within 30 days of the date of the clerk's notice—petition the Court to allow oral argument. This petition must contain specific reasons why oral argument is desired.

75.3. Oral Argument

Unless extended in a special case, the total maximum time for oral argument is 20 minutes per side. Counsel for the appellant or petitioner is entitled to open and conclude the argument. Counsel should not read at length from the briefs, records, or authorities. Counsel may orally correct a brief, but multiple additional citations should not be given orally; instead, these citations should be filed in writing with the clerk.

Eff. Sept. 1, 1997.

76. Submissions En Banc

The Court will sit en banc to consider the following types of cases:

(a) direct appeals;

(b) cases of discretionary review;

(c) cases in which leave to file was granted under Rule 72[1];

(d) cases that were docketed under Code of Criminal Procedure articles 11.07 or 11.071;

(e) certified questions; and

(f) rehearings under Rule 79.[2]

Eff. Sept. 1, 1997.

[1] Vernon's Ann.Rules App.Proc., rule 72.1 et seq.
[2] Vernon's Ann.Rules App.Proc., rule 79.1 et seq.

Notes and Comments

Comment to 1997 change: This is former Rule 222. The rule is expanded to include other kinds of cases. Internal procedures of the Court are deleted. Other nonsubstantive changes are made.

Rule 77. Opinions

Notes and Comments

Comment to 1997 change: This is former Rule 223. The rule is amended without substantive change.

77.1. Generally

In each case that is argued or submitted without argument to the Court of Criminal Appeals, the Court will hand down a written opinion setting forth the reasons for its decision and any germane precedent. Any judge may file an opinion dissenting from or concurring in the Court's judgment.

Eff. Sept. 1, 1997.

77.2. Signing; Publication

A majority of the judges will determine whether an opinion will be signed by a judge or issued per curiam, and whether the opinion (or a portion of the opinion) will be published.

Eff. Sept. 1, 1997.

77.3. Unpublished Opinions

Unpublished opinions have no precedential value and must not be cited as authority by counsel or by a court.

Eff. Sept. 1, 1997.

77.4. Copies

On the date when an opinion is handed down or an order rendered, the clerk of the Court of Criminal Appeals must mail copies of the opinion or order to:

(a) the parties;

(b) the State Prosecuting Attorney;

(c) the trial court clerk; and

(d) if the case is of discretionary review, the court of appeals clerk.

Eff. Sept. 1, 1997.

Rule 78. Judgments in the Court of Criminal Appeals

Notes and Comments

Comment to 1997 change: The rule is new.

78.1. Types of Judgment

The Court of Criminal Appeals may:

(a) affirm the lower court's judgment in whole or in part;

(b) modify the lower court's judgment and affirm it as modified;

(c) reverse the court's judgment in whole or in part and render the judgment that the lower court should have rendered;

(d) reverse the lower court's judgment and remand the case for further proceedings;

(e) vacate the judgments of the lower courts and dismiss the case;

(f) vacate the lower court's judgment and remand the case for further proceedings in light of changes in the law; or

(g) dismiss the appeal.

Eff. Sept. 1, 1997.

78.2. Remand in the Interests of Justice

When reversing the court of appeals' judgment, the Court of Criminal Appeals may, in the interests of justice, remand the case to the trial court even if a rendition of judgment is otherwise appropriate.

Eff. Sept. 1, 1997.

78.3. Other Orders

The Court of Criminal Appeals may make any other appropriate order required by the law and the nature of the case.

Eff. Sept. 1, 1997.

Rule 79. Rehearings

Notes and Comments

Comment to 1997 change: This is former Rule 230, and the portion of former Rule 213 that prohibited motions for rehearing. The Court may now permit oral argument after granting rehearing, although it is disfavored. A further motion for rehearing may now be filed by any party, rather than only the losing party. Other nonsubstantive changes are made.

79.1. Motion for Rehearing

A motion for rehearing may be filed with the Court of Criminal Appeals clerk within 15 days from the date of the judgment or order. In exceptional cases, if justice requires, the Court may shorten the time within which the motion may be filed or even deny the right to file it altogether.

Eff. Sept. 1, 1997.

79.2. Contents

(a) The motion must briefly and distinctly state the grounds and arguments relied on for rehearing.

(b) A motion for rehearing an order that grants discretionary review may not be filed.

(c) A motion for rehearing an order that refuses a petition for discretionary review may be grounded only on substantial intervening circumstances or on other significant circumstances which are specified in the motion. Counsel must certify that the motion is so grounded and that the motion is made in good faith and not for delay.

(d) A motion for rehearing an order that denies habeas corpus relief or dismisses a habeas corpus application under Code of Criminal Procedure, articles 11.07 or 11.071, may not be filed. The Court may on its own initiative reconsider the case.

Eff. Sept. 1, 1997. Amended by Court of Criminal Appeals July 12, 2011, eff. September 1, 2011. Amended by orders of Supreme Court February 16, 2016, and Court of Criminal Appeals December 7, 2015, and February 29, 2016, eff. January 1, 2016.

79.3. Amendments

A motion for rehearing may be amended anytime before the period allowed for filing the motion expires, and with leave of the court, anytime before the Court decides the motion.

Eff. Sept. 1, 1997.

79.4. Decision

If the Court grants rehearing, the case will be set for submission. Oral argument may, but normally will not, be permitted.

Eff. Sept. 1, 1997.

79.5. Further Motion for Rehearing

The Court will not consider a second motion for rehearing after rehearing is denied. If rehearing is granted and the Court delivers an opinion on rehearing, a party may file a further motion for rehearing.

Eff. Sept. 1, 1997.

79.6. Extension of Time

The Court may extend the time for filing a motion or a further motion for rehearing if a party files a motion complying with Rule 10.5(b) within the time for filing a motion or further motion for rehearing.

Eff. Sept. 1, 1997.

79.7. Service

The requirements of Rule 68.11 apply.

Eff. Sept. 1, 1997.

STANDARDS FOR APPELLATE CONDUCT

Lawyers are an indispensable part of the pursuit of justice. They are officers of courts charged with safeguarding, interpreting, and applying the law through which justice is achieved. Appellate courts rely on counsel to present opposing views of how the law should be applied to facts established in other proceedings. The appellate lawyer's role is to present the law controlling the disposition of a case in a manner that clearly reveals the legal issues raised by the record while persuading the court that an interpretation or application favored by the lawyer's clients is in the best interest of the administration of equal justice under law.

The duties lawyers owe to the justice system, other officers of the court, and lawyers' clients are generally well-defined and understood by the appellate bar. Problems that arise when duties conflict can be resolved through understanding the nature and extent of a lawyer's respective duties, avoiding the tendency to emphasize a particular duty at the expense of others, and detached common sense. To that end, the following standards of conduct for appellate lawyers are set forth by reference to the duties owed by every appellate practitioner.

Use of these standards for appellate conduct as a basis for motions for sanctions, civil liability or litigation would be contrary to their intended purpose and shall not be permitted. Nothing in these standards alters existing standards of conduct under the Texas Disciplinary Rules of Professional Conduct, the Texas Rules of Disciplinary Procedure or the Code of Judicial Conduct.

LAWYERS' DUTIES TO CLIENTS

A lawyer owes to a client allegiance, learning, skill, and industry. A lawyer shall employ all appropriate means to protect and advance the client's legitimate rights, claims, and objectives. A lawyer shall not be deterred by a real or imagined fear of judicial disfavor or public unpopularity, nor be influenced by mere self-interest. The lawyer's duty to a client does not militate against the concurrent obligation to treat with consideration all persons involved in the legal process and to avoid the infliction of harm on the appellate process, the courts, and the law itself.

1. Counsel will advise their clients of the contents of these Standards of Conduct when undertaking representation.

2. Counsel will explain the fee agreement and cost expectation to their clients. Counsel will then endeavor to achieve the client's lawful appellate objectives as quickly, efficiently, and economically as possible.

3. Counsel will maintain sympathetic detachment, recognizing that lawyers should not become so closely associated with clients that the lawyer's objective judgment is impaired.

4. Counsel will be faithful to their clients' lawful objectives, while mindful of their concurrent duties to the legal system and the public good.

5. Counsel will explain the appellate process to their clients. Counsel will advise clients of the range of potential outcomes, likely costs, timetables, effect of the judgment pending appeal, and the availability of alternative dispute resolution.

6. Counsel will not foster clients' unrealistic expectations.

7. Negative opinions of the court or opposing counsel shall not be expressed unless relevant to a client's decision process.

8. Counsel will keep clients informed and involved in decisions and will promptly respond to inquiries.

9. Counsel will advise their clients of proper behavior, including that civility and courtesy are expected.

10. Counsel will advise their clients that counsel reserves the right to grant accommodations to opposing counsel in matters that do not adversely affect the client's lawful objectives. A client has no right to instruct a lawyer to refuse reasonable requests made by other counsel.

11. A client has no right to demand that counsel abuse anyone or engage in any offensive conduct.

12. Counsel will advise clients that an appeal should only be pursued in a good faith belief that the trial court has committed error or that there is a reasonable basis for the extension, modification, or reversal of existing law, or that an appeal is otherwise warranted.

13. Counsel will advise clients that they will not take frivolous positions in an appellate court, explaining the penalties associated therewith. Appointed appellate counsel in criminal cases shall be deemed to have complied with this standard of conduct if they comply with the requirements imposed on appointed counsel by courts and statutes.

LAWYERS' DUTIES TO THE COURT

As professionals and advocates, counsel assist the Court in the administration of justice at the appellate level. Through briefs and oral submissions, counsel provide a fair and accurate understanding of the facts and law applicable to their case. Counsel also serve the Court by respecting and maintaining the dignity and integrity of the appellate process.

1. An appellate remedy should not be pursued unless counsel believes in good faith that error has been committed, that there is a reasonable basis for the extension, modification, or reversal of existing law, or that an appeal is otherwise warranted.

2. An appellate remedy should not be pursued primarily for purposes of delay or harassment.

3. Counsel should not misrepresent, mischaracterize, misquote, or miscite the factual record or legal authorities.

4. Counsel will advise the Court of controlling legal authorities, including those adverse to their position, and should not cite authority that has been reversed, overruled, or restricted without informing the court of those limitations.

5. Counsel will present the Court with a thoughtful, organized, and clearly written brief.

6. Counsel will not submit reply briefs on issues previously briefed in order to obtain the last word.

7. Counsel will conduct themselves before the Court in a professional manner, respecting the decorum and integrity of the judicial process.

8. Counsel will be civil and respectful in all communications with the judges and staff.

9. Counsel will be prepared and punctual for all Court appearances, and will be prepared to assist the Court in understanding the record, controlling authority, and the effect of the court's decision.

10. Counsel will not permit a client's or their own ill feelings toward the opposing party, opposing counsel, trial judges or members of the appellate court to influence their conduct or demeanor in dealings with the judges, staff, other counsel, and parties.

LAWYERS' DUTIES TO LAWYERS

Lawyers bear a responsibility to conduct themselves with dignity towards and respect for each other, for the sake of maintaining the effectiveness and credibility of the system they serve. The duty that lawyers owe their clients and the system can be most effectively carried out when lawyers treat each other honorably.

1. Counsel will treat each other and all parties with respect.

2. Counsel will not unreasonably withhold consent to a reasonable request for cooperation or scheduling accommodation by opposing counsel.

3. Counsel will not request an extension of time solely for the purpose of unjustified delay.

4. Counsel will be punctual in communications with opposing counsel.

5. Counsel will not make personal attacks on opposing counsel or parties.

6. Counsel will not attribute bad motives or improper conduct to other counsel without good cause, or make unfounded accusations of impropriety.

7. Counsel will not lightly seek court sanctions.

8. Counsel will adhere to oral or written promises and agreements with other counsel.

9. Counsel will neither ascribe to another counsel or party a position that counsel or the party has not taken, nor seek to create an unjustified inference based on counsel's statements or conduct.

10. Counsel will not attempt to obtain an improper advantage by manipulation of margins and type size in a manner to avoid court rules regarding page limits.

11. Counsel will not serve briefs or other communications in a manner or at a time that unfairly limits another party's opportunity to respond.

THE COURT'S RELATIONSHIP WITH COUNSEL

Unprofessionalism can exist only to the extent it is tolerated by the court. Because courts grant the right to practice law, they control the manner in which the practice is conducted. The right to practice requires counsel to conduct themselves in a manner compatible with the role of the appellate courts in administering justice. Likewise, no one more surely sets the tone and the pattern for the conduct of appellate lawyers than appellate judges. Judges must practice civility in order to foster professionalism in those appearing before them.

1. Inappropriate conduct will not be rewarded, while exemplary conduct will be appreciated.

2. The court will take special care not to reward departures from the record.

3.   The court will be courteous, respectful, and civil to counsel.

4.   The court will not disparage the professionalism or integrity of counsel based upon the conduct or reputation of counsel's client or co-counsel.

5.   The court will endeavor to avoid the injustice that can result from delay after submission of a case.

6.   The court will abide by the same standards of professionalism that it expects of counsel in its treatment of the facts, the law, and the arguments.

7.   Members of the court will demonstrate respect for other judges and courts.

IN THE SUPREME COURT OF TEXAS

Misc. Docket No. 13-**912 7**

**FEES CHARGED IN THE SUPREME COURT,
IN CIVIL CASES IN THE COURTS OF APPEALS, AND
BEFORE THE JUDICIAL PANEL ON MULTI-DISTRICT LITIGATION**

ORDERED that:

Effective September 1, 2013, the following fees apply except to persons exempt by law.

In the Supreme Court:

petition for review	$145
additional fee if petition for review is granted	$75
original proceeding	$145
additional fee if original proceeding is granted	$75
certified question from a federal court of appeals	$170
direct appeal to the Supreme Court	$195
any other proceeding filed in the Supreme Court	$170
administering an oath with sealed certificate of oath	$5
certified copy including certificate and seal	$0.50 per page, $5 minimum
comparing and certifying copy of document	$0.50 per page, $5 minimum
motion for rehearing	$15
motion not otherwise listed	$10
exhibit tendered for oral argument	$25

In the Courts of Appeals:

appeal from a district or county court	$195
petition for permissive appeal (no additional fee if petition is granted)	$195
original proceeding	$145
administering an oath with sealed certificate of oath	$5
certified copy including certificate and seal certification	$1.00 per page, $5 minimum

comparing and certifying copy of document .... $1.00 per page, $5 minimum
motion for rehearing or for en banc reconsideration $15
motion not otherwise listed $10
exhibit tendered for oral argument $25

In the Supreme Court and the Courts of Appeals:

paper copy, no certificate or seal* .... $0.10 per printed side of page or part of side of page
audio tape of oral argument (if available)* .... $1 per tape
VHS video tape of oral argument (if available)* .... $2.50 per tape
digital video disc of oral argument (if available)* .... $3 per DVD
personnel, overhead, and document retrieval charges .... see 1 Tex. Admin. Code § 70.3

   *A Court may authorize additional, reasonable charges for personnel, overhead, or document
   retrieval for services provided by the clerk or by contract with an outside entity.

Before the Judicial Panel on Multi-District Litigation

motion to transfer to pretrial court $275
appeal of a pretrial court order by motion for rehearing $275
any other motion or document $50

   This Order is promulgated in accordance with: the Act of May 16, 2013, 83rd Leg., R.S., (HB
2302), amending Texas Gov't Code § 51.851; Tex. Gov't Code §§ 51.005, 51.0051, 51.207, 51.208,
51.941, & 552.262; Rule of Judicial Administration 13.3(g); and 1 Tex. Admin. Code § 70.3 (2007).
The Order supersedes the fee provisions in Misc. Docket Nos. 98-9120 (July 21, 1998), 03-9151
(September 10, 2003), and 07-9138 (August 28, 2007).

Dated: August 16 , 2013

Misc. Docket No. 13-9127   Page 2

Wallace B. Jefferson, Chief Justice

Nathan L. Hecht, Justice

Paul W. Green, Justice

Phil Johnson, Justice

Don R. Willett, Justice

Eva M. Guzman, Justice

Debra H. Lehrmann, Justice

Jeffrey S. Boyd, Justice

John P. Devine, Justice

Misc. Docket No. 13- **912 7**

Page 3

Adopted Aug. 15, 1997, eff. Sept. 1, 1997. Amended July 21, 1998, eff. Sept. 1, 1998; Sept. 10, 2003, eff. Sept. 10, 2003; Aug. 28, 2007, eff. Sept. 1, 2007; Aug. 16, 2013, eff. Sept. 1, 2013; Aug. 28, 2015, eff. Sept. 1, 2015.

APPENDIX B

IN THE SUPREME COURT OF TEXAS

ORDER REGARDING DISPOSITION OF COURT PAPERS IN CIVIL CASES

ORDERED that:

A. Definitions.

1. *Court records* or *records* means:

(a) the clerk's record;

(b) the reporter's record; and

(c) any other documents or items filed, or presented for filing and received in an appellate court in a particular case.

2. *Appellate record* means the clerk's record and the reporter's record and any supplements.

B. In the Courts of Appeals.
The following paragraphs govern disposing of court records by the courts of appeals:

1. *Determination of permanent preservation.* Before any court records are destroyed, the court of appeals must—under Section 51.205 of the Government Code and State Archives guidelines—determine whether the records should be permanently preserved.

2. *Initial determination.* Immediately after final disposition of an appeal or other proceeding, the panel that decided the case must determine whether the case's records should be permanently preserved and must file with the records a statement declaring that the records should or should not be permanently preserved.

3. *Later determination.* After its initial determination, but before any court records are destroyed, the court of appeals may reexamine its initial determination under 2. and may change its designation.

4. *Original papers and exhibits in appeals.* Whatever the court determines concerning permanent preservation of a case's records, any original documents or exhibits must, within 30 days after final disposition of an appeal or other proceeding, be returned to the trial court in accordance with any trial court order entered under Rules 34.5(f) and 34.6(g). The court of appeals may, but need not, copy those documents and exhibits before returning them to the trial court. The court of appeals may dispose of copies of nondocumentary exhibits after the case is final on appeal.

5. *All other papers and exhibits.* Subject to paragraph 4., the court of appeals must keep and preserve all records of a case (except duplicates) until they are ultimately disposed of under this rule.

6. *Ultimate disposition.* After the period prescribed by Section 51.204 of the Government Code or other applicable statute has expired, the court of appeals must:

(a) destroy those records the court has determined need not be permanently preserved; and

(b) turn over to the State Archives or other repository allowed by law those records the court has determined should be permanently preserved.

C. In the Supreme Court.
The following paragraphs govern disposing of court records by the Supreme Court:

1. *If case reversed and remanded to court of appeals.* If the Supreme Court grants review and remands the case to the court of appeals, the Supreme Court will return the appellate record to the court of appeals. The court of appeals will then dispose of the court records in accordance with subdivision B. The Supreme Court will keep and preserve all remaining items (except duplicates) until they are turned over to the State Archives as provided by law.

2. *If case affirmed or reversed and remanded to trial court.* If the Supreme Court grants review and either affirms the court of appeals or reverses and remands to the trial court, the Supreme Court will not return the appellate record but will keep and preserve all records of the case (except duplicates) until those records are turned over to the State Archives as provided by law.

3. *In all other cases.* In all other cases, the Supreme court will return the appellate record to the court of appeals and keep and preserve all remaining records of the case (except duplicates) until they are turned over to the State Archives as provided by law.

APPENDIX C

IN THE SUPREME COURT OF TEXAS

IN THE COURT OF CRIMINAL APPEALS

ORDER DIRECTING

THE FORM OF THE APPELLATE RECORD

RULE 1   CLERK'S RECORD

1.1.   Preparation of Electronic or Paper Clerk's Record.

The trial court clerk must prepare and file the clerk's record in accordance with Rules of Appellate Procedure 34.5 and 35. Even if more than one notice of appeal or request for inclusion of items is filed, the clerk should prepare only one consolidated record in a case. To prepare the clerk's record, the trial court clerk must:

(a) gather the documents required by Rule of Appellate Procedure 34.5(a) and those requested by a party under Rule of Appellate Procedure 34.5(b);

(b) start each document on a new page;

(c) include the date of filing on each document;

(d) arrange the documents in ascending chronological order, by date of filing or occurrence;

(e) start the page numbering on the front cover of the first volume of the clerk's record and continue to number all pages consecutively—including the front and back covers, tables of contents, certification page, and separator pages, if any—until the final page of the clerk's record, without regard for the number of volumes in the clerk's record, and place each page number at the bottom of each page;

(f) prepare, label, and certify the clerk's record as required by this rule;

(g) as far as practicable, include the date of signing by the judge on each order and judgment;

(h) include on the front cover of the first volume, and any subsequent volumes, of the clerk's record, whether filed in paper or electronic form, the following information, in substantially the following form:

CLERK'S RECORD

VOLUME ___ of _____

Trial Court Cause No. _____

In the _____ (District or County) Court of _____ County, Texas,

Honorable _____, Judge Presiding

_____, Plaintiff(s)

vs.

_____, Defendant(s)

Appealed to the
(Supreme Court of Texas at Austin, Texas,
or Court of Criminal Appeals of Texas at Austin, Texas,
or Court of Appeals for the _____ District of Texas, at _____, Texas).

Attorney for Appellant(s):

Name _____

Address _____

_____

Telephone no.: _____

Fax no.: _____

E–mail address: _____

SBOT no.: _____

Attorney for: _____, Appellant(s)

_____

Name of clerk preparing the clerk's record: _____

(i) prepare and include after the front cover of the clerk's record a detailed table of contents identifying each document in the entire record (including sealed documents), the date each document was filed, and, except for sealed documents, the page on which each document begins. The table of contents must be double-spaced and conform to the order in which documents appear in the clerk's record, rather than in alphabetical order. If the clerk's record consists of multiple volumes, the table of contents must indicate the page on which each volume begins. If the clerk's record is filed in electronic form, the clerk must use bookmarks to link each document description in the table of contents, except descriptions of sealed documents, to the page on which each document begins; and

(j) conclude the clerk's record with a certificate in substantially the following form:

The State of Texas)
County of _____)

I, _____, Clerk of the _____ Court of _____ County, Texas do hereby certify that the documents contained in this record to which this certification is attached are all of the documents specified by Texas Rule of Appellate Procedure 34.5(a) and all other documents timely requested by a party to this proceeding under Texas Rule of Appellate Procedure 34.5(b).

GIVEN UNDER MY HAND AND SEAL at my office in _____, County, Texas this ___ day of _____.

signature of clerk _____

name of clerk _____

title _____

If the clerk's record is filed in electronic form, the trial court clerk must include either a scanned image of the clerk's signature or "/s/" and the clerk's name typed in the space where the signature would otherwise appear.

1.2. Filing an Electronic Clerk's Record.

Unless the clerk receives permission from the appellate court to file the record in paper form, the clerk must file the record electronically. When filing a clerk's record in electronic form, the trial court clerk must:

(a) file each computer file in text-searchable Portable Document Format (PDF);

(b) create electronic bookmarks to mark the first page of each document in the clerk's record;

(c) limit the size of each computer file to 100 MB or less, if possible;

(d) directly convert, rather than scan, the record to PDF, if possible;

(e) comply with the Technology Standards set by the Judicial Committee on Information Technology;

(f) include the following elements in the computer file name, exemplified as CR (01 of 02).pdf:

(1) "CR";

(2) the volume number, using at least two digits, with leading zeroes if needed; "of"; and the total number of volumes;

(3) a period; and

(4) "pdf";

(g) file each sealed document separately from the remainder of the clerk's record and include the word "sealed" in the computer file name;

(h) if filing a supplement to the clerk's record, include the number of the supplement and "Supp";

(i) submit each computer file to the Texas Appeals Management and E–filing System (TAMES) web portal using the instructions provided on the appellate court's website; and

(j) not lock any document that is part of the record.

1.3. Filing a Paper Clerk's Record.

When filing a paper record with the appellate court, the trial court clerk must:

(a) bind the documents together in one or more volumes with a top bound, two-inch capacity, two-and-three-quarter-inch, center-to-center removable fastener and no other binding materials, like wax, ribbon, glue, staples, tape, etc.;

(b) include no more than 500 pages in each volume, or limit the thickness of each volume to a maximum of two inches;

(c) include only one-sided copies in the clerk's record;

(d) number the first volume "1" and each succeeding volume sequentially;

(e) if practicable, make a legible copy of the documents on opaque, white, 8 1/2 × 11 inch paper; and

(f) place each sealed document in a securely sealed, manila envelope that is not bound with the other documents in the clerk's record.

1.4. Non–Conforming Records and Supplements.

In the event of a material violation of this rule in the preparation or filing of the clerk's record, on motion of a party or on its own initiative, the appellate court may require the trial court clerk to amend the clerk's record or to prepare a new clerk's record in proper form—and provide it to any party who has previously made a copy of the original, defective clerk's record—at the trial clerk's expense. A supplement to a clerk's record must also be prepared in conformity with this rule.

RULE 2. ELECTRONIC REPORTER'S RECORD.

(a) The court reporter or court recorder must prepare and file the reporter's record in accordance with Rules of Appellate Procedure 34.6 and 35 and the Uniform Format Manual for Texas Reporters' Records [1], and the court's local rules. Even if more than one notice of appeal or request for preparation of the record is filed, the court reporter or court recorder should prepare only one consolidated record in the case.

(b) If proceedings were recorded stenographically, the court reporter or recorder must file the reporter's record in an electronic format via the Texas Appeals Management and E–filing System (TAMES) web portal and in accordance with Section 8 of the Uniform Format Manual for Texas Reporters' Records, the court's local rules, and any guidelines posted on the appellate court's website.

(c) If the record is filed in electronic format, the court reporter or recorder must include either a scanned image of any required signature or "/s/" and name typed in the space where the signature would otherwise appear.

(d) A court reporter or recorder must not lock any document that is part of the record.

(e) In exhibit volumes, the court reporter or recorder must create bookmarks to mark the first page of each exhibit document.

(f) In the event of a material violation of this rule in the preparation of a reporter's record, on motion of a party or on the court's own initiative, the appellate court may require the court reporter or court recorder to amend the reporter's record or to prepare a new reporter's record in proper form—and provide it to any party who has previously made a copy of the original, defective reporter's record—at the reporter's or recorder's expense. A court reporter who fails to comply with the requirements of the Uniform Format Manual for Texas Reporters' Records is also subject to discipline by the Court Reporters Certification Board.

Amended April 8, 1999, effective May 1, 1999. Amended by Supreme Court Dec. 11, 2013, eff. Jan. 1, 2014. Approved by Court of Criminal Appeals Dec. 11, 2013, eff. Jan. 1, 2014.

[1] Publisher's Note: The text of the Manual is not included.

APPENDIX D

Appendix: Certification of Defendant's Right of Appeal

No. _____

The State of Texas	In the _____ Court
v.	of
_____	_____ County, Texas
Defendant	

TRIAL COURT'S CERTIFICATION OF DEFENDANT'S RIGHT OF APPEAL *

I, judge of the trial court, certify this criminal case:

[] is not a plea-bargain case, and the defendant has the right of appeal, [or]

[] is a plea-bargain case, but matters were raised by written motion filed and ruled on before trial and not withdrawn or waived, and the defendant has the right of appeal. [or]

[] is a plea-bargain case, but the trial court has given permission to appeal, and the defendant has the right of appeal. [or]

[] is a plea-bargain case, and the defendant has NO right of appeal. [or]

[] the defendant has waived the right of appeal.

_____   _____
Judge   Date Signed

I have received a copy of this certification. I have also been informed of my rights concerning any appeal of this criminal case, including any right to file a *pro se* petition for discretionary review pursuant to Rule 68 of the Texas Rules of Appellate Procedure. I have been admonished that my attorney must mail a copy of the court of appeals's judgment and opinion to my last known address and that I have only 30 days in which to file a *pro se* petition for discretionary review in the Court of Criminal Appeals. TEX. R. APP. P. 68.2. I acknowledge that, if I wish to appeal this case and if I am entitled to do so. it is my duty to inform my appellate attorney, by written communication, of any change in the address at which I am currently living or any change in my current prison unit. I understand that, because of appellate deadlines, if I fail to timely inform my appellate attorney of any change in my address, I may lose the opportunity to file a *pro se* petition for discretionary review.

_____   _____

Defendant   Defendant's Counsel
Mailing address: State Bar of Texas ID number
Telephone number: Mailing address:
Fax number (if any):   Telephone number:
                                                           Fax number (if any):

Amended May 2, 2007 and Aug. 20, 2007, eff. Sept. 1, 2007; Sept. 30, 2011, eff. Sept. 30, 2011; Oct. 17, 2011, eff. Oct. 17, 2011.

---

* "A defendant in a criminal case has the right of appeal under these rules. The trial court shall enter a certification of the defendant's right to appeal in every case in which it enters a judgment of guilt or other appealable order. In a plea bargain case—that is, a case in which a defendant's plea was guilty or nolo contendere and the punishment did not exceed the punishment recommended by the prosecutor and agreed to by the defendant—a defendant may appeal only: (A) those matters that were raised by written motion filed and ruled on before trial, or (B) after getting the trial court's permission to appeal." TEXAS RULE OF APPELLATE PROCEDURE 25.2(a)(2)

APPENDIX E

COURT OF CRIMINAL APPEALS OF TEXAS
APPLICATION FOR A WRIT OF HABEAS CORPUS
SEEKING RELIEF FROM FINAL FELONY CONVICTION
UNDER CODE OF CRIMINAL PROCEDURE, ARTICLE 11.07

INSTRUCTIONS

1. You must use the complete form, which begins on the following page, to file an application for a writ of habeas corpus seeking relief from a final felony conviction under Article 11.07 of the Code of Criminal Procedure. (This form is not for death-penalty cases, probated sentences which have not been revoked, or misdemeanors.)

2. The district clerk of the county in which you were convicted will make this form available to you on request, without charge.

3. You must file the entire writ application form, including those sections that do not apply to you. If any pages are missing from the form, or if the questions have been renumbered or omitted, your entire application may be dismissed as non-compliant.

4. You must make a separate application on a separate form for each judgment of conviction you seek relief from. Even if the judgments were entered in the same court on the same day, you must make a separate application for each one.

5. Answer every item that applies to you on the form. Do not attach any additional pages for any item.

6. You must include all grounds for relief on the application form as provided by the instructions under item 17. You must also briefly summarize the facts of your claim on the application form as provided by the instructions under item 17. Each ground shall begin on a new page, and the recitation of the facts supporting the ground shall be no longer than the two pages provided for the claim in the form.

7. Legal citations and arguments may be made in a separate memorandum that complies with Texas Rule of Appellate Procedure 73 and does not exceed 15,000 words if computer-generated or 50 pages if not.

8. You must verify the application by signing either the Oath Before Notary Public or the Inmate's Declaration, which are at the end of this form on pages 11 and 12. You may be prosecuted and convicted for aggravated perjury if you make any false statement of a material fact in this application.

9. When the application is fully completed, mail the original to the district clerk of the county of conviction. Keep a copy of the application for your records.

10. You must notify the district clerk of the county of conviction of any change in address after you have filed your application.

RULES OF APPELLATE PROCEDURE

Case No. _____

(The Clerk of the convicting court will fill this line in.)

IN THE COURT OF CRIMINAL APPEALS OF TEXAS

APPLICATION FOR A WRIT OF HABEAS CORPUS SEEKING RELIEF FROM FINAL FELONY CONVICTION UNDER CODE OF CRIMINAL PROCEDURE, ARTICLE 11.07

NAME: _____

DATE OF BIRTH: _____

PLACE OF CONFINEMENT: _____

TDCJ–CID NUMBER: _____ SID NUMBER: _____

(1) **This application concerns** (check all that apply):

_____

☐ a conviction   ☐ parole

☐ a sentence   ☐ mandatory supervision

☐ time credit   ☐ out–of–time appeal or petition
                                 for discretionary review

(2) **What district court entered the judgment of the conviction you want relief from?** (Include the court number and county.)

_____

(3) **What was the case number in the trial court?**

_____

(4) **What was the name of the trial judge?**

(5) **Were you represented by counsel? If yes, provide the attorney's name:**

_____

(6) **What was the date that the judgment was entered?**

_____

(7) **For what offense were you convicted and what was the sentence?**

_____

(8) **If you were sentenced on more than one count of an indictment in the same court at the same time, what counts were you convicted of and what was the sentence in each count?**

_____

_____

(9) **What was the plea you entered?** (Check one.)

☐ guilty–open plea   ☐ guilty–plea bargain
☐ not guilty   ☐ *nolo contendere*/no contest

If you entered different pleas to counts in a multi-count indictment, please explain:

_____

_____

(10) **What kind of trial did you have?**

☐   no jury   ☐   jury for guilt and punishment

☐   jury for guilt, judge for punishment

(11) Did you testify at trial? If yes, at what phase of the trial did you testify?

_____

(12) Did you appeal from the judgment of conviction?

☐   yes   ☐   no

If you did appeal, answer the following questions:

(A) What court of appeals did you appeal to? _____

(B) What was the case number? _____

(C) Were you represented by counsel on appeal? If yes, provide the attorney's name:

_____

(D) What was the decision and the date of the decision? _____

(13) Did you file a petition for discretionary review in the Court of Criminal Appeals?

☐   yes   ☐   no

If you did file a petition for discretionary review, answer the following questions:

(A) What was the case number? _____

(B) What was the decision and the date of the decision? _____

(14) Have you previously filed an application for a writ of habeas corpus under Article 11.07 of the Texas Code of Criminal Procedure challenging *this conviction?*

☐   yes   ☐   no

If you answered yes, answer the following questions:

(A) What was the Court of Criminal Appeals' writ number?

(B) What was the decision and the date of the decision? _____

(C) Please identify the reason that the current claims were not presented and could not have been presented on your previous application.

_____

_____

_____

_____

(15) Do you currently have any petition or appeal pending in any other state or federal court?

☐   yes   ☐   no

If you answered yes, please provide the name of the court and the case number:

_____

(16) If you are presenting a claim for time credit, have you exhausted your administrative remedies by presenting your claim to the time credit resolution system of the Texas Department of Criminal Justice? (This requirement applies to any final felony conviction, including state jail felonies)

☐   yes   ☐   no

If you answered yes, answer the following questions:

   (A) What date did you present the claim? _____

   (B) Did you receive a decision and, if yes, what was the date of the decision?

_____

If you answered no, please explain why you have not submitted your claim:

_____
_____
_____
_____
_____

(17) Beginning on page 6, state *concisely* every legal ground for your claim that you are being unlawfully restrained, and then briefly summarize the facts supporting each ground. You must present each ground on the form application and a brief summary of the facts. *If your grounds and brief summary of the facts have not been presented on the form application, the Court will not consider your grounds.*

If you have more than four grounds, use pages 14 and 15 of the form, which you may copy as many times as needed to give you a separate page for each ground, with each ground numbered in sequence. The recitation of the facts supporting each ground must be no longer than the two pages provided for the ground in the form.

You may include with the form a memorandum of law if you want to present legal authorities, but the Court will *not* consider grounds for relief set out in a memorandum of law that were not raised on the form. The citations and argument must be in a memorandum that complies with Texas Rule of Appellate Procedure 73 and does not exceed 15,000 words if computer-generated or 50 pages if not. If you are challenging the validity of your conviction, please include a summary of the facts pertaining to your offense and trial in your memorandum.

GROUND ONE:

_____
_____

FACTS SUPPORTING GROUND ONE:

_____
_____
_____
_____
_____
_____
_____
_____
_____
_____
_____
_____
_____

GROUND TWO:

FACTS SUPPORTING GROUND TWO:

_____
_____
_____
_____
_____

GROUND THREE:
_____

FACTS SUPPORTING GROUND THREE:
_____
_____
_____
_____
_____
_____
_____
_____
_____
_____
_____
_____
_____
_____
_____
_____
_____
_____
_____
_____
_____
_____
_____

GROUND FOUR:
_____

FACTS SUPPORTING GROUND FOUR:
_____
_____
_____

GROUND:

FACTS SUPPORTING GROUND:

_____
_____
_____
_____
_____
_____
_____
_____
_____
_____
_____
_____
_____
_____

WHEREFORE, APPLICANT PRAYS THAT THE COURT GRANT APPLICANT RELIEF TO WHICH HE MAY BE ENTITLED IN THIS PROCEEDING.

VERIFICATION

This application must be verified or it will be dismissed for non-compliance. For verification purposes, an applicant is a person filing the application on his or her own behalf. A petitioner is a person filing the application on behalf of an applicant, for example, an applicant's attorney. An inmate is a person who is in custody.

The inmate applicant must sign either the "Oath Before a Notary Public" before a notary public or the "Inmate's Declaration" without a notary public. If the inmate is represented by a licensed attorney, the attorney may sign the "Oath Before a Notary Public" as petitioner and then complete "Petitioner's Information." A non-inmate applicant must sign the "Oath Before a Notary Public" before a notary public unless he is represented by a licensed attorney, in which case the attorney may sign the verification as petitioner.

A non-inmate non-attorney petitioner must sign the "Oath Before a Notary Public" before a notary public and must also complete "Petitioner's Information." An inmate petitioner must sign either the "Oath Before a Notary Public" before a notary public or the "Inmate's Declaration" without a notary public and must also complete the appropriate "Petitioner's Information."

OATH BEFORE A NOTARY PUBLIC

STATE OF TEXAS
COUNTY OF _____

_____, being duly sworn, under oath says: "I am the applicant / petitioner (circle one) in this action and know the contents of the above application for a writ of habeas corpus and, according to my belief, the facts stated in the application are true."

_____
Signature of Applicant / Petitioner (circle one)

SUBSCRIBED AND SWORN TO BEFORE ME THIS ___ DAY OF _____,
20 ___.

_____
Signature of Notary Public

PETITIONER'S INFORMATION

Petitioner's printed name: _____

State bar number, if applicable: _____

Address: _____

_____

_____

Telephone: _____

Fax: _____

INMATE'S DECLARATION

I, _____, am the applicant / petitioner (circle one) and being presently
incarcerated in _____, declare under penalty of perjury that, according to my
belief, the facts stated in the above application are true and correct.

Signed on _____, 20 ___.

_____
Signature of Applicant / Petitioner (circle
one)

PETITIONER'S INFORMATION

Petitioner's printed name: _____

Address: _____

_____

_____

Telephone: _____

Fax: _____

Signed on _____, 20 ___.

_____
Signature of Petitioner

Former Appendix F amended March 5, 2007, eff. March 5, 2007; July 12, 2011, eff. Sept. 1,
2011. Renumbered as Appendix E and amended Dec. 11, 2013, eff. Jan. 1, 2014.

APPENDIX F

IN THE COURT OF CRIMINAL APPEALS OF TEXAS

ORDER ADOPTING SUMMARY SHEET
FOR POSTCONVICTION APPLICATIONS FOR
WRIT OF HABEAS CORPUS

Application for Writ of Habeas Corpus

Ex Parte _____   from _____ County
(Name of Applicant)   _____ Court

TRIAL COURT WRIT NO. _____

CLERK'S SUMMARY SHEET

APPLICANT'S NAME: _____

(As reflected in judgment)

OFFENSE: _____

(As reflected in judgment)

CAUSE NO: _____

(As reflected in judgment)

PLEA: _____ GUILTY _____ NOT GUILTY

SENTENCE: _____ DATE: _____

(Terms of years reflected in judgment)

TRIAL DATE: _____

JUDGE'S NAME: _____

(Judge presiding at trial)

APPEAL NO: _____

(If applicable)

CITATION TO OPINION: _____ S.W.3d _____

(If applicable)

HEARING HELD: _____ YES _____ NO

(Pertaining to the application for writ of habeas corpus)

FINDINGS & CONCLUSIONS FILED: _____ YES _____ NO

(Pertaining to the application for writ of habeas corpus)

RECOMMENDATION: _____ GRANT _____ DENY _____ NONE

(Trial court's recommendation regarding application for writ of habeas corpus)

JUDGE'S NAME:

(Judge presiding over habeas corpus proceeding)

NAME OF COUNSEL IF APPLICANT IS REPRESENTED: _____

Former Appendix G renumbered as Appendix F and amended by Court of Criminal Appeals Dec. 11, 2013, eff. Jan. 1, 2014.

APPENDIX G [Renumbered as Appendix F by Order of Dec. 11, 2013, eff. Jan. 1, 2014]

APPENDIX H [Repealed by Order of Dec. 11, 2013, eff. Jan. 1, 2014]

INDEX

Abbreviations

Index

ACCUSED—Cont'd

Confession, generally, this index

Continuance. Trial, this index

Former Jeopardy, generally, this index

Indictment and Information, this index

ACKNOWLEDGED DOCUMENTS

Self authentication, **Evid Rule 902**

ACKNOWLEDGMENTS

Subpoenas, **CCrP 24.04**

ACQUIRED IMMUNE DEFICIENCY SYNDROME

AIDS, generally, this index

ACQUITTAL

Crimes and Offenses, this index

Former Jeopardy, generally, this index

Judgments and decrees, **App Pro Rule 51.2**

ACT WITH INTENT TO COMMIT OFFENSE

Indictment or information, **CCrP 21.13**

ACTIONS AND PROCEEDINGS

Administrative Law and Procedure, generally, this index

Appeal and Review, generally, this index

Appearance, generally, this index

Attachment, generally, this index

Autopsies, person performing autopsy, **CCrP 49.12**

Citation, generally, this index

Communications, interception, **CCrP 18A.502, 18A.503, 18B.551 et seq.**

Community supervision, deferred adjudication, **CCrP 42A.110**

Complaints, generally, this index

Compromise and Settlement, generally, this index

Contempt, generally, this index

Contraband, forfeitures, **CCrP 59.023**

Correctional Institutions, this index

Costs, generally, this index

Crime victims, compensation, **CCrP 56.52**

Damages, generally, this index

Dismissal and Nonsuit, generally, this index

Electronic communications, **CCrP 18.21**

Communications interception, **CCrP 18B.551 et seq.**

Evidence, generally, this index

ACTIONS AND PROCEEDINGS—Cont'd

Executions, generally, this index

Forfeitures, contraband, **CCrP 59.023**

Frivolous actions and proceedings, habeas corpus, community supervision, **CCrP 11.072**

Habeas corpus, frivolous actions and proceedings, community supervision, **CCrP 11.072**

Holidays, religious holidays, **CCrP 29.011**

Injunctions, generally, this index

Interception, communications, **CCrP 18A.502, 18A.503, 18B.551 et seq.**

Interrogatories, generally, this index

Judgments and Decrees, generally, this index

Jurisdiction, generally, this index

Justices of the Peace, generally, this index

Libel and Slander, generally, this index

Limitation of Actions, generally, this index

Mandamus, generally, this index

Motions, generally, this index

Nolo contendere plea, admission, **CCrP 27.02**

Nonsuit. Dismissal and Nonsuit, generally, this index

Parentage and Parentage Determination, generally, this index

Parties, generally, this index

Paternity suits. Parentage and Parentage Determination, generally, this index

Pending Actions, generally, this index

Pleadings, generally, this index

Privileges and Immunities, generally, this index

Probate Proceedings, generally, this index

Process, generally, this index

Religious holidays, **CCrP 29.011**

Review. Appeal and Review, generally, this index

Security to keep the peace, bonds (officers and fiduciaries), **CCrP 7.16**

Slander. Libel and Slander, generally, this index

Statute of limitations. Limitation of Actions, generally, this index

Stay of proceedings. Supersedeas or Stay, generally, this index

Subpoenas, generally, this index

Supersedeas or Stay, generally, this index

ACTIONS AND PROCEEDINGS—Cont'd

Third Parties, generally, this index

Trial, generally, this index

Venue, generally, this index

Wireless telecommunications, communications interception, **CCrP 18B.551 et seq.**

Wiretapping, **CCrP 18A.502, 18A.503, 18B.551 et seq.**

Witnesses, generally, this index

ACTIVE TRUSTS

Trusts and Trustees, generally, this index

ACTS

Statutes, generally, this index

ADDICTS

Alcoholics and Intoxicated Persons, generally, this index

Chemically Dependent Persons, generally, this index

ADDITIONAL FORENSIC TESTING

Definitions, habeas corpus, **CCrP 11.07**

ADDRESS

Attachment,

County residents, failure to appear, **CCrP 24.12**

Resident material witness about to move out of county, **CCrP 24.14**

Change of address, sexual offenses, registration, **CCrP 62.055**

Crime victims, confidential or privileged information, domestic violence, sexual offenses, stalking, **CCrP 56.81 et seq.**

Crimes and offenses, identity and identification, fraud, venue, **CCrP 13.29**

Foster care, domestic violence, investigations and investigators, **CCrP 5.04**

Fraud, identity and identification, venue, **CCrP 13.29**

Grand jury, confidential or privileged information, **CCrP 19.42**

Identity and identification, fraud, venue, **CCrP 13.29**

Juvenile delinquents and dependents, providing, **CCrP 45.057**

Probationer, changing, **CCrP 42A.153**

Sexual abuse, confidential or privileged information, **CCrP 56.81 et seq.**

Sexual assault, confidential or privileged information, crime victims, **CCrP 56.81 et seq.**

Index

Index

I-4

Index

Index

Index

Index

Index

Index

I-13

Index

Index

Index

Index

Index

Index

CHILD SUPPORT

Support, generally, this index

CHILDREN AND MINORS

Abduction, restitution, **CCrP 42.0371**

Abuse of children,
 Alerts, investigations and investigators, lists, safety, peace officers, response, **CCrP 2.272**
 Costs, sexual abuse, convictions, **CCrP 102.0186**
 Counselors and counseling, fees, **CCrP 42.151**
 Crimes and offenses, sexual abuse, rights, **CCrP 56.021**
 Cross examination, sexual abuse, **CCrP 38.071**
 Evidence, hearsay, **CCrP 38.072**
 Family violence prevention, **CCrP 5.01 et seq.**
 Fees, counseling, **CCrP 42.151**
 Investigations and investigators,
  Missing persons, **CCrP 63.009**
  Reports, **CCrP 2.27**
 Missing persons, investigations and investigators, **CCrP 63.009**
 Prevention, funds, **CCrP 102.014**
 Protective orders, sexual abuse, **CCrP 7A.01**
  Hearsay, **CCrP 7A.035**
 Removal, missing persons, **CCrP 63.009**
 Reports, investigations and investigators, **CCrP 2.27**
 Sexual abuse,
  Costs, convictions, **CCrP 102.0186**
  Cross examination, **CCrP 38.071**
  Limitation of prosecutions, **CCrP 12.01**
  Protective orders, **CCrP 7A.01**
   Hearsay, **CCrP 7A.035**
  Rights, **CCrP 56.021**
  Tests, AIDS, **CCrP 21.31**
 Tests, AIDS, sexual abuse, **CCrP 21.31**
 Victims, hearsay statement, **CCrP 38.072**

Actions affecting parent child relationship. Parentage and Parentage Determination, generally, this index

Actions and proceedings. Parentage and Parentage Determination, generally, this index

Alcohol and drug abuse prevention programs, funds, **CCrP 102.014**

Application of law, crimes and offenses, witnesses, **CCrP 38.074**

CHILDREN AND MINORS—Cont'd

Arrest, capias pro fine, **CCrP 45.045**

Athletics,
 Community supervision, violent offenses, safety zones, **CCrP 42A.502**
 Parole, safety zones, violent crimes, **Gov 508.225**

Autopsies, parental rights, **CCrP 49.52**

Bail bonds, sureties, **CCrP 17.10**

Child Day Care, generally, this index

Children born out of wedlock. Parentage and Parentage Determination, generally, this index

Citation, schools and school districts, **CCrP 45.058**

Clearinghouse, missing persons, **CCrP 63.001 et seq.**

Community service, fines and penalties,
 Elections, **CCrP 42.15, 45.041**
 Satisfaction, **CCrP 42.15, 45.0492**

Community Supervision, this index

Confidential or privileged information,
 Criminal history record information, **CCrP 44.2811, 45.0217**
 Missing persons, **CCrP 63.015, 63.017**

Costs, waiver, **CCrP 43.091, 45.0491**

Crime victims,
 Compensation, filing, **CCrP 56.37**
 Human trafficking, protective orders, **CCrP 56.021**
 Medical records, seals, **CCrP 57C.01, 57C.02**
 Restitution, **CCrP 42.0371**
 Rights, **CCrP 56.01 et seq.**
 Testimony, **CCrP 38.071, 38.072**

Crimes and offenses,
 Delinquency. Juvenile Delinquents and Dependents, generally, this index
 Exploitation, limitation of prosecutions, **CCrP 12.01**
 Juvenile Delinquents and Dependents, generally, this index
 Obscenity, this index
 Pornography, restitution, **CCrP 42.037**
 Records and recordation, expunction, **CCrP 45.0216**
 Witnesses, **CCrP 38.074**

Criminal history record information, **CCrP 44.2811, 45.0217**

Cross examination, crime victims, **CCrP 38.071**

Custody, definitions, nonsecure custody, **CCrP 45.058**

CHILDREN AND MINORS—Cont'd

Day care. Child Day Care, generally, this index

Death, inquest, **CCrP 49.25**

Death certificates, missing persons, **CCrP 63.018**

Definitions,
 Autopsies, parental rights, **CCrP 49.51**
 Crime victims,
  Compensation, **CCrP 56.32**
  Medical records, seals, **CCrP 57C.01**
 Juvenile delinquents and dependents, fines and penalties, **CCrP 45.050**
 Missing, **CCrP 63.001**
 Organized crime, information, compilation, **CCrP 61.01**

Dentists and dentistry, missing persons, records and recordation, **CCrP 63.006**

Drugs and medicine, abuse prevention programs, funds, **CCrP 102.014**

Electronic communications, obscenity,
 Community supervision, **CCrP 42A.512**
 Restitution, **CCrP 42.037**

Electronic records, victims, testimony, **CCrP 38.071**

Evidence,
 Electronic recordings, victims, **CCrP 38.071**
 Hearsay, **CCrP 38.072**
  Protective orders, sexual abuse, **CCrP 7A.035**

Exploitation, limitation of prosecutions, **CCrP 12.01**

Expunction, records and recordation, crimes and offenses, **CCrP 45.0216**

Fees,
 Abuse, counseling, **CCrP 42.151**
 Records and recordation, expungement, **CCrP 45.0216**

Fines and penalties,
 Pornography, restitution, **CCrP 42.037**
 Waiver, **CCrP 43.091, 45.0491**

Forms, missing persons, **CCrP 63.004**

Foster Care, generally, this index

Gifts, missing persons, clearinghouse, **CCrP 63.016**

Grand jury, care, excuse from service, **CCrP 19.25**

Guardian and Ward, generally, this index

Homicide, cross examination, **CCrP 38.071**

Index

Index

COLLECTIONS

Costs, CCrP 103.001 et seq.

County courts, crimes and offenses, **CCrP 103.0033**

Criminal district courts, **CCrP 103.0033**

Municipal Courts, this index

COLLEGES AND UNIVERSITIES

Athletics,

  Illegal recruitment, venue, **CCrP 13.24**

  Recruitment, illegal recruitment, venue, **CCrP 13.24**

Cemeteries and dead bodies, DNA, database, University of North Texas system, **CCrP 63.051 et seq.**

Commissioned officers, peace officers, **CCrP 2.12**

Community colleges and districts, school marshals, **CCrP 2.127**

Counties of less than 200,000, adjunct police officers, private university, **CCrP 2.123**

Courses of study, law enforcement, financial aid, **CCrP 59.06**

Criminal justice, agents and agencies, University of North Texas system, health science center, **CCrP 63.0515**

Damages, adjunct police officers, **CCrP 2.123**

Definitions, law enforcement, financial aid, **CCrP 59.06**

DNA, missing persons, database, University of North Texas system, **CCrP 63.051 et seq.**

Domicile and residence, housing, sexual offenses, registration, **CCrP 62.064**

Financial assistance, law enforcement, **CCrP 59.06**

Grand jury service, excuses, **CCrP 19.25**

Housing, sexual offenses, registration, **CCrP 62.064**

Law enforcement, financial aid, **CCrP 59.06**

Missing persons, DNA, database, University of North Texas system, **CCrP 63.051 et seq.**

Police, adjunct police officers, private institutions, **CCrP 2.123**

Private postsecondary educational institutions,

  Adjunct police officers, **CCrP 2.123**

  Degrees and diplomas,

    Fraud, venue, **CCrP 13.30**

    Venue, fraud, **CCrP 13.30**

  Fraud, degrees and diplomas, venue, **CCrP 13.30**

COLLEGES AND UNIVERSITIES —Cont'd

Private postsecondary educational institutions—Cont'd

  Venue, degrees and diplomas, fraud, **CCrP 13.30**

Sexual offenses, registration, **CCrP 62.053, 62.151 et seq.**

  Housing, **CCrP 62.064**

  Transfers, notice, **CCrP 62.057**

Texas State Technical College system, peace officers, **CCrP 2.12**

University of North Texas system,

  Cemeteries and dead bodies, DNA, database, **CCrP 63.051 et seq.**

  Criminal justice agencies, health science center, **CCrP 63.0515**

  DNA, database, missing persons, **CCrP 63.051 et seq.**

  Health science center,

    Cemeteries and dead bodies, DNA, database, **CCrP 63.051 et seq.**

    Criminal justice agencies, **CCrP 63.0515**

    Missing persons, DNA, database, **CCrP 63.051 et seq.**

  Missing persons, DNA, database, **CCrP 63.051 et seq.**

Venue,

  Private postsecondary educational institutions, degrees and diplomas, fraud, **CCrP 13.30**

  Recruitment, athletes, **CCrP 13.24**

COLOR

Discrimination, generally, this index

COMBINATION

Definitions, organized crime, information, compilation, **CCrP 61.01**

COMMENCEMENT OF ACTIONS AND PROCEEDINGS

Limitation of Actions, generally, this index

COMMENTS

Privileges and immunities, **Evid Rule 513**

COMMERCE

Business and Commerce, generally, this index

COMMERCIAL CODE

Negotiable Instruments, generally, this index

Sales, generally, this index

COMMERCIAL PAPER

Negotiable Instruments, generally, this index

COMMERCIAL PUBLICATIONS

Admissibility, **Evid Rule 803**

COMMERCIAL SOCIAL NETWORKING SITES

Definitions, sexual offenses, online identifiers, **CCrP 62.0061**

COMMISSIONERS

Boards and Commissions, generally, this index

COMMISSIONERS COURTS

Attorneys, indigent persons,

  Appointment, **CCrP 26.044**

  Supervision, **CCrP 26.045**

Audits and auditors, costs, collections, **CCrP 103.0033**

Collections, costs, **CCrP 103.003, 103.0033**

Contracts, **CCrP 103.0031**

Community service, privileges and immunities, **CCrP 42.20, 43.131**

Computers, justice court technology fund, **CCrP 102.0173**

Contracts,

  Costs, collections, **CCrP 103.0031, 103.0033**

  Managers and management, attorneys, indigent persons, **CCrP 26.047**

Costs,

  Collections, **CCrP 103.003, 103.0033**

  Contracts, **CCrP 103.0031**

Juvenile delinquency prevention fund, **CCrP 102.0171**

Technology, **CCrP 102.0173**

Death investigator office, **CCrP 49.23**

Definitions, costs, collections, **CCrP 103.0033**

Deposits, justice court technology fund, **CCrP 102.0173**

Fees, technology, **CCrP 102.0173**

Fines and penalties, collections, contracts, **CCrP 103.0031**

Funds, justice court technology fund, **CCrP 102.0173**

Justice court technology fund, **CCrP 102.0173**

Juvenile delinquency prevention fund, **CCrP 102.0171**

Managers and management, attorneys, indigent persons, **CCrP 26.047**

Notice, fines and penalties, payments, **CCrP 103.0031**

Open records. Records and Recordation, this index

Privileges and immunities,

  Community corrections, **CCrP 42.03**

I-26

Index

Index

Index

Index

Index

Index

Index

Index

Index

Index

Index

Index

Index

Index

I-49

Index

Index

Index

CRIMES AND OFFENSES—Cont'd

Recommitment, defendant on quashing indictment, **CCrP 28.05**

Records and recordation,

Criminal History Record Information, generally, this index

Expunction of Criminal Record, generally, this index

Fees, **CCrP 103.009**

Fine only misdemeanors, confidential or privileged information, **CCrP 44.2812, 45.0218**

Restitution, liens, **CCrP 42.22**

Sentence suspension proceedings, **CCrP 42A.202**

Signatures, digital signature, **CCrP 2.26**

Videoconferences, **CCrP 27.18**

Recruitment, athletes, **CCrP 28.05**

Venue, **CCrP 13.24**

Reformation, sentence, capital offenses, confinement, **CCrP 44.251, 44.2511**

Registered or certified mail, criminal records, expunction, notice, **CCrP 55.02**

Registration. Sexual Offenses, this index

Rehearing, sentence suspension, **CCrP 42A.202**

Release, stolen property, **CCrP 47.01**

Religious holidays, **CCrP 29.011**

Remission of fines, **CCrP 48.01 et seq.**

Rendition, prisoners in criminal proceedings, **CCrP 24.29**

Reports,

Criminal and social history, **CCrP 42A.253, 42A.256**

Transfers, **CCrP 42.09**

Reprieves. Pardons and Reprieves, generally, this index

Restitution, generally, this index

Restoration, civil rights, **CCrP 48.05**

Rewards,

Fugitives from justice, **CCrP 51.11**

Repayment, **CCrP 37.073, 42.152**

Rights, victims, **CCrP 56.01 et seq.**

Rights of accused, **CCrP 1.05**

Bail, **CCrP 1.07**

Jury trial, **CCrP 1.12**

Riots and Mobs, generally, this index

Robbery, generally, this index

Searches and Seizures, generally, this index

Second and subsequent offenses, **CCrP 42.08**

Evidence,

Deferred adjudication of guilt, dismissal, **CCrP 42A.111**

CRIMES AND OFFENSES—Cont'd

Second and subsequent offenses —Cont'd

Evidence—Cont'd

Hearing on punishment, **CCrP 37.07**

Indictments, reading to jury, **CCrP 36.01**

Sentences, **CCrP 42.08**

Sexual offenses, capital offenses, **CCrP 37.072**

Sedition. Insurrection and Sedition, generally, this index

Seizures. Searches and Seizures, generally, this index

Self Incrimination, generally, this index

Separate hearing on punishment, **CCrP 37.07**

Service, process, rights of accused, **CCrP 1.05**

Severability clause, **CCrP 54.01**

Sexual Abuse, generally, this index

Sexual Assault, generally, this index

Sexual Offenses, generally, this index

Sexually Violent Predators, generally, this index

Shock probation, **CCrP 42A.302**

Felonies, **CCrP 42A.555**

Short title, **CCrP 1.01**

Signatures, records and recordation, digital signature, **CCrP 2.26**

Smuggling of persons. Human Trafficking, generally, this index

Social history, presentence report, **CCrP 42A.253, 42A.256**

Speedy Trial, generally, this index

Stalking, generally, this index

State jail felonies,

Community supervision, **CCrP 42A.551 et seq.**

Diligent participation credit, **CCrP 42A.559**

Vocational training, **CCrP 42A.562**

Statements of Accused, generally, this index

Stay of proceedings. Supersedeas or Stay, generally, this index

Subpoenas, **CCrP 24.01 et seq.**

Application, **CCrP 24.03**

Attachment for witnesses,

Examining courts, **CCrP 16.10**

Refusal, fines and penalties, **CCrP 2.16**

Autopsies, **CCrP 24.01**

Change of venue, **CCrP 31.07**

Coroners inquest, **CCrP 24.01**

Courts of inquiry, **CCrP 52.03**

Examining courts,

Attachment for witnesses, **CCrP 16.10**

CRIMES AND OFFENSES—Cont'd

Subpoenas—Cont'd

Examining courts—Cont'd

Persons to testify, **CCrP 24.01**

Failure to execute, **CCrP 2.16**

Fees,

Execution, **CCrP 24.18**

Refusal of witness to obey, **CCrP 24.22**

Service, **CCrP 24.19**

Habeas corpus, persons to testify, **CCrP 24.01**

Inquests, **CCrP 49.14**

Mail and mailing, **CCrP 24.04**

Names, **CCrP 24.03**

Neglect to execute, **CCrP 2.16**

Out of county witnesses, **CCrP 24.16**

Peace officers, **CCrP 24.01**

Refusal, **CCrP 2.16, 24.05**

Returns, **CCrP 24.04**

Seals, **CCrP 24.01**

Service, **CCrP 24.04**

Body attachment and failure of witness to appear, **CCrP 24.11 et seq.**

Certificate of officer, **CCrP 24.19**

Duty of officer receiving, **CCrP 24.17**

Fees, **CCrP 24.18, 24.19**

Future date, **CCrP 24.20**

Property, **CCrP 24.17, 24.18**

Returnable forthwith, **CCrP 24.18**

Sheriffs, **CCrP 24.01**

Signatures, **CCrP 24.01**

Time, **CCrP 24.01, 24.04**

Suicide, generally, this index

Supersedeas or Stay, generally, this index

Supervision, mandatory supervision. Parole, this index

Tape and sound recordings, income, forfeitures, **CCrP 59.06**

Telecommunications, this index

Tests. DNA, this index

Theft, generally, this index

Threats, generally, this index

Time,

DNA, evidence, destruction, **CCrP 38.43**

Dockets, notice, posting, **CCrP 17.085**

Jurisdiction of court over convicted felons, **CCrP 42A.202, 42A.203**

Release of defendant, delay in trial, **CCrP 17.151**

Weapons, felonies, **CCrP 42A.204**

Torture, prisoners, **CCrP 43.24**

I-53

Index

Index

Index

Index

ELECTRONIC MAIL—Cont'd

Evidence,

Certificates of analysis, laboratories, **CCrP 38.41**

Chain of custody, affidavits, **CCrP 38.41**

Habeas corpus, **CCrP 11.07 et seq.**

ELECTRONIC MONITORING

Generally, **Gov 508.221, 508.315**

Bail and recognizances,

Condition, **CCrP 17.44**

Personal bond, **CCrP 17.43**

Cessation, notice, crime victims, **CCrP 56.11**

Community supervision, **CCrP 42A.301**

Gangs, **CCrP 42A.507**

Definitions, community supervision, **CCrP 42A.001**

Drug testing as condition, **CCrP 17.44**

Gangs, **Gov 508.227**

Community supervision, **CCrP 42A.507**

Good conduct, punishment mitigation factor, **CCrP 37.07**

Indigent defendants, inability to pay fine, alternative, **CCrP 43.09**

Jails, alternative, **CCrP 42.035**

Medically recommended intensive supervision, **Gov 508.146**

ELECTRONIC RECORDS

Children and minors, victims of crimes, testimony, **CCrP 38.071**

Customers, searches and seizures, warrants, **CCrP 18.02, 18.21**

District clerks, **CCrP 2.21**

Victims of crimes, children and minors, testimony, **CCrP 38.071**

ELECTRONIC SIGNATURES

Papers, **App Pro Rule 9.1**

ELECTRONIC SURVEILLANCE

Communications Interception, generally, this index

ELECTRONIC TRANSACTIONS

Communications. Electronic Communications, generally, this index

ELEMENTARY SCHOOLS

Schools and School Districts, generally, this index

EMAIL

Electronic Mail, generally, this index

EMBARRASSMENT

Witnesses, **Evid Rule 611**

EMBEZZLEMENT

Bank officer or employee, limitation of criminal prosecution, **CCrP 12.01**

Limitation of criminal prosecution, **CCrP 12.01**

EMERGENCIES

Communications Interception, this index

Crime victims, compensation, awards, **CCrP 56.50**

Crimes and offenses, interference, emergency calls, warrantless arrests, **CCrP 14.03**

Criminal Code, application of law, **CCrP 54.03**

Electronic communications, interception, installation, **CCrP 18.20, 18.21**

Interception, communications. Communications Interception, this index

Medical care and treatment. Emergency Medical Services, generally, this index

Telecommunications, this index

Trap and trace devices, telecommunications, interception, **CCrP 18.21**

Wiretapping. Communications Interception, this index

EMERGENCY CARE ATTENDANTS

Emergency Medical Services, generally, this index

EMERGENCY MEDICAL SERVICES

Assault and battery, bodily fluids, diseases, tests, **CCrP 18.22**

Diseases, assault and battery, tests, bodily fluids, **CCrP 18.22**

Tests, assault and battery, diseases, **CCrP 18.22**

EMERGENCY SERVICES DISTRICTS

Fire marshal, peace officers, **CCrP 2.12**

Investigations and investigators, peace officers, **CCrP 2.12**

Peace officers, investigations and investigators, **CCrP 2.12**

EMMA'S LAW

Parole, **Gov 508.141**

EMOTIONAL CONDITION

Hearsay, **Evid Rule 803**

EMOTIONAL ILLNESS

Mental Health, generally, this index

EMPLOYEES

Labor and Employment, generally, this index

EMPLOYERS

Labor and Employment, generally, this index

EMPLOYMENT

Labor and Employment, generally, this index

EN BANC COURTS

Generally, **App Pro Rule 41.2**

Court of criminal appeals, **App Pro Rule 76**

Opinions and decisions, **App Pro Rule 47.6**

Reconsideration, **App Pro Rule 49.6**

ENCUMBRANCES

Liens and Incumbrances, generally, this index

ENDORSEMENTS

Indorsements, generally, this index

ENFORCEMENT OF JUDGMENTS

Judgments and Decrees, this index

ENTERTAINMENT

Motion Pictures, generally, this index

ENTRAPMENT

Defenses, pretrial hearings, **CCrP 28.01 et seq.**

Pretrial hearings, **CCrP 28.01**

ENTRY ON PROPERTY

Communications interception, orders of court, **CCrP 18A.104**

Interception, communications, orders of court, **CCrP 18A.104**

Wiretapping, orders of court, **CCrP 18A.104**

ERRORS

Corrections, generally, this index

ESCAPE

Appeal and review, escapes pending, **CCrP 44.10**

Arrest without warrant, felonies, **CCrP 14.04**

Bail, time to procure, **CCrP 2.18**

Citizens to aid in preventing, **CCrP 43.26**

Condemned prisoner, **CCrP 43.21, 43.22**

Crime victims, notice, **CCrP 56.11, 56.12**

Death sentence, **CCrP 43.22**

Guards to prevent, **CCrP 16.21**

Habeas corpus applicant, **CCrP 11.37**

Index

EVIDENCE—Cont'd

Hearsay—Cont'd

Prostitution, compelling prostitution, children and minors, **CCrP 38.072**

Stolen property, restoration, **CCrP 47.01a**

Homicide, **CCrP 38.36**

Husband and wife, privilege, **Evid Rule 504**

Identity and identification, **Evid Rule 901 et seq.**

In camera hearings, preliminary questions, **Evid Rule 104**

Indictment and information, **CCrP 21.03**

Inference, claim of privilege, **Evid Rule 513**

Informers, identity and identification, **Evid Rule 508**

Inquests, this index

Insanity defense, notice, **CCrP 46C.051, 46C.052**

Insurance, **Evid Rule 411**

Interception, communications. Communications Interception, this index

Internet, solicitations, children and minors, investigations and investigators, **CCrP 24A.051**

Investigations and investigators. Private Investigators, generally, this index

Jailhouse witnesses, **CCrP 2.023**

Judgment debtors, affidavits, superseding judgments, **App Pro Rule 24.2**

Judicial Notice, generally, this index

Justices of the Peace, this index

Laboratories, certificates of analysis, **CCrP 38.41**

Lawyer client privilege, **Evid Rule 503**

Waiver, **Evid Rule 511**

Lay witnesses, opinion testimony, **Evid Rule 701**

Lesser included offenses, **CCrP 37.09**

Limited admissibility, **Evid Rule 105**

Material evidence, new trial, **CCrP 40.001**

Medical assistance, fraud, **CCrP 37.07**

Medical expenses, payment, **Evid Rule 409**

Medicare, fraud, **CCrP 38.47**

Motions, **App Pro Rule 10.2**

Municipal Courts, this index

New trial, material evidence, **CCrP 40.001**

Oaths and affirmations,

Chain of custody, affidavits, **CCrP 38.42**

EVIDENCE—Cont'd

Oaths and affirmations—Cont'd

Laboratories, certificates of analysis, **CCrP 38.41**

Objections and exceptions, erroneous rulings, **Evid Rule 103**

Obscenity, children and minors, **CCrP 38.45, 39.15**

Privacy, **CCrP 38.451, 39.151**

Offer of proof, **Evid Rule 103**

Opinion and expert testimony, **Evid Rule 701 et seq.**

Opposing parties, statements, hearsay, **Evid Rule 801**

Optional completeness, **Evid Rule 107**

Oral communications, interception, **CCrP 18.20**

Ordinances, judicial notice, **Evid Rule 204**

Original documents, **Evid Rule 1002**

Parties, admission or testimony, **Evid Rule 1007**

Perjury, generally, this index

Photography and pictures,

Content, **Evid Rule 1001 et seq.**

Theft cases, **CCrP 38.34**

Physician patient privilege, **Evid Rule 509**

Pleas and plea discussions, **Evid Rule 410**

Political vote, privilege, **Evid Rule 506**

Pregnancy, crimes and offenses, **CCrP 38.40**

Preliminary questions, **Evid Rule 104**

Presentation, **Evid Rule 611**

Presumptions,

Death, **CCrP 38.32**

Habeas corpus, innocence, **CCrP 11.43**

Indictment, stating presumptions of law, **CCrP 21.18**

Indigent persons, perfection of appeal, **App Pro Rule 25.1**

Innocence, **CCrP 2.03, 38.03**

Justices of the peace, indigent persons, waiver, costs, fines and penalties, **CCrP 43.091**

Law, statements in indictment, **CCrP 21.18**

Municipal courts, indigent persons, waiver, costs, fines and penalties, **CCrP 43.091**

Presence of defendant at trial, **CCrP 33.03**

Proof of other facts, **CCrP 38.04**

Self authentication, **Evid Rule 902**

Trial, competency, **CCrP 46B.003**

EVIDENCE—Cont'd

Previous sexual conduct, **Evid Rule 412**

Private Investigators, generally, this index

Privileged communications. Confidential or Privileged Information, generally, this index

Privileges, **Evid Rule 501 et seq.**

Probable Cause, generally, this index

Production of Books and Papers, generally, this index

Public health, offenses injurious to, action on bond, **CCrP 9.05**

Punishment, character evidence, relevancy, **Evid Rule 404**

Records and recordation, content, **Evid Rule 1001 et seq.**

Related writings or recorded statements, **Evid Rule 106**

Relevancy, **Evid Rule 401 et seq.**

Preliminary questions, **Evid Rule 104**

Remainder, related writings or recorded statements, **Evid Rule 106**

Remedial measures, **Evid Rule 407**

Reports,

Forensic science commission, **CCrP 38.01**

Organizations, disclosure, privilege, **Evid Rule 502**

Reputation and character. Private Investigators, generally, this index

Restitution, this index

Rights of accused, **CCrP 1.05**

Routine practice, admissibility, **Evid Rule 406**

Rulings, **Evid Rule 103**

Scope of rules, **Evid Rule 101**

Search warrants, description of property, **CCrP 18.01, 18.02**

Security on bail bond, sufficiency, **CCrP 17.11**

Self authentication, **Evid Rule 902**

Self incrimination, failure of defendant to testify, comments, **CCrP 38.08**

Sexual Offenses, this index

Social services, medical assistance, fraud, **CCrP 37.07, 38.47**

Special grounds, exclusion of relevant evidence, exclusion, **Evid Rule 403**

Stalking, **CCrP 38.46**

Subpoenas, generally, this index

Subsequent remedial measures, **Evid Rule 407**

Summaries, documents, **Evid Rule 1006**

Index

Index

Index

Index

Index

Index

Index

Index

Index

Index

Index

Index

Index

Index

Index

Index

Index

Index

Index

Index

Index

Index

MENTAL HEALTH—Cont'd
Retarded persons—Cont'd
Jails, early identification, **CCrP 16.22**
Sexual abuse, evidence, hearsay, **CCrP 38.072**
Sentence, **CCrP 42.07**
Television and radio, competency, **CCrP 46B.013**
Return, **CCrP 46B.084**
Transportation, detention, **CCrP 46.04**
Treatment, insanity defense, acquittal, commitments, **CCrP 46C.254, 46C.256 et seq.**
Verdicts, jury belief on guilty plea, **CCrP 37.13**
Video recordings, competency, **CCrP 46B.013**
Return, **CCrP 46B.084**
Weapons, searches and seizures, disposition, **CCrP 18.191**
Witnesses, competency, **Evid Rule 601**

MENTAL HEALTH CODE
Mental Health, generally, this index

MENTAL ILLNESS
Mental Health, generally, this index

MENTAL RETARDATION
Retarded persons. Mental Health, this index

MENTALLY DEFICIENT AND MENTALLY ILL PERSONS
Mental Health, generally, this index

MENTALLY ILL PERSONS
Mental Health, generally, this index

MENTALLY RETARDED PERSONS
Retarded persons. Mental Health, this index

MERCY
Sentence and punishment, **CCrP 48.01**

METROPOLITAN RAPID TRANSIT AUTHORITIES
Officers and employees, commissions, peace officers, **CCrP 2.12**

MICHAEL MORTON ACT
Production of books and papers, **CCrP 39.14**

MIDDLE SCHOOLS
Schools and School Districts, generally, this index

MILEAGE
Traveling Expenses, generally, this index

MILITARY FORCES
Application of rules, **Evid Rule 101**
Crimes and offenses, presentence investigations, **CCrP 42A.253**
Depositions, **CCrP 39.09**
Domestic violence,
Notice, **CCrP 42.0183**
Reports, **CCrP 5.05**
Escapes, preventing, **CCrP 43.26**
Evidence, rules, application, **Evid Rule 101**
Executing process, aid, **CCrP 8.01, 8.02**
Habeas corpus, federal custody, **CCrP 11.63**
Militia, generally, this index
Naval facilities, criminal justice planning fund, appropriations to local units of government, **CCrP 102.056**
Notice, domestic violence, **CCrP 42.0183**
Posttraumatic stress disorder, presentence investigations, **CCrP 42A.253**
Presentence investigations, **CCrP 42A.253**
Prisoners of war, habeas corpus, **CCrP 11.63**
Process, aiding execution, **CCrP 8.01, 8.02**
Records and recordation, presentence investigations, **CCrP 42A.253**
Registration, sexual offenses, **CCrP 62.003, 62.052**
Reports, domestic violence, **CCrP 5.05**
Rescues, correctional institutions, prevention, **CCrP 43.26**
Riots, aid in suppressing, **CCrP 8.03**
Sexual offenses, registration, **CCrP 62.003, 62.052**
State. Militia, generally, this index
State militia. Militia, generally, this index
Unlawful assemblies, aid in suppressing, **CCrP 8.03**
Veterans, generally, this index

MILITARY SERVICE
Military Forces, generally, this index

MILITIA
Depositions, **CCrP 39.09**
Escapes, preventing, **CCrP 43.26**
Executing process, aid, **CCrP 8.01, 8.02**
Habeas corpus, federal custody, **CCrP 11.63**
Prisoner of war, habeas corpus, **CCrP 11.63**
Process, aid in execution, **CCrP 8.01, 8.02**

MILITIA—Cont'd
Rescue, correctional institutions, prevention, **CCrP 43.26**
Riots, aid in suppressing, **CCrP 8.03**
Unlawful assemblies, aid in suppressing, **CCrP 8.03**

MINISTERS
Clergy, generally, this index

MINORITIES
Discrimination, generally, this index
Profiling, racial profiling, **CCrP 2.131 et seq.**
Racial profiling, **CCrP 2.131 et seq.**

MINORS
Children and Minors, generally, this index

MINUTES
Courts, this index

MIRANDA WARNINGS
Generally, **CCrP 38.22**
Arraignment, **CCrP 16.03**
Deaf persons, interpreters, **CCrP 15.17**
Hearing impaired persons, interpreters, **CCrP 15.17**
Magistrates, **CCrP 14.06, 15.17**

MISDEMEANORS
Crimes and Offenses, generally, this index

MISFEASANCE
Jurisdiction, **CCrP 4.05**

MISLEADING EVIDENCE
Exclusion, **Evid Rule 403**

MISREPRESENTATION
Fraud, generally, this index

MISSING PERSONS
Generally, **CCrP 63.001 et seq.**
Absence and Absentees, generally, this index

MISSIONS
Hearsay, **Evid Rule 801**

MISTAKES
Corrections, generally, this index

MISTRIAL
Trial, this index
Witnesses, statements, production, **Evid Rule 615**

MOBILE TELEPHONES
Wireless telecommunications. Telecommunications, this index

MOBILE TRACKING DEVICES
Global Positioning Systems, generally, this index

Index

Index

Index

Index

Index

Index

Index

Index

PETIT LARCENY
Theft, generally, this index

PETITIONER
Definitions, **App Pro Rule 3.1**

PETITIONS
Adoption by reference, **App Pro Rule 9.7**

Court of criminal appeals, discretionary review, **App Pro Rules 67.1 et seq., 68.1 et seq.**

Discretionary review, court of criminal appeals, **App Pro Rules 67.1 et seq., 68.1 et seq.**

Expunction of criminal records, **CCrP 55.02**

Habeas corpus, **CCrP 11.12 et seq.**

Length, **App Pro Rule 9.4**

Original proceedings, **App Pro Rule 52.1 et seq.**

Permissive appeals, **App Pro Rule 28.3**

Sexual offenses, registration, children and minors, exemptions, **CCrP 62.301**

Stolen property, restoration, **CCrP 47.01a**

PETS
Dogs, generally, this index

PHARMACIES
Pharmacists, generally, this index

PHARMACISTS
Boards and commissions,
Criminal history record system, **CCrP 66.104**

Information, criminal history record system, **CCrP 66.104**

Officers, peace officers, designation, **CCrP 2.12**

PHARMACY BOARD
Boards and commissions.
Pharmacists, this index

PHONOGRAPHS AND PHONOGRAPH RECORDS
Tape and Sound Recordings, generally, this index

PHOTOCOPIES
Authentication or identification, **Evid Rule 901 et seq.**

Originals, **Evid Rule 1001 et seq.**

PHOTOGRAPHY AND PICTURES
Chemical dispensing devices, disposition, **CCrP 18.181**

Children and Minors, this index

Courtrooms, **App Pro Rule 14.1 et seq.**

Crimes and offenses,
Lineups, **CCrP 38.20**

PHOTOGRAPHY AND PICTURES
—Cont'd
Crimes and offenses—Cont'd
Sexual Offenses, this index

Definitions, **Evid Rule 1001**

Discovery, **CCrP 39.14**

Explosive weapons, disposition, **CCrP 18.181**

Jury, deliberations, **CCrP 36.215**

Originals, **Evid Rule 1001 et seq.**

Parole, release, summary, **CCrP 42.09**

Searches and seizures, **CCrP 18.01**

Sexual Offenses, this index

Theft cases, evidence, **CCrP 38.34**

PHRASES
Words and Phrases, generally, this index

PHYSICAL CONDITION
Hearsay, **Evid Rule 803**

PHYSICAL EVIDENCE
Definitions, crimes and offenses, **CCrP 38.35**

PHYSICAL EXAMINATIONS
Crime victims, compensation, **CCrP 56.38, 56.39**

Sexual Assault, this index

PHYSICAL SUFFERING
Prisoners, **CCrP 1.09, 16.21, 43.24**

PHYSICALLY DISABLED PERSONS
Handicapped Persons, generally, this index

PHYSICIAN PATIENT PRIVILEGE
Generally, **Evid Rule 509**

PHYSICIANS AND SURGEONS
See, also, Medical Care and Treatment, generally, this index

Autopsies,
Conflict of interest, **CCrP 49.35**

Consent, **CCrP 49.13**

Inquests, **CCrP 49.10 et seq.**

Boards and commissions. Medical Board, generally, this index

Conflict of interest, autopsies, **CCrP 49.35**

Consent, autopsies, **CCrP 49.13**

Correctional institutions, visitation, **CCrP 43.17**

County medical examiners, **CCrP 49.25**

Death, without attendance, inquests, **CCrP 49.01 et seq.**

Definitions, inquests and autopsies, **CCrP 49.01**

PHYSICIANS AND SURGEONS
—Cont'd
Examinations and examiners.
Medical Board, generally, this index

Inquests, dead bodies, **CCrP 49.01 et seq.**

Licenses and permits. Medical Board, generally, this index

Medical Board, generally, this index

Medical Care and Treatment, generally, this index

Prisoner sentenced to death, visitor, **CCrP 43.17**

Privileges and immunities, **Evid Rule 509**

Mental health, information, **Evid Rule 510**

Sexual assault, medical examinations, **CCrP 56.065**

PICKUP TRUCKS
Motor Vehicles, generally, this index

PICTURES
Photography and Pictures, generally, this index

PISTOLS
Weapons, generally, this index

PLAINTIFFS
Parties, generally, this index

PLANES
Aircraft, generally, this index

PLANS AND SPECIFICATIONS
Character and reputation, **Evid Rules 404, 405**

Crimes and offenses, client supervision plan, use, **CCrP 42.09**

Criminal history record information, **CCrP 60.21**

Jury, excuses, determination, **CCrP 35.03**

Law enforcement agencies, lineups, **CCrP 38.20**

Parole, **Gov 508.044**

PLAYGROUNDS
Parks and Playgrounds, generally, this index

PLAYING CARDS
Gambling, generally, this index

PLEA BARGAINING
Crime victims rights, **CCrP 26.13, 56.02**

PLEADINGS
See, also, Petitions, generally, this index

Generally, **App Pro Rule 9.1 et seq.**

Index

Index

Index

Index

PURCHASES AND PURCHASING
Sales, generally, this index

PURPOSE
Rules, **Evid Rule 102**

QUALIFIED INTERPRETER
Definitions, court interpreter for deaf person, **CCrP 38.31**

QUASHING
Communications interception, orders of court, service providers, **CCrP 18A.153**
Indictments, **CCrP 28.04, 28.05**

QUESTIONS
Preliminary questions, **Evid Rule 104**
Witnesses, leading questions, **Evid Rule 611**

QUO WARRANTO
Generally, **App Pro Rule 52.1 et seq.**
Accelerated appeals, **App Pro Rule 28.2**

RABBIS
Clergy, generally, this index

RACE
Discrimination, generally, this index

RACIAL PROFILING
Generally, **CCrP 2.131 et seq.**
Definitions, **CCrP 3.05**

RADIO
Television and Radio, generally, this index

RAILROADS
Certificates and certification, peace officers, **CCrP 2.121**
Damages, peace officers, **CCrP 2.121**
Labor disputes, peace officers, **CCrP 2.12**
Licenses and permits, peace officers, **CCrP 2.123**
Peace officers, **CCrP 2.121, 2.123**

RANGERS
Texas Rangers, generally, this index

RAPE
Sexual Assault, generally, this index
Shield Law, **Evid Rule 412**
Victims, previous sexual conduct, **Evid Rule 412**

RAPE SHIELD LAW
Generally, **Evid Rule 412**

READILY ACCESSIBLE TO THE GENERAL PUBLIC
Definitions, communication interception, **CCrP 18.20**

REAL ESTATE
Attachment, generally, this index
Buildings, generally, this index
Contraband, forfeitures, **CCrP 59.02**
Conveyances. Deeds and Conveyances, generally, this index
Crimes and offenses,
    False statements to obtain property or credit, limitation of criminal prosecutions, **CCrP 12.01**
    Liens and incumbrances, fraud, venue, **CCrP 13.27**
Deeds and Conveyances, generally, this index
Entry on Property, generally, this index
False statements to obtain property or credit, limitation of criminal prosecutions, **CCrP 12.01**
Fines and penalties, liens and incumbrances, fraud, venue, **CCrP 13.27**
Forfeitures, convictions, **CCrP 1.19**
Fraud,
    Liens and incumbrances, release, venue, **CCrP 13.27**
    Venue, **CCrP 13.271**
Hearsay, **Evid Rule 803**
Indictment and information, description, **CCrP 21.09**
Landlord and Tenant, generally, this index
Leases, generally, this index
Liens and incumbrances. Mortgages, generally, this index
Limitation of criminal prosecutions, false statements to obtain property or credit, **CCrP 12.01**
Loans. Mortgages, generally, this index
Mortgages, generally, this index
Records and Recordation, generally, this index
Release, liens and incumbrances, refusal, venue, **CCrP 13.27**
Sales. Deeds and Conveyances, generally, this index
Title to Property, generally, this index
Transfers. Deeds and Conveyances, generally, this index
Venue, fraud, **CCrP 13.271**

REAL ESTATE BROKERS AND SALESPERSONS
Sexual offenses, registration, disclosure, **CCrP 62.056**

REAL PROPERTY
Real Estate, generally, this index

REASONABLE DOUBT
Weight of evidence, **CCrP 38.03**

REBUTTAL TESTIMONY
Order of proceedings, jury trial, **CCrP 36.01**

RECIDIVISM
Second and subsequent offenses. Crimes and Offenses, this index

RECKLESS CONDUCT
Indictment and information, allegation, **CCrP 21.15**

RECOGNIZANCES
Bail and Recognizances, generally, this index

RECORDED RECOLLECTION
Hearsay, **Evid Rule 803**

RECORDINGS
Tape and Sound Recordings, generally, this index
Video Recordings, generally, this index

RECORDS AND RECORDATION
Generally, **App Pro Rule 34.1 et seq.**
Accelerated appeals, **App Pro Rule 28.3**
Administrative law and procedure, **App Pro Rule 36.1 et seq.**
Admissibility, evidence, **Evid Rule 1001 et seq.**
Audio recordings. Tape and Sound Recordings, generally, this index
Authentication or identification, **Evid Rule 901 et seq.**
Bail, **CCrP 17.39**
Broadcasting, courtroom proceedings, **App Pro Rule 14.1 et seq.**
Certified questions of law, transmission, **App Pro Rules 58.4, 74.4**
Change of venue, transfer of records, **CCrP 31.05**
Chemical dispensing devices, **CCrP 18.181**
Children and Minors, this index
Clerks of Courts, this index
Closed circuit television, victims of crimes, children and minors, **CCrP 38.071**
Communications interception, **CCrP 18A.451 et seq.**
    Service providers, subpoenas, **CCrP 18B.451 et seq.**
Communications of jury to court, **CCrP 36.27**
Community Supervision, this index
Computers. Electronic Records, generally, this index
Confidential or Privileged Information, generally, this index

Index

Index

Index

SCHOOLS AND SCHOOL DISTRICTS—Cont'd

Truancy—Cont'd

Funds, **CCrP 102.015**

Hearings, records and recordation, expunction, **CCrP 45.055**

Managers and management, case managers, **CCrP 45.056**

Parents, crimes and offenses, dismissal and nonsuit, **CCrP 45.0531**

Records and recordation, expunction, **CCrP 45.055**

Reimbursement, case managers, **CCrP 45.056**

Reports, case managers, **CCrP 45.056**

Training, case managers, **CCrP 45.056**

Trusts and trustees, open records. Records and Recordation, this index

Vocational Education, generally, this index

Weapons, notice, crimes and offenses, **CCrP 15.27**

SCHOOLTEACHERS

See, also, School Officers and Employees, generally, this index

Certificates and certification, crimes and offenses, notice, **CCrP 42.018**

Crimes and offenses, notice, boards and commissions, certificates and certification, **CCrP 42.018**

SCIENCE

Forensic science commission, **CCrP 38.01**

SCIENTIFIC EXPERTS

Generally, **Evid Rule 702 et seq.**

SCIRE FACIAS

Bail, forfeiture, docket, **CCrP 22.10**

SCOPE OF RULES

Limited admissibility, **Evid Rule 101**

SCOTCH

Alcoholic Beverages, generally, this index

SEALED FILES AND RECORDS

Criminal cases, **App Pro Rule 9.10**

SEALS

Affidavits, search warrants, **CCrP 18.011**

Attachment for witnesses, **CCrP 24.11**

Communications Interception, this index

SEALS—Cont'd

Depositions, **CCrP 39.08**

Governor, pardons, remission of fines and forfeitures, reprieves and commutation of sentence, **CCrP 48.03**

Habeas corpus writ, **CCrP 11.02**

Interception. Communications Interception, this index

Obscenity, children and minors, **CCrP 38.45**

Pardons, remission of fines and forfeitures, reprieves and commutation of sentence, **CCrP 48.03**

Search warrants, affidavits, **CCrP 18.011**

Self authentication, **Evid Rule 902**

State, this index

Subpoena, **CCrP 24.01**

Wiretapping. Communications Interception, this index

SEARCH AND RESCUE

Correctional institutions, prevention, **CCrP 43.26**

SEARCH WARRANTS

Warrants. Searches and Seizures, this index

SEARCHES AND SEIZURES

Generally, **CCrP 1.06, 18.01 et seq.**

Abandoned or unclaimed property, disposition, **CCrP 18.17**

Adulterated medicine, **CCrP 9.06**

Arraignment, **CCrP 18.14**

Buildings, warrants, **CCrP 18.05**

Business nuisance, **CCrP 9.02**

Children and minors, injuries, photographs, **CCrP 18.021**

Computers, warrants, duration, **CCrP 18.07**

Contraband, this index

Copies, warrants, inspection and inspectors, **CCrP 18.01**

Courts authorized to issue warrants, **CCrP 18.01**

Custody of property, **CCrP 18.11**

Definitions, **CCrP 18.01, 18.09**

Contraband, forfeitures, **CCrP 59.01**

Delivery, unclaimed property, **CCrP 18.17**

Deposits, disposition of stolen property, **CCrP 18.183**

Description of property, **CCrP 18.01, 18.02**

Discharge, defendant, **CCrP 18.13**

Disposition of property, **CCrP 18.09**

Abandoned or unclaimed property, **CCrP 18.17**

SEARCHES AND SEIZURES—Cont'd

DNA, warrants, **CCrP 18.065**

Evidence, description of property, warrants, **CCrP 18.01, 18.02**

Executions, warrants, **CCrP 18.06 et seq.**

Service providers, customer data, disclosure, **CCrP 18B.355**

Extension, warrants, seals, affidavits, **CCrP 18.011**

Food, unwholesome food, **CCrP 9.06**

Forfeitures,

Aircraft, contraband, **CCrP 59.04, 59.11**

Contraband, **CCrP 18.18**

Deadly weapons, **CCrP 18.19**

Gambling, this index

Good faith reliance upon search warrant, admissibility, **CCrP 38.23**

Illegally obtained evidence, use in prosecution, **CCrP 38.23**

Inspection and inspectors, warrants, **CCrP 18.01**

Inventory, seized property, **CCrP 18.06, 18.10**

Investigations,

Discharge of defendant, **CCrP 18.13**

Warrants, **CCrP 18.12**

Magazine offices, **CCrP 18.01**

Magistrates, search warrants, authority to issue, **CCrP 18.01**

News magazine offices, **CCrP 18.01**

Newspaper offices, warrants, **CCrP 18.01**

Nuclear power plants, security officers and employees, **CCrP 2.122**

Orders of court, warrants, affidavits, seals, **CCrP 18.011**

Photographs,

Affidavits, **CCrP 18.01**

Children, injuries, **CCrP 18.021**

Preventing theft of property, **CCrP 18.16**

Probable cause, warrants, service providers, customer data, disclosure, **CCrP 18B.354**

Production of property, disposition, **CCrP 18.09**

Public health, offenses injurious to, **CCrP 9.02, 9.06**

Radio stations, warrants, **CCrP 18.01**

Records, **CCrP 18.15**

Registered or certified mail, sale, notice, **CCrP 18.17**

Restitution, discharge of defendant, **CCrP 18.13**

Index

SEXUAL OFFENSES—Cont'd

Evidence,

Capital offenses, second and subsequent offenses, children and minors, **CCrP 37.072**

Children and minors, extraneous offenses or acts, **CCrP 38.37**

Corroboration, **CCrP 38.07**

Photography and pictures, children and minors, **CCrP 38.451, 39.151**

Registration, **CCrP 62.051**

Expiration, registration, **CCrP 62.101**

Information, removal, **CCrP 62.251**

Extraneous offenses or acts, children and minors, evidence, **CCrP 38.37**

Failure to comply, registration,

Civil commitment, **CCrP 62.203**

Venue, **CCrP 13.31**

Federal law, registration, **CCrP 62.003, 62.052**

Fees, community supervision, **CCrP 42A.653**

Findings of law or fact, victims, age, **CCrP 42.015**

Foreign countries, registration, **CCrP 62.003, 62.052**

Forms, registration, **CCrP 62.051**

Guilty pleas, registration, **CCrP 26.13**

Hearings,

Children and minors, exemptions, **CCrP 62.301**

Early termination, motions, **CCrP 62.405**

Extraneous offenses or acts, evidence, **CCrP 38.37**

Juvenile delinquents and dependents, exemptions, **CCrP 62.351 et seq.**

Hearsay statement, child abuse victim, **CCrP 38.072**

High schools or secondary schools, registration, **CCrP 62.151, 62.152**

Housing, registration,

Colleges and universities, **CCrP 62.064**

Disclosure, **CCrP 62.056**

Information, release, **CCrP 42A.256**

Inspection and inspectors, electronic devices, community supervision, **CCrP 42A.454**

Internet,

Access, social networking sites, **CCrP 42A.454; Gov 508.1861**

Children and minors, solicitations, orders of court, subpoenas, **CCrP 24A.001 et seq.**

SEXUAL OFFENSES—Cont'd

Internet—Cont'd

Community supervision, **CCrP 42A.454**

Online identifiers, social networking sites,

Changes, **CCrP 62.0551**

Requests, **CCrP 62.0061**

Orders of court, **CCrP 24A.001 et seq.**

Parole, **Gov 508.1861**

Social networking sites,

Access, **CCrP 42A.454; Gov 508.1861**

Online identifiers,

Changes, **CCrP 62.0551**

Requests, **CCrP 62.0061**

Subpoenas, **CCrP 24A.001 et seq.**

Investigations and investigators,

Presentence investigations, reports, community supervision, **CCrP 42A.251 et seq.**

Texas Rangers, public officers and employees, **CCrP 2.022**

Judgments and decrees, registration, **CCrP 42.01**

Jury, instructions,

Capital offenses, second and subsequent offenses, children and minors, **CCrP 37.072**

Corroboration, **CCrP 38.07**

Juvenile delinquents and dependents,

Education, sexting, **CCrP 6.10**

Registration, exemptions, **CCrP 62.351 et seq.**

Sexting, education, **CCrP 6.10**

Labor and employment, **CCrP 62.053**

Registration, **CCrP 62.063, 62.151 et seq.**

Reports, **CCrP 62.057**

Landlord and tenant, registration, disclosure, **CCrP 62.056**

Law enforcement officers, registration, information, **CCrP 62.006**

Licenses and permits, registration, notice, **CCrP 62.005**

Life imprisonment, second and subsequent offenses, **CCrP 37.072**

Limitation of prosecutions, **CCrP 12.01**

Limousines, registration, labor and employment, **CCrP 62.063**

Mail and mailing, crime victims, address, **CCrP 56.81 et seq.**

Medical care and treatment, registration, reports, **CCrP 62.057**

Medical records, release, **CCrP 42A.256**

Military forces, registration, **CCrP 62.003, 62.052**

SEXUAL OFFENSES—Cont'd

Motions,

Early termination, **CCrP 62.404**

Hearings, **CCrP 62.405**

Juvenile delinquents and dependents, exemptions, **CCrP 62.351 et seq.**

Names, change of name, registration, **CCrP 62.057**

Newspapers, notice, registration, **CCrP 62.062**

Nolo contendere plea, registration, **CCrP 26.13**

Notice,

Extraneous offenses or acts, evidence, **CCrP 38.37**

Parole, **Gov 508.181**

Victims, **CCrP 56.11**

Obscenity, generally, this index

Officers and employees, registration, privileges and immunities, **CCrP 62.008**

Orchiectomy,

Community supervision, condition, **CCrP 42A.307**

Evidence, **CCrP 37.07**

Parole, **Gov 508.226**

Orders of court,

Children and minors, exemptions, **CCrP 62.301**

State, appeal and review, **CCrP 44.01**

Early termination, **CCrP 62.407**

State, appeal and review, **CCrP 44.01**

Internet, **CCrP 24A.001 et seq.**

Juvenile delinquents and dependents, exemptions, **CCrP 62.351 et seq.**

State, appeal and review, **CCrP 44.01**

Parole,

Internet, use, limitations, **Gov 508.1861**

Mandatory supervision,

Notice, **Gov 508.181**

Registration, **CCrP 62.051**

Treatment, **Gov 508.1862, 508.228**

Notice, **Gov 508.181**

Registration, **CCrP 62.051; Gov 508.186**

Treatment, **Gov 508.1862, 508.228**

Peace officers, registration, information, **CCrP 62.006**

Personal identification cards, registration, **CCrP 42.016, 62.053, 62.060**

Petitions, registration, children and minors, exemptions, **CCrP 62.301**

I-143

Index

Index

Index

Index

I-159

Index

Index

Index

Index

Index

Index

Index

Index

Index

Index